INTRODUCTION TO
JAVA™

PROGRAMMING AND
DATA STRUCTURES

COMPREHENSIVE VERSION

Eleventh Edition

Y. Daniel Liang

Armstrong State University

330 Hudson Street, NY NY 10013

To Samantha, Michael, and Michelle

Senior Vice President Courseware Portfolio
    Management: Marcia J. Horton
Director, Portfolio Management: Engineering,
    Computer Science & Global Editions: Julian
    Partridge
Higher Ed Portfolio Management: Tracy Johnson
    (Dunkelberger)
Portfolio Management Assistant: Kristy Alaura
Managing Content Producer: Scott Disanno
Content Producer: Robert Engelhardt
Web Developer: Steve Wright

Rights and Permissions Manager: Ben Ferrini
Manufacturing Buyer, Higher Ed, Lake Side
    Communications Inc (LSC): Maura Zaldivar-Garcia
Inventory Manager: Ann Lam
Marketing Manager: Demetrius Hall
Product Marketing Manager: Bram Van Kempen
Marketing Assistant: Jon Bryant
Cover Designer: Marta Samsel
Cover Photography: Germano Poli/123RF.com
Full-Service Project Management: Shylaja Gattupalli,
    SPi Global

Java™ and Netbeans™ screenshots ©2017 by Oracle Corporation, all rights reserved. Reprinted with permission.

Credits and acknowledgments borrowed from other sources and reproduced, with permission, in this textbook appear on the appropriate page within text.

Library of Congress Cataloging-in-Publication Data

Names: Liang, Y. Daniel, author.
Title: Introduction to Java programming and data structures / Y. Daniel
    Liang, Armstrong State University.
Other titles: Introduction to Java programming
Description: Eleventh edition. Comprehensive version. | New York, NY :
    Pearson Education, 2017. | Revised edition of: Introduction to Java
    programming / Y. Daniel Liang, Armstrong Atlantic State University. Tenth
    edition. Comprehensive version. 2015. | Includes index.
Identifiers: LCCN 2017002082| ISBN 9780134670942 | ISBN 0134670949
Subjects: LCSH: Java (Computer program language)
Classification: LCC QA76.73.J38 L52 2017 | DDC 005.13/3--dc23 LC record available at https://lccn.loc.gov/2017002082

4 17

Pearson

ISBN-10: 0-13-467094-9
ISBN-13: 978-0-13-467094-2

PREFACE

Dear Reader,

Many of you have provided feedback on earlier editions of this book, and your comments and suggestions have greatly improved the book. This edition has been substantially enhanced in presentation, organization, examples, exercises, and supplements.

The book is fundamentals first by introducing basic programming concepts and techniques before designing custom classes. The fundamental concepts and techniques of selection statements, loops, methods, and arrays are the foundation for programming. Building this strong foundation prepares students to learn object-oriented programming and advanced Java programming.

fundamentals-first

This book teaches programming in a problem-driven way that focuses on problem solving rather than syntax. We make introductory programming interesting by using thought-provoking problems in a broad context. The central thread of early chapters is on problem solving. Appropriate syntax and library are introduced to enable readers to write programs for solving the problems. To support the teaching of programming in a problem-driven way, the book provides a wide variety of problems at various levels of difficulty to motivate students. To appeal to students in all majors, the problems cover many application areas, including math, science, business, financial, gaming, animation, and multimedia.

problem-driven

The book seamlessly integrates programming, data structures, and algorithms into one text. It employs a practical approach to teach data structures. We first introduce how to use various data structures to develop efficient algorithms, and then show how to implement these data structures. Through implementation, students gain a deep understanding on the efficiency of data structures and on how and when to use certain data structures. Finally, we design and implement custom data structures for trees and graphs.

data structures

The book is widely used in the introductory programming, data structures, and algorithms courses in the universities around the world. This *comprehensive version* covers fundamentals of programming, object-oriented programming, GUI programming, data structures, algorithms, concurrency, networking, database, and Web programming. It is designed to prepare students to become proficient Java programmers. A *brief version* (*Introduction to Java Programming*, Brief Version, Eleventh Edition) is available for a first course on programming, commonly known as CS1. The brief version contains the first 18 chapters of the comprehensive version. An AP version of the book is also available for high school students taking an AP Computer Science course.

comprehensive version

brief version

AP Computer Science

The best way to teach programming is *by example*, and the only way to learn programming is *by doing*. Basic concepts are explained by example and a large number of exercises with various levels of difficulty are provided for students to practice. For our programming courses, we assign programming exercises after each lecture.

examples and exercises

Our goal is to produce a text that teaches problem solving and programming in a broad context using a wide variety of interesting examples. If you have any comments on and suggestions for improving the book, please email me.

Sincerely,

Y. Daniel Liang
y.daniel.liang@gmail.com
www.cs.armstrong.edu/liang
www.pearsonhighered.com/liang

ACM/IEEE Curricular 2013 and ABET Course Assessment

The new ACM/IEEE Computer Science Curricular 2013 defines the Body of Knowledge organized into 18 Knowledge Areas. To help instructors design the courses based on this book, we provide sample syllabi to identify the Knowledge Areas and Knowledge Units. The sample syllabi are for a three semester course sequence and serve as an example for institutional customization. The sample syllabi are accessible from the Instructor Resource Website.

Many of our users are from the ABET-accredited programs. A key component of the ABET accreditation is to identify the weakness through continuous course assessment against the course outcomes. We provide sample course outcomes for the courses and sample exams for measuring course outcomes on the Instructor Resource Website.

What's New in This Edition?

This edition is completely revised in every detail to enhance clarity, presentation, content, examples, and exercises. The major improvements are as follows:

- The book's title is changed to Introduction to Java Programming and Data Structures with new enhancements on data structures. The book uses a practical approach to introduce design, implement, and use data structures and covers all topics in a typical data structures course. Additionally, it provides bonus chapters that cover advanced data structures such as 2-4 trees, B-trees, and red-black trees.

- Updated to the latest Java technology. Examples and exercises are improved and simplified by using the new features in Java 8.

- The default and static methods are introduced for interfaces in Chapter 13.

- The GUI chapters are updated to JavaFX 8. The examples are revised. The user interfaces in the examples and exercises are now resizable and displayed in the center of the window.

- Inner classes, anonymous inner classes, and lambda expressions are covered using practical examples in Chapter 15.

- More examples and exercises in the data structures chapters use lambda expressions to simplify coding. Method references are introduced along with the `Comparator` interface in Section 20.6.

- The `forEach` method is introduced in Chapter 20 as a simple alternative to the foreach loop for applying an action to each element in a collection.

- Use the default methods for interfaces in Java 8 to redesign and simplify `MyList`, `MyArrayList`, `MyLinkedList`, `Tree`, `BST`, `AVLTree`, `MyMap`, `MyHashMap`, `MySet`, `MyHashSet`, `Graph`, `UnweightedGraph`, and `WeightedGraph` in Chapters 24–29.

- Chapter 30 is brand new to introduce aggregate operations for collection streams.

- FXML and the Scene Builder visual tool are introduced in Chapter 31.

- The Companion Website has been redesigned with new interactive quiz, CheckPoint questions, animations, and live coding.

- More than 200 additional programming exercises with solutions are provided to the instructor on the Instructor Resource Website. These exercises are not printed in the text.

Please visit www.pearsonhighered.com/liang for a complete list of new features as well as correlations to the previous edition.

Pedagogical Features

The book uses the following elements to help students get the most from the material:

- The **Objectives** at the beginning of each chapter list what students should learn from the chapter. This will help them determine whether they have met the objectives after completing the chapter.

- The **Introduction** opens the discussion with a thought-provoking question to motivate the reader to delve into the chapter.

- **Key Points** highlight the important concepts covered in each section.

- **Check Points** provide review questions to help students track their progress as they read through the chapter and evaluate their learning.

- **Problems and Case Studies**, carefully chosen and presented in an easy-to-follow style, teach problem solving and programming concepts. The book uses many small, simple, and stimulating examples to demonstrate important ideas.

- The **Chapter Summary** reviews the important subjects that students should understand and remember. It helps them reinforce the key concepts they have learned in the chapter.

- **Quizzes** are accessible online, grouped by sections, for students to do self-test on programming concepts and techniques.

- **Programming Exercises** are grouped by sections to provide students with opportunities to apply the new skills they have learned on their own. The level of difficulty is rated as easy (no asterisk), moderate (*), hard (**), or challenging (***). The trick of learning programming is practice, practice, and practice. To that end, the book provides a great many exercises. Additionally, more than 200 programming exercises with solutions are provided to the instructors on the Instructor Resource Website. These exercises are not printed in the text.

- **Notes**, **Tips**, **Cautions**, and **Design Guides** are inserted throughout the text to offer valuable advice and insight on important aspects of program development.

Note
Provides additional information on the subject and reinforces important concepts.

Tip
Teaches good programming style and practice.

Caution
Helps students steer away from the pitfalls of programming errors.

Design Guide
Provides guidelines for designing programs.

Flexible Chapter Orderings

The book is designed to provide flexible chapter orderings to enable GUI, exception handling, recursion, generics, and the Java Collections Framework to be covered earlier or later. The diagram on the next page shows the chapter dependencies.

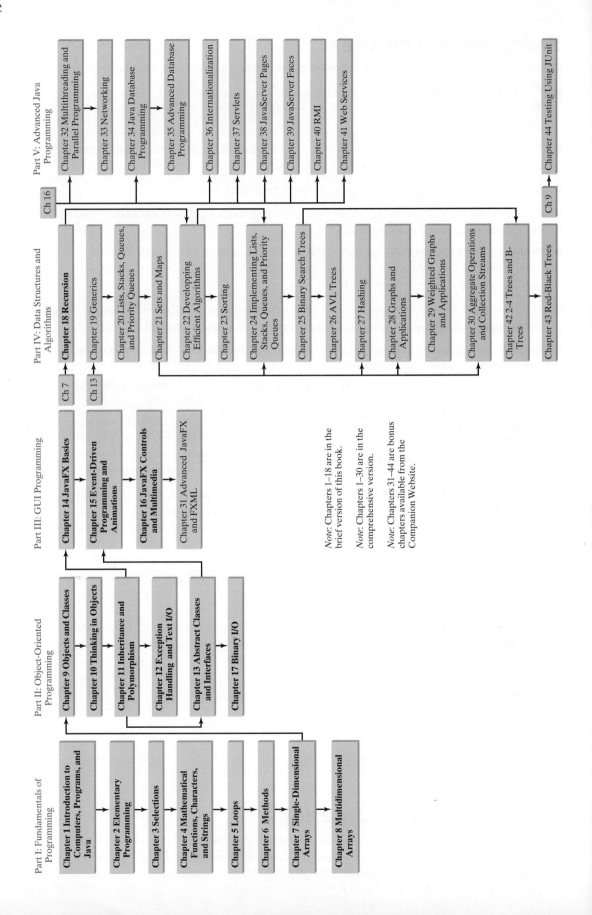

Part I: Fundamentals of Programming

Chapter 1 Introduction to Computers, Programs, and Java

Chapter 2 Elementary Programming

Chapter 3 Selections

Chapter 4 Mathematical Functions, Characters, and Strings

Chapter 5 Loops

Chapter 6 Methods

Chapter 7 Single-Dimensional Arrays

Chapter 8 Multidimensional Arrays

Part II: Object-Oriented Programming

Chapter 9 Objects and Classes

Chapter 10 Thinking in Objects

Chapter 11 Inheritance and Polymorphism

Chapter 12 Exception Handling and Text I/O

Chapter 13 Abstract Classes and Interfaces

Chapter 17 Binary I/O

Part III: GUI Programming

Chapter 14 JavaFX Basics

Chapter 15 Event-Driven Programming and Animations

Chapter 16 JavaFX Controls and Multimedia

Chapter 31 Advanced JavaFX and FXML

Part IV: Data Structures and Algorithms

Ch 7

Ch 13

Chapter 18 Recursion

Chapter 19 Generics

Chapter 20 Lists, Stacks, Queues, and Priority Queues

Chapter 21 Sets and Maps

Chapter 22 Developping Efficient Algorithms

Chapter 23 Sorting

Chapter 24 Implementing Lists, Stacks, Queues, and Priority Queues

Chapter 25 Binary Search Trees

Chapter 26 AVL Trees

Chapter 27 Hashing

Chapter 28 Graphs and Applications

Chapter 29 Weighted Graphs and Applications

Chapter 30 Aggregate Operations and Collection Streams

Chapter 42 2-4 Trees and B-Trees

Chapter 43 Red-Black Trees

Part V: Advanced Java Programming

Ch 16

Ch 9

Chapter 32 Multithreading and Parallel Programming

Chapter 33 Networking

Chapter 34 Java Database Programming

Chapter 35 Advanced Database Programming

Chapter 36 Internationalization

Chapter 37 Servlets

Chapter 38 JavaServer Pages

Chapter 39 JavaServer Faces

Chapter 40 RMI

Chapter 41 Web Services

Chapter 44 Testing Using JUnit

Note: Chapters 1–18 are in the brief version of this book.

Note: Chapters 1–30 are in the comprehensive version.

Note: Chapters 31–44 are bonus chapters available from the Companion Website.

Organization of the Book

The chapters can be grouped into five parts that, taken together, form a comprehensive introduction to Java programming, data structures and algorithms, and database and Web programming. Because knowledge is cumulative, the early chapters provide the conceptual basis for understanding programming and guide students through simple examples and exercises; subsequent chapters progressively present Java programming in detail, culminating with the development of comprehensive Java applications. The appendixes contain a mixed bag of topics, including an introduction to number systems, bitwise operations, regular expressions, and enumerated types.

Part I: Fundamentals of Programming (Chapters 1–8)

The first part of the book is a stepping stone, preparing you to embark on the journey of learning Java. You will begin to learn about Java (Chapter 1) and fundamental programming techniques with primitive data types, variables, constants, assignments, expressions, and operators (Chapter 2), selection statements (Chapter 3), mathematical functions, characters, and strings (Chapter 4), loops (Chapter 5), methods (Chapter 6), and arrays (Chapters 7–8). After Chapter 7, you can jump to Chapter 18 to learn how to write recursive methods for solving inherently recursive problems.

Part II: Object-Oriented Programming (Chapters 9–13, and 17)

This part introduces object-oriented programming. Java is an object-oriented programming language that uses abstraction, encapsulation, inheritance, and polymorphism to provide great flexibility, modularity, and reusability in developing software. You will learn programming with objects and classes (Chapters 9–10), class inheritance (Chapter 11), polymorphism (Chapter 11), exception handling (Chapter 12), abstract classes (Chapter 13), and interfaces (Chapter 13). Text I/O is introduced in Chapter 12 and binary I/O is discussed in Chapter 17.

Part III: GUI Programming (Chapters 14–16 and Bonus Chapter 31)

JavaFX is a new framework for developing Java GUI programs. It is not only useful for developing GUI programs, but also an excellent pedagogical tool for learning object-oriented programming. This part introduces Java GUI programming using JavaFX in Chapters 14–16. Major topics include GUI basics (Chapter 14), container panes (Chapter 14), drawing shapes (Chapter 14), event-driven programming (Chapter 15), animations (Chapter 15), and GUI controls (Chapter 16), and playing audio and video (Chapter 16). You will learn the architecture of JavaFX GUI programming and use the controls, shapes, panes, image, and video to develop useful applications. Chapter 31 covers advanced features in JavaFX.

Part IV: Data Structures and Algorithms (Chapters 18–30 and Bonus Chapters 42–43)

This part covers the main subjects in a typical data structures and algorithms course. Chapter 18 introduces recursion to write methods for solving inherently recursive problems. Chapter 19 presents how generics can improve software reliability. Chapters 20 and 21 introduce the Java Collection Framework, which defines a set of useful API for data structures. Chapter 22 discusses measuring algorithm efficiency in order to choose an appropriate algorithm for applications. Chapter 23 describes classic sorting algorithms. You will learn how to implement several classic data structures lists, queues, and priority queues in Chapter 24. Chapters 25 and 26 introduce binary search trees and AVL trees. Chapter 27 presents hashing and implementing maps and sets using hashing. Chapters 28 and 29 introduce graph applications. Chapter 30 introduces aggregate operations for collection streams. The 2-4 trees, B-trees, and red-black trees are covered in Bonus Chapters 42–43.

Part V: Advanced Java Programming (Chapters 32-41, 44)

This part of the book is devoted to advanced Java programming. Chapter 32 treats the use of multithreading to make programs more responsive and interactive and introduces parallel programming. Chapter 33 discusses how to write programs that talk with each other from different hosts over the Internet. Chapter 34 introduces the use of Java to develop database projects. Chapter 35 delves into advanced Java database programming. Chapter 36 covers the use of internationalization support to develop projects for international audiences. Chapters 37 and 38 introduce how to use Java servlets and JavaServer Pages to generate dynamic content from Web servers. Chapter 39 introduces modern Web application development using JavaServer Faces. Chapter 40 introduces remote method invocation and Chapter 41 discusses Web services. Chapter 44 introduces testing Java programs using JUnit.

Appendixes

This part of the book covers a mixed bag of topics. Appendix A lists Java keywords. Appendix B gives tables of ASCII characters and their associated codes in decimal and in hex. Appendix C shows the operator precedence. Appendix D summarizes Java modifiers and their usage. Appendix E discusses special floating-point values. Appendix F introduces number systems and conversions among binary, decimal, and hex numbers. Finally, Appendix G introduces bitwise operations. Appendix H introduces regular expressions. Appendix I covers enumerated types.

Java Development Tools

You can use a text editor, such as the Windows Notepad or WordPad, to create Java programs and to compile and run the programs from the command window. You can also use a Java development tool, such as NetBeans or Eclipse. These tools support an integrated development environment (IDE) for developing Java programs quickly. Editing, compiling, building, executing, and debugging programs are integrated in one graphical user interface. Using these tools effectively can greatly increase your programming productivity. NetBeans and Eclipse are easy to use if you follow the tutorials. Tutorials on NetBeans and Eclipse can be found in the supplements on the Companion Website www.pearsonhighered.com/liang.

IDE tutorials

Student Resource Website

The Student Resource Website (www.pearsonhighered.com/liang) contains the following resources:

- Answers to CheckPoint questions

- Solutions to majority of even-numbered programming exercises

- Source code for the examples in the book

- Interactive quiz (organized by sections for each chapter)

- Supplements

- Debugging tips

- Video notes

- Algorithm animations

- Errata

Supplements

The text covers the essential subjects. The supplements extend the text to introduce additional topics that might be of interest to readers. The supplements are available from the Companion Website.

Instructor Resource Website

The Instructor Resource Website, accessible from www.pearsonhighered.com/liang, contains the following resources:

- Microsoft PowerPoint slides with interactive buttons to view full-color, syntax-highlighted source code and to run programs without leaving the slides.

- Solutions to majority of odd-numbered programming exercises.

- More than 200 additional programming exercises and 300 quizzes organized by chapters. These exercises and quizzes are available only to the instructors. Solutions to these exercises and quizzes are provided.

- Web-based quiz generator. (Instructors can choose chapters to generate quizzes from a large database of more than two thousand questions.)

- Sample exams. Most exams have four parts:

    - Multiple-choice questions or short-answer questions

    - Correct programming errors

    - Trace programs

    - Write programs

- Sample exams with ABET course assessment.

- Projects. In general, each project gives a description and asks students to analyze, design, and implement the project.

    Some readers have requested the materials from the Instructor Resource Website. Please understand that these are for instructors only. Such requests will not be answered.

Online Practice and Assessment with MyProgrammingLab

MyProgrammingLab™

MyProgrammingLab helps students fully grasp the logic, semantics, and syntax of programming. Through practice exercises and immediate, personalized feedback, MyProgrammingLab improves the programming competence of beginning students who often struggle with the basic concepts and paradigms of popular high-level programming languages.

A self-study and homework tool, a MyProgrammingLab course consists of hundreds of small practice problems organized around the structure of this textbook. For students, the system automatically detects errors in the logic and syntax of their code submissions and offers targeted hints that enable students to figure out what went wrong—and why. For instructors, a comprehensive gradebook tracks correct and incorrect answers and stores the code inputted by students for review.

MyProgrammingLab is offered to users of this book in partnership with Turing's Craft, the makers of the CodeLab interactive programming exercise system. For a full demonstration, to see feedback from instructors and students, or to get started using MyProgrammingLab in your course, visit www.myprogramminglab.com.

Video Notes

VideoNote

We are excited about the new Video Notes feature that is found in this new edition. These videos provide additional help by presenting examples of key topics and showing how to solve problems completely from design through coding. Video Notes are available from www.pearsonhighered.com/liang.

Animation

Algorithm Animations

We have provided numerous animations for algorithms. These are valuable pedagogical tools to demonstrate how algorithms work. Algorithm animations can be accessed from the Companion Website.

Acknowledgments

I would like to thank Armstrong State University for enabling me to teach what I write and for supporting me in writing what I teach. Teaching is the source of inspiration for continuing to improve the book. I am grateful to the instructors and students who have offered comments, suggestions, corrections, and praise. My special thanks go to Stefan Andrei of Lamar University and William Bahn of University of Colorado Colorado Spring for their help to improve the data structures part of this book.

This book has been greatly enhanced thanks to outstanding reviews for this and previous editions. The reviewers are: Elizabeth Adams (James Madison University), Syed Ahmed (North Georgia College and State University), Omar Aldawud (Illinois Institute of Technology), Stefan Andrei (Lamar University), Yang Ang (University of Wollongong, Australia), Kevin Bierre (Rochester Institute of Technology), Aaron Braskin (Mira Costa High School), David Champion (DeVry Institute), James Chegwidden (Tarrant County College), Anup Dargar (University of North Dakota), Daryl Detrick (Warren Hills Regional High School), Charles Dierbach (Towson University), Frank Ducrest (University of Louisiana at Lafayette), Erica Eddy (University of Wisconsin at Parkside), Summer Ehresman (Center Grove High School), Deena Engel (New York University), Henry A. Etlinger (Rochester Institute of Technology), James Ten Eyck (Marist College), Myers Foreman (Lamar University), Olac Fuentes (University of Texas at El Paso), Edward F. Gehringer (North Carolina State University), Harold Grossman (Clemson University), Barbara Guillot (Louisiana State University), Stuart Hansen (University of Wisconsin, Parkside), Dan Harvey (Southern Oregon University), Ron Hofman (Red River College, Canada), Stephen Hughes (Roanoke College), Vladan Jovanovic (Georgia Southern University), Deborah Kabura Kariuki (Stony Point High School), Edwin Kay (Lehigh University), Larry King (University of Texas at Dallas), Nana Kofi (Langara College, Canada), George Koutsogiannakis (Illinois Institute of Technology), Roger Kraft (Purdue University at Calumet), Norman Krumpe (Miami University), Hong Lin (DeVry Institute), Dan Lipsa (Armstrong State University), James Madison (Rensselaer Polytechnic Institute), Frank Malinowski (Darton College), Tim Margush (University of Akron), Debbie Masada (Sun Microsystems), Blayne Mayfield (Oklahoma State University), John McGrath (J.P. McGrath Consulting), Hugh McGuire (Grand Valley State), Shyamal Mitra (University of Texas at Austin), Michel Mitri (James Madison University), Kenrick Mock (University of Alaska Anchorage), Frank Murgolo (California State University, Long Beach), Jun Ni (University of Iowa), Benjamin Nystuen (University of Colorado at Colorado Springs), Maureen Opkins (CA State University, Long Beach), Gavin Osborne (University of Saskatchewan), Kevin Parker (Idaho State University), Dale Parson (Kutztown University), Mark Pendergast (Florida Gulf Coast University), Richard Povinelli (Marquette University), Roger Priebe (University of Texas at Austin), Mary Ann Pumphrey (De Anza Junior College), Pat Roth (Southern Polytechnic State University), Amr Sabry (Indiana University), Ben Setzer (Kennesaw State University), Carolyn Schauble (Colorado State University), David Scuse (University of Manitoba), Ashraf Shirani (San Jose State University), Daniel Spiegel (Kutztown University), Joslyn A. Smith (Florida Atlantic University), Lixin Tao (Pace University), Ronald F. Taylor (Wright State University), Russ Tront (Simon Fraser University), Deborah Trytten (University of Oklahoma), Michael Verdicchio (Citadel), Kent Vidrine (George Washington University), and Bahram Zartoshty (California State University at Northridge).

It is a great pleasure, honor, and privilege to work with Pearson. I would like to thank Tracy Johnson and her colleagues Marcia Horton, Demetrius Hall, Yvonne Vannatta, Kristy Alaura, Carole Snyder, Scott Disanno, Bob Engelhardt, Shylaja Gattupalli, and their colleagues for organizing, producing, and promoting this project.

As always, I am indebted to my wife, Samantha, for her love, support, and encouragement.

BRIEF CONTENTS

CONTENTS

Chapter 31–44 are available from the Companion Website at www.pearsonhighered.com/liang

VideoNotes

Locations of VideoNotes

http://www.pearsonhighered.com/liang

VideoNote

Animations

Introduction to Computers, Programs, and Java™

Objectives

- To understand computer basics, programs, and operating systems (§§1.2–1.4).

- To describe the relationship between Java and the World Wide Web (§1.5).

- To understand the meaning of Java language specification, API, JDK™, JRE™, and IDE (§1.6).

- To write a simple Java program (§1.7).

- To display output on the console (§1.7).

- To explain the basic syntax of a Java program (§1.7).

- To create, compile, and run Java programs (§1.8).

- To use sound Java programming style and document programs properly (§1.9).

- To explain the differences between syntax errors, runtime errors, and logic errors (§1.10).

- To develop Java programs using NetBeans™ (§1.11).

- To develop Java programs using Eclipse™ (§1.12).

1.1 Introduction

The central theme of this book is to learn how to solve problems by writing a program.

what is programming?
programming
program

This book is about programming. So, what is programming? The term *programming* means to create (or develop) software, which is also called a *program.* In basic terms, software contains instructions that tell a computer—or a computerized device—what to do.

Software is all around you, even in devices you might not think would need it. Of course, you expect to find and use software on a personal computer, but software also plays a role in running airplanes, cars, cell phones, and even toasters. On a personal computer, you use word processors to write documents, web browsers to explore the Internet, and e-mail programs to send and receive messages. These programs are all examples of software. Software developers create software with the help of powerful tools called *programming languages.*

This book teaches you how to create programs by using the Java programming language. There are many programming languages, some of which are decades old. Each language was invented for a specific purpose—to build on the strengths of a previous language, for example, or to give the programmer a new and unique set of tools. Knowing there are so many programming languages available, it would be natural for you to wonder which one is best. However, in truth, there is no "best" language. Each one has its own strengths and weaknesses. Experienced programmers know one language might work well in some situations, whereas a different language may be more appropriate in other situations. For this reason, seasoned programmers try to master as many different programming languages as they can, giving them access to a vast arsenal of software-development tools.

If you learn to program using one language, you should find it easy to pick up other languages. The key is to learn how to solve problems using a programming approach. That is the main theme of this book.

You are about to begin an exciting journey: learning how to program. At the outset, it is helpful to review computer basics, programs, and operating systems (OSs). If you are already familiar with such terms as central processing unit (CPU), memory, disks, operating systems, and programming languages, you may skip Sections 1.2–1.4.

1.2 What Is a Computer?

A computer is an electronic device that stores and processes data.

hardware
software

A computer includes both *hardware* and *software.* In general, hardware comprises the visible, physical elements of the computer, and software provides the invisible instructions that control the hardware and make it perform specific tasks. Knowing computer hardware isn't essential to learning a programming language, but it can help you better understand the effects that a program's instructions have on the computer and its components. This section introduces computer hardware components and their functions.

A computer consists of the following major hardware components (see Figure 1.1):

- A central processing unit (CPU)

- Memory (main memory)

- Storage devices (such as disks and CDs)

- Input devices (such as the mouse and the keyboard)

- Output devices (such as monitors and printers)

- Communication devices (such as modems and network interface cards (NIC))

bus

A computer's components are interconnected by a subsystem called a *bus.* You can think of a bus as a sort of system of roads running among the computer's components; data and power travel along the bus from one part of the computer to another. In personal computers,

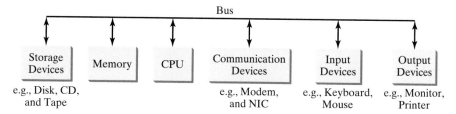

FIGURE 1.1 A computer consists of a CPU, memory, storage devices, input devices, output devices, and communication devices.

the bus is built into the computer's *motherboard*, which is a circuit case that connects all of the parts of a computer together. motherboard

1.2.1 Central Processing Unit

The *central processing unit (CPU)* is the computer's brain. It retrieves instructions from the memory and executes them. The CPU usually has two components: a *control unit* and an *arithmetic/logic unit.* The control unit controls and coordinates the actions of the other components. The arithmetic/logic unit performs numeric operations (addition, subtraction, multiplication, and division) and logical operations (comparisons). CPU

Today's CPUs are built on small silicon semiconductor chips that contain millions of tiny electric switches, called *transistors*, for processing information.

Every computer has an internal clock that emits electronic pulses at a constant rate. These pulses are used to control and synchronize the pace of operations. A higher clock *speed* enables more instructions to be executed in a given period of time. The unit of measurement of clock speed is the *hertz (Hz)*, with 1 Hz equaling 1 pulse per second. In the 1990s, computers measured clock speed in *megahertz (MHz)*, but CPU speed has been improving continuously; the clock speed of a computer is now usually stated in *gigahertz (GHz)*. Intel's newest processors run at about 3 GHz. speed
hertz
megahertz
gigahertz

CPUs were originally developed with only one core. The *core* is the part of the processor that performs the reading and executing of instructions. In order to increase the CPU processing power, chip manufacturers are now producing CPUs that contain multiple cores. A multicore CPU is a single component with two or more independent cores. Today's consumer computers typically have two, three, and even four separate cores. Soon, CPUs with dozens or even hundreds of cores will be affordable. core

1.2.2 Bits and Bytes

Before we discuss memory, let's look at how information (data and programs) are stored in a computer.

A computer is really nothing more than a series of switches. Each switch exists in two states: on or off. Storing information in a computer is simply a matter of setting a sequence of switches on or off. If the switch is on, its value is 1. If the switch is off, its value is 0. These 0s and 1s are interpreted as digits in the binary number system and are called *bits* (binary digits). bits

The minimum storage unit in a computer is a *byte*. A byte is composed of eight bits. A small number such as 3 can be stored as a single byte. To store a number that cannot fit into a single byte, the computer uses several bytes. byte

Data of various kinds, such as numbers and characters, are encoded as a series of bytes. As a programmer, you don't need to worry about the encoding and decoding of data, which the computer system performs automatically, based on the encoding scheme. An *encoding scheme* is a set of rules that govern how a computer translates characters and numbers into data with which the computer can actually work. Most schemes translate each character into a encoding scheme predetermined string of bits. In the popular ASCII encoding scheme, for example, the character C is represented as `01000011` in 1 byte.

A computer's storage capacity is measured in bytes and multiples of the byte, as follows:

- A *kilobyte (KB)* is about 1,000 bytes.

- A *megabyte (MB)* is about 1 million bytes.

- A *gigabyte (GB)* is about 1 billion bytes.

- A *terabyte (TB)* is about 1 trillion bytes.

A typical one-page word document might take 20 KB. Therefore, 1 MB can store 50 pages of documents, and 1 GB can store 50,000 pages of documents. A typical two-hour high-resolution movie might take 8 GB, so it would require 160 GB to store 20 movies.

1.2.3 Memory

memory

A computer's *memory* consists of an ordered sequence of bytes for storing programs as well as data with which the program is working. You can think of memory as the computer's work area for executing a program. A program and its data must be moved into the computer's memory before they can be executed by the CPU.

unique address

RAM

Every byte in the memory has a *unique address*, as shown in Figure 1.2. The address is used to locate the byte for storing and retrieving the data. Since the bytes in the memory can be accessed in any order, the memory is also referred to as *random-access memory (RAM)*.

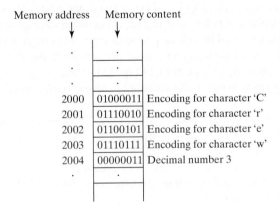

FIGURE 1.2 Memory stores data and program instructions in uniquely addressed memory locations.

Today's personal computers usually have at least 4 GB of RAM, but they more commonly have 6 to 8 GB installed. Generally speaking, the more RAM a computer has, the faster it can operate, but there are limits to this simple rule of thumb.

A memory byte is never empty, but its initial content may be meaningless to your program. The current content of a memory byte is lost whenever new information is placed in it.

Like the CPU, memory is built on silicon semiconductor chips that have millions of transistors embedded on their surface. Compared to CPU chips, memory chips are less complicated, slower, and less expensive.

1.2.4 Storage Devices

storage devices

A computer's memory (RAM) is a volatile form of data storage: Any information that has been saved in memory is lost when the system's power is turned off. Programs and data are permanently stored on *storage devices* and are moved, when the computer actually uses them, to memory, which operates at much faster speeds than permanent storage devices can.

There are three main types of storage devices:

- Magnetic disk drives
- Optical disc drives (CD and DVD)
- Universal serial bus (USB) flash drives

Drives are devices for operating a medium, such as disks and CDs. A storage medium physically stores data and program instructions. The drive reads data from the medium and writes data onto the medium.

drive

Disks

A computer usually has at least one hard disk drive. *Hard disks* are used for permanently storing data and programs. Newer computers have hard disks that can store from 500 GB to 1 TB of data. Hard disk drives are usually encased inside the computer, but removable hard disks are also available.

hard disk

CDs and DVDs

CD stands for compact disc. There are three types of CDs: CD-ROM, CD-R, and CD-RW. A CD-ROM is a prepressed disc. It was popular for distributing software, music, and video. Software, music, and video are now increasingly distributed on the Internet without using CDs. A *CD-R* (CD-Recordable) is a write-once medium. It can be used to record data once and read any number of times. A *CD-RW* (CD-ReWritable) can be used like a hard disk; that is, you can write data onto the disc, then overwrite that data with new data. A single CD can hold up to 700 MB.

CD-ROM
CD-R

CD-RW

DVD stands for digital versatile disc or digital video disc. DVDs and CDs look alike, and you can use either to store data. A DVD can hold more information than a CD; a standard DVD's storage capacity is 4.7 GB. There are two types of DVDs: DVD-R (Recordable) and DVD-RW (ReWritable).

DVD

USB Flash Drives

Universal serial bus (USB) connectors allow the user to attach many kinds of peripheral devices to the computer. You can use an USB to connect a printer, digital camera, mouse, external hard disk drive, and other devices to the computer.

An USB *flash drive* is a device for storing and transporting data. A flash drive is small—about the size of a pack of gum. It acts like a portable hard drive that can be plugged into your computer's USB port. USB flash drives are currently available with up to 256 GB storage capacity.

1.2.5 Input and Output Devices

Input and output devices let the user communicate with the computer. The most common input devices are the *keyboard* and *mouse*. The most common output devices are *monitors* and *printers*.

The Keyboard

A keyboard is a device for entering input. Compact keyboards are available without a numeric keypad.

Function keys are located across the top of the keyboard and are prefaced with the letter *F*. Their functions depend on the software currently being used.

function key

A *modifier key* is a special key (such as the *Shift*, *Alt*, and *Ctrl* keys) that modifies the normal action of another key when the two are pressed simultaneously.

modifier key

numeric keypad

The *numeric keypad*, located on the right side of most keyboards, is a separate set of keys styled like a calculator to use for quickly entering numbers.

arrow keys

Arrow keys, located between the main keypad and the numeric keypad, are used to move the mouse pointer up, down, left, and right on the screen in many kinds of programs.

Insert key
Delete key
Page Up key
Page Down key

The *Insert*, *Delete*, *Page Up*, and *Page Down keys* are used in word processing and other programs for inserting text and objects, deleting text and objects, and moving up or down through a document one screen at a time.

The Mouse

A *mouse* is a pointing device. It is used to move a graphical pointer (usually in the shape of an arrow) called a *cursor* around the screen, or to click on-screen objects (such as a button) to trigger them to perform an action.

The Monitor

The *monitor* displays information (text and graphics). The screen resolution and dot pitch determine the quality of the display.

screen resolution
pixels

The *screen resolution* specifies the number of pixels in horizontal and vertical dimensions of the display device. *Pixels* (short for "picture elements") are tiny dots that form an image on the screen. A common resolution for a 17-inch screen, for example, is 1,024 pixels wide and 768 pixels high. The resolution can be set manually. The higher the resolution, the sharper and clearer the image is.

dot pitch

The *dot pitch* is the amount of space between pixels, measured in millimeters. The smaller the dot pitch, the sharper is the display.

1.2.6 Communication Devices

Computers can be networked through communication devices, such as a dial-up modem (*mo*dulator/*dem*odulator), a digital subscriber line (DSL) or cable modem, a wired network interface card, or a wireless adapter.

dial-up modem

- A *dial-up modem* uses a phone line to dial a phone number to connect to the Internet and can transfer data at a speed up to 56,000 bps (bits per second).

digital subscriber line (DSL)

- A *digital subscriber line (DSL)* connection also uses a standard phone line, but it can transfer data 20 times faster than a standard dial-up modem.

cable modem

- A *cable modem* uses the cable line maintained by the cable company and is generally faster than DSL.

network interface card (NIC)
local area network (LAN)
million bits per second (mbps)

- A *network interface card (NIC)* is a device that connects a computer to a *local area network (LAN)*. LANs are commonly used to connect computers within a limited area such as a school, a home, and an office. A high-speed NIC called *1000BaseT* can transfer data at 1,000 million bits per second (mbps).

- Wireless networking is now extremely popular in homes, businesses, and schools. Every laptop computer sold today is equipped with a wireless adapter that enables the computer to connect to the LAN and the Internet.

Note
Answers to the CheckPoint questions are available at **www.pearsonhighered.com/liang**. Choose this book and click Companion Website to select CheckPoint.

 Check Point

1.2.1 What are hardware and software?

1.2.2 List the five major hardware components of a computer.

1.2.3   What does the acronym CPU stand for? What unit is used to measure CPU speed?

1.2.4   What is a bit? What is a byte?

1.2.5   What is memory for? What does RAM stand for? Why is memory called RAM?

1.2.6   What unit is used to measure memory size? What unit is used to measure disk size?

1.2.7   What is the primary difference between memory and a storage device?

1.3 Programming Languages

Computer programs, known as software, are instructions that tell a computer what to do.

Key
Point

Computers do not understand human languages, so programs must be written in a language a computer can use. There are hundreds of programming languages, and they were developed to make the programming process easier for people. However, all programs must be converted into the instructions the computer can execute.

1.3.1   Machine Language

A computer's native language, which differs among different types of computers, is its *machine language*—a set of built-in primitive instructions. These instructions are in the form of binary code, so if you want to give a computer an instruction in its native language, you have to enter the instruction as binary code. For example, to add two numbers, you might have to write an instruction in binary code as follows:

machine language

    1101101010011010

1.3.2   Assembly Language

Programming in machine language is a tedious process. Moreover, programs written in machine language are very difficult to read and modify. For this reason, *assembly language* was created in the early days of computing as an alternative to machine languages. Assembly language uses a short descriptive word, known as a *mnemonic*, to represent each of the machine-language instructions. For example, the mnemonic **add** typically means to add numbers, and **sub** means to subtract numbers. To add the numbers **2** and **3** and get the result, you might write an instruction in assembly code as follows:

assembly language

```
add 2, 3, result
```

Assembly languages were developed to make programming easier. However, because the computer cannot execute assembly language, another program—called an *assembler*—is used to translate assembly-language programs into machine code, as shown in Figure 1.3.

assembler

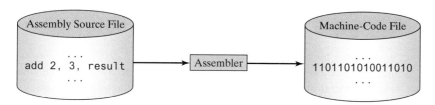

FIGURE 1.3   An assembler translates assembly-language instructions into machine code.

Writing code in assembly language is easier than in machine language. However, it is still tedious to write code in assembly language. An instruction in assembly language essentially corresponds to an instruction in machine code. Writing in assembly language requires that you

low-level language

know how the CPU works. Assembly language is referred to as a *low-level language*, because assembly language is close in nature to machine language and is machine dependent.

1.3.3 High-Level Language

high-level language

In the 1950s, a new generation of programming languages known as *high-level languages* emerged. They are platform independent, which means that you can write a program in a high-level language and run it in different types of machines. High-level languages are similar to English and easy to learn and use. The instructions in a high-level programming language are called *statements*. Here, for example, is a high-level language statement that computes the area of a circle with a radius of 5:

statement

```
area = 5 * 5 * 3.14159;
```

There are many high-level programming languages, and each was designed for a specific purpose. Table 1.1 lists some popular ones.

TABLE 1.1 Popular High-Level Programming Languages

Language	Description
Ada	Named for Ada Lovelace, who worked on mechanical general-purpose computers. Developed for the Department of Defense and used mainly in defense projects.
BASIC	Beginner's All-purpose Symbolic Instruction Code. Designed to be learned and used easily by beginners.
C	Developed at Bell Laboratories. Combines the power of an assembly language with the ease of use and portability of a high-level language.
C++	An object-oriented language, based on C
C#	Pronounced "C Sharp." An object-oriented programming language developed by Microsoft.
COBOL	COmmon Business Oriented Language. Used for business applications.
FORTRAN	FORmula TRANslation. Popular for scientific and mathematical applications.
Java	Developed by Sun Microsystems, now part of Oracle. An object-oriented programming language, widely used for developing platform-independent Internet applications.
JavaScript	A Web programming language developed by Netscape
Pascal	Named for Blaise Pascal, who pioneered calculating machines in the seventeenth century. A simple, structured, general-purpose language primarily for teaching programming.
Python	A simple general-purpose scripting language good for writing short programs.
Visual Basic	Visual Basic was developed by Microsoft. Enables the programmers to rapidly develop Windows-based applications.

source program
source code

A program written in a high-level language is called a *source program* or *source code*. Because a computer cannot execute a source program, a source program must be translated into machine code for execution. The translation can be done using another programming tool called an *interpreter* or a *compiler*.

interpreter
compiler

- An interpreter reads one statement from the source code, translates it to the machine code or virtual machine code, then executes it right away, as shown in Figure 1.4a. Note a statement from the source code may be translated into several machine instructions.

- A compiler translates the entire source code into a machine-code file, and the machine-code file is then executed, as shown in Figure 1.4b.

1.3.1 What language does the CPU understand?

1.3.2 What is an assembly language? What is an assembler?

1.3.3 What is a high-level programming language? What is a source program?

1.3.4 What is an interpreter? What is a compiler?

1.3.5 What is the difference between an interpreted language and a compiled language?

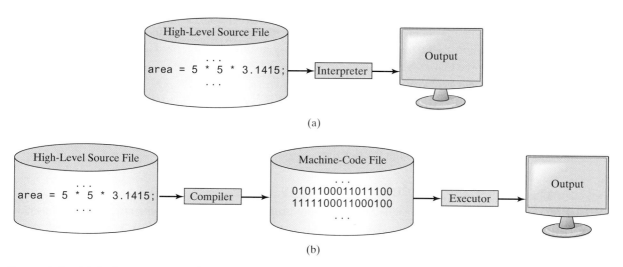

FIGURE 1.4   (a) An interpreter translates and executes a program one statement at a time. (b) A compiler translates the entire source program into a machine-language file for execution.

1.4 Operating Systems

The operating system (OS) is the most important program that runs on a computer. The OS manages and controls a computer's activities.

operating system (OS)

The popular *operating systems* for general-purpose computers are Microsoft Windows, Mac OS, and Linux. Application programs, such as a web browser or a word processor, cannot run unless an operating system is installed and running on the computer. Figure 1.5 shows the interrelationship of hardware, operating system, application software, and the user.

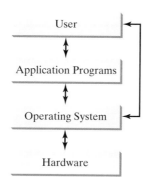

FIGURE 1.5   Users and applications access the computer's hardware via the operating system.

The major tasks of an operating system are as follows:

■ Controlling and monitoring system activities

■ Allocating and assigning system resources

■ Scheduling operations

1.4.1 Controlling and Monitoring System Activities

Operating systems perform basic tasks, such as recognizing input from the keyboard, sending output to the monitor, keeping track of files and folders on storage devices, and controlling peripheral devices such as disk drives and printers. An operating system must also ensure different programs and users working at the same time do not interfere with each other. In addition, the OS is responsible for security, ensuring unauthorized users and programs are not allowed to access the system.

1.4.2 Allocating and Assigning System Resources

The operating system is responsible for determining what computer resources a program needs (such as CPU time, memory space, disks, and input and output devices) and for allocating and assigning them to run the program.

1.4.3 Scheduling Operations

The OS is responsible for scheduling programs' activities to make efficient use of system resources. Many of today's operating systems support techniques such as *multiprogramming*, *multithreading*, and *multiprocessing* to increase system performance.

multiprogramming
multithreading
multiprocessing

Multiprogramming allows multiple programs such as Microsoft Word, E-mail, and web browser to run simultaneously by sharing the same CPU. The CPU is much faster than the computer's other components. As a result, it is idle most of the time—for example, while waiting for data to be transferred from a disk or waiting for other system resources to respond. A multiprogramming OS takes advantage of this situation by allowing multiple programs to use the CPU when it would otherwise be idle. For example, multiprogramming enables you to use a word processor to edit a file at the same time as your web browser is downloading a file.

Multithreading allows a single program to execute multiple tasks at the same time. For instance, a word-processing program allows users to simultaneously edit text and save it to a disk. In this example, editing and saving are two tasks within the same program. These two tasks may run concurrently.

Multiprocessing is similar to multithreading. The difference is that multithreading is for running multithreads concurrently within one program, but multiprocessing is for running multiple programs concurrently using multiple processors.

1.4.1 What is an operating system? List some popular operating systems.

1.4.2 What are the major responsibilities of an operating system?

1.4.3 What are multiprogramming, multithreading, and multiprocessing?

1.5 Java, the World Wide Web, and Beyond

Java is a powerful and versatile programming language for developing software running on mobile devices, desktop computers, and servers.

This book introduces Java programming. Java was developed by a team led by James Gosling at Sun Microsystems. Sun Microsystems was purchased by Oracle in 2010. Originally called *Oak,* Java was designed in 1991 for use in embedded chips in consumer electronic appliances.

In 1995, renamed *Java*, it was redesigned for developing web applications. For the history of Java, see www.java.com/en/javahistory/index.jsp.

Java has become enormously popular. Its rapid rise and wide acceptance can be traced to its design characteristics, particularly its promise that you can write a program once and run it anywhere. As stated by its designer, Java is *simple, object oriented, distributed, interpreted, robust, secure, architecture neutral, portable, high performance, multithreaded,* and *dynamic.* For the anatomy of Java characteristics, see liveexample.pearsoncmg.com/etc/JavaCharacteristics.pdf.

Java is a full-featured, general-purpose programming language that can be used to develop robust mission-critical applications. Today, it is employed not only for web programming but also for developing stand-alone applications across platforms on servers, desktop computers, and mobile devices. It was used to develop the code to communicate with and control the robotic rover on Mars. Many companies that once considered Java to be more hype than substance are now using it to create distributed applications accessed by customers and partners across the Internet. For every new project being developed today, companies are asking how they can use Java to make their work easier.

The World Wide Web is an electronic information repository that can be accessed on the Internet from anywhere in the world. The Internet, the Web's infrastructure, has been around for more than 40 years. The colorful World Wide Web and sophisticated web browsers are the major reason for the Internet's popularity.

Java initially became attractive because Java programs can run from a web browser. Such programs are called *applets.* Today applets are no longer allowed to run from a Web browser in the latest version of Java due to security issues. Java, however, is now very popular for developing applications on web servers. These applications process data, perform computations, and generate dynamic webpages. Many commercial Websites are developed using Java on the backend.

Java is a versatile programming language: You can use it to develop applications for desktop computers, servers, and small handheld devices. The software for Android cell phones is developed using Java.

1.5.1 Who invented Java? Which company owns Java now?

1.5.2 What is a Java applet?

1.5.3 What programming language does Android use?

Check
Point

1.6 The Java Language Specification, API, JDK, JRE, and IDE

Java syntax is defined in the Java language specification, and the Java library is defined in the Java application program interface (API). The JDK is the software for compiling and running Java programs. An IDE is an integrated development environment for rapidly developing programs.

Key
Point

Computer languages have strict rules of usage. If you do not follow the rules when writing a program, the computer will not be able to understand it. The Java language specification and the Java API define the Java standards.

The *Java language specification* is a technical definition of the Java programming language's syntax and semantics. You can find the complete Java language specification at docs.oracle.com/javase/specs/.

Java language specification

The *application program interface (API)*, also known as *library*, contains predefined classes and interfaces for developing Java programs. The API is still expanding. You can view and download the latest version of the Java API at download.java.net/jdk8/docs/api/.

API
library

Java is a full-fledged and powerful language that can be used in many ways. It comes in three editions:

Java SE, EE, and ME

- *Java Standard Edition (Java SE)* to develop client-side applications. The applications can run on desktop.

- *Java Enterprise Edition (Java EE)* to develop server-side applications, such as Java servlets, JavaServer Pages (JSP), and JavaServer Faces (JSF).

- *Java Micro Edition (Java ME)* to develop applications for mobile devices, such as cell phones.

Java Development
Toolkit (JDK)

JDK 1.8 = JDK 8

Java Runtime Environment
(JRE)

Integrated development
environment

This book uses Java SE to introduce Java programming. Java SE is the foundation upon which all other Java technology is based. There are many versions of Java SE. The latest, Java SE 8, is used in this book. Oracle releases each version with a *Java Development Toolkit (JDK)*. For Java SE 8, the Java Development Toolkit is called *JDK 1.8* (also known as *Java 8* or *JDK 8*).

The JDK consists of a set of separate programs, each invoked from a command line, for compiling, running, and testing Java programs. The program for running Java programs is known as *JRE (Java Runtime Environment)*. Instead of using the JDK, you can use a Java development tool (e.g., NetBeans, Eclipse, and TextPad)—software that provides an *integrated development environment (IDE)* for developing Java programs quickly. Editing, compiling, building, debugging, and online help are integrated in one graphical user interface. You simply enter source code in one window or open an existing file in a window, and then click a button or menu item or press a function key to compile and run the program.

1.6.1 What is the Java language specification?

1.6.2 What does JDK stand for? What does JRE stand for?

1.6.3 What does IDE stand for?

1.6.4 Are tools like NetBeans and Eclipse different languages from Java, or are they dialects or extensions of Java?

1.7 A Simple Java Program

A Java program is executed from the main *method in the class.*

Let's begin with a simple Java program that displays the message `Welcome to Java!` on the console. (The word *console* is an old computer term that refers to the text entry and display device of a computer. *Console input* means to receive input from the keyboard, and *console output* means to display output on the monitor.) The program is given in Listing 1.1.

what is a console?
console input
console output

LISTING 1.1 Welcome.java

class
main method
display message

```
1  public class Welcome {
2    public static void main(String[] args) {
3      // Display message Welcome to Java! on the console
4      System.out.println("Welcome to Java!");
5    }
6  }
```

VideoNote
Your first Java program

```
Welcome to Java!
```

line numbers

Note the *line numbers* are for reference purposes only; they are not part of the program. So, don't type line numbers in your program.

Line 1 defines a class. Every Java program must have at least one class. Each class has a name. By convention, *class names* start with an uppercase letter. In this example, the class name is `Welcome`.

class name

Line 2 defines the `main` method. The program is executed from the `main` method. A class may contain several methods. The `main` method is the entry point where the program begins execution.

main method

A method is a construct that contains statements. The `main` method in this program contains the `System.out.println` statement. This statement displays the string `Welcome to Java!` on the console (line 4). *String* is a programming term meaning a sequence of characters. A string must be enclosed in double quotation marks. Every statement in Java ends with a semicolon (;), known as the *statement terminator.*

string

statement terminator

Reserved words, or *keywords*, have a specific meaning to the compiler and cannot be used for other purposes in the program. For example, when the compiler sees the word `class`, it understands that the word after `class` is the name for the class. Other reserved words in this program are `public`, `static`, and `void`.

reserved word

keyword

Line 3 is a *comment* that documents what the program is and how it is constructed. Comments help programmers to communicate and understand the program. They are not programming statements, and thus are ignored by the compiler. In Java, comments are preceded by two slashes (//) on a line, called a *line comment,* or enclosed between /* and */ on one or several lines, called a *block comment* or *paragraph comment.* When the compiler sees //, it ignores all text after // on the same line. When it sees /*, it scans for the next */ and ignores any text between /* and */. Here are examples of comments:

comment

line comment

block comment

```
// This application program displays Welcome to Java!
/* This application program displays Welcome to Java! */
/* This application program
   displays Welcome to Java! */
```

A pair of braces in a program forms a *block* that groups the program's components. In Java, each block begins with an opening brace ({) and ends with a closing brace (}). Every class has a *class block* that groups the data and methods of the class. Similarly, every method has a *method block* that groups the statements in the method. Blocks can be *nested*, meaning that one block can be placed within another, as shown in the following code:

block

```
public class Welcome {
    public static void main(String[] args) {                Class block
        System.out.println("Welcome to Java!");  Method block
    }
}
```

Tip
An opening brace must be matched by a closing brace. Whenever you type an opening brace, immediately type a closing brace to prevent the missing-brace error. Most Java IDEs automatically insert the closing brace for each opening brace.

match braces

Caution
Java source programs are case sensitive. It would be wrong, for example, to replace `main` in the program with `Main`.

case sensitive

You have seen several special characters (e.g., { }, //, ;) in the program. They are used in almost every program. Table 1.2 summarizes their uses.

special characters

The most common errors you will make as you learn to program will be syntax errors. Like any programming language, Java has its own syntax, and you need to write code that conforms

common errors

TABLE 1.2 Special Characters

Character	Name	Description
{}	Opening and closing braces	Denote a block to enclose statements.
()	Opening and closing parentheses	Used with methods.
[]	Opening and closing brackets	Denote an array.
//	Double slashes	Precede a comment line.
""	Opening and closing quotation marks	Enclose a string (i.e., sequence of characters).
;	Semicolon	Mark the end of a statement.

syntax rules

to the *syntax rules.* If your program violates a rule—for example, if the semicolon is missing, a brace is missing, a quotation mark is missing, or a word is misspelled—the Java compiler will report syntax errors. Try to compile the program with these errors and see what the compiler reports.

Note
You are probably wondering why the `main` method is defined this way and why `System.out.println(...)` is used to display a message on the console. *For the time being, simply accept that this is how things are done.* Your questions will be fully answered in subsequent chapters.

The program in Listing 1.1 displays one message. Once you understand the program, it is easy to extend it to display more messages. For example, you can rewrite the program to display three messages, as shown in Listing 1.2.

LISTING 1.2 WelcomeWithThreeMessages.java

class
main method
display message

```
1  public class WelcomeWithThreeMessages {
2    public static void main(String[] args) {
3      System.out.println("Programming is fun!");
4      System.out.println("Fundamentals First");
5      System.out.println("Problem Driven");
6    }
7  }
```

```
Programming is fun!
Fundamentals First
Problem Driven
```

Further, you can perform mathematical computations and display the result on the console. Listing 1.3 gives an example of evaluating $\frac{10.5 + 2 \times 3}{45 - 3.5}$.

LISTING 1.3 ComputeExpression.java

class
main method
compute expression

```
1  public class ComputeExpression {
2    public static void main(String[] args) {
3      System.out.print("(10.5 + 2 * 3) / (45 - 3.5) = ");
4      System.out.println((10.5 + 2 * 3) / (45 - 3.5));
5    }
6  }
```

```
(10.5 + 2 * 3) / (45 - 3.5) = 0.39759036144578314
```

The `print` method in line 3

print vs. println

```
System.out.print("(10.5 + 2 * 3) / (45 - 3.5) = ");
```

is identical to the `println` method except that `println` moves to the beginning of the next line after displaying the string, but `print` does not advance to the next line when completed.

The multiplication operator in Java is `*`. As you can see, it is a straightforward process to translate an arithmetic expression to a Java expression. We will discuss Java expressions further in Chapter 2.

1.7.1 What is a keyword? List some Java keywords.

Check Point

1.7.2 Is Java case sensitive? What is the case for Java keywords?

1.7.3 What is a comment? Is the comment ignored by the compiler? How do you denote a comment line and a comment paragraph?

1.7.4 What is the statement to display a string on the console?

1.7.5 Show the output of the following code:

```java
public class Test {
  public static void main(String[] args) {
    System.out.println("3.5 * 4 / 2 - 2.5 is ");
    System.out.println(3.5 * 4 / 2 - 2.5);
  }
}
```

1.8 Creating, Compiling, and Executing a Java Program

You save a Java program in a .java file and compile it into a .class file. The .class file is executed by the Java Virtual Machine (JVM).

Key Point

You have to create your program and compile it before it can be executed. This process is repetitive, as shown in Figure 1.6. If your program has compile errors, you have to modify the program to fix them, then recompile it. If your program has runtime errors or does not produce the correct result, you have to modify the program, recompile it, and execute it again.

You can use any text editor or IDE to create and edit a Java source-code file. This section demonstrates how to create, compile, and run Java programs from a command window. Sections 1.11 and 1.12 will introduce developing Java programs using NetBeans and Eclipse. From the command window, you can use a text editor such as Notepad to create the Java source-code file, as shown in Figure 1.7.

command window

Note
The source file must end with the extension `.java` and must have the same exact name as the public class name. For example, the file for the source code in Listing 1.1 should be named **Welcome.java**, since the public class name is `Welcome`.

file name Welcome.java,

A Java compiler translates a Java source file into a Java bytecode file. The following command compiles **Welcome.java**:

compile

```
javac Welcome.java
```

Note
You must first install and configure the JDK before you can compile and run programs. See Supplement I.B, Installing and Configuring JDK 8, for how to install the JDK and set up the environment to compile and run Java programs. If you have trouble compiling and running programs, see Supplement I.C, Compiling and Running Java from the Command Window. This supplement also explains how to use basic DOS commands and how to use Windows Notepad to create and edit files. All the supplements are accessible from the Companion Website.

Supplement I.B

Supplement I.C

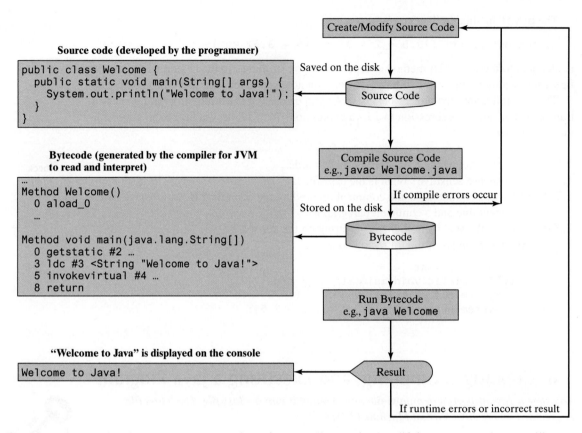

FIGURE 1.6 The Java program-development process consists of repeatedly creating/modifying source code, compiling, and executing programs.

FIGURE 1.7 You can create a Java source file using Windows Notepad.

.class bytecode file

bytecode
Java Virtual Machine (JVM)

interpret bytecode

If there aren't any syntax errors, the *compiler* generates a bytecode file with a `.class` extension. Thus, the preceding command generates a file named **Welcome.class**, as shown in Figure 1.8a. The Java language is a high-level language, but Java bytecode is a low-level language. The *bytecode* is similar to machine instructions but is architecture neutral and can run on any platform that has a *Java Virtual Machine (JVM)*, as shown in Figure 1.8b. Rather than a physical machine, the virtual machine is a program that interprets Java bytecode. This is one of Java's primary advantages: *Java bytecode can run on a variety of hardware platforms and operating systems.* Java source code is compiled into Java bytecode, and Java bytecode is interpreted by the JVM. Your Java code may use the code in the Java library. The JVM executes your code along with the code in the library.

To execute a Java program is to run the program's bytecode. You can execute the bytecode on any platform with a JVM, which is an interpreter. It translates the individual instructions in the bytecode into the target machine language code one at a time, rather than the whole program as a single unit. Each step is executed immediately after it is translated.

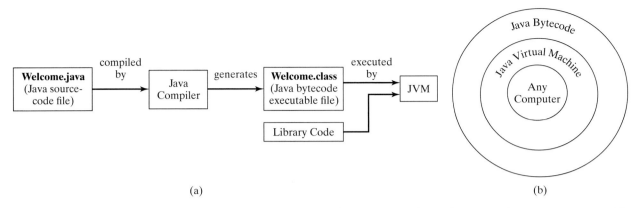

FIGURE 1.8 (a) Java source code is translated into bytecode. (b) Java bytecode can be executed on any computer with a Java Virtual Machine.

The following command runs the bytecode for Listing 1.1:

`run`

```
java Welcome
```

Figure 1.9 shows the `javac` command for compiling **Welcome.java**. The compiler generates the **Welcome.class** file, and this file is executed using the `java` command.

`javac command`
`java command`

 Note
For simplicity and consistency, all source-code and class files used in this book are placed under **c:\book** unless specified otherwise.

`c:\book`

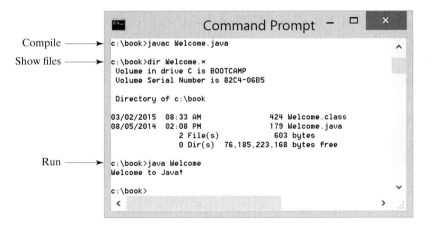

VideoNote

Compile and run a Java program

FIGURE 1.9 The output of Listing 1.1 displays the message "Welcome to Java!"

 Caution
Do not use the extension `.class` in the command line when executing the program. Use `java ClassName` to run the program. If you use `java ClassName.class` in the command line, the system will attempt to fetch `ClassName.class.class`.

`java ClassName`

 Tip
If you execute a class file that does not exist, a `NoClassDefFoundError` will occur. If you execute a class file that does not have a `main` method or you mistype the `main` method (e.g., by typing `Main` instead of `main`), a `NoSuchMethodError` will occur.

`NoClassDefFoundError`

`NoSuchMethodError`

class loader

bytecode verifier

Note

When executing a Java program, the JVM first loads the bytecode of the class to memory using a program called the *class loader*. If your program uses other classes, the class loader dynamically loads them just before they are needed. After a class is loaded, the JVM uses a program called the *bytecode verifier* to check the validity of the bytecode and to ensure that the bytecode does not violate Java's security restrictions. Java enforces strict security to make sure Java class files are not tampered with and do not harm your computer.

use package

Pedagogical Note

Your instructor may require you to use packages for organizing programs. For example, you may place all programs in this chapter in a package named *chapter1*. For instructions on how to use packages, see Supplement I.F, Using Packages to Organize the Classes in the Text.

Check Point

1.8.1 What is the Java source filename extension, and what is the Java bytecode filename extension?

1.8.2 What are the input and output of a Java compiler?

1.8.3 What is the command to compile a Java program?

1.8.4 What is the command to run a Java program?

1.8.5 What is the JVM?

1.8.6 Can Java run on any machine? What is needed to run Java on a computer?

1.8.7 If a `NoClassDefFoundError` occurs when you run a program, what is the cause of the error?

1.8.8 If a `NoSuchMethodError` occurs when you run a program, what is the cause of the error?

1.9 Programming Style and Documentation

Key Point

Good programming style and proper documentation make a program easy to read and help programmers prevent errors.

programming style
documentation

Programming style deals with what programs look like. A program can compile and run properly even if written on only one line, but writing it all on one line would be bad programming style because it would be hard to read. *Documentation* is the body of explanatory remarks and comments pertaining to a program. Programming style and documentation are as important as coding. Good programming style and appropriate documentation reduce the chance of errors and make programs easy to read. This section gives several guidelines. For more detailed guidelines, see Supplement I.D, Java Coding Style Guidelines, on the Companion Website.

1.9.1 Appropriate Comments and Comment Styles

Include a summary at the beginning of the program that explains what the program does, its key features, and any unique techniques it uses. In a long program, you should also include comments that introduce each major step and explain anything that is difficult to read. It is important to make comments concise so that they do not crowd the program or make it difficult to read.

javadoc comment

In addition to line comments (beginning with `//`) and block comments (beginning with `/*`), Java supports comments of a special type, referred to as *javadoc comments*. javadoc comments begin with `/**` and end with `*/`. They can be extracted into an HTML file using the JDK's `javadoc` command. For more information, see Supplement III.Y, javadoc Comments, on the Companion Website.

Use javadoc comments (/** . . . */) for commenting on an entire class or an entire method. These comments must precede the class or the method header in order to be extracted into a javadoc HTML file. For commenting on steps inside a method, use line comments (//). To see an example of a javadoc HTML file, check out liveexample.pearsoncmg.com/javadoc/Exercise1.html. Its corresponding Java code is shown in liveexample.pearsoncmg.com/java-doc/Exercise1.txt.

1.9.2 Proper Indentation and Spacing

A consistent indentation style makes programs clear and easy to read, debug, and maintain. *Indentation* is used to illustrate the structural relationships between a program's components or statements. Java can read the program even if all of the statements are on the same long line, but humans find it easier to read and maintain code that is aligned properly. Indent each subcomponent or statement at least *two* spaces more than the construct within which it is nested.

indent code

A single space should be added on both sides of a binary operator, as shown in (a), rather in (b).

```
System.out.println(3 + 4 * 4);
```
(a) Good style

```
System.out.println(3+4*4);
```
(b) Bad style

1.9.3 Block Styles

A *block* is a group of statements surrounded by braces. There are two popular styles, *next-line* style and *end-of-line* style, as shown below.

```
public class Test
{
  public static void main(String[] args)
  {
    System.out.println("Block Styles");
  }
}
```
Next-line style

```
public class Test {
  public static void main(String[] args) {
    System.out.println("Block Styles");
  }
}
```
End-of-line style

The next-line style aligns braces vertically and makes programs easy to read, whereas the end-of-line style saves space and may help avoid some subtle programming errors. Both are acceptable block styles. The choice depends on personal or organizational preference. You should use a block style consistently—mixing styles is not recommended. This book uses the *end-of-line* style to be consistent with the Java API source code.

1.9.1 Reformat the following program according to the programming style and documentation guidelines. Use the end-of-line brace style.

Check Point

```
public class Test
{
  // Main method
  public static void main(String[] args) {
  /** Display output */
  System.out.println("Welcome to Java");
  }
}
```

1.10 Programming Errors

Programming errors can be categorized into three types: syntax errors, runtime errors, and logic errors.

1.10.1 Syntax Errors

syntax errors

compile errors

Errors that are detected by the compiler are called *syntax errors* or *compile errors*. Syntax errors result from errors in code construction, such as mistyping a keyword, omitting some necessary punctuation, or using an opening brace without a corresponding closing brace. These errors are usually easy to detect because the compiler tells you where they are and what caused them. For example, the program in Listing 1.4 has a syntax error, as shown in Figure 1.10.

LISTING 1.4 ShowSyntaxErrors.java

```
1  public class ShowSyntaxErrors {
2    public static main(String[] args) {
3      System.out.println("Welcome to Java);
4    }
5  }
```

Four errors are reported, but the program actually has two errors:

- The keyword `void` is missing before `main` in line 2.

- The string `Welcome to Java` should be closed with a closing quotation mark in line 3.

Since a single error will often display many lines of compile errors, it is a good practice to fix errors from the top line and work downward. Fixing errors that occur earlier in the program may also fix additional errors that occur later.

Compile

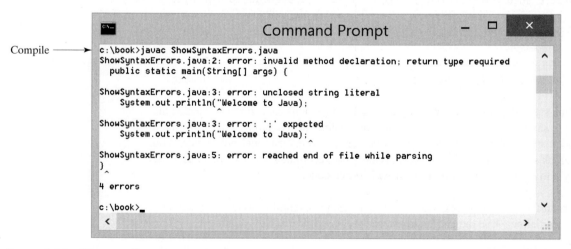

FIGURE 1.10 The compiler reports syntax errors.

Tip

fix syntax errors

If you don't know how to correct an error, compare your program closely, character by character, with similar examples in the text. In the first few weeks of this course, you will probably spend a lot of time fixing syntax errors. Soon you will be familiar with Java syntax, and can quickly fix syntax errors.

1.10.2 Runtime Errors

Runtime errors are errors that cause a program to terminate abnormally. They occur while a program is running if the environment detects an operation that is impossible to carry out. Input mistakes typically cause runtime errors. An *input error* occurs when the program is waiting for the user to enter a value, but the user enters a value that the program cannot handle. For instance, if the program expects to read in a number, but instead the user enters a string, this causes data-type errors to occur in the program.

runtime errors

Another example of runtime errors is division by zero. This happens when the divisor is zero for integer divisions. For instance, the program in Listing 1.5 would cause a runtime error, as shown in Figure 1.11.

LISTING 1.5 ShowRuntimeErrors.java

```
1  public class ShowRuntimeErrors {
2    public static void main(String[] args) {
3      System.out.println(1 / 0);
4    }
5  }
```

runtime error

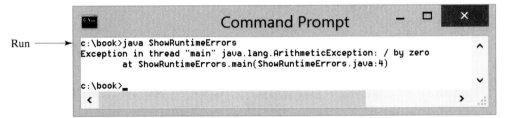

Run ⟶

FIGURE 1.11 The runtime error causes the program to terminate abnormally.

1.10.3 Logic Errors

Logic errors occur when a program does not perform the way it was intended to. Errors of this kind occur for many different reasons. For example, suppose you wrote the program in Listing 1.6 to convert Celsius 35 degrees to a Fahrenheit degree:

logic errors

LISTING 1.6 ShowLogicErrors.java

```
1  public class ShowLogicErrors {
2    public static void main(String[] args) {
3      System.out.print("Celsius 35 is Fahrenheit degree ");
4      System.out.println((9 / 5) * 35 + 32);
5    }
6  }
```

```
Celsius 35 is Fahrenheit degree 67
```

You will get Fahrenheit 67 degrees, which is wrong. It should be 95.0. In Java, the division for integers is the quotient—the fractional part is truncated—so in Java 9 / 5 is 1. To get the correct result, you need to use 9.0 / 5, which results in 1.8.

In general, syntax errors are easy to find and easy to correct because the compiler gives indications as to where the errors came from and why they are wrong. Runtime errors are not difficult to find, either, since the reasons and locations for the errors are displayed on the console when the program aborts. Finding logic errors, on the other hand, can be very challenging. In the upcoming chapters, you will learn the techniques of tracing programs and finding logic errors.

1.10.4 Common Errors

Missing a closing brace, missing a semicolon, missing quotation marks for strings, and misspelling names are common errors for new programmers.

Common Error 1: Missing Braces

The braces are used to denote a block in the program. Each opening brace must be matched by a closing brace. A common error is missing the closing brace. To avoid this error, type a closing brace whenever an opening brace is typed, as shown in the following example:

```
public class Welcome {

}          Type this closing brace right away to match the opening brace.
```

If you use an IDE such as NetBeans and Eclipse, the IDE automatically inserts a closing brace for each opening brace typed.

Common Error 2: Missing Semicolons

Each statement ends with a statement terminator (;). Often, a new programmer forgets to place a statement terminator for the last statement in a block, as shown in the following example:

```
public static void main(String[] args) {
   System.out.println("Programming is fun!");
   System.out.println("Fundamentals First");
   System.out.println("Problem Driven")
}                                       ↑
                               Missing a semicolon
```

Common Error 3: Missing Quotation Marks

A string must be placed inside the quotation marks. Often, a new programmer forgets to place a quotation mark at the end of a string, as shown in the following example:

```
System.out.println("Problem Driven);
                          ↑
                  Missing a quotation mark
```

If you use an IDE such as NetBeans and Eclipse, the IDE automatically inserts a closing quotation mark for each opening quotation mark typed.

Common Error 4: Misspelling Names

Java is case sensitive. Misspelling names is a common error for new programmers. For example, the word `main` is misspelled as `Main` and `String` is misspelled as `string` in the following code:

```
1  public class Test {
2    public static void Main(string[] args) {
3      System.out.println((10.5 + 2 * 3) / (45 - 3.5));
4    }
5  }
```

Check Point

1.10.1 What are syntax errors (compile errors), runtime errors, and logic errors?

1.10.2 Give examples of syntax errors, runtime errors, and logic errors.

1.10.3 If you forget to put a closing quotation mark on a string, what kind error of will be raised?

1.10.4 If your program needs to read integers, but the user entered strings, an error would occur when running this program. What kind of error is this?

1.10.5 Suppose you write a program for computing the perimeter of a rectangle and you mistakenly write your program so it computes the area of a rectangle. What kind of error is this?

1.10.6 Identify and fix the errors in the following code:

```
1  public class Welcome {
2    public void Main(String[] args) {
3      System.out.println('Welcome to Java!);
4    }
5  )
```

Note

Section 1.8 introduced developing programs from the command line. Many of our readers also use an IDE. The following two sections introduce two most popular Java IDEs: NetBeans and Eclipse. These two sections may be skipped.

1.11 Developing Java Programs Using NetBeans

You can edit, compile, run, and debug Java Programs using NetBeans.

NetBeans and Eclipse are two free popular integrated development environments for developing Java programs. They are easy to learn if you follow simple instructions. We recommend that you use either one for developing Java programs. This section gives the essential instructions to guide new users to create a project, create a class, compile, and run a class in NetBeans. The use of Eclipse will be introduced in the next section. For instructions on downloading and installing latest version of NetBeans, see Supplement II.B.

Key Point

VideoNote

NetBeans brief tutorial

1.11.1 Creating a Java Project

Before you can create Java programs, you need to first create a project. A project is like a folder to hold Java programs and all supporting files. You need to create a project only once. Here are the steps to create a Java project:

1. Choose *File*, *New Project* to display the New Project dialog box, as shown in Figure 1.12.

2. Select Java in the Categories section and Java Application in the Projects section, and then click *Next* to display the New Java Application dialog box, as shown in Figure 1.13.

3. Type demo in the Project Name field and c:\michael in Project Location field. Uncheck *Use Dedicated Folder for Storing Libraries* and uncheck *Create Main Class*.

4. Click *Finish* to create the project, as shown in Figure 1.14.

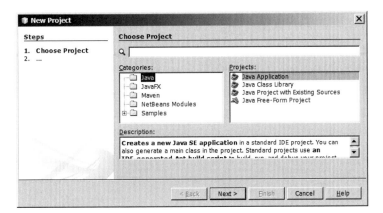

FIGURE 1.12 The New Project dialog is used to create a new project and specify a project type. *Source*: Copyright © 1995–2016 Oracle and/or its affiliates. All rights reserved. Used with permission.

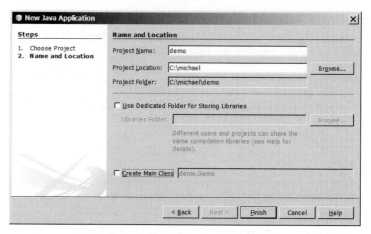

FIGURE 1.13 The New Java Application dialog is for specifying a project name and location. *Source*: Copyright © 1995–2016 Oracle and/or its affiliates. All rights reserved. Used with permission.

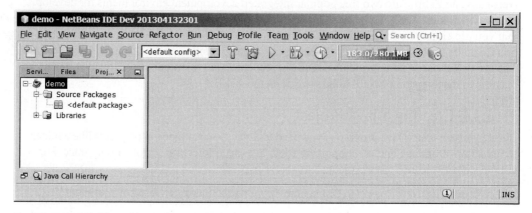

FIGURE 1.14 A New Java project named demo is created. *Source*: Copyright © 1995–2016 Oracle and/or its affiliates. All rights reserved. Used with permission.

1.11.2 Creating a Java Class

After a project is created, you can create Java programs in the project using the following steps:

1. Right-click the demo node in the project pane to display a context menu. Choose *New*, *Java Class* to display the New Java Class dialog box, as shown in Figure 1.15.

2. Type `Welcome` in the Class Name field and select the Source Packages in the Location field. Leave the Package field blank. This will create a class in the default package.

3. Click *Finish* to create the Welcome class. The source-code file **Welcome.java** is placed under the <default package> node.

4. Modify the code in the Welcome class to match Listing 1.1 in the text, as shown in Figure 1.16.

1.11.3 Compiling and Running a Class

To run **Welcome.java**, right-click **Welcome.java** to display a context menu and choose *Run File*, or simply press Shift + F6. The output is displayed in the Output pane, as shown in Figure 1.16. The *Run File* command automatically compiles the program if the program has been changed.

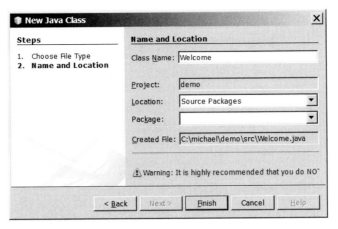

FIGURE 1.15 The New Java Class dialog box is used to create a new Java class. *Source*: Copyright © 1995–2016 Oracle and/or its affiliates. All rights reserved. Used with permission.

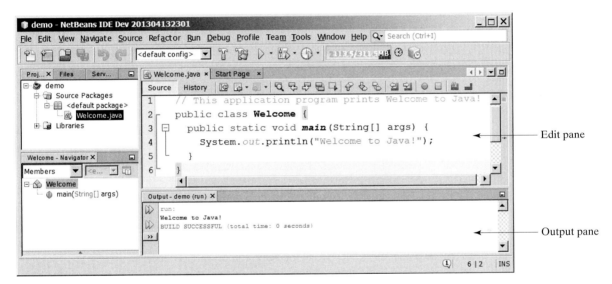

FIGURE 1.16 You can edit a program and run it in NetBeans. *Source*: Copyright © 1995–2016 Oracle and/or its affiliates. All rights reserved. Used with permission.

1.12 Developing Java Programs Using Eclipse

You can edit, compile, run, and debug Java Programs using Eclipse.

The preceding section introduced developing Java programs using NetBeans. You can also use Eclipse to develop Java programs. This section gives the essential instructions to guide new users to create a project, create a class, and compile/run a class in Eclipse. For instructions on downloading and installing latest version of Eclipse, see Supplement II.D.

Key Point

1.12.1 Creating a Java Project

Before creating Java programs in Eclipse, you need to first create a project to hold all files. Here are the steps to create a Java project in Eclipse:

1. Choose *File*, *New*, *Java Project* to display the New Project wizard, as shown in Figure 1.17.

2. Type demo in the Project name field. As you type, the Location field is automatically set by default. You may customize the location for your project.

VideoNote

Eclipse brief tutorial

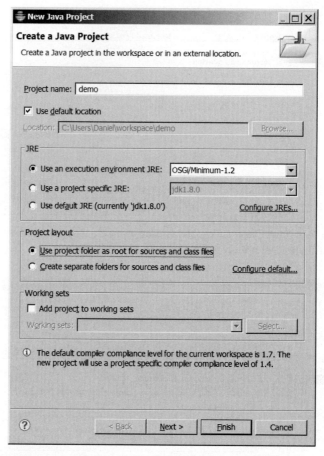

FIGURE 1.17 The New Java Project dialog is for specifying a project name and the properties. *Source*: Eclipse Foundation, Inc.

3. Make sure you selected the options *Use project folder as root for sources and class files* so the .java and .class files are in the same folder for easy access.

4. Click *Finish* to create the project, as shown in Figure 1.18.

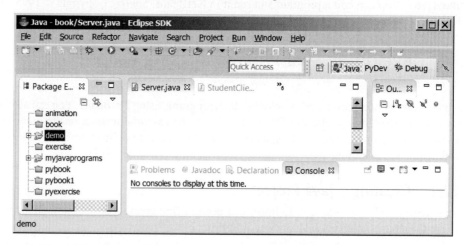

FIGURE 1.18 A New Java project named demo is created. *Source*: Eclipse Foundation, Inc.

1.12.2   Creating a Java Class

After a project is created, you can create Java programs in the project using the following steps:

1. Choose *File*, *New*, *Class* to display the New Java Class wizard.

2. Type `Welcome` in the Name field.

3. Check the option *public static void main(String[] args)*.

4. Click *Finish* to generate the template for the source code **Welcome.java**, as shown in Figure 1.19.

1.12.3   Compiling and Running a Class

To run the program, right-click the class in the project to display a context menu. Choose *Run*, *Java Application* in the context menu to run the class. The output is displayed in the Console pane, as shown in Figure 1.20. The *Run* command automatically compiles the program if the program has been changed.

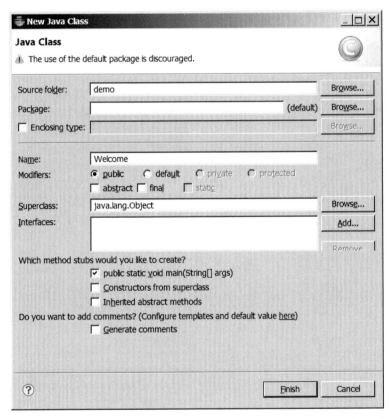

FIGURE 1.19   The New Java Class dialog box is used to create a new Java class. *Source*: Eclipse Foundation, Inc.

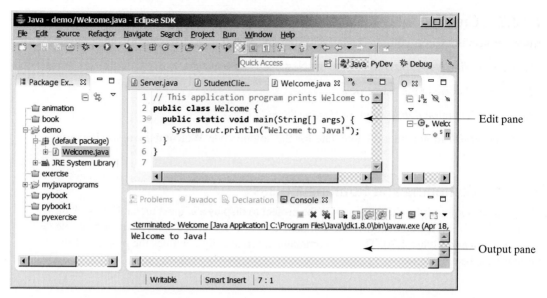

FIGURE 1.20 You can edit a program and run it in Eclipse. *Source*: Eclipse Foundation, Inc.

KEY TERMS

Application Program Interface (API) 11	Java Runtime Environment (JRE) 12
assembler 7	Java Virtual Machine (JVM) 16
assembly language 7	`javac` command 17
bit 3	keyword (or reserved word) 13
block 13	library 11
block comment 13	line comment 13
bus 2	logic error 21
byte 3	low-level language 8
bytecode 16	machine language 7
bytecode verifier 18	`main` method 13
cable modem 6	memory 4
central processing unit (CPU) 3	dial-up modem 6
class loader 18	motherboard 3
comment 13	network interface card (NIC) 6
compiler 8	operating system (OS) 9
console 12	pixel 6
dot pitch 6	program 2
DSL (digital subscriber line) 6	programming 2
encoding scheme 3	runtime error 21
hardware 2	screen resolution 6
high-level language 8	software 2
integrated development environment (IDE) 12	source code 8
	source program 8
interpreter 8	statement 8
`java` command 17	statement terminator 13
Java Development Toolkit (JDK) 12	storage devices 4
Java language specification 11	syntax error 20

Supplement I.A

Note
The above terms are defined in this chapter. Supplement I.A, Glossary, lists all the key terms and descriptions in the book, organized by chapters.

CHAPTER SUMMARY

1. A computer is an electronic device that stores and processes data.

2. A computer includes both *hardware* and *software.*

3. Hardware is the physical aspect of the computer that can be touched.

4. Computer *programs*, known as *software*, are the invisible instructions that control the hardware and make it perform tasks.

5. Computer *programming* is the writing of instructions (i.e., code) for computers to perform.

6. The *central processing unit (CPU)* is a computer's brain. It retrieves instructions from *memory* and executes them.

7. Computers use zeros and ones because digital devices have two stable states, referred to by convention as zero and one.

8. A *bit* is a binary digit 0 or 1.

9. A *byte* is a sequence of 8 bits.

10. A kilobyte is about 1,000 bytes, a megabyte about 1 million bytes, a gigabyte about 1 billion bytes, and a terabyte about 1,000 gigabytes.

11. Memory stores data and program instructions for the CPU to execute.

12. A memory unit is an ordered sequence of bytes.

13. Memory is volatile, because information is lost when the power is turned off.

14. Programs and data are permanently stored on *storage devices* and are moved to memory when the computer actually uses them.

15. The *machine language* is a set of primitive instructions built into every computer.

16. *Assembly language* is a *low-level programming language* in which a mnemonic is used to represent each machine-language instruction.

17. *High-level languages* are English-like and easy to learn and program.

18. A program written in a high-level language is called a *source program.*

19. A *compiler* is a software program that translates the source program into a *machine-language program.*

20. The *operating system (OS)* is a program that manages and controls a computer's activities.

21. Java is platform independent, meaning you can write a program once and run it on any computer.

22. The Java source file name must match the public class name in the program. Java source-code files must end with the `.java` extension.

23. Every class is compiled into a separate bytecode file that has the same name as the class and ends with the `.class` extension.

24. To compile a Java source-code file from the command line, use the `javac` command.

25. To run a Java class from the command line, use the `java` command.

26. Every Java program is a set of class definitions. The keyword `class` introduces a class definition. The contents of the class are included in a *block*.

27. A block begins with an opening brace (`{`) and ends with a closing brace (`}`).

28. Methods are contained in a class. To run a Java program, the program must have a `main` method. The `main` method is the entry point where the program starts when it is executed.

29. Every *statement* in Java ends with a semicolon (`;`), known as the *statement terminator*.

30. *Reserved words,* or *keywords,* have a specific meaning to the compiler and cannot be used for other purposes in the program.

31. In Java, comments are preceded by two slashes (`//`) on a line, called a *line comment,* or enclosed between `/*` and `*/` on one or several lines, called a *block comment* or *paragraph comment.* Comments are ignored by the compiler.

32. Java source programs are case sensitive.

33. Programming errors can be categorized into three types: *syntax errors*, *runtime errors*, and *logic errors.* Errors reported by a compiler are called syntax errors or *compile errors.* Runtime errors are errors that cause a program to terminate abnormally. Logic errors occur when a program does not perform the way it was intended to.

QUIZ

Answer the quiz for this chapter at www.pearsonhighered.com/liang. Choose this book and click Companion Website to select Quiz.

MyProgrammingLab™   **PROGRAMMING EXERCISES**

 Pedagogical Note

We cannot stress enough the importance of learning programming through exercises. For this reason, the book provides a large number of programming exercises at various levels of difficulty. The problems cover many application areas, including math, science, business, financial, gaming, animation, and multimedia. Solutions to most even-numbered programming exercises are on the Companion Website. Solutions to most odd-numbered programming exercises are on the Instructor Resource Website. The level

level of difficulty   of difficulty is rated easy (no star), moderate (*****), hard (******), or challenging (*******).

1.1   (*Display three messages*) Write a program that displays `Welcome to Java`, `Welcome to Computer Science`, and `Programming is fun`.

1.2   (*Display five messages*) Write a program that displays `Welcome to Java` five times.

*1.3   (*Display a pattern*) Write a program that displays the following pattern:

1.4 (*Print a table*) Write a program that displays the following table:

```
a       a^2     a^3
1       1       1
2       4       8
3       9       27
4       16      64
```

1.5 (*Compute expressions*) Write a program that displays the result of
$$\frac{9.5 \times 4.5 - 2.5 \times 3}{45.5 - 3.5}.$$

1.6 (*Summation of a series*) Write a program that displays the result of
$$1 + 2 + 3 + 4 + 5 + 6 + 7 + 8 + 9.$$

1.7 (*Approximate* π) π can be computed using the following formula:
$$\pi = 4 \times \left(1 - \frac{1}{3} + \frac{1}{5} - \frac{1}{7} + \frac{1}{9} - \frac{1}{11} + \cdots\right)$$

Write a program that displays the result of $4 \times \left(1 - \frac{1}{3} + \frac{1}{5} - \frac{1}{7} + \frac{1}{9} - \frac{1}{11}\right)$
and $4 \times \left(1 - \frac{1}{3} + \frac{1}{5} - \frac{1}{7} + \frac{1}{9} - \frac{1}{11} + \frac{1}{13}\right)$. Use `1.0` instead of `1` in your program.

1.8 (*Area and perimeter of a circle*) Write a program that displays the area and perimeter of a circle that has a radius of `5.5` using the following formulas:
$$perimeter = 2 \times radius \times \pi$$
$$area = radius \times radius \times \pi$$

1.9 (*Area and perimeter of a rectangle*) Write a program that displays the area and perimeter of a rectangle with a width of `4.5` and a height of `7.9` using the following formula:
$$area = width \times height$$

1.10 (*Average speed in miles*) Assume that a runner runs `14` kilometers in `45` minutes and `30` seconds. Write a program that displays the average speed in miles per hour. (Note `1` mile is equal to `1.6` kilometers.)

*1.11 (*Population projection*) The U.S. Census Bureau projects population based on the following assumptions:

- One birth every 7 seconds
- One death every 13 seconds
- One new immigrant every 45 seconds

Write a program to display the population for each of the next five years. Assume that the current population is 312,032,486, and one year has 365 days. *Hint*: In Java, if two integers perform division, the result is an integer. The fractional part is truncated. For example, `5 / 4` is `1` (not `1.25`) and `10 / 4` is `2` (not `2.5`). To get an accurate result with the fractional part, one of the values involved in the division must be a number with a decimal point. For example, `5.0 / 4` is `1.25` and `10 / 4.0` is `2.5`.

1.12 (*Average speed in kilometers*) Assume that a runner runs `24` miles in `1` hour, `40` minutes, and `35` seconds. Write a program that displays the average speed in kilometers per hour. (Note `1` mile is equal to `1.6` kilometers.)

*1.13 (*Algebra: solve 2 × 2 linear equations*) You can use Cramer's rule to solve the following 2 × 2 system of linear equation provided that *ad* − *bc* is not 0:

$$ax + by = e \qquad x = \frac{ed - bf}{ad - bc} \qquad y = \frac{af - ec}{ad - bc}$$
$$cx + dy = f$$

Write a program that solves the following equation and displays the value for *x* and *y*: (Hint: replace the symbols in the formula with numbers to compute *x* and *y*. This exercise can be done in Chapter 1 without using materials in later chapters.)

$$3.4x + 50.2y = 44.5$$
$$2.1x + .55y = 5.9$$

Note
More than 200 additional programming exercises with solutions are provided to the instructors on the Instructor Resource Website.

ELEMENTARY PROGRAMMING

Objectives

- To write Java programs to perform simple computations (§2.2).
- To obtain input from the console using the `Scanner` class (§2.3).
- To use identifiers to name variables, constants, methods, and classes (§2.4).
- To use variables to store data (§§2.5 and 2.6).
- To program with assignment statements and assignment expressions (§2.6).
- To use constants to store permanent data (§2.7).
- To name classes, methods, variables, and constants by following their naming conventions (§2.8).
- To explore Java numeric primitive data types: `byte`, `short`, `int`, `long`, `float`, and `double` (§2.9.1).

- To read a `byte`, `short`, `int`, `long`, `float`, or `double` value from the keyboard (§2.9.2).
- To perform operations using operators `+`, `-`, `*`, `/`, and `%` (§2.9.3).
- To perform exponent operations using `Math.pow(a, b)` (§2.9.4).
- To write integer literals, floating-point literals, and literals in scientific notation (§2.10).
- To write and evaluate numeric expressions (§2.11).
- To obtain the current system time using `System.currentTimeMillis()` (§2.12).
- To use augmented assignment operators (§2.13).
- To distinguish between postincrement and preincrement and between postdecrement and predecrement (§2.14).
- To cast the value of one type to another type (§2.15).
- To describe the software development process and apply it to develop the loan payment program (§2.16).
- To write a program that converts a large amount of money into smaller units (§2.17).
- To avoid common errors and pitfalls in elementary programming (§2.18).

2.1 Introduction

The focus of this chapter is on learning elementary programming techniques to solve problems.

In Chapter 1, you learned how to create, compile, and run very basic Java programs. You will learn how to solve problems by writing programs. Through these problems, you will learn elementary programming using primitive data types, variables, constants, operators, expressions, and input and output.

Suppose, for example, you need to take out a student loan. Given the loan amount, loan term, and annual interest rate, can you write a program to compute the monthly payment and total payment? This chapter shows you how to write programs like this. Along the way, you will learn the basic steps that go into analyzing a problem, designing a solution, and implementing the solution by creating a program.

2.2 Writing a Simple Program

Writing a program involves designing a strategy for solving the problem then using a programming language to implement that strategy.

Let's first consider the simple *problem* of computing the area of a circle. How do we write a program for solving this problem?

problem

algorithm

pseudocode

Writing a program involves designing algorithms and translating algorithms into programming instructions, or code. An *algorithm* lists the steps you can follow to solve a problem. Algorithms can help the programmer plan a program before writing it in a programming language. Algorithms can be described in natural languages or in *pseudocode* (natural language mixed with some programming code). The algorithm for calculating the area of a circle can be described as follows:

1. Read in the circle's radius.

2. Compute the area using the following formula:

$$area = radius \times radius \times \pi$$

3. Display the result.

Tip

It's always a good practice to outline your program (or its underlying problem) in the form of an algorithm before you begin coding.

When you *code*—that is, when you write a program—you translate an algorithm into a program. You already know every Java program begins with a class definition in which the keyword `class` is followed by the class name. Assume you have chosen `ComputeArea` as the class name. The outline of the program would look as follows:

```java
public class ComputeArea {
    // Details to be given later
}
```

As you know, every Java program must have a `main` method where program execution begins. The program is then expanded as follows:

```java
public class ComputeArea {
    public static void main(String[] args) {
        // Step 1: Read in radius

        // Step 2: Compute area
```

```
    // Step 3: Display the area
  }
}
```

The program needs to read the radius entered by the user from the keyboard. This raises two important issues:

- Reading the radius

- Storing the radius in the program

Let's address the second issue first. In order to store the radius, the program needs to declare a symbol called a *variable*. A variable represents a value stored in the computer's memory.

Rather than using x and y as variable names, choose *descriptive names*: in this case, `radius` for radius and `area` for area. To let the compiler know what `radius` and `area` are, specify their *data types*. That is the kind of data stored in a variable, whether an integer, real number, or something else. This is known as *declaring variables*. Java provides simple data types for representing integers, real numbers, characters, and Boolean types. These types are known as *primitive data types* or *fundamental types*.

Real numbers (i.e., numbers with a decimal point) are represented using a method known as *floating-point* in computers. Therefore, the real numbers are also called *floating-point numbers*. In Java, you can use the keyword `double` to declare a floating-point variable. Declare `radius` and `area` as `double`. The program can be expanded as follows:

variable

descriptive names

data type
declare variables
primitive data types

floating-point

```java
public class ComputeArea {
  public static void main(String[] args) {
    double radius;
    double area;

    // Step 1: Read in radius

    // Step 2: Compute area

    // Step 3: Display the area
  }
}
```

The program declares `radius` and `area` as variables. The reserved word `double` indicates that `radius` and `area` are floating-point values stored in the computer.

The first step is to prompt the user to designate the circle's `radius`. You will soon learn how to prompt the user for information. For now, to learn how variables work, you can assign a fixed value to `radius` in the program as you write the code. Later, you'll modify the program to prompt the user for this value.

The second step is to compute `area` by assigning the result of the expression `radius * radius * 3.14159` to `area`.

In the final step, the program will display the value of `area` on the console by using the `System.out.println` method.

Listing 2.1 shows the complete program, and a sample run of the program is shown in Figure 2.1.

LISTING 2.1 ComputeArea.java

```java
1  public class ComputeArea {
2    public static void main(String[] args) {
3      double radius; // Declare radius
4      double area; // Declare area
5
6      // Assign a radius
7      radius = 20; // radius is now 20
```

```
8
9      // Compute area
10     area = radius * radius * 3.14159;
11
12     // Display results
13     System.out.println("The area for the circle of radius " +
14       radius + " is " + area);
15   }
16 }
```

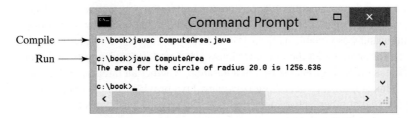

Compile ⟶

Run ⟶

```
c:\book>javac ComputeArea.java

c:\book>java ComputeArea
The area for the circle of radius 20.0 is 1256.636

c:\book>
```

FIGURE 2.1 The program displays the area of a circle.

declare variable
assign value

Variables such as `radius` and `area` correspond to memory locations. Every variable has a name, a type, and a value. Line 3 declares that `radius` can store a `double` value. The value is not defined until you assign a value. Line 7 assigns 20 into the variable `radius`. Similarly, line 4 declares the variable `area`, and line 10 assigns a value into `area`. The following table shows the value in the memory for `area` and `radius` as the program is executed. Each row in the table shows the values of variables after the statement in the corresponding line in the program is executed. This method of reviewing how a program works is called *tracing a program.* Tracing programs are helpful for understanding how programs work, and they are useful tools for finding errors in programs.

tracing program

line#	radius	area
3	no value	
4		no value
7	20	
10		1256.636

concatenate strings

concatenate strings with numbers

The plus sign (+) has two meanings: one for addition, and the other for concatenating (combining) strings. The plus sign (+) in lines 13–14 is called a *string concatenation operator.* It combines two strings into one. If a string is combined with a number, the number is converted into a string and concatenated with the other string. Therefore, the plus signs (+) in lines 13–14 concatenate strings into a longer string, which is then displayed in the output. Strings and string concatenation will be discussed further in Chapter 4.

 Caution

A string cannot cross lines in the source code. Thus, the following statement would result in a compile error:

```
System.out.println("Introduction to Java Programming,
by Y. Daniel Liang");
```

break a long string

To fix the error, break the string into separate substrings, and use the concatenation operator (+) to combine them:

```
System.out.println("Introduction to Java Programming, " +
  "by Y. Daniel Liang");
```

2.2.1 Identify and fix the errors in the following code:

```
1  public class Test {
2    public void main(string[] args) {
3      double i = 50.0;
4      double k = i + 50.0;
5      double j = k + 1;
6
7      System.out.println("j is " + j + " and
8        k is " + k);
9    }
10 }
```

2.3 Reading Input from the Console

Reading input from the console enables the program to accept input from the user.

Key Point

VideoNote

Obtain input

In Listing 2.1, the radius is fixed in the source code. To use a different radius, you have to modify the source code and recompile it. Obviously, this is not convenient, so instead you can use the Scanner class for console input.

Java uses System.out to refer to the standard output device, and System.in to the standard input device. By default, the output device is the display monitor, and the input device is the keyboard. To perform console output, you simply use the println method to display a primitive value or a string to the console. To perform console input, you need to use the Scanner class to create an object to read input from System.in, as follows:

```
Scanner input = new Scanner(System.in);
```

The syntax new Scanner(System.in) creates an object of the Scanner type. The syntax Scanner input declares that input is a variable whose type is Scanner. The whole line Scanner input = new Scanner(System.in) creates a Scanner object and assigns its reference to the variable input. An object may invoke its methods. To invoke a method on an object is to ask the object to perform a task. You can invoke the nextDouble() method to read a double value as follows:

```
double radius = input.nextDouble();
```

This statement reads a number from the keyboard and assigns the number to radius. Listing 2.2 rewrites Listing 2.1 to prompt the user to enter a radius.

LISTING 2.2 ComputeAreaWithConsoleInput.java

```
1  import java.util.Scanner; // Scanner is in the java.util package    import class
2
3  public class ComputeAreaWithConsoleInput {
4    public static void main(String[] args) {
5      // Create a Scanner object
6      Scanner input = new Scanner(System.in);                         create a Scanner
7
8      // Prompt the user to enter a radius
9      System.out.print("Enter a number for radius: ");
10     double radius = input.nextDouble();                             read a double
11
12     // Compute area
13     double area = radius * radius * 3.14159;
14
15     // Display results
16     System.out.println("The area for the circle of radius " +
```

```
17            radius + " is " + area);
18    }
19  }
```

```
Enter a number for radius: 2.5 ⏎Enter
The area for the circle of radius 2.5 is 19.6349375
```

```
Enter a number for radius: 23 ⏎Enter
The area for the circle of radius 23.0 is 1661.90111
```

The `Scanner` class is in the `java.util` package. It is imported in line 1. Line 6 creates a `Scanner` object. Note the `import` statement can be omitted if you replace `Scanner` by `java.util.Scanner` in line 6.

Line 9 displays a string `"Enter a number for radius: "` to the console. This is known
prompt
as a *prompt*, because it directs the user to enter an input. Your program should always tell the user what to enter when expecting input from the keyboard.

Recall that the `print` method in line 9 is identical to the `println` method, except that `println` moves to the beginning of the next line after displaying the string, but `print` does not advance to the next line when completed.

Line 6 creates a `Scanner` object. The statement in line 10 reads input from the keyboard.

```
double radius = input.nextDouble();
```

After the user enters a number and presses the *Enter* key, the program reads the number and assigns it to `radius`.

More details on objects will be introduced in Chapter 9. *For the time being, simply accept that this is how we obtain input from the console.*

The `Scanner` class is in the `java.util` package. It is imported in line 1. There are two
specific import
types of `import` statements: *specific import* and *wildcard import*. The *specific import* specifies a single class in the import statement. For example, the following statement imports `Scanner` from the package `java.util`.

```
import java.util.Scanner;
```

wildcard import
The *wildcard import* imports all the classes in a package by using the asterisk as the wildcard. For example, the following statement imports all the classes from the package `java.util`.

```
import java.util.*;
```

The information for the classes in an imported package is not read in at compile time or runtime unless the class is used in the program. The import statement simply tells the compiler
no performance difference
where to locate the classes. There is no performance difference between a specific import and a wildcard import declaration.

Listing 2.3 gives an example of reading multiple inputs from the keyboard. The program reads three numbers and displays their average.

LISTING 2.3 ComputeAverage.java

import class

```
1  import java.util.Scanner; // Scanner is in the java.util package
2
3  public class ComputeAverage {
4    public static void main(String[] args) {
5      // Create a Scanner object
6      Scanner input = new Scanner(System.in);
7
8      // Prompt the user to enter three numbers
9      System.out.print("Enter three numbers: ");
```
create a Scanner

```
10      double number1 = input.nextDouble();
11      double number2 = input.nextDouble();
12      double number3 = input.nextDouble();
13
14      // Compute average
15      double average = (number1 + number2 + number3) / 3;
16
17      // Display results
18      System.out.println("The average of " + number1 + " " + number2
19        + " " + number3 + " is " + average);
20    }
21  }
```

read a double

```
Enter three numbers: 1 2 3 ⏎Enter
The average of 1.0 2.0 3.0 is 2.0
```

enter input in one line

```
Enter three numbers: 10.5 ⏎Enter
11 ⏎Enter
11.5 ⏎Enter
The average of 10.5 11.0 11.5 is 11.0
```

enter input in multiple lines

The codes for importing the Scanner class (line 1) and creating a Scanner object (line 6) are the same as in the preceding example, as well as in all new programs you will write for reading input from the keyboard.

Line 9 prompts the user to enter three numbers. The numbers are read in lines 10–12. You may enter three numbers separated by spaces, then press the *Enter* key, or enter each number followed by a press of the *Enter* key, as shown in the sample runs of this program.

If you entered an input other than a numeric value, a runtime error would occur. In Chapter 12, you will learn how to handle the exception so the program can continue to run.

runtime error

> **Note**
> Most of the programs in the early chapters of this book perform three steps— input, process, and output—called *IPO*. Input is receiving input from the user; process is producing results using the input; and output is displaying the results.

IPO

> **Note**
> If you use an IDE such as Eclipse or NetBeans, you will get a warning to ask you to close the input for preventing a potential resource leak. Ignore the warning for the time being because the input is automatically closed when your program is terminated. In this case, there will be no resource leaking.

Warning in IDE

2.3.1 How do you write a statement to let the user enter a double value from the keyboard? What happens if you entered 5a when executing the following code?

Check
Point

```
double radius = input.nextDouble();
```

2.3.2 Are there any performance differences between the following two import statements?

```
import java.util.Scanner;
import java.util.*;
```

2.4 Identifiers

Identifiers are the names that identify the elements such as classes, methods, and variables in a program.

identifiers
identifier naming rules

As you see in Listing 2.3, `ComputeAverage`, `main`, `input`, `number1`, `number2`, `number3`, and so on are the names of things that appear in the program. In programming terminology, such names are called *identifiers*. All identifiers must obey the following rules:

- An identifier is a sequence of characters that consists of letters, digits, underscores (_), and dollar signs ($).

- An identifier must start with a letter, an underscore (_), or a dollar sign ($). It cannot start with a digit.

- An identifier cannot be a reserved word. (See Appendix A for a list of reserved words.)

- An identifier cannot be `true`, `false`, or `null`.

- An identifier can be of any length.

For example, `$2`, `ComputeArea`, `area`, `radius`, and `print` are legal identifiers, whereas `2A` and `d+4` are not because they do not follow the rules. The Java compiler detects illegal identifiers and reports syntax errors.

case sensitive

Note
Since Java is case sensitive, `area`, `Area`, and `AREA` are all different identifiers.

Tip
Identifiers are for naming variables, methods, classes, and other items in a program. Descriptive identifiers make programs easy to read. Avoid using abbreviations for identifiers. Using complete words is more descriptive. For example, `numberOfStudents` is better than `numStuds`, `numOfStuds`, or `numOfStudents`. We use descriptive names for complete programs in the text. However, we will occasionally use variable names such as `i`, `j`, `k`, `x`, and `y` in the code snippets for brevity. These names also provide a generic tone to the code snippets.

descriptive names

the $ character

Tip
Do not name identifiers with the `$` character. By convention, the `$` character should be used only in mechanically generated source code.

2.4.1 Which of the following identifiers are valid? Which are Java keywords?

```
miles, Test, a++, --a, 4#R, $4, #44, apps
class, public, int, x, y, radius
```

2.5 Variables

Variables are used to represent values that may be changed in the program.

why called variables?

As you see from the programs in the preceding sections, variables are used to store values to be used later in a program. They are called variables because their values can be changed. In the program in Listing 2.2, `radius` and `area` are variables of the `double` type. You can assign any numerical value to `radius` and `area`, and the values of `radius` and `area` can be reassigned. For example, in the following code, `radius` is initially `1.0` (line 2) then changed to `2.0` (line 7), and area is set to `3.14159` (line 3) then reset to `12.56636` (line 8).

```
1   // Compute the first area
2   radius = 1.0;                                  radius:  1.0
3   area = radius * radius * 3.14159;                area:  3.14159
4   System.out.println("The area is " + area + " for radius " + radius);
5
6   // Compute the second area
7   radius = 2.0;                                  radius:  2.0
8   area = radius * radius * 3.14159;                area:  12.56636
9   System.out.println("The area is " + area + " for radius " + radius);
```

Variables are for representing data of a certain type. To use a variable, you declare it by telling the compiler its name as well as what type of data it can store. The *variable declaration* tells the compiler to allocate appropriate memory space for the variable based on its data type. The syntax for declaring a variable is

```
datatype variableName;
```

Here are some examples of variable declarations:

declare variable

```
int count;            // Declare count to be an integer variable
double radius;        // Declare radius to be a double variable
double interestRate;  // Declare interestRate to be a double variable
```

These examples use the data types `int` and `double`. Later you will be introduced to additional data types, such as `byte`, `short`, `long`, `float`, `char`, and `boolean`.

If variables are of the same type, they can be declared together, as follows:

```
datatype variable1, variable2, ..., variablen;
```

The variables are separated by commas. For example,

```
int i, j, k; // Declare i, j, and k as int variables
```

Variables often have initial values. You can declare a variable and initialize it in one step. Consider, for instance, the following code:

initialize variables

```
int count = 1;
```

This is equivalent to the next two statements:

```
int count;
count = 1;
```

You can also use a shorthand form to declare and initialize variables of the same type together. For example,

```
int i = 1, j = 2;
```

Tip

A variable must be declared before it can be assigned a value. A variable declared in a method must be assigned a value before it can be used.

Whenever possible, declare a variable and assign its initial value in one step. This will make the program easy to read and avoid programming errors.

Every variable has a scope. The *scope of a variable* is the part of the program where the variable can be referenced. The rules that define the scope of a variable will be gradually introduced later in the book. For now, all you need to know is that a variable must be declared and initialized before it can be used.

2.5.1 Identify and fix the errors in the following code:

```
1  public class Test {
2    public static void main(String[] args) {
3      int i = k + 2;
4      System.out.println(i);
5    }
6  }
```

2.6 Assignment Statements and Assignment Expressions

Key Point

An assignment statement designates a value for a variable. An assignment statement can be used as an expression in Java.

assignment statement
assignment operator

After a variable is declared, you can assign a value to it by using an *assignment statement*. In Java, the equal sign (=) is used as the *assignment operator*. The syntax for assignment statements is as follows:

```
variable = expression;
```

expression

An *expression* represents a computation involving values, variables, and operators that, taking them together, evaluates to a value. For example, consider the following code:

```
int y = 1;                          // Assign 1 to variable y
double radius = 1.0;                // Assign 1.0 to variable radius
int x = 5 * (3 / 2);                // Assign the value of the expression to x
x = y + 1;                          // Assign the addition of y and 1 to x
double area = radius * radius * 3.14159;    // Compute area
```

You can use a variable in an expression. A variable can also be used in both sides of the = operator. For example,

```
x = x + 1;
```

In this assignment statement, the result of x + 1 is assigned to x. If x is 1 before the statement is executed, then it becomes 2 after the statement is executed.

To assign a value to a variable, you must place the variable name to the left of the assignment operator. Thus, the following statement is wrong:

```
1 = x; // Wrong
```

Note

In mathematics, x = 2 * x + 1 denotes an equation. However, in Java, x = 2 * x + 1 is an assignment statement that evaluates the expression 2 * x + 1 and assigns the result to x.

In Java, an assignment statement is essentially an expression that evaluates to the value to be assigned to the variable on the left side of the assignment operator. For this reason, an assignment statement is also known as an *assignment expression*. For example, the following statement is correct:

assignment expression

```
System.out.println(x = 1);
```

which is equivalent to

```
x = 1;
System.out.println(x);
```

If a value is assigned to multiple variables, you can use the following syntax:

```
i = j = k = 1;
```

which is equivalent to

```
k = 1;
j = k;
i = j;
```

Note

In an assignment statement, the data type of the variable on the left must be compatible with the data type of the value on the right. For example, `int x = 1.0` would be illegal, because the data type of `x` is `int`. You cannot assign a `double` value (`1.0`) to an `int` variable without using type casting. Type casting will be introduced in Section 2.15.

2.6.1 Identify and fix the errors in the following code:

```
1  public class Test {
2    public static void main(String[] args) {
3      int i = j = k = 2;
4      System.out.println(i + " " + j + " " + k);
5    }
6  }
```

2.7 Named Constants

A named constant is an identifier that represents a permanent value.

The value of a variable may change during the execution of a program, but a *named constant*, or simply *constant*, represents permanent data that never changes. A constant is also known as a *final variable* in Java. In our `ComputeArea` program, π is a constant. If you use it frequently, you don't want to keep typing `3.14159`; instead, you can declare a constant for π. Here is the syntax for declaring a constant:

Key
Point

constant

```
final datatype CONSTANTNAME = value;
```

A constant must be declared and initialized in the same statement. The word `final` is a Java keyword for declaring a constant. By convention, all letters in a constant are in uppercase. For example, you can declare π as a constant and rewrite Listing 2.2, as in Listing 2.4.

final keyword

LISTING 2.4 `ComputeAreaWithConstant.java`

```
1  import java.util.Scanner; // Scanner is in the java.util package
2
3  public class ComputeAreaWithConstant {
4    public static void main(String[] args) {
5      final double PI = 3.14159; // Declare a constant
6
7      // Create a Scanner object
8      Scanner input = new Scanner(System.in);
9
10     // Prompt the user to enter a radius
11     System.out.print("Enter a number for radius: ");
12     double radius = input.nextDouble();
13
14     // Compute area
```

```
15        double area = radius * radius * PI;
16
17        // Display result
18        System.out.println("The area for the circle of radius " +
19          radius + " is " + area);
20    }
21 }
```

benefits of constants

There are three benefits of using constants: (1) you don't have to repeatedly type the same value if it is used multiple times; (2) if you have to change the constant value (e.g., from `3.14` to `3.14159` for `PI`), you need to change it only in a single location in the source code; and (3) a descriptive name for a constant makes the program easy to read.

2.7.1 What are the benefits of using constants? Declare an `int` constant `SIZE` with value `20`.

2.8 Naming Conventions

Sticking with the Java naming conventions makes your programs easy to read and avoids errors.

Make sure you choose descriptive names with straightforward meanings for the variables, constants, classes, and methods in your program. As mentioned earlier, names are case sensitive. Listed below are the conventions for naming variables, methods, and classes.

name variables and methods

■ Use lowercase for variables and methods—for example, the variables `radius` and `area`, and the method `print`. If a name consists of several words, concatenate them into one, making the first word lowercase and capitalizing the first letter of each subsequent word—for example, the variable `numberOfStudents`. This naming style is known as the *camelCase* because the uppercase characters in the name resemble a camel's humps.

name classes

■ Capitalize the first letter of each word in a class name—for example, the class names `ComputeArea` and `System`.

name constants

■ Capitalize every letter in a constant, and use underscores between words—for example, the constants `PI` and `MAX_VALUE`.

It is important to follow the naming conventions to make your programs easy to read.

Caution

name classes

Do not choose class names that are already used in the Java library. For example, since the `System` class is defined in Java, you should not name your class `System`.

2.8.1 What are the naming conventions for class names, method names, constants, and variables? Which of the following items can be a constant, a method, a variable, or a class according to the Java naming conventions?

`MAX_VALUE`, `Test`, `read`, `readDouble`

2.8.2 Translate the following algorithm into Java code:

Step 1: Declare a `double` variable named `miles` with an initial value `100`.

Step 2: Declare a `double` constant named `KILOMETERS_PER_MILE` with value `1.609`.

Step 3: Declare a `double` variable named `kilometers`, multiply `miles` and `KILOMETERS_PER_MILE`, and assign the result to `kilometers`.

Step 4: Display `kilometers` to the console.

What is `kilometers` after Step 4?

2.9 Numeric Data Types and Operations

Java has six numeric types for integers and floating-point numbers with operators +, -, *, /, and %.

Key Point

2.9.1 Numeric Types

Every data type has a range of values. The compiler allocates memory space for each variable or constant according to its data type. Java provides eight primitive data types for numeric values, characters, and Boolean values. This section introduces numeric data types and operators.

Table 2.1 lists the six numeric data types, their ranges, and their storage sizes.

TABLE 2.1 Numeric Data Types

Name	Range	Storage Size	
byte	-2^7 to 2^7-1 (-128 to 127)	8-bit signed	byte type
short	-2^{15} to $2^{15}-1$ (-32768 to 32767)	16-bit signed	short type
int	-2^{31} to $2^{31}-1$ (-2147483648 to 2147483647)	32-bit signed	int type
long	-2^{63} to $2^{63}-1$	64-bit signed	long type
	(i.e., -9223372036854775808 to 9223372036854775807)		
float	Negative range: $-3.4028235E+38$ to $-1.4E-45$	32-bit IEEE 754	float type
	Positive range: $1.4E-45$ to $3.4028235E+38$		
double	Negative range: $-1.7976931348623157E+308$ to $-4.9E-324$	64-bit IEEE 754	double type
	Positive range: $4.9E-324$ to $1.7976931348623157E+308$		

Note

IEEE 754 is a standard approved by the Institute of Electrical and Electronics Engineers for representing floating-point numbers on computers. The standard has been widely adopted. Java uses the 32-bit **IEEE 754** for the `float` type and the 64-bit **IEEE 754** for the `double` type. The **IEEE 754** standard also defines special floating-point values, which are listed in Appendix E.

Java uses four types for integers: `byte`, `short`, `int`, and `long`. Choose the type that is most appropriate for your variable. For example, if you know an integer stored in a variable is within a range of a byte, declare the variable as a `byte`. For simplicity and consistency, we will use `int` for integers most of the time in this book.

integer types

Java uses two types for floating-point numbers: `float` and `double`. The `double` type is twice as big as `float`, so the `double` is known as *double precision*, and `float` as *single precision*. Normally, you should use the `double` type, because it is more accurate than the `float` type.

floating-point types

2.9.2 Reading Numbers from the Keyboard

You know how to use the `nextDouble()` method in the `Scanner` class to read a double value from the keyboard. You can also use the methods listed in Table 2.2 to read a number of the `byte`, `short`, `int`, `long`, and `float` type.

TABLE 2.2 Methods for Scanner Objects

Method	Description
nextByte()	reads an integer of the byte type.
nextShort()	reads an integer of the short type.
nextInt()	reads an integer of the int type.
nextLong()	reads an integer of the long type.
nextFloat()	reads a number of the float type.
nextDouble()	reads a number of the double type.

Here are examples for reading values of various types from the keyboard:

```
1  Scanner input = new Scanner(System.in);
2  System.out.print("Enter a byte value: ");
3  byte byteValue = input.nextByte();
4
5  System.out.print("Enter a short value: ");
6  short shortValue = input.nextShort();
7
8  System.out.print("Enter an int value: ");
9  int intValue = input.nextInt();
10
11 System.out.print("Enter a long value: ");
12 long longValue = input.nextLong();
13
14 System.out.print("Enter a float value: ");
15 float floatValue = input.nextFloat();
```

If you enter a value with an incorrect range or format, a runtime error would occur. For example, if you enter a value 128 for line 3, an error would occur because 128 is out of range for a byte type integer.

2.9.3 Numeric Operators

operators +, -, *, /, and %

The operators for numeric data types include the standard arithmetic operators: addition (+), subtraction (−), multiplication (*), division (/), and remainder (%), as listed in Table 2.3. The

operands

operands are the values operated by an operator.

TABLE 2.3 Numeric Operators

Name	Meaning	Example	Result
+	Addition	34 + 1	35
-	Subtraction	34.0 − 0.1	33.9
*	Multiplication	300*30	9000
/	Division	1.0 / 2.0	0.5
%	Remainder	20 % 3	2

When both operands of a division are integers, the result of the division is the quotient and the fractional part is truncated. For example, 5 / 2 yields 2, not 2.5, and −5 / 2 yields −2,

integer division

not −2.5. To perform a floating-point division, one of the operands must be a floating-point number. For example, 5.0 / 2 yields 2.5.

The % operator, known as *remainder*, yields the remainder after division. The operand on the left is the dividend, and the operand on the right is the divisor. Therefore, 7 % 3 yields 1, 3 % 7 yields 3, 12 % 4 yields 0, 26 % 8 yields 2, and 20 % 13 yields 7.

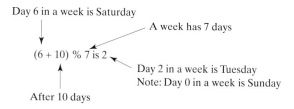

The % operator is often used for positive integers, but it can also be used with negative integers and floating-point values. The remainder is negative only if the dividend is negative. For example, -7 % 3 yields -1, -12 % 4 yields 0, -26 % -8 yields -2, and 20 % -13 yields 7.

Remainder is very useful in programming. For example, an even number % 2 is always 0 and a positive odd number % 2 is always 1. Thus, you can use this property to determine whether a number is even or odd. If today is Saturday, it will be Saturday again in 7 days. Suppose you and your friends are going to meet in 10 days. What will be the day in 10 days? You can find that the day is Tuesday using the following expression:

Day 6 in a week is Saturday

A week has 7 days

(6 + 10) % 7 is 2

Day 2 in a week is Tuesday
Note: Day 0 in a week is Sunday

After 10 days

The program in Listing 2.5 obtains minutes and remaining seconds from an amount of time in seconds. For example, 500 seconds contains 8 minutes and 20 seconds.

LISTING 2.5 DisplayTime.java

```
 1  import java.util.Scanner;
 2
 3  public class DisplayTime {
 4    public static void main(String[] args) {
 5      Scanner input = new Scanner(System.in);
 6      // Prompt the user for input
 7      System.out.print("Enter an integer for seconds: ");
 8      int seconds = input.nextInt();
 9
10      int minutes = seconds / 60; // Find minutes in seconds
11      int remainingSeconds = seconds % 60; // Seconds remaining
12      System.out.println(seconds + " seconds is " + minutes +
13        " minutes and " + remainingSeconds + " seconds");
14    }
15  }
```

import Scanner

create a Scanner

read an integer

divide
remainder

```
Enter an integer for seconds: 500 ↵Enter
500 seconds is 8 minutes and 20 seconds
```

line#	seconds	minutes	remainingSeconds
8	500		
10		8	
11			20

The nextInt() method (line 8) reads an integer for seconds. Line 10 obtains the minutes using seconds / 60. Line 11 (seconds % 60) obtains the remaining seconds after taking away the minutes.

unary operator
binary operator

The + and - operators can be both unary and binary. A *unary operator* has only one operand; a *binary operator* has two. For example, the – operator in –5 is a unary operator to negate number 5, whereas the – operator in 4 – 5 is a binary operator for subtracting 5 from 4.

2.9.4 Exponent Operations

Math.pow(a, b) method

The Math.pow(a, b) method can be used to compute a^b. The pow method is defined in the Math class in the Java API. You invoke the method using the syntax Math.pow(a, b) (e.g., Math.pow(2, 3)), which returns the result of a^b (2^3). Here, a and b are parameters for the pow method and the numbers 2 and 3 are actual values used to invoke the method. For example,

```
System.out.println(Math.pow(2, 3)); // Displays 8.0
System.out.println(Math.pow(4, 0.5)); // Displays 2.0
System.out.println(Math.pow(2.5, 2)); // Displays 6.25
System.out.println(Math.pow(2.5, -2)); // Displays 0.16
```

Chapter 6 introduces more details on methods. For now, all you need to know is how to invoke the pow method to perform the exponent operation.

Check Point

2.9.1 Find the largest and smallest byte, short, int, long, float, and double. Which of these data types requires the least amount of memory?

2.9.2 Show the result of the following remainders:

```
56  %  6
78  %  -4
-34 %  5
-34 %  -5
5   %  1
1   %  5
```

2.9.3 If today is Tuesday, what will be the day in 100 days?

2.9.4 What is the result of 25 / 4? How would you rewrite the expression if you wished the result to be a floating-point number?

2.9.5 Show the result of the following code:

```
System.out.println(2 * (5 / 2 + 5 / 2));
System.out.println(2 * 5 / 2 + 2 * 5 / 2);
System.out.println(2 * (5 / 2));
System.out.println(2 * 5 / 2);
```

2.9.6 Are the following statements correct? If so, show the output.

```
System.out.println("25 / 4 is " + 25 / 4);
System.out.println("25 / 4.0 is " + 25 / 4.0);
System.out.println("3 * 2 / 4 is " + 3 * 2 / 4);
System.out.println("3.0 * 2 / 4 is " + 3.0 * 2 / 4);
```

2.9.7 Write a statement to display the result of $2^{3.5}$.

2.9.8 Suppose m and r are integers. Write a Java expression for mr^2 to obtain a floating-point result.

Key Point

2.10 Numeric Literals

A literal is a constant value that appears directly in a program.

literal

For example, 34 and 0.305 are literals in the following statements:

```
int numberOfYears = 34;
double weight = 0.305;
```

2.10.1   Integer Literals

An integer literal can be assigned to an integer variable as long as it can fit into the variable. A compile error will occur if the literal is too large for the variable to hold. The statement `byte b = 128`, for example, will cause a compile error, because `128` cannot be stored in a variable of the `byte` type. (Note the range for a byte value is from `-128` to `127`.)

An integer literal is assumed to be of the `int` type, whose value is between -2^{31} (-2147483648) and $2^{31} -1$ (2147483647). To denote an integer literal of the `long` type, append the letter L or l to it. For example, to write integer `2147483648` in a Java program, you have to write it as `2147483648L` or `2147483648l`, because `2147483648` exceeds the range for the `int` value. L is preferred because l (lowercase L) can easily be confused with 1 (the digit one).

Note

By default, an integer literal is a decimal integer number. To denote a binary integer literal, use a leading **0b** or **0B** (zero B); to denote an octal integer literal, use a leading **0** (zero); and to denote a hexadecimal integer literal, use a leading **0x** or **0X** (zero X). For example,

binary, octal, and hex literals

```
System.out.println(0B1111); // Displays 15
System.out.println(07777); // Displays 4095
System.out.println(0XFFFF); // Displays 65535
```

Hexadecimal numbers, binary numbers, and octal numbers will be introduced in Appendix F.

Note

To improve readability, Java allows you to use underscores between two digits in a number literal. For example, the following literals are correct.

```
long ssn = 232_45_4519;
long creditCardNumber = 2324_4545_4519_3415L;
```

However, `45_` or `_45` is incorrect. The underscore must be placed between two digits.

underscores in numbers

2.10.2   Floating-Point Literals

Floating-point literals are written with a decimal point. By default, a floating-point literal is treated as a `double` type value. For example, `5.0` is considered a `double` value, not a `float` value. You can make a number a `float` by appending the letter `f` or `F`, and you can make a number a `double` by appending the letter `d` or `D`. For example, you can use `100.2f` or `100.2F` for a `float` number, and `100.2d` or `100.2D` for a `double` number.

suffix f or F
suffix d or D

Note

The `double` type values are more accurate than the `float` type values. For example,

double vs. float

```
System.out.println("1.0 / 3.0 is " + 1.0 / 3.0);
```

displays `1.0 / 3.0 is 0`.$\underbrace{3333333333333333}_{\text{16 digits}}$

```
System.out.println("1.0F / 3.0F is " + 1.0F / 3.0F);
```

displays `1.0F / 3.0F is 0`.$\underbrace{33333334}_{\text{8 digits}}$

A float value has `7-8` numbers of significant digits, and a double value has `15-17` numbers of significant digits.

2.10.3 Scientific Notation

Floating-point literals can be written in scientific notation in the form of $a \times 10^b$. For example, the scientific notation for 123.456 is 1.23456×10^2 and for 0.0123456 is 1.23456×10^{-2}. A special syntax is used to write scientific notation numbers. For example, 1.23456×10^2 is written as `1.23456E2` or `1.23456E+2` and 1.23456×10^{-2} as `1.23456E-2`. E (or e) represents an exponent, and can be in either lowercase or uppercase.

why called floating-point?

Note
The `float` and `double` types are used to represent numbers with a decimal point. Why are they called *floating-point numbers*? These numbers are stored in scientific notation internally. When a number such as `50.534` is converted into scientific notation, such as `5.0534E+1`, its decimal point is moved (i.e., floated) to a new position.

Check Point

2.10.1 How many accurate digits are stored in a `float` or `double` type variable?

2.10.2 Which of the following are correct literals for floating-point numbers?
`12.3`, `12.3e+2`, `23.4e-2`, `-334.4`, `20.5`, `39F`, `40D`

2.10.3 Which of the following are the same as `52.534`?
`5.2534e+1`, `0.52534e+2`, `525.34e-1`, `5.2534e+0`

2.10.4 Which of the following are correct literals?
`5_2534e+1`, `_2534`, `5_2`, `5_`

2.11 Evaluating Expressions and Operator Precedence

Java expressions are evaluated in the same way as arithmetic expressions.

Key Point

Writing a numeric expression in Java involves a straightforward translation of an arithmetic expression using Java operators. For example, the arithmetic expression

$$\frac{3 + 4x}{5} - \frac{10(y - 5)(a + b + c)}{x} + 9\left(\frac{4}{x} + \frac{9 + x}{y}\right)$$

can be translated into a Java expression as follows:

```
(3 + 4 * x) / 5 - 10 * (y - 5) * (a + b + c) / x +
  9 * (4 / x + (9 + x) / y)
```

evaluating an expression

Although Java has its own way to evaluate an expression behind the scene, the result of a Java expression and its corresponding arithmetic expression is the same. Therefore, you can safely apply the arithmetic rule for evaluating a Java expression. Operators contained within pairs of parentheses are evaluated first. Parentheses can be nested, in which case the expression in the inner parentheses is evaluated first. When more than one operator is used in an expression, the following operator precedence rule is used to determine the order of evaluation:.

operator precedence rule

- Multiplication, division, and remainder operators are applied first. If an expression contains several multiplication, division, and remainder operators, they are applied from left to right.

- Addition and subtraction operators are applied last. If an expression contains several addition and subtraction operators, they are applied from left to right.

Here is an example of how an expression is evaluated:

```
3 + 4 * 4 + 5 * (4 + 3) - 1
```
———— (1) inside parentheses first
```
3 + 4 * 4 + 5 * 7 - 1
```
———— (2) multiplication
```
3 + 16 + 5 * 7 - 1
```
———— (3) multiplication
```
3 + 16 + 35 - 1
```
———— (4) addition
```
19 + 35 - 1
```
———— (5) addition
```
54 - 1
```
———— (6) subtraction
```
53
```

Listing 2.6 gives a program that converts a Fahrenheit degree to Celsius using the formula Celsius $= (\frac{5}{9})$(Fahrenheit $-$ 32).

LISTING 2.6 FahrenheitToCelsius.java

```java
1   import java.util.Scanner;
2
3   public class FahrenheitToCelsius {
4     public static void main(String[] args) {
5       Scanner input = new Scanner(System.in);
6
7       System.out.print("Enter a degree in Fahrenheit: ");
8       double fahrenheit = input.nextDouble();
9
10      // Convert Fahrenheit to Celsius
11      double celsius = (5.0 / 9) * (fahrenheit - 32);          divide
12      System.out.println("Fahrenheit " + fahrenheit + " is " +
13        celsius + " in Celsius");
14    }
15  }
```

```
Enter a degree in Fahrenheit: 100 ⏎Enter
Fahrenheit 100.0 is 37.77777777777778 in Celsius
```

line#	fahrenheit	celsius
8	100	
11		37.77777777777778

Be careful when applying division. Division of two integers yields an integer in Java. $\frac{5}{9}$ is coded `5.0 / 9` instead of `5 / 9` in line 11, because `5 / 9` yields `0` in Java.

integer vs. floating-point division

2.11.1 How would you write the following arithmetic expressions in Java?

✔ **Check Point**

a. $\dfrac{4}{3(r + 34)} - 9(a + bc) + \dfrac{3 + d(2 + a)}{a + bd}$

b. $5.5 \times (r + 2.5)^{2.5+t}$

2.12 Case Study: Displaying the Current Time

Key Point

VideoNote

Use operators / and %

currentTimeMillis
UNIX epoch

You can invoke `System.currentTimeMillis()` *to return the current time.*

The problem is to develop a program that displays the current time in GMT (Greenwich Mean Time) in the format hour:minute:second, such as 13:19:8.

The `currentTimeMillis` method in the `System` class returns the current time in milliseconds elapsed since the time midnight, January 1, 1970 GMT, as shown in Figure 2.2. This time is known as the *UNIX epoch*. The epoch is the point when time starts, and 1970 was the year when the UNIX operating system was formally introduced.

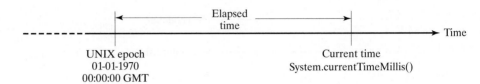

FIGURE 2.2 The `System.currentTimeMillis()` returns the number of milliseconds since the UNIX epoch.

You can use this method to obtain the current time, then compute the current second, minute, and hour as follows:

1. Obtain the total milliseconds since midnight, January 1, 1970, in `totalMilliseconds` by invoking `System.currentTimeMillis()` (e.g., 1203183068328 milliseconds).

2. Obtain the total seconds `totalSeconds` by dividing `totalMilliseconds` by 1000 (e.g., 1203183068328 milliseconds / 1000 = 1203183068 seconds).

3. Compute the current second from `totalSeconds % 60` (e.g., 1203183068 seconds % 60 = 8, which is the current second).

4. Obtain the total minutes `totalMinutes` by dividing `totalSeconds` by 60 (e.g., 1203183068 seconds / 60 = 20053051 minutes).

5. Compute the current minute from `totalMinutes % 60` (e.g., 20053051 minutes % 60 = 31, which is the current minute).

6. Obtain the total hours `totalHours` by dividing `totalMinutes` by 60 (e.g., 20053051 minutes / 60 = 334217 hours).

7. Compute the current hour from `totalHours % 24` (e.g., 334217 hours % 24 = 17, which is the current hour).

Listing 2.7 gives the complete program.

LISTING 2.7 ShowCurrentTime.java

```
1  public class ShowCurrentTime {
2    public static void main(String[] args) {
3      // Obtain the total milliseconds since midnight, Jan 1, 1970
4      long totalMilliseconds = System.currentTimeMillis();
5
6      // Obtain the total seconds since midnight, Jan 1, 1970
7      long totalSeconds = totalMilliseconds / 1000;
8
9      // Compute the current second in the minute in the hour
10     long currentSecond = totalSeconds % 60;
11
```

totalMilliseconds

totalSeconds

currentSecond

```
12        // Obtain the total minutes
13        long totalMinutes = totalSeconds / 60;                              totalMinutes
14
15        // Compute the current minute in the hour
16        long currentMinute = totalMinutes % 60;                             currentMinute
17
18        // Obtain the total hours
19        long totalHours = totalMinutes / 60;                                totalHours
20
21        // Compute the current hour
22        long currentHour = totalHours % 24;                                 currentHour
23
24        // Display results
25        System.out.println("Current time is " + currentHour + ":"           display output
26          + currentMinute + ":" + currentSecond + " GMT");
27    }
28  }
```

```
Current time is 17:31:8 GMT
```

Line 4 invokes `System.currentTimeMillis()` to obtain the current time in milliseconds as a `long` value. Thus, all the variables are declared as the long type in this program. The seconds, minutes, and hours are extracted from the current time using the `/` and `%` operators (lines 6–22).

variables	line# 4	7	10	13	16	19	22
totalMilliseconds	1203183068328						
totalSeconds		1203183068					
currentSecond			8				
totalMinutes				20053051			
currentMinute					31		
totalHours						334217	
currentHour							17

In the sample run, a single digit 8 is displayed for the second. The desirable output would be 08. This can be fixed by using a method that formats a single digit with a prefix 0 (see Programming Exercise 6.37).

The hour displayed in this program is in GMT. Programming Exercise 2.8 enables to display the hour in any time zone.

Java also provides the `System.nanoTime()` method that returns the elapse time in nano-seconds. `nanoTime()` is more precise and accurate than `currentTimeMillis()`.

nanoTime

Check
Point

2.12.1 How do you obtain the current second, minute, and hour?

Key
Point

2.13 Augmented Assignment Operators

The operators +, -, *, /, and % can be combined with the assignment operator to form augmented operators.

Very often, the current value of a variable is used, modified, then reassigned back to the same variable. For example, the following statement increases the variable count by 1:

```
count = count + 1;
```

Java allows you to combine assignment and addition operators using an augmented (or compound) assignment operator. For example, the preceding statement can be written as

```
count += 1;
```

addition assignment operator

The += is called the *addition assignment operator.* Table 2.4 shows other augmented assignment operators.

TABLE 2.4 Augmented Assignment Operators

Operator	Name	Example	Equivalent
+=	Addition assignment	i += 8	i = i + 8
-=	Subtraction assignment	i -= 8	i = i - 8
*=	Multiplication assignment	i *= 8	i = i * 8
/=	Division assignment	i /= 8	i = i / 8
%=	Remainder assignment	i %= 8	i = i % 8

The augmented assignment operator is performed last after all the other operators in the expression are evaluated. For example,

```
x /= 4 + 5.5 * 1.5;
```

is same as

```
x = x / (4 + 5.5 * 1.5);
```

Caution

There are no spaces in the augmented assignment operators. For example, + = should be +=.

Note

Like the assignment operator (=), the operators (+=, -=, *=, /=, and %=) can be used to form an assignment statement as well as an expression. For example, in the following code, x += 2 is a statement in the first line, and an expression in the second line:

```
x += 2; // Statement
System.out.println(x += 2); // Expression
```

Check
Point

2.13.1 Show the output of the following code:

```
double a = 6.5;
a += a + 1;
```

```
System.out.println(a);
a = 6;
a /= 2;
System.out.println(a);
```

2.14 Increment and Decrement Operators

The increment operator (+ +) and decrement operator (− −) are for incrementing and decrementing a variable by 1.

Key Point

The `++` and `−−` are two shorthand operators for incrementing and decrementing a variable by `1`. These are handy because that's often how much the value needs to be changed in many programming tasks. For example, the following code increments `i` by `1` and decrements `j` by `1`.

increment operator (++)
decrement operator (−−)

```
int i = 3, j = 3;
i++; // i becomes 4
j--; // j becomes 2
```

`i++` is pronounced as "i plus plus" and `i−−` as "i minus minus." These operators are known as *postfix increment* (or *postincrement*) and *postfix decrement* (or *postdecrement*), because the operators `++` and `−−` are placed after the variable. These operators can also be placed before the variable. For example,

postincrement
postdecrement

```
int i = 3, j = 3;
++i; // i becomes 4
--j; // j becomes 2
```

`++i` increments `i` by `1` and `−−j` decrements `j` by `1`. These operators are known as *prefix increment* (or *preincrement*) and *prefix decrement* (or *predecrement*).

preincrement
predecrement

As you see, the effect of `i++` and `++i` or `i−−` and `−−i` are the same in the preceding examples. However, their effects are different when they are used in statements that do more than just increment and decrement. Table 2.5 describes their differences and gives examples.

TABLE 2.5 Increment and Decrement Operators

Operator	Name	Description	Example (assume i = 1)
++var	preincrement	Increment var by 1, and use the new var value in the statement	`int j = ++i;` // j is 2, i is 2
var++	postincrement	Increment var by 1, but use the original var value in the statement	`int j = i++;` // j is 1, i is 2
−−var	predecrement	Decrement var by 1, and use the new var value in the statement	`int j = --i;` // j is 0, i is 0
var−−	postdecrement	Decrement var by 1, and use the original var value in the statement	`int j = i--;` // j is 1, i is 0

Here are additional examples to illustrate the differences between the prefix form of `++` (or `−−`) and the postfix form of `++` (or `−−`). Consider the following code:

```
int i = 10;
int newNum = 10 * i++;
System.out.print("i is " + i
   + ", newNum is " + newNum);
```

Same effect as →

```
int newNum = 10 * i;
i = i + 1;
```

```
i is 11, newNum is 100
```

In this case, i is incremented by 1, then the *old* value of i is used in the multiplication. Thus, newNum becomes 100. If i++ is replaced by ++i, then it becomes as follows:

```
int i = 10;
int newNum = 10 * (++i);
System.out.print("i is " + i
    + ", newNum is " + newNum);
```

Same effect as →

```
i = i + 1;
int newNum = 10 * i;
```

```
i is 11, newNum is 110
```

i is incremented by 1, and the new value of i is used in the multiplication. Thus, newNum becomes 110.

Here is another example:

```
double x = 1.0;
double y = 5.0;
double z = x-- + (++y);
```

After all three lines are executed, y becomes 6.0, z becomes 7.0, and x becomes 0.0.

Operands are evaluated from left to right in Java. The left-hand operand of a binary operator is evaluated before any part of the right-hand operand is evaluated. This rule takes precedence over any other rules that govern expressions. Here is an example:

```
int i = 1;
int k = ++i + i * 3;
```

++i is evaluated and returns 2. When evaluating i * 3, i is now 2. Therefore, k becomes 8.

Tip
Using increment and decrement operators makes expressions short, but it also makes them complex and difficult to read. Avoid using these operators in expressions that modify multiple variables or the same variable multiple times, such as this one: int k = ++i + i * 3.

2.14.1 Which of these statements are true?

    a. Any expression can be used as a statement.

    b. The expression x++ can be used as a statement.

    c. The statement x = x + 5 is also an expression.

    d. The statement x = y = x = 0 is illegal.

2.14.2 Show the output of the following code:

```
int a = 6;
int b = a++;
System.out.println(a);
System.out.println(b);
a = 6;
b = ++a;
System.out.println(a);
System.out.println(b);
```

2.15 Numeric Type Conversions

Floating-point numbers can be converted into integers using explicit casting.

Key Point

Can you perform binary operations with two operands of different types? Yes. If an integer and a floating-point number are involved in a binary operation, Java automatically converts the integer to a floating-point value. Therefore, `3 * 4.5` is the same as `3.0 * 4.5`.

You can always assign a value to a numeric variable whose type supports a larger range of values; thus, for instance, you can assign a `long` value to a `float` variable. You cannot, how-ever, assign a value to a variable of a type with a smaller range unless you use *type casting*. *Casting* is an operation that converts a value of one data type into a value of another data type. Casting a type with a small range to a type with a larger range is known as *widening a type*. Casting a type with a large range to a type with a smaller range is known as *narrowing a type*. Java will automatically widen a type, but you must narrow a type explicitly.

casting

widening a type
narrowing a type

The syntax for casting a type is to specify the target type in parentheses, followed by the variable's name or the value to be cast. For example, the following statement

```java
System.out.println((int)1.7);
```

displays `1`. When a `double` value is cast into an `int` value, the fractional part is truncated. The following statement

```java
System.out.println((double)1 / 2);
```

displays `0.5`, because `1` is cast to `1.0` first, then `1.0` is divided by `2`. However, the statement

```java
System.out.println(1 / 2);
```

displays `0`, because `1` and `2` are both integers and the resulting value should also be an integer.

Caution

Casting is necessary if you are assigning a value to a variable of a smaller type range, such as assigning a `double` value to an `int` variable. A compile error will occur if casting is not used in situations of this kind. However, be careful when using casting, as loss of information might lead to inaccurate results.

possible loss of precision

Note

Casting does not change the variable being cast. For example, `d` is not changed after casting in the following code:

```java
double d = 4.5;
int i = (int)d; // i becomes 4, but d is still 4.5
```

Note

In Java, an augmented expression of the form `x1 op= x2` is implemented as `x1 = (T)(x1 op x2)`, where `T` is the type for `x1`. Therefore, the following code is correct:

casting in an augmented expression

```java
int sum = 0;
sum += 4.5; // sum becomes 4 after this statement
```

`sum += 4.5` is equivalent to `sum = (int)(sum + 4.5)`.

Note

To assign a variable of the `int` type to a variable of the `short` or `byte` type, explicit casting must be used. For example, the following statements have a compile error:

```java
int i = 1;
byte b = i; // Error because explicit casting is required
```

However, so long as the integer literal is within the permissible range of the target variable, explicit casting is not needed to assign an integer literal to a variable of the **short** or **byte** type (see Section 2.10, Numeric Literals).

The program in Listing 2.8 displays the sales tax with two digits after the decimal point.

LISTING 2.8 SalesTax.java

```
1  import java.util.Scanner;
2
3  public class SalesTax {
4    public static void main(String[] args) {
5      Scanner input = new Scanner(System.in);
6
7      System.out.print("Enter purchase amount: ");
8      double purchaseAmount = input.nextDouble();
9
10     double tax = purchaseAmount * 0.06;
11     System.out.println("Sales tax is $" + (int)(tax * 100) / 100.0);
12   }
13 }
```

casting (line 10-11)

```
Enter purchase amount: 197.55 ↵Enter
Sales tax is $11.85
```

line#	purchaseAmount	tax	Output
8	197.55		
10		11.853	
11			11.85

formatting numbers

Using the input in the sample run, the variable `purchaseAmount` is `197.55` (line 8). The sales tax is `6%` of the purchase, so the `tax` is evaluated as `11.853` (line 10). Note

```
tax * 100 is 1185.3
(int)(tax * 100) is 1185
(int)(tax * 100) / 100.0 is 11.85
```

Thus, the statement in line 11 displays the tax `11.85` with two digits after the decimal point. Note the expression `(int)(tax * 100) / 100.0` rounds down `tax` to two decimal places. If `tax` is `3.456`, `(int)(tax * 100) / 100.0` would be `3.45`. Can it be rounded up to two decimal places? Note any double value x can be rounded up to an integer using `(int)(x + 0.5)`. Thus, `tax` can be rounded up to two decimal places using `(int)(tax * 100 + 0.5) / 100.0`.

Check Point

2.15.1 Can different types of numeric values be used together in a computation?

2.15.2 What does an explicit casting from a **double** to an **int** do with the fractional part of the **double** value? Does casting change the variable being cast?

2.15.3 Show the following output:

```
float f = 12.5F;
int i = (int)f;
System.out.println("f is " + f);
System.out.println("i is " + i);
```

2.15.4 If you change `(int)(tax * 100) / 100.0` to `(int)(tax * 100) / 100` in line 11 in Listing 2.8, what will be the output for the input purchase amount of `197.556`?

2.15.5 Show the output of the following code:

```java
double amount = 5;
System.out.println(amount / 2);
System.out.println(5 / 2);
```

2.15.6 Write an expression that rounds up a `double` value in variable `d` to an integer.

2.16 Software Development Process

The software development life cycle is a multistage process that includes requirements specification, analysis, design, implementation, testing, deployment, and maintenance.

Developing a software product is an engineering process. Software products, no matter how large or how small, have the same life cycle: requirements specification, analysis, design, implementation, testing, deployment, and maintenance, as shown in Figure 2.3.

Key Point

VideoNote

Software development process

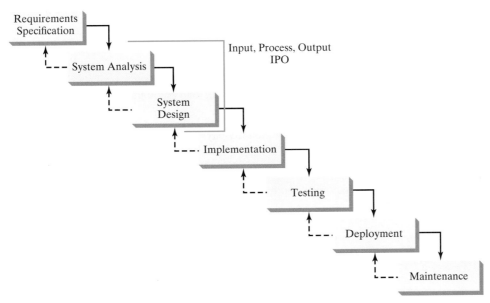

Figure 2.3 At any stage of the software development life cycle, it may be necessary to go back to a previous stage to correct errors or deal with other issues that might prevent the software from functioning as expected.

Requirements specification is a formal process that seeks to understand the problem the software will address, and to document in detail what the software system needs to do. This phase involves close interaction between users and developers. Most of the examples in this book are simple, and their requirements are clearly stated. In the real world, however, problems are not always well defined. Developers need to work closely with their customers (the individuals or organizations that will use the software) and study the problem carefully to identify what the software needs to do.

System analysis seeks to analyze the data flow and to identify the system's input and output. When you perform analysis, it helps to identify what the output is first, then figure out what input data you need in order to produce the output.

requirements specification

system analysis

system design

IPO
implementation

testing

deployment

maintenance

VideoNote

Compute loan payments

System design is to design a process for obtaining the output from the input. This phase involves the use of many levels of abstraction to break down the problem into manageable components and design strategies for implementing each component. You can view each component as a subsystem that performs a specific function of the system. The essence of system analysis and design is input, process, and output (IPO).

Implementation involves translating the system design into programs. Separate programs are written for each component then integrated to work together. This phase requires the use of a programming language such as Java. The implementation involves coding, self-testing, and debugging (that is, finding errors, called *bugs*, in the code).

Testing ensures the code meets the requirements specification and weeds out bugs. An independent team of software engineers not involved in the design and implementation of the product usually conducts such testing.

Deployment makes the software available for use. Depending on the type of software, it may be installed on each user's machine, or installed on a server accessible on the Internet.

Maintenance is concerned with updating and improving the product. A software product must continue to perform and improve in an ever-evolving environment. This requires periodic upgrades of the product to fix newly discovered bugs and incorporate changes.

To see the software development process in action, we will now create a program that computes loan payments. The loan can be a car loan, a student loan, or a home mortgage loan. For an introductory programming course, we focus on requirements specification, analysis, design, implementation, and testing.

Stage 1: Requirements Specification

The program must satisfy the following requirements:

- It must let the user enter the interest rate, the loan amount, and the number of years for which payments will be made.

- It must compute and display the monthly payment and total payment amounts.

Stage 2: System Analysis

The output is the monthly payment and total payment, which can be obtained using the following formulas:

$$monthlyPayment = \frac{loanAmount \times monthlyInterestRate}{1 - \dfrac{1}{(1 + monthlyInterestRate)^{numberOfYears \times 12}}}$$

$$totalPayment = monthlyPayment \times numberOfYears \times 12$$

Therefore, the input needed for the program is the monthly interest rate, the length of the loan in years, and the loan amount.

 Note

The requirements specification says the user must enter the annual interest rate, the loan amount, and the number of years for which payments will be made. During analysis, however, it is possible you may discover that input is not sufficient or some values are unnecessary for the output. If this happens, you can go back and modify the requirements specification.

 Note

In the real world, you will work with customers from all walks of life. You may develop software for chemists, physicists, engineers, economists, and psychologists, and of course you will not have (or need) complete knowledge of all these fields. Therefore, you don't have to know how formulas are derived, but given the monthly interest rate, the number of years, and the loan amount, you can compute the monthly payment in this program. You will, however, need to communicate with customers and understand how a mathematical model works for the system.

Stage 3: System Design

During system design, you identify the steps in the program.

Step 3.1. Prompt the user to enter the annual interest rate, the number of years, and the loan amount.

(The interest rate is commonly expressed as a percentage of the principal for a period of one year. This is known as the *annual interest rate*.)

Step 3.2. The input for the annual interest rate is a number in percent format, such as 4.5%. The program needs to convert it into a decimal by dividing it by 100. To obtain the monthly interest rate from the annual interest rate, divide it by 12, since a year has 12 months. Thus, to obtain the monthly interest rate in decimal format, you need to divide the annual interest rate in percentage by 1200. For example, if the annual interest rate is 4.5%, then the monthly interest rate is 4.5/1200 = 0.00375.

Step 3.3. Compute the monthly payment using the preceding formula.

Step 3.4. Compute the total payment, which is the monthly payment multiplied by 12 and multiplied by the number of years.

Step 3.5. Display the monthly payment and total payment.

Stage 4: Implementation

Implementation is also known as *coding* (writing the code). In the formula, you have to compute $(1 + \text{monthlyInterestRate})^{\text{numberOfYears} \times 12}$, which can be obtained using `Math.` `Math.pow(a, b)` method `pow(1 + monthlyInterestRate, numberOfYears * 12)`.

Listing 2.9 gives the complete program.

LISTING 2.9 `ComputeLoan.java`

```java
1  import java.util.Scanner;
2
3  public class ComputeLoan {
4    public static void main(String[] args) {
5      // Create a Scanner
6      Scanner input = new Scanner(System.in);
7
8      // Enter annual interest rate in percentage, e.g., 7.25
9      System.out.print("Enter annual interest rate, e.g., 7.25: ");
10     double annualInterestRate = input.nextDouble();
11
12     // Obtain monthly interest rate
13     double monthlyInterestRate = annualInterestRate / 1200;
14
15     // Enter number of years
16     System.out.print(
17       "Enter number of years as an integer, e.g., 5: ");
18     int numberOfYears = input.nextInt();
19
20     // Enter loan amount
21     System.out.print("Enter loan amount, e.g., 120000.95: ");
```

import class

create a Scanner

enter interest rate

enter years

enter loan amount

```
22    double loanAmount = input.nextDouble();
23
24    // Calculate payment
25    double monthlyPayment = loanAmount * monthlyInterestRate / (1
26      - 1 / Math.pow(1 + monthlyInterestRate, numberOfYears * 12));
27    double totalPayment = monthlyPayment * numberOfYears * 12;
28
29    // Display results
30    System.out.println("The monthly payment is $" +
31      (int)(monthlyPayment * 100) / 100.0);
32    System.out.println("The total payment is $" +
33      (int)(totalPayment * 100) / 100.0);
34    }
35  }
```

monthlyPayment (line 25)

totalPayment (line 27)

casting (line 30)

casting (line 32)

```
Enter annual interest rate, for example, 7.25: 5.75 ↵Enter
Enter number of years as an integer, for example, 5: 15 ↵Enter
Enter loan amount, for example, 120000.95: 250000 ↵Enter
The monthly payment is $2076.02
The total payment is $373684.53
```

variables \ line#	10	13	18	22	25	27
annualInterestRate	5.75					
monthlyInterestRate		0.0047916666666				
numberOfYears			15			
loanAmount				250000		
monthlyPayment					2076.0252175	
totalPayment						373684.539

Line 10 reads the annual interest rate, which is converted into the monthly interest rate in line 13.

Choose the most appropriate data type for the variable. For example, numberOfYears is best declared as an int (line 18), although it could be declared as a long, float, or double. Note byte might be the most appropriate for numberOfYears. For simplicity, however, the examples in this book will use int for integer and double for floating-point values.

The formula for computing the monthly payment is translated into Java code in lines 25–27.

Casting is used in lines 31 and 33 to obtain a new monthlyPayment and totalPayment with two digits after the decimal points.

java.lang package

The program uses the Scanner class, imported in line 1. The program also uses the Math class, and you might be wondering why that class isn't imported into the program. The Math class is in the java.lang package, and all classes in the java.lang package are implicitly imported. Therefore, you don't need to explicitly import the Math class.

Stage 5: Testing

After the program is implemented, test it with some sample input data and verify whether the output is correct. Some of the problems may involve many cases, as you will see in later chapters. For these types of problems, you need to design test data that cover all cases.

Tip
The system design phase in this example identified several steps. It is a good approach to code and test these steps incrementally by adding them one at a time. This approach makes it much easier to pinpoint problems and debug the program.

incremental code and test

2.16.1 How would you write the following arithmetic expression?

$$\frac{-b + \sqrt{b^2 - 4ac}}{2a}$$

Check Point

2.17 Case Study: Counting Monetary Units

This section presents a program that breaks a large amount of money into smaller units.

Key Point

Suppose you want to develop a program that changes a given amount of money into smaller monetary units. The program lets the user enter an amount as a `double` value representing a total in dollars and cents, and outputs a report listing the monetary equivalent in the maximum number of dollars, quarters, dimes, nickels, and pennies, in this order, to result in the minimum number of coins.

Here are the steps in developing the program:

1. Prompt the user to enter the amount as a decimal number, such as `11.56`.

2. Convert the amount (e.g., `11.56`) into cents (`1156`).

3. Divide the cents by `100` to find the number of dollars. Obtain the remaining cents using the cents remainder `100`.

4. Divide the remaining cents by `25` to find the number of quarters. Obtain the remaining cents using the remaining cents remainder `25`.

5. Divide the remaining cents by `10` to find the number of dimes. Obtain the remaining cents using the remaining cents remainder `10`.

6. Divide the remaining cents by `5` to find the number of nickels. Obtain the remaining cents using the remaining cents remainder `5`.

7. The remaining cents are the pennies.

8. Display the result.

The complete program is given in Listing 2.10.

LISTING 2.10 ComputeChange.java

```
1  import java.util.Scanner;
2
3  public class ComputeChange {
4    public static void main(String[] args) {
5      // Create a Scanner
6      Scanner input = new Scanner(System.in);
7
8      // Receive the amount
9      System.out.print(
10       "Enter an amount in double, for example 11.56: ");
11     double amount = input.nextDouble();
12
13     int remainingAmount = (int)(amount * 100);
14
15     // Find the number of one dollars
```

import class

enter input

dollars

quarters

dimes

nickels

pennies

output

```
16          int numberOfOneDollars = remainingAmount / 100;
17          remainingAmount = remainingAmount % 100;
18
19          // Find the number of quarters in the remaining amount
20          int numberOfQuarters = remainingAmount / 25;
21          remainingAmount = remainingAmount % 25;
22
23          // Find the number of dimes in the remaining amount
24          int numberOfDimes = remainingAmount / 10;
25          remainingAmount = remainingAmount % 10;
26
27          // Find the number of nickels in the remaining amount
28          int numberOfNickels = remainingAmount / 5;
29          remainingAmount = remainingAmount % 5;
30
31          // Find the number of pennies in the remaining amount
32          int numberOfPennies = remainingAmount;
33
34          // Display results
35          System.out.println("Your amount " + amount + " consists of");
36          System.out.println("    " + numberOfOneDollars + " dollars");
37          System.out.println("    " + numberOfQuarters + " quarters ");
38          System.out.println("    " + numberOfDimes + " dimes");
39          System.out.println("    " + numberOfNickels + " nickels");
40          System.out.println("    " + numberOfPennies + " pennies");
41      }
42  }
```

```
Enter an amount in double, for example, 11.56: 11.56 ⏎Enter
Your amount 11.56 consists of
        11 dollars
        2 quarters
        0 dimes
        1 nickels
        1 pennies
```

variables \ line#	11	13	16	17	20	21	24	25	28	29	32
amount	11.56										
remainingAmount		1156		56		6		6		1	
numberOfOneDollars			11								
numberOfQuarters					2						
numberOfDimes							0				
numberOfNickels									1		
numberOfPennies											1

The variable amount stores the amount entered from the console (line 11). This variable is not changed, because the amount has to be used at the end of the program to display the results. The program introduces the variable remainingAmount (line 13) to store the changing remaining amount.

The variable `amount` is a `double` decimal representing dollars and cents. It is converted to an `int` variable `remainingAmount`, which represents all the cents. For instance, if `amount` is `11.56`, then the initial `remainingAmount` is `1156`. The division operator yields the integer part of the division, so `1156 / 100` is `11`. The remainder operator obtains the remainder of the division, so `1156 % 100` is `56`.

The program extracts the maximum number of singles from the remaining amount and obtains a new remaining amount in the variable `remainingAmount` (lines 16–17). It then extracts the maximum number of quarters from `remainingAmount` and obtains a new `remainingAmount` (lines 20–21). Continuing the same process, the program finds the maximum number of dimes, nickels, and pennies in the remaining amount.

One serious problem with this example is the possible loss of precision when casting a `double` amount to an `int remainingAmount`. This could lead to an inaccurate result. If you try to enter the amount `10.03`, `10.03 * 100` becomes `1002.9999999999999`. You will find that the program displays `10` dollars and `2` pennies. To fix the problem, enter the amount as an integer value representing cents (see Programming Exercise 2.22).

loss of precision

2.17.1 Show the output of Listing 2.10 with the input value `1.99`.

Check
Point

2.18 Common Errors and Pitfalls

Common elementary programming errors often involve undeclared variables, uninitialized variables, integer overflow, unintended integer division, and round-off errors.

Key
Point

Common Error 1: Undeclared/Uninitialized Variables and Unused Variables

A variable must be declared with a type and assigned a value before using it. A common error is not declaring a variable or initializing a variable. Consider the following code:

```
double interestRate = 0.05;
double interest = interestrate * 45;
```

This code is wrong, because `interestRate` is assigned a value `0.05`; but `interestrate` has not been declared and initialized. Java is case sensitive, so it considers `interestRate` and `interestrate` to be two different variables.

If a variable is declared, but not used in the program, it might be a potential programming error. Therefore, you should remove the unused variable from your program. For example, in the following code, `taxRate` is never used. It should be removed from the code.

```
double interestRate = 0.05;
double taxRate = 0.05;
double interest = interestRate * 45;
System.out.println("Interest is " + interest);
```

If you use an IDE such as Eclipse and NetBeans, you will receive a warning on unused variables.

Common Error 2: Integer Overflow

Numbers are stored with a limited numbers of digits. When a variable is assigned a value that is too large (*in size*) to be stored, it causes *overflow*. For example, executing the following statement causes overflow, because the largest value that can be stored in a variable of the `int` type is `2147483647`. `2147483648` will be too large for an `int` value:

what is overflow?

```
int value = 2147483647 + 1;
// value will actually be -2147483648
```

Likewise, executing the following statement also causes overflow, because the smallest value that can be stored in a variable of the `int` type is `-2147483648`. `-2147483649` is too large in size to be stored in an `int` variable.

```
int value = −2147483648 − 1;
// value will actually be 2147483647
```

Java does not report warnings or errors on overflow, so be careful when working with integers close to the maximum or minimum range of a given type.

what is underflow?

When a floating-point number is too small (i.e., too close to zero) to be stored, it causes *underflow*. Java approximates it to zero, so normally you don't need to be concerned about underflow.

Common Error 3: Round-off Errors

floating-point approximation

A *round-off error*, also called a *rounding error*, is the difference between the calculated approximation of a number and its exact mathematical value. For example, 1/3 is approximately 0.333 if you keep three decimal places, and is 0.3333333 if you keep seven decimal places. Since the number of digits that can be stored in a variable is limited, round-off errors are inevitable. Calculations involving floating-point numbers are approximated because these numbers are not stored with complete accuracy. For example,

```
System.out.println(1.0 - 0.1 - 0.1 - 0.1 - 0.1 - 0.1);
```

displays `0.5000000000000001`, not `0.5`, and

```
System.out.println(1.0 - 0.9);
```

displays `0.09999999999999998`, not `0.1`. Integers are stored precisely. Therefore, calculations with integers yield a precise integer result.

Common Error 4: Unintended Integer Division

Java uses the same divide operator, namely `/`, to perform both integer and floating-point division. When two operands are integers, the `/` operator performs an integer division. The result of the operation is an integer. The fractional part is truncated. To force two integers to perform a floating-point division, make one of the integers into a floating-point number. For example, the code in (a) displays that `average` as `1` and the code in (b) displays that `average` as `1.5`.

```
int number1 = 1;
int number2 = 2;
double average = (number1 + number2) / 2;
System.out.println(average);
```

```
int number1 = 1;
int number2 = 2;
double average = (number1 + number2) / 2.0;
System.out.println(average);
```

(a)   (b)

Common Pitfall 1: Redundant Input Objects

New programmers often write the code to create multiple input objects for each input. For example, the following code reads an integer and a double value:

```
Scanner input = new Scanner(System.in);
System.out.print("Enter an integer: ");
int v1 = input.nextInt();

Scanner input1 = new Scanner(System.in);     BAD CODE
System.out.print("Enter a double value: ");
double v2 = input1.nextDouble();
```

The code is not good. It creates two input objects unnecessarily and may lead to some subtle errors. You should rewrite the code as follows:

```
Scanner input = new Scanner(System.in);    GOOD CODE
System.out.print("Enter an integer: ");
int v1 = input.nextInt();
System.out.print("Enter a double value: ");
double v2 = input.nextDouble();
```

2.18.1 Can you declare a variable as `int` and later redeclare it as `double`?

2.18.2 What is an integer overflow? Can floating-point operations cause overflow?

2.18.3 Will overflow cause a runtime error?

2.18.4 What is a round-off error? Can integer operations cause round-off errors? Can floating-point operations cause round-off errors?

✓**Check Point**

Key Terms

algorithm 34	narrowing a type 57
assignment operator (=) 42	operand 46
assignment statement 42	operator 46
byte type 45	overflow 65
casting 57	postdecrement 55
constant 43	postincrement 55
data type 35	predecrement 55
declare variables 35	preincrement 55
decrement operator (−−) 55	primitive data type 35
double type 45	pseudocode 34
expression 42	requirements specification 59
final keyword 43	scope of a variable 41
float type 45	**short** type 45
floating-point number 35	specific import 38
identifier 40	system analysis 59
increment operator (++) 55	system design 60
incremental code and testing 63	underflow 66
int type 45	UNIX epoch 52
IPO 39	variable 35
literal 48	widening a type 57
long type 45	wildcard import 38

Chapter Summary

1. *Identifiers* are names for naming elements such as variables, constants, methods, classes, and packages in a program.

2. An identifier is a sequence of characters that consists of letters, digits, underscores (_), and dollar signs ($). An identifier must start with a letter or an underscore. It cannot start with a digit. An identifier cannot be a reserved word. An identifier can be of any length.

3. *Variables* are used to store data in a program. To declare a variable is to tell the compiler what type of data a variable can hold.

4. There are two types of `import` statements: *specific import* and *wildcard import*. The specific import specifies a single class in the import statement. The wildcard import imports all the classes in a package.

5. In Java, the equal sign (=) is used as the *assignment operator*.

6. A variable declared in a method must be assigned a value before it can be used.

7. A *named constant* (or simply a *constant*) represents permanent data that never changes.

8. A named constant is declared by using the keyword `final`.

9. Java provides four integer types (`byte`, `short`, `int`, and `long`) that represent integers of four different sizes.

10. Java provides two *floating-point types* (`float` and `double`) that represent floating-point numbers of two different precisions.

11. Java provides *operators* that perform numeric operations: + (addition), – (subtraction), * (multiplication), / (division), and % (remainder).

12. Integer arithmetic (/) yields an integer result.

13. The numeric operators in a Java expression are applied the same way as in an arithmetic expression.

14. Java provides the augmented assignment operators += (addition assignment), –= (subtraction assignment), *= (multiplication assignment), /= (division assignment), and %= (remainder assignment).

15. The *increment operator* (++) and the *decrement operator* (--) increment or decrement a variable by 1.

16. When evaluating an expression with values of mixed types, Java automatically converts the operands to appropriate types.

17. You can explicitly convert a value from one type to another using the `(type)value` notation.

18. *Casting* a variable of a type with a small range to a type with a larger range is known as *widening a type*.

19. Casting a variable of a type with a large range to a type with a smaller range is known as *narrowing a type*.

20. Widening a type can be performed automatically without explicit casting. Narrowing a type must be performed explicitly.

21. In computer science, midnight of January 1, 1970, is known as the *UNIX epoch*.

 # QUIZ

Answer the quiz for this chapter online at the Companion Website.

PROGRAMMING EXERCISES

MyProgrammingLab™

Debugging Tip
The compiler usually gives a reason for a syntax error. If you don't know how to correct it, compare your program closely, character by character, with similar examples in the text.

learn from examples

Pedagogical Note
Instructors may ask you to document your analysis and design for selected exercises. Use your own words to analyze the problem, including the input, output, and what needs to be computed, and describe how to solve the problem in pseudocode.

document analysis and design

Pedagogical Note
The solution to most even-numbered programming exercises are provided to students. These exercises serve as additional examples for a variety of programs. To maximize the benefits of these solutions, students should first attempt to complete the even-numbered exercises and then compare their solutions with the solutions provided in the book. Since the book provides a large number of programming exercises, it is sufficient if you can complete all even-numbered programming exercises.

even-numbered programming exercises

Sections 2.2–2.12

2.1   (*Convert Celsius to Fahrenheit*) Write a program that reads a Celsius degree in a `double` value from the console, then converts it to Fahrenheit, and displays the result. The formula for the conversion is as follows:

```
fahrenheit = (9 / 5) * celsius + 32
```

Hint: In Java, `9 / 5` is `1`, but `9.0 / 5` is `1.8`.

Here is a sample run:

```
Enter a degree in Celsius: 43.5 ⏎Enter
43.5 Celsius is 110.3 Fahrenheit
```

2.2   (*Compute the volume of a cylinder*) Write a program that reads in the radius and length of a cylinder and computes the area and volume using the following formulas:

```
area = radius * radius * π
volume = area * length
```

Here is a sample run:

```
Enter the radius and length of a cylinder: 5.5 12 ⏎Enter
The area is 95.0331
The volume is 1140.4
```

2.3   (*Convert feet into meters*) Write a program that reads a number in feet, converts it to meters, and displays the result. One foot is `0.305` meter. Here is a sample run:

```
Enter a value for feet: 16.5 ⏎Enter
16.5 feet is 5.0325 meters
```

2.4 (*Convert pounds into kilograms*) Write a program that converts pounds into kilograms. The program prompts the user to enter a number in pounds, converts it to kilograms, and displays the result. One pound is 0.454 kilogram. Here is a sample run:

```
Enter a number in pounds: 55.5  ↵Enter
55.5 pounds is 25.197 kilograms
```

*2.5 (*Financial application: calculate tips*) Write a program that reads the subtotal and the gratuity rate, then computes the gratuity and total. For example, if the user enters 10 for subtotal and 15% for gratuity rate, the program displays $1.5 as gratuity and $11.5 as total. Here is a sample run:

```
Enter the subtotal and a gratuity rate: 10 15  ↵Enter
The gratuity is $1.5 and total is $11.5
```

**2.6 (*Sum the digits in an integer*) Write a program that reads an integer between 0 and 1000 and adds all the digits in the integer. For example, if an integer is 932, the sum of all its digits is 14.

Hint: Use the % operator to extract digits, and use the / operator to remove the extracted digit. For instance, 932 % 10 = 2 and 932 / 10 = 93.

Here is a sample run:

```
Enter a number between 0 and 1000: 999  ↵Enter
The sum of the digits is 27
```

*2.7 (*Find the number of years*) Write a program that prompts the user to enter the minutes (e.g., 1 billion), and displays the number of years and remaining days for the minutes. For simplicity, assume that a year has 365 days. Here is a sample run:

```
Enter the number of minutes: 1000000000  ↵Enter
1000000000 minutes is approximately 1902 years and 214 days
```

*2.8 (*Current time*) Listing 2.7, ShowCurrentTime.java, gives a program that displays the current time in GMT. Revise the program so it prompts the user to enter the time zone offset to GMT and displays the time in the specified time zone. Here is a sample run:

```
Enter the time zone offset to GMT: -5  ↵Enter
The current time is 4:50:34
```

2.9 (*Physics: acceleration*) Average acceleration is defined as the change of velocity divided by the time taken to make the change, as given by the following formula:

$$a = \frac{v_1 - v_0}{t}$$

Write a program that prompts the user to enter the starting velocity v_0 in meters/second, the ending velocity v_1 in meters/second, and the time span t in seconds, then displays the average acceleration. Here is a sample run:

```
Enter v0, v1, and t: 5.5 50.9 4.5
The average acceleration is 10.0889
```

2.10   (*Science: calculating energy*) Write a program that calculates the energy needed to heat water from an initial temperature to a final temperature. Your program should prompt the user to enter the amount of water in kilograms and the initial and final temperatures of the water. The formula to compute the energy is

```
Q = M * (finalTemperature - initialTemperature) * 4184
```

where M is the weight of water in kilograms, initial and final temperatures are in degrees Celsius, and energy Q is measured in joules. Here is a sample run:

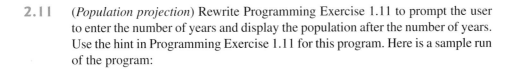

```
Enter the amount of water in kilograms: 55.5  ↵Enter
Enter the initial temperature: 3.5  ↵Enter
Enter the final temperature: 10.5  ↵Enter
The energy needed is 1625484.0
```

2.11   (*Population projection*) Rewrite Programming Exercise 1.11 to prompt the user to enter the number of years and display the population after the number of years. Use the hint in Programming Exercise 1.11 for this program. Here is a sample run of the program:

```
Enter the number of years: 5  ↵Enter
The population in 5 years is 325932969
```

2.12   (*Physics: finding runway length*) Given an airplane's acceleration a and take-off speed v, you can compute the minimum runway length needed for an airplane to take off using the following formula:

$$\text{length} = \frac{v^2}{2a}$$

Write a program that prompts the user to enter v in meters/second (m/s) and the acceleration a in meters/second squared (m/s^2), then, displays the minimum runway length. Here is a sample run:

```
Enter speed and acceleration: 60 3.5  ↵Enter
The minimum runway length for this airplane is 514.286
```

**2.13   (*Financial application: compound value*) Suppose you save $100 *each* month into a savings account with an annual interest rate 5%. Thus, the monthly interest rate is 0.05/12 = 0.00417. After the first month, the value in the account becomes

```
100 * (1 + 0.00417) = 100.417
```

After the second month, the value in the account becomes

```
(100 + 100.417) * (1 + 0.00417) = 201.252
```

After the third month, the value in the account becomes

```
(100 + 201.252) * (1 + 0.00417) = 302.507
```

and so on.

Write a program that prompts the user to enter a monthly saving amount and displays the account value after the sixth month. (In Programming Exercise 5.30, you will use a loop to simplify the code and display the account value for any month.)

```
Enter the monthly saving amount: 100 ↵Enter
After the sixth month, the account value is $608.81
```

VideoNote

Compute BMI

*2.14 (*Health application: computing BMI*) Body Mass Index (BMI) is a measure of health on weight. It can be calculated by taking your weight in kilograms and dividing, by the square of your height in meters. Write a program that prompts the user to enter a weight in pounds and height in inches and displays the BMI. Note one pound is `0.45359237` kilograms and one inch is `0.0254` meters. Here is a sample run:

```
Enter weight in pounds: 95.5 ↵Enter
Enter height in inches: 50 ↵Enter
BMI is 26.8573
```

2.15 (*Geometry: distance of two points*) Write a program that prompts the user to enter two points (`x1, y1`) and (`x2, y2`) and displays their distance. The formula for computing the distance is $\sqrt{(x_2 - x_1)^2 + (y_2 - y_1)^2}$. Note you can use `Math.pow(a, 0.5)` to compute $\sqrt{a}$. Here is a sample run:

```
Enter x1 and y1: 1.5 -3.4 ↵Enter
Enter x2 and y2: 4 5 ↵Enter
The distance between the two points is 8.764131445842194
```

2.16 (*Geometry: area of a hexagon*) Write a program that prompts the user to enter the side of a hexagon and displays its area. The formula for computing the area of a hexagon is

$$\text{Area} = \frac{3\sqrt{3}}{2} s^2,$$

where s is the length of a side. Here is a sample run:

```
Enter the length of the side: 5.5 ⏎Enter
The area of the hexagon is 78.5918
```

*2.17 (*Science: wind-chill temperature*) How cold is it outside? The temperature alone is not enough to provide the answer. Other factors including wind speed, relative humidity, and sunshine play important roles in determining coldness outside. In 2001, the National Weather Service (NWS) implemented the new wind-chill temperature to measure the coldness using temperature and wind speed. The formula is

$$t_{wc} = 35.74 + 0.6215t_a - 35.75v^{0.16} + 0.4275t_av^{0.16}$$

where t_a is the outside temperature measured in degrees Fahrenheit, v is the speed measured in miles per hour, and t_{wc} is the wind-chill temperature. The formula cannot be used for wind speeds below 2 mph or temperatures below −58°F or above 41°F.

Write a program that prompts the user to enter a temperature between −58°F and 41°F and a wind speed greater than or equal to 2 then displays the wind-chill temperature. Use Math.pow(a, b) to compute $v^{0.16}$. Here is a sample run:

```
Enter the temperature in Fahrenheit between −58°F and 41°F:
5.3 ⏎Enter
Enter the wind speed (>= 2) in miles per hour: 6 ⏎Enter
The wind chill index is −5.56707
```

2.18 (*Print a table*) Write a program that displays the following table. Cast floating-point numbers into integers.

a	b	pow(a, b)
1	2	1
2	3	8
3	4	81
4	5	1024
5	6	15625

*2.19 (*Geometry: area of a triangle*) Write a program that prompts the user to enter three points, (x1, y1), (x2, y2), and (x3, y3), of a triangle then displays its area. The formula for computing the area of a triangle is

$$s = (side1 + side2 + side3)/2;$$

$$area = \sqrt{s(s - side1)(s - side2)(s - side3)}$$

Here is a sample run:

```
Enter the coordinates of three points separated by spaces
like x1 y1 x2 y2 x3 y3: 1.5 -3.4 4.6 5 9.5 -3.4 ⏎Enter
The area of the triangle is 33.6
```

Sections 2.13–2.17

*2.20 (*Financial application: calculate interest*) If you know the balance and the annual percentage interest rate, you can compute the interest on the next monthly payment using the following formula:

interest = balance × (annualInterestRate/1200)

Write a program that reads the balance and the annual percentage interest rate and displays the interest for the next month. Here is a sample run:

```
Enter balance and interest rate (e.g., 3 for 3%): 1000 3.5  ↵Enter
The interest is 2.91667
```

*2.21 (*Financial application: calculate future investment value*) Write a program that reads in investment amount, annual interest rate, and number of years and displays the future investment value using the following formula:

futureInvestmentValue =

investmentAmount × (1 + monthlyInterestRate)^{numberOfYears*12}

For example, if you enter amount **1000**, annual interest rate **3.25%**, and number of years **1**, the future investment value is **1032.98**.

Here is a sample run:

```
Enter investment amount: 1000.56  ↵Enter
Enter annual interest rate in percentage: 4.25  ↵Enter
Enter number of years: 1  ↵Enter
Future value is $1043.92
```

*2.22 (*Financial application: monetary units*) Rewrite Listing 2.10, ComputeChange.java, to fix the possible loss of accuracy when converting a double value to an int value. Enter the input as an integer whose last two digits represent the cents. For example, the input **1156** represents **11** dollars and **56** cents.

*2.23 (*Cost of driving*) Write a program that prompts the user to enter the distance to drive, the fuel efficiency of the car in miles per gallon, and the price per gallon then displays the cost of the trip. Here is a sample run:

```
Enter the driving distance: 900.5  ↵Enter
Enter miles per gallon: 25.5  ↵Enter
Enter price per gallon: 3.55  ↵Enter
The cost of driving is $125.36
```

Note
More than 200 additional programming exercises with solutions are provided to the instructors on the Instructor Resource Website.

CHAPTER

3

SELECTIONS

Objectives

- To declare `boolean` variables and write Boolean expressions using relational operators (§3.2).

- To implement selection control using one-way `if` statements (§3.3).

- To implement selection control using two-way `if-else` statements (§3.4).

- To implement selection control using nested `if` and multi-way `if` statements (§3.5).

- To avoid common errors and pitfalls in `if` statements (§3.6).

- To generate random numbers using the `Math.random()` method (§3.7).

- To program using selection statements for a variety of examples (`SubtractionQuiz`, `BMI`, `ComputeTax`) (§§3.7–3.9).

- To combine conditions using logical operators (`!`, `&&`, `||`, and `^`) (§3.10).

- To program using selection statements with combined conditions (`LeapYear`, `Lottery`) (§§3.11 and 3.12).

- To implement selection control using `switch` statements (§3.13).

- To write expressions using the conditional operator (§3.14).

- To examine the rules governing operator precedence and associativity (§3.15).

- To apply common techniques to debug errors (§3.16).

3.1 Introduction

problem

The program can decide which statements to execute based on a condition.

If you enter a negative value for `radius` in Listing 2.2, ComputeAreaWithConsoleInput.java, the program displays an invalid result. If the radius is negative, you don't want the program to compute the area. How can you deal with this situation?

selection statements

Like all high-level programming languages, Java provides *selection statements*: statements that let you choose actions with alternative courses. You can use the following selection statement to replace lines 12–17 in Listing 2.2:

```java
if (radius < 0) {
  System.out.println("Incorrect input");
}
else {
  double area = radius * radius * 3.14159;
  System.out.println("Area is " + area);
}
```

Boolean expression
Boolean value

Selection statements use conditions that are Boolean expressions. A *Boolean expression* is an expression that evaluates to a *Boolean value*: `true` or `false`. We now introduce the `boolean` type and relational operators.

3.2 `boolean` Data Type

The `boolean` data type declares a variable with the value either `true` or `false`.

How do you compare two values, such as whether a radius is greater than `0`, equal to `0`, or less than `0`? Java provides six *relational operators* (also known as *comparison operators*), shown in Table 3.1, which can be used to compare two values (assume radius is `5` in the table).

`boolean` data type
relational operators

TABLE 3.1 Relational Operators

Java Operator	Mathematics Symbol	Name	Example (radius is 5)	Result
<	<	Less than	radius < 0	false
<=	≤	Less than or equal to	radius <= 0	false
>	>	Greater than	radius > 0	true
>=	≥	Greater than or equal to	radius >= 0	true
==	=	Equal to	radius == 0	false
!=	≠	Not equal to	radius != 0	true

== vs. =

 Caution

The equality testing operator is two equal signs (==), not a single equal sign (=). The latter symbol is for assignment.

The result of the comparison is a Boolean value: `true` or `false`. For example, the following statement displays `true`:

```java
double radius = 1;
System.out.println(radius > 0);
```

Boolean variable

A variable that holds a Boolean value is known as a *Boolean variable*. The `boolean` data type is used to declare Boolean variables. A `boolean` variable can hold one of the two values: `true` or `false`. For example, the following statement assigns `true` to the variable `lightsOn`:

```
boolean lightsOn = true;
```

Boolean literals

`true` and `false` are literals, just like a number such as `10`. They are treated as reserved words and cannot be used as identifiers in the program.

VideoNote

Program addition quiz

Suppose you want to develop a program to let a first-grader practice addition. The program randomly generates two single-digit integers, `number1` and `number2`, and displays to the student a question such as "What is 1 + 7?, " as shown in the sample run in Listing 3.1. After the student types the answer, the program displays a message to indicate whether it is true or false.

There are several ways to generate random numbers. For now, generate the first integer using `System.currentTimeMillis() % 10` (i.e., the last digit in the current time) and the second using `System.currentTimeMillis() / 10 % 10` (i.e., the second last digit in the current time). Listing 3.1 gives the program. Lines 5–6 generate two numbers, `number1` and `number2`. Line 14 obtains an answer from the user. The answer is graded in line 18 using a Boolean expression `number1 + number2 == answer`.

LISTING 3.1 AdditionQuiz.java

```java
1  import java.util.Scanner;
2
3  public class AdditionQuiz {
4    public static void main(String[] args) {
5      int number1 = (int)(System.currentTimeMillis() % 10);          generate number1
6      int number2 = (int)(System.currentTimeMillis() / 10 % 10);     generate number2
7
8      // Create a Scanner
9      Scanner input = new Scanner(System.in);
10
11     System.out.print(                                              show question
12       "What is " + number1 + " + " + number2 + "? ");
13
14     int answer = input.nextInt();                                  receive answer
15
16     System.out.println(                                            display result
17       number1 + " + " + number2 + " = " + answer + " is " +
18       (number1 + number2 == answer));
19   }
20 }
```

```
What is 1 + 7? 8 ⏎Enter
1 + 7 = 8 is true
```

```
What is 4 + 8? 9 ⏎Enter
4 + 8 = 9 is false
```

line#	number1	number2	answer	output
5	4			
6		8		
14			9	
16				4 + 8 = 9 is false

3.2.1 List six relational operators.

3.2.2 Assuming x is 1, show the result of the following Boolean expressions:

```
(x > 0)
(x < 0)
(x != 0)
(x >= 0)
(x != 1)
```

3.2.3 Can the following conversions involving casting be allowed? Write a test program to verify it.

```
boolean b = true;
i = (int)b;

int i = 1;
boolean b = (boolean)i;
```

3.3 **if** Statements

An if statement is a construct that enables a program to specify alternative paths of execution.

why if statement?

The preceding program displays a message such as "6 + 2 = 7 is false." If you wish the message to be "6 + 2 = 7 is incorrect," you have to use a selection statement to make this minor change.

Java has several types of selection statements: one-way if statements, two-way if-else statements, nested if statements, multi-way if-else statements, switch statements, and conditional operators.

A one-way if statement executes an action if and only if the condition is true. The syntax for a one-way if statement is as follows:

if statement

```
if (boolean-expression) {
    statement(s);
}
```

flowchart

The flowchart in Figure 3.1a illustrates how Java executes the syntax of an if statement. A *flowchart* is a diagram that describes an algorithm or process, showing the steps as boxes of various kinds, and their order by connecting these with arrows. Process operations are represented in these boxes, and the arrows connecting them represent the flow of control. A diamond box denotes a Boolean condition, and a rectangle box represents statements.

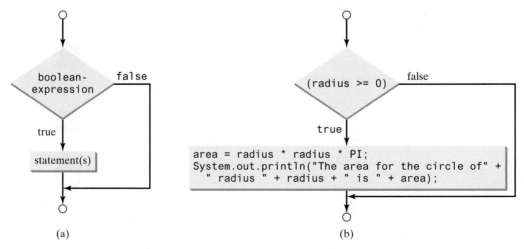

(a)   (b)

FIGURE 3.1 An if statement executes statements if the boolean-expression evaluates to true.

If the `boolean-expression` evaluates to `true`, the statements in the block are executed. As an example, see the following code:

```
if (radius >= 0) {
  area = radius * radius * PI;
  System.out.println("The area for the circle of radius " +
    radius + " is " + area);
}
```

The flowchart of the preceding statement is shown in Figure 3.1b. If the value of `radius` is greater than or equal to `0`, then the `area` is computed and the result is displayed; otherwise, the two statements in the block will not be executed.

The `boolean-expression` is enclosed in parentheses. For example, the code in (a) is wrong. It should be corrected, as shown in (b).

```
if  i > 0  {
  System.out.println("i is positive");
}
```

(a) Wrong

```
if (i > 0) {
  System.out.println("i is positive");
}
```

(b) Correct

The block braces can be omitted if they enclose a single statement. For example, the following statements are equivalent:

```
if (i > 0) {
  System.out.println("i is positive");
}
```

(a)

Equivalent

```
if (i > 0)
  System.out.println("i is positive");
```

(b)

Caution

Omitting braces makes the code shorter, but it is prone to errors. It is a common mistake to forget the braces when you go back to modify the code that omits the braces.

Omitting braces or not

Listing 3.2 gives a program that prompts the user to enter an integer. If the number is a multiple of `5`, the program displays `HiFive`. If the number is divisible by `2`, it displays `HiEven`.

LISTING 3.2 SimpleIfDemo.java

```
 1  import java.util.Scanner;
 2
 3  public class SimpleIfDemo {
 4    public static void main(String[] args) {
 5      Scanner input = new Scanner(System.in);
 6      System.out.print("Enter an integer: ");
 7      int number = input.nextInt();
 8
 9      if (number % 5 == 0)
10        System.out.println("HiFive");
11
12      if (number % 2 == 0)
13        System.out.println("HiEven");
14    }
15  }
```

enter input

check 5

check even

```
Enter an integer: 4  ↵Enter
HiEven
```

```
Enter an integer: 30  ↵Enter
HiFive
HiEven
```

The program prompts the user to enter an integer (lines 6–7) and displays `HiFive` if it is divisible by **5** (lines 9–10) and `HiEven` if it is divisible by **2** (lines 12–13).

3.3.1 Write an `if` statement that assigns **1** to `x` if `y` is greater than **0**.

3.3.2 Write an `if` statement that increases pay by 3% if `score` is greater than **90**.

3.3.3 What is wrong in the following code?

```
if radius >= 0
{
  area = radius * radius * PI;
  System.out.println("The area for the circle of " +
    " radius " + radius + " is " + area);
}
```

3.4 Two-Way `if-else` Statements

An `if-else` statement decides the execution path based on whether the condition is true or false.

A one-way `if` statement performs an action if the specified condition is `true`. If the condition is `false`, nothing is done. But what if you want to take alternative actions when the condition is `false`? You can use a two-way `if-else` statement. The actions that a two-way `if-else` statement specifies differ based on whether the condition is `true` or `false`.

Here is the syntax for a two-way `if-else` statement:

```
if (boolean-expression) {
  statement(s)-for-the-true-case;
}
else {
  statement(s)-for-the-false-case;
}
```

The flowchart of the statement is shown in Figure 3.2.

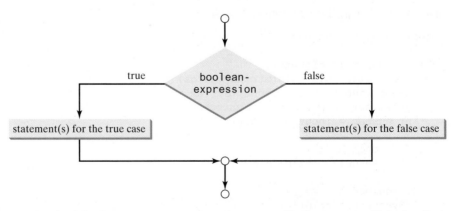

FIGURE 3.2 An `if-else` statement executes statements for the true case if the `boolean-expression` evaluates to `true`; otherwise, statements for the `false` case are executed.

If the `boolean-expression` evaluates to `true`, the statement(s) for the true case are executed; otherwise, the statement(s) for the `false` case are executed. For example, consider the following code:

```
if (radius >= 0) {
  area = radius * radius * PI;
  System.out.println("The area for the circle of radius " +
    radius + " is " + area);
}
else {
  System.out.println("Negative input");
}
```

 two-way **if-else** statement

If `radius >= 0` is `true`, `area` is computed and displayed; if it is `false`, the message `"Negative input"` is displayed.

As usual, the braces can be omitted if there is only one statement within them. The braces enclosing the `System.out.println("Negative input")` statement can therefore be omitted in the preceding example.

Here is another example of using the `if-else` statement. The example checks whether a number is even or odd, as follows:

```
if (number % 2 == 0)
  System.out.println(number + " is even.");
else
  System.out.println(number + " is odd.");
```

3.4.1 Write an `if` statement that increases `pay` by 3% if `score` is greater than `90`, otherwise increases `pay` by 1%.

3.4.2 What is the output of the code in (a) and (b) if `number` is `30`? What if `number` is `35`?

```
if (number % 2 == 0)
  System.out.println(number + " is even.");

System.out.println(number + " is odd.");
```
(a)

```
if (number % 2 == 0)
  System.out.println(number + " is even.");
else
  System.out.println(number + " is odd.");
```
(b)

3.5 Nested **if** and Multi-Way **if-else** Statements

An if *statement can be inside another* if *statement to form a nested* if *statement.*

The statement in an `if` or `if-else` statement can be any legal Java statement, including another `if` or `if-else` statement. The inner `if` statement is said to be *nested* inside the outer `if` statement. The inner `if` statement can contain another `if` statement; in fact, there is no limit to the depth of the nesting. For example, the following is a nested `if` statement:

 Key Point

nested **if** statement

```
if (i > k) {
  if (j > k)
    System.out.println("i and j are greater than k");
}
else
  System.out.println("i is less than or equal to k");
```

The `if (j > k)` statement is nested inside the `if (i > k)` statement.

The nested `if` statement can be used to implement multiple alternatives. The statement given in Figure 3.3a, for instance, prints a letter grade according to the score, with multiple alternatives.

```
if (score >= 90)
  System.out.print("A");
else
  if (score >= 80)
    System.out.print("B");
  else
    if (score >= 70)
      System.out.print("C");
    else
      if (score >= 60)
        System.out.print("D");
      else
        System.out.print("F");
```
(a)

Equivalent

This is better

```
if (score >= 90)
  System.out.print("A");
else if (score >= 80)
  System.out.print("B");
else if (score >= 70)
  System.out.print("C");
else if (score >= 60)
  System.out.print("D");
else
  System.out.print("F");
```
(b)

FIGURE 3.3 A preferred format for multiple alternatives is shown in (b) using a multi-way if-else statement.

The execution of this if statement proceeds as shown in Figure 3.4. The first condition (score >= 90) is tested. If it is true, the grade is A. If it is false, the second condition (score >= 80) is tested. If the second condition is true, the grade is B. If that condition is false, the third condition and the rest of the conditions (if necessary) are tested until a condition is met or all of the conditions prove to be false. If all of the conditions are false, the grade is F. Note a condition is tested only when all of the conditions that come before it are false.

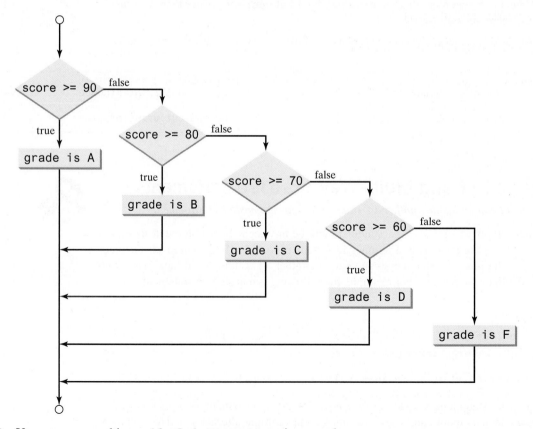

FIGURE 3.4 You can use a multi-way if-else statement to assign a grade.

The `if` statement in Figure 3.3a is equivalent to the `if` statement in Figure 3.3b. In fact, Figure 3.3b is the preferred coding style for multiple alternative `if` statements. This style, called *multi-way `if-else` statements*, avoids deep indentation and makes the program easy to read.

multi-way `if` statement

3.5.1 Suppose `x = 3` and `y = 2`; show the output, if any, of the following code. What is the output if `x = 3` and `y = 4`? What is the output if `x = 2` and `y = 2`? Draw a flowchart of the code.

✓Check Point

```
if (x > 2) {
  if (y > 2) {
    z = x + y;
    System.out.println("z is " + z);
  }
}
else
  System.out.println("x is " + x);
```

3.5.2 Suppose `x = 2` and `y = 3`. Show the output, if any, of the following code. What is the output if `x = 3` and `y = 2`? What is the output if `x = 3` and `y = 3`?

```
if (x > 2)
  if (y > 2) {
    int z = x + y;
    System.out.println("z is " + z);
  }
else
  System.out.println("x is " + x);
```

3.5.3 What is wrong in the following code?

```
if (score >= 60)
  System.out.println("D");
else if (score >= 70)
  System.out.println("C");
else if (score >= 80)
  System.out.println("B");
else if (score >= 90)
  System.out.println("A");
else
  System.out.println("F");
```

3.6 Common Errors and Pitfalls

Forgetting necessary braces, ending an `if` statement in the wrong place, mistaking `==` for `=`, and dangling `else` clauses are common errors in selection statements. Duplicated statements in `if-else` statements and testing equality of double values are common pitfalls.

Key Point

The following errors are common among new programmers.

Common Error 1: Forgetting Necessary Braces

The braces can be omitted if the block contains a single statement. However, forgetting the braces when they are needed for grouping multiple statements is a common programming error. If you modify the code by adding new statements in an `if` statement without braces, you will have to insert the braces. For example, the following code in (a) is wrong. It should be written with braces to group multiple statements, as shown in (b).

```
if (radius >= 0)
    area = radius * radius * PI;
    System.out.println("The area "
        + " is " + area);
```
(a) Wrong

```
if (radius >= 0) {
    area = radius * radius * PI;
    System.out.println("The area "
        + " is " + area);
}
```
(b) Correct

In (a), the console output statement is not part of the `if` statement. It is the same as the following code:

```
if (radius >= 0)
    area = radius * radius * PI;

System.out.println("The area "
    + " is " + area);
```

Regardless of the condition in the `if` statement, the console output statement is always executed.

Common Error 2: Wrong Semicolon at the `if` Line

Adding a semicolon at the end of an `if` line, as shown in (a) below, is a common mistake.

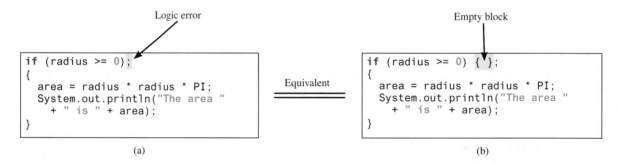

Logic error

```
if (radius >= 0);
{
    area = radius * radius * PI;
    System.out.println("The area "
        + " is " + area);
}
```
(a)

Equivalent

Empty block

```
if (radius >= 0) { };
{
    area = radius * radius * PI;
    System.out.println("The area "
        + " is " + area);
}
```
(b)

This mistake is hard to find, because it is neither a compile error nor a runtime error; it is a logic error. The code in (a) is equivalent to that in (b) with an empty block.

This error often occurs when you use the next-line block style. Using the end-of-line block style can help prevent this error.

Common Error 3: Redundant Testing of Boolean Values

To test whether a `boolean` variable is `true` or `false` in a test condition, it is redundant to use the equality testing operator like the code in (a):

```
if (even == true)
    System.out.println(
        "It is even.");
```
(a)

Equivalent

This is better

```
if (even)
    System.out.println(
        "It is even.");
```
(b)

Instead, it is better to test the `boolean` variable directly, as shown in (b). Another good reason for doing this is to avoid errors that are difficult to detect. Using the `=` operator instead of the `==` operator to compare the equality of two items in a test condition is a common error. It could lead to the following erroneous statement:

```
if (even = true)
    System.out.println("It is even.");
```

This statement does not have compile errors. It assigns `true` to `even`, so `even` is always `true`.

Common Error 4: Dangling `else` Ambiguity

dangling `else` ambiguity

The code in (a) below has two `if` clauses and one `else` clause. Which `if` clause is matched by the `else` clause? The indentation indicates that the `else` clause matches the first `if` clause. However, the `else` clause actually matches the second `if` clause. This situation is known as the *dangling else ambiguity*. The `else` clause always matches the most recent unmatched `if` clause in the same block. Therefore, the statement in (a) is equivalent to the code in (b).

```
int i = 1, j = 2, k = 3;

if (i > j)
  if (i > k)
      System.out.println("A");
else
      System.out.println("B");
```

Equivalent

This is better
with correct
indentation

```
int i = 1, j = 2, k = 3;

if (i > j)
  if (i > k)
      System.out.println("A");
  else
      System.out.println("B");
```

(a)   (b)

Since `(i > j)` is false, nothing is displayed from the statements in (a) and (b). To force the `else` clause to match the first `if` clause, you must add a pair of braces:

```
int i = 1, j = 2, k = 3;

if (i > j) {
  if (i > k)
     System.out.println("A");
}
else
  System.out.println("B");
```

This statement displays `B`.

Common Error 5: Equality Test of Two Floating-Point Values

As discussed in Common Error 3 in Section 2.8, floating-point numbers have a limited precision and calculations; involving floating-point numbers can introduce round-off errors. Therefore, equality test of two floating-point values is not reliable. For example, you expect the following code to display `true`, but surprisingly, it displays `false`:

```
double x = 1.0 - 0.1 - 0.1 - 0.1 - 0.1 - 0.1;
System.out.println(x == 0.5);
```

Here, `x` is not exactly `0.5`, but is `0.500000000000001`. You cannot reliably test equality of two floating-point values. However, you can compare whether they are close enough by testing whether the difference of the two numbers is less than some threshold. That is, two numbers x and y are very close if $|x - y| < \varepsilon$, for a very small value, ε. ε, a Greek letter pronounced "epsilon", is commonly used to denote a very small value. Normally, you set ε to 10^{-14} for comparing two values of the `double` type, and to 10^{-7} for comparing two values of the `float` type. For example, the following code

```
final double EPSILON = 1E-14;
double x = 1.0 - 0.1 - 0.1 - 0.1 - 0.1 - 0.1;
if (Math.abs(x - 0.5) < EPSILON)
  System.out.println(x + " is approximately 0.5");
```

will display

```
0.5000000000000001 is approximately 0.5.
```

The `Math.abs(a)` method can be used to return the absolute value of `a`.

Common Pitfall 1: Simplifying Boolean Variable Assignment

Often, new programmers write the code that assigns a test condition to a `boolean` variable like the code in (a):

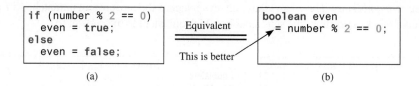

```
if (number % 2 == 0)
    even = true;
else
    even = false;
```
(a)

Equivalent

This is better

```
boolean even
    = number % 2 == 0;
```
(b)

This is not an error, but it should be better written as shown in (b).

Common Pitfall 2: Avoiding Duplicate Code in Different Cases

Often, new programmers write the duplicate code in different cases that should be combined in one place. For example, the highlighted code in the following statement is duplicated:

```
if (inState) {
    tuition = 5000;
    System.out.println("The tuition is " + tuition);
}
else {
    tuition = 15000;
    System.out.println("The tuition is " + tuition);
}
```

This is not an error, but it should be better written as follows:

```
if (inState) {
    tuition = 5000;
}
else {
    tuition = 15000;
}
System.out.println("The tuition is " + tuition);
```

The new code removes the duplication and makes the code easy to maintain, because you only need to change in one place if the print statement is modified.

 Check Point

3.6.1 Which of the following statements are equivalent? Which ones are correctly indented?

```
if (i > 0) if
(j > 0)
x = 0; else
if (k > 0) y = 0;
else z = 0;
```
(a)

```
if (i > 0) {
    if (j > 0)
        x = 0;
    else if (k > 0)
        y = 0;
}
else
    z = 0;
```
(b)

```
if (i > 0)
    if (j > 0)
        x = 0;
    else if (k > 0)
        y = 0;
    else
        z = 0;
```
(c)

```
if (i > 0)
    if (j > 0)
        x = 0;
    else if (k > 0)
        y = 0;
else
    z = 0;
```
(d)

3.6.2 Rewrite the following statement using a Boolean expression:

```
if (count % 10 == 0)
    newLine = true;
else
    newLine = false;
```

3.6.3 Are the following statements correct? Which one is better?

```
if (age < 16)
  System.out.println
    ("Cannot get a driver's license");
if (age >= 16)
  System.out.println
    ("Can get a driver's license");
```
(a)

```
if (age < 16)
  System.out.println
    ("Cannot get a driver's license");
else
  System.out.println
    ("Can get a driver's license");
```
(b)

3.6.4 What is the output of the following code if number is 14, 15, or 30?

```
if (number % 2 == 0)
  System.out.println
    (number + " is even");
if (number % 5 == 0)
  System.out.println
    (number + " is multiple of 5");
```
(a)

```
if (number % 2 == 0)
  System.out.println
    (number + " is even");
else if (number % 5 == 0)
  System.out.println
    (number + " is multiple of 5");
```
(b)

3.7 Generating Random Numbers

You can use Math.random() *to obtain a random double value between* 0.0 *and* 1.0, *excluding* 1.0.

Suppose you want to develop a program for a first-grader to practice subtraction. The program randomly generates two single-digit integers, number1 and number2, with number1 >= number2, and it displays to the student a question such as "What is 9 − 2?" After the student enters the answer, the program displays a message indicating whether it is correct.

VideoNote

Program subtraction quiz

The previous programs generate random numbers using System.currentTimeMillis(). A better approach is to use the random() method in the Math class. Invoking this method returns a random double value d such that 0.0 ≤ d < 1.0. Thus, (int)(Math.random() * 10) returns a random single-digit integer (i.e., a number between 0 and 9).

random() method

The program can work as follows:

1. Generate two single-digit integers into number1 and number2.

2. If number1 < number2, swap number1 with number2.

3. Prompt the student to answer, "What is number1 − number2?"

4. Check the student's answer and display whether the answer is correct.

The complete program is given in Listing 3.3.

LISTING 3.3 SubtractionQuiz.java

```
1 import java.util.Scanner;
2
3 public class SubtractionQuiz {
4   public static void main(String[] args) {
5     // 1. Generate two random single-digit integers
6     int number1 = (int)(Math.random() * 10);
7     int number2 = (int)(Math.random() * 10);
8
9     // 2. If number1 < number2, swap number1 with number2
10    if (number1 < number2) {
11      int temp = number1;
```

random number

```
12        number1 = number2;
13        number2 = temp;
14      }
15
16      // 3. Prompt the student to answer "What is number1 - number2?"
17      System.out.print
18        ("What is " + number1 + " - " + number2 + "? ");
19      Scanner input = new Scanner(System.in);
20      int answer = input.nextInt();
21
22      // 4. Grade the answer and display the result
23      if (number1 - number2 == answer)
24        System.out.println("You are correct!");
25      else {
26        System.out.println("Your answer is wrong.");
27        System.out.println(number1 + " - " + number2 +
28          " should be " + (number1 - number2));
29      }
30    }
31 }
```

get answer (line 20)

check the answer (line 23)

```
What is 6 - 6? 0 ⏎Enter
You are correct!
```

```
What is 9 - 2? 5 ⏎Enter
Your answer is wrong
9 - 2 is 7
```

line#	number1	number2	temp	answer	output
6	2				
7		9			
11			2		
12	9				
13		2			
20				5	
26					Your answer is wrong 9 - 2 should be 7

To swap two variables `number1` and `number2`, a temporary variable `temp` (line 11) is used to first hold the value in `number1`. The value in `number2` is assigned to `number1` (line 12), and the value in `temp` is assigned to `number2` (line 13).

Check
Point

3.7.1 Which of the following is a possible output from invoking `Math.random()`?

`323.4, 0.5, 34, 1.0, 0.0, 0.234`

3.7.2 a. How do you generate a random integer `i` such that $0 \le i < 20$?

b. How do you generate a random integer `i` such that $10 \le i < 20$?

c. How do you generate a random integer `i` such that $10 \le i \le 50$?

d. Write an expression that returns `0` or `1` randomly.

3.8 Case Study: Computing Body Mass Index

You can use nested `if` *statements to write a program that interprets body mass index.*

Key
Point

Body mass index (BMI) is a measure of health based on height and weight. It can be calculated by taking your weight in kilograms and dividing it by the square of your height in meters. The interpretation of BMI for people 20 years or older is as follows:

BMI	Interpretation
BMI < 18.5	Underweight
18.5 ≤ BMI < 25.0	Normal
25.0 ≤ BMI < 30.0	Overweight
30.0 ≤ BMI	Obese

Write a program that prompts the user to enter a weight in pounds and height in inches and displays the BMI. Note that one pound is 0.45359237 kilograms, and one inch is 0.0254 meters. Listing 3.4 gives the program.

LISTING 3.4 ComputeAndInterpretBMI.java

```java
 1 import java.util.Scanner;
 2
 3 public class ComputeAndInterpretBMI {
 4   public static void main(String[] args) {
 5     Scanner input = new Scanner(System.in);
 6
 7     // Prompt the user to enter weight in pounds
 8     System.out.print("Enter weight in pounds: ");
 9     double weight = input.nextDouble();                         input weight
10
11     // Prompt the user to enter height in inches
12     System.out.print("Enter height in inches: ");
13     double height = input.nextDouble();                         input height
14
15     final double KILOGRAMS_PER_POUND = 0.45359237; // Constant
16     final double METERS_PER_INCH = 0.0254; // Constant
17
18     // Compute BMI
19     double weightInKilograms = weight * KILOGRAMS_PER_POUND;
20     double heightInMeters = height * METERS_PER_INCH;
21     double bmi = weightInKilograms /                            compute bmi
22       (heightInMeters * heightInMeters);
23
24     // Display result
25     System.out.println("BMI is " + bmi);                        display output
26     if (bmi < 18.5)
27       System.out.println("Underweight");
28     else if (bmi < 25)
29       System.out.println("Normal");
30     else if (bmi < 30)
31       System.out.println("Overweight");
32     else
33       System.out.println("Obese");
34   }
35 }
```

```
Enter weight in pounds: 146 ↵Enter
Enter height in inches: 70 ↵Enter
BMI is 20.948603801493316
Normal
```

line#	weight	height	weightInKilograms	heightInMeters	bmi	output
9	146					
13		70				
19			66.22448602			
20				1.778		
21					20.9486	
25						BMI is 20.95
29						Normal

The constants `KILOGRAMS_PER_POUND` and `METERS_PER_INCH` are defined in lines 15–16. Using constants here makes programs easy to read.

test all cases   You should test the input that covers all possible cases for BMI to ensure that the program works for all cases.

3.9 Case Study: Computing Taxes

You can use nested `if` statements to write a program for computing taxes.

Key Point

VideoNote
Use multi-way `if-else` statements

The U.S. federal personal income tax is calculated based on filing status and taxable income. There are four filing statuses: single filers, married filing jointly or qualified widow(er), married filing separately, and head of household. The tax rates vary every year. Table 3.2 shows the rates for 2009. If you are single with a taxable income of $10,000, for example, the first $8,350 is taxed at 10% and the other $1,650 is taxed at 15%, so your total tax is $1,082.50.

TABLE 3.2 2009 U.S. Federal Personal Tax Rates

Marginal Tax Rate	Single	Married Filing Jointly or Qualifying Widow(er)	Married Filing Separately	Head of Household
10%	$0–$8,350	$0–$16,700	$0–$8,350	$0–$11,950
15%	$8,351–$33,950	$16,701–$67,900	$8,351–$33,950	$11,951–$45,500
25%	$33,951–$82,250	$67,901–$137,050	$33,951–$68,525	$45,501–$117,450
28%	$82,251–$171,550	$137,051–$208,850	$68,526–$104,425	$117,451–$190,200
33%	$171,551–$372,950	$208,851–$372,950	$104,426–$186,475	$190,201–$372,950
35%	$372,951+	$372,951+	$186,476+	$372,951+

You are to write a program to compute personal income tax. Your program should prompt the user to enter the filing status and taxable income and compute the tax. Enter 0 for single filers, 1 for married filing jointly or qualified widow(er), 2 for married filing separately, and 3 for head of household.

Your program computes the tax for the taxable income based on the filing status. The filing status can be determined using `if` statements outlined as follows:

```
if (status == 0) {
  // Compute tax for single filers
}
else if (status == 1) {
  // Compute tax for married filing jointly or qualifying widow(er)
}
else if (status == 2) {
  // Compute tax for married filing separately
}
else if (status == 3) {
  // Compute tax for head of household
}
else  {
  // Display wrong status
}
```

For each filing status there are six tax rates. Each rate is applied to a certain amount of taxable income. For example, of a taxable income of \$400,000 for single filers, \$8,350 is taxed at 10%, (33,950 − 8,350) at 15%, (82,250 − 33,950) at 25%, (171,550 − 82,250) at 28%, (372,950 − 171,550) at 33%, and (400,000 − 372,950) at 35%.

Listing 3.5 gives the solution for computing taxes for single filers. The complete solution is left as an exercise.

LISTING 3.5 ComputeTax.java

```java
 1  import java.util.Scanner;
 2
 3  public class ComputeTax {
 4    public static void main(String[] args) {
 5      // Create a Scanner
 6      Scanner input = new Scanner(System.in);
 7
 8      // Prompt the user to enter filing status
 9      System.out.print("(0-single filer, 1-married jointly or " +
10        "qualifying widow(er), 2-married separately, 3-head of " +
11        "household) Enter the filing status: ");
12
13      int status = input.nextInt();                                    input status
14
15      // Prompt the user to enter taxable income
16      System.out.print("Enter the taxable income: ");                  input income
17      double income = input.nextDouble();
18
19      // Compute tax
20      double tax = 0;                                                  compute tax
21
22      if (status == 0) { // Compute tax for single filers
23        if (income <= 8350)
24          tax = income * 0.10;
25        else if (income <= 33950)
26          tax = 8350 * 0.10 + (income - 8350) * 0.15;
27        else if (income <= 82250)
28          tax = 8350 * 0.10 + (33950 - 8350) * 0.15 +
29            (income - 33950) * 0.25;
30        else if (income <= 171550)
31          tax = 8350 * 0.10 + (33950 - 8350) * 0.15 +
32            (82250 - 33950) * 0.25 + (income - 82250) * 0.28;
```

```
33        else if (income <= 372950)
34          tax = 8350 * 0.10 + (33950 - 8350) * 0.15 +
35            (82250 - 33950) * 0.25 + (171550 - 82250) * 0.28 +
36            (income - 171550) * 0.33;
37        else
38          tax = 8350 * 0.10 + (33950 - 8350) * 0.15 +
39            (82250 - 33950) * 0.25 + (171550 - 82250) * 0.28 +
40            (372950 - 171550) * 0.33 + (income - 372950) * 0.35;
41      }
42    else if (status == 1) { // Left as an exercise
43        // Compute tax for married file jointly or qualifying widow(er)
44    }
45    else if (status == 2) { // Compute tax for married separately
46        // Left as an exercise in Programming Exercise 3.13
47    }
48    else if (status == 3) { // Compute tax for head of household
49        // Left as an exercise in Programming Exercise 3.13
50    }
51    else {
52      System.out.println("Error: invalid status");
53      System.exit(1);
54    }
55
56    // Display the result
57    System.out.println("Tax is " + (int)(tax * 100) / 100.0);
58  }
59 }
```

exit program (line 53)

display output (line 57)

```
(0-single filer, 1-married jointly or qualifying widow(er),
2-married separately, 3-head of household)
Enter the filing status: 0  ↵Enter
Enter the taxable income: 400000  ↵Enter
Tax is 117683.5
```

line#	status	income	Tax	output
13	0			
17		400000		
20			0	
38			117683.5	
57				Tax is 117683.5

The program receives the filing status and taxable income. The multi-way `if-else` statements (lines 22, 42, 45, 48, and 51) check the filing status and compute the tax based on the filing status.

System.exit(status)

`System.exit(status)` (line 53) is defined in the `System` class. Invoking this method terminates the program. The status `0` indicates that the program is terminated normally. A nonzero status code indicates abnormal termination.

An initial value of `0` is assigned to `tax` (line 20). A compile error would occur if it had no initial value, because all of the other statements that assign values to `tax` are within the `if` statement. The compiler thinks these statements may not be executed, and therefore reports a compile error.

To test a program, you should provide the input that covers all cases. For this program, your input should cover all statuses (0, 1, 2, 3). For each status, test the tax for each of the six brackets. Thus, there are a total of 24 cases.

test all cases

Tip
For all programs, you should write a small amount of code and test it before moving on to add more code. This is called *incremental development and testing*. This approach makes testing easier, because the errors are likely in the new code you just added.

incremental development and testing

3.9.1 Are the following two statements equivalent?

Check Point

```
if (income <= 10000)
  tax = income * 0.1;
else if (income <= 20000)
  tax = 1000 +
    (income - 10000) * 0.15;
```

```
if (income <= 10000)
  tax = income * 0.1;
else if (income > 10000 &&
          income <= 20000)
  tax = 1000 +
    (income - 10000) * 0.15;
```

3.10 Logical Operators

The logical operators !, &&, ||, and ^ can be used to create a compound Boolean expression.

Key Point

Sometimes, whether a statement is executed is determined by a combination of several conditions. You can use logical operators to combine these conditions to form a compound Boolean expression. *Logical operators*, also known as *Boolean operators*, operate on Boolean values to create a new Boolean value. Table 3.3 lists the Boolean operators. Table 3.4 defines the not (!) operator, which negates true to false and false to true. Table 3.5 defines the and (&&) operator. The and (&&) of two Boolean operands is true if and only if both the operands are true. Table 3.6 defines the or (||) operator. The or (||) of two Boolean operands is true if at least one of the operands is true. Table 3.7 defines the exclusive or (^) operator. The exclusive or (^) of two Boolean operands is true if and only if the two operands have different Boolean values. Note p1 ^ p2 is the same as p1 != p2.

TABLE 3.3 Boolean Operators

Operator	Name	Description
!	not	Logical negation
&&	and	Logical conjunction
||	or	Logical disjunction
^	exclusive or	Logical exclusion

TABLE 3.4 Truth Table for Operator !

p	!p	Example (assume age = 24, weight = 140)
true	false	!(age > 18) is false, because (age > 18) is true.
false	true	!(weight == 150) is true, because (weight == 150) is false.

TABLE 3.5 Truth Table for Operator &&

p₁	p₂	p₁ && p₂	*Example (assume* **age = 24, weight = 140***)*
false	false	false	
false	true	false	(age > 28) && (weight <= 140) is false, because (age > 28) is false.
true	false	false	
true	true	true	(age > 18) && (weight >= 140) is true, because (age > 18) and (weight >= 140) are both true.

TABLE 3.6 Truth Table for Operator ||

p₁	p₂	p₁ || p₂	*Example (assume* **age = 24, weight = 140***)*
false	false	false	(age > 34) || (weight >= 150) is false, because (age > 34) and (weight >= 150) are both false.
false	true	true	
true	false	true	(age > 18) || (weight < 140) is true, because (age > 18) is true.
true	true	true	

TABLE 3.7 Truth Table for Operator ^

p₁	p₂	p₁ ^ p₂	*Example (assume* **age = 24, weight = 140***)*
false	false	false	(age > 34) ^ (weight > 140) is false, because (age > 34) and (weight > 140) are both false.
false	true	true	(age > 34) ^ (weight >= 140) is true, because (age > 34) is false but (weight >= 140) is true.
true	false	true	
true	true	false	

Listing 3.6 gives a program that checks whether a number is divisible by 2 and 3, by 2 or 3, and by 2 or 3 but not both.

LISTING 3.6 TestBooleanOperators.java

```java
import java.util.Scanner;

public class TestBooleanOperators {
  public static void main(String[] args) {
    // Create a Scanner
    Scanner input = new Scanner(System.in);

    // Receive an input
    System.out.print("Enter an integer: ");
    int number = input.nextInt();

    if (number % 2 == 0 && number % 3 == 0)
      System.out.println(number + " is divisible by 2 and 3.");

```

import class

input

and

```
15       if (number % 2 == 0 || number % 3 == 0)
16         System.out.println(number + " is divisible by 2 or 3.");
17
18       if (number % 2 == 0 ^ number % 3 == 0)
19         System.out.println(number +
20           " is divisible by 2 or 3, but not both.");
21   }
22 }
```

or

exclusive or

```
Enter an integer: 4 ↵Enter
4 is divisible by 2 or 3.
4 is divisible by 2 or 3, but not both.
```

```
Enter an integer: 18 ↵Enter
18 is divisible by 2 and 3.
18 is divisible by 2 or 3.
```

(number % 2 == 0 && number % 3 == 0) (line 12) checks whether the number is divisible by both 2 and 3. (number % 2 == 0 || number % 3 == 0) (line 15) checks whether the number is divisible by 2 or by 3. (number % 2 == 0 ^ number % 3 == 0) (line 18) checks whether the number is divisible by 2 or 3, but not both.

> ⚠️ **Caution**
>
> In mathematics, the expression
>
> 28 <= numberOfDaysInAMonth <= 31
>
> is correct. However, it is incorrect in Java, because 28 <= numberOfDaysInAMonth is evaluated to a boolean value, which cannot be compared with 31. Here, two operands (a boolean value and a numeric value) are *incompatible*. The correct expression in Java is
>
> 28 <= numberOfDaysInAMonth && numberOfDaysInAMonth <= 31

incompatible operands

> 📝 **Note**
>
> De Morgan's law, named after Indian-born British mathematician and logician Augustus De Morgan (1806–1871), can be used to simplify Boolean expressions. The law states the following:
>
> !(condition1 && condition2) is the same as
>   !condition1 || !condition2
> !(condition1 || condition2) is the same as
>   !condition1 && !condition2
>
> For example,
>
> !(number % 2 == 0 && number % 3 == 0)
>
> can be simplified using an equivalent expression:
>
> number % 2 != 0 || number % 3 != 0
>
> As another example,
>
> !(number == 2 || number == 3)
>
> is better written as
>
> number != 2 && number != 3

De Morgan's law

If one of the operands of an `&&` operator is `false`, the expression is `false`; if one of the operands of an `||` operator is `true`, the expression is `true`. Java uses these properties to improve the performance of these operators. When evaluating `p1 && p2`, Java first evaluates `p1` then, if `p1` is `true`, evaluates `p2`; if `p1` is `false`, it does not evaluate `p2`. When evaluating `p1 || p2`, Java first evaluates `p1` then, if `p1` is `false`, evaluates `p2`; if `p1` is `true`, it does not evaluate `p2`. In programming language terminology, `&&` and `||` are known as the *short-circuit* or *lazy* operators. Java also provides the `&` and `|` operators, which are covered in Supplement III.C for advanced readers.

short-circuit operator

lazy operator

Check
Point

3.10.1 Assuming that `x` is `1`, show the result of the following Boolean expressions:

```
(true) && (3 > 4)
!(x > 0) && (x > 0)
(x > 0) || (x < 0)
(x != 0) || (x == 0)
(x >= 0) || (x < 0)
(x != 1) == !(x == 1)
```

3.10.2 (a) Write a Boolean expression that evaluates to `true` if a number stored in variable `num` is between `1` and `100`. (b) Write a Boolean expression that evaluates to `true` if a number stored in variable `num` is between `1` and `100` or the number is negative.

3.10.3 (a) Write a Boolean expression for $|x - 5| < 4.5$. (b) Write a Boolean expression for $|x - 5| > 4.5$.

3.10.4 Assume `x` and `y` are `int` type. Which of the following are legal Java expressions?

```
x > y > 0
x = y && y
x /= y
x or y
x and y
(x != 0) || (x = 0)
```

3.10.5 Are the following two expressions the same?

(a) `x % 2 == 0 && x % 3 == 0`

(b) `x % 6 == 0`

3.10.6 What is the value of the expression `x >= 50 && x <= 100` if `x` is `45`, `67`, or `101`?

3.10.7 Suppose, when you run the following program, you enter the input `2 3 6` from the console. What is the output?

```java
public class Test {
  public static void main(String[] args) {
    java.util.Scanner input = new java.util.Scanner(System.in);
    double x = input.nextDouble();
    double y = input.nextDouble();
    double z = input.nextDouble();

    System.out.println("(x < y && y < z) is " + (x < y && y < z));
    System.out.println("(x < y || y < z) is " + (x < y || y < z));
    System.out.println("!(x < y) is " + !(x < y));
    System.out.println("(x + y < z) is " + (x + y < z));
    System.out.println("(x + y > z) is " + (x + y > z));
  }
}
```

3.10.8 Write a Boolean expression that evaluates to `true` if `age` is greater than `13` and less than `18`.

3.10.9   Write a Boolean expression that evaluates to true if weight is greater than 50 pounds or height is greater than 60 inches.

3.10.10   Write a Boolean expression that evaluates to true if weight is greater than 50 pounds and height is greater than 60 inches.

3.10.11   Write a Boolean expression that evaluates to true if either weight is greater than 50 pounds or height is greater than 60 inches, but not both.

3.11 Case Study: Determining Leap Year

A year is a leap year if it is divisible by 4 but not by 100, or if it is divisible by 400.

Key
Point

A leap year has 366 days. The February of a leap year has 29 days. You can use the following Boolean expressions to check whether a year is a leap year:

```
// A leap year is divisible by 4
boolean isLeapYear = (year % 4 == 0);

// A leap year is divisible by 4 but not by 100
isLeapYear = isLeapYear && (year % 100 != 0);

// A leap year is divisible by 4 but not by 100 or divisible by 400
isLeapYear = isLeapYear || (year % 400 == 0);
```

Or you can combine all these expressions into one as follows:

```
isLeapYear = (year % 4 == 0 && year % 100 != 0) || (year % 400 == 0);
```

Listing 3.7 gives the program that lets the user enter a year and checks whether it is a leap year.

LISTING 3.7   LeapYear.java

```
 1  import java.util.Scanner;
 2
 3  public class LeapYear {
 4    public static void main(String[] args) {
 5      // Create a Scanner
 6      Scanner input = new Scanner(System.in);
 7      System.out.print("Enter a year: ");
 8      int year = input.nextInt();                                    input
 9
10      // Check if the year is a leap year
11      boolean isLeapYear =                                           leap year?
12        (year % 4 == 0 && year % 100 != 0) || (year % 400 == 0);
13
14      // Display the result
15      System.out.println(year + " is a leap year? " + isLeapYear);   display result
16    }
17  }
```

```
Enter a year: 2008 ⏎Enter
2008 is a leap year? true
```

```
Enter a year: 1900 ⏎Enter
1900 is a leap year? false
```

```
Enter a year: 2002 ⏎Enter
2002 is a leap year? false
```

Check
Point

3.11.1 How many days in the February of a leap year? Which of the following is a leap year? 500, 1000, 2000, 2016, and 2020?

3.12 Case Study: Lottery

Key
Point

The lottery program involves generating random numbers, comparing digits, and using Boolean operators.

Suppose you want to develop a program to play lottery. The program randomly generates a lottery of a two-digit number, prompts the user to enter a two-digit number, and determines whether the user wins according to the following rules:

1. If the user input matches the lottery number in the exact order, the award is $10,000.

2. If all digits in the user input match all digits in the lottery number, the award is $3,000.

3. If one digit in the user input matches a digit in the lottery number, the award is $1,000.

Note the digits of a two-digit number may be 0. If a number is less than 10, we assume that the number is preceded by a 0 to form a two-digit number. For example, number 8 is treated as 08, and number 0 is treated as 00 in the program. Listing 3.8 gives the complete program.

LISTING 3.8 Lottery.java

```java
1  import java.util.Scanner;
2
3  public class Lottery {
4    public static void main(String[] args) {
5      // Generate a lottery number
6      int lottery = (int)(Math.random() * 100);
7
8      // Prompt the user to enter a guess
9      Scanner input = new Scanner(System.in);
10     System.out.print("Enter your lottery pick (two digits): ");
11     int guess = input.nextInt();
12
13     // Get digits from lottery
14     int lotteryDigit1 = lottery / 10;
15     int lotteryDigit2 = lottery % 10;
16
17     // Get digits from guess
18     int guessDigit1 = guess / 10;
19     int guessDigit2 = guess % 10;
20
21     System.out.println("The lottery number is " + lottery);
22
23     // Check the guess
24     if (guess == lottery)
25       System.out.println("Exact match: you win $10,000");
26     else if (guessDigit2 == lotteryDigit1
27             && guessDigit1 == lotteryDigit2)
28       System.out.println("Match all digits: you win $3,000");
29     else if (guessDigit1 == lotteryDigit1
30             || guessDigit1 == lotteryDigit2
31             || guessDigit2 == lotteryDigit1
```

generate a lottery number

enter a guess

exact match?

match all digits?

match one digit?

```
32              || guessDigit2 == lotteryDigit2)
33          System.out.println("Match one digit: you win $1,000");
34      else
35          System.out.println("Sorry, no match");
36      }
37   }
```

```
Enter your lottery pick (two digits): 15 ↵Enter
The lottery number is 15
Exact match: you win $10,000
```

```
Enter your lottery pick (two digits): 45 ↵Enter
The lottery number is 54
Match all digits: you win $3,000
```

```
Enter your lottery pick: 23 ↵Enter
The lottery number is 34
Match one digit: you win $1,000
```

```
Enter your lottery pick: 23 ↵Enter
The lottery number is 14
Sorry: no match
```

line# variable	6	11	14	15	18	19	33
lottery	34						
guess		23					
lotteryDigit1			3				
lotteryDigit2				4			
guessDigit1					2		
guessDigit2						3	
Output							Match one digit: you win $1,000

The program generates a lottery using the random() method (line 6) and prompts the user to enter a guess (line 11). Note guess % 10 obtains the last digit from guess and guess /10 obtains the first digit from guess, since guess is a two-digit number (lines 18 and 19).

The program checks the guess against the lottery number in this order:

1. First, check whether the guess matches the lottery exactly (line 24).

2. If not, check whether the reversal of the guess matches the lottery (lines 26 and 27).

3. If not, check whether one digit is in the lottery (lines 29–32).

4. If not, nothing matches and display "Sorry, no match" (lines 34 and 35).

3.12.1 What happens if you enter an integer as 05?

Check
Point

Key
Point

3.13 switch Statements

A switch *statement executes statements based on the value of a variable or an expression.*

The if statement in Listing 3.5, ComputeTax.java, makes selections based on a single true or false condition. There are four cases for computing taxes, which depend on the value of status. To fully account for all the cases, nested if statements were used. Overuse of nested if statements makes a program difficult to read. Java provides a switch statement to simplify coding for multiple conditions. You can write the following switch statement to replace the nested if statement in Listing 3.5:

```
switch (status) {
  case 0:  compute tax for single filers;
           break;
  case 1:  compute tax for married jointly or qualifying widow(er);
           break;
  case 2:  compute tax for married filing separately;
           break;
  case 3:  compute tax for head of household;
           break;
  default: System.out.println("Error: invalid status");
           System.exit(1);
}
```

The flowchart of the preceding switch statement is shown in Figure 3.5.

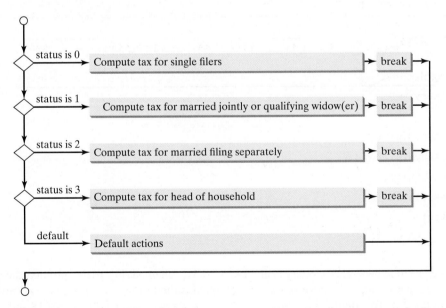

FIGURE 3.5 The switch statement checks all cases and executes the statements in the matched case.

This statement checks to see whether the status matches the value 0, 1, 2, or 3, in that order. If matched, the corresponding tax is computed; if not matched, a message is displayed. Here is the full syntax for the switch statement:

switch statement

```
switch (switch-expression) {
  case value1: statement(s)1;
               break;
```

```
   case value2: statement(s)2;
                break;
   ...
   case valueN: statement(s)N;
                break;
   default:    statement(s)-for-default;
}
```

The `switch` statement observes the following rules:

■ The `switch-expression` must yield a value of `char`, `byte`, `short`, `int`, or `String` type and must always be enclosed in parentheses. (The `char` and `String` types will be introduced in Chapter 4.)

■ The `value1`, . . ., and `valueN` must have the same data type as the value of the `switch-expression`. Note that `value1`, . . ., and `valueN` are constant expressions, meaning they cannot contain variables, such as `1 + x`.

■ When the value in a `case` statement matches the value of the `switch-expression`, the statements *starting from this case* are executed until either a `break` statement or the end of the `switch` statement is reached.

■ The `default` case, which is optional, can be used to perform actions when none of the specified cases matches the `switch-expression`.

■ The keyword `break` is optional. The `break` statement immediately ends the `switch` statement.

Caution

Do not forget to use a `break` statement when one is needed. Once a case is matched, the statements starting from the matched case are executed until a `break` statement or the end of the `switch` statement is reached. This is referred to as *fall-through behavior*. For example, the following code displays `Weekday` for days `1`–`5` and `Weekend` for day `0` and day `6`.

without break

fall-through behavior

```
switch (day) {
  case 1:
  case 2:
  case 3:
  case 4:
  case 5: System.out.println("Weekday"); break;
  case 0:
  case 6: System.out.println("Weekend");
}
```

Tip

To avoid programming errors and improve code maintainability, it is a good idea to put a comment in a case clause if `break` is purposely omitted.

Now let us write a program to find out the Chinese Zodiac sign for a given year. The Chinese Zodiac is based on a 12-year cycle, with each year represented by an animal—monkey, rooster, dog, pig, rat, ox, tiger, rabbit, dragon, snake, horse, or sheep—in this cycle, as shown in Figure 3.6.

Note `year % 12` determines the Zodiac sign. 1900 is the year of the rat because `1900 % 12` is `4`. Listing 3.9 gives a program that prompts the user to enter a year and displays the animal for the year.

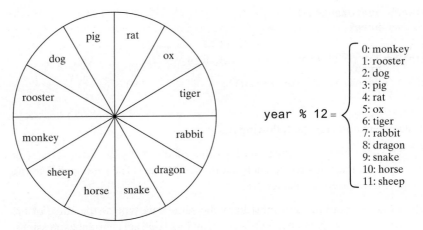

FIGURE 3.6 The Chinese Zodiac is based on a 12-year cycle.

LISTING 3.9 ChineseZodiac.java

```
1  import java.util.Scanner;
2
3  public class ChineseZodiac {
4    public static void main(String[] args) {
5      Scanner input = new Scanner(System.in);
6
7      System.out.print("Enter a year: ");
8      int year = input.nextInt();
9
10     switch (year % 12) {
11       case 0: System.out.println("monkey"); break;
12       case 1: System.out.println("rooster"); break;
13       case 2: System.out.println("dog"); break;
14       case 3: System.out.println("pig"); break;
15       case 4: System.out.println("rat"); break;
16       case 5: System.out.println("ox"); break;
17       case 6: System.out.println("tiger"); break;
18       case 7: System.out.println("rabbit"); break;
19       case 8: System.out.println("dragon"); break;
20       case 9: System.out.println("snake"); break;
21       case 10: System.out.println("horse"); break;
22       case 11: System.out.println("sheep");
23     }
24   }
25 }
```

enter year

determine Zodiac sign

```
Enter a year: 1963  ⏎Enter
rabbit
```

```
Enter a year: 1877  ⏎Enter
ox
```

3.13.1 What data types are required for a `switch` variable? If the keyword `break` is not used after a case is processed, what is the next statement to be executed? Can you convert a `switch` statement to an equivalent `if` statement, or vice versa? What are the advantages of using a `switch` statement?

3.13.2 What is `y` after the following `switch` statement is executed? Rewrite the code using an `if-else` statement.

```
x = 3; y = 3;
switch (x +  3) {
  case 6: y = 1;
  default: y += 1;
}
```

3.13.3 What is `x` after the following `if-else` statement is executed? Use a `switch` statement to rewrite it and draw the flowchart for the new `switch` statement.

```
int x = 1, a = 3;
if (a == 1)
  x += 5;
else if (a == 2)
  x += 10;
else if (a == 3)
  x += 16;
else if (a == 4)
  x += 34;
```

3.13.4 Write a `switch` statement that displays Sunday, Monday, Tuesday, Wednesday, Thursday, Friday, Saturday, if `day` is `0`, `1`, `2`, `3`, `4`, `5`, `6`, respectively.

3.13.5 Rewrite Listing 3.9 using an `if-else` statement.

3.14 Conditional Operators

A conditional operator evaluates an expression based on a condition.

You might want to assign a value to a variable that is restricted by certain conditions. For example, the following statement assigns `1` to `y` if `x` is greater than `0` and `-1` to `y` if `x` is less than or equal to `0`:

```
if (x > 0)
  y = 1;
else
  y = -1;
```

Alternatively, as in the following example, you can use a *conditional operator* to achieve the same result.

conditional operator

```
y = (x > 0) ? 1 : -1;
```

The symbols `?` and `:` appearing together is called a conditional operator (also known as a *ternary operator* because it uses three operands. It is the only ternary operator in Java. The conditional operator is in a completely different style, with no explicit `if` in the statement. The syntax to use the operator is as follows:

ternary operator

```
boolean-expression ? expression1 : expression2
```

The result of this expression is `expression1` if `boolean-expression` is true; otherwise the result is `expression2`.

Suppose you want to assign the larger number of variable `num1` and `num2` to `max`. You can simply write a statement using the conditional operator:

```
max = (num1 > num2) ? num1 : num2;
```

For another example, the following statement displays the message "num is even" if `num` is even, and otherwise displays "num is odd."

```
System.out.println((num % 2 == 0) ? "num is even" : "num is odd");
```

As you can see from these examples, the conditional operator enables you to write short and concise code.

3.14.1 Suppose when you run the following program, you enter the input `2 3 6` from the console. What is the output?

```java
public class Test {
  public static void main(String[] args) {
    java.util.Scanner input = new java.util.Scanner(System.in);
    double x = input.nextDouble();
    double y = input.nextDouble();
    double z = input.nextDouble();

    System.out.println((x < y && y < z) ? "sorted" : "not sorted");
  }
}
```

3.14.2 Rewrite the following `if` statements using the conditional operator.

```
if (ages >= 16)
   ticketPrice = 20;
else
   ticketPrice = 10;
```

3.14.3 Rewrite the following codes using `if-else` statements.

a. `score = (x > 10) ? 3 * scale : 4 * scale;`
b. `tax = (income > 10000) ? income * 0.2 : income * 0.17 + 1000;`
c. `System.out.println((number % 3 == 0) ? i : j);`

3.14.4 Write an expression using a conditional operator that returns randomly `-1` or `1`.

3.15 Operator Precedence and Associativity

Operator precedence and associativity determine the order in which operators are evaluated.

Section 2.11 introduced operator precedence involving arithmetic operators. This section discusses operator precedence in more detail. Suppose you have this expression:

```
3 + 4 * 4 > 5 * (4 + 3) − 1 && (4 − 3 > 5)
```

What is its value? What is the execution order of the operators?

The expression within parentheses is evaluated first. (Parentheses can be nested, in which case the expression within the inner parentheses is executed first.) When evaluating an expression without parentheses, the operators are applied according to the precedence rule and the associativity rule.

The precedence rule defines precedence for operators, as shown in Table 3.8, which contains the operators you have learned so far. Operators are listed in decreasing order of precedence from top to bottom. The logical operators have lower precedence than the relational operators, and the relational operators have lower precedence than the arithmetic operators. Operators with the same precedence appear in the same group. (See Appendix C, *Operator Precedence Chart*, for a complete list of Java operators and their precedence.)

operator precedence

TABLE 3.8 Operator Precedence Chart

Precedence	Operator
	`var++` and `var--` (Postfix)
	`+`, `-` (Unary plus and minus), `++var` and `--var` (Prefix)
	`(type)` (Casting)
	`!`(Not)
	`*`, `/`, `%` (Multiplication, division, and remainder)
	`+`, `-` (Binary addition and subtraction)
	`<`, `<=`, `>`, `>=` (Relational)
	`==`, `!=` (Equality)
	`^` (Exclusive OR)
	`&&` (AND)
	`||` (OR)
	`=`, `+=`, `-=`, `*=`, `/=`, `%=` (Assignment operators)

If operators with the same precedence are next to each other, their *associativity* determines the order of evaluation. All binary operators except assignment operators are *left associative*. For example, since `+` and `-` are of the same precedence and are left associative, the expression

operator associativity

$$a - b + c - d \quad \underset{\text{is equivalent to}}{=\!=\!=\!=\!=} \quad ((a - b) + c) - d$$

Assignment operators are *right associative*. Therefore, the expression

$$a = b \mathrel{+\!=} c = d \quad \underset{\text{is equivalent to}}{=\!=\!=\!=\!=} \quad a = (b \mathrel{+\!=} (c = 5))$$

Suppose a, b, and c are 1 before the assignment; after the whole expression is evaluated, a becomes 6, b becomes 6, and c becomes 5. Note left associativity for the assignment operator would not make sense.

 Note

Java has its own way to evaluate an expression internally. The result of a Java evaluation is the same as that of its corresponding arithmetic evaluation. Advanced readers may refer to Supplement III.B for more discussions on how an expression is evaluated in Java *behind the scenes*.

behind the scenes

3.15.1 List the precedence order of the Boolean operators. Evaluate the following expressions:

✓ **Check Point**

```
true || true && false
true && true || false
```

3.15.2 True or false? All the binary operators except `=` are left associative.

3.15.3 Evaluate the following expressions:

```
2 * 2 - 3 > 2 && 4 - 2 > 5
2 * 2 - 3 > 2 || 4 - 2 > 5
```

3.15.4 Is `(x > 0 && x < 10)` the same as `((x > 0) && (x < 10))`?
Is `(x > 0 || x < 10)` the same as `((x > 0) || (x < 10))`?
Is `(x > 0 || x < 10 && y < 0)` the same as `(x > 0 || (x < 10 && y < 0))`?

Key
Point

3.16 Debugging

Debugging is the process of finding and fixing errors in a program.

As mentioned in Section 1.10, syntax errors are easy to find and easy to correct because the compiler gives indications as to where the errors came from and why they are there. Runtime errors are not difficult to find either, because the Java interpreter displays them on the console when the program aborts. Finding logic errors, on the other hand, can be very challenging.

bugs
debugging
hand-traces

Logic errors are called *bugs*. The process of finding and correcting errors is called *debugging*. A common approach to debugging is to use a combination of methods to help pinpoint the part of the program where the bug is located. You can *hand-trace* the program (i.e., catch errors by reading the program), or you can insert print statements in order to show the values of the variables or the execution flow of the program. These approaches might work for debugging a short, simple program, but for a large, complex program, the most effective approach is to use a debugger utility.

JDK includes a command-line debugger, jdb, which is invoked with a class name. jdb is itself a Java program, running its own copy of Java interpreter. All the Java IDE tools, such as Eclipse and NetBeans, include integrated debuggers. The debugger utilities let you follow the execution of a program. They vary from one system to another, but they all support most of the following helpful features.

- **Executing a single statement at a time:** The debugger allows you to execute one statement at a time so that you can see the effect of each statement.

- **Tracing into or stepping over a method:** If a method is being executed, you can ask the debugger to enter the method and execute one statement at a time in the method, or you can ask it to step over the entire method. You should step over the entire method if you know that the method works. For example, always step over system-supplied methods, such as `System.out.println`.

- **Setting breakpoints:** You can also set a breakpoint at a specific statement. Your program pauses when it reaches a breakpoint. You can set as many breakpoints as you want. Breakpoints are particularly useful when you know where your programming error starts. You can set a breakpoint at that statement, and have the program execute until it reaches the breakpoint.

- **Displaying variables:** The debugger lets you select several variables and display their values. As you trace through a program, the content of a variable is continuously updated.

- **Displaying call stacks:** The debugger lets you trace all of the method calls. This feature is helpful when you need to see a large picture of the program-execution flow.

- **Modifying variables:** Some debuggers enable you to modify the value of a variable when debugging. This is convenient when you want to test a program with different samples, but do not want to leave the debugger.

debugging in IDE

Tip

If you use an IDE such as Eclipse or NetBeans, please refer to *Learning Java Effectively with Eclipse/NetBeans* in Supplements II.C and II.E on the Companion Website. The supplement shows you how to use a debugger to trace programs, and how debugging can help in learning Java effectively.

KEY TERMS

Boolean expression   76
boolean data type   76
Boolean value   76
conditional operator   103
dangling else ambiguity   85
debugging   106
fall-through behavior   101

flowchart   78
lazy operator   96
operator associativity   105
operator precedence   104
selection statement   76
short-circuit operator   96

CHAPTER SUMMARY

1. A `boolean`-type variable can store a `true` or `false` value.

2. The relational operators (`<`, `<=`, `==`, `!=`, `>`, and `>=`) yield a Boolean value.

3. *Selection statements* are used for programming with alternative courses of actions. There are several types of selection statements: one-way `if` statements, two-way `if-else` statements, nested `if` statements, multi-way `if-else` statements, `switch` statements, and conditional operators.

4. The various `if` statements all make control decisions based on a *Boolean expression*. Based on the `true` or `false` evaluation of the expression, these statements take one of the two possible courses.

5. The Boolean operators `&&`, `||`, `!`, and `^` operate with Boolean values and variables.

6. When evaluating `p1 && p2`, Java first evaluates `p1` then evaluates `p2` if `p1` is `true`; if `p1` is `false`, it does not evaluate `p2`. When evaluating `p1 || p2`, Java first evaluates `p1` then evaluates `p2` if `p1` is `false`; if `p1` is `true`, it does not evaluate `p2`. Therefore, `&&` is referred to as the *short-circuit* or *lazy AND operator*, and `||` is referred to as the *short-circuit* or *lazy OR operator*.

7. The `switch` statement makes control decisions based on a switch expression of type `char`, `byte`, `short`, `int`, or `String`.

8. The keyword `break` is optional in a `switch` statement, but it is normally used at the end of each case in order to skip the remainder of the `switch` statement. If the `break` statement is not present, the next `case` statement will be executed.

9. The operators in expressions are evaluated in the order determined by the rules of parentheses, *operator precedence*, and *operator associativity*.

10. Parentheses can be used to force the order of evaluation to occur in any sequence.

11. Operators with higher precedence are evaluated earlier. For operators of the same precedence, their associativity determines the order of evaluation.

12. All binary operators except assignment operators are left associative; assignment operators are right associative.

QUIZ

Answer the quiz for this chapter online at the Companion Website.

MyProgrammingLab™ ## PROGRAMMING EXERCISES

think before coding

Pedagogical Note

For each exercise, carefully analyze the problem requirements and design strategies for solving the problem before coding.

Debugging Tip

Before you ask for help, read and explain the program to yourself, and trace it using several representative inputs by hand or using an IDE debugger. You learn how to program by debugging your own mistakes.

learn from mistakes

Section 3.2

*3.1 (*Algebra: solve quadratic equations*) The two roots of a quadratic equation $ax^2 + bx + c = 0$ can be obtained using the following formula:

$$r_1 = \frac{-b + \sqrt{b^2 - 4ac}}{2a} \quad \text{and} \quad r_2 = \frac{-b - \sqrt{b^2 - 4ac}}{2a}$$

$b^2 - 4ac$ is called the discriminant of the quadratic equation. If it is positive, the equation has two real roots. If it is zero, the equation has one root. If it is negative, the equation has no real roots.

Write a program that prompts the user to enter values for a, b, and c and displays the result based on the discriminant. If the discriminant is positive, display two roots. If the discriminant is 0, display one root. Otherwise, display "The equation has no real roots."

Note you can use `Math.pow(x, 0.5)` to compute $\sqrt{x}$. Here are some sample runs:

```
Enter a, b, c: 1.0 3 1  ↵Enter
The equation has two roots -0.381966 and -2.61803
```

```
Enter a, b, c: 1 2.0 1  ↵Enter
The equation has one root -1.0
```

```
Enter a, b, c: 1 2 3  ↵Enter
The equation has no real roots
```

3.2 (*Game: add three numbers*) The program in Listing 3.1, AdditionQuiz.java, generates two integers and prompts the user to enter the sum of these two integers. Revise the program to generate three single-digit integers and prompt the user to enter the sum of these three integers.

Sections 3.3–3.7

*3.3   (*Algebra: solve* 2 × 2 *linear equations*) A linear equation can be solved using Cramer's rule given in Programming Exercise 1.13. Write a program that prompts the user to enter *a, b, c, d, e,* and *f* and displays the result. If *ad* − *bc* is 0, report that "The equation has no solution."

```
Enter a, b, c, d, e, f: 9.0 4.0 3.0 -5.0 -6.0 -21.0  ↵Enter
x is -2.0 and y is 3.0
```

```
Enter a, b, c, d, e, f: 1.0 2.0 2.0 4.0 4.0 5.0  ↵Enter
The equation has no solution
```

**3.4   **(*Random month*) Write a program that randomly generates an integer between 1 and 12 and displays the English month names January, February, . . . , December for the numbers 1, 2, . . . , 12, accordingly.

*3.5   (*Find future dates*) Write a program that prompts the user to enter an integer for today's day of the week (Sunday is 0, Monday is 1, . . . , and Saturday is 6). Also prompt the user to enter the number of days after today for a future day and display the future day of the week. Here is a sample run:

```
Enter today's day: 1  ↵Enter
Enter the number of days elapsed since today: 3  ↵Enter
Today is Monday and the future day is Thursday
```

```
Enter today's day: 0  ↵Enter
Enter the number of days elapsed since today: 31  ↵Enter
Today is Sunday and the future day is Wednesday
```

*3.6   (*Health application: BMI*) Revise Listing 3.4, ComputeAndInterpretBMI.java, to let the user enter weight, feet, and inches. For example, if a person is 5 feet and 10 inches, you will enter 5 for feet and 10 for inches. Here is a sample run:

```
Enter weight in pounds: 140  ↵Enter
Enter feet: 5  ↵Enter
Enter inches: 10  ↵Enter
BMI is 20.087702275404553
Normal
```

3.7   (*Financial application: monetary units*) Modify Listing 2.10, ComputeChange. java, to display the nonzero denominations only, using singular words for single units such as 1 dollar and 1 penny, and plural words for more than one unit such as 2 dollars and 3 pennies.

VideoNote

Sort three integers

*3.8 (*Sort three integers*) Write a program that prompts the user to enter three integers and display the integers in non-decreasing order.

**3.9 (*Business: check ISBN-10*) An ISBN-10 (International Standard Book Number) consists of 10 digits: $d_1d_2d_3d_4d_5d_6d_7d_8d_9d_{10}$. The last digit, d_{10}, is a checksum, which is calculated from the other 9 digits using the following formula:

$$(d_1 \times 1 + d_2 \times 2 + d_3 \times 3 + d_4 \times 4 + d_5 \times 5 +$$
$$d_6 \times 6 + d_7 \times 7 + d_8 \times 8 + d_9 \times 9)\%11$$

If the checksum is 10, the last digit is denoted as X according to the ISBN-10 convention. Write a program that prompts the user to enter the first 9 digits and displays the 10-digit ISBN (including leading zeros). Your program should read the input as an integer. Here are sample runs:

```
Enter the first 9 digits of an ISBN as integer: 013601267 ↵Enter
The ISBN-10 number is 0136012671
```

```
Enter the first 9 digits of an ISBN as integer: 013031997 ↵Enter
The ISBN-10 number is 013031997X
```

3.10 (*Game: addition quiz*) Listing 3.3, SubtractionQuiz.java, randomly generates a subtraction question. Revise the program to randomly generate an addition question with two integers less than 100.

Sections 3.8–3.16

*3.11 (*Find the number of days in a month*) Write a program that prompts the user to enter the month and year and displays the number of days in the month. For example, if the user entered month 2 and year 2012, the program should display that February 2012 has 29 days. If the user entered month 3 and year 2015, the program should display that March 2015 has 31 days.

3.12 (*Palindrome integer*) Write a program that prompts the user to enter a three-digit integer and determines whether it is a palindrome *integer*. An *integer* is palindrome if it reads the same from right to left and from left to right. A negative integer is treated the same as a positive integer. Here are sample runs of this program:

```
Enter a three-digit integer: 121 ↵Enter
121 is a palindrome
```

```
Enter a three-digit integer: 123 ↵Enter
123 is not a palindrome
```

*3.13 (*Financial application: compute taxes*) Listing 3.5, ComputeTax.java, gives the source code to compute taxes for single filers. Complete this program to compute taxes for all filing statuses.

3.14 (*Game: heads or tails*) Write a program that lets the user guess whether the flip of a coin results in heads or tails. The program randomly generates an integer 0 or 1, which represents head or tail. The program prompts the user to enter a guess, and reports whether the guess is correct or incorrect.

**3.15 (*Game: lottery*) Revise Listing 3.8, Lottery.java, to generate a lottery of a three-digit integer. The program prompts the user to enter a three-digit integer and determines whether the user wins according to the following rules:

1. If the user input matches the lottery number in the exact order, the award is $10,000.
2. If all digits in the user input match all digits in the lottery number, the award is $3,000.
3. If one digit in the user input matches a digit in the lottery number, the award is $1,000.

3.16 (*Random point*) Write a program that displays a random coordinate in a rectangle. The rectangle is centered at (0, 0) with width 100 and height 200.

*3.17 (*Game: scissor, rock, paper*) Write a program that plays the popular scissor–rock–paper game. (A scissor can cut a paper, a rock can knock a scissor, and a paper can wrap a rock.) The program randomly generates a number 0, 1, or 2 representing scissor, rock, and paper. The program prompts the user to enter a number 0, 1, or 2 and displays a message indicating whether the user or the computer wins, loses, or draws. Here are sample runs:

```
scissor (0), rock (1), paper (2): 1  ↵ Enter
The computer is scissor. You are rock. You won
```

```
scissor (0), rock (1), paper (2): 2  ↵ Enter
The computer is paper. You are paper too. It is a draw
```

*3.18 (*Cost of shipping*) A shipping company uses the following function to calculate the cost (in dollars) of shipping based on the weight of the package (in pounds).

$$c(w) = \begin{cases} 3.5, \text{ if } 0 < w <= 1 \\ 5.5, \text{ if } 1 < w <= 3 \\ 8.5, \text{ if } 3 < w <= 10 \\ 10.5, \text{ if } 10 < w <= 20 \end{cases}$$

Write a program that prompts the user to enter the weight of the package and displays the shipping cost. If the weight is negative or zero, display a message "Invalid input." If the weight is greater than 20, display a message "The package cannot be shipped."

**3.19 (*Compute the perimeter of a triangle*) Write a program that reads three edges for a triangle and computes the perimeter if the input is valid. Otherwise, display that the input is invalid. The input is valid if the sum of every pair of two edges is greater than the remaining edge.

*3.20 (*Science: wind-chill temperature*) Programming Exercise 2.17 gives a formula to compute the wind-chill temperature. The formula is valid for temperatures in the range between −58°F and 41°F and wind speed greater than or equal to 2. Write a program that prompts the user to enter a temperature and a wind speed. The program displays the wind-chill temperature if the input is valid; otherwise, it displays a message indicating whether the temperature and/or wind speed is invalid.

Comprehensive

**3.21 (*Science: day of the week*) Zeller's congruence is an algorithm developed by Christian Zeller to calculate the day of the week. The formula is

$$h = \left(q + \frac{26(m + 1)}{10} + k + \frac{k}{4} + \frac{j}{4} + 5j \right) \% 7$$

where

- h is the day of the week (0: Saturday, 1: Sunday, 2: Monday, 3: Tuesday, 4: Wednesday, 5: Thursday, and 6: Friday).
- q is the day of the month.
- m is the month (3: March, 4: April, . . ., 12: December). January and February are counted as months 13 and 14 of the previous year.
- j is $\frac{year}{100}$.
- k is the year of the century (i.e., *year* % 100).

Note all divisions in this exercise perform an integer division. Write a program that prompts the user to enter a year, month, and day of the month, and displays the name of the day of the week. Here are some sample runs:

```
Enter year: (e.g., 2012): 2015 ↵Enter
Enter month: 1-12: 1 ↵Enter
Enter the day of the month: 1-31: 25 ↵Enter
Day of the week is Sunday
```

```
Enter year: (e.g., 2012): 2012 ↵Enter
Enter month: 1-12: 5 ↵Enter
Enter the day of the month: 1-31: 12 ↵Enter
Day of the week is Saturday
```

(*Hint:* January and February are counted as 13 and 14 in the formula, so you need to convert the user input 1 to 13 and 2 to 14 for the month and change the year to the previous year. For example, if the user enters 1 for m and 2015 for year, m will be 13 and year will be 2014 used in the formula.)

VideoNote

Check point location

**3.22 (*Geometry: point in a circle?*) Write a program that prompts the user to enter a point (x, y) and checks whether the point is within the circle centered at (0, 0) with radius 10. For example, (4, 5) is inside the circle and (9, 9) is outside the circle, as shown in Figure 3.7a.

(*Hint:* A point is in the circle if its distance to (0, 0) is less than or equal to 10. The formula for computing the distance is $\sqrt{(x_2 - x_1)^2 + (y_2 - y_1)^2}$. Test your program to cover all cases.) Two sample runs are shown below:

```
Enter a point with two coordinates: 4 5 ↵Enter
Point (4.0, 5.0) is in the circle
```

```
Enter a point with two coordinates: 9 9 ↵Enter
Point (9.0, 9.0) is not in the circle
```

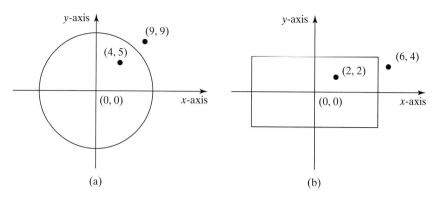

FIGURE 3.7 (a) Points inside and outside of the circle. (b) Points inside and outside of the rectangle.

**3.23 (*Geometry: point in a rectangle?*) Write a program that prompts the user to enter a point (x, y) and checks whether the point is within the rectangle centered at (0, 0) with width 10 and height 5. For example, (2, 2) is inside the rectangle and (6, 4) is outside the rectangle, as shown in Figure 3.7b. (*Hint*: A point is in the rectangle if its horizontal distance to (0, 0) is less than or equal to 10 / 2 and its vertical distance to (0, 0) is less than or equal to 5.0 / 2. Test your program to cover all cases.) Here are two sample runs:

```
Enter a point with two coordinates: 2 2  ↵Enter
Point (2.0, 2.0) is in the rectangle
```

```
Enter a point with two coordinates: 6 4  ↵Enter
Point (6.0, 4.0) is not in the rectangle
```

**3.24 (*Game: pick a card*) Write a program that simulates picking a card from a deck of 52 cards. Your program should display the rank (Ace, 2, 3, 4, 5, 6, 7, 8, 9, 10, Jack, Queen, King) and suit (Clubs, Diamonds, Hearts, Spades) of the card. Here is a sample run of the program:

```
The card you picked is Jack of Hearts
```

*3.25 (*Geometry: intersecting point*) Two points on line 1 are given as (x1, y1) and (x2, y2) and on line 2 as (x3, y3) and (x4, y4), as shown in Figure 3.8a and b.

The intersecting point of the two lines can be found by solving the following linear equations:

$$(y_1 - y_2)x - (x_1 - x_2)y = (y_1 - y_2)x_1 - (x_1 - x_2)y_1$$
$$(y_3 - y_4)x - (x_3 - x_4)y = (y_3 - y_4)x_3 - (x_3 - x_4)y_3$$

This linear equation can be solved using Cramer's rule (see Programming Exercise 3.3). If the equation has no solutions, the two lines are parallel (see Figure 3.8c).

Write a program that prompts the user to enter four points and displays the intersecting point. Here are sample runs:

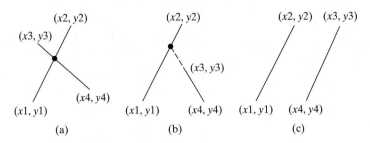

FIGURE 3.8 Two lines intersect in (a and b) and two lines are parallel in (c).

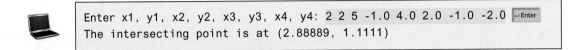

```
Enter x1, y1, x2, y2, x3, y3, x4, y4: 2 2 5 -1.0 4.0 2.0 -1.0 -2.0 ⏎Enter
The intersecting point is at (2.88889, 1.1111)
```

```
Enter x1, y1, x2, y2, x3, y3, x4, y4: 2 2 7 6.0 4.0 2.0 -1.0 -2.0 ⏎Enter
The two lines are parallel
```

3.26 (*Use the &&, ||, and ^ operators*) Write a program that prompts the user to enter an integer and determines whether it is divisible by 5 and 6, whether it is divisible by 5 or 6, and whether it is divisible by 5 or 6, but not both. Here is a sample run of this program:

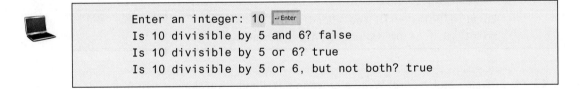

```
Enter an integer: 10 ⏎Enter
Is 10 divisible by 5 and 6? false
Is 10 divisible by 5 or 6? true
Is 10 divisible by 5 or 6, but not both? true
```

**3.27 (*Geometry: points in triangle?*) Suppose a right triangle is placed in a plane as shown below. The right-angle point is placed at (0, 0), and the other two points are placed at (200, 0) and (0, 100). Write a program that prompts the user to enter a point with *x*- and *y*-coordinates and determines whether the point is inside the triangle. Here are the sample runs:

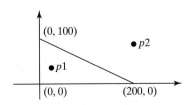

```
Enter a point's x- and y-coordinates: 100.5 25.5 ⏎Enter
The point is in the triangle
```

```
Enter a point's x- and y-coordinates: 100.5 50.5 ↵Enter
The point is not in the triangle
```

**3.28 (*Geometry: two rectangles*) Write a program that prompts the user to enter the center *x*-, *y*-coordinates, width, and height of two rectangles and determines whether the second rectangle is inside the first or overlaps with the first, as shown in Figure 3.9. Test your program to cover all cases.

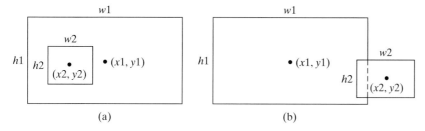

(a)   (b)

FIGURE 3.9   (a) A rectangle is inside another one. (b) A rectangle overlaps another one.

Here are the sample runs:

```
Enter r1's center x-, y-coordinates, width, and height: 2.5 4 2.5 43 ↵Enter
Enter r2's center x-, y-coordinates, width, and height: 1.5 5 0.5 3 ↵Enter
r2 is inside r1
```

```
Enter r1's center x-, y-coordinates, width, and height: 1 2 3 5.5 ↵Enter
Enter r2's center x-, y-coordinates, width, and height: 3 4 4.5 5 ↵Enter
r2 overlaps r1
```

```
Enter r1's center x-, y-coordinates, width, and height: 1 2 3 3 ↵Enter
Enter r2's center x-, y-coordinates, width, and height: 40 45 3 2 ↵Enter
r2 does not overlap r1
```

**3.29 (*Geometry: two circles*) Write a program that prompts the user to enter the center coordinates and radii of two circles and determines whether the second circle is inside the first or overlaps with the first, as shown in Figure 3.10. (*Hint:* circle2 is inside circle1 if the distance between the two centers <= r1 - r2 and circle2 overlaps circle1 if the distance between the two centers <= r1 + r2. Test your program to cover all cases.)

Here are the sample runs:

```
Enter circle1's center x-, y-coordinates, and radius: 0.5 5.1 13 ↵Enter
Enter circle2's center x-, y-coordinates, and radius: 1 1.7 4.5 ↵Enter
circle2 is inside circle1
```

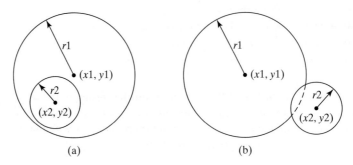

FIGURE 3.10 (a) A circle is inside another circle. (b) A circle overlaps another circle.

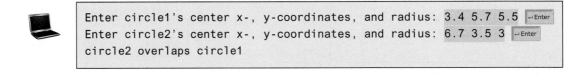

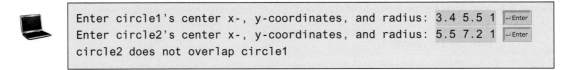

*3.30 (*Current time*) Revise Programming Exercise 2.8 to display the hour using a 12-hour clock. Here is a sample run:

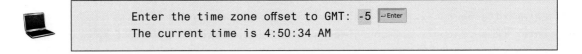

*3.31 (*Financials: currency exchange*) Write a program that prompts the user to enter the exchange rate from currency in U.S. dollars to Chinese RMB. Prompt the user to enter 0 to convert from U.S. dollars to Chinese RMB and 1 to convert from Chinese RMB to U.S. dollars. Prompt the user to enter the amount in U.S. dollars or Chinese RMB to convert it to Chinese RMB or U.S. dollars, respectively. Here are the sample runs:

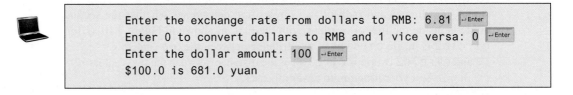

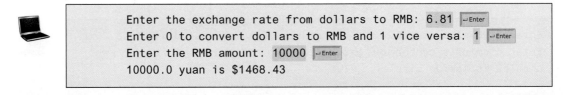

```
Enter the exchange rate from dollars to RMB: 6.81  ↵Enter
Enter 0 to convert dollars to RMB and 1 vice versa: 5  ↵Enter
Incorrect input
```

*3.32 (*Geometry: point position*) Given a directed line from point $p0(x0, y0)$ to $p1(x1, y1)$, you can use the following condition to decide whether a point $p2(x2, y2)$ is on the left of the line, on the right, or on the same line (see Figure 3.11):

$$(x1 - x0)*(y2 - y0) - (x2 - x0)*(y1 - y0) \begin{cases} >0 \ \text{p2 is on the left side of the line} \\ =0 \ \text{p2 is on the same line} \\ <0 \ \text{p2 is on the right side of the line} \end{cases}$$

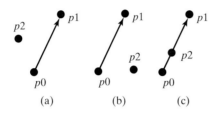

FIGURE 3.11 (a) $p2$ is on the left of the line. (b) $p2$ is on the right of the line. (c) $p2$ is on the same line.

Write a program that prompts the user to enter the three points for $p0$, $p1$, and $p2$ and displays whether $p2$ is on the left of the line from $p0$ to $p1$, to the right, or on the same line. Here are some sample runs:

```
Enter three points for p0, p1, and p2: 4.4 2 6.5 9.5 -5 4  ↵Enter
p2 is on the left side of the line
```

```
Enter three points for p0, p1, and p2: 1 1 5 5 2 2  ↵Enter
p2 is on the same line
```

```
Enter three points for p0, p1, and p2: 3.4 2 6.5 9.5 5 2.5  ↵Enter
p2 is on the right side of the line
```

*3.33 (*Financial: compare costs*) Suppose you shop for rice in two different packages. You would like to write a program to compare the cost. The program prompts the user to enter the weight and price of each package and displays the one with the better price. Here is a sample run:

```
Enter weight and price for package 1: 50 24.59  ↵Enter
Enter weight and price for package 2: 25 11.99  ↵Enter
Package 2 has a better price.
```

```
Enter weight and price for package 1: 50 25  ↵Enter
Enter weight and price for package 2: 25 12.5  ↵Enter
Two packages have the same price.
```

*3.34 (*Geometry: point on line segment*) Exercise 3.32 shows how to test whether a point is on an unbounded line. Revise Exercise 3.32 to test whether a point is on a line segment. Write a program that prompts the user to enter the three points for *p*0, *p*1, and *p*2 and displays whether *p*2 is on the line segment from *p*0 to *p*1. Here are some sample runs:

```
Enter three points for p0, p1, and p2: 1 1 2.5 2.5 1.5 1.5  ↵Enter
(1.5, 1.5) is on the line segment from (1.0, 1.0) to (2.5, 2.5)  ↵Enter
```

```
Enter three points for p0, p1, and p2: 1 1 2 2 3.5 3.5  ↵Enter
(3.5, 3.5) is not on the line segment from (1.0, 1.0) to (2.0, 2.0)
```

Note
More than 200 additional programming exercises with solutions are provided to the instructors on the Instructor Resource Website.

CHAPTER

4

MATHEMATICAL FUNCTIONS, CHARACTERS, AND STRINGS

Objectives

- To solve mathematical problems by using the methods in the `Math` class (§4.2).
- To represent characters using the `char` type (§4.3).
- To encode characters using ASCII and Unicode (§4.3.1).
- To represent special characters using the escape sequences (§4.3.2).
- To cast a numeric value to a character and cast a character to an integer (§4.3.3).
- To compare and test characters using the static methods in the `Character` class (§4.3.4).

- To introduce objects and instance methods (§4.4).
- To represent strings using the `String` object (§4.4).
- To return the string length using the `length()` method (§4.4.1).
- To return a character in the string using the `charAt(i)` method (§4.4.2).
- To use the `+` operator to concatenate strings (§4.4.3).
- To return an uppercase string or a lowercase string and to trim a string (§4.4.4).
- To read strings from the console (§4.4.5).
- To read a character from the console (§4.4.6).
- To compare strings using the `equals` and the `compareTo` methods (§4.4.7).
- To obtain substrings (§4.4.8).
- To find a character or a substring in a string using the `indexOf` method (§4.4.9).
- To program using characters and strings (`GuessBirthday`) (§4.5.1).
- To convert a hexadecimal character to a decimal value (`HexDigit2Dec`) (§4.5.2).
- To revise the lottery program using strings (`LotteryUsingStrings`) (§4.5.3).
- To format output using the `System.out.printf` method (§4.6).

4.1 Introduction

Key
Point

The focus of this chapter is to introduce mathematical functions, characters, string objects, and use them to develop programs.

The preceding chapters introduced fundamental programming techniques and taught you how to write simple programs to solve basic problems using selection statements. This chapter introduces methods for performing common mathematical operations. You will learn how to create custom methods in Chapter 6.

problem

Suppose you need to estimate the area enclosed by four cities, given the GPS locations (latitude and longitude) of these cities, as shown in the following diagram. How would you write a program to solve this problem? You will be able to write such a program in this chapter.

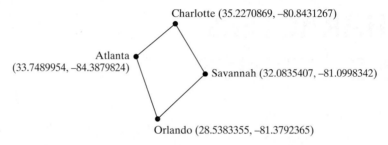

Because strings are frequently used in programming, it is beneficial to introduce strings early so that you can begin to use them to develop useful programs. This chapter also gives a brief introduction to string objects; you will learn more on objects and strings in Chapters 9 and 10.

4.2 Common Mathematical Functions

Key
Point

Java provides many useful methods in the Math class for performing common mathematical functions.

A method is a group of statements that performs a specific task. You have already used the `pow(a, b)` method to compute a^b in Section 2.9.4, Exponent Operations and the `random()` method for generating a random number in Section 3.7. This section introduces other useful methods in the `Math` class. They can be categorized as *trigonometric methods*, *exponent methods*, and *service methods*. Service methods include the rounding, min, max, absolute, and random methods. In addition to methods, the `Math` class provides two useful `double` constants, `PI` and `E` (the base of natural logarithms). You can use these constants as `Math.PI` and `Math.E` in any program.

4.2.1 Trigonometric Methods

VideoNote
Introduce Math functions

The `Math` class contains the following methods as listed in Table 4.1 for performing trigonometric functions:

TABLE 4.1 Trigonometric Methods in the Math Class

Method	Description
`sin(radians)`	Returns the trigonometric sine of an angle in radians.
`cos(radians)`	Returns the trigonometric cosine of an angle in radians.
`tan(radians)`	Returns the trigonometric tangent of an angle in radians.
`toRadians(degree)`	Returns the angle in radians for the angle in degrees.
`toDegrees(radians)`	Returns the angle in degrees for the angle in radians.
`asin(a)`	Returns the angle in radians for the inverse of sine.
`acos(a)`	Returns the angle in radians for the inverse of cosine.
`atan(a)`	Returns the angle in radians for the inverse of tangent.

The parameter for `sin`, `cos`, and `tan` is an angle in radians. The return value for `asin` and `atan` is an angle in radians in the range between $-\pi/2$ and $\pi/2$, and for `acos` is between 0 and π. One degree is equal to $\pi/180$ in radians, 90 degrees is equal to $\pi/2$ in radians, and 30 degrees is equal to $\pi/6$ in radians.

For example,

```
Math.toDegrees(Math.PI / 2) returns 90.0
Math.toRadians(30) returns 0.5236 (same as π/6)
Math.sin(0) returns 0.0
Math.sin(Math.toRadians(270)) returns -1.0
Math.sin(Math.PI / 6) returns 0.5
Math.sin(Math.PI / 2) returns 1.0
Math.cos(0) returns 1.0
Math.cos(Math.PI / 6) returns 0.866
Math.cos(Math.PI / 2) returns 0
Math.asin(0.5) returns 0.523598333 (same as π/6)
Math.acos(0.5) returns 1.0472 (same as π/3)
Math.atan(1.0) returns 0.785398 (same as π/4)
```

4.2.2 Exponent Methods

There are five methods related to exponents in the `Math` class as listed in Table 4.2.

TABLE 4.2 Exponent Methods in the Math Class

Method	Description
`exp(x)`	Returns e raised to power of x (e^x).
`log(x)`	Returns the natural logarithm of x ($\ln(x) = \log_e(x)$).
`log10(x)`	Returns the base 10 logarithm of x ($\log_{10}(x)$).
`pow(a, b)`	Returns a raised to the power of b (a^b).
`sqrt(x)`	Returns the square root of x ($\sqrt{x}$) for $x >= 0$.

For example,

```
e^3.5 is Math.exp(3.5), which returns 33.11545
ln(3.5) is Math.log(3.5), which returns 1.25276
log₁₀ (3.5) is Math.log10(3.5), which returns 0.544
2³ is Math.pow(2, 3), which returns 8.0
3² is Math.pow(3, 2), which returns 9.0
4.5^2.5 is Math.pow(4.5, 2.5), which returns 42.9567
√4 is Math.sqrt(4), which returns 2.0
√10.5 is Math.sqrt(10.5), which returns 3.24
```

4.2.3 The Rounding Methods

The `Math` class contains four rounding methods as listed in Table 4.3.

TABLE 4.3 Rounding Methods in the Math Class

Method	Description
`ceil(x)`	x is rounded up to its nearest integer. This integer is returned as a double value.
`floor(x)`	x is rounded down to its nearest integer. This integer is returned as a double value.
`rint(x)`	x is rounded to its nearest integer. If x is equally close to two integers, the even one is returned as a double value.
`round(x)`	Returns `(int)Math.floor(x + 0.5)` if x is a float and returns `(long)Math.floor(x + 0.5)` if x is a double.

For example,

```
Math.ceil(2.1) returns 3.0
Math.ceil(2.0) returns 2.0
Math.ceil(-2.0) returns -2.0
Math.ceil(-2.1) returns -2.0
Math.floor(2.1) returns 2.0
Math.floor(2.0) returns 2.0
Math.floor(-2.0) returns -2.0
Math.floor(-2.1) returns -3.0
Math.rint(2.1) returns 2.0
Math.rint(-2.0) returns -2.0
Math.rint(-2.1) returns -2.0
Math.rint(2.5) returns 2.0
Math.rint(4.5) returns 4.0
Math.rint(-2.5) returns -2.0
Math.round(2.6f) returns 3 // Returns int
Math.round(2.0) returns 2 // Returns long
Math.round(-2.0f) returns -2 // Returns int
Math.round(-2.6) returns -3 // Returns long
Math.round(-2.4) returns -2 // Returns long
```

4.2.4 The min, max, and abs Methods

The min and max methods return the minimum and maximum numbers of two numbers (int, long, float, or double). For example, max(4.4, 5.0) returns 5.0, and min(3, 2) returns 2.

The abs method returns the absolute value of the number (int, long, float, or double). For example,

```
Math.max(2, 3) returns 3
Math.min(2.5, 4.6) returns 2.5
Math.max(Math.max(2.5, 4.6), Math.min(3, 5.6)) returns 4.6
Math.abs(-2) returns 2
Math.abs(-2.1) returns 2.1
```

4.2.5 The random Method

You used the random() method in the preceding chapter. This method generates a random double value greater than or equal to 0.0 and less than 1.0 (0 <= Math.random() < 1.0). You can use it to write a simple expression to generate random numbers in any range. For example,

`(int)(Math.random() * 10)` → Returns a random integer between 0 and 9.

`50 + (int)(Math.random() * 50)` → Returns a random integer between 50 and 99.

In general,

`a + Math.random() * b` → Returns a random number between a and a + b, excluding a + b.

4.2.6 Case Study: Computing Angles of a Triangle

You can use the math methods to solve many computational problems. Given the three sides of a triangle, for example, you can compute the angles by using the following formulas:

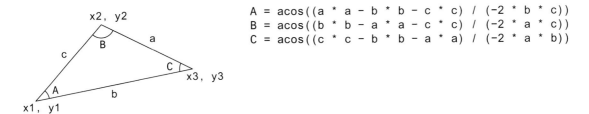

```
A = acos((a * a - b * b - c * c) / (-2 * b * c))
B = acos((b * b - a * a - c * c) / (-2 * a * c))
C = acos((c * c - b * b - a * a) / (-2 * a * b))
```

Don't be intimidated by the mathematical formula. As we discussed early in Listing 2.9, ComputeLoan.java, you don't have to know how the mathematical formula is derived in order to write a program for computing the loan payments. Here, in this example, given the length of three sides, you can use this formula to write a program to compute the angles without having to know how the formula is derived. In order to compute the lengths of the sides, we need to know the coordinates of three corner points and compute the distances between the points.

Listing 4.1 is an example of a program that prompts the user to enter the *x*- and *y*-coordinates of the three corner points in a triangle then displays the three angles.

LISTING 4.1   ComputeAngles.java

```java
 1 import java.util.Scanner;
 2
 3 public class ComputeAngles {
 4   public static void main(String[] args) {
 5     Scanner input = new Scanner(System.in);
 6
 7     // Prompt the user to enter three points
 8     System.out.print("Enter three points: ");
 9     double x1 = input.nextDouble();
10     double y1 = input.nextDouble();
11     double x2 = input.nextDouble();
12     double y2 = input.nextDouble();
13     double x3 = input.nextDouble();
14     double y3 = input.nextDouble();
15
16     // Compute three sides
17     double a = Math.sqrt((x2 - x3) * (x2 - x3)
18       + (y2 - y3) * (y2 - y3));
19     double b = Math.sqrt((x1 - x3) * (x1 - x3)
20       + (y1 - y3) * (y1 - y3));
21     double c = Math.sqrt((x1 - x2) * (x1 - x2)
22       + (y1 - y2) * (y1 - y2));
23
24     // Compute three angles
25     double A = Math.toDegrees(Math.acos((a * a - b * b - c * c)
26       / (-2 * b * c)));
27     double B = Math.toDegrees(Math.acos((b * b - a * a - c * c)
28       / (-2 * a * c)));
29     double C = Math.toDegrees(Math.acos((c * c - b * b - a * a)
30       / (-2 * a * b)));
31
```

enter three points

compute sides

display result

```
32       // Display results
33       System.out.println("The three angles are " +
34          Math.round(A * 100) / 100.0 + " " +
35          Math.round(B * 100) / 100.0 + " " +
36          Math.round(C * 100) / 100.0);
37    }
38 }
```

```
Enter three points: 1 1 6.5 1 6.5 2.5  ↵Enter
The three angles are 15.26 90.0 74.74
```

The program prompts the user to enter three points (line 8). This prompting message is not clear. You should give the user explicit instructions on how to enter these points as follows:

```
System.out.print("Enter the coordinates of three points separated "
   + "by spaces like x1 y1 x2 y2 x3 y3: ");
```

Note that the <u>distance between two points</u> (x1, y1) and (x2, y2) can be computed using the formula $\sqrt{(x_2 - x_1)^2 + (y_2 - y_1)^2}$. The program computes the distances between two points (lines 17–22), and applies the formula to compute the angles (lines 25–30). The angles are rounded to display up to two digits after the decimal point (lines 34–36).

The `Math` class is used in the program, but not imported, because it is in the `java.lang` package. All the classes in the `java.lang` package are *implicitly* imported in a Java program.

4.2.1 Evaluate the following method calls:

(a) `Math.sqrt(4)`   (j) `Math.floor(-2.5)`

(b) `Math.sin(2 * Math.PI)`   (k) `Math.round(-2.5f)`

(c) `Math.cos(2 * Math.PI)`   (l) `Math.round(-2.5)`

(d) `Math.pow(2, 2)`   (m) `Math.rint(2.5)`

(e) `Math.log(Math.E)`   (n) `Math.ceil(2.5)`

(f) `Math.exp(1)`   (o) `Math.floor(2.5)`

(g) `Math.max(2,Math.min(3, 4))`   (p) `Math.round(2.5f)`

(h) `Math.rint(-2.5)`   (q) `Math.round(2.5)`

(i) `Math.ceil(-2.5)`   (r) `Math.round(Math.abs(-2.5))`

4.2.2 True or false? The argument for trigonometric methods is an angle in radians.

4.2.3 Write a statement that converts 47 degrees to radians and assigns the result to a variable.

4.2.4 Write a statement that converts `PI` to an angle in degrees and assigns the result to a variable.

4.2.5 Write an expression that obtains a random integer between 34 and 55. Write an expression that obtains a random integer between 0 and 999. Write an expression that obtains a random number between 5.5 and 55.5.

4.2.6 Why does the `Math` class not need to be imported?

4.2.7 What is `Math.log(Math.exp(5.5))`?
What is `Math.exp(Math.log(5.5))`?
What is `Math.asin(Math.sin(Math.PI / 6))`?
What is `Math.sin(Math.asin(Math.PI / 6))`?

4.3 Character Data Type and Operations

A character data type represents a single character.

In addition to processing numeric values, you can process characters in Java. The character data type, `char`, is used to represent a single character. A character literal is enclosed in single quotation marks. Consider the following code:

Key Point

char type

```
char letter = 'A';
char numChar = '4';
```

The first statement assigns character `A` to the `char` variable `letter`. The second statement assigns digit character `4` to the `char` variable `numChar`.

> **Caution**
>
> A string literal must be enclosed in double quotation marks (`" "`). A character literal is a single character enclosed in single quotation marks (`' '`). Therefore, `"A"` is a string, but `'A'` is a character.

char literal

4.3.1 Unicode and ASCII code

Computers use binary numbers internally. A character is stored in a computer as a sequence of 0s and 1s. Mapping a character to its binary representation is called *encoding*. There are different ways to encode a character. How characters are encoded is defined by an *encoding scheme*.

encoding

Java supports *Unicode*, an encoding scheme established by the Unicode Consortium to support the interchange, processing, and display of written texts in the world's diverse languages. Unicode was originally designed as a 16-bit character encoding. The primitive data type `char` was intended to take advantage of this design by providing a simple data type that could hold any character. However, it turned out that the 65,536 characters possible in a 16-bit encoding are not sufficient to represent all the characters in the world. The Unicode standard therefore has been extended to allow up to 1,112,064 characters. Those characters that go beyond the original 16-bit limit are called *supplementary characters*. Java supports the supplementary characters. The processing and representing of supplementary characters are beyond the scope of this book. For simplicity, this book considers only the original 16-bit Unicode characters. These characters can be stored in a `char` type variable.

Unicode

original Unicode

supplementary Unicode

A 16-bit Unicode takes two bytes, preceded by `\u`, expressed in four hexadecimal digits that run from `\u0000` to `\uFFFF`. Hexadecimal numbers are introduced in Appendix F, Number Systems. For example, the English word `welcome` is translated into Chinese using two characters, 欢迎. The Unicodes of these two characters are `\u6B22\u8FCE`. The Unicodes for the Greek letters α β γ are `\u03b1 \u03b2 \u03b4` respectively.

ASCII

Most computers use *ASCII* (*American Standard Code for Information Interchange*), an 8-bit encoding scheme, for representing all uppercase and lowercase letters, digits, punctuation marks, and control characters. Unicode includes ASCII code, with `\u0000` to `\u007F` corresponding to the 128 ASCII characters. Table 4.4 shows the ASCII code for some commonly used characters. Appendix B, "The ASCII Character Set," gives a complete list of ASCII characters and their decimal and hexadecimal codes.

TABLE 4.4 ASCII Code for Commonly Used Characters

Characters	Code Value in Decimal	Unicode Value
`'0'` to `'9'`	48 to 57	\u0030 to \u0039
`'A'` to `'Z'`	65 to 90	\u0041 to \u005A
`'a'` to `'z'`	97 to 122	\u0061 to \u007A

You can use ASCII characters such as `'X'`, `'1'`, and `'$'` in a Java program as well as Unicodes. Thus, for example, the following statements are equivalent:

```java
char letter = 'A';
char letter = '\u0041'; // Character A's Unicode is 0041
```

Both statements assign character `A` to the `char` variable `letter`.

char increment and
decrement

 Note

The increment and decrement operators can also be used on `char` variables to get the next or preceding Unicode character. For example, the following statements display character `b`:

```java
char ch = 'a';
System.out.println(++ch);
```

4.3.2 Escape Sequences for Special Characters

Suppose you want to print a message with quotation marks in the output. Can you write a statement like this?

```java
System.out.println("He said "Java is fun"");
```

No, this statement has a compile error. The compiler thinks the second quotation character is the end of the string and does not know what to do with the rest of the characters.

escape sequence

To overcome this problem, Java uses a special notation to represent special characters, as listed in Table 4.5. This special notation, called an *escape sequence*, consists of a backslash (\) followed by a character or a combination of digits. For example, `\t` is an escape sequence for the Tab character, and an escape sequence such as `\u03b1` is used to represent a Unicode. The symbols in an escape sequence are interpreted as a whole rather than individually. An escape sequence is considered as a single character.

So, now you can print the quoted message using the following statement:

```java
System.out.println("He said \"Java is fun\"");
```

The output is

```
He said "Java is fun"
```

Note the symbols \ and " together represent one character.

TABLE 4.5 Escape Sequences

Escape Sequence	Name	Unicode Code	Decimal Value
\b	Backspace	\u0008	8
\t	Tab	\u0009	9
\n	Linefeed	\u000A	10
\f	Formfeed	\u000C	12
\r	Carriage Return	\u000D	13
\\	Backslash	\u005C	92
\"	Double Quote	\u0022	34

escape character

The backslash \ is called an *escape character*. It is a special character. To display this character, you have to use an escape sequence \\. For example, the following code

```java
System.out.println("\\t is a tab character");
```

displays

```
\t is a tab character
```

4.3.3 Casting between char and Numeric Types

A char can be cast into any numeric type, and vice versa. When an integer is cast into a char, only its lower 16 bits of data are used; the other part is ignored. For example:

```
// Note a hex integer is written using prefix 0X
char ch = (char)0XAB0041; // The lower 16 bits hex code 0041 is
                          // assigned to ch
System.out.println(ch);   // ch is character A
```

When a floating-point value is cast into a char, the floating-point value is first cast into an int, which is then cast into a char.

```
char ch = (char)65.25;    // Decimal 65 is assigned to ch
System.out.println(ch);   // ch is character A
```

When a char is cast into a numeric type, the character's Unicode is cast into the specified numeric type.

```
int i = (int)'A'; // The Unicode of character A is assigned to i
System.out.println(i);  // i is 65
```

Implicit casting can be used if the result of a casting fits into the target variable. Otherwise, explicit casting must be used. For example, since the Unicode of 'a' is 97, which is within the range of a byte, these implicit castings are fine:

```
byte b = 'a';
int i = 'a';
```

But the following statement is incorrect, because the Unicode \uFFF4 cannot fit into a byte:

```
byte b = '\uFFF4';
```

To force this assignment, use explicit casting, as follows:

```
byte b = (byte)'\uFFF4';
```

Any positive integer between 0 and FFFF in hexadecimal can be cast into a character implicitly. Any number not in this range must be cast into a char explicitly.

All numeric operators can be applied to char operands. A char operand is automatically cast into a number if the other operand is a number or a character. If the other operand is a string, the character is concatenated with the string. For example, the following statements

numeric operators on characters

```
int i = '2' + '3'; // (int)'2' is 50 and (int)'3' is 51
System.out.println("i is " + i); // i is 101
int j = 2 + 'a'; // (int)'a' is 97
System.out.println("j is " + j); // j is 99
System.out.println(j + " is the Unicode for character ")
  + (char)j); // 99 is the Unicode for character c
System.out.println("Chapter " + '2');
```

display

```
i is 101
j is 99
99 is the Unicode for character c
Chapter 2
```

4.3.4 Comparing and Testing Characters

Two characters can be compared using the relational operators just like comparing two numbers. This is done by comparing the Unicodes of the two characters. For example,

'a' < 'b' is true because the Unicode for 'a' (97) is less than the Unicode for 'b' (98).

'a' > 'A' is false because the Unicode for 'a' (97) is greater than the Unicode for 'A' (65).

'1' < '8' is true because the Unicode for '1' (49) is less than the Unicode for '8' (56).

Often in the program, you need to test whether a character is a number, a letter, an uppercase letter, or a lowercase letter. As given in Appendix B, the ASCII character set, that the Unicodes for lowercase letters are consecutive integers starting from the Unicode for 'a', then for 'b', 'c', . . . , and 'z'. The same is true for the uppercase letters and for numeric characters. This property can be used to write the code to test characters. For example, the following code tests whether a character ch is an uppercase letter, a lowercase letter, or a digital character:

```
if (ch >= 'A' && ch <= 'Z')
  System.out.println(ch + " is an uppercase letter");
else if (ch >= 'a' && ch <= 'z')
  System.out.println(ch + " is a lowercase letter");
else if (ch >= '0' && ch <= '9')
  System.out.println(ch + " is a numeric character");
```

For convenience, Java provides the following methods in the Character class for testing characters as listed in Table 4.6. The Character class is defined in the java.lang package.

TABLE 4.6 Methods in the Character Class

Method	Description
isDigit(ch)	Returns true if the specified character is a digit.
isLetter(ch)	Returns true if the specified character is a letter.
isLetterOrDigit(ch)	Returns true if the specified character is a letter or digit.
isLowerCase(ch)	Returns true if the specified character is a lowercase letter.
isUpperCase(ch)	Returns true if the specified character is an uppercase letter.
toLowerCase(ch)	Returns the lowercase of the specified character.
toUpperCase(ch)	Returns the uppercase of the specified character.

For example,

```
System.out.println("isDigit('a') is " + Character.isDigit('a'));
System.out.println("isLetter('a') is " + Character.isLetter('a'));
System.out.println("isLowerCase('a') is "
  + Character.isLowerCase('a'));
System.out.println("isUpperCase('a') is "
  + Character.isUpperCase('a'));
System.out.println("toLowerCase('T') is "
  + Character.toLowerCase('T'));
System.out.println("toUpperCase('q') is "
  + Character.toUpperCase('q'));
```

displays

```
isDigit('a') is false
isLetter('a') is true
```

```
isLowerCase('a') is true
isUpperCase('a') is false
toLowerCase('T') is t
toUpperCase('q') is Q
```

4.3.1 Use print statements to find out the ASCII code for `'1'`, `'A'`, `'B'`, `'a'`, and `'b'`. Use print statements to find out the character for the decimal codes 40, 59, 79, 85, and 90. Use print statements to find out the character for the hexadecimal code 40, 5A, 71, 72, and 7A.

Check Point

4.3.2 Which of the following are correct literals for characters?

```
'1', '\u345dE', '\u3fFa', '\b', '\t'
```

4.3.3 How do you display the characters \ and "?

4.3.4 Evaluate the following:

```
int i = '1';
int j = '1' + '2' * ('4' - '3') + 'b' / 'a';
int k = 'a';
char c = 90;
```

4.3.5 Can the following conversions involving casting be allowed? If so, find the converted result.

```
char c = 'A';
int i = (int)c;

float f = 1000.34f;
int i = (int)f;

double d = 1000.34;
int i = (int)d;

int i = 97;
char c = (char)i;
```

4.3.6 Show the output of the following program:

```
public class Test {
  public static void main(String[] args) {
    char x = 'a';
    char y = 'c';
    System.out.println(++x);
    System.out.println(y++);
    System.out.println(x - y);
  }
}
```

4.3.7 Write the code that generates a random lowercase letter.

4.3.8 Show the output of the following statements:

```
System.out.println('a' < 'b');
System.out.println('a' <= 'A');
System.out.println('a' > 'b');
System.out.println('a' >= 'A');
System.out.println('a' == 'a');
System.out.println('a' != 'b');
```

4.4 The String Type

A string is a sequence of characters.

Key
Point

VideoNote

Introduce strings and objects

The `char` type represents only one character. To represent a string of characters, use the data type called `String`. For example, the following code declares `message` to be a string with the value `"Welcome to Java"`.

```java
String message = "Welcome to Java";
```

`String` is a predefined class in the Java library, just like the classes `System` and `Scanner`. The `String` type is not a primitive type. It is known as a *reference type*. Any Java class can be used as a reference type for a variable. The variable declared by a reference type is known as a reference variable that references an object. Here, `message` is a reference variable that references a string object with contents `Welcome to Java`.

Reference data types will be discussed in detail in Chapter 9, Objects and Classes. For the time being, you need to know only how to declare a `String` variable, how to assign a string to the variable, and how to use the methods in the `String` class. More details on using strings will be covered in Chapter 10.

Table 4.7 lists the `String` methods for obtaining string length, for accessing characters in the string, for concatenating string, for converting string to uppercases or lowercases, and for trimming a string.

TABLE 4.7 Simple Methods for `String` Objects

Method	Description
`length()`	Returns the number of characters in this string.
`charAt(index)`	Returns the character at the specified index from this string.
`concat(s1)`	Returns a new string that concatenates this string with string `s1`.
`toUpperCase()`	Returns a new string with all letters in uppercase.
`toLowerCase()`	Returns a new string with all letters in lowercase.
`trim()`	Returns a new string with whitespace characters trimmed on both sides.

instance method
static method

Strings are objects in Java. The methods listed in Table 4.7 can only be invoked from a specific string instance. For this reason, these methods are called *instance methods*. A noninstance method is called a *static method*. A static method can be invoked without using an object. All the methods defined in the `Math` class are static methods. They are not tied to a specific object instance. The syntax to invoke an instance method is `referenceVariable.methodName(arguments)`. A method may have many arguments or no arguments. For example, the `charAt(index)` method has one argument, but the `length()` method has no arguments. Recall that the syntax to invoke a static method is `ClassName.methodName(arguments)`. For example, the `pow` method in the `Math` class can be invoked using `Math.pow(2, 2.5)`.

4.4.1 Getting String Length

You can use the `length()` method to return the number of characters in a string. For example, the following code

```java
String message = "Welcome to Java";
System.out.println("The length of " + message + " is "
  + message.length());
```

displays

```
The length of Welcome to Java is 15
```

 Note

When you use a string, you often know its literal value. For convenience, Java allows you to use the *string literal* to refer directly to strings without creating new variables. Thus, `"Welcome to Java".length()` is correct and returns `15`. Note that `""` denotes an *empty string* and `"".length()` is `0`.

string literal

empty string

4.4.2 Getting Characters from a String

The `s.charAt(index)` method can be used to retrieve a specific character in a string `s`, where the index is between `0` and `s.length()-1`. For example, `message.charAt(0)` returns the character `W`, as shown in Figure 4.1. Note that the index for the first character in the string is `0`.

charAt(index)

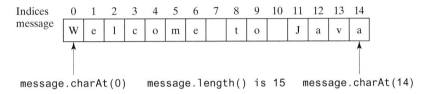

FIGURE 4.1 The characters in a `String` object can be accessed using its index.

 Caution

Attempting to access characters in a string `s` out of bounds is a common programming error. To avoid it, make sure that you do not use an index beyond `s.length()-1`. For example, `s.charAt(s.length())` would cause a `StringIndexOutOfBoundsException`.

string index range

4.4.3 Concatenating Strings

You can use the `concat` method to concatenate two strings. The statement given below, for example, concatenates strings `s1` and `s2` into `s3`:

```
String s3 = s1.concat(s2);
```

s1.concat(s2)

Because string concatenation is heavily used in programming, Java provides a convenient way to accomplish it. You can use the plus (+) operator to concatenate two strings, so the previous statement is equivalent to

```
String s3 = s1 + s2;
```

s1 + s2

The following code combines the strings `message`, `" and "`, and `"HTML"` into one string:

```
String myString = message + " and " + "HTML";
```

Recall that the + operator can also concatenate a number with a string. In this case, the number is converted into a string then concatenated. Note at least one of the operands must be a string in order for concatenation to take place. If one of the operands is a nonstring (e.g., a

concatenate strings and numbers

number), the nonstring value is converted into a string and concatenated with the other string. Here are some examples:

```
// Three strings are concatenated
String message = "Welcome " + "to " + "Java";

// String Chapter is concatenated with number 2
String s = "Chapter" + 2; // s becomes Chapter2

// String Supplement is concatenated with character B
String s1 = "Supplement" + 'B'; // s1 becomes SupplementB
```

If neither of the operands is a string, the plus sign (+) is the addition operator that adds two numbers.

The augmented += operator can also be used for string concatenation. For example, the following code appends the string " and Java is fun" with the string "Welcome to Java" in message.

```
message += " and Java is fun";
```

So the new message is "Welcome to Java and Java is fun."
If i = 1 and j = 2, what is the output of the following statement?

```
System.out.println("i + j is " + i + j);
```

The output is "i + j is 12" because "i + j is" is concatenated with the value of i first. To force i + j to be executed first, enclose i + j in the parentheses, as follows:

```
System.out.println("i + j is " + (i + j));
```

4.4.4 Converting Strings

The toLowerCase() method returns a new string with all lowercase letters, and the toUpperCase() method returns a new string with all uppercase letters. For example,

toLowerCase()
toUpperCase()

"Welcome".toLowerCase() returns a new string welcome.
"Welcome".toUpperCase() returns a new string WELCOME.

whitespace character

The trim() method returns a new string by eliminating whitespace characters from both ends of the string. The characters ' ', \t, \f, \r, or \n are known as *whitespace characters*. For example,

trim()

"\t Good Night \n".trim() returns a new string Good Night.

4.4.5 Reading a String from the Console

read strings

To read a string from the console, invoke the next() method on a Scanner object. For example, the following code reads three strings from the keyboard:

```
Scanner input = new Scanner(System.in);
System.out.print("Enter three words separated by spaces: ");
String s1 = input.next();
String s2 = input.next();
String s3 = input.next();
System.out.println("s1 is " + s1);
System.out.println("s2 is " + s2);
System.out.println("s3 is " + s3);
```

```
Enter three words separated by spaces: Welcome to Java ↵Enter
s1 is Welcome
s2 is to
s3 is Java
```

The `next()` method reads a string that ends with a whitespace character. You can use the `nextLine()` method to read an entire line of text. The `nextLine()` method reads a string that ends with the *Enter* key pressed. For example, the following statements read a line of text:

```
Scanner input = new Scanner(System.in);
System.out.println("Enter a line: ");
String s = input.nextLine();
System.out.println("The line entered is " + s);
```

```
Enter a line: Welcome to Java ↵Enter
The line entered is Welcome to Java
```

For convenience, we call the input using the methods `next()`, `nextByte()`, `nextShort()`, `nextInt()`, `nextLong()`, `nextFloat()`, and `nextDouble()` the token-based input, because they read individual elements separated by whitespace characters rather than an entire line. The `nextLine()` method is called a line-based input.

token-based input

line-based input

 Important Caution

To *avoid input errors*, do not use a line-based input after a token-based input in the program. The reasons will be explained in Section 12.11.4, "How Does Scanner Work?"

avoid input errors

4.4.6 Reading a Character from the Console

To read a character from the console, use the `nextLine()` method to read a string and then invoke the `charAt(0)` method on the string to return a character. For example, the following code reads a character from the keyboard:

```
Scanner input = new Scanner(System.in);
System.out.print("Enter a character: ");
String s = input.nextLine();
char ch = s.charAt(0);
System.out.println("The character entered is " + ch);
```

4.4.7 Comparing Strings

The `String` class contains the methods, as listed in Table 4.8, for comparing two strings.

TABLE 4.8 Comparison Methods for `String` Objects

Method	Description
equals(s1)	Returns true if this string is equal to string s1.
equalsIgnoreCase(s1)	Returns true if this string is equal to string s1; it is case insensitive.
compareTo(s1)	Returns an integer greater than 0, equal to 0, or less than 0 to indicate whether this string is greater than, equal to, or less than s1.
compareToIgnoreCase(s1)	Same as compareTo except that the comparison is case insensitive.
startsWith(prefix)	Returns true if this string starts with the specified prefix.
endsWith(suffix)	Returns true if this string ends with the specified suffix.
contains(s1)	Returns true if s1 is a substring in this string.

How do you compare the contents of two strings? You might attempt to use the `==` operator, as follows:

==

```
if (string1 == string2)
    System.out.println("string1 and string2 are the same object");
else
    System.out.println("string1 and string2 are different objects");
```

However, the `==` operator checks only whether `string1` and `string2` refer to the same object; it does not tell you whether they have the same contents. Therefore, you cannot use the `==` operator to find out whether two string variables have the same contents. Instead, you should use the `equals` method. The following code, for instance, can be used to compare two strings:

string1.equals(string2)

```
if (string1.equals(string2))
    System.out.println("string1 and string2 have the same contents");
else
    System.out.println("string1 and string2 are not equal");
```

For example, the following statements display `true` then `false`:

```
String s1 = "Welcome to Java";
String s2 = "Welcome to Java";
String s3 = "Welcome to C++";
System.out.println(s1.equals(s2)); // true
System.out.println(s1.equals(s3)); // false
```

The `compareTo` method can also be used to compare two strings. For example, consider the following code:

s1.compareTo(s2)

```
s1.compareTo(s2)
```

The method returns the value `0` if `s1` is equal to `s2`, a value less than `0` if `s1` is lexicographically (i.e., in terms of Unicode ordering) less than `s2`, and a value greater than `0` if `s1` is lexicographically greater than `s2`.

The actual value returned from the `compareTo` method depends on the offset of the first two distinct characters in `s1` and `s2` from left to right. For example, suppose `s1` is `abc` and `s2` is `abg`, and `s1.compareTo(s2)` returns `-4`. The first two characters (`a` vs. `a`) from `s1` and `s2` are compared. Because they are equal, the second two characters (`b` vs. `b`) are compared. Because they are also equal, the third two characters (`c` vs. `g`) are compared. Since the character `c` is `4` less than `g`, the comparison returns `-4`.

 Caution

Syntax errors will occur if you compare strings by using relational operators `>`, `>=`, `<`, or `<=`. Instead, you have to use `s1.compareTo(s2)`.

 Note

The `equals` method returns `true` if two strings are equal, and `false` if they are not. The `compareTo` method returns `0`, a positive integer, or a negative integer, depending on whether one string is equal to, greater than, or less than the other string.

The `String` class also provides the `equalsIgnoreCase` and `compareToIgnoreCase` methods for comparing strings. The `equalsIgnoreCase` and `compareToIgnoreCase` methods ignore the case of the letters when comparing two strings. You can also use `str.startsWith(prefix)` to check whether string `str` starts with a specified prefix, `str.endsWith(suffix)` to check whether string `str` ends with a specified suffix, and `str.contains(s1)` to check whether string `str` contains string `s1`. For example,

```
"Welcome to Java".startsWith("We") returns true.
"Welcome to Java".startsWith("we") returns false.
"Welcome to Java".endsWith("va") returns true.
```

```
"Welcome to Java".endsWith("v") returns false.
"Welcome to Java".contains("to") returns true.
"Welcome to Java".contains("To") returns false.
```

Listing 4.2 gives a program that prompts the user to enter two cities and displays them in alphabetical order.

LISTING 4.2 OrderTwoCities.java

```
 1  import java.util.Scanner;
 2
 3  public class OrderTwoCities {
 4    public static void main(String[] args) {
 5      Scanner input = new Scanner(System.in);
 6
 7      // Prompt the user to enter two cities
 8      System.out.print("Enter the first city: ");
 9      String city1 = input.nextLine();                              input city1
10      System.out.print("Enter the second city: ");
11      String city2 = input.nextLine();                              input city2
12
13      if (city1.compareTo(city2) < 0)                               compare two cities
14        System.out.println("The cities in alphabetical order are " +
15          city1 + " " + city2);
16      else
17        System.out.println("The cities in alphabetical order are " +
18          city2 + " " + city1);
19    }
20  }
```

```
Enter the first city: New York ⏎Enter
Enter the second city: Boston ⏎Enter
The cities in alphabetical order are Boston New York
```

The program reads two strings for two cities (lines 9 and 11). If `input.nextLine()` is replaced by `input.next()` (line 9), you cannot enter a string with spaces for `city1`. Since a city name may contain multiple words separated by spaces, the program uses the `nextLine` method to read a string (lines 9 and 11). Invoking `city1.compareTo(city2)` compares two strings `city1` with `city2` (line 13). A negative return value indicates that `city1` is less than `city2`.

4.4.8 Obtaining Substrings

You can obtain a single character from a string using the `charAt` method. You can also obtain a substring from a string using the `substring` method (see Figure 4.2) in the `String` class, as given in Table 4.9.

For example,

```
String message = "Welcome to Java";
String message = message.substring(0,11) + "HTML";
The string message now becomes Welcome to HTML.
```

TABLE 4.9 The String Class Contains the Methods for Obtaining Substrings

Method	Description
substring(beginIndex)	Returns this string's substring that begins with the character at the specified beginIndex and extends to the end of the string, as shown in Figure 4.2.
substring(beginIndex, endIndex)	Returns this string's substring that begins at the specified beginIndex and extends to the character at index endIndex − 1, as shown in Figure 4.2. Note the character at endIndex is not part of the substring.

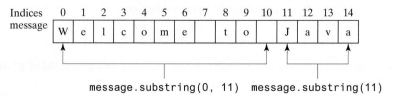

FIGURE 4.2 The substring method obtains a substring from a string.

> **Note**
>
> If beginIndex is endIndex, substring(beginIndex, endIndex) returns an empty string with length 0. If beginIndex > endIndex, it would be a runtime error.

beginIndex <= endIndex

4.4.9 Finding a Character or a Substring in a String

The String class provides several versions of indexOf and lastIndexOf methods to find a character or a substring in a string, as listed in Table 4.10.

TABLE 4.10 The String Class Contains the Methods for Finding Substrings

Method	Description
index Of (ch)	Returns the index of the first occurrence of ch in the string. Returns −1 if not matched.
indexOf(ch, fromIndex)	Returns the index of the first occurrence of ch after fromIndex in the string. Returns −1 if not matched.
indexOf(s)	Returns the index of the first occurrence of string s in this string. Returns −1 if not matched.
indexOf(s, fromIndex)	Returns the index of the first occurrence of string s in this string after fromIndex. Returns −1 if not matched.
lastIndexOf(ch)	Returns the index of the last occurrence of ch in the string. Returns −1 if not matched.
lastIndexOf(ch, fromIndex)	Returns the index of the last occurrence of ch before fromIndex in this string. Returns −1 if not matched.
lastIndexOf(s)	Returns the index of the last occurrence of string s. Returns −1 if not matched.
lastIndexOf(s, fromIndex)	Returns the index of the last occurrence of string s before fromIndex. Returns −1 if not matched.

For example,

indexOf

```
"Welcome to Java".indexOf('W') returns 0.
"Welcome to Java".indexOf('o') returns 4.
"Welcome to Java".indexOf('o', 5) returns 9.
"Welcome to Java".indexOf("come") returns 3.
"Welcome to Java".indexOf("Java", 5) returns 11.
"Welcome to Java".indexOf("java", 5) returns -1.
```

lastIndexOf

```
"Welcome to Java".lastIndexOf('W') returns 0.
"Welcome to Java".lastIndexOf('o') returns 9.
"Welcome to Java".lastIndexOf('o', 5) returns 4.
"Welcome to Java".lastIndexOf("come") returns 3.
"Welcome to Java".lastIndexOf("Java", 5) returns -1.
"Welcome to Java".lastIndexOf("Java") returns 11.
```

Suppose that a string s contains the first name and last name separated by a space. You can use the following code to extract the first name and last name from the string:

```
int k = s.indexOf(' ');
String firstName = s.substring(0, k);
String lastName = s.substring(k + 1);
```

For example, if s is Kim Jones, the following diagram illustrates how the first name and last name are extracted.

```
                        012345678
  s.substring(0, k) →  Kim Jones  ← s.substring(k + 1)
  is Kim                   ↑           is Jones
                        k is 3
```

4.4.10 Conversion between Strings and Numbers

You can convert a numeric string into a number. To convert a string into an int value, use the Integer.parseInt method, as follows:

Integer.parseInt method

```
int intValue = Integer.parseInt(intString);
```

where intString is a numeric string such as "123".

To convert a string into a double value, use the Double.parseDouble method, as follows:

Double.parseDouble method

```
double doubleValue = Double.parseDouble(doubleString);
```

where doubleString is a numeric string such as "123.45".

If the string is not a numeric string, the conversion would cause a runtime error. The Integer and Double classes are both included in the java.lang package, and thus they are automatically imported.

You can convert a number into a string; simply use the string concatenating operator as follows:

```
String s = number + "";
```

number to string

4.4.1 Suppose s1, s2, and s3 are three strings, given as follows:

Check Point

```
String s1 = "Welcome to Java";
String s2 = "Programming is fun";
String s3 = "Welcome to Java";
```

What are the results of the following expressions?

(a) s1 == s2

(b) s2 == s3

(c) s1.equals(s2)

(d) s2.equals(s3)

(e) s1.compareTo(s2)

(f) s2.compareTo(s3)

(g) s2.compareTo(s2)

(h) s1.charAt(0)

(i) s1.indexOf('j')

(j) s1.indexOf("to")

(k) s1.lastIndexOf('a')

(l) s1.lastIndexOf("o", 15)

(m) s1.length()

(n) s1.substring(5)

(o) s1.substring(5, 11)

(p) s1.startsWith("Wel")

(q) s1.endsWith("Java")

(r) s1.toLowerCase()

(s) s1.toUpperCase()

(t) s1.concat(s2)

(u) s1.contain(s2)

(v) "\t Wel \t".trim()

4.4.2 Suppose `s1` and `s2` are two strings. Which of the following statements or expressions are incorrect?

```java
String s = "Welcome to Java";
String s3 = s1 + s2;
String s3 = s1 - s2;
s1 == s2;
s1 >= s2;
s1.compareTo(s2);
int i = s1.length();
char c = s1(0);
char c = s1.charAt(s1.length());
```

4.4.3 Show the output of the following statements (write a program to verify your results):

```java
System.out.println("1" + 1);
System.out.println('1' + 1);
System.out.println("1" + 1 + 1);
System.out.println("1" + (1 + 1));
System.out.println('1' + 1 + 1);
```

4.4.4 Evaluate the following expressions (write a program to verify your results):

```java
1 + "Welcome " + 1 + 1
1 + "Welcome " + (1 + 1)
1 + "Welcome " + ('\u0001' + 1)
1 + "Welcome " + 'a' + 1
```

4.4.5 Let `s1` be " Welcome " and `s2` be " welcome ". Write the code for the following statements:

(a) Check whether `s1` is equal to `s2` and assign the result to a Boolean variable `isEqual`.

(b) Check whether `s1` is equal to `s2`, ignoring case, and assign the result to a Boolean variable `isEqual`.

(c) Compare `s1` with `s2` and assign the result to an `int` variable `x`.

(d) Compare `s1` with `s2`, ignoring case, and assign the result to an `int` variable `x`.

(e) Check whether `s1` has the prefix `AAA` and assign the result to a Boolean variable `b`.

(f) Check whether `s1` has the suffix `AAA` and assign the result to a Boolean variable `b`.

(g) Assign the length of `s1` to an `int` variable `x`.

(h) Assign the first character of `s1` to a `char` variable `x`.

(i) Create a new string `s3` that combines `s1` with `s2`.

(j) Create a substring of `s1` starting from index `1`.

(k) Create a substring of `s1` from index `1` to index `4`.

(l) Create a new string `s3` that converts `s1` to lowercase.

(m) Create a new string `s3` that converts `s1` to uppercase.

(n) Create a new string `s3` that trims whitespaces on both ends of `s1`.

(o) Assign the index of the first occurrence of the character `e` in `s1` to an `int` variable `x`.

(p) Assign the index of the last occurrence of the string `abc` in `s1` to an `int` variable `x`.

4.4.6 Write one statement to return the number of digits in an integer `i`.

4.4.7 Write one statement to return the number of digits in a double value `d`.

4.5 Case Studies

Strings are fundamental in programming. The ability to write programs using strings is essential in learning Java programming.

Key Point

You will frequently use strings to write useful programs. This section presents three examples of solving problems using strings.

4.5.1 Case Study: Guessing Birthdays

You can find out the date of the month when your friend was born by asking five questions. Each question asks whether the day is in one of the five sets of numbers.

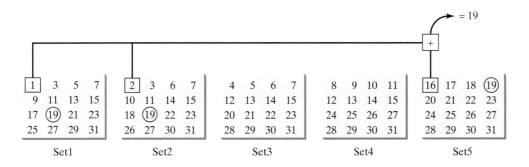

The birthday is the sum of the first numbers in the sets where the day appears. For example, if the birthday is 19, it appears in Set1, Set2, and Set5. The first numbers in these three sets are 1, 2, and 16. Their sum is 19.

Listing 4.3 gives a program that prompts the user to answer whether the day is in Set1 (lines 41–44), in Set2 (lines 50–53), in Set3 (lines 59–62), in Set4 (lines 68–71), and in Set5 (lines 77–80). If the number is in the set, the program adds the first number in the set to day (lines 47, 56, 65, 74, and 83).

LISTING 4.3 GuessBirthday.java

```
1  import java.util.Scanner;
2
3  public class GuessBirthday {
4    public static void main(String[] args) {
5      String set1 =
6        " 1  3  5  7\n" +
7        " 9 11 13 15\n" +
8        "17 19 21 23\n" +
9        "25 27 29 31";
10
11     String set2 =
12        " 2  3  6  7\n" +
```

```
13            "10 11 14 15\n" +
14            "18 19 22 23\n" +
15            "26 27 30 31";
16
17       String set3 =
18            " 4  5  6  7\n" +
19            "12 13 14 15\n" +
20            "20 21 22 23\n" +
21            "28 29 30 31";
22
23       String set4 =
24            " 8  9 10 11\n" +
25            "12 13 14 15\n" +
26            "24 25 26 27\n" +
27            "28 29 30 31";
28
29       String set5 =
30            "16 17 18 19\n" +
31            "20 21 22 23\n" +
32            "24 25 26 27\n" +
33            "28 29 30 31";
34
```

day to be determined
```
35       int day = 0;
36
37       // Create a Scanner
38       Scanner input = new Scanner(System.in);
39
40       // Prompt the user to answer questions
41       System.out.print("Is your birthday in Set1?\n");
42       System.out.print(set1);
43       System.out.print("\nEnter 0 for No and 1 for Yes: ");
44       int answer = input.nextInt();
45
```

in Set1?
```
46       if (answer == 1)
47          day += 1;
48
49       // Prompt the user to answer questions
50       System.out.print("\nIs your birthday in Set2?\n");
51       System.out.print(set2);
52       System.out.print("\nEnter 0 for No and 1 for Yes: ");
53       answer = input.nextInt();
54
```

in Set2?
```
55       if (answer == 1)
56          day += 2;
57
58       // Prompt the user to answer questions
59       System.out.print("\nIs your birthday in Set3?\n");
60       System.out.print(set3);
61       System.out.print("\nEnter 0 for No and 1 for Yes: ");
62       answer = input.nextInt();
63
```

in Set3?
```
64       if (answer == 1)
65          day += 4;
66
67       // Prompt the user to answer questions
68       System.out.print("\nIs your birthday in Set4?\n");
69       System.out.print(set4);
70       System.out.print("\nEnter 0 for No and 1 for Yes: ");
71       answer = input.nextInt();
72
```

```
73        if (answer == 1)                                              in Set4?
74           day += 8;
75
76        // Prompt the user to answer questions
77        System.out.print("\nIs your birthday in Set5?\n");
78        System.out.print(set5);
79        System.out.print("\nEnter 0 for No and 1 for Yes: ");
80        answer = input.nextInt();
81
82        if (answer == 1)                                              in Set5?
83           day += 16;
84
85        System.out.println("\nYour birthday is " + day + "!");
86     }
87  }
```

```
Is your birthday in Set1?
 1  3  5  7
 9 11 13 15
17 19 21 23
25 27 29 31
Enter 0 for No and 1 for Yes: 1 ↵Enter

Is your birthday in Set2?
 2  3  6  7
10 11 14 15
18 19 22 23
26 27 30 31
Enter 0 for No and 1 for Yes: 1 ↵Enter

Is your birthday in Set3?
 4  5  6  7
12 13 14 15
20 21 22 23
28 29 30 31
Enter 0 for No and 1 for Yes: 0 ↵Enter

Is your birthday in Set4?
 8  9 10 11
12 13 14 15
24 25 26 27
28 29 30 31
Enter 0 for No and 1 for Yes: 0 ↵Enter

Is your birthday in Set5?
16 17 18 19
20 21 22 23
24 25 26 27
28 29 30 31
Enter 0 for No and 1 for Yes: 1 ↵Enter
Your birthday is 19!
```

line#	day	answer	output
35	0		
44		1	
47	1		
53		1	
56	3		
62		0	
71		0	
80		1	
83	19		
85			Your birthday is 19!

mathematics behind the game   This game is easy to program. You may wonder how the game was created. The mathematics behind the game is actually quite simple. The numbers are not grouped together by accident—the way they are placed in the five sets is deliberate. The starting numbers in the five sets are 1, 2, 4, 8, and 16, which correspond to 1, 10, 100, 1000, and 10000 in binary (binary numbers are introduced in Appendix F, Number Systems). A binary number for decimal integers between 1 and 31 has at most five digits, as shown in Figure 4.3a. Let it be $b_5b_4b_3b_2b_1$. Thus, $b_5b_4b_3b_2b_1 = b_5\,0000 + b_4\,000 + b_3\,00 + b_2\,0 + b_1$, as shown in Figure 4.3b. If a day's binary number has a digit 1 in b_k, the number should appear in Set$k$. For example, number 19 is binary 10011, so it appears in Set1, Set2, and Set5. It is binary 1 + 10 + 10000 = 10011 or decimal 1 + 2 + 16 = 19. Number 31 is binary 11111, so it appears in Set1, Set2, Set3, Set4, and Set5. It is binary 1 + 10 + 100 + 1000 + 10000 = 11111 or decimal 1 + 2 + 4 + 8 + 16 = 31.

Decimal	Binary
1	00001
2	00010
3	00011
...	
19	10011
...	
31	11111

$$
\begin{array}{r}
b_5\ 0\ 0\ 0\ 0 \\
b_4\ 0\ 0\ 0 \\
b_3\ 0\ 0 \\
b_2\ 0 \\
+\ \underline{\hspace{1cm} b_1} \\
b_5\,b_4\,b_3\,b_2\,b_1
\end{array}
\qquad
\begin{array}{r}
10000 \\
10 \\
+\ \underline{\hspace{0.8cm}1} \\
10011 \\
19
\end{array}
\qquad
\begin{array}{r}
10000 \\
1000 \\
100 \\
10 \\
+\ \underline{\hspace{0.8cm}1} \\
11111 \\
31
\end{array}
$$

(a)   (b)

FIGURE 4.3   (a) A number between 1 and 31 can be represented using a five-digit binary number. (b) A five-digit binary number can be obtained by adding binary numbers 1, 10, 100, 1000, or 10000.

4.5.2   Case Study: Converting a Hexadecimal Digit to a Decimal Value

The hexadecimal number system has 16 digits: 0–9, A–F. The letters A, B, C, D, E, and F correspond to the decimal numbers 10, 11, 12, 13, 14, and 15. We now write a program that prompts the user to enter a hex digit and display its corresponding decimal value, as given in Listing 4.4.

LISTING 4.4 HexDigit2Dec.java

VideoNote

Convert hex to decimal

```
 1  import java.util.Scanner;
 2
 3  public class HexDigit2Dec {
 4    public static void main(String[] args) {
 5      Scanner input = new Scanner(System.in);
 6      System.out.print("Enter a hex digit: ");
 7      String hexString = input.nextLine();
 8
 9      // Check if the hex string has exactly one character
10      if (hexString.length() != 1) {
11        System.out.println("You must enter exactly one character");
12        System.exit(1);
13      }
14
15      // Display decimal value for the hex digit
16      char ch = Character.toUpperCase(hexString.charAt(0));
17      if ('A' <= ch && ch <= 'F') {
18        int value = ch - 'A' + 10;
19        System.out.println("The decimal value for hex digit "
20          + ch + " is " + value);
21      }
22      else if (Character.isDigit(ch)) {
23        System.out.println("The decimal value for hex digit "
24          + ch + " is " + ch);
25      }
26      else {
27        System.out.println(ch + " is an invalid input");
28      }
29    }
30  }
```

input string

check length

is A–F?

is 0–9?

```
Enter a hex digit: AB7C  ↵Enter
You must enter exactly one character
```

```
Enter a hex digit: B  ↵Enter
The decimal value for hex digit B is 11
```

```
Enter a hex digit: 8  ↵Enter
The decimal value for hex digit 8 is 8
```

```
Enter a hex digit: T  ↵Enter
T is an invalid input
```

The program reads a string from the console (line 7) and checks if the string contains a single character (line 10). If not, report an error and exit the program (line 12).

The program invokes the Character.toUpperCase method to obtain the character ch as an uppercase letter (line 16). If ch is between 'A' and 'F' (line 17), the corresponding decimal value is ch - 'A' + 10 (line 18). Note ch - 'A' is 0 if ch is 'A', ch - 'A' is

1 if `ch` is `'B'`, and so on. When two characters perform a numerical operation, the characters' Unicodes are used in the computation.

The program invokes the `Character.isDigit(ch)` method to check if `ch` is between `'0'` and `'9'` (line 22). If so, the corresponding decimal digit is the same as `ch` (lines 23 and 24).

If `ch` is not between `'A'` and `'F'` nor a digit character, the program displays an error message (line 27).

4.5.3 Case Study: Revising the Lottery Program Using Strings

The lottery program in Listing 3.8, Lottery.java, generates a random two-digit number, prompts the user to enter a two-digit number, and determines whether the user wins according to the following rule:

1. If the user input matches the lottery number in the exact order, the award is $10,000.

2. If all the digits in the user input match all the digits in the lottery number, the award is $3,000.

3. If one digit in the user input matches a digit in the lottery number, the award is $1,000.

The program in Listing 3.8 uses an integer to store the number. Listing 4.5 gives a new program that generates a random two-digit string instead of a number, and receives the user input as a string instead of a number.

LISTING 4.5 `LotteryUsingStrings.java`

```
1  import java.util.Scanner;
2
3  public class LotteryUsingStrings {
4    public static void main(String[] args) {
5      // Generate a lottery as a two-digit string
6      String lottery = "" + (int)(Math.random() * 10)
7        + (int)(Math.random() * 10);
8
9      // Prompt the user to enter a guess
10     Scanner input = new Scanner(System.in);
11     System.out.print("Enter your lottery pick (two digits): ");
12     String guess = input.nextLine();
13
14     // Get digits from lottery
15     char lotteryDigit1 = lottery.charAt(0);
16     char lotteryDigit2 = lottery.charAt(1);
17
18     // Get digits from guess
19     char guessDigit1 = guess.charAt(0);
20     char guessDigit2 = guess.charAt(1);
21
22     System.out.println("The lottery number is " + lottery);
23
24     // Check the guess
25     if (guess.equals(lottery))
26       System.out.println("Exact match: you win $10,000");
27     else if (guessDigit2 == lotteryDigit1
28              && guessDigit1 == lotteryDigit2)
29       System.out.println("Match all digits: you win $3,000");
30     else if (guessDigit1 == lotteryDigit1
31              || guessDigit1 == lotteryDigit2
32              || guessDigit2 == lotteryDigit1
33              || guessDigit2 == lotteryDigit2)
34       System.out.println("Match one digit: you win $1,000");
```

generate a lottery — lines 6–7

enter a guess — line 12

exact match? — line 25

match all digits? — line 27

match one digit? — line 30

```
35       else
36          System.out.println("Sorry, no match");
37    }
38  }
```

```
Enter your lottery pick (two digits): 00 ↵Enter
The lottery number is 00
Exact match: you win $10,000
```

```
Enter your lottery pick (two digits): 45 ↵Enter
The lottery number is 54
Match all digits: you win $3,000
```

```
Enter your lottery pick: 23 ↵Enter
The lottery number is 34
Match one digit: you win $1,000
```

```
Enter your lottery pick: 23 ↵Enter
The lottery number is 14
Sorry: no match
```

The program generates two random digits and concatenates them into the string `lottery` (lines 6 and 7). After this, `lottery` contains two random digits.

The program prompts the user to enter a guess as a two-digit string (line 12) and checks the guess against the lottery number in this order:

- First, check whether the guess matches the lottery exactly (line 25).

- If not, check whether the reversal of the guess matches the lottery (line 27).

- If not, check whether one digit is in the lottery (lines 30–33).

- If not, nothing matches and display "Sorry, no match" (line 36).

4.5.1 If you run Listing 4.3 GuessBirthday.java with input 1 for Set1, Set3, and Set4 and 0 for Set2 and Set5, what will be the birthday?

4.5.2 If you enter a lowercase letter such as b, the program in Listing 4.4 displays B is 11. Revise the code as to display b is 11.

4.5.3 What would be wrong if lines 6 and 7 are in Listing 4.5 replaced by the following code?

```
String lottery = "" + (int)(Math.random() * 100);
```

4.6 Formatting Console Output

You can use the `System.out.printf` *method to display formatted output on the console.*

Often, it is desirable to display numbers in a certain format. For example, the following code computes interest, given the amount and the annual interest rate:

```
double amount = 12618.98;
double interestRate = 0.0013;
double interest = amount * interestRate;
System.out.println("Interest is $" + interest);
```

```
Interest is $16.404674
```

Because the interest amount is currency, it is desirable to display only two digits after the decimal point. To do this, you can write the code as follows:

```
double amount = 12618.98;
double interestRate = 0.0013;
double interest = amount * interestRate;
System.out.println("Interest is $"
  + (int)(interest * 100) / 100.0);
```

```
Interest is $16.4
```

However, the format is still not correct. There should be two digits after the decimal point: `16.40` rather than `16.4`. You can fix it by using the `printf` method, as follows:

printf

```
double amount = 12618.98;
double interestRate = 0.0013;
double interest = amount * interestRate;
System.out.printf("Interest is $%4.2f",
  interest);
```

% 4 . 2 f ◄— format specifier

field width   conversion code

precision

```
Interest is $16.40
```

The `f` in the `printf` stands for formatted, implying that the method prints an item in some format. The syntax to invoke this method is

```
System.out.printf(format, item1, item2, ..., itemk);
```

where `format` is a string that may consist of substrings and format specifiers.

format specifier

A *format specifier* specifies how an item should be formatted. An item may be a numeric value, a character, a Boolean value, or a string. A simple format specifier consists of a percent sign (%) followed by a conversion code. Table 4.11 lists some frequently used simple format specifiers.

TABLE 4.11 Frequently Used Format Specifiers

Format Specifier	Output	Example
%b	A Boolean value	True or false
%c	A character	'a'
%d	A decimal integer	200
%f	A floating-point number	45.460000
%e	A number in standard scientific notation	4.556000e+01
%s	A string	"Java is cool"

Here is an example:

```
                                                        items
int count = 5;
double amount = 45.56;
System.out.printf("count is %d and amount is %f", count, amount);
```

display   count is 5 and amount is 45.560000

Items must match the format specifiers in order, in number, and in exact type. For example, the format specifier for `count` is `%d` and for `amount` is `%f`. By default, a floating-point value is displayed with six digits after the decimal point. You can specify the width and precision in a format specifier, as shown in the examples in Table 4.12.

TABLE 4.12 Examples of Specifying Width and Precision

Example	Output
`%5c`	Output the character and add four spaces before the character item, because the width is 5.
`%6b`	Output the Boolean value and add one space before the false value and two spaces before the true value.
`%5d`	Output the integer item with width 5. If the number of digits in the item is < 5, add spaces before the number. If the number of digits in the item is > 5, the width is automatically increased.
`%10.2f`	Output the floating-point item with width 10 including a decimal point and two digits after the point. Thus, there are seven digits allocated before the decimal point. If the number of digits before the decimal point in the item is < 7, add spaces before the number. If the number of digits before the decimal point in the item is > 7, the width is automatically increased.
`%10.2e`	Output the floating-point item with width 10 including a decimal point, two digits after the point and the exponent part. If the displayed number in scientific notation has width < 10, add spaces before the number.
`%12s`	Output the string with width 12 characters. If the string item has fewer than 12 characters, add spaces before the string. If the string item has more than 12 characters, the width is automatically increased.

If an item requires more spaces than the specified width, the width is automatically increased. For example, the following code

```
System.out.printf("%3d#%2s#%4.2f\n", 1234, "Java", 51.6653);
```

displays

```
1234#Java#51.67
```

The specified width for `int` item `1234` is `3`, which is smaller than its actual size `4`. The width is automatically increased to `4`. The specified width for string item `Java` is `2`, which is smaller than its actual size `4`. The width is automatically increased to `4`. The specified width for `double` item `51.6653` is `4`, but it needs width `5` to display `51.67`, so the width is automatically increased to `5`.

You can display a number with comma separators by adding a comma in front of a number specifier. For example, the following code   comma separators

```
System.out.printf("%,8d %,10.1f\n", 12345678, 12345678.263);
```

displays

```
12,345,678 12,345,678.3
```

You can pad a number with leading zeros rather than spaces by adding a `0` in front of a   leading zeros
number specifier. For example, the following code

```
System.out.printf("%08d %08.1f\n", 1234, 5.63);
```

displays

```
00001234 000005.6
```

right justify
left justify

By default, the output is right justified. You can put the minus sign (−) in the format specifier to specify that the item is left justified in the output within the specified field. For example, the following statements

```
System.out.printf("%8d%8s%8.1f\n", 1234, "Java", 5.63);
System.out.printf("%-8d%-8s%-8.1f \n", 1234, "Java", 5.63);
```

display

```
|← 8 →|← 8 →|← 8 →|
□□□□ 1234 □□□□ Java □□□□□ 5.6
1234 □□□□ Java □□□ 5.6 □□□□□
```

where the square box (□) denotes a blank space.

Caution

The items must match the format specifiers in exact type. The item for the format specifier %f or %e must be a floating-point type value such as 40.0, not 40. Thus, an int variable cannot match %f or %e. You can use %.2f to specify a floating-point value with two digits after the decimal point. However, %0.2f would be incorrect.

%%

Tip

The % sign denotes a format specifier. To output a literal % in the format string, use %%. For example, the following code

```
System.out.printf("%.2f%%\n", 75.234);
```

displays

```
75.23%
```

Listing 4.6 gives a program that uses printf to display a table.

LISTING 4.6 FormatDemo.java

```
1  public class FormatDemo {
2    public static void main(String[] args) {
3      // Display the header of the table
4      System.out.printf("%-10s%-10s%-10s%-10s%-10s\n", "Degrees",
5        "Radians", "Sine", "Cosine", "Tangent");
6
7      // Display values for 30 degrees
8      int degrees = 30;
9      double radians = Math.toRadians(degrees);
10     System.out.printf("%-10d%-10.4f%-10.4f%-10.4f%-10.4f\n", degrees,
11       radians, Math.sin(radians), Math.cos(radians),
12       Math.tan(radians));
13
14     // Display values for 60 degrees
15     degrees = 60;
16     radians = Math.toRadians(degrees);
17     System.out.printf("%-10d%-10.4f%-10.4f%-10.4f%-10.4f\n", degrees,
18       radians, Math.sin(radians), Math.cos(radians),
19       Math.tan(radians));
20   }
21 }
```

display table header

values for 30 degrees

values for 60 degrees

Degrees	Radians	Sine	Cosine	Tangent
30	0.5236	0.5000	0.8660	0.5774
60	1.0472	0.8660	0.5000	1.7321

The statements in lines 4 and 5 display the column names of the table. The column names are strings. Each string is displayed using the specifier `%-10s`, which left-justifies the string. The statements in lines 10–12 display the degrees as an integer and four float values. The integer is displayed using the specifier `%-10d`, and each float is displayed using the specifier `%-10.4f`, which specifies four digits after the decimal point.

4.6.1 What are the format specifiers for outputting a Boolean value, a character, a decimal integer, a floating-point number, and a string?

4.6.2 What is wrong in the following statements?

(a) `System.out.printf("%5d %d", 1, 2, 3);`

(b) `System.out.printf("%5d %f", 1);`

(c) `System.out.printf("%5d %f", 1, 2);`

(d) `System.out.printf("%.2f\n%0.3f\n", 1.23456, 2.34);`

(e) `System.out.printf("%08s\n", "Java");`

4.6.3 Show the output of the following statements:

(a) `System.out.printf("amount is %f %e\n", 32.32, 32.32);`

(b) `System.out.printf("amount is %5.2f%% %5.4e\n", 32.327, 32.32);`

(c) `System.out.printf("%6b\n", (1 > 2));`

(d) `System.out.printf("%6s\n", "Java");`

(e) `System.out.printf("%-6b%s\n", (1 > 2), "Java");`

(f) `System.out.printf("%6b%-8s\n", (1 > 2), "Java");`

(g) `System.out.printf("%,5d %,6.1f\n", 312342, 315562.932);`

(h) `System.out.printf("%05d %06.1f\n", 32, 32.32);`

KEY TERMS

char type   125
encoding   125
escape character   126
escape sequence   126
format specifier   146
instance method   130
line-based input   133

specific import   130
static method   130
supplementary Unicode   125
token-based input   133
Unicode   125
whitespace character   132

CHAPTER SUMMARY

1. Java provides the mathematical methods `sin`, `cos`, `tan`, `asin`, `acos`, `atan`, `toRadians`, `toDegrees`, `exp`, `log`, `log10`, `pow`, `sqrt`, `ceil`, `floor`, `rint`, `round`, `min`, `max`, `abs`, and `random` in the `Math` class for performing mathematical functions.

2. The character type `char` represents a single character.

3. An escape sequence consists of a backslash (\) followed by a character or a combination of digits.

4. The character \ is called the escape character.

5. The characters ' ', \t, \f, \r, and \n are known as the whitespace characters.

6. Characters can be compared based on their Unicode using the relational operators.

7. The `Character` class contains the methods `isDigit`, `isLetter`, `isLetterOrDigit`, `isLowerCase`, and `isUpperCase` for testing whether a character is a digit, letter, lowercase, or uppercase. It also contains the `toLowerCase` and `toUpperCase` methods for returning a lowercase or uppercase letter.

8. A *string* is a sequence of characters. A string value is enclosed in matching double quotes ("). A character value is enclosed in matching single quotes (').

9. Strings are objects in Java. A method that can only be invoked from a specific object is called an *instance method*. A noninstance method is called a *static method*, which can be invoked without using an object.

10. You can get the length of a string by invoking its `length()` method, retrieve a character at the specified index in the string using the `charAt(index)` method, and use the `indexOf` and `lastIndexOf` methods to find a character or a substring in a string.

11. You can use the `concat` method to concatenate two strings or the plus (+) operator to concatenate two or more strings.

12. You can use the `substring` method to obtain a substring from the string.

13. You can use the `equals` and `compareTo` methods to compare strings. The `equals` method returns `true` if two strings are equal, and `false` if they are not equal. The `compareTo` method returns `0`, a positive integer, or a negative integer, depending on whether one string is equal to, greater than, or less than the other string.

14. The `printf` method can be used to display a formatted output using format specifiers.

Quiz

Answer the quiz for this chapter online at the Companion Website.

MyProgrammingLab™ **PROGRAMMING EXERCISES**

Section 4.2

4.1 (*Geometry: area of a pentagon*) Write a program that prompts the user to enter the length from the center of a pentagon to a vertex and computes the area of the pentagon, as shown in the following figure.

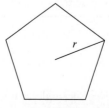

The formula for computing the area of a pentagon is $Area = \dfrac{5 \times s^2}{4 \times \tan\left(\dfrac{\pi}{5}\right)}$, where

s is the length of a side. The side can be computed using the formula $s = 2r\sin\dfrac{\pi}{5}$, where r is the length from the center of a pentagon to a vertex. Round up two digits after the decimal point. Here is a sample run:

```
Enter the length from the center to a vertex: 5.5  ↵Enter
The area of the pentagon is 71.92
```

*4.2 *(Geometry: great circle distance)* The great circle distance is the distance between two points on the surface of a sphere. Let $(x1, y1)$ and $(x2, y2)$ be the geographical latitude and longitude of two points. The great circle distance between the two points can be computed using the following formula:

VideoNote

Compute great circle distance

$$d = radius \times \arccos(\sin(x_1) \times \sin(x_2) + \cos(x_1) \times \cos(x_2) \times \cos(y_1 - y_2))$$

Write a program that prompts the user to enter the latitude and longitude of two points on the earth in degrees and displays its great circle distance. The average radius of the earth is 6,371.01 km. Note you need to convert the degrees into radians using the `Math.toRadians` method since the Java trigonometric methods use radians. The latitude and longitude degrees in the formula are for north and west. Use negative to indicate south and east degrees. Here is a sample run:

```
Enter point 1 (latitude and longitude) in degrees: 39.55 -116.25  ↵Enter
Enter point 2 (latitude and longitude) in degrees: 41.5 87.37  ↵Enter
The distance between the two points is 10691.79183231593 km
```

*4.3 *(Geography: estimate areas)* Use the GPS locations for Atlanta, Georgia; Orlando, Florida; Savannah, Georgia; and Charlotte, North Carolina in the figure in Section 4.1 to compute the estimated area enclosed by these four cities. (*Hint*: Use the formula in Programming Exercise 4.2 to compute the distance between two cities. Divide the polygon into two triangles and use the formula in Programming Exercise 2.19 to compute the area of a triangle.)

4.4 *(Geometry: area of a hexagon)* The area of a hexagon can be computed using the following formula (s is the length of a side):

$$Area = \dfrac{6 \times s^2}{4 \times \tan(\dfrac{\pi}{6})}$$

Write a program that prompts the user to enter the side of a hexagon and displays its area. Here is a sample run:

```
Enter the side: 5.5  ↵Enter
The area of the hexagon is 78.59
```

*4.5 (*Geometry: area of a regular polygon*) A regular polygon is an *n*-sided polygon in which all sides are of the same length and all angles have the same degree (i.e., the polygon is both equilateral and equiangular). The formula for computing the area of a regular polygon is

$$Area = \frac{n \times s^2}{4 \times \tan(\frac{\pi}{n})}$$

Here, *s* is the length of a side. Write a program that prompts the user to enter the number of sides and their length of a regular polygon and displays its area. Here is a sample run:

```
Enter the number of sides: 5  ↵Enter
Enter the side: 6.5  ↵Enter
The area of the polygon is 72.69017017488385
```

*4.6 (*Random points on a circle*) Write a program that generates three random points on a circle centered at (0, 0) with radius 40 and displays three angles in a triangle formed by these three points, as shown in Figure 4.4a. (*Hint*: Generate a random angle α in radians between 0 and 2π, as shown in Figure 4.4b and the point determined by this angle is ($r^x\cos(\alpha)$, $r^x\sin(\alpha)$).)

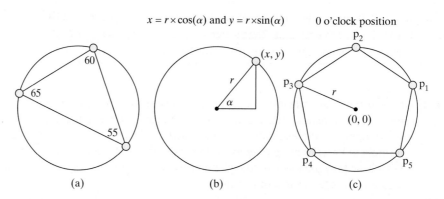

FIGURE 4.4 (a) A triangle is formed from three random points on the circle. (b) A random point on the circle can be generated using a random angle α. (c) A pentagon is centered at (0, 0) with one point at the 0 o'clock position.

*4.7 (*Corner point coordinates*) Suppose a pentagon is centered at (0, 0) with one point at the 0 o'clock position, as shown in Figure 4.4c. Write a program that prompts the user to enter the radius of the bounding circle of a pentagon and displays the coordinates of the five corner points on the pentagon from p1 to p5 in this order.

Use console format to display two digits after the decimal point. Here is a sample run:

```
Enter the radius of the bounding circle: 100.52  ↵Enter
The coordinates of five points on the pentagon are
(95.60, 31.06)
(0.00, 100.52)
(-95.60, 31.06)
(-58.08, -81.32)
(59.08, -81.32)
```

Sections 4.3–4.6

*4.8   (*Find the character of an ASCII code*) Write a program that receives an ASCII code (an integer between 0 and 127) and displays its character. Here is a sample run:

```
Enter an ASCII code: 69  ↵Enter
The character for ASCII code 69 is E
```

*4.9   (*Find the Unicode of a character*) Write a program that receives a character and displays its Unicode. Here is a sample run:

```
Enter a character: E  ↵Enter
The Unicode for the character E is 69
```

*4.10   (*Guess birthday*) Rewrite Listing 4.3, GuessBirthday.java, to prompt the user to enter the character Y for Yes and N for No, rather than entering 1 for Yes and 0 for No.

*4.11   (*Decimal to hex*) Write a program that prompts the user to enter an integer between 0 and 15 and displays its corresponding hex number. For an incorrect input number, display invalid input. Here are some sample runs:

```
Enter a decimal value (0 to 15): 11  ↵Enter
The hex value is B
```

```
Enter a decimal value (0 to 15): 5  ↵Enter
The hex value is 5
```

```
Enter a decimal value (0 to 15): 31  ↵Enter
31 is an invalid input
```

VideoNote

Convert hex to binary

4.12 (*Hex to binary*) Write a program that prompts the user to enter a hex digit and displays its corresponding binary number. For an incorrect input, display invalid input. Here is a sample run:

```
Enter a hex digit: B  ↵Enter
The binary value is 1011
```

```
Enter a hex digit: G  ↵Enter
G is an invalid input
```

*4.13 (*Vowel or consonant?*) Write a program that prompts the user to enter a letter and check whether the letter is a vowel or consonant. For a nonletter input, display invalid input. Here is a sample run:

```
Enter a letter: B  ↵Enter
B is a consonant
```

```
Enter a letter: a  ↵Enter
a is a vowel
```

```
Enter a letter: #  ↵Enter
# is an invalid input
```

*4.14 (*Convert letter grade to number*) Write a program that prompts the user to enter a letter grade A, B, C, D, or F and displays its corresponding numeric value 4, 3, 2, 1, or 0. For other input, display invalid grade. Here is a sample run:

```
Enter a letter grade: B  ↵Enter
The numeric value for grade B is 3
```

```
Enter a letter grade: T  ↵Enter
T is an invalid grade
```

*4.15 (*Phone key pads*) The international standard letter/number mapping found on the telephone is shown below:

Write a program that prompts the user to enter a lowercase or uppercase letter and displays its corresponding number. For a nonletter input, display invalid input.

```
Enter a letter: A  ↵Enter
The corresponding number is 2
```

```
Enter a letter: a  ↵Enter
The corresponding number is 2
```

```
Enter a letter: +  ↵Enter
+ is an invalid input
```

4.16 (*Random character*) Write a program that displays a random uppercase letter using the `Math.random()` method.

*4.17 (*Days of a month*) Write a program that prompts the user to enter the year and the first three letters of a month name (with the first letter in uppercase) and displays the number of days in the month. If the input for month is incorrect, display a message as presented in the following sample runs:

```
Enter a year: 2001  ↵Enter
Enter a month: Jan  ↵Enter
Jan 2001 has 31 days
```

```
Enter a year: 2016  ↵Enter
Enter a month: jan  ↵Enter
jan is not a correct month name
```

*4.18 (*Student major and status*) Write a program that prompts the user to enter two characters and displays the major and status represented in the characters. The first character indicates the major and the second is a number character 1, 2, 3, or 4, which indicates whether a student is a freshman, sophomore, junior, or senior. Suppose that the following characters are used to denote the majors:

M: Mathematics
C: Computer Science
I: Information Technology

Here are sample runs:

```
Enter two characters: M1  ↵Enter
Mathematics Freshman
```

```
Enter two characters: C3  ↵Enter
Computer Science Junior
```

```
Enter two characters: T3  ↵Enter
Invalid input
```

4.19 (*Business: check ISBN-10*) Rewrite Programming Exercise 3.9 by entering the ISBN number as a string.

4.20 (*Process a string*) Write a program that prompts the user to enter a string and displays its length and its first character.

*4.21 (*Check SSN*) Write a program that prompts the user to enter a Social Security number in the format DDD-DD-DDDD, where D is a digit. Your program should check whether the input is valid. Here are sample runs:

```
Enter a SSN: 232-23-5435  ↵Enter
232-23-5435 is a valid social security number
```

```
Enter a SSN: 23-23-5435  ↵Enter
23-23-5435 is an invalid social security number
```

4.22 (*Check substring*) Write a program that prompts the user to enter two strings, and reports whether the second string is a substring of the first string.

```
Enter string s1: ABCD  ↵Enter
Enter string s2: BC  ↵Enter
BC is a substring of ABCD
```

```
Enter string s1: ABCD  ↵Enter
Enter string s2: BDC  ↵Enter
BDC is not a substring of ABCD
```

*4.23 (*Financial application: payroll*) Write a program that reads the following information and prints a payroll statement:

Employee's name (e.g., Smith)
Number of hours worked in a week (e.g., 10)
Hourly pay rate (e.g., 9.75)

Federal tax withholding rate (e.g., 20%)
State tax withholding rate (e.g., 9%)

A sample run is as follows:

```
Enter employee's name: Smith ⏎Enter
Enter number of hours worked in a week: 10 ⏎Enter
Enter hourly pay rate: 9.75 ⏎Enter
Enter federal tax withholding rate: 0.20 ⏎Enter
Enter state tax withholding rate: 0.09 ⏎Enter

Employee Name: Smith
Hours Worked: 10.0
Pay Rate: $9.75
Gross Pay: $97.5
Deductions:
   Federal Withholding (20.0%): $19.5
   State Withholding (9.0%): $8.77
   Total Deduction: $28.27
Net Pay: $69.22
```

*4.24   (*Order three cities*) Write a program that prompts the user to enter three cities and displays them in ascending order. Here is a sample run:

```
Enter the first city: Chicago ⏎Enter
Enter the second city: Los Angeles ⏎Enter
Enter the third city: Atlanta ⏎Enter
The three cities in alphabetical order are Atlanta Chicago Los
Angeles
```

*4.25   (*Generate vehicle plate numbers*) Assume that a vehicle plate number consists of three uppercase letters followed by four digits. Write a program to generate a plate number.

*4.26   (*Financial application: monetary units*) Rewrite Listing 2.10, ComputeChange.java, to fix the possible loss of accuracy when converting a float value to an `int` value. Read the input as a string such as `"11.56"`. Your program should extract the dollar amount before the decimal point, and the cents after the decimal amount using the `indexOf` and `substring` methods.

Note
More than 200 additional programming exercises with solutions are provided to the instructors on the Instructor Resource Website.

LOOPS

Objectives

- To write programs for executing statements repeatedly using a `while` loop (§5.2).

- To write loops for the guessing number problem (§5.3).

- To follow the loop design strategy to develop loops (§5.4).

- To control a loop with the user confirmation or a sentinel value (§5.5).

- To obtain large input from a file using input redirection rather than typing from the keyboard (§5.5).

- To write loops using `do-while` statements (§5.6).

- To write loops using `for` statements (§5.7).

- To discover the similarities and differences of three types of loop statements (§5.8).

- To write nested loops (§5.9).

- To learn the techniques for minimizing numerical errors (§5.10).

- To learn loops from a variety of examples (`GCD`, `FutureTuition`, and `Dec2Hex`) (§5.11).

- To implement program control with `break` and `continue` (§5.12).

- To process characters in a string using a loop in a case study for checking palindrome (§5.13).

- To write a program that displays prime numbers (§5.14).

5.1 Introduction

Key
Point

problem

A loop can be used to tell a program to execute statements repeatedly.

Suppose you need to display a string (e.g., `Welcome to Java!`) a hundred times. It would be tedious to have to write the following statement a hundred times:

100 times $\left\{\begin{array}{l}\end{array}\right.$
```
System.out.println("Welcome to Java!");
System.out.println("Welcome to Java!");
...
System.out.println("Welcome to Java!");
```

So, how do you solve this problem?

loop

Java provides a powerful construct called a *loop* that controls how many times an operation or a sequence of operations is performed in succession. Using a loop statement, you can simply tell the computer to display a string a hundred times without having to code the print statement a hundred times, as follows:

```
int count = 0;
while (count < 100) {
  System.out.println("Welcome to Java!");
  count++;
}
```

The variable `count` is initially `0`. The loop checks whether `count < 100` is `true`. If so, it executes the loop body to display the message `Welcome to Java!` and increments `count` by `1`. It repeatedly executes the loop body until `count < 100` becomes `false`. When `count < 100` is `false` (i.e., when `count` reaches `100`), the loop terminates, and the next statement after the loop statement is executed.

Loops are constructs that control repeated executions of a block of statements. The concept of looping is fundamental to programming. Java provides three types of loop statements: `while` loops, `do-while` loops, and `for` loops.

5.2 The `while` Loop

Key
Point

A `while` loop executes statements repeatedly while the condition is true.

The syntax for the `while` loop is as follows:

```
while (loop-continuation-condition) {
  // Loop body
  Statement(s);
}
```

while loop

VideoNote
Use while loop
loop body
iteration
loop-continuation-condition

Figure 5.1a shows the `while` loop flowchart. The part of the loop that contains the statements to be repeated is called the *loop body*. A one-time execution of a loop body is referred to as an *iteration (or repetition) of the loop*. Each loop contains a `loop-continuation-condition`, a Boolean expression that controls the execution of the body. It is evaluated each time to determine if the loop body is executed. If its evaluation is `true`, the loop body is executed; if its evaluation is `false`, the entire loop terminates and the program control turns to the statement that follows the `while` loop.

The loop for displaying `Welcome to Java!` a hundred times introduced in the preceding section is an example of a `while` loop. Its flowchart is shown in Figure 5.1b.

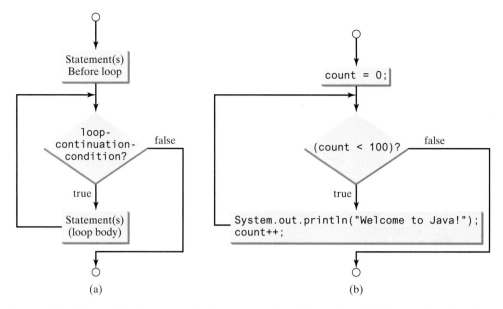

FIGURE 5.1   The while loop repeatedly executes the statements in the loop body when the loop-continuation-condition evaluates to true.

The loop-continuation-condition is count < 100 and the loop body contains two statements in the following code:

```
                              loop-continuation-condition
  int count = 0;
  while (count < 100) {
     System.out.println("Welcome to Java!");    loop body
     count++;
  }
```

In this example, you know exactly how many times the loop body needs to be executed because the control variable count is used to count the number of iterations. This type of loop is known as a *counter-controlled loop*.

counter-controlled loop

 Note

> The loop-continuation-condition must always appear inside the parentheses. The braces enclosing the loop body can be omitted only if the loop body contains one or no statement.

Here is another example to help understand how a loop works.

```
  int sum = 0, i = 1;
  while (i < 10) {
     sum = sum + i;
     i++;
  }
  System.out.println("sum is " + sum); // sum is 45
```

If i < 10 is true, the program adds i to sum. Variable i is initially set to 1, then is incremented to 2, 3, and up to 10. When i is 10, i < 10 is false, so the loop exits. Therefore, the sum is 1 + 2 + 3 + ... + 9 = 45.

What happens if the loop is mistakenly written as follows?

```
int sum = 0, i = 1;
while (i < 10) {
  sum = sum + i;
}
```

This loop is infinite, because i is always 1 and i < 10 will always be true.

Note

infinite loop

Make sure that the loop-continuation-condition eventually becomes false so that the loop will terminate. A common programming error involves *infinite loops* (i.e., the loop runs forever). If your program takes an unusually long time to run and does not stop, it may have an infinite loop. If you are running the program from the command window, press *CTRL+C* to stop it.

Caution

off-by-one error

Programmers often make the mistake of executing a loop one more or less time. This is commonly known as the *off-by-one error*. For example, the following loop displays Welcome to Java 101 times rather than 100 times. The error lies in the condition, which should be count < 100 rather than count <= 100.

```
int count = 0;
while (count <= 100) {
  System.out.println("Welcome to Java!");
  count++;
}
```

Recall that Listing 3.1, AdditionQuiz.java, gives a program that prompts the user to enter an answer for a question on addition of two single digits. Using a loop, you can now rewrite the program to let the user repeatedly enter a new answer until it is correct, as given in Listing 5.1.

LISTING 5.1 RepeatAdditionQuiz.java

generate number1
generate number2

show question

get first answer

check answer

read an answer

```
1  import java.util.Scanner;
2
3  public class RepeatAdditionQuiz {
4    public static void main(String[] args) {
5      int number1 = (int)(Math.random() * 10);
6      int number2 = (int)(Math.random() * 10);
7
8      // Create a Scanner
9      Scanner input = new Scanner(System.in);
10
11     System.out.print(
12       "What is " + number1 + " + " + number2 + "? ");
13     int answer = input.nextInt();
14
15     while (number1 + number2 != answer)  {
16       System.out.print("Wrong answer. Try again. What is "
17         + number1 + " + " + number2 + "? ");
18       answer = input.nextInt();
19     }
20
21     System.out.println("You got it!");
22   }
23 }
```

```
What is 5 + 9? 12 [↵Enter]
Wrong answer. Try again. What is 5 + 9? 34 [↵Enter]
Wrong answer. Try again. What is 5 + 9? 14 [↵Enter]
You got it!
```

The loop in lines 15–19 repeatedly prompts the user to enter an `answer` when `number1 + number2 != answer` is `true`. Once `number1 + number2 != answer` is `false`, the loop exits.

5.2.1 Analyze the following code. Is `count < 100` always `true`, always `false`, or sometimes `true` or sometimes `false` at Point A, Point B, and Point C?

Check Point

```
int count = 0;
while (count < 100) {
  // Point A
  System.out.println("Welcome to Java!");
  count++;
  // Point B
}
// Point C
```

5.2.2 How many times are the following loop bodies repeated? What is the output of each loop?

```
int i = 1;
while (i < 10)
  if (i % 2 == 0)
    System.out.println(i);
```
(a)

```
int i = 1;
while (i < 10)
  if (i % 2 == 0)
    System.out.println(i++);
```
(b)

```
int i = 1;
while (i < 10)
  if ((i++) % 2 == 0)
    System.out.println(i);
```
(c)

5.2.3 What is the output of the following code? Explain the reason.

```
int x = 80000000;

while (x > 0)
  x++;

System.out.println("x is " + x);
```

5.3 Case Study: Guessing Numbers

This case study generates a random number and lets the user repeatedly guess a number until it is correct.

Key Point

The problem is to guess what number a computer has in mind. You will write a program that randomly generates an integer between `0` and `100`, inclusive. The program prompts the user to enter a number continuously until the number matches the randomly generated number. For each user input, the program tells the user whether the input is too low or too high, so the user can make the next guess intelligently. Here is a sample run:

VideoNote

Guess a number

```
Guess a magic number between 0 and 100
Enter your guess: 50 ⏎Enter
Your guess is too high
Enter your guess: 25 ⏎Enter
Your guess is too low
Enter your guess: 42 ⏎Enter
Your guess is too high
Enter your guess: 39 ⏎Enter
Yes, the number is 39
```

intelligent guess

The magic number is between 0 and 100. To minimize the number of guesses, enter 50 first. If your guess is too high, the magic number is between 0 and 49. If your guess is too low, the magic number is between 51 and 100. Thus, you can eliminate half of the numbers from further consideration after one guess.

How do you write this program? Do you immediately begin coding? No. It is important to *think before coding*. Think how you would solve the problem without writing a program. You need first to generate a random number between 0 and 100, inclusive, then to prompt the user to enter a guess, then to compare the guess with the random number.

think before coding

It is a good practice to *code incrementally* one step at a time. For programs involving loops, if you don't know how to write a loop right away, you may first write the code for executing the loop one time, then figure out how to repeatedly execute the code in a loop. For this program, you may create an initial draft, as given in Listing 5.2.

code incrementally

LISTING 5.2 GuessNumberOneTime.java

```
1  import java.util.Scanner;
2
3  public class GuessNumberOneTime {
4    public static void main(String[] args) {
5      // Generate a random number to be guessed
6      int number = (int)(Math.random() * 101);
7
8      Scanner input = new Scanner(System.in);
9      System.out.println("Guess a magic number between 0 and 100");
10
11     // Prompt the user to guess the number
12     System.out.print("\nEnter your guess: ");
13     int guess = input.nextInt();
14
15     if (guess == number)
16       System.out.println("Yes, the number is " + number);
17     else if (guess > number)
18       System.out.println("Your guess is too high");
19     else
20       System.out.println("Your guess is too low");
21   }
22 }
```

generate a number

enter a guess

correct guess

too high

too low

When you run this program, it prompts the user to enter a guess only once. To let the user enter a guess repeatedly, you may wrap the code in lines 11–20 in a loop as follows:

```
while (true) {
  // Prompt the user to guess the number
  System.out.print("\nEnter your guess: ");
  guess = input.nextInt();

  if (guess == number)
    System.out.println("Yes, the number is " + number);
  else if (guess > number)
    System.out.println("Your guess is too high");
  else
    System.out.println("Your guess is too low");
} // End of loop
```

This loop repeatedly prompts the user to enter a guess. However, this loop is not correct, because it never terminates. When guess matches number, the loop should end. Thus, the loop can be revised as follows:

```
while (guess != number) {
  // Prompt the user to guess the number
```

```
      System.out.print("\nEnter your guess: ");
      guess = input.nextInt();

      if (guess == number)
        System.out.println("Yes, the number is " + number);
      else if (guess > number)
        System.out.println("Your guess is too high");
      else
        System.out.println("Your guess is too low");
    } // End of loop
```

The complete code is given in Listing 5.3.

LISTING 5.3 GuessNumber.java

```
 1  import java.util.Scanner;
 2
 3  public class GuessNumber {
 4    public static void main(String[] args) {
 5      // Generate a random number to be guessed
 6      int number = (int)(Math.random() * 101);          generate a number
 7
 8      Scanner input = new Scanner(System.in);
 9      System.out.println("Guess a magic number between 0 and 100");
10
11      int guess = -1;
12      while (guess != number) {
13        // Prompt the user to guess the number
14        System.out.print("\nEnter your guess: ");
15        guess = input.nextInt();                        enter a guess
16
17        if (guess == number)
18          System.out.println("Yes, the number is " + number);
19        else if (guess > number)
20          System.out.println("Your guess is too high");   too high
21        else
22          System.out.println("Your guess is too low");     too low
23      } // End of loop
24    }
25  }
```

	line#	number	guess	output
	6	39		
	11		-1	
iteration 1	15		50	
iteration 1	20			Your guess is too high
iteration 2	15		25	
iteration 2	22			Your guess is too low
iteration 3	15		42	
iteration 3	20			Your guess is too high
iteration 4	15		39	
iteration 4	18			Yes, the number is 39

The program generates the magic number in line 6 and prompts the user to enter a guess
continuously in a loop (lines 12–23). For each guess, the program checks whether the guess is

correct, too high, or too low (lines 17–22). When the guess is correct, the program exits the loop (line 12). Note that `guess` is initialized to `-1`. Initializing it to a value between `0` and `100` would be wrong, because that could be the number to be guessed.

5.3.1 What is wrong if `guess` is initialized to `0` in line 11 in Listing 5.3?

5.4 Loop Design Strategies

The key to designing a loop is to identify the code that needs to be repeated and write a condition for terminating the loop.

Writing a correct loop is not an easy task for novice programmers. Consider three steps when writing a loop.

Step 1: Identify the statements that need to be repeated.

Step 2: Wrap these statements in a loop as follows:

```
while (true) {
  Statements;
}
```

Step 3: Code the `loop-continuation-condition` and add appropriate statements for controlling the loop.

```
while (loop-continuation-condition) {
  Statements;
  Additional statements for controlling the loop;
}
```

The Math subtraction learning tool program in Listing 3.3, SubtractionQuiz.java, generates just one question for each run. You can use a loop to generate questions repeatedly. How do you write the code to generate five questions? Follow the loop design strategy. First, identify the statements that need to be repeated. These are the statements for obtaining two random numbers, prompting the user with a subtraction question, and grading the question. Second, wrap the statements in a loop. Third, add a loop control variable and the `loop-continuation-condition` to execute the loop five times.

Listing 5.4 gives a program that generates five questions and, after a student answers all five, reports the number of correct answers. The program also displays the time spent on the test and lists all the questions.

VideoNote

Multiple subtraction quiz

LISTING 5.4 SubtractionQuizLoop.java

```java
 1  import java.util.Scanner;
 2
 3  public class SubtractionQuizLoop {
 4    public static void main(String[] args) {
 5      final int NUMBER_OF_QUESTIONS = 5; // Number of questions
 6      int correctCount = 0; // Count the number of correct answers
 7      int count = 0; // Count the number of questions
 8      long startTime = System.currentTimeMillis();
 9      String output = " "; // output string is initially empty
10      Scanner input = new Scanner(System.in);
11
12      while (count < NUMBER_OF_QUESTIONS) {
13        // 1. Generate two random single-digit integers
14        int number1 = (int)(Math.random() * 10);
15        int number2 = (int)(Math.random() * 10);
16
17        // 2. If number1 < number2, swap number1 with number2
18        if (number1 < number2) {
```

get start time

loop

```
19              int temp = number1;
20              number1 = number2;
21              number2 = temp;
22          }
23
24          // 3. Prompt the student to answer "What is number1 - number2?"
25          System.out.print(                                          display a question
26              "What is " + number1 + " - " + number2 + "? ");
27          int answer = input.nextInt();
28
29          // 4. Grade the answer and display the result
30          if (number1 - number2 == answer) {                         grade an answer
31              System.out.println("You are correct!");
32              correctCount++; // Increase the correct answer count    increase correct count
33          }
34          else
35              System.out.println("Your answer is wrong.\n" + number1
36                  + " - " + number2 + " should be " + (number1 - number2));
37
38          // Increase the question count
39          count++;                                                   increase control variable
40
41          output += "\n" + number1 + "-" + number2 + "=" + answer +   prepare output
42              ((number1 - number2 == answer) ? " correct": " wrong");
43      }                                                              end loop
44
45      long endTime = System.currentTimeMillis();                     get end time
46      long testTime = endTime - startTime;                           test time
47
48      System.out.println("Correct count is " + correctCount +        display result
49          "\nTest time is " + testTime / 1000 + " seconds\n" + output);
50  }
51 }
```

```
What is 9 - 2?  7  [↵Enter]
You are correct!

What is 3 - 0?  3  [↵Enter]
You are correct!

What is 3 - 2?  1  [↵Enter]
You are correct!

What is 7 - 4?  4  [↵Enter]
Your answer is wrong.
7 - 4 should be 3

What is 7 - 5?  4  [↵Enter]
Your answer is wrong.
7 - 5 should be 2

Correct count is 3
Test time is 1021 seconds

9-2=7 correct
3-0=3 correct
3-2=1 correct
7-4=4 wrong
7-5=4 wrong
```

The program uses the control variable count to control the execution of the loop. count is initially 0 (line 7) and is increased by 1 in each iteration (line 39). A subtraction question is displayed and processed in each iteration. The program obtains the time before the test starts in line 8 and the time after the test ends in line 45, then computes the test time in line 46. The test time is in milliseconds and is converted to seconds in line 49.

5.4.1 Revise the code using the System.nanoTime() to measure the time in nano seconds.

5.5 Controlling a Loop with User Confirmation or a Sentinel Value

It is a common practice to use a sentinel value to terminate the input.

The preceding example executes the loop five times. If you want the user to decide whether to continue, you can offer a user *confirmation*. The template of the program can be coded as follows:

```
char continueLoop = 'Y';
while (continueLoop == 'Y') {
  // Execute the loop body once
  ...
  // Prompt the user for confirmation
  System.out.print("Enter Y to continue and N to quit: ");
  continueLoop = input.getLine().charAt(0);
}
```

You can rewrite the program given in Listing 5.4 with user confirmation to let the user decide whether to advance to the next question.

sentinel value

sentinel-controlled loop

Another common technique for controlling a loop is to designate a special value when reading and processing a set of values. This special input value, known as a *sentinel value*, signifies the end of the input. A loop that uses a sentinel value to control its execution is called a *sentinel-controlled loop*.

Listing 5.5 gives a program that reads and calculates the sum of an unspecified number of integers. The input 0 signifies the end of the input. Do you need to declare a new variable for each input value? No. Just use one variable named data (line 12) to store the input value, and use a variable named sum (line 15) to store the total. Whenever a value is read, assign it to data and, if it is not zero, add it to sum (line 17).

LISTING 5.5 SentinelValue.java

input

loop

```
1  import java.util.Scanner;
2
3  public class SentinelValue {
4    /** Main method */
5    public static void main(String[] args) {
6      // Create a Scanner
7      Scanner input = new Scanner(System.in);
8
9      // Read an initial data
10     System.out.print(
11       "Enter an integer (the input ends if it is 0): ");
12     int data = input.nextInt();
13
14     // Keep reading data until the input is 0
15     int sum = 0;
16     while (data != 0) {
```

```
17              sum += data;
18
19              // Read the next data
20              System.out.print(
21                "Enter an integer (the input ends if it is 0): ");
22              data = input.nextInt();
23            }
24
25            System.out.println("The sum is " + sum);
26          }
27        }
```

end of loop

display result

```
Enter an integer (the input ends if it is 0): 2 ⏎Enter
Enter an integer (the input ends if it is 0): 3 ⏎Enter
Enter an integer (the input ends if it is 0): 4 ⏎Enter
Enter an integer (the input ends if it is 0): 0 ⏎Enter
The sum is 9
```

	line#	data	sum	output
	12	2		
	15		0	
iteration 1	17		2	
	22	3		
iteration 2	17		5	
	22	4		
iteration 3	17		9	
	22	0		
	25			The sum is 9

If data is not 0, it is added to sum (line 17) and the next item of input data is read (lines 20–22). If data is 0, the loop body is no longer executed and the while loop terminates. The input value 0 is the sentinel value for this loop. Note if the first input read is 0, the loop body never executes, and the resulting sum is 0.

⚠ Caution

Don't use floating-point values for equality checking in a loop control. Because floating-point values are approximations for some values, using them could result in imprecise counter values and inaccurate results.

Consider the following code for computing 1 + 0.9 + 0.8 + ... + 0.1:

```
double item = 1; double sum = 0;
while (item != 0) { // No guarantee item will be 0
  sum += item;
  item -= 0.1;
}
System.out.println(sum);
```

Variable item starts with 1 and is reduced by 0.1 every time the loop body is executed. The loop should terminate when item becomes 0. However, there is no guarantee that item will be exactly 0, because the floating-point arithmetic is approximated. This loop seems okay on the surface, but it is actually an infinite loop.

numeric error

In the preceding example, if you have a large number of data to enter, it would be cumbersome to type from the keyboard. You can store the data separated by whitespaces in a text file, say **input.txt**, and run the program using the following command:

```
java SentinelValue < input.txt
```

input redirection

This command is called *input redirection*. The program takes the input from the file **input. txt** rather than having the user type the data from the keyboard at runtime. Suppose the contents of the file are as follows:

```
2 3 4 5 6 7 8 9 12 23 32
23 45 67 89 92 12 34 35 3 1 2 4 0
```

The program should get sum to be 518.

output redirection

Similarly, there is *output redirection,* which sends the output to a file rather than displaying it on the console. The command for output redirection is

```
java ClassName > output.txt
```

Input and output redirections can be used in the same command. For example, the following command gets input from **input.txt** and sends output to **output.txt**:

```
java SentinelValue < input.txt > output.txt
```

Try running the program to see what contents are in **output.txt**.

5.5.1 Suppose the input is 2 3 4 5 0. What is the output of the following code?

```java
import java.util.Scanner;

public class Test {
  public static void main(String[] args) {
    Scanner input = new Scanner(System.in);

    int number, max;
    number = input.nextInt();
    max = number;

    while (number != 0) {
      number = input.nextInt();
      if (number > max)
        max = number;
    }

    System.out.println("max is " + max);
    System.out.println("number " + number);
  }
}
```

5.6 The **do-while** Loop

A do-while *loop is the same as a* while *loop except that it executes the loop body first then checks the loop continuation condition.*

VideoNote
Use do-while loop
do-while loop

Key Point

The do-while loop is a variation of the while loop. Its syntax is as follows:

```java
do {
  // Loop body;
  Statement(s);
} while (loop-continuation-condition);
```

Its execution flowchart is shown in Figure 5.2a.

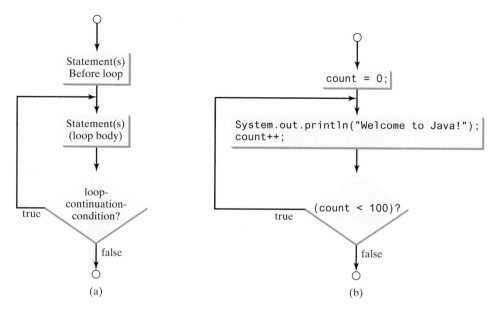

FIGURE 5.2 The do-while loop executes the loop body first then checks the loop-continuation-condition to determine whether to continue or terminate the loop.

The loop body is executed first, then the loop-continuation-condition is evaluated. If the evaluation is true, the loop body is executed again; if it is false, the do-while loop terminates. For example, the following while loop statement

```
int count = 0;
while (count < 100) {
  System.out.println("Welcome to Java!");
  count++;
}
```

can be written using a do-while loop as follows:

```
int count = 0;
do {
  System.out.println("Welcome to Java!");
  count++;
} while (count < 100);
```

The flowchart of this do-while loop is shown in Figure 5.2b.

The difference between a while loop and a do-while loop is the order in which the loop-continuation-condition is evaluated and the loop body is executed. In the case of a do-while loop, the loop body is executed at least once. You can write a loop using either the while loop or the do-while loop. Sometimes one is a more convenient choice than the other. For example, you can rewrite the while loop in Listing 5.5 using a do-while loop, as given in Listing 5.6.

LISTING 5.6 TestDoWhile.java

```
1  import java.util.Scanner;
2
3  public class TestDoWhile {
4    /** Main method */
5    public static void main(String[] args) {
6      int data;
7      int sum = 0;
```

```
      8
      9      // Create a Scanner
     10      Scanner input = new Scanner(System.in);
     11
     12      // Keep reading data until the input is 0
loop 13      do {
     14        // Read the next data
     15        System.out.print(
     16          "Enter an integer (the input ends if it is 0): ");
     17        data = input.nextInt();
     18
     19        sum += data;
end loop 20   } while (data != 0);
     21
     22      System.out.println("The sum is " + sum);
     23    }
     24  }
```

```
Enter an integer (the input ends if it is 0): 3  ↵Enter
Enter an integer (the input ends if it is 0): 5  ↵Enter
Enter an integer (the input ends if it is 0): 6  ↵Enter
Enter an integer (the input ends if it is 0): 0  ↵Enter
The sum is 14
```

Tip

Use a do-while loop if you have statements inside the loop that must be executed *at least once*, as in the case of the do-while loop in the preceding TestDoWhile program. These statements must appear before the loop as well as inside it if you use a while loop.

5.6.1 Suppose the input is 2 3 4 5 0. What is the output of the following code?

```java
import java.util.Scanner;

public class Test {
  public static void main(String[] args) {
    Scanner input = new Scanner(System.in);

    int number, max;
    number = input.nextInt();
    max = number;

    do {
      number = input.nextInt();
      if (number > max)
        max = number;
    } while (number != 0);

    System.out.println("max is " + max);
    System.out.println("number " + number);
  }
}
```

5.6.2 What are the differences between a `while` loop and a `do-while` loop? Convert the following `while` loop into a `do-while` loop:

```
Scanner input = new Scanner(System.in);
int sum = 0;
System.out.println("Enter an integer " +
    "(the input ends if it is 0)");
int number = input.nextInt();
while (number != 0) {
  sum += number;
  System.out.println("Enter an integer " +
      "(the input ends if it is 0)");
  number = input.nextInt();
}
```

5.7 The **for** Loop

A `for` *loop has a concise syntax for writing loops.*

Often you write a loop in the following common form:

```
i = initialValue; // Initialize loop control variable
while (i < endValue) {
  // Loop body
  ...
  i++; // Adjust loop control variable
}
```

This loop is intuitive and easy for beginners to grasp. However, programmers often forget to adjust the control variable, which leads to an infinite loop. A `for` loop can be used to simplify the preceding loop as shown in (a), which is equivalent to (b)

```
for (i = initialValue; i < endValue; i++) {
  // Loop body
  ...
}
```

(a)

```
i = initialValue;
while (i < endValue) {
  // Loop body
  ...
  i++;
}
```

(b)

In general, the syntax of a `for` loop is as follows:

```
for (initial-action; loop-continuation-condition;
    action-after-each-iteration) {
  // Loop body;
  Statement(s);
}
```

for loop

The flowchart of the `for` loop is shown in Figure 5.3a.

The `for` loop statement starts with the keyword `for`, followed by a pair of parentheses enclosing the control structure of the loop. This structure consists of `initial-action`, `loop-continuation-condition`, and `action-after-each-iteration`. The control structure is followed by the loop body enclosed inside braces. The `initial-action`, `loop-continuation-condition`, and `action-after-each-iteration` are separated by semicolons.

A `for` loop generally uses a variable to control how many times the loop body is executed and when the loop terminates. This variable is referred to as a *control variable*. The `initial-action` often initializes a control variable, the `action-after-each-iteration` usually increments or decrements the control variable, and the `loop-continuation-condition`

control variable

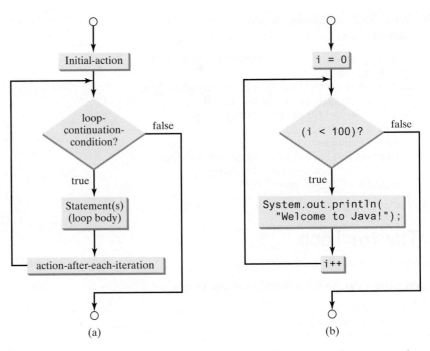

FIGURE 5.3 A `for` loop performs an initial action once, then repeatedly executes the statements in the loop body, and performs an action after an iteration when the `loop-continuation-condition` evaluates to `true`.

tests whether the control variable has reached a termination value. For example, the following `for` loop prints `Welcome to Java!` a hundred times:

```java
int i;
for (i = 0; i < 100; i++) {
  System.out.println("Welcome to Java!");
}
```

The flowchart of the statement is shown in Figure 5.3b. The `for` loop initializes `i` to `0`, then repeatedly executes the `println` statement and evaluates `i++` while `i` is less than `100`.

initial-action

The `initial-action`, `i = 0`, initializes the control variable, `i`. The `loop-continuation-condition`, `i < 100`, is a Boolean expression. The expression is evaluated right after the initialization and at the beginning of each iteration. If this condition is `true`, the loop body is executed. If it is `false`, the loop terminates and the program control turns to the line following the loop.

action-after-each-iteration

The `action-after-each-iteration`, `i++`, is a statement that adjusts the control variable. This statement is executed after each iteration and increments the control variable. Eventually, the value of the control variable should force the `loop-continuation-condition` to become `false`; otherwise, the loop is infinite.

The loop control variable can be declared and initialized in the `for` loop. Here is an example:

```java
for (int i = 0; i < 100; i++) {
  System.out.println("Welcome to Java!");
}
```

omitting braces

If there is only one statement in the loop body, as in this example, the braces can be omitted.

Tip

declare control variable

The control variable must be declared inside the control structure of the loop or before the loop. If the loop control variable is used only in the loop, and not elsewhere, it is a good programming practice to declare it in the `initial-action` of the `for` loop. If the variable is declared inside the loop control structure, it cannot be referenced outside the loop. In the preceding code, for example, you cannot reference i outside the for loop, because it is declared inside the for loop.

 Note

The initial-action in a for loop can be a list of zero or more comma-separated variable declaration statements or assignment expressions. For example:

for loop variations

```
for (int i = 0, j = 0; i + j < 10; i++, j++) {
    // Do something
}
```

The action-after-each-iteration in a for loop can be a list of zero or more comma-separated statements. For example:

```
for (int i = 1; i < 100; System.out.println(i), i++) ;
```

This example is correct, but it is a bad example, because it makes the code difficult to read. Normally, you declare and initialize a control variable as an initial action, and increment or decrement the control variable as an action after each iteration.

 Note

If the loop-continuation-condition in a for loop is omitted, it is implicitly true. Thus, the statement given below in (a), which is an infinite loop, is the same as in (b). To avoid confusion, though, it is better to use the equivalent loop in (c).

```
for ( ; ; ) {
    // Do something
}
```
(a)

Equivalent

```
for ( ; true; ) {
    // Do something
}
```
(b)

Equivalent

This is better

```
while (true) {
    // Do something
}
```
(c)

Check Point

5.7.1 Do the following two loops result in the same value in sum?

```
for (int i = 0; i < 10; ++i) {
    sum += i;
}
```
(a)

```
for (int i = 0; i < 10; i++) {
    sum += i;
}
```
(b)

5.7.2 What are the three parts of a for loop control? Write a for loop that prints the numbers from 1 to 100.

5.7.3 Suppose the input is 2 3 4 5 0. What is the output of the following code?

```
import java.util.Scanner;

public class Test {
  public static void main(String[] args) {
    Scanner input = new Scanner(System.in);

    int number, sum = 0, count;

    for (count = 0; count < 5; count++) {
      number = input.nextInt();
      sum += number;
    }

    System.out.println("sum is " + sum);
    System.out.println("count is " + count);
  }
}
```

5.7.4 What does the following statement do?

```
for ( ; ; ) {
    // Do something
}
```

5.7.5 If a variable is declared in a `for` loop control, can it be used after the loop exits?

5.7.6 Convert the following `for` loop statement to a `while` loop and to a `do-while` loop:

```
long sum = 0;
for (int i = 0; i <= 1000; i++)
    sum = sum + i;
```

5.7.7 Count the number of iterations in the following loops.

```
int count = 0;
while (count < n) {
    count++;
}
```
(a)

```
for (int count = 0;
    count <= n; count++) {
}
```
(b)

```
int count = 5;
while (count < n) {
    count++;
}
```
(c)

```
int count = 5;
while (count < n) {
    count = count + 3;
}
```
(d)

5.8 Which Loop to Use?

Key
Point

You can use a `for` *loop, a* `while` *loop, or a* `do-while` *loop, whichever is convenient.*

The `while` loop and `do-while` loop are easier to learn than the `for` loop. However, you will learn the `for` loop quickly after some practice. A `for` loop places control variable initialization, loop continuation condition, and adjustment after each iteration all together. It is more concise and enables you to write the code with less errors than the other two loops.

pretest loop
posttest loop

The `while` loop and `for` loop are called *pretest loops* because the continuation condition is checked before the loop body is executed. The `do-while` loop is called a *posttest loop* because the condition is checked after the loop body is executed. The three forms of loop statements—`while`, `do-while`, and `for`—are expressively equivalent; that is, you can write a loop in any of these three forms. For example, a `while` loop in (a) in the following figure can always be converted into the `for` loop in (b).

```
while (loop-continuation-condition) {
    // Loop body
}
```
(a)

Equivalent

```
for ( ; loop-continuation-condition; ) {
    // Loop body
}
```
(b)

A `for` loop in (a) in the next figure can generally be converted into the `while` loop in (b) except in certain special cases (see CheckPoint Question 5.12.2 in Section 5.12 for such a case).

```
for (initial-action;
    loop-continuation-condition;
    action-after-each-iteration) {
    // Loop body;
}
```
(a)

Equivalent

```
initial-action;
while (loop-continuation-condition) {
    // Loop body;
    action-after-each-iteration;
}
```
(b)

Use the loop statement that is most intuitive and comfortable for you. In general, a `for` loop may be used if the number of repetitions is known in advance, as, for example, when you need to display a message a hundred times. A `while` loop may be used if the number of repetitions is not fixed, as in the case of reading the numbers until the input is `0`. A `do-while` loop can be used to replace a `while` loop if the loop body has to be executed before the continuation condition is tested.

 Caution

Adding a semicolon at the end of the `for` clause before the loop body is a common mistake, as shown below in (a). In (a), the semicolon signifies the end of the loop prematurely. The loop body is actually empty, as shown in (b). (a) and (b) are equivalent. Both are incorrect.

Error

Empty body

```
for (int i = 0; i < 10; i++);
{
   System.out.println("i is " + i);
}
```

```
for (int i = 0; i < 10; i++) { };
{
   System.out.println("i is " + i);
}
```

(a)   (b)

Similarly, the loop in (c) is also wrong. (c) is equivalent to (d). Both are incorrect.

Error

Empty body

```
int i = 0;
while (i < 10);
{
   System.out.println("i is " + i);
   i++;
}
```

```
int i = 0;
while (i < 10) { };
{
   System.out.println("i is " + i);
   i++;
}
```

(c)   (d)

These errors often occur when you use the next-line block style. Using the end-of-line block style can avoid errors of this type.

In the case of the `do-while` loop, the semicolon is needed to end the loop.

```
int i = 0;
do {
   System.out.println("i is " + i);
   i++;
} while (i < 10);
```

Correct

5.8.1 Can you convert a `for` loop to a `while` loop? List the advantages of using `for` loops.

5.8.2 Can you always convert a `while` loop into a `for` loop? Convert the following `while` loop into a `for` loop:

```
int i = 1;
int sum = 0;
while (sum < 10000) {
   sum = sum + i;
   i++;
}
```

Check Point

5.8.3 Identify and fix the errors in the following code:

```
1  public class Test {
2    public void main(String[] args) {
3      for (int i = 0; i < 10; i++);
4        sum += i;
5
6      if (i < j);
7        System.out.println(i)
8      else
9        System.out.println(j);
10
11     while (j < 10);
12     {
13       j++;
14     }
15
16     do {
17       j++;
18     } while (j < 10)
19   }
20  }
```

5.8.4 What is wrong with the following programs?

```
1  public class ShowErrors {
2    public static void main(String[] args) {
3      int i = 0;
4      do  {
5        System.out.println(i + 4);
6        i++;
7      }
8      while (i < 10)
8    }
9  }
```

(a)

```
1  public class ShowErrors {
2    public static void main(String[] args) {
3      for (int i = 0; i < 10; i++);
4        System.out.println(i + 4);
5    }
6  }
```

(b)

5.9 Nested Loops

Key Point

A loop can be nested inside another loop.

Nested loops consist of an outer loop and one or more inner loops. Each time the outer loop is repeated, the inner loops are reentered, and started anew.

nested loop

Listing 5.7 presents a program that uses nested `for` loops to display a multiplication table.

LISTING 5.7 `MultiplicationTable.java`

```
1  public class MultiplicationTable {
2    /** Main method */
3    public static void main(String[] args) {
4      // Display the table heading
5      System.out.println("          Multiplication Table");
6
7      // Display the number title
8      System.out.print("    ");
9      for (int j = 1; j <= 9; j++)
10       System.out.print("    " + j);
```

table title

```
11
12          System.out.println("\n ------------------------------");
13
14          // Display table body
15          for (int i = 1; i <= 9; i++) {                          outer loop
16            System.out.print(i + " | ");
17            for (int j = 1; j <= 9; j++) {                        inner loop
18              // Display the product and align properly
19              System.out.printf("%4d", i * j);
20            }
21            System.out.println();
22          }
23        }
24      }
```

```
Multiplication Table
          1   2   3   4   5   6   7   8   9
     ------------------------------------------
1 |       1   2   3   4   5   6   7   8   9
2 |       2   4   6   8  10  12  14  16  18
3 |       3   6   9  12  15  18  21  24  27
4 |       4   8  12  16  20  24  28  32  36
5 |       5  10  15  20  25  30  35  40  45
6 |       6  12  18  24  30  36  42  48  54
7 |       7  14  21  28  35  42  49  56  63
8 |       8  16  24  32  40  48  56  64  72
9 |       9  18  27  36  45  54  63  72  81
```

The program displays a title (line 5) on the first line in the output. The first `for` loop (lines 9 and 10) displays the numbers 1–9 on the second line. A dashed (–) line is displayed on the third line (line 12).

The next loop (lines 15–22) is a nested `for` loop with the control variable `i` in the outer loop and `j` in the inner loop. For each `i`, the product `i * j` is displayed on a line in the inner loop, with `j` being 1, 2, 3, ..., 9.

> **Note**
>
> Be aware that a nested loop may take a long time to run. Consider the following loop nested in three levels:
>
> ```
> for (int i = 0; i < 10000; i++)
>   for (int j = 0; j < 10000; j++)
>     for (int k = 0; k < 10000; k++)
>       Perform an action
> ```
>
> The action is performed one trillion times. If it takes 1 microsecond to perform the action, the total time to run the loop would be more than 277 hours. Note 1 microsecond is one-millionth (10^{-6}) of a second.

5.9.1 How many times is the `println` statement executed?

```
for (int i = 0; i < 10; i++)
  for (int j = 0; j < i; j++)
    System.out.println(i * j)
```

Check Point

5.9.2 Show the output of the following programs. (*Hint*: Draw a table and list the variables in the columns to trace these programs.)

```java
public class Test {
  public static void main(String[] args) {
    for (int i = 1; i < 5; i++) {
      int j = 0;
      while (j < i) {
        System.out.print(j + " ");
        j++;
      }
    }
  }
}
```
(a)

```java
public class Test {
  public static void main(String[] args) {
    int i = 0;
    while (i < 5) {
      for (int j = i; j > 1; j--)
        System.out.print(j + " ");
      System.out.println("*****");
      i++;
    }
  }
}
```
(b)

```java
public class Test {
  public static void main(String[] args) {
    int i = 5;
    while (i >= 1) {
      int num = 1;
      for (int j = 1; j <= i; j++) {
        System.out.print(num + "xxx");
        num *= 2;
      }

      System.out.println();
      i--;
    }
  }
}
```
(c)

```java
public class Test {
  public static void main(String[] args) {
    int i = 1;
    do {
      int num = 1;
      for (int j = 1; j <= i; j++) {
        System.out.print(num + "G");
        num += 2;
      }

      System.out.println();
      i++;
    } while (i <= 5);
  }
}
```
(d)

5.10 Minimizing Numeric Errors

Key Point

Using floating-point numbers in the loop continuation condition may cause numeric errors.

Numeric errors involving floating-point numbers are inevitable, because floating-point numbers are represented in approximation in computers by nature. This section discusses how to minimize such errors through an example.

Listing 5.8 presents an example summing a series that starts with 0.01 and ends with 1.0. The numbers in the series will increment by 0.01, as follows: 0.01 + 0.02 + 0.03, and so on.

LISTING 5.8 TestSum.java

loop

```java
 1  public class TestSum {
 2    public static void main(String[] args) {
 3      // Initialize sum
 4      float sum = 0;
 5
 6      // Add 0.01, 0.02, ..., 0.99, 1 to sum
 7      for (float i = 0.01f; i <= 1.0f; i = i + 0.01f)
 8        sum += i;
 9
10      // Display result
```

```
11        System.out.println("The sum is " + sum);
12    }
13  }
```

```
The sum is 50.499985
```

The `for` loop (lines 7 and 8) repeatedly adds the control variable `i` to `sum`. This variable, which begins with `0.01`, is incremented by `0.01` after each iteration. The loop terminates when `i` exceeds `1.0`.

The `for` loop initial action can be any statement, but it is often used to initialize a control variable. From this example, you can see a control variable can be a `float` type. In fact, it can be any data type.

The exact `sum` should be `50.50`, but the answer is `50.499985`. The result is imprecise because computers use a fixed number of bits to represent floating-point numbers, and thus they cannot represent some floating-point numbers exactly. If you change `float` in the program to `double`, as follows, you should see a slight improvement in precision, because a `double` variable holds 64 bits, whereas a `float` variable holds 32 bits.

double precision

```
// Initialize sum
double sum = 0;

// Add 0.01, 0.02, ..., 0.99, 1 to sum
for (double i = 0.01; i <= 1.0; i = i + 0.01)
  sum += i;
```

However, you will be stunned to see the result is actually `49.50000000000003`. What went wrong? If you display `i` for each iteration in the loop, you will see that the last `i` is slightly larger than `1` (not exactly `1`). This causes the last `i` not to be added into `sum`. The fundamental problem is the floating-point numbers are represented by approximation. To fix the problem, use an integer count to ensure all the numbers are added to `sum`. Here is the new loop:

numeric error

```
double currentValue = 0.01;

for (int count = 0; count < 100; count++) {
  sum += currentValue;
  currentValue += 0.01;
}
```

After this loop, `sum` is `50.50000000000003`. This loop adds the numbers from smallest to biggest. What happens if you add numbers from biggest to smallest (i.e., `1.0`, `0.99`, `0.98`, ..., `0.02`, `0.01` in this order) is as follows:

```
double currentValue = 1.0;

for (int count = 0; count < 100; count++) {
  sum += currentValue;
  currentValue -= 0.01;
}
```

After this loop, `sum` is `50.49999999999995`. Adding from biggest to smallest is less accurate than adding from smallest to biggest. This phenomenon is an artifact of the finite-precision arithmetic. Adding a very small number to a very big number can have no effect if the result requires more precision than the variable can store. For example, the inaccurate result of `100000000.0 + 0.000000001` is `100000000.0`. To obtain more accurate results, carefully select the order of computation. Adding smaller numbers before bigger numbers to sum is one way to minimize errors.

avoiding numeric error

5.11 Case Studies

Loops are fundamental in programming. The ability to write loops is essential in learning Java programming.

If you can write programs using loops, you know how to program! For this reason, this section presents three additional examples of solving problems using loops.

5.11.1 Case Study: Finding the Greatest Common Divisor

gcd

The greatest common divisor (gcd) of the two integers 4 and 2 is 2. The greatest common divisor of the two integers 16 and 24 is 8. How would you write this program to find the greatest common divisor? Would you immediately begin to write the code? No. It is important to *think before you code*. Thinking enables you to generate a logical solution for the problem without concern about how to write the code.

think before you code

Let the two input integers be n1 and n2. You know that number 1 is a common divisor, but it may not be the greatest common divisor. Therefore, you can check whether k (for k = 2, 3, 4, and so on) is a common divisor for n1 and n2, until k is greater than n1 or n2. Store the common divisor in a variable named gcd. Initially, gcd is 1. Whenever a new common divisor is found, it becomes the new gcd. When you have checked all the possible common divisors from 2 up to n1 or n2, the value in variable gcd is the greatest common divisor.

logical solution

Once you have a *logical solution*, type the code to translate the solution into a Java program as follows:

```
int gcd = 1; // Initial gcd is 1
int k = 2; // Possible gcd

while (k <= n1 && k <= n2) {
  if (n1 % k == 0 && n2 % k == 0)
    gcd = k; // Update gcd
  k++; // Next possible gcd
}

// After the loop, gcd is the greatest common divisor for n1 and n2
```

Listing 5.9 presents the program that prompts the user to enter two positive integers and finds their greatest common divisor.

LISTING 5.9 GreatestCommonDivisor.java

```
1  import java.util.Scanner;
2
3  public class GreatestCommonDivisor {
4    /** Main method */
5    public static void main(String[] args) {
6      // Create a Scanner
7      Scanner input = new Scanner(System.in);
8
9      // Prompt the user to enter two integers
10     System.out.print("Enter first integer: ");
11     int n1 = input.nextInt();
12     System.out.print("Enter second integer: ");
13     int n2 = input.nextInt();
14
15     int gcd = 1; // Initial gcd is 1
16     int k = 2; // Possible gcd
17     while (k <= n1 && k <= n2) {
18       if (n1 % k == 0 && n2 % k == 0)
19         gcd = k; // Update gcd
20       k++;
```

input
input
gcd
check divisor

```
21      }
22
23      System.out.println("The greatest common divisor for " + n1 +
24          " and " + n2 + " is " + gcd);
25   }
26 }
```

output

```
Enter first integer: 125  ↵Enter
Enter second integer: 2525  ↵Enter
The greatest common divisor for 125 and 2525 is 25
```

Translating a logical solution to Java code is not unique. For example, you could use a `for` loop to rewrite the code as follows:

think before you type

```
for (int k = 2; k <= n1 && k <= n2; k++) {
  if (n1 % k == 0 && n2 % k == 0)
    gcd = k;
}
```

A problem often has multiple solutions, and the gcd problem can be solved in many ways. Programming Exercise 5.14 suggests another solution. A more efficient solution is to use the classic Euclidean algorithm (see Section 22.6).

multiple solutions

You might think that a divisor for a number `n1` cannot be greater than `n1 / 2` and would attempt to improve the program using the following loop:

erroneous solutions

```
for (int k = 2; k <= n1 / 2 && k <= n2 / 2; k++) {
  if (n1 % k == 0 && n2 % k == 0)
    gcd = k;
}
```

This revision is wrong. Can you find the reason? See Checkpoint Question 5.11.1 for the answer.

5.11.2   Case Study: Predicting the Future Tuition

Suppose the tuition for a university is $10,000 this year and tuition increases 7% every year. In how many years will the tuition be doubled?

Before you can write a program to solve this problem, first consider how to solve it by hand. The tuition for the second year is the tuition for the first year * 1.07. The tuition for a future year is the tuition of its preceding year * 1.07. Thus, the tuition for each year can be computed as follows:

think before you code

```
double tuition = 10000; int year = 0; // Year 0
tuition = tuition * 1.07; year++;      // Year 1
tuition = tuition * 1.07; year++;      // Year 2
tuition = tuition * 1.07; year++;      // Year 3
...
```

Keep computing the tuition for a new year until it is at least 20000. By then, you will know how many years it will take for the tuition to be doubled. You can now translate the logic into the following loop:

```
double tuition = 10000; // Year 0
int year = 0;
while (tuition < 20000) {
  tuition = tuition * 1.07;
  year++;
}
```

The complete program is given in Listing 5.10.

LISTING 5.10 FutureTuition.java

```java
1  public class FutureTuition {
2    public static void main(String[] args) {
3      double tuition = 10000; // Year 0
4      int year = 0;
5      while (tuition < 20000) {
6        tuition = tuition * 1.07;
7        year++;
8      }
9
10     System.out.println("Tuition will be doubled in "
11       + year + " years");
12     System.out.printf("Tuition will be $%.2f in %1d years",
13       tuition, year);
14   }
15 }
```

loop
next year's tuition

```
Tuition will be doubled in 11 years
Tuition will be $21048.52 in 11 years
```

The `while` loop (lines 5–8) is used to repeatedly compute the tuition for a new year. The loop terminates when the tuition is greater than or equal to `20000`.

5.11.3 Case Study: Converting Decimals to Hexadecimals

Hexadecimals are often used in computer systems programming (see Appendix F for an introduction to number systems). How do you convert a decimal number to a hexadecimal number? To convert a decimal number d to a hexadecimal number is to find the hexadecimal digits $h_n, h_{n-1}, h_{n-2}, \ldots, h_2, h_1,$ and h_0 such that

$$d = h_n \times 16^n + h_{n-1} \times 16^{n-1} + h_{n-2} \times 16^{n-2} + \cdots$$
$$+ h_2 \times 16^2 + h_1 \times 16^1 + h_0 \times 16^0$$

These hexadecimal digits can be found by successively dividing d by 16 until the quotient is 0. The remainders are $h_0, h_1, h_2, \ldots, h_{n-2}, h_{n-1},$ and h_n. The hexadecimal digits include the decimal digits 0, 1, 2, 3, 4, 5, 6, 7, 8, and 9, plus A, which is the decimal value 10; B, which is the decimal value 11; C, which is 12; D, which is 13; E, which is 14; and F, which is 15.

For example, the decimal number `123` is `7B` in hexadecimal. The conversion is done as follows. Divide `123` by `16`. The remainder is `11` (`B` in hexadecimal) and the quotient is `7`. Continue to divide `7` by `16`. The remainder is `7` and the quotient is `0`. Therefore, `7B` is the hexadecimal number for `123`.

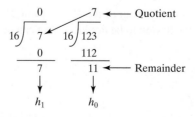

Listing 5.11 gives a program that prompts the user to enter a decimal number and converts it into a hex number as a string.

LISTING 5.11 Dec2Hex.java

```
1  import java.util.Scanner;
2
3  public class Dec2Hex {
4    /** Main method */
5    public static void main(String[] args) {
6      // Create a Scanner
7      Scanner input = new Scanner(System.in);
8
9      // Prompt the user to enter a decimal integer
10     System.out.print("Enter a decimal number: ");
11     int decimal = input.nextInt();                                        input decimal
12
13     // Convert decimal to hex
14     String hex = "";                                                      decimal to hex
15
16     while (decimal != 0) {
17       int hexValue = decimal % 16;
18
19       // Convert a decimal value to a hex digit
20       char hexDigit = (0 <= hexValue && hexValue <= 9) ?                   get a hex char
21         (char)(hexValue + '0') : (char)(hexValue - 10 + 'A');
22
23       hex = hexDigit + hex;                                               add to hex string
24       decimal = decimal / 16;
25     }
26
27     System.out.println("The hex number is " + hex);
28   }
29 }
```

```
Enter a decimal number: 1234 ⏎Enter
The hex number is 4D2
```

	line#	decimal	hex	hexValue	hexDigit
	14	1234	""		
iteration 1	17			2	
	23		"2"		2
	24	77			
iteration 2	17			13	
	23		"D2"		D
	24	4			
iteration 3	17			4	
	23		"4D2"		4
	24	0			

The program prompts the user to enter a decimal integer (line 11), converts it to a hex number as a string (lines 14–25), and displays the result (line 27). To convert a decimal to a hex number, the program uses a loop to successively divide the decimal number by 16 and obtain its remainder (line 17). The remainder is converted into a hex character (lines 20 and 21). The character is then appended to the hex string (line 23). The hex string is initially empty (line 14). Divide the decimal number by 16 to remove a hex digit from the number (line 24). The loop ends when the remaining decimal number becomes 0.

The program converts a `hexValue` between 0 and 15 into a hex character. If `hexValue` is between 0 and 9, it is converted to `(char)(hexValue +'0')` (line 21). Recall that when adding a character with an integer, the character's Unicode is used in the evaluation. For example, if `hexValue` is 5, `(char)(hexValue + '0')` returns 5. Similarly, if `hexValue` is between 10 and 15, it is converted to `(char)(hexValue - 10 + 'A')` (line 21). For instance, if `hexValue` is 11, `(char),(hexValue - 10 + 'A')` returns B.

5.11.1 Will the program work if `n1` and `n2` are replaced by `n1 / 2` and `n2 / 2` in line 17 in Listing 5.9?

5.11.2 In Listing 5.11, why is it wrong if you change the code `(char)(hexValue + '0')` to `hexValue + '0'` in line 21?

5.11.3 In Listing 5.11, how many times the loop body is executed for a decimal number 245, and how many times the loop body is executed for a decimal number 3245?

5.11.4 What is the hex number after E? What is the hex number after F?

5.11.5 Revise line 27 in Listing 5.11 so the program displays hex number 0 if the input decimal is 0.

5.12 Keywords *break* and *continue*

The break *and* continue *keywords provide additional controls in a loop.*

> **Pedagogical Note**
>
> Two keywords, break and continue, can be used in loop statements to provide additional controls. Using break and continue can simplify programming in some cases. Overusing or improperly using them, however, can make programs difficult to read and debug. (*Note to instructors*: You may skip this section without affecting students' understanding of the rest of the book.)

break statement

You have used the keyword break in a switch statement. You can also use break in a loop to immediately terminate the loop. Listing 5.12 presents a program to demonstrate the effect of using break in a loop.

break

LISTING 5.12 TestBreak.java

```java
1  public class TestBreak {
2    public static void main(String[] args) {
3      int sum = 0;
4      int number = 0;
5
6      while (number < 20) {
7        number++;
8        sum += number;
9        if (sum >= 100)
10         break;
11     }
12
13     System.out.println("The number is " + number);
14     System.out.println("The sum is " + sum);
15   }
16 }
```

```
The number is 14
The sum is 105
```

The program in Listing 5.12 adds integers from 1 to 20 in this order to sum until sum is greater than or equal to 100. Without the if statement (line 9), the program calculates the sum of the numbers from 1 to 20. However, with the if statement, the loop terminates when sum becomes greater than or equal to 100. Without the if statement, the output would be as follows:

```
The number is 20
The sum is 210
```

You can also use the continue keyword in a loop. When it is encountered, it ends the current iteration and program control goes to the end of the loop body. In other words, continue breaks out of an iteration, while the break keyword breaks out of a loop. Listing 5.13 presents a program to demonstrate the effect of using continue in a loop.

continue statement

Listing 5.13 TestContinue.java

```java
1  public class TestContinue {
2    public static void main(String[] args) {
3      int sum = 0;
4      int number = 0;
5
6      while (number < 20) {
7        number++;
8        if (number == 10 || number == 11)
9          continue;
10       sum += number;
11     }
12
13     System.out.println("The sum is " + sum);
14   }
15 }
```

continue

```
The sum is 189
```

The program in Listing 5.13 adds integers from 1 to 20 except 10 and 11 to sum. With the if statement in the program (line 8), the continue statement is executed when number becomes 10 or 11. The continue statement ends the current iteration so that the rest of the statement in the loop body is not executed; therefore, number is not added to sum when it is 10 or 11. Without the if statement in the program, the output would be as follows:

```
The sum is 210
```

In this case, all of the numbers are added to sum, even when number is 10 or 11. Therefore, the result is 210, which is 21 more than it was with the if statement.

Note
The continue statement is always inside a loop. In the while and do-while loops, the loop-continuation-condition is evaluated immediately after the continue statement. In the for loop, the action-after-each-iteration is performed, then the loop-continuation-condition is evaluated immediately after the continue statement.

goto

Note

Some programming languages have a `goto` statement. The `goto` statement indiscrimi-
nately transfers control to any statement in the program and executes it. This makes your
program vulnerable to errors. The `break` and `continue` statements in Java are different
from `goto` statements. They operate only in a loop or a `switch` statement. The `break`
statement breaks out of the loop, and the `continue` statement breaks out of the current
iteration in the loop.

You can always write a program without using `break` or `continue` in a loop (see Check-
Point Question 5.12.3). In general, though, using `break` and `continue` is appropriate if it
simplifies coding and makes programs easier to read.

Suppose you need to write a program to find the smallest factor other than 1 for an integer
n (assume n >= 2). You can write a simple and intuitive code using the `break` statement as
follows:

```
int factor = 2;
while (factor <= n) {
  if (n % factor == 0)
    break;
  factor++;
}
System.out.println("The smallest factor other than 1 for "
  + n + " is " + factor);
```

You may rewrite the code without using `break` as follows:

```
boolean found = false;
int factor = 2;
while (factor <= n && !found) {
  if (n % factor == 0)
    found = true;
  else
    factor++;
}
System.out.println("The smallest factor other than 1 for "
  + n + " is " + factor);
```

Obviously, the `break` statement makes this program simpler and easier to read in this
case. However, you should use `break` and `continue` with caution. Too many `break` and
`continue` statements will produce a loop with many exit points and make the program difficult to read.

Note

Programming is a creative endeavor. There are many different ways to write code. In fact,
you can find a smallest factor using a rather simple code as follows:

```
int factor = 2;
while (n % factor != 0)
  factor++;
```

or

```
for (int factor = 2; n % factor != 0; factor++);
```

The code here finds the smallest factor for an integer n. Programming Exercise 5.16 writes
a program that finds all smallest factors in n.

Check Point

5.12.1 What is the keyword `break` for? What is the keyword `continue` for? Will the following programs terminate? If so, give the output.

```
int balance = 10;
while (true) {
  if (balance < 9)
    break;
  balance = balance - 9;
}

System.out.println("Balance is "
  + balance);
```
(a)

```
int balance = 10;
while (true) {
  if (balance < 9)
    continue;
  balance = balance - 9;
}

System.out.println("Balance is "
  + balance);
```
(b)

5.12.2 The `for` loop on the left is converted into the `while` loop on the right. What is wrong? Correct it.

```
int sum = 0;
for (int i = 0; i < 4; i++) {
  if (i % 3 == 0) continue;
  sum += i;
}
```
Converted
→ Wrong conversion
```
int i = 0, sum = 0;
while (i < 4) {
  if (i % 3 == 0) continue;
  sum += i;
  i++;
}
```

5.12.3 Rewrite the programs `TestBreak` and `TestContinue` in Listings 5.12 and 5.13 without using `break` and `continue`.

5.12.4 After the `break` statement in (a) is executed in the following loop, which statement is executed? Show the output. After the `continue` statement in (b) is executed in the following loop, which statement is executed? Show the output.

```
for (int i = 1; i < 4; i++) {
  for (int j = 1; j < 4; j++) {
    if (i * j > 2)
      break;

    System.out.println(i * j);
  }

  System.out.println(i);
}
```
(a)

```
for (int i = 1; i < 4; i++) {
  for (int j = 1; j < 4; j++) {
    if (i * j > 2)
      continue;

    System.out.println(i * j);
  }

  System.out.println(i);
}
```
(b)

5.13 Case Study: Checking Palindromes

This section presents a program that checks whether a string is a palindrome.

Key
Point

A string is a palindrome if it reads the same forward and backward. The words "mom," "dad," and "noon," for instance, are all palindromes.

The problem is to write a program that prompts the user to enter a string and reports whether the string is a palindrome. One solution is to check whether the first character in the string is the same as the last character. If so, check whether the second character is the same as the second-to-last

think before you code

character. This process continues until a mismatch is found or all the characters in the string are checked, except for the middle character if the string has an odd number of characters.

Listing 5.14 gives the program.

LISTING 5.14 Palindrome.java

```java
 1  import java.util.Scanner;
 2
 3  public class Palindrome {
 4    /** Main method */
 5    public static void main(String[] args) {
 6      // Create a Scanner
 7      Scanner input = new Scanner(System.in);
 8
 9      // Prompt the user to enter a string
10      System.out.print("Enter a string: ");
11      String s = input.nextLine();
12
13      // The index of the first character in the string
14      int low = 0;
15
16      // The index of the last character in the string
17      int high = s.length() - 1;
18
19      boolean isPalindrome = true;
20      while (low < high) {
21        if (s.charAt(low) != s.charAt(high)) {
22          isPalindrome = false;
23          break;
24        }
25
26        low++;
27        high--;
28      }
29
30      if (isPalindrome)
31        System.out.println(s + " is a palindrome");
32      else
33        System.out.println(s + " is not a palindrome");
34    }
35  }
```

input string

low index

high index

update indices

```
Enter a string: noon  ↵Enter
noon is a palindrome
```

```
Enter a string: abcdefgnhgfedcba  ↵Enter
abcdefgnhgfedcba is not a palindrome
```

The program uses two variables, `low` and `high`, to denote the positions of the two characters at the beginning and the end in a string `s` (lines 14 and 17), as shown in the following figure.

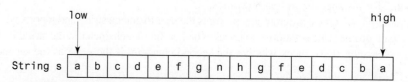

Initially, `low` is `0` and `high` is `s.length() - 1`. If the two characters at these positions match, increment `low` by `1` and decrement `high` by `1` (lines 26–27). This process continues until (`low >= high`) or a mismatch is found (line 21).

The program uses a `boolean` variable `isPalindrome` to denote whether the string `s` is a palindrome. Initially, it is set to `true` (line 19). When a mismatch is discovered (line 21), `isPalindrome` is set to `false` (line 22) and the loop is terminated with a break statement (line 23).

5.13.1 What happens to the program if (`low < high`) in line 20 is changed to (`low <= high`)?

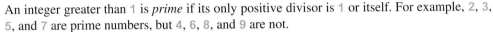

Check Point

5.14 Case Study: Displaying Prime Numbers

This section presents a program that displays the first 50 prime numbers in 5 lines, each containing 10 numbers.

Key Point

An integer greater than `1` is *prime* if its only positive divisor is `1` or itself. For example, `2`, `3`, `5`, and `7` are prime numbers, but `4`, `6`, `8`, and `9` are not.

The problem is to display the first 50 prime numbers in 5 lines, each of which contains 10 numbers. The problem can be broken into the following tasks:

- Determine whether a given number is prime.

- For `number = 2, 3, 4, 5, 6, …`, test whether it is prime.

- Count the prime numbers.

- Display each prime number and display 10 numbers per line.

Obviously, you need to write a loop and repeatedly test whether a new `number` is prime. If the `number` is prime, increase the count by `1`. The `count` is `0` initially. When it reaches `50`, the loop terminates.

Here is the algorithm for the problem:

```
Set the number of prime numbers to be printed as
  a constant NUMBER_OF_PRIMES;
Use count to track the number of prime numbers and
  set an initial count to 0;
Set an initial number to 2;

while (count < NUMBER_OF_PRIMES) {
  Test whether number is prime;

  if number is prime {
    Display the prime number and increase the count;
  }

  Increment number by 1;
}
```

To test whether a number is prime, check whether it is divisible by `2`, `3`, `4`, and so on up to `number/2`. If a divisor is found, the number is not a prime. The algorithm can be described as follows:

```
Use a boolean variable isPrime to denote whether
  the number is prime; Set isPrime to true initially;

for (int divisor = 2; divisor <= number / 2; divisor++) {
  if (number % divisor == 0) {
    Set isPrime to false
    Exit the loop;
  }
}
```

The complete program is given in Listing 5.15.

LISTING 5.15 PrimeNumber.java

count prime numbers

check primeness

exit loop

display if prime

```java
1  public class PrimeNumber {
2    public static void main(String[] args) {
3      final int NUMBER_OF_PRIMES = 50; // Number of primes to display
4      final int NUMBER_OF_PRIMES_PER_LINE = 10; // Display 10 per line
5      int count = 0; // Count the number of prime numbers
6      int number = 2; // A number to be tested for primeness
7
8      System.out.println("The first 50 prime numbers are \n");
9
10     // Repeatedly find prime numbers
11     while (count < NUMBER_OF_PRIMES) {
12       // Assume the number is prime
13       boolean isPrime = true; // Is the current number prime?
14
15       // Test whether number is prime
16       for (int divisor = 2; divisor <= number / 2; divisor++) {
17         if (number % divisor == 0) {  // If true, number is not prime
18           isPrime = false; // Set isPrime to false
19           break; // Exit the for loop
20         }
21       }
22
23       // Display the prime number and increase the count
24       if (isPrime) {
25         count++; // Increase the count
26
27         if (count % NUMBER_OF_PRIMES_PER_LINE == 0) {
28           // Display the number and advance to the new line
29           System.out.println(number);
30         }
31         else
32           System.out.print(number + " ");
33       }
34
35       // Check if the next number is prime
36       number++;
37     }
38   }
39 }
```

```
The first 50 prime numbers are
2 3 5 7 11 13 17 19 23 29
31 37 41 43 47 53 59 61 67 71
73 79 83 89 97 101 103 107 109 113
127 131 137 139 149 151 157 163 167 173
179 181 191 193 197 199 211 223 227 229
```

subproblem

This is a complex program for novice programmers. The key to developing a programmatic solution for this problem, and for many other problems, is to break it into subproblems and develop solutions for each of them in turn. Do not attempt to develop a complete solution in the first trial. Instead, begin by writing the code to determine whether a given number is prime, then expand the program to test whether other numbers are prime in a loop.

To determine whether a number is prime, check whether it is divisible by a number between 2 and number/2 inclusive (lines 16–21). If so, it is not a prime number (line 18); otherwise, it is a prime number. For a prime number, display it (lines 27–33). If the count is divisible by 10, display the number followed by a newline (lines 27–30). The program ends when the count reaches 50.

The program uses the break statement in line 19 to exit the for loop as soon as the number is found to be a nonprime. You can rewrite the loop (lines 16–21) without using the break statement, as follows:

```
for (int divisor = 2; divisor <= number / 2 && isPrime;
    divisor++) {
  // If true, the number is not prime
  if (number % divisor == 0) {
    // Set isPrime to false, if the number is not prime
    isPrime = false;
  }
}
```

However, using the break statement makes the program simpler and easier to read in this case.

Prime numbers have many applications in computer science. Section 22.7 will study several efficient algorithms for finding prime numbers.

5.14.1 Simplify the code in lines 27–32 using a conditional operator.

Check
Point

KEY TERMS

break statement 186	loop body 160
continue statement 187	nested loop 178
do-while loop 170	off-by-one error 162
for loop 173	output redirection 170
infinite loop 162	posttest loop 176
input redirection 170	pretest loop 176
iteration 160	sentinel value 168
loop 160	while loop 160

CHAPTER SUMMARY

1. There are three types of repetition statements: the while loop, the do-while loop, and the for loop.

2. The part of the loop that contains the statements to be repeated is called the *loop body*.

3. A one-time execution of a loop body is referred to as an *iteration of the loop*.

4. An *infinite loop* is a loop statement that executes infinitely.

5. In designing loops, you need to consider both the *loop control structure* and the loop body.

6. The while loop checks the loop-continuation-condition first. If the condition is true, the loop body is executed; if it is false, the loop terminates.

7. The do-while loop is similar to the while loop, except the do-while loop executes the loop body first then checks the loop-continuation-condition to decide whether to continue or to terminate.

8. The while loop and the do-while loop often are used when the number of repetitions is not predetermined.

9. A *sentinel value* is a special value that signifies the end of the loop.

10. The `for` loop generally is used to execute a loop body a fixed number of times.

11. The `for` loop control has three parts. The first part is an initial action that often initializes a control variable. The second part, the `loop-continuation-condition`, determines whether the loop body is to be executed. The third part is executed after each iteration and is often used to adjust the control variable. Usually, the loop control variables are initialized and changed in the control structure.

12. The `while` loop and `for` loop are called *pretest loops* because the continuation condition is checked before the loop body is executed.

13. The `do-while` loop is called a *posttest loop* because the condition is checked after the loop body is executed.

14. Two keywords `break` and `continue` can be used in a loop.

15. The `break` keyword immediately ends the innermost loop, which contains the break.

16. The `continue` keyword only ends the current iteration.

QUIZ

Answer the quiz for this chapter online at the Companion Website.

MyProgrammingLab™

PROGRAMMING EXERCISES

read and think before coding

Pedagogical Note

Read each problem several times until you understand it. Think how to solve the problem before starting to write code. Translate your logic into a program.

explore solutions

A problem often can be solved in many different ways. Students are encouraged to explore various solutions.

Sections 5.2–5.7

*5.1   (*Count positive and negative numbers and compute the average of numbers*) Write a program that reads an unspecified number of integers, determines how many positive and negative values have been read, and computes the total and average of the input values (not counting zeros). Your program ends with the input 0. Display the average as a floating-point number. Here are sample runs:

```
Enter an integer, the input ends if it is 0: 1 2 -1 3 0 ↵Enter
The number of positives is 3
The number of negatives is 1
The total is 5.0
The average is 1.25
```

```
Enter an integer, the input ends if it is 0: 0 ↵Enter
No numbers are entered except 0
```

5.2 (*Repeat additions*) Listing 5.4, SubtractionQuizLoop.java, generates five random subtraction questions. Revise the program to generate 10 random addition questions for two integers between 1 and 15. Display the correct count and test time.

5.3 (*Conversion from kilograms to pounds*) Write a program that displays the following table (note 1 kilogram is 2.2 pounds):

```
Kilograms        Pounds
1                   2.2
3                   6.6
. . .
197               433.4
199               437.8
```

5.4 (*Conversion from miles to kilometers*) Write a program that displays the following table (note 1 mile is 1.609 kilometers):

```
Miles       Kilometers
1            1.609
2            3.218
. . .
9           14.481
10          16.090
```

5.5 (*Conversion from kilograms to pounds and pounds to kilograms*) Write a program that displays the following two tables side by side:

```
Kilograms      Pounds    |   Pounds      Kilograms
1                 2.2    |   20             9.09
3                 6.6    |   25            11.36
. . .
197             433.4    |   510          231.82
199             437.8    |   515          234.09
```

5.6 (*Conversion from miles to kilometers*) Write a program that displays the following two tables side by side:

```
Miles       Kilometers   |   Kilometers    Miles
1            1.609        |   20            12.430
2            3.218        |   25            15.538
. . .
9           14.481        |   60            37.290
10          16.090        |   65            40.398
```

**5.7 (*Financial application: compute future tuition*) Suppose the tuition for a university is $10,000 this year and increases 5% every year. In one year, the tuition will be $10,500. Write a program that displays the tuition in 10 years, and the total cost of four years' worth of tuition after the tenth year.

5.8 (*Find the highest score*) Write a program that prompts the user to enter the number of students and each student's name and score, and finally displays the name of the student with the highest score. Use the next() method in the Scanner class to read a name, rather than using the nextLine() method.

*5.9 (*Find the two highest scores*) Write a program that prompts the user to enter the number of students and each student's name and score, and finally displays the student with the highest score and the student with the second-highest score. Use the next() method in the Scanner class to read a name rather than using the nextLine() method.

5.10 (*Find numbers divisible by 5 and 6*) Write a program that displays all the numbers from 100 to 1,000 (10 per line) that are divisible by 5 and 6. Numbers are separated by exactly one space.

5.11 (*Find numbers divisible by 5 or 6, but not both*) Write a program that displays all the numbers from 100 to 200 (10 per line) that are divisible by 5 or 6, but not both. Numbers are separated by exactly one space.

5.12 (*Find the smallest n such that $n^2 > 12,000$*) Use a `while` loop to find the smallest integer n such that n^2 is greater than 12,000.

5.13 (*Find the largest n such that $n^3 < 12,000$*) Use a `while` loop to find the largest integer n such that n^3 is less than 12,000.

Sections 5.8–5.10

*5.14 (*Compute the greatest common divisor*) Another solution for Listing 5.9 to find the greatest common divisor of two integers n1 and n2 is as follows: First find d to be the minimum of n1 and n2, then check whether d, d−1, d−2, ..., 2, or 1 is a divisor for both n1 and n2 in this order. The first such common divisor is the greatest common divisor for n1 and n2. Write a program that prompts the user to enter two positive integers and displays the gcd.

*5.15 (*Display the ASCII character table*) Write a program that prints the characters in the ASCII character table from ! to ~. Display 10 characters per line. The ASCII table is given in Appendix B. Characters are separated by exactly one space.

*5.16 (*Find the factors of an integer*) Write a program that reads an integer and displays all its smallest factors in an increasing order. For example, if the input integer is 120, the output should be as follows: 2, 2, 2, 3, 5.

**5.17 (*Display pyramid*) Write a program that prompts the user to enter an integer from 1 to 15 and displays a pyramid, as presented in the following sample run:

```
Enter the number of lines: 7 ↵Enter
            1
          2 1 2
        3 2 1 2 3
      4 3 2 1 2 3 4
    5 4 3 2 1 2 3 4 5
  6 5 4 3 2 1 2 3 4 5 6
7 6 5 4 3 2 1 2 3 4 5 6 7
```

*5.18 (*Display four patterns using loops*) Use nested loops that display the following patterns in four separate programs:

```
Pattern A        Pattern B        Pattern C        Pattern D
1                1 2 3 4 5 6                1      1 2 3 4 5 6
1 2              1 2 3 4 5               2 1        1 2 3 4 5
1 2 3            1 2 3 4              3 2 1           1 2 3 4
1 2 3 4          1 2 3             4 3 2 1              1 2 3
1 2 3 4 5        1 2            5 4 3 2 1                 1 2
1 2 3 4 5 6      1           6 5 4 3 2 1                    1
```

**5.19 (*Display numbers in a pyramid pattern*) Write a nested `for` loop that prints the following output:

```
                        1
                    1   2   1
                1   2   4   2   1
            1   2   4   8   4   2   1
        1   2   4   8  16   8   4   2   1
      1   2   4   8  16  32  16   8   4   2   1
    1   2   4   8  16  32  64  32  16   8   4   2   1
  1   2   4   8  16  32  64 128  64  32  16   8   4   2   1
```

*5.20 (*Display prime numbers between 2 and 1,000*) Modify the program given in Listing 5.15 to display all the prime numbers between 2 and 1,000, inclusive. Display eight prime numbers per line. Numbers are separated by exactly one space.

Comprehensive

**5.21 (*Financial application: compare loans with various interest rates*) Write a program that lets the user enter the loan amount and loan period in number of years, and displays the monthly and total payments for each interest rate starting from 5% to 8%, with an increment of 1/8. Here is a sample run:

```
Loan Amount: 10000 ↵Enter
Number of Years: 5 ↵Enter
Interest Rate     Monthly Payment      Total Payment
5.000%            188.71               11322.74
5.125%            189.29               11357.13
5.250%            189.86               11391.59
...
7.875%            202.17               12129.97
8.000%            202.76               12165.84
```

For the formula to compute monthly payment, see Listing 2.9, ComputeLoan.java.

**5.22 (*Financial application: loan amortization schedule*) The monthly payment for a given loan pays the principal and the interest. The monthly interest is computed by multiplying the monthly interest rate and the balance (the remaining principal). The principal paid for the month is therefore the monthly payment minus the monthly interest. Write a program that lets the user enter the loan amount, number of years, and interest rate then displays the amortization schedule for the loan. Here is a sample run:

VideoNote
Display loan schedule

```
Loan Amount: 10000 ↵Enter
Number of Years: 1 ↵Enter
Annual Interest Rate: 7 ↵Enter

Monthly Payment: 865.26
Total Payment: 10383.21

Payment#      Interest      Principal      Balance
1             58.33         806.93         9193.07
2             53.62         811.64         8381.43
...
11            10.00         855.26         860.27
12             5.01         860.25           0.01
```

> ✏️ **Note**
> The balance after the last payment may not be zero. If so, the last payment should be the normal monthly payment plus the final balance.
>
> *Hint*: Write a loop to display the table. Since the monthly payment is the same for each month, it should be computed before the loop. The balance is initially the loan amount. For each iteration in the loop, compute the interest and principal, and update the balance. The loop may look as follows:
>
> ```
> for (i = 1; i <= numberOfYears * 12; i++) {
>     interest = monthlyInterestRate * balance;
>     principal = monthlyPayment - interest;
>     balance = balance - principal;
>     System.out.println(i + "\t\t" + interest
>         + "\t\t" + principal + "\t\t" + balance);
> }
> ```

*5.23 (*Demonstrate cancellation errors*) A cancellation error occurs when you are manipulating a very large number with a very small number. The large number may cancel out the smaller number. For example, the result of `100000000.0 + 0.000000001` is equal to `100000000.0`. To avoid cancellation errors and obtain more accurate results, carefully select the order of computation. For example, in computing the following summation, you will obtain more accurate results by computing from right to left rather than from left to right:

$$1 + \frac{1}{2} + \frac{1}{3} + \ \cdots \ + \frac{1}{n}$$

Write a program that compares the results of the summation of the preceding series, computing from left to right and from right to left with `n = 50000`.

*5.24 (*Sum a series*) Write a program to compute the following summation:

$$\frac{1}{3} + \frac{3}{5} + \frac{5}{7} + \frac{7}{9} + \frac{9}{11} + \frac{11}{13} + \ \cdots \ + \frac{95}{97} + \frac{97}{99}$$

VideoNote

Sum a series

**5.25 (*Compute π*) You can approximate π by using the following summation:

$$\pi = 4\left(1 - \frac{1}{3} + \frac{1}{5} - \frac{1}{7} + \frac{1}{9} - \frac{1}{11} + \ \cdots \ + \frac{(-)^{i+1}}{2i - 1}\right)$$

Write a program that displays the π value for `i = 10000, 20000, ...,` and `100000`.

**5.26 (*Compute e*) You can approximate e using the following summation:

$$e = 1 + \frac{1}{1!} + \frac{1}{2!} + \frac{1}{3!} + \frac{1}{4!} + \ \cdots \ + \frac{1}{i!}$$

Write a program that displays the e value for `i = 10000, 20000, ...,` and `100000`. (*Hint*: Because $i! = i \times (i - 1) \times \ \ldots \ \times 2 \times 1$, then

$$\frac{1}{i!} \text{ is } \frac{1}{i(i - 1)!}$$

Initialize e and `item` to be `1`, and keep adding a new `item` to e. The new item is the previous item divided by `i`, for `i >= 2`.)

**5.27 (*Display leap years*) Write a program that displays all the leap years, 10 per line, from 101 to 2100, separated by exactly one space. Also display the number of leap years in this period.

**5.28 (*Display the first days of each month*) Write a program that prompts the user to enter the year and first day of the year, then displays the first day of each month in the year. For example, if the user entered the year 2013, and 2 for Tuesday, January 1, 2013, your program should display the following output:

```
January 1, 2013 is Tuesday
...
December 1, 2013 is Sunday
```

**5.29 (*Display calendars*) Write a program that prompts the user to enter the year and first day of the year and displays the calendar table for the year on the console. For example, if the user entered the year 2013, and 2 for Tuesday, January 1, 2013, your program should display the calendar for each month in the year, as follows:

January 2013

Sun	Mon	Tue	Wed	Thu	Fri	Sat
		1	2	3	4	5
6	7	8	9	10	11	12
13	14	15	16	17	18	19
20	21	22	23	24	25	26
27	28	29	30	31		

. . .

December 2013

Sun	Mon	Tue	Wed	Thu	Fri	Sat
1	2	3	4	5	6	7
8	9	10	11	12	13	14
15	16	17	18	19	20	21
22	23	24	25	26	27	28
29	30	31				

*5.30 (*Financial application: compound value*) Suppose you save $100 *each* month into a savings account with the annual interest rate 5%. Thus, the monthly interest rate is 0.05 / 12 = 0.00417. After the first month, the value in the account becomes

$$100 * (1 + 0.00417) = 100.417$$

After the second month, the value in the account becomes

$$(100 + 100.417) * (1 + 0.00417) = 201.252$$

After the third month, the value in the account becomes

$$(100 + 201.252) * (1 + 0.00417) = 302.507$$

and so on.

Write a program that prompts the user to enter an amount (e.g., 100), the annual interest rate (e.g., 5), and the number of months (e.g., 6) then displays the amount in the savings account after the given month.

*5.31 (*Financial application: compute CD value*) Suppose you put $10,000 into a CD with an annual percentage yield of 5.75%. After one month, the CD is worth

$$10000 + 10000 * 5.75 / 1200 = 10047.92$$

After two months, the CD is worth

$$10047.91 + 10047.91 * 5.75 / 1200 = 10096.06$$

After three months, the CD is worth

$$10096.06 + 10096.06 * 5.75 / 1200 = 10144.44$$

and so on.

Write a program that prompts the user to enter an amount (e.g., 10000), the annual percentage yield (e.g., 5.75), and the number of months (e.g., 18) and displays a table as presented in the sample run.

```
Enter the initial deposit amount: 10000 ↵Enter
Enter annual percentage yield: 5.75 ↵Enter
Enter maturity period (number of months): 18 ↵Enter

Month    CD Value
1        10047.92
2        10096.06
...
17       10846.57
18       10898.54
```

**5.32 (*Game: lottery*) Revise Listing 3.8, Lottery.java, to generate a lottery of a two-digit number. The two digits in the number are distinct. (*Hint*: Generate the first digit. Use a loop to continuously generate the second digit until it is different from the first digit.)

**5.33 (*Perfect number*) A positive integer is called a *perfect number* if it is equal to the sum of all of its positive divisors, excluding itself. For example, 6 is the first perfect number because 6 = 3 + 2 + 1. The next is 28 = 14 + 7 + 4 + 2 + 1. There are four perfect numbers < 10,000. Write a program to find all these four numbers.

***5.34 (*Game: scissor, rock, paper*) Programming Exercise 3.17 gives a program that plays the scissor–rock–paper game. Revise the program to let the user continuously play until either the user or the computer wins more than two times than its opponent.

*5.35 (*Summation*) Write a program to compute the following summation:

$$\frac{1}{1 + \sqrt{2}} + \frac{1}{\sqrt{2} + \sqrt{3}} + \frac{1}{\sqrt{3} + \sqrt{4}} + \dots + \frac{1}{\sqrt{624} + \sqrt{625}}$$

**5.36 (*Business application: checking ISBN*) Use loops to simplify Programming Exercise 3.9.

**5.37 (*Decimal to binary*) Write a program that prompts the user to enter a decimal integer then displays its corresponding binary value. Don't use Java's `Integer.toBinaryString(int)` in this program.

**5.38 (*Decimal to octal*) Write a program that prompts the user to enter a decimal integer and displays its corresponding octal value. Don't use Java's `Integer.toOctalString(int)` in this program.

*5.39   (*Financial application: find the sales amount*) You have just started a sales job in a department store. Your pay consists of a base salary and a commission. The base salary is $5,000. The scheme shown below is used to determine the commission rate.

Sales Amount	Commission Rate
$0.01–$5,000	8%
$5,000.01–$10,000	10%
$10,000.01 and above	12%

Note this is a graduated rate. The rate for the first $5,000 is at 8%, the next $5,000 is at 10%, and the rest is at 12%. If the sales amount is 25,000, the commission is 5,000 * 8% + 5,000 * 10% + 15,000 * 12% = $2,700.

Your goal is to earn $30,000 a year. Write a program that finds out the minimum number of sales you have to generate in order to make $30,000.

5.40   (*Simulation: heads or tails*) Write a program that simulates flipping a coin one million times and displays the number of heads and tails.

*5.41   (*Occurrence of max numbers*) Write a program that reads integers, finds the largest of them, and counts its occurrences. Assume the input ends with number 0. Suppose you entered 3 5 2 5 5 5 0; the program finds that the largest is 5 and the occurrence count for 5 is 4.

(*Hint*: Maintain two variables, max and count. max stores the current max number and count stores its occurrences. Initially, assign the first number to max and 1 to count. Compare each subsequent number with max. If the number is greater than max, assign it to max and reset count to 1. If the number is equal to max, increment count by 1.)

```
Enter numbers: 3 5 2 5 5 5 0  ↵Enter
The largest number is 5
The occurrence count of the largest number is 4
```

*5.42   (*Financial application: find the sales amount*) Rewrite Programming Exercise 5.39 as follows:

- Use a for loop instead of a do-while loop.
- Let the user enter COMMISSION_SOUGHT instead of fixing it as a constant.

*5.43   (*Math: combinations*) Write a program that displays all possible combinations for picking two numbers from integers 1 to 7. Also display the total number of all combinations.

```
1 2
1 3
. . .
. . .

The total number of all combinations is 21
```

*5.44 (*Computer architecture: bit-level operations*) A short value is stored in 16 bits. Write a program that prompts the user to enter a short integer and displays the 16 bits for the integer. Here are sample runs:

```
Enter an integer: 5 ↵Enter
The bits are 0000000000000101
```

```
Enter an integer: −5 ↵Enter
The bits are 1111111111111011
```

(*Hint*: You need to use the bitwise right shift operator (>>) and the bitwise AND operator (&), which are covered in Appendix G, Bitwise Operations.)

**5.45 (*Statistics: compute mean and standard deviation*) In business applications, you are often asked to compute the mean and standard deviation of data. The mean is simply the average of the numbers. The standard deviation is a statistic that tells you how tightly all the various data are clustered around the mean in a set of data. For example, what is the average age of the students in a class? How close are the ages? If all the students are the same age, the deviation is 0.

Write a program that prompts the user to enter 10 numbers and displays the mean and standard deviations of these numbers using the following formula:

$$\text{mean} = \frac{\sum_{i=1}^{n} x_i}{n} = \frac{x_1 + x_2 + \cdots + x_n}{n} \qquad \text{deviation} = \sqrt{\frac{\sum_{i=1}^{n} x_i^2 - \frac{\left(\sum_{i=1}^{n} x_i\right)^2}{n}}{n-1}}$$

Here is a sample run:

```
Enter 10 numbers: 1 2 3 4.5 5.6 6 7 8 9 10 ↵Enter
The mean is 5.61
The standard deviation is 2.99794
```

*5.46 (*Reverse a string*) Write a program that prompts the user to enter a string and displays the string in reverse order.

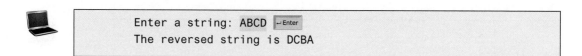

```
Enter a string: ABCD ↵Enter
The reversed string is DCBA
```

*5.47   (*Business: check ISBN-13*) **ISBN-13** is a new standard for identifying books. It uses 13 digits $d_1d_2d_3d_4d_5d_6d_7d_8d_9d_{10}d_{11}d_{12}d_{13}$. The last digit d_{13} is a checksum, which is calculated from the other digits using the following formula:

$$10 - (d_1 + 3d_2 + d_3 + 3d_4 + d_5 + 3d_6 + d_7 + 3d_8 + d_9 + 3d_{10} + d_{11} + 3d_{12})\%10$$

If the checksum is **10**, replace it with **0**. Your program should read the input as a string. Here are sample runs:

```
Enter the first 12 digits of an ISBN-13 as a string: 978013213080 ⏎Enter
The ISBN-13 number is 9780132130806
```

```
Enter the first 12 digits of an ISBN-13 as a string: 978013213079 ⏎Enter
The ISBN-13 number is 9780132130790
```

```
Enter the first 12 digits of an ISBN-13 as a string: 97801320 ⏎Enter
97801320 is an invalid input
```

*5.48   (*Process string*) Write a program that prompts the user to enter a string and displays the characters at odd positions. Here is a sample run:

```
Enter a string: Beijing Chicago ⏎Enter
BiigCiao
```

*5.49   (*Count vowels and consonants*) Assume that the letters A, E, I, O, and U are vowels. Write a program that prompts the user to enter a string, and displays the number of vowels and consonants in the string.

```
Enter a string: Programming is fun ⏎Enter
The number of vowels is 5
The number of consonants is 11
```

*5.50   (*Count uppercase letters*) Write a program that prompts the user to enter a string and displays the number of the uppercase letters in the string.

```
Enter a string: Welcome to Java ⏎Enter
The number of uppercase letters is 2
```

*5.51 (*Longest common prefix*) Write a program that prompts the user to enter two strings and displays the largest common prefix of the two strings. Here are some sample runs:

```
Enter the first string: Welcome to C++ ⏎Enter
Enter the second string: Welcome to programming ⏎Enter
The common prefix is Welcome to
```

```
Enter the first string: Atlanta ⏎Enter
Enter the second string: Macon ⏎Enter
Atlanta and Macon have no common prefix
```

METHODS

Objectives

- To define methods with formal parameters (§6.2).

- To invoke methods with actual parameters (i.e., arguments) (§6.2).

- To define methods with a return value (§6.3).

- To define methods without a return value and distinguish the differences between void methods and value-returning methods (§6.4).

- To pass arguments by value (§6.5).

- To develop reusable code that is modular, easy to read, easy to debug, and easy to maintain (§6.6).

- To write a method that converts hexadecimals to decimals (§6.7).

- To use method overloading and understand ambiguous overloading (§6.8).

- To determine the scope of variables (§6.9).

- To apply the concept of method abstraction in software development (§6.10).

- To design and implement methods using stepwise refinement (§6.11).

6.1 Introduction

Methods can be used to define reusable code and organize and simplify coding.

Suppose you need to find the sum of integers from 1 to 10, 20 to 37, and 35 to 49, respectively. You may write the code as follows:

```
int sum = 0;
for (int i = 1; i <= 10; i++)
  sum += i;
System.out.println("Sum from 1 to 10 is " + sum);

sum = 0;
for (int i = 20; i <= 37; i++)
  sum += i;
System.out.println("Sum from 20 to 37 is " + sum);

sum = 0;
for (int i = 35; i <= 49; i++)
  sum += i;
System.out.println("Sum from 35 to 49 is " + sum);
```

You may have observed that computing these sums from 1 to 10, 20 to 37, and 35 to 49 are very similar, except that the starting and ending integers are different. Wouldn't it be nice if we could write the common code once and reuse it? We can do so by defining a method and invoking it.

The preceding code can be simplified as follows:

```
1  public static int sum(int i1, int i2) {
2    int result = 0;
3    for (int i = i1; i <= i2; i++)
4      result += i;
5
6    return result;
7  }
8
9  public static void main(String[] args) {
10   System.out.println("Sum from 1 to 10 is " + sum(1, 10));
11   System.out.println("Sum from 20 to 37 is " + sum(20, 37));
12   System.out.println("Sum from 35 to 49 is " + sum(35, 49));
13 }
```

Lines 1–7 define the method named sum with two parameters i1 and i2. The statements in the main method invoke sum(1, 10) to compute the sum from 1 to 10, sum(20, 37) to compute the sum from 20 to 37, and sum(35, 49) to compute the sum from 35 to 49.

A *method* is a collection of statements grouped together to perform an operation. In earlier chapters you have used predefined methods such as System.out.println, System.exit, Math.pow, and Math.random. These methods are defined in the Java library. In this chapter, you will learn how to define your own methods and apply method abstraction to solve complex problems.

6.2 Defining a Method

A method definition consists of method name, parameters, return value type, and body.

The syntax for defining a method is as follows:

```
modifier returnValueType methodName(list of parameters) {
  // Method body;
}
```

Key margin notes: problem; why methods?; define sum method; main method; invoke sum; method; Key Point; Key Point

Let's look at a method defined to find the larger between two integers. This method, named `max`, has two `int` parameters, `num1` and `num2`, the larger of which is returned by the method. Figure 6.1 illustrates the components of this method.

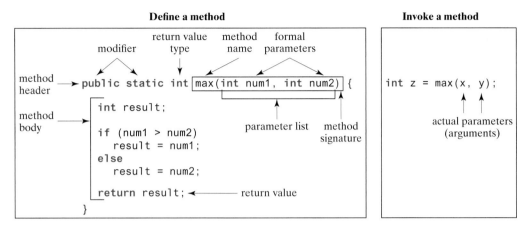

FIGURE 6.1 A method definition consists of a method header and a method body.

The *method header* specifies the *modifiers*, *return value type*, *method name*, and *parameters* of the method. The `static` modifier is used for all the methods in this chapter. The reason for using it will be discussed in Chapter 9, Objects and Classes.

method header
modifier

A method may return a value. The `returnValueType` is the data type of the value the method returns. Some methods perform desired operations without returning a value. In this case, the `returnValueType` is the keyword `void`. For example, the `returnValueType` is `void` in the `main` method, as well as in `System.exit`, and `System.out.println`. If a method returns a value, it is called a *value-returning method;* otherwise, it is called a *void method.*

value-returning method
void method

The variables defined in the method header are known as *formal parameters* or simply *parameters.* A parameter is like a placeholder: when a method is invoked, you pass a value to the parameter. This value is referred to as an *actual parameter or argument.* The *parameter list* refers to the method's type, order, and the number of parameters. The method name and the parameter list together constitute the *method signature.* Parameters are optional; that is, a method may contain no parameters. For example, the `Math.random()` method has no parameters.

formal parameter
parameter
actual parameter
argument
parameter list
method signature

The method body contains a collection of statements that implement the method. The method body of the `max` method uses an `if` statement to determine which number is larger and return the value of that number. In order for a value-returning method to return a result, a return statement using the keyword `return` is *required.* The method terminates when a return statement is executed.

Note
Some programming languages refer to methods as *procedures* and *functions.* In those languages, a value-returning method is called a *function* and a void method is called a *procedure.*

Caution
In the method header, you need to declare each parameter separately. For instance, `max(int num1, int num2)` is correct, but `max(int num1, num2)` is wrong.

define vs. declare

 Note
We say "*define* a method" and "*declare* a variable." We are making a subtle distinction here. A definition defines what the defined item is, but a declaration usually involves allocating memory to store data for the declared item.

6.3 Calling a Method

Calling a method executes the code in the method.

caller

In a method definition, you define what the method is to do. To execute the method, you have to *call* or *invoke* it. The program that calls the function is called a *caller*. There are two ways to call a method, depending on whether the method returns a value or not.

If a method returns a value, a call to the method is usually treated as a value. For example,

```java
int larger = max(3, 4);
```

calls `max(3, 4)` and assigns the result of the method to the variable `larger`. Another example of a call that is treated as a value is

```java
System.out.println(max(3, 4));
```

which prints the return value of the method call `max(3, 4)`.

If a method returns `void`, a call to the method must be a statement. For example, the method `println` returns `void`. The following call is a statement:

```java
System.out.println("Welcome to Java!");
```

 Note
A value-returning method can also be invoked as a statement in Java. In this case, the caller simply ignores the return value. This is not often done, but it is permissible if the caller is not interested in the return value.

When a program calls a method, program control is transferred to the called method. A called method returns control to the caller when its return statement is executed or when its method-ending closing brace is reached.

Listing 6.1 presents a complete program that is used to test the `max` method.

VideoNote

Define/invoke `max` method

LISTING 6.1 TestMax.java

main method

invoke max

define method

```java
 1  public class TestMax {
 2    /** Main method */
 3    public static void main(String[] args) {
 4      int i = 5;
 5      int j = 2;
 6      int k = max(i, j);
 7      System.out.println("The maximum of " + i +
 8        " and " + j + " is " + k);
 9    }
10
11    /** Return the max of two numbers */
12    public static int max(int num1, int num2) {
13      int result;
14
15      if (num1 > num2)
16        result = num1;
17      else
18        result = num2;
19
20      return result;
21    }
22  }
```

```
The maximum of 5 and 2 is 5
```

	line#	i	j	k	num1	num2	result
	4	5					
	5		2				
Invoking max	12				5	2	
	13						undefined
	16						5
	6			5			

main method

This program contains the `main` method and the `max` method. The `main` method is just like any other method, except that it is invoked by the JVM to start the program.

The `main` method's header is always the same. Like the one in this example, it includes the modifiers `public` and `static`, return value type `void`, method name `main`, and a parameter of the `String[]` type. `String[]` indicates the parameter is an array of `String`, a subject addressed in Chapter 7.

The statements in `main` may invoke other methods that are defined in the class that contains the `main` method or in other classes. In this example, the `main` method invokes `max(i, j)`, which is defined in the same class with the `main` method.

max method

When the `max` method is invoked (line 6), variable `i`'s value 5 is passed to `num1` and variable `j`'s value 2 is passed to `num2` in the `max` method. The flow of control transfers to the `max` method and the `max` method is executed. When the `return` statement in the `max` method is executed, the `max` method returns the control to its caller (in this case, the caller is the `main` method). This process is illustrated in Figure 6.2.

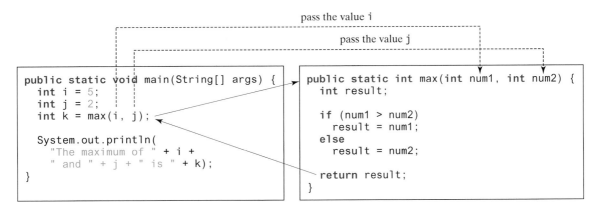

```
pass the value i
pass the value j

public static void main(String[] args) {          public static int max(int num1, int num2) {
  int i = 5;                                          int result;
  int j = 2;
  int k = max(i, j);                                  if (num1 > num2)
                                                        result = num1;
  System.out.println(                               else
    "The maximum of " + i +                           result = num2;
    " and " + j + " is " + k);
}                                                     return result;
                                                  }
```

FIGURE 6.2 When the `max` method is invoked, the flow of control transfers to it. Once the `max` method is finished, it returns control back to the caller.

Caution

A `return` statement is required for a value-returning method. The method given in (a) is logically correct, but it has a compile error because the Java compiler thinks this method might not return a value.

```
public static int sign(int n) {
  if (n > 0)
    return 1;
  else if (n == 0)
    return 0;
  else if (n < 0)
    return -1;
}
```

Should be →

```
public static int sign(int n) {
  if (n > 0)
    return 1;
  else if (n == 0)
    return 0;
  else
    return -1;
}
```

(a)   (b)

To fix this problem, delete `if (n < 0)` in (a), so the compiler will see a `return` statement to be reached regardless of how the `if` statement is evaluated.

reusing method

Note

Methods enable code sharing and reuse. The `max` method can be invoked from any class, not just `TestMax`. If you create a new class, you can invoke the `max` method using `ClassName.methodName` (i.e., `TestMax.max`).

activation record

call stack

Each time a method is invoked, the system creates an *activation record* (also called an *activation frame*) that stores parameters and variables for the method and places the activation record in an area of memory known as a *call stack*. A call stack is also known as an *execution stack*, *runtime stack*, or *machine stack* and it is often shortened to just "the stack." When a method calls another method, the caller's activation record is kept intact and a new activation record is created for the new method called. When a method finishes its work and returns to its caller, its activation record is removed from the call stack.

A call stack stores the activation records in a last-in, first-out fashion: The activation record for the method that is invoked last is removed first from the stack. For example, suppose method `m1` calls method `m2`, and `m2` calls method `m3`. The runtime system pushes `m1`'s activation record into the stack, then `m2`'s, and then `m3`'s. After `m3` is finished, its activation record is removed from the stack. After `m2` is finished, its activation record is removed from the stack. After `m1` is finished, its activation record is removed from the stack.

Understanding call stacks helps you to comprehend how methods are invoked. The variables defined in the `main` method in Listing 6.1 are `i`, `j`, and `k`. The variables defined in the `max` method are `num1`, `num2`, and `result`. The variables `num1` and `num2` are defined in the method signature and are parameters of the `max` method. Their values are passed through method invocation. Figure 6.3 illustrates the activation records for method calls in the stack.

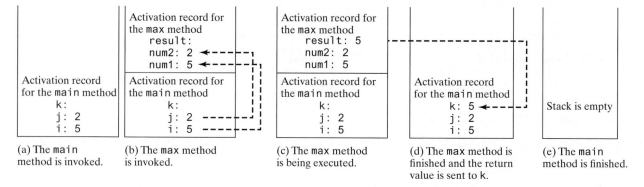

(a) The `main` method is invoked.

(b) The `max` method is invoked.

(c) The `max` method is being executed.

(d) The `max` method is finished and the return value is sent to k.

(e) The `main` method is finished.

FIGURE 6.3 When the `max` method is invoked, the flow of control transfers to the `max` method. Once the `max` method is finished, it returns control back to the caller.

6.4 `void` vs. Value-Returning Methods

A void *method does not return a value.*

The preceding section gives an example of a value-returning method. This section shows how to define and invoke a void method. Listing 6.2 gives a program that defines a method named printGrade and invokes it to print the grade for a given score.

Key Point

VideoNote
Use void method

LISTING 6.2 `TestVoidMethod.java`

```
1  public class TestVoidMethod {
2    public static void main(String[] args) {
3      System.out.print("The grade is ");
4      printGrade(78.5);
5
6      System.out.print("The grade is ");
7      printGrade(59.5);
8    }
9
10   public static void printGrade(double score) {
11     if (score >= 90.0) {
12       System.out.println('A');
13     }
14     else if (score >= 80.0) {
15       System.out.println('B');
16     }
17     else if (score >= 70.0) {
18       System.out.println('C');
19     }
20     else if (score >= 60.0) {
21       System.out.println('D');
22     }
23     else {
24       System.out.println('F');
25     }
26   }
27 }
```

main method

invoke printGrade

printGrade method

```
The grade is C
The grade is F
```

The printGrade method is a void method because it does not return any value. A call to a void method must be a statement. Therefore, it is invoked as a statement in line 4 in the main method. Like any Java statement, it is terminated with a semicolon.

invoke void method

To see the differences between a void and value-returning method, let's redesign the printGrade method to return a value. The new method, which we call getGrade, returns the grade as given in Listing 6.3.

void vs. value-returned

LISTING 6.3 `TestReturnGradeMethod.java`

```
1  public class TestReturnGradeMethod {
2    public static void main(String[] args) {
3      System.out.print("The grade is " + getGrade(78.5));
4      System.out.print("\nThe grade is " + getGrade(59.5));
5    }
6
```

main method

invoke getGrade

getGrade method

```
7   public static char getGrade(double score) {
8     if (score >= 90.0)
9       return 'A';
10    else if (score >= 80.0)
11      return 'B';
12    else if (score >= 70.0)
13      return 'C';
14    else if (score >= 60.0)
15      return 'D';
16    else
17      return 'F';
18   }
19 }
```

```
The grade is C
The grade is F
```

The getGrade method defined in lines 7–18 returns a character grade based on the numeric score value. The caller invokes this method in lines 3 and 4.

The getGrade method can be invoked by a caller wherever a character may appear. The printGrade method does not return any value, so it must be invoked as a statement.

return in void method

Note

A return statement is not needed for a void method, but it can be used for terminating the method and returning to the method's caller. The syntax is simply

```
return;
```

This is not often done, but sometimes it is useful for circumventing the normal flow of control in a void method. For example, the following code has a return statement to terminate the method when the score is invalid:

```
public static void printGrade(double score) {
  if (score < 0 || score > 100) {
    System.out.println("Invalid score");
    return;
  }

  if (score >= 90.0) {
    System.out.println('A');
  }
  else if (score >= 80.0) {
    System.out.println('B');
  }
  else if (score >= 70.0) {
    System.out.println('C');
  }
  else if (score >= 60.0) {
    System.out.println('D');
  }
  else {
    System.out.println('F');
  }
}
```

6.4.1   What are the benefits of using a method?

6.4.2   How do you define a method? How do you invoke a method?

6.4.3   How do you simplify the `max` method in Listing 6.1 using the conditional operator?

6.4.4   True or false? A call to a method with a `void` return type is always a statement itself, but a call to a value-returning method cannot be a statement by itself.

6.4.5   What is the `return` type of a `main` method?

6.4.6   What would be wrong with not writing a `return` statement in a value-returning method? Can you have a `return` statement in a `void` method? Does the `return` statement in the following method cause syntax errors?

```
public static void xMethod(double x, double y) {
  System.out.println(x + y);
  return x + y;
}
```

6.4.7   Define the terms parameter, argument, and method signature.

6.4.8   Write method headers (not the bodies) for the following methods:

    a. Return a sales commission, given the sales amount and the commission rate.

    b. Display the calendar for a month, given the month and year.

    c. Return a square root of a number.

    d. Test whether a number is even, and returning `true` if it is.

    e. Display a message a specified number of times.

    f. Return the monthly payment, given the loan amount, number of years, and annual interest rate.

    g. Return the corresponding uppercase letter, given a lowercase letter.

6.4.9   Identify and correct the errors in the following program:

```
 1  public class Test {
 2    public static method1(int n, m) {
 3      n += m;
 4      method2(3.4);
 5    }
 6
 7    public static int method2(int n) {
 8      if (n > 0) return 1;
 9      else if (n == 0) return 0;
10      else if (n < 0) return -1;
11    }
12  }
```

6.4.10   Reformat the following program according to the programming style and documentation guidelines proposed in Section 1.9, Programming Style and Documentation. Use the next-line brace style.

```
public class Test {
  public static double method(double i, double j)
  {
  while (i < j) {
    j--;
  }

  return j;
  }
}
```

6.5 Passing Parameters by Values

Key Point

The arguments are passed by value to parameters when invoking a method.

The power of a method is its ability to work with parameters. You can use `println` to print any string, and `max` to find the maximum of any two `int` values. When calling a method, you need to provide arguments, which must be given in the same order as their respective parameters in the method signature. This is known as *parameter order association*. For example, the following method prints a message n times:

parameter order association

```
public static void nPrintln(String message, int n) {
  for (int i = 0; i < n; i++)
    System.out.println(message);
}
```

You can use `nPrintln("Hello", 3)` to print `Hello` three times. The `nPrintln("Hello", 3)` statement passes the actual string parameter `Hello` to the parameter `message`, passes `3` to n, and prints `Hello` three times. However, the statement `nPrintln(3, "Hello")` would be wrong. The data type of `3` does not match the data type for the first parameter, `message`, nor does the second argument, `Hello`, match the second parameter, n.

> ⚠ **Caution**
>
> The arguments must match the parameters in *order, number,* and *compatible type,* as defined in the method signature. Compatible type means you can pass an argument to a parameter without explicit casting, such as passing an `int` value argument to a `double` value parameter.

pass-by-value

When you invoke a method with an argument, the value of the argument is passed to the parameter. This is referred to as *pass-by-value*. If the argument is a variable rather than a literal value, the value of the variable is passed to the parameter. The variable is not affected, regardless of the changes made to the parameter inside the method. As given in Listing 6.4, the value of x (1) is passed to the parameter n to invoke the `increment` method (line 5). The parameter n is incremented by 1 in the method (line 10), but x is not changed no matter what the method does.

LISTING 6.4 Increment.java

```
 1  public class Increment {
 2    public static void main(String[] args) {
 3      int x = 1;
 4      System.out.println("Before the call, x is " + x);
 5      increment(x);
 6      System.out.println("After the call, x is " + x);
 7    }
 8
 9    public static void increment(int n) {
10      n++;
11      System.out.println("n inside the method is " + n);
12    }
13  }
```

invoke increment

increment n

```
Before the call, x is 1
n inside the method is 2
After the call, x is 1
```

Listing 6.5 gives another program that demonstrates the effect of passing by value. The program creates a method for swapping two variables. The swap method is invoked by passing two arguments. Interestingly, the values of the arguments are not changed after the method is invoked.

LISTING 6.5 TestPassByValue.java

```java
 1  public class TestPassByValue {
 2    /** Main method */
 3    public static void main(String[] args) {
 4      // Declare and initialize variables
 5      int num1 = 1;
 6      int num2 = 2;
 7
 8      System.out.println("Before invoking the swap method, num1 is " +
 9        num1 + " and num2 is " + num2);
10
11      // Invoke the swap method to attempt to swap two variables
12      swap(num1, num2);                                              false swap
13
14      System.out.println("After invoking the swap method, num1 is " +
15        num1 + " and num2 is " + num2);
16    }
17
18    /** Swap two variables */
19    public static void swap(int n1, int n2) {
20      System.out.println("\tInside the swap method");
21      System.out.println("\t\tBefore swapping, n1 is " + n1
22        + " and n2 is " + n2);
23
24      // Swap n1 with n2
25      int temp = n1;
26      n1 = n2;
27      n2 = temp;
28
29      System.out.println("\t\tAfter swapping, n1 is " + n1
30        + " and n2 is " + n2);
31    }
32  }
```

```
Before invoking the swap method, num1 is 1 and num2 is 2
  Inside the swap method
    Before swapping, n1 is 1 and n2 is 2
    After swapping, n1 is 2 and n2 is 1
After invoking the swap method, num1 is 1 and num2 is 2
```

Before the swap method is invoked (line 12), num1 is 1 and num2 is 2. After the swap method is invoked, num1 is still 1 and num2 is still 2. Their values have not been swapped. As shown in Figure 6.4, the values of the arguments num1 and num2 are passed to n1 and n2, but n1 and n2 have their own memory locations independent of num1 and num2. Therefore, changes in n1 and n2 do not affect the contents of num1 and num2.

Another twist is to change the parameter name n1 in swap to num1. What effect does this have? No change occurs, because it makes no difference whether the parameter and the argument have the same name. The parameter is a variable in the method with its own memory space. The variable is allocated when the method is invoked, and it disappears when the method is returned to its caller.

The values of num1 and num2 are
passed to n1 and n2.

The values for n1 and n2 are
swapped, but it does not affect
num1 and num2.

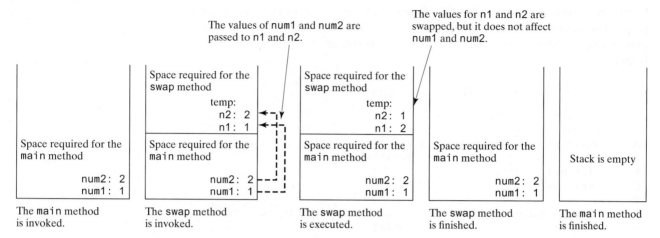

FIGURE 6.4 The values of the variables are passed to the method's parameters.

Note

For simplicity, Java programmers often say *passing* x to y, which actually means *passing the value of argument* x *to parameter* y.

6.5.1 How is an argument passed to a method? Can the argument have the same name as its parameter?

6.5.2 Identify and correct the errors in the following program:

```
1  public class Test {
2    public static void main(String[] args) {
3      nPrintln(5, "Welcome to Java!");
4    }
5
6    public static void nPrintln(String message, int n) {
7      int n = 1;
8      for (int i = 0; i < n; i++)
9        System.out.println(message);
10   }
11 }
```

6.5.3 What is pass-by-value? Show the result of the following programs.

```
public class Test {
  public static void main(String[] args) {
    int max = 0;
    max(1, 2, max);
    System.out.println(max);
  }

  public static void max(
      int value1, int value2, int max) {
    if (value1 > value2)
      max = value1;
    else
      max = value2;
  }
}
```

(a)

```
public class Test {
  public static void main(String[] args) {
    int i = 1;
    while (i <= 6) {
      method1(i, 2);
      i++;
    }
  }

  public static void method1(
      int i, int num) {
    for (int j = 1; j <= i; j++) {
      System.out.print(num + " ");
      num *= 2;
    }

    System.out.println();
  }
}
```

(b)

```
public class Test {
  public static void main(String[] args) {
    // Initialize times
    int times = 3;
    System.out.println("Before the call,"
      + " variable times is " + times);

    // Invoke nPrintln and display times
    nPrintln("Welcome to Java!", times);
    System.out.println("After the call,"
      + " variable times is " + times);
  }

  // Print the message n times
  public static void nPrintln(
      String message, int n) {
    while (n > 0) {
      System.out.println("n = " + n);
      System.out.println(message);
      n--;
    }
  }
}
```

(c)

```
public class Test {
  public static void main(String[] args) {
    int i = 0;
    while (i <= 4) {
      method1(i);
      i++;
    }

    System.out.println("i is " + i);
  }

  public static void method1(int i) {
    do {
      if (i % 3 != 0)
        System.out.print(i + " ");
      i--;
    }
    while (i >= 1);

    System.out.println();
  }
}
```

(d)

6.5.4 For (a) in the preceding question, show the contents of the activation records in the call stack just before the method `max` is invoked, just as `max` is entered, just before `max` is returned, and right after `max` is returned.

6.6 Modularizing Code

Modularizing makes the code easy to maintain and debug and enables the code to be reused.

Methods can be used to reduce redundant code and enable code reuse. Methods can also be used to modularize code and improve the quality of the program.

Listing 5.9 gives a program that prompts the user to enter two integers and displays their greatest common divisor. You can rewrite the program using a method, as given in Listing 6.6.

VideoNote

Modularize code

LISTING 6.6 GreatestCommonDivisorMethod.java

```
1  import java.util.Scanner;
2
3  public class GreatestCommonDivisorMethod {
4    /** Main method */
5    public static void main(String[] args) {
6      // Create a Scanner
7      Scanner input = new Scanner(System.in);
8
9      // Prompt the user to enter two integers
10     System.out.print("Enter first integer: ");
11     int n1 = input.nextInt();
12     System.out.print("Enter second integer: ");
13     int n2 = input.nextInt();
14
```

Key Point

invoke gcd

```
15      System.out.println("The greatest common divisor for " + n1 +
16        " and " + n2 + " is " + gcd(n1, n2));
17    }
18
19    /** Return the gcd of two integers */
```

compute gcd

```
20    public static int gcd(int n1,int n2) {
21      int gcd = 1; // Initial gcd is 1
22      int k = 2; // Possible gcd
23
24      while (k <= n1 && k <= n2) {
25        if (n1 % k == 0 && n2 % k == 0)
26          gcd = k; // Update gcd
27        k++;
28      }
29
```

return gcd

```
30      return gcd; // Return gcd
31    }
32  }
```

```
Enter first integer: 45  ↵Enter
Enter second integer: 75  ↵Enter
The greatest common divisor for 45 and 75 is 15
```

By encapsulating the code for obtaining the gcd in a method, this program has several advantages:

1. It isolates the problem for computing the gcd from the rest of the code in the main method. Thus, the logic becomes clear, and the program is easier to read.

2. The errors on computing the gcd are confined in the gcd method, which narrows the scope of debugging.

3. The gcd method now can be reused by other programs.

Listing 6.7 applies the concept of code modularization to improve Listing 5.15, Prime-Number.java.

LISTING 6.7 PrimeNumberMethod.java

```
1  public class PrimeNumberMethod {
2    public static void main(String[] args) {
3      System.out.println("The first 50 prime numbers are \n");
```

invoke printPrimeNumbers

```
4      printPrimeNumbers(50);
5    }
6
```

printPrimeNumbers method

```
7    public static void printPrimeNumbers(int numberOfPrimes) {
8      final int NUMBER_OF_PRIMES_PER_LINE = 10; // Display 10 per line
9      int count = 0; // Count the number of prime numbers
10     int number = 2; // A number to be tested for primeness
11
12     // Repeatedly find prime numbers
13     while (count < numberOfPrimes) {
14       // Print the prime number and increase the count
```

invoke isPrime

```
15       if (isPrime(number)) {
16         count++; // Increase the count
17
```

```
18              if (count % NUMBER_OF_PRIMES_PER_LINE == 0) {
19                  // Print the number and advance to the new line
20                  System.out.printf("%-5d\n", number);
21              }
22              else
23                  System.out.printf("%-5d", number);
24          }
25
26          // Check whether the next number is prime
27          number++;
28      }
29  }
30
31  /** Check whether number is prime */
32  public static boolean isPrime(int number) {                    isPrime method
33      for (int divisor = 2; divisor <= number / 2; divisor++) {
34          if (number % divisor == 0) { // If true, number is not prime
35              return false; // Number is not a prime
36          }
37      }
38
39      return true; // Number is prime
40  }
41 }
```

```
The first 50 prime numbers are

2    3    5    7    11   13   17   19   23   29
31   37   41   43   47   53   59   61   67   71
73   79   83   89   97   101  103  107  109  113
127  131  137  139  149  151  157  163  167  173
179  181  191  193  197  199  211  223  227  229
```

We divided a large problem into two subproblems: determining whether a number is a prime, and printing the prime numbers. As a result, the new program is easier to read and easier to debug. Moreover, the methods `printPrimeNumbers` and `isPrime` can be reused by other programs.

6.6.1 Trace the `gcd` method to find the return value for `gcd(4, 6)`.

6.6.2 Trace the `isPrime` method to find the return value for `isPrime(25)`.

6.7 Case Study: Converting Hexadecimals to Decimals

This section presents a program that converts a hexadecimal number into a decimal number.

Listing 5.11, Dec2Hex.java, gives a program that converts a decimal to a hexadecimal. How would you convert a hex number into a decimal?

Given a hexadecimal number $h_n h_{n-1} h_{n-2} \ldots h_2 h_1 h_0$, the equivalent decimal value is

$$h_n \times 16^n + h_{n-1} \times 16^{n-1} + h_{n-2} \times 16^{n-2} + \cdots + h_2 \times 16^2 + h_1 \times 16^1 + h_0 \times 16^0$$

For example, the hex number AB8C is

$$10 \times 16^3 + 11 \times 16^2 + 8 \times 16^1 + 12 \times 16^0 = 43916$$

Our program will prompt the user to enter a hex number as a string and convert it into a decimal using the following method:

```
public static int hexToDecimal(String hex)
```

A brute-force approach is to convert each hex character into a decimal number, multiply it by 16^i for a hex digit at the i's position, and then add all the items together to obtain the equivalent decimal value for the hex number.

Note that

$$h_n \times 16^n + h_{n-1} \times 16^{n-1} + h_{n-2} \times 16^{n-2} + \cdots + h_1 \times 16^1 + h_0 \times 16^0$$
$$= (\ldots ((h_n \times 16 + h_{n-1}) \times 16 + h_{n-2}) \times 16 + \cdots + h_1) \times 16 + h_0$$

This observation, known as the Horner's algorithm, leads to the following efficient code for converting a hex string to a decimal number:

```
int decimalValue = 0;
for (int i = 0; i < hex.length(); i++) {
  char hexChar = hex.charAt(i);
  decimalValue = decimalValue * 16 + hexCharToDecimal(hexChar);
}
```

Here is a trace of the algorithm for hex number AB8C:

	i	hexChar	hexCharToDecimal (hexChar)	decimalValue
Before the loop				0
After the 1st iteration	0	A	10	10
After the 2nd iteration	1	B	11	10 * 16 + 11
After the 3rd iteration	2	8	8	(10 * 16 + 11) * 16 + 8
After the 4th iteration	3	C	12	((10 * 16 + 11) * 16 + 8) * 16 + 12

Listing 6.8 gives the complete program.

LISTING 6.8 Hex2Dec.java

```
1  import java.util.Scanner;
2
3  public class Hex2Dec {
4    /** Main method */
5    public static void main(String[] args) {
6      // Create a Scanner
7      Scanner input = new Scanner(System.in);
8
9      // Prompt the user to enter a string
10     System.out.print("Enter a hex number: ");
11     String hex = input.nextLine();
12
13     System.out.println("The decimal value for hex number "
14       + hex + " is " + hexToDecimal(hex.toUpperCase()));
15   }
16
17   public static int hexToDecimal(String hex) {
18     int decimalValue = 0;
19     for (int i = 0; i < hex.length(); i++) {
20       char hexChar = hex.charAt(i);
21       decimalValue = decimalValue * 16 + hexCharToDecimal(hexChar);
```

input string

hex to decimal

```
22      }
23
24      return decimalValue;
25    }
26
27    public static int hexCharToDecimal(char ch) {
28      if (ch >= 'A' && ch <= 'F')
29        return 10 + ch - 'A';
30      else // ch is '0', '1', ..., or '9'
31        return ch - '0';
32    }
33  }
```

hex char to decimal
check uppercase

```
Enter a hex number: AB8C  ↵Enter
The decimal value for hex number AB8C is 43916
```

```
Enter a hex number: af71  ↵Enter
The decimal value for hex number af71 is 44913
```

The program reads a string from the console (line 11) and invokes the hexToDecimal method to convert a hex string to decimal number (line 14). The characters can be in either lowercase or uppercase. They are converted to uppercase before invoking the hexToDecimal method.

The hexToDecimal method is defined in lines 17–25 to return an integer. The length of the string is determined by invoking hex.length() in line 19.

The hexCharToDecimal method is defined in lines 27–32 to return a decimal value for a hex character. The character can be in either lowercase or uppercase. Recall that to subtract two characters is to subtract their Unicodes. For example, '5' - '0' is 5.

6.7.1 What is hexCharToDecimal('B')?
       What is hexCharToDecimal('7')?
       What is hexToDecimal("A9")?

Check
Point

6.8 Overloading Methods

Overloading methods enable you to define the methods with the same name as long as their parameter lists are different.

Key
Point

The max method used earlier works only with the int data type. But what if you need to determine which of the two floating-point numbers has the maximum value? The solution is to create another method with the same name but different parameters, as shown in the following code:

```
public static double max(double num1, double num2) {
  if (num1 > num2)
    return num1;
  else
    return num2;
}
```

If you call max with int parameters, the max method that expects int parameters will be invoked; and if you call max with double parameters, the max method that expects double parameters will be invoked. This is referred to as *method overloading*; that is, two methods have the same name but different parameter lists within one class. The Java compiler determines which method to use based on the method signature.

method overloading

Listing 6.9 is a program that creates three methods. The first finds the maximum integer, the second finds the maximum double, and the third finds the maximum among three double values. All three methods are named `max`.

LISTING 6.9 TestMethodOverloading.java

```
1   public class TestMethodOverloading {
2     /** Main method */
3     public static void main(String[] args) {
4       // Invoke the max method with int parameters
5       System.out.println("The maximum of 3 and 4 is "
6         + max(3, 4));
7
8       // Invoke the max method with the double parameters
9       System.out.println("The maximum of 3.0 and 5.4 is "
10        + max(3.0, 5.4));
11
12      // Invoke the max method with three double parameters
13      System.out.println("The maximum of 3.0, 5.4, and 10.14 is "
14        + max(3.0, 5.4, 10.14));
15    }
16
17    /** Return the max of two int values */
```

overloaded max

```
18    public static int max(int num1, int num2) {
19      if (num1 > num2)
20        return num1;
21      else
22        return num2;
23    }
24
25    /** Find the max of two double values */
```

overloaded max

```
26    public static double max(double num1, double num2) {
27      if (num1 > num2)
28        return num1;
29      else
30        return num2;
31    }
32
33    /** Return the max of three double values */
```

overloaded max

```
34    public static double max(double num1, double num2, double num3) {
35      return max(max(num1, num2), num3);
36    }
37  }
```

```
The maximum of 3 and 4 is 4
The maximum of 3.0 and 5.4 is 5.4
The maximum of 3.0, 5.4, and 10.14 is 10.14
```

When calling `max(3, 4)` (line 6), the `max` method for finding the maximum of two integers is invoked. When calling `max(3.0, 5.4)` (line 10), the `max` method for finding the maximum of two doubles is invoked. When calling `max(3.0, 5.4, 10.14)` (line 14), the `max` method for finding the maximum of three double values is invoked.

Can you invoke the `max` method with an `int` value and a `double` value, such as `max(2, 2.5)`? If so, which of the `max` methods is invoked? The answer to the first question is yes. The answer to the second question is that the `max` method for finding the maximum of two `double` values is invoked. The argument value `2` is automatically converted into a `double` value and passed to this method.

You may be wondering why the method `max(double, double)` is not invoked for the call `max(3, 4)`. Both `max(double, double)` and `max(int, int)` are possible matches for `max(3, 4)`. The Java compiler finds the method that best matches a method invocation. Since the method `max(int, int)` is a better match for `max(3, 4)` than `max(double, double)`, `max(int, int)` is used to invoke `max(3, 4)`.

Tip
Overloading methods can make programs clearer and more readable. Methods that perform the same function with different types of parameters should be given the same name.

Note
Overloaded methods must have different parameter lists. You cannot overload methods based on different modifiers or return types.

Note
Sometimes there are two or more possible matches for the invocation of a method, but the compiler cannot determine the most specific match. This is referred to as *ambiguous invocation*. Ambiguous invocation causes a compile error. Consider the following code:

ambiguous invocation

```java
public class AmbiguousOverloading {
  public static void main(String[] args) {
    System.out.println(max(1, 2));
  }

  public static double max(int num1, double num2) {
    if (num1 > num2)
      return num1;
    else
      return num2;
  }

  public static double max(double num1, int num2) {
    if (num1 > num2)
      return num1;
    else
      return num2;
  }
}
```

Both `max(int, double)` and `max(double, int)` are possible candidates to match `max(1, 2)`. Because neither is more specific than the other, the invocation is ambiguous, resulting in a compile error.

6.8.1 What is method overloading? Is it permissible to define two methods that have the same name but different parameter types? Is it permissible to define two methods in a class that have identical method names and parameter lists, but different return value types or different modifiers?

Check Point

6.8.2 What is wrong in the following program?

```java
public class Test {
  public static void method(int x) {
  }

  public static int method(int y) {
```

```
                return y;
        }
    }
```

6.8.3 Given two method definitions,

```
public static double m(double x, double y)

public static double m(int x, double y)
```

tell which of the two methods is invoked for:

a. **double** z = m(4, 5);

b. **double** z = m(4, 5.4);

c. **double** z = m(4.5, 5.4);

6.9 The Scope of Variables

Key
Point

The scope of a variable is the part of the program where the variable can be referenced.

scope of variables
local variable

Section 2.5 introduced the scope of a variable. This section discusses the scope of variables in detail. A variable defined inside a method is referred to as a *local variable*. The scope of a local variable starts from its declaration and continues to the end of the block that contains the variable. A local variable must be declared and assigned a value before it can be used.

A parameter is actually a local variable. The scope of a method parameter covers the entire method. A variable declared in the initial-action part of a `for`-loop header has its scope in the entire loop. However, a variable declared inside a `for`-loop body has its scope limited in the loop body from its declaration to the end of the block that contains the variable, as shown in Figure 6.5.

```
                              public static void method1() {
                                  .
                                  .
                              for (int i = 1; i < 10; i++) {
                                  .
    The scope of i ─────────→      .
                                   int j;
                                  .
    The scope of j ─────────→      .
                                  .
                                  }
                              }
```

FIGURE 6.5 A variable declared in the initial-action part of a `for`-loop header has its scope in the entire loop.

You can declare a local variable with the same name in different blocks in a method, but you cannot declare a local variable twice in the same block or in nested blocks, as shown in Figure 6.6.

It is fine to declare i in two
nonnested blocks.

```
public static void method1() {
   int x = 1;
   int y = 1;

   for (int i = 1; i < 10; i++) {
     x += i;
   }

   for (int i = 1; i < 10; i++) {
     y += i;
   }
}
```

It is wrong to declare i in two
nested blocks.

```
public static void method2() {

   int i = 1;
   int sum = 0;

   for (int i = 1; i < 10; i++) {
     sum += i;
   }

}
```

FIGURE 6.6 A variable can be declared multiple times in nonnested blocks, but only once in nested blocks.

 Caution

A common mistake is to declare a variable in a `for` loop and then attempt to use it outside the loop. As shown in the following code, `i` is declared in the `for` loop, but it is accessed from the outside of the `for` loop, which causes a syntax error.

```
for (int i = 0; i < 10; i++) {
}
System.out.println(i); // Causes a syntax error on i
```

The last statement would cause a syntax error, because variable `i` is not defined outside of the `for` loop.

6.9.1 What is a local variable?

6.9.2 What is the scope of a local variable?

6.10 Case Study: Generating Random Characters

A character is coded using an integer. Generating a random character is to generate an integer.

Computer programs process numerical data and characters. You have seen many examples that involve numerical data. It is also important to understand characters and how to process them. This section presents an example of generating random characters.

As introduced in Section 4.3, every character has a unique Unicode between 0 and FFFF in hexadecimal (65535 in decimal). To generate a random character is to generate a random integer between 0 and 65535 using the following expression (note since 0 <= Math .random() < 1.0, you have to add 1 to 65535):

```
(int)(Math.random() * (65535 + 1))
```

Now let's consider how to generate a random lowercase letter. The Unicodes for lowercase letters are consecutive integers starting from the Unicode for a, then for b, c, . . . , and z. The Unicode for a is

```
(int)'a'
```

Thus, a random integer between `(int)'a'` and `(int)'z'` is

```
(int)((int)'a' + Math.random() * ((int)'z' - (int)'a' + 1))
```

As discussed in Section 4.3.3, all numeric operators can be applied to the `char` operands. The `char` operand is cast into a number if the other operand is a number or a character. Therefore, the preceding expression can be simplified as follows:

```
'a' + Math.random() * ('z' - 'a' + 1)
```

and a random lowercase letter is

```
(char)('a' + Math.random() * ('z' - 'a' + 1))
```

Hence, a random character between any two characters `ch1` and `ch2` with `ch1 < ch2` can be generated as follows:

```
(char)(ch1 + Math.random() * (ch2 - ch1 + 1))
```

This is a simple but useful discovery. Listing 6.10 defines a class named `RandomCharacter` with overloaded methods to get a certain type of random character. You can use these methods in your future projects.

LISTING 6.10 RandomCharacter.java

getRandomCharacter

getRandomLower
  CaseLetter()

getRandomUpper
  CaseLetter()

getRandomDigit
  Character()

getRandomCharacter()

```java
 1  public class RandomCharacter {
 2    /** Generate a random character between ch1 and ch2 */
 3    public static char getRandomCharacter(char ch1, char ch2) {
 4      return (char)(ch1 + Math.random() * (ch2 - ch1 + 1));
 5    }
 6
 7    /** Generate a random lowercase letter */
 8    public static char getRandomLowerCaseLetter() {
 9      return getRandomCharacter('a', 'z');
10    }
11
12    /** Generate a random uppercase letter */
13    public static char getRandomUpperCaseLetter() {
14      return getRandomCharacter('A', 'Z');
15    }
16
17    /** Generate a random digit character */
18    public static char getRandomDigitCharacter() {
19      return getRandomCharacter('0', '9');
20    }
21
22    /** Generate a random character */
23    public static char getRandomCharacter() {
24      return getRandomCharacter('\u0000', '\uFFFF');
25    }
26  }
```

Listing 6.11 gives a test program that displays 175 random lowercase letters.

LISTING 6.11 TestRandomCharacter.java

constants

lowercase letter

```java
 1  public class TestRandomCharacter {
 2    /** Main method */
 3    public static void main(String[] args) {
 4      final int NUMBER_OF_CHARS = 175;
 5      final int CHARS_PER_LINE = 25;
 6
 7      // Print random characters between 'a' and 'z', 25 chars per line
 8      for (int i = 0; i < NUMBER_OF_CHARS; i++) {
 9        char ch = RandomCharacter.getRandomLowerCaseLetter();
10        if ((i + 1) % CHARS_PER_LINE == 0)
11          System.out.println(ch);
```

```
12          else
13              System.out.print(ch);
14          }
15      }
16  }
```

```
gmjsohezfkgtazqgmswfclrao
pnrunulnwmaztlfjedmpchcif
lalqdgivxkxpbzulrmqmbhikr
lbnrjlsopfxahssqhwuuljvbe
xbhdotzhpehbqmuwsfktwsoli
cbuwkzgxpmtzihgatdslvbwbz
bfesoklwbhnooygiigzdxuqni
```

Line 9 invokes `getRandomLowerCaseLetter()` defined in the `RandomCharacter` class. Note `getRandomLowerCaseLetter()` does not have any parameters, but you still have to use the parentheses when defining and invoking the method.

parentheses required

6.11 Method Abstraction and Stepwise Refinement

The key to developing software is to apply the concept of abstraction.

Key Point

VideoNote

Stepwise refinement

method abstraction

information hiding

You will learn many levels of abstraction from this book. *Method abstraction* is achieved by separating the use of a method from its implementation. The client can use a method without knowing how it is implemented. The details of the implementation are encapsulated in the method and hidden from the client who invokes the method. This is also known as *information hiding* or *encapsulation*. If you decide to change the implementation, the client program will not be affected, provided that you do not change the method signature. The implementation of the method is hidden from the client in a "black box," as shown in Figure 6.7.

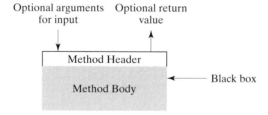

FIGURE 6.7 The method body can be thought of as a black box that contains the detailed implementation for the method.

You have already used the `System.out.print` method to display a string and the `max` method to find the maximum number. You know how to write the code to invoke these methods in your program, but as a user of these methods, you are not required to know how they are implemented.

The concept of method abstraction can be applied to the process of developing programs. When writing a large program, you can use the *divide-and-conquer* strategy, also known as *stepwise refinement*, to decompose it into subproblems. The subproblems can be further decomposed into smaller, more manageable problems.

divide and conquer

stepwise refinement

Suppose that you write a program that displays the calendar for a given month of the year. The program prompts the user to enter the year and the month, and then displays the entire calendar for the month, as presented in the following sample run:

```
Enter full year (e.g., 2012):  2012  ↵Enter
Enter month as number between 1 and 12:  3  ↵Enter

         March 2012
-----------------------------
 Sun Mon Tue Wed Thu Fri Sat
                   1   2   3
  4   5   6   7   8   9  10
 11  12  13  14  15  16  17
 18  19  20  21  22  23  24
 25  26  27  28  29  30
```

Let us use this example to demonstrate the divide-and-conquer approach.

6.11.1 Top-Down Design

How would you get started on such a program? Would you immediately start coding? Beginning programmers often start by trying to work out the solution to every detail. Although details are important in the final program, concern for detail in the early stages may block the problem-solving process. To make problem solving flow as smoothly as possible, this example begins by using method abstraction to isolate details from design and only later implements the details.

For this example, the problem is first broken into two subproblems: get input from the user, and print the calendar for the month. At this stage, you should be concerned with what the subproblems will achieve, not with how to get input and print the calendar for the month. You can draw a structure chart to help visualize the decomposition of the problem (see Figure 6.8a).

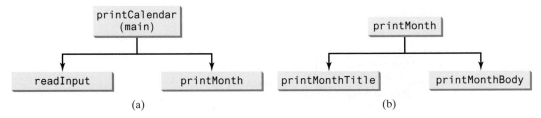

(a)   (b)

FIGURE 6.8 The structure chart shows the `printCalendar` problem is divided into two subproblems, `readInput` and `printMonth` in (a), and `printMonth` is divided into two smaller subproblems, `printMonthTitle` and `printMonthBody` in (b).

You can use Scanner to read input for the year and the month. The problem of printing the calendar for a given month can be broken into two subproblems: print the month title, and print the month body, as shown in Figure 6.8b. The month title consists of three lines: month and year, a dashed line, and the names of the seven days of the week. You need to get the month name (e.g., January) from the numeric month (e.g., 1). This is accomplished in getMonthName (see Figure 6.9a).

In order to print the month body, you need to know which day of the week is the first day of the month (getStartDay) and how many days the month has (getNumberOfDaysInMonth),

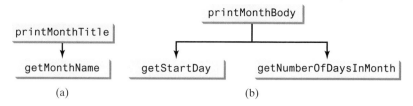

FIGURE 6.9 (a) To `printMonthTitle`, you need `getMonthName`. (b) The `printMonthBody` problem is refined into several smaller problems.

as shown in Figure 6.9b. For example, December 2013 has 31 days, and December 1, 2013 is a Sunday.

How would you get the start day for the first date in a month? There are several ways to do so. For now, we'll use an alternative approach. Assume you know that the start day for January 1, 1800 was a Wednesday (`START_DAY_FOR_JAN_1_1800 = 3`). You could compute the total number of days (`totalNumberOfDays`) between January 1, 1800 and the first date of the calendar month. The start day for the calendar month is (`totalNumberOfDays + START_DAY_FOR_JAN_1_1800) % 7`, since every week has seven days. Thus, the `getStartDay` problem can be further refined as `getTotalNumberOfDays`, as shown in Figure 6.10a.

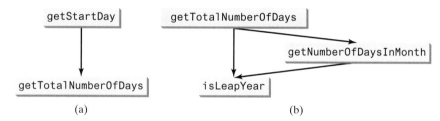

FIGURE 6.10 (a) To `getStartDay`, you need `getTotalNumberOfDays`. (b) The `getTotalNumberOfDays` problem is refined into two smaller problems.

To get the total number of days, you need to know whether the year is a leap year and the number of days in each month. Thus, `getTotalNumberOfDays` can be further refined into two subproblems: `isLeapYear` and `getNumberOfDaysInMonth`, as shown in Figure 6.10b. The complete structure chart is shown in Figure 6.11.

6.11.2 Top-Down and/or Bottom-Up Implementation

Now we turn our attention to implementation. In general, a subproblem corresponds to a method in the implementation, although some are so simple that this is unnecessary. You would need to decide which modules to implement as methods and which to combine with other methods. Decisions of this kind should be based on whether the overall program will be easier to read as a result of your choice. In this example, the subproblem `readInput` can be simply implemented in the `main` method.

You can use either a "top-down" or a "bottom-up" approach. The top-down approach implements one method in the structure chart at a time from the top to the bottom. *Stubs*—a simple but incomplete version of a method—can be used for the methods waiting to be implemented. The use of stubs enables you to quickly build the framework of the program. Implement the `main`

top-down approach

stub

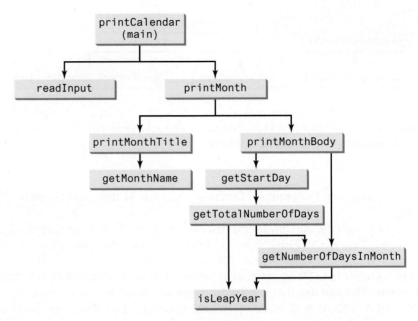

FIGURE 6.11 The structure chart shows the hierarchical relationship of the subproblems in the program.

method first then use a stub for the `printMonth` method. For example, let `printMonth` display the year and the month in the stub. Thus, your program may begin as follows:

```java
public class PrintCalendar {
  /** Main method */
  public static void main(String[] args) {
    Scanner input = new Scanner(System.in);

    // Prompt the user to enter year
    System.out.print("Enter full year (e.g., 2012): ");
    int year = input.nextInt();

    // Prompt the user to enter month
    System.out.print("Enter month as a number between 1 and 12: ");
    int month = input.nextInt();

    // Print calendar for the month of the year
    printMonth(year, month);
  }

  /** A stub for printMonth may look like this */
  public static void printMonth(int year, int month) {
    System.out.print(month + " " + year);
  }

  /** A stub for printMonthTitle may look like this */
  public static void printMonthTitle(int year, int month)  {
  }

  /** A stub for printMonthBody may look like this */
  public static void printMonthBody(int year, int month) {
  }
```

```
/** A stub for getMonthName may look like this */
public static String getMonthName(int month) {
  return "January"; // A dummy value
}

/** A stub for getStartDay may look like this */
public static int getStartDay(int year, int month) {
  return 1; // A dummy value
}

/** A stub for getTotalNumberOfDays may look like this */
public static int getTotalNumberOfDays(int year, int month) {
  return 10000; // A dummy value
}

/** A stub for getNumberOfDaysInMonth may look like this */
public static int getNumberOfDaysInMonth(int year, int month) {
  return 31; // A dummy value
}

/** A stub for isLeapYear may look like this */
public static boolean isLeapYear(int year) {
  return true; // A dummy value
}
}
```

Compile and test the program, and fix any errors. You can now implement the printMonth method. For methods invoked from the printMonth method, you can again use stubs.

The bottom-up approach implements one method in the structure chart at a time from the bottom to the top. For each method implemented, write a test program, known as the *driver*, to test it. The top-down and bottom-up approaches are equally good: Both approaches implement methods incrementally, help to isolate programming errors, and make debugging easy. They can be used together.

bottom-up approach

driver

6.11.3 Implementation Details

The isLeapYear(int year) method can be implemented using the following code from Section 3.11:

```
return year % 400 == 0 || (year % 4 == 0 && year % 100 != 0);
```

Use the following facts to implement getTotalNumberOfDaysInMonth(int year, int month):

- January, March, May, July, August, October, and December have 31 days.

- April, June, September, and November have 30 days.

- February has 28 days during a regular year, and 29 days during a leap year. A regular year, therefore, has 365 days, and a leap year has 366 days.

To implement getTotalNumberOfDays(int year, int month), you need to compute the total number of days (totalNumberOfDays) between January 1, 1800 and the first day of the calendar month. You could find the total number of days between the year 1800 and the calendar year then figure out the total number of days prior to the calendar month in the calendar year. The sum of these two totals is totalNumberOfDays.

To print a body, first pad some space before the start day then print the lines for every week.

The complete program is given in Listing 6.12.

LISTING 6.12 PrintCalendar.java

```
1   import java.util.Scanner;
2
3   public class PrintCalendar {
4     /** Main method */
5     public static void main(String[] args) {
6       Scanner input = new Scanner(System.in);
7
8       // Prompt the user to enter year
9       System.out.print("Enter full year (e.g., 2012): ");
10      int year = input.nextInt();
11
12      // Prompt the user to enter month
13      System.out.print("Enter month as a number between 1 and 12: ");
14      int month = input.nextInt();
15
16      // Print calendar for the month of the year
17      printMonth(year, month);
18    }
19
20    /** Print the calendar for a month in a year */
21    public static void printMonth(int year, int month) {
22      // Print the headings of the calendar
23      printMonthTitle(year, month);
24
25      // Print the body of the calendar
26      printMonthBody(year, month);
27    }
28
29    /** Print the month title, e.g., March 2012 */
30    public static void printMonthTitle(int year, int month) {
31      System.out.println("          " + getMonthName(month)
32        + " " + year);
33      System.out.println("-----------------------------");
34      System.out.println(" Sun Mon Tue Wed Thu Fri Sat");
35    }
36
37    /** Get the English name for the month */
38    public static String getMonthName(int month) {
39      String monthName = "";
40      switch (month) {
41        case 1: monthName = "January"; break;
42        case 2: monthName = "February"; break;
43        case 3: monthName = "March"; break;
44        case 4: monthName = "April"; break;
45        case 5: monthName = "May"; break;
46        case 6: monthName = "June"; break;
47        case 7: monthName = "July"; break;
48        case 8: monthName = "August"; break;
49        case 9: monthName = "September"; break;
50        case 10: monthName = "October"; break;
51        case 11: monthName = "November"; break;
52        case 12: monthName = "December";
53      }
54
55      return monthName;
56    }
57
58    /** Print month body */
```

printMonth (line 21)

printMonthTitle (line 30)

getMonthName (line 38)

```
59   public static void printMonthBody(int year, int month) {              printMonthBody
60     // Get start day of the week for the first date in the month
61     int startDay = getStartDay(year, month);
62
63     // Get number of days in the month
64     int numberOfDaysInMonth = getNumberOfDaysInMonth(year, month);
65
66     // Pad space before the first day of the month
67     int i = 0;
68     for (i = 0; i < startDay; i++)
69       System.out.print("    ");
70
71     for (i = 1; i <= numberOfDaysInMonth; i++) {
72       System.out.printf("%4d", i);
73
74       if ((i + startDay) % 7 == 0)
75         System.out.println();
76     }
77
78     System.out.println();
79   }
80
81   /** Get the start day of month/1/year */
82   public static int getStartDay(int year, int month) {                   getStartDay
83     final int START_DAY_FOR_JAN_1_1800 = 3;
84     // Get total number of days from 1/1/1800 to month/1/year
85     int totalNumberOfDays = getTotalNumberOfDays(year, month);
86
87     // Return the start day for month/1/year
88     return (totalNumberOfDays + START_DAY_FOR_JAN_1_1800) % 7;
89   }
90
91   /** Get the total number of days since January 1, 1800 */
92   public static int getTotalNumberOfDays(int year, int month) {          getTotalNumberOfDays
93     int total = 0;
94
95     // Get the total days from 1800 to 1/1/year
96     for (int i = 1800; i < year; i++)
97       if (isLeapYear(i))
98         total = total + 366;
99       else
100        total = total + 365;
101
102    // Add days from Jan to the month prior to the calendar month
103    for (int i = 1; i < month; i++)
104      total = total + getNumberOfDaysInMonth(year, i);
105
106    return total;
107  }
108
109  /** Get the number of days in a month */
110  public static int getNumberOfDaysInMonth(int year, int month) {        getNumberOfDaysInMonth
111    if (month == 1 || month == 3 || month == 5 || month == 7 ||
112      month == 8 || month == 10 || month == 12)
113      return 31;
114
115    if (month == 4 || month == 6 || month == 9 || month == 11)
116      return 30;
117
118    if (month == 2) return isLeapYear(year) ? 29 : 28;
```

```
119
120       return 0; // If month is incorrect
121   }
122
123   /** Determine if it is a leap year */
124   public static boolean isLeapYear(int year) {
125       return year % 400 == 0 || (year % 4 == 0 && year % 100 != 0);
126   }
127 }
```

isLeapYear

The program does not validate user input. For instance, if the user enters either a month not in the range between 1 and 12 or a year before 1800, the program displays an erroneous calendar. To avoid this error, add an if statement to check the input before printing the calendar.

This program prints calendars for a month, but could easily be modified to print calendars for a whole year. Although it can print months only after January 1800, it could be modified to print months before 1800.

6.11.4 Benefits of Stepwise Refinement

Stepwise refinement breaks a large problem into smaller manageable subproblems. Each subproblem can be implemented using a method. This approach makes the program easier to write, reuse, debug, test, modify, and maintain.

Simpler Program

The print calendar program is long. Rather than writing a long sequence of statements in one method, stepwise refinement breaks it into smaller methods. This simplifies the program and makes the whole program easier to read and understand.

Reusing Methods

Stepwise refinement promotes code reuse within a program. The isLeapYear method is defined once and invoked from the getTotalNumberOfDays and getNumberOfDaysInMonth methods. This reduces redundant code.

Easier Developing, Debugging, and Testing

Since each subproblem is solved in a method, a method can be developed, debugged, and tested individually. This isolates the errors and makes developing, debugging, and testing easier.

incremental development and testing

When implementing a large program, use the top-down and/or bottom-up approach. Do not write the entire program at once. Using these approaches seems to take more development time (because you repeatedly compile and run the program), but it actually saves time and makes debugging easier.

Better Facilitating Teamwork

When a large problem is divided into subprograms, subproblems can be assigned to different programmers. This makes it easier for programmers to work in teams.

KEY TERMS

actual parameter   207
ambiguous invocation   223
argument   207
divide and conquer   227
formal parameter (i.e., parameter)   207
information hiding   227
method   206
method abstraction   227

method overloading   221
method signature   207
modifier   207
parameter   207
pass-by-value   214
scope of a variable   224
stepwise refinement   227
stub   229

CHAPTER SUMMARY

1. Making programs modular and reusable is one of the central goals in software engineering. Java provides many powerful constructs that help to achieve this goal. *Methods* are one such construct.

2. The method header specifies the *modifiers, return value type, method name,* and *parameters* of the method. The `static` modifier is used for all the methods in this chapter.

3. A method may return a value. The `returnValueType` is the data type of the value the method returns. If the method does not return a value, the `returnValueType` is the keyword `void`.

4. The *parameter list* refers to the type, order, and number of a method's parameters. The method name and the parameter list together constitute the *method signature.* Parameters are optional; that is, a method doesn't need to contain any parameters.

5. A return statement can also be used in a `void` method for terminating the method and returning to the method's caller. This is useful occasionally for circumventing the normal flow of control in a method.

6. The arguments that are passed to a method should have the same number, type, and order as the parameters in the method signature.

7. When a program calls a method, program control is transferred to the called method. A called method returns control to the caller when its return statement is executed, or when its method-ending closing brace is reached.

8. A value-returning method can also be invoked as a statement in Java. In this case, the caller simply ignores the return value.

9. A method can be overloaded. This means that two methods can have the same name, as long as their method parameter lists differ.

10. A variable declared in a method is called a local variable. The *scope of a local variable* starts from its declaration and continues to the end of the block that contains the variable. A local variable must be declared and initialized before it is used.

11. *Method abstraction* is achieved by separating the use of a method from its implementation. The client can use a method without knowing how it is implemented. The details of the implementation are encapsulated in the method and hidden from the client who invokes the method. This is known as *information hiding* or *encapsulation.*

12. Method abstraction modularizes programs in a neat, hierarchical manner. Programs written as collections of concise methods are easier to write, debug, maintain, and modify than would otherwise be the case. This writing style also promotes method reusability.

13. When implementing a large program, use the top-down and/or bottom-up coding approach. Do not write the entire program at once. This approach may seem to take more time for coding (because you are repeatedly compiling and running the program), but it actually saves time and makes debugging easier.

Quiz

Answer the quiz for this chapter online at the Companion Website.

MyProgrammingLab™ **Programming Exercises**

Note

A common error for the exercises in this chapter is that students don't implement the methods to meet the requirements even though the output from the main program is correct. For an example of this type of error, see liveexample.pearsoncmg.com/etc/CommonMethodErrorJava.pdf.

Sections 6.2–6.9

6.1 (*Math: pentagonal numbers*) A pentagonal number is defined as $n(3n-1)/2$ for $n = 1, 2, ...$, and so on. Therefore, the first few numbers are 1, 5, 12, 22, ... Write a method with the following header that returns a pentagonal number:

```
public static int getPentagonalNumber(int n)
```

For example, `getPentagonalNumber(1)` returns `1` and `getPentagonal-Number(2)` returns `5`. Write a test program that uses this method to display the first 100 pentagonal numbers with 10 numbers on each line. Use the `%7d` format to display each number.

*6.2 (*Sum the digits in an integer*) Write a method that computes the sum of the digits in an integer. Use the following method header:

```
public static int sumDigits(long n)
```

For example, `sumDigits(234)` returns `9` (= 2 + 3 + 4). (*Hint*: Use the `%` operator to extract digits and the `/` operator to remove the extracted digit. For instance, to extract 4 from 234, use `234 % 10` (= 4). To remove 4 from 234, use `234 / 10` (= 23). Use a loop to repeatedly extract and remove the digit until all the digits are extracted. Write a test program that prompts the user to enter an integer then displays the sum of all its digits.

**6.3 (*Palindrome integer*) Write the methods with the following headers:

```
// Return the reversal of an integer, e.g., reverse(456) returns 654
public static int reverse(int number)
```

```
// Return true if number is a palindrome
public static boolean isPalindrome(int number)
```

Use the `reverse` method to implement `isPalindrome`. A number is a palindrome if its reversal is the same as itself. Write a test program that prompts the user to enter an integer and reports whether the integer is a palindrome.

*6.4 (*Display an integer reversed*) Write a method with the following header to display an integer in reverse order:

```
public static void reverse(int number)
```

For example, `reverse(3456)` displays `6543`. Write a test program that prompts the user to enter an integer then displays its reversal.

VideoNote

Reverse an integer

*6.5 (*Sort three numbers*) Write a method with the following header to display three
numbers in increasing order:

```
public static void displaySortedNumbers(
    double num1, double num2, double num3)
```

Write a test program that prompts the user to enter three numbers and invokes the
method to display them in increasing order.

*6.6 (*Display patterns*) Write a method to display a pattern as follows:

```
        1
      2 1
    3 2 1
...
n n-1 ... 3 2 1
```

The method header is

```
public static void displayPattern(int n)
```

*6.7 (*Financial application: compute the future investment value*) Write a method that
computes future investment value at a given interest rate for a specified number
of years. The future investment is determined using the formula in Programming
Exercise 2.21.

Use the following method header:

```
public static double futureInvestmentValue(
    double investmentAmount, double monthlyInterestRate, int years)
```

For example, `futureInvestmentValue(10000, 0.05/12, 5)` returns
`12833.59`.

Write a test program that prompts the user to enter the investment amount (e.g.,
1,000) and the interest rate (e.g., 9%) and prints a table that displays future value
for the years from 1 to 30, as shown below:

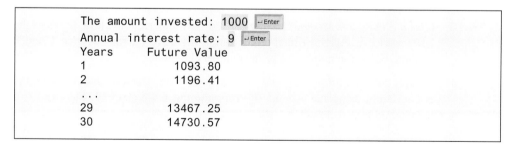

```
The amount invested: 1000  ↵Enter
Annual interest rate: 9  ↵Enter
Years       Future Value
1              1093.80
2              1196.41
...
29            13467.25
30            14730.57
```

6.8 (*Conversions between Celsius and Fahrenheit*) Write a class that contains the
following two methods:

```
/** Convert from Celsius to Fahrenheit */
public static double celsiusToFahrenheit(double celsius)

/** Convert from Fahrenheit to Celsius */
public static double fahrenheitToCelsius(double fahrenheit)
```

The formula for the conversion is as follows:

```
fahrenheit = (9.0 / 5) * celsius + 32
celsius = (5.0 / 9) * (fahrenheit - 32)
```

Write a test program that invokes these methods to display the following tables:

Celsius	Fahrenheit		Fahrenheit	Celsius
40.0	104.0		120.0	48.89
39.0	102.2		110.0	43.33
...				
32.0	89.6		40.0	4.44
31.0	87.8		30.0	-1.11

6.9 (*Conversions between feet and meters*) Write a class that contains the following two methods:

```
/** Convert from feet to meters */
public static double footToMeter(double foot)

/** Convert from meters to feet */
public static double meterToFoot(double meter)
```

The formula for the conversion is:

```
meter = 0.305 * foot
foot = 3.279 * meter
```

Write a test program that invokes these methods to display the following tables:

Feet	Meters		Meters	Feet
1.0	0.305		20.0	65.574
2.0	0.610		25.0	81.967
...				
9.0	2.745		60.0	196.721
10.0	3.050		65.0	213.115

6.10 (*Use the* isPrime *Method*) Listing 6.7, PrimeNumberMethod.java, provides the isPrime(int number) method for testing whether a number is prime. Use this method to find the number of prime numbers less than 10000.

6.11 (*Financial application: compute commissions*) Write a method that computes the commission, using the scheme in Programming Exercise 5.39. The header of the method is as follows:

```
public static double computeCommission(double salesAmount)
```

Write a test program that displays the following table:

Sales Amount	Commission
10000	900.0
15000	1500.0
...	
95000	11100.0
100000	11700.0

6.12 (*Display characters*) Write a method that prints characters using the following header:

```
public static void printChars(char ch1, char ch2, int
   numberPerLine)
```

This method prints the characters between `ch1` and `ch2` with the specified numbers per line. Write a test program that prints 10 characters per line from `1` to `Z`. Characters are separated by exactly one space.

*6.13 (*Sum series*) Write a method to compute the following summation:

$$m(i) = \frac{1}{2} + \frac{2}{3} + \cdots + \frac{i}{i+1}$$

Write a test program that displays the following table:

i	m(i)
1	0.5000
2	1.1667
...	
19	16.4023
20	17.3546

*6.14 (*Estimate* π) π can be computed using the following summation:

$$m(i) = 4\left(1 - \frac{1}{3} + \frac{1}{5} - \frac{1}{7} + \frac{1}{9} - \frac{1}{11} + \cdots + \frac{(-1)^{i+1}}{2i-1}\right)$$

VideoNote

Estimate π

Write a method that returns `m(i)` for a given `i` and write a test program that displays the following table:

i	m(i)
1	4.0000
101	3.1515
201	3.1466
301	3.1449
401	3.1441
501	3.1436
601	3.1433
701	3.1430
801	3.1428
901	3.1427

*6.15 (*Financial application: print a tax table*) Listing 3.5 gives a program to compute tax. Write a method for computing tax using the following header:

```
public static double computeTax(int status, double
   taxableIncome)
```

Use this method to write a program that prints a tax table for taxable income from $50,000 to $60,000 with intervals of $50 for all the following statuses:

Taxable Income	Single	Married Joint or Qualifying Widow(er)	Married Separate	Head of House hold
50000	8688	6665	8688	7353
50050	8700	6673	8700	7365
...				
59950	11175	8158	11175	9840
60000	11188	8165	11188	9853

Hint: round the tax into integers using `Math.round` (i.e., `Math.round(computeTax(status, taxableIncome))`).

*6.16 (*Number of days in a year*) Write a method that returns the number of days in a year using the following header:

```
public static int numberOfDaysInAYear(int year)
```

Write a test program that displays the number of days in year from 2000 to 2020.

Sections 6.10 and 6.11

*6.17 (*Display matrix of 0s and 1s*) Write a method that displays an *n*-by-*n* matrix using the following header:

```
public static void printMatrix(int n)
```

Each element is 0 or 1, which is generated randomly. Write a test program that prompts the user to enter n and displays an *n*-by-*n* matrix. Here is a sample run:

```
Enter n: 3 ⏎Enter
0 1 0
0 0 0
1 1 1
```

**6.18 (*Check password*) Some Websites impose certain rules for passwords. Write a method that checks whether a string is a valid password. Suppose the password rules are as follows:

- A password must have at least eight characters.
- A password must contain only letters and digits.
- A password must contain at least two digits.

Write a program that prompts the user to enter a password and displays `Valid Password` if the rules are followed, or `Invalid Password` otherwise.

*6.19 (*Triangles*) Implement the following two methods:

```
/** Return true if the sum of every two sides is
 * greater than the third side. */
public static boolean isValid(
  double side1, double side2, double side3)
```

```
/** Return the area of the triangle. */
public static double area(
  double side1, double side2, double side3)
```

Write a test program that reads three sides for a triangle and uses the `isValid` method to test if the input is valid and uses the `area` method to obtain the area. The program displays the area if the input is valid. Otherwise, it displays that the input is invalid. The formula for computing the area of a triangle is given in Programming Exercise 2.19.

*6.20 (*Count the letters in a string*) Write a method that counts the number of letters in a string using the following header:

```
public static int countLetters(String s)
```

Write a test program that prompts the user to enter a string and displays the number of letters in the string.

*6.21 (*Phone keypads*) The international standard letter/number mapping for telephones is given in Programming Exercise 4.15. Write a method that returns a number, given an uppercase letter, as follows:

```
public static int getNumber(char uppercaseLetter)
```

Write a test program that prompts the user to enter a phone number as a string. The input number may contain letters. The program translates a letter (uppercase or lowercase) to a digit and leaves all other characters intact. Here are sample runs of the program:

```
Enter a string: 1-800-Flowers  ↵Enter
1-800-3569377
```

```
Enter a string: 1800flowers  ↵Enter
18003569377
```

**6.22 (*Math: approximate the square root*) There are several techniques for implementing the `sqrt` method in the `Math` class. One such technique is known as the *Babylonian method*. It approximates the square root of a number, n, by repeatedly performing the calculation using the following formula:

```
nextGuess = (lastGuess + n / lastGuess) / 2
```

When `nextGuess` and `lastGuess` are almost identical, `nextGuess` is the approximated square root. The initial guess can be any positive value (e.g., `1`). This value will be the starting value for `lastGuess`. If the difference between `nextGuess` and `lastGuess` is less than a very small number, such as `0.0001`, you can claim that `nextGuess` is the approximated square root of n. If not, `nextGuess` becomes `lastGuess` and the approximation process continues. Implement the following method that returns the square root of n:

```
public static double sqrt(long n)
```

*6.23 (*Occurrences of a specified character*) Write a method that finds the number of occurrences of a specified character in a string using the following header:

```
public static int count(String str, char a)
```

For example, `count("Welcome", 'e')` returns `2`. Write a test program that prompts the user to enter a string followed by a character then displays the number of occurrences of the character in the string.

Sections 6.10–6.12

**6.24 (*Display current date and time*) Listing 2.7, ShowCurrentTime.java, displays the current time. Revise this example to display the current date and time. The calendar example in Listing 6.12, PrintCalendar.java, should give you some ideas on how to find the year, month, and day.

**6.25 (*Convert milliseconds to hours, minutes, and seconds*) Write a method that converts milliseconds to hours, minutes, and seconds using the following header:

```
public static String convertMillis(long millis)
```

The method returns a string as *hours:minutes:seconds*. For example, `convertMillis(5500)` returns a string `0:0:5`, `convertMillis(100000)` returns a string `0:1:40`, and `convertMillis(555550000)` returns a string `154:19:10`. Write a test program that prompts the user to enter a long integer for milliseconds and displays a string in the format of hours:minutes:seconds.

Comprehensive

**6.26 (*Palindromic prime*) A *palindromic prime* is a prime number and also palindromic. For example, 131 is a prime and also a palindromic prime, as are 313 and 757. Write a program that displays the first 100 palindromic prime numbers. Display 10 numbers per line, separated by exactly one space, as follows:

```
2 3 5 7 11 101 131 151 181 191
313 353 373 383 727 757 787 797 919 929
. . .
```

**6.27 (*Emirp*) An *emirp* (prime spelled backward) is a nonpalindromic prime number whose reversal is also a prime. For example, 17 is a prime and 71 is a prime, so 17 and 71 are emirps. Write a program that displays the first 100 emirps. Display 10 numbers per line, separated by exactly one space, as follows:

```
13 17 31 37 71 73 79 97 107 113
149 157 167 179 199 311 337 347 359 389
. . .
```

**6.28 (*Mersenne prime*) A prime number is called a *Mersenne prime* if it can be written in the form $2^p - 1$ for some positive integer p. Write a program that finds all Mersenne primes with $p \leq 31$ and displays the output as follows:

p	2^p – 1
2	3
3	7
5	31
. . .	

**6.29 (*Twin primes*) Twin primes are a pair of prime numbers that differ by 2. For example, 3 and 5 are twin primes, 5 and 7 are twin primes, and 11 and 13 are twin primes. Write a program to find all twin primes less than 1,000. Display the output as follows:

```
(3, 5)
(5, 7)
. . .
```

**6.30 (*Game: craps*) Craps is a popular dice game played in casinos. Write a program to play a variation of the game, as follows:

Roll two dice. Each die has six faces representing values 1, 2, . . ., and 6, respectively. Check the sum of the two dice. If the sum is 2, 3, or 12 (called *craps*), you lose; if the sum is 7 or 11 (called *natural*), you win; if the sum is another value (i.e., 4, 5, 6, 8, 9, or 10), a point is established. Continue to roll the dice until either a 7 or the same point value is rolled. If 7 is rolled, you lose. Otherwise, you win.

Your program acts as a single player. Here are some sample runs.

```
You rolled 5 + 6 = 11
You win
```

```
You rolled 1 + 2 = 3
You lose
```

```
You rolled 4 + 4 = 8
point is 8
You rolled 6 + 2 = 8
You win
```

```
You rolled 3 + 2 = 5
point is 5
You rolled 2 + 5 = 7
You lose
```

**6.31 (*Financial: credit card number validation*) Credit card numbers follow certain patterns. A credit card number must have between 13 and 16 digits. It must start with

- 4 for Visa cards
- 5 for Master cards
- 37 for American Express cards
- 6 for Discover cards

In 1954, Hans Luhn of IBM proposed an algorithm for validating credit card numbers. The algorithm is useful to determine whether a card number is entered correctly, or whether a credit card is scanned correctly by a scanner. Credit card numbers are generated following this validity check, commonly known as the *Luhn check* or the *Mod 10 check,* which can be described as follows (for illustration, consider the card number 4388576018402626):

1. Double every second digit from right to left. If doubling of a digit results in a two-digit number, add up the two digits to get a single-digit number.

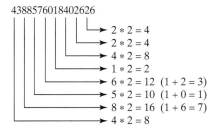

4388576018402626

$2 * 2 = 4$
$2 * 2 = 4$
$4 * 2 = 8$
$1 * 2 = 2$
$6 * 2 = 12 \ (1 + 2 = 3)$
$5 * 2 = 10 \ (1 + 0 = 1)$
$8 * 2 = 16 \ (1 + 6 = 7)$
$4 * 2 = 8$

2. Now add all single-digit numbers from Step 1.

$$4 + 4 + 8 + 2 + 3 + 1 + 7 + 8 = 37$$

3. Add all digits in the odd places from right to left in the card number.

$$6 + 6 + 0 + 8 + 0 + 7 + 8 + 3 = 38$$

4. Sum the results from Step 2 and Step 3.

$$37 + 38 = 75$$

5. If the result from Step 4 is divisible by 10, the card number is valid; otherwise, it is invalid. For example, the number 4388576018402626 is invalid, but the number 4388576018410707 is valid.

Write a program that prompts the user to enter a credit card number as a `long` integer. Display whether the number is valid or invalid. Design your program to use the following methods:

```
/** Return true if the card number is valid */
public static boolean isValid(long number)

/** Get the result from Step 2 */
public static int sumOfDoubleEvenPlace(long number)

/** Return this number if it is a single digit, otherwise,
 * return the sum of the two digits */
public static int getDigit(int number)

/** Return sum of odd-place digits in number */
public static int sumOfOddPlace(long number)

/** Return true if the number d is a prefix for number */
public static boolean prefixMatched(long number, int d)

/** Return the number of digits in d */
public static int getSize(long d)

/** Return the first k number of digits from number. If the
 * number of digits in number is less than k, return number. */
public static long getPrefix(long number, int k)
```

Here are sample runs of the program: (You may also implement this program by reading the input as a string and processing the string to validate the credit card.)

```
Enter a credit card number as a long integer:
4388576018410707  ↵Enter
4388576018410707 is valid
```

```
Enter a credit card number as a long integer:
4388576018402626  ↵Enter
4388576018402626 is invalid
```

**6.32 (*Game: chance of winning at craps*) Revise Programming Exercise 6.30 to run it 10,000 times and display the number of winning games.

**6.33 (*Current date and time*) Invoking `System.currentTimeMillis()` returns the elapsed time in milliseconds since midnight of January 1, 1970. Write a program that displays the date and time. Here is a sample run:

```
Current date and time is May 16, 2012 10:34:23
```

**6.34 (*Print calendar*) Programming Exercise 3.21 uses Zeller's congruence to calculate the day of the week. Simplify Listing 6.12, PrintCalendar.java, using Zeller's algorithm to get the start day of the month.

6.35 (*Geometry: area of a pentagon*) The area of a pentagon can be computed using the following formula:

$$Area = \frac{5 \times s^2}{4 \times \tan\left(\dfrac{\pi}{5}\right)}$$

Write a method that returns the area of a pentagon using the following header:

```
public static double area(double side)
```

Write a main method that prompts the user to enter the side of a pentagon and displays its area. Here is a sample run:

```
Enter the side: 5.5 ↵Enter
The area of the pentagon is 52.04444136781625
```

*6.36 (*Geometry: area of a regular polygon*) A regular polygon is an *n*-sided polygon in which all sides are of the same length and all angles have the same degree (i.e., the polygon is both equilateral and equiangular). The formula for computing the area of a regular polygon is

$$Area = \frac{n \times s^2}{4 \times \tan\left(\dfrac{\pi}{n}\right)}$$

Write a method that returns the area of a regular polygon using the following header:

```
public static double area(int n, double side)
```

Write a main method that prompts the user to enter the number of sides and the side of a regular polygon and displays its area. Here is a sample run:

```
Enter the number of sides: 5 ↵Enter
Enter the side: 6.5 ↵Enter
The area of the polygon is 72.69017017488385
```

6.37 (*Format an integer*) Write a method with the following header to format the integer with the specified width.

```
public static String format(int number, int width)
```

The method returns a string for the number with one or more prefix 0s. The size of the string is the width. For example, `format(34, 4)` returns `0034` and `format(34, 5)` returns `00034`. If the number is longer than the width, the method returns the string representation for the number. For example, `format(34, 1)` returns `34`.

Write a test program that prompts the user to enter a number and its width, and displays a string returned by invoking `format(number, width)`.

*6.38 (*Generate random characters*) Use the methods in `RandomCharacter` in Listing 6.10 to print 100 uppercase letters then 100 single digits, printing 10 per line.

6.39 (*Geometry: point position*) Programming Exercise 3.32 shows how to test whether a point is on the left side of a directed line, on the right, or on the same line. Write the methods with the following headers:

```
/** Return true if point (x2, y2) is on the left side of the
 * directed line from (x0, y0) to (x1, y1) */
public static boolean leftOfTheLine(double x0, double y0,
  double x1, double y1, double x2, double y2)

/** Return true if point (x2, y2) is on the same
 * line from (x0, y0) to (x1, y1) */
public static boolean onTheSameLine(double x0, double y0,
  double x1, double y1, double x2, double y2)

/** Return true if point (x2, y2) is on the
 * line segment from (x0, y0) to (x1, y1) */
public static boolean onTheLineSegment(double x0, double y0,
  double x1, double y1, double x2, double y2)
```

Write a program that prompts the user to enter the three points for p0, p1, and p2 and displays whether p2 is on the left side of the line from p0 to p1, right side, the same line, or on the line segment. Here are some sample runs:

```
Enter three points for p0, p1, and p2: 1 1 2 2 1.5 1.5 ↵Enter
(1.5, 1.5) is on the line segment from (1.0, 1.0) to (2.0, 2.0)
```

```
Enter three points for p0, p1, and p2: 1 1 2 2 3 3 ↵Enter
(3.0, 3.0) is on the same line from (1.0, 1.0) to (2.0, 2.0)
```

```
Enter three points for p0, p1, and p2: 1 1 2 2 1 1.5 ↵Enter
(1.0, 1.5) is on the left side of the line
   from (1.0, 1.0) to (2.0, 2.0)
```

```
Enter three points for p0, p1, and p2: 1 1 2 2 1 −1 ↵Enter
(1.0, -1.0) is on the right side of the line
   from (1.0, 1.0) to (2.0, 2.0)
```

SINGLE-DIMENSIONAL ARRAYS

Objectives

- To describe why arrays are necessary in programming (§7.1).

- To declare array reference variables and create arrays (§§7.2.1 and 7.2.2).

- To obtain array size using `arrayRefVar.length` and know default values in an array (§7.2.3).

- To access array elements using indexes (§7.2.4).

- To declare, create, and initialize an array using an array initializer (§7.2.5).

- To program common array operations (displaying arrays, summing all elements, finding the minimum and maximum elements, random shuffling, and shifting elements) (§7.2.6).

- To simplify programming using the foreach loops (§7.2.7).

- To apply arrays in application development (`AnalyzeNumbers`, and `DeckOfCards`) (§§7.3 and 7.4).

- To copy contents from one array to another (§7.5).

- To develop and invoke methods with array arguments and return values (§§7.6–7.8).

- To define a method with a variable-length argument list (§7.9).

- To search elements using the linear (§7.10.1) or binary (§7.10.2) search algorithm.

- To sort an array using the selection sort approach (§7.11).

- To use the methods in the `java.util.Arrays` class (§7.12).

- To pass arguments to the main method from the command line (§7.13).

7.1 Introduction

A single array variable can reference a large collection of data.

Often you will have to store a large number of values during the execution of a program. Suppose, for instance, that you need to read 100 numbers, compute their average, and find out how many numbers are above the average. Your program first reads the numbers and computes their average, then compares each number with the average to determine whether it is above the average. In order to accomplish this task, the numbers must all be stored in variables. You have to declare 100 variables and repeatedly write almost identical code 100 times. Writing a program this way would be impractical. So, how do you solve this problem?

An efficient, organized approach is needed. Java and most other high-level languages provide a data structure, the *array*, which stores a fixed-size sequential collection of elements of the same type. In the present case, you can store all 100 numbers into an array and access them through a single array variable.

This chapter introduces single-dimensional arrays. The next chapter will introduce two-dimensional and multidimensional arrays.

7.2 Array Basics

Once an array is created, its size is fixed. An array reference variable is used to access the elements in an array using an index.

An array is used to store a collection of data, but often we find it more useful to think of an array as a collection of variables of the same type. Instead of declaring individual variables, such as `number0`, `number1`, . . . , and `number99`, you declare one array variable such as `numbers` and use `numbers[0]`, `numbers[1]`, . . . , and `numbers[99]` to represent individual variables. This section introduces how to declare array variables, create arrays, and process arrays using indexes.

7.2.1 Declaring Array Variables

To use an array in a program, you must declare a variable to reference the array and specify the array's *element type*. Here is the syntax for declaring an array variable:

```
elementType[] arrayRefVar;
```

or

```
elementType arrayRefVar[]; // Allowed, but not preferred
```

The `elementType` can be any data type, and all elements in the array will have the same data type. For example, the following code declares a variable `myList` that references an array of double elements.

```
double[] myList;
```

or

```
double myList[]; // Allowed, but not preferred
```

> **Note**
> You can use `elementType arrayRefVar[]` to declare an array variable. This style comes from the C/C++ language and was adopted in Java to accommodate C/C++ programmers. The style `elementType[] arrayRefVar` is preferred.

7.2.2 Creating Arrays

Unlike declarations for primitive data type variables, the declaration of an array variable does not allocate any space in memory for the array. It creates only a storage location for the reference to an array. If a variable does not contain a reference to an array, the value of the variable is `null`. You cannot assign elements to an array unless it has already been created. After an array variable is declared, you can create an array by using the `new` operator and assign its reference to the variable with the following syntax:

```
arrayRefVar = new elementType[arraySize];
```

This statement does two things: (1) it creates an array using `new elementType[arraySize]` and (2) it assigns the reference of the newly created array to the variable `arrayRefVar`.

Declaring an array variable, creating an array, and assigning the reference of the array to the variable can be combined in one statement as

```
elementType[] arrayRefVar = new elementType[arraySize];
```

or

```
elementType arrayRefVar[] = new elementType[arraySize];
```

Here is an example of such a statement:

```
double[] myList = new double[10];
```

This statement declares an array variable, `myList`, creates an array of 10 elements of `double` type, and assigns its reference to `myList`. To assign values to the elements, use the syntax

```
arrayRefVar[index] = value;
```

For example, the following code initializes the array:

```
myList[0] = 5.6;
myList[1] = 4.5;
myList[2] = 3.3;
myList[3] = 13.2;
myList[4] = 4.0;
myList[5] = 34.33;
myList[6] = 34.0;
myList[7] = 45.45;
myList[8] = 99.993;
myList[9] = 11123;
```

This array is illustrated in Figure 7.1.

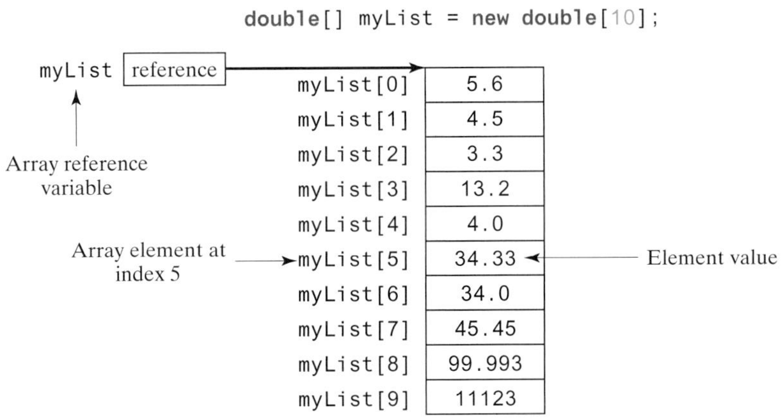

FIGURE 7.1 The array `myList` has 10 elements of `double` type and `int` indices from `0` to `9`.

array vs. array variable

 Note
An array variable that appears to hold an array actually contains a reference to that array. Strictly speaking, an array variable and an array are different, but most of the time the distinction can be ignored. Thus, it is all right to say, for simplicity, that `myList` is an array, instead of stating, at greater length, that `myList` is a variable that contains a reference to an array of double elements.

7.2.3 Array Size and Default Values

array length

When space for an array is allocated, the array size must be given, specifying the number of elements that can be stored in it. The size of an array cannot be changed after the array is created. Size can be obtained using `arrayRefVar.length`. For example, `myList.length` is 10.

default values

When an array is created, its elements are assigned the default value of 0 for the numeric primitive data types, `\u0000` for `char` types, and `false` for `boolean` types.

7.2.4 Accessing Array Elements

0 based index

The array elements are accessed through the index. Array indices are 0 based; that is, they range from 0 to `arrayRefVar.length` − 1. In the example in Figure 7.1, `myList` holds 10 `double` values, and the indices are from 0 to 9.

indexed variable

Each element in the array is represented using the following syntax, known as an *indexed variable*:

```
arrayRefVar[index];
```

For example, `myList[9]` represents the last element in the array `myList`.

 Caution
Some programming languages use parentheses to reference an array element, as in `myList(9)`, but Java uses brackets, as in `myList[9]`.

An indexed variable can be used in the same way as a regular variable. For example, the following code adds the values in `myList[0]` and `myList[1]` to `myList[2]`:

```
myList[2] = myList[0] + myList[1];
```

The following loop assigns 0 to `myList[0]`, 1 to `myList[1]`, . . . , and 9 to `myList[9]`:

```
for (int i = 0; i < myList.length; i++) {
  myList[i] = i;
}
```

7.2.5 Array Initializers

array initializer

Java has a shorthand notation, known as the *array initializer*, which combines the declaration, creation, and initialization of an array in one statement using the following syntax:

```
elementType[] arrayRefVar = {value0, value1, ..., valuek};
```

For example, the statement

```
double[] myList = {1.9, 2.9, 3.4, 3.5};
```

declares, creates, and initializes the array `myList` with four elements, which is equivalent to the following statements:

```
double[] myList = new double[4];
myList[0] = 1.9;
myList[1] = 2.9;
```

```
myList[2] = 3.4;
myList[3] = 3.5;
```

 Caution

The new operator is not used in the array-initializer syntax. Using an array initializer, you have to declare, create, and initialize the array all in one statement. Splitting it would cause a syntax error. Thus, the next statement is wrong:

```
double[] myList;
myList = {1.9, 2.9, 3.4, 3.5}; // Wrong
```

7.2.6 Processing Arrays

When processing array elements, you will often use a `for` loop for one of two reasons:

1. All of the elements in an array are of the same type. They are evenly processed in the same fashion repeatedly using a loop.

2. Since the size of the array is known, it is natural to use a `for` loop.

Assume that the array is created as follows:

```
double[] myList = new double[10];
```

The following are some examples of processing arrays:

1. *Initializing arrays with input values:* The following loop initializes the array `myList` with user input values:

```
java.util.Scanner input = new java.util.Scanner(System.in);
System.out.print("Enter " + myList.length + " values: ");
for (int i = 0; i < myList.length; i++)
  myList[i] = input.nextDouble();
```

2. *Initializing arrays with random values:* The following loop initializes the array `myList` with random values between `0.0` and `100.0`, but less than `100.0`:

```
for (int i = 0; i < myList.length; i++) {
  myList[i] = Math.random() * 100;
}
```

3. *Displaying arrays:* To print an array, you have to print each element in the array using a loop such as the following:

```
for (int i = 0; i < myList.length; i++) {
  System.out.print(myList[i] + " ");
}
```

 Tip

For an array of the `char[]` type, it can be printed using one print statement. For   print character array
example, the following code displays `Dallas`:

```
char[] city = {'D', 'a', 'l', 'l', 'a', 's'};
System.out.println(city);
```

4. *Summing all elements:* Use a variable named `total` to store the sum. Initially `total` is `0`. Add each element in the array to `total` using a loop such as the following:

```
double total = 0;
for (int i = 0; i < myList.length; i++) {
  total += myList[i];
}
```

5. *Finding the largest element:* Use a variable named `max` to store the largest element. Initially `max` is `myList[0]`. To find the largest element in the array `myList`, compare each element with `max`, and update `max` if the element is greater than `max`.

```
double max = myList[0];
for (int i = 1; i < myList.length; i++) {
  if (myList[i] > max) max = myList[i];
}
```

6. *Finding the smallest index of the largest element:* Often you need to locate the largest element in an array. If an array has multiple elements with the same largest value, find the smallest index of such an element. Suppose that the array `myList` is {1, 5, 3, 4, 5, 5}. The largest element is 5, and the smallest index for 5 is 1. Use a variable named `max` to store the largest element, and a variable named `indexOfMax` to denote the index of the largest element. Initially `max` is `myList[0]` and `indexOfMax` is 0. Compare each element in `myList` with `max` and update `max` and `indexOfMax` if the element is greater than `max`.

```
double max = myList[0];
int indexOfMax = 0;
for (int i = 1; i < myList.length; i++) {
  if (myList[i] > max) {
    max = myList[i];
    indexOfMax = i;
  }
}
```

random shuffling

VideoNote

Random shuffling

7. *Random shuffling:* In many applications, you need to randomly reorder the elements in an array. This is called *shuffling*. To accomplish this, for each element `myList[i]`, randomly generate an index `j` and swap `myList[i]` with `myList[j]`, as follows:

```
for (int i = 0; i < myList.length - 1; i++) {
  // Generate an index j randomly
  int j = (int)(Math.random()
    * myList.length);

  // Swap myList[i] with myList[j]
  double temp = myList[i];
  myList[i] = myList[j];
  myList[j] = temp;
}
```

8. *Shifting elements:* Sometimes you need to shift the elements left or right. Here is an example of shifting the elements one position to the left and filling the last element with the first element:

```
double temp = myList[0]; // Retain the first element

// Shift elements left
for (int i = 1; i < myList.length; i++) {
  myList[i - 1] = myList[i];
}

// Move the first element to fill in the last position
myList[myList.length - 1] = temp;
```

9. *Simplifying coding:* Arrays can be used to greatly simplify coding for certain tasks. For example, suppose you wish to obtain the English name of a given month by its number. If the month names are stored in an array, the month name for a given month can be

accessed simply via the index. The following code prompts the user to enter a month number and displays its month name:

```
String[] months = {"January", "February",..., "December"};
System.out.print("Enter a month number (1 to 12): ");
int monthNumber = input.nextInt();
System.out.println("The month is " + months[monthNumber - 1]);
```

If you didn't use the months array, you would have to determine the month name using a lengthy multiway if-else statement as follows:

```
if (monthNumber == 1)
  System.out.println("The month is January");
else if (monthNumber == 2)
  System.out.println("The month is February");
...
else
  System.out.println("The month is December");
```

7.2.7 Foreach Loops

Java supports a convenient for loop, known as a *foreach loop*, which enables you to traverse the array sequentially without using an index variable. For example, the following code displays all the elements in the array myList:

```
for (double e: myList) {
  System.out.println(e);
}
```

You can read the code as "for each element e in myList, do the following." Note that the variable, e, must be declared as the same type as the elements in myList.

In general, the syntax for a foreach loop is

```
for (elementType element: arrayRefVar) {
  // Process the element
}
```

You still have to use an index variable if you wish to traverse the array in a different order or change the elements in the array.

 Caution

Accessing an array out of bounds is a common programming error that throws a runtime ArrayIndexOutOfBoundsException. To avoid it, make sure you do not use an index beyond arrayRefVar.length − 1 or simply using a foreach loop if possible.

ArrayIndexOutOfBounds-
   Exception

Programmers often mistakenly reference the first element in an array with index 1, but it should be 0. This is called the *off-by-one error*. Another common off-by-one error in a loop is using <= where < should be used. For example, the following loop is wrong:

off-by-one error

```
for (int i = 0; i <= list.length; i++)
  System.out.print(list[i] + " ");
```

The <= should be replaced by <. Using a foreach loop can avoid the off-by-one error in this case.

7.2.1   How do you declare an array reference variable and how do you create an array?

7.2.2   When is the memory allocated for an array?

Check Point

7.2.3 What is the output of the following code?

```
int x = 30;
int[] numbers = new int[x];
x = 60;
System.out.println("x is " + x);
System.out.println("The size of numbers is " + numbers.length);
```

7.2.4 Indicate true or false for the following statements:

a. Every element in an array has the same type.
b. The array size is fixed after an array reference variable is declared.
c. The array size is fixed after it is created.
d. The elements in an array must be of a primitive data type.

7.2.5 Which of the following statements are valid?

a. **int** i = **new int**(30);
b. **double** d[] = **new double**[30];
c. **char**[] r = **new char**(1..30);
d. **int** i[] = (3, 4, 3, 2);
e. **float** f[] = {2.3, 4.5, 6.6};
f. **char**[] c = **new char**();

7.2.6 How do you access elements in an array?

7.2.7 What is the array index type? What is the lowest index? What is the representation of the third element in an array named a?

7.2.8 Write statements to do the following:

a. Create an array to hold 10 double values.

b. Assign the value 5.5 to the last element in the array.

c. Display the sum of the first two elements.

d. Write a loop that computes the sum of all elements in the array.

e. Write a loop that finds the minimum element in the array.

f. Randomly generate an index and display the element of this index in the array.

g. Use an array initializer to create another array with the initial values 3.5, 5.5, 4.52, and 5.6.

7.2.9 What happens when your program attempts to access an array element with an invalid index?

7.2.10 Identify and fix the errors in the following code:

```
1  public class Test {
2    public static void main(String[] args) {
3      double[100] r;
4
5      for (int i = 0; i < r.length(); i++);
6        r(i) = Math.random * 100;
7    }
8  }
```

7.2.11 What is the output of the following code?

```
1  public class Test {
2    public static void main(String[] args) {
3      int list[] = {1, 2, 3, 4, 5, 6};
```

```
4      for (int i = 1; i < list.length; i++)
5        list[i] = list[i - 1];
6
7      for (int i = 0; i < list.length; i++)
8        System.out.print(list[i] + " ");
9    }
10 }
```

7.3 Case Study: Analyzing Numbers

The problem is to write a program that finds the number of items above the average of all items.

Key
Point

Now you can write a program using arrays to solve the problem proposed at the beginning of this chapter. The problem is to read 100 numbers, get the average of these numbers, and find the number of the items greater than the average. To be flexible for handling any number of inputs, we will let the user enter the number of inputs, rather than fixing it to 100. Listing 7.1 gives a solution.

LISTING 7.1 AnalyzeNumbers.java

```
1  public class AnalyzeNumbers {
2    public static void main(String[] args) {
3      java.util.Scanner input = new java.util.Scanner(System.in);
4      System.out.print("Enter the number of items: ");
5      int n = input.nextInt();
6      double[] numbers = new double[n];
7      double sum = 0;
8
9      System.out.print("Enter the numbers: ");
10     for (int i = 0; i < n; i++) {
11       numbers[i] = input.nextDouble();
12       sum += numbers[i];
13     }
14
15     double average = sum / n;
16
17     int count = 0; // The number of elements above average
18     for (int i = 0; i < n; i++)
19       if (numbers[i] > average)
20         count++;
21
22     System.out.println("Average is " + average);
23     System.out.println("Number of elements above the average is "
24       + count);
25   }
26 }
```

numbers[0]:
numbers[1]:
numbers[2]:

create array

numbers[i]:

numbers[n-3]:
numbers[n-2]:   store number in array
numbers[n-1]:

get average

above average?

```
Enter the number of items: 10 ↵Enter
Enter the numbers: 3.4 5 6 1 6.5 7.8 3.5 8.5 6.3 9.5 ↵Enter
Average is 5.75
Number of elements above the average is 6
```

The program prompts the user to enter the array size (line 5) and creates an array with the specified size (line 6). The program reads the input, stores numbers into the array (line 11), adds each number to `sum` in line 11, and obtains the average (line 15). It then compares each number in the array with the average to count the number of values above the average (lines 7–20).

7.4 Case Study: Deck of Cards

Key Point

The problem is to create a program that will randomly select four cards from a deck of cards.

Say you want to write a program that will pick four cards at random from a deck of 52 cards. All the cards can be represented using an array named deck, filled with initial values 0–51, as follows:

VideoNote

Deck of cards

```
int[] deck = new int[52];

// Initialize cards
for (int i = 0; i < deck.length; i++)
  deck[i] = i;
```

Card numbers 0–12, 13–25, 26–38, and 39–51 represent 13 Spades, 13 Hearts, 13 Diamonds, and 13 Clubs, respectively, as shown in Figure 7.2. cardNumber / 13 determines the suit of the card, and cardNumber % 13 determines the rank of the card, as shown in Figure 7.3. After shuffling the array deck, pick the first four cards from deck. The program displays the cards from these four card numbers.

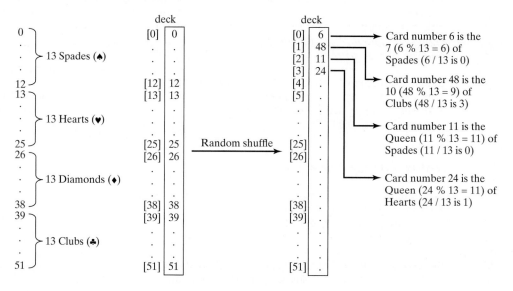

FIGURE 7.2 52 cards are stored in an array named deck.

cardNumber / 13 =
- 0 → Spades
- 1 → Hearts
- 2 → Diamonds
- 3 → Clubs

cardNumber % 13 =
- 0 → Ace
- 1 → 2
- .
- .
- 10 → Jack
- 11 → Queen
- 12 → King

FIGURE 7.3 cardNumber identifies a card's suit and rank number.

Listing 7.2 gives the solution to the problem.

LISTING 7.2 DeckOfCards.java

```java
 1  public class DeckOfCards {
 2    public static void main(String[] args) {
 3      int[] deck = new int[52];                                    // create array deck
 4      String[] suits = {"Spades", "Hearts", "Diamonds", "Clubs"};  // array of strings
 5      String[] ranks = {"Ace", "2", "3", "4", "5", "6", "7", "8", "9",  // array of strings
 6        "10", "Jack", "Queen", "King"};
 7
 8      // Initialize the cards
 9      for (int i = 0; i < deck.length; i++)                        // initialize deck
10        deck[i] = i;
11
12      // Shuffle the cards
13      for (int i = 0; i < deck.length; i++) {                      // shuffle deck
14        // Generate an index randomly
15        int index = (int)(Math.random() * deck.length);
16        int temp = deck[i];
17        deck[i] = deck[index];
18        deck[index] = temp;
19      }
20
21      // Display the first four cards
22      for (int i = 0; i < 4; i++) {
23        String suit = suits[deck[i] / 13];                         // suit of a card
24        String rank = ranks[deck[i] % 13];                         // rank of a card
25        System.out.println("Card number " + deck[i] + ": "
26          + rank + " of " + suit);
27      }
28    }
29  }
```

```
Card number 6: 7 of Spades
Card number 48: 10 of Clubs
Card number 11: Queen of Spades
Card number 24: Queen of Hearts
```

The program creates an array `suits` for four suits (line 4) and an array `ranks` for 13 cards in a suit (lines 5 and 6). Each element in these arrays is a string.

The program initializes `deck` with values 0–51 in lines 9 and 10. The `deck` value 0 represents the Ace of Spades, 1 represents the card 2 of Spades, 13 represents the Ace of Hearts, and 14 represents the 2 of Hearts.

Lines 13–19 randomly shuffle the deck. After a deck is shuffled, `deck[i]` contains an arbitrary value. `deck[i] / 13` is 0, 1, 2, or 3, which determines the suit (line 23). `deck[i] % 13` is a value between 0 and 12, which determines the rank (line 24). If the `suits` array is not defined, you would have to determine the suit using a lengthy multiway `if-else` statement as follows:

```java
if (deck[i] / 13 == 0)
  System.out.print("suit is Spades");
else if (deck[i] / 13 == 1)
  System.out.print("suit is Hearts");
else if (deck[i] / 13 == 2)
  System.out.print("suit is Diamonds");
else
  System.out.print("suit is Clubs");
```

With `suits = {"Spades", "Hearts", "Diamonds", "Clubs"}` created in an array, `suits[deck[i] / 13]` gives the suit for `deck[i]`. Using arrays greatly simplifies the solution for this program.

7.4.1 Will the program pick four random cards if you replace lines 22–27 in Listing 7.2, DeckOfCards.java, with the following code?

```
for (int i = 0; i < 4; i++) {
  int cardNumber = (int)(Math.random() * deck.length);
  String suit = suits[cardNumber / 13];
  String rank = ranks[cardNumber % 13];
  System.out.println("Card number " + cardNumber + ": "
    + rank + " of " + suit);
}
```

7.5 Copying Arrays

To copy the contents of one array into another, you have to copy the array's individual elements into the other array.

Often, in a program, you need to duplicate an array or a part of an array. In such cases you could attempt to use the assignment statement (=), as follows:

```
list2 = list1;
```

copy reference

However, this statement does not copy the contents of the array referenced by `list1` to `list2`, but instead merely copies the reference value from `list1` to `list2`. After this statement, `list1` and `list2` reference the same array, as shown in Figure 7.4. The array previously referenced by `list2` is no longer referenced; it becomes garbage, which will be automatically collected by the Java Virtual Machine. This process is called *garbage collection*.

garbage collection

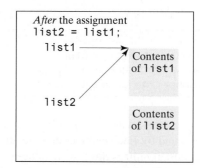

FIGURE 7.4 Before the assignment statement, `list1` and `list2` point to separate memory locations. After the assignment, the reference of the `list1` array is passed to `list2`.

In Java, you can use assignment statements to copy primitive data type variables, but not arrays. Assigning one array variable to another array variable actually copies one reference to another and makes both variables point to the same memory location.

There are three ways to copy arrays:

1. Use a loop to copy individual elements one by one.

2. Use the static `arraycopy` method in the `System` class.

3. Use the `clone` method to copy arrays; this will be introduced in Chapter 13, Abstract Classes and Interfaces.

You can write a loop to copy every element from the source array to the corresponding element in the target array. The following code, for instance, copies sourceArray to targetArray using a for loop:

```
int[] sourceArray = {2, 3, 1, 5, 10};
int[] targetArray = new int[sourceArray.length];
for (int i = 0; i < sourceArray.length; i++) {
  targetArray[i] = sourceArray[i];
}
```

Another approach is to use the arraycopy method in the java.lang.System class to copy arrays instead of using a loop. The syntax for arraycopy is:

arraycopy method

```
arraycopy(sourceArray, srcPos, targetArray, tarPos, length);
```

The parameters srcPos and tarPos indicate the starting positions in sourceArray and targetArray, respectively. The number of elements copied from sourceArray to targetArray is indicated by length. For example, you can rewrite the loop using the following statement:

```
System.arraycopy(sourceArray, 0, targetArray, 0, sourceArray.length);
```

The arraycopy method does not allocate memory space for the target array. The target array must have already been created with its memory space allocated. After the copying takes place, targetArray and sourceArray have the same content but independent memory locations.

Note

The arraycopy method violates the Java naming convention. By convention, this method should be named arrayCopy (i.e., with an uppercase C).

7.5.1 Use the arraycopy method to copy the following array to a target array t:

```
int[] source = {3, 4, 5};
```

7.5.2 Once an array is created, its size cannot be changed. Does the following code resize the array?

```
int[] myList;
myList = new int[10];
// Sometime later you want to assign a new array to myList
myList = new int[20];
```

7.6 Passing Arrays to Methods

When passing an array to a method, the reference of the array is passed to the method.

Just as you can pass primitive type values to methods, you can also pass arrays to methods. For example, the following method displays the elements in an int array:

```
public static void printArray(int[] array) {
  for (int i = 0; i < array.length; i++) {
    System.out.print(array[i] + " ");
  }
}
```

You can invoke it by passing an array. For example, the following statement invokes the printArray method to display 3, 1, 2, 6, 4, and 2.

```
printArray(new int[]{3, 1, 2, 6, 4, 2});
```

> **Note**
>
> The preceding statement creates an array using the following syntax:
>
> ```
> new elementType[]{value0, value1, ..., valuek};
> ```

anonymous array

There is no explicit reference variable for the array. Such array is called an *anonymous array*.

pass-by-value

Java uses *pass-by-value* to pass arguments to a method. There are important differences between passing the values of variables of primitive data types and passing arrays.

- For an argument of a primitive type, the argument's value is passed.

pass-by-sharing

- For an argument of an array type, the value of the argument is a reference to an array; this reference value is passed to the method. Semantically, it can be best described as *pass-by-sharing*, that is, the array in the method is the same as the array being passed. Thus, if you change the array in the method, you will see the change outside the method.

Take the following code, for example:

```java
public class TestArrayArguments {
  public static void main(String[] args) {
    int x = 1; // x represents an int value
    int[] y = new int[10]; // y represents an array of int values

    m(x, y); // Invoke m with arguments x and y

    System.out.println("x is " + x);
    System.out.println("y[0] is " + y[0]);
  }

  public static void m(int number, int[] numbers) {
    number = 1001; // Assign a new value to number
    numbers[0] = 5555; // Assign a new value to numbers[0]
  }
}
```

```
x is 1
y[0] is 5555
```

You may wonder why after m is invoked, x remains 1, but y[0] becomes 5555. This is because y and numbers, although they are independent variables, reference the same array, as illustrated in Figure 7.5. When m(x, y) is invoked, the values of x and y are passed to number and numbers. Since y contains the reference value to the array, numbers now contains the same reference value to the same array.

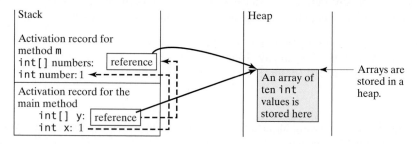

FIGURE 7.5 The primitive type value in x is passed to number, and the reference value in y is passed to numbers.

> **Note**
> Arrays are objects in Java (objects are introduced in Chapter 9). The JVM stores the objects in an area of memory called the *heap*, which is used for dynamic memory allocation.

heap

Listing 7.3 gives another program that shows the difference between passing a primitive data type value and an array reference variable to a method.

The program contains two methods for swapping elements in an array. The first method, named `swap`, fails to swap two `int` arguments. The second method, named `swapFirst-TwoInArray`, successfully swaps the first two elements in the array argument.

LISTING 7.3 TestPassArray.java

```
 1  public class TestPassArray {
 2    /** Main method */
 3    public static void main(String[] args) {
 4      int[] a = {1, 2};
 5
 6      // Swap elements using the swap method
 7      System.out.println("Before invoking swap");
 8      System.out.println("array is {" + a[0] + ", " + a[1] + "}");
 9      swap(a[0], a[1]);
10      System.out.println("After invoking swap");
11      System.out.println("array is {" + a[0] + ", " + a[1] + "}");
12
13      // Swap elements using the swapFirstTwoInArray method
14      System.out.println("Before invoking swapFirstTwoInArray");
15      System.out.println("array is {" + a[0] + ", " + a[1] + "}");
16      swapFirstTwoInArray(a);
17      System.out.println("After invoking swapFirstTwoInArray");
18      System.out.println("array is {" + a[0] + ", " + a[1] + "}");
19    }
20
21    /** Swap two variables */
22    public static void swap(int n1, int n2) {
23      int temp = n1;
24      n1 = n2;
25      n2 = temp;
26    }
27
28    /** Swap the first two elements in the array */
29    public static void swapFirstTwoInArray(int[] array) {
30      int temp = array[0];
31      array[0] = array[1];
32      array[1] = temp;
33    }
34  }
```

false swap

swap array elements

```
Before invoking swap
array is {1, 2}
After invoking swap
array is {1, 2}
Before invoking swapFirstTwoInArray
array is {1, 2}
After invoking swapFirstTwoInArray
array is {2, 1}
```

As shown in Figure 7.6, the two elements are not swapped using the `swap` method. However, they are swapped using the `swapFirstTwoInArray` method. Since the parameters in the `swap` method are primitive type, the values of `a[0]` and `a[1]` are passed to `n1` and `n2` inside the method when invoking `swap(a[0], a[1])`. The memory locations for `n1` and `n2` are independent of the ones for `a[0]` and `a[1]`. The contents of the array are not affected by this call.

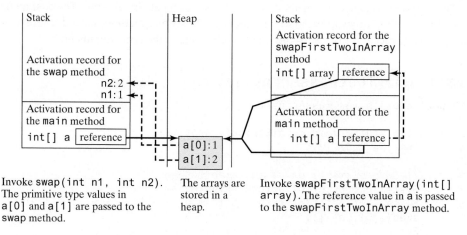

Invoke `swap(int n1, int n2)`. The primitive type values in `a[0]` and `a[1]` are passed to the `swap` method.

The arrays are stored in a heap.

Invoke `swapFirstTwoInArray(int[] array)`. The reference value in a is passed to the `swapFirstTwoInArray` method.

FIGURE 7.6 When passing an array to a method, the reference of the array is passed to the method.

The parameter in the `swapFirstTwoInArray` method is an array. As shown in Figure 7.6, the reference of the array is passed to the method. Thus, the variables `a` (outside the method) and `array` (inside the method) both refer to the same array in the same memory location. Therefore, swapping `array[0]` with `array[1]` inside the method `swapFirstTwoInArray` is the same as swapping `a[0]` with `a[1]` outside of the method.

7.7 Returning an Array from a Method

*Key
Point*

When a method returns an array, the reference of the array is returned.

You can pass arrays when invoking a method. A method may also return an array. For example, the following method returns an array that is the reversal of another array.

create array

return array

```
1  public static int[] reverse(int[] list) {
2    int[] result = new int[list.length];
3
4    for (int i = 0, j = result.length - 1;
5         i < list.length; i++, j--) {
6      result[j] = list[i];
7    }
8
9    return result;
10 }
```

Line 2 creates a new array `result`. Lines 4–7 copy elements from array `list` to array `result`. Line 9 returns the array. For example, the following statement returns a new array `list2` with elements 6, 5, 4, 3, 2, 1:

```
int[] list1 = {1, 2, 3, 4, 5, 6};
int[] list2 = reverse(list1);
```

7.7.1 Suppose the following code is written to reverse the contents in an array, explain why it is wrong. How do you fix it?

```
int[] list = {1, 2, 3, 5, 4};

for (int i = 0, j = list.length - 1; i < list.length; i++, j--) {
  // Swap list[i] with list[j]
  int temp = list[i];
  list[i] = list[j];
  list[j] = temp;
}
```

7.8 Case Study: Counting the Occurrences of Each Letter

This section presents a program to count the occurrences of each letter in an array of characters.

The program given in Listing 7.4 does the following:

1. Generates 100 lowercase letters randomly and assigns them to an array of characters, as shown in Figure 7.7a. You can obtain a random letter by using the getRandomLower-CaseLetter() method in the RandomCharacter class in Listing 6.10.

2. Count the occurrences of each letter in the array. To do so, create an array, say counts, of 26 int values, each of which counts the occurrences of a letter, as shown in Figure 7.7b. That is, counts[0] counts the number of a's, counts[1] counts the number of b's, and so on.

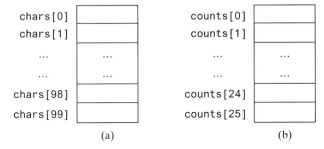

(a)   (b)

FIGURE 7.7 The chars array stores 100 characters, and the counts array stores 26 counts, each of which counts the occurrences of a letter.

LISTING 7.4 CountLettersInArray.java

```
1  public class CountLettersInArray {
2    /** Main method */
3    public static void main(String[] args) {
4      // Declare and create an array
5      char[] chars = createArray();
6
7      // Display the array
8      System.out.println("The lowercase letters are:");
9      displayArray(chars);
10
```

create array

pass array

```
11        // Count the occurrences of each letter
12        int[] counts = countLetters(chars);
13
14        // Display counts
15        System.out.println();
16        System.out.println("The occurrences of each letter are:");
17        displayCounts(counts);
18      }
19
20      /** Create an array of characters */
21      public static char[] createArray() {
22        // Declare an array of characters and create it
23        char[] chars = new char[100];
24
25        // Create lowercase letters randomly and assign
26        // them to the array
27        for (int i = 0; i < chars.length; i++)
28          chars[i] = RandomCharacter.getRandomLowerCaseLetter();
29
30        // Return the array
31        return chars;
32      }
33
34      /** Display the array of characters */
35      public static void displayArray(char[] chars) {
36        // Display the characters in the array 20 on each line
37        for (int i = 0; i < chars.length; i++) {
38          if ((i + 1) % 20 == 0)
39            System.out.println(chars[i]);
40          else
41            System.out.print(chars[i] + " ");
42        }
43      }
44
45      /** Count the occurrences of each letter */
46      public static int[] countLetters(char[] chars) {
47        // Declare and create an array of 26 int
48        int[] counts = new int[26];
49
50        // For each lowercase letter in the array, count it
51        for (int i = 0; i < chars.length; i++)
52          counts[chars[i] - 'a']++;
53
54        return counts;
55      }
56
57      /** Display counts */
58      public static void displayCounts(int[] counts) {
59        for (int i = 0; i < counts.length; i++) {
60          if ((i + 1) % 10 == 0)
61            System.out.println(counts[i] + " " + (char)(i + 'a'));
62          else
63            System.out.print(counts[i] + " " + (char)(i + 'a') + " ");
64        }
65      }
66    }
```

return array

pass array

increase count

```
The lowercase letters are:
e y l s r i b k j v j h a b z n w b t v
s c c k r d w a m p w v u n q a m p l o
a z g d e g f i n d x m z o u l o z j v
h w i w n t g x w c d o t x h y v z y z
q e a m f w p g u q t r e n n w f c r f

The occurrences of each letter are:
5 a 3 b 4 c 4 d 4 e 4 f 4 g 3 h 3 i 3 j
2 k 3 l 4 m 6 n 4 o 3 p 3 q 4 r 2 s 4 t
3 u 5 v 8 w 3 x 3 y 6 z
```

The `createArray` method (lines 21–32) generates an array of `100` random lowercase letters. Line 5 invokes the method and assigns the array to `chars`. What would be wrong if you rewrote the code as follows?

```java
char[] chars = new char[100];
chars = createArray();
```

You would be creating two arrays. The first line would create an array by using `new char[100]`. The second line would create an array by invoking `createArray()` and assign the reference of the array to `chars`. The array created in the first line would be garbage because it is no longer referenced, and as mentioned earlier, Java automatically collects garbage behind the scenes. Your program would compile and run correctly, but it would create an array unnecessarily.

Invoking `getRandomLowerCaseLetter()` (line 28) returns a random lowercase letter. This method is defined in the `RandomCharacter` class in Listing 6.10.

The `countLetters` method (lines 46–55) returns an array of `26` `int` values, each of which stores the number of occurrences of a letter. The method processes each letter in the array and increases its count by one. A brute-force approach to count the occurrences of each letter might be as follows:

```java
for (int i = 0; i < chars.length; i++)
  if (chars[i] == 'a')
    counts[0]++;
  else if (chars[i] == 'b')
    counts[1]++;
  . . .
```

However, a better solution is given in lines 51 and 52.

```java
for (int i = 0; i < chars.length; i++)
  counts[chars[i] - 'a']++;
```

If the letter (`chars[i]`) is `a`, the corresponding count is `counts['a' - 'a']` (i.e., `counts[0]`). If the letter is `b`, the corresponding count is `counts['b' - 'a']` (i.e., `counts[1]`), since the Unicode of `b` is one more than that of `a`. If the letter is `z`, the corresponding count is `counts['z' - 'a']` (i.e., `counts[25]`), since the Unicode of `z` is `25` more than that of `a`.

Figure 7.8 shows the call stack and heap *during* and *after* executing `createArray`. See CheckPoint Question 7.8.3 to show the call stack and heap for other methods in the program.

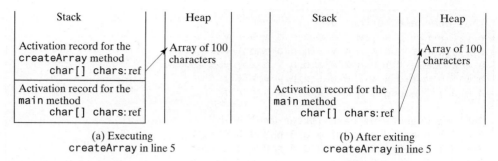

FIGURE 7.8 (a) An array of 100 characters is created when executing `createArray`. (b) This array is returned and assigned to the variable `chars` in the `main` method.

Check Point

7.8.1 True or false? When an array is passed to a method, a new array is created and passed to the method.

7.8.2 Show the output of the following two programs:

```
public class Test {
  public static void main(String[] args) {
    int number = 0;
    int[] numbers = new int[1];

    m(number, numbers);

    System.out.println("number is " + number
      + " and numbers[0] is " + numbers[0]);
  }

  public static void m(int x, int[] y) {
    x = 3;
    y[0] = 3;
  }
}
```

(a)

```
public class Test {
  public static void main(String[] args) {
    int[] list = {1, 2, 3, 4, 5};
    reverse(list);
    for (int i = 0; i < list.length; i++)
      System.out.print(list[i] + " ");
  }

  public static void reverse(int[] list) {
    int[] newList = new int[list.length];

    for (int i = 0; i < list.length; i++)
      newList[i] = list[list.length - 1 - i];

    list = newList;
  }
}
```

(b)

7.8.3 Where are the arrays stored during execution? Show the contents of the stack and heap during and after executing `displayArray`, `countLetters`, and `display-Counts` in Listing 7.4.

7.9 Variable-Length Argument Lists

Key Point

A variable number of arguments of the same type can be passed to a method and treated as an array.

You can pass a variable number of arguments of the same type to a method. The parameter in the method is declared as follows:

```
typeName... parameterName
```

In the method declaration, you specify the type followed by an ellipsis (...). Only one variable-length parameter may be specified in a method, and this parameter must be the last parameter. Any regular parameters must precede it.

Java treats a variable-length parameter as an array. You can pass an array or a variable number of arguments to a variable-length parameter. When invoking a method with a variable number of arguments, Java creates an array and passes the arguments to it. Listing 7.5 presents a method that prints the maximum value in a list of an unspecified number of values.

LISTING 7.5   VarArgsDemo.java

```
1  public class VarArgsDemo {
2    public static void main(String[] args) {
3      printMax(34, 3, 3, 2, 56.5);                    pass variable-length arg list
4      printMax(new double[]{1, 2, 3});                pass an array arg
5    }
6
7    public static void printMax(double... numbers) {  a variable-length arg
8      if (numbers.length == 0) {                          parameter
9        System.out.println("No argument passed");
10       return;
11     }
12
13     double result = numbers[0];
14
15     for (int i = 1; i < numbers.length; i++)
16       if (numbers[i] > result)
17         result = numbers[i];
18
19     System.out.println("The max value is " + result);
20   }
21 }
```

Line 3 invokes the `printMax` method with a variable-length argument list passed to the array `numbers`. If no arguments are passed, the length of the array is `0` (line 8).

Line 4 invokes the `printMax` method with an array.

7.9.1   What is wrong with each of the following method headers?

Check Point

```
a. public static void print(String... strings, double... numbers)
b. public static void print(double... numbers, String name)
c. public static double... print(double d1, double d2)
```

7.9.2   Can you invoke the `printMax` method in Listing 7.5 using the following statements?

```
a. printMax(1, 2, 2, 1, 4);
b. printMax(new double[]{1, 2, 3});
c. printMax(new int[]{1, 2, 3});
```

7.10 Searching Arrays

If an array is sorted, binary search is more efficient than linear search for finding an element in the array.

Key Point

Searching is the process of looking for a specific element in an array—for example, discovering whether a certain score is included in a list of scores. Searching is a common task in computer programming. Many algorithms and data structures are devoted to searching. This section discusses two commonly used approaches, *linear search* and *binary search*.

linear search
binary search

7.10.1   The Linear Search Approach

The linear search approach compares the key element `key` sequentially with each element in the array. It continues to do so until the key matches an element in the array, or the array is exhausted without a match being found. If a match is made, the linear search returns the index

linear search animation on
Companion Website

of the element in the array that matches the key. If no match is found, the search returns −1. The `linearSearch` method in Listing 7.6 gives the solution.

LISTING 7.6 LinearSearch.java

```
 1 public class LinearSearch {
 2    /** The method for finding a key in the list */
 3    public static int linearSearch(int[] list, int key) {
 4       for (int i = 0; i < list.length; i++) {
 5          if (key == list[i])
 6             return i;
 7       }
 8       return -1;
 9    }
10 }
```

[0] [1] [2] ...

list

key   Compare key with `list[i]` for i = 0, 1, ...

To better understand this method, trace it with the following statements:

```
 1  int[] list = {1, 4, 4, 2, 5, -3, 6, 2};
 2  int i = linearSearch(list, 4);  // Returns 1
 3  int j = linearSearch(list, -4); // Returns -1
 4  int k = linearSearch(list, -3); // Returns 5
```

The linear search method compares the key with each element in the array. The elements can be in any order. On average, the algorithm will have to examine half of the elements in an array before finding the key, if it exists. Since the execution time of a linear search increases linearly as the number of array elements increases, linear search is inefficient for a large array.

7.10.2 The Binary Search Approach

Binary search is the other common search approach for a list of values. For binary search to work, the elements in the array must already be ordered. Assume that the array is in ascending order. The binary search first compares the key with the element in the middle of the array. Consider the following three cases:

1. If the key is less than the middle element, you need to continue to search for the key only in the first half of the array.

2. If the key is equal to the middle element, the search ends with a match.

3. If the key is greater than the middle element, you need to continue to search for the key only in the second half of the array.

binary search animation on
Companion Website

Clearly, the binary search method eliminates at least half of the array after each comparison. Sometimes you eliminate half of the elements, and sometimes you eliminate half plus one. Suppose the array has n elements. For convenience, let n be a power of 2. After the first comparison, $n/2$ elements are left for further search; after the second comparison, $(n/2)/2$ elements are left. After the kth comparison, $n/2^k$ elements are left for further search. When $k = \log_2 n$, only one element is left in the array, and you need only one more comparison. Therefore, in the worst case when using the binary search approach, you need $\log_2 n + 1$ comparisons to find an element in the sorted array. In the worst case for a list of 1024 (2^{10}) elements, binary search requires only 11 comparisons, whereas a linear search requires 1023 comparisons in the worst case.

The portion of the array being searched shrinks by half after each comparison. Let `low` and `high` denote, respectively, the first index and last index of the array that is currently being searched. Initially, `low` is `0` and `high` is `list.length - 1`. Let `mid` denote the index of the middle element, so `mid` is `(low + high)/2`. Figure 7.9 shows how to find key `11` in the list {$2, 4, 7, 10, 11, 45, 50, 59, 60, 66, 69, 70, 79$} using binary search.

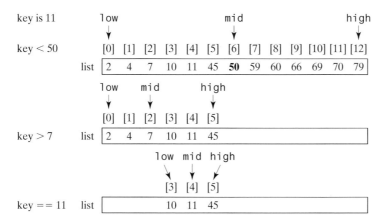

key is 11

key < 50

key > 7

key == 11

FIGURE 7.9 Binary search eliminates half of the list from further consideration after each comparison.

You now know how the binary search works. The next task is to implement it in Java. Don't rush to give a complete implementation. Implement it incrementally, one step at a time. You may start with the first iteration of the search, as shown in Figure 7.10a. It compares the key with the middle element in the list whose `low` index is `0` and `high` index is `list.length - 1`. If `key < list[mid]`, set the `high` index to `mid - 1`; if `key == list[mid]`, a match is found and return `mid`; if `key > list[mid]`, set the `low` index to `mid + 1`.

Next, consider implementing the method to perform the search repeatedly by adding a loop, as shown in Figure 7.10b. The search ends if the key is found, or if the key is not found when `low > high`.

why not −1?

```
public static int binarySearch(
    int[] list, int key) {
  int low = 0;
  int high = list.length - 1;

  int mid = (low + high) / 2;
  if (key < list[mid])
    high = mid - 1;
  else if (key == list[mid])
    return mid;
  else
    low = mid + 1;

}
```

```
public static int binarySearch(
    int[] list, int key) {
  int low = 0;
  int high = list.length - 1;

  while (high >= low) {
    int mid = (low + high) / 2;
    if (key < list[mid])
      high = mid - 1;
    else if (key == list[mid])
      return mid;
    else
      low = mid + 1;
  }

  return -1; // Not found
}
```

(a) Version 1   (b) Version 2

FIGURE 7.10 Binary search is implemented incrementally.

When the key is not found, `low` is the insertion point where a key would be inserted to maintain the order of the list. It is more useful to return the insertion point than −1. The method must return a negative value to indicate that the key is not in the list. Can it simply return −`low`? No. If the key is less than `list[0]`, `low` would be 0. −0 is 0. This would indicate the key matches `list[0]`. A good choice is to let the method return −`low` − 1 if the key is not in the list. Returning −`low` − 1 indicates not only that the key is not in the list, but also where the key would be inserted.

The complete program is given in Listing 7.7.

LISTING 7.7   BinarySearch.java

```java
public class BinarySearch {
  /** Use binary search to find the key in the list */
  public static int binarySearch(int[] list, int key) {
    int low = 0;
    int high = list.length - 1;

    while (high >= low) {
      int mid = (low + high) / 2;
      if (key < list[mid])
        high = mid - 1;
      else if (key == list[mid])
        return mid;
      else
        low = mid + 1;
    }

    return -low - 1; // Now high < low, key not found
  }
}
```

first half (line 10)

second half (line 14)

The binary search returns the index of the search key if it is contained in the list (line 12). Otherwise, it returns −low − 1 (line 17).

What would happen if we replaced (high >= low) in line 7 with (high > low)? The search would miss a possible matching element. Consider a list with just one element. The search would miss the element.

Does the method still work if there are duplicate elements in the list? Yes, as long as the elements are sorted in increasing order. The method returns the index of one of the matching elements if the element is in the list.

The precondition for the binary search method is that the list must be sorted in increasing order. The postcondition is that the method returns the index of the element that matches the key if the key is in the list or a negative integer k such that −k − 1 is the position for inserting the key. Precondition and postcondition are the terms often used to describe the properties of a method. Preconditions are the things that are true before the method is invoked, and postconditions are the things that are true after the method is returned:

precondition
postcondition

To better understand this method, trace it with the following statements and identify low and high when the method returns.

```java
int[] list = {2, 4, 7, 10, 11, 45, 50, 59, 60, 66, 69, 70, 79};
int i = BinarySearch.binarySearch(list, 2);  // Returns 0
int j = BinarySearch.binarySearch(list, 11); // Returns 4
int k = BinarySearch.binarySearch(list, 12); // Returns −6
int l = BinarySearch.binarySearch(list, 1);  // Returns −1
int m = BinarySearch.binarySearch(list, 3);  // Returns −2
```

Here is the table that lists the low and high values when the method exits, and the value returned from invoking the method.

Method	Low	High	Value Returned
binarySearch(list, 2)	0	1	0 (mid)
binarySearch(list, 11)	3	5	4 (mid)
binarySearch(list, 12)	5	4	−6
binarySearch(list, 1)	0	−1	−1
binarySearch(list, 3)	1	0	−2

Note

Linear search is useful for finding an element in a small array or an unsorted array, but it is inefficient for large arrays. Binary search is more efficient, but it requires that the array be presorted.

binary search benefits

7.10.1 If `high` is a very large integer such as the maximum `int` value 2147483647, `(low + high) / 2` may cause overflow. How do you fix it to avoid overflow?

✓ **Check Point**

7.10.2 Use Figure 7.9 as an example to show how to apply the binary search approach to a search for key 10 and key 12 in list {2, 4, 7, 10, 11, 45, 50, 59, 60, 66, 69, 70, 79}.

7.10.3 If the binary search method returns −4, is the key in the list? Where should the key be inserted if you wish to insert the key into the list?

7.11 Sorting Arrays

Sorting, like searching, is a common task in computer programming. Many different algorithms have been developed for sorting. This section introduces an intuitive sorting algorithm: selection sort.

 Key Point

VideoNote

Selection sort

Suppose you want to sort a list in ascending order. Selection sort finds the smallest number in the list and swaps it with the first element. It then finds the smallest number remaining and swaps it with the second element, and so on, until only a single number remains. Figure 7.11 shows how to sort the list {2, 9, 5, 4, 8, 1, 6} using selection sort.

selection sort

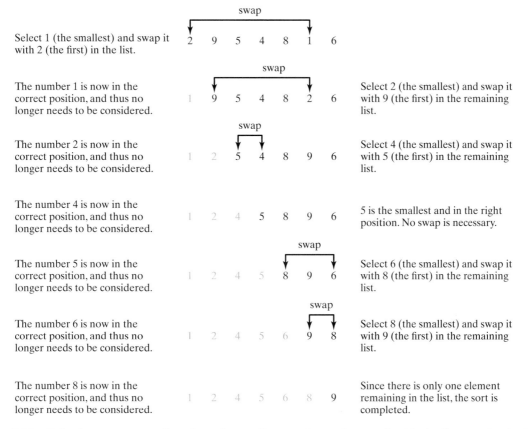

FIGURE 7.11 Selection sort repeatedly selects the smallest number and swaps it with the first number in the list.

You know how the selection-sort approach works. The task now is to implement it in Java. Beginners find it difficult to develop a complete solution on the first attempt. Start by writing the code for the first iteration to find the smallest element in the list and swap it with the first element, then observe what would be different for the second iteration, the third, and so on. The insight this gives will enable you to write a loop that generalizes all the iterations.

selection sort animation on Companion Website

The solution can be described as follows:

```
for (int i = 0; i < list.length - 1; i++) {
  select the smallest element in list[i..list.length-1];
  swap the smallest with list[i], if necessary;
  // list[i] is in its correct position.
  // The next iteration applies on list[i+1..list.length-1]
}
```

Listing 7.8 implements the solution.

LISTING 7.8 SelectionSort.java

```
1  public class SelectionSort {
2    /** The method for sorting the numbers */
3    public static void selectionSort(double[] list) {
4      for (int i = 0; i < list.length - 1; i++) {
5        // Find the minimum in the list[i..list.length-1]
6        double currentMin = list[i];
7        int currentMinIndex = i;
8
9        for (int j = i + 1; j < list.length; j++) {
10         if (currentMin > list[j]) {
11           currentMin = list[j];
12           currentMinIndex = j;
13         }
14       }
15
16       // Swap list[i] with list[currentMinIndex] if necessary
17       if (currentMinIndex != i) {
18         list[currentMinIndex] = list[i];
19         list[i] = currentMin;
20       }
21     }
22   }
23 }
```

select (line 9)

swap (line 17)

The `selectionSort(double[] list)` method sorts any array of `double` elements. The method is implemented with a nested `for` loop. The outer loop (with the loop control variable `i` in line 4) is iterated in order to find the smallest element in the list, which ranges from `list[i]` to `list[list.length-1]`, and exchanges it with `list[i]`.

The variable `i` is initially `0`. After each iteration of the outer loop, `list[i]` is in the right place. Eventually, all the elements are put in the right place; therefore, the whole list is sorted. To understand this method better, trace it with the following statements:

```
double[] list = {1, 9, 4.5, 6.6, 5.7, -4.5};
SelectionSort.selectionSort(list);
```

7.11.1 Use Figure 7.11 as an example to show how to apply the selection-sort approach to sort {3.4, 5, 3, 3.5, 2.2, 1.9, 2}.

7.11.2 How do you modify the `selectionSort` method in Listing 7.8 to sort numbers in decreasing order?

7.12 The Arrays Class

The `java.util.Arrays` class contains useful methods for common array operations such as sorting and searching.

The `java.util.Arrays` class contains various static methods for sorting and searching arrays, comparing arrays, filling array elements, and returning a string representation of the array. These methods are overloaded for all primitive types.

You can use the `sort` or `parallelSort` method to sort a whole array or a partial array. For example, the following code sorts an array of numbers and an array of characters:

sort
parallelSort

```java
double[] numbers = {6.0, 4.4, 1.9, 2.9, 3.4, 3.5};
java.util.Arrays.sort(numbers); // Sort the whole array
java.util.Arrays.parallelSort(numbers); // Sort the whole array

char[] chars = {'a', 'A', '4', 'F', 'D', 'P'};
java.util.Arrays.sort(chars, 1, 3); // Sort part of the array
java.util.Arrays.parallelSort(chars, 1, 3); // Sort part of the array
```

Invoking `sort(numbers)` sorts the whole array `numbers`. Invoking `sort(chars, 1, 3)` sorts a partial array from `chars[1]` to `chars[3-1]`. `parallelSort` is more efficient if your computer has multiple processors.

You can use the `binarySearch` method to search for a key in an array. The array must be pre-sorted in increasing order. If the key is not in the array, the method returns $-($insertionIndex $+ 1)$. For example, the following code searches the keys in an array of integers and an array of characters:

binarySearch

```java
int[] list = {2, 4, 7, 10, 11, 45, 50, 59, 60, 66, 69, 70, 79};
System.out.println("1. Index is " +
  java.util.Arrays.binarySearch(list, 11));
System.out.println("2. Index is " +
  java.util.Arrays.binarySearch(list, 12));

char[] chars = {'a', 'c', 'g', 'x', 'y', 'z'};
System.out.println("3. Index is " +
  java.util.Arrays.binarySearch(chars, 'a'));
System.out.println("4. Index is " +
  java.util.Arrays.binarySearch(chars, 't'));
```

The output of the preceding code is as follows:

```
Index is 4
Index is -6
Index is 0
Index is -4
```

You can use the `equals` method to check whether two arrays are strictly equal. Two arrays are strictly equal if their corresponding elements are the same. In the following code, `list1` and `list2` are equal, but `list2` and `list3` are not.

equals

```java
int[] list1 = {2, 4, 7, 10};
int[] list2 = {2, 4, 7, 10};
int[] list3 = {4, 2, 7, 10};
System.out.println(java.util.Arrays.equals(list1, list2)); // true
System.out.println(java.util.Arrays.equals(list2, list3)); // false
```

You can use the `fill` method to fill in all or part of the array. For example, the following code fills `list1` with 5 and fills 8 into elements `list2[1]` through `list2[5-1]`.

fill

```java
int[] list1 = {2, 4, 7, 10};
int[] list2 = {2, 4, 7, 7, 7, 10};
java.util.Arrays.fill(list1, 5); // Fill 5 to the whole array
java.util.Arrays.fill(list2, 1, 5, 8); // Fill 8 to a partial array
```

toString

You can also use the `toString` method to return a string that represents all elements in the array. This is a quick and simple way to display all elements in the array. For example, the following code:

```
int[] list = {2, 4, 7, 10};
System.out.println(java.util.Arrays.toString(list));
```

displays `[2, 4, 7, 10]`.

7.12.1 What types of array can be sorted using the `java.util.Arrays.sort` method? Does this `sort` method create a new array?

7.12.2 To apply `java.util.Arrays.binarySearch(array, key)`, should the array be sorted in increasing order, in decreasing order, or neither?

7.12.3 Show the output of the following code:

```
int[] list1 = {2, 4, 7, 10};
java.util.Arrays.fill(list1, 7);
System.out.println(java.util.Arrays.toString(list1));

int[] list2 = {2, 4, 7, 10};
System.out.println(java.util.Arrays.toString(list2));
System.out.print(java.util.Arrays.equals(list1, list2));
```

7.13 Command-Line Arguments

The main method can receive string arguments from the command line.

Perhaps you have already noticed the unusual header for the `main` method, which has the parameter `args` of the `String[]` type. It is clear that `args` is an array of strings. The `main` method is just like a regular method with a parameter. You can call a regular method by passing actual parameters. Can you pass arguments to `main`? Yes, of course you can. In the following examples, the `main` method in class `TestMain` is invoked by a method in `A`:

```
public class A {
  public static void main(String[] args) {
    String[] strings = {"New York",
      "Boston", "Atlanta"};
    TestMain.main(strings);
  }
}
```

```
public class TestMain {
  public static void main(String[] args) {
    for (int i = 0; i < args.length; i++)
      System.out.println(args[i]);
  }
}
```

A `main` method is just like a regular method. Furthermore, you can pass arguments to a main method from the command line.

7.13.1 Passing Strings to the **main** Method

You can pass strings to a `main` method from the command line when you run the program. The following command line, for example, starts the program `TestMain` with three strings: `arg0`, `arg1`, and `arg2`:

```
java TestMain arg0 arg1 arg2
```

`arg0`, `arg1`, and `arg2` are strings, but they don't have to appear in double quotes on the command line. The strings are separated by a space. A string that contains a space must be enclosed in double quotes. Consider the following command line:

```
java TestMain "First num" alpha 53
```

It starts the program with three strings: First num, alpha, and 53. Since First num is a string, it is enclosed in double quotes. Note 53 is actually treated as a string. You can use "53" instead of 53 in the command line.

When the main method is invoked, the Java interpreter creates an array to hold the command-line arguments and pass the array reference to args. For example, if you invoke a program with n arguments, the Java interpreter creates an array such as the one that follows:

```
args = new String[n];
```

The Java interpreter then passes args to invoke the main method.

> **Note**
> If you run the program with no strings passed, the array is created with new String[0]. In this case, the array is empty with length 0. args references to this empty array. Therefore, args is not null, but args.length is 0.

7.13.2 Case Study: Calculator

Suppose you are to develop a program that performs arithmetic operations on integers. The program receives an expression. The expression consists of an integer followed by an operator and another integer. For example, to add two integers, use this command:

VideoNote
Command-line arguments

```
java Calculator 2 + 3
```

The program will display the following output:

```
2 + 3 = 5
```

Figure 7.12 shows sample runs of the program.

The strings passed to the main program are stored in args, which is an array of strings. The first string is stored in args[0], and args.length is the number of strings passed.

Here are the steps in the program:

1. Use args.length to determine whether the expression has been provided as three arguments in the command line. If not, terminate the program using System.exit(1).

2. Perform a binary arithmetic operation on the operands args[0] and args[2] using the operator in args[1].

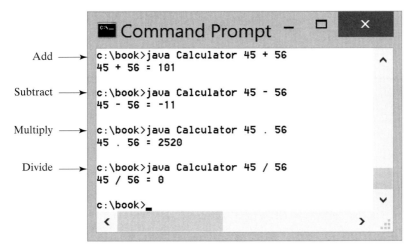

FIGURE 7.12 The program takes three arguments (operand1 operator operand2) from the command line and displays the expression and the result of the arithmetic operation.

The program is given in Listing 7.9.

Listing 7.9 Calculator.java

check argument

check operator

```
 1  public class Calculator {
 2    /** Main method */
 3    public static void main(String[] args) {
 4      // Check number of strings passed
 5      if (args.length != 3) {
 6        System.out.println(
 7          "Usage: java Calculator operand1 operator operand2");
 8        System.exit(1);
 9      }
10
11      // The result of the operation
12      int result = 0;
13
14      // Determine the operator
15      switch (args[1].charAt(0)) {
16        case '+': result = Integer.parseInt(args[0]) +
17                           Integer.parseInt(args[2]);
18               break;
19        case '-': result = Integer.parseInt(args[0]) -
20                           Integer.parseInt(args[2]);
21               break;
22        case '.': result = Integer.parseInt(args[0]) *
23                           Integer.parseInt(args[2]);
24               break;
25        case '/': result = Integer.parseInt(args[0]) /
26                           Integer.parseInt(args[2]);
27      }
28
29      // Display result
30      System.out.println(args[0] + ' ' + args[1] + ' ' + args[2]
31        + " = " + result);
32    }
33  }
```

`Integer.parseInt(args[0])` (line 16) converts a digital string into an integer. The string must consist of digits. If not, the program will terminate abnormally.

We used the . symbol for multiplication, not the common * symbol. The reason for this is the * symbol refers to all the files in the current directory when it is used on a command line. The following program displays all the files in the current directory when issuing the command `java Test *`:

```
public class Test {
  public static void main(String[] args) {
    for (int i = 0; i < args.length; i++)
      System.out.println(args[i]);
  }
}
```

To circumvent this problem, we will have to use a different symbol for the multiplication operator.

7.13.1 This book declares the `main` method as

`public static void main(String[] args)`

Can it be replaced by one of the following lines?

a. `public static void main(String args[])`
b. `public static void main(String[] x)`

    c. **public static void** main(String x[])
    d. **static void** main(String x[])

7.13.2   Show the output of the following program when invoked using

    1. **java Test I have a dream**

    2. **java Test "1 2 3"**

    3. **java Test**

```java
public class Test {
  public static void main(String[] args) {
    System.out.println("Number of strings is " + args.length);
    for (int i = 0; i < args.length; i++)
      System.out.println(args[i]);
  }
}
```

KEY TERMS

anonymous array 260	indexed variable 250
array 248	linear search 267
array initializer 250	off-by-one error 253
binary search 267	postcondition 270
garbage collection 258	precondition 270
index 248	selection sort 271

CHAPTER SUMMARY

1. A variable is declared as an *array* type using the syntax `elementType[] arrayRefVar` or `elementType arrayRefVar[]`. The style `elementType[] arrayRefVar` is preferred, although `elementType arrayRefVar[]` is legal.

2. Unlike declarations for primitive data type variables, the declaration of an array variable does not allocate any space in memory for the array. An array variable is not a primitive data type variable. An array variable contains a reference to an array.

3. You cannot assign elements to an array unless it has already been created. You can create an array by using the `new` operator with the following syntax: `new elementType[arraySize]`.

4. Each element in the array is represented using the syntax `arrayRefVar[index]`. An *index* must be an integer or an integer expression.

5. After an array is created, its size becomes permanent and can be obtained using `arrayRefVar.length`. Since the index of an array always begins with `0`, the last index is always `arrayRefVar.length - 1`. An out-of-bounds error will occur if you attempt to reference elements beyond the bounds of an array.

6. Programmers often mistakenly reference the first element in an array with index `1`, but it should be `0`. This is called the index *off-by-one error*.

7. When an array is created, its elements are assigned the default value of 0 for the numeric primitive data types, \u0000 for char types, and `false` for `boolean` types.

8. Java has a shorthand notation, known as the *array initializer*, which combines declaring an array, creating an array, and initializing an array in one statement, using the syntax `elementType[] arrayRefVar = {value0, value1, . . . , valuek}`.

9. When you pass an array argument to a method, you are actually passing the reference of the array; that is, the called method can modify the elements in the caller's original array.

10. If an array is sorted, *binary search* is more efficient than *linear search* for finding an element in the array.

11. *Selection sort* finds the smallest number in the list and swaps it with the first element. It then finds the smallest number remaining and swaps it with the first element in the remaining list, and so on, until only a single number remains.

QUIZ

Answer the quiz for this chapter online at the Companion Website.

MyProgrammingLab™ **PROGRAMMING EXERCISES**

Sections 7.2–7.5

*7.1 (*Assign grades*) Write a program that reads student scores, gets the best score, and then assigns grades based on the following scheme:

Grade is A if score is ≥ best −10;
Grade is B if score is ≥ best −20;
Grade is C if score is ≥ best −30;
Grade is D if score is ≥ best −40;
Grade is F otherwise.

The program prompts the user to enter the total number of students, then prompts the user to enter all of the scores, and concludes by displaying the grades. Here is a sample run:

```
Enter the number of students: 4 ↵Enter
Enter 4 scores: 40 55 70 58 ↵Enter
Student 0 score is 40 and grade is C
Student 1 score is 55 and grade is B
Student 2 score is 70 and grade is A
Student 3 score is 58 and grade is B
```

7.2 (*Reverse the numbers entered*) Write a program that reads 10 integers then displays them in the reverse of the order in which they were read.

**7.3 (*Count occurrence of numbers*) Write a program that reads the integers between 1 and 100 and counts the occurrences of each. Assume the input ends with 0. Here is a sample run of the program:

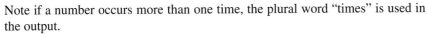

```
Enter the integers between 1 and 100: 2 5 6 5 4 3 23 43 2 0  ↵Enter
2 occurs 2 times
3 occurs 1 time
4 occurs 1 time
5 occurs 2 times
6 occurs 1 time
23 occurs 1 time
43 occurs 1 time
```

Note if a number occurs more than one time, the plural word "times" is used in the output.

7.4 (*Analyze scores*) Write a program that reads an unspecified number of scores and determines how many scores are above or equal to the average, and how many scores are below the average. Enter a negative number to signify the end of the input. Assume the maximum number of scores is 100.

**7.5 (*Print distinct numbers*) Write a program that reads in 10 numbers and displays the number of distinct numbers and the distinct numbers in their input order and separated by exactly one space (i.e., if a number appears multiple times, it is displayed only once). (*Hint*: Read a number and store it to an array if it is new. If the number is already in the array, ignore it.) After the input, the array contains the distinct numbers. Here is the sample run of the program:

```
Enter 10 numbers: 1 2 3 2 1 6 3 4 5 2  ↵Enter
The number of distinct numbers is 6
The distinct numbers are: 1 2 3 6 4 5
```

*7.6 (*Revise Listing 5.15, PrimeNumber.java*) Listing 5.15 determines whether a number n is prime by checking whether 2, 3, 4, 5, 6, . . . , n / 2 is a divisor. If a divisor is found, n is not prime. A more efficient approach is to check whether any of the prime numbers less than or equal to $\sqrt{n}$ can divide n evenly. If not, n is prime. Rewrite Listing 5.15 to display the first 50 prime numbers using this approach. You need to use an array to store the prime numbers, and later use them to check whether they are possible divisors for n.

*7.7 (*Count single digits*) Write a program that generates 100 random integers between 0 and 9 and displays the count for each number. (*Hint*: Use an array of 10 integers, say counts, to store the counts for the number of 0s, 1s, . . . , 9s.)

Sections 7.6–7.8

7.8 (*Average an array*) Write two overloaded methods that return the average of an array with the following headers:

```
public static int average(int[] array)
public static double average(double[] array)
```

Write a test program that prompts the user to enter 10 double values, invokes this method, then displays the average value.

7.9 (*Find the smallest element*) Write a method that finds the smallest element in an array of double values using the following header:

```
public static double min(double[] array)
```

Write a test program that prompts the user to enter 10 numbers, invokes this method to return the minimum value, and displays the minimum value. Here is a sample run of the program:

```
Enter 10 numbers: 1.9 2.5 3.7 2 1.5 6 3 4 5 2 ↵Enter
The minimum number is 1.5
```

7.10 (*Find the index of the smallest element*) Write a method that returns the index of the smallest element in an array of integers. If the number of such elements is greater than 1, return the smallest index. Use the following header:

```
public static int indexOfSmallestElement(double[] array)
```

Write a test program that prompts the user to enter 10 numbers, invokes this method to return the index of the smallest element, and displays the index.

*7.11 (*Statistics: compute deviation*) Programming Exercise 5.45 computes the standard deviation of numbers. This exercise uses a different but equivalent formula to compute the standard deviation of n numbers.

$$\text{mean} = \frac{\sum_{i=1}^{n} x_i}{n} = \frac{x_1 + x_2 + \cdots + x_n}{n} \qquad \text{deviation} = \sqrt{\frac{\sum_{i=1}^{n}(x_i - \text{mean})^2}{n - 1}}$$

To compute the standard deviation with this formula, you have to store the individual numbers using an array, so they can be used after the mean is obtained.

Your program should contain the following methods:

```
/** Compute the deviation of double values */
public static double deviation(double[] x)

/** Compute the mean of an array of double values */
public static double mean(double[] x)
```

Write a test program that prompts the user to enter 10 numbers and displays the mean and standard deviation, as presented in the following sample run:

```
Enter 10 numbers: 1.9 2.5 3.7 2 1 6 3 4 5 2 ↵Enter
The mean is 3.11
The standard deviation is 1.55738
```

*7.12 (*Reverse an array*) The `reverse` method in Section 7.7 reverses an array by copying it to a new array. Rewrite the method that reverses the array passed in the argument and returns this array. Write a test program that prompts the user to enter 10 numbers, invokes the method to reverse the numbers, and displays the numbers.

Section 7.9

*7.13 (*Random number chooser*) Write a method that returns a random number between 1 and 54, excluding the numbers passed in the argument. The method header is specified as follows:

```
public static int getRandom(int... numbers)
```

7.14 (*Computing gcd*) Write a method that returns the gcd of an unspecified number of integers. The method header is specified as follows:

```
public static int gcd(int... numbers)
```

Write a test program that prompts the user to enter five numbers, invokes the method to find the gcd of these numbers, and displays the gcd.

Sections 7.10–7.12

7.15 (*Eliminate duplicates*) Write a method that returns a new array by eliminating the duplicate values in the array using the following method header:

```
public static int[] eliminateDuplicates(int[] list)
```

Write a test program that reads in 10 integers, invokes the method, and displays the distinct numbers separated by exactly one space. Here is a sample run of the program:

```
Enter 10 numbers: 1 2 3 2 1 6 3 4 5 2  ↵Enter
The distinct numbers are: 1 2 3 6 4 5
```

7.16 (*Execution time*) Write a program that randomly generates an array of 100,000 integers and a key. Estimate the execution time of invoking the `linearSearch` method in Listing 7.6. Sort the array and estimate the execution time of invoking the `binarySearch` method in Listing 7.7. You can use the following code template to obtain the execution time:

```
long startTime = System.nanoTime();
perform the task;
long endTime = System.nanoTime();
long executionTime = endTime - startTime;
```

**7.17 (*Sort students*) Write a program that prompts the user to enter the number of students, the students' names, and their scores and prints student names in decreasing order of their scores. Assume the name is a string without spaces, use the `Scanner`'s `next()` method to read a name.

**7.18 (*Bubble sort*) Write a sort method that uses the bubble-sort algorithm. The bubble-sort algorithm makes several passes through the array. On each pass, successive neighboring pairs are compared. If a pair is not in order, its values are swapped; otherwise, the values remain unchanged. The technique is called a *bubble sort* or *sinking sort* because the smaller values gradually "bubble" their way to the top, and the larger values "sink" to the bottom. Write a test program that reads in 10 double numbers, invokes the method, and displays the sorted numbers.

**7.19 (*Sorted?*) Write the following method that returns true if the list is already sorted in nondecreasing order:

```
public static boolean isSorted(int[] list)
```

Write a test program that prompts the user to enter a list and displays whether the list is sorted or not. Here is a sample run. Note that the program first prompts the user to enter the size of the list.

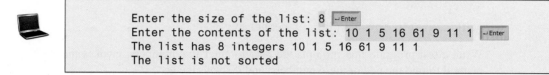

```
Enter the size of the list: 8 ↵Enter
Enter the contents of the list: 10 1 5 16 61 9 11 1 ↵Enter
The list has 8 integers 10 1 5 16 61 9 11 1
The list is not sorted
```

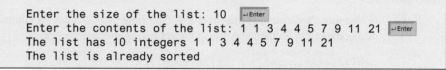

```
Enter the size of the list: 10 ↵Enter
Enter the contents of the list: 1 1 3 4 4 5 7 9 11 21 ↵Enter
The list has 10 integers 1 1 3 4 4 5 7 9 11 21
The list is already sorted
```

*7.20 (*Revise selection sort*) In Listing 7.8, you used selection sort to sort an array. The selection-sort method repeatedly finds the smallest number in the current array and swaps it with the first. Rewrite this program by finding the largest number and swapping it with the last. Write a test program that reads in 10 double numbers, invokes the method, and displays the sorted numbers.

Section 7.13

*7.21 (*Sum integers*) Write a program that passes an unspecified number of integers from command line and displays their total.

*7.22 (*Find the number of uppercase letters in a string*) Write a program that passes a string to the command line and displays the number of uppercase letters in the string.

Comprehensive

**7.23 (*Game: locker puzzle*) A school has 100 lockers and 100 students. All lockers are closed on the first day of school. As the students enter, the first student, denoted as S1, opens every locker. Then the second student, S2, begins with the second locker, denoted as L2, and closes every other locker. Student S3 begins with the third locker and changes every third locker (closes it if it was open and opens it if it was closed). Student S4 begins with locker L4 and changes every fourth locker. Student S5 starts with L5 and changes every fifth locker, and so on, until student S100 changes L100.

After all the students have passed through the building and changed the lockers, which lockers are open? Write a program to find your answer and display all open locker numbers separated by exactly one space.

(*Hint*: Use an array of 100 Boolean elements, each of which indicates whether a locker is open (`true`) or closed (`false`). Initially, all lockers are closed.)

**7.24 (*Simulation: coupon collector's problem*) Coupon collector is a classic statistics problem with many practical applications. The problem is to repeatedly pick objects from a set of objects and find out how many picks are needed for all the objects to be picked at least once. A variation of the problem is to pick cards from a shuffled deck of 52 cards repeatedly, and find out how many picks are needed before you see one of each suit. Assume a picked card is placed back in the deck before picking another. Write a program to simulate the number of picks needed to get four cards from each suit and display the four cards picked (it is possible a card may be picked twice). Here is a sample run of the program:

```
Queen of Spades
5 of Clubs
Queen of Hearts
4 of Diamonds
Number of picks: 12
```

7.25 (*Algebra: solve quadratic equations*) Write a method for solving a quadratic equation using the following header:

```
public static int solveQuadratic(double[] eqn, double[] roots)
```

The coefficients of a quadratic equation $ax^2 + bx + c = 0$ are passed to the array eqn and the real roots are stored in roots. The method returns the number of real roots. See Programming Exercise 3.1 on how to solve a quadratic equation.

Write a program that prompts the user to enter values for a, b, and c and displays the number of real roots and all real roots.

7.26 (*Strictly identical arrays*) The arrays list1 and list2 are *strictly identical* if their corresponding elements are equal. Write a method that returns true if list1 and list2 are strictly identical, using the following header:

```
public static boolean equals(int[] list1, int[] list2)
```

Write a test program that prompts the user to enter two lists of integers and displays whether the two are strictly identical. Here are the sample runs. Note the first number in the input indicates the number of the elements in the list. This number is not part of the list.

```
Enter list1 size and contents: 5 2 5 6 1 6  ↵ Enter
Enter list2 size and contents: 5 2 5 6 1 6  ↵ Enter
Two lists are strictly identical
```

```
Enter list1 size and contents: 5 2 5 6 6 1  ↵ Enter
Enter list2 size and contents: 5 2 5 6 1 6  ↵ Enter
Two lists are not strictly identical
```

7.27 (*Identical arrays*) The arrays list1 and list2 are *identical* if they have the same contents. Write a method that returns true if list1 and list2 are identical, using the following header:

```
public static boolean equals(int[] list1, int[] list2)
```

Write a test program that prompts the user to enter two lists of integers and displays whether the two are identical. Here are the sample runs. Note the first number in the input indicates the number of the elements in the list. This number is not part of the list.

```
Enter list1 size and contents: 5 2 5 6 6 1  ↵ Enter
Enter list2 size and contents: 5 5 2 6 1 6  ↵ Enter
Two lists are identical
```

```
Enter list1: 5 5 5 6 6 1  ↵ Enter
Enter list2: 5 2 5 6 1 6  ↵ Enter
Two lists are not identical
```

*7.28 (*Math: combinations*) Write a program that prompts the user to enter 10 integers and displays all combinations of picking two numbers from the 10 numbers.

*7.29 (*Game: pick four cards*) Write a program that picks four cards from a deck of 52 cards and computes their sum. An Ace, King, Queen, and Jack represent 1, 13, 12, and 11, respectively. Your program should display the number of picks that yields the sum of 24.

*7.30 (*Pattern recognition: consecutive four equal numbers*) Write the following method that tests whether the array has four consecutive numbers with the same value:

```java
public static boolean isConsecutiveFour(int[] values)
```

Write a test program that prompts the user to enter a series of integers and displays it if the series contains four consecutive numbers with the same value. Your program should first prompt the user to enter the input size—i.e., the number of values in the series. Here are sample runs:

```
Enter the number of values: 8  ↵ Enter
Enter the values: 3 4 5 5 5 5 4 5  ↵ Enter
The list has consecutive fours
```

```
Enter the number of values: 9  ↵ Enter
Enter the values: 3 4 5 5 6 5 5 4 5  ↵ Enter
The list has no consecutive fours
```

**7.31 (*Merge two sorted lists*) Write the following method that merges two sorted lists into a new sorted list:

```java
public static int[] merge(int[] list1, int[] list2)
```

Implement the method in a way that takes at most `list1.length + list2.length` comparisons. See liveexample.pearsoncmg.com/dsanimation/ MergeSortNeweBook.html for an animation of the implementation. Write a test program that prompts the user to enter two sorted lists and displays the merged list. Here is a sample run. Note the first number in the input indicates the number of the elements in the list. This number is not part of the list.

```
Enter list1 size and contents: 5 1 5 16 61 111  ↵ Enter
Enter list2 size and contents: 4 2 4 5 6  ↵ Enter
list1 is 1 5 16 61 111
list2 is 2 4 5 6
The merged list is 1 2 4 5 5 6 16 61 111
```

**7.32 (*Partition of a list*) Write the following method that partitions the list using the first element, called a *pivot*:

```
public static int partition(int[] list)
```

After the partition, the elements in the list are rearranged so all the elements before the pivot are less than or equal to the pivot, and the elements after the pivot are greater than the pivot. The method returns the index where the pivot is located in the new list. For example, suppose the list is {5, 2, 9, 3, 6, 8}. After the partition, the list becomes {3, 2, 5, 9, 6, 8}. Implement the method in a way that takes at most `list.length` comparisons. See liveexample.pearsoncmg.com/dsanimation/QuickSortNeweBook.html for an animation of the implementation. Write a test program that prompts the user to enter the size of the list and the contents of the list and displays the list after the partition. Here is a sample run.

```
Enter list size: 8 ↵Enter
Enter list content: 10 1 5 16 61 9 11 1 ↵Enter
After the partition, the list is 9 1 5 1 10 61 11 16
```

*7.33 (*Culture: Chinese Zodiac*) Simplify Listing 3.9 using an array of strings to store the animal names.

**7.34 (*Sort characters in a string*) Write a method that returns a sorted string using the following header:

```
public static String sort(String s)
```

For example, `sort("acb")` returns abc.

Write a test program that prompts the user to enter a string and displays the sorted string.

***7.35 (*Game: hangman*) Write a hangman game that randomly generates a word and prompts the user to guess one letter at a time, as presented in the sample run. Each letter in the word is displayed as an asterisk. When the user makes a correct guess, the actual letter is then displayed. When the user finishes a word, display the number of misses and ask the user whether to continue to play with another word. Declare an array to store words, as follows:

```
// Add any words you wish in this array
String[] words = {"write", "that",...};
```

```
(Guess) Enter a letter in word ******* > p ↵Enter
(Guess) Enter a letter in word p****** > r ↵Enter
(Guess) Enter a letter in word pr**r** > p ↵Enter
        p is already in the word
(Guess) Enter a letter in word pr**r** > o ↵Enter
(Guess) Enter a letter in word pro*r** > g ↵Enter
(Guess) Enter a letter in word progr** > n ↵Enter
        n is not in the word
(Guess) Enter a letter in word progr** > m ↵Enter
(Guess) Enter a letter in word progr*m > a ↵Enter
The word is program. You missed 1 time
Do you want to guess another word? Enter y or n>
```

***7.36 (*Game: Eight Queens*) The classic Eight Queens puzzle is to place eight queens on a chessboard such that no two queens can attack each other (i.e., no two queens are on the same row, same column, or same diagonal). There are many possible solutions. Write a program that displays one such solution. A sample output is shown below:

```
|Q| | | | | | | |
| | | | |Q| | | |
| | | | | | | |Q|
| | | | |Q| | | |
| | |Q| | | | | |
| | | | | | |Q| |
| |Q| | | | | | |
| | | |Q| | | | |
```

***7.37 (*Game: bean machine*) The bean machine, also known as a quincunx or the Galton box, is a device for statistics experiments named after English scientist Sir Francis Galton. It consists of an upright board with evenly spaced nails (or pegs) in a triangular form, as shown in Figure 7.13.

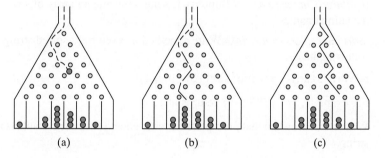

| (a) | (b) | (c) |

FIGURE 7.13 Each ball takes a random path and falls into a slot.

Balls are dropped from the opening of the board. Every time a ball hits a nail, it has a 50% chance of falling to the left or to the right. The piles of balls are accumulated in the slots at the bottom of the board.

Write a program that simulates the bean machine. Your program should prompt the user to enter the number of the balls and the number of the slots in the machine. Simulate the falling of each ball by printing its path. For example, the path for the ball in Figure 7.13b is LLRRLLR and the path for the ball in Figure 7.13c is RLRRLRR. Display the final buildup of the balls in the slots in a histogram. Here is a sample run of the program:

(*Hint*: Create an array named `slots`. Each element in `slots` stores the number of balls in a slot. Each ball falls into a slot via a path. The number of Rs in a path is the position of the slot where the ball falls. For example, for the path LRLR-LRR, the ball falls into `slots[4]`, and for the path RRLLLLL, the ball falls into `slots[2]`.)

```
Enter the number of balls to drop: 5 [↵Enter]
Enter the number of slots in the bean machine: 8 [↵Enter]

LRLRLRR
RRLLLRR
LLRLLRR
RRLLLLL
LRLRRLR

      O
      O
    OOO
```

MULTIDIMENSIONAL ARRAYS

Objectives

- To give examples of representing data using two-dimensional arrays (§8.1).

- To declare variables for two-dimensional arrays, create arrays, and access array elements in a two-dimensional array using row and column indices (§8.2).

- To program common operations for two-dimensional arrays (displaying arrays, summing all elements, finding the minimum and maximum elements, and random shuffling) (§8.3).

- To pass two-dimensional arrays to methods (§8.4).

- To write a program for grading multiple-choice questions using two-dimensional arrays (§8.5).

- To solve the closest pair problem using two-dimensional arrays (§8.6).

- To check a Sudoku solution using two-dimensional arrays (§8.7).

- To use multidimensional arrays (§8.8).

8.1 Introduction

Data in a table or a matrix can be represented using a two-dimensional array.

The preceding chapter introduced how to use one-dimensional arrays to store linear collections of elements. You can use a two-dimensional array to store a matrix or a table. For example, the following table that lists the distances between cities can be stored using a two-dimensional array named `distances`.

problem

Distance Table (in miles)							
	Chicago	**Boston**	**New York**	**Atlanta**	**Miami**	**Dallas**	**Houston**
Chicago	0	983	787	714	1375	967	1087
Boston	983	0	214	1102	1763	1723	1842
New York	787	214	0	888	1549	1548	1627
Atlanta	714	1102	888	0	661	781	810
Miami	1375	1763	1549	661	0	1426	1187
Dallas	967	1723	1548	781	1426	0	239
Houston	1087	1842	1627	810	1187	239	0

```
double[][] distances = {
  {0, 983, 787, 714, 1375, 967, 1087},
  {983, 0, 214, 1102, 1763, 1723, 1842},
  {787, 214, 0, 888, 1549, 1548, 1627},
  {714, 1102, 888, 0, 661, 781, 810},
  {1375, 1763, 1549, 661, 0, 1426, 1187},
  {967, 1723, 1548, 781, 1426, 0, 239},
  {1087, 1842, 1627, 810, 1187, 239, 0},
};
```

8.2 Two-Dimensional Array Basics

An element in a two-dimensional array is accessed through a row and a column index.

How do you declare a variable for two-dimensional arrays? How do you create a two-dimensional array? How do you access elements in a two-dimensional array? This section will address these issues.

8.2.1 Declaring Variables of Two-Dimensional Arrays and Creating Two-Dimensional Arrays

The syntax for declaring a two-dimensional array is as follows:

```
elementType[][] arrayRefVar;
```

or

```
elementType arrayRefVar[][]; // Allowed, but not preferred
```

As an example, here is how you would declare a two-dimensional array variable `matrix` of `int` values:

```
int[][] matrix;
```

or

```
int matrix[][]; // This style is allowed, but not preferred
```

You can create a two-dimensional array of 5-by-5 `int` values and assign it to `matrix` using this syntax:

```
matrix = new int[5][5];
```

Two subscripts are used in a two-dimensional array: one for the row, and the other for the column. As in a one-dimensional array, the index for each subscript is of the `int` type and starts from `0`, as shown in Figure 8.1a.

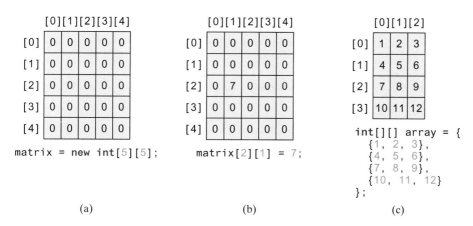

FIGURE 8.1 The index of each subscript of a two-dimensional array is an `int` value, starting from `0`.

To assign the value `7` to a specific element at row index `2` and column index `1`, as shown in Figure 8.1b, you can use the following syntax:

```
matrix[2][1] = 7;
```

 Caution

It is a common mistake to use `matrix[2, 1]` to access the element at row `2` and column `1`. In Java, each subscript must be enclosed in a pair of square brackets.

You can also use an array initializer to declare, create, and initialize a two-dimensional array. For example, the following code in (a) creates an array with the specified initial values, as shown in Figure 8.1c. This is equivalent to the code in (b).

int[][] array = {
  {1, 2, 3},
  {4, 5, 6},
  {7, 8, 9},
  {10, 11, 12}
};
	Equivalent	int[][] array = new int[4][3];
		array[0][0] = 1; array[0][1] = 2; array[0][2] = 3;
		array[1][0] = 4; array[1][1] = 5; array[1][2] = 6;
		array[2][0] = 7; array[2][1] = 8; array[2][2] = 9;
		array[3][0] = 10; array[3][1] = 11; array[3][2] = 12;

(a)		(b)

8.2.2 Obtaining the Lengths of Two-Dimensional Arrays

A two-dimensional array is actually an array in which each element is a one-dimensional array. The length of an array `x` is the number of elements in the array, which can be obtained using `x.length`. `x[0]`, `x[1]`, ..., and `x[x.length - 1]` are arrays. Their lengths can be obtained using `x[0].length`, `x[1].length`, ..., and `x[x.length - 1].length`.

292 Chapter 8 Multidimensional Arrays

For example, suppose that `x = new int[3][4]`, `x[0]`, `x[1]`, and `x[2]` are one-dimensional arrays and each contains four elements, as shown in Figure 8.2. `x.length` is 3, and `x[0].length`, `x[1].length`, and `x[2].length` are 4.

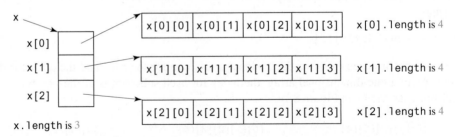

FIGURE 8.2 A two-dimensional array is a one-dimensional array in which each element is another one-dimensional array.

8.2.3 Ragged Arrays

ragged array

Each row in a two-dimensional array is itself an array. Thus, the rows can have different lengths. An array of this kind is known as a *ragged array*. Here is an example of creating a ragged array:

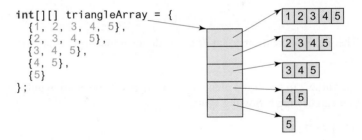

As you can see, `triangleArray[0].length` is 5, `triangleArray[1].length` is 4, `triangleArray[2].length` is 3, `triangleArray[3].length` is 2, and `triangle-Array[4].length` is 1.

If you don't know the values in a ragged array in advance, but do know the sizes—say, the same as in the preceding figure—you can create a ragged array using the following syntax:

```
int[][] triangleArray = new int[5][];
triangleArray[0] = new int[5];
triangleArray[1] = new int[4];
triangleArray[2] = new int[3];
triangleArray[3] = new int[2];
triangleArray[4] = new int[1];
```

You can now assign values to the array. For example,

```
triangleArray[0][3] = 4;
triangleArray[4][0] = 5;
```

Note

The syntax `new int[5][]` for creating an array requires the first index to be specified. The syntax `new int[][]` would be wrong.

8.2.1 Declare an array reference variable for a two-dimensional array of `int` values, create a 4-by-5 `int` matrix, and assign it to the variable.

Check
Point

8.2.2 Can the rows in a two-dimensional array have different lengths?

8.2.3 What is the output of the following code?

```
int[][] array = new int[5][6];
int[] x = {1, 2};
array[0] = x;
System.out.println("array[0][1] is " + array[0][1]);
```

8.2.4 Which of the following statements are valid?

```
int[][] r = new int[2];
int[] x = new int[];
int[][] y = new int[3][];
int[][] z = {{1, 2}};
int[][] m = {{1, 2}, {2, 3}};
int[][] n = {{1, 2}, {2, 3}, };
```

8.3 Processing Two-Dimensional Arrays

Nested `for` *loops are often used to process a two-dimensional array.*

Suppose an array `matrix` is created as follows:

Key
Point

```
int[][] matrix = new int[10][10];
```

The following are some examples of processing two-dimensional arrays.

1. *Initializing arrays with input values.* The following loop initializes the array with user input values:

```
java.util.Scanner input = new java.util.Scanner(System.in);
System.out.println("Enter " + matrix.length + " rows and " +
  matrix[0].length + " columns: ");
for (int row = 0; row < matrix.length; row++) {
  for (int column = 0; column < matrix[row].length; column++) {
    matrix[row][column] = input.nextInt();
  }
}
```

2. *Initializing arrays with random values.* The following loop initializes the array with random values between 0 and 99:

```
for (int row = 0; row < matrix.length; row++) {
  for (int column = 0; column < matrix[row].length; column++) {
    matrix[row][column] = (int)(Math.random() * 100);
  }
}
```

3. *Printing arrays.* To print a two-dimensional array, you have to print each element in the array using a loop like the following loop:

```
for (int row = 0; row < matrix.length; row++) {
  for (int column = 0; column < matrix[row].length; column++) {
    System.out.print(matrix[row][column] + " ");
  }

  System.out.println();
}
```

4. *Summing all elements.* Use a variable named `total` to store the sum. Initially `total` is 0. Add each element in the array to `total` using a loop like this:

```
int total = 0;
for (int row = 0; row < matrix.length; row++) {
  for (int column = 0; column < matrix[row].length; column++) {
    total += matrix[row][column];
  }
}
```

5. *Summing elements by column.* For each column, use a variable named `total` to store its sum. Add each element in the column to `total` using a loop like this:

```
for (int column = 0; column < matrix[0].length; column++) {
  int total = 0;
  for (int row = 0; row < matrix.length; row++)
    total += matrix[row][column];
  System.out.println("Sum for column " + column + " is "
    + total);
}
```

VideoNote

Find the row with the largest sum

6. *Which row has the largest sum?* Use variables `maxRow` and `indexOfMaxRow` to track the largest sum and index of the row. For each row, compute its sum and update `maxRow` and `indexOfMaxRow` if the new sum is greater.

```
int maxRow = 0;
int indexOfMaxRow = 0;

// Get sum of the first row in maxRow
for (int column = 0; column < matrix[0].length; column++) {
  maxRow += matrix[0][column];
}

for (int row = 1; row < matrix.length; row++) {
  int totalOfThisRow = 0;
  for (int column = 0; column < matrix[row].length; column++)
    totalOfThisRow += matrix[row][column];

  if (totalOfThisRow > maxRow) {
    maxRow = totalOfThisRow;
    indexOfMaxRow = row;
  }
}

System.out.println("Row " + indexOfMaxRow
  + " has the maximum sum of " + maxRow);
```

7. *Random shuffling.* Shuffling the elements in a one-dimensional array was introduced in Section 7.2.6. How do you shuffle all the elements in a two-dimensional array? To accomplish this, for each element `matrix[i][j]`, randomly generate indices `i1` and `j1` and swap `matrix[i][j]` with `matrix[i1][j1]`, as follows:

```
for (int i = 0; i < matrix.length; i++) {
  for (int j = 0; j < matrix[i].length; j++) {
    int i1 = (int)(Math.random() * matrix.length);
    int j1 = (int)(Math.random() * matrix[i].length);

    // Swap matrix[i][j] with matrix[i1][j1]
```

```
      int temp = matrix[i][j];
      matrix[i][j] = matrix[i1][j1];
      matrix[i1][j1] = temp;
    }
  }
}
```

8.3.1 Show the output of the following code:

Check
Point

```
int[][] array = {{1, 2}, {3, 4}, {5, 6}};
for (int i = array.length - 1; i >= 0; i--) {
  for (int j = array[i].length - 1; j >= 0; j--)
    System.out.print(array[i][j] + " ");
  System.out.println();
}
```

8.3.2 Show the output of the following code:

```
int[][] array = {{1, 2}, {3, 4}, {5, 6}};
int sum = 0;
for (int i = 0; i < array.length; i++)
  sum += array[i][0];
System.out.println(sum);
```

8.4 Passing Two-Dimensional Arrays to Methods

When passing a two-dimensional array to a method, the reference of the array is passed to the method.

Key
Point

You can pass a two-dimensional array to a method just as you pass a one-dimensional array. You can also return an array from a method. Listing 8.1 gives an example with two methods. The first method, `getArray()`, returns a two-dimensional array and the second method, `sum(int[][] m)`, returns the sum of all the elements in a matrix.

LISTING 8.1   PassTwoDimensionalArray.java

```
 1  import java.util.Scanner;
 2
 3  public class PassTwoDimensionalArray {
 4    public static void main(String[] args) {
 5      int[][] m = getArray(); // Get an array
 6
 7      // Display sum of elements
 8      System.out.println("\nSum of all elements is " + sum(m));
 9    }
10
11    public static int[][] getArray() {
12      // Create a Scanner
13      Scanner input = new Scanner(System.in);
14
15      // Enter array values
16      int[][] m = new int[3][4];
17      System.out.println("Enter " + m.length + " rows and "
18        + m[0].length + " columns: ");
19      for (int i = 0; i < m.length; i++)
20        for (int j = 0; j < m[i].length; j++)
21          m[i][j] = input.nextInt();
22
```

get array

pass array

getArray method

return array

```
23        return m;
24    }
25
```

sum method

```
26    public static int sum(int[][] m) {
27      int total = 0;
28      for (int row = 0; row < m.length; row++) {
29        for (int column = 0; column < m[row].length; column++) {
30          total += m[row][column];
31        }
32      }
33
34      return total;
35    }
36  }
```

```
Enter 3 rows and 4 columns:
1 2 3 4  ↵Enter
5 6 7 8  ↵Enter
9 10 11 12  ↵Enter

Sum of all elements is 78
```

The method `getArray` prompts the user to enter values for the array (lines 11–24) and returns the array (line 23).

The method `sum` (lines 26–35) has a two-dimensional array argument. You can obtain the number of rows using `m.length` (line 28), and the number of columns in a specified row using `m[row].length` (line 29).

8.4.1 Show the output of the following code:

```
public class Test {
  public static void main(String[] args) {
    int[][] array = {{1, 2, 3, 4}, {5, 6, 7, 8}};
    System.out.println(m1(array)[0]);
    System.out.println(m1(array)[1]);
  }

  public static int[] m1(int[][] m) {
    int[] result = new int[2];
    result[0] = m.length;
    result[1] = m[0].length;
    return result;
  }
}
```

8.5 Case Study: Grading a Multiple-Choice Test

The problem is to write a program that will grade multiple-choice tests.

VideoNote

Grade multiple-choice test

Key Point

Suppose you need to write a program that grades multiple-choice tests. Assume there are eight students and ten questions, and the answers are stored in a two-dimensional array. Each row records a student's answers to the questions, as shown in the following array:

Students' Answers to the Questions:

```
           0 1 2 3 4 5 6 7 8 9
Student 0  A B A C C D E E A D
Student 1  D B A B C A E E A D
Student 2  E D D A C B E E A D
Student 3  C B A E D C E E A D
Student 4  A B D C C D E E A D
Student 5  B B E C C D E E A D
Student 6  B B A C C D E E A D
Student 7  E B E C C D E E A D
```

The key is stored in a one-dimensional array:

Key to the Questions:

```
    0 1 2 3 4 5 6 7 8 9
Key D B D C C D A E A D
```

Your program grades the test and displays the result. It compares each student's answers with the key, counts the number of correct answers, and displays it. Listing 8.2 gives the program.

LISTING 8.2 GradeExam.java

```java
1  public class GradeExam {
2    /** Main method */
3    public static void main(String[] args) {
4      // Students' answers to the questions
5      char[][] answers = {                                    2-D array
6        {'A', 'B', 'A', 'C', 'C', 'D', 'E', 'E', 'A', 'D'},
7        {'D', 'B', 'A', 'B', 'C', 'A', 'E', 'E', 'A', 'D'},
8        {'E', 'D', 'D', 'A', 'C', 'B', 'E', 'E', 'A', 'D'},
9        {'C', 'B', 'A', 'E', 'D', 'C', 'E', 'E', 'A', 'D'},
10       {'A', 'B', 'D', 'C', 'C', 'D', 'E', 'E', 'A', 'D'},
11       {'B', 'B', 'E', 'C', 'C', 'D', 'E', 'E', 'A', 'D'},
12       {'B', 'B', 'A', 'C', 'C', 'D', 'E', 'E', 'A', 'D'},
13       {'E', 'B', 'E', 'C', 'C', 'D', 'E', 'E', 'A', 'D'}};
14
15     // Key to the questions
16     char[] keys = {'D', 'B', 'D', 'C', 'C', 'D', 'A', 'E', 'A', 'D'};   1-D array
17
18     // Grade all answers
19     for (int i = 0; i < answers.length; i++) {
20       // Grade one student
21       int correctCount = 0;
22       for (int j = 0; j < answers[i].length; j++) {
23         if (answers[i][j] == keys[j])                        compare with key
24           correctCount++;
25       }
26
27       System.out.println("Student " + i + "'s correct count is " +
28         correctCount);
29     }
30   }
31 }
```

```
Student 0's correct count is 7
Student 1's correct count is 6
Student 2's correct count is 5
Student 3's correct count is 4
Student 4's correct count is 8
Student 5's correct count is 7
Student 6's correct count is 7
Student 7's correct count is 7
```

The statement in lines 5–13 declares, creates, and initializes a two-dimensional array of characters and assigns the reference to answers of the char[][] type.

The statement in line 16 declares, creates, and initializes an array of char values and assigns the reference to keys of the char[] type.

Each row in the array answers stores a student's answer, which is graded by comparing it with the key in the array keys. The result is displayed immediately after a student's answer is graded.

8.5.1 How do you modify the code so it also displays the highest count and the student with the highest count?

8.6 Case Study: Finding the Closest Pair

This section presents a geometric problem for finding the closest pair of points.

closest-pair animation on the Companion Website

Given a set of points, the closest-pair problem is to find the two points that are nearest to each other. In Figure 8.3, for example, points (1, 1) and (2, 0.5) are closest to each other. There are several ways to solve this problem. An intuitive approach is to compute the distances between all pairs of points and find the one with the minimum distance, as implemented in Listing 8.3.

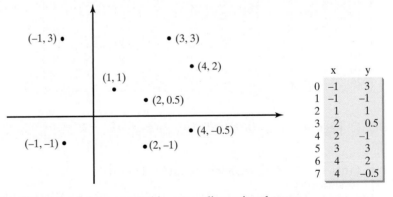

FIGURE 8.3 Points can be represented in a two-dimensional array.

LISTING 8.3 FindNearestPoints.java

```
1  import java.util.Scanner;
2
3  public class FindNearestPoints {
4    public static void main(String[] args) {
5      Scanner input = new Scanner(System.in);
6      System.out.print("Enter the number of points: ");
7      int numberOfPoints = input.nextInt();
8
9      // Create an array to store points
```

number of points

```
10        double[][] points = new double[numberOfPoints][2];              2-D array
11        System.out.print("Enter " + numberOfPoints + " points: ");
12        for (int i = 0; i < points.length; i++) {                       read points
13          points[i][0] = input.nextDouble();
14          points[i][1] = input.nextDouble();
15        }
16
17        // p1 and p2 are the indices in the points' array
18        int p1 = 0, p2 = 1; // Initial two points                       track two points
19        double shortestDistance = distance(points[p1][0], points[p1][1], track shortestDistance
20          points[p2][0], points[p2][1]); // Initialize shortestDistance
21
22        // Compute distance for every two points
23        for (int i = 0; i < points.length; i++) {                       for each point i
24          for (int j = i + 1; j < points.length; j++) {                 for each point j
25            double distance = distance(points[i][0], points[i][1],       distance between i and j
26              points[j][0], points[j][1]); // Find distance             distance between two points
27
28            if (shortestDistance > distance) {
29              p1 = i; // Update p1
30              p2 = j; // Update p2
31              shortestDistance = distance; // Update shortestDistance    update shortestDistance
32            }
33          }
34        }
35
36        // Display result
37        System.out.println("The closest two points are " +
38          "(" + points[p1][0] + ", " + points[p1][1] + ") and (" +
39          points[p2][0] + ", " + points[p2][1] + ")");
40      }
41
42      /** Compute the distance between two points (x1, y1) and (x2, y2)*/
43      public static double distance(
44          double x1, double y1, double x2, double y2) {
45        return Math.sqrt((x2 - x1) * (x2 - x1) + (y2 - y1) * (y2 - y1));
46      }
47    }
```

```
Enter the number of points: 8 ↵Enter
Enter 8 points: -1 3 -1 -1 1 1 2 0.5 2 -1 3 3 4 2 4 -0.5 ↵Enter
The closest two points are (1, 1) and (2, 0.5)
```

The program prompts the user to enter the number of points (lines 6 and 7). The points are read from the console and stored in a two-dimensional array named points (lines 12–15). The program uses the variable shortestDistance (line 19) to store the distance between the two nearest points, and the indices of these two points in the points array are stored in p1 and p2 (line 18).

For each point at index i, the program computes the distance between points[i] and points[j] for all j > i (lines 23–34). Whenever a shorter distance is found, the variable shortestDistance and p1 and p2 are updated (lines 28–32).

The distance between two points (x1, y1) and (x2, y2) can be computed using the formula $\sqrt{(x_2 - x_1)^2 + (y_2 - y_1)^2}$ (lines 43–46).

The program assumes the plane has at least two points. You can easily modify the program to handle the case if the plane has zero or one point.

multiple closest pairs

Note that there might be more than one closest pair of points with the same minimum distance. The program finds one such pair. You may modify the program to find all closest pairs in Programming Exercise 8.8.

input file

Tip
It is cumbersome to enter all points from the keyboard. You may store the input in a file, say **FindNearestPoints.txt**, and run the program using the following command:

```
java FindNearestPoints < FindNearestPoints.txt
```

8.6.1 What happens if the input has only one point?

VideoNote
Sudoku

fixed cells
free cells

representing a grid

8.7 Case Study: Sudoku

The problem is to check whether a given Sudoku solution is correct.

This section presents an interesting problem of a sort that appears in the newspaper every day. It is a number-placement puzzle, commonly known as *Sudoku*. This is a very challenging problem. To make it accessible to the novice, this section presents a simplified version of the Sudoku problem, which is to verify whether a Sudoku solution is correct. The complete program for finding a Sudoku solution is presented in Supplement VI.C.

Sudoku is a 9 × 9 grid divided into smaller 3 × 3 boxes (also called *regions* or *blocks*), as shown in Figure 8.4a. Some cells, called *fixed cells*, are populated with numbers from 1 to 9. The objective is to fill the empty cells, also called *free cells*, with the numbers 1 to 9 so every row, every column, and every 3 × 3 box contains the numbers 1 to 9, as shown in Figure 8.4b.

5	3			7				
6			1	9	5			
	9	8					6	
8				6				3
4			8		3			1
7				2				6
	6					4	1	9
				8			7	9

Solution →

5	3	4	6	7	8	9	1	2
6	7	2	1	9	5	3	4	8
1	9	8	3	4	2	5	6	7
8	5	9	7	6	1	4	2	3
4	2	6	8	5	3	7	9	1
7	1	3	9	2	4	8	5	6
9	6	1	5	3	7	2	8	4
2	8	7	4	1	9	6	3	5
3	4	5	2	8	6	1	7	9

(a) Puzzle   (b) Solution

FIGURE 8.4 The Sudoku puzzle in (a) is solved in (b).

For convenience, we use value 0 to indicate a free cell, as shown in Figure 8.5a. The grid can be naturally represented using a two-dimensional array, as shown in Figure 8.5b.

5	3	0	0	7	0	0	0	0
6	0	0	1	9	5	0	0	0
0	9	8	0	0	0	0	6	0
8	0	0	0	6	0	0	0	3
4	0	0	8	0	3	0	0	1
7	0	0	0	2	0	0	0	6
0	6	0	0	0	0	2	8	0
0	0	0	4	1	9	0	0	5
0	0	0	0	8	0	0	7	9

```
int[][] grid =
  {{5, 3, 0, 0, 7, 0, 0, 0, 0},
   {6, 0, 0, 1, 9, 5, 0, 0, 0},
   {0, 9, 8, 0, 0, 0, 0, 6, 0},
   {8, 0, 0, 0, 6, 0, 0, 0, 3},
   {4, 0, 0, 8, 0, 3, 0, 0, 1},
   {7, 0, 0, 0, 2, 0, 0, 0, 6},
   {0, 6, 0, 0, 0, 0, 2, 8, 0},
   {0, 0, 0, 4, 1, 9, 0, 0, 5},
   {0, 0, 0, 0, 8, 0, 0, 7, 9}
  };
```

(a)   (b)

FIGURE 8.5 A grid can be represented using a two-dimensional array.

To find a solution for the puzzle, we must replace each 0 in the grid with an appropriate number from 1 to 9. For the solution to the puzzle in Figure 8.5, the grid should be as shown in Figure 8.6.

Once a solution to a Sudoku puzzle is found, how do you verify that it is correct? Here are two approaches:

1. Check if every row has numbers from 1 to 9, every column has numbers from 1 to 9, and every small box has numbers from 1 to 9.

2. Check each cell. Each cell must be a number from 1 to 9 and the cell must be unique on every row, every column, and every small box.

```
A solution grid is
  {{5, 3, 4, 6, 7, 8, 9, 1, 2},
   {6, 7, 2, 1, 9, 5, 3, 4, 8},
   {1, 9, 8, 3, 4, 2, 5, 6, 7},
   {8, 5, 9, 7, 6, 1, 4, 2, 3},
   {4, 2, 6, 8, 5, 3, 7, 9, 1},
   {7, 1, 3, 9, 2, 4, 8, 5, 6},
   {9, 6, 1, 5, 3, 7, 2, 8, 4},
   {2, 8, 7, 4, 1, 9, 6, 3, 5},
   {3, 4, 5, 2, 8, 6, 1, 7, 9}
  };
```

FIGURE 8.6   A solution is stored in `grid`.

The program in Listing 8.4 prompts the user to enter a solution and reports whether it is valid. We use the second approach in the program to check whether the solution is correct.

LISTING 8.4   CheckSudokuSolution.java

```java
 1  import java.util.Scanner;
 2
 3  public class CheckSudokuSolution {
 4    public static void main(String[] args) {
 5      // Read a Sudoku solution
 6      int[][] grid = readASolution();                          // read input
 7
 8      System.out.println(isValid(grid) ? "Valid solution" :    // solution valid?
 9        "Invalid solution");
10    }
11
12    /** Read a Sudoku solution from the console */
13    public static int[][] readASolution() {                    // read solution
14      // Create a Scanner
15      Scanner input = new Scanner(System.in);
16
17      System.out.println("Enter a Sudoku puzzle solution:");
18      int[][] grid = new int[9][9];
19      for (int i = 0; i < 9; i++)
20        for (int j = 0; j < 9; j++)
21          grid[i][j] = input.nextInt();
22
23      return grid;
24    }
25
26    /** Check whether a solution is valid */
27    public static boolean isValid(int[][] grid) {              // check solution
```

```
28        for (int i = 0; i < 9; i++)
29          for (int j = 0; j < 9; j++)
30            if (grid[i][j] < 1 || grid[i][j] > 9
31                || !isValid(i, j, grid))
32              return false;
33        return true; // The solution is valid
34    }
35
36    /** Check whether grid[i][j] is valid in the grid */
37    public static boolean isValid(int i, int j, int[][] grid) {
38      // Check whether grid[i][j] is unique in i's row
39      for (int column = 0; column < 9; column++)
40        if (column != j && grid[i][column] == grid[i][j])
41          return false;
42
43      // Check whether grid[i][j] is unique in j's column
44      for (int row = 0; row < 9; row++)
45        if (row != i && grid[row][j] == grid[i][j])
46          return false;
47
48      // Check whether grid[i][j] is unique in the 3-by-3 box
49      for (int row = (i / 3) * 3; row < (i / 3) * 3 + 3; row++)
50        for (int col = (j / 3) * 3; col < (j / 3) * 3 + 3; col++)
51          if (!(row == i && col == j) && grid[row][col] == grid[i][j])
52            return false;
53
54      return true; // The current value at grid[i][j] is valid
55    }
56  }
```

check rows (line 39)
check columns (line 44)
check small boxes (line 49)

```
Enter a Sudoku puzzle solution:
9 6 3 1 7 4 2 5 8 ↵Enter
1 7 8 3 2 5 6 4 9 ↵Enter
2 5 4 6 8 9 7 3 1 ↵Enter
8 2 1 4 3 7 5 9 6 ↵Enter
4 9 6 8 5 2 3 1 7 ↵Enter
7 3 5 9 6 1 8 2 4 ↵Enter
5 8 9 7 1 3 4 6 2 ↵Enter
3 1 7 2 4 6 9 8 5 ↵Enter
6 4 2 5 9 8 1 7 3 ↵Enter
Valid solution
```

The program invokes the readASolution() method (line 6) to read a Sudoku solution and return a two-dimensional array representing a Sudoku grid.

isValid method

The isValid(grid) method checks whether the values in the grid are valid by verifying that each value is between 1 and 9, and that each value is valid in the grid (lines 27–34).

overloaded isValid method

The isValid(i, j, grid) method checks whether the value at grid[i][j] is valid. It checks whether grid[i][j] appears more than once in row i (lines 39–41), in column j (lines 44–46), and in the 3 × 3 box (lines 49–52).

How do you locate all the cells in the same box? For any grid[i][j], the starting cell of the 3 × 3 box that contains it is grid[(i / 3) * 3][(j / 3) * 3], as illustrated in Figure 8.7.

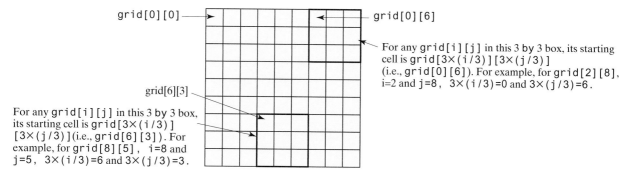

FIGURE 8.7 The location of the first cell in a 3 × 3 box determines the locations of other cells in the box.

With this observation, you can easily identify all the cells in the box. For instance, if `grid[r][c]` is the starting cell of a 3 × 3 box, the cells in the box can be traversed in a nested loop as follows:

```
// Get all cells in a 3-by-3 box starting at grid[r][c]
for (int row = r; row < r + 3; row++)
  for (int col = c; col < c + 3; col++)
    // grid[row][col] is in the box
```

It is cumbersome to enter 81 numbers from the console. When you test the program, you may store the input in a file, say **CheckSudokuSolution.txt** (see liveexample.pearsoncmg. com/data/CheckSudokuSolution.txt) and run the program using the following command:

input file

```
java CheckSudokuSolution < CheckSudokuSolution.txt
```

8.7.1 What happens if the code in line 51 in Listing 8.4 is changed to

```
if (row != i && col != j && grid[row][col] == grid[i][j])
```

✓ **Check Point**

8.8 Multidimensional Arrays

A two-dimensional array is an array of one-dimensional arrays, and a three-dimensional array is an array of two-dimensional arrays.

Key Point

In the preceding section, you used a two-dimensional array to represent a matrix or a table. Occasionally, you will need to represent *n*-dimensional data structures. In Java, you can create *n*-dimensional arrays for any positive integer *n*.

The way to declare two-dimensional array variables and create two-dimensional arrays can be generalized to declare *n*-dimensional array variables and create *n*-dimensional arrays for $n >= 3$. For example, you may use a three-dimensional array to store exam scores for a class of six students with five exams, and each exam has two parts (multiple-choice and essay type questions). The following syntax declares a three-dimensional array variable `scores`, creates an array, and assigns its reference to `scores`.

```
double[][][] scores = new double[6][5][2];
```

You can also use the array initializer to create and initialize the array as follows:

```
double[][][] scores = {
  {{7.5, 20.5}, {9.0, 22.5}, {15, 33.5}, {13, 21.5}, {15, 2.5}},
  {{4.5, 21.5}, {9.0, 22.5}, {15, 34.5}, {12, 20.5}, {14, 9.5}},
  {{6.5, 30.5}, {9.4, 10.5}, {11, 33.5}, {11, 23.5}, {10, 2.5}},
  {{6.5, 23.5}, {9.4, 32.5}, {13, 34.5}, {11, 20.5}, {16, 7.5}},
  {{8.5, 26.5}, {9.4, 52.5}, {13, 36.5}, {13, 24.5}, {16, 2.5}},
  {{9.5, 20.5}, {9.4, 42.5}, {13, 31.5}, {12, 20.5}, {16, 6.5}}};
```

`scores[0][1][0]` refers to the multiple-choice score for the first student's second exam, which is `9.0`. `scores[0][1][1]` refers to the essay score for the first student's second exam, which is `22.5`. This is depicted in the following figure:

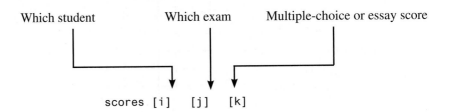

A multidimensional array is actually an array in which each element is another array. A three-dimensional array is an array of two-dimensional arrays. A two-dimensional array is an array of one-dimensional arrays. For example, suppose that `x = new int[2][2][5]` and `x[0]` and `x[1]` are two-dimensional arrays. `x[0][0]`, `x[0][1]`, `x[1][0]`, and `x[1][1]` are one-dimensional arrays and each contains five elements. `x.length` is `2`, `x[0].length` and `x[1].length` are `2`, and `x[0][0].length`, `x[0][1].length`, `x[1][0].length`, and `x[1][1].length` are `5`.

8.8.1 Case Study: Daily Temperature and Humidity

Suppose a meteorology station records the temperature and humidity every hour of every day, and stores the data for the past 10 days in a text file named **Weather.txt** (see liveexample.pearsoncmg.com/data/Weather.txt). Each line of the file consists of four numbers that indicate the day, hour, temperature, and humidity. The contents of the file may look like those in (a).

Day	Hour	Temperature	Humidity
1	1	76.4	0.92
1	2	77.7	0.93
...			
10	23	97.7	0.71
10	24	98.7	0.74

(a)

Day	Hour	Temperature	Humidity
10	24	98.7	0.74
1	2	77.7	0.93
...			
10	23	97.7	0.71
1	1	76.4	0.92

(b)

Note the lines in the file are not necessarily in increasing order of day and hour. For example, the file may appear as shown in (b).

Your task is to write a program that calculates the average daily temperature and humidity for the `10` days. You can use the input redirection to read the file and store the data in a three-dimensional array named `data`. The first index of `data` ranges from `0` to `9` and represents `10` days, the second index ranges from `0` to `23` and represents `24` hours, and the third index ranges from `0` to `1` and represents temperature and humidity, as depicted in the following figure:

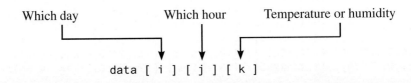

Note the days are numbered from 1 to 10 and the hours from 1 to 24 in the file. Because the array index starts from 0, `data[0][0][0]` stores the temperature in day 1 at hour 1 and `data[9][23][1]` stores the humidity in day 10 at hour 24.

The program is given in Listing 8.5.

LISTING 8.5 Weather.java

```
1   import java.util.Scanner;
2
3   public class Weather {
4     public static void main(String[] args) {
5       final int NUMBER_OF_DAYS = 10;
6       final int NUMBER_OF_HOURS = 24;
7       double[][][] data
8         = new double[NUMBER_OF_DAYS][NUMBER_OF_HOURS][2];       three-dimensional array
9
10      Scanner input = new Scanner(System.in);
11      // Read input using input redirection from a file
12      for (int k = 0; k < NUMBER_OF_DAYS * NUMBER_OF_HOURS; k++) {
13        int day = input.nextInt();
14        int hour = input.nextInt();
15        double temperature = input.nextDouble();
16        double humidity = input.nextDouble();
17        data[day - 1][hour - 1][0] = temperature;
18        data[day - 1][hour - 1][1] = humidity;
19      }
20
21      // Find the average daily temperature and humidity
22      for (int i = 0; i < NUMBER_OF_DAYS; i++) {
23        double dailyTemperatureTotal = 0, dailyHumidityTotal = 0;
24        for (int j = 0; j < NUMBER_OF_HOURS; j++) {
25          dailyTemperatureTotal += data[i][j][0];
26          dailyHumidityTotal += data[i][j][1];
27        }
28
29        // Display result
30        System.out.println("Day " + i + "'s average temperature is "
31          + dailyTemperatureTotal / NUMBER_OF_HOURS);
32        System.out.println("Day " + i + "'s average humidity is "
33          + dailyHumidityTotal / NUMBER_OF_HOURS);
34      }
35    }
36  }
```

```
Day 0's average temperature is 77.7708
Day 0's average humidity is 0.929583
Day 1's average temperature is 77.3125
Day 1's average humidity is 0.929583
...
Day 9's average temperature is 79.3542
Day 9's average humidity is 0.9125
```

You can use the following command to run the program:

```
java Weather < Weather.txt
```

A three-dimensional array for storing temperature and humidity is created in line 8. The loop in lines 12–19 reads the input to the array. You can enter the input from the keyboard, but doing so will be awkward. For convenience, we store the data in a file and use input redirection to read the data from the file. The loop in lines 24–27 adds all temperatures for each hour in a day to `dailyTemperatureTotal`, and all humidity for each hour to `dailyHumidityTotal`. The average daily temperature and humidity are displayed in lines 30–33.

8.8.2 Case Study: Guessing Birthdays

Listing 4.3, GuessBirthday.java, gives a program that guesses a birthday. The program can be simplified by storing the numbers in five sets in a three-dimensional array and it prompts the user for the answers using a loop, as given in Listing 8.6. The sample run of the program can be the same as given in Listing 4.3.

LISTING 8.6 `GuessBirthdayUsingArray.java`

three-dimensional array

Set i

add to day

```
 1  import java.util.Scanner;
 2
 3  public class GuessBirthdayUsingArray {
 4    public static void main(String[] args) {
 5      int day = 0; // Day to be determined
 6      int answer;
 7
 8      int[][][] dates = {
 9        {{ 1,  3,  5,  7},
10         { 9, 11, 13, 15},
11         {17, 19, 21, 23},
12         {25, 27, 29, 31}},
13        {{ 2,  3,  6,  7},
14         {10, 11, 14, 15},
15         {18, 19, 22, 23},
16         {26, 27, 30, 31}},
17        {{ 4,  5,  6,  7},
18         {12, 13, 14, 15}},
19         {20, 21, 22, 23},
20         {28, 29, 30, 31}},
21        {{ 8,  9, 10, 11},
22         {12, 13, 14, 15},
23         {24, 25, 26, 27},
24         {28, 29, 30, 31}},
25        {{16, 17, 18, 19},
26         {20, 21, 22, 23},
27         {24, 25, 26, 27},
28         {28, 29, 30, 31}}};
29
30      // Create a Scanner
31      Scanner input = new Scanner(System.in);
32
33      for (int i = 0; i < 5; i++) {
34        System.out.println("Is your birthday in Set" + (i + 1) + "?");
35        for (int j = 0; j < 4; j++) {
36          for (int k = 0; k < 4; k++)
37            System.out.printf("%4d", dates[i][j][k]);
38          System.out.println();
39        }
40
41        System.out.print("\nEnter 0 for No and 1 for Yes: ");
42        answer = input.nextInt();
43
44        if (answer == 1)
45          day += dates[i][0][0];
```

```
46        }
47
48        System.out.println("Your birthday is " + day);
49    }
50 }
```

A three-dimensional array `dates` is created in lines 8–28. This array stores five sets of numbers. Each set is a 4-by-4 two-dimensional array.

The loop starting from line 33 displays the numbers in each set and prompts the user to answer whether the birthday is in the set (lines 41 and 42). If the day is in the set, the first number (`dates[i][0][0]`) in the set is added to variable `day` (line 45).

8.8.1 Declare an array variable for a three-dimensional array, create a 4 × 6 × 5 `int` array, and assign its reference to the variable.

8.8.2 Assume `char[][][] x = new char[12][5][2]`, how many elements are in the array? What are `x.length`, `x[2].length`, and `x[0][0].length`?

8.8.3 Show the output of the following code:

```
int[][][] array = {{{1, 2}, {3, 4}}, {{5, 6},{7, 8}}};
System.out.println(array[0][0][0]);
System.out.println(array[1][1][1]);
```

 Check Point

CHAPTER SUMMARY

1. A two-dimensional array can be used to store a table.

2. A variable for two-dimensional arrays can be declared using the syntax: `elementType[][] arrayVar`.

3. A two-dimensional array can be created using the syntax: `new elementType[ROW_SIZE][COLUMN_SIZE]`.

4. Each element in a two-dimensional array is represented using the syntax: `arrayVar[rowIndex][columnIndex]`.

5. You can create and initialize a two-dimensional array using an array initializer with the syntax: `elementType[][] arrayVar = {{row values}, . . ., {row values}}`.

6. You can use arrays of arrays to form multidimensional arrays. For example, a variable for three-dimensional arrays can be declared as `elementType[][][] arrayVar` and a three-dimensional array can be created using `new elementType[size1][size2][size3]`.

QUIZ

Answer the quiz for this chapter online at the book Companion Website.

PROGRAMMING EXERCISES

MyProgrammingLab™

*8.1 (*Sum elements column by column*) Write a method that returns the sum of all the elements in a specified column in a matrix using the following header:

```
public static double sumColumn(double[][] m, int columnIndex)
```

Write a test program that reads a 3-by-4 matrix and displays the sum of each column. Here is a sample run:

```
Enter a 3-by-4 matrix row by row:
1.5 2 3 4  ↵Enter
5.5 6 7 8  ↵Enter
9.5 1 3 1  ↵Enter
Sum of the elements at column 0 is 16.5
Sum of the elements at column 1 is 9.0
Sum of the elements at column 2 is 13.0
Sum of the elements at column 3 is 13.0
```

*8.2   (*Sum the major diagonal in a matrix*) Write a method that sums all the numbers in the major diagonal in an $n \times n$ matrix of `double` values using the following header:

```
public static double sumMajorDiagonal(double[][] m)
```

Write a test program that reads a 4-by-4 matrix and displays the sum of all its elements on the major diagonal. Here is a sample run:

```
Enter a 4-by-4 matrix row by row:
1 2 3 4.0  ↵Enter
5 6.5 7 8  ↵Enter
9 10 11 12  ↵Enter
13 14 15 16  ↵Enter
Sum of the elements in the major diagonal is 34.5
```

*8.3   (*Sort students on grades*) Rewrite Listing 8.2, GradeExam.java, to display the students in increasing order of the number of correct answers.

**8.4   (*Compute the weekly hours for each employee*) Suppose the weekly hours for all employees are stored in a two-dimensional array. Each row records an employee's seven-day work hours with seven columns. For example, the following array stores the work hours for eight employees. Write a program that displays employees and their total hours in decreasing order of the total hours.

	Su	M	T	W	Th	F	Sa
Employee 0	2	4	3	4	5	8	8
Employee 1	7	3	4	3	3	4	4
Employee 2	3	3	4	3	3	2	2
Employee 3	9	3	4	7	3	4	1
Employee 4	3	5	4	3	6	3	8
Employee 5	3	4	4	6	3	4	4
Employee 6	3	7	4	8	3	8	4
Employee 7	6	3	5	9	2	7	9

8.5   (*Algebra: add two matrices*) Write a method to add two matrices. The header of the method is as follows:

```
public static double[][] addMatrix(double[][] a, double[][] b)
```

In order to be added, the two matrices must have the same dimensions and the same or compatible types of elements. Let c be the resulting matrix. Each element c_{ij} is $a_{ij} + b_{ij}$. For example, for two 3×3 matrices a and b, c is

$$\begin{pmatrix} a_{11} & a_{12} & a_{13} \\ a_{21} & a_{22} & a_{23} \\ a_{31} & a_{32} & a_{33} \end{pmatrix} + \begin{pmatrix} b_{11} & b_{12} & b_{13} \\ b_{21} & b_{22} & b_{23} \\ b_{31} & b_{32} & b_{33} \end{pmatrix} = \begin{pmatrix} a_{11} + b_{11} & a_{12} + b_{12} & a_{13} + b_{13} \\ a_{21} + b_{21} & a_{22} + b_{22} & a_{23} + b_{23} \\ a_{31} + b_{31} & a_{32} + b_{32} & a_{33} + b_{33} \end{pmatrix}$$

Write a test program that prompts the user to enter two 3×3 matrices and displays their sum. Here is a sample run:

```
Enter matrix1: 1 2 3 4 5 6 7 8 9  ↵Enter
Enter matrix2: 0 2 4 1 4.5 2.2 1.1 4.3 5.2  ↵Enter
The matrices are added as follows
   1.0 2.0 3.0      0.0 2.0 4.0       1.0 4.0 7.0
   4.0 5.0 6.0  +   1.0 4.5 2.2   =   5.0 9.5 8.2
   7.0 8.0 9.0      1.1 4.3 5.2       8.1 12.3 14.2
```

**8.6 (*Algebra: multiply two matrices*) Write a method to multiply two matrices. The header of the method is:

VideoNote
Multiply two matrices

```
public static double[][]
    multiplyMatrix(double[][] a, double[][] b)
```

To multiply matrix a by matrix b, the number of columns in a must be the same as the number of rows in b, and the two matrices must have elements of the same or compatible types. Let c be the result of the multiplication. Assume the column size of matrix a is n. Each element c_{ij} is $a_{i1} \times b_{1j} + a_{i2} \times b_{2j} + \cdots + a_{in} \times b_{nj}$. For example, for two 3×3 matrices a and b, c is

$$\begin{pmatrix} a_{11} & a_{12} & a_{13} \\ a_{21} & a_{22} & a_{23} \\ a_{31} & a_{32} & a_{33} \end{pmatrix} \times \begin{pmatrix} b_{11} & b_{12} & b_{13} \\ b_{21} & b_{22} & b_{23} \\ b_{31} & b_{32} & b_{33} \end{pmatrix} = \begin{pmatrix} c_{11} & c_{12} & c_{13} \\ c_{21} & c_{22} & c_{23} \\ c_{31} & c_{32} & c_{33} \end{pmatrix}$$

where $c_{ij} = a_{i1} \times b_{1j} + a_{i2} \times b_{2j} + a_{i3} \times b_{3j}$.

Write a test program that prompts the user to enter two 3×3 matrices and displays their product. Here is a sample run:

```
Enter matrix1: 1 2 3 4 5 6 7 8 9  ↵Enter
Enter matrix2: 0 2 4 1 4.5 2.2 1.1 4.3 5.2  ↵Enter
The multiplication of the matrices is
   1 2 3      0 2.0 4.0        5.3 23.9 24
   4 5 6  *   1 4.5 2.2    =   11.6 56.3 58.2
   7 8 9      1.1 4.3 5.2      17.9 88.7 92.4
```

*8.7 (*Points nearest to each other*) Listing 8.3 gives a program that finds two points in a two-dimensional space nearest to each other. Revise the program so it finds two points in a three-dimensional space nearest to each other. Use a two-dimensional array to represent the points. Test the program using the following points:

```
double[][] points = {{-1, 0, 3}, {-1, -1, -1}, {4, 1, 1},
   {2, 0.5, 9}, {3.5, 2, -1}, {3, 1.5, 3}, {-1.5, 4, 2},
   {5.5, 4, -0.5}};
```

The formula for computing the distance between two points (x1, y1, z1) and (x2, y2, z2) is $\sqrt{(x_2 - x_1)^2 + (y_2 - y_1)^2 + (z_2 - z_1)^2}$.

**8.8 (*All closest pairs of points*) Revise Listing 8.3, FindNearestPoints.java, to display all closest pairs of points with the same minimum distance. Here is a sample run:

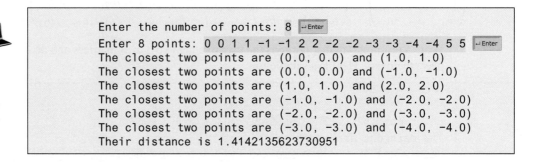

```
Enter the number of points: 8  ↵Enter
Enter 8 points: 0 0 1 1 -1 -1 2 2 -2 -2 -3 -3 -4 -4 5 5  ↵Enter
The closest two points are (0.0, 0.0) and (1.0, 1.0)
The closest two points are (0.0, 0.0) and (-1.0, -1.0)
The closest two points are (1.0, 1.0) and (2.0, 2.0)
The closest two points are (-1.0, -1.0) and (-2.0, -2.0)
The closest two points are (-2.0, -2.0) and (-3.0, -3.0)
The closest two points are (-3.0, -3.0) and (-4.0, -4.0)
Their distance is 1.4142135623730951
```

***8.9 (*Game: play a tic-tac-toe game*) In a game of tic-tac-toe, two players take turns marking an available cell in a 3 × 3 grid with their respective tokens (either X or O). When one player has placed three tokens in a horizontal, vertical, or diagonal row on the grid, the game is over and that player has won. A draw (no winner) occurs when all the cells on the grid have been filled with tokens and neither player has achieved a win. Create a program for playing a tic-tac-toe game.

The program prompts two players to alternately enter an X token and O token. Whenever a token is entered, the program redisplays the board on the console and determines the status of the game (win, draw, or continue). Here is a sample run:

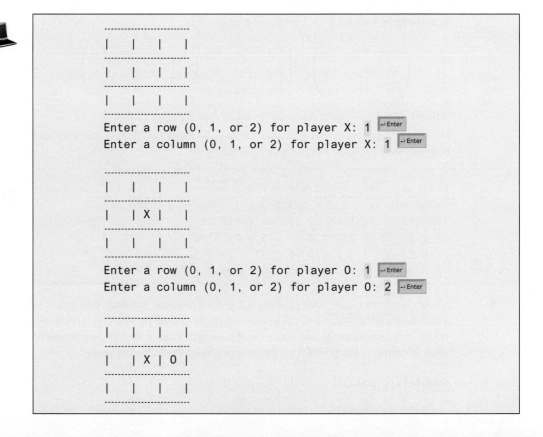

```
-------------------
|   |   |   |
-------------------
|   |   |   |
-------------------
|   |   |   |
-------------------
Enter a row (0, 1, or 2) for player X: 1  ↵Enter
Enter a column (0, 1, or 2) for player X: 1  ↵Enter

-------------------
|   |   |   |
-------------------
|   | X |   |
-------------------
|   |   |   |
-------------------
Enter a row (0, 1, or 2) for player O: 1  ↵Enter
Enter a column (0, 1, or 2) for player O: 2  ↵Enter

-------------------
|   |   |   |
-------------------
|   | X | O |
-------------------
|   |   |   |
-------------------
```

```
Enter a row (0, 1, or 2) for player X:

. . .

-------------------------
| X |   |   |
-------------------------
| O | X | O |
-------------------------
|   |   | X |
-------------------------
X player won
```

*8.10   (*Largest row and column*) Write a program that randomly fills in 0s and 1s into a 4-by-4 matrix, prints the matrix, and finds the first row and column with the most 1s. Here is a sample run of the program:

```
0011
0011
1101
1010
The largest row index: 2
The largest column index: 2
```

**8.11   (*Game: nine heads and tails*) Nine coins are placed in a 3-by-3 matrix with some face up and some face down. You can represent the state of the coins using a 3-by-3 matrix with values 0 (heads) and 1 (tails). Here are some examples:

```
0 0 0    1 0 1    1 1 0    1 0 1    1 0 0
0 1 0    0 0 1    1 0 0    1 1 0    1 1 1
0 0 0    1 0 0    0 0 1    1 0 0    1 1 0
```

Each state can also be represented using a binary number. For example, the preceding matrices correspond to the numbers

000010000 101001100 110100001 101110100 100111110

There are a total of 512 possibilities, so you can use decimal numbers 0, 1, 2, 3, . . . , and 511 to represent all states of the matrix. Write a program that prompts the user to enter a number between 0 and 511 and displays the corresponding matrix with the characters H and T. Here is a sample run:

```
Enter a number between 0 and 511: 7  ↵Enter
H H H
H H H
T T T
```

The user entered 7, which corresponds to 000000111. Since 0 stands for H and 1 for T, the output is correct.

**8.12   (*Financial application: compute tax*) Rewrite Listing 3.5, ComputeTax.java, using arrays. For each filing status, there are six tax rates. Each rate is applied to a certain amount of taxable income. For example, from the taxable income of $400,000 for a single filer, $8,350 is taxed at 10%, (33,950 − 8,350) at 15%,

(82,250 − 33,950) at 25%, (171,550 − 82,550) at 28%, (372,550 − 82,250) at 33%, and (400,000 − 372,950) at 36%. The six rates are the same for all filing statuses, which can be represented in the following array:

```
double[] rates = {0.10, 0.15, 0.25, 0.28, 0.33, 0.35};
```

The brackets for each rate for all the filing statuses can be represented in a two-dimensional array as follows:

```
int[][] brackets = {
  {8350, 33950, 82250, 171550, 372950},    // Single filer
  {16700, 67900, 137050, 20885, 372950},   // Married jointly
                                           // -or qualifying widow(er)
  {8350, 33950, 68525, 104425, 186475},    // Married separately
  {11950, 45500, 117450, 190200, 372950}   // Head of household
};
```

Suppose the taxable income is $400,000 for single filers. The tax can be computed as follows:

```
tax = brackets[0][0] * rates[0] +
  (brackets[0][1] - brackets[0][0]) * rates[1] +
  (brackets[0][2] - brackets[0][1]) * rates[2] +
  (brackets[0][3] - brackets[0][2]) * rates[3] +
  (brackets[0][4] - brackets[0][3]) * rates[4] +
  (400000 - brackets[0][4]) * rates[5];
```

*8.13   (*Locate the largest element*) Write the following method that returns the location of the largest element in a two-dimensional array:

```
public static int[] locateLargest(double[][] a)
```

The return value is a one-dimensional array that contains two elements. These two elements indicate the row and column indices of the largest element in the two-dimensional array. Write a test program that prompts the user to enter a two-dimensional array and displays the location of the largest element in the array. Here is a sample run:

```
Enter the number of rows and columns of the array: 3 4 ⏎Enter
Enter the array:
23.5 35 2 10 ⏎Enter
4.5 3 45 3.5 ⏎Enter
35 44 5.5 9.6 ⏎Enter
The location of the largest element is at (1, 2)
```

**8.14   (*Explore matrix*) Write a program that prompts the user to enter the length of a square matrix, randomly fills in 0s and 1s into the matrix, prints the matrix, and finds the rows, columns, and diagonals with all 0s or 1s. Here is a sample run of the program:

```
Enter the size for the matrix: 4  ↵Enter
0111
0000
0100
1111
All 0s on row 2
All 1s on row 4
No same numbers on a column
No same numbers on the major diagonal
No same numbers on the sub-diagonal
```

*8.15   (*Geometry: same line?*) Programming Exercise 6.39 gives a method for testing whether three points are on the same line.

Write the following method to test whether all the points in the array `points` are on the same line:

public static boolean sameLine(**double**[][] points)

Write a program that prompts the user to enter five points and displays whether they are on the same line. Here are sample runs:

```
Enter five points: 3.4 2 6.5 9.5 2.3 2.3 5.5 5 -5 4  ↵Enter
The five points are not on the same line
```

```
Enter five points: 1 1 2 2 3 3 4 4 5 5  ↵Enter
The five points are on the same line
```

*8.16   (*Sort two-dimensional array*) Write a method to sort a two-dimensional array using the following header:

public static void sort(**int** m[][])

The method performs a primary sort on rows, and a secondary sort on columns. For example, the following array

{{4, 2},{1, 7},{4, 5},{1, 2},{1, 1},{4, 1}}

will be sorted to

{{1, 1},{1, 2},{1, 7},{4, 1},{4, 2},{4, 5}}.

***8.17   (*Financial tsunami*) Banks lend money to each other. In tough economic times, if a bank goes bankrupt, it may not be able to pay back the loan. A bank's total assets are its current balance plus its loans to other banks. The diagram in Figure 8.8 shows five banks. The banks' current balances are 25, 125, 175, 75, and 181 million dollars, respectively. The directed edge from node 1 to node 2 indicates that bank 1 lends 40 million dollars to bank 2.

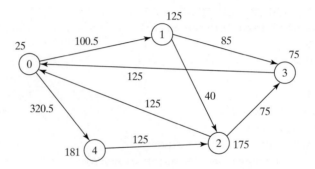

FIGURE 8.8   Banks lend money to each other.

If a bank's total assets are under a certain limit, the bank is unsafe. The money it borrowed cannot be returned to the lender, and the lender cannot count the loan in its total assets. Consequently, the lender may also be unsafe, if its total assets are under the limit. Write a program to find all the unsafe banks. Your program reads the input as follows. It first reads two integers n and limit, where n indicates the number of banks and limit is the minimum total assets for keeping a bank safe. It then reads n lines that describe the information for n banks with IDs from 0 to n−1.

The first number in the line is the bank's balance, the second number indicates the number of banks that borrowed money from the bank, and the rest are pairs of two numbers. Each pair describes a borrower. The first number in the pair is the borrower's ID and the second is the amount borrowed. For example, the input for the five banks in Figure 8.8 is as follows (note the limit is 201):

```
5 201
25 2 1 100.5 4 320.5
125 2 2 40 3 85
175 2 0 125 3 75
75 1 0 125
181 1 2 125
```

The total assets of bank 3 are (75 + 125), which is under 201, so bank 3 is unsafe. After bank 3 becomes unsafe, the total assets of bank 1 fall below (125 + 40). Thus, bank 1 is also unsafe. The output of the program should be

```
Unsafe banks are 3 1
```

(*Hint*: Use a two-dimensional array borrowers to represent loans. borrowers[i][j] indicates the loan that bank i provides to bank j. Once bank j becomes unsafe, borrowers[i][j] should be set to 0.)

*8.18   (*Shuffle rows*) Write a method that shuffles the rows in a two-dimensional int array using the following header:

```
public static void shuffle(int[][] m)
```

Write a test program that shuffles the following matrix:

```
int[][] m = {{1, 2}, {3, 4}, {5, 6}, {7, 8}, {9, 10}};
```

**8.19   (*Pattern recognition: four consecutive equal numbers*) Write the following method that tests whether a two-dimensional array has four consecutive numbers of the same value, either horizontally, vertically, or diagonally:

```
public static boolean isConsecutiveFour(int[][] values)
```

Write a test program that prompts the user to enter the number of rows and columns of a two-dimensional array then the values in the array, and displays true if the array contains four consecutive numbers with the same value. Otherwise, the program displays false. Here are some examples of the true cases:

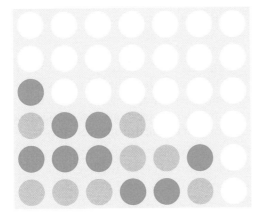

0	1	0	3	1	6	1
0	1	6	8	6	0	1
5	6	2	1	8	2	9
6	5	6	1	1	9	1
1	3	6	1	4	0	7
3	3	3	3	4	0	7

0	1	0	3	1	6	1
0	1	6	8	6	0	1
5	5	2	1	8	2	9
6	5	6	1	1	9	1
1	5	6	1	4	0	7
3	5	3	3	4	0	7

0	1	0	3	1	6	1
0	1	6	8	6	0	1
5	6	2	1	6	2	9
6	5	6	6	1	9	1
1	3	6	1	4	0	7
3	6	3	3	4	0	7

0	1	0	3	1	6	1
0	1	6	8	6	0	1
9	6	2	1	8	2	9
6	9	6	1	1	9	1
1	3	9	1	4	0	7
3	3	3	9	4	0	7

***8.20 (*Game: connect four*) Connect four is a two-player board game in which the players alternately drop colored disks into a seven-column, six-row vertically suspended grid, as shown below.

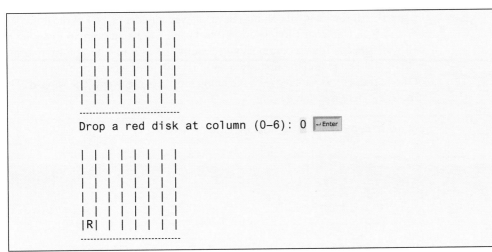

The objective of the game is to connect four same-colored disks in a row, a column, or a diagonal before your opponent can do likewise. The program prompts two players to drop a red or yellow disk alternately. In the preceding figure, the red disk is shown in a dark color and the yellow in a light color. Whenever a disk is dropped, the program redisplays the board on the console and determines the status of the game (win, draw, or continue). Here is a sample run:

```
| | | | | | | |
| | | | | | | |
| | | | | | | |
| | | | | | | |
| | | | | | | |
| | | | | | | |
---------------------------------
Drop a red disk at column (0-6): 0 ↵Enter

| | | | | | | |
| | | | | | | |
| | | | | | | |
| | | | | | | |
| | | | | | | |
|R| | | | | | |
---------------------------------
```

```
Drop a yellow disk at column (0-6): 3 ⏎Enter

| | | | | | | |
| | | | | | | |
| | | | | | | |
| | | | | | | |
| | | | | | | |
|R| | |Y| | | |

        . . .
        . . .
        . . .

Drop a yellow disk at column (0-6): 6 ⏎Enter

| | | | | | | |
| | | | | | | |
| | | |R| | | |
| | | |Y|R|Y| |
| | |R|Y|Y|Y|Y|
|R|Y|R|Y|R|R|R|
-------------------------------
The yellow player won
```

*8.21   (*Central city*) Given a set of cities, the central city is the city that has the shortest total distance to all other cities. Write a program that prompts the user to enter the number of cities and the locations of the cities (coordinates), and finds the central city and its total distance to all other cities.

```
Enter the number of cities: 5 ⏎Enter
Enter the coordinates of the cities:
  2.5 5 5.1 3 1 9 5.4 54 5.5 2.1 ⏎Enter
The central city is at (2.5, 5.0)
The total distance to all other cities is 60.81
```

*8.22   (*Even number of 1s*) Write a program that generates a 6-by-6 two-dimensional matrix filled with 0s and 1s, displays the matrix, and checks if every row and every column have an even number of 1s.

*8.23   (*Game: find the flipped cell*) Suppose you are given a 6-by-6 matrix filled with 0s and 1s. All rows and all columns have an even number of 1s. Let the user flip one cell (i.e., flip from 1 to 0 or from 0 to 1) and write a program to find which cell was flipped. Your program should prompt the user to enter a 6-by-6 array with 0s and 1s and find the first row r and first column c where the even number of the 1s property is violated (i.e., the number of 1s is not even). The flipped cell is at (r, c). Here is a sample run:

```
Enter a 6-by-6 matrix row by row:
1 1 1 0 1 1 ⏎Enter
1 1 1 1 0 0 ⏎Enter
0 1 0 1 1 1 ⏎Enter
1 1 1 1 1 1 ⏎Enter
0 1 1 1 1 0 ⏎Enter
1 0 0 0 0 1 ⏎Enter
The flipped cell is at (0, 1)
```

*8.24   (*Check Sudoku solution*) Listing 8.4 checks whether a solution is valid by checking whether every number is valid in the board. Rewrite the program by checking
whether every row, every column, and every small box has the numbers 1 to 9.

*8.25   (*Markov matrix*) An $n \times n$ matrix is called a *positive Markov matrix* if each
element is positive and the sum of the elements in each column is 1. Write the
following method to check whether a matrix is a Markov matrix:

```
public static boolean isMarkovMatrix(double[][] m)
```

Write a test program that prompts the user to enter a 3×3 matrix of double
values and tests whether it is a Markov matrix. Here are sample runs:

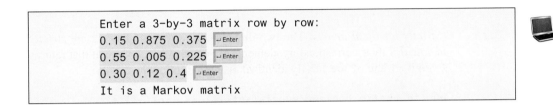

```
Enter a 3-by-3 matrix row by row:
0.15 0.875 0.375 ↵Enter
0.55 0.005 0.225 ↵Enter
0.30 0.12 0.4 ↵Enter
It is a Markov matrix
```

```
Enter a 3-by-3 matrix row by row:
0.95 -0.875 0.375 ↵Enter
0.65 0.005 0.225 ↵Enter
0.30 0.22 -0.4 ↵Enter
It is not a Markov matrix
```

*8.26   (*Row sorting*) Implement the following method to sort the rows in a two-
dimensional array. A new array is returned and the original array is intact.

```
public static double[][] sortRows(double[][] m)
```

Write a test program that prompts the user to enter a 3×3 matrix of double
values and displays a new row-sorted matrix. Here is a sample run:

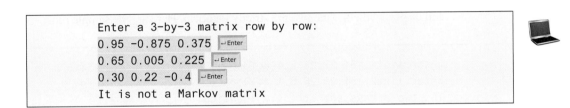

```
Enter a 3-by-3 matrix row by row:
0.15 0.875 0.375 ↵Enter
0.55 0.005 0.225 ↵Enter
0.30 0.12 0.4 ↵Enter

The row-sorted array is
0.15 0.375 0.875
0.005 0.225 0.55
0.12 0.30 0.4
```

*8.27   (*Column sorting*) Implement the following method to sort the columns in a two-
dimensional array. A new array is returned and the original array is intact.

```
public static double[][] sortColumns(double[][] m)
```

Write a test program that prompts the user to enter a 3 × 3 matrix of double values and displays a new column-sorted matrix. Here is a sample run:

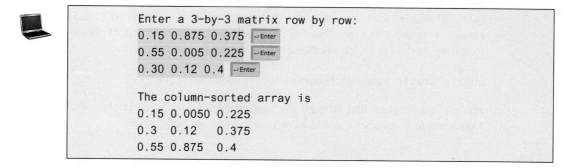

```
Enter a 3-by-3 matrix row by row:
0.15 0.875 0.375  ↵Enter
0.55 0.005 0.225  ↵Enter
0.30 0.12 0.4  ↵Enter

The column-sorted array is
0.15 0.0050 0.225
0.3  0.12   0.375
0.55 0.875  0.4
```

8.28 (*Strictly identical arrays*) The two-dimensional arrays m1 and m2 are *strictly identical* if their corresponding elements are equal. Write a method that returns true if m1 and m2 are strictly identical, using the following header:

```
public static boolean equals(int[][] m1, int[][] m2)
```

Write a test program that prompts the user to enter two 3 × 3 arrays of integers and displays whether the two are strictly identical. Here are the sample runs:

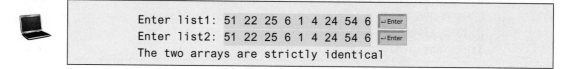

```
Enter list1: 51 22 25 6 1 4 24 54 6  ↵Enter
Enter list2: 51 22 25 6 1 4 24 54 6  ↵Enter
The two arrays are strictly identical
```

```
Enter list1: 51 25 22 6 1 4 24 54 6  ↵Enter
Enter list2: 51 22 25 6 1 4 24 54 6  ↵Enter
The two arrays are not strictly identical
```

8.29 (*Identical arrays*) The two-dimensional arrays m1 and m2 are *identical* if they have the same contents. Write a method that returns true if m1 and m2 are identical, using the following header:

```
public static boolean equals(int[][] m1, int[][] m2)
```

Write a test program that prompts the user to enter two 3 × 3 arrays of integers and displays whether the two are identical. Here are the sample runs:

```
Enter list1: 51 25 22 6 1 4 24 54 6  ↵Enter
Enter list2: 51 22 25 6 1 4 24 54 6  ↵Enter
The two arrays are identical
```

```
Enter list1: 51 5 22 6 1 4 24 54 6  ↵Enter
Enter list2: 51 22 25 6 1 4 24 54 6  ↵Enter
The two arrays are not identical
```

*8.30 (*Algebra: solve linear equations*) Write a method that solves the following 2×2 system of linear equations:

$$a_{00}x + a_{01}y = b_0 \qquad x = \frac{b_0 a_{11} - b_1 a_{01}}{a_{00} a_{11} - a_{01} a_{10}} \qquad y = \frac{b_1 a_{00} - b_0 a_{10}}{a_{00} a_{11} - a_{01} a_{10}}$$
$$a_{10}x + a_{11}y = b_1$$

The method header is:

```
public static double[] linearEquation(double[][] a, double[] b)
```

The method returns `null` if $a_{00}a_{11} - a_{01}a_{10}$ is `0`. Write a test program that prompts the user to enter a_{00}, a_{01}, a_{10}, a_{11}, b_0, and b_1 and displays the result. If $a_{00}a_{11} - a_{01}a_{10}$ is `0`, report that "The equation has no solution." A sample run is similar to Programming Exercise 3.3.

*8.31 (*Geometry: intersecting point*) Write a method that returns the intersecting point of two lines. The intersecting point of the two lines can be found by using the formula given in Programming Exercise 3.25. Assume that (x1, y1) and (x2, y2) are the two points on line 1 and (x3, y3) and (x4, y4) are on line 2. The method header is:

```
public static double[] getIntersectingPoint(double[][] points)
```

The points are stored in a 4-by-2 two-dimensional array points with (points [0][0], points[0][1]) for (x1, y1). The method returns the intersecting point or null if the two lines are parallel. Write a program that prompts the user to enter four points and displays the intersecting point. See Programming Exercise 3.25 for a sample run.

*8.32 (*Geometry: area of a triangle*) Write a method that returns the area of a triangle using the following header:

```
public static double getTriangleArea(double[][] points)
```

The points are stored in a 3-by-2 two-dimensional array points with points [0][0] and points[0][1] for (x1, y1). The triangle area can be computed using the formula in Programming Exercise 2.19. The method returns `0` if the three points are on the same line. Write a program that prompts the user to enter three points of a triangle and displays the triangle's area. Here are the sample runs:

```
Enter x1, y1, x2, y2, x3, y3: 2.5 2 5 -1.0 4.0 2.0 ↵Enter
The area of the triangle is 2.25
```

```
Enter x1, y1, x2, y2, x3, y3: 2 2 4.5 4.5 6 6 ↵Enter
The three points are on the same line
```

*8.33 (*Geometry: polygon subareas*) A convex four-vertex polygon is divided into four triangles, as shown in Figure 8.9.

Write a program that prompts the user to enter the coordinates of four vertices and displays the areas of the four triangles in increasing order. Here is a sample run:

```
Enter x1, y1, x2, y2, x3, y3, x4, y4:
  -2.5 2 4 4 3 -2 -2 -3.5 ↵Enter
The areas are 6.17 7.96 8.08 10.42
```

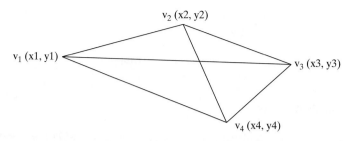

FIGURE 8.9 A four-vertex polygon is defined by four vertices.

*8.34 (*Geometry: rightmost lowest point*) In computational geometry, often you need to find the rightmost lowest point in a set of points. Write the following method that returns the rightmost lowest point in a set of points:

```
public static double[]
    getRightmostLowestPoint(double[][] points)
```

Write a test program that prompts the user to enter the coordinates of six points and displays the rightmost lowest point. Here is a sample run:

```
Enter 6 points: 1.5 2.5 -3 4.5 5.6 -7 6.5 -7 8 1 10 2.5 ⏎Enter
The rightmost lowest point is (6.5, -7.0)
```

**8.35 (*Largest block*) Given a square matrix with the elements 0 or 1, write a program to find a maximum square submatrix whose elements are all 1s. Your program should prompt the user to enter the number of rows in the matrix. The program then displays the location of the first element in the maximum square submatrix and the number of rows in the submatrix. Here is a sample run:

```
Enter the number of rows in the matrix: 5 ⏎Enter
Enter the matrix row by row:
1 0 1 0 1 ⏎Enter
1 1 1 0 1 ⏎Enter
1 0 1 1 1 ⏎Enter
1 0 1 1 1 ⏎Enter
1 0 1 1 1 ⏎Enter

The maximum square submatrix is at (2, 2) with size 3
```

Your program should implement and use the following method to find the maximum square submatrix:

```
public static int[] findLargestBlock(int[][] m)
```

The return value is an array that consists of three values. The first two values are the row and column indices for the first element in the submatrix, and the third value is the number of the rows in the submatrix.

8.36 (*Latin square*) A Latin square is an *n*-by-*n* array filled with *n* different Latin letters, each occurring exactly once in each row and once in each column. Write a program that prompts the user to enter the number **n and the array of characters, as shown in the sample output, and checks if the input array is a Latin square. The characters are the first **n** characters starting from **A**.

```
Enter number n: 4 ↵Enter
Enter 4 rows of letters separated by spaces:
A B C D ↵Enter
B A D C ↵Enter
C D B A ↵Enter
D C A B ↵Enter
The input array is a Latin square
```

```
Enter number n: 3 ↵Enter
Enter 3 rows of letters separated by spaces:
A F D ↵Enter
Wrong input: the letters must be from A to C
```

8.37 (*Guess the capitals*) Write a program that repeatedly prompts the user to enter a capital for a state. Upon receiving the user input, the program reports whether the answer is correct. Assume that **50 states and their capitals are stored in a two-dimensional array, as shown in Figure 8.10. The program prompts the user to answer all states' capitals and displays the total correct count. The user's answer is not case-sensitive.

```
Alabama      Montgomery
Alaska       Juneau
Arizona      Phoenix
...          ...
...          ...
```

FIGURE 8.10 A two-dimensional array stores states and their capitals.

Here is a sample run:

```
What is the capital of Alabama? Montogomery ↵Enter
The correct answer should be Montgomery
What is the capital of Alaska? Juneau ↵Enter
Your answer is correct
What is the capital of Arizona? ...
...
The correct count is 35
```

OBJECTS AND CLASSES

Objectives

- To describe objects and classes, and use classes to model objects (§9.2).
- To use UML graphical notation to describe classes and objects (§9.2).
- To demonstrate how to define classes and create objects (§9.3).
- To create objects using constructors (§9.4).
- To access objects via object reference variables (§9.5).
- To define a reference variable using a reference type (§9.5.1).
- To access an object's data and methods using the object member access operator (.) (§9.5.2).
- To define data fields of reference types and assign default values for an object's data fields (§9.5.3).
- To distinguish between object reference variables and primitive-data-type variables (§9.5.4).

- To use the Java library classes Date, Random, and Point2D (§9.6).
- To distinguish between instance and static variables and methods (§9.7).
- To define private data fields with appropriate getter and setter methods (§9.8).
- To encapsulate data fields to make classes easy to maintain (§9.9).
- To develop methods with object arguments and differentiate between primitive-type arguments and object-type arguments (§9.10).
- To store and process objects in arrays (§9.11).
- To create immutable objects from immutable classes to protect the contents of objects (§9.12).
- To determine the scope of variables in the context of a class (§9.13).
- To use the keyword this to refer to the calling object itself (§9.14).

9.1 Introduction

Object-oriented programming enables you to develop large-scale software and GUIs effectively.

Object-oriented programming is essentially a technology for developing reusable software. Having learned the material in the preceding chapters, you are able to solve many programming problems using selections, loops, methods, and arrays. However, these Java features are not sufficient for developing graphical user interfaces and large-scale software systems. Suppose you want to develop a graphical user interface (GUI, pronounced *goo-ee*) as shown in Figure 9.1. How would you program it?

why OOP?

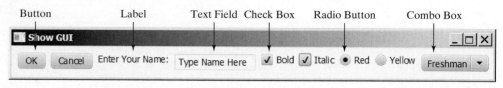

FIGURE 9.1 The GUI objects are created from classes.

This chapter introduces object-oriented programming, which you can use to develop GUI and large-scale software systems.

9.2 Defining Classes for Objects

A class defines the properties and behaviors for objects.

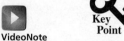

VideoNote

Define classes and objects

Object-oriented programming (OOP) involves programming using objects. An *object* represents an entity in the real world that can be distinctly identified. For example, a student, a desk, a circle, a button, and even a loan can all be viewed as objects. An object has a unique identity, state, and behavior.

object
state of an object
properties
attributes
data fields
behavior
actions

- The *state* of an object (also known as its *properties* or *attributes*) is represented by *data fields* with their current values. A circle object, for example, has a data field `radius`, which is the property that characterizes a circle. A rectangle object, for example, has the data fields `width` and `height`, which are the properties that characterize a rectangle.

- The *behavior* of an object (also known as its *actions*) is defined by methods. To invoke a method on an object is to ask the object to perform an action. For example, you may define methods named `getArea()` and `getPerimeter()` for circle objects. A circle object may invoke `getArea()` to return its area and `getPerimeter()` to return its perimeter. You may also define the `setRadius(radius)` method. A circle object can invoke this method to change its radius.

class
contract

instantiation
instance

Objects of the same type are defined using a common class. A *class* is a template, blueprint, or *contract* that defines what an object's data fields and methods will be. An object is an instance of a class. You can create many instances of a class. Creating an instance is referred to as *instantiation*. The terms *object* and *instance* are often interchangeable. The relationship between classes and objects is analogous to that between an apple-pie recipe and apple pies: You can make as many apple pies as you want from a single recipe. Figure 9.2 shows a class named `Circle` and its three objects.

data field
method
constructors

A Java class uses variables to define data fields and methods to define actions. In addition, a class provides methods of a special type, known as *constructors*, which are invoked to create a new object. A constructor can perform any action, but constructors are designed to perform initializing actions, such as initializing the data fields of objects. Figure 9.3 shows an example of defining the class for circle objects.

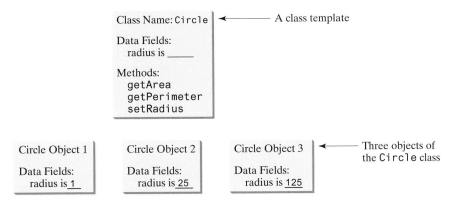

FIGURE 9.2 A class is a template for creating objects.

```
class Circle {
  /** The radius of this circle */
  double radius = 1;                              Data field

  /** Construct a circle object */
  Circle() {
  }

  /** Construct a circle object */             Constructors
  Circle(double newRadius) {
    radius = newRadius;
  }

  /** Return the area of this circle */
  double getArea() {
    return radius * radius * Math.PI;
  }

  /** Return the perimeter of this circle */
  double getPerimeter() {                        Method
    return 2 * radius * Math.PI;
  }

  /** Set a new radius for this circle */
  void setRadius(double newRadius) {
    radius = newRadius;
  }
}
```

FIGURE 9.3 A class is a construct that defines objects of the same type.

The Circle class is different from all of the other classes you have seen thus far. It does not have a main method, and therefore cannot be run; it is merely a definition for circle objects. The class that contains the main method will be referred to in this book, for convenience, as the *main class*.

The illustration of class templates and objects in Figure 9.2 can be standardized using *Unified Modeling Language (UML)* notation. This notation, as shown in Figure 9.4, is called a *UML class diagram*, or simply a *class diagram*. In the class diagram, the data field is denoted as

main class

Unified Modeling Language (UML)

class diagram

```
dataFieldName: dataFieldType
```

The constructor is denoted as

```
ClassName(parameterName: parameterType)
```

UML Class Diagram

Circle	◄—— Class name
radius: double	◄—— Data fields
Circle()	◄—— Constructors and methods
Circle(newRadius: double)	
getArea(): double	
getPerimeter(): double	
setRadius(newRadius: double): void	

circle1: Circle	circle2: Circle	circle3: Circle	◄—— UML notation for objects
radius = 1	radius = 25	radius = 125	

FIGURE 9.4 Classes and objects can be represented using UML notation.

The method is denoted as

```
methodName(parameterName: parameterType): returnType
```

9.3 Example: Defining Classes and Creating Objects

Key
Point

Classes are definitions for objects and objects are created from classes.

This section gives two examples of defining classes and uses the classes to create objects. Listing 9.1 is a program that defines the `Circle` class and uses it to create objects. The program constructs three circle objects with radius `1`, `25`, and `125` and displays the `radius` and `area` of each of the three circles. It then changes the radius of the second object to `100` and displays its new radius and area.

LISTING 9.1   TestCircle.java

main class

main method

create object

create object

create object

create object

```
 1  public class TestCircle {
 2    /** Main method */
 3    public static void main(String[] args) {
 4      // Create a circle with radius 1
 5      Circle circle1 = new Circle();
 6      System.out.println("The area of the circle of radius "
 7        + circle1.radius + " is " + circle1.getArea());
 8
 9      // Create a circle with radius 25
10      Circle circle2 = new Circle(25);
11      System.out.println("The area of the circle of radius "
12        + circle2.radius + " is " + circle2.getArea());
13
14      // Create a circle with radius 125
15      Circle circle3 = new Circle(125);
16      System.out.println("The area of the circle of radius "
17        + circle3.radius + " is " + circle3.getArea());
18
19      // Modify circle radius
20      circle2.radius = 100; // or circle2.setRadius(100)
21      System.out.println("The area of the circle of radius "
22        + circle2.radius + " is " + circle2.getArea());
23    }
24  }
25
```

```
26   // Define the circle class with two constructors
27   class Circle {
28     double radius;
29
30     /** Construct a circle with radius 1 */
31     Circle() {
32       radius = 1;
33     }
34
35     /** Construct a circle with a specified radius */
36     Circle(double newRadius) {
37       radius = newRadius;
38     }
39
40     /** Return the area of this circle */
41     double getArea() {
42       return radius * radius * Math.PI;
43     }
44
45     /** Return the perimeter of this circle */
46     double getPerimeter() {
47       return 2 * radius * Math.PI;
48     }
49
50     /** Set a new radius for this circle */
51     void setRadius(double newRadius) {
52       radius = newRadius;
53     }
54   }
```

class Circle
data field

no-arg constructor

second constructor

getArea

getPerimeter

setRadius

```
The area of the circle of radius 1.0 is 3.141592653589793
The area of the circle of radius 25.0 is 1963.4954084936207
The area of the circle of radius 125.0 is 49087.385212340516
The area of the circle of radius 100.0 is 31415.926535897932
```

The program contains two classes. The first of these, `TestCircle`, is the main class. Its sole purpose is to test the second class, `Circle`. Such a program that uses the class is often referred to as a *client* of the class. When you run the program, the Java runtime system invokes the `main` method in the main class.

    You can put the two classes into one file, but only one class in the file can be a *public class*. Furthermore, the public class must have the same name as the file name. Therefore, the file name is **TestCircle.java**, since `TestCircle` is public. Each class in the source code is compiled into a **.class** file. When you compile **TestCircle.java**, two class files **TestCircle.class** and **Circle.class** are generated, as shown in Figure 9.5.

client

public class

```
// File TestCircle.java

public class TestCircle {
  ...
}

class Circle {
  ...
}
```

compiled by → Java Compiler

generates → TestCircle.class

generates → Circle.class

FIGURE 9.5 Each class in the source code file is compiled into a **.class** file.

The main class contains the `main` method (line 3) that creates three objects. As in creating an array, the `new` operator is used to create an object from the constructor: `new Circle()` creates an object with radius 1 (line 5), `new Circle(25)` creates an object with radius 25 (line 10), and `new Circle(125)` creates an object with radius 125 (line 15).

These three objects (referenced by `circle1`, `circle2`, and `circle3`) have different data but the same methods. Therefore, you can compute their respective areas by using the `getArea()` method. The data fields can be accessed via the reference of the object using `circle1.radius`, `circle2.radius`, and `circle3.radius`, respectively. The object can invoke its method via the reference of the object using `circle1.getArea()`, `circle2.getArea()`, and `circle3.getArea()`, respectively.

These three objects are independent. The radius of `circle2` is changed to `100` in line 20. The object's new radius and area are displayed in lines 21 and 22.

There are many ways to write Java programs. For instance, you can combine the two classes in the preceding example into one, as given in Listing 9.2.

LISTING 9.2 Circle.java (AlternativeCircle.java)

```
1  public class Circle {
2    /** Main method */
3    public static void main(String[] args) {
4      // Create a circle with radius 1
5      Circle circle1 = new Circle();
6      System.out.println("The area of the circle of radius "
7        + circle1.radius + " is " + circle1.getArea());
8
9      // Create a circle with radius 25
10     Circle circle2 = new Circle(25);
11     System.out.println("The area of the circle of radius "
12       + circle2.radius + " is " + circle2.getArea());
13
14     // Create a circle with radius 125
15     Circle circle3 = new Circle(125);
16     System.out.println("The area of the circle of radius "
17       + circle3.radius + " is " + circle3.getArea());
18
19     // Modify circle radius
20     circle2.radius = 100;
21     System.out.println("The area of the circle of radius "
22       + circle2.radius + " is " + circle2.getArea());
23   }
24
25   double radius;
26
27   /** Construct a circle with radius 1 */
28   Circle() {
29     radius = 1;
30   }
31
32   /** Construct a circle with a specified radius */
33   Circle(double newRadius) {
34     radius = newRadius;
35   }
36
37   /** Return the area of this circle */
38   double getArea() {
39     return radius * radius * Math.PI;
40   }
41
```

main method — line 3
data field — line 25
no-arg constructor — line 28
second constructor — line 33
method — line 38

```
42      /** Return the perimeter of this circle */
43      double getPerimeter() {
44        return 2 * radius * Math.PI;
45      }
46
47      /** Set a new radius for this circle */
48      void setRadius(double newRadius) {
49        radius = newRadius;
50      }
51    }
```

Since the combined class has a `main` method, it can be executed by the Java interpreter. The `main` method is the same as that in Listing 9.1. This demonstrates that you can test a class by simply adding a `main` method in the same class.

As another example, consider television sets. Each TV is an object with states (current channel, current volume level, and power on or off) and behaviors (change channels, adjust volume, and turn on/off). You can use a class to model TV sets. The UML diagram for the class is shown in Figure 9.6.

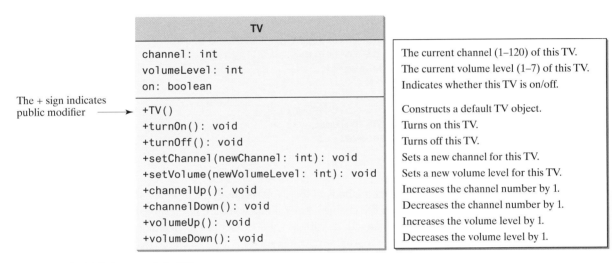

FIGURE 9.6 The TV class models TV sets.

Listing 9.3 gives a program that defines the TV class.

LISTING 9.3 TV.java

```
1   public class TV {
2     int channel = 1; // Default channel is 1                          data fields
3     int volumeLevel = 1; // Default volume level is 1
4     boolean on = false; // TV is off
5
6     public TV() {                                                      constructor
7     }
8
9     public void turnOn() {                                             turn on TV
10       on = true;
11     }
12
13     public void turnOff() {                                           turn off TV
```

```
14        on = false;
15      }
16
17  public void setChannel(int newChannel) {
18      if (on && newChannel >= 1 && newChannel <= 120)
19        channel = newChannel;
20  }
21
22  public void setVolume(int newVolumeLevel) {
23      if (on && newVolumeLevel >= 1 && newVolumeLevel <= 7)
24        volumeLevel = newVolumeLevel;
25  }
26
27  public void channelUp() {
28      if (on && channel < 120)
29        channel++;
30  }
31
32  public void channelDown() {
33      if (on && channel > 1)
34        channel--;
35  }
36
37  public void volumeUp() {
38      if (on && volumeLevel < 7)
39        volumeLevel++;
40  }
41
42  public void volumeDown() {
43      if (on && volumeLevel > 1)
44        volumeLevel--;
45  }
46 }
```

set a new channel (17), set a new volume (22), increase channel (27), decrease channel (32), increase volume (37), decrease volume (42)

The constructor and methods in the TV class are defined public so they can be accessed from other classes. Note the channel and volume level are not changed if the TV is not on. Before either of these is changed, its current value is checked to ensure it is within the correct range.

Listing 9.4 gives a program that uses the TV class to create two objects.

LISTING 9.4 TestTV.java

```
1  public class TestTV {
2    public static void main(String[] args) {
3      TV tv1 = new TV();
4      tv1.turnOn();
5      tv1.setChannel(30);
6      tv1.setVolume(3);
7
8      TV tv2 = new TV();
9      tv2.turnOn();
10     tv2.channelUp();
11     tv2.channelUp();
12     tv2.volumeUp();
13
14     System.out.println("tv1's channel is " + tv1.channel
15       + " and volume level is " + tv1.volumeLevel);
16     System.out.println("tv2's channel is " + tv2.channel
17       + " and volume level is " + tv2.volumeLevel);
18   }
19 }
```

main method (2), create a TV (3), turn on (4), set a new channel (5), set a new volume (6), create a TV (8), turn on (9), increase channel (10), increase volume (12), display state (14)

```
tv1's channel is 30 and volume level is 3
tv2's channel is 3 and volume level is 2
```

The program creates two objects in lines 3 and 8 and invokes the methods on the objects to perform actions for setting channels and volume levels and for increasing channels and volumes. The program displays the state of the objects in lines 14–17. The methods are invoked using syntax such as `tv1.turnOn()` (line 4). The data fields are accessed using syntax such as `tv1.channel` (line 14).

These examples have given you a glimpse of classes and objects. You may have many questions regarding constructors, objects, reference variables, accessing data fields, and invoking object's methods. The sections that will follow discuss these issues in detail.

9.3.1 Describe the relationship between an object and its defining class.

9.3.2 How do you define a class?

9.3.3 How do you declare an object's reference variable?

9.3.4 How do you create an object?

9.4 Constructing Objects Using Constructors

A constructor is invoked to create an object using the new *operator.*

Constructors are a special kind of method. They have three peculiarities:

- A constructor must have the same name as the class itself. ·constructor's name

- Constructors do not have a return type—not even `void`. ·no return type

- Constructors are invoked using the `new` operator when an object is created. ·new operator
  Constructors play the role of initializing objects.

The constructor has exactly the same name as its defining class. Like regular methods, constructors can be overloaded (i.e., multiple constructors can have the same name but different ·overloaded constructors
signatures), making it easy to construct objects with different initial data values.

It is a common mistake to put the `void` keyword in front of a constructor. For example,

```
public void Circle() {      ·no void
}
```

In this case, `Circle()` is a method, not a constructor.

Constructors are used to construct objects. To construct an object from a class, invoke a ·constructing objects
constructor of the class using the `new` operator, as follows:

```
new ClassName(arguments);
```

For example, `new Circle()` creates an object of the `Circle` class using the first constructor defined in the `Circle` class, and `new Circle(25)` creates an object using the second constructor defined in the `Circle` class.

A class normally provides a constructor without arguments (e.g., `Circle()`). Such a constructor is referred to as a *no-arg* or *no-argument constructor*. ·no-arg constructor

A class may be defined without constructors. In this case, a public no-arg constructor with an empty body is implicitly defined in the class. This constructor, called a *default constructor*, ·default constructor
is provided automatically *only if no constructors are explicitly defined in the class*.

9.4.5 What are the differences between constructors and methods?

9.4.6 When will a class have a default constructor?

9.5 Accessing Objects via Reference Variables

An object's data and methods can be accessed through the dot (.) operator via the object's reference variable.

Newly created objects are allocated in the memory. They can be accessed via reference variables.

9.5.1 Reference Variables and Reference Types

reference variable

Objects are accessed via the object's *reference variables*, which contain references to the objects. Such variables are declared using the following syntax:

```
ClassName objectRefVar;
```

reference type

A class is essentially a programmer-defined type. A class is a *reference type*, which means that a variable of the class type can reference an instance of the class. The following statement declares the variable `myCircle` to be of the `Circle` type:

```
Circle myCircle;
```

The variable `myCircle` can reference a `Circle` object. The next statement creates an object and assigns its reference to `myCircle`:

```
myCircle = new Circle();
```

You can write a single statement that combines the declaration of an object reference variable, the creation of an object, and the assigning of an object reference to the variable with the following syntax:

```
ClassName objectRefVar = new ClassName();
```

Here is an example:

```
Circle myCircle = new Circle();
```

The variable `myCircle` holds a reference to a `Circle` object.

object vs. object reference variable

Note
An object reference variable that appears to hold an object actually contains a reference to that object. Strictly speaking, an object reference variable and an object are different, but most of the time the distinction can be ignored. Therefore, it is fine, for simplicity, to say that `myCircle` is a `Circle` object rather than use the long-winded description that `myCircle` is a variable that contains a reference to a `Circle` object.

array object

Note
Arrays are treated as objects in Java. Arrays are created using the `new` operator. An array variable is actually a variable that contains a reference to an array.

9.5.2 Accessing an Object's Data and Methods

In OOP terminology, an object's member refers to its data fields and methods. After an object is created, its data can be accessed and its methods can be invoked using the *dot operator* (.), also known as the *object member access operator*:

dot operator (.)

- `objectRefVar.dataField` references a data field in the object.

- `objectRefVar.method(arguments)` invokes a method on the object.

For example, `myCircle.radius` references the radius in `myCircle` and `myCircle`
`.getArea()` invokes the `getArea` method on `myCircle`. Methods are invoked as operations
on objects.

The data field `radius` is referred to as an *instance variable* because it is dependent on a
specific instance. For the same reason, the method `getArea` is referred to as an *instance
method* because you can invoke it only on a specific instance. The object on which an instance
method is invoked is called a *calling object*.

instance variable
instance method

calling object

Caution
Recall that you use `Math.methodName(arguments)` (e.g., `Math.pow(3, 2.5)`)
to invoke a method in the `Math` class. Can you invoke `getArea()` using `Circle.`
`getArea()`? The answer is no. All the methods in the `Math` class are static methods,
which are defined using the `static` keyword. However, `getArea()` is an instance
method, and thus nonstatic. It must be invoked from an object using `objectRefVar.`
`methodName(arguments)` (e.g., `myCircle.getArea()`). Further explanation will
be given in Section 9.7, Static Variables, Constants, and Methods.

invoking methods

Note
Usually you create an object and assign it to a variable, then later you can use the
variable to reference the object. Occasionally, an object does not need to be referenced
later. In this case, you can create an object without explicitly assigning it to a variable
using the syntax:

```java
new Circle();
```

or

```java
System.out.println("Area is " + new Circle(5).getArea());
```

The former statement creates a `Circle` object. The latter creates a `Circle` object and
invokes its `getArea` method to return its area. An object created in this way is known
as an *anonymous object*.

anonymous object

9.5.3 Reference Data Fields and the `null` Value

The data fields can be of reference types. For example, the following `Student` class contains
a data field `name` of the `String` type. `String` is a predefined Java class.

reference data fields

```java
class Student {
  String name; // name has the default value null
  int age; // age has the default value 0
  boolean isScienceMajor; // isScienceMajor has default value false
  char gender; // gender has default value '\u0000'
}
```

If a data field of a reference type does not reference any object, the data field holds a special
Java value, `null`. `null` is a literal just like `true` and `false`. While `true` and `false` are
Boolean literals, `null` is a literal for a reference type.

null value

The default value of a data field is `null` for a reference type, `0` for a numeric type, `false`
for a `boolean` type, and `\u0000` for a `char` type. However, Java assigns no default value to
a local variable inside a method. The following code displays the default values of the data
fields `name`, `age`, `isScienceMajor`, and `gender` for a `Student` object:

default field values

```java
class TestStudent {
  public static void main(String[] args) {
    Student student = new Student();
    System.out.println("name? " + student.name);
```

```
System.out.println("age? " + student.age);
System.out.println("isScienceMajor? " + student.isScienceMajor);
System.out.println("gender? " + student.gender);
  }
}
```

The following code has a compile error, because the local variables x and y are not initialized:

```
class TestLocalVariables {
  public static void main(String[] args) {
    int x; // x has no default value
    String y; // y has no default value
    System.out.println("x is " + x);
    System.out.println("y is " + y);
  }
}
```

NullPointerException

> **Caution**
>
> NullPointerException is a common runtime error. It occurs when you invoke a method on a reference variable with a null value. Make sure you assign an object reference to the variable before invoking the method through the reference variable (see CheckPoint Question 9.5.5c).

9.5.4   Differences between Variables of Primitive Types and Reference Types

Every variable represents a memory location that holds a value. When you declare a variable, you are telling the compiler what type of value the variable can hold. For a variable of a primitive type, the value is of the primitive type. For a variable of a reference type, the value is a reference to where an object is located. For example, as shown in Figure 9.7, the value of int variable i is int value 1, and the value of Circle object c holds a reference to where the contents of the Circle object are stored in memory.

Created using new Circle()

Primitive type	int i = 1 i	1
Object type	Circle c c	reference ┄┄┄┄► c: Circle / radius = 1

FIGURE 9.7   A variable of a primitive type holds a value of the primitive type, and a variable of a reference type holds a reference to where an object is stored in memory.

When you assign one variable to another, the other variable is set to the same value. For a variable of a primitive type, the real value of one variable is assigned to the other variable. For a variable of a reference type, the reference of one variable is assigned to the other variable. As shown in Figure 9.8, the assignment statement i = j copies the contents of j into i

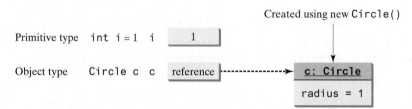

Primitive type assignment i = j

Before i = j   After i = j

i   1   i   2

j   2   j   2

FIGURE 9.8   Primitive variable j is copied to variable i.

for primitive variables. As shown in Figure 9.9, the assignment statement `c1 = c2` copies the reference of `c2` into `c1` for reference variables. After the assignment, variables `c1` and `c2` refer to the same object.

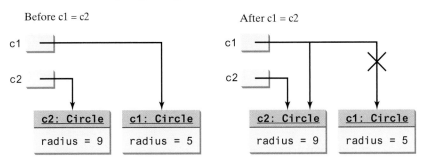

FIGURE 9.9 Reference variable `c2` is copied to variable `c1`.

Note

As illustrated in Figure 9.9, after the assignment statement `c1 = c2`, `c1` points to the same object referenced by `c2`. The object previously referenced by `c1` is no longer useful and therefore is now known as *garbage*. Garbage occupies memory space, so the Java runtime system detects garbage and automatically reclaims the space it occupies. This process is called *garbage collection*.

garbage

garbage collection

Tip

If you know that an object is no longer needed, you can explicitly assign `null` to a reference variable for the object. The JVM will automatically collect the space if the object is not referenced by any reference variable.

9.5.1 Which operator is used to access a data field or invoke a method from an object?

9.5.2 What is an anonymous object?

9.5.3 What is `NullPointerException`?

9.5.4 Is an array an object or a primitive-type value? Can an array contain elements of an object type? Describe the default value for the elements of an array.

9.5.5 What is wrong with each of the following programs?

Check
Point

```
1  public class ShowErrors {
2    public static void main(String[] args) {
3      ShowErrors t = new ShowErrors(5);
4    }
5  }
```
(a)

```
1  public class ShowErrors {
2    public static void main(String[] args) {
3      ShowErrors t = new ShowErrors();
4      t.x();
5    }
6  }
```
(b)

```
1  public class ShowErrors {
2    public void method1() {
3      Circle c;
4      System.out.println("What is radius "
5        + c.getRadius());
6      c = new Circle();
7    }
8  }
```
(c)

```
1   public class ShowErrors {
2     public static void main(String[] args) {
3       C c = new C(5.0);
4       System.out.println(c.value);
5     }
6   }
7
8   class C {
9     int value = 2;
10  }
```
(d)

9.5.6 What is wrong in the following code?

```
1  class Test {
2    public static void main(String[] args) {
3      A a = new A();
4      a.print();
5    }
6  }
7
8  class A {
9    String s;
10
11   A(String newS) {
12     s = newS;
13   }
14
15   public void print() {
16     System.out.print(s);
17   }
18 }
```

9.5.7 What is the output of the following code?

```
public class A {
  boolean x;

  public static void main(String[] args) {
    A a = new A();
    System.out.println(a.x);
  }
}
```

9.6 Using Classes from the Java Library

The Java API contains a rich set of classes for developing Java programs.

Key Point

VideoNote

Use classes

Listing 9.1 defined the `Circle` class and created objects from the class. You will frequently use the classes in the Java library to develop programs. This section gives some examples of the classes in the Java library.

9.6.1 The `Date` Class

java.util.Date class

In Listing 2.7, ShowCurrentTime.java, you learned how to obtain the current time using `System.currentTimeMillis()`. You used the division and remainder operators to extract the current second, minute, and hour. Java provides a system-independent encapsulation of date and time in the `java.util.Date` class, as shown in Figure 9.10.

java.util.Date	
+Date()	Constructs a `Date` object for the current time.
+Date(elapseTime: long)	Constructs a `Date` object for a given time in milliseconds elapsed since January 1, 1970, GMT.
+toString(): String	Returns a string representing the date and time.
+getTime(): long	Returns the number of milliseconds since January 1, 1970, GMT.
+setTime(elapseTime: long): void	Sets a new elapse time in the object.

FIGURE 9.10 A `Date` object represents a specific date and time.

You can use the no-arg constructor in the `Date` class to create an instance for the current date and time, the `getTime()` method to return the elapsed time in milliseconds since January 1, 1970, GMT, and the `toString()` method to return the date and time as a string. For example, the following code

```
java.util.Date date = new java.util.Date();                    create object
System.out.println("The elapsed time since Jan 1, 1970 is " +
  date.getTime() + " milliseconds");                           get elapsed time
System.out.println(date.toString());                           invoke toString
```

displays the output as follows:

```
The elapsed time since Jan 1, 1970 is 1324903419651 milliseconds
Mon Dec 26 07:43:39 EST 2011
```

The `Date` class has another constructor, `Date(long elapseTime)`, which can be used to construct a `Date` object for a given time in milliseconds elapsed since January 1, 1970, GMT.

9.6.2 The `Random` Class

You have used `Math.random()` to obtain a random `double` value between `0.0` and `1.0` (excluding `1.0`). Another way to generate random numbers is to use the `java.util.Random` class, as shown in Figure 9.11, which can generate a random `int`, `long`, `double`, `float`, and `boolean` value.

java.util.Random	
+Random()	Constructs a Random object with the current time as its seed.
+Random(seed: long)	Constructs a Random object with a specified seed.
+nextInt(): int	Returns a random int value.
+nextInt(n: int): int	Returns a random int value between 0 and n (excluding n).
+nextLong(): long	Returns a random long value.
+nextDouble(): double	Returns a random double value between 0.0 and 1.0 (excluding 1.0).
+nextFloat(): float	Returns a random float value between 0.0F and 1.0F (excluding 1.0F).
+nextBoolean(): boolean	Returns a random boolean value.

FIGURE 9.11   A `Random` object can be used to generate random values.

When you create a `Random` object, you have to specify a seed or use the default seed. A seed is a number used to initialize a random number generator. The no-arg constructor creates a `Random` object using the current elapsed time as its seed. If two `Random` objects have the same seed, they will generate identical sequences of numbers. For example, the following code creates two `Random` objects with the same seed, `3`:

```
Random generator1 = new Random(3);
System.out.print("From generator1: ");
for (int i = 0; i < 10; i++)
  System.out.print(generator1.nextInt(1000) + " ");

Random generator2 = new Random(3);
System.out.print("\nFrom generator2: ");
for (int i = 0; i < 10; i++)
  System.out.print(generator2.nextInt(1000) + " ");
```

The code generates the same sequence of random `int` values:

```
From generator1: 734 660 210 581 128 202 549 564 459 961
From generator2: 734 660 210 581 128 202 549 564 459 961
```

same sequence

Note
The ability to generate the same sequence of random values is useful in software testing and many other applications. In software testing, often you need to reproduce the test cases from a fixed sequence of random numbers.

SecureRandom

Note
You can generate random numbers using the `java.security.SecureRandom` class rather than the `Random` class. The random numbers generated from the `Random` are deterministic and they can be predicated by hackers. The random numbers generated from the `SecureRandom` class are nondeterministic and are secure.

9.6.3 The `Point2D` Class

Java API has a convenient `Point2D` class in the `javafx.geometry` package for representing a point in a two-dimensional plane. The UML diagram for the class is shown in Figure 9.12.

javafx.geometry.Point2D	
+Point2D(x: double, y: double)	Constructs a Point2D object with the specified *x*- and *y*-coordinates.
+distance(x: double, y: double): double	Returns the distance between this point and the specified point (*x*, *y*).
+distance(p: Point2D): double	Returns the distance between this point and the specified point p.
+getX(): double	Returns the *x*-coordinate from this point.
+getY(): double	Returns the *y*-coordinate from this point.
+midpoint(p: Point2D): Point2D	Returns the midpoint between this point and point p.
+toString(): String	Returns a string representation for the point.

FIGURE 9.12 A `Point2D` object represents a point with *x*- and *y*-coordinates.

You can create a `Point2D` object for a point with the specified *x*- and *y*-coordinates, use the `distance` method to compute the distance from this point to another point, and use the `toString()` method to return a string representation of the point. Listing 9.5 gives an example of using this class.

LISTING 9.5 TestPoint2D.java

```
1  import java.util.Scanner;
2  import javafx.geometry.Point2D;
3
4  public class TestPoint2D {
5    public static void main(String[] args) {
6      Scanner input = new Scanner(System.in);
7
8      System.out.print("Enter point1's x-, y-coordinates: ");
9      double x1 = input.nextDouble();
10     double y1 = input.nextDouble();
11     System.out.print("Enter point2's x-, y-coordinates: ");
12     double x2 = input.nextDouble();
13     double y2 = input.nextDouble();
14
15     Point2D p1 = new Point2D(x1, y1);
16     Point2D p2 = new Point2D(x2, y2);
17     System.out.println("p1 is " + p1.toString());
18     System.out.println("p2 is " + p2.toString());
19     System.out.println("The distance between p1 and p2 is " +
20       p1.distance(p2));
```

create an object

invoke toString()

get distance

```
21        System.out.println("The midpoint between p1 and p2 is " +
22            p1.midpoint(p2).toString());
23    }
24  }
```

get midpoint

```
Enter point1's x-, y-coordinates: 1.5 5.5 ↵Enter
Enter point2's x-, y-coordinates: -5.3 -4.4 ↵Enter
p1 is Point2D [x = 1.5, y = 5.5]
p2 is Point2D [x = -5.3, y = -4.4]
The distance between p1 and p2 is 12.010412149464313
The midpoint between p1 and p2 is
Point2D [x = -1.9, y = 0.5499999999999998]
```

This program creates two objects of the `Point2D` class (lines 15 and 16). The `toString()` method returns a string that describes the object (lines 17 and 18). Invoking `p1.distance(p2)` returns the distance between the two points (line 20). Invoking `p1.midpoint(p2)` returns the midpoint between the two points (line 22).

9.6.1 How do you create a `Date` for the current time? How do you display the current time?

9.6.2 How do you create a `Point2D`? Suppose `p1` and `p2` are two instances of `Point2D`, how do you obtain the distance between the two points? How do you obtain the midpoint between the two points?

9.6.3 Which packages contain the classes `Date`, `Random`, `Point2D`, `System`, and `Math`?

Check Point

9.7 Static Variables, Constants, and Methods

A static variable is shared by all objects of the class. A static method cannot access instance members (i.e., instance data fields and methods) of the class.

Key Point

The data field `radius` in the circle class is known as an *instance variable*. An instance variable is tied to a specific instance of the class; it is not shared among objects of the same class. For example, suppose that you create the following objects:

Static vs. instance
instance variable

```
Circle circle1 = new Circle();
Circle circle2 = new Circle(5);
```

VideoNote
Static vs. instance

The `radius` in `circle1` is independent of the `radius` in `circle2` and is stored in a different memory location. Changes made to `circle1`'s `radius` do not affect `circle2`'s `radius`, and vice versa.

If you want all the instances of a class to share data, use *static variables*, also known as *class variables*. Static variables store values for the variables in a common memory location. Because of this common location, if one object changes the value of a static variable, all objects of the same class are affected. Java supports static methods as well as static variables. *Static methods* can be called without creating an instance of the class.

static variable

static method

Let's modify the `Circle` class by adding a static variable `numberOfObjects` to count the number of circle objects created. When the first object of this class is created, `numberOfObjects` is `1`. When the second object is created, `numberOfObjects` becomes `2`. The UML of the new circle class is shown in Figure 9.13. The `Circle` class defines the instance variable `radius` and the static variable `numberOfObjects`, the instance methods `getRadius`, `setRadius`, and `getArea`, and the static method `getNumberOfObjects`. (Note static variables and methods are underlined in the UML class diagram.)

UML Notation:
  underline: static variables or methods

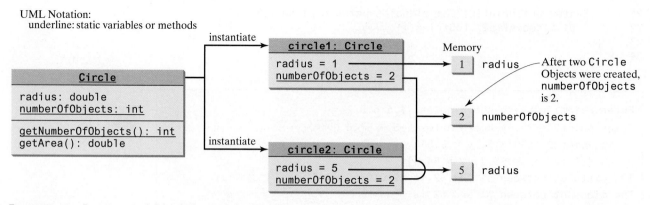

FIGURE 9.13 Instance variables belong to the instances and have memory storage independent of one another. Static variables are shared by all the instances of the same class.

To declare a static variable or define a static method, put the modifier `static` in the variable or method declaration. The static variable `numberOfObjects` and the static method `getNumberOfObjects()` can be declared as follows:

declare static variable

```
static int numberOfObjects;
```

define static method

```
static int getNumberObjects() {
  return numberOfObjects;
}
```

declare constant

Constants in a class are shared by all objects of the class. Thus, constants should be declared as `final static`. For example, the constant `PI` in the `Math` class is defined as follows:

```
final static double PI = 3.14159265358979323846;
```

The new circle class is defined in Listing 9.6.

LISTING 9.6 Circle.java (for CircleWithStaticMembers)

```
1  public class Circle {
2    /** The radius of the circle */
3    double radius;
4
5    /** The number of objects created */
6    static int numberOfObjects = 0;
7
8    /** Construct a circle with radius 1 */
9    Circle() {
10     radius = 1;
11     numberOfObjects++;
12   }
13
14   /** Construct a circle with a specified radius */
15   Circle(double newRadius) {
16     radius = newRadius;
17     numberOfObjects++;
18   }
19
20   /** Return numberOfObjects */
21   static int getNumberOfObjects() {
22     return numberOfObjects;
23   }
24
25   /** Return the area of this circle */
```

static variable (line 6)

increase by 1 (line 11)

increase by 1 (line 17)

static method (line 21)

```
26      double getArea() {
27        return radius * radius * Math.PI;
28      }
29  }
```

Method `getNumberOfObjects()` in `Circle` is a static method. All the methods in the `Math` class are static. The `main` method is static, too.

Instance methods (e.g., `getArea()`) and instance data (e.g., `radius`) belong to instances and can be used only after the instances are created. They are accessed via a reference variable. Static methods (e.g., `getNumberOfObjects()`) and static data (e.g., `numberOfObjects`) can be accessed from a reference variable or from their class name.

The program in Listing 9.7 demonstrates how to use instance and static variables and methods and illustrates the effects of using them.

LISTING 9.7   TestCircleWithStaticMembers.java

```
1   public class TestCircleWithStaticMembers {
2     /** Main method */
3     public static void main(String[] args) {
4       System.out.println("Before creating objects");
5       System.out.println("The number of Circle objects is " +
6         Circle.numberOfObjects);                                static variable
7
8       // Create c1
9       Circle c1 = new Circle(); // Use the Circle class in Listing 9.6
10
11      // Display c1 BEFORE c2 is created
12      System.out.println("\nAfter creating c1");
13      System.out.println("c1: radius (" + c1.radius +          instance variable
14        ") and number of Circle objects (" +
15        c1.numberOfObjects + ")");                             static variable
16
17      // Create c2
18      Circle c2 = new Circle(5);
19
20      // Modify c1
21      c1.radius = 9;                                           instance variable
22
23      // Display c1 and c2 AFTER c2 was created
24      System.out.println("\nAfter creating c2 and modifying c1");
25      System.out.println("c1: radius (" + c1.radius +
26        ") and number of Circle objects (" +
27        c1.numberOfObjects + ")");                             static variable
28      System.out.println("c2: radius (" + c2.radius +
29        ") and number of Circle objects (" +
30        c2.numberOfObjects + ")");                             static variable
31    }
32  }
```

```
Before creating objects
The number of Circle objects is 0
After creating c1
c1: radius (1.0) and number of Circle objects (1)
After creating c2 and modifying c1
c1: radius (9.0) and number of Circle objects (2)
c2: radius (5.0) and number of Circle objects (2)
```

When you compile `TestCircleWithStaticMembers.java`, the Java compiler automatically compiles `Circle.java` if it has not been compiled since the last change.

Static variables and methods can be accessed without creating objects. Line 6 displays the number of objects, which is `0`, since no objects have been created.

The `main` method creates two circles, `c1` and `c2` (lines 9 and18). The instance variable `radius` in `c1` is modified to become `9` (line 21). This change does not affect the instance variable `radius` in `c2`, since these two instance variables are independent. The static variable `numberOfObjects` becomes `1` after `c1` is created (line 9), and it becomes `2` after `c2` is created (line 18).

Note `PI` is a constant defined in `Math` and `Math.PI` references the constant. `c1.numberOfObjects` (line 27) and `c2.numberOfObjects` (line 30) are better replaced by `Circle.numberOfObjects`. This improves readability because other programmers can easily recognize the static variable. You can also replace `Circle.numberOfObjects` with `Circle.getNumberOfObjects()`.

use class name

Tip
Use `ClassName.methodName(arguments)` to invoke a static method and `ClassName.staticVariable` to access a static variable. This improves readability because this makes static methods and data easy to spot.

An instance method can invoke an instance or static method, and access an instance or static data field. A static method can invoke a static method and access a static data field. However, a static method cannot invoke an instance method or access an instance data field, since static methods and static data fields don't belong to a particular object. The relationship between static and instance members is summarized in the following diagram:

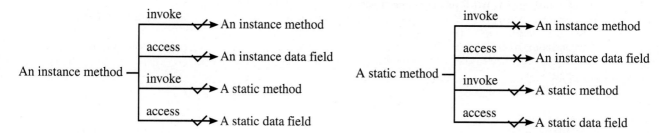

For example, the following code is wrong.

```
1  public class A {
2    int i = 5;
3    static int k = 2;
4
5    public static void main(String[] args) {
6      int j = i; // Wrong because i is an instance variable
7      m1(); // Wrong because m1() is an instance method
8    }
9
10   public void m1() {
11     // Correct since instance and static variables and methods
12     // can be used in an instance method
13     i = i + k + m2(i, k);
14   }
15
16   public static int m2(int i, int j) {
17     return (int)(Math.pow(i, j));
18   }
19 }
```

Note if you replace the preceding code with the following new code, the program would be fine, because the instance data field `i` and method `m1` are now accessed from an object `a` (lines 7 and 8):

```
1  public class A {
2    int i = 5;
3    static int k = 2;
4
5    public static void main(String[] args) {
6      A a = new A();
7      int j = a.i; // OK, a.i accesses the object's instance variable
8      a.m1(); // OK, a.m1() invokes the object's instance method
9    }
10
11   public void m1() {
12     i = i + k + m2(i, k);
13   }
14
15   public static int m2(int i, int j) {
16     return (int)(Math.pow(i, j));
17   }
18 }
```

Design Guide

How do you decide whether a variable or a method should be instance or static? A variable or a method that is dependent on a specific instance of the class should be an instance variable or method. A variable or a method that is not dependent on a specific instance of the class should be a static variable or method. For example, every circle has its own radius, so the radius is dependent on a specific circle. Therefore, `radius` is an instance variable of the `Circle` class. Since the `getArea` method is dependent on a specific circle, it is an instance method. None of the methods in the `Math` class, such as `random`, `pow`, `sin`, and `cos`, is dependent on a specific instance. Therefore, these methods are static methods. The `main` method is static and can be invoked directly from a class.

instance or static?

Caution

It is a common design error to define an instance method that should have been defined as static. For example, the method `factorial(int n)` should be defined as static, as shown next, because it is independent of any specific instance.

common design error

```
public class Test {
  public int factorial(int n) {
    int result = 1;
    for (int i = 1; i <= n; i++)
      result *= i;

    return result;
  }
}
```
(a) Wrong design

```
public class Test {
  public static int factorial(int n) {
    int result = 1;
    for (int i = 1; i <= n; i++)
      result *= i;

    return result;
  }
}
```
(b) Correct design

9.7.1 Suppose the class `F` is defined in (a). Let `f` be an instance of `F`. Which of the statements in (b) are correct?

Check
Point

```
public class F {
  int i;
  static String s;

  void imethod() {
  }

  static void smethod() {
  }
}
```

```
System.out.println(f.i);
System.out.println(f.s);
f.imethod();
f.smethod();
System.out.println(F.i);
System.out.println(F.s);
F.imethod();
F.smethod();
```

(a)   (b)

9.7.2 Add the `static` keyword in the place of **?** if appropriate.

```
public class Test {
  int count;

  public ? void main(String[] args) {
    ...
  }

  public ? int getCount() {
    return count;
  }

  public ? int factorial(int n) {
    int result = 1;
    for (int i = 1; i <= n; i++)
      result *= i;

    return result;
  }
}
```

9.7.3 Can you invoke an instance method or reference an instance variable from a static method? Can you invoke a static method or reference a static variable from an instance method? What is wrong in the following code?

```
1  public class C {
2    public static void main(String[] args) {
3      method1();
4    }
5
6    public void method1() {
7      method2();
8    }
9
10   public static void method2() {
11     System.out.println("What is radius " + c.getRadius());
12   }
13
14   Circle c = new Circle();
15 }
```

9.8 Visibility Modifiers

Visibility modifiers can be used to specify the visibility of a class and its members.

You can use the `public` visibility modifier for classes, methods, and data fields to denote they can be accessed from any other classes. If no visibility modifier is used, then by default the classes, methods, and data fields are accessible by any class in the same package. This is known as *package-private* or *package-access*.

package-private (or
package-access)

Note

Packages can be used to organize classes. To do so, you need to add the following line as the first noncomment and nonblank statement in the program:

using packages

```
package packageName;
```

If a class is defined without the package statement, it is said to be placed in the *default package*.

Java recommends that you place classes into packages rather than using a default package. For simplicity, however, this book uses default packages. For more information on packages, see Supplement III.E, Packages.

In addition to the `public` and default visibility modifiers, Java provides the `private` and `protected` modifiers for class members. This section introduces the `private` modifier. The `protected` modifier will be introduced in Section 11.14, The `protected` Data and Methods.

The `private` modifier makes methods and data fields accessible only from within its own class. Figure 9.14 illustrates how a public, default, and private data field or method in class C1 can be accessed from a class C2 in the same package, and from a class C3 in a different package.

```
package p1;

public class C1 {
  public int x;
  int y;
  private int z;

  public void m1() {
  }
  void m2() {
  }
  private void m3() {
  }
}
```

```
package p1;

public class C2 {
  void aMethod() {
    C1 c1 = new C1();
    can access c1.x;
    can access c1.y;
    cannot access o.z;

    can invoke c1.m1();
    can invoke c1.m2();
    cannot invoke c1.m3();
  }
}
```

```
package p2;

public class C3 {
  void aMethod() {
    C1 c1 = new C1();
    can access c1.x;
    cannot access c1.y;
    cannot access c1.z;

    can invoke c1.m1();
    cannot invoke c1.m2();
    cannot invoke c1.m3();
  }
}
```

FIGURE 9.14 The private modifier restricts access to its defining class, the default modifier restricts access to a package, and the public modifier enables unrestricted access.

If a class is not defined as public, it can be accessed only within the same package. As shown in Figure 9.15, C1 can be accessed from C2, but not from C3.

```
package p1;

class  C1 {
  ...
}
```

```
package p1;

public class C2 {
  can access C1
}
```

```
package p2;

public class C3 {
  cannot access p1.C1;
  can access p1.C2;
}
```

FIGURE 9.15 A nonpublic class has package access.

A visibility modifier specifies how data fields and methods in a class can be accessed from outside the class. There is no restriction on accessing data fields and methods from inside the class. As shown in Figure 9.16b, an object c of class C cannot access its private members, because c is in the Test class. As shown in Figure 9.16a, an object c of class C can access its private members, because c is defined inside its own class.

inside access

```
public class C {
  private boolean x;

  public static void main(string[] args) {
    C c = new C();
    system.out.println(c.x);
    system.out.println(c.convert());
  }

  private int convert() {
    return x ? 1 : -1;
  }
}
```

```
public class Test {
  public static void main(string[] args) {
    C c = new C();
    system.out.println(c.x);
    system.out.println(c.convert());
  }
}
```

(a) This is okay because object c is used inside the class C.   (b) This is wrong because x and convert are private in class C.

FIGURE 9.16 An object can access its private members if it is defined in its own class.

>
> **Caution**
> The `private` modifier applies only to the members of a class. The `public` modifier can apply to a class or members of a class. Using the modifiers `public` and `private` on local variables would cause a compile error.

private constructor

>
> **Note**
> In most cases, the constructor should be public. However, if you want to prohibit the user from creating an instance of a class, use a *private constructor*. For example, there is no reason to create an instance from the `Math` class, because all of its data fields and methods are static. To prevent the user from creating objects from the `Math` class, the constructor in `java.lang.Math` is defined as follows:

```
private Math() {
}
```

9.9 Data Field Encapsulation

Key Point

Making data fields private protects data and makes the class easy to maintain.

Data field encapsulation

VideoNote

Data field encapsulation

The data fields `radius` and `numberOfObjects` in the `Circle` class in Listing 9.6 can be modified directly (e.g., `c1.radius = 5` or `Circle.numberOfObjects = 10`). This is not a good practice—for two reasons:

1. Data may be tampered with. For example, `numberOfObjects` is to count the number of objects created, but it may be mistakenly set to an arbitrary value (e.g., `Circle.numberOfObjects = 10`).

2. The class becomes difficult to maintain and vulnerable to bugs. Suppose that you want to modify the `Circle` class to ensure that the radius is nonnegative after other programs have already used the class. You have to change not only the `Circle` class but also the programs that use it because the clients may have modified the radius directly (e.g., `c1.radius = -5`).

data field encapsulation

To prevent direct modifications of data fields, you should declare the data fields private, using the `private` modifier. This is known as *data field encapsulation*.

A private data field cannot be accessed by an object from outside the class that defines the private field. However, a client often needs to retrieve and modify a data field. To make a private data field accessible, provide a *getter* method to return its value. To enable a private data field to be updated, provide a *setter* method to set a new value. A getter method is also referred to as an *accessor* and a setter to a *mutator*. A getter method has the following signature:

getter (or accessor)
setter (or mutator)

```
public returnType getPropertyName()
```

If the returnType is boolean, the getter method should be defined as follows by convention:

boolean accessor

```
public boolean isPropertyName()
```

A setter method has the following signature:

```
public void setPropertyName(dataType propertyValue)
```

Let's create a new circle class with a private data-field radius and its associated accessor and mutator methods. The class diagram is shown in Figure 9.17. The new circle class is defined in Listing 9.8:

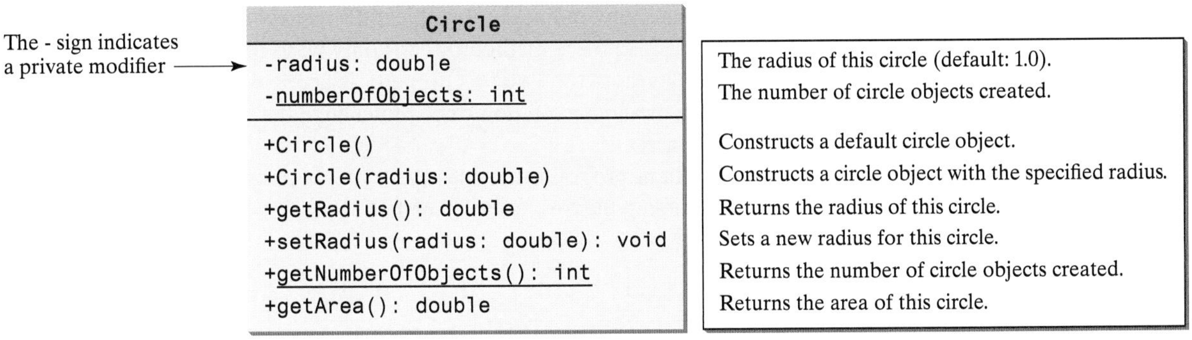

FIGURE 9.17 The Circle class encapsulates circle properties and provides getter/setter and other methods.

LISTING 9.8 Circle.java (for CircleWithPrivateDataFields)

```
 1  public class Circle {
 2    /** The radius of the circle */
 3    private double radius = 1;                    encapsulate radius
 4
 5    /** The number of objects created */
 6    private static int numberOfObjects = 0;       encapsulate
 7                                                     numberOfObjects
 8    /** Construct a circle with radius 1 */
 9    public Circle() {
10      numberOfObjects++;
11    }
12
13    /** Construct a circle with a specified radius */
14    public Circle(double newRadius) {
15      radius = newRadius;
16      numberOfObjects++;
```

```
17      }
18
19      /** Return radius */
20      public double getRadius() {
21        return radius;
22      }
23
24      /** Set a new radius */
25      public void setRadius(double newRadius) {
26        radius = (newRadius >= 0) ? newRadius : 0;
27      }
28
29      /** Return numberOfObjects */
30      public static int getNumberOfObjects() {
31        return numberOfObjects;
32      }
33
34      /** Return the area of this circle */
35      public double getArea() {
36        return radius * radius * Math.PI;
37      }
38    }
```

(*accessor method* — line 20; *mutator method* — line 25; *accessor method* — line 30)

The getRadius() method (lines 20–22) returns the radius and the setRadius(newRadius) method (lines 25–27) sets a new radius for the object. If the new radius is negative, 0 is set as the radius for the object. Since these methods are the only ways to read and modify the radius, you have total control over how the radius property is accessed. If you have to change the implementation of these methods, you don't need to change the client programs. This makes the class easy to maintain.

Listing 9.9 gives a client program that uses the Circle class to create a Circle object, and modifies the radius using the setRadius method.

LISTING 9.9 TestCircleWithPrivateDataFields.java

```
1   public class TestCircleWithPrivateDataFields {
2     /** Main method */
3     public static void main(String[] args) {
4       // Create a circle with radius 5.0
5       Circle myCircle = new Circle(5.0);
6       System.out.println("The area of the circle of radius "
7         + myCircle.getRadius() + " is " + myCircle.getArea());
8
9       // Increase myCircle's radius by 10%
10      myCircle.setRadius(myCircle.getRadius() * 1.1);
11      System.out.println("The area of the circle of radius "
12        + myCircle.getRadius() + " is " + myCircle.getArea());
13
14      System.out.println("The number of objects created is "
15        + Circle.getNumberOfObjects());
16    }
17  }
```

(*invoke public method* — lines 7, 12, 15)

The data field radius is declared private. Private data can be accessed only within their defining class, so you cannot use myCircle.radius in the client program. A compile error would occur if you attempted to access private data from a client.

Since numberOfObjects is private, it cannot be modified. This prevents tampering. For example, the user cannot set numberOfObjects to 100. The only way to make it 100 is to create 100 objects of the Circle class.

Suppose you combined `TestCircleWithPrivateDataFields` and `Circle` into one class by moving the `main` method in `TestCircleWithPrivateDataFields` into `Circle`. Could you use `myCircle.radius` in the `main` method? See CheckPoint Question 9.9.3 for the answer.

Design Guide

To prevent data from being tampered with and to make the class easy to maintain, declare data fields private.

Note

From now on, all data fields should be declared private, and all constructors and methods should be defined public, unless specified otherwise.

9.9.1 What is an accessor method? What is a mutator method? What are the naming conventions for accessor methods and mutator methods?

9.9.2 What are the benefits of data field encapsulation?

9.9.3 In the following code, `radius` is private in the `Circle` class, and `myCircle` is an object of the `Circle` class. Does the highlighted code cause any problems? If so, explain why.

```java
public class Circle {
  private double radius = 1;

  /** Find the area of this circle */
  public double getArea() {
    return radius * radius * Math.PI;
  }

  public static void main(String[] args) {
    Circle myCircle = new Circle();
    System.out.println("Radius is " + myCircle.radius);
  }
}
```

9.10 Passing Objects to Methods

Passing an object to a method is to pass the reference of the object.

You can pass objects to methods. Like passing an array, passing an object is actually passing the reference of the object. The following code passes the `myCircle` object as an argument to the `printCircle` method:

```java
1  public class Test {
2    public static void main(String[] args) {
3      // Circle is defined in Listing 9.8
4      Circle myCircle = new Circle(5.0);
5      printCircle(myCircle);
6    }
7
8    public static void printCircle(Circle c) {
9      System.out.println("The area of the circle of radius "
10        + c.getRadius() + " is " + c.getArea());
11    }
12  }
```

pass an object

Java uses exactly one mode of passing arguments: pass-by-value. In the preceding code, the value of `myCircle` is passed to the `printCircle` method. This value is a reference to a `Circle` object.

pass-by-value

The program in Listing 9.10 demonstrates the difference between passing a primitive-type value and passing a reference value.

LISTING 9.10 TestPassObject.java

```
1   public class TestPassObject {
2     /** Main method */
3     public static void main(String[] args) {
4       // Create a Circle object with radius 1
5       Circle myCircle =
6         new Circle(1); // Use the Circle class in Listing 9.8
7
8       // Print areas for radius 1, 2, 3, 4, and 5.
9       int n = 5;
10      printAreas(myCircle, n);
11
12      // See myCircle.radius and times
13      System.out.println("\n" + "Radius is " + myCircle.getRadius());
14      System.out.println("n is " + n);
15    }
16
17    /** Print a table of areas for radius */
18    public static void printAreas(Circle c, int times) {
19      System.out.println("Radius \t\tArea");
20      while (times >= 1) {
21        System.out.println(c.getRadius() + "\t\t" + c.getArea());
22        c.setRadius(c.getRadius() + 1);
23        times--;
24      }
25    }
26  }
```

pass object (line 10)

object parameter (line 18)

```
Radius        Area
1.0           3.141592653589793
2.0           12.566370614359172
3.0           28.274333882308138
4.0           50.26548245743669
5.0           78.53981633974483
Radius is 6.0
n is 5
```

The Circle class is defined in Listing 9.8. The program passes a Circle object myCircle and an integer value from n to invoke printAreas(myCircle, n) (line 10), which prints a table of areas for radii 1, 2, 3, 4, and 5, as presented in the sample output.

Figure 9.18 shows the call stack for executing the methods in the program. Note the objects are stored in a heap (see Section 7.6).

When passing an argument of a primitive data type, the value of the argument is passed. In this case, the value of n (5) is passed to times. Inside the printAreas method, the content of times is changed; this does not affect the content of n.

When passing an argument of a reference type, the reference of the object is passed. In this case, c contains a reference for the object that is also referenced via myCircle. Therefore, changing the properties of the object through c inside the printAreas method has the same effect as doing so outside the method through the variable myCircle. Pass-by-value on references can be best described semantically as *pass-by-sharing*; that is, the object referenced in the method is the same as the object being passed.

pass-by-sharing

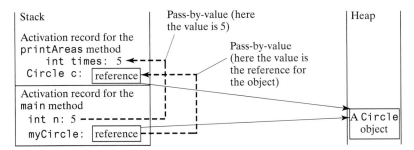

FIGURE 9.18 The value of n is passed to `times`, and the reference to `myCircle` is passed to c in the `printAreas` method.

9.10.1 Describe the difference between passing a parameter of a primitive type and passing a parameter of a reference type. Show the output of the following programs:

```java
public class Test {
  public static void main(String[] args) {
    Count myCount = new  Count();
    int times = 0;

    for (int i = 0; i < 100; i++)
      increment(myCount, times);

    System.out.println("count is " + myCount.count);
    System.out.println("times is " + times);
  }

  public static void increment(Count c, int times) {
    c.count++;
    times++;
  }
}
```

```java
public class Count {
  public int count;

  public Count (int c) {
    count = c;
  }

  public Count () {
    count = 1;
  }
}
```

9.10.2 Show the output of the following program:

```java
public class Test {
  public static void main(String[] args) {
    Circle circle1 = new Circle(1);
    Circle circle2 = new Circle(2);

    swap1(circle1, circle2);
    System.out.println("After swap1: circle1 = " +
      circle1.radius + " circle2 = " + circle2.radius);

    swap2(circle1, circle2);
    System.out.println("After swap2: circle1 = " +
      circle1.radius + " circle2 = " + circle2.radius);
  }

  public static void swap1(Circle x, Circle y) {
    Circle temp = x;
    x = y;
    y = temp;
  }
```

```
                    public static void swap2(Circle x, Circle y) {
                      double temp = x.radius;
                      x.radius = y.radius;
                      y.radius = temp;
                    }
                  }

                  class Circle {
                    double radius;

                    Circle(double newRadius) {
                      radius = newRadius;
                    }
                  }
```

9.10.3 Show the output of the following code:

```
public class Test {
  public static void main(String[] args) {
    int[] a = {1, 2};
    swap(a[0], a[1]);
    System.out.println("a[0] = " + a[0]
      + " a[1] = " + a[1]);
  }

  public static void swap(int n1, int n2) {
    int temp = n1;
    n1 = n2;
    n2 = temp;
  }
}
```
(a)

```
public class Test {
  public static void main(String[] args) {
    int[] a = {1, 2};
    swap(a);
    System.out.println("a[0] = " + a[0]
      + " a[1] = " + a[1]);
  }

  public static void swap(int[] a) {
    int temp = a[0];
    a[0] = a[1];
    a[1] = temp;
  }
}
```
(b)

```
public class Test {
  public static void main(String[] args) {
    T t = new T();
    swap(t);
    System.out.println("e1 = " + t.e1
      + " e2 = " + t.e2);
  }

  public static void swap(T t) {
    int temp = t.e1;
    t.e1 = t.e2;
    t.e2 = temp;
  }
}

class T {
  int e1 = 1;
  int e2 = 2;
}
```
(c)

```
public class Test {
  public static void main(String[] args) {
    T t1 = new T();
    T t2 = new T();
    System.out.println("t1's i = " +
      t1.i + " and j = " + t1.j);
    System.out.println("t2's i = " +
      t2.i + " and j = " + t2.j);
  }
}

class T {
  static int i = 0;
  int j = 0;

  T() {
    i++;
    j = 1;
  }
}
```
(d)

9.10.4 What is the output of the following programs?

```java
import java.util.Date;

public class Test {
  public static void main(String[] args) {
    Date date = null;
    m1(date);
    System.out.println(date);
  }

  public static void m1(Date date) {
    date = new Date();
  }
}
```
(a)

```java
import java.util.Date;

public class Test {
  public static void main(String[] args) {
    Date date = new Date(1234567);
    m1(date);
    System.out.println(date.getTime());
  }

  public static void m1(Date date) {
    date = new Date(7654321);
  }
}
```
(b)

```java
import java.util.Date;

public class Test {
  public static void main(String[] args) {
    Date date = new Date(1234567);
    m1(date);
    System.out.println(date.getTime());
  }

  public static void m1(Date date) {
    date.setTime(7654321);
  }
}
```
(c)

```java
import java.util.Date;

public class Test {
  public static void main(String[] args) {
    Date date = new Date(1234567);
    m1(date);
    System.out.println(date.getTime());
  }

  public static void m1(Date date) {
    date = null;
  }
}
```
(d)

9.11 Array of Objects

An array can hold objects as well as primitive-type values.

Chapter 7, Single-Dimensional Arrays, described how to create arrays of primitive-type elements. You can also create arrays of objects. For example, the following statement declares and creates an array of 10 `Circle` objects:

```java
Circle[] circleArray = new Circle[10];
```

To initialize `circleArray`, you can use a `for` loop as follows:

```java
for (int i = 0; i < circleArray.length; i++) {
  circleArray[i] = new Circle();
}
```

An array of objects is actually an *array of reference variables*. Thus, invoking `circleArray[1].getArea()` involves two levels of referencing, as shown in Figure 9.19. `circleArray` references the entire array, and `circleArray[1]` references a `Circle` object.

Note

When an array of objects is created using the `new` operator, each element in the array is a reference variable with a default value of `null`.

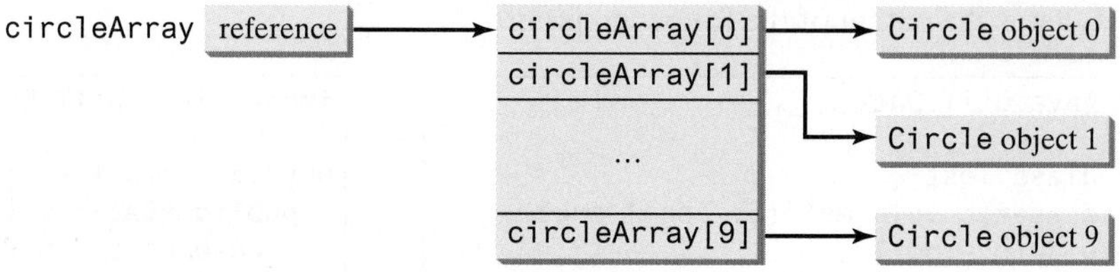

FIGURE 9.19 In an array of objects, an element of the array contains a reference to an object.

Listing 9.11 gives an example that demonstrates how to use an array of objects. The program summarizes the areas of an array of circles. The program creates circleArray, an array composed of five Circle objects; it then initializes circle radii with random values and displays the total area of the circles in the array.

LISTING 9.11   TotalArea.java

array of objects

return array of objects

pass array of objects

```java
1  public class TotalArea {
2    /** Main method */
3    public static void main(String[] args) {
4      // Declare circleArray
5      Circle[] circleArray;
6
7      // Create circleArray
8      circleArray = createCircleArray();
9
10     // Print circleArray and total areas of the circles
11     printCircleArray(circleArray);
12   }
13
14   /** Create an array of Circle objects */
15   public static Circle[] createCircleArray() {
16     Circle[] circleArray = new Circle[5];
17
18     for (int i = 0; i < circleArray.length; i++) {
19       circleArray[i] = new Circle(Math.random() * 100);
20     }
21
22     // Return Circle array
23     return circleArray;
24   }
25
26   /** Print an array of circles and their total area */
27   public static void printCircleArray(Circle[] circleArray) {
28     System.out.printf("%-30s%-15s\n", "Radius", "Area");
29     for (int i = 0; i < circleArray.length; i++) {
30       System.out.printf("%-30f%-15f\n", circleArray[i].getRadius(),
31         circleArray[i].getArea());
32     }
33
34     System.out.println("_____");
35
36     // Compute and display the result
37     System.out.printf("%-30s%-15f\n", "The total area of circles is",
38       sum(circleArray));
39   }
40
```

```
41    /** Add circle areas */
42    public static double sum(Circle[] circleArray) {
43      // Initialize sum
44      double sum = 0;
45
46      // Add areas to sum
47      for (int i = 0; i < circleArray.length; i++)
48        sum += circleArray[i].getArea();
49
50      return sum;
51    }
52  }
```

pass array of objects

```
Radius                  Area
70.577708               15649.941866
44.152266                6124.291736
24.867853                1942.792644
 5.680718                 101.380949
36.734246                4239.280350
_____

The total area of circles is 28056.687544
```

The program invokes createCircleArray() (line 8) to create an array of five circle objects. Several circle classes were introduced in this chapter. This example uses the Circle class introduced in Section 9.9, Data Field Encapsulation.

The circle radii are randomly generated using the Math.random() method (line 19). The createCircleArray method returns an array of Circle objects (line 23). The array is passed to the printCircleArray method, which displays the radius and area of each circle and the total area of the circles.

The sum of the circle areas is computed by invoking the sum method (line 38), which takes the array of Circle objects as the argument and returns a double value for the total area.

9.11.1 What is wrong in the following code?

```
1  public class Test {
2    public static void main(String[] args) {
3      java.util.Date[] dates = new java.util.Date[10];
4      System.out.println(dates[0]);
5      System.out.println(dates[0].toString());
6    }
7  }
```

9.12 Immutable Objects and Classes

You can define immutable classes to create immutable objects. The contents of immutable objects cannot be changed.

Key Point

VideoNote
Immutable objects and this keyword

Normally, you create an object and allow its contents to be changed later. However, occasionally it is desirable to create an object whose contents cannot be changed once the object has been created. We call such an object as *immutable object* and its class as *immutable class*. The String class, for example, is immutable. If you deleted the setter method in the Circle class in Listing 9.8, the class would be immutable because radius is private and cannot be changed without a setter method.

If a class is immutable, then all its data fields must be private and it cannot contain public setter methods for any data fields. A class with all private data fields and no mutators is not

immutable object
immutable class

Student class

necessarily immutable. For example, the following `Student` class has all private data fields and no setter methods, but it is not an immutable class:

```
1  public class Student {
2    private int id;
3    private String name;
4    private java.util.Date dateCreated;
5
6    public Student(int ssn, String newName) {
7      id = ssn;
8      name = newName;
9      dateCreated = new java.util.Date();
10   }
11
12   public int getId() {
13     return id;
14   }
15
16   public String getName() {
17     return name;
18   }
19
20   public java.util.Date getDateCreated() {
21     return dateCreated;
22   }
23 }
```

As shown in the following code, the data field `dateCreated` is returned using the `get-DateCreated()` method. This is a reference to a `Date` object. Through this reference, the content for `dateCreated` can be changed.

```
public class Test {
  public static void main(String[] args) {
    Student student = new Student(111223333, "John");
    java.util.Date dateCreated = student.getDateCreated();
    dateCreated.setTime(200000); // Now dateCreated field is changed!
  }
}
```

For a class to be immutable, it must meet the following requirements:

■ All data fields must be private.

■ There can't be any mutator methods for data fields.

■ No accessor methods can return a reference to a data field that is mutable.

Interested readers may refer to Supplement III.U for an extended discussion on immutable objects.

9.12.1 If a class contains only private data fields and no setter methods, is the class immutable?

9.12.2 If all the data fields in a class are private and of primitive types, and the class doesn't contain any setter methods, is the class immutable?

9.12.3 Is the following class immutable?

```
public class A {
  private int[] values;

  public int[] getValues() {
```

```
      return values;
    }
  }
```

9.13 The Scope of Variables

The scope of instance and static variables is the entire class, regardless of where the variables are declared.

Section 6.9 discussed local variables and their scope rules. Local variables are declared and used inside a method locally. This section discusses the scope rules of all the variables in the context of a class.

Instance and static variables in a class are referred to as the *class's variables* or *data fields*. A variable defined inside a method is referred to as a *local variable*. The scope of a class's variables is the entire class, regardless of where the variables are declared. A class's variables and methods can appear in any order in the class, as shown in Figure 9.20a. The exception is when a data field is initialized based on a reference to another data field. In such cases, the other data field must be declared first, as shown in Figure 9.20b. For consistency, this book declares data fields at the beginning of the class.

class's variables

```
public class Circle {
  public double getArea() {
    return radius * radius * Math.PI;
  }

  private double radius = 1;
}
```

```
public class F {
  private int i;
  private int j = i + 1;
}
```

(a) The variable `radius` and method `getArea()` can be declared in any order.

(b) `i` has to be declared before `j` because `j`'s initial value is dependent on `i`.

FIGURE 9.20 Members of a class can be declared in any order, with one exception.

You can declare a class's variable only once, but you can declare the same variable name in a method many times in different nonnesting blocks.

If a local variable has the same name as a class's variable, the local variable takes precedence and the class's variable with the same name is *hidden*. For example, in the following program, `x` is defined both as an instance variable and as a local variable in the method:

hidden variables

```
public class F {
  private int x = 0; // Instance variable
  private int y = 0;

  public F() {
  }

  public void p() {
    int x = 1; // Local variable
    System.out.println("x = " + x);
    System.out.println("y = " + y);
  }
}
```

What is the output for `f.p()`, where `f` is an instance of `F`? The output for `f.p()` is `1` for `x` and `0` for `y`. Here is why:

■ `x` is declared as a data field with the initial value of `0` in the class, but it is also declared in the method `p()` with an initial value of `1`. The latter `x` is referenced in the `System.out.println` statement.

■ `y` is declared outside the method `p()`, but `y` is accessible inside the method.

Tip
To avoid confusion and mistakes, do not use the names of instance or static variables as local variable names, except for method parameters. We will discuss hidden data fields by method parameters in the next section.

9.13.1 What is the output of the following program?

```java
public class Test {
  private static int i = 0;
  private static int j = 0;

  public static void main(String[] args) {
    int i = 2;
    int k = 3;

    {
      int j = 3;
      System.out.println("i + j is " + i + j);
    }

    k = i + j;
    System.out.println("k is " + k);
    System.out.println("j is " + j);
  }
}
```

9.14 The this Reference

The keyword this *refers to the object itself. It can also be used inside a constructor to invoke another constructor of the same class.*

this keyword

VideoNote
The this keyword

The this *keyword* is the name of a reference that an object can use to refer to itself. You can use the this *keyword* to reference the object's instance members. For example, the following code in (a) uses this to reference the object's radius and invokes its getArea() method explicitly. The this reference is normally omitted for brevity as shown in (b). However, the this reference is needed to reference a data field hidden by a method or constructor parameter, or to invoke an overloaded constructor.

```java
public class Circle {
  private double radius;

  ...

  public double getArea() {
    return this.radius * this.radius * Math.PI;
  }

  public String toString() {
    return "radius: " + this.radius
      + "area: " + this.getArea();
  }
}
```

Equivalent

```java
public class Circle {
  private double radius;

  ...

  public double getArea() {
    return radius * radius * Math.PI;
  }

  public String toString() {
    return "radius: " + radius
      + "area: " + getArea();
  }
}
```

(a)   (b)

9.14.1 Using **this** to Reference Data Fields

It is a good practice to use the data field as the parameter name in a setter method or a constructor to make the code easy to read and to avoid creating unnecessary names. In this case, you need to use the `this` keyword to reference the data field in the setter method. For example, the `setRadius` method can be implemented as shown in (a). It would be wrong if it is implemented as shown in (b).

Refers to data field `radius` in this object.

```
private double radius;

public void setRadius(double radius) {
    this.radius = radius;
}
```

(a) this.radius refers the radius data field in this object.

Here, `radius` is the parameter in the method.

```
private double radius = 1;

public void setRadius(double radius) {
    radius = radius;
}
```

(b) radius is the parameter defined in the method header.

The data field `radius` is hidden by the parameter `radius` in the setter method. You need to reference the data field name in the method using the syntax `this.radius`. A hidden static variable can be accessed simply by using the `ClassName.staticVariable` reference. A hidden instance variable can be accessed by using the keyword `this`, as shown in Figure 9.21a.

reference data fields

```
public class F {
  private int i = 5;
  private static double k = 0;

  public void setI(int i) {
    this.i = i;
  }

  public static void setK(double k) {
    F.k = k;
  }

  // other methods omitted
}
```

(a)

```
Suppose that f1 and f2 are two objects of F.

Invoking f1.setI(10) is to execute
    this.i = 10, where this refers f1

Invoking f2.setI(45) is to execute
    this.i = 45, where this refers f2

Invoking F.setK(33) is to execute
    F.k = 33. setK is a static method
```

(b)

FIGURE 9.21 The keyword `this` refers to the calling object that invokes the method.

The `this` keyword gives us a way to reference the object that invokes an instance method. To invoke `f1.setI(10)`, `this.i = i` is executed, which assigns the value of parameter `i` to the data field `i` of this calling object `f1`. The keyword `this` refers to the object that invokes the instance method `setI`, as shown in Figure 9.21b. The line `F.k = k` means the value in parameter `k` is assigned to the static data field `k` of the class, which is shared by all the objects of the class.

9.14.2 Using `this` to Invoke a Constructor

The `this` keyword can be used to invoke another constructor of the same class. For example, you can rewrite the `Circle` class as follows:

```java
public class Circle {
  private double radius;
  public Circle(double radius) {
    this.radius = radius;
  }

  public Circle() {
    this(1.0);
  }

  ...
}
```

The `this` keyword is used to reference the data field radius of the object being constructed.

The `this` keyword is used to invoke another constructor.

The line `this(1.0)` in the second constructor invokes the first constructor with a `double` value argument.

Note
Java requires that the `this(arg-list)` statement appear first in the constructor before any other executable statements.

Tip
If a class has multiple constructors, it is better to implement them using `this(arg-list)` as much as possible. In general, a constructor with no or fewer arguments can invoke a constructor with more arguments using `this(arg-list)`. This syntax often simplifies coding and makes the class easier to read and to maintain.

Check
Point

9.14.1 Describe the role of the `this` keyword.

9.14.2 What is wrong in the following code?

```java
1  public class C {
2    private int p;
3
4    public C() {
5      System.out.println("C's no-arg constructor invoked");
6      this(0);
7    }
8
9    public C(int p) {
10     p = p;
11   }
12
13   public void setP(int p) {
14     p = p;
15   }
16 }
```

9.14.3 What is wrong in the following code?

```java
public class Test {
  private int id;

  public void m1() {
    this.id = 45;
  }
```

```
      public void m2() {
        Test.id = 45;
      }
    }
```

KEY TERMS

action 324	immutable object 355
anonymous object 333	no-arg constructor 327
attribute 324	null value 333
behavior 324	object 324
class 324	object-oriented programming (OOP)
class's variable 357	package-private (or package-access) 344
client 327	private constructor 346
constructor 324	property 324
data field 324	public class 327
data field encapsulation 346	reference type 332
default constructor 331	reference variable 332
dot operator (.) 332	setter (or mutator) 347
getter (or accessor) 347	state 324
instance 324	static method 339
instance method 333	static variable 339
instance variable 333	this keyword 358
instantiation 324	Unified Modeling Language (UML) 325
immutable class 355	

CHAPTER SUMMARY

1. A *class* is a template for *objects*. It defines the *properties* of objects and provides *constructors* for creating objects and methods for manipulating them.

2. A class is also a data type. You can use it to declare object *reference variables*. An object reference variable that appears to hold an object actually contains a reference to that object. Strictly speaking, an object reference variable and an object are different, but most of the time the distinction can be ignored.

3. An object is an *instance* of a class. You use the new operator to create an object and the *dot operator* (.) to access members of that object through its reference variable.

4. An *instance variable* or *method* belongs to an instance of a class. Its use is associated with individual instances. A *static variable* is a variable shared by all instances of the same class. A *static method* is a method that can be invoked without using instances.

5. Every instance of a class can access the class's static variables and methods. For clarity, however, it is better to invoke static variables and methods using ClassName .variable and ClassName.method.

6. Visibility modifiers specify how the class, method, and data are accessed. A public class, method, or data is accessible to all clients. A private method or data is accessible only inside the class.

7. You can provide a getter (accessor) method or a setter (mutator) method to enable clients to see or modify the data.

8. A getter method has the signature `public returnType getPropertyName()`. If the `returnType` is `boolean`, the getter method should be defined as `public boolean isPropertyName()`. A setter method has the signature `public void setPropertyName(dataType propertyValue)`.

9. All parameters are passed to methods using pass-by-value. For a parameter of a primitive type, the actual value is passed; for a parameter of a *reference type*, the reference for the object is passed.

10. A Java array is an object that can contain primitive-type values or object-type values. When an array of objects is created, its elements are assigned the default value of `null`.

11. Once it is created, an *immutable object* cannot be modified. To prevent users from modifying an object, you can define *immutable classes*.

12. The scope of instance and static variables is the entire class, regardless of where the variables are declared. Instance and static variables can be declared anywhere in the class. For consistency, they are declared at the beginning of the class in this book.

13. The keyword `this` can be used to refer to the calling object. It can also be used inside a constructor to invoke another constructor of the same class.

QUIZ

Answer the quiz for this chapter online at the book Companion Website.

MyProgrammingLab™

PROGRAMMING EXERCISES

three objectives

Pedagogical Note

The exercises in Chapters 9–13 help you to achieve three objectives:

1. Design classes and draw UML class diagrams.
2. Implement classes from the UML.
3. Use classes to develop applications.

Students can download solutions for the UML diagrams for the even-numbered exercises from the Companion Website and instructors can download all solutions from the same site.

Starting from Section 9.7, all data fields should be declared private and all constructors and methods should be defined public unless specified otherwise.

Sections 9.2–9.5

9.1 (*The Rectangle class*) Following the example of the `Circle` class in Section 9.2, design a class named `Rectangle` to represent a rectangle. The class contains:

- Two `double` data fields named `width` and `height` that specify the width and height of the rectangle. The default values are `1` for both `width` and `height`.
- A no-arg constructor that creates a default rectangle.
- A constructor that creates a rectangle with the specified `width` and `height`.
- A method named `getArea()` that returns the area of this rectangle.
- A method named `getPerimeter()` that returns the perimeter.

Draw the UML diagram for the class then implement the class. Write a test program that creates two `Rectangle` objects—one with width 4 and height 40, and the other with width 3.5 and height 35.9. Display the width, height, area, and perimeter of each rectangle in this order.

9.2 (*The Stock class*) Following the example of the Circle class in Section 9.2, design a class named Stock that contains:

- A string data field named symbol for the stock's symbol.
- A string data field named name for the stock's name.
- A double data field named previousClosingPrice that stores the stock price for the previous day.
- A double data field named currentPrice that stores the stock price for the current time.
- A constructor that creates a stock with the specified symbol and name.
- A method named getChangePercent() that returns the percentage changed from previousClosingPrice to currentPrice.

Draw the UML diagram for the class then implement the class. Write a test program that creates a Stock object with the stock symbol ORCL, the name Oracle Corporation, and the previous closing price of 34.5. Set a new current price to 34.35 and display the price-change percentage.

Section 9.6

*9.3 (*Use the Date class*) Write a program that creates a Date object, sets its elapsed time to 10000, 100000, 1000000, 10000000, 100000000, 1000000000, 10000000000, and 100000000000, and displays the date and time using the toString() method, respectively.

*9.4 (*Use the Random class*) Write a program that creates a Random object with seed 1000 and displays the first 50 random integers between 0 and 100 using the nextInt(100) method.

*9.5 (*Use the GregorianCalendar class*) Java API has the GregorianCalendar class in the java.util package, which you can use to obtain the year, month, and day of a date. The no-arg constructor constructs an instance for the current date, and the methods get(GregorianCalendar.YEAR), get(GregorianCalendar.MONTH), and get(GregorianCalendar.DAY_OF_MONTH) return the year, month, and day. Write a program to perform two tasks:

1. Display the current year, month, and day.
2. The GregorianCalendar class has the setTimeInMillis(long), which can be used to set a specified elapsed time since January 1, 1970. Set the value to 1234567898765L and display the year, month, and day.

Sections 9.7–9.9

*9.6 (*Stopwatch*) Design a class named StopWatch. The class contains:

- Private data fields startTime and endTime with getter methods.
- A no-arg constructor that initializes startTime with the current time.
- A method named start() that resets the startTime to the current time.
- A method named stop() that sets the endTime to the current time.
- A method named getElapsedTime() that returns the elapsed time for the stopwatch in milliseconds.

Draw the UML diagram for the class then implement the class. Write a test program that measures the execution time of sorting 100,000 numbers using selection sort.

9.7 (*The Account class*) Design a class named Account that contains:

- A private int data field named id for the account (default 0).
- A private double data field named balance for the account (default 0).

- A private `double` data field named `annualInterestRate` that stores the current interest rate (default `0`). Assume that all accounts have the same interest rate.
- A private `Date` data field named `dateCreated` that stores the date when the account was created.
- A no-arg constructor that creates a default account.
- A constructor that creates an account with the specified id and initial balance.
- The accessor and mutator methods for `id`, `balance`, and `annualInterestRate`.
- The accessor method for `dateCreated`.
- A method named `getMonthlyInterestRate()` that returns the monthly interest rate.
- A method named `getMonthlyInterest()` that returns the monthly interest.
- A method named `withdraw` that withdraws a specified amount from the account.
- A method named `deposit` that deposits a specified amount to the account.

Draw the UML diagram for the class then implement the class. (*Hint*: The method `getMonthlyInterest()` is to return monthly interest, not the interest rate. Monthly interest is `balance * monthlyInterestRate`. `monthlyInterestRate` is `annualInterestRate / 12`. Note `annualInterestRate` is a percentage, for example 4.5%. You need to divide it by 100.)

Write a test program that creates an `Account` object with an account ID of 1122, a balance of $20,000, and an annual interest rate of 4.5%. Use the `withdraw` method to withdraw $2,500, use the `deposit` method to deposit $3,000, and print the balance, the monthly interest, and the date when this account was created.

VideoNote

The Fan class

9.8 (*The Fan class*) Design a class named `Fan` to represent a fan. The class contains:

- Three constants named `SLOW`, `MEDIUM`, and `FAST` with the values `1`, `2`, and `3` to denote the fan speed.
- A private `int` data field named `speed` that specifies the speed of the fan (the default is `SLOW`).
- A private `boolean` data field named `on` that specifies whether the fan is on (the default is `false`).
- A private `double` data field named `radius` that specifies the radius of the fan (the default is `5`).
- A string data field named `color` that specifies the color of the fan (the default is `blue`).
- The accessor and mutator methods for all four data fields.
- A no-arg constructor that creates a default fan.
- A method named `toString()` that returns a string description for the fan. If the fan is on, the method returns the fan speed, color, and radius in one combined string. If the fan is not on, the method returns the fan color and radius along with the string "fan is off" in one combined string.

Draw the UML diagram for the class then implement the class. Write a test program that creates two `Fan` objects. Assign maximum speed, radius `10`, color `yellow`, and turn it on to the first object. Assign medium speed, radius `5`, color `blue`, and turn it off to the second object. Display the objects by invoking their `toString` method.

**9.9 (*Geometry: n-sided regular polygon*) In an *n*-sided regular polygon, all sides have the same length and all angles have the same degree (i.e., the polygon is both equilateral and equiangular). Design a class named `RegularPolygon` that contains:

- A private `int` data field named `n` that defines the number of sides in the polygon with default value `3`.

- A private `double` data field named `side` that stores the length of the side with default value `1`.
- A private `double` data field named `x` that defines the *x*-coordinate of the polygon's center with default value `0`.
- A private `double` data field named `y` that defines the *y*-coordinate of the polygon's center with default value `0`.
- A no-arg constructor that creates a regular polygon with default values.
- A constructor that creates a regular polygon with the specified number of sides and length of side, centered at (`0`, `0`).
- A constructor that creates a regular polygon with the specified number of sides, length of side, and *x*- and *y*-coordinates.
- The accessor and mutator methods for all data fields.
- The method `getPerimeter()` that returns the perimeter of the polygon.
- The method `getArea()` that returns the area of the polygon. The formula for computing the area of a regular polygon is

$$\text{Area} = \frac{n \times s^2}{4 \times \tan\left(\dfrac{\pi}{n}\right)}.$$

Draw the UML diagram for the class then implement the class. Write a test program that creates three `RegularPolygon` objects, created using the no-arg constructor, using `RegularPolygon(6, 4)`, and using `RegularPolygon(10, 4, 5.6, 7.8)`. For each object, display its perimeter and area.

*9.10 (*Algebra: quadratic equations*) Design a class named `QuadraticEquation` for a quadratic equation $ax^2 + bx + c = 0$. The class contains:

- Private data fields `a`, `b`, and `c` that represent three coefficients.
- A constructor with the arguments for `a`, `b`, and `c`.
- Three getter methods for `a`, `b`, and `c`.
- A method named `getDiscriminant()` that returns the discriminant, which is $b^2 - 4ac$.
- The methods named `getRoot1()` and `getRoot2()` for returning two roots of the equation

$$r_1 = \frac{-b + \sqrt{b^2 - 4ac}}{2a} \quad \text{and} \quad r_2 = \frac{-b - \sqrt{b^2 - 4ac}}{2a}$$

These methods are useful only if the discriminant is nonnegative. Let these methods return `0` if the discriminant is negative.

Draw the UML diagram for the class then implement the class. Write a test program that prompts the user to enter values for *a*, *b*, and *c* and displays the result based on the discriminant. If the discriminant is positive, display the two roots. If the discriminant is 0, display the one root. Otherwise, display "The equation has no roots." See Programming Exercise 3.1 for sample runs.

*9.11 (*Algebra: 2 × 2 linear equations*) Design a class named `LinearEquation` for a 2 × 2 system of linear equations:

$$\begin{matrix} ax + by = e \\ cx + dy = f \end{matrix} \quad x = \frac{ed - bf}{ad - bc} \quad y = \frac{af - ec}{ad - bc}$$

The class contains:

- Private data fields a, b, c, d, e, and f.
- A constructor with the arguments for a, b, c, d, e, and f.
- Six getter methods for a, b, c, d, e, and f.
- A method named isSolvable() that returns true if $ad - bc$ is not 0.
- Methods getX() and getY() that return the solution for the equation.

Draw the UML diagram for the class then implement the class. Write a test program that prompts the user to enter a, b, c, d, e, and f and displays the result. If $ad - bc$ is 0, report that "The equation has no solution." See Programming Exercise 3.3 for sample runs.

**9.12 (*Geometry: intersecting point*) Suppose two line segments intersect. The two endpoints for the first line segment are (x1, y1) and (x2, y2) and for the second line segment are (x3, y3) and (x4, y4). Write a program that prompts the user to enter these four endpoints and displays the intersecting point. As discussed in Programming Exercise 3.25, the intersecting point can be found by solving a linear equation. Use the LinearEquation class in Programming Exercise 9.11 to solve this equation. See Programming Exercise 3.25 for sample runs.

**9.13 (*The Location class*) Design a class named Location for locating a maximal value and its location in a two-dimensional array. The class contains public data fields row, column, and maxValue that store the maximal value and its indices in a two-dimensional array with row and column as int types and maxValue as a double type.

Write the following method that returns the location of the largest element in a two-dimensional array:

```
public static Location locateLargest(double[][] a)
```

The return value is an instance of Location. Write a test program that prompts the user to enter a two-dimensional array and displays the location of the largest element in the array. Here is a sample run:

```
Enter the number of rows and columns in the array: 3 4 ↵Enter
Enter the array:
23.5 35 2 10 ↵Enter
4.5 3 45 3.5 ↵Enter
35 44 5.5 9.6 ↵Enter
The location of the largest element is 45 at (1, 2)
```

OBJECT-ORIENTED THINKING

Objectives

- To apply class abstraction to develop software (§10.2).
- To explore the differences between the procedural paradigm and object-oriented paradigm (§10.3).
- To discover the relationships between classes (§10.4).
- To design programs using the object-oriented paradigm (§§10.5 and 10.6).
- To create objects for primitive values using the wrapper classes (`Byte`, `Short`, `Integer`, `Long`, `Float`, `Double`, `Character`, and `Boolean`) (§10.7).
- To simplify programming using automatic conversion between primitive types and wrapper class types (§10.8).
- To use the `BigInteger` and `BigDecimal` classes for computing very large numbers with arbitrary precisions (§10.9).
- To use the `String` class to process immutable strings (§10.10).
- To use the `StringBuilder` and `StringBuffer` classes to process mutable strings (§10.11).

CHAPTER 10

10.1 Introduction

The focus of this chapter is on class design and to explore the differences between procedural programming and object-oriented programming.

The preceding chapter introduced objects and classes. You learned how to define classes, create objects, and use objects. This book's approach is to teach problem solving and fundamental programming techniques before object-oriented programming. This chapter shows how procedural and object-oriented programming differ. You will see the benefits of object-oriented programming and learn to use it effectively.

Our focus here is on class design. We will use several examples to illustrate the advantages of the object-oriented approach. The examples involve designing new classes and using them in applications and introducing new classes in the Java API.

10.2 Class Abstraction and Encapsulation

Class abstraction is separation of class implementation from the use of a class. The details of implementation are encapsulated and hidden from the user. This is known as class encapsulation.

class abstraction

In Chapter 6, you learned about method abstraction and used it in stepwise refinement. Java provides many levels of abstraction, and *class abstraction* separates class implementation from how the class is used. The creator of a class describes the functions of the class and lets the user know how the class can be used. The collection of public constructors, methods, and fields that are accessible from outside the class, together with the description of how these members are expected to behave, serves as the *class's contract*. As shown in Figure 10.1, the user of the class does not need to know how the class is implemented. The details of implementation are encapsulated and hidden from the user. This is called *class encapsulation*. For example, you can create a `Circle` object and find the area of the circle without knowing how the area is computed. For this reason, a class is also known as an *abstract data type* (ADT).

class's contract

class encapsulation

abstract data type

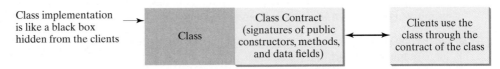

FIGURE 10.1 Class abstraction separates class implementation from the use of the class.

Class abstraction and encapsulation are two sides of the same coin. Many real-life examples illustrate the concept of class abstraction. Consider, for instance, building a computer system. Your personal computer has many components—a CPU, memory, disk, motherboard, fan, and so on. Each component can be viewed as an object that has properties and methods. To get the components to work together, you need to know only how each component is used and how it interacts with the others. You don't need to know how the components work internally. The internal implementation is encapsulated and hidden from you. You can build a computer without knowing how a component is implemented.

The computer-system analogy precisely mirrors the object-oriented approach. Each component can be viewed as an object of the class for the component. For example, you might have a class that models all kinds of fans for use in a computer, with properties such as fan size and speed and methods such as start and stop. A specific fan is an instance of this class with specific property values.

As another example, consider getting a loan. A specific loan can be viewed as an object of a `Loan` class. The interest rate, loan amount, and loan period are its data properties and computing the monthly and total payments are its methods. When you buy a car, a loan object is created by instantiating the class with your loan interest rate, loan amount, and loan period. You can then use the methods to find the monthly payment and total payment of your loan. As a user of the `Loan` class, you don't need to know how these methods are implemented.

VideoNote

The Loan class

Listing 2.9, ComputeLoan.java, presented a program for computing loan payments. That program cannot be reused in other programs because the code for computing the payments is in the `main` method. One way to fix this problem is to define static methods for computing the monthly payment and the total payment. However, this solution has limitations. Suppose that you wish to associate a date with the loan. There is no good way to tie a date with a loan without using objects. The traditional procedural programming paradigm is action-driven, and data are separated from actions. The object-oriented programming paradigm focuses on objects, and actions are defined along with the data in objects. To tie a date with a loan, you can define a loan class with a date along with the loan's other properties as data fields. A loan object now contains data and actions for manipulating and processing data, and the loan data and actions are integrated in one object. Figure 10.2 shows the UML class diagram for the `Loan` class.

Loan	
−annualInterestRate: double	The annual interest rate of the loan (default: 2.5).
−numberOfYears: int	The number of years for the loan (default: 1).
−loanAmount: double	The loan amount (default: 1000).
−loanDate: java.util.Date	The date this loan was created.
+Loan()	Constructs a default Loan object.
+Loan(annualInterestRate: double, numberOfYears: int, loanAmount: double)	Constructs a loan with specified interest rate, years, and loan amount.
+getAnnualInterestRate(): double	Returns the annual interest rate of this loan.
+getNumberOfYears(): int	Returns the number of years of this loan.
+getLoanAmount(): double	Returns the amount of this loan.
+getLoanDate(): java.util.Date	Returns the date of the creation of this loan.
+setAnnualInterestRate(annualInterestRate: double): void	Sets a new annual interest rate for this loan.
+setNumberOfYears(numberOfYears: int): void	Sets a new number of years for this loan.
+setLoanAmount(loanAmount: double): void	Sets a new amount for this loan.
+getMonthlyPayment(): double	Returns the monthly payment for this loan.
+getTotalPayment(): double	Returns the total payment for this loan.

FIGURE 10.2 The Loan class models the properties and behaviors of loans.

The UML diagram in Figure 10.2 serves as the contract for the `Loan` class. Throughout this book, you will play the roles of both class user and class developer. Remember that a class user can use the class without knowing how the class is implemented.

Assume the `Loan` class is available. The program in Listing 10.1 uses that class.

LISTING 10.1 TestLoanClass.java

```
1  import java.util.Scanner;
2
3  public class TestLoanClass {
4    /** Main method */
5    public static void main(String[] args) {
```

```
 6       // Create a Scanner
 7       Scanner input = new Scanner(System.in);
 8
 9       // Enter annual interest rate
10       System.out.print(
11         "Enter annual interest rate, for example, 8.25: ");
12       double annualInterestRate = input.nextDouble();
13
14       // Enter number of years
15       System.out.print("Enter number of years as an integer: ");
16       int numberOfYears = input.nextInt();
17
18       // Enter loan amount
19       System.out.print("Enter loan amount, for example, 120000.95: ");
20       double loanAmount = input.nextDouble();
21
22       // Create a Loan object
23       Loan loan =
24         new Loan(annualInterestRate, numberOfYears, loanAmount);
25
26       // Display loan date, monthly payment, and total payment
27       System.out.printf("The loan was created on %s\n" +
28         "The monthly payment is %.2f\nThe total payment is %.2f\n",
29         loan.getLoanDate().toString(), loan.getMonthlyPayment(),
30         loan.getTotalPayment());
31   }
32 }
```

create loan object *(line 24)*

invoke instance method *(line 29)*
invoke instance method *(line 30)*

```
Enter annual interest rate, for example, 8.25: 2.5 [↵Enter]
Enter number of years as an integer: 5 [↵Enter]
Enter loan amount, for example, 120000.95: 1000 [↵Enter]
The loan was created on Sat Jun 16 21:12:50 EDT 2012
The monthly payment is 17.75
The total payment is 1064.84
```

The `main` method reads the interest rate, the payment period (in years), and the loan amount; creates a `Loan` object; then obtains the monthly payment (line 29) and the total payment (line 30) using the instance methods in the `Loan` class.

The `Loan` class can be implemented as in Listing 10.2.

LISTING 10.2   Loan.java

```
 1 public class Loan {
 2   private double annualInterestRate;
 3   private int numberOfYears;
 4   private double loanAmount;
 5   private java.util.Date loanDate;
 6
 7   /** Default constructor */
 8   public Loan() {
 9     this(2.5, 1, 1000);
10   }
11
```

no-arg constructor *(line 8)*

```java
12     /** Construct a loan with specified annual interest rate,
13         number of years, and loan amount
14      */
15     public Loan(double annualInterestRate, int numberOfYears,      constructor
16         double loanAmount) {
17       this.annualInterestRate = annualInterestRate;
18       this.numberOfYears = numberOfYears;
19       this.loanAmount = loanAmount;
20       loanDate = new java.util.Date();
21     }
22
23     /** Return annualInterestRate */
24     public double getAnnualInterestRate() {
25       return annualInterestRate;
26     }
27
28     /** Set a new annualInterestRate */
29     public void setAnnualInterestRate(double annualInterestRate) {
30       this.annualInterestRate = annualInterestRate;
31     }
32
33     /** Return numberOfYears */
34     public int getNumberOfYears() {
35       return numberOfYears;
36     }
37
38     /** Set a new numberOfYears */
39     public void setNumberOfYears(int numberOfYears) {
40       this.numberOfYears = numberOfYears;
41     }
42
43     /** Return loanAmount */
44     public double getLoanAmount() {
45       return loanAmount;
46     }
47
48     /** Set a new loanAmount */
49     public void setLoanAmount(double loanAmount) {
50       this.loanAmount = loanAmount;
51     }
52
53     /** Find monthly payment */
54     public double getMonthlyPayment() {
55       double monthlyInterestRate = annualInterestRate / 1200;
56       double monthlyPayment = loanAmount * monthlyInterestRate / (1 -
57         (1 / Math.pow(1 + monthlyInterestRate, numberOfYears * 12)));
58       return monthlyPayment;
59     }
60
61     /** Find total payment */
62     public double getTotalPayment() {
63       double totalPayment = getMonthlyPayment() * numberOfYears * 12;
64       return totalPayment;
65     }
66
67     /** Return loan date */
68     public java.util.Date getLoanDate() {
69       return loanDate;
70     }
71   }
```

From a class developer's perspective, a class is designed for use by many different customers. In order to be useful in a wide range of applications, a class should provide a variety of ways for customization through constructors, properties, and methods.

The `Loan` class contains two constructors, four getter methods, three setter methods, and the methods for finding the monthly payment and the total payment. You can construct a `Loan` object by using the no-arg constructor or the constructor with three parameters: annual interest rate, number of years, and loan amount. When a loan object is created, its date is stored in the `loanDate` field. The `getLoanDate` method returns the date. The methods—`getAnnualInterest`, `getNumberOfYears`, and `getLoanAmount`—return the annual interest rate, payment years, and loan amount, respectively. All the data properties and methods in this class are tied to a specific instance of the `Loan` class. Therefore, they are instance variables and methods.

Important Pedagogical Tip

Use the UML diagram for the `Loan` class shown in Figure 10.2 to write a test program that uses the `Loan` class even though you don't know how the `Loan` class is implemented. This has three benefits:

■ It demonstrates that developing a class and using a class are two separate tasks.

■ It enables you to skip the complex implementation of certain classes without interrupting the sequence of this book.

■ It is easier to learn how to implement a class if you are familiar with it by using the class.

For all the class examples from now on, create an object from the class and try using its methods before turning your attention to its implementation.

10.2.1 If you redefine the `Loan` class in Listing 10.2 without setter methods, is the class immutable?

10.3 Thinking in Objects

The procedural paradigm focuses on designing methods. The object-oriented paradigm couples data and methods together into objects. Software design using the object-oriented paradigm focuses on objects and operations on objects.

Chapters 1 through 8 introduced fundamental programming techniques for problem solving using loops, methods, and arrays. Knowing these techniques lays a solid foundation for object-oriented programming. Classes provide more flexibility and modularity for building reusable software. This section improves the solution for a problem introduced in Chapter 3 using the object-oriented approach. From these improvements, you will gain insight into the differences between procedural and object-oriented programming, and see the benefits of developing reusable code using objects and classes.

Listing 3.4, ComputeAndInterpretBMI.java, presented a program for computing the body mass index (BMI). The code cannot be reused in other programs, because the code is in the `main` method. To make it reusable, define a static method to compute body mass index as follows:

```
public static double getBMI(double weight, double height)
```

This method is useful for computing body mass index for a specified weight and height. However, it has limitations. Suppose you need to associate the weight and height with a person's name and birth date. You could declare separate variables to store these values, but these values would not be tightly coupled. The ideal way to couple them is to create an object that contains them all. Since these values are tied to individual objects, they should be stored in instance data fields. You can define a class named `BMI` as shown in Figure 10.3.

VideoNote

The `BMI` class

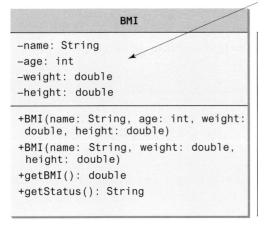

The getter methods for these data fields are provided in the class, but omitted in the UML diagram for brevity.

BMI	
−name: String	The name of the person.
−age: int	The age of the person.
−weight: double	The weight of the person in pounds.
−height: double	The height of the person in inches.
+BMI(name: String, age: int, weight: double, height: double)	Creates a BMI object with the specified name, age, weight, and height.
+BMI(name: String, weight: double, height: double)	Creates a BMI object with the specified name, weight, height, and a default age 20.
+getBMI(): double	Returns the BMI.
+getStatus(): String	Returns the BMI status (e.g., normal, overweight, etc.).

FIGURE 10.3 The BMI class encapsulates BMI information.

Assume the BMI class is available. Listing 10.3 gives a test program that uses this class.

LISTING 10.3 UseBMIClass.java

```
1  public class UseBMIClass {
2    public static void main(String[] args) {
3      BMI bmi1 = new BMI("Kim Yang", 18, 145, 70);          create an object
4      System.out.println("The BMI for " + bmi1.getName() + " is "   invoke instance method
5        + bmi1.getBMI() + " " + bmi1.getStatus());
6
7      BMI bmi2 = new BMI("Susan King", 215, 70);            create an object
8      System.out.println("The BMI for " + bmi2.getName() + " is "   invoke instance method
9        + bmi2.getBMI() + " " + bmi2.getStatus());
10   }
11 }
```

```
The BMI for Kim Yang is 20.81 Normal
The BMI for Susan King is 30.85 Obese
```

Line 3 creates the object bmi1 for Kim Yang, and line 7 creates the object bmi2 for Susan King. You can use the instance methods getName(), getBMI(), and getStatus() to return the BMI information in a BMI object.

The BMI class can be implemented as in Listing 10.4.

LISTING 10.4 BMI.java

```
1  public class BMI {
2    private String name;
3    private int age;
4    private double weight; // in pounds
5    private double height; // in inches
6    public static final double KILOGRAMS_PER_POUND = 0.45359237;
7    public static final double METERS_PER_INCH = 0.0254;
8
9    public BMI(String name, int age, double weight, double height) {   constructor
10     this.name = name;
```

```
11        this.age = age;
12        this.weight = weight;
13        this.height = height;
14      }
15
16      public BMI(String name, double weight, double height) {
17        this(name, 20, weight, height);
18      }
19
20      public double getBMI() {
21        double bmi = weight * KILOGRAMS_PER_POUND /
22          ((height * METERS_PER_INCH) * (height * METERS_PER_INCH));
23        return Math.round(bmi * 100) / 100.0;
24      }
25
26      public String getStatus() {
27        double bmi = getBMI();
28        if (bmi < 18.5)
29          return "Underweight";
30        else if (bmi < 25)
31          return "Normal";
32        else if (bmi < 30)
33          return "Overweight";
34        else
35          return "Obese";
36      }
37
38      public String getName() {
39        return name;
40      }
41
42      public int getAge() {
43        return age;
44      }
45
46      public double getWeight() {
47        return weight;
48      }
49
50      public double getHeight() {
51        return height;
52      }
53    }
```

margin notes:
constructor (line 16)
getBMI (line 20)
getStatus (line 26)

The mathematical formula for computing the BMI using weight and height is given in Section 3.8. The instance method getBMI() returns the BMI. Since the weight and height are instance data fields in the object, the getBMI() method can use these properties to compute the BMI for the object.

The instance method getStatus() returns a string that interprets the BMI. The interpretation is also given in Section 3.8.

procedural vs. object-oriented paradigms

This example demonstrates the advantages of the object-oriented paradigm over the procedural paradigm. The procedural paradigm focuses on designing methods. The object-oriented paradigm couples data and methods together into objects. Software design using the object-oriented paradigm focuses on objects and operations on objects. The object-oriented approach combines the power of the procedural paradigm with an added dimension that integrates data with operations into objects.

In procedural programming, data and operations on the data are separate, and this methodology requires passing data to methods. Object-oriented programming places data and the operations that pertain to them in an object. This approach solves many of the problems inherent in procedural programming. The object-oriented programming approach organizes programs in a way that mirrors the real world, in which all objects are associated with both attributes and activities. Using objects improves software reusability and makes programs easier to develop and easier to maintain. Programming in Java involves thinking in terms of objects; a Java program can be viewed as a collection of cooperating objects.

10.3.1 Is the `BMI` class defined in Listing 10.4 immutable?

Check Point

10.4 Class Relationships

To design classes, you need to explore the relationships among classes. The common relationships among classes are association, aggregation, composition, *and* inheritance.

Key Point

This section explores association, aggregation, and composition. The inheritance relationship will be introduced in Chapter 11.

10.4.1 Association

Association is a general binary relationship that describes an activity between two classes. For example, a student taking a course is an association between the `Student` class and the `Course` class, and a faculty member teaching a course is an association between the `Faculty` class and the `Course` class. These associations can be represented in UML graphical notation, as shown in Figure 10.4.

association

FIGURE 10.4 This UML diagram shows that a student may take any number of courses, a faculty member may teach at most three courses, a course may have from 5 to 60 students, and a course is taught by only one faculty member.

An association is illustrated by a solid line between two classes with an optional label that describes the relationship. In Figure 10.4, the labels are *Take* and *Teach*. Each relationship may have an optional small black triangle that indicates the direction of the relationship. In this figure, the ▶ indicates that a student takes a course (as opposed to a course taking a student).

Each class involved in the relationship may have a role name that describes the role it plays in the relationship. In Figure 10.4, *teacher* is the role name for `Faculty`.

Each class involved in an association may specify a *multiplicity*, which is placed at the side of the class to specify how many of the class's objects are involved in the relationship in UML. A multiplicity could be a number or an interval that specifies how many of the class's objects are involved in the relationship. The character `*` means an unlimited number of objects, and the interval `m..n` indicates that the number of objects is between `m` and `n`, inclusively. In Figure 10.4, each student may take any number of courses, and each course must have at least 5 and at most 60 students. Each course is taught by only one faculty member, and a faculty member may teach from 0 to 3 courses per semester.

In Java code, you can implement associations by using data fields and methods. For example, the relationships in Figure 10.4 may be implemented using the classes in Figure 10.5.

multiplicity

The relation "a student takes a course" is implemented using the `addCourse` method in the `Student` class and the `addStudent` method in the `Course` class. The relation "a faculty teaches a course" is implemented using the `addCourse` method in the `Faculty` class and the `setFaculty` method in the `Course` class. The `Student` class may use a list to store the courses that the student is taking, the `Faculty` class may use a list to store the courses that the faculty is teaching, and the `Course` class may use a list to store students enrolled in the course and a data field to store the instructor who teaches the course.

```
public class Student {
  private Course[]
    courseList;

  public void addCourse(
    Course c) { ... }
}
```

```
public class Course {
  private Student[]
    classList;
  private Faculty faculty;

  public void addStudent(
    Student s) { ... }

  public void setFaculty(
    Faculty faculty) { ... }
}
```

```
public class Faculty {
  private Course[]
    courseList;

  public void addCourse(
    Course c) { ... }
}
```

FIGURE 10.5 The association relations are implemented using data fields and methods in classes.

many possible
implementations

Note
There are many possible ways to implement relationships. For example, the student and faculty information in the `Course` class can be omitted, since they are already in the `Student` and `Faculty` class. Likewise, if you don't need to know the courses a student takes or a faculty member teaches, the data field `courseList` and the `addCourse` method in `Student` or `Faculty` can be omitted.

10.4.2 Aggregation and Composition

aggregation
aggregating object
aggregating class
aggregated object
aggregated class
composition

Aggregation is a special form of association that represents an ownership relationship between two objects. Aggregation models *has-a* relationships. The owner object is called an *aggregating object*, and its class is called an *aggregating class*. The subject object is called an *aggregated object*, and its class is called an *aggregated class*.

We refer aggregation between two objects as *composition* if the existence of the aggregated object is dependent on the aggregating object. In other words, if a relationship is composition, the aggregated object cannot exist on its own. For example, "a student has a name" is a composition relationship between the `Student` class and the `Name` class because `Name` is dependent on `Student`, whereas "a student has an address" is an aggregation relationship between the `Student` class and the `Address` class because an address can exist by itself. Composition implies exclusive ownership. One object owns another object. When the owner object is destroyed, the dependent object is destroyed as well. In UML, a filled diamond is attached to an aggregating class (in this case, `Student`) to denote the composition relationship with an aggregated class (`Name`), and an empty diamond is attached to an aggregating class (`Student`) to denote the aggregation relationship with an aggregated class (`Address`), as shown in Figure 10.6.

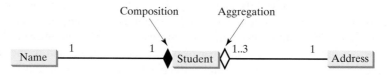

FIGURE 10.6 Each student has a name and an address.

In Figure 10.6, each student has only one multiplicity—address—and each address can be shared by up to **3** students. Each student has one name, and the name is unique for each student.

An aggregation relationship is usually represented as a data field in the aggregating class. For example, the relationships in Figure 10.6 may be implemented using the classes in Figure 10.7. The relation "a student has a name" and "a student has an address" are implemented in the data field `name` and `address` in the `Student` class.

```
public class Name {
    ...
}
```
Aggregated class

```
public class Student {
    private Name name;
    private Address address;
    ...
}
```
Aggregating class

```
public class Address {
    ...
}
```
Aggregated class

FIGURE 10.7 The composition relations are implemented using data fields in classes.

Aggregation may exist between objects of the same class. For example, a person may have a supervisor. This is illustrated in Figure 10.8.

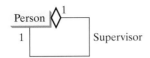

FIGURE 10.8 A person may have a supervisor.

In the relationship "a person has a supervisor," a supervisor can be represented as a data field in the `Person` class, as follows:

```
public class Person {
    // The type for the data is the class itself
    private Person supervisor;

    ...
}
```

If a person can have several supervisors, as shown in Figure 10.9a, you may use an array to store supervisors, as shown in Figure 10.9b.

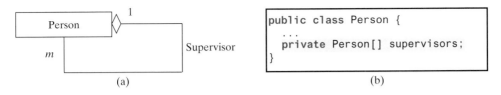

(a)

```
public class Person {
    ...
    private Person[] supervisors;
}
```
(b)

FIGURE 10.9 A person can have several supervisors.

 Important Note

Since aggregation and composition relationships are represented using classes in the same way, we will not differentiate them and call both compositions for simplicity.

aggregation or composition

10.4.1 What are common relationships among classes?

10.4.2 What is association? What is aggregation? What is composition?

10.4.3 What is UML notation of aggregation and composition?

10.4.4 Why both aggregation and composition are together referred to as composition?

Check
Point

10.5 Case Study: Designing the Course Class

This section designs a class for modeling courses.

This book's philosophy is *teaching by example and learning by doing*. The book provides a wide variety of examples to demonstrate object-oriented programming. This section and the next offer additional examples on designing classes.

Suppose you need to process course information. Each course has a name and has students enrolled. You should be able to add/drop a student to/from the course. You can use a class to model the courses, as shown in Figure 10.10.

Course	
−courseName: String	The name of the course.
−students: String[]	An array to store the students for the course.
−numberOfStudents: int	The number of students (default: 0).
+Course(courseName: String)	Creates a course with the specified name.
+getCourseName(): String	Returns the course name.
+addStudent(student: String): void	Adds a new student to the course.
+dropStudent(student: String): void	Drops a student from the course.
+getStudents(): String[]	Returns the students for the course.
+getNumberOfStudents(): int	Returns the number of students for the course.

FIGURE 10.10 The Course class models the courses.

A Course object can be created using the constructor Course(String name) by passing a course name. You can add students to the course using the addStudent(String student) method, drop a student from the course using the dropStudent(String student) method, and return all the students in the course using the getStudents() method. Suppose that the Course class is available; Listing 10.5 gives a test class that creates two courses and adds students to them.

LISTING 10.5 TestCourse.java

```java
1  public class TestCourse {
2    public static void main(String[] args) {
3      Course course1 = new Course("Data Structures");
4      Course course2 = new Course("Database Systems");
5
6      course1.addStudent("Peter Jones");
7      course1.addStudent("Kim Smith");
8      course1.addStudent("Anne Kennedy");
9
10     course2.addStudent("Peter Jones");
11     course2.addStudent("Steve Smith");
12
13     System.out.println("Number of students in course1: "
14       + course1.getNumberOfStudents());
15     String[] students = course1.getStudents();
16     for (int i = 0; i < course1.getNumberOfStudents(); i++)
17       System.out.print(students[i] + ", ");
18
19     System.out.println();
20     System.out.print("Number of students in course2: "
21       + course2.getNumberOfStudents());
22   }
23 }
```

create a Course

add a Student

number of students
return students

```
Number of students in course1: 3
Peter Jones, Kim Smith, Anne Kennedy,
Number of students in course2: 2
```

The Course class is implemented in Listing 10.6. It uses an array to store the students in the course. For simplicity, assume the maximum course enrollment is 100. The array is created using new String[100] in line 3. The addStudent method (line 10) adds a student to the array. Whenever a new student is added to the course, numberOfStudents is increased (line 12). The getStudents method returns the array. The dropStudent method (line 27) is left as an exercise.

LISTING 10.6 Course.java

```
1  public class Course {
2    private String courseName;
3    private String[] students = new String[100];     create students
4    private int numberOfStudents;
5
6    public Course(String courseName) {               add a course
7      this.courseName = courseName;
8    }
9
10   public void addStudent(String student) {
11     students[numberOfStudents] = student;
12     numberOfStudents++;
13   }
14
15   public String[] getStudents() {                   return students
16     return students;
17   }
18
19   public int getNumberOfStudents() {                number of students
20     return numberOfStudents;
21   }
22
23   public String getCourseName() {
24     return courseName;
25   }
26
27   public void dropStudent(String student) {
28     // Left as an exercise in Programming Exercise 10.9
29   }
30 }
```

The array size is fixed to be 100 (line 3), so you cannot have more than 100 students in the course. You can improve the class by automatically increasing the array size in Programming Exercise 10.9.

When you create a Course object, an array object is created. A Course object contains a reference to the array. For simplicity, you can say the Course object contains the array.

The user can create a Course object and manipulate it through the public methods addStudent, dropStudent, getNumberOfStudents, and getStudents. However, the user doesn't need to know how these methods are implemented. The Course class encapsulates the internal implementation. This example uses an array to store students, but you could use a different data structure to store students. The program that uses Course does not need to change as long as the contract of the public methods remains unchanged.

10.5.1 Replace the statement in line 17 in Listing 10.5, TestCourse.java, so the loop displays each student name followed by a comma except the last student name.

10.6 Case Study: Designing a Class for Stacks

This section designs a class for modeling stacks.

stack

Key
Point

Recall that a *stack* is a data structure that holds data in a last-in, first-out fashion, as shown in Figure 10.11.

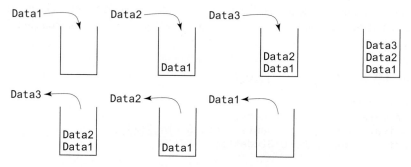

FIGURE 10.11 A stack holds data in a last-in, first-out fashion.

Stacks have many applications. For example, the compiler uses a stack to process method invocations. When a method is invoked, its parameters and local variables are pushed into a stack. When a method calls another method, the new method's parameters and local variables are pushed into the stack. When a method finishes its work and returns to its caller, its associated space is released from the stack.

You can define a class to model stacks. For simplicity, assume the stack holds the `int` values. Thus, name the stack class `StackOfIntegers`. The UML diagram for the class is shown in Figure 10.12.

VideoNote

The `StackOfIntegers` class

StackOfIntegers	
−elements: int[]	An array to store integers in the stack.
−size: int	The number of integers in the stack.
+StackOfIntegers()	Constructs an empty stack with a default capacity of 16.
+StackOfIntegers(capacity: int)	Constructs an empty stack with a specified capacity.
+empty(): boolean	Returns true if the stack is empty.
+peek(): int	Returns the integer at the top of the stack without removing it from the stack.
+push(value: int): void	Stores an integer into the top of the stack.
+pop(): int	Removes the integer at the top of the stack and returns it.
+getSize(): int	Returns the number of elements in the stack.

FIGURE 10.12 The `StackOfIntegers` class encapsulates the stack storage and provides the operations for manipulating the stack.

Suppose the class is available. The test program in Listing 10.7 uses the class to create a stack (line 3), store 10 integers 0, 1, 2, . . . , and 9 (line 6), and displays them in reverse order (line 9).

LISTING 10.7 TestStackOfIntegers.java

```
1  public class TestStackOfIntegers {
2    public static void main(String[] args) {
3      StackOfIntegers stack = new StackOfIntegers();
```

create a stack

```
 4
 5      for (int i = 0; i < 10; i++)
 6        stack.push(i);                              push to stack
 7
 8      while (!stack.empty())
 9        System.out.print(stack.pop() + " ");        pop from stack
10    }
11  }
```

```
9 8 7 6 5 4 3 2 1 0
```

How do you implement the `StackOfIntegers` class? The elements in the stack are stored in an array named `elements`. When you create a stack, the array is also created. The no-arg constructor creates an array with the default capacity of `16`. The variable `size` counts the number of elements in the stack, and `size – 1` is the index of the element at the top of the stack, as shown in Figure 10.13. For an empty stack, `size` is `0`.

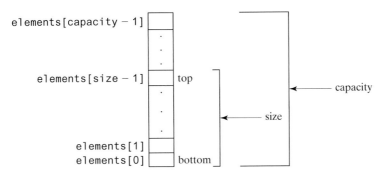

FIGURE 10.13 The `StackOfIntegers` uses an array to store the elements in a stack.

The `StackOfIntegers` class is implemented in Listing 10.8. The methods `empty()`, `peek()`, `pop()`, and `getSize()` are easy to implement. To implement `push(int value)`, assign `value` to `elements[size]` if `size < capacity` (line 24). If the stack is full (i.e., `size >= capacity`), create a new array of twice the current capacity (line 19), copy the contents of the current array to the new array (line 20), and assign the reference of the new array to the current array in the stack (line 21). Now you can add the new value to the array (line 24).

LISTING 10.8 StackOfIntegers.java

```
 1  public class StackOfIntegers {
 2    private int[] elements;
 3    private int size;
 4    public static final int DEFAULT_CAPACITY = 16;      max capacity 16
 5
 6    /** Construct a stack with the default capacity 16 */
 7    public StackOfIntegers() {
 8      this(DEFAULT_CAPACITY);
 9    }
10
11    /** Construct a stack with the specified maximum capacity */
12    public StackOfIntegers(int capacity) {
13      elements = new int[capacity];
14    }
15
```

```
16    /** Push a new integer to the top of the stack */
17    public void push(int value) {
18      if (size >= elements.length) {
19        int[] temp = new int[elements.length * 2];
20        System.arraycopy(elements, 0, temp, 0, elements.length);
21        elements = temp;
22      }
23
24      elements[size++] = value;
25    }
26
27    /** Return and remove the top element from the stack */
28    public int pop() {
29      return elements[--size];
30    }
31
32    /** Return the top element from the stack */
33    public int peek() {
34      return elements[size - 1];
35    }
36
37    /** Test whether the stack is empty */
38    public boolean empty() {
39      return size == 0;
40    }
41
42    /** Return the number of elements in the stack */
43    public int getSize() {
44      return size;
45    }
46  }
```

double the capacity (line 19)

add to stack (line 24)

10.7 Processing Primitive Data Type Values as Objects

Key Point

A primitive-type value is not an object, but it can be wrapped in an object using a wrapper class in the Java API.

Owing to performance considerations, primitive data type values are not objects in Java. Because of the overhead of processing objects, the language's performance would be adversely affected if primitive data type values were treated as objects. However, many Java methods require the use of objects as arguments. Java offers a convenient way to incorporate, or wrap, a primitive data type value into an object (e.g., wrapping an `int` into an `Integer` object, wrapping a `double` into a `Double` object, and wrapping a `char` into a `Character` object). By using a wrapper class, you can process primitive data type values as objects. Java provides `Boolean`, `Character`, `Double`, `Float`, `Byte`, `Short`, `Integer`, and `Long` wrapper classes in the `java.lang` package for primitive data types. The `Boolean` class wraps a Boolean value `true` or `false`. This section uses `Integer` and `Double` as examples to introduce the numeric wrapper classes.

why wrapper class?

 Note

Most wrapper class names for a primitive type are the same as the primitive data type name with the first letter capitalized. The exceptions are `Integer` for `int` and `Character` for `char`.

naming convention

Numeric wrapper classes are very similar to each other. Each contains the methods `doubleValue()`, `floatValue()`, `intValue()`, `longValue()`, `shortValue()`, and `byteValue()`. These methods "convert" objects into primitive-type values. The key features of `Integer` and `Double` are shown in Figure 10.14.

java.lang.Integer
−value: int
+MAX_VALUE: int
+MIN_VALUE: int
+Integer(value: int)
+Integer(s: String)
+byteValue(): byte
+shortValue(): short
+intValue(): int
+longValue(): long
+floatValue(): float
+doubleValue(): double
+compareTo(o: Integer): int
+toString(): String
+valueOf(s: String): Integer
+valueOf(s: String, radix: int): Integer
+parseInt(s: String): int
+parseInt(s: String, radix: int): int

java.lang.Double
−value: double
+MAX_VALUE: double
+MIN_VALUE: double
+Double(value: double)
+Double(s: String)
+byteValue(): byte
+shortValue(): short
+intValue(): int
+longValue(): long
+floatValue(): float
+doubleValue(): double
+compareTo(o: Double): int
+toString(): String
+valueOf(s: String): Double
+valueOf(s: String, radix: int): Double
+parseDouble(s: String): double
+parseDouble(s: String, radix: int): double

FIGURE 10.14 The wrapper classes provide constructors, constants, and conversion methods for manipulating various data types.

constructors

You can construct a wrapper object either from a primitive data type value or from a string representing the numeric value—for example, new Double(5.0), new Double("5.0"), new Integer(5), and new Integer("5").

no no-arg constructor
immutable

The wrapper classes do not have no-arg constructors. The instances of all wrapper classes are immutable; this means that, once the objects are created, their internal values cannot be changed.

constants

Each numeric wrapper class has the constants MAX_VALUE and MIN_VALUE. MAX_VALUE represents the maximum value of the corresponding primitive data type. For Byte, Short, Integer, and Long, MIN_VALUE represents the minimum byte, short, int, and long values. Float and Double, MIN_VALUE represents the minimum *positive* float and double values. The following statements display the maximum integer (2,147,483,647), the minimum positive float (1.4E–45), and the maximum double floating-point number (1.79769313486231570e + 308d):

```
System.out.println("The maximum integer is " + Integer.MAX_VALUE);
System.out.println("The minimum positive float is " +
  Float.MIN_VALUE);
System.out.println(
  "The maximum double-precision floating-point number is " +
  Double.MAX_VALUE);
```

conversion methods

Each numeric wrapper class contains the methods doubleValue(), floatValue(), intValue(), longValue(), and shortValue() for returning a double, float, int, long, or short value for the wrapper object. For example,

```
new Double(12.4).intValue() returns 12;
new Integer(12).doubleValue() returns 12.0;
```

compareTo method

Recall the String class contains the compareTo method for comparing two strings. The numeric wrapper classes contain the compareTo method for comparing two numbers and returns 1, 0, or −1, if this number is greater than, equal to, or less than the other number. For example,

```
new Double(12.4).compareTo(new Double(12.3)) returns 1;
new Double(12.3).compareTo(new Double(12.3)) returns 0;
new Double(12.3).compareTo(new Double(12.51)) returns −1;
```

static valueOf methods

The numeric wrapper classes have a useful static method, valueOf(String s). This method creates a new object initialized to the value represented by the specified string. For example,

```
Double doubleObject = Double.valueOf("12.4");
Integer integerObject = Integer.valueOf("12");
```

static parsing methods

You have used the parseInt method in the Integer class to parse a numeric string into an int value and the parseDouble method in the Double class to parse a numeric string into a double value. Each numeric wrapper class has two overloaded parsing methods to parse a numeric string into an appropriate numeric value based on 10 (decimal) or any specified radix (e.g., 2 for binary, 8 for octal, and 16 for hexadecimal).

```
// These two methods are in the Byte class
public static byte parseByte(String s)
public static byte parseByte(String s, int radix)

// These two methods are in the Short class
public static short parseShort(String s)
public static short parseShort(String s, int radix)

// These two methods are in the Integer class
public static int parseInt(String s)
public static int parseInt(String s, int radix)

// These two methods are in the Long class
public static long parseLong(String s)
public static long parseLong(String s, int radix)

// These two methods are in the Float class
public static float parseFloat(String s)
public static float parseFloat(String s, int radix)

// These two methods are in the Double class
public static double parseDouble(String s)
public static double parseDouble(String s, int radix)
```

For example,

```
Integer.parseInt("11", 2) returns 3;
Integer.parseInt("12", 8) returns 10;
Integer.parseInt("13", 10) returns 13;
Integer.parseInt("1A", 16) returns 26;
```

Integer.parseInt("12", 2) would raise a runtime exception because 12 is not a binary number.

converting decimal to hex

Note you can convert a decimal number into a hex number using the format method. For example,

```
String.format("%x", 26) returns 1A;
```

10.7.1 Describe primitive-type wrapper classes.

10.7.2 Can each of the following statements be compiled?

a. `Integer i = new Integer("23");`

b. `Integer i = new Integer(23);`

c. `Integer i = Integer.valueOf("23");`

d. `Integer i = Integer.parseInt("23", 8);`

e. `Double d = new Double();`

f. `Double d = Double.valueOf("23.45");`

g. `int i = (Integer.valueOf("23")).intValue();`

h. `double d = (Double.valueOf("23.4")).doubleValue();`

i. `int i = (Double.valueOf("23.4")).intValue();`

j. `String s = (Double.valueOf("23.4")).toString();`

10.7.3 How do you convert an integer into a string? How do you convert a numeric string into an integer? How do you convert a double number into a string? How do you convert a numeric string into a double value?

10.7.4 Show the output of the following code:

```
public class Test {
  public static void main(String[] args) {
    Integer x = new Integer(3);
    System.out.println(x.intValue());
    System.out.println(x.compareTo(new Integer(4)));
  }
}
```

10.7.5 What is the output of the following code?

```
public class Test {
  public static void main(String[] args) {
    System.out.println(Integer.parseInt("10"));
    System.out.println(Integer.parseInt("10", 10));
    System.out.println(Integer.parseInt("10", 16));
    System.out.println(Integer.parseInt("11"));
    System.out.println(Integer.parseInt("11", 10));
    System.out.println(Integer.parseInt("11", 16));
  }
}
```

10.8 Automatic Conversion between Primitive Types and Wrapper Class Types

A primitive-type value can be automatically converted to an object using a wrapper class, and vice versa, depending on the context.

Converting a primitive value to a wrapper object is called *boxing*. The reverse conversion is called *unboxing*. Java allows primitive types and wrapper classes to be converted automatically. The compiler will automatically box a primitive value that appears in a context requiring an object, and unbox an object that appears in a context requiring a primitive value. This is called *autoboxing* and *autounboxing*.

boxing
unboxing
autoboxing
autounboxing

For instance, the following statement in (a) can be simplified as in (b) using autoboxing.

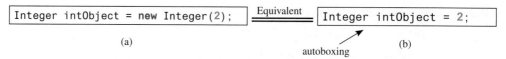

```
Integer intObject = new Integer(2);
```
(a)

Equivalent

```
Integer intObject = 2;
```
(b)

autoboxing

The following statement in (a) is the same as in (b) due to autounboxing.

```
int i = 1;
```
(a)

(a) and (b) are
Equivalent

```
int i = new Integer(1);
```
(b)

Consider the following example:

```
1 Integer[] intArray = {1, 2, 3};
2 System.out.println(intArray[0] + intArray1] + intArray[2]);
```

In line 1, the primitive values 1, 2, and 3 are automatically boxed into objects new Integer(1), new Integer(2), and new Integer(3). In line 2, the objects intArray[0], intArray[1], and intArray[2] are automatically unboxed into int values that are added together.

10.8.1   What are autoboxing and autounboxing? Are the following statements correct?

a. Integer x = 3 + new Integer(5);
b. Integer x = 3;
c. Double x = 3;
d. Double x = 3.0;
e. int x = new Integer(3);
f. int x = new Integer(3) + new Integer(4);

10.8.2   Show the output of the following code.

```
public class Test {
  public static void main(String[] args) {
    Double x = 3.5;
    System.out.println(x.intValue());
    System.out.println(x.compareTo(4.5));
  }
}
```

10.9 The BigInteger and BigDecimal Classes

The BigInteger and BigDecimal classes can be used to represent integers or decimal numbers of any size and precision.

Key Point

immutable

VideoNote

Process large numbers

If you need to compute with very large integers or high-precision floating-point values, you can use the BigInteger and BigDecimal classes in the java.math package. Both are *immutable*. The largest integer of the long type is Long.MAX_VALUE (i.e., 9223372036854775807). An instance of BigInteger can represent an integer of any size. You can use new BigInteger(String) and new BigDecimal(String) to create an instance of BigInteger and BigDecimal, use the add, subtract, multiply, divide, and remainder methods to perform arithmetic operations, and use the compareTo method to compare two big numbers. For example, the following code creates two BigInteger objects and multiplies them:

```
BigInteger a = new BigInteger("9223372036854775807");
BigInteger b = new BigInteger("2");
BigInteger c = a.multiply(b); // 9223372036854775807 * 2
System.out.println(c);
```

The output is 18446744073709551614.

There is no limit to the precision of a `BigDecimal` object. The `divide` method may throw an `ArithmeticException` if the result cannot be terminated. However, you can use the overloaded `divide(BigDecimal d, int scale, int roundingMode)` method to specify a scale and a rounding mode to avoid this exception, where `scale` is the maximum number of digits after the decimal point. For example, the following code creates two `BigDecimal` objects and performs division with scale 20 and rounding mode `BigDecimal.ROUND_UP`:

```
BigDecimal a = new BigDecimal(1.0);
BigDecimal b = new BigDecimal(3);
BigDecimal c = a.divide(b, 20, BigDecimal.ROUND_UP);
System.out.println(c);
```

The output is 0.33333333333333333334.

Note the factorial of an integer can be very large. Listing 10.9 gives a method that can return the factorial of any integer.

LISTING 10.9   LargeFactorial.java

```
1  import java.util.Scanner;
2  import java.math.*;
3
4  public class LargeFactorial {
5    public static void main(String[] args) {
6      Scanner input = new Scanner(System.in);
7      System.out.print("Enter an integer: ");
8      int n = input.nextInt();
9      System.out.println(n +"! is \n" + factorial(n));
10   }
11
12   public static BigInteger factorial(long n) {
13     BigInteger result = BigInteger.ONE;          constant
14     for (int i = 1; i <= n; i++)
15       result = result.multiply(new BigInteger(i + ""));    multiply
16
17     return result;
18   }
19 }
```

```
Enter an integer: 50 ↵Enter
50! is
30414093201713378043612608166064768844377641568960512000000000000
```

`BigInteger.ONE` (line 13) is a constant defined in the `BigInteger` class. `BigInteger.ONE` is the same as `new BigInteger("1")`.

A new result is obtained by invoking the `multiply` method (line 15).

10.9.1   What is the output of the following code?

```
public class Test {
  public static void main(String[] args) {
    java.math.BigInteger x = new java.math.BigInteger("3");
    java.math.BigInteger y = new java.math.BigInteger("7");
    java.math.BigInteger z = x.add(y);
    System.out.println("x is " + x);
    System.out.println("y is " + y);
    System.out.println("z is " + z);
  }
}
```

10.10 The String Class

A `String` *object is immutable; its contents cannot be changed once the string is created.*

VideoNote

The `String` class

Strings were introduced in Section 4.4. You know strings are objects. You can invoke the `charAt(index)` method to obtain a character at the specified index from a string, the `length()` method to return the size of a string, the `substring` method to return a substring in a string, the `indexOf` and `lastIndexOf` methods to return the first or last index of a matching character or a substring, the `equals` and `compareTo` methods to compare two strings, and the `trim()` method to trim whitespace characters from the two ends of a string, and the `toLowerCase()` and `toUpperCase()` methods to return the lowercase and uppercase from a string. We will take a closer look at strings in this section.

The `String` class has 13 constructors and more than 40 methods for manipulating strings. Not only is it very useful in programming, but it is also a good example for learning classes and objects.

10.10.1 Constructing a String

You can create a string object from a string literal or from an array of characters. To create a string from a string literal, use the syntax:

```
String newString = new String(stringLiteral);
```

The argument `stringLiteral` is a sequence of characters enclosed in double quotes. The following statement creates a `String` object `message` for the string literal `"Welcome to Java"`:

```
String message = new String("Welcome to Java");
```

string literal object

Java treats a string literal as a `String` object. Thus, the following statement is valid:

```
String message = "Welcome to Java";
```

You can also create a string from an array of characters. For example, the following statements create the string `"Good Day"`:

```
char[] charArray = {'G', 'o', 'o', 'd', ' ', 'D', 'a', 'y'};
String message = new String(charArray);
```

String variable, string
object, string value

> **Note**
> A `String` variable holds a reference to a `String` object that stores a string value. Strictly speaking, the terms `String` *variable*, `String` *object*, and *string value* are different, but most of the time the distinctions between them can be ignored. For simplicity, the term *string* will often be used to refer to `String` variable, `String` object, and string value.

10.10.2 Immutable Strings and Interned Strings

immutable

A `String` object is immutable; its contents cannot be changed. Does the following code change the contents of the string?

```
String s = "Java";
s = "HTML";
```

The answer is no. The first statement creates a `String` object with the content `"Java"` and assigns its reference to `s`. The second statement creates a new `String` object with the content `"HTML"` and assigns its reference to `s`. The first `String` object still exists after the assignment, but it can no longer be accessed, because variable `s` now points to the new object, as shown in Figure 10.15.

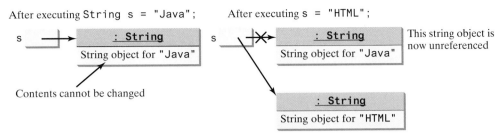

FIGURE 10.15 Strings are immutable; once created, their contents cannot be changed.

Because strings are immutable and are ubiquitous in programming, the JVM uses a unique instance for string literals with the same character sequence in order to improve efficiency and save memory. Such an instance is called an *interned string*. For example, the following statements: interned string

```
String s1 = "Welcome to Java";

String s2 = new String("Welcome to Java");

String s3 = "Welcome to Java";

System.out.println("s1 == s2 is " + (s1 == s2));
System.out.println("s1 == s3 is " + (s1 == s3));
```

display

```
s1 == s2 is false
s1 == s3 is true
```

In the preceding statements, s1 and s3 refer to the same interned string—"Welcome to Java"—so s1 == s3 is true. However, s1 == s2 is false, because s1 and s2 are two different string objects, even though they have the same contents.

10.10.3 Replacing and Splitting Strings

The String class provides the methods for replacing and splitting strings, as shown in Figure 10.16.

java.lang.String	
+replace(oldChar: char, newChar: char): String	Returns a new string that replaces all matching characters in this string with the new character.
+replaceFirst(oldString: String, newString: String): String	Returns a new string that replaces the first matching substring in this string with the new substring.
+replaceAll(oldString: String, newString: String): String	Returns a new string that replaces all matching substrings in this string with the new substring.
+split(delimiter: String): String[]	Returns an array of strings consisting of the substrings split by the delimiter.

FIGURE 10.16 The String class contains the methods for replacing and splitting strings.

Once a string is created, its contents cannot be changed. The methods `replace`, `replaceFirst`, and `replaceAll` return a new string derived from the original string (without changing the original string!). Several versions of the `replace` methods are provided to replace a character or a substring in the string with a new character or a new substring.

For example,

replace
replaceFirst
replace
replace

`"Welcome".replace('e', 'A')` returns a new string, WAlcomA.
`"Welcome".replaceFirst("e", "AB")` returns a new string, WABlcome.
`"Welcome".replace("e", "AB")` returns a new string, WABlcomAB.
`"Welcome".replace("el", "AB")` returns a new string, WABcome.

split

The `split` method can be used to extract tokens from a string with the specified delimiters. For example, the following code

```
String[] tokens = "Java#HTML#Perl".split("#");
for (int i = 0; i < tokens.length; i++)
  System.out.print(tokens[i] + " ");
```

displays

```
Java HTML Perl
```

10.10.4 Matching, Replacing, and Splitting by Patterns

why regular expression?

Often you will need to write code that validates user input, such as to check whether the input is a number, a string with all lowercase letters, or a Social Security number. How do you write this type of code? A simple and effective way to accomplish this task is to use the regular expression.

regular expression
regex

A *regular expression* (abbreviated *regex*) is a string that describes a pattern for matching a set of strings. You can match, replace, or split a string by specifying a pattern. This is an extremely useful and powerful feature.

matches(regex)

Let us begin with the `matches` method in the `String` class. At first glance, the `matches` method is very similar to the `equals` method. For example, the following two statements both evaluate to `true`:

```
"Java".matches("Java");
"Java".equals("Java");
```

However, the `matches` method is more powerful. It can match not only a fixed string, but also a set of strings that follow a pattern. For example, the following statements all evaluate to `true`:

```
"Java is fun".matches("Java.*")
"Java is cool".matches("Java.*")
"Java is powerful".matches("Java.*")
```

`Java.*` in the preceding statements is a regular expression. It describes a string pattern that begins with Java followed by *any* zero or more characters. Here, the substring matches any zero or more characters.

The following statement evaluates to `true`:

```
"440-02-4534".matches("\\d{3}-\\d{2}-\\d{4}")
```

Here, `\\d` represents a single digit, and `\\d{3}` represents three digits.

The `replaceAll`, `replaceFirst`, and `split` methods can be used with a regular expression. For example, the following statement returns a new string that replaces $, +, or # in a+b$#c with the string NNN.

```
String s = "a+b$#c".replaceAll("[$+#]", "NNN");
System.out.println(s);
```

replaceAll(regex)

Here, the regular expression `[$+#]` specifies a pattern that matches $, +, or #. Thus, the output is aNNNbNNNNNNc.

The following statement splits the string into an array of strings delimited by punctuation marks.

```
String[] tokens = "Java,C?C#,C++".split("[.,:;?]");

for (int i = 0; i < tokens.length; i++)
  System.out.println(tokens[i]);
```

split(regex)

In this example, the regular expression `[.,:;?]` specifies a pattern that matches ., ,, :, ;, or ?. Each of these characters is a delimiter for splitting the string. Thus, the string is split into Java, C, C#, and C++, which are stored in array tokens.

further studies

Regular expression patterns are complex for beginning students to understand. For this reason, simple patterns are introduced in this section. Please refer to Appendix H, Regular Expressions, to learn more about these patterns.

10.10.5 Conversion between Strings and Arrays

Strings are not arrays, but a string can be converted into an array and vice versa. To convert a string into an array of characters, use the `toCharArray` method. For example, the following statement converts the string Java to an array:

toCharArray

```
char[] chars = "Java".toCharArray();
```

Thus, chars[0] is J, chars[1] is a, chars[2] is v, and chars[3] is a.

You can also use the `getChars(int srcBegin, int srcEnd, char[] dst, int dstBegin)` method to copy a substring of the string from index srcBegin to index srcEnd–1 into a character array dst starting from index dstBegin. For example, the following code copies a substring "3720" in "CS3720" from index 2 to index 6–1 into the character array dst starting from index 4:

```
char[] dst = {'J', 'A', 'V', 'A', '1', '3', '0', '1'};
"CS3720".getChars(2, 6, dst, 4);
```

getChars

Thus, dst becomes {'J', 'A', 'V', 'A', '3', '7', '2', '0'}.

To convert an array of characters into a string, use the `String(char[])` constructor or the `valueOf(char[])` method. For example, the following statement constructs a string from an array using the `String` constructor:

```
String str = new String(new char[]{'J', 'a', 'v', 'a'});
```

The next statement constructs a string from an array using the `valueOf` method.

valueOf

```
String str = String.valueOf(new char[]{'J', 'a', 'v', 'a'});
```

10.10.6 Converting Characters and Numeric Values to Strings

Recall that you can use `Double.parseDouble(str)` or `Integer.parseInt(str)` to convert a string to a `double` value or an `int` value", and you can convert a character or a number into a string by using the string concatenating operator. Another way of converting a

overloaded valueOf

number into a string is to use the overloaded static `valueOf` method. This method can also be used to convert a character or an array of characters into a string, as shown in Figure 10.17.

java.lang.String	
+valueOf(c: char): String	Returns a string consisting of the character c.
+valueOf(data: char[]): String	Returns a string consisting of the characters in the array.
+valueOf(d: double): String	Returns a string representing the double value.
+valueOf(f: float): String	Returns a string representing the float value.
+valueOf(i: int): String	Returns a string representing the int value.
+valueOf(l: long): String	Returns a string representing the long value.
+valueOf(b: boolean): String	Returns a string representing the boolean value.

FIGURE 10.17 The `String` class contains the static methods for creating strings from primitive-type values.

For example, to convert a `double` value `5.44` to a string, use `String.valueOf(5.44)`. The return value is a string consisting of the characters `'5'`, `'.'`, `'4'`, and `'4'`.

10.10.7 Formatting Strings

The `String` class contains the static `format` method to return a formatted string. The syntax to invoke this method is

```
String.format(format, item1, item2, ..., itemk);
```

This method is similar to the `printf` method except that the `format` method returns a formatted string, whereas the `printf` method displays a formatted string. For example,

```
String s = String.format("%7.2f%6d%-4s", 45.556, 14, "AB");
System.out.println(s);
```

displays

　□□45.56□□□□14AB□□

where the square box (□) denotes a blank space.

Note

```
System.out.printf(format, item1, item2, ..., itemk);
```

is equivalent to

```
System.out.print(
  String.format(format, item1, item2, ..., itemk));
```

Check
Point

10.10.1 Suppose s1, s2, s3, and s4 are four strings, given as follows:

```
String s1 = "Welcome to Java";
String s2 = s1;
String s3 = new String("Welcome to Java");
String s4 = "Welcome to Java";
```

What are the results of the following expressions?

```
a. s1 == s2
b. s1 == s3
```

```
  c. s1 == s4
  d. s1.equals(s3)
  e. s1.equals(s4)
  f. "Welcome to Java".replace("Java", "HTML")
  g. s1.replace('o', 'T')
  h. s1.replaceAll("o", "T")
  i. s1.replaceFirst("o", "T")
  j. s1.toCharArray()
```

10.10.2 To create the string `Welcome to Java`, you may use a statement like this:

```
String s = "Welcome to Java";
```

or

```
String s = new String("Welcome to Java");
```

Which one is better? Why?

10.10.3 What is the output of the following code?

```
String s1 = "Welcome to Java";
String s2 = s1.replace("o", "abc");
System.out.println(s1);
System.out.println(s2);
```

10.10.4 Let `s1` be `" Welcome "` and `s2` be `" welcome "`. Write the code for the following statements:

a. Replace all occurrences of the character `e` with `E` in `s1` and assign the new string to `s3`.

b. Split `Welcome to Java and HTML` into an array `tokens` delimited by a space and assign the first two tokens into `s1` and `s2`.

10.10.5 Does any method in the `String` class change the contents of the string?

10.10.6 Suppose string `s` is created using `new String()`; what is `s.length()`?

10.10.7 How do you convert a `char`, an array of characters, or a number to a string?

10.10.8 Why does the following code cause a `NullPointerException`?

```
1  public class Test {
2    private String text;
3
4    public Test(String s) {
5      String text = s;
6    }
7
8    public static void main(String[] args) {
9      Test test = new Test("ABC");
10     System.out.println(test.text.toLowerCase());
11   }
12 }
```

10.10.9 What is wrong in the following program?

```
1  public class Test {
2    String text;
3
```

```
 4      public void Test(String s) {
 5        text = s;
 6      }
 7
 8      public static void main(String[] args) {
 9        Test test = new Test("ABC");
10        System.out.println(test);
11      }
12  }
```

10.10.10 Show the output of the following code:

```
public class Test {
  public static void main(String[] args) {
    System.out.println("Hi, ABC, good".matches("ABC "));
    System.out.println("Hi, ABC, good".matches(".*ABC.*"));
    System.out.println("A,B;C".replaceAll(",;", "#"));
    System.out.println("A,B;C".replaceAll("[,;]", "#"));

    String[] tokens = "A,B;C".split("[,;]");
    for (int i = 0; i < tokens.length; i++)
      System.out.print(tokens[i] + " ");
  }
}
```

10.10.11 Show the output of the following code:

```
public class Test {
  public static void main(String[] args) {
    String s = "Hi, Good Morning";
    System.out.println(m(s));
  }

  public static int m(String s) {
    int count = 0;
    for (int i = 0; i < s.length(); i++)
      if (Character.isUpperCase(s.charAt(i)))
        count++;

    return count;
  }
}
```

10.11 The StringBuilder and StringBuffer Classes

Key Point

The StringBuilder and StringBuffer classes are similar to the String class except that the String class is immutable.

In general, the StringBuilder and StringBuffer classes can be used wherever a string is used. StringBuilder and StringBuffer are more flexible than String. You can add, insert, or append new contents into StringBuilder and StringBuffer objects, whereas the value of a String object is fixed once the string is created.

StringBuilder

The StringBuilder class is similar to StringBuffer except that the methods for modifying the buffer in StringBuffer are *synchronized*, which means that only one task is allowed to execute the methods. Use StringBuffer if the class might be accessed by multiple tasks concurrently, because synchronization is needed in this case to prevent corruptions to

StringBuffer. Concurrent programming will be introduced in Chapter 32. Using String-Builder is more efficient if it is accessed by just a single task, because no synchronization is needed in this case. The constructors and methods in StringBuffer and StringBuilder are almost the same. This section covers StringBuilder. You can replace StringBuilder in all occurrences in this section by StringBuffer. The program can compile and run without any other changes.

The StringBuilder class has three constructors and more than 30 methods for managing the builder and modifying strings in the builder. You can create an empty string builder or a string builder from a string using the constructors, as shown in Figure 10.18.

StringBuilder constructors

java.lang.StringBuilder	
+StringBuilder()	Constructs an empty string builder with capacity 16.
+StringBuilder(capacity: int)	Constructs a string builder with the specified capacity.
+StringBuilder(s: String)	Constructs a string builder with the specified string.

FIGURE 10.18 The StringBuilder class contains the constructors for creating instances of StringBuilder.

10.11.1 Modifying Strings in the StringBuilder

You can append new contents at the end of a string builder, insert new contents at a specified position in a string builder, and delete or replace characters in a string builder, using the methods listed in Figure 10.19.

java.lang.StringBuilder	
+append(data: char[]): StringBuilder	Appends a char array into this string builder.
+append(data: char[], offset: int, len: int): StringBuilder	Appends a subarray in data into this string builder.
+append(v: *aPrimitiveType*): StringBuilder	Appends a primitive-type value as a string to this builder.
+append(s: String): StringBuilder	Appends a string to this string builder.
+delete(startIndex: int, endIndex: int): StringBuilder	Deletes characters from startIndex to endIndex−1.
+deleteCharAt(index: int): StringBuilder	Deletes a character at the specified index.
+insert(index: int, data: char[], offset: int, len: int): StringBuilder	Inserts a subarray of the data in the array into the builder at the specified index.
+insert(offset: int, data: char[]): StringBuilder	Inserts data into this builder at the position offset.
+insert(offset: int, b: *aPrimitiveType*): StringBuilder	Inserts a value converted to a string into this builder.
+insert(offset: int, s: String): StringBuilder	Inserts a string into this builder at the position offset.
+replace(startIndex: int, endIndex: int, s: String): StringBuilder	Replaces the characters in this builder from startIndex to endIndex − 1 with the specified string.
+reverse(): StringBuilder	Reverses the characters in the builder.
+setCharAt(index: int, ch: char): void	Sets a new character at the specified index in this builder.

FIGURE 10.19 The StringBuilder class contains the methods for modifying string builders.

The `StringBuilder` class provides several overloaded methods to append `boolean`, `char`, `char[]`, `double`, `float`, `int`, `long`, and `String` into a string builder. For example, the following code appends strings and characters into `stringBuilder` to form a new string, `Welcome to Java`:

append

```
StringBuilder stringBuilder = new StringBuilder();
stringBuilder.append("Welcome");
stringBuilder.append(' ');
stringBuilder.append("to");
stringBuilder.append(' ');
stringBuilder.append("Java");
```

The `StringBuilder` class also contains overloaded methods to insert `boolean`, `char`, `char array`, `double`, `float`, `int`, `long`, and `String` into a string builder. Consider the following code:

insert

```
stringBuilder.insert(11, "HTML and ");
```

Suppose `stringBuilder` contains `Welcome to Java` before the `insert` method is applied. This code inserts `"HTML and "` at position 11 in `stringBuilder` (just before the `J`). The new `stringBuilder` is `Welcome to HTML and Java`.

You can also delete characters from a string in the builder using the two `delete` methods, reverse the string using the `reverse` method, replace characters using the `replace` method, or set a new character in a string using the `setCharAt` method.

For example, suppose `stringBuilder` contains `Welcome to Java` before each of the following methods is applied:

delete
deleteCharAt
reverse
replace
setCharAt

```
stringBuilder.delete(8, 11) changes the builder to Welcome Java.
stringBuilder.deleteCharAt(8) changes the builder to Welcome o Java.
stringBuilder.reverse() changes the builder to avaJ ot emocleW.
stringBuilder.replace(11, 15, "HTML") changes the builder to Welcome to HTML.
stringBuilder.setCharAt(0, 'w') sets the builder to welcome to Java.
```

All these modification methods except `setCharAt` do two things:

1. Change the contents of the string builder

ignore return value

2. Return the reference of the string builder

For example, the following statement:

```
StringBuilder stringBuilder1 = stringBuilder.reverse();
```

reverses the string in the builder and assigns the builder's reference to `stringBuilder1`. Thus, `stringBuilder` and `stringBuilder1` both point to the same `StringBuilder` object. Recall that a value-returning method can be invoked as a statement, if you are not interested in the return value of the method. In this case, the return value is simply ignored. For example, in the following statement:

```
stringBuilder.reverse():
```

the return value is ignored. Returning the reference of a `StringBuilder` enables the `StringBuilder` methods to be invoked in a chain such as the following:

```
stringBuilder.reverse().delete(8, 11).replace(11, 15, "HTML");
```

String or StringBuilder?

Tip

If a string does not require any change, use `String` rather than `StringBuilder`. `String` is more efficient than `StringBuilder`.

10.11.2 The `toString`, `capacity`, `length`, `setLength`, and `charAt` Methods

The `StringBuilder` class provides the additional methods for manipulating a string builder and obtaining its properties, as shown in Figure 10.20.

java.lang.StringBuilder	
+toString(): String	Returns a string object from the string builder.
+capacity(): int	Returns the capacity of this string builder.
+charAt(index: int): char	Returns the character at the specified index.
+length(): int	Returns the number of characters in this builder.
+setLength(newLength: int): void	Sets a new length in this builder.
+substring(startIndex: int): String	Returns a substring starting at startIndex.
+substring(startIndex: int, endIndex: int): String	Returns a substring from startIndex to endIndex − 1.
+trimToSize(): void	Reduces the storage size used for the string builder.

FIGURE 10.20 The `StringBuilder` class contains the methods for modifying string builders.

The `capacity()` method returns the current capacity of the string builder. The capacity is the number of characters the string builder is able to store without having to increase its size.

The `length()` method returns the number of characters actually stored in the string builder. The `setLength(newLength)` method sets the length of the string builder. If the `newLength` argument is less than the current length of the string builder, the string builder is truncated to contain exactly the number of characters given by the `newLength` argument. If the `newLength` argument is greater than or equal to the current length, sufficient null characters (`\u0000`) are appended to the string builder so `length` becomes the `newLength` argument. The `newLength` argument must be greater than or equal to `0`.

The `charAt(index)` method returns the character at a specific `index` in the string builder. The index is `0` based. The first character of a string builder is at index `0`, the next at index `1`, and so on. The `index` argument must be greater than or equal to `0`, and less than the length of the string builder.

Note

The length of the string builder is always less than or equal to the capacity of the builder. The length is the actual size of the string stored in the builder, and the capacity is the current size of the builder. The builder's capacity is automatically increased if more characters are added to exceed its capacity. Internally, a string builder is an array of characters, so the builder's capacity is the size of the array. If the builder's capacity is exceeded, the array is replaced by a new array. The new array size is `2 * (the previous array size + 1)`.

Tip

You can use `new StringBuilder(initialCapacity)` to create a `StringBuilder` with a specified initial capacity. By carefully choosing the initial capacity, you can make your program more efficient. If the capacity is always larger than the actual length of the builder, the JVM will never need to reallocate memory for the builder. On the other hand, if the capacity is too large, you will waste memory space. You can use the `trimToSize()` method to reduce the capacity to the actual size.

capacity()

length()
setLength(int)

charAt(int)

length and capacity

initial capacity

trimToSize()

10.11.3 Case Study: Ignoring Nonalphanumeric Characters When Checking Palindromes

Listing 5.14, Palindrome.java, considered all the characters in a string to check whether it is a palindrome. Write a new program that ignores nonalphanumeric characters in checking whether a string is a palindrome.

Here are the steps to solve the problem:

1. Filter the string by removing the nonalphanumeric characters. This can be done by creating an empty string builder, adding each alphanumeric character in the string to a string builder, and returning the string from the string builder. You can use the isLetterOrDigit(ch) method in the Character class to check whether character ch is a letter or a digit.

2. Obtain a new string that is the reversal of the filtered string. Compare the reversed string with the filtered string using the equals method.

The complete program is shown in Listing 10.10.

LISTING 10.10 PalindromeIgnoreNonAlphanumeric.java

```
1   import java.util.Scanner;
2
3   public class PalindromeIgnoreNonAlphanumeric {
4     /** Main method */
5     public static void main(String[] args) {
6       // Create a Scanner
7       Scanner input = new Scanner(System.in);
8
9       // Prompt the user to enter a string
10      System.out.print("Enter a string: ");
11      String s = input.nextLine();
12
13      // Display result
14      System.out.println("Ignoring nonalphanumeric characters, \nis "
15        + s + " a palindrome? " + isPalindrome(s));
16    }
17
18    /** Return true if a string is a palindrome */
19    public static boolean isPalindrome(String s) {
20      // Create a new string by eliminating nonalphanumeric chars
21      String s1 = filter(s);
22
23      // Create a new string that is the reversal of s1
24      String s2 = reverse(s1);
25
26      // Check if the reversal is the same as the original string
27      return s2.equals(s1);
28    }
29
30    /** Create a new string by eliminating nonalphanumeric chars */
31    public static String filter(String s) {
32      // Create a string builder
33      StringBuilder stringBuilder = new StringBuilder();
34
35      // Examine each char in the string to skip alphanumeric char
36      for (int i = 0; i < s.length(); i++) {
37        if (Character.isLetterOrDigit(s.charAt(i))) {
38          stringBuilder.append(s.charAt(i));
39        }
```

check palindrome (line 19)

add letter or digit (line 38)

```
40        }
41
42        // Return a new filtered string
43        return stringBuilder.toString();
44    }
45
46    /** Create a new string by reversing a specified string */
47    public static String reverse(String s) {
48        StringBuilder stringBuilder = new StringBuilder(s);
49        stringBuilder.reverse(); // Invoke reverse in StringBuilder
50        return stringBuilder.toString();
51    }
52 }
```

```
Enter a string: ab<c>cb?a  ↵Enter
Ignoring nonalphanumeric characters,
is ab<c>cb?a a palindrome? true
```

```
Enter a string: abcc><?cab  ↵Enter
Ignoring nonalphanumeric characters,
is abcc><?cab a palindrome? false
```

The `filter(String s)` method (lines 31–44) examines each character in string `s` and copies it to a string builder if the character is a letter or a numeric character. The `filter` method
returns the string in the builder. The `reverse(String s)` method (lines 47–51) creates a
new string that reverses the specified string `s`. The `filter` and `reverse` methods both return
a new string. The original string is not changed.

The program in Listing 5.14 checks whether a string is a palindrome by comparing pairs
of characters from both ends of the string. Listing 10.10 uses the `reverse` method in the
`StringBuilder` class to reverse the string, then compares whether the two strings are equal
to determine whether the original string is a palindrome.

10.11.1 What is the difference between `StringBuilder` and `StringBuffer`?

10.11.2 How do you create a string builder from a string? How do you return a string
from a string builder?

10.11.3 Write three statements to reverse a string `s` using the `reverse` method in the
`StringBuilder` class.

10.11.4 Write three statements to delete a substring from a string `s` of `20` characters,
starting at index `4` and ending with index `10`. Use the `delete` method in the
`StringBuilder` class.

10.11.5 What is the internal storage for characters in a string and a string builder?

10.11.6 Suppose `s1` and `s2` are given as follows:

```
StringBuilder s1 = new StringBuilder("Java");
StringBuilder s2 = new StringBuilder("HTML");
```

Show the value of `s1` after each of the following statements. Assume the
statements are independent.

```
a. s1.append(" is fun");
b. s1.append(s2);
```

```
      c. s1.insert(2, "is fun");
      d. s1.insert(1, s2);
      e. s1.charAt(2);
      f. s1.length();
      g. s1.deleteCharAt(3);
      h. s1.delete(1, 3);
      i. s1.reverse();
      j. s1.replace(1, 3, "Computer");
      k. s1.substring(1, 3);
      l. s1.substring(2);
```

10.11.7 Show the output of the following program:

```
public class Test {
  public static void main(String[] args) {
    String s = "Java";
    StringBuilder builder = new StringBuilder(s);
    change(s, builder);

    System.out.println(s);
    System.out.println(builder);
  }

  private static void change(String s, StringBuilder builder) {
    s = s + " and HTML";
    builder.append(" and HTML");
  }
}
```

KEY TERMS

abstract data type (ADT) 368
aggregation 376
boxing 385
class abstraction 368
class encapsulation 368
class's contract 368
composition 376
has-a relationship 376
multiplicity 375
stack 380
unboxing 385

CHAPTER SUMMARY

1. The procedural paradigm focuses on designing methods. The object-oriented paradigm couples data and methods together into objects. Software design using the object-oriented paradigm focuses on objects and operations on objects. The object-oriented approach combines the power of the procedural paradigm with an added dimension that integrates data with operations into objects.

2. Many Java methods require the use of objects as arguments. Java offers a convenient way to incorporate, or wrap, a primitive data type into an object (e.g., wrapping `int` into the `Integer` class, and wrapping `double` into the `Double` class).

3. Java can automatically convert a primitive-type value to its corresponding wrapper object in the context and vice versa.

4. The `BigInteger` class is useful for computing and processing integers of any size. The `BigDecimal` class can be used to compute and process floating-point numbers with any arbitrary precision.

5. A `String` object is immutable; its contents cannot be changed. To improve efficiency and save memory, the JVM stores two literal strings that have the same character sequence in a unique object. This unique object is called an *interned string object*.

6. A *regular expression* (abbreviated *regex*) is a string that describes a pattern for matching a set of strings. You can match, replace, or split a string by specifying a pattern.

7. The `StringBuilder` and `StringBuffer` classes can be used to replace the `String` class. The `String` object is immutable, but you can add, insert, or append new contents into `StringBuilder` and `StringBuffer` objects. Use `String` if the string contents do not require any change and use `StringBuilder` or `StringBuffer` if they might change.

QUIZ

Answer the quiz for this chapter online at the book Companion Website.

PROGRAMMING EXERCISES

MyProgrammingLab™

Sections 10.2 and 10.3

*10.1 (*The* `Time` *class*) Design a class named `Time`. The class contains:

- The data fields `hour`, `minute`, and `second` that represent a time.
- A no-arg constructor that creates a `Time` object for the current time. (The values of the data fields will represent the current time.)
- A constructor that constructs a `Time` object with a specified elapsed time since midnight, January 1, 1970, in milliseconds. (The values of the data fields will represent this time.)
- A constructor that constructs a `Time` object with the specified hour, minute, and second.
- Three getter methods for the data fields `hour`, `minute`, and `second`, respectively.
- A method named `setTime(long elapseTime)` that sets a new time for the object using the elapsed time. For example, if the elapsed time is `555550000` milliseconds, the hour is `10`, the minute is `19`, and the second is `10`.

Draw the UML diagram for the class then implement the class. Write a test program that creates three `Time` objects (using `new Time()`, `new Time(555550000)`, and `new Time(5, 23, 55)`) and displays their hour, minute, and second in the format hour:minute:second.

(*Hint*: The first two constructors will extract the hour, minute, and second from the elapsed time. For the no-arg constructor, the current time can be obtained using `System.currentTimeMillis()`, as shown in Listing 2.7, ShowCurrentTime.java. Assume the time is in GMT.)

10.2 (*The* BMI *class*) Add the following new constructor in the BMI class:

```
/** Construct a BMI with the specified name, age, weight,
 * feet, and inches
 */
public BMI(String name, int age, double weight, double feet,
    double inches)
```

10.3 (*The* MyInteger *class*) Design a class named MyInteger. The class contains:

■ An int data field named value that stores the int value represented by this object.
■ A constructor that creates a MyInteger object for the specified int value.
■ A getter method that returns the int value.
■ The methods isEven(), isOdd(), and isPrime() that return true if the value in this object is even, odd, or prime, respectively.
■ The static methods isEven(int), isOdd(int), and isPrime(int) that return true if the specified value is even, odd, or prime, respectively.
■ The static methods isEven(MyInteger), isOdd(MyInteger), and isPrime(MyInteger) that return true if the specified value is even, odd, or prime, respectively.
■ The methods equals(int) and equals(MyInteger) that return true if the value in this object is equal to the specified value.
■ A static method parseInt(char[]) that converts an array of numeric characters to an int value.
■ A static method parseInt(String) that converts a string into an int value.

Draw the UML diagram for the class then implement the class. Write a client program that tests all methods in the class.

10.4 (*The* MyPoint *class*) Design a class named MyPoint to represent a point with x- and y-coordinates. The class contains:

■ The data fields x and y that represent the coordinates with getter methods.
■ A no-arg constructor that creates a point (0, 0).
■ A constructor that constructs a point with specified coordinates.
■ A method named distance that returns the distance from this point to a specified point of the MyPoint type.
■ A method named distance that returns the distance from this point to another point with specified x- and y-coordinates.
■ A static method named distance that returns the distance from two MyPoint objects.

VideoNote
The MyPoint class

Draw the UML diagram for the class then implement the class. Write a test program that creates the two points (0, 0) and (10, 30.5) and displays the distance between them.

Sections 10.4–10.8

*10.5 (*Display the prime factors*) Write a program that prompts the user to enter a positive integer and displays all its smallest factors in decreasing order. For example, if the integer is 120, the smallest factors are displayed as 5, 3, 2, 2, 2. Use the StackOfIntegers class to store the factors (e.g., 2, 2, 2, 3, 5) and retrieve and display them in reverse order.

*10.6 (*Display the prime numbers*) Write a program that displays all the prime numbers less than 120 in decreasing order. Use the StackOfIntegers class to store the prime numbers (e.g., 2, 3, 5, . . .) and retrieve and display them in reverse order.

**10.7 (*Game: ATM machine*) Use the `Account` class created in Programming Exercise 9.7 to simulate an ATM machine. Create 10 accounts in an array with id `0`, `1, . . . , 9`, and an initial balance of $100. The system prompts the user to enter an id. If the id is entered incorrectly, ask the user to enter a correct id. Once an id is accepted, the main menu is displayed as shown in the sample run. You can enter choice `1` for viewing the current balance, `2` for withdrawing money, `3` for depositing money, and `4` for exiting the main menu. Once you exit, the system will prompt for an id again. Thus, once the system starts, it will not stop.

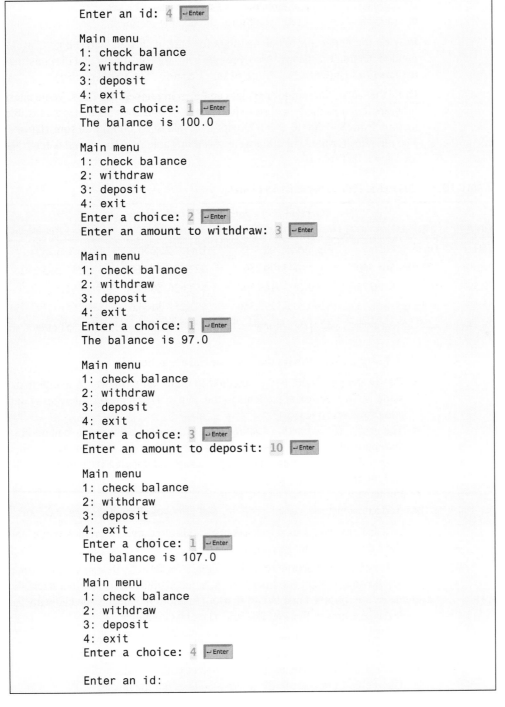

```
Enter an id: 4 ↵Enter

Main menu
1: check balance
2: withdraw
3: deposit
4: exit
Enter a choice: 1 ↵Enter
The balance is 100.0

Main menu
1: check balance
2: withdraw
3: deposit
4: exit
Enter a choice: 2 ↵Enter
Enter an amount to withdraw: 3 ↵Enter

Main menu
1: check balance
2: withdraw
3: deposit
4: exit
Enter a choice: 1 ↵Enter
The balance is 97.0

Main menu
1: check balance
2: withdraw
3: deposit
4: exit
Enter a choice: 3 ↵Enter
Enter an amount to deposit: 10 ↵Enter

Main menu
1: check balance
2: withdraw
3: deposit
4: exit
Enter a choice: 1 ↵Enter
The balance is 107.0

Main menu
1: check balance
2: withdraw
3: deposit
4: exit
Enter a choice: 4 ↵Enter

Enter an id:
```

***10.8   (*Financial: the* Tax *class*) Programming Exercise 8.12 writes a program for computing taxes using arrays. Design a class named Tax to contain the following instance data fields:

- int filingStatus: One of the four tax-filing statuses: 0—single filer, 1—married filing jointly or qualifying widow(er), 2—married filing separately, and 3—head of household. Use the public static constants SINGLE_FILER (0), MARRIED_JOINTLY_OR_QUALIFYING_WIDOW(ER) (1), MARRIED_SEPARATELY (2), HEAD_OF_HOUSEHOLD (3) to represent the statuses.
- int[][] brackets: Stores the tax brackets for each filing status.
- double[] rates: Stores the tax rates for each bracket.
- double taxableIncome: Stores the taxable income.

Provide the getter and setter methods for each data field and the getTax() method that returns the tax. Also, provide a no-arg constructor and the constructor Tax(filingStatus, brackets, rates, taxableIncome).

Draw the UML diagram for the class and then implement the class. Write a test program that uses the Tax class to print the 2001 and 2009 tax tables for taxable income from $50,000 to $60,000 with intervals of $1,000 for all four statuses. The tax rates for the year 2009 were given in Table 3.2. The tax rates for 2001 are shown in Table 10.1.

TABLE 10.1   2001 U.S. Federal Personal Tax Rates

Tax Rate	Single Filers	Married—Filing Jointly or Qualifying Widow(er)	Married—Filing Separately	Head of Household
15%	Up to $27,050	Up to $45,200	Up to $22,600	Up to $36,250
27.5%	$27,051–$65,550	$45,201–$109,250	$22,601–$54,625	$36,251–$93,650
30.5%	$65,551–$136,750	$109,251–$166,500	$54,626–$83,250	$93,651–$151,650
35.5%	$136,751–$297,350	$166,501–$297,350	$83,251–$148,675	$151,651–$297,350
39.1%	$297,351 or more	$297,351 or more	$ 148,676 or more	$297,351 or more

**10.9   (*The* Course *class*) Revise the Course class as follows:

- Revise the getStudents() method to return an array whose length is the same as the number of students in the course. (*Hint*: create a new array and copy students to it.)
- The array size is fixed in Listing 10.6. Revise the addStudent method to automatically increase the array size if there is no room to add more students. This is done by creating a new larger array and copying the contents of the current array to it.
- Implement the dropStudent method.
- Add a new method named clear() that removes all students from the course.

Write a test program that creates a course, adds three students, removes one, and displays the students in the course.

*10.10   (*The* Queue *class*) Section 10.6 gives a class for Stack. Design a class named Queue for storing integers. Like a stack, a queue holds elements. In a stack, the elements are retrieved in a last-in first-out fashion. In a queue, the elements are retrieved in a first-in first-out fashion. The class contains:

- An int[] data field named elements that stores the int values in the queue.
- A data field named size that stores the number of elements in the queue.
- A constructor that creates a Queue object with default capacity 8.
- The method enqueue(int v) that adds v into the queue.

- The method `dequeue()` that removes and returns the element from the queue.
- The method `empty()` that returns true if the queue is empty.
- The method `getSize()` that returns the size of the queue.

Draw an UML diagram for the class. Implement the class with the initial array size set to 8. The array size will be doubled once the number of the elements exceeds the size. After an element is removed from the beginning of the array, you need to shift all elements in the array one position the left. Write a test program that adds 20 numbers from 1 to 20 into the queue then removes these numbers and displays them.

*10.11 (*Geometry: the* `Circle2D` *class*) Define the `Circle2D` class that contains:

- Two `double` data fields named `x` and `y` that specify the center of the circle with getter methods.
- A data field `radius` with a getter method.
- A no-arg constructor that creates a default circle with (0, 0) for (x, y) and 1 for `radius`.
- A constructor that creates a circle with the specified `x`, `y`, and `radius`.
- A method `getArea()` that returns the area of the circle.
- A method `getPerimeter()` that returns the perimeter of the circle.
- A method `contains(double x, double y)` that returns `true` if the specified point (x, y) is inside this circle (see Figure 10.21a).
- A method `contains(Circle2D circle)` that returns `true` if the specified circle is inside this circle (see Figure 10.21b).
- A method `overlaps(Circle2D circle)` that returns `true` if the specified circle overlaps with this circle (see Figure 10.21c).

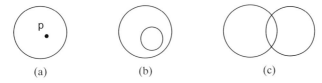

(a)	(b)	(c)

Figure 10.21 (a) A point is inside the circle. (b) A circle is inside another circle. (c) A circle overlaps another circle.

Draw the UML diagram for the class then implement the class. Write a test program that creates a `Circle2D` object c1 (`new Circle2D(2, 2, 5.5)`), displays its area and perimeter, and displays the result of `c1.contains(3, 3)`, `c1.contains(new Circle2D(4, 5, 10.5))`, and `c1.overlaps(new Circle2D(3, 5, 2.3))`.

***10.12 (*Geometry: the* `Triangle2D` *class*) Define the `Triangle2D` class that contains:

- Three points named `p1`, `p2`, and `p3` of the type `MyPoint` with getter and setter methods. `MyPoint` is defined in Programming Exercise 10.4.
- A no-arg constructor that creates a default triangle with the points (0, 0), (1, 1), and (2, 5).
- A constructor that creates a triangle with the specified points.
- A method `getArea()` that returns the area of the triangle.
- A method `getPerimeter()` that returns the perimeter of the triangle.
- A method `contains(MyPoint p)` that returns `true` if the specified point p is inside this triangle (see Figure 10.22a).

- A method `contains(Triangle2D t)` that returns `true` if the specified triangle is inside this triangle (see Figure 10.22b).
- A method `overlaps(Triangle2D t)` that returns `true` if the specified triangle overlaps with this triangle (see Figure 10.22c).

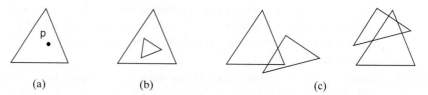

(a)   (b)   (c)

FIGURE 10.22 (a) A point is inside the triangle. (b) A triangle is inside another triangle. (c) A triangle overlaps another triangle.

Draw the UML diagram for the class and then implement the class. Write a test program that creates a `Triangle2D` object `t1` using the constructor `new Triangle2D(new MyPoint(2.5, 2), new MyPoint(4.2, 3), new MyPoint(5, 3.5))`, displays its area and perimeter, and displays the result of `t1.contains(3, 3)`, `r1.contains(new Triangle2D(new MyPoint(2.9, 2), new MyPoint(4, 1), MyPoint(1, 3.4)))`, and `t1.overlaps(new Triangle2D(new MyPoint(2, 5.5), new MyPoint(4, -3), MyPoint(2, 6.5)))`.

(*Hint:* For the formula to compute the area of a triangle, see Programming Exercise 2.19. To detect whether a point is inside a triangle, draw three dashed lines, as shown in Figure 10.23. If the point is inside a triangle, each dashed line should intersect a side only once. If a dashed line intersects a side twice, then the point must be outside the triangle. For the algorithm of finding the intersecting point of two lines, see Programming Exercise 3.25.)

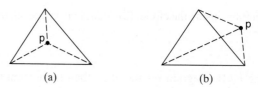

(a)   (b)

FIGURE 10.23 (a) A point is inside the triangle. (b) A point is outside the triangle.

*10.13 (*Geometry: the* `MyRectangle2D` *class*) Define the `MyRectangle2D` class that contains:

- Two `double` data fields named `x` and `y` that specify the center of the rectangle with getter and setter methods. (Assume the rectangle sides are parallel to `x`- or `y`-axis.)
- The data fields `width` and `height` with getter and setter methods.
- A no-arg constructor that creates a default rectangle with (0, 0) for (`x`, `y`) and 1 for both `width` and `height`.
- A constructor that creates a rectangle with the specified `x`, `y`, `width`, and `height`.

- A method `getArea()` that returns the area of the rectangle.
- A method `getPerimeter()` that returns the perimeter of the rectangle.
- A method `contains(double x, double y)` that returns `true` if the specified point (x, y) is inside this rectangle (see Figure 10.24a).
- A method `contains(MyRectangle2D r)` that returns `true` if the specified rectangle is inside this rectangle (see Figure 10.24b).
- A method `overlaps(MyRectangle2D r)` that returns `true` if the specified rectangle overlaps with this rectangle (see Figure 10.24c).

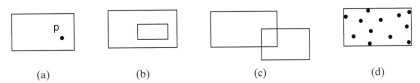

    (a)   (b)   (c)   (d)

FIGURE 10.24 A point is inside the rectangle. (b) A rectangle is inside another rectangle. (c) A rectangle overlaps another rectangle. (d) Points are enclosed inside a rectangle.

Draw the UML diagram for the class then implement the class. Write a test program that creates a `MyRectangle2D` object r1 (`new MyRectangle2D (2, 2, 5.5, 4.9)`), displays its area and perimeter, and displays the result of `r1.contains(3, 3)`, `r1.contains(new MyRectangle2D(4, 5, 10.5, 3.2))`, and `r1.overlaps(new MyRectangle2D(3, 5, 2.3, 5.4))`.

*10.14   (*The* `MyDate` *class*) Design a class named `MyDate`. The class contains:

- The data fields `year`, `month`, and `day` that represent a date. `month` is 0-based, i.e., `0` is for January.
- A no-arg constructor that creates a `MyDate` object for the current date.
- A constructor that constructs a `MyDate` object with a specified elapsed time since midnight, January 1, 1970, in milliseconds.
- A constructor that constructs a `MyDate` object with the specified year, month, and day.
- Three getter methods for the data fields `year`, `month`, and `day`, respectively.
- A method named `setDate(long elapsedTime)` that sets a new date for the object using the elapsed time.

Draw the UML diagram for the class then implement the class. Write a test program that creates two `MyDate` objects (using `new MyDate()` and `new MyDate(34355555133101L)`) and displays their year, month, and day.

(*Hint*: The first two constructors will extract the year, month, and day from the elapsed time. For example, if the elapsed time is `561555550000` milliseconds, the year is `1987`, the month is `9`, and the day is `18`. You may use the `GregorianCalendar` class discussed in Programming Exercise 9.5 to simplify coding.)

*10.15   (*Geometry: the bounding rectangle*) A bounding rectangle is the minimum rectangle that encloses a set of points in a two-dimensional plane, as shown in Figure 10.24d. Write a method that returns a bounding rectangle for a set of points in a two-dimensional plane, as follows:

```
public static MyRectangle2D getRectangle(double[][] points)
```

The `Rectangle2D` class is defined in Programming Exercise 10.13. Write a test program that prompts the user to enter five points and displays the bounding rectangle's center, width, and height. Here is a sample run:

```
Enter five points: 1.0 2.5 3 4 5 6 7 8 9 10  ⏎Enter
The bounding rectangle's center (5.0, 6.25), width 8.0, height 7.5
```

Section 10.9

*10.16 (*Divisible by 2 or 3*) Find the first 10 numbers with 50 decimal digits that are divisible by 2 or 3.

*10.17 (*Square numbers*) Find the first 10 square numbers that are greater than `Long.MAX_VALUE`. A square number is a number in the form of n^2. For example, 4, 9, and 16 are square numbers. Find an efficient approach to run your program fast.

*10.18 (*Large prime numbers*) Write a program that finds five prime numbers larger than `Long.MAX_VALUE`.

*10.19 (*Mersenne prime*) A prime number is called a *Mersenne prime* if it can be written in the form $2^p - 1$ for some positive integer p. Write a program that finds all Mersenne primes with $p \le 100$ and displays the output as shown below. (*Hint*: You have to use `BigInteger` to store the number because it is too big to be stored in `long`. Your program may take several hours to run.)

```
p            2^p - 1
--------------------
2            3
3            7
5            31
...
```

*10.20 (*Approximate e*) Programming Exercise 5.26 approximates *e* using the following series:

$$e = 1 + \frac{1}{1!} + \frac{1}{2!} + \frac{1}{3!} + \frac{1}{4!} + \cdots + \frac{1}{i!}$$

In order to get better precision, use `BigDecimal` with 25 digits of precision in the computation. Write a program that displays the e value for i = 100, 200, . . . , and 1000.

10.21 (*Divisible by 5 or 6*) Find the first 10 numbers greater than `Long.MAX_VALUE` that are divisible by 5 or 6.

Sections 10.10 and 10.11

**10.22 (*Implement the* `String` *class*) The `String` class is provided in the Java library. Provide your own implementation for the following methods (name the new class `MyString1`):

```
public MyString1(char[] chars);
public char charAt(int index);
public int length();
public MyString1 substring(int begin, int end);
public MyString1 toLowerCase();
public boolean equals(MyString1 s);
public static MyString1 valueOf(int i);
```

**10.23 (*Implement the* `String` *class*) The `String` class is provided in the Java library. Provide your own implementation for the following methods (name the new class `MyString2`):

```
public MyString2(String s);
public int compare(String s);
public MyString2 substring(int begin);
public MyString2 toUpperCase();
public char[] toChars();
public static MyString2 valueOf(boolean b);
```

10.24 (*Implement the* `Character` *class*) The `Character` class is provided in the Java library. Provide your own implementation for this class. Name the new class `MyCharacter`.

**10.25 (*New string* `split` *method*) The `split` method in the `String` class returns an array of strings consisting of the substrings split by the delimiters. However, the delimiters are not returned. Implement the following new method that returns an array of strings consisting of the substrings split by the matching delimiters, including the matching delimiters.

```
public static String[] split(String s, String regex)
```

For example, `split("ab#12#453", "#")` returns `ab`, `#`, `12`, `#`, and `453` in an array of `String` and `split("a?b?gf#e", "[?#]")` returns `a`, `?`, `b`, `?`, `gf`, `#`, and `e` in an array of `String`.

*10.26 (*Calculator*) Revise Listing 7.9, Calculator.java, to accept an expression as a string in which the operands and operator are separated by zero or more spaces. For example, `3+4` and `3 + 4` are acceptable expressions. Here is a sample run:

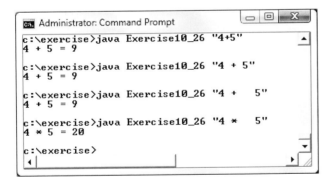

**10.27 (*Implement the* `StringBuilder` *class*) The `StringBuilder` class is provided in the Java library. Provide your own implementation for the following methods (name the new class `MyStringBuilder1`):

```
public MyStringBuilder1(String s);
public MyStringBuilder1 append(MyStringBuilder1 s);
public MyStringBuilder1 append(int i);
public int length();
public char charAt(int index);
public MyStringBuilder1 toLowerCase();
public MyStringBuilder1 substring(int begin, int end);
public String toString();
```

**10.28 (*Implement the StringBuilder class*) The StringBuilder class is provided
in the Java library. Provide your own implementation for the following methods
(name the new class MyStringBuilder2):

```
public MyStringBuilder2();
public MyStringBuilder2(char[] chars);
public MyStringBuilder2(String s);
public MyStringBuilder2 insert(int offset, MyStringBuilder2 s);
public MyStringBuilder2 reverse();
public MyStringBuilder2 substring(int begin);
public MyStringBuilder2 toUpperCase();
```

CHAPTER

11

INHERITANCE AND POLYMORPHISM

Objectives

■ To define a subclass from a superclass through inheritance (§11.2).

■ To invoke the superclass's constructors and methods using the `super` keyword (§11.3).

■ To override instance methods in the subclass (§11.4).

■ To distinguish differences between overriding and overloading (§11.5).

■ To explore the `toString()` method in the `Object` class (§11.6).

■ To discover polymorphism and dynamic binding (§§11.7 and 11.8).

■ To describe casting and explain why explicit downcasting is necessary (§11.9).

■ To explore the `equals` method in the `Object` class (§11.10).

■ To store, retrieve, and manipulate objects in an `ArrayList` (§11.11).

■ To construct an array list from an array, to sort and shuffle a list, and to obtain max and min element from a list (§11.12).

■ To implement a `Stack` class using `ArrayList` (§11.13).

■ To enable data and methods in a superclass accessible from subclasses using the `protected` visibility modifier (§11.14).

■ To prevent class extending and method overriding using the `final` modifier (§11.15).

11.1 Introduction

Object-oriented programming allows you to define new classes from existing classes. This is called inheritance.

inheritance

As discussed in the preceding chapter, the procedural paradigm focuses on designing methods, and the object-oriented paradigm couples data and methods together into objects. Software design using the object-oriented paradigm focuses on objects and operations on objects. The object-oriented approach combines the power of the procedural paradigm with an added dimension that integrates data with operations into objects.

why inheritance?

Inheritance is an important and powerful feature for reusing software. Suppose you need to define classes to model circles, rectangles, and triangles. These classes have many common features. What is the best way to design these classes so as to avoid redundancy and make the system easy to comprehend and easy to maintain? The answer is to use inheritance.

11.2 Superclasses and Subclasses

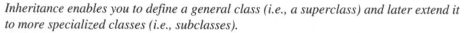

Inheritance enables you to define a general class (i.e., a superclass) and later extend it to more specialized classes (i.e., subclasses).

VideoNote

Geometric class hierarchy

You use a class to model objects of the same type. Different classes may have some common properties and behaviors, which can be generalized in a class that can be shared by other classes. You can define a specialized class that extends the generalized class. The specialized classes inherit the properties and methods from the general class.

Consider geometric objects. Suppose you want to design the classes to model geometric objects such as circles and rectangles. Geometric objects have many common properties and behaviors. They can be drawn in a certain color and be filled or unfilled. Thus, a general class `GeometricObject` can be used to model all geometric objects. This class contains the properties `color` and `filled` and their appropriate getter and setter methods. Assume this class also contains the `dateCreated` property, and the `getDateCreated()` and `toString()` methods. The `toString()` method returns a string representation of the object. Since a circle is a special type of geometric object, it shares common properties and methods with other geometric objects. Thus, it makes sense to define the `Circle` class that extends the `GeometricObject` class. Likewise, `Rectangle` can also be defined as a special type of `GeometricObject`. Figure 11.1 shows the relationship among these classes. A triangular arrow pointing to the generalized class is used to denote the inheritance relationship between the two classes involved.

subclass

superclass

In Java terminology, a class `C1` extended from another class `C2` is called a *subclass*, and `C2` is called a *superclass*. A superclass is also referred to as a *parent class* or a *base class*, and a subclass as a *child class*, an *extended class*, or a *derived class*. A subclass inherits accessible data fields and methods from its superclass and may also add new data fields and methods. Therefore, `Circle` and `Rectangle` are subclasses of `GeometricObject`, and `GeometricObject` is the superclass for `Circle` and `Rectangle`. A class defines a type. A type defined by a subclass is called a *subtype*, and a type defined by its superclass is called a *supertype*. Therefore, you can say that `Circle` is a subtype of `GeometricObject`, and `GeometricObject` is a supertype for `Circle`.

subtype

supertype

is-a relationship

The subclass and its superclass are said to form a *is-a* relationship. A `Circle` object is a special type of general `GeometricObject`. The `Circle` class inherits all accessible data fields and methods from the `GeometricObject` class. In addition, it has a new data field, `radius`, and its associated getter and setter methods. The `Circle` class also contains the `getArea()`, `getPerimeter()`, and `getDiameter()` methods for returning the area, perimeter, and diameter of the circle.

width and height

The `Rectangle` class inherits all accessible data fields and methods from the `GeometricObject` class. In addition, it has the data fields `width` and `height` and their associated getter and setter methods. It also contains the `getArea()` and `getPerimeter()`

GeometricObject	
−color: String	The color of the object (default: white).
−filled: boolean	Indicates whether the object is filled with a color (default: false).
−dateCreated: java.util.Date	The date when the object was created.
+GeometricObject()	Creates a GeometricObject.
+GeometricObject(color: String, filled: boolean)	Creates a GeometricObject with the specified color and filled values.
+getColor(): String	Returns the color.
+setColor(color: String): void	Sets a new color.
+isFilled(): boolean	Returns the filled property.
+setFilled(filled: boolean): void	Sets a new filled property.
+getDateCreated(): java.util.Date	Returns the dateCreated.
+toString(): String	Returns a string representation of this object.

Circle
−radius: double
+Circle()
+Circle(radius: double)
+Circle(radius: double, color: String, filled: boolean)
+getRadius(): double
+setRadius(radius: double): void
+getArea(): double
+getPerimeter(): double
+getDiameter(): double
+printCircle(): void

Rectangle
−width: double
−height: double
+Rectangle()
+Rectangle(width: double, height: double)
+Rectangle(width: double, height: double color: String, filled: boolean)
+getWidth(): double
+setWidth(width: double): void
+getHeight(): double
+setHeight(height: double): void
+getArea(): double
+getPerimeter(): double

FIGURE 11.1 The GeometricObject class is the superclass for Circle and Rectangle.

methods for returning the area and perimeter of the rectangle. Note that you may have used the terms width and length to describe the sides of a rectangle in geometry. The common terms used in computer science are width and height, where width refers to the horizontal length, and height to the vertical length.

The GeometricObject, Circle, and Rectangle classes are shown in Listings 11.1, 11.2, and 11.3, respectively.

LISTING 11.1   GeometricObject.java

```
1  public class GeometricObject {
2    private String color = "white";                          data fields
3    private boolean filled;
4    private java.util.Date dateCreated;
5
6    /** Construct a default geometric object */
7    public GeometricObject() {                                constructor
8      dateCreated = new java.util.Date();                     date constructed
9    }
10
```

```
11    /** Construct a geometric object with the specified color
12     *   and filled value */
13    public GeometricObject(String color, boolean filled) {
14      dateCreated = new java.util.Date();
15      this.color = color;
16      this.filled = filled;
17    }
18
19    /** Return color */
20    public String getColor() {
21      return color;
22    }
23
24    /** Set a new color */
25    public void setColor(String color) {
26      this.color = color;
27    }
28
29    /** Return filled. Since filled is boolean,
30       its getter method is named isFilled */
31    public boolean isFilled() {
32      return filled;
33    }
34
35    /** Set a new filled */
36    public void setFilled(boolean filled) {
37      this.filled = filled;
38    }
39
40    /** Get dateCreated */
41    public java.util.Date getDateCreated() {
42      return dateCreated;
43    }
44
45    /** Return a string representation of this object */
46    public String toString() {
47      return "created on " + dateCreated + "\ncolor: " + color +
48        " and filled: " + filled;
49    }
50  }
```

LISTING 11.2 Circle.java

extends superclass
data fields

constructor

```
1   public class Circle extends GeometricObject {
2     private double radius;
3
4     public Circle() {
5     }
6
7     public Circle(double radius) {
8       this.radius = radius;
9     }
10
11    public Circle(double radius,
12        String color, boolean filled) {
13      this.radius = radius;
14      setColor(color);
15      setFilled(filled);
16    }
17
```

```
18      /** Return radius */
19      public double getRadius() {
20        return radius;
21      }
22
23      /** Set a new radius */
24      public void setRadius(double radius) {
25        this.radius = radius;
26      }
27
28      /** Return area */
29      public double getArea() {
30        return radius * radius * Math.PI;
31      }
32
33      /** Return diameter */
34      public double getDiameter() {
35        return 2 * radius;
36      }
37
38      /** Return perimeter */
39      public double getPerimeter() {
40        return 2 * radius * Math.PI;
41      }
42
43      /** Print the circle info */
44      public void printCircle() {
45        System.out.println("The circle is created " + getDateCreated() +
46          " and the radius is " + radius);
47      }
48    }
```

methods

The `Circle` class (Listing 11.2) extends the `GeometricObject` class (Listing 11.1) using the following syntax:

The keyword `extends` (lines 1 and 2) tells the compiler that the `Circle` class extends the `GeometricObject` class, thus inheriting the methods `getColor`, `setColor`, `isFilled`, `setFilled`, and `toString`.

The overloaded constructor `Circle(double radius, String color, boolean filled)` is implemented by invoking the `setColor` and `setFilled` methods to set the `color` and `filled` properties (lines 14 and 15). The public methods defined in the superclass `GeometricObject` are inherited in `Circle`, so they can be used in the `Circle` class.

You might attempt to use the data fields `color` and `filled` directly in the constructor as follows:

```
public Circle(double radius, String color, boolean filled) {
  this.radius = radius;
  this.color = color; // Illegal
  this.filled = filled; // Illegal
}
```

private member in superclass

This is wrong because the private data fields `color` and `filled` in the `GeometricObject` class cannot be accessed in any class other than in the `GeometricObject` class itself. The only way to read and modify `color` and `filled` is through their getter and setter methods.

The `Rectangle` class (Listing 11.3) extends the `GeometricObject` class (Listing 11.1) using the following syntax:

Subclass   Superclass

public class Rectangle **extends** GeometricObject

The keyword `extends` (lines 1 and 2) tells the compiler the `Rectangle` class extends the `GeometricObject` class, thus inheriting the methods `getColor`, `setColor`, `isFilled`, `setFilled`, and `toString`.

LISTING 11.3   Rectangle.java

```
1  public class Rectangle extends GeometricObject {
2    private double width;
3    private double height;
4
5    public Rectangle() {
6    }
7
8    public Rectangle(double width, double height) {
9      this.width = width;
10     this.height = height;
11   }
12
13   public Rectangle(
14       double width, double height, String color, boolean filled) {
15     this.width = width;
16     this.height = height;
17     setColor(color);
18     setFilled(filled);
19   }
20
21   /** Return width */
22   public double getWidth() {
23     return width;
24   }
25
26   /** Set a new width */
27   public void setWidth(double width) {
28     this.width = width;
29   }
30
31   /** Return height */
32   public double getHeight() {
33     return height;
34   }
35
36   /** Set a new height */
37   public void setHeight(double height) {
38     this.height = height;
39   }
40
```

extends superclass

data fields

constructor

methods

```
41    /** Return area */
42    public double getArea() {
43      return width * height;
44    }
45
46    /** Return perimeter */
47    public double getPerimeter() {
48      return 2 * (width + height);
49    }
50  }
```

The code in Listing 11.4 creates objects of `Circle` and `Rectangle` and invokes the methods on these objects. The `toString()` method is inherited from the `GeometricObject` class and is invoked from a `Circle` object (line 4) and a `Rectangle` object (line 11).

LISTING 11.4 TestCircleRectangle.java

```
1   public class TestCircleRectangle {
2     public static void main(String[] args) {
3       Circle circle = new Circle(1);                                    Circle object
4       System.out.println("A circle " + circle.toString());             invoke toString
5       System.out.println("The color is " + circle.getColor());         invoke getColor
6       System.out.println("The radius is " + circle.getRadius());
7       System.out.println("The area is " + circle.getArea());
8       System.out.println("The diameter is " + circle.getDiameter());
9
10      Rectangle rectangle = new Rectangle(2, 4);                        Rectangle object
11      System.out.println("\nA rectangle " + rectangle.toString());      invoke toString
12      System.out.println("The area is " + rectangle.getArea());
13      System.out.println("The perimeter is " +
14        rectangle.getPerimeter());
15    }
16  }
```

```
A circle created on Thu Feb 10 19:54:25 EST 2011
color: white and filled: false
The color is white
The radius is 1.0
The area is 3.141592653589793
The diameter is 2.0
A rectangle created on Thu Feb 10 19:54:25 EST 2011
color: white and filled: false
The area is 8.0
The perimeter is 12.0
```

Note the following points regarding inheritance:

- Contrary to the conventional interpretation, a subclass is not a subset of its superclass. In fact, a subclass usually contains more information and methods than its superclass.   *more in subclass*

- Private data fields in a superclass are not accessible outside the class. Therefore, they cannot be used directly in a subclass. They can, however, be accessed/mutated through public accessors/mutators if defined in the superclass.   *private data fields*

nonextensible is-a

■ Not all is-a relationships should be modeled using inheritance. For example, a square is a rectangle, but you should not extend a `Square` class from a `Rectangle` class, because the `width` and `height` properties are not appropriate for a square. Instead, you should define a `Square` class to extend the `GeometricObject` class and define the `side` property for the side of a square.

no blind extension

■ Inheritance is used to model the is-a relationship. Do not blindly extend a class just for the sake of reusing methods. For example, it makes no sense for a `Tree` class to extend a `Person` class, even though they share common properties such as `height` and `weight`. A subclass and its superclass must have the is-a relationship.

multiple inheritance

single inheritance

■ Some programming languages allow you to derive a subclass from several classes. This capability is known as *multiple inheritance*. Java, however, does not allow multiple inheritance. A Java class may inherit directly from only one superclass. This restriction is known as *single inheritance*. If you use the `extends` keyword to define a subclass, it allows only one parent class. Nevertheless, multiple inheritance can be achieved through interfaces, which will be introduced in Section 13.5.

11.2.1 True or false? A subclass is a subset of a superclass.

11.2.2 What keyword do you use to define a subclass?

11.2.3 What is single inheritance? What is multiple inheritance? Does Java support multiple inheritance?

11.3 Using the `super` Keyword

The keyword `super` *refers to the superclass and can be used to invoke the superclass's methods and constructors.*

A subclass inherits accessible data fields and methods from its superclass. Does it inherit constructors? Can the superclass's constructors be invoked from a subclass? This section addresses these questions and their ramifications.

Section 9.14, The `this` Reference, introduced the use of the keyword `this` to reference the calling object. The keyword `super` refers to the superclass of the class in which `super` appears. It can be used in two ways:

1. To call a superclass constructor

2. To call a superclass method

11.3.1 Calling Superclass Constructors

A constructor is used to construct an instance of a class. Unlike properties and methods, the constructors of a superclass are not inherited by a subclass. They can only be invoked from the constructors of the subclasses using the keyword `super`.

The syntax to call a superclass's constructor is:

super() or **super**(arguments);

The statement `super()` invokes the no-arg constructor of its superclass, and the statement `super(arguments)` invokes the superclass constructor that matches the `arguments`. The statement `super()` or `super(arguments)` must be the first statement of the subclass's constructor; this is the only way to explicitly invoke a superclass constructor. For example, the constructor in lines 11–16 in Listing 11.2 can be replaced by the following code:

```java
public Circle(double radius, String color, boolean filled) {
  super(color, filled);
  this.radius = radius;
}
```

Caution

You must use the keyword super to call the superclass constructor, and the call must be the first statement in the constructor. Invoking a superclass constructor's name in a subclass causes a syntax error.

11.3.2 Constructor Chaining

A constructor may invoke an overloaded constructor or its superclass constructor. If neither is invoked explicitly, the compiler automatically puts super() as the first statement in the constructor. For example:

```
public ClassName() {
  // some statements
}
```

Equivalent

```
public ClassName() {
  super();
  // some statements
}
```

```
public ClassName(parameters) {
  // some statements
}
```

Equivalent

```
public ClassName(parameters) {
  super();
  // some statements
}
```

In any case, constructing an instance of a class invokes the constructors of all the super-classes along the inheritance chain. When constructing an object of a subclass, the subclass constructor first invokes its superclass constructor before performing its own tasks. If the superclass is derived from another class, the superclass constructor invokes its parent-class constructor before performing its own tasks. This process continues until the last constructor along the inheritance hierarchy is called. This is called *constructor chaining.*

constructor chaining

Consider the following code:

```
1   public class Faculty extends Employee {
2     public static void main(String[] args) {
3       new Faculty();
4     }
5
6     public Faculty() {
7       System.out.println("(4) Performs Faculty's tasks");
8     }
9   }
10
11  class Employee extends Person {
12    public Employee() {
13      this("(2) Invoke Employee's overloaded constructor");
14      System.out.println("(3) Performs Employee's tasks ");
15    }
16
17    public Employee(String s) {
18      System.out.println(s);
19    }
20  }
21
22  class Person {
23    public Person() {
24      System.out.println("(1) Performs Person's tasks");
25    }
26  }
```

invoke overloaded constructor

```
(1) Performs Person's tasks
(2) Invoke Employee's overloaded constructor
(3) Performs Employee's tasks
(4) Performs Faculty's tasks
```

The program produces the preceding output. Why? Let us discuss the reason. In line 3, new Faculty() invokes Faculty's no-arg constructor. Since Faculty is a subclass of Employee, Employee's no-arg constructor is invoked before any statements in Faculty's constructor are executed. Employee's no-arg constructor invokes Employee's second constructor (line 13). Since Employee is a subclass of Person, Person's no-arg constructor is invoked before any statements in Employee's second constructor are executed. This process is illustrated in the following figure.

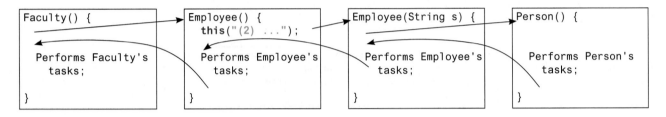

no-arg constructor

 Caution

If a class is designed to be extended, it is better to provide a no-arg constructor to avoid programming errors. Consider the following code:

```
1  public class Apple extends Fruit {
2  }
3
4  class Fruit {
5    public Fruit(String name) {
6      System.out.println("Fruit's constructor is invoked");
7    }
8  }
```

Since no constructor is explicitly defined in Apple, Apple's default no-arg constructor is defined implicitly. Since Apple is a subclass of Fruit, Apple's default constructor automatically invokes Fruit's no-arg constructor. However, Fruit does not have a no-arg constructor, because Fruit has an explicit constructor defined. Therefore, the program cannot be compiled.

no-arg constructor

 Design Guide

If possible, you should provide a no-arg constructor for every class to make the class easy to extend and to avoid errors.

11.3.3 Calling Superclass Methods

The keyword super can also be used to reference a method other than the constructor in the superclass. The syntax is

```
super.method(arguments);
```

You could rewrite the printCircle() method in the Circle class as follows:

```
public void printCircle() {
  System.out.println("The circle is created " +
    super.getDateCreated() + " and the radius is " + radius);
}
```

It is not necessary to put `super` before `getDateCreated()` in this case, however, because `getDateCreated` is a method in the `GeometricObject` class and is inherited by the `Circle` class. Nevertheless, in some cases, as shown in the next section, the keyword `super` is needed.

11.3.1 What is the output of running the class `C` in (a)? What problem arises in compiling the program in (b)?

Check
Point

```
class A {
  public A() {
    System.out.println(
      "A's no-arg constructor is invoked");
  }
}

class B extends A {
}

public class C {
  public static void main(String[] args) {
    B b = new B();
  }
}
```
(a)

```
class A {
  public A(int x) {
  }
}

class B extends A {
  public B() {
  }
}

public class C {
  public static void main(String[] args) {
    B b = new B();
  }
}
```
(b)

11.3.2 How does a subclass invoke its superclass's constructor?

11.3.3 True or false? When invoking a constructor from a subclass, its superclass's no-arg constructor is always invoked.

11.4 Overriding Methods

To override a method, the method must be defined in the subclass using the same signature as in its superclass.

Key
Point

A subclass inherits methods from a superclass. Sometimes, it is necessary for the subclass to modify the implementation of a method defined in the superclass. This is referred to as *method overriding*.

method overriding

The `toString` method in the `GeometricObject` class (lines 46–49 in Listing 11.1) returns the string representation of a geometric object. This method can be overridden to return the string representation of a circle. To override it, add the following new method in the `Circle` class in Listing 11.2:

```
1  public class Circle extends GeometricObject {
2    // Other methods are omitted
3
4    // Override the toString method defined in the superclass
5    public String toString() {
6      return super.toString() + "\nradius is " + radius;
7    }
8  }
```

toString in superclass

The `toString()` method is defined in the `GeometricObject` class and modified in the `Circle` class. Both methods can be used in the `Circle` class. To invoke the `toString` method defined in the `GeometricObject` class from the `Circle` class, use `super.toString()` (line 6).

no super.super.methodName()

override accessible instance
method

cannot override static method

Can a subclass of `Circle` access the `toString` method defined in the `GeometricObject` class using syntax such as `super.super.toString()`? No. This is a syntax error.

Several points are worth noting:

- The overriding method must have the same signature as the overridden method and same or compatible return type. Compatible means that the overriding method's return type is a subtype of the overridden method's return type.

- An instance method can be overridden only if it is accessible. Thus, a private method cannot be overridden, because it is not accessible outside its own class. If a method defined in a subclass is private in its superclass, the two methods are completely unrelated.

- Like an instance method, a static method can be inherited. However, a static method cannot be overridden. If a static method defined in the superclass is redefined in a subclass, the method defined in the superclass is hidden. The hidden static methods can be invoked using the syntax `SuperClassName.staticMethodName`.

11.4.1 True or false? You can override a private method defined in a superclass.

11.4.2 True or false? You can override a static method defined in a superclass.

11.4.3 How do you explicitly invoke a superclass's constructor from a subclass?

11.4.4 How do you invoke an overridden superclass method from a subclass?

11.5 Overriding vs. Overloading

Overloading means to define multiple methods with the same name but different signatures. Overriding means to provide a new implementation for a method in the subclass.

You learned about overloading methods in Section 6.8. To override a method, the method must be defined in the subclass using the same signature and the same or compatible return type.

Let us use an example to show the differences between overriding and overloading. In (a) below, the method `p(double i)` in class `A` overrides the same method defined in class `B`. In (b), however, the class `A` has two overloaded methods: `p(double i)` and `p(int i)`. The method `p(double i)` is inherited from `B`.

```
public class TestOverriding {
  public static void main(String[] args) {
    A a = new A();
    a.p(10);
    a.p(10.0);
  }
}

class B {
  public void p(double i) {
    System.out.println(i * 2);
  }
}

class A extends B {
  // This method overrides the method in B
  public void p(double i) {
    System.out.println(i);
  }
}
```

(a)

```
public class TestOverloading {
  public static void main(String[] args) {
    A a = new A();
    a.p(10);
    a.p(10.0);
  }
}

class B {
  public void p(double i) {
    System.out.println(i * 2);
  }
}

class A extends B {
  // This method overloads the method in B
  public void p(int i) {
    System.out.println(i);
  }
}
```

(b)

When you run the `TestOverriding` class in (a), both `a.p(10)` and `a.p(10.0)` invoke the `p(double i)` method defined in class A to display `10.0`. When you run the `TestOverloading` class in (b), `a.p(10)` invokes the `p(int i)` method defined in class A to display `10` and `a.p(10.0)` invokes the `p(double i)` method defined in class B to display `20.0`.

Note the following:

- Overridden methods are in different classes related by inheritance; overloaded methods can be either in the same class, or in different classes related by inheritance.

- Overridden methods have the same signature; overloaded methods have the same name but different parameter lists.

To avoid mistakes, you can use a special Java syntax, called *override annotation*, to place `@Override` before the overriding method in the subclass. For example,

override annotation

```
1  public class Circle extends GeometricObject {
2    // Other methods are omitted
3
4    @Override
5    public String toString() {
6      return super.toString() + "\nradius is " + radius;
7    }
8  }
```

toString in superclass

This annotation denotes that the annotated method is required to override a method in its superclass. If a method with this annotation does not override its superclass's method, the compiler will report an error. For example, if `toString` is mistyped as `tostring`, a compile error is reported. If the `@Override` annotation isn't used, the compiler won't report an error. Using the `@Override` annotation avoids mistakes.

11.5.1 Identify the problems in the following code:

Check Point

```
1  public class Circle {
2    private double radius;
3
4    public Circle(double radius) {
5      radius = radius;
6    }
7
8    public double getRadius() {
9      return radius;
10   }
11
12   public double getArea() {
13     return radius * radius * Math.PI;
14   }
15 }
16
17 class B extends Circle {
18   private double length;
19
20   B(double radius, double length) {
21     Circle(radius);
22     length = length;
23   }
24
25   @Override
26   public double getArea() {
27     return getArea() * length;
28   }
29 }
```

11.5.2 Explain the difference between method overloading and method overriding.

11.5.3 If a method in a subclass has the same signature as a method in its superclass with the same return type, is the method overridden or overloaded?

11.5.4 If a method in a subclass has the same signature as a method in its superclass with a different return type, will this be a problem?

11.5.5 If a method in a subclass has the same name as a method in its superclass with different parameter types, is the method overridden or overloaded?

11.5.6 What is the benefit of using the @Override annotation?

11.6 The Object Class and Its toString() Method

Key Point

Every class in Java is descended from the java.lang.Object class.

If no inheritance is specified when a class is defined, the superclass of the class is Object by default. For example, the following two class definitions are the same:

```public class ClassName { . . . }```	```public class ClassName extends Object { . . . }```

Equivalent

Classes such as String, StringBuilder, Loan, and GeometricObject are implicitly subclasses of Object (as are all the main classes you have seen in this book so far). It is important to be familiar with the methods provided by the Object class so that you can use them in your classes. This section introduces the toString method in the Object class.

toString()

The signature of the toString() method is:

```
public String toString()
```

string representation

Invoking toString() on an object returns a string that describes the object. By default, it returns a string consisting of a class name of which the object is an instance, an at sign (@), and the object's memory address in hexadecimal. For example, consider the following code for the Loan class defined in Listing 10.2:

```
Loan loan = new Loan();
System.out.println(loan.toString());
```

The output for this code displays something like Loan@15037e5. This message is not very helpful or informative. Usually you should override the toString method so that it returns a descriptive string representation of the object. For example, the toString method in the Object class was overridden in the GeometricObject class in lines 46–49 in Listing 11.1 as follows:

```
public String toString() {
  return "created on " + dateCreated + "\ncolor: " + color +
    " and filled: " + filled;
}
```

print object

 Note
You can also pass an object to invoke System.out.println(object) or System.out.print(object). This is equivalent to invoking System.out.println(object.toString()) or System.out.print(object.toString()). Thus, you could replace System.out.println(loan.toString()) with System.out.println(loan).

11.7 Polymorphism

Polymorphism means that a variable of a supertype can refer to a subtype object.

The three pillars of object-oriented programming are encapsulation, inheritance, and polymorphism. You have already learned the first two. This section introduces polymorphism.

The inheritance relationship enables a subclass to inherit features from its superclass with additional new features. A subclass is a specialization of its superclass; every instance of a subclass is also an instance of its superclass, but not vice versa. For example, every circle is a geometric object, but not every geometric object is a circle. Therefore, you can always pass an instance of a subclass to a parameter of its superclass type. Consider the code in Listing 11.5.

LISTING 11.5 `PolymorphismDemo.java`

```
1   public class PolymorphismDemo {
2     /** Main method */
3     public static void main(String[] args) {
4       // Display circle and rectangle properties
5       displayObject(new Circle(1, "red", false));
6       displayObject(new Rectangle(1, 1, "black", true));
7     }
8
9     /** Display geometric object properties */
10    public static void displayObject(GeometricObject object) {
11      System.out.println("Created on " + object.getDateCreated() +
12        ". Color is " + object.getColor());
13    }
14  }
```

polymorphic call
polymorphic call

```
Created on Mon Mar 09 19:25:20 EDT 2011. Color is white
Created on Mon Mar 09 19:25:20 EDT 2011. Color is black
```

The method `displayObject` (line 10) takes a parameter of the `GeometricObject` type. You can invoke `displayObject` by passing any instance of `GeometricObject` (e.g., `new Circle(1, "red", false)` and `new Rectangle(1, 1, "black", false)` in lines 5 and 6). An object of a subclass can be used wherever its superclass object is used. This is commonly known as *polymorphism* (from a Greek word meaning "many forms"). In simple terms, polymorphism means that a variable of a supertype can refer to a subtype object.

what is polymorphism?

11.7.1 What are the three pillars of object-oriented programming? What is polymorphism?

11.8 Dynamic Binding

A method can be implemented in several classes along the inheritance chain. The JVM decides which method is invoked at runtime.

A method can be defined in a superclass and overridden in its subclass. For example, the `toString()` method is defined in the `Object` class and overridden in `GeometricObject`. Consider the following code:

```
Object o = new GeometricObject();
System.out.println(o.toString());
```

declared type

actual type

dynamic binding

Which `toString()` method is invoked by o? To answer this question, we first introduce two terms: declared type and actual type. A variable must be declared a type. The type that declares a variable is called the variable's *declared type*. Here, o's declared type is `Object`. A variable of a reference type can hold a `null` value or a reference to an instance of the declared type. The instance may be created using the constructor of the declared type or its subtype. The *actual type* of the variable is the actual class for the object referenced by the variable. Here, o's actual type is `GeometricObject`, because o references an object created using `new GeometricObject()`. Which `toString()` method is invoked by o is determined by o's actual type. This is known as *dynamic binding*.

Dynamic binding works as follows: Suppose that an object o is an instance of classes C_1, $C_2, \ldots, C_{n-1}$, and C_n, where C_1 is a subclass of C_2, C_2 is a subclass of $C_3, \ldots$, and C_{n-1} is a subclass of C_n, as shown in Figure 11.2. That is, C_n is the most general class, and C_1 is the most specific class. In Java, C_n is the `Object` class. If o invokes a method p, the JVM searches for the implementation of the method p in C_1, $C_2, \ldots, C_{n-1}$, and C_n, in this order, until it is found. Once an implementation is found, the search stops and the first-found implementation is invoked.

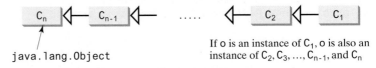

java.lang.Object

If o is an instance of C_1, o is also an instance of $C_2, C_3, \ldots, C_{n-1}$, and C_n.

FIGURE 11.2 The method to be invoked is dynamically bound at runtime.

VideoNote

Polymorphism and dynamic binding demo

polymorphic call

dynamic binding

override toString()

override toString()

Listing 11.6 gives an example to demonstrate dynamic binding.

LISTING 11.6 `DynamicBindingDemo.java`

```java
1  public class DynamicBindingDemo {
2    public static void main(String[] args) {
3      m(new GraduateStudent());
4      m(new Student());
5      m(new Person());
6      m(new Object());
7    }
8
9    public static void m(Object x) {
10     System.out.println(x.toString());
11   }
12 }
13
14 class GraduateStudent extends Student {
15 }
16
17 class Student extends Person {
18   @Override
19   public String toString() {
20     return "Student";
21   }
22 }
23
24 class Person extends Object {
25   @Override
```

```
26    public String toString() {
27      return "Person";
28    }
29  }
```

```
Student
Student
Person
java.lang.Object@130c19b
```

Method m (line 9) takes a parameter of the Object type. You can invoke m with any object (e.g., new GraduateStudent(), new Student(), new Person(), and new Object()) in lines 3–6).

When the method m(Object x) is executed, the argument x's toString method is invoked. x may be an instance of GraduateStudent, Student, Person, or Object. The toString method is implemented in Student, Person, and Object. Which implementation is used will be determined by x's actual type at runtime. Invoking m(new GraduateStudent()) (line 3) causes the toString method defined in the Student class to be invoked.

Invoking m(new Student()) (line 4) causes the toString method defined in the Student class to be invoked; invoking m(new Person()) (line 5) causes the toString method defined in the Person class to be invoked; and invoking m(new Object()) (line 6) causes the toString method defined in the Object class to be invoked.

Matching a method signature and binding a method implementation are two separate issues. The *declared type* of the reference variable decides which method to match at compile time. The compiler finds a matching method according to the parameter type, number of parameters, and order of the parameters at compile time. A method may be implemented in several classes along the inheritance chain. The JVM dynamically binds the implementation of the method at runtime, decided by the actual type of the variable.

matching vs. binding

11.8.1 What is polymorphism? What is dynamic binding?

11.8.2 Describe the difference between method matching and method binding.

11.8.3 Can you assign new int[50], new Integer[50], new String[50], or new Object[50] into a variable of Object[] type?

11.8.4 What is wrong in the following code?

```
1   public class Test {
2     public static void main(String[] args) {
3       Integer[] list1 = {12, 24, 55, 1};
4       Double[] list2 = {12.4, 24.0, 55.2, 1.0};
5       int[] list3 = {1, 2, 3};
6       printArray(list1);
7       printArray(list2);
8       printArray(list3);
9     }
10
11    public static void printArray(Object[] list) {
12      for (Object o: list)
13        System.out.print(o + " ");
14      System.out.println();
15    }
16  }
```

11.8.5 Show the output of the following code:

```
public class Test {
  public static void main(String[] args) {
    new Person().printPerson();
    new Student().printPerson();
  }
}

class Student extends Person {
  @Override
  public String getInfo() {
    return "Student";
  }
}

class Person {
  public String getInfo() {
    return "Person";
  }

  public void printPerson() {
    System.out.println(getInfo());
  }
}
```

(a)

```
public class Test {
  public static void main(String[] args) {
    new Person().printPerson();
    new Student().printPerson();
  }
}

class Student extends Person {
  private String getInfo() {
    return "Student";
  }
}

class Person {
  private String getInfo() {
    return "Person";
  }

  public void printPerson() {
    System.out.println(getInfo());
  }
}
```

(b)

11.8.6 Show the output of following program:

```
1   public class Test {
2     public static void main(String[] args) {
3       A a = new A(3);
4     }
5   }
6
7   class A extends B {
8     public A(int t) {
9       System.out.println("A's constructor is invoked");
10    }
11  }
12
13  class B {
14    public B() {
15      System.out.println("B's constructor is invoked");
16    }
17  }
```

Is the no-arg constructor of `Object` invoked when `new A(3)` is invoked?

11.8.7 Show the output of following program:

```
public class Test {
  public static void main(String[] args) {
    new A();
    new B();
  }
}
```

```
class A {
  int i = 7;

  public A() {
    setI(20);
    System.out.println("i from A is " + i);
  }

  public void setI(int i) {
    this.i = 2 * i;
  }
}

class B extends A {
  public B() {
    System.out.println("i from B is " + i);
  }

  public void setI(int i) {
    this.i = 3 * i;
  }
}
```

11.9 Casting Objects and the `instanceof` Operator

One object reference can be typecast into another object reference. This is called casting object.

In the preceding section, the statement

```
m(new Student());
```

assigns the object `new Student()` to a parameter of the `Object` type. This statement is equivalent to

```
Object o = new Student(); // Implicit casting
m(o);
```

The statement `Object o = new Student()`, known as *implicit casting*, is legal because an instance of `Student` is an instance of `Object`.

Suppose you want to assign the object reference o to a variable of the `Student` type using the following statement:

```
Student b = o;
```

In this case a compile error would occur. Why does the statement `Object o = new Student()` work, but `Student b = o` doesn't? The reason is that a `Student` object is always an instance of `Object`, but an `Object` is not necessarily an instance of `Student`. Even though you can see that o is really a `Student` object, the compiler is not clever enough to know it. To tell the compiler o is a `Student` object, use *explicit casting*. The syntax is similar to the one used for casting among primitive data types. Enclose the target object type in parentheses and place it before the object to be cast, as follows:

```
Student b = (Student)o; // Explicit casting
```

It is always possible to cast an instance of a subclass to a variable of a superclass (known as *upcasting*) because an instance of a subclass is *always* an instance of its superclass. When casting an instance of a superclass to a variable of its subclass (known as *downcasting*), explicit casting must be used to confirm your intention to the compiler with the (SubclassName) cast notation. For the casting to be successful, you must make sure the object to be cast is an instance of the subclass. If the superclass object is not an instance of the subclass, a runtime *ClassCastException* occurs. For example, if an object is not an instance of Student, it cannot be cast into a variable of Student. It is a good practice, therefore, to ensure the object is an instance of another object before attempting a casting. This can be accomplished by using the *instanceof* operator. Consider the following code:

```
void someMethod(Object myObjet) {
  ... // Some lines of code
  /** Perform casting if myObject is an instance of Circle */
  if (myObject instanceof Circle) {
    System.out.println("The circle diameter is " +
      ((Circle)myObject).getDiameter());
    ...
  }
}
```

You may be wondering why casting is necessary. The variable myObject is declared Object. The *declared type* decides which method to match at compile time. Using myObject.getDiameter() would cause a compile error, because the Object class does not have the getDiameter method. The compiler cannot find a match for myObject.getDiameter(). Therefore, it is necessary to cast myObject into the Circle type to tell the compiler that myObject is also an instance of Circle.

Why not declare myObject as a Circle type in the first place? To enable generic programming, it is a good practice to declare a variable with a supertype that can accept an object of any subtype.

> **Note**
>
> instanceof is a Java keyword. Every letter in a Java keyword is in lowercase.

> **Tip**
>
> To help understand casting, you may also consider the analogy of fruit, apple, and orange, with the Fruit class as the superclass for Apple and Orange. An apple is a fruit, so you can always safely assign an instance of Apple to a variable for Fruit. However, a fruit is not necessarily an apple, so you have to use explicit casting to assign an instance of Fruit to a variable of Apple.

Listing 11.7 demonstrates polymorphism and casting. The program creates two objects (lines 5 and 6), a circle and a rectangle, and invokes the displayObject method to display them (lines 9 and 10). The displayObject method displays the area and diameter if the object is a circle (line 15), and the area if the object is a rectangle (line 21).

LISTING 11.7 CastingDemo.java

```
 1  public class CastingDemo {
 2    /** Main method */
 3    public static void main(String[] args) {
 4      // Create and initialize two objects
 5      Object object1 = new Circle(1);
 6      Object object2 = new Rectangle(1, 1);
 7
 8      // Display circle and rectangle
 9      displayObject(object1);
10      displayObject(object2);
11    }
12
```

```
13    /** A method for displaying an object */
14    public static void displayObject(Object object) {
15      if (object instanceof Circle) {
16        System.out.println("The circle area is " +
17          ((Circle)object).getArea());                            polymorphic call
18        System.out.println("The circle diameter is " +
19          ((Circle)object).getDiameter());
20      }
21      else if (object instanceof Rectangle) {
22        System.out.println("The rectangle area is " +
23          ((Rectangle)object).getArea());                         polymorphic call
24      }
25    }
26  }
```

```
The circle area is 3.141592653589793
The circle diameter is 2.0
The rectangle area is 1.0
```

The `displayObject(Object object)` method is an example of generic programming. It can be invoked by passing any instance of `Object`.

The program uses implicit casting to assign a `Circle` object to `object1` and a `Rectangle` object to `object2` (lines 5 and 6), then invokes the `displayObject` method to display the information on these objects (lines 9–10).

In the `displayObject` method (lines 14–25), explicit casting is used to cast the object to `Circle` if the object is an instance of `Circle`, and the methods `getArea` and `getDiameter` are used to display the area and diameter of the circle.

Casting can be done only when the source object is an instance of the target class. The program uses the `instanceof` operator to ensure that the source object is an instance of the target class before performing a casting (line 15).

Explicit casting to `Circle` (lines 17 and 19) and to `Rectangle` (line 23) is necessary because the `getArea` and `getDiameter` methods are not available in the `Object` class.

> ⚠ **Caution**
> The object member access operator (.) precedes the casting operator. Use parentheses   precedes casting
> to ensure that casting is done before the . operator, as in
>
> ```
>               ((Circle)object).getArea();
> ```

Casting a primitive-type value is different from casting an object reference. Casting a primitive-type value returns a new value. For example:

```
int age = 45;
byte newAge = (byte)age; // A new value is assigned to newAge
```

However, casting an object reference does not create a new object. For example:

```
Object o = new Circle();
Circle c = (Circle)o; // No new object is created
```

Now, reference variables `o` and `c` point to the same object.

11.9.1 Indicate true or false for the following statements:

a. You can always successfully cast an instance of a subclass to a superclass.

b. You can always successfully cast an instance of a superclass to a subclass.

11.9.2 For the `GeometricObject` and `Circle` classes in Listings 11.1 and 11.2, answer the following questions:

a. Assume that `circle` and `object1` are created as follows:

```
Circle circle = new Circle(1);
GeometricObject object1 = new GeometricObject();
```

Are the following Boolean expressions true or false?
```
(circle instanceof GeometricObject)
(object instanceof GeometricObject)
(circle instanceof Circle)
(object instanceof Circle)
```

b. Can the following statements be compiled?
```
Circle circle = new Circle(5);
GeometricObject object = circle;
```

c. Can the following statements be compiled?
```
GeometricObject object = new GeometricObject();
Circle circle = (Circle)object;
```

11.9.3 Suppose `Fruit`, `Apple`, `Orange`, `GoldenDelicious`, and `McIntosh` are defined in the following inheritance hierarchy:

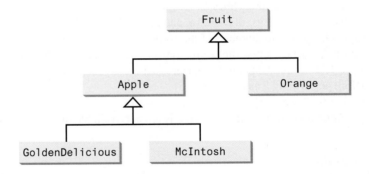

Assume the following code is given:

```
Fruit fruit = new GoldenDelicious();
Orange orange = new Orange();
```

Answer the following questions:

a. Is `fruit instanceof Fruit`?

b. Is `fruit instanceof Orange`?

c. Is `fruit instanceof Apple`?

d. Is `fruit instanceof GoldenDelicious`?

e. Is `fruit instanceof McIntosh`?

f. Is `orange instanceof Orange`?

g. Is orange instanceof Fruit?

h. Is orange instanceof Apple?

i. Suppose the method makeAppleCider is defined in the Apple class. Can Fruit invoke this method? Can orange invoke this method?

j. Suppose the method makeOrangeJuice is defined in the Orange class. Can orange invoke this method? Can Fruit invoke this method?

k. Is the statement Orange p = new Apple() legal?

l. Is the statement McIntosh p = new Apple() legal?

m. Is the statement Apple p = new McIntosh() legal?

11.9.4 What is wrong in the following code?

```
1  public class Test {
2    public static void main(String[] args) {
3      Object fruit = new Fruit();
4      Object apple = (Apple)fruit;
5    }
6  }
7
8  class Apple extends Fruit {
9  }
10
11  class Fruit {
12  }
```

11.10 The Object's equals Method

Like the toString() method, the equals(Object) method is another useful method defined in the Object class.

Key Point

Another method defined in the Object class that is often used is the equals method. Its signature is

```
public boolean equals(Object o)
```

This method tests whether two objects are equal. The syntax for invoking it is

```
object1.equals(object2);
```

The default implementation of the equals method in the Object class is

```
public boolean equals(Object obj) {
  return this == obj;
}
```

This implementation checks whether two reference variables point to the same object using the == operator. You should override this method in your custom class to test whether two distinct objects have the same content.

The equals method is overridden in many classes in the Java API, such as java.lang.String and java.util.Date, to compare whether the contents of two objects are equal. You have already used the equals method to compare two strings in Section 4.4.7, The String Class. The equals method in the String class is inherited from the Object class, and is overridden in the String class to test whether two strings are identical in content.

You can override the `equals` method in the `Circle` class to compare whether two circles are equal based on their radius as follows:

```
@Override
public boolean equals(Object o) {
  if (o instanceof Circle)
    return radius == ((Circle)o).radius;
  else
    return false;
}
```

== vs. equals

 Note
The `==` comparison operator is used for comparing two primitive-data-type values or for determining whether two objects have the same references. The `equals` method is intended to test whether two objects have the same contents, provided the method is overridden in the defining class of the objects. The `==` operator is stronger than the `equals` method in that the `==` operator checks whether the two reference variables refer to the same object.

 Caution
Using the signature `equals(SomeClassName obj)` (e.g., `equals(Circle c)`) to override the `equals` method in a subclass is a common mistake. You should use `equals(Object obj)`. See CheckPoint Question 11.10.2.

equals(Object)

 11.10.1 Does every object have a `toString` method and an `equals` method? Where do they come from? How are they used? Is it appropriate to override these methods?

11.10.2 When overriding the `equals` method, a common mistake is mistyping its signature in the subclass. For example, the `equals` method is incorrectly written as `equals(Circle circle)`, as shown in (a) in the following code; instead, it should be `equals(Object circle)`, as shown in (b). Show the output of running class `Test` with the `Circle` class in (a) and in (b), respectively.

```
public class Test {
  public static void main(String[] args) {
    Object circle1 = new Circle();
    Object circle2 = new Circle();
    System.out.println(circle1.equals(circle2));
  }
}
```

```
class Circle {
  double radius;

  public boolean equals(Circle circle) {
    return this.radius == circle.radius;
  }
}
```
(a)

```
class Circle {
  double radius;

  public boolean equals(Object circle) {
    return this.radius ==
      ((Circle)circle).radius;
  }
}
```
(b)

If `Object` is replaced by `Circle` in the `Test` class, what would be the output to run `Test` using the `Circle` class in (a) and (b), respectively?

11.11 The ArrayList Class

An ArrayList object can be used to store a list of objects.

VideoNote
The ArrayList class

Now we are ready to introduce a very useful class for storing objects. You can create an array to store objects. However, once the array is created, its size is fixed. Java provides the ArrayList class, which can be used to store an unlimited number of objects. Figure 11.3 shows some methods in `ArrayList`.

java.util.ArrayList<E>	
+ArrayList()	Creates an empty list.
+add(e: E): void	Appends a new element e at the end of this list.
+add(index: int, e: E): void	Adds a new element e at the specified index in this list.
+clear(): void	Removes all elements from this list
+contains(o: Object): boolean	Returns true if this list contains the element o.
+get(index: int): E	Returns the element from this list at the specified index.
+indexOf(o: Object): int	Returns the index of the first matching element in this list.
+isEmpty(): boolean	Returns true if this list contains no elements.
+lastIndexOf(o: Object): int	Returns the index of the last matching element in this list.
+remove(o: Object): boolean	Removes the first element CDT from this list. Returns true if an element is removed.
+size(): int	Returns the number of elements in this list.
+remove(index: int): E	Removes the element at the specified index. Returns the removed element.
+set(index: int, e: E): E	Sets the element at the specified index.

FIGURE 11.3   An `ArrayList` stores an unlimited number of objects.

`ArrayList` is known as a generic class with a generic type `E`. You can specify a concrete type to replace `E` when creating an `ArrayList`. For example, the following statement creates an `ArrayList` and assigns its reference to variable `cities`. This `ArrayList` object can be used to store strings.

```
ArrayList<String> cities = new ArrayList<String>();
```

The following statement creates an `ArrayList` and assigns its reference to variable `dates`. This `ArrayList` object can be used to store dates.

```
ArrayList<java.util.Date> dates = new ArrayList<java.util.Date>();
```

> **Note**
> Since JDK 7, the statement
>
> ```
> ArrayList <AConcreteType> list = new ArrayList<AConcreteType>();
> ```
>
> can be simplified by
>
> ```
> ArrayList<AConcreteType> list = new ArrayList<>();
> ```
>
> The concrete type is no longer required in the constructor, thanks to a feature called *type inference*. The compiler is able to infer the type from the variable declaration. More discussions on generics including how to define custom generic classes and methods will be introduced in Chapter 19, Generics.

type inference

Listing 11.8 gives an example of using `ArrayList` to store objects.

LISTING 11.8 TestArrayList.java

import ArrayList	1	`import java.util.ArrayList;`
	2	
	3	`public class TestArrayList {`
	4	`  public static void main(String[] args) {`
	5	`    // Create a list to store cities`
create ArrayList	6	`    ArrayList<String> cityList = new ArrayList<>();`
	7	
	8	`    // Add some cities in the list`
add element	9	`    cityList.add("London");`
	10	`    // cityList now contains [London]`
	11	`    cityList.add("Denver");`
	12	`    // cityList now contains [London, Denver]`
	13	`    cityList.add("Paris");`
	14	`    // cityList now contains [London, Denver, Paris]`
	15	`    cityList.add("Miami");`
	16	`    // cityList now contains [London, Denver, Paris, Miami]`
	17	`    cityList.add("Seoul");`
	18	`    // Contains [London, Denver, Paris, Miami, Seoul]`
	19	`    cityList.add("Tokyo");`
	20	`    // Contains [London, Denver, Paris, Miami, Seoul, Tokyo]`
	21	
list size	22	`    System.out.println("List size? " + cityList.size());`
	23	`    System.out.println("Is Miami in the list? " +`
contains element?	24	`      cityList.contains("Miami"));`
	25	`    System.out.println("The location of Denver in the list? "`
element index	26	`      + cityList.indexOf("Denver"));`
	27	`    System.out.println("Is the list empty? " +`
is empty?	28	`      cityList.isEmpty()); // Print false`
	29	
	30	`    // Insert a new city at index 2`
	31	`    cityList.add(2, "Xian");`
	32	`    // Contains [London, Denver, Xian, Paris, Miami, Seoul, Tokyo]`
	33	
	34	`    // Remove a city from the list`
remove element	35	`    cityList.remove("Miami");`
	36	`    // Contains [London, Denver, Xian, Paris, Seoul, Tokyo]`
	37	
	38	`    // Remove a city at index 1`
remove element	39	`    cityList.remove(1);`
	40	`    // Contains [London, Xian, Paris, Seoul, Tokyo]`
	41	
	42	`    // Display the contents in the list`
toString()	43	`    System.out.println(cityList.toString());`
	44	
	45	`    // Display the contents in the list in reverse order`
	46	`    for (int i = cityList.size() - 1; i >= 0; i--)`
get element	47	`      System.out.print(cityList.get(i) + " ");`
	48	`    System.out.println();`
	49	
	50	`    // Create a list to store two circles`
create ArrayList	51	`    ArrayList<Circle> list = new ArrayList<>();`
	52	
	53	`    // Add two circles`
	54	`    list.add(new Circle(2));`
	55	`    list.add(new Circle(3));`
	56	
	57	`    // Display the area of the first circle in the list`
	58	`    System.out.println("The area of the circle? " +`

```
59            list.get(0).getArea());
60      }
61   }
```

```
List size? 6
Is Miami in the list? true
The location of Denver in the list? 1
Is the list empty? false
[London, Xian, Paris, Seoul, Tokyo]
Tokyo Seoul Paris Xian London
The area of the circle? 12.566370614359172
```

Since the `ArrayList` is in the `java.util` package, it is imported in line 1. The program creates an `ArrayList` of strings using its no-arg constructor and assigns the reference to `cityList` (line 6). The `add` method (lines 9–19) adds strings to the end of list. Thus, after `cityList.add("London")` (line 9), the list contains

    `[London]`

add(Object)

After `cityList.add("Denver")` (line 11), the list contains

    `[London, Denver]`

After adding `Paris`, `Miami`, `Seoul`, and `Tokyo` (lines 13–19), the list contains

    `[London, Denver, Paris, Miami, Seoul, Tokyo]`

Invoking `size()` (line 22) returns the size of the list, which is currently `6`. Invoking `contains("Miami")` (line 24) checks whether the object is in the list. In this case, it returns `true`, since `Miami` is in the list. Invoking `indexOf("Denver")` (line 26) returns the index of `Denver` in the list, which is `1`. If `Denver` were not in the list, it would return `–1`. The `isEmpty()` method (line 28) checks whether the list is empty. It returns `false`, since the list is not empty.

size()

    The statement `cityList.add(2, "Xian")` (line 31) inserts an object into the list at the specified index. After this statement, the list becomes

add(index, Object)

    `[London, Denver, Xian, Paris, Miami, Seoul, Tokyo]`

The statement `cityList.remove("Miami")` (line 35) removes the object from the list. After this statement, the list becomes

remove(Object)

    `[London, Denver, Xian, Paris, Seoul, Tokyo]`

The statement `cityList.remove(1)` (line 39) removes the object at the specified index from the list. After this statement, the list becomes

remove(index)

    `[London, Xian, Paris, Seoul, Tokyo]`

The statement in line 43 is same as

    `System.out.println(cityList);`

The `toString()` method returns a string representation of the list in the form of `[e0.toString(), e1.toString(), ..., ek.toString()]`, where `e0`, `e1`,..., and `ek` are the elements in the list.

toString()

    The `get(index)` method (line 47) returns the object at the specified index.

get(index)

    `ArrayList` objects can be used like arrays, but there are many differences. Table 11.1 lists their similarities and differences.

array vs. ArrayList

    Once an array is created, its size is fixed. You can access an array element using the square-bracket notation (e.g., `a[index]`). When an `ArrayList` is created, its size is `0`.

TABLE 11.1 Differences and Similarities between Arrays and `ArrayList`

Operation	Array	ArrayList
Creating an array/ArrayList	`String[] a = new String[10]`	`ArrayList<String> list = new ArrayList<>();`
Accessing an element	`a[index]`	`list.get(index);`
Updating an element	`a[index] = "London";`	`list.set(index, "London");`
Returning size	`a.length`	`list.size();`
Adding a new element		`list.add("London");`
Inserting a new element		`list.add(index, "London");`
Removing an element		`list.remove(index);`
Removing an element		`list.remove(Object);`
Removing all elements		`list.clear();`

You cannot use the `get(index)` and `set(index, element)` methods if the element is not in the list. It is easy to add, insert, and remove elements in a list, but it is rather complex to add, insert, and remove elements in an array. You have to write code to manipulate the array in order to perform these operations. Note you can sort an array using the `java.util.Arrays.sort(array)` method. To sort an array list, use the `java.util.Collections.sort(arraylist)` method.

Suppose you want to create an `ArrayList` for storing integers. Can you use the following code to create a list?

```
ArrayList<int> listOfIntegers = new ArrayList<>();
```

No. This will not work because the elements stored in an `ArrayList` must be of an object type. You cannot use a primitive data type such as `int` to replace a generic type. However, you can create an `ArrayList` for storing `Integer` objects as follows:

```
ArrayList<Integer> listOfIntegers = new ArrayList<>();
```

remove(int) vs. remove(Integer)

Note the `remove(int index)` method removes an element at the specified index. To remove an integer value v from `listOfIntegers`, you need to use `listOfIntegers.remove(new Integer(v))`. This is not a good design in the Java API because it could easily lead to mistakes. It would be much better if `remove(int)` is renamed `removeAt(int)`.

Listing 11.9 gives a program that prompts the user to enter a sequence of numbers and displays the distinct numbers in the sequence. Assume the input ends with 0, and 0 is not counted as a number in the sequence.

LISTING 11.9 `DistinctNumbers.java`

create an array list

```
1  import java.util.ArrayList;
2  import java.util.Scanner;
3
4  public class DistinctNumbers {
5    public static void main(String[] args) {
6      ArrayList<Integer> list = new ArrayList<>();
7
8      Scanner input = new Scanner(System.in);
9      System.out.print("Enter integers (input ends with 0): ");
10     int value;
11
12     do {
13       value = input.nextInt(); // Read a value from the input
14
```

```
15              if (!list.contains(value) && value != 0)                     contained in list?
16                list.add(value); // Add the value if it is not in the list  add to list
17           } while (value != 0);
18
19           // Display the distinct numbers
20           for (int i = 0; i < list.size(); i++)
21             System.out.print(list.get(i) + " ");
22       }
23   }
```

```
Enter numbers (input ends with 0): 1 2 3 2 1 6 3 4 5 4 5 1 2 3 0 ↵Enter
The distinct numbers are: 1 2 3 6 4 5
```

The program creates an `ArrayList` for `Integer` objects (line 6) and repeatedly reads a value in the loop (lines 12–17). For each value, if it is not in the list (line 15), add it to the list (line 16). You can rewrite this program using an array to store the elements rather than using an `ArrayList`. However, it is simpler to implement this program using an `ArrayList` for two reasons.

1. The size of an `ArrayList` is flexible so you don't have to specify its size in advance. When creating an array, its size must be specified.

2. `ArrayList` contains many useful methods. For example, you can test whether an element is in the list using the `contains` method. If you use an array, you have to write additional code to implement this method.

You can traverse the elements in an array using a foreach loop. The elements in an array list   foreach loop
can also be traversed using a foreach loop using the following syntax:

```
for (elementType element: arrayList) {
  // Process the element
}
```

For example, you can replace the code in lines 20 and 21 using the following code:

```
for (Integer number: list)
  System.out.print(number + " ");
```

or

```
for (int number: list)
  System.out.print(number + " ");
```

Note the elements in `list` are `Integer` objects. They are automatically unboxed into `int` in this foreach loop.

11.11.1   How do you do the following?

    a. Create an `ArrayList` for storing double values?

    b. Append an object to a list?

    c. Insert an object at the beginning of a list?

    d. Find the number of objects in a list?

    e. Remove a given object from a list?

    f. Remove the last object from a list?

    g. Check whether a given object is in a list?

    h. Retrieve an object at a specified index from a list?

11.11.2 Identify the errors in the following code.

```
ArrayList<String> list = new ArrayList<>();
list.add("Denver");
list.add("Austin");
list.add(new java.util.Date());
String city = list.get(0);
list.set(3, "Dallas");
System.out.println(list.get(3));
```

11.11.3 Suppose the `ArrayList list` contains {"Dallas", "Dallas", "Houston", "Dallas"}. What is the list after invoking `list.remove("Dallas")` one time? Does the following code correctly remove all elements with value "Dallas" from the list? If not, correct the code.

```
for (int i = 0; i < list.size(); i++)
  list.remove("Dallas");
```

11.11.4 Explain why the following code displays [1, 3] rather than [2, 3].

```
ArrayList<Integer> list = new ArrayList<>();
list.add(1);
list.add(2);
list.add(3);
list.remove(1);
System.out.println(list);
```
How do you remove integer value 3 from the list?

11.11.5 Explain why the following code is wrong:

```
ArrayList<Double> list = new ArrayList<>();
list.add(1);
```

11.12 Useful Methods for Lists

Key Point

Java provides the methods for creating a list from an array, for sorting a list, and for finding maximum and minimum element in a list, and for shuffling a list.

array to array list

Often you need to create an array list from an array of objects or vice versa. You can write the code using a loop to accomplish this, but an easy way is to use the methods in the Java API. Here is an example to create an array list from an array:

```
String[] array = {"red", "green", "blue"};
ArrayList<String> list = new ArrayList<>(Arrays.asList(array));
```

array list to array

The static method `asList` in the `Arrays` class returns a list that is passed to the `ArrayList` constructor for creating an `ArrayList`. Conversely, you can use the following code to create an array of objects from an array list:

```
String[] array1 = new String[list.size()];
list.toArray(array1);
```

sort a list

Invoking `list.toArray(array1)` copies the contents from `list` to `array1`. If the elements in a list are comparable, such as integers, double, or strings, you can use the static `sort` method in the `java.util.Collections` class to sort the elements. Here are some examples:

```
Integer[] array = {3, 5, 95, 4, 15, 34, 3, 6, 5};
ArrayList<Integer> list = new ArrayList<>(Arrays.asList(array));
java.util.Collections.sort(list);
System.out.println(list);
```

You can use the static `max` and `min` in the `java.util.Collections` class to return the maximum and minimal element in a list. Here are some examples:

max and min methods

```
Integer[] array = {3, 5, 95, 4, 15, 34, 3, 6, 5};
ArrayList<Integer> list = new ArrayList<>(Arrays.asList(array));
System.out.println(java.util.Collections.max(list));
System.out.println(java.util.Collections.min(list));
```

You can use the static `shuffle` method in the `java.util.Collections` class to perform a random shuffle for the elements in a list. Here are some examples:

shuffle method

```
Integer[] array = {3, 5, 95, 4, 15, 34, 3, 6, 5};
ArrayList<Integer> list = new ArrayList<>(Arrays.asList(array));
java.util.Collections.shuffle(list);
System.out.println(list);
```

11.12.1 Correct errors in the following statements:

```
int[] array = {3, 5, 95, 4, 15, 34, 3, 6, 5};
ArrayList<Integer> list = new ArrayList<>(Arrays.asList(array));
```

11.12.2 Correct errors in the following statements:

```
int[] array = {3, 5, 95, 4, 15, 34, 3, 6, 5};
System.out.println(java.util.Collections.max(array));
```

11.13 Case Study: A Custom Stack Class

This section designs a stack class for holding objects.

Section 10.6 presented a stack class for storing `int` values. This section introduces a stack class to store objects. You can use an `ArrayList` to implement `Stack`, as shown in Listing 11.10. The UML diagram for the class is shown in Figure 11.4.

VideoNote
The `MyStack` class

MyStack	
-list: ArrayList<Object>	A list to store elements.
+isEmpty(): boolean	Returns true if this stack is empty.
+getSize(): int	Returns the number of elements in this stack.
+peek(): Object	Returns the top element in this stack without removing it.
+pop(): Object	Returns and removes the top element in this stack.
+push(o: Object): void	Adds a new element to the top of this stack.

FIGURE 11.4 The `MyStack` class encapsulates the stack storage and provides the operations for manipulating the stack.

LISTING 11.10 MyStack.java

```
1  import java.util.ArrayList;
2
3  public class MyStack {
4    private ArrayList<Object> list = new ArrayList<>();
5
6    public boolean isEmpty() {
7      return list.isEmpty();
```

array list

stack empty?

```
 8    }
 9
10    public int getSize() {
11      return list.size();
12    }
13
14    public Object peek() {
15      return list.get(getSize() - 1);
16    }
17
18    public Object pop() {
19      Object o = list.get(getSize() - 1);
20      list.remove(getSize() - 1);
21      return o;
22    }
23
24    public void push(Object o) {
25      list.add(o);
26    }
27
28    @Override
29    public String toString() {
30      return "stack: " + list.toString();
31    }
32  }
```

get stack size

peek stack

remove

push

An array list is created to store the elements in the stack (line 4). The `isEmpty()` method (lines 6–8) returns `list.isEmpty()`. The `getSize()` method (lines 10–12) returns `list.size()`. The `peek()` method (lines 14–16) retrieves the element at the top of the stack without removing it. The end of the list is the top of the stack. The `pop()` method (lines 18–22) removes the top element from the stack and returns it. The `push(Object element)` method (lines 24–26) adds the specified element to the stack. The `toString()` method (lines 28–31) defined in the `Object` class is overridden to display the contents of the stack by invoking `list.toString()`. The `toString()` method implemented in `ArrayList` returns a string representation of all the elements in an array list.

Design Guide

In Listing 11.10, `MyStack` contains `ArrayList`. The relationship between `MyStack` and `ArrayList` is *composition*. Composition essentially means declaring an instance variable for referencing an object. This object is said to be composed. While inheritance models an *is-a* relationship, composition models a *has-a* relationship. You could also implement `MyStack` as a subclass of `ArrayList` (see Programming Exercise 11.10). Using composition is better, however, because it enables you to define a completely new stack class without inheriting the unnecessary and inappropriate methods from `ArrayList`.

composition

has-a

11.13.1 Write statements that create a `MyStack` and add number `11` to the stack.

11.14 The protected Data and Methods

A protected member of a class can be accessed from a subclass.

So far you have used the `private` and `public` keywords to specify whether data fields and methods can be accessed from outside of the class. Private members can be accessed only from inside of the class, and public members can be accessed from any other classes.

Often it is desirable to allow subclasses to access data fields or methods defined in the superclass, but not to allow nonsubclasses in different packages to access these data fields and methods. To accomplish this, you can use the `protected` keyword. This way you can access protected data fields or methods in a superclass from its subclasses.

why protected?

The modifiers `private`, `protected`, and `public` are known as *visibility* or *accessibility modifiers* because they specify how classes and class members are accessed. The visibility of these modifiers increases in this order:

Visibility increases

private, default (no modifier), protected, public

Table 11.2 summarizes the accessibility of the members in a class. Figure 11.5 illustrates how a public, protected, default, and private datum or method in class `C1` can be accessed from a class `C2` in the same package, a subclass `C3` in the same package, a subclass `C4` in a different package, and a class `C5` in a different package.

Use the `private` modifier to hide the members of the class completely so they cannot be accessed directly from outside the class. Use no modifiers (the default) in order to allow the members of the class to be accessed directly from any class within the same package but not from other packages. Use the `protected` modifier to enable the members of the class to be

TABLE 11.2 Data and Methods Visibility

Modifier on Members in a Class	Accessed from the Same Class	Accessed from the Same Package	Accessed from a Subclass in a Different Package	Accessed from a Different Package
Public	✓	✓	✓	✓
Protected	✓	✓	✓	–
Default (no modifier)	✓	✓	–	–
Private	✓	–	–	–

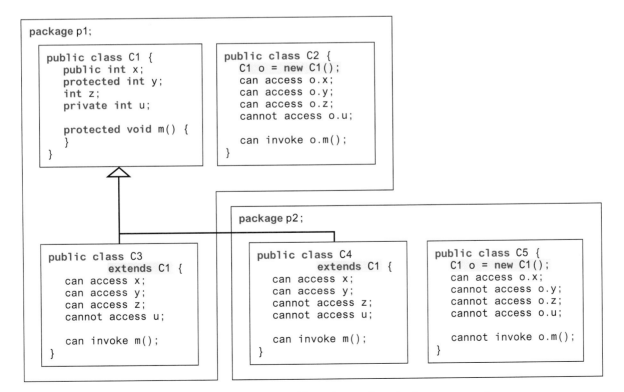

FIGURE 11.5 Visibility modifiers are used to control how data and methods are accessed.

accessed by the subclasses in any package or classes in the same package. Use the `public` modifier to enable the members of the class to be accessed by any class.

Your class can be used in two ways: (1) for creating instances of the class and (2) for defining subclasses by extending the class. Make the members `private` if they are not intended for use from outside the class. Make the members `public` if they are intended for the users of the class. Make the fields or methods `protected` if they are intended for the extenders of the class but not for the users of the class.

The `private` and `protected` modifiers can be used only for members of the class. The `public` modifier and the default modifier (i.e., no modifier) can be used on members of the class as well as on the class. A class with no modifier (i.e., not a public class) is not accessible by classes from other packages.

change visibility

 Note

A subclass may override a protected method defined in its superclass and change its visibility to public. However, a subclass cannot weaken the accessibility of a method defined in the superclass. For example, if a method is defined as public in the superclass, it must be defined as public in the subclass.

 Check Point

11.14.1 What modifier should you use on a class so a class in the same package can access it, but a class in a different package cannot access it?

11.14.2 What modifier should you use so a class in a different package cannot access the class, but its subclasses in any package can access it?

11.14.3 In the following code, the classes A and B are in the same package. If the question marks in (a) are replaced by blanks, can class B be compiled? If the question marks are replaced by `private`, can class B be compiled? If the question marks are replaced by `protected`, can class B be compiled?

```
package p1;

public class A {
    ?    int i;

    ?    void m() {
       ...
    }
}
```
(a)

```
package p1;

public class B extends A {
    public void m1(String[] args) {
        System.out.println(i);
        m();
    }
}
```
(b)

11.14.4 In the following code, the classes A and B are in different packages. If the question marks in (a) are replaced by blanks, can class B be compiled? If the question marks are replaced by `private`, can class B be compiled? If the question marks are replaced by `protected`, can class B be compiled?

```
package p1;

public class A {
    ?    int i;

    ?    void m() {
       ...
    }
}
```
(a)

```
package p2;

public class B extends A {
    public void m1(String[] args) {
        System.out.println(i);
        m();
    }
}
```
(b)

11.15 Preventing Extending and Overriding

Key
Point

Neither a final class nor a final method can be extended. A final data field is a constant.

You may occasionally want to prevent classes from being extended. In such cases, use the `final` modifier to indicate a class is final and cannot be a parent class. The `Math` class is a final class. The `String`, `StringBuilder`, and `StringBuffer` classes, and all wrapper classes for primitive data types are also final classes. For example, the following class `A` is final and cannot be extended:

```
public final class A {
   // Data fields, constructors, and methods omitted
}
```

You also can define a method to be final; a final method cannot be overridden by its subclasses. For example, the following method `m` is final and cannot be overridden:

```
public class Test {
   // Data fields, constructors, and methods omitted

   public final void m() {
      // Do something
   }
}
```

 Note

The modifiers `public`, `protected`, `private`, `static`, `abstract`, and `final` are used on classes and class members (data and methods), except that the `final` modifier can also be used on local variables in a method. A `final` local variable is a constant inside a method.

Check
Point

11.15.1 How do you prevent a class from being extended? How do you prevent a method from being overridden?

11.15.2 Indicate true or false for the following statements:

a. A protected datum or method can be accessed by any class in the same package.

b. A protected datum or method can be accessed by any class in different packages.

c. A protected datum or method can be accessed by its subclasses in any package.

d. A final class can have instances.

e. A final class can be extended.

f. A final method can be overridden.

KEY TERMS

actual type   426
casting objects   429
constructor chaining   419
declared type   426
dynamic binding   426
inheritance   412
`instanceof`   430
is-a relationship   412
method overriding   421
multiple inheritance   418

override   421
polymorphism   425
`protected`   442
single inheritance   418
subclass   412
subtype   412
superclass   412
supertype   412
type inference   435

CHAPTER SUMMARY

1. You can define a new class from an existing class. This is known as class *inheritance*. The new class is called a *subclass*, *child class*, or *extended class*. The existing class is called a *superclass*, *parent class*, or *base class*.

2. A constructor is used to construct an instance of a class. Unlike properties and methods, the constructors of a superclass are not inherited in the subclass. They can be invoked only from the constructors of the subclasses, using the keyword `super`.

3. A constructor may invoke an overloaded constructor or its superclass's constructor. The call must be the first statement in the constructor. If none of them is invoked explicitly, the compiler puts `super()` as the first statement in the constructor, which invokes the superclass's no-arg constructor.

4. To *override* a method, the method must be defined in the subclass using the same signature and the same or compatible return type as in its superclass.

5. An instance method can be overridden only if it is accessible. Thus, a private method cannot be overridden because it is not accessible outside its own class. If a method defined in a subclass is private in its superclass, the two methods are completely unrelated.

6. Like an instance method, a static method can be inherited. However, a static method cannot be overridden. If a static method defined in the superclass is redefined in a subclass, the method defined in the superclass is hidden.

7. Every class in Java is descended from the `java.lang.Object` class. If no superclass is specified when a class is defined, its superclass is `Object`.

8. If a method's parameter type is a superclass (e.g., `Object`), you may pass an object to this method of any of the parameter's subclasses (e.g., `Circle` or `String`). This is known as polymorphism.

9. It is always possible to cast an instance of a subclass to a variable of a superclass because an instance of a subclass is *always* an instance of its superclass. When casting an instance of a superclass to a variable of its subclass, explicit casting must be used to confirm your intention to the compiler with the `(SubclassName)` cast notation.

10. A class defines a type. A type defined by a subclass is called a *subtype*, and a type defined by its superclass is called a *supertype*.

11. When invoking an instance method from a reference variable, the *actual type of* the variable decides which implementation of the method is used *at runtime*. This is known as dynamic binding.

12. You can use `obj instanceof AClass` to test whether an object is an instance of a class.

13. You can use the `ArrayList` class to create an object to store a list of objects.

14. You can use the `protected` modifier to prevent the data and methods from being accessed by nonsubclasses from a different package.

15. You can use the `final` modifier to indicate a class is final and cannot be extended and to indicate a method is final and cannot be overridden.

QUIZ

Answer the quiz for this chapter online at the book Companion Website.

PROGRAMMING EXERCISES

MyProgrammingLab™

Sections 11.2–11.4

11.1 (*The Triangle class*) Design a class named `Triangle` that extends `GeometricObject`. The class contains:

- Three `double` data fields named `side1`, `side2`, and `side3` with default values `1.0` to denote three sides of a triangle.
- A no-arg constructor that creates a default triangle.
- A constructor that creates a triangle with the specified `side1`, `side2`, and `side3`.
- The accessor methods for all three data fields.
- A method named `getArea()` that returns the area of this triangle.
- A method named `getPerimeter()` that returns the perimeter of this triangle.
- A method named `toString()` that returns a string description for the triangle.

For the formula to compute the area of a triangle, see Programming Exercise 2.19. The `toString()` method is implemented as follows:

```
return "Triangle: side1 = " + side1 + " side2 = " + side2 +
  " side3 = " + side3;
```

Draw the UML diagrams for the classes `Triangle` and `GeometricObject` and implement the classes. Write a test program that prompts the user to enter three sides of the triangle, a color, and a Boolean value to indicate whether the triangle is filled. The program should create a `Triangle` object with these sides and set the `color` and `filled` properties using the input. The program should display the area, perimeter, color, and true or false to indicate whether it is filled or not.

Sections 11.5–11.14

11.2 (*The Person, Student, Employee, Faculty, and Staff classes*) Design a class named `Person` and its two subclasses named `Student` and `Employee`. Make `Faculty` and `Staff` subclasses of `Employee`. A person has a name, address, phone number, and e-mail address. A student has a class status (freshman, sophomore, junior, or senior). Define the status as a constant. An employee has an office, salary, and date hired. Use the `MyDate` class defined in Programming Exercise 10.14 to create an object for date hired. A faculty member has office hours and a rank. A staff member has a title. Override the `toString` method in each class to display the class name and the person's name.

Draw the UML diagram for the classes and implement them. Write a test program that creates a `Person`, `Student`, `Employee`, `Faculty`, and `Staff`, and invokes their `toString()` methods.

11.3 (*Subclasses of Account*) In Programming Exercise 9.7, the `Account` class was defined to model a bank account. An account has the properties account number, balance, annual interest rate, and date created, and methods to deposit and withdraw funds. Create two subclasses for checking and saving accounts. A checking account has an overdraft limit, but a savings account cannot be overdrawn.

Draw the UML diagram for the classes and implement them. Write a test program that creates objects of `Account`, `SavingsAccount`, and `CheckingAccount` and invokes their `toString()` methods.

11.4 (*Maximum element in* `ArrayList`) Write the following method that returns the maximum value in an `ArrayList` of integers. The method returns `null` if the list is `null` or the list size is `0`.

```
public static Integer max(ArrayList<Integer> list)
```

Write a test program that prompts the user to enter a sequence of numbers ending with `0` and invokes this method to return the largest number in the input.

11.5 (*The* `Course` *class*) Rewrite the `Course` class in Listing 10.6. Use an `Array-List` to replace an array to store students. Draw the new UML diagram for the class. You should not change the original contract of the `Course` class (i.e., the definition of the constructors and methods should not be changed, but the private members may be changed.)

11.6 (*Use* `ArrayList`) Write a program that creates an `ArrayList` and adds a `Loan` object, a `Date` object, a string, and a `Circle` object to the list, and use a loop to display all the elements in the list by invoking the object's `toString()` method.

11.7 (*Shuffle* `ArrayList`) Write the following method that shuffles the elements in an `ArrayList` of integers:

```
public static void shuffle(ArrayList<Integer> list)
```

**11.8 (*New* `Account` *class*) An `Account` class was specified in Programming Exercise 9.7. Design a new `Account` class as follows:

- Add a new data field `name` of the `String` type to store the name of the customer.
- Add a new constructor that constructs an account with the specified name, id, and balance.
- Add a new data field named `transactions` whose type is `ArrayList` that stores the transaction for the accounts. Each transaction is an instance of the `Transaction` class, which is defined as shown in Figure 11.6.

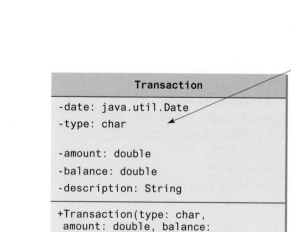

The get and set methods for these data fields are provided in the class, but omitted in the UML diagram for brevity.

Transaction
-date: java.util.Date
-type: char
-amount: double
-balance: double
-description: String
+Transaction(type: char, amount: double, balance: double, description: String)

The date of this transaction.
The type of the transaction, such as "W" for withdrawal, "D" for deposit.
The amount of the transaction.
The new balance after this transaction.
The description of this transaction.

Construct a `Transaction` with the specified date, type, balance, and description.

FIGURE 11.6 The `Transaction` class describes a transaction for a bank account.

- Modify the `withdraw` and `deposit` methods to add a transaction to the `transactions` array list.
- All other properties and methods are the same as in Programming Exercise 9.7.

VideoNote

New Account class

Write a test program that creates an `Account` with annual interest rate `1.5%`, balance `1000`, id `1122`, and name `George`. Deposit $30, $40, and $50 to the account and withdraw $5, $4, and $2 from the account. Print an account summary that shows the account holder name, interest rate, balance, and all transactions.

*11.9 (*Largest rows and columns*) Write a program that randomly fills in `0`s and `1`s into an n-by-n matrix, prints the matrix, and finds the rows and columns with the most `1`s. (*Hint*: Use two `ArrayLists` to store the row and column indices with the most `1`s.) Here is a sample run of the program:

```
Enter the array size n: 4 ⏎Enter
The random array is
0011
0011
1101
1010
The largest row index: 2
The largest column index: 2, 3
```

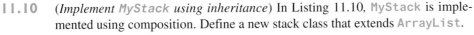

11.10 (*Implement MyStack using inheritance*) In Listing 11.10, `MyStack` is implemented using composition. Define a new stack class that extends `ArrayList`.

Draw the UML diagram for the classes then implement `MyStack`. Write a test program that prompts the user to enter five strings and displays them in reverse order.

11.11 (*Sort ArrayList*) Write the following method that sorts an `ArrayList` of numbers:

```
public static void sort(ArrayList<Integer> list)
```

Write a test program that prompts the user to enter five numbers, stores them in an array list, and displays them in increasing order.

11.12 (*Sum ArrayList*) Write the following method that returns the sum of all numbers in an `ArrayList`:

```
public static double sum(ArrayList<Double> list)
```

Write a test program that prompts the user to enter five numbers, stores them in an array list, and displays their sum.

*11.13 (*Remove duplicates*) Write a method that removes the duplicate elements from an array list of integers using the following header:

```
public static void removeDuplicate(ArrayList<Integer> list)
```

Write a test program that prompts the user to enter 10 integers to a list and displays the distinct integers in their input order and separated by exactly one space. Here is a sample run:

```
Enter 10 integers: 34 5 3 5 6 4 33 2 2 4 ⏎Enter
The distinct integers are 34 5 3 6 4 33 2
```

11.14 (*Combine two lists*) Write a method that returns the union of two array lists of integers using the following header:

```
public static ArrayList<Integer> union(
   ArrayList<Integer> list1, ArrayList<Integer> list2)
```

For example, the addition of two array lists {2, 3, 1, 5} and {3, 4, 6} is {2, 3, 1, 5, 3, 4, 6}. Write a test program that prompts the user to enter two lists, each with five integers, and displays their union. The numbers are separated by exactly one space. Here is a sample run:

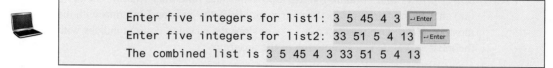

```
Enter five integers for list1: 3 5 45 4 3  ↵Enter
Enter five integers for list2: 33 51 5 4 13  ↵Enter
The combined list is 3 5 45 4 3 33 51 5 4 13
```

*11.15 (*Area of a convex polygon*) A polygon is convex if it contains any line segments that connects two points of the polygon. Write a program that prompts the user to enter the number of points in a convex polygon, enter the points clockwise, then displays the area of the polygon. For the formula for computing the area of a polygon, see http://www.mathwords.com/a/area_convex_polygon.htm. Here is a sample run of the program:

```
Enter the number of points: 7  ↵Enter
Enter the coordinates of the points:
 -12 0 -8.5 10 0 11.4 5.5 7.8 6 -5.5 0 -7 -3.5 -13.5  ↵Enter
The total area is 292.575
```

**11.16 (*Addition quiz*) Rewrite Listing 5.1, RepeatAdditionQuiz.java, to alert the user if an answer is entered again. (*Hint:* use an array list to store answers.) Here is a sample run:

```
What is 5 + 9? 12  ↵Enter
Wrong answer. Try again. What is 5 + 9? 34  ↵Enter
Wrong answer. Try again. What is 5 + 9? 12  ↵Enter
You already entered 12
Wrong answer. Try again. What is 5 + 9? 14  ↵Enter
You got it!
```

**11.17 (*Algebra: perfect square*) Write a program that prompts the user to enter an integer m and find the smallest integer n such that $m * n$ is a perfect square. (*Hint:* Store all smallest factors of m into an array list. n is the product of the factors that appear an odd number of times in the array list. For example, consider $m = 90$, store the factors 2, 3, 3, and 5 in an array list. 2 and 5 appear an odd number of times in the array list. Thus, n is 10.) Here are some sample runs:

```
Enter an integer m: 1500  ↵Enter
The smallest number n for m * n to be a perfect square is 15
m * n is 22500
```

```
Enter an integer m: 63  ↵Enter
The smallest number n for m * n to be a perfect square is 7
m * n is 441
```

**11.18 (*ArrayList of Character*) Write a method that returns an array list of `Charac-ter` from a string using the following header:

```
public static ArrayList<Character> toCharacterArray(String s)
```

For example, `toCharacterArray("abc")` returns an array list that contains characters `'a'`, `'b'`, and `'c'`.

**11.19 (*Bin packing using first fit*) The bin packing problem is to pack the objects of various weights into containers. Assume each container can hold a maximum of 10 pounds. The program uses an algorithm that places an object into the first bin in which it would fit. Your program should prompt the user to enter the total number of objects and the weight of each object. The program displays the total number of containers needed to pack the objects and the contents of each container. Here is a sample run of the program:

```
Enter the number of objects: 6
Enter the weights of the objects: 7 5 2 3 5 8
Container 1 contains objects with weight 7 2
Container 2 contains objects with weight 5 3
Container 3 contains objects with weight 5
Container 4 contains objects with weight 8
```

Does this program produce an optimal solution, that is, finding the minimum number of containers to pack the objects?

EXCEPTION HANDLING AND TEXT I/O

Objectives

- To get an overview of exceptions and exception handling (§12.2).

- To explore the advantages of using exception handling (§12.2).

- To distinguish exception types: `Error` (fatal) vs. `Exception` (nonfatal) and checked vs. unchecked (§12.3).

- To declare exceptions in a method header (§12.4.1).

- To throw exceptions in a method (§12.4.2).

- To write a `try-catch` block to handle exceptions (§12.4.3).

- To explain how an exception is propagated (§12.4.3).

- To obtain information from an exception object (§12.4.4).

- To develop applications with exception handling (§12.4.5).

- To use the `finally` clause in a `try-catch` block (§12.5).

- To use exceptions only for unexpected errors (§12.6).

- To rethrow exceptions in a `catch` block (§12.7).

- To create chained exceptions (§12.8).

- To define custom exception classes (§12.9).

- To discover file/directory properties, to delete and rename files/directories, and to create directories using the `File` class (§12.10).

- To write data to a file using the `PrintWriter` class (§12.11.1).

- To use try-with-resources to ensure that the resources are closed automatically (§12.11.2).

- To read data from a file using the `Scanner` class (§12.11.3).

- To understand how data is read using a `Scanner` (§12.11.4).

- To develop a program that replaces text in a file (§12.11.5).

- To read data from the Web (§12.12).

- To develop a Web crawler (§12.13).

12.1 Introduction

Key Point

Exceptions are runtime errors. Exception handling enables a program to deal with runtime errors and continue its normal execution.

Runtime errors occur while a program is running if the JVM detects an operation that is impossible to carry out. For example, if you access an array using an index that is out of bounds, you will get a runtime error with an `ArrayIndexOutOfBoundsException`. If you enter a `double` value when your program expects an integer, you will get a runtime error with an `InputMismatchException`.

exception

In Java, runtime errors are thrown as exceptions. An *exception* is an object that represents an error or a condition that prevents execution from proceeding normally. If the exception is not handled, the program will terminate abnormally. How can you handle the exception so the program can continue to run or else terminate gracefully? This chapter introduces this subject, and text input and output.

12.2 Exception-Handling Overview

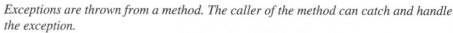

Key Point

Exceptions are thrown from a method. The caller of the method can catch and handle the exception.

VideoNote

Exception-handling advantages

To demonstrate exception handling, including how an exception object is created and thrown, let's begin with the example in Listing 12.1, which reads in two integers and displays their quotient.

LISTING 12.1 Quotient.java

```java
1  import java.util.Scanner;
2
3  public class Quotient {
4    public static void main(String[] args) {
5      Scanner input = new Scanner(System.in);
6
7      // Prompt the user to enter two integers
8      System.out.print("Enter two integers: ");
9      int number1 = input.nextInt();
10     int number2 = input.nextInt();
11
12     System.out.println(number1 + " / " + number2 + " is " +
13       (number1 / number2));
14   }
15 }
```

read two integers

integer division

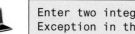

```
Enter two integers: 5 2 ↵Enter
5 / 2 is 2
```

```
Enter two integers: 3 0 ↵Enter
Exception in thread "main" java.lang.ArithmeticException: / by zero
at Quotient.main(Quotient.java:13)
```

If you entered 0 for the second number, a runtime error would occur, because you cannot divide an integer by 0. (*Note a floating-point number divided by 0 does not raise an exception.*) A simple way to fix this error is to add an `if` statement to test the second number, as shown in Listing 12.2.

LISTING 12.2 QuotientWithIf.java

```java
1   import java.util.Scanner;
2
3   public class QuotientWithIf {
4     public static void main(String[] args) {
5       Scanner input = new Scanner(System.in);
6
7       // Prompt the user to enter two integers
8       System.out.print("Enter two integers: ");
9       int number1 = input.nextInt();
10      int number2 = input.nextInt();
11
12      if (number2 != 0)
13        System.out.println(number1 + " / " + number2
14          + " is " + (number1 / number2));
15      else
16        System.out.println("Divisor cannot be zero ");
17    }
18  }
```

read two integers

test number2

```
Enter two integers: 5 0 ↵Enter
Divisor cannot be zero
```

Before introducing exception handling, let us rewrite Listing 12.2 to compute a quotient using a method, as shown in Listing 12.3.

LISTING 12.3 QuotientWithMethod.java

```java
1   import java.util.Scanner;
2
3   public class QuotientWithMethod {
4     public static int quotient(int number1, int number2) {
5       if (number2 == 0) {
6         System.out.println("Divisor cannot be zero");
7         System.exit(1);
8       }
9
10      return number1 / number2;
11    }
12
13    public static void main(String[] args) {
14      Scanner input = new Scanner(System.in);
15
16      // Prompt the user to enter two integers
17      System.out.print("Enter two integers: ");
18      int number1 = input.nextInt();
19      int number2 = input.nextInt();
20
21      int result = quotient(number1, number2);
22      System.out.println(number1 + " / " + number2 + " is "
23        + result);
24    }
25  }
```

quotient method

terminate the program

read two integers

invoke method

```
Enter two integers: 5 3 ↵Enter
5 / 3 is 1
```

```
Enter two integers: 5 0 ↵Enter
Divisor cannot be zero
```

The method `quotient` (lines 4–11) returns the quotient of two integers. If `number2` is `0`, it cannot return a value, so the program is terminated in line 7. This is clearly a problem. You should not let the method terminate the program—the *caller* should decide whether to terminate the program.

How can a method notify its caller an exception has occurred? Java enables a method to throw an exception that can be caught and handled by the caller. Listing 12.3 can be rewritten, as shown in Listing 12.4.

LISTING 12.4 QuotientWithException.java

```java
 1  import java.util.Scanner;
 2
 3  public class QuotientWithException {
 4    public static int quotient(int number1, int number2) {
 5      if (number2 == 0)
 6        throw new ArithmeticException("Divisor cannot be zero");
 7
 8      return number1 / number2;
 9    }
10
11    public static void main(String[] args) {
12      Scanner input = new Scanner(System.in);
13
14      // Prompt the user to enter two integers
15      System.out.print("Enter two integers: ");
16      int number1 = input.nextInt();
17      int number2 = input.nextInt();
18
19      try {
20        int result = quotient(number1, number2);
21        System.out.println(number1 + " / " + number2 + " is "
22          + result);
23      }
24      catch (ArithmeticException ex) {
25        System.out.println("Exception: an integer " +
26          "cannot be divided by zero ");
27      }
28
29      System.out.println("Execution continues ...");
30    }
31  }
```

quotient method

throw exception

read two integers

try block
invoke method
If an Arithmetic Exception occurs

catch block

```
Enter two integers: 5 3 ↵Enter
5 / 3 is 1
Execution continues ...
```

```
Enter two integers: 5 0 ↲Enter
Exception: an integer cannot be divided by zero
Execution continues ...
```

If `number2` is `0`, the method throws an exception (line 6) by executing

> `throw new ArithmeticException("Divisor cannot be zero");`   throw statement

The value thrown, in this case `new ArithmeticException("Divisor cannot be zero")`, is called an *exception*. The execution of a `throw` statement is called *throwing an exception*. The exception is an object created from an exception class. In this case, the exception class is `java.lang.ArithmeticException`. The constructor `ArithmeticException(str)` is invoked to construct an exception object, where `str` is a message that describes the exception.

     exception
     throw exception

When an exception is thrown, the normal execution flow is interrupted. As the name suggests, to "throw an exception" is to pass the exception from one place to another. The statement for invoking the method is contained in a `try` block. The `try` block (lines 19–23) contains the code that is executed in normal circumstances. The exception is caught by the `catch` block. The code in the `catch` block is executed to *handle the exception*. Afterward, the statement (line 29) after the `catch` block is executed.

     handle exception

The `throw` statement is analogous to a method call, but instead of calling a method, it calls a `catch` block. In this sense, a `catch` block is like a method definition with a parameter that matches the type of the value being thrown. Unlike a method, however, after the `catch` block is executed, the program control does not return to the `throw` statement; instead, it executes the next statement after the `catch` block.

The identifier `ex` in the `catch`–block header

> `catch (ArithmeticException ex)`

acts very much like a parameter in a method. Thus, this parameter is referred to as a `catch`–block parameter. The type (e.g., `ArithmeticException`) preceding `ex` specifies what kind of exception the `catch` block can catch. Once the exception is caught, you can access the thrown value from this parameter in the body of a `catch` block.

     catch–block parameter

In summary, a template for a `try`-`throw`-`catch` block may look as follows:

```
try {
  Code to run;
  A statement or a method that may throw an exception;
  More code to run;
}
catch (type ex) {
  Code to process the exception;
}
```

An exception may be thrown directly by using a `throw` statement in a `try` block, or by invoking a method that may throw an exception.

The main method invokes `quotient` (line 20). If the quotient method executes normally, it returns a value to the caller. If the `quotient` method encounters an exception, it throws the exception back to its caller. The caller's `catch` block handles the exception.

Now you can see the *advantage* of using exception handling: It enables a method to throw an exception to its caller, enabling the caller to handle the exception. Without this capability, the called method itself must handle the exception or terminate the program. Often the called method does not know what to do in case of error. This is typically the case for the library methods. The library method can detect the error, but only the caller knows what needs to be

     advantage

done when an error occurs. The key benefit of exception handling is separating the detection of an error (done in a called method) from the handling of an error (done in the calling method).

Many library methods throw exceptions. Listing 12.5 gives an example that handles an InputMismatchException when reading an input.

LISTING 12.5   InputMismatchExceptionDemo.java

```
 1  import java.util.*;
 2
 3  public class InputMismatchExceptionDemo {
 4    public static void main(String[] args) {
 5      Scanner input = new Scanner(System.in);
 6      boolean continueInput = true;
 7
 8      do {
 9        try {
10          System.out.print("Enter an integer: ");
11          int number = input.nextInt();
12
13          // Display the result
14          System.out.println(
15            "The number entered is " + number);
16
17          continueInput = false;
18        }
19        catch (InputMismatchException ex) {
20          System.out.println("Try again. (" +
21            "Incorrect input: an integer is required)");
22          input.nextLine(); // Discard input
23        }
24      } while (continueInput);
25    }
26  }
```

create a Scanner (line 5)

try block (line 9)

If an InputMismatch Exception occurs (lines 11–14)

catch block (line 19)

```
Enter an integer: 3.5 ⏎Enter
Try again. (Incorrect input: an integer is required)
Enter an integer: 4 ⏎Enter
The number entered is 4
```

When executing input.nextInt() (line 11), an InputMismatchException occurs if the input entered is not an integer. Suppose 3.5 is entered. An InputMismatchException occurs and the control is transferred to the catch block. The statements in the catch block are now executed. The statement input.nextLine() in line 22 discards the current input line so the user can enter a new line of input. The variable continueInput controls the loop. Its initial value is true (line 6) and it is changed to false (line 17) when a valid input is received. Once a valid input is received, there is no need to continue the input.

✔ Check Point

12.2.1 What is the advantage of using exception handling?

12.2.2 Which of the following statements will throw an exception?

```
System.out.println(1 / 0);
System.out.println(1.0 / 0);
```

12.2.3 Point out the problem in the following code. Does the code throw any exceptions?

```
long value = Long.MAX_VALUE + 1;
System.out.println(value);
```

12.2.4 What does the JVM do when an exception occurs? How do you catch an exception?

12.2.5 What is the output of the following code?

```
public class Test {
  public static void main(String[] args) {
    try {
      int value = 30;
      if (value < 40)
        throw new Exception("value is too small");
    }
    catch (Exception ex) {
      System.out.println(ex.getMessage());
    }
    System.out.println("Continue after the catch block");
  }
}
```

What would be the output if the line

```
int value = 30;
```

were changed to

```
int value = 50;
```

12.2.6 Show the output of the following code:

```
public class Test {
  public static void main(String[] args) {
    for (int i = 0; i < 2; i++) {
      System.out.print(i + " ");
      try {
        System.out.println(1 / 0);
      }
      catch (Exception ex) {
      }
    }
  }
}
```
(a)

```
public class Test {
  public static void main(String[] args) {
    try {
      for (int i = 0; i < 2; i++) {
        System.out.print(i + " ");
        System.out.println(1 / 0);
      }
    }
    catch (Exception ex) {
    }
  }
}
```
(b)

12.3 Exception Types

Exceptions are objects, and objects are defined using classes. The root class for exceptions is java.lang.Throwable.

Key Point

The preceding section used the classes ArithmeticException and InputMismatch-Exception. Are there any other types of exceptions you can use? Can you define your own exception classes? Yes. There are many predefined exception classes in the Java API. Figure 12.1 shows some of them, and in Section 12.9, you will learn how to define your own exception classes.

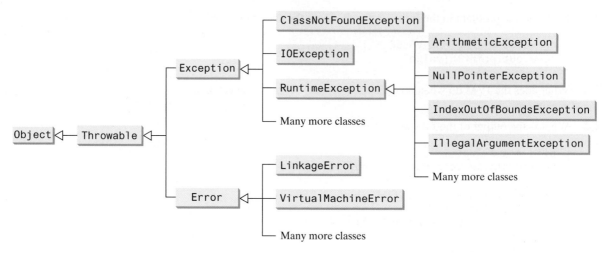

FIGURE 12.1 Exceptions thrown are instances of the classes shown in this diagram, or of subclasses of one of these classes.

 Note

The class names `Error`, `Exception`, and `RuntimeException` are somewhat confusing. All three of these classes are exceptions and all of the errors occur at runtime.

The `Throwable` class is the root of exception classes. All Java exception classes inherit directly or indirectly from `Throwable`. You can create your own exception classes by extending `Exception` or a subclass of `Exception`.

The exception classes can be classified into three major types: system errors, exceptions, and runtime exceptions.

system error

- *System errors* are thrown by the JVM and are represented in the `Error` class. The `Error` class describes internal system errors, though such errors rarely occur. If one does, there is little you can do beyond notifying the user and trying to terminate the program gracefully. Examples of subclasses of `Error` are listed in Table 12.1.

TABLE 12.1 Examples of Subclasses of `Error`

Class	Reasons for Exception
LinkageError	A class has some dependency on another class, but the latter class has changed incompatibly after the compilation of the former class.
VirtualMachineError	The JVM is broken or has run out of the resources it needs in order to continue operating.

exception

- *Exceptions* are represented in the `Exception` class, which describes errors caused by your program and by external circumstances. These errors can be caught and handled by your program. Examples of subclasses of `Exception` are listed in Table 12.2.

TABLE 12.2 Examples of Subclasses of `Exception`

Class	Reasons for Exception
ClassNotFoundException	Attempt to use a class that does not exist. This exception would occur, for example, if you tried to run a nonexistent class using the `java` command or if your program were composed of, say, three class files, only two of which could be found.
IOException	Related to input/output operations, such as invalid input, reading past the end of a file, and opening a nonexistent file. Examples of subclasses of `IOException` are `InterruptedIOException`, `EOFException` (EOF is short for End of File), and `FileNotFoundException`.

■ *Runtime exceptions* are represented in the `RuntimeException` class, which describes programming errors, such as bad casting, accessing an out-of-bounds array, and numeric errors. Runtime exceptions normally indicate programming errors. Examples of subclasses are listed in Table 12.3.

runtime exception

TABLE 12.3 Examples of Subclasses of `RuntimeException`

Class	Reasons for Exception
`ArithmeticException`	Dividing an integer by zero. Note floating-point arithmetic does not throw exceptions (see Appendix E, Special Floating-Point Values).
`NullPointerException`	Attempt to access an object through a `null` reference variable.
`IndexOutOfBoundsException`	Index to an array is out of range.
`IllegalArgumentException`	A method is passed an argument that is illegal or inappropriate.

`RuntimeException`, `Error`, and their subclasses are known as *unchecked exceptions*. All other exceptions are known as *checked exceptions*, meaning the compiler forces the programmer to check and deal with them in a `try-catch` block or declare it in the method header. Declaring an exception in the method header will be covered in Section 12.4.

unchecked exception
checked exception

In most cases, unchecked exceptions reflect programming logic errors that are unrecoverable. For example, a `NullPointerException` is thrown if you access an object through a reference variable before an object is assigned to it; an `IndexOutOfBoundsException` is thrown if you access an element in an array outside the bounds of the array. These are logic errors that should be corrected in the program. Unchecked exceptions can occur anywhere in a program. To avoid cumbersome overuse of `try-catch` blocks, Java does not mandate that you write code to catch or declare unchecked exceptions.

12.3.1 Describe the Java `Throwable` class, its subclasses, and the types of exceptions.

12.3.2 What `RuntimeException` will the following programs throw, if any?

Check
Point

```java
public class Test {
  public static void main(String[] args) {
    System.out.println(1 / 0);
  }
}
```
(a)

```java
public class Test {
  public static void main(String[] args) {
    int[] list = new int[5];
    System.out.println(list[5]);
  }
}
```
(b)

```java
public class Test {
  public static void main(String[] args) {
    String s = "abc";
    System.out.println(s.charAt(3));
  }
}
```
(c)

```java
public class Test {
  public static void main(String[] args) {
    Object o = new Object();
    String d = (String)o;
  }
}
```
(d)

```java
public class Test {
  public static void main(String[] args) {
    Object o = null;
    System.out.println(o.toString());
  }
}
```
(e)

```java
public class Test {
  public static void main(String[] args) {
    System.out.println(1.0 / 0);
  }
}
```
(f)

12.4 More on Exception Handling

A handler for an exception is found by propagating the exception backward through a chain of method calls, starting from the current method.

The preceding sections gave you an overview of exception handling and introduced several predefined exception types. This section provides an in-depth discussion of exception handling.

Java's exception-handling model is based on three operations: *declaring an exception*, *throwing an exception*, and *catching an exception*, as shown in Figure 12.2.

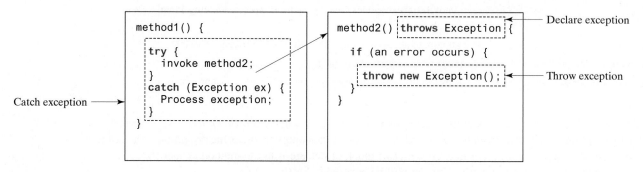

FIGURE 12.2 Exception handling in Java consists of declaring exceptions, throwing exceptions, and catching and processing exceptions.

12.4.1 Declaring Exceptions

declare exception

In Java, the statement currently being executed belongs to a method. The Java interpreter invokes the `main` method to start executing a program. Every method must state the types of checked exceptions it might throw. This is known as *declaring exceptions*. Because system errors and runtime errors can happen to any code, Java does not require that you declare `Error` and `RuntimeException` (unchecked exceptions) explicitly in the method. However, all other exceptions thrown by the method must be explicitly declared in the method header so the caller of the method is informed of the exception.

To declare an exception in a method, use the `throws` keyword in the method header, as in this example:

```
public void myMethod() throws IOException
```

The `throws` keyword indicates `myMethod` might throw an `IOException`. If the method might throw multiple exceptions, add a list of the exceptions, separated by commas, after `throws`:

```
public void myMethod()
  throws Exception1, Exception2, ..., ExceptionN
```

Note
If a method does not declare exceptions in the superclass, you cannot override it to declare exceptions in the subclass.

12.4.2 Throwing Exceptions

throw exception

A program that detects an error can create an instance of an appropriate exception type and throw it. This is known as *throwing an exception*. Here is an example: Suppose the program detects that an argument passed to the method violates the method contract (e.g., the argument must be nonnegative, but a negative argument is passed); the program can create an instance of IllegalArgumentException and throw it, as follows:

```
IllegalArgumentException ex =
  new IllegalArgumentException("Wrong Argument");
throw ex;
```

Or, if you prefer, you can use the following:

```
throw new IllegalArgumentException("Wrong Argument");
```

Note

IllegalArgumentException is an exception class in the Java API. In general, each exception class in the Java API has at least two constructors: a no-arg constructor and a constructor with a String argument that describes the exception. This argument is called the *exception message*, which can be obtained by invoking getMessage() from an exception object.

exception message

Tip

The keyword to declare an exception is throws, and the keyword to throw an exception is throw.

throws vs. throw

12.4.3 Catching Exceptions

You now know how to declare an exception and how to throw an exception. When an exception is thrown, it can be caught and handled in a try-catch block, as follows:

catch exception

```
try {
  statements; // Statements that may throw exceptions
}
catch (Exception1 exVar1) {
  handler for exception1;
}
catch (Exception2 exVar2) {
  handler for exception2;
}
...
catch (ExceptionN exVarN) {
  handler for exceptionN;
}
```

If no exceptions arise during the execution of the try block, the catch blocks are skipped.

If one of the statements inside the try block throws an exception, Java skips the remaining statements in the try block and starts the process of finding the code to handle the exception. The code that handles the exception is called the *exception handler*; it is found by *propagating the exception* backward through a chain of method calls, starting from the current method. Each catch block is examined in turn, from first to last, to see whether the type of the exception object is an instance of the exception class in the catch block. If so, the exception object is assigned to the variable declared and the code in the catch block is executed. If no handler is found, Java exits this method, passes the exception to the method's caller, and continues the same process to find a handler. If no handler is found in the chain of methods being invoked, the program terminates and prints an error message on the console. The process of finding a handler is called *catching an exception*.

exception handler
exception propagation

Suppose the `main` method invokes `method1`, `method1` invokes `method2`, `method2` invokes `method3`, and `method3` throws an exception, as shown in Figure 12.3. Consider the following scenario:

- If the exception type is `Exception3`, it is caught by the `catch` block for handling exception `ex3` in `method2`. `statement5` is skipped and `statement6` is executed.

- If the exception type is `Exception2`, `method2` is aborted, the control is returned to `method1`, and the exception is caught by the `catch` block for handling exception `ex2` in `method1`. `statement3` is skipped and `statement4` is executed.

- If the exception type is `Exception1`, `method1` is aborted, the control is returned to the `main` method, and the exception is caught by the `catch` block for handling exception `ex1` in the `main` method. `statement1` is skipped and `statement2` is executed.

- If the exception type is not caught in `method2`, `method1`, or `main`, the program terminates and `statement1` and `statement2` are not executed.

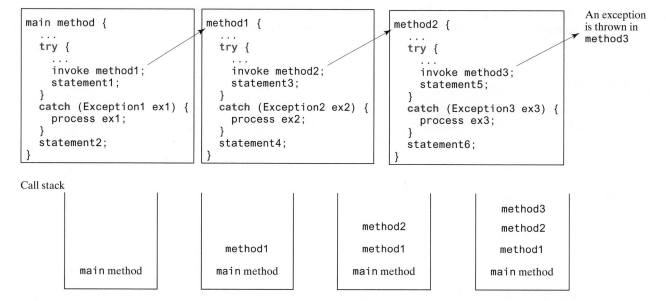

FIGURE 12.3 If an exception is not caught in the current method, it is passed to its caller. The process is repeated until the exception is caught or passed to the `main` method.

catch block

 Note
Various exception classes can be derived from a common superclass. If a `catch` block catches exception objects of a superclass, it can catch all the exception objects of the subclasses of that superclass.

order of exception handlers

 Note
The order in which exceptions are specified in `catch` blocks is important. A compile error will result if a catch block for a superclass type appears before a catch block for a subclass type. For example, the ordering in (a) below is erroneous, because `RuntimeException` is a subclass of `Exception`. The correct ordering should be as shown in (b).

```
try {
  ...
}
catch (Exception ex) {
  ...
}
catch (RuntimeException ex) {
  ...
}
```

(a) Wrong order

```
try {
  ...
}
catch (RuntimeException ex) {
  ...
}
catch (Exception ex) {
  ...
}
```

(b) Correct order

Note

Java forces you to deal with checked exceptions. If a method declares a checked exception (i.e., an exception other than `Error` or `RuntimeException`), you must invoke it in a `try-catch` block or declare to throw the exception in the calling method. For example, suppose method `p1` invokes method `p2` and `p2` may throw a checked exception (e.g., `IOException`); you have to write the code as shown in (a) or (b) below.

catch or declare checked exceptions

```
void p1() {
  try {
    p2();
  }
  catch (IOException ex) {
    ...
  }
}
```

(a) Catch exception

```
void p1() throws IOException {

  p2();

}
```

(b) Throw exception

Note

You can use the new JDK 7 multicatch feature to simplify coding for the exceptions with the same handling code. The syntax is:

JDK 7 multicatch

```
catch (Exception1 | Exception2 | ... | Exceptionk ex) {
  // Same code for handling these exceptions
}
```

Each exception type is separated from the next with a vertical bar (|). If one of the exceptions is caught, the handling code is executed.

12.4.4 Getting Information from Exceptions

An exception object contains valuable information about the exception. You may use the following instance methods in the `java.lang.Throwable` class to get information regarding the exception, as shown in Figure 12.4. The `printStackTrace()` method prints stack trace

methods in Throwable

java.lang.Throwable	
+getMessage(): String	Returns the message that describes this exception object.
+toString(): String	Returns the concatenation of three strings: (1) the full name of the exception class; (2) ":" (a colon and a space); and (3) the getMessage() method.
+printStackTrace(): void	Prints the Throwable object and its call stack trace information on the console.
+getStackTrace(): StackTraceElement[]	Returns an array of stack trace elements representing the stack trace pertaining to this exception object.

FIGURE 12.4 Throwable is the root class for all exception objects.

information on the console. The stack trace lists all the methods in the call stack, which provides valuable information for debugging runtime errors. The `getStackTrace()` method provides programmatic access to the stack trace information printed by `printStackTrace()`.

Listing 12.6 gives an example that uses the methods in `Throwable` to display exception information. Line 4 invokes the `sum` method to return the sum of all the elements in the array. There is an error in line 23 that causes the `ArrayIndexOutOfBoundsException`, a subclass of `IndexOutOfBoundsException`. This exception is caught in the `try-catch` block. Lines 7, 8, and 9 display the stack trace, exception message, and exception object and message using the `printStackTrace()`, `getMessage()`, and `toString()` methods, as shown in Figure 12.5. Line 12 brings stack trace elements into an array. Each element represents a method call. You can obtain the method (line 14), class name (line 15), and exception line number (line 16) for each element.

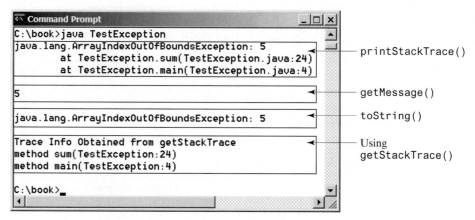

FIGURE 12.5 You can use the `printStackTrace()`, `getMessage()`, `toString()`, and `getStackTrace()` methods to obtain information from exception objects.

LISTING 12.6 TestException.java

```
 1  public class TestException {
 2    public static void main(String[] args) {
 3      try {
 4        System.out.println(sum(new int[] {1, 2, 3, 4, 5}));
 5      }
 6      catch (Exception ex) {
 7        ex.printStackTrace();
 8        System.out.println("\n" + ex.getMessage());
 9        System.out.println("\n" + ex.toString());
10
11        System.out.println("\nTrace Info Obtained from getStackTrace");
12        StackTraceElement[] traceElements = ex.getStackTrace();
13        for (int i = 0; i < traceElements.length; i++) {
14          System.out.print("method " + traceElements[i].getMethodName());
15          System.out.print("(" + traceElements[i].getClassName() + ":");
16          System.out.println(traceElements[i].getLineNumber() + ")");
17        }
18      }
19    }
20
21    private static int sum(int[] list) {
22      int result = 0;
23      for (int i = 0; i <= list.length; i++)
```

invoke sum

printStackTrace()
getMessage()
toString()

getStackTrace()

cause an exception

```
24          result += list[i];
25       return result;
26    }
27  }
```

12.4.5 Example: Declaring, Throwing, and Catching Exceptions

This example demonstrates declaring, throwing, and catching exceptions by modifying the setRadius method in the Circle class in Listing 9.8, Circle.java (CircleWithPrivate DataField). The new setRadius method throws an exception if the radius is negative.

Listing 12.7 defines a new circle class named CircleWithException, which is the same as Circle in Listing 9.8 except that the setRadius(double newRadius) method throws an IllegalArgumentException if the argument newRadius is negative.

LISTING 12.7 CircleWithException.java

```
1  public class CircleWithException {
2    /** The radius of the circle */
3    private double radius;
4
5    /** The number of the objects created */
6    private static int numberOfObjects = 0;
7
8    /** Construct a circle with radius 1 */
9    public CircleWithException() {
10     this(1.0);
11   }
12
13   /** Construct a circle with a specified radius */
14   public CircleWithException(double newRadius) {
15     setRadius(newRadius);
16     numberOfObjects++;
17   }
18
19   /** Return radius */
20   public double getRadius() {
21     return radius;
22   }
23
24   /** Set a new radius */
25   public void setRadius(double newRadius)
26       throws IllegalArgumentException {        declare exception
27     if (newRadius >= 0)
28       radius = newRadius;
29     else
30       throw new IllegalArgumentException(      throw exception
31         "Radius cannot be negative");
32   }
33
34   /** Return numberOfObjects */
35   public static int getNumberOfObjects() {
36     return numberOfObjects;
37   }
38
39   /** Return the area of this circle */
40   public double findArea() {
41     return radius * radius * 3.14159;
42   }
43 }
```

A test program that uses the new `Circle` class is given in Listing 12.8.

LISTING 12.8 TestCircleWithException.java

try

catch

```java
 1  public class TestCircleWithException {
 2    public static void main(String[] args) {
 3      try {
 4        CircleWithException c1 = new CircleWithException(5);
 5        CircleWithException c2 = new CircleWithException(-5);
 6        CircleWithException c3 = new CircleWithException(0);
 7      }
 8      catch (IllegalArgumentException ex) {
 9        System.out.println(ex);
10      }
11
12      System.out.println("Number of objects created: " +
13        CircleWithException.getNumberOfObjects());
14    }
15  }
```

```
java.lang.IllegalArgumentException: Radius cannot be negative
Number of objects created: 1
```

The original `Circle` class remains intact except that the class name is changed to `CircleWithException`, a new constructor `CircleWithException(newRadius)` is added, and the `setRadius` method now declares an exception and throws it if the radius is negative.

The `setRadius` method declares to throw `IllegalArgumentException` in the method header (lines 25–32 in Listing 12.7 CircleWithException.java). The `CircleWithException` class would still compile if the `throws IllegalArgumentException` clause (line 26) were removed from the method declaration, since it is a subclass of `RuntimeException` and every method can throw `RuntimeException` (an unchecked exception) regardless of whether it is declared in the method header.

The test program creates three `CircleWithException` objects—c1, c2, and c3—to test how to handle exceptions. Invoking new `CircleWithException(-5)` (line 5 in Listing 12.8) causes the `setRadius` method to be invoked, which throws an `IllegalArgumentException`, because the radius is negative. In the `catch` block, the type of the object `ex` is `IllegalArgumentException`, which matches the exception object thrown by the `setRadius` method, so this exception is caught by the `catch` block.

The exception handler prints a short message, `ex.toString()` (line 9 in Listing 12.8), about the exception, using `System.out.println(ex)`.

Note that the execution continues in the event of the exception. If the handlers had not caught the exception, the program would have abruptly terminated.

The test program would still compile if the `try` statement were not used, because the method throws an instance of `IllegalArgumentException`, a subclass of `RuntimeException` (an unchecked exception).

Check Point

12.4.1 What is the purpose of declaring exceptions? How do you declare an exception and where? Can you declare multiple exceptions in a method header?

12.4.2 What is a checked exception and what is an unchecked exception?

12.4.3 How do you throw an exception? Can you throw multiple exceptions in one `throw` statement?

12.4.4 What is the keyword `throw` used for? What is the keyword `throws` used for?

12.4.5 Suppose `statement2` causes an exception in the following `try-catch` block:

```
try {
  statement1;
  statement2;
  statement3;
}
catch (Exception1 ex1) {
}
catch (Exception2 ex2) {
}

statement4;
```

Answer the following questions:

■ Will `statement3` be executed?

■ If the exception is not caught, will `statement4` be executed?

■ If the exception is caught in the `catch` block, will `statement4` be executed?

12.4.6 What is displayed when running the following program?

```
public class Test {
  public static void main(String[] args) {
    try {
      int[] list = new int[10];
      System.out.println("list[10] is " + list[10]);
    }
    catch (ArithmeticException ex) {
      System.out.println("ArithmeticException");
    }
    catch (RuntimeException ex) {
      System.out.println("RuntimeException");
    }
    catch (Exception ex) {
      System.out.println("Exception");
    }
  }
}
```

12.4.7 What is displayed when running the following program?

```
public class Test {
  public static void main(String[] args) {
    try {
      method();
      System.out.println("After the method call");
    }
    catch (ArithmeticException ex) {
      System.out.println("ArithmeticException");
    }
    catch (RuntimeException ex) {
      System.out.println("RuntimeException");
    }
    catch (Exception e) {
      System.out.println("Exception");
    }
  }

  static void method() throws Exception {
```

```
        System.out.println(1 / 0);
      }
    }
```

12.4.8 What is displayed when running the following program?

```java
public class Test {
  public static void main(String[] args) {
    try {
      method();
      System.out.println("After the method call");
    }
    catch (RuntimeException ex) {
      System.out.println("RuntimeException in main");
    }
    catch (Exception ex) {
      System.out.println("Exception in main");
    }
  }

  static void method() throws Exception {
    try {
      String s ="abc";
      System.out.println(s.charAt(3));
    }
    catch (RuntimeException ex) {
      System.out.println("RuntimeException in method()");
    }
    catch (Exception ex) {
     System.out.println("Exception in method()");
    }
  }
}
```

12.4.9 What does the method `getMessage()` do?

12.4.10 What does the method `printStackTrace()` do?

12.4.11 Does the presence of a `try-catch` block impose overhead when no exception occurs?

12.4.12 Correct a compile error in the following code:

```java
public void m(int value) {
  if (value < 40)
    throw new Exception("value is too small");
}
```

12.5 The `finally` Clause

Key
Point

The `finally` clause is always executed regardless of whether an exception occurred or not.

Occasionally, you may want some code to be executed regardless of whether an exception occurs or is caught. Java has a `finally` clause that can be used to accomplish this objective. The syntax for the `finally` clause might look like this:

```java
try {
  statements;
}
catch (TheException ex) {
  handling ex;
}
```

```
finally {
   finalStatements;
}
```

The code in the `finally` block is executed under all circumstances, regardless of whether an exception occurs in the `try` block or is caught. Consider three possible cases:

1. If no exception arises in the `try` block, `finalStatements` is executed and the next statement after the `try` statement is executed.

2. If a statement causes an exception in the `try` block that is caught in a `catch` block, the rest of the statements in the `try` block are skipped, the `catch` block is executed, and the `finally` clause is executed. The next statement after the `try` statement is executed.

3. If one of the statements causes an exception that is not caught in any `catch` block, the other statements in the `try` block are skipped, the `finally` clause is executed, and the exception is passed to the caller of this method.

The `finally` block executes even if there is a `return` statement prior to reaching the `finally` block.

Note
The `catch` block may be omitted when the `finally` clause is used.

omit catch block

Check Point

12.5.1 Suppose `statement2` may cause an exception in the following statement:

```
try {
   statement1;
   statement2;
   statement3;
}
catch (Exception1 ex1) {
}
finally {
   statement4;
}
statement5;
```

Answer the following questions:

a. If no exception occurs, will `statement4` or `statement5` be executed?

b. If the exception is of type `Exception1`, will `statement4` or `statement5` be executed?

c. If the exception is not of type `Exception1`, will `statement4` or `statement5` be executed?

12.6 When to Use Exceptions

A method should throw an exception if the error needs to be handled by its caller.

Key Point

The `try` block contains the code that is executed in normal circumstances. The `catch` block contains the code that is executed in exceptional circumstances. Exception handling separates error-handling code from normal programming tasks, thus making programs easier to read and to modify. Be aware, however, that exception handling usually requires more time and resources, because it requires instantiating a new exception object, rolling back the call stack, and propagating the exception through the chain of method calls to search for the handler.

An exception occurs in a method. If you want the exception to be processed by its caller, you should create an exception object and throw it. If you can handle the exception in the method where it occurs, there is no need to throw or use exceptions.

In general, common exceptions that may occur in multiple classes in a project are candidates for exception classes. Simple errors that may occur in individual methods are best handled without throwing exceptions. This can be done by using `if` statements to check for errors.

When should you use a `try-catch` block in the code? Use it when you have to deal with unexpected error conditions. Do not use a `try-catch` block to deal with simple, expected situations. For example, the following code:

```
try {
  System.out.println(refVar.toString());
}
catch (NullPointerException ex) {
  System.out.println("refVar is null");
}
```

is better replaced by

```
if (refVar != null)
  System.out.println(refVar.toString());
else
  System.out.println("refVar is null");
```

Which situations are exceptional and which are expected is sometimes difficult to decide. The point is not to abuse exception handling as a way to deal with a simple logic test.

12.6.1   The following method checks whether a string is a numeric string:

```
public static boolean isNumeric(String token) {
  try {
    Double.parseDouble(token);
    return true;
  }
  catch (java.lang.NumberFormatException ex) {
    return false;
  }
}
```

Is it correct? Rewrite it without using exceptions.

12.7 Rethrowing Exceptions

Java allows an exception handler to rethrow the exception if the handler cannot process the exception, or simply wants to let its caller be notified of the exception.

The syntax for rethrowing an exception may look like this:

```
try {
  statements;
}
catch (TheException ex) {
  perform operations before exits;
  throw ex;
}
```

The statement `throw ex` rethrows the exception to the caller so other handlers in the caller get a chance to process the exception `ex`.

12.7.1 Suppose that `statement2` may cause an exception in the following code:

```
try {
  statement1;
  statement2;
  statement3;
}
catch (Exception1 ex1) {
}
catch (Exception2 ex2) {
  throw ex2;
}
finally {
  statement4;
}
statement5;
```

Answer the following questions:

a. If no exception occurs, will `statement4` or `statement5` be executed?

b. If the exception is of type `Exception1`, will `statement4` or `statement5` be executed?

c. If the exception is of type `Exception2`, will `statement4` or `statement5` be executed?

d. If the exception is not `Exception1` nor `Exception2`, will `statement4` or `statement5` be executed?

12.8 Chained Exceptions

Throwing an exception along with another exception forms a chained exception.

In the preceding section, the `catch` block rethrows the original exception. Sometimes, you may need to throw a new exception (with additional information) along with the original exception. This is called *chained exceptions*. Listing 12.9 illustrates how to create and throw chained exceptions.

chained exception

LISTING 12.9 `ChainedExceptionDemo.java`

```
1  public class ChainedExceptionDemo {
2    public static void main(String[] args) {
3      try {
4        method1();
5      }
6      catch (Exception ex) {
7        ex.printStackTrace();
8      }
9    }
10
11   public static void method1() throws Exception {
12     try {
13       method2();
14     }
15     catch (Exception ex) {
16       throw new Exception("New info from method1", ex);
17     }
18   }
```

stack trace

chained exception

throw exception

```
19
20    public static void method2() throws Exception {
21      throw new Exception("New info from method2");
22    }
23  }
```

```
java.lang.Exception: New info from method1
  at ChainedExceptionDemo.method1(ChainedExceptionDemo.java:16)
  at ChainedExceptionDemo.main(ChainedExceptionDemo.java:4)
Caused by: java.lang.Exception: New info from method2
  at ChainedExceptionDemo.method2(ChainedExceptionDemo.java:21)
  at ChainedExceptionDemo.method1(ChainedExceptionDemo.java:13)
  ... 1 more
```

The `main` method invokes `method1` (line 4), `method1` invokes `method2` (line 13), and `method2` throws an exception (line 21). This exception is caught in the `catch` block in `method1` and is wrapped in a new exception in line 16. The new exception is thrown and caught in the catch block in the `main` method in line 6. The sample output shows the output from the `printStackTrace()` method in line 7. The new exception thrown from `method1` is displayed first, followed by the original exception thrown from `method2`.

12.8.1   What would be the output if line 16 of Listing 12.9 is replaced by the following line?

```
throw new Exception("New info from method1");
```

12.9 Defining Custom Exception Classes

You can define a custom exception class by extending the `java.lang.Exception` *class.*

VideoNote

Create custom exception classes

Java provides quite a few exception classes. Use them whenever possible instead of defining your own exception classes. However, if you run into a problem that cannot be adequately described by the predefined exception classes, you can create your own exception class, derived from `Exception` or from a subclass of `Exception`, such as `IOException`.

In Listing 12.7, CircleWithException.java, the `setRadius` method throws an exception if the radius is negative. Suppose you wish to pass the radius to the handler. In that case, you can define a custom exception class, as shown in Listing 12.10.

LISTING 12.10   `InvalidRadiusException.java`

extends Exception

```
1   public class InvalidRadiusException extends Exception {
2     private double radius;
3
4     /** Construct an exception */
5     public InvalidRadiusException(double radius) {
6       super("Invalid radius " + radius);
7       this.radius = radius;
8     }
9
10    /** Return the radius */
11    public double getRadius() {
12      return radius;
13    }
14  }
```

This custom exception class extends `java.lang.Exception` (line 1). The `Exception` class extends `java.lang.Throwable`. All the methods (e.g., `getMessage()`, `toString()`, and `printStackTrace()`) in `Exception` are inherited from `Throwable`. The `Exception` class contains four constructors. Among them, the following constructors are often used:

java.lang.Exception	
+Exception()	Constructs an exception with no message.
+Exception(message: String)	Constructs an exception with the specified message.
+Exception(message: String, cause: Exception)	Constructs an exception with the specified message and a cause. This forms a chained exception.

Line 6 invokes the superclass's constructor with a message. This message will be set in the exception object and can be obtained by invoking `getMessage()` on the object.

Tip
Most exception classes in the Java API contain two constructors: a no-arg constructor and a constructor with a message parameter.

To create an `InvalidRadiusException`, you have to pass a radius. Therefore, the `setRadius` method in Listing 12.7 can be modified as shown in Listing 12.11.

LISTING 12.11 TestCircleWithCustomException.java

```java
1  public class TestCircleWithCustomException {
2    public static void main(String[] args) {
3      try {
4        new CircleWithCustomException(5);
5        new CircleWithCustomException(-5);
6        new CircleWithCustomException(0);
7      }
8      catch (InvalidRadiusException ex) {
9        System.out.println(ex);
10     }
11
12     System.out.println("Number of objects created: " +
13       CircleWithCustomException.getNumberOfObjects());
14   }
15 }
16
17 class CircleWithCustomException {
18   /** The radius of the circle */
19   private double radius;
20
21   /** The number of objects created */
22   private static int numberOfObjects = 0;
23
24   /** Construct a circle with radius 1 */
25   public CircleWithCustomException() throws InvalidRadiusException {          declare exception
26     this(1.0);
27   }
28
29   /** Construct a circle with a specified radius */
30   public CircleWithCustomException(double newRadius)
31       throws InvalidRadiusException {
32     setRadius(newRadius);
33     numberOfObjects++;
34   }
35
36   /** Return radius */
```

```
37    public double getRadius() {
38      return radius;
39    }
40
41    /** Set a new radius */
42    public void setRadius(double newRadius)
43        throws InvalidRadiusException {
44      if (newRadius >= 0)
45        radius = newRadius;
46      else
47        throw new InvalidRadiusException(newRadius);
48    }
49
50    /** Return numberOfObjects */
51    public static int getNumberOfObjects() {
52      return numberOfObjects;
53    }
54
55    /** Return the area of this circle */
56    public double findArea() {
57      return radius * radius * 3.14159;
58    }
59  }
```

throw exception

```
InvalidRadiusException: Invalid radius -5.0
Number of objects created: 1
```

The `setRadius` method in `CircleWithCustomException` throws an `InvalidRadius-Exception` when radius is negative (line 47). Since `InvalidRadiusException` is a checked exception, the `setRadius` method must declare it in the method header (line 43). Since the constructors for `CircleWithCustomException` invoke the `setRadius` method to set a new radius, and it may throw an `InvalidRadiusException`, the constructors are declared to throw `InvalidRadiusException` (lines 25 and 31).

Invoking `new CircleWithCustomException(-5)` (line 5) throws an `InvalidRadius-Exception`, which is caught by the handler. The handler displays the radius in the exception object `ex`.

checked custom exception

Tip

Can you define a custom exception class by extending `RuntimeException`? Yes, but it is not a good way to go because it makes your custom exception unchecked. It is better to make a custom exception checked, so the compiler can force these exceptions to be caught in your program.

12.9.1 How do you define a custom exception class?

12.9.2 Suppose that the `setRadius` method throws the `InValidRadiusException` defined in Listing 12.10. What is displayed when running the following program?

```
public class Test {
  public static void main(String[] args) {
    try {
      method();
      System.out.println("After the method call");
    }
    catch (RuntimeException ex) {
      System.out.println("RuntimeException in main");
    }
```

```
        catch (Exception ex) {
          System.out.println("Exception in main");
        }
      }

      static void method() throws Exception {
        try {
          Circle c1 = new Circle(1);
          c1.setRadius(-1);
          System.out.println(c1.getRadius());
        }
        catch (RuntimeException ex) {
          System.out.println("RuntimeException in method()");
        }
        catch (Exception ex) {
          System.out.println("Exception in method()");
          throw ex;
        }
      }
    }
```

12.10 The `File` Class

The `File` class contains the methods for obtaining the properties of a file/directory, and for renaming and deleting a file/directory.

Key Point

Having learned exception handling, you are ready to step into file processing. Data stored in the program are temporary; they are lost when the program terminates. To permanently store the data created in a program, you need to save them in a file on a disk or other permanent storage device. The file can then be transported and read later by other programs. Since data are stored in files, this section introduces how to use the `File` class to obtain file/directory properties, to delete and rename files/directories, and to create directories. The next section introduces how to read/write data from/to text files.

why file?

Every file is placed in a directory in the file system. An *absolute file name* (or *full name*) contains a file name with its complete path and drive letter. For example, **c:\book\ Welcome.java** is the absolute file name for the file **Welcome.java** on the Windows operating system. Here, **c:\book** is referred to as the *directory path* for the file. Absolute file names are machine dependent. On the UNIX platform, the absolute file name may be **/home/liang/book/Welcome.java**, where **/home/liang/book** is the directory path for the file **Welcome.java**.

absolute file name

directory path

A *relative file name* is in relation to the current working directory. The complete directory path for a relative file name is omitted. For example, **Welcome.java** is a relative file name. If the current working directory is **c:\book**, the absolute file name would be **c:\book\Welcome.java**.

relative file name

The `File` class is intended to provide an abstraction that deals with most of the machine-dependent complexities of files and path names in a machine-independent fashion. The `File` class contains the methods for obtaining file and directory properties, and for renaming and deleting files and directories, as shown in Figure 12.6. However, *the `File` class does not contain the methods for reading and writing file contents*.

The file name is a string. The `File` class is a wrapper class for the file name and its directory path. For example, `new File("c:\\book")` creates a `File` object for the directory **c:\book** and `new File("c:\\book\\test.dat")` creates a `File` object for the file **c:\book\test.dat**, both on Windows. You can use the `File` class's `isDirectory()` method to check whether the object represents a directory, and the `isFile()` method to check whether the object represents a file.

java.io.File	
+File(pathname: String)	Creates a File object for the specified path name. The path name may be a directory or a file.
+File(parent: String, child: String)	Creates a File object for the child under the directory parent. The child may be a file name or a subdirectory.
+File(parent: File, child: String)	Creates a File object for the child under the directory parent. The parent is a File object. In the preceding constructor, the parent is a string.
+exists(): boolean	Returns true if the file or the directory represented by the File object exists.
+canRead(): boolean	Returns true if the file represented by the File object exists and can be read.
+canWrite(): boolean	Returns true if the file represented by the File object exists and can be written.
+isDirectory(): boolean	Returns true if the File object represents a directory.
+isFile(): boolean	Returns true if the File object represents a file.
+isAbsolute(): boolean	Returns true if the File object is created using an absolute path name.
+isHidden(): boolean	Returns true if the file represented in the File object is hidden. The exact definition of *hidden* is system dependent. On Windows, you can mark a file hidden in the File Properties dialog box. On Unix systems, a file is hidden if its name begins with a period (.) character.
+getAbsolutePath(): String	Returns the complete absolute file or directory name represented by the File object.
+getCanonicalPath(): String	Returns the same as getAbsolutePath() except that it removes redundant names, such as "." and "..", from the path name, resolves symbolic links (on Unix), and converts drive letters to standard uppercase (on Windows).
+getName(): String	Returns the last name of the complete directory and file name represented by the File object. For example, new File("c:\\book\\test.dat").getName() returns test.dat.
+getPath(): String	Returns the complete directory and file name represented by the File object. For example, new File("c:\\book\\test.dat").getPath() returns c:\book\test.dat.
+getParent(): String	Returns the complete parent directory of the current directory or the file represented by the File object. For example, new File("c:\\book\\test.dat").getParent() returns c:\book.
+lastModified(): long	Returns the time that the file was last modified.
+length(): long	Returns the size of the file, or 0 if it does not exist or if it is a directory.
+listFile(): File[]	Returns the files under the directory for a directory File object.
+delete(): boolean	Deletes the file or directory represented by this File object. The method returns true if the deletion succeeds.
+renameTo(dest: File): boolean	Renames the file or directory represented by this File object to the specified name represented in dest. The method returns true if the operation succeeds.
+mkdir(): boolean	Creates a directory represented in this File object. Returns true if the the directory is created successfully.
+mkdirs(): boolean	Same as mkdir() except that it creates directory along with its parent directories if the parent directories do not exist.

FIGURE 12.6 The File class can be used to obtain file and directory properties, to delete and rename files and directories, and to create directories.

\ in file names

Caution
The directory separator for Windows is a backslash (\). The backslash is a special character in Java and should be written as \\ in a string literal (see Table 4.5).

Note
Constructing a File instance does not create a file on the machine. You can create a File instance for any file name regardless of whether it exists or not. You can invoke the exists() method on a File instance to check whether the file exists.

Do not use absolute file names in your program. If you use a file name such as c:\\book\\Welcome.java, it will work on Windows but not on other platforms. You should use a file name relative to the current directory. For example, you may create a File object using new File("Welcome.java") for the file **Welcome.java** in the current directory. You may create a File object using new File("image/us.gif") for the file **us.gif** under the **image** directory in the current directory. The forward slash (/) is the Java directory separator, which

relative file name

Java directory separator (/)

is the same as on UNIX. The statement `new File("image/us.gif")` works on Windows, UNIX, and any other platform.

Listing 12.12 demonstrates how to create a `File` object and use the methods in the `File` class to obtain its properties. The program creates a `File` object for the file **us.gif**. This file is stored under the **image** directory in the current directory.

LISTING 12.12 TestFileClass.java

```
1  public class TestFileClass {
2    public static void main(String[] args) {
3      java.io.File file = new java.io.File("image/us.gif");     create a File
4      System.out.println("Does it exist? " + file.exists());     exists()
5      System.out.println("The file has " + file.length() + " bytes");     length()
6      System.out.println("Can it be read? " + file.canRead());     canRead()
7      System.out.println("Can it be written? " + file.canWrite());     canWrite()
8      System.out.println("Is it a directory? " + file.isDirectory());     isDirectory()
9      System.out.println("Is it a file? " + file.isFile());     isFile()
10     System.out.println("Is it absolute? " + file.isAbsolute());     isAbsolute()
11     System.out.println("Is it hidden? " + file.isHidden());     isHidden()
12     System.out.println("Absolute path is " +
13       file.getAbsolutePath());     getAbsolutePath()
14     System.out.println("Last modified on " +
15       new java.util.Date(file.lastModified()));     lastModified()
16   }
17 }
```

The `lastModified()` method returns the date and time when the file was last modified, measured in milliseconds since the beginning of UNIX time (00:00:00 GMT, January 1, 1970). The `Date` class is used to display it in a readable format in lines 14 and 15.

Figure 12.7a shows a sample run of the program on Windows and Figure 12.7b, a sample run on UNIX. As shown in the figures, the path-naming conventions on Windows are different from those on UNIX.

(a) On Windows   (b) On UNIX

FIGURE 12.7 The program creates a `File` object and displays file properties.

12.10.1 What is wrong about creating a `File` object using the following statement?
`new File("c:\book\test.dat");`

Check Point

12.10.2 How do you check whether a file already exists? How do you delete a file? How do you rename a file? Can you find the file size (the number of bytes) using the `File` class? How do you create a directory?

12.10.3 Can you use the `File` class for I/O? Does creating a `File` object create a file on the disk?

VideoNote

Write and read data

12.11 File Input and Output

Use the Scanner *class for reading text data from a file, and the* PrintWriter *class for writing text data to a file.*

A File object encapsulates the properties of a file or a path, but it does not contain the methods for writing/reading data to/from a file (referred to as data *input* and *output*, or *I/O* for short). In order to perform I/O, you need to create objects using appropriate Java I/O classes. The objects contain the methods for reading/writing data from/to a file. There are two types of files: text and binary. Text files are essentially characters on disk. This section introduces how to read/write strings and numeric values from/to a text file using the Scanner and PrintWriter classes. Binary files will be introduced in Chapter 17.

12.11.1 Writing Data Using PrintWriter

The java.io.PrintWriter class can be used to create a file and write data to a text file. First, you have to create a PrintWriter object for a text file as follows:

```
PrintWriter output = new PrintWriter(filename);
```

Then, you can invoke the print, println, and printf methods on the PrintWriter object to write data to a file. Figure 12.8 summarizes frequently used methods in PrintWriter.

java.io.PrintWriter	
+PrintWriter(file: File)	Creates a PrintWriter object for the specified file object.
+PrintWriter(filename: String)	Creates a PrintWriter object for the specified file name string.
+print(s: String): void	Writes a string to the file.
+print(c: char): void	Writes a character to the file.
+print(cArray: char[]): void	Writes an array of characters to the file.
+print(i: int): void	Writes an int value to the file.
+print(l: long): void	Writes a long value to the file.
+print(f: float): void	Writes a float value to the file.
+print(d: double): void	Writes a double value to the file.
+print(b: boolean): void	Writes a boolean value to the file.
Also contains the overloaded println methods.	A println method acts like a print method; additionally, it prints a line separator. The line-separator string is defined by the system. It is \r\n on Windows and \n on Unix.
Also contains the overloaded printf methods.	The printf method was introduced in §4.6, "Formatting Console Output."

FIGURE 12.8 The PrintWriter class contains the methods for writing data to a text file.

Listing 12.13 gives an example that creates an instance of PrintWriter and writes two lines to the file **scores.txt**. Each line consists of a first name (a string), a middle-name initial (a character), a last name (a string), and a score (an integer).

LISTING 12.13 WriteData.java

throws an exception
create File object
file exist?

```
1  public class WriteData {
2    public static void main(String[] args) throws java.io.IOException {
3      java.io.File file = new java.io.File("scores.txt");
4      if (file.exists()) {
5        System.out.println("File already exists");
6        System.exit(1);
7      }
8
```

```
 9        // Create a file
10        java.io.PrintWriter output = new java.io.PrintWriter(file);          create PrintWriter
11
12        // Write formatted output to the file
13        output.print("John T Smith ");                                       print data
14        output.println(90);
15        output.print("Eric K Jones ");
16        output.println(85);
17
18        // Close the file
19        output.close();                                                      close file
20    }
21 }
```

John T Smith 90   scores.txt
Eric K Jones 85

Lines 4–7 check whether the file **scores.txt** exists. If so, exit the program (line 6).

Invoking the constructor of `PrintWriter` will create a new file if the file does not exist. If the   create a file
file already exists, the current content in the file will be discarded without verifying with the user.

Invoking the constructor of `PrintWriter` may throw an I/O exception. Java forces you to
write the code to deal with this type of exception. For simplicity, we declare `throws`   throws IOException
`IOException` in the main method header (line 2).

You have used the `System.out.print`, `System.out.println`, and `System.out`   print method
`.printf` methods to write text to the console output. `System.out` is a standard Java object
for the console. You can create `PrintWriter` objects for writing text to any file using `print`,
`println`, and `printf` (lines 13–16).

The `close()` method must be used to close the file (line 19). If this method is not invoked,   close file
the data may not be saved properly in the file.

12.11.2 Closing Resources Automatically Using try-with-resources

Programmers often forget to close the file. JDK 7 provides the followings new try-with-
resources syntax that automatically closes the files.

```
try (declare and create resources) {
  Use the resource to process the file;
}
```

Using the try-with-resources syntax, we rewrite the code in Listing 12.13 as shown in
Listing 12.14.

LISTING 12.14   WriteDataWithAutoClose.java

```
 1  public class WriteDataWithAutoClose {
 2    public static void main(String[] args) throws Exception {
 3      java.io.File file = new java.io.File("scores.txt");
 4      if (file.exists()) {
 5        System.out.println("File already exists");
 6        System.exit(0);
 7      }
 8
 9      try (
10        // Create a file
11        java.io.PrintWriter output = new java.io.PrintWriter(file);          declare/create resource
12      ) {
13        // Write formatted output to the file
14        output.print("John T Smith ");                                       use the resource
15        output.println(90);
16        output.print("Eric K Jones ");
17        output.println(85);
18      }
19    }
20  }
```

A resource is declared and created followed by the keyword `try`. Note the resources are enclosed in the parentheses (lines 9–12). The resources must be a subtype of `AutoCloseable` such as a `PrinterWriter` that has the `close()` method. A resource must be declared and created in the same statement, and multiple resources can be declared and created inside the parentheses. The statements in the block (lines 12–18) immediately following the resource declaration use the resource. After the block is finished, the resource's `close()` method is automatically invoked to close the resource. Using try-with-resources can not only avoid errors, but also make the code simpler. Note the catch clause may be omitted in a try-with-resources statement.

12.11.3 Reading Data Using **Scanner**

The `java.util.Scanner` class was used to read strings and primitive values from the console in Section 2.3, Reading Input from the Console. A `Scanner` breaks its input into tokens delimited by whitespace characters. To read from the keyboard, you create a `Scanner` for `System.in`, as follows:

```
Scanner input = new Scanner(System.in);
```

To read from a file, create a `Scanner` for a file, as follows:

```
Scanner input = new Scanner(new File(filename));
```

Figure 12.9 summarizes frequently used methods in `Scanner`.

java.util.Scanner	
+Scanner(source: File)	Creates a Scanner that produces values scanned from the specified file.
+Scanner(source: String)	Creates a Scanner that produces values scanned from the specified string.
+close()	Closes this scanner.
+hasNext(): boolean	Returns true if this scanner has more data to be read.
+next(): String	Returns next token as a string from this scanner.
+nextLine(): String	Returns a line ending with the line separator from this scanner.
+nextByte(): byte	Returns next token as a byte from this scanner.
+nextShort(): short	Returns next token as a short from this scanner.
+nextInt(): int	Returns next token as an int from this scanner.
+nextLong(): long	Returns next token as a long from this scanner.
+nextFloat(): float	Returns next token as a float from this scanner.
+nextDouble(): double	Returns next token as a double from this scanner.
+useDelimiter(pattern: String): Scanner	Sets this scanner's delimiting pattern and returns this scanner.

FIGURE 12.9   The Scanner class contains the methods for scanning data.

Listing 12.15 gives an example that creates an instance of Scanner and reads data from the file **scores.txt**.

LISTING 12.15   ReadData.java

```
1 import java.util.Scanner;
2
3 public class ReadData {
4   public static void main(String[] args) throws Exception {
5     // Create a File instance
6     java.io.File file = new java.io.File("scores.txt");
7
8     // Create a Scanner for the file
9     Scanner input = new Scanner(file);
```

create a File

create a Scanner

```
10
11       // Read data from a file                                    scores.txt
12       while (input.hasNext()) {                                                      has next?
13         String firstName = input.next();                 John T Smith 90            read items
14         String mi = input.next();                        Eric K Jones 85
15         String lastName = input.next();
16         int score = input.nextInt();
17         System.out.println(
18           firstName + " " + mi + " " + lastName + " " + score);
19       }
20
21       // Close the file
22       input.close();                                                                 close file
23     }
24 }
```

Note `new Scanner(String)` creates a `Scanner` for a given string. To create a `Scanner` to read data from a file, you have to use the `java.io.File` class to create an instance of the `File` using the constructor `new File(filename)` (line 6) and use `new Scanner(File)` to create a `Scanner` for the file (line 9).

`File` class

Invoking the constructor `new Scanner(File)` may throw an I/O exception, so the `main` method declares `throws Exception` in line 4.

`throws Exception`

Each iteration in the `while` loop reads the first name, middle initial, last name, and score from the text file (lines 12–19). The file is closed in line 22.

It is not necessary to close the input file (line 22), but it is a good practice to do so to release the resources occupied by the file. You can rewrite this program using the try-with-resources syntax. See liveexample.pearsoncmg.com/html/ReadDataWithAutoClose.html.

close file

12.11.4 How Does **Scanner** Work?

Section 4.5.5 introduced token-based and line-based input. The token-based input methods `nextByte()`, `nextShort()`, `nextInt()`, `nextLong()`, `nextFloat()`, `nextDouble()`, and `next()` read input separated by delimiters. By default, the delimiters are whitespace characters. You can use the `useDelimiter(String regex)` method to set a new pattern for delimiters.

change delimiter

How does an input method work? A token-based input first skips any delimiters (whitespace characters by default) then reads a token ending at a delimiter. The token is then automatically converted into a value of the `byte`, `short`, `int`, `long`, `float`, or `double` type for `nextByte()`, `nextShort()`, `nextInt()`, `nextLong()`, `nextFloat()`, and `nextDouble()`, respectively. For the `next()` method, no conversion is performed. If the token does not match the expected type, a runtime exception `java.util.InputMismatchException` will be thrown.

InputMismatchException

Both methods `next()` and `nextLine()` read a string. The `next()` method reads a string separated by delimiters and `nextLine()` reads a line ending with a line separator.

next() vs. nextLine()

Note

The line-separator string is defined by the system. It is `\r\n` on Windows and `\n` on UNIX. To get the line separator on a particular platform, use

line separator

```
String lineSeparator = System.getProperty("line.separator");
```

If you enter input from a keyboard, a line ends with the *Enter* key, which corresponds to the `\n` character.

The token-based input method does not read the delimiter after the token. If the `nextLine()` method is invoked after a token-based input method, this method reads characters that start from this delimiter and end with the line separator. The line separator is read, but it is not part of the string returned by `nextLine()`.

behavior of nextLine()

Suppose a text file named **test.txt** contains a line

```
34 567
```

After the following code is executed,

```
Scanner input = new Scanner(new File("test.txt"));
int intValue = input.nextInt();
String line = input.nextLine();
```

`intValue` contains `34` and `line` contains the characters `' '`, `5`, `6`, and `7`.

What happens if the input is *entered from the keyboard*? Suppose you enter `34`, press the *Enter* key, then enter `567` and press the *Enter* key for the following code:

```
Scanner input = new Scanner(System.in);
int intValue = input.nextInt();
String line = input.nextLine();
```

You will get `34` in `intValue` and an empty string in `line`. Why? Here is the reason. The token-based input method `nextInt()` reads in `34` and stops at the delimiter, which in this case is a line separator (the *Enter* key). The `nextLine()` method ends after reading the line separator and returns the string read before the line separator. Since there are no characters before the line separator, `line` is empty. For this reason, *you should not use a line-based input after a token-based input.*

You can read data from a file or from the keyboard using the `Scanner` class. You can also scan data from a string using the `Scanner` class. For example, the following code:

```
Scanner input = new Scanner("13 14");
int sum = input.nextInt() + input.nextInt();
System.out.println("Sum is " + sum);
```

displays

```
Sum is 27
```

12.11.5   Case Study: Replacing Text

Suppose you are to write a program named `ReplaceText` that replaces all occurrences of a string in a text file with a new string. The file name and strings are passed as command-line arguments as follows:

```
java ReplaceText sourceFile targetFile oldString newString
```

For example, invoking

```
java ReplaceText FormatString.java t.txt StringBuilder StringBuffer
```

replaces all the occurrences of `StringBuilder` by `StringBuffer` in the file **FormatString.java** and saves the new file in **t.txt**.

Listing 12.16 gives the program. The program checks the number of arguments passed to the `main` method (lines 7–11), checks whether the source and target files exist (lines 14–25), creates a `Scanner` for the source file (line 29), creates a `PrintWriter` for the target file (line 30), and repeatedly reads a line from the source file (line 33), replaces the text (line 34), and writes a new line to the target file (line 35).

LISTING 12.16   `ReplaceText.java`

```
1  import java.io.*;
2  import java.util.*;
3
```

```
4   public class ReplaceText {
5     public static void main(String[] args) throws Exception {
6       // Check command line parameter usage
7       if (args.length != 4) {                                              check command usage
8         System.out.println(
9           "Usage: java ReplaceText sourceFile targetFile oldStr newStr");
10        System.exit(1);
11      }
12
13      // Check if source file exists
14      File sourceFile = new File(args[0]);
15      if (!sourceFile.exists()) {                                          source file exists?
16        System.out.println("Source file " + args[0] + " does not exist");
17        System.exit(2);
18      }
19
20      // Check if target file exists
21      File targetFile = new File(args[1]);
22      if (targetFile.exists()) {                                           target file exists?
23        System.out.println("Target file " + args[1] + " already exists");
24        System.exit(3);
25      }
26
27      try (                                                                try-with-resources
28        // Create input and output files
29        Scanner input = new Scanner(sourceFile);                           create a Scanner
30        PrintWriter output = new PrintWriter(targetFile);                  create a PrintWriter
31      ) {
32        while (input.hasNext()) {                                          has next?
33          String s1 = input.nextLine();                                    read a line
34          String s2 = s1.replaceAll(args[2], args[3]);
35          output.println(s2);
36        }
37      }
38    }
39  }
```

In a normal situation, the program is terminated after a file is copied. The program is terminated abnormally if the command-line arguments are not used properly (lines 7–11), if the source file does not exist (lines 14–18), or if the target file already exists (lines 22–25). The exit status codes 1, 2, and 3 are used to indicate these abnormal terminations (lines 10, 17, and 24).

12.11.1 How do you create a `PrintWriter` to write data to a file? What is the reason to declare `throws Exception` in the main method in Listing 12.13, WriteData.java? What would happen if the `close()` method were not invoked in Listing 12.13?

Check Point

12.11.2 Show the contents of the file **temp.txt** after the following program is executed:

```
public class Test {
  public static void main(String[] args) throws Exception {
    java.io.PrintWriter output = new
      java.io.PrintWriter("temp.txt");
    output.printf("amount is %f %e\r\n", 32.32, 32.32);
    output.printf("amount is %5.4f %5.4e\r\n", 32.32, 32.32);
    output.printf("%6b\r\n", (1 > 2));
    output.printf("%6s\r\n", "Java");
    output.close();
  }
}
```

12.11.3   Rewrite the code in the preceding question using a try-with-resources syntax.

12.11.4   How do you create a Scanner to read data from a file? What is the reason to define throws Exception in the main method in Listing 12.15, ReadData.java? What would happen if the close() method were not invoked in Listing 12.15?

12.11.5   What will happen if you attempt to create a Scanner for a nonexistent file? What will happen if you attempt to create a PrintWriter for an existing file?

12.11.6   Is the line separator the same on all platforms? What is the line separator on Windows?

12.11.7   Suppose you enter 45 57.8 789, then press the *Enter* key. Show the contents of the variables after the following code is executed:

```
Scanner input = new Scanner(System.in);
int intValue = input.nextInt();
double doubleValue = input.nextDouble();
String line = input.nextLine();
```

12.11.8   Suppose you enter 45, press the *Enter* key, enter 57.8, press the *Enter* key, and enter 789, press the *Enter* key. Show the contents of the variables after the following code is executed:

```
Scanner input = new Scanner(System.in);
int intValue = input.nextInt();
double doubleValue = input.nextDouble();
String line = input.nextLine();
```

12.12 Reading Data from the Web

Key Point

Just like you can read data from a file on your computer, you can read data from a file on the Web.

In addition to reading data from a local file on a computer or file server, you can also access data from a file that is on the Web if you know the file's URL (Uniform Resource Locator—the unique address for a file on the Web). For example, www.google.com/index.html is the URL for the file **index.html** located on the Google web server. When you enter the URL in a Web browser, the Web server sends the data to your browser, which renders the data graphically. Figure 12.10 illustrates how this process works.

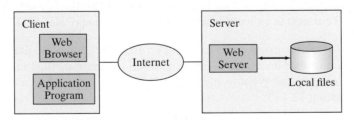

FIGURE 12.10   The client retrieves files from a Web server.

For an application program to read data from a URL, you first need to create a URL object using the java.net.URL class with this constructor:

```
public URL(String spec) throws MalformedURLException
```

For example, the following statement creates a URL object for http://www.google.com/index.html.

```
1  try {
2    URL url = new URL("http://www.google.com/index.html");
3  }
```

```
4  catch (MalformedURLException ex) {
5    ex.printStackTrace();
6  }
```

A `MalformedURLException` is thrown if the URL string has a syntax error. For example, the URL string http:www.google.com/index.html would cause a `MalformedURLException` runtime error because two slashes (`//`) are required after the colon (`:`). Note the `http://` prefix is required for the `URL` class to recognize a valid URL. It would be wrong if you replace line 2 with the following code:

```
URL url = new URL("www.google.com/index.html");
```

After a `URL` object is created, you can use the `openStream()` method defined in the `URL` class to open an input stream and use this stream to create a `Scanner` object as follows:

```
Scanner input = new Scanner(url.openStream());
```

Now you can read the data from the input stream just like from a local file. The example in Listing 12.17 prompts the user to enter a URL and displays the size of the file.

LISTING 12.17 ReadFileFromURL.java

```
1   import java.util.Scanner;
2
3   public class ReadFileFromURL {
4     public static void main(String[] args) {
5       System.out.print("Enter a URL: ");
6       String URLString = new Scanner(System.in).next();         enter a URL
7
8       try {
9         java.net.URL url = new java.net.URL(URLString);          create a URL object
10        int count = 0;
11        Scanner input = new Scanner(url.openStream());           create a Scanner object
12        while (input.hasNext()) {                                more to read?
13          String line = input.nextLine();                        read a line
14          count += line.length();
15        }
16
17        System.out.println("The file size is " + count + " characters");
18      }
19      catch (java.net.MalformedURLException ex) {                MalformedURLException
20        System.out.println("Invalid URL");
21      }
22      catch (java.io.IOException ex) {                           IOException
23        System.out.println("I/O Errors: no such file");
24      }
25    }
26  }
```

```
Enter a URL: http://liveexample.pearsoncmg.com/data/Lincoln.txt  ↵Enter
The file size is 1469 characters
```

```
Enter a URL: http://www.yahoo.com  ↵Enter
The file size is 190006 characters
```

The program prompts the user to enter a URL string (line 6) and creates a `URL` object (line 9). The constructor will throw a `java.net.MalformedURLException` (line 19) if the URL isn't formed correctly.

The program creates a `Scanner` object from the input stream for the URL (line 11). If the URL is formed correctly but does not exist, an `IOException` will be thrown (line 22). For example, http://google.com/index1.html uses the appropriate form, but the URL itself does not exist. An `IOException` would be thrown if this URL was used for this program.

12.12.1 How do you create a `Scanner` object for reading text from a URL?

12.13 Case Study: Web Crawler

This case study develops a program that travels the Web by following hyperlinks.

web crawler

The World Wide web, abbreviated as WWW, W3, or Web, is a system of interlinked hypertext documents on the Internet. With a web browser, you can view a document and follow the hyperlinks to view other documents. In this case study, we will develop a program that automatically traverses the documents on the Web by following the hyperlinks. This type of program is commonly known as a *web crawler*. For simplicity, our program follows the hyperlink that starts with `http://`. Figure 12.11 shows an example of traversing the Web. We start from a Webpage that contains three URLs named URL1, URL2, and URL3. Following URL1 leads to the page that contains three URLs named URL11, URL12, and URL13. Following URL2 leads to the page that contains two URLs named URL21 and URL22. Following URL3 leads to the page that contains four URLs named URL31, URL32, URL33, and URL34. Continue to traverse the Web following the new hyperlinks. As you see, this process may continue forever, but we will exit the program once we have traversed 100 pages.

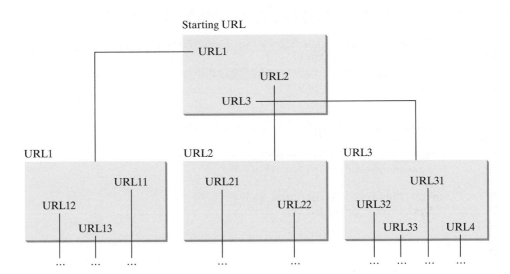

FIGURE 12.11 Web crawler explores the web through hyperlinks.

The program follows the URLs to traverse the Web. To ensure that each URL is traversed only once, the program maintains two lists of URLs. One list stores the URLs pending for traversing, and the other stores the URLs that have already been traversed. The algorithm for this program can be described as follows:

```
Add the starting URL to a list named listOfPendingURLs;
while listOfPendingURLs is not empty and size of listOfTraversedURLs
<= 100 {
```

```
      Remove a URL from listOfPendingURLs;
      if this URL is not in listOfTraversedURLs {
        Add it to listOfTraversedURLs;
        Display this URL;
        Read the page from this URL and for each URL contained in the page {
          Add it to listOfPendingURLs if it is not in listOfTraversedURLs;
        }
      }
    }
  }
```

Listing 12.18 gives the program that implements this algorithm.

LISTING 12.18 WebCrawler.java

```
1   import java.util.Scanner;
2   import java.util.ArrayList;
3
4   public class WebCrawler {
5     public static void main(String[] args) {
6       Scanner input = new Scanner(System.in);
7       System.out.print("Enter a URL: ");
8       String url = input.nextLine();
9       crawler(url); // Traverse the Web from the a starting url
10    }
11
12    public static void crawler(String startingURL) {
13      ArrayList<String> listOfPendingURLs = new ArrayList<>();
14      ArrayList<String> listOfTraversedURLs = new ArrayList<>();
15
16      listOfPendingURLs.add(startingURL);
17      while (!listOfPendingURLs.isEmpty() &&
18          listOfTraversedURLs.size() <= 100) {
19        String urlString = listOfPendingURLs.remove(0);
20        if (!listOfTraversedURLs.contains(urlString)) {
21          listOfTraversedURLs.add(urlString);
22          System.out.println("Crawl " + urlString);
23
24          for (String s: getSubURLs(urlString)) {
25            if (!listOfTraversedURLs.contains(s))
26              listOfPendingURLs.add(s);
27          }
28        }
29      }
30    }
31
32    public static ArrayList<String> getSubURLs(String urlString) {
33      ArrayList<String> list = new ArrayList<>();
34
35      try {
36        java.net.URL url = new java.net.URL(urlString);
37        Scanner input = new Scanner(url.openStream());
38        int current = 0;
39        while (input.hasNext()) {
40          String line = input.nextLine();
41          current = line.indexOf("http:", current);
42          while (current > 0) {
43            int endIndex = line.indexOf("\"", current);
44            if (endIndex > 0) { // Ensure that a correct URL is found
45              list.add(line.substring(current, endIndex));
46              current = line.indexOf("http:", endIndex);
47            }
```

enter a URL
crawl from this URL

list of pending URLs
list of traversed URLs

add starting URL

get the first URL

URL traversed

add a new URL

read a line
search for a URL
end of a URL

URL ends with "
extract a URL
search for next URL

```
48              else
49                  current = –1;
50            }
51        }
52    }
53    catch (Exception ex) {
54        System.out.println("Error: " + ex.getMessage());
55    }
56
```
return URLs
```
57    return list;
58  }
59 }
```

```
Enter a URL: http://cs.armstrong.edu/liang  ↵Enter
Crawl http://www.cs.armstrong.edu/liang
Crawl http://www.cs.armstrong.edu
Crawl http://www.armstrong.edu
Crawl http://www.pearsonhighered.com/liang
...
```

The program prompts the user to enter a starting URL (lines 7 and 8) and invokes the crawler(url) method to traverse the Web (line 9).

The crawler(url) method adds the starting url to listOfPendingURLs (line 16) and repeatedly process each URL in listOfPendingURLs in a while loop (lines 17–29). It removes the first URL in the list (line 19) and processes the URL if it has not been processed (lines 20–28). To process each URL, the program first adds the URL to listOfTraversedURLs (line 21). This list stores all the URLs that have been processed. The getSubURLs(url) method returns a list of URLs in the webpage for the specified URL (line 24). The program uses a foreach loop to add each URL in the page into listOfPendingURLs if it is not in listOfTraversedURLs (lines 24–27).

The getSubURLs(url) method reads each line from the webpage (line 40) and searches for the URLs in the line (line 41). Note a correct URL cannot contain line break characters. Therefore, it is sufficient to limit the search for a URL in one line of the text in a webpage. For simplicity, we assume that a URL ends with a quotation mark " (line 43). The method obtains a URL and adds it to a list (line 45). A line may contain multiple URLs. The method continues to search for the next URL (line 46). If no URL is found in the line, current is set to –1 (line 49). The URLs contained in the page are returned in the form of a list (line 57).

The program terminates when the number of traversed URLs reaches 100 (line 18).

This is a simple program to traverse the Web. Later, you will learn the techniques to make the program more efficient and robust.

Check Point

12.13.1 Before a URL is added to listOfPendingURLs, line 25 checks whether it has been traversed. Is it possible that listOfPendingURLs contains duplicate URLs? If so, give an example.

12.13.2 Simplify the code in lines 20-28 as follows: 1. Delete lines 20 and 28; 2. Add an additional condition !listOfPendingURLs.contains(s) to the if statement in line 25. Write the complete new code for the while loop in lines 20-29. Does this revision work?

KEY TERMS

absolute file name 477	exception 454
chained exception 473	exception propagation 463
checked exception 461	relative file name 477
declare exception 462	throw exception 457
directory path 477	unchecked exception 461

CHAPTER SUMMARY

1. Exception handling enables a method to throw an exception to its caller.

2. A Java *exception* is an instance of a class derived from `java.lang.Throwable`. Java provides a number of predefined exception classes, such as `Error`, `Exception`, `RuntimeException`, `ClassNotFoundException`, `NullPointerException`, and `ArithmeticException`. You can also define your own exception class by extending `Exception`.

3. Exceptions occur during the execution of a method. `RuntimeException` and `Error` are *unchecked exceptions*; all other exceptions are *checked*.

4. When *declaring a method*, you have to declare a checked exception if the method might throw it, thus telling the compiler what can go wrong.

5. The keyword for declaring an exception is `throws`, and the keyword for throwing an exception is `throw`.

6. To invoke the method that declares checked exceptions, enclose it in a `try` statement. When an exception occurs during the execution of the method, the `catch` block catches and handles the exception.

7. If an exception is not caught in the current method, it is passed to its caller. The process is repeated until the exception is caught or passed to the `main` method.

8. Various exception classes can be derived from a common superclass. If a `catch` block catches the exception objects of a superclass, it can also catch all the exception objects of the subclasses of that superclass.

9. The order in which exceptions are specified in a `catch` block is important. A compile error will result if you specify an exception object of a class after an exception object of the superclass of that class.

10. When an exception occurs in a method, the method exits immediately if it does not catch the exception. If the method is required to perform some task before exiting, you can catch the exception in the method and then rethrow it to its caller.

11. The code in the `finally` block is executed under all circumstances, regardless of whether an exception occurs in the `try` block, or whether an exception is caught if it occurs.

12. Exception handling separates error-handling code from normal programming tasks, thus making programs easier to read and to modify.

13. Exception handling should not be used to replace simple tests. You should perform simple test using `if` statements whenever possible and reserve exception handling for dealing with situations that cannot be handled with `if` statements.

14. The `File` class is used to obtain file properties and manipulate files. It does not contain the methods for creating a file or for reading/writing data from/to a file.

15. You can use `Scanner` to read string and primitive data values from a text file and use `PrintWriter` to create a file and write data to a text file.

16. You can read from a file on the Web using the `URL` class.

QUIZ

Answer the quiz for this chapter online at the Companion Website.

MyProgrammingLab™ **PROGRAMMING EXERCISES**

Sections 12.2–12.9

*12.1 (*NumberFormatException*) Listing 7.9, Calculator.java, is a simple command-line calculator. Note the program terminates if any operand is nonnumeric. Write a program with an exception handler that deals with nonnumeric operands; then write another program without using an exception handler to achieve the same objective. Your program should display a message that informs the user of the wrong operand type before exiting (see Figure 12.12).

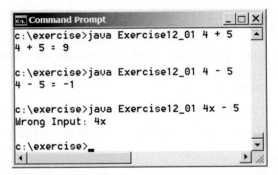

FIGURE 12.12 The program performs arithmetic operations and detects input errors.

*12.2 (*InputMismatchException*) Write a program that prompts the user to read two integers and displays their sum. Your program should prompt the user to read the number again if the input is incorrect.

*12.3 (*ArrayIndexOutOfBoundsException*) Write a program that meets the following requirements:

- Creates an array with 100 randomly chosen integers.
- Prompts the user to enter the index of the array, then displays the corresponding element value. If the specified index is out of bounds, display the message "Out of Bounds".

*12.4 (*IllegalArgumentException*) Modify the Loan class in Listing 10.2 to throw IllegalArgumentException if the loan amount, interest rate, or number of years is less than or equal to zero.

*12.5 (*IllegalTriangleException*) Programming Exercise 11.1 defined the Triangle class with three sides. In a triangle, the sum of any two sides is greater than the other side. The Triangle class must adhere to this rule. Create the IllegalTriangleException class, and modify the constructor of the Triangle class to throw an IllegalTriangleException object if a triangle is created with sides that violate the rule, as follows:

```
/** Construct a triangle with the specified sides */
public Triangle(double side1, double side2, double side3)
  throws IllegalTriangleException {
  // Implement it
}
```

*12.6 (*NumberFormatException*) Listing 6.8 implements the `hex2Dec(String hexString)` method, which converts a hex string into a decimal number. Implement the `hex2Dec` method to throw a `NumberFormatException` if the string is not a hex string.

*12.7 (*NumberFormatException*) Write the `bin2Dec(String binaryString)` method to convert a binary string into a decimal number. Implement the `bin2Dec` method to throw a `NumberFormatException` if the string is not a binary string.

*12.8 (*HexFormatException*) Programming Exercise 12.6 implements the `hex2Dec` method to throw a `NumberFormatException` if the string is not a hex string. Define a custom exception called `HexFormatException`. Implement the `hex2Dec` method to throw a `HexFormatException` if the string is not a hex string.

VideoNote

HexFormatException

*12.9 (*BinaryFormatException*) Exercise 12.7 implements the `bin2Dec` method to throw a `BinaryFormatException` if the string is not a binary string. Define a custom exception called `BinaryFormatException`. Implement the `bin2Dec` method to throw a `BinaryFormatException` if the string is not a binary string.

*12.10 (*OutOfMemoryError*) Write a program that causes the JVM to throw an `OutOfMemoryError` and catches and handles this error.

Sections 12.10–12.12

**12.11 (*Remove text*) Write a program that removes all the occurrences of a specified string from a text file. For example, invoking

```
java Exercise12_11 John filename
```

removes the string John from the specified file. Your program should get the arguments from the command line.

**12.12 (*Reformat Java source code*) Write a program that converts the Java source code from the next-line brace style to the end-of-line brace style. For example, the following Java source in (a) uses the next-line brace style. Your program converts it to the end-of-line brace style in (b).

```
public class Test
{
  public static void main(String[] args)
  {
    // Some statements
  }
}
```

```
public class Test {
  public static void main(String[] args) {
    // Some statements
  }
}
```

(a) Next-line brace style   (b) End-of-line brace style

Your program can be invoked from the command line with the Java source-code file as the argument. It converts the Java source code to a new format. For example, the following command converts the Java source-code file **Test.java** to the end-of-line brace style.

```
java Exercise12_12 Test.java
```

*12.13 (*Count characters, words, and lines in a file*) Write a program that will count the number of characters, words, and lines in a file. Words are separated by whitespace characters. The file name should be passed as a command-line argument, as shown in Figure 12.13.

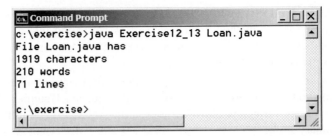

FIGURE 12.13 The program displays the number of characters, words, and lines in the given file.

*12.14 (*Process scores in a text file*) Suppose a text file contains an unspecified number of scores separated by spaces. Write a program that prompts the user to enter the file, reads the scores from the file, and displays their total and average.

*12.15 (*Write/read data*) Write a program to create a file named **Exercise12_15.txt** if it does not exist. Write 100 integers created randomly into the file using text I/O. Integers are separated by spaces in the file. Read the data back from the file and display the data in increasing order.

**12.16 (*Replace text*) Listing 12.16, ReplaceText.java, gives a program that replaces text in a source file and saves the change into a new file. Revise the program to save the change into the original file. For example, invoking

```
java Exercise12_16 file oldString newString
```

replaces oldString in the source file with newString.

***12.17 (*Game: hangman*) Rewrite Programming Exercise 7.35. The program reads the words stored in a text file named **hangman.txt**. Words are delimited by spaces.

**12.18 (*Add package statement*) Suppose you have Java source files under the directories chapter1, chapter2, ..., chapter34. Write a program to insert the statement package chapteri; as the first line for each Java source file under the directory chapteri. Suppose chapter1, chapter2, ..., chapter34 are under the root directory srcRootDirectory. The root directory and chapteri directory may contain other folders and files. Use the following command to run the program:

```
java Exercise12_18 srcRootDirectory
```

*12.19 (*Count words*) Write a program that counts the number of words in President Abraham Lincoln's Gettysburg address from https://liveexample.pearsoncmg.com/data/Lincoln.txt.

**12.20 (*Remove package statement*) Suppose you have Java source files under the directories chapter1, chapter2, ..., chapter34. Write a program to remove the statement package chapteri; in the first line for each Java source file under the directory chapteri. Suppose chapter1, chapter2, ..., chapter34 are under the root directory srcRootDirectory. The root directory and chapteri directory may contain other folders and files. Use the following command to run the program:

```
java Exercise12_20 srcRootDirectory
```

*12.21 (*Data sorted?*) Write a program that reads the strings from file **SortedStrings.txt** and reports whether the strings in the files are stored in increasing order. If the strings are not sorted in the file, it displays the first two strings that are out of the order.

**12.22 (*Replace text*) Revise Programming Exercise 12.16 to replace a string in a file with a new string for all files in the specified directory using the following command:

```
java Exercise12_22 dir oldString newString
```

**12.23 (*Process scores in a text file on the Web*) Suppose the text file on the Web http://liveexample.pearsoncmg.com/data/Scores.txt contains an unspecified number of scores separated by spaces. Write a program that reads the scores from the file and displays their total and average.

*12.24 (*Create large dataset*) Create a data file with 1,000 lines. Each line in the file consists of a faculty member's first name, last name, rank, and salary. The faculty member's first name and last name for the *i*th line are FirstName*i* and LastName*i*. The rank is randomly generated as assistant, associate, and full. The salary is randomly generated as a number with two digits after the decimal point. The salary for an assistant professor should be in the range from 50,000 to 80,000, for associate professor from 60,000 to 110,000, and for full professor from 75,000 to 130,000. Save the file in **Salary.txt**. Here are some sample data:

FirstName1 LastName1 assistant 60055.95

FirstName2 LastName2 associate 81112.45

. . .

FirstName1000 LastName1000 full 92255.21

*12.25 (*Process large dataset*) A university posts its employees' salaries at http://liveexample.pearsoncmg.com/data/Salary.txt. Each line in the file consists of a faculty member's first name, last name, rank, and salary (see Programming Exercise 12.24). Write a program to display the total salary for assistant professors, associate professors, full professors, and faculty, respectively, and display the average salary for assistant professors, associate professors, full professors, and faculty, respectively.

**12.26 (*Create a directory*) Write a program that prompts the user to enter a directory name and creates a directory using the `File`'s `mkdirs` method. The program displays the message "Directory created successfully" if a directory is created or "Directory already exists" if the directory already exists.

12.27 (*Replace words*) Suppose you have a lot of files in a directory that contain words **Exercise*i*_*j*, where *i* and *j* are digits. Write a program that pads a 0 before *i* if *i* is a single digit and 0 before *j* if *j* is a single digit. For example, the word **Exercise2_1** in a file will be replaced by **Exercise02_01**. In Java, when you pass the symbol * from the command line, it refers to all files in the directory (see Supplement III.V). Use the following command to run your program:

```
java Exercise12_27 *
```

12.28 (*Rename files*) Suppose you have a lot of files in a directory named **Exercise*i*_*j*, where *i* and *j* are digits. Write a program that pads a 0 before *i* if *i* is a single digit. For example, a file named **Exercise2_1** in a directory will be renamed to **Exercise02_1**. In Java, when you pass the symbol * from the command line, it refers to all files in the directory (see Supplement III.V). Use the following command to run your program:

```
java Exercise12_28 *
```

12.29 (*Rename files*) Suppose you have several files in a directory named **Exercise*i_j*, where *i* and *j* are digits. Write a program that pads a 0 before *j* if *j* is a single digit. For example, a file named **Exercise2_1** in a directory will be renamed to **Exercise2_01**. In Java, when you pass the symbol * from the command line, it refers to all files in the directory (see Supplement III.V). Use the following command to run your program:

```
java Exercise12_29 *
```

**12.30 (*Occurrences of each letter*) Write a program that prompts the user to enter a file name and displays the occurrences of each letter in the file. Letters are case insensitive. Here is a sample run:

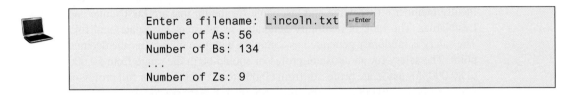

```
Enter a filename: Lincoln.txt  ↵Enter
Number of As: 56
Number of Bs: 134
...
Number of Zs: 9
```

*12.31 (*Baby name popularity ranking*) The popularity ranking of baby names from years 2001 to 2010 is downloaded from www.ssa.gov/oact/babynames and stored in files named **babynameranking2001.txt**, **babynameranking2002.txt**, . . . , **babynameranking2010.txt**. You can download these files using the URL such as http://liveexample.pearsoncmg.com/data/babynamesranking2001.txt. Each file contains 1,000 lines. Each line contains a ranking, a boy's name, number for the boy's name, a girl's name, and number for the girl's name. For example, the first two lines in the file **babynameranking2010.txt** are as follows:

1	Jacob	21,875	Isabella	22,731
2	Ethan	17,866	Sophia	20,477

Therefore, the boy's name Jacob and girl's name Isabella are ranked #1 and the boy's name Ethan and girl's name Sophia are ranked #2; 21,875 boys are named Jacob, and 22,731 girls are named Isabella. Write a program that prompts the user to enter the year, gender, followed by a name, and displays the ranking of the name for the year. Here is a sample run:

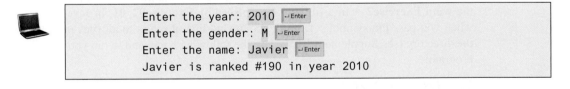

```
Enter the year: 2010  ↵Enter
Enter the gender: M  ↵Enter
Enter the name: Javier  ↵Enter
Javier is ranked #190 in year 2010
```

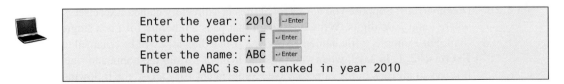

```
Enter the year: 2010  ↵Enter
Enter the gender: F  ↵Enter
Enter the name: ABC  ↵Enter
The name ABC is not ranked in year 2010
```

*12.32   (*Ranking summary*) Write a program that uses the files described in Programming Exercise 12.31 and displays a ranking summary table for the first five girl's and boy's names as follows:

Year	Rank 1	Rank 2	Rank 3	Rank 4	Rank 5	Rank 1	Rank 2	Rank 3	Rank 4	Rank 5
2010	Isabella	Sophia	Emma	Olivia	Ava	Jacob	Ethan	Michael	Jayden	William
2009	Isabella	Emma	Olivia	Sophia	Ava	Jacob	Ethan	Michael	Alexander	William
...										
2001	Emily	Madison	Hannah	Ashley	Alexis	Jacob	Michael	Matthew	Joshua	Christopher

**12.33   (*Search Web*) Modify Listing 12.18 WebCrawler.java to search for the word (e.g., Computer Programming) starting from a URL (e.g., http://cs.armstrong .edu/liang). Your program prompts the user to enter the word and the starting URL and terminates once the word is found. Display the URL for the page that contains the word.

ABSTRACT CLASSES AND INTERFACES

Objectives

- To design and use abstract classes (§13.2).

- To generalize numeric wrapper classes `BigInteger` and `BigDecimal` using the abstract `Number` class (§13.3).

- To process a calendar using the `Calendar` and `GregorianCalendar` classes (§13.4).

- To specify common behavior for objects using interfaces (§13.5).

- To define interfaces and define classes that implement interfaces (§13.5).

- To define a natural order using the `Comparable` interface (§13.6).

- To make objects cloneable using the `Cloneable` interface (§13.7).

- To explore the similarities and differences among concrete classes, abstract classes, and interfaces (§13.8).

- To design the `Rational` class for processing rational numbers (§13.9).

- To design classes that follow the class-design guidelines (§13.10).

13.1 Introduction

A superclass defines common behavior for related subclasses. An interface can be used to define common behavior for classes (including unrelated classes).

problem
interface

You can use the `java.util.Arrays.sort` method to sort an array of numbers or strings. Can you apply the same `sort` method to sort an array of geometric objects? In order to write such code, you have to know about interfaces. An *interface* is for defining common behavior for classes (including unrelated classes). Before discussing interfaces, we introduce a closely related subject: abstract classes.

13.2 Abstract Classes

An abstract class cannot be used to create objects. An abstract class can contain abstract methods that are implemented in concrete subclasses.

In the inheritance hierarchy, classes become more specific and concrete *with each new subclass*. If you move from a subclass back up to a superclass, the classes become more general and less specific. Class design should ensure a superclass contains common features of its subclasses. Sometimes, a superclass is so abstract it cannot be used to create any specific instances. Such a class is referred to as an *abstract class*.

abstract class

VideoNote

Abstract GeometricObject class

abstract method

abstract modifier

In Chapter 11, `GeometricObject` was defined as the superclass for `Circle` and `Rectangle`. `GeometricObject` models common features of geometric objects. Both `Circle` and `Rectangle` contain the `getArea()` and `getPerimeter()` methods for computing the area and perimeter of a circle and a rectangle. Since you can compute areas and perimeters for all geometric objects, it is better to define the `getArea()` and `getPerimeter()` methods in the `GeometricObject` class. However, these methods cannot be implemented in the `GeometricObject` class because their implementation depends on the specific type of geometric object. Such methods are referred to as *abstract methods* and are denoted using the `abstract` modifier in the method header. After you define the methods in `GeometricObject`, it becomes an abstract class. Abstract classes are denoted using the `abstract` modifier in the class header. In UML graphic notation, the names of abstract classes and their abstract methods are italicized, as shown in Figure 13.1. Listing 13.1 gives the source code for the new `GeometricObject` class.

abstract class

LISTING 13.1 GeometricObject.java

```java
1  public abstract class GeometricObject {
2    private String color = "white";
3    private boolean filled;
4    private java.util.Date dateCreated;
5
6    /** Construct a default geometric object */
7    protected GeometricObject() {
8      dateCreated = new java.util.Date();
9    }
10
11   /** Construct a geometric object with color and filled value */
12   protected GeometricObject(String color, boolean filled) {
13     dateCreated = new java.util.Date();
14     this.color = color;
15     this.filled = filled;
16   }
17
18   /** Return color */
19   public String getColor() {
20     return color;
```

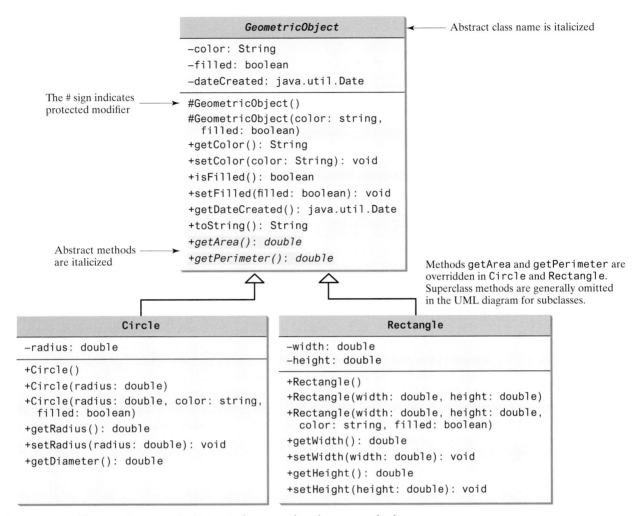

The # sign indicates
protected modifier

Abstract methods
are italicized

Abstract class name is italicized

Methods getArea and getPerimeter are
overridden in Circle and Rectangle.
Superclass methods are generally omitted
in the UML diagram for subclasses.

FIGURE 13.1 The new GeometricObject class contains abstract methods.

```
21    }
22
23    /** Set a new color */
24    public void setColor(String color) {
25      this.color = color;
26    }
27
28    /** Return filled. Since filled is boolean,
29     *  the getter method is named isFilled */
30    public boolean isFilled() {
31      return filled;
32    }
33
34    /** Set a new filled */
35    public void setFilled(boolean filled) {
36      this.filled = filled;
37    }
38
39    /** Get dateCreated */
40    public java.util.Date getDateCreated() {
41      return dateCreated;
42    }
```

```
43
44    @Override
45    public String toString() {
46      return "created on " + dateCreated + "\ncolor: " + color +
47        " and filled: " + filled;
48    }
49
50    /** Abstract method getArea */
```

abstract method
```
51    public abstract double getArea();
52
53    /** Abstract method getPerimeter */
```

abstract method
```
54    public abstract double getPerimeter();
55 }
```

Abstract classes are like regular classes, but you cannot create instances of abstract classes using the new operator. An abstract method is defined without implementation. Its implementation is provided by the subclasses. A class that contains abstract methods must be defined as abstract.

why protected constructor?

The constructor in the abstract class is defined as protected because it is used only by subclasses. When you create an instance of a concrete subclass, its superclass's constructor is invoked to initialize data fields defined in the superclass.

The GeometricObject abstract class defines the common features (data and methods) for geometric objects and provides appropriate constructors. Because you don't know how to compute areas and perimeters of geometric objects, getArea() and getPerimeter() are defined as abstract methods. These methods are implemented in the subclasses. The implementation of Circle and Rectangle is the same as in Listings 11.2 and 11.3, except they extend the GeometricObject class defined in this chapter. You can see the complete code for these two programs at liveexample.pearsoncmg.com/html/Circle.html and liveexample. pearsoncmg.com/html/Rectangle.html, respectively.

implement Circle
implement Rectangle

LISTING 13.2 Circle.java

extends abstract
  GeometricObject
```
1  public class Circle extends GeometricObject {
2    // Same as lines 2-47 in Listing 11.2, so omitted
3  }
```

LISTING 13.3 Rectangle.java

extends abstract
  GeometricObject
```
1  public class Rectangle extends GeometricObject {
2    // Same as lines 2-49 in Listing 11.3, so omitted
3  }
```

13.2.1 Why Abstract Methods?

You may be wondering what advantage is gained by defining the methods getArea() and getPerimeter() as abstract in the GeometricObject class. The example in Listing 13.4 shows the benefits of defining them in the GeometricObject class. The program creates two geometric objects, a circle and a rectangle, invokes the equalArea method to check whether they have equal areas, and invokes the displayGeometricObject method to display them.

LISTING 13.4 TestGeometricObject.java

```
1  public class TestGeometricObject {
2    /** Main method */
3    public static void main(String[] args) {
4      // Create two geometric objects
```

create a circle
create a rectangle
```
5      GeometricObject geoObject1 = new Circle(5);
6      GeometricObject geoObject2 = new Rectangle(5, 3);
```

```
 7
 8        System.out.println("The two objects have the same area? " +
 9          equalArea(geoObject1, geoObject2));
10
11        // Display circle
12        displayGeometricObject(geoObject1);
13
14        // Display rectangle
15        displayGeometricObject(geoObject2);
16      }
17
18      /** A method for comparing the areas of two geometric objects */
19      public static boolean equalArea(GeometricObject object1,                equalArea
20          GeometricObject object2) {
21        return object1.getArea() == object2.getArea();
22      }
23
24      /** A method for displaying a geometric object */
25      public static void displayGeometricObject(GeometricObject object) {     displayGeometricObject
26        System.out.println();
27        System.out.println("The area is " + object.getArea());
28        System.out.println("The perimeter is " + object.getPerimeter());
29      }
30    }
```

```
The two objects have the same area? false

The area is 78.53981633974483
The perimeter is 31.41592653589793

The area is 13.0
The perimeter is 16.0
```

The methods `getArea()` and `getPerimeter()` defined in the `GeometricObject` class are overridden in the `Circle` class and the `Rectangle` class. The statements (lines 5–6)

```
GeometricObject geoObject1 = new Circle(5);
GeometricObject geoObject2 = new Rectangle(5, 3);
```

create a new circle and rectangle and assign them to the variables `geoObject1` and `geoObject2`. These two variables are of the `GeometricObject` type.

When invoking `equalArea(geoObject1, geoObject2)` (line 9), the `getArea()` method defined in the `Circle` class is used for `object1.getArea()`, since `geoObject1` is a circle, and the `getArea()` method defined in the `Rectangle` class is used for `object2.getArea()`, since `geoObject2` is a rectangle.

Similarly, when invoking `displayGeometricObject(geoObject1)` (line 12), the methods `getArea()` and `getPerimeter()` defined in the `Circle` class are used, and when invoking `displayGeometricObject(geoObject2)` (line 15), the methods `getArea` and `getPerimeter` defined in the `Rectangle` class are used. The JVM dynamically determines which of these methods to invoke at runtime, depending on the actual object that invokes the method.

Note you could not define the `equalArea` method for comparing whether two geometric objects have the same area if the `getArea` method were not defined in `GeometricObject`. Now you have seen the benefits of defining the abstract methods in `GeometricObject`.   why abstract methods?

13.2.2 Interesting Points about Abstract Classes

The following points about abstract classes are worth noting:

abstract method in abstract class

- An abstract method cannot be contained in a nonabstract class. If a subclass of an abstract superclass does not implement all the abstract methods, the subclass must be defined as abstract. In other words, in a nonabstract subclass extended from an abstract class, all the abstract methods must be implemented. Also note abstract methods are nonstatic.

object cannot be created from abstract class

- An abstract class cannot be instantiated using the new operator, but you can still define its constructors, which are invoked in the constructors of its subclasses. For instance, the constructors of GeometricObject are invoked in the Circle class and the Rectangle class.

abstract class without abstract method

- A class that contains abstract methods must be abstract. However, it is possible to define an abstract class that doesn't contain any abstract methods. This abstract class is used as a base class for defining subclasses.

concrete method overridden to be abstract

- A subclass can override a method from its superclass to define it as abstract. This is *very unusual*, but it is useful when the implementation of the method in the superclass becomes invalid in the subclass. In this case, the subclass must be defined as abstract.

concrete method overridden to be abstract

- A subclass can be abstract even if its superclass is concrete. For example, the Object class is concrete, but its subclasses, such as GeometricObject, may be abstract.

abstract class as type

- You cannot create an instance from an abstract class using the new operator, but an abstract class can be used as a data type. Therefore, the following statement, which creates an array whose elements are of the GeometricObject type, is correct:

```
GeometricObject[] objects = new GeometricObject[10];
```

You can then create an instance of GeometricObject and assign its reference to the array like this:

```
objects[0] = new Circle();
```

Check Point

13.2.1 Which of the following classes defines a legal abstract class?

```
class A {
  abstract void unfinished() {
  }
}
```
(a)

```
public class abstract A {
  abstract void unfinished();
}
```
(b)

```
class A {
  abstract void unfinished();
}
```
(c)

```
abstract class A {
  protected void unfinished();
}
```
(d)

```
abstract class A {
  abstract void unfinished();
}
```
(e)

```
abstract class A {
  abstract int unfinished();
}
```
(f)

13.2.2   The `getArea()` and `getPerimeter()` methods may be removed from the `GeometricObject` class. What are the benefits of defining `getArea()` and `getPerimeter()` as abstract methods in the `GeometricObject` class?

13.2.3   True or false?

    a. An abstract class can be used just like a nonabstract class except that you cannot use the `new` operator to create an instance from the abstract class.

    b. An abstract class can be extended.

    c. A subclass of a nonabstract superclass cannot be abstract.

    d. A subclass cannot override a concrete method in a superclass to define it as abstract.

    e. An abstract method must be nonstatic.

13.3 Case Study: the Abstract **Number** Class

`Number` is an abstract superclass for numeric wrapper classes `BigInteger` and `BigDecimal`.

Key Point

Section 10.7 introduced numeric wrapper classes and Section 10.9 introduced the `BigInteger` and `BigDecimal` classes. These classes have common methods `byteValue()`, `shortValue()`, `intValue()`, `longValue()`, `floatValue()`, and `doubleValue()` for returning a `byte`, `short`, `int`, `long`, `float`, and `double` value from an object of these classes. These common methods are actually defined in the `Number` class, which is a superclass for the numeric wrapper classes `BigInteger` and `BigDecimal`, as shown in Figure 13.2.

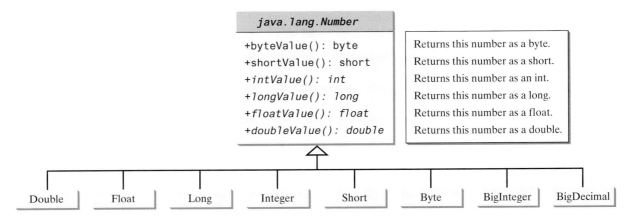

FIGURE 13.2   The `Number` class is an abstract superclass for `Double`, `Float`, `Long`, `Integer`, `Short`, `Byte`, `BigInteger`, and `BigDecimal`.

Since the `intValue()`, `longValue()`, `floatValue()`, and `doubleValue()` methods cannot be implemented in the `Number` class, they are defined as abstract methods in the `Number` class. The `Number` class is therefore an abstract class. The `byteValue()` and `shortValue()` method are implemented from the `intValue()` method as follows:

```java
public byte byteValue() {
  return (byte)intValue();
}

public short shortValue() {
  return (short)intValue();
}
```

With `Number` defined as the superclass for the numeric classes, we can define methods to perform common operations for numbers. Listing 13.5 gives a program that finds the largest number in a list of `Number` objects.

LISTING 13.5 LargestNumber.java

```
1   import java.util.ArrayList;
2   import java.math.*;
3
4   public class LargestNumber {
5     public static void main(String[] args) {
6       ArrayList<Number> list = new ArrayList<>();
7       list.add(45); // Add an integer
8       list.add(3445.53); // Add a double
9       // Add a BigInteger
10      list.add(new BigInteger("3432323234344343101"));
11      // Add a BigDecimal
12      list.add(new BigDecimal("2.0909090989091343433344343"));
13
14      System.out.println("The largest number is " +
15        getLargestNumber(list));
16    }
17
18    public static Number getLargestNumber(ArrayList<Number> list) {
19      if (list == null || list.size() == 0)
20        return null;
21
22      Number number = list.get(0);
23      for (int i = 1; i < list.size(); i++)
24        if (number.doubleValue() < list.get(i).doubleValue())
25          number = list.get(i);
26
27      return number;
28    }
29  }
```

create an array list
add number to list

invoke getLargestNumber

doubleValue

```
The largest number is 3432323234344343101
```

The program creates an `ArrayList` of `Number` objects (line 6). It adds an `Integer` object, a `Double` object, a `BigInteger` object, and a `BigDecimal` object to the list (lines 7–12). Note `45` is automatically converted into an `Integer` object and added to the list in line 7, and `3445.53` is automatically converted into a `Double` object and added to the list in line 8 using autoboxing.

Invoking the `getLargestNumber` method returns the largest number in the list (line 15). The `getLargestNumber` method returns `null` if the list is `null` or the list size is `0` (lines 19 and 20). To find the largest number in the list, the numbers are compared by invoking their `doubleValue()` method (line 24). The `doubleValue()` method is defined in the `Number` class and implemented in the concrete subclass of `Number`. If a number is an `Integer` object, the `Integer`'s `doubleValue()` is invoked. If a number is a `BigDecimal` object, the `BigDecimal`'s `doubleValue()` is invoked.

If the `doubleValue()` method were not defined in the `Number` class, you will not be able to find the largest number among different types of numbers using the `Number` class.

Check Point

13.3.1 Why do the following two lines of code compile but cause a runtime error?

```
Number numberRef = new Integer(0);
Double doubleRef = (Double)numberRef;
```

13.3.2 Why do the following two lines of code compile but cause a runtime error?

```
Number[] numberArray = new Integer[2];
numberArray[0] = new Double(1.5);
```

13.3.3 Show the output of the following code:

```
public class Test {
  public static void main(String[] args) {
    Number x = 3;
    System.out.println(x.intValue());
    System.out.println(x.doubleValue());
  }
}
```

13.3.4 What is wrong in the following code? (Note the compareTo method for the Integer and Double classes was introduced in Section 10.7.)

```
public class Test {
  public static void main(String[] args) {
    Number x = new Integer(3);
    System.out.println(x.intValue());
    System.out.println(x.compareTo(new Integer(4)));
  }
}
```

13.3.5 What is wrong in the following code?

```
public class Test {
  public static void main(String[] args) {
    Number x = new Integer(3);
    System.out.println(x.intValue());
    System.out.println((Integer)x.compareTo(new Integer(4)));
  }
}
```

13.4 Case Study: `Calendar` and `GregorianCalendar`

`GregorianCalendar` is a concrete subclass of the abstract class `Calendar`.

An instance of `java.util.Date` represents a specific instant in time with millisecond precision. `java.util.Calendar` is an abstract base class for extracting detailed calendar information, such as the year, month, date, hour, minute, and second. Subclasses of `Calendar` can implement specific calendar systems, such as the Gregorian calendar, the lunar calendar, and the Jewish calendar. Currently, `java.util.GregorianCalendar` for the Gregorian calendar is supported in Java, as shown in Figure 13.3. The add method is abstract in the `Calendar` class because its implementation is dependent on a concrete calendar system.

You can use `new GregorianCalendar()` to construct a default `GregorianCalendar` with the current time and `new GregorianCalendar(year, month, date)` to construct a `GregorianCalendar` with the specified year, month, and date. The month parameter is 0-based—that is, 0 is for January.

The `get(int field)` method defined in the `Calendar` class is useful for extracting the date and time information from a `Calendar` object. The fields are defined as constants, as shown in Table 13.1.

Listing 13.6 gives an example that displays the date and time information for the current time.

Key Point

VideoNote

Calendar and GregorianCalendar classes

abstract add method

construct calendar

get(field)

java.util.Calendar	
#Calendar()	Constructs a default calendar.
+get(field: int): int	Returns the value of the given calendar field.
+set(field: int, value: int): void	Sets the given calendar to the specified value.
+set(year: int, month: int, dayOfMonth: int): void	Sets the calendar with the specified year, month, and date. The month parameter is 0-based; that is, 0 is for January.
+getActualMaximum(field: int): int	Returns the maximum value that the specified calendar field could have.
+add(field: int, amount: int): void	Adds or subtracts the specified amount of time to the given calendar field.
+getTime(): java.util.Date	Returns a Date object representing this calendar's time value (million second offset from the UNIX epoch).
+setTime(date: java.util.Date): void	Sets this calendar's time with the given Date object.

java.util.GregorianCalendar	
+GregorianCalendar()	Constructs a GregorianCalendar for the current time.
+GregorianCalendar(year: int, month: int, dayOfMonth: int)	Constructs a GregorianCalendar for the specified year, month, and date.
+GregorianCalendar(year: int, month: int, dayOfMonth: int, hour:int, minute: int, second: int)	Constructs a GregorianCalendar for the specified year, month, date, hour, minute, and second. The month parameter is 0-based, that is, 0 is for January.

Figure 13.3 The abstract Calendar class defines common features of various calendars.

Table 13.1 Field Constants in the Calendar Class

Constant	Description
YEAR	The year of the calendar.
MONTH	The month of the calendar, with 0 for January.
DATE	The day of the calendar.
HOUR	The hour of the calendar (12-hour notation).
HOUR_OF_DAY	The hour of the calendar (24-hour notation).
MINUTE	The minute of the calendar.
SECOND	The second of the calendar.
DAY_OF_WEEK	The day number within the week, with 1 for Sunday.
DAY_OF_MONTH	Same as DATE.
DAY_OF_YEAR	The day number in the year, with 1 for the first day of the year.
WEEK_OF_MONTH	The week number within the month, with 1 for the first week.
WEEK_OF_YEAR	The week number within the year, with 1 for the first week.
AM_PM	Indicator for AM or PM (0 for AM and 1 for PM).

Listing 13.6 TestCalendar.java

```
1  import java.util.*;
2
3  public class TestCalendar {
4    public static void main(String[] args) {
5      // Construct a Gregorian calendar for the current date and time
6      Calendar calendar = new GregorianCalendar();
7      System.out.println("Current time is " + new Date());
8      System.out.println("YEAR: " + calendar.get(Calendar.YEAR));
```

calendar for current time

extract fields in calendar

```java
 9       System.out.println("MONTH: " + calendar.get(Calendar.MONTH));
10       System.out.println("DATE: " + calendar.get(Calendar.DATE));
11       System.out.println("HOUR: " + calendar.get(Calendar.HOUR));
12       System.out.println("HOUR_OF_DAY: " +
13         calendar.get(Calendar.HOUR_OF_DAY));
14       System.out.println("MINUTE: " + calendar.get(Calendar.MINUTE));
15       System.out.println("SECOND: " + calendar.get(Calendar.SECOND));
16       System.out.println("DAY_OF_WEEK: " +
17         calendar.get(Calendar.DAY_OF_WEEK));
18       System.out.println("DAY_OF_MONTH: " +
19         calendar.get(Calendar.DAY_OF_MONTH));
20       System.out.println("DAY_OF_YEAR: " +
21         calendar.get(Calendar.DAY_OF_YEAR));
22       System.out.println("WEEK_OF_MONTH: " +
23         calendar.get(Calendar.WEEK_OF_MONTH));
24       System.out.println("WEEK_OF_YEAR: " +
25         calendar.get(Calendar.WEEK_OF_YEAR));
26       System.out.println("AM_PM: " + calendar.get(Calendar.AM_PM));
27
28       // Construct a calendar for December 25, 1997
29       Calendar calendar1 = new GregorianCalendar(1997, 11, 25);     create a calendar
30       String[] dayNameOfWeek = {"Sunday", "Monday", "Tuesday", "Wednesday",
31         "Thursday", "Friday", "Saturday"};
32       System.out.println("December 25, 1997 is a " +
33         dayNameOfWeek[calendar1.get(Calendar.DAY_OF_WEEK) - 1]);
34     }
35   }
```

```
Current time is Tue Sep 22 12:55:56 EDT 2015
YEAR: 2015
MONTH: 8
DATE: 22
HOUR: 0
HOUR_OF_DAY: 12
MINUTE: 55
SECOND: 56
DAY_OF_WEEK: 3
DAY_OF_MONTH: 22
DAY_OF_YEAR: 265
WEEK_OF_MONTH: 4
WEEK_OF_YEAR: 39
AM_PM: 1
December 25, 1997 is a Thursday
```

The `set(int field, value)` method defined in the `Calendar` class can be used to set a field. For example, you can use `calendar.set(Calendar.DAY_OF_MONTH, 1)` to set the `calendar` to the first day of the month.   `set(field, value)`

The `add(field, value)` method adds the specified amount to a given field. For example, `add(Calendar.DAY_OF_MONTH, 5)` adds five days to the current time of the calendar. `add(Calendar.DAY_OF_MONTH, -5)` subtracts five days from the current time of the calendar.   `add(field, amount)`

To obtain the number of days in a month, use `calendar.getActualMaximum(Calendar.DAY_OF_MONTH)`. For example, if the `calendar` were for March, this method would return `31`.   `getActualMaximum(field)`

setTime(date)
getTime()

You can set a time represented in a `Date` object for the `calendar` by invoking `calendar.setTime(date)` and retrieve the time by invoking `calendar.getTime()`.

13.4.1 Can you create a `Calendar` object using the `Calendar` class?

13.4.2 Which method in the `Calendar` class is abstract?

13.4.3 How do you create a `Calendar` object for the current time?

13.4.4 For a `Calendar` object `c`, how do you get its year, month, date, hour, minute, and second?

13.5 Interfaces

An interface is a class-like construct for defining common operations for objects.

VideoNote

The concept of interface

In many ways an interface is similar to an abstract class, but its intent is to specify common behavior for objects of related classes or unrelated classes. For example, using appropriate interfaces, you can specify that the objects are comparable, edible, and/or cloneable.

To distinguish an interface from a class, Java uses the following syntax to define an interface:

```
modifier interface InterfaceName {
  /** Constant declarations */
  /** Abstract method signatures */
}
```

Here is an example of an interface:

```
public interface Edible {
  /** Describe how to eat */
  public abstract String howToEat();
}
```

An interface is treated like a special class in Java. Each interface is compiled into a separate bytecode file, just like a regular class. You can use an interface more or less the same way you use an abstract class. For example, you can use an interface as a data type for a reference variable, as the result of casting, and so on. As with an abstract class, you cannot create an instance from an interface using the `new` operator.

You can use the `Edible` interface to specify whether an object is edible. This is accomplished by letting the class for the object implement this interface using the `implements` keyword. For example, the classes `Chicken` and `Fruit` in Listing 13.7 (lines 30 and 49) implement the `Edible` interface. The relationship between the class and the interface is known as *interface inheritance*. Since interface inheritance and class inheritance are essentially the same, we will simply refer to both as *inheritance*.

interface inheritance

LISTING 13.7 `TestEdible.java`

```
1  public class TestEdible {
2    public static void main(String[] args) {
3      Object[] objects = {new Tiger(), new Chicken(), new Apple()};
4      for (int i = 0; i < objects.length; i++) {
5        if (objects[i] instanceof Edible)
6          System.out.println(((Edible)objects[i]).howToEat());
7
8        if (objects[i] instanceof Animal) {
9          System.out.println(((Animal)objects[i]).sound());
10       }
11     }
12   }
13 }
```

```
14
15   abstract class Animal {                              Animal class
16     private double weight;
17
18     public double getWeight() {
19       return weight;
20     }
21
22     public void setWeight(double weight) {
23       this.weight = weight;
24     }
25
26     /** Return animal sound */
27     public abstract String sound();
28   }
29
30   class Chicken extends Animal implements Edible {      implements Edible
31     @Override
32     public String howToEat() {                          howToEat()
33       return "Chicken: Fry it";
34     }
35
36     @Override
37     public String sound() {
38       return "Chicken: cock-a-doodle-doo";
39     }
40   }
41
42   class Tiger extends Animal {                          Tiger class
43     @Override
44     public String sound() {
45       return "Tiger: RROOAARR";
46     }
47   }
48
49   abstract class Fruit implements Edible {              implements Edible
50     // Data fields, constructors, and methods omitted here
51   }
52
53   class Apple extends Fruit {                           Apple class
54     @Override
55     public String howToEat() {
56       return "Apple: Make apple cider";
57     }
58   }
59
60   class Orange extends Fruit {                          Orange class
61     @Override
62     public String howToEat() {
63       return "Orange: Make orange juice";
64     }
65   }
```

```
Tiger: RROOAARR
Chicken: Fry it
Chicken: cock-a-doodle-doo
Apple: Make apple cider
```

This example uses several classes and interfaces. Their inheritance relationship is shown in Figure 13.4.

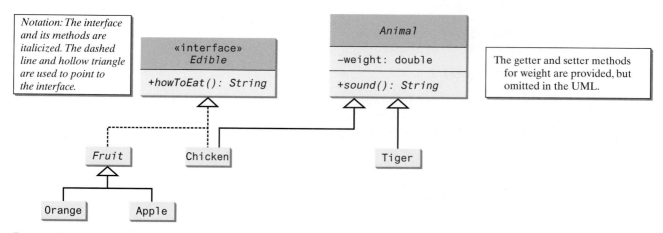

FIGURE 13.4 Edible is a supertype for Chicken and Fruit. Animal is a supertype for Chicken and Tiger. Fruit is a supertype for Orange and Apple.

The Animal class defines the weight property with its getter and setter methods (lines 16–24) and the sound method (line 27). The sound method is an abstract method and will be implemented by a concrete animal class.

The Chicken class implements Edible to specify that chickens are edible. When a class implements an interface, it implements all the methods defined in the interface. The Chicken class implements the howToEat method (lines 32–34). Chicken also extends Animal to implement the sound method (lines 37–39).

The Fruit class implements Edible. Since it does not implement the howToEat method, Fruit must be defined as abstract (line 49). The concrete subclasses of Fruit must implement the howToEat method. The Apple and Orange classes implement the howToEat method (lines 55 and 62).

The main method creates an array with three objects for Tiger, Chicken, and Apple (line 3) and invokes the howToEat method if the element is edible (line 6), and the sound method if the element is an animal (line 9).

common behavior

In essence, the Edible interface defines common behavior for edible objects. All edible objects have the howToEat method.

 Note

omit modifiers

The modifiers *public static final* on data fields and the modifiers *public abstract* on methods can be omitted in an interface. Therefore, the following interface definitions are equivalent:

```
public interface T {
  public static final int K = 1;

  public abstract void p();
}
```

Equivalent

```
public interface T {
  int K = 1;

  void p();
}
```

Although the public modifier may be omitted for a method defined in the interface, the method must be defined public when it is implemented in a subclass.

 Note

default methods

Java 8 introduced default interface methods using the keyword default. A default method provides a default implementation for the method in the interface. A class that implements the interface may simply use the default implementation for the method or override the method with a new implementation. This feature enables you to add a new method to an existing interface with a default implementation without having to rewrite the code for the existing classes that implement this interface.

Java 8 also permits public static methods in an interface. A public static method in an interface can be used just like a public static method in a class. Here is an example of defining default methods and static methods in an interface:

public static methods

```
public interface A {
  /** default method */
  public default void doSomething() {
    System.out.println("Do something");
  }

  /** static method */
  public static int getAValue() {
    return 0;
  }
}
```

13.5.1 Suppose A is an interface. Can you create an instance using new A()?

Check Point

13.5.2 Suppose A is an interface. Can you declare a reference variable x with type A like this?

A x;

13.5.3 Which of the following is a correct interface?

```
interface A {
  void print() { }
}
```
(a)

```
abstract interface A {
  abstract void print() { }
}
```
(b)

```
abstract interface A {
  print();
}
```
(c)

```
interface A {
  void print();
}
```
(d)

```
interface A {
  default void print() {
  }
}
```
(e)

```
interface A {
  static int get() {
    return 0;
  }
}
```
(f)

13.5.4 Show the error in the following code:

```
interface A {
  void m1();
}

class B implements A {
  void m1() {
    System.out.println("m1");
  }
}
```

13.6 The **Comparable** Interface

The Comparable *interface defines the* compareTo *method for comparing objects.*

Key Point

Suppose you want to design a generic method to find the larger of two objects of the same type, such as two students, two dates, two circles, two rectangles, or two squares. In order to accomplish this, the two objects must be comparable, so the common behavior for the objects must be comparable. Java provides the `Comparable` interface for this purpose. The interface is defined as follows:

```java
// Interface for comparing objects, defined in java.lang
package java.lang;

public interface Comparable<E> {
  public int compareTo(E o);
}
```

The `compareTo` method determines the order of this object with the specified object `o` and returns a negative integer, zero, or a positive integer if this object is less than, equal to, or greater than `o`.

The `Comparable` interface is a generic interface. The generic type `E` is replaced by a concrete type when implementing this interface. Many classes in the Java library implement `Comparable` to define a natural order for objects. The classes `Byte`, `Short`, `Integer`, `Long`, `Float`, `Double`, `Character`, `BigInteger`, `BigDecimal`, `Calendar`, `String`, and `Date` all implement the `Comparable` interface. For example, the `Integer`, `BigInteger`, `String`, and `Date` classes are defined as follows in the Java API:

```java
public final class Integer extends Number
    implements Comparable<Integer> {
  // class body omitted

  @Override
  public int compareTo(Integer o) {
    // Implementation omitted
  }
}
```

```java
public class BigInteger extends Number
    implements Comparable<Biginteger> {
  // class body omitted

  @Override
  public int compareTo(BigInteger o) {
    // Implementation omitted
  }
}
```

```java
public final class String extends Object
    implements Comparable<String> {
  // class body omitted

  @Override
  public int compareTo(String o) {
    // Implementation omitted
  }
}
```

```java
public class Date extends Object
    implements Comparable<Date> {
  // class body omitted

  @Override
  public int compareTo(Date o) {
    // Implementation omitted
  }
}
```

Thus, numbers are comparable, strings are comparable, and so are dates. You can use the `compareTo` method to compare two numbers, two strings, and two dates. For example, the following code:

```java
1  System.out.println(new Integer(3).compareTo(new Integer(5)));
2  System.out.println("ABC".compareTo("ABC"));
3  java.util.Date date1 = new java.util.Date(2013, 1, 1);
4  java.util.Date date2 = new java.util.Date(2012, 1, 1);
5  System.out.println(date1.compareTo(date2));
```

displays

```
-1
 0
 1
```

Line 1 displays a negative value since 3 is less than 5. Line 2 displays zero since ABC is equal to ABC. Line 5 displays a positive value since date1 is greater than date2.

Let n be an Integer object, s be a String object, and d be a Date object. All the following expressions are true:

```
n instanceof Integer
n instanceof Object
n instanceof Comparable
```

```
s instanceof String
s instanceof Object
s instanceof Comparable
```

```
d instanceof java.util.Date
d instanceof Object
d instanceof Comparable
```

Since all Comparable objects have the compareTo method, the java.util.Arrays.sort(Object[]) method in the Java API uses the compareTo method to compare and sorts the objects in an array, provided the objects are instances of the Comparable interface. Listing 13.8 gives an example of sorting an array of strings and an array of BigInteger objects.

LISTING 13.8 SortComparableObjects.java

```
1  import java.math.*;
2
3  public class SortComparableObjects {
4    public static void main(String[] args) {
5      String[] cities = {"Savannah", "Boston", "Atlanta", "Tampa"};   create an array
6      java.util.Arrays.sort(cities);                                   sort the array
7      for (String city: cities)
8        System.out.print(city + " ");
9      System.out.println();
10
11     BigInteger[] hugeNumbers = {new BigInteger("2323231092923992"),  create an array
12       new BigInteger("432232323239292"),
13       new BigInteger("54623239292")};
14     java.util.Arrays.sort(hugeNumbers);                              sort the array
15     for (BigInteger number: hugeNumbers)
16       System.out.print(number + " ");
17   }
18 }
```

```
Atlanta Boston Savannah Tampa
54623239292 432232323239292 2323231092923992
```

The program creates an array of strings (line 5) and invokes the sort method to sort the strings (line 6). The program creates an array of BigInteger objects (lines 11–13) and invokes the sort method to sort the BigInteger objects (line 14).

You cannot use the sort method to sort an array of Rectangle objects because Rectangle does not implement Comparable. However, you can define a new rectangle class that implements Comparable. The instances of this new class are comparable. Let this new class be named ComparableRectangle, as shown in Listing 13.9.

LISTING 13.9 ComparableRectangle.java

```
1  public class ComparableRectangle extends Rectangle
2      implements Comparable<ComparableRectangle> {              implements Comparable
3    /** Construct a ComparableRectangle with specified properties */
4    public ComparableRectangle(double width, double height) {
5      super(width, height);
6    }
7
8    @Override // Implement the compareTo method defined in Comparable
```

implement compareTo

```
 9    public int compareTo(ComparableRectangle o) {
10      if (getArea() > o.getArea())
11        return 1;
12      else if (getArea() < o.getArea())
13        return -1;
14      else
15        return 0;
16    }
17
18    @Override // Implement the toString method in GeometricObject
19    public String toString() {
20      return super.toString() + " Area: " + getArea();
21    }
22  }
```

implement toString

`ComparableRectangle` extends `Rectangle` and implements `Comparable`, as shown in Figure 13.5. The keyword `implements` indicates that `ComparableRectangle` inherits all the constants from the `Comparable` interface and implements the methods in the interface. The `compareTo` method compares the areas of two rectangles. An instance of `ComparableRectangle` is also an instance of `Rectangle`, `GeometricObject`, `Object`, and `Comparable`.

Notation:
The interface name and the method names are italicized. The dashed line and hollow triangle are used to point to the interface.

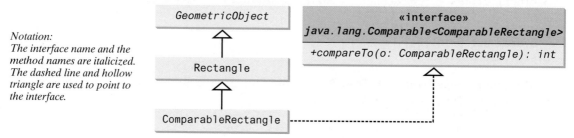

FIGURE 13.5   `ComparableRectangle` extends `Rectangle` and implements `Comparable`.

You can now use the `sort` method to sort an array of `ComparableRectangle` objects, as in Listing 13.10.

LISTING 13.10   SortRectangles.java

create an array

sort the array

```
 1  public class SortRectangles {
 2    public static void main(String[] args) {
 3      ComparableRectangle[] rectangles = {
 4        new ComparableRectangle(3.4, 5.4),
 5        new ComparableRectangle(13.24, 55.4),
 6        new ComparableRectangle(7.4, 35.4),
 7        new ComparableRectangle(1.4, 25.4)};
 8      java.util.Arrays.sort(rectangles);
 9      for (Rectangle rectangle: rectangles) {
10        System.out.print(rectangle + " ");
11        System.out.println();
12      }
13    }
14  }
```

```
Width: 3.4 Height: 5.4 Area: 18.36
Width: 1.4 Height: 25.4 Area: 35.559999999999995
Width: 7.4 Height: 35.4 Area: 261.96
Width: 13.24 Height: 55.4 Area: 733.496
```

An interface provides another form of generic programming. It would be difficult to use a generic `sort` method to sort the objects without using an interface in this example, because multiple inheritance would be necessary to inherit `Comparable` and another class, such as `Rectangle`, at the same time.

benefits of interface

The `Object` class contains the `equals` method, which is intended for the subclasses of the `Object` class to override in order to compare whether the contents of the objects are the same. Suppose the `Object` class contains the `compareTo` method, as defined in the `Comparable` interface; the `sort` method can be used to compare a list of *any* objects. Whether a `compareTo` method should be included in the `Object` class is debatable. Since the `compareTo` method is not defined in the `Object` class, the `Comparable` interface is defined in Java to enable objects to be compared if they are instances of the `Comparable` interface. `compareTo` should be consistent with `equals`. That is, for two objects o1 and o2, o1.compareTo(o2) == 0 if and only if o1.equals(o2) is `true`. Therefore, you should also override the `equals` method in the `ComparableRectangle` class to return `true` if two rectangles have the same area.

13.6.1 True or false? If a class implements `Comparable`, the object of the class can invoke the `compareTo` method.

13.6.2 Which of the following is the correct method header for the `compareTo` method in the `String` class?

```
public int compareTo(String o)
public int compareTo(Object o)
```

13.6.3 Can the following code be compiled? Why?

```
Integer n1 = new Integer(3);
Object n2 = new Integer(4);
System.out.println(n1.compareTo(n2));
```

13.6.4 You can define the `compareTo` method in a class without implementing the `Comparable` interface. What are the benefits of implementing the `Comparable` interface?

13.6.5 What is wrong in the following code?

```
public class Test {
  public static void main(String[] args) {
    Person[] persons = {new Person(3), new Person(4), new Person(1)};
    java.util.Arrays.sort(persons);
  }
}

class Person {
  private int id;

  Person(int id) {
    this.id = id;
  }
}
```

13.6.6 Simplify the code in lines 10–15 in Listing 13.9 using one line of code. Also override the `equals` method in this class.

13.6.7 Listing 13.5 has an error. If you add `list.add(new BigInteger ("34323232343443343102"));` in line 11, you will see the result is incorrect. This is due to the fact that a double value can have up to 17 significant digits. When invoking `doubleValue()` on a `BigInteger` object in line 24, precision is lost. Fix the error by converting the numbers into `BigDecimal`, and compare them using the `compareTo` method in line 24.

13.7 The Cloneable Interface

**Key
Point**

The Cloneable interface specifies that an object can be cloned.

Often, it is desirable to create a copy of an object. To do this, you need to use the clone method and understand the Cloneable interface.

An interface contains constants and abstract methods, but the Cloneable interface is a special case. The Cloneable interface in the java.lang package is defined as follows:

java.lang.Cloneable

```
package java.lang;

public interface Cloneable {
}
```

marker interface

This interface is empty. An interface with an empty body is referred to as a *marker interface*. A marker interface is used to denote that a class possesses certain desirable properties. A class that implements the Cloneable interface is marked cloneable, and its objects can be cloned using the clone() method defined in the Object class.

Many classes in the Java library (e.g., Date, Calendar and ArrayList) implement Cloneable. Thus, the instances of these classes can be cloned. For example, the following code:

```
1  Calendar calendar = new GregorianCalendar(2013, 2, 1);
2  Calendar calendar1 = calendar;
3  Calendar calendar2 = (Calendar)calendar.clone();
4  System.out.println("calendar == calendar1 is " +
5    (calendar == calendar1));
6  System.out.println("calendar == calendar2 is " +
7    (calendar == calendar2));
8  System.out.println("calendar.equals(calendar2) is " +
9    calendar.equals(calendar2));
```

displays

```
calendar == calendar1 is true
calendar == calendar2 is false
calendar.equals(calendar2) is true
```

In the preceding code, line 2 copies the reference of calendar to calendar1, so calendar and calendar1 point to the same Calendar object. Line 3 creates a new object that is the clone of calendar and assigns the new object's reference to calendar2. calendar2 and calendar are different objects with the same contents.

The following code:

```
1   ArrayList<Double> list1 = new ArrayList<>();
2   list1.add(1.5);
3   list1.add(2.5);
4   list1.add(3.5);
5   ArrayList<Double> list2 = (ArrayList<Double>)list1.clone();
6   ArrayList<Double> list3 = list1;
7   list2.add(4.5);
8   list3.remove(1.5);
9   System.out.println("list1 is " + list1);
10  System.out.println("list2 is " + list2);
11  System.out.println("list3 is " + list3);
```

displays

```
list1 is [2.5, 3.5]
list2 is [1.5, 2.5, 3.5, 4.5]
list3 is [2.5, 3.5]
```

In the preceding code, line 5 creates a new object that is the clone of `list1` and assigns the new object's reference to `list2`. `list2` and `list1` are different objects with the same contents. Line 6 copies the reference of `list1` to `list3`, so `list1` and `list3` point to the same `ArrayList` object. Line 7 adds `4.5` into `list2`. Line 8 removes `1.5` from `list3`. Since `list1` and `list3` point to the same `ArrayList`, line 9 and 11 display the same content.

You can clone an array using the `clone` method. For example, the following code:

clone arrays

```
1  int[] list1 = {1, 2};
2  int[] list2 = list1.clone();
3  list1[0] = 7;
4  list2[1] = 8;
5  System.out.println("list1 is " + list1[0] + ", " + list1[1]);
6  System.out.println("list2 is " + list2[0] + ", " + list2[1]);
```

displays

```
list1 is 7, 2
list2 is 1, 8
```

Note the return type of the `clone()` method for an array is the same as the type of the array. For example, the return type for `list1.clone()` is `int[]` since `list1` is of the type `int[]`.

To define a custom class that implements the `Cloneable` interface, the class must override the `clone()` method in the `Object` class. Listing 13.11 defines a class named `House` that implements `Cloneable` and `Comparable`.

how to implement `Cloneable`

Listing 13.11   House.java

```
1   public class House implements Cloneable, Comparable<House> {
2     private int id;
3     private double area;
4     private java.util.Date whenBuilt;
5
6     public House(int id, double area) {
7       this.id = id;
8       this.area = area;
9       whenBuilt = new java.util.Date();
10    }
11
12    public int getId() {
13      return id;
14    }
15
16    public double getArea() {
17      return area;
18    }
19
20    public java.util.Date getWhenBuilt() {
21      return whenBuilt;
22    }
```

```
23
24    @Override /** Override the protected clone method defined in
25      the Object class, and strengthen its accessibility */
26    public Object clone() {
27      try {
28        return super.clone();
29      }
30      catch (CloneNotSupportedException ex) {
31        return null;
32      }
33    }
34
35    @Override // Implement the compareTo method defined in Comparable
36    public int compareTo(House o) {
37      if (area > o.area)
38        return 1;
39      else if (area < o.area)
40        return -1;
41      else
42        return 0;
43    }
44  }
```

This exception is thrown if House does not implement Cloneable

CloneNotSupported-Exception

The House class implements the clone method (lines 26–33) defined in the Object class. The header for the clone method defined in the Object class is:

```
protected native Object clone() throws CloneNotSupportedException;
```

The keyword native indicates that this method is not written in Java, but is implemented in the JVM for the native platform. The keyword protected restricts the method to be accessed in the same package or in a subclass. For this reason, the House class must override the method and change the visibility modifier to public so the method can be used in any package. Since the clone method implemented for the native platform in the Object class performs the task of cloning objects, the clone method in the House class simply invokes super.clone(). The clone method defined in the Object class throws CloneNotSupportedException if the object is not a type of Cloneable. Since we catch the exception in the method (lines 30–32), there is no need to declare it in the clone() method header.

The House class implements the compareTo method (lines 36–43) defined in the Comparable interface. The method compares the areas of two houses.

You can now create an object of the House class and create an identical copy from it, as follows:

```
House house1 = new House(1, 1750.50);
House house2 = (House)house1.clone();
```

shallow copy
deep copy

house1 and house2 are two different objects with identical contents. The clone method in the Object class copies each field from the original object to the target object. If the field is of a primitive type, its value is copied. For example, the value of area (double type) is copied from house1 to house2. If the field is of an object, the reference of the field is copied. For example, the field whenBuilt is of the Date class, so its reference is copied into house2, as shown in Figure 13.6a. Therefore, house1.whenBuilt == house2.whenBuilt is true, although house1 == house2 is false. This is referred to as a *shallow copy* rather than a *deep copy*, meaning if the field is of an object type, the object's reference is copied rather than its contents.

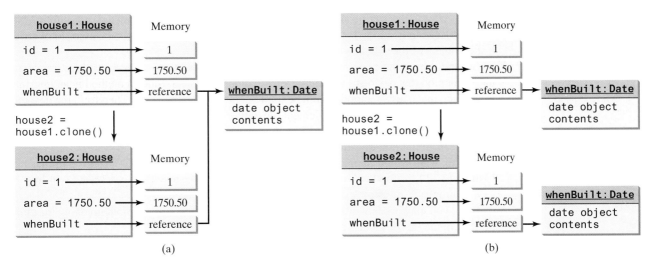

FIGURE 13.6 (a) The default `clone` method performs a shallow copy. (b) The custom `clone` method performs a deep copy.

To perform a deep copy for a House object, replace the `clone()` method in lines 26–33 with the following code: (For the complete code, see liveexample.pearsoncmg.com/text/House.txt.)   deep copy

```
public Object clone() throws CloneNotSupportedException {
  // Perform a shallow copy
  House houseClone = (House)super.clone();
  // Deep copy on whenBuilt
  houseClone.whenBuilt = (java.util.Date)(whenBuilt.clone());
  return houseClone;
}
```

or

```
public Object clone() {
  try {
    // Perform a shallow copy
    House houseClone = (House)super.clone();
    // Deep copy on whenBuilt
    houseClone.whenBuilt = (java.util.Date)(whenBuilt.clone());
    return houseClone;
  }
  catch (CloneNotSupportedException ex) {
    return null;
  }
}
```

Now, if you clone a House object in the following code:

```
House house1 = new House(1, 1750.50);
House house2 = (House)house1.clone();
```

house1.whenBuilt == house2.whenBuilt will be false. house1 and house2 contain two different Date objects, as shown in Figure 13.6b.

Several questions arise from the clone method and Cloneable interface.

First, why is the `clone` method in the `Object` class defined protected, not public? Not every object can be cloned. The designer of Java purposely forces the subclasses to override it if an object of the subclass is cloneable.

Second, why is the `clone` method not defined in the `Cloneable` interface? Java provides a native method that performs a shallow copy to clone an object. Since a method in an interface is abstract, this native method cannot be implemented in the interface. Therefore, the designer of Java decided to define and implement the native `clone` method in the `Object` class.

Third, why doesn't the `Object` class implement the `Cloneable` interface? The answer is the same as in the first question.

Fourth, what would happen if the `House` class did not implement `Cloneable` in line 1 of Listing 13.11? `house1.clone()` would return `null` because `super.clone()` in line 28 would throw a `CloneNotSupportedException`.

Fifth, you may implement the `clone` method in the `House` class without invoking the clone method in the `Object` class as follows:

```java
public Object clone() {
  // Perform a shallow copy
  House houseClone = new House(id, area);

  // Deep copy on whenBuilt
  houseClone.whenBuilt = new Date();
  houseClone.getWhenBuilt().setTime(whenBuilt.getTime());

  return houseClone;
}
```

In this case, the `House` class does not need to implement the `Cloneable` interface, and you have to make sure all the data fields are copied correctly. Using the `clone()` method in the `Object` class relieves you from manually copying the data fields. The `clone` method in the `Object` class automatically performs a shallow copy of all the data fields.

 Check Point

13.7.1 Can a class invoke the `super.clone()` when implementing the `clone()` method if the class does not implement the `java.lang.Cloneable`? Does the `Date` class implement `Cloneable`?

13.7.2 What would happen if the `House` class (defined in Listing 13.11) did not override the `clone()` method or if `House` did not implement `java.lang.Cloneable`?

13.7.3 Show the output of the following code:

```java
java.util.Date date = new java.util.Date();
java.util.Date date1 = date;
java.util.Date date2 = (java.util.Date)(date.clone());
System.out.println(date == date1);
System.out.println(date == date2);
System.out.println(date.equals(date2));
```

13.7.4 Show the output of the following code:

```java
ArrayList<String> list = new ArrayList<>();
list.add("New York");
ArrayList<String> list1 = list;
ArrayList<String> list2 = (ArrayList<String>)(list.clone());
list.add("Atlanta");
System.out.println(list == list1);
System.out.println(list == list2);
System.out.println("list is " + list);
System.out.println("list1 is " + list1);
System.out.println("list2.get(0) is " + list2.get(0));
System.out.println("list2.size() is " + list2.size());
```

13.7.5 What is wrong in the following code?

```
public class Test {
  public static void main(String[] args) {
    GeometricObject x = new Circle(3);
    GeometricObject y = x.clone();
    System.out.println(x == y);
  }
}
```

13.7.6 Show the output of the following code:

```
public class Test {
  public static void main(String[] args) {
    House house1 = new House(1, 1750, 50);
    House house2 = (House)house1.clone();
    System.out.println(house1.equals(house2);
  }
}
```

13.8 Interfaces vs. Abstract Classes

A class can implement multiple interfaces, but it can only extend one superclass.

An interface can be used more or less the same way as an abstract class, but defining an interface is different from defining an abstract class. Table 13.2 summarizes the differences.

Key
Point

TABLE 13.2 Interfaces vs. Abstract Classes

	Variables	*Constructors*	*Methods*
Abstract class	No restrictions.	Constructors are invoked by subclasses through constructor chaining. An abstract class cannot be instantiated using the new operator.	No restrictions.
Interface	All variables must be `public static final`.	No constructors. An interface cannot be instantiated using the new operator.	May contain public abstract instance methods, public default, and public static methods.

Java allows only *single inheritance* for class extension, but allows *multiple extensions* for interfaces. For example,

single inheritance
multiple inheritance

```
public class NewClass extends BaseClass
    implements Interface1, ... , InterfaceN {
  ...
}
```

An interface can inherit other interfaces using the `extends` keyword. Such an interface is called a *subinterface*. For example, `NewInterface` in the following code is a subinterface of `Interface1,...,` and `InterfaceN`.

subinterface

```
public interface NewInterface extends Interface1, ... , InterfaceN {
  // constants and abstract methods
}
```

A class implementing `NewInterface` must implement the abstract methods defined in `NewInterface`, `Interface1,...,` and `InterfaceN`. An interface can extend other interfaces, but not classes. A class can extend its superclass and implement multiple interfaces.

All classes share a single root, the `Object` class, but there is no single root for interfaces. Like a class, an interface also defines a type. A variable of an interface type can reference any instance of the class that implements the interface. If a class implements an interface, the interface is like a superclass for the class. You can use an interface as a data type and cast a variable of an interface type to its subclass, and vice versa. For example, suppose `c` is an instance of `Class2` in Figure 13.7. `c` is also an instance of `Object`, `Class1`, `Interface1`, `Interface1_1`, `Interface1_2`, `Interface2_1`, and `Interface2_2`.

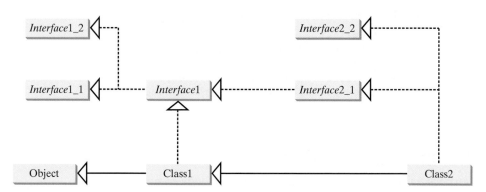

FIGURE 13.7 `Class1` implements `Interface1`; `Interface1` extends `Interface1_1` and `Interface1_2`. `Class2` extends `Class1` and implements `Interface2_1` and `Interface2_2`.

Note

naming convention

Class names are nouns. Interface names may be adjectives or nouns.

Design Guide

Abstract classes and interfaces can both be used to specify common behavior of objects. How do you decide whether to use an interface or a class? In general, a *strong is-a relationship* that clearly describes a parent–child relationship should be modeled using classes. For example, Gregorian calendar is a calendar, so the relationship between the class `java.util.GregorianCalendar` and `java.util.Calendar` is modeled

is-a relationship
is-kind-of relationship

using class inheritance. A *weak is-a relationship*, also known as an *is-kind-of relationship*, indicates that an object possesses a certain property. A weak is-a relationship can be modeled using interfaces. For example, all strings are comparable, so the `String` class implements the `Comparable` interface.

interface preferred

In general, interfaces are preferred over abstract classes because an interface can define a common supertype for unrelated classes. Interfaces are more flexible than classes. Consider the `Animal` class. Suppose the `howToEat` method is defined in the `Animal` class as follows:

Animal class

```
abstract class Animal {
  public abstract String howToEat();
}
```

Two subclasses of `Animal` are defined as follows:

Chicken class

```
class Chicken extends Animal {
  @Override
  public String howToEat() {
    return "Fry it";
  }
}
```

```
class Duck extends Animal {                                              Duck class
  @Override
  public String howToEat() {
    return "Roast it";
  }
}
```

Given this inheritance hierarchy, polymorphism enables you to hold a reference to a Chicken object or a Duck object in a variable of type Animal, as in the following code:

```
public static void main(String[] args) {
  Animal animal = new Chicken();
  eat(animal);

  animal = new Duck();
  eat(animal);
}

public static void eat(Animal animal) {
  System.out.println(animal.howToEat());
}
```

The JVM dynamically decides which howToEat method to invoke based on the actual object that invokes the method.

You can define a subclass of Animal. However, there is a restriction: The subclass must be for another animal (e.g., Turkey). Another issue arises: If an animal (e.g., Tiger) is not edible, it will not be appropriate to extend the Animal class.

Interfaces don't have these problems. Interfaces give you more flexibility than classes because you don't have to make everything fit into one type of class. You may define the howToEat() method in an interface, and let it serve as a common supertype for other classes. For example,

```
public class DesignDemo {
  public static void main(String[] args) {
    Edible stuff = new Chicken();
    eat(stuff);

    stuff = new Duck();
    eat(stuff);

    stuff = new Broccoli();
    eat(stuff);
  }

  public static void eat(Edible stuff) {
    System.out.println(stuff.howToEat()):
  }
}

interface Edible {                                                       Edible interface
  public String howToEat();
}

class Chicken implements Edible {                                        Chicken class
  @Override
  public String howToEat() {
    return "Fry it";
  }
}
```

Duck class

```
class Duck implements Edible {
  @Override
  public String howToEat() {
    return "Roast it";
  }
}
```

Broccoli class

```
class Broccoli implements Edible {
  @Override
  public String howToEat() {
    return "Stir-fry it";
  }
}
```

To define a class that represents edible objects, simply let the class implement the `Edible` interface. The class is now a subtype of the `Edible` type, and any `Edible` object can be passed to invoke the `howToEat` method.

13.8.1 Give an example to show why interfaces are preferred over abstract classes.

13.8.2 Define the terms abstract classes and interfaces. What are the similarities and differences between abstract classes and interfaces?

13.8.3 True or false?

   a. An interface is compiled into a separate bytecode file.

   b. An interface can have static methods.

   c. An interface can extend one or more interfaces.

   d. An interface can extend an abstract class.

   e. An interface can have default methods.

13.9 Case Study: The `Rational` Class

This section shows how to design the `Rational` class for representing and processing rational numbers.

A rational number has a numerator and a denominator in the form a / b, where a is the numerator and b the denominator. For example, 1 / 3, 3 / 4, and 10 / 4 are rational numbers.

A rational number cannot have a denominator of 0, but a numerator of 0 is fine. Every integer i is equivalent to a rational number i / 1. Rational numbers are used in exact computations involving fractions—for example, 1 / 3 = 0.33333.... This number cannot be precisely represented in floating-point format using either the data type `double` or `float`. To obtain the exact result, we must use rational numbers.

Java provides data types for integers and floating-point numbers, but not for rational numbers. This section shows how to design a class to represent rational numbers.

Since rational numbers share many common features with integers and floating-point numbers, and `Number` is the root class for numeric wrapper classes, it is appropriate to define `Rational` as a subclass of `Number`. Since rational numbers are comparable, the `Rational` class should also implement the `Comparable` interface. Figure 13.8 illustrates the `Rational` class and its relationship to the `Number` class and the `Comparable` interface.

A rational number consists of a numerator and a denominator. There are many equivalent rational numbers—for example, 1 / 3 = 2 / 6 = 3 / 9 = 4 / 12. The numerator and the denominator of 1 / 3 have no common divisor except 1, so 1 / 3 is said to be in *lowest terms*.

To reduce a rational number to its lowest terms, you need to find the greatest common divisor (GCD) of the absolute values of its numerator and denominator, then divide both the numerator and denominator by this value. You can use the method for computing the GCD of

```
java.lang.Number

java.lang.Comparable<Rational>
```

```
                        1
                    Rational
                        1
```
Add, Subtract, Multiply, Divide

Rational
–numerator: long –denominator: long

+Rational()
+Rational(numerator: long,
  denominator: long)
+getNumerator(): long
+getDenominator(): long
+add(secondRational: Rational):
  Rational
+subtract(secondRational:
  Rational): Rational
+multiply(secondRational:
  Rational): Rational
+divide(secondRational:
  Rational): Rational
+toString(): String
 	
–gcd(n: long, d: long): long

The numerator of this rational number.
The denominator of this rational number.

Creates a rational number with numerator 0 and denominator 1.
Creates a rational number with a specified numerator and denominator.

Returns the numerator of this rational number.
Returns the denominator of this rational number.
Returns the addition of this rational number with another.

Returns the subtraction of this rational number with another.

Returns the multiplication of this rational number with another.

Returns the division of this rational number with another.

Returns a string in the form "numerator/denominator." Returns the numerator if denominator is 1.
Returns the greatest common divisor of n and d.

FIGURE 13.8 The properties, constructors, and methods of the `Rational` class are illustrated in UML.

two integers n and d, as suggested in Listing 5.9, GreatestCommonDivisor.java. The numerator and denominator in a `Rational` object are reduced to their lowest terms.

As usual, let us first write a test program to create two `Rational` objects and test its methods. Listing 13.12 is a test program.

LISTING 13.12 TestRationalClass.java

```java
1  public class TestRationalClass {
2    /** Main method */
3    public static void main(String[] args) {
4      // Create and initialize two rational numbers r1 and r2
5      Rational r1 = new Rational(4, 2);                                    create a Rational
6      Rational r2 = new Rational(2, 3);                                    create a Rational
7
8      // Display results
9      System.out.println(r1 + " + " + r2 + " = " + r1.add(r2));           add
10     System.out.println(r1 + " - " + r2 + " = " + r1.subtract(r2));
11     System.out.println(r1 + " * " + r2 + " = " + r1.multiply(r2));
12     System.out.println(r1 + " / " + r2 + " = " + r1.divide(r2));
13     System.out.println(r2 + " is " + r2.doubleValue());
14   }
15 }
```

```
2 + 2/3 = 8/3
2 - 2/3 = 4/3
2 * 2/3 = 4/3
2 / 2/3 = 3
2/3 is 0.6666666666666666
```

The `main` method creates two rational numbers, `r1` and `r2` (lines 5 and 6), and displays the results of `r1 + r2`, `r1 - r2`, `r1 x r2`, and `r1 / r2` (lines 9–12). To perform `r1 + r2`, invoke `r1.add(r2)` to return a new `Rational` object. Similarly, invoke `r1.subtract(r2)` for `r1 - r2`, `r1.multiply(r2)` for `r1 x r2`, and `r1.divide(r2)` for `r1 / r2`.

The `doubleValue()` method displays the double value of `r2` (line 13). The `doubleValue()` method is defined in `java.lang.Number` and overridden in `Rational`.

Note when a string is concatenated with an object using the plus sign (+), the object's string representation from the `toString()` method is used to concatenate with the string. Thus, `r1 + " + " + r2 + " = " + r1.add(r2)` is equivalent to `r1.toString() + " + " + r2.toString() + " = " + r1.add(r2).toString()`.

The `Rational` class is implemented in Listing 13.13.

LISTING 13.13   `Rational.java`

```java
 1  public class Rational extends Number implements Comparable<Rational> {
 2    // Data fields for numerator and denominator
 3    private long numerator = 0;
 4    private long denominator = 1;
 5
 6    /** Construct a rational with default properties */
 7    public Rational() {
 8      this(0, 1);
 9    }
10
11    /** Construct a rational with specified numerator and denominator */
12    public Rational(long numerator, long denominator) {
13      long gcd = gcd(numerator, denominator);
14      this.numerator = (denominator > 0 ? 1 : -1) * numerator / gcd;
15      this.denominator = Math.abs(denominator) / gcd;
16    }
17
18    /** Find GCD of two numbers */
19    private static long gcd(long n, long d) {
20      long n1 = Math.abs(n);
21      long n2 = Math.abs(d);
22      int gcd = 1;
23
24      for (int k = 1; k <= n1 && k <= n2; k++) {
25        if (n1 % k == 0 && n2 % k == 0) {
26          gcd = k;
27      }
28
29      return gcd;
30    }
31
32    /** Return numerator */
33    public long getNumerator() {
34      return numerator;
35    }
36
37    /** Return denominator */
38    public long getDenominator() {
39      return denominator;
40    }
41
42    /** Add a rational number to this rational */
43    public Rational add(Rational secondRational) {
44      long n = numerator * secondRational.getDenominator() +
45        denominator * secondRational.getNumerator();
```

$$\frac{a}{b} + \frac{c}{d} = \frac{ad + bc}{bd}$$

```
46       long d = denominator * secondRational.getDenominator();
47       return new Rational(n, d);
48     }
49
50     /** Subtract a rational number from this rational */
51     public Rational subtract(Rational secondRational) {
52       long n = numerator * secondRational.getDenominator()
53         - denominator * secondRational.getNumerator();
54       long d = denominator * secondRational.getDenominator();
55       return new Rational(n, d);
56     }
57
58     /** Multiply a rational number by this rational */
59     public Rational multiply(Rational secondRational) {
60       long n = numerator * secondRational.getNumerator();
61       long d = denominator * secondRational.getDenominator();
62       return new Rational(n, d);
63     }
64
65     /** Divide a rational number by this rational */
66     public Rational divide(Rational secondRational) {
67       long n = numerator * secondRational.getDenominator();
68       long d = denominator * secondRational.numerator;
69       return new Rational(n, d);
70     }
71
72     @Override
73     public String toString() {
74       if (denominator == 1)
75         return numerator + "";
76       else
77         return numerator + "/" + denominator;
78     }
79
80     @Override // Override the equals method in the Object class
81     public boolean equals(Object other) {
82       if ((this.subtract((Rational)(other))).getNumerator() == 0)
83         return true;
84       else
85         return false;
86     }
87
88     @Override // Implement the abstract intValue method in Number
89     public int intValue() {
90       return (int)doubleValue();
91     }
92
93     @Override // Implement the abstract floatValue method in Number
94     public float floatValue() {
95       return (float)doubleValue();
96     }
97
98     @Override // Implement the doubleValue method in Number
99     public double doubleValue() {
100      return numerator * 1.0 / denominator;
101    }
102
103    @Override // Implement the abstract longValue method in Number
104    public long longValue() {
105      return (long)doubleValue();
```

$\frac{a}{b} - \frac{c}{d} = \frac{ad-bc}{bd}$

$\frac{a}{b} \times \frac{c}{d} = \frac{ac}{bd}$

$\frac{a}{b} \div \frac{c}{d} = \frac{ad}{bc}$

```
106     }
107
108     @Override // Implement the compareTo method in Comparable
109     public int compareTo(Rational o) {
110       if (this.subtract(o).getNumerator() > 0)
111         return 1;
112       else if (this.subtract(o).getNumerator() < 0)
113         return -1;
114       else
115         return 0;
116     }
117   }
```

The rational number is encapsulated in a `Rational` object. Internally, a rational number is represented in its lowest terms (line 13) and the numerator determines its sign (line 14). The denominator is always positive (line 15).

The `gcd` method (lines 19–30 in the `Rational` class) is private; it is not intended for use by clients. The `gcd` method is only for internal use by the `Rational` class. The `gcd` method is also static, since it is not dependent on any particular `Rational` object.

The `abs(x)` method (lines 20 and 21 in the `Rational` class) is defined in the `Math` class and returns the absolute value of `x`.

Two `Rational` objects can interact with each other to perform add, subtract, multiply, and divide operations. These methods return a new `Rational` object (lines 43–70).

The methods `toString` and `equals` in the `Object` class are overridden in the `Rational` class (lines 72–86). The `toString()` method returns a string representation of a `Rational` object in the form `numerator/denominator`, or simply `numerator` if `denominator` is 1. The `equals(Object other)` method returns true if this rational number is equal to the other rational number.

The abstract methods `intValue`, `longValue`, `floatValue`, and `doubleValue` in the `Number` class are implemented in the `Rational` class (lines 88–106). These methods return the `int`, `long`, `float`, and `double` value for this rational number.

The `compareTo(Rational other)` method in the `Comparable` interface is implemented in the `Rational` class (lines 108–116) to compare this rational number to the other rational number.

Note

immutable

The getter methods for the properties `numerator` and `denominator` are provided in the `Rational` class, but the setter methods are not provided, so, once a `Rational` object is created, its contents cannot be changed. The `Rational` class is immutable. The `String` class and the wrapper classes for primitive-type values are also immutable.

Note

encapsulation

The numerator and denominator are represented using two variables. It is possible to use an array of two integers to represent the numerator and denominator (see Programming Exercise 13.14). The signatures of the public methods in the `Rational` class are not changed, although the internal representation of a rational number is changed. This is a good example to illustrate the idea that the data fields of a class should be kept private so as to encapsulate the implementation of the class from the use of the class.

overflow

The `Rational` class has serious limitations and can easily overflow. For example, the following code will display an incorrect result, because the denominator is too large:

```
public class Test {
  public static void main(String[] args) {
    Rational r1 = new Rational(1, 123456789);
```

```
    Rational r2 = new Rational(1, 123456789);
    Rational r3 = new Rational(1, 123456789);
    System.out.println("r1 * r2 * r3 is " +
      r1.multiply(r2.multiply(r3)));
  }
}
```

```
r1 * r2 * r3 is -1/2204193661661244627
```

To fix it, you can implement the `Rational` class using the `BigInteger` for numerator and denominator (see Programming Exercise 13.15).

13.9.1 Show the output of the following code:

```
Rational r1 = new Rational(-2, 6);
System.out.println(r1.getNumerator());
System.out.println(r1.getDenominator());
System.out.println(r1.intValue());
System.out.println(r1.doubleValue());
```

13.9.2 Why is the following code wrong?

```
Rational r1 = new Rational(-2, 6);
Object r2 = new Rational(1, 45);
System.out.println(r2.compareTo(r1));
```

13.9.3 Why is the following code wrong?

```
Object r1 = new Rational(-2, 6);
Rational r2 = new Rational(1, 45);
System.out.println(r2.compareTo(r1));
```

13.9.4 Simplify the code in lines 82–85 in Listing 13.13 Rational.java using one line of code without using the if statement. Simply the code in lines 110-115 using a conditional operator.

13.9.5 Trace the program carefully and show the output of the following code:

```
Rational r1 = new Rational(1, 2);
Rational r2 = new Rational(1, -2);
System.out.println(r1.add(r2));
```

13.9.6 The preceding question shows a bug in the `toString` method. Revise the `toString()` method to fix the error.

13.10 Class-Design Guidelines

Class-design guidelines are helpful for designing sound classes.

You have learned how to design classes from the preceding example and from many other examples in the previous chapters. This section summarizes some of the guidelines.

13.10.1 Cohesion

A class should describe a single entity, and all the class operations should logically fit together to support a coherent purpose. You can use a class for students, for example, but you should not combine students and staff in the same class, because students and staff are different entities.

coherent purpose

separate responsibilities

A single entity with many responsibilities can be broken into several classes to separate the responsibilities. The classes `String`, `StringBuilder`, and `StringBuffer` all deal with strings, for example, but have different responsibilities. The `String` class deals with immutable strings, the `StringBuilder` class is for creating mutable strings, and the `String-Buffer` class is similar to `StringBuilder`, except that `StringBuffer` contains synchronized methods for updating strings.

13.10.2 Consistency

naming conventions

Follow standard Java programming style and naming conventions. Choose informative names for classes, data fields, and methods. A popular style is to place the data declaration before the constructor, and place constructors before methods.

naming consistency

Make the names consistent. It is not a good practice to choose different names for similar operations. For example, the `length()` method returns the size of a `String`, a `StringBuilder`, and a `StringBuffer`. It would be inconsistent if different names were used for this method in these classes.

no-arg constructor

In general, you should consistently provide a public no-arg constructor for constructing a default instance. If a class does not support a no-arg constructor, document the reason. If no constructors are defined explicitly, a public default no-arg constructor with an empty body is assumed.

If you want to prevent users from creating an object for a class, you can declare a private constructor in the class, as is the case for the `Math` class and the `GuessDate` class.

13.10.3 Encapsulation

encapsulate data fields

A class should use the `private` modifier to hide its data from direct access by clients. This makes the class easy to maintain.

Provide a getter method only if you want the data field to be readable and provide a setter method only if you want the data field to be updateable. For example, the `Rational` class provides a getter method for `numerator` and `denominator`, but no setter method, because a `Rational` object is immutable.

13.10.4 Clarity

easy to explain

Cohesion, consistency, and encapsulation are good guidelines for achieving design clarity. In addition, a class should have a clear contract that is easy to explain and easy to understand.

Users can incorporate classes in many different combinations, orders, and environments. Therefore, you should design a class that imposes no restrictions on how or when the user can use it, design the properties in a way that lets the user set them in any order and with any combination of values, and design methods that function independently of their order of occur-

independent methods
intuitive meaning

rence. For example, the `Loan` class contains the properties `loanAmount`, `numberOfYears`, and `annualInterestRate`. The values of these properties can be set in any order.

Methods should be defined intuitively without causing confusion. For example, the `substring(int beginIndex, int endIndex)` method in the `String` class is somewhat confusing. The method returns a substring from `beginIndex` to `endIndex - 1`, rather than to `endIndex`. It would be more intuitive to return a substring from `beginIndex` to `endIndex`.

independent properties

You should not declare a data field that can be derived from other data fields. For example, the following `Person` class has two data fields: `birthDate` and `age`. Since `age` can be derived from `birthDate`, `age` should not be declared as a data field.

```java
public class Person {
  private java.util.Date birthDate;
  private int age;

  . . .
}
```

13.10.5   Completeness

Classes are designed for use by many different customers. In order to be useful in a wide range of applications, a class should provide a variety of ways for customization through properties and methods. For example, the `String` class contains more than 40 methods that are useful for a variety of applications.

13.10.6   Instance vs. Static

A variable or method that is dependent on a specific instance of the class must be an instance variable or method. A variable that is shared by all the instances of a class should be declared static. For example, the variable `numberOfObjects` in `Circle` in Listing 9.8 is shared by all the objects of the `Circle` class, and therefore is declared static. A method that is not dependent on a specific instance should be defined as a static method. For instance, the `getNumberOfObjects()` method in `Circle` is not tied to any specific instance and therefore is defined as a static method.

Always reference static variables and methods from a class name (rather than a reference variable) to improve readability and avoid errors.

Do not pass a parameter from a constructor to initialize a static data field. It is better to use a setter method to change the static data field. Thus, the following class in (a) is better replaced by (b):

```java
public class SomeThing {
  private int t1;
  private static int t2;

  public SomeThing(int t1, int t2) {
    ...
  }
}
```
(a)

```java
public class SomeThing {
  private int t1;
  private static int t2;

  public SomeThing(int t1) {
    ...
  }

  public static void setT2(int t2) {
    SomeThing.t2 = t2;
  }
}
```
(b)

Instance and static are integral parts of object-oriented programming. A data field or method is either instance or static. Do not mistakenly overlook static data fields or methods. It is a common design error to define an instance method that should have been static. For example, the `factorial(int n)` method for computing the factorial of n should be defined static because it is independent of any specific instance.

common design error

A constructor is always instance because it is used to create a specific instance. A static variable or method can be invoked from an instance method, but an instance variable or method cannot be invoked from a static method.

13.10.7   Inheritance vs. Aggregation

The difference between inheritance and aggregation is the difference between an is-a and a has-a relationship. For example, an apple is a fruit; thus, you would use inheritance to model the relationship between the classes `Apple` and `Fruit`. A person has a name; thus, you would use aggregation to model the relationship between the classes `Person` and `Name`.

13.10.8 Interfaces vs. Abstract Classes

Both interfaces and abstract classes can be used to specify common behavior for objects. How do you decide whether to use an interface or a class? In general, a strong is-a relationship that clearly describes a parent–child relationship should be modeled using classes. For example, since an orange is a fruit, their relationship should be modeled using class inheritance. A weak is-a relationship, also known as an is-kind-of relationship, indicates that an object possesses a certain property. A weak is-a relationship can be modeled using interfaces. For example, all strings are comparable, so the `String` class implements the `Comparable` interface. A circle or a rectangle is a geometric object, so `Circle` can be designed as a subclass of `GeometricObject`. Circles are different and comparable based on their radii, so `Circle` can implement the `Comparable` interface.

Interfaces are more flexible than abstract classes because a subclass can extend only one superclass, but can implement any number of interfaces. However, interfaces cannot contain data fields. In Java 8, interfaces can contain default methods and static methods, which are very useful to simplify class design. We will give examples of this type of design in Chapter 20, Lists, Stacks, Queues, and Priority Queues.

13.10.1 Describe class-design guidelines.

KEY TERMS

abstract class 500	marker interface 518
abstract method 500	shallow copy 520
deep copy 520	subinterface 523
interface 500	

CHAPTER SUMMARY

1. *Abstract classes* are like regular classes with data and methods, but you cannot create instances of abstract classes using the `new` operator.

2. An *abstract method* cannot be contained in a nonabstract class. If a subclass of an abstract superclass does not implement all the inherited abstract methods of the superclass, the subclass must be defined as abstract.

3. A class that contains abstract methods must be abstract. However, it is possible to define an abstract class that doesn't contain any abstract methods.

4. A subclass can be abstract even if its superclass is concrete.

5. An *interface* is a class-like construct that contains only constants, abstract methods, default methods, and static methods. In many ways, an interface is similar to an abstract class, but an abstract class can contain data fields.

6. An interface is treated like a special class in Java. Each interface is compiled into a separate bytecode file, just like a regular class.

7. The `java.lang.Comparable` interface defines the `compareTo` method. Many classes in the Java library implement `Comparable`.

8. The `java.lang.Cloneable` interface is a *marker interface*. An object of the class that implements the `Cloneable` interface is cloneable.

9. A class can extend only one superclass but can implement one or more interfaces.

10. An interface can extend one or more interfaces.

QUIZ

Answer the quiz for this chapter online at the book Companion Website.

PROGRAMMING EXERCISES

MyProgrammingLab™

Sections 13.2 and 13.3

**13.1 (*Triangle class*) Design a new `Triangle` class that extends the abstract `GeometricObject` class. Draw the UML diagram for the classes `Triangle` and `GeometricObject` then implement the `Triangle` class. Write a test program that prompts the user to enter three sides of the triangle, a color, and a Boolean value to indicate whether the triangle is filled. The program should create a `Triangle` object with these sides, and set the `color` and `filled` properties using the input. The program should display the area, perimeter, color, and true or false to indicate whether it is filled or not.

*13.2 (*Shuffle ArrayList*) Write the following method that shuffles an `ArrayList` of numbers:

```
public static void shuffle(ArrayList<Number> list)
```

*13.3 (*Sort ArrayList*) Write the following method that sorts an `ArrayList` of numbers:

```
public static void sort(ArrayList<Number> list)
```

**13.4 (*Display calendars*) Rewrite the `PrintCalendar` class in Listing 6.12 to display a calendar for a specified month using the `Calendar` and `GregorianCalendar` classes. Your program receives the month and year from the command line. For example:

```
java Exercise13_04 5 2016
```

This displays the calendar shown in Figure 13.9.

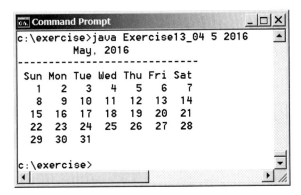

FIGURE 13.9 The program displays a calendar for May 2016.

You can also run the program without the year. In this case, the year is the current year. If you run the program without specifying a month and a year, the month is the current month.

Sections 13.4–13.8

*13.5 (*Enable GeometricObject comparable*) Modify the GeometricObject class to implement the Comparable interface and define a static max method in the GeometricObject class for finding the larger of two GeometricObject objects. Draw the UML diagram and implement the new GeometricObject class. Write a test program that uses the max method to find the larger of two circles, the larger of two rectangles.

*13.6 (*The ComparableCircle class*) Define a class named ComparableCircle that extends Circle and implements Comparable. Draw the UML diagram and implement the compareTo method to compare the circles on the basis of area. Write a test class to find the larger of two instances of ComparableCircle objects, and the larger between a circle and a rectangle.

*13.7 (*The Colorable interface*) Design an interface named Colorable with a void method named howToColor(). Every class of a colorable object must implement the Colorable interface. Design a class named Square that extends GeometricObject and implements Colorable. Implement howToColor to display the message Color all four sides. The Square class contains a data field side with getter and setter methods, and a constructor for constructing a Square with a specified side. The Square class has a private double data field named side with its getter and setter methods. It has a no-arg constructor to create a Square with side 0, and another constructor that creates a Square with the specified side.

Draw a UML diagram that involves Colorable, Square, and GeometricObject. Write a test program that creates an array of five GeometricObjects. For each object in the array, display its area and invoke its howToColor method if it is colorable.

*13.8 (*Revise the MyStack class*) Rewrite the MyStack class in Listing 11.10 to perform a deep copy of the list field.

*13.9 (*Enable Circle comparable*) Rewrite the Circle class in Listing 13.2 to extend GeometricObject and implement the Comparable interface. Override the equals method in the Object class. Two Circle objects are equal if their radii are the same. Draw the UML diagram that involves Circle, GeometricObject, and Comparable.

VideoNote

Redesign the Rectangle class

*13.10 (*Enable Rectangle comparable*) Rewrite the Rectangle class in Listing 13.3 to extend GeometricObject and implement the Comparable interface. Override the equals method in the Object class. Two Rectangle objects are equal if their areas are the same. Draw the UML diagram that involves Rectangle, GeometricObject, and Comparable.

*13.11 (*The Octagon class*) Write a class named Octagon that extends GeometricObject and implements the Comparable and Cloneable interfaces. Assume all eight sides of the octagon are of equal length. The area can be computed using the following formula:

$$area = \left(2 + 4/\sqrt{2}\right) * side * side$$

The `Octagon` class has a private double data field named side with its getter and setter methods. The class has a no-arg constructor that creates an `Octagon` with side 0, and a constructor to create an `Octagon` with a specified side.

Draw the UML diagram that involves `Octagon`, `GeometricObject`, `Comparable`, and `Cloneable`. Write a test program that creates an `Octagon` object with side value 5 and displays its area and perimeter. Create a new object using the `clone` method, and compare the two objects using the `compareTo` method.

*13.12 (*Sum the areas of geometric objects*) Write a method that sums the areas of all the geometric objects in an array. The method signature is:

```
public static double sumArea(GeometricObject[] a)
```

Write a test program that creates an array of four objects (two circles and two rectangles) and computes their total area using the `sumArea` method.

*13.13 (*Enable the Course class cloneable*) Rewrite the `Course` class in Listing 10.6 to add a `clone` method to perform a deep copy on the `students` field.

Section 13.9

*13.14 (*Demonstrate the benefits of encapsulation*) Rewrite the `Rational` class in Listing 13.13 using a new internal representation for the numerator and denominator. Create an array of two integers as follows:

```
private long[] r = new long[2];
```

Use `r[0]` to represent the numerator and `r[1]` to represent the denominator. The signatures of the methods in the `Rational` class are not changed, so a client application that uses the previous `Rational` class can continue to use this new `Rational` class without being recompiled.

*13.15 (*Use BigInteger for the Rational class*) Redesign and implement the `Rational` class in Listing 13.13 using `BigInteger` for the numerator and denominator. Write a test program that prompts the user to enter two rational numbers and display the results as shown in the following sample run:

```
Enter the first rational number: 3 454  ↵Enter
Enter the second second number: 7 2389  ↵Enter
3/454 + 7/2389 = 10345/1084606
3/454 - 7/2389 = 3989/1084606
3/454 * 7/2389 = 21/1084606
3/454 / 7/2389 = 7167/3178
7/2389 is 0.0029300962745918793
```

*13.16 (*Create a rational-number calculator*) Write a program similar to Listing 7.9, Calculator.java. Instead of using integers, use rationals, as shown in Figure 13.10. You will need to use the `split` method in the `String` class, introduced in Section 10.10.3, Replacing and Splitting Strings, to retrieve the numerator string and denominator string, and convert strings into integers using the `Integer.parseInt` method.

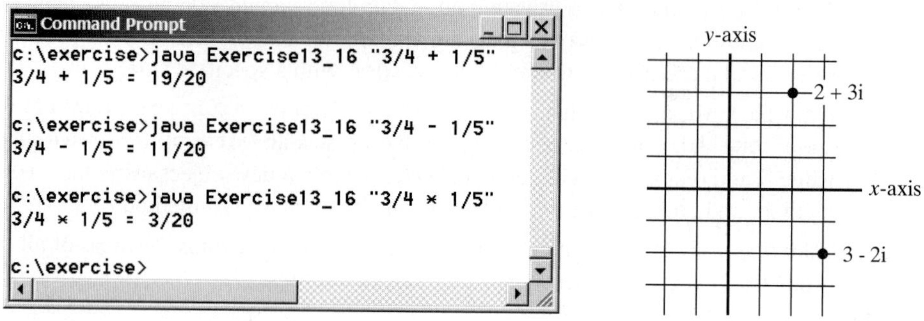

(a) (b)

FIGURE 13.10 (a) The program takes a string argument that consists of operand1, operator, and operand2 from the command line and displays the expression and the result of the arithmetic operation. (b) A complex number can be interpreted as a point in a plane.

*13.17 (*Math: The* Complex *class*) A complex number is a number in the form $a + bi$, where a and b are real numbers and i is $\sqrt{-1}$. The numbers a and b are known as the real part and imaginary part of the complex number, respectively. You can perform addition, subtraction, multiplication, and division for complex numbers using the following formulas:

$$a + bi + c + di = (a + c) + (b + d)i$$

$$a + bi - (c + di) = (a - c) + (b - d)i$$

$$(a + bi) * (c + di) = (ac - bd) + (bc + ad)i$$

$$(a + bi)/(c + di) = (ac + bd)/(c^2 + d^2) + (bc - ad)i/(c^2 + d^2)$$

You can also obtain the absolute value for a complex number using the following formula:

$$|a + bi| = \sqrt{a^2 + b^2}$$

(A complex number can be interpreted as a point on a plane by identifying the (a,b) values as the coordinates of the point. The absolute value of the complex number corresponds to the distance of the point to the origin, as shown in Figure 13.10.)

Design a class named Complex for representing complex numbers and the methods add, subtract, multiply, divide, and abs for performing complex-number operations, and override toString method for returning a string representation for a complex number. The toString method returns (a + bi) as a string. If b is 0, it simply returns a. Your Complex class should also implement Cloneable and Comparable. Compare two complex numbers using their absolute values.

Provide three constructors Complex(a, b), Complex(a), and Complex(). Complex() creates a Complex object for number 0, and Complex(a) creates a Complex object with 0 for b. Also provide the getRealPart() and getImaginaryPart() methods for returning the real part and the imaginary part of the complex number, respectively.

Draw the UML class diagram and implement the class. Write a test program that prompts the user to enter two complex numbers and displays the result of their addition, subtraction, multiplication, division, and absolute value. Here is a sample run:

```
Enter the first complex number: 3.5 5.5  ↵Enter
Enter the second complex number: -3.5 1  ↵Enter
(3.5 + 5.5i) + (-3.5 + 1.0i) = 0.0 + 6.5i
(3.5 + 5.5i) - (-3.5 + 1.0i) = 7.0 + 4.5i
(3.5 + 5.5i) * (-3.5 + 1.0i) = -17.75 + -15.75i
(3.5 + 5.5i) / (-3.5 + 1.0i) = -0.5094 + -1.7i
|(3.5 + 5.5i)| = 6.519202405202649
```

13.18 (*Use the `Rational` class*) Write a program that computes the following summation series using the `Rational` class:

$$\frac{1}{2} + \frac{2}{3} + \frac{3}{4} + \cdots + \frac{98}{99} + \frac{99}{100}$$

You will discover that the output is incorrect because of integer overflow (too large). To fix this problem, see Programming Exercise 13.15.

13.19 (*Convert decimals to fractions*) Write a program that prompts the user to enter a decimal number and displays the number in a fraction. (*Hint*: read the decimal number as a string, extract the integer part and fractional part from the string, and use the `BigInteger` implementation of the `Rational` class in Programming Exercise 13.15 to obtain a rational number for the decimal number.) Here are some sample runs:

```
Enter a decimal number: 3.25  ↵Enter
The fraction number is 13/4
```

```
Enter a decimal number: -0.45452  ↵Enter
The fraction number is -11363/25000
```

13.20 (*Algebra: solve quadratic equations*) Rewrite Programming Exercise 3.1 to obtain imaginary roots if the determinant is less than 0 using the `Complex` class in Programming Exercise 13.17. Here are some sample runs:

```
Enter a, b, c: 1 3 1  ↵Enter
The roots are -0.381966 and -2.61803
```

```
Enter a, b, c: 1 2 1  ↵Enter
The root is -1
```

```
Enter a, b, c: 1 2 3  ↵Enter
The roots are -1.0 + 1.4142i and -1.0 + -1.4142i
```

13.21   (*Algebra: vertex form equations*) The equation of a parabola can be expressed in either standard form ($y = ax^2 + bx + c$) or vertex form ($y = a(x - h)^2 + k$). Write a program that prompts the user to enter a, b, and c as integers in standard form and displays $h\left(= \dfrac{-b}{2a}\right)$ and $k\left(= \dfrac{4ac - b^2}{4a}\right)$ in the vertex form. Display h and k as rational numbers. Here are some sample runs:

```
Enter a, b, c: 1 3 1  ↵Enter
h is -3/2 k is -5/4
```

```
Enter a, b, c: 2 3 4  ↵Enter
h is -3/4 k is 23/8
```

JavaFX Basics

Objectives

- To distinguish between JavaFX, Swing, and AWT (§14.2).

- To write a simple JavaFX program and understand the relationship among stages, scenes, and nodes (§14.3).

- To create user interfaces using panes, groups, UI controls, and shapes (§14.4).

- To update property values automatically through property binding (§14.5).

- To use the common properties `style` and `rotate` for nodes (§14.6).

- To create colors using the `Color` class (§14.7).

- To create fonts using the `Font` class (§14.8).

- To create images using the `Image` class, and to create image views using the `ImageView` class (§14.9).

- To layout nodes using `Pane`, `StackPane`, `FlowPane`, `GridPane`, `BorderPane`, `HBox`, and `VBox` (§14.10).

- To display text using the `Text` class, and create shapes using the `Line`, `Circle`, `Rectangle`, `Ellipse`, `Arc`, `Polygon`, and `Polyline` classes (§14.11).

- To develop the reusable GUI component `ClockPane` for displaying an analog clock (§14.12).

14.1 Introduction

JavaFX is an excellent pedagogical tool for learning object-oriented programming.

JavaFX is a new framework for developing Java GUI programs. The JavaFX API is an excellent example of how the object-oriented principles are applied. This chapter serves two purposes. First, it presents the basics of JavaFX programming. Second, it uses JavaFX to demonstrate object-oriented design and programming. Specifically, this chapter introduces the framework of JavaFX and discusses JavaFX GUI components and their relationships. You will learn how to develop simple GUI programs using layout panes, groups, buttons, labels, text fields, colors, fonts, images, image views, and shapes.

14.2 JavaFX vs. Swing and AWT

Swing and AWT are replaced by the JavaFX platform for developing rich GUI applications.

AWT

Swing

JavaFX

When Java was introduced, the GUI classes were bundled in a library known as the *Abstract Windows Toolkit (AWT)*. AWT is fine for developing simple graphical user interfaces, but not for developing comprehensive GUI projects. In addition, AWT is prone to platform-specific bugs. The AWT user-interface components were replaced by a more robust, versatile, and flexible library known as *Swing*. Swing components are painted directly on canvases using Java code. Swing components depend less on the target platform, and use less of the native GUI resources. Swing is designed for developing desktop GUI applications. It is now replaced by a completely new GUI platform known as *JavaFX*. JavaFX incorporates modern GUI technologies to enable you to develop rich GUI applications. In addition, JavaFX provides a multitouch support for touch-enabled devices such as tablets and smart phones. JavaFX has a built-in 2D, 3D, animation support, and video and audio playback. Using third-party software, you can develop JavaFX programs to be deployed on devices running iOS or Android.

why teaching JavaFX

    This book teaches Java GUI programming using JavaFX for three reasons. First, JavaFX is much simpler to learn and use for new Java programmers. Second, JavaFX is a better pedagogical tool for demonstrating object-oriented programming than Swing. Third, Swing is essentially dead because it will not receive any further enhancement. JavaFX is the new GUI tool for developing cross-platform rich GUI applications on desktop computers and on handheld devices.

14.2.1 Explain the evolution of Java GUI technologies.

14.2.2 Explain why this book teaches Java GUI using JavaFX.

14.3 The Basic Structure of a JavaFX Program

The `javafx.application.Application` *class defines the essential framework for writing JavaFX programs.*

VideoNote

Getting started with JavaFX

We begin by writing a simple JavaFX program that illustrates the basic structure of a JavaFX program. Every JavaFX program is defined in a class that extends `javafx.application.Application`, as shown in Listing 14.1.

LISTING 14.1   `MyJavaFX.java`

```
1  import javafx.application.Application;
2  import javafx.scene.Scene;
3  import javafx.scene.control.Button;
4  import javafx.stage.Stage;
```

```
 5
 6   public class MyJavaFX extends Application {                          extend Application
 7     @Override // Override the start method in the Application class
 8     public void start(Stage primaryStage) {                           override start
 9       // Create a scene and place a button in the scene
10       Button btOK = new Button("OK");                                 create a button
11       Scene scene = new Scene(btOK, 200, 250);                        create a scene
12       primaryStage.setTitle("MyJavaFX"); // Set the stage title       set stage title
13       primaryStage.setScene(scene); // Place the scene in the stage   set a scene
14       primaryStage.show(); // Display the stage                       display stage
15     }
16
17     /**
18      * The main method is only needed for the IDE with limited
19      * JavaFX support. Not needed for running from the command line.
20      */
21     public static void main(String[] args) {                          main method
22       Application.launch(args);                                       launch application
23     }
24   }
```

You can test and run your program from a command window or from an IDE such as NetBeans or Eclipse. A sample run of the program is shown in Figure 14.1. Supplements II.F–H give the tips for running JavaFX programs from a command window, NetBeans, and Eclipse.

JavaFX on NetBeans and Eclipse

FIGURE 14.1   A simple JavaFX displays a button in the window.

The `launch` method (line 22) is a static method defined in the `Application` class for launching a stand-alone JavaFX application. The `main` method (lines 21–23) is not needed if you run the program from the command line. It may be needed to launch a JavaFX program from an IDE with a limited JavaFX support. When you run a JavaFX application without a main method, JVM automatically invokes the `launch` method to run the application.

launch

The main class overrides the `start` method defined in `javafx.application` `.Application` (line 8). After a JavaFX application is launched, the JVM constructs an instance of the class using its `no-arg` constructor and invokes its `start` method. The `start` method normally places UI controls in a scene and displays the scene in a stage, as shown in Figure 14.2a.

construct application
start application

Line 10 creates a `Button` object and places it in a `Scene` object (line 11). A `Scene` object can be created using the constructor `Scene(node, width, height)`. This constructor specifies the width and height of the scene and places the node in the scene.

scene

A `Stage` object is a window. A `Stage` object called *primary stage* is automatically created by the JVM when the application is launched. Line 13 sets the scene to the primary stage and line 14 displays the primary stage. JavaFX names the `Stage` and `Scene` classes using the analogy from the theater. You may think of stage as the platform to support scenes, and nodes as actors to perform in the scenes.

primary stage

You can create additional stages if needed. The JavaFX program in Listing 14.2 displays two stages, as shown in Figure 14.2b.

FIGURE 14.2 (a) Stage is a window for displaying a scene that contains nodes. (b) Multiple stages can be displayed in a JavaFX program.

LISTING 14.2 MultipleStageDemo.java

```
1  import javafx.application.Application;
2  import javafx.scene.Scene;
3  import javafx.scene.control.Button;
4  import javafx.stage.Stage;
5
6  public class MultipleStageDemo extends Application {
7    @Override // Override the start method in the Application class
8    public void start(Stage primaryStage) {
9      // Create a scene and place a button in the scene
10     Scene scene = new Scene(new Button("OK"), 200, 250);
11     primaryStage.setTitle("MyJavaFX"); // Set the stage title
12     primaryStage.setScene(scene); // Place the scene in the stage
13     primaryStage.show(); // Display the stage
14
15     Stage stage = new Stage(); // Create a new stage
16     stage.setTitle("Second Stage"); // Set the stage title
17     // Set a scene with a button in the stage
18     stage.setScene(new Scene(new Button("New Stage"), 200, 250));
19     stage.show(); // Display the stage
20   }
21 }
```

primary stage in start

display primary stage

create second stage

display second stage

main method omitted

main method omitted

Note the main method is omitted in the listing since it is identical for every JavaFX application. From now on, we will not list the main method in our JavaFX source code for brevity.

By default, the user can resize the stage. To prevent the user from resizing the stage, invoke `stage.setResizable(false)`.

prevent stage resizing

Check Point

14.3.1 How do you define a JavaFX main class? What is the signature of the start method? What is a stage? What is a primary stage? Is a primary stage automatically created? How do you display a stage? Can you prevent the user from resizing the stage? Can you replace `Application.launch(args)` by `launch(args)` in line 22 in Listing 14.1?

14.3.2 Show the output of the following JavaFX program:

```
import javafx.application.Application;
import javafx.stage.Stage;

public class Test extends Application {
  public Test() {
    System.out.println("Test constructor is invoked");
  }
```

```
@Override // Override the start method in the Application class
public void start(Stage primaryStage) {
    System.out.println("start method is invoked");
}

public static void main(String[] args) {
    System.out.println("launch application");
    Application.launch(args);
}
}
```

14.4 Panes, Groups, UI Controls, and Shapes

Panes, Groups, UI controls, and shapes are subtypes of Node.

Key Point

When you run MyJavaFX in Listing 14.1, the window is displayed as shown in Figure 14.1. The button is always centered in the scene and occupies the entire window no matter how you resize it. You can fix the problem by setting the position and size properties of a button. However, a better approach is to use container classes, called *panes*, for automatically laying out the nodes in a desired location and size. You place nodes inside a pane then place the pane into a scene. A *node* is a visual component such as a shape, an image view, a UI control, a group, or a pane. A *shape* refers to a text, line, circle, ellipse, rectangle, arc, polygon, polyline, and so on. A *UI control* refers to a label, button, check box, radio button, text field, text area, and so on. A group is a container that groups a collection of nodes. You can apply transformations or effects to a group, which automatically apply to all the children in the group. A scene can be displayed in a stage, as shown in Figure 14.3a. The relationship among Stage, Scene, Node, Control, Group, and Pane is illustrated in the UML diagram, as shown in Figure 14.3b. Note a Scene can contain a Control, Group, or a Pane, but not a Shape or an ImageView. A Pane or a Group can contain any subtype of Node. You can create a Scene using the constructor Scene(Parent, width, height) or Scene(Parent). The dimension of the scene is automatically decided in the latter constructor. Every subclass of Node has a no-arg constructor for creating a default node.

pane

node

shape

UI control

group

Listing 14.3 gives a program that places a button in a pane, as shown in Figure 14.4.

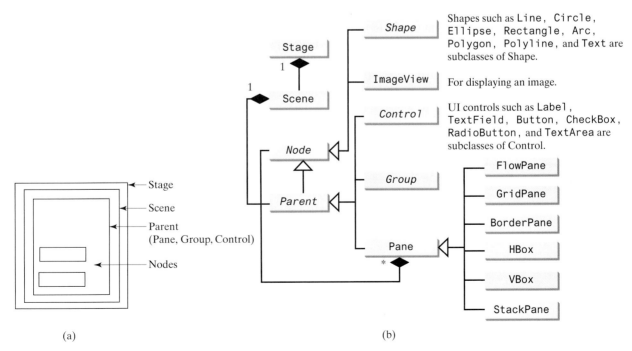

(a) (b)

FIGURE 14.3 (a) Panes and groups are used to hold nodes. (b) Nodes can be shapes, image views, UI controls, groups, and panes.

LISTING 14.3 ButtonInPane.java

```
1   import javafx.application.Application;
2   import javafx.scene.Scene;
3   import javafx.scene.control.Button;
4   import javafx.stage.Stage;
5   import javafx.scene.layout.StackPane;
6
7   public class ButtonInPane extends Application {
8     @Override // Override the start method in the Application class
9     public void start(Stage primaryStage) {
10      // Create a scene and place a button in the scene
11      StackPane pane = new StackPane();
12      pane.getChildren().add(new Button("OK"));
13      Scene scene = new Scene(pane, 200, 50);
14      primaryStage.setTitle("Button in a pane"); // Set the stage title
15      primaryStage.setScene(scene); // Place the scene in the stage
16      primaryStage.show(); // Display the stage
17    }
18  }
```

create a pane (line 11)
add a button (line 12)
add pane to scene (line 13)

display stage (line 16)

main method omitted (line 18)

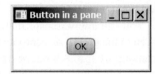

FIGURE 14.4   A button is placed in the center of the pane.

The program creates a StackPane (line 11) and adds a button as a child of the pane (line 12). The getChildren() method returns an instance of javafx.collections .ObservableList. ObservableList behaves very much like an ArrayList for storing a collection of elements. Invoking add(e) adds an element to the list. The StackPane places the nodes in the center of the pane on top of each other. Here, there is only one node in the pane. The StackPane respects a node's preferred size. Therefore, you see the button displayed in its preferred size.

ObservableList

Along with many other constructors, each pane and group have a no-arg constructor, and also a contractor that adds one or more children to the pane or group. Thus, the code in lines 11 and 12 can be replaced using one statement:

```
StackPane pane = new StackPane(new Button("OK"));
```

Listing 14.4 gives an example that displays a circle in the center of the pane, as shown in Figure 14.5a.

LISTING 14.4   ShowCircle.java

```
1   import javafx.application.Application;
2   import javafx.scene.Scene;
3   import javafx.scene.layout.Pane;
4   import javafx.scene.paint.Color;
5   import javafx.scene.shape.Circle;
6   import javafx.stage.Stage;
7
8   public class ShowCircle extends Application {
9     @Override // Override the start method in the Application class
10    public void start(Stage primaryStage) {
```

```
11        // Create a circle and set its properties
12        Circle circle = new Circle();                                create a circle
13        circle.setCenterX(100);                                      set circle properties
14        circle.setCenterY(100);
15        circle.setRadius(50);
16        circle.setStroke(Color.BLACK);
17        circle.setFill(Color.WHITE);
18
19        // Create a pane to hold the circle
20        Pane pane = new Pane();                                      create a pane
21        pane.getChildren().add(circle);                              add circle to pane
22
23        // Create a scene and place it in the stage
24        Scene scene = new Scene(pane, 200, 200);                     add pane to scene
25        primaryStage.setTitle("ShowCircle"); // Set the stage title
26        primaryStage.setScene(scene); // Place the scene in the stage
27        primaryStage.show(); // Display the stage                    display stage
28      }
29  }                                                                  main method omitted
```

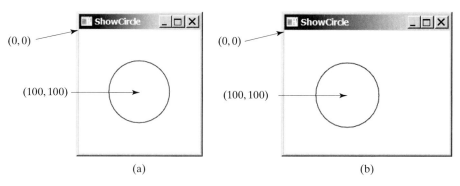

FIGURE 14.5 (a) A circle is displayed in the center of the scene. (b) The circle is not centered after the window is resized.

The program creates a `Circle` (line 12) and sets its center at (100, 100) (lines 13 and 14), which is also the center for the scene, since the scene is created with the width and height of 200 (line 24). The radius of the circle is set to 50 (line 15). Note the measurement units for graphics in Java are all in *pixels*. pixels

The stroke color (i.e., the color to draw the circle) is set to black (line 16). The fill color (i.e., the color to fill the circle) is set to white (line 17). You may set the color to `null` to set color specify that no color is set.

The program creates a `Pane` (line 20) and places the circle in the pane (line 21). Note the coordinates of the upper-left corner of the pane is (0, 0) in the Java coordinate system, as shown in Figure 14.6a, as opposed to the conventional coordinate system, where (0, 0) is at the center of the window, as shown in Figure 14.6b. The *x*-coordinate increases from left to right, and the *y*-coordinate increases downward in the Java coordinate system.

The pane is placed in the scene (line 24) and the scene is set in the stage (line 26). The circle is displayed in the center of the stage, as shown in Figure 14.5a. However, if you resize the window, the circle is not centered, as shown in Figure 14.5b. In order to display the circle centered as the window resizes, the *x*- and *y*-coordinates of the circle center need to be reset to the center of the pane. This can be done by using property binding, introduced in the next section.

FIGURE 14.6 The Java coordinate system is measured in pixels, with $(0, 0)$ at its upper-left corner.

Check Point

14.4.1 How do you create a Scene object? How do you set a scene in a stage? How do you place a circle into a scene?

14.4.2 What is a pane? What is a node? How do you place a node in a pane? Can you directly place a Shape or an ImageView into a Scene? Can you directly place a Control or a Pane into a Scene?

14.4.3 How do you create a Circle? How do you set its center location and radius? How do you set its stroke color and fill color?

14.4.4 How do you replace the code in lines 20 and 21 in Listing 14.4 using one statement?

14.5 Property Binding

You can bind a target object to a source object. A change in the source object will be automatically reflected in the target object.

JavaFX introduces a new concept called *property binding* that enables a *target object* to be bound to a *source object*. If the value in the source object changes, the target object is also automatically changed. The target object is called a *binding object* or a *binding property*, and the source object is called a *bindable object* or *observable object*. As discussed in Listing 14.4 ShowCircle.java, the circle is not centered after the window is resized. In order to display the circle centered as the window resizes, the *x*- and *y*-coordinates of the circle center need to be reset to the center of the pane. This can be done by binding the centerX with pane's width/2 and centerY with pane's height/2, as given in lines 16–17 Listing 14.5.

target object
source object
binding object
binding property
bindable object
observable object

VideoNote

Understand property binding

LISTING 14.5   ShowCircleCentered.java

```
1   import javafx.application.Application;
2   import javafx.scene.Scene;
3   import javafx.scene.layout.Pane;
4   import javafx.scene.paint.Color;
5   import javafx.scene.shape.Circle;
6   import javafx.stage.Stage;
7
8   public class ShowCircleCentered extends Application {
9     @Override // Override the start method in the Application class
10      public void start(Stage primaryStage) {
```

```
11        // Create a pane to hold the circle
12        Pane pane = new Pane();                                              create a pane
13
14        // Create a circle and set its properties
15        Circle circle = new Circle();                                        create a circle
16        circle.centerXProperty().bind(pane.widthProperty().divide(2));       bind properties
17        circle.centerYProperty().bind(pane.heightProperty().divide(2));
18        circle.setRadius(50);
19        circle.setStroke(Color.BLACK);
20        circle.setFill(Color.WHITE);
21        pane.getChildren().add(circle); // Add circle to the pane            add circle to pane
22
23        // Create a scene and place it in the stage
24        Scene scene = new Scene(pane, 200, 200);                             add pane to scene
25        primaryStage.setTitle("ShowCircleCentered"); // Set the stage title
26        primaryStage.setScene(scene); // Place the scene in the stage
27        primaryStage.show(); // Display the stage                            display stage
28      }
29  }
```

The `Circle` class has the `centerX` property for representing the *x*-coordinate of the circle center. This property like many properties in JavaFX classes can be used both as target and source in a property binding. A binding property is an object that can be bound to a source object. A target listens to the changes in the source and automatically updates itself once a change is made in the source. A target binds with a source using the `bind` method as follows:

```
target.bind(source);
```

The `bind` method is defined in the `javafx.beans.property.Property` interface. A binding property is an instance of `javafx.beans.property.Property`. An observable source object is an instance of the `javafx.beans.value.ObservableValue` interface. An `ObservableValue` is an entity that wraps a value and allows to observe the value for changes.

A binding property is an object. JavaFX defines binding properties for primitive types and strings. For a `double`/`float`/`long`/`int`/`boolean` value, its binding property type is `Double Property`/`FloatProperty`/`LongProperty`/`IntegerProperty`/`BooleanProperty` respectively. For a string, its binding property type is `StringProperty`. These properties are also subtypes of `ObservableValue`. Therefore, they can be used as both source and target in a binding.

By convention, each binding property (e.g., `centerX`) in a JavaFX class (e.g., `Circle`) has a getter (e.g., `getCenterX()`) and setter (e.g., `setCenterX(double)`) method for returning and setting the property's value. It also has a getter method for returning the property itself. The naming convention for this method is the property name followed by the word `Property`. For example, the property getter method for `centerX` is `centerXProperty()`. We call the `getCenterX()` method as the *value getter method*, the `setCenterX(double)` method as the *value setter method*, and `centerXProperty()` as the *property getter method*. Note `getCenterX()` returns a `double` value, and `centerXProperty()` returns an object of the `DoubleProperty` type. Figure 14.7a shows the convention for defining a binding property in a class, and Figure 14.7b shows a concrete example in which `centerX` is a binding property of the type `DoubleProperty`.

The program in Listing 14.5 is the same as in Listing 14.4 except that it binds `circle`'s `centerX` and `centerY` properties to half of `pane`'s width and height (lines 16 and 17). Note `circle.centerXProperty()` returns `centerX` and `pane.widthProperty()` returns

the `Property` interface

the `ObservableValue` interface

common binding properties

common `ObservableValue` objects

value getter method
value setter method
property getter method

```
public class SomeClassName {

  private PropertyType x;

  /** Value getter method */
  public propertyValueType getX() { ... }

  /** Value setter method */
  public void setX(propertyValueType value) { ... }

  /** Property getter method */
  public PropertyType
    xProperty() { ... }
}
```

```
public class Circle {

  private DoubleProperty centerX;

  /** Value getter method */
  public double getCenterX() { ... }

  /** Value setter method */
  public void setCenterX(double value) { ... }

  /** Property getter method */
  public DoubleProperty centerXProperty() { ... }
}
```

(a) x is a binding property

(b) centerX is binding property in the Circle class

FIGURE 14.7 A binding property has a value getter method, setter method, and property getter method.

width. Both centerX and width are binding properties of the DoubleProperty type. The numeric binding property classes such as DoubleProperty and IntegerProperty contain the add, subtract, multiply, and divide methods for adding, subtracting, multiplying, and dividing a value in a binding property and returning a new observable property. Therefore, pane.widthProperty().divide(2) returns a new observable property that represents half of the pane's width. The statement

```
circle.centerXProperty().bind(pane.widthProperty().divide(2));
```

is the same as

```
DoubleProperty centerX = circle.centerXProperty();
DoubleProperty width = pane.widthProperty();
centerX.bind(width.divide(2));
```

Since centerX is bound to width.divide(2), when pane's width is changed, centerX automatically updates itself to match pane's width / 2.

Listing 14.6 gives another example that demonstrates bindings.

LISTING 14.6 BindingDemo.java

```
 1  import javafx.beans.property.DoubleProperty;
 2  import javafx.beans.property.SimpleDoubleProperty;
 3
 4  public class BindingDemo {
 5    public static void main(String[] args) {
 6      DoubleProperty d1 = new SimpleDoubleProperty(1);
 7      DoubleProperty d2 = new SimpleDoubleProperty(2);
 8      d1.bind(d2);
 9      System.out.println("d1 is " + d1.getValue()
10        + " and d2 is " + d2.getValue());
11      d2.setValue(70.2);
12      System.out.println("d1 is " + d1.getValue()
13        + " and d2 is " + d2.getValue());
14    }
15  }
```

create a DoubleProperty
create a DoubleProperty
bind property

set a new source value

```
d1 is 2.0 and d2 is 2.0
d1 is 70.2 and d2 is 70.2
```

The program creates an instance of `DoubleProperty` using `SimpleDoubleProperty(1)` (line 6). Note that `DoubleProperty`, `FloatProperty`, `LongProperty`, `IntegerProperty`, and `BooleanProperty` are abstract classes. Their concrete subclasses `SimpleDoubleProperty`, `SimpleFloatProperty`, `SimpleLongProperty`, `SimpleIntegerProperty`, and `SimpleBooleanProperty` are used to create instances of these properties. These classes are very much like wrapper classes `Double`, `Float`, `Long`, `Integer`, and `Boolean` with additional features for property binding.

The program binds `d1` with `d2` (line 8). Now the values in `d1` and `d2` are the same. After setting `d2` to `70.2` (line 11), `d1` also becomes `70.2` (line 13).

The binding demonstrated in this example is known as *unidirectional binding*. Occasionally, it is useful to synchronize two properties so a change in one property is reflected in another object, and vice versa. This is called a *bidirectional binding*. If the target and source are both binding properties and observable properties, they can be bound bidirectionally using the `bindBidirectional` method.

unidirectional binding
bidirectional binding

14.5.1 What is a binding property? What interface defines a binding property? What interface defines a source object? What are the binding object types for `int`, `long`, `float`, `double`, and `boolean`? Are `Integer` and `Double` binding properties? Can `Integer` and `Double` be used as source objects in a binding?

14.5.2 Following the JavaFX binding property naming convention, for a binding property named `age` of the `IntegerProperty` type, what is its value getter method, value setter method, and property getter method?

14.5.3 Can you create an object of `IntegerProperty` using `new IntegerProperty(3)`? If not, what is the correct way to create it? What will be the output if line 8 is replaced by `d1.bind(d2.multiply(2))` in Listing 14.6? What will be the output if line 8 is replaced by `d1.bind(d2.add(2))` in Listing 14.6?

14.5.4 What is unidirectional binding and what is bidirectional binding? Are all binding properties capable of bidirectional binding? Write a statement to bind property `d1` with property `d2` bidirectionally.

Check Point

14.6 Common Properties and Methods for Nodes

The Node class defines many properties and methods that are common to all nodes.

Key Point

Nodes share many common properties. This section introduces two such properties: `style` and `rotate`.

JavaFX style properties are similar to cascading style sheets (CSS) used to specify the styles for HTML elements in a Web page. Therefore, the style properties in JavaFX are called *JavaFX CSS*. In JavaFX, a style property is defined with a prefix `-fx-`. Each node has its own style properties. You can find these properties at docs.oracle.com/javafx/2/api/javafx/scene/doc-files/cssref.html. For information on HTML and CSS, see Supplements V.A and V.B. If you are not familiar with HTML and CSS, you can still use JavaFX CSS.

JavaFX CSS

The syntax for setting a style is `styleName:value`. Multiple style properties for a node can be set together separated by semicolon (`;`). For example, the following statement:

```
circle.setStyle("-fx-stroke: black; -fx-fill: red;");
```

setStyle

sets two JavaFX CSS properties for a circle. This statement is equivalent to the following two statements:

```
circle.setStroke(Color.BLACK);
circle.setFill(Color.RED);
```

If an incorrect JavaFX CSS is used, your program will still compile and run, but the style will be ignored.

The `rotate` property enables you to specify an angle in degrees for rotating a node from its center. If the degree is positive, the rotation is performed clockwise; otherwise, it is performed counterclockwise. For example, the following code rotates a button 80 degrees:

```
button.setRotate(80);
```

Listing 14.7 gives an example that creates a button, sets its style, and adds it to a pane. It then rotates the pane 45 degrees and sets its style with border color red and background color light gray, as shown in Figure 14.8.

LISTING 14.7 NodeStyleRotateDemo.java

```
 1  import javafx.application.Application;
 2  import javafx.scene.Scene;
 3  import javafx.scene.control.Button;
 4  import javafx.stage.Stage;
 5  import javafx.scene.layout.StackPane;
 6
 7  public class NodeStyleRotateDemo extends Application {
 8    @Override // Override the start method in the Application class
 9    public void start(Stage primaryStage) {
10      // Create a scene and place a button in the scene
11      StackPane pane = new StackPane();
12      Button btOK = new Button("OK");
13      btOK.setStyle("-fx-border-color: blue;");
14      pane.getChildren().add(btOK);
15
16      pane.setRotate(45);
17      pane.setStyle(
18        "-fx-border-color: red; -fx-background-color: lightgray;");
19
20      Scene scene = new Scene(pane, 200, 250);
21      primaryStage.setTitle("NodeStyleRotateDemo"); // Set the stage title
22      primaryStage.setScene(scene); // Place the scene in the stage
23      primaryStage.show(); // Display the stage
24    }
25  }
```

rotate the pane
set style for pane

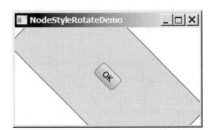

FIGURE 14.8 A pane's style is set and the pane is rotated 45 degrees.

As seen in Figure 14.8, rotating a pane causes all its containing nodes rotated as well.

The `Node` class contains many useful methods that can be applied to all nodes. For example, you can use the `contains(double x, double y)` method to test whether a point (x, y) is inside the boundary of a node and use the `setScaleX(double scale)` and `setScaleY(double scale)` methods to scale a node.

contains method
setScaleX method
setScaleY method

14.6.1 How do you set a style of a node with border color red? Modify the code to set the text color for the button to red.

14.6.2 Can you rotate a pane, a text, or a button? Modify the code to rotate the button 15 degrees counterclockwise? How do you test if a point is inside a node? How do you scale up or down a node?

14.7 The **Color** Class

The Color *class can be used to create colors.*

JavaFX defines the abstract Paint class for painting a node. The javafx.scene.paint.Color is a concrete subclass of Paint, which is used to encapsulate colors, as shown in Figure 14.9.

Key Point

> The getter methods for property values are provided in the class, but omitted in the UML diagram for brevity.

javafx.scene.paint.Color	
−red: double	The red value of this color (between 0.0 and 1.0).
−green: double	The green value of this color (between 0.0 and 1.0).
−blue: double	The blue value of this color (between 0.0 and 1.0).
−opacity: double	The opacity of this color (between 0.0 and 1.0).
+Color(r: double, g: double, b: double, opacity: double)	Creates a Color with the specified red, green, blue, and opacity values.
+brighter(): Color	Creates a Color that is a brighter version of this Color.
+darker(): Color	Creates a Color that is a darker version of this Color.
+color(r: double, g: double, b: double): Color	Creates an opaque Color with the specified red, green, and blue values.
+color(r: double, g: double, b: double, opacity: double): Color	Creates a Color with the specified red, green, blue, and opacity values.
+rgb(r: int, g: int, b: int): Color	Creates a Color with the specified red, green, and blue values in the range from 0 to 255.
+rgb(r: int, g: int, b: int, opacity: double): Color	Creates a Color with the specified red, green, and blue values in the range from 0 to 255 and a given opacity.

FIGURE 14.9 Color encapsulates information about colors.

A color instance can be constructed using the following constructor:

```
public Color(double r, double g, double b, double opacity);
```

in which r, g, and b specify a color by its red, green, and blue components with values in the range from 0.0 (darkest shade) to 1.0 (lightest shade). The opacity value defines the transparency of a color within the range from 0.0 (completely transparent) to 1.0 (completely opaque). This is known as the RGBA model, where RGBA stands for red, green, blue, and alpha. The alpha value indicates the opacity. For example,

RBGA model

```
Color color = new Color(0.25, 0.14, 0.333, 0.51);
```

For an interactive demo, see liveexample.pearsoncmg.com/dsanimation/FigureSection14_7 .html.

The Color class is immutable. Once a Color object is created, its properties cannot be changed. The brighter() method returns a new Color with a larger red, green, and blue values, and the darker() method returns a new Color with a smaller red, green, and blue values. The opacity value is the same as in the original Color object.

You can also create a Color object using the static methods color(r, g, b), color(r, g, b, opacity), rgb(r, g, b), and rgb(r, g, b, opacity).

Alternatively, you can use one of the many standard colors such as BEIGE, BLACK, BLUE, BROWN, CYAN, DARKGRAY, GOLD, GRAY, GREEN, LIGHTGRAY, MAGENTA, NAVY, ORANGE, PINK, RED, SILVER, WHITE, and YELLOW defined as constants in the Color class. The following code, for instance, sets the fill color of a circle to red:

```
circle.setFill(Color.RED);
```

14.7.1 How do you create a color? What is wrong about creating a `Color` using `new Color(1.2, 2.3, 3.5, 4)`? Which of two colors is darker, `new Color(0, 0, 0, 1)` or `new Color(1, 1, 1, 1)`? Does invoking `c.darker()` change the color value in `c`?

14.7.2 How do you create a `Color` object with a random color?

14.7.3 How do you set a circle object `c` with blue fill color using the `setFill` method and the `setStyle` method?

14.8 The Font Class

A Font describes font name, weight, and size.

You can set fonts for rendering the text. The `javafx.scene.text.Font` class is used to create fonts, as shown in Figure 14.10.

A `Font` instance can be constructed using its constructors or using its static methods. A `Font` is defined by its name, weight, posture, and size. Times New Roman, Courier, and Arial are examples of font names. You can obtain a list of available font family names by invoking the static `getFontNames()` method. This method returns `List<String>`. `List` is an interface that defines common methods for lists. `ArrayList`, introduced in Section 11.11, is a concrete class that implements `List`. There are two font postures defined as constants in the `FontPosture` class: `FontPosture.ITALIC` and `FontPosture.REGULAR`.

```
Font font1 = new Font("SansSerif", 16);
Font font2 = Font.font("Times New Roman", FontWeight.BOLD,
  FontPosture.ITALIC, 12);
```

Listing 14.8 gives a program that displays a label using the font (Times New Roman, bold, italic, and size 20), as shown in Figure 14.11.

The `getter` methods for property values are provided in the class, but omitted in the UML diagram for brevity.

javafx.scene.text.Font	
-size: double	The size of this font.
-name: String	The name of this font.
-family: String	The family of this font.
+Font(size: double)	Creates a Font with the specified size.
+Font(name: String, size: double)	Creates a Font with the specified full font name and size.
+font(name: String, size: double)	Creates a Font with the specified name and size.
+font(name: String, w: FontWeight, size: double)	Creates a Font with the specified name, weight, and size.
+font(name: String, w: FontWeight, p: FontPosture, size: double)	Creates a Font with the specified name, weight, posture, and size.
+getFontNames(): List<String>	Returns a list of all font names installed on the user system.

FIGURE 14.10 `Font` encapsulates information about fonts.

LISTING 14.8 FontDemo.java

```
1  import javafx.application.Application;
2  import javafx.scene.Scene;
3  import javafx.scene.layout.*;
4  import javafx.scene.paint.Color;
```

```
 5  import javafx.scene.shape.Circle;
 6  import javafx.scene.text.*;
 7  import javafx.scene.control.*;
 8  import javafx.stage.Stage;
 9
10  public class FontDemo extends Application {
11    @Override // Override the start method in the Application class
12    public void start(Stage primaryStage) {
13      // Create a pane to hold the circle
14      Pane pane = new StackPane();                              create a StackPane
15
16      // Create a circle and set its properties
17      Circle circle = new Circle();                            create a Circle
18      circle.setRadius(50);
19      circle.setStroke(Color.BLACK);
20      circle.setFill(new Color(0.5, 0.5, 0.5, 0.1));           create a Color
21      pane.getChildren().add(circle); // Add circle to the pane  add circle to the pane
22
23      // Create a label and set its properties
24      Label label = new Label("JavaFX");                       create a label
25      label.setFont(Font.font("Times New Roman",               create a font
26        FontWeight.BOLD, FontPosture.ITALIC, 20));
27      pane.getChildren().add(label);                           add label to the pane
28
29      // Create a scene and place it in the stage
30      Scene scene = new Scene(pane);
31      primaryStage.setTitle("FontDemo"); // Set the stage title
32      primaryStage.setScene(scene); // Place the scene in the stage
33      primaryStage.show(); // Display the stage
34    }
35  }
```

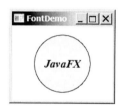

FIGURE 14.11 A label is on top of a circle displayed in the center of the scene.

The program creates a StackPane (line 14) and adds a circle and a label to it (lines 21 and 27). These two statements can be combined using the following one statement:

```
pane.getChildren().addAll(circle, label);
```

A StackPane places the nodes in the center and nodes are placed on top of each other. A custom color is created and set as a fill color for the circle (line 20). The program creates a label and sets a font (line 25) so that the text in the label is displayed in Times New Roman, bold, italic, and 20 pixels.

As you resize the window, the circle and label are displayed in the center of the window because the circle and label are placed in the stack pane. Stack pane automatically places nodes in the center of the pane.

A Font object is immutable. Once a Font object is created, its properties cannot be changed.

14.8.1 How do you create a Font object with font name Courier, size 20, and weight bold?

14.8.2 How do you find all available fonts on your system?

Check Point

14.9 The **Image** and **ImageView** Classes

VideoNote

Use Image and ImageView

The Image *class represents a graphical image, and the* ImageView *class can be used to display an image.*

The javafx.scene.image.Image class represents a graphical image and is used for loading an image from a specified filename or a URL. For example, new Image("image/us.gif") creates an Image object for the image file us.gif under the directory image in the Java class directory and new Image("http://liveexample.pearsoncmg.com/book/image/us.gif") creates an Image object for the image file in the URL on the Web.

The javafx.scene.image.ImageView is a node for displaying an image. An ImageView can be created from an Image object. For example, the following code creates an ImageView from an image file:

```
Image image = new Image("image/us.gif");
ImageView imageView = new ImageView(image);
```

Alternatively, you can create an ImageView directly from a file or a URL as follows:

```
ImageView imageView = new ImageView("image/us.gif");
```

The UML diagrams for the Image class and ImageView classes are illustrated in Figures 14.12 and 14.13.

The getter methods for property values are provided in the class, but omitted in the UML diagram for brevity.

---

javafx.scene.image.Image

-error: ReadOnlyBooleanProperty
-height: ReadOnlyDoubleProperty
-width: ReadOnlyDoubleProperty
-progress: ReadOnlyDoubleProperty

+Image(filenameOrURL: String)

Indicates whether the image is loaded correctly?
The height of the image.
The width of the image.
The approximate percentage of image's loading that is completed.

Creates an Image with contents loaded from a file or a URL.

FIGURE 14.12 Image encapsulates information about images.

The getter and setter methods for property values and a getter for property itself are provided in the class, but omitted in the UML diagram for brevity.

---

javafx.scene.image.ImageView

-fitHeight: DoubleProperty
-fitWidth: DoubleProperty
-x: DoubleProperty
-y: DoubleProperty
-image: ObjectProperty<Image>

+ImageView()
+ImageView(image: Image)
+ImageView(filenameOrURL: String)

The height of the bounding box within which the image is resized to fit.
The width of the bounding box within which the image is resized to fit.
The *x*-coordinate of the ImageView origin.
The *y*-coordinate of the ImageView origin.
The image to be displayed in the image view.

Creates an ImageView.
Creates an ImageView with the specified image.
Creates an ImageView with image loaded from the specified file or URL.

FIGURE 14.13 ImageView is a node for displaying an image.

Listing 14.9 displays an image in three image views, as shown in Figure 14.14.

LISTING 14.9 ShowImage.java

```
1  import javafx.application.Application;
2  import javafx.scene.Scene;
3  import javafx.scene.layout.HBox;
4  import javafx.scene.layout.Pane;
5  import javafx.geometry.Insets;
6  import javafx.stage.Stage;
7  import javafx.scene.image.Image;
8  import javafx.scene.image.ImageView;
9
10 public class ShowImage extends Application {
11   @Override // Override the start method in the Application class
12   public void start(Stage primaryStage) {
13     // Create a pane to hold the image views
14     Pane pane = new HBox(10);                              create an HBox
15     pane.setPadding(new Insets(5, 5, 5, 5));
16     Image image = new Image("image/us.gif");              create an image
17     pane.getChildren().add(new ImageView(image));         add an image view to pane
18
19     ImageView imageView2 = new ImageView(image);          create an image view
20     imageView2.setFitHeight(100);                         set image view properties
21     imageView2.setFitWidth(100);
22     pane.getChildren().add(imageView2);                   add an image to pane
23
24     ImageView imageView3 = new ImageView(image);          create an image view
25     imageView3.setRotate(90);                             rotate an image view
26     pane.getChildren().add(imageView3);                   add an image to pane
27
28     // Create a scene and place it in the stage
29     Scene scene = new Scene(pane);
30     primaryStage.setTitle("ShowImage"); // Set the stage title
31     primaryStage.setScene(scene); // Place the scene in the stage
32     primaryStage.show(); // Display the stage
33   }
34 }
```

FIGURE 14.14 An image is displayed in three image views placed in a pane. *Source*: booka/ Fotolia.

The program creates an HBox (line 14). An HBox is a pane that places all nodes horizontally in one row. The program creates an Image, then an ImageView for displaying the image, and places the ImageView in the HBox (line 17).

The program creates the second ImageView (line 19), sets its fitHeight and fitWidth properties (lines 20 and 21), and places the ImageView into the HBox (line 22). The program creates the third ImageView (line 24), rotates it 90 degrees (line 25), and places it into the HBox (line 26). The setRotate method is defined in the Node class and can be used for any node. Note an Image object can be shared by multiple nodes. In this case, it is shared by three ImageView. However, a node such as ImageView cannot be shared. You cannot place an ImageView multiple times into a pane or scene.

Note you must place the image file in the same directory as the class file, as shown in the following figure.

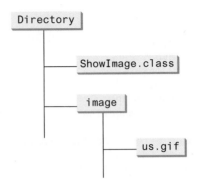

If you use the URL to locate the image file, the URL protocol `http://` must be present. Therefore, the following code is wrong:

```
new Image("liveexample.pearsoncmg.com/book/image/us.gif");
```

It must be replaced by

```
new Image("http://liveexample.pearsoncmg.com/book/image/us.gif");
```

Check Point

14.9.1 How do you create an `Image` from a URL or a filename?

14.9.2 How do you create an `ImageView` from an `Image` or directly from a file or a URL?

14.9.3 Can you set an `Image` to multiple `ImageViews`? Can you display the same `ImageView` multiple times?

14.10 Layout Panes and Groups

Key Point

VideoNote
Use layout panes

JavaFX provides many types of panes for automatically laying out nodes in a desired location and size.

Panes and groups are the containers for holding nodes. The `Group` class is often used to group nodes and to perform transformation and scale as a group. Panes and UI control objects are resizable, but group, shape, and text objects are not resizable. JavaFX provides many types of panes for organizing nodes in a container, as shown in Table 14.1. You have used the layout panes `Pane`, `StackPane`, and `HBox` in the preceding sections for containing nodes. This section introduces the panes in more details.

TABLE 14.1 Panes for Containing and Organizing Nodes

Class	Description
Pane	Base class for layout panes. It contains the `getChildren()` method for returning a list of nodes in the pane.
StackPane	Places the nodes on top of each other in the center of the pane.
FlowPane	Places the nodes row-by-row horizontally or column-by-column vertically.
GridPane	Places the nodes in the cells in a two-dimensional grid.
BorderPane	Places the nodes in the top, right, bottom, left, and center regions.
HBox	Places the nodes in a single row.
VBox	Places the nodes in a single column.

You have used the Pane in Listing 14.4, ShowCircle.java. A Pane is usually used as a canvas for displaying shapes. Pane is the base class for all specialized panes. You have used a specialized pane StackPane in Listing 14.3, ButtonInPane.java. Nodes are placed in the center of a StackPane. Each pane contains a list for holding nodes in the pane. This list is an instance of ObservableList, which can be obtained using pane's getChildren() method. You can use add(node) to add an element to the list and addAll(node1, node2, ...) to add a variable number of nodes.

ObservableList
getChildren()

14.10.1 FlowPane

FlowPane arranges the nodes in the pane horizontally from left to right, or vertically from top to bottom, in the order in which they were added. When one row or one column is filled, a new row or column is started. You can specify the way the nodes are placed horizontally or vertically using one of two constants: Orientation.HORIZONTAL or Orientation.VERTICAL. You can also specify the gap between the nodes in pixels. The class diagram for FlowPane is shown in Figure 14.15.

Data fields alignment, orientation, hgap, and vgap are binding properties. Recall that each binding property in JavaFX has a getter method (e.g., getGap()) that returns its value, a setter method (e.g., setHGap(double)) for setting a value, and a getter method that returns the property itself (e.g., hgapProperty()). For a data field of ObjectProperty<T> type, the value getter method returns a value of type T, and the property getter method returns a property value of type ObjectProperty<T>.

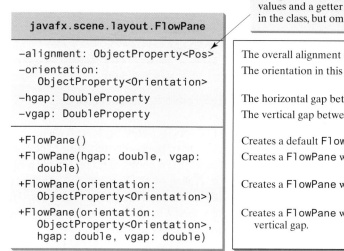

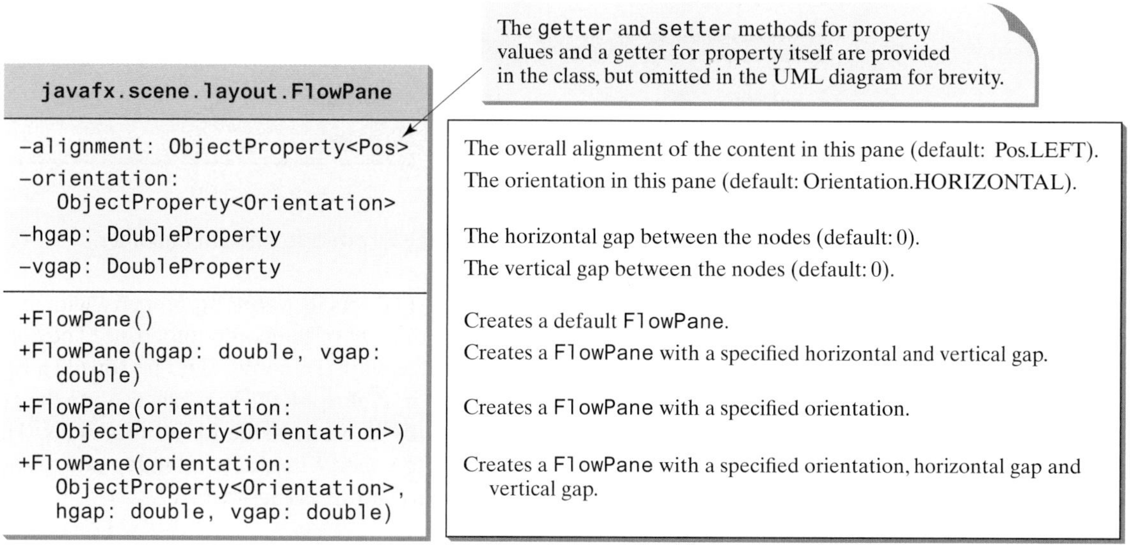

FIGURE 14.15 FlowPane lays out nodes row-by-row horizontally or column-by-column vertically.

Listing 14.10 gives a program that demonstrates FlowPane. The program adds labels and text fields to a FlowPane, as shown in Figure 14.16.

LISTING 14.10 ShowFlowPane.java

```
1  import javafx.application.Application;
2  import javafx.geometry.Insets;
3  import javafx.scene.Scene;
4  import javafx.scene.control.Label;
5  import javafx.scene.control.TextField;
6  import javafx.scene.layout.FlowPane;
7  import javafx.stage.Stage;
```

extend Application

create FlowPane

add UI controls to pane

add pane to scene

place scene to stage
display stage

```
8
9   public class ShowFlowPane extends Application {
10     @Override // Override the start method in the Application class
11     public void start(Stage primaryStage) {
12       // Create a pane and set its properties
13       FlowPane pane = new FlowPane();
14       pane.setPadding(new Insets(11, 12, 13, 14));
15       pane.setHgap(5);
16       pane.setVgap(5);
17
18       // Place nodes in the pane
19       pane.getChildren().addAll(new Label("First Name:"),
20         new TextField(), new Label("MI:"));
21       TextField tfMi = new TextField();
22       tfMi.setPrefColumnCount(1);
23       pane.getChildren().addAll(tfMi, new Label("Last Name:"),
24         new TextField());
25
26       // Create a scene and place it in the stage
27       Scene scene = new Scene(pane, 200, 250);
28       primaryStage.setTitle("ShowFlowPane"); // Set the stage title
29       primaryStage.setScene(scene); // Place the scene in the stage
30       primaryStage.show(); // Display the stage
31     }
32   }
```

(a)　　　　　　　　　　(b)

FIGURE 14.16 The nodes fill in the rows in the FlowPane one after another.

The program creates a FlowPane (line 13) and sets its padding property with an Insets object (line 14). An Insets object specifies the size of the border of a pane. The constructor Insets(11, 12, 13, 14) creates an Insets with the border sizes for top (11), right (12), bottom (13), and left (14) in pixels, as shown in Figure 14.17. You can also use the constructor Insets(value) to create an Insets with the same value for all four sides. The hGap and vGap properties are in lines 15 and 16 to specify the horizontal gap and vertical gap, respectively, between two nodes in the pane, as shown in Figure 14.17.

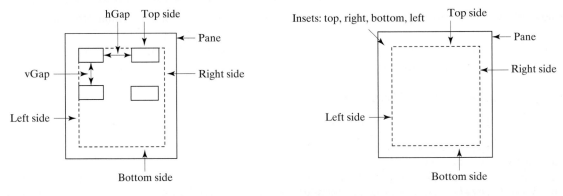

FIGURE 14.17 You can specify hGap and vGap between the nodes in a FlowLPane.

Each `FlowPane` contains an object of `ObservableList` for holding the nodes. This list can be obtained using the `getChildren()` method (line 19). To add a node into a `FlowPane` is to add it to this list using the `add(node)` or `addAll(node1, node2, ...)` method. You can also remove a node from the list using the `remove(node)` method, or use the `removeAll()` method to remove all nodes from the pane. The program adds the labels and text fields into the pane (lines 19–24). Invoking `tfMi.setPrefColumnCount(1)` sets the preferred column count to `1` for the MI text field (line 22). The program declares an explicit reference `tfMi` for a `TextField` object for MI. The explicit reference is necessary because we need to reference the object directly to set its `prefColumnCount` property.

The program adds the pane to the scene (line 27), sets the scene in the stage (line 29), and displays the stage (line 30). Note if you resize the window, the nodes are automatically rearranged to fit in the pane. In Figure 14.16a, the first row has three nodes, but in Figure 14.16b, the first row has four nodes because the width has been increased.

Suppose you wish to add the object `tfMi` to a pane 10 times; will 10 text fields appear in the pane? No, a node such as a text field can be added to only one pane and once. Adding a node to a pane multiple times or to different panes will cause a runtime error.

14.10.2 GridPane

A `GridPane` arranges nodes in a grid (matrix) formation. The nodes are placed in the specified column and row indices. The class diagram for `GridPane` is shown in Figure 14.18.

The `getter` and `setter` methods for property values and a getter for property itself are provided in the class, but omitted in the UML diagram for brevity.

javafx.scene.layout.GridPane	
-alignment: ObjectProperty<Pos>	The overall alignment of the content in this pane (default: Pos.LEFT).
-gridLinesVisible: BooleanProperty	Is the grid line visible? (default: false)
-hgap: DoubleProperty	The horizontal gap between the nodes (default: 0).
-vgap: DoubleProperty	The vertical gap between the nodes (default: 0).
+GridPane()	Creates a GridPane.
+add(child: Node, columnIndex: int, rowIndex: int): void	Adds a node to the specified column and row.
+addColumn(columnIndex: int, children: Node...): void	Adds multiple nodes to the specified column.
+addRow(rowIndex: int, children: Node...): void	Adds multiple nodes to the specified row.
+getColumnIndex(child: Node): int	Returns the column index for the specified node.
+setColumnIndex(child: Node, columnIndex: int): void	Sets a node to a new column. This method repositions the node.
+getRowIndex(child:Node): int	Returns the row index for the specified node.
+setRowIndex(child: Node, rowIndex: int): void	Sets a node to a new row. This method repositions the node.
+setHalighnment(child: Node, value: HPos): void	Sets the horizontal alignment for the child in the cell.
+setValighnment(child: Node, value: VPos): void	Sets the vertical alignment for the child in the cell.

FIGURE 14.18 `GridPane` lays out nodes in the specified cell in a grid.

Listing 14.11 gives a program that demonstrates `GridPane`. The program is similar to the one in Listing 14.10, except that it adds three labels and three text fields, and a button to the specified location in a grid, as shown in Figure 14.19.

FIGURE 14.19 The GridPane places the nodes in a grid with a specified column and row indices.

LISTING 14.11 ShowGridPane.java

```
1  import javafx.application.Application;
2  import javafx.geometry.HPos;
3  import javafx.geometry.Insets;
4  import javafx.geometry.Pos;
5  import javafx.scene.Scene;
6  import javafx.scene.control.Button;
7  import javafx.scene.control.Label;
8  import javafx.scene.control.TextField;
9  import javafx.scene.layout.GridPane;
10 import javafx.stage.Stage;
11
12 public class ShowGridPane extends Application {
13   @Override // Override the start method in the Application class
14   public void start(Stage primaryStage) {
15     // Create a pane and set its properties
16     GridPane pane = new GridPane();
17     pane.setAlignment(Pos.CENTER);
18     pane.setPadding(new Insets(11.5, 12.5, 13.5, 14.5));
19     pane.setHgap(5.5);
20     pane.setVgap(5.5);
21
22     // Place nodes in the pane
23     pane.add(new Label("First Name:"), 0, 0);
24     pane.add(new TextField(), 1, 0);
25     pane.add(new Label("MI:"), 0, 1);
26     pane.add(new TextField(), 1, 1);
27     pane.add(new Label("Last Name:"), 0, 2);
28     pane.add(new TextField(), 1, 2);
29     Button btAdd = new Button("Add Name");
30     pane.add(btAdd, 1, 3);
31     GridPane.setHalignment(btAdd, HPos.RIGHT);
32
33     // Create a scene and place it in the stage
34     Scene scene = new Scene(pane);
35     primaryStage.setTitle("ShowGridPane"); // Set the stage title
36     primaryStage.setScene(scene); // Place the scene in the stage
37     primaryStage.show(); // Display the stage
38   }
39 }
```

Margin notes:
- create a grid pane (line 16)
- set properties (line 17)
- add label (line 23)
- add text field (line 24)
- add button (line 30)
- align button right (line 31)
- create a scene (line 34)
- display stage (line 37)

The program creates a GridPane (line 16) and sets its properties (line 17–20). The alignment is set to the center position (line 17), which causes the nodes to be placed in the center of the grid pane. If you resize the window, you will see the nodes remained in the center of the grid pane.

The program adds the label in column 0 and row 0 (line 23). The column and row index starts from 0. The `add` method places a node in the specified column and row. Not every cell in the grid needs to be filled. A button is placed in column 1 and row 3 (line 30), but there are no nodes placed in column 0 and row 3. To remove a node from a `GridPane`, use `pane.getChildren().remove(node)`. To remove all nodes, use `pane.getChildren().removeAll()`.

remove nodes

The program invokes the static `setHalignment` method to align the button right in the cell (line 31).

Note the scene size is not set (line 34). In this case, the scene size is automatically computed according to the sizes of the nodes placed inside the scene.

By default, the grid pane will resize rows and columns to the preferred sizes of its contents, even if the grid pane is resized larger than its preferred size. You may purposely set a large value for the preferred width and height of its contents by invoking the `setPrefWidth` and `setPrefHeight` methods, so the contents will be automatically stretched to fill in the grid pane when the grid pane is enlarged (see Programming Exercise 14.8).

remove nodes

setPrefWidth

setPrefHeight

14.10.3 BorderPane

A `BorderPane` can place nodes in five regions: top, bottom, left, right, and center, using the `setTop(node)`, `setBottom(node)`, `setLeft(node)`, `setRight(node)`, and `setCenter(node)` methods. The class diagram for `BorderPane` is shown in Figure 14.20.

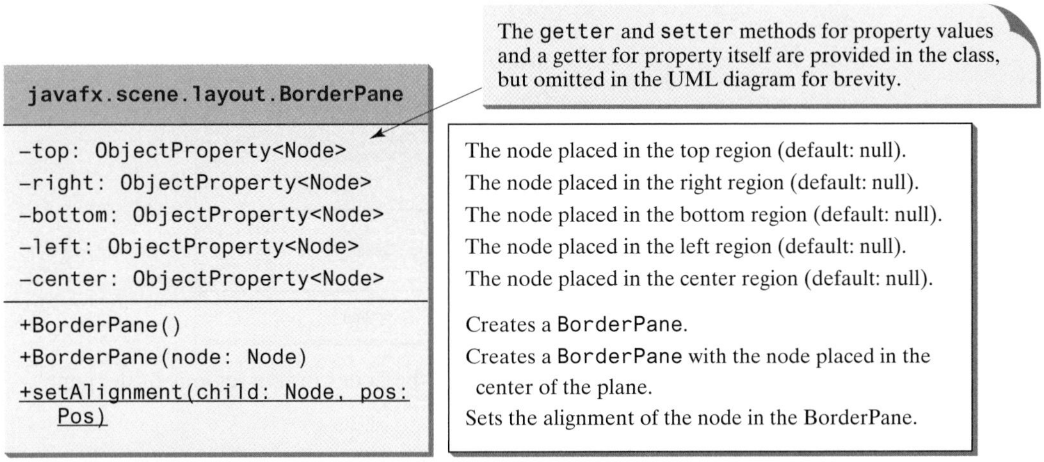

The getter and setter methods for property values and a getter for property itself are provided in the class, but omitted in the UML diagram for brevity.

```
javafx.scene.layout.BorderPane
```

```
-top: ObjectProperty<Node>
-right: ObjectProperty<Node>
-bottom: ObjectProperty<Node>
-left: ObjectProperty<Node>
-center: ObjectProperty<Node>

+BorderPane()
+BorderPane(node: Node)
+setAlignment(child: Node, pos:
    Pos)
```

The node placed in the top region (default: null).
The node placed in the right region (default: null).
The node placed in the bottom region (default: null).
The node placed in the left region (default: null).
The node placed in the center region (default: null).

Creates a BorderPane.
Creates a BorderPane with the node placed in the center of the plane.
Sets the alignment of the node in the BorderPane.

FIGURE 14.20 BorderPane places the nodes in top, bottom, left, right, and center regions.

Listing 14.12 gives a program that demonstrates `BorderPane`. The program places five buttons in the five regions of the pane, as shown in Figure 14.21.

LISTING 14.12 ShowBorderPane.java

```java
1  import javafx.application.Application;
2  import javafx.geometry.Insets;
3  import javafx.scene.Scene;
4  import javafx.scene.control.Label;
5  import javafx.scene.layout.BorderPane;
6  import javafx.scene.layout.StackPane;
7  import javafx.stage.Stage;
8
9  public class ShowBorderPane extends Application {
10   @Override // Override the start method in the Application class
```

```
11    public void start(Stage primaryStage) {
12      // Create a border pane
13      BorderPane pane = new BorderPane();
14
15      // Place nodes in the pane
16      pane.setTop(new CustomPane("Top"));
17      pane.setRight(new CustomPane("Right"));
18      pane.setBottom(new CustomPane("Bottom"));
19      pane.setLeft(new CustomPane("Left"));
20      pane.setCenter(new CustomPane("Center"));
21
22      // Create a scene and place it in the stage
23      Scene scene = new Scene(pane);
24      primaryStage.setTitle("ShowBorderPane"); // Set the stage title
25      primaryStage.setScene(scene); // Place the scene in the stage
26      primaryStage.show(); // Display the stage
27    }
28  }
29
30  // Define a custom pane to hold a label in the center of the pane
31  class CustomPane extends StackPane {
32    public CustomPane(String title) {
33      getChildren().add(new Label(title));
34      setStyle("-fx-border-color: red");
35      setPadding(new Insets(11.5, 12.5, 13.5, 14.5));
36    }
37  }
```

Margin notes:
- create a border pane (line 13)
- add to top (line 16)
- add to right (line 17)
- add to bottom (line 18)
- add to left (line 19)
- add to center (line 20)
- define a custom pane (line 31)
- add a label to pane (line 33)
- set style (line 34)
- set padding (line 35)

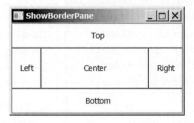

FIGURE 14.21 The BorderPane places the nodes in five regions of the pane.

The program defines CustomPane that extends StackPane (line 31). The constructor of CustomPane adds a label with the specified title (line 33), sets a style for the border color, and sets a padding using insets (line 35).

The program creates a BorderPane (line 13) and places five instances of CustomPane into five regions of the border pane (lines 16–20). Note a pane is a node. Therefore, a pane can be added into another pane. To remove a node from the top region, invoke setTop(null). If a region is not occupied, no space will be allocated for this region.

14.10.4 HBox and VBox

An HBox lays out its children in a single horizontal row. A VBox lays out its children in a single vertical column. Recall that a FlowPane can lay out its children in multiple rows or multiple columns, but an HBox or a VBox can lay out children only in one row or one column. The class diagrams for HBox and VBox are shown in Figures 14.22 and 14.23.

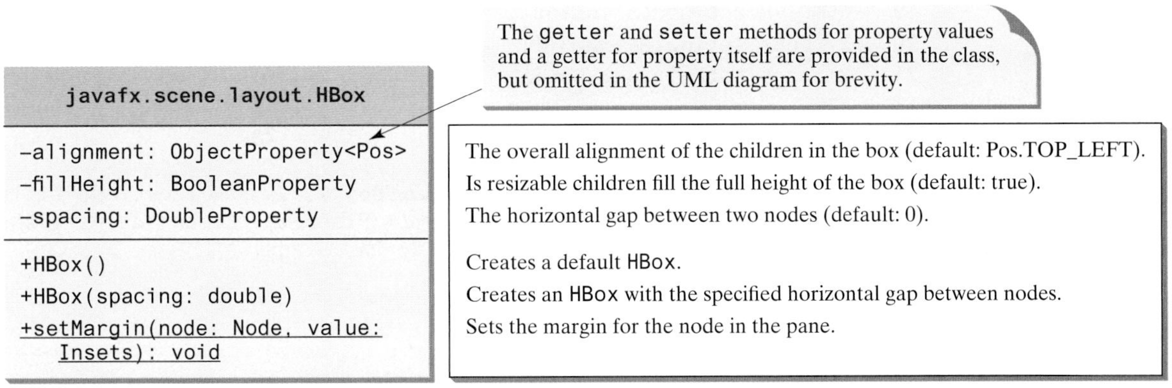

The `getter` and `setter` methods for property values and a getter for property itself are provided in the class, but omitted in the UML diagram for brevity.

javafx.scene.layout.HBox
–alignment: ObjectProperty<Pos>
–fillHeight: BooleanProperty
–spacing: DoubleProperty
+HBox()
+HBox(spacing: double)
+setMargin(node: Node, value: Insets): void

The overall alignment of the children in the box (default: Pos.TOP_LEFT).
Is resizable children fill the full height of the box (default: true).
The horizontal gap between two nodes (default: 0).

Creates a default HBox.
Creates an HBox with the specified horizontal gap between nodes.
Sets the margin for the node in the pane.

FIGURE 14.22 HBox places the nodes in one row.

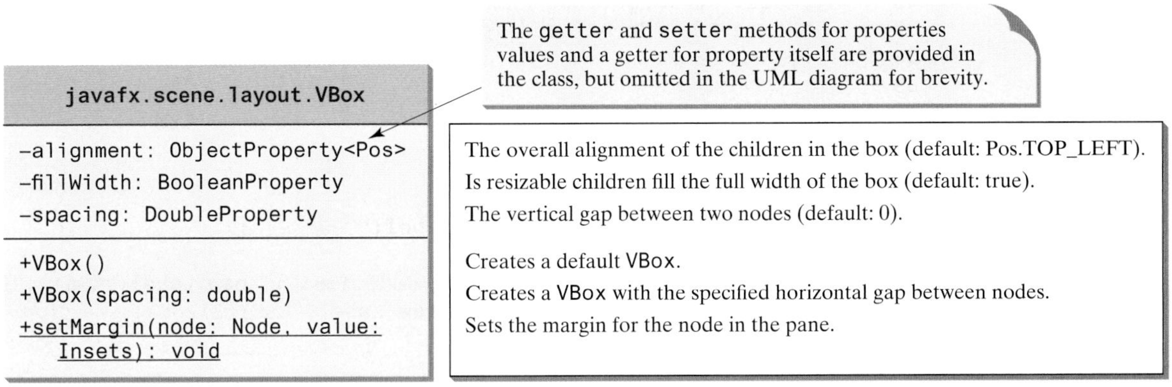

The `getter` and `setter` methods for properties values and a getter for property itself are provided in the class, but omitted in the UML diagram for brevity.

javafx.scene.layout.VBox
–alignment: ObjectProperty<Pos>
–fillWidth: BooleanProperty
–spacing: DoubleProperty
+VBox()
+VBox(spacing: double)
+setMargin(node: Node, value: Insets): void

The overall alignment of the children in the box (default: Pos.TOP_LEFT).
Is resizable children fill the full width of the box (default: true).
The vertical gap between two nodes (default: 0).

Creates a default VBox.
Creates a VBox with the specified horizontal gap between nodes.
Sets the margin for the node in the pane.

FIGURE 14.23 VBox places the nodes in one column.

Listing 14.13 gives a program that demonstrates HBox and VBox. The program places two buttons and an image view in an HBox and five labels in a VBox, as shown in Figure 14.24.

LISTING 14.13 ShowHBoxVBox.java

```java
1  import javafx.application.Application;
2  import javafx.geometry.Insets;
3  import javafx.scene.Scene;
4  import javafx.scene.control.Button;
5  import javafx.scene.control.Label;
6  import javafx.scene.layout.BorderPane;
7  import javafx.scene.layout.HBox;
8  import javafx.scene.layout.VBox;
9  import javafx.stage.Stage;
10 import javafx.scene.image.Image;
11 import javafx.scene.image.ImageView;
12
13 public class ShowHBoxVBox extends Application {
14   @Override // Override the start method in the Application class
15   public void start(Stage primaryStage) {
16     // Create a border pane
17     BorderPane pane = new BorderPane();          create a border pane
18
```

add an HBox to top
add a VBox to left

create a scene

display stage

getHBox

add buttons to HBox

return an HBox

getVBox

add a label

set margin
add a label

return vBox

```
19        // Place nodes in the pane
20        pane.setTop(getHBox());
21        pane.setLeft(getVBox());
22
23        // Create a scene and place it in the stage
24        Scene scene = new Scene(pane);
25        primaryStage.setTitle("ShowHBoxVBox"); // Set the stage title
26        primaryStage.setScene(scene); // Place the scene in the stage
27        primaryStage.show(); // Display the stage
28      }
29
30      private HBox getHBox() {
31        HBox hBox = new HBox(15);
32        hBox.setPadding(new Insets(15, 15, 15, 15));
33        hBox.setStyle("-fx-background-color: gold");
34        hBox.getChildren().add(new Button("Computer Science"));
35        hBox.getChildren().add(new Button("Chemistry"));
36        ImageView imageView = new ImageView(new Image("image/us.gif"));
37        hBox.getChildren().add(imageView);
38        return hBox;
39      }
40
41      private VBox getVBox() {
42        VBox vBox = new VBox(15);
43        vBox.setPadding(new Insets(15, 5, 5, 5));
44        vBox.getChildren().add(new Label("Courses"));
45
46        Label[] courses = {new Label("CSCI 1301"), new Label("CSCI 1302"),
47            new Label("CSCI 2410"), new Label("CSCI 3720")};
48
49        for (Label course: courses) {
50          VBox.setMargin(course, new Insets(0, 0, 0, 15));
51          vBox.getChildren().add(course);
52        }
53
54        return vBox;
55      }
56    }
```

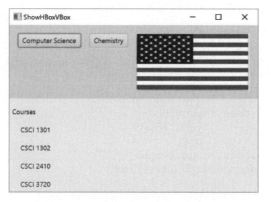

Figure 14.24 The HBox places the nodes in one row, and the VBox places the nodes in one column. *Source*: booka/Fotolia.

The program defines the getHBox() method. This method returns an HBox that contains two buttons and an image view (lines 30–39). The background color of the HBox is set to gold using Java CSS (line 33). The program defines the getVBox() method. This method returns a VBox that contains five labels (lines 41–55). The first label is added to the VBox in line 44 and the other four are added in line 51. The `setMargin` method is used to set a node's margin when placed inside the `VBox` (line 50).

14.10.1 How do you add a node to a `Pane`, `StackPane`, `FlowPane`, `GridPane`, `BorderPane`, `HBox`, and `VBox`? How do you remove a node from these panes?

14.10.2 How do you set the alignment to right for nodes in a `FlowPane`, `GridPane`, `HBox`, and `VBox`?

14.10.3 How do you set the horizontal gap and vertical gap between nodes in 8 pixels in a `FlowPane` and `GridPane` and set spacing in 8 pixels in an `HBox` and `VBox`?

14.10.4 How do you get the column and row index of a node in a `GridPane`? How do you reposition a node in a `GridPane`?

14.10.5 What are the differences between a `FlowPane` and an `HBox` or a `VBox`?

14.11 Shapes

JavaFX provides many shape classes for drawing texts, lines, circles, rectangles, ellipses, arcs, polygons, and polylines.

Key Point

VideoNote
Use shapes

`fill` property
`stroke` property
`strokeWidth` property

The `Shape` class is the abstract base class that defines the common properties for all shapes. Among them are the `fill`, `stroke`, and `strokeWidth` properties. The `fill` property specifies a color that fills the interior of a shape. The `stroke` property specifies a color that is used to draw the outline of a shape. The `strokeWidth` property specifies the width of the outline of a shape. This section introduces the classes `Text`, `Line`, `Rectangle`, `Circle`, `Ellipse`, `Arc`, `Polygon`, and `Polyline` for drawing texts and simple shapes. All these are subclasses of `Shape`, as shown in Figure 14.25.

14.11.1 Text

The `Text` class defines a node that displays a string at a starting point (x, y), as shown in Figure 14.27a. A `Text` object is usually placed in a pane. The pane's upper-left corner point is (0, 0) and the bottom-right point is (`pane.getWidth()`, `pane.getHeight()`). A string may be displayed in multiple lines separated by \n. The UML diagram for the `Text` class is shown in Figure 14.26. Listing 14.14 gives an example that demonstrates text, as shown in Figure 14.27b.

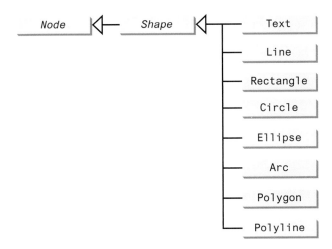

FIGURE 14.25 A shape is a node. The `Shape` class is the root of all shape classes.

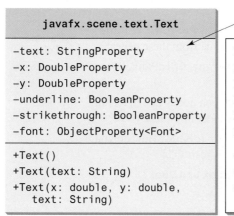

> The getter and setter methods for property value and a getter for property itself are provided in the class, but omitted in the UML diagram for brevity.

javafx.scene.text.Text
-text: StringProperty
-x: DoubleProperty
-y: DoubleProperty
-underline: BooleanProperty
-strikethrough: BooleanProperty
-font: ObjectProperty<Font>
+Text()
+Text(text: String)
+Text(x: double, y: double, text: String)

Defines the text to be displayed.
Defines the *x*-coordinate of text (default 0).
Defines the *y*-coordinate of text (default 0).
Defines if each line has an underline below it (default false).
Defines if each line has a line through it (default false).
Defines the font for the text.

Creates an empty Text.
Creates a Text with the specified text.
Creates a Text with the specified *x*-, *y*-coordinates and text.

FIGURE 14.26 Text defines a node for displaying a text.

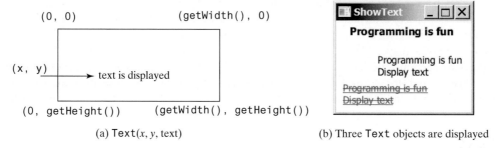

(a) Text(*x*, *y*, text)

(b) Three Text objects are displayed

FIGURE 14.27 A Text object is created to display a text.

LISTING 14.14 ShowText.java

```
1  import javafx.application.Application;
2  import javafx.scene.Scene;
3  import javafx.scene.layout.Pane;
4  import javafx.scene.paint.Color;
5  import javafx.geometry.Insets;
6  import javafx.stage.Stage;
7  import javafx.scene.text.Text;
8  import javafx.scene.text.Font;
9  import javafx.scene.text.FontWeight;
10 import javafx.scene.text.FontPosture;
11
12 public class ShowText extends Application {
13   @Override // Override the start method in the Application class
14   public void start(Stage primaryStage) {
15     // Create a pane to hold the texts
16     Pane pane = new Pane();
17     pane.setPadding(new Insets(5, 5, 5, 5));
18     Text text1 = new Text(20, 20, "Programming is fun");
19     text1.setFont(Font.font("Courier", FontWeight.BOLD,
20       FontPosture.ITALIC, 15));
21     pane.getChildren().add(text1);
```

create a pane

create a Text
set text font

add text to pane

```
22
23       Text text2 = new Text(60, 60, "Programming is fun\nDisplay text");    create a two-line Text
24       pane.getChildren().add(text2);                                        add text to pane
25
26       Text text3 = new Text(10, 100, "Programming is fun\nDisplay text");   create a Text
27       text3.setFill(Color.RED);                                             set text color
28       text3.setUnderline(true);                                             set underline
29       text3.setStrikethrough(true);                                         set strike line
30       pane.getChildren().add(text3);                                        add text to pane
31
32       // Create a scene and place it in the stage
33       Scene scene = new Scene(pane);
34       primaryStage.setTitle("ShowText"); // Set the stage title
35       primaryStage.setScene(scene); // Place the scene in the stage
36       primaryStage.show(); // Display the stage
37     }
38 }
```

The program creates a Text (line 18), sets its font (line 19), and places it to the pane (line 21). The program creates another Text with multiple lines (line 23) and places it to the pane (line 24). The program creates the third Text (line 26), sets its color (line 27), sets an underline and a strike through line (lines 28 and 29), and places it to the pane (line 30).

14.11.2 Line

A line connects two points with four parameters startX, startY, endX, and endY, as shown in Figure 14.29a. The Line class defines a line. The UML diagram for the Line class is shown in Figure 14.28. Listing 14.15 gives an example that demonstrates the line shape, as shown in Figure 14.29b.

LISTING 14.15 ShowLine.java

```
1  import javafx.application.Application;
2  import javafx.scene.Scene;
3  import javafx.scene.layout.Pane;
4  import javafx.scene.paint.Color;
5  import javafx.stage.Stage;
6  import javafx.scene.shape.Line;
7
8  public class ShowLine extends Application {
9    @Override // Override the start method in the Application class
10   public void start(Stage primaryStage) {
11     // Create a scene and place it in the stage
12     Scene scene = new Scene(new LinePane(), 200, 200);          create a pane in scene
13     primaryStage.setTitle("ShowLine"); // Set the stage title
14     primaryStage.setScene(scene); // Place the scene in the stage
15     primaryStage.show(); // Display the stage
16   }
17 }
18
19 class LinePane extends Pane {                                    define a custom pane
20   public LinePane() {
21     Line line1 = new Line(10, 10, 10, 10);                       create a line
22     line1.endXProperty().bind(widthProperty().subtract(10));
23     line1.endYProperty().bind(heightProperty().subtract(10));
24     line1.setStrokeWidth(5);                                     set stroke width
25     line1.setStroke(Color.GREEN);                                set stroke
26     getChildren().add(line1);                                    add line to pane
```

create a line

```
27
28        Line line2 = new Line(10, 10, 10, 10);
29        line2.startXProperty().bind(widthProperty().subtract(10));
30        line2.endYProperty().bind(heightProperty().subtract(10));
31        line2.setStrokeWidth(5);
32        line2.setStroke(Color.GREEN);
33        getChildren().add(line2);
34      }
35    }
```

add line to pane

> The getter and setter methods for property value and a getter for property itself are provided in the class, but omitted in the UML diagram for brevity.

javafx.scene.shape.Line

−startX: DoubleProperty	The *x*-coordinate of the start point.
−startY: DoubleProperty	The *y*-coordinate of the start point.
−endX: DoubleProperty	The *x*-coordinate of the end point.
−endY: DoubleProperty	The *y*-coordinate of the end point.
+Line()	Creates an empty Line.
+Line(startX: double, startY: double, endX: double, endY: double)	Creates a Line with the specified starting and ending points.

FIGURE 14.28 The Line class defines a line.

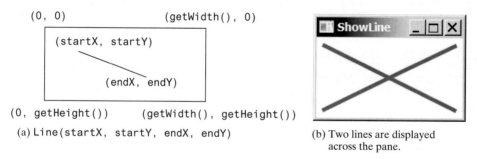

(a) Line(startX, startY, endX, endY)

(b) Two lines are displayed across the pane.

FIGURE 14.29 A Line object is created to display a line.

The program defines a custom pane class named LinePane (line 19). The custom pane class creates two lines and binds the starting and ending points of the line with the width and height of the pane (lines 22 and 23 and 29 and 30) so the two points of the lines are changed as the pane is resized.

14.11.3 Rectangle

A rectangle is defined by the parameters x, y, width, height, arcWidth, and arcHeight, as shown in Figure 14.31a. The rectangle's upper-left corner point is at (x, y), parameter aw (arcWidth) is the horizontal diameter of the arcs at the corner, and ah (arcHeight) is the vertical diameter of the arcs at the corner.

The Rectangle class defines a rectangle. The UML diagram for the Rectangle class is shown in Figure 14.30. Listing 14.16 gives an example that demonstrates rectangles, as shown in Figure 14.31b.

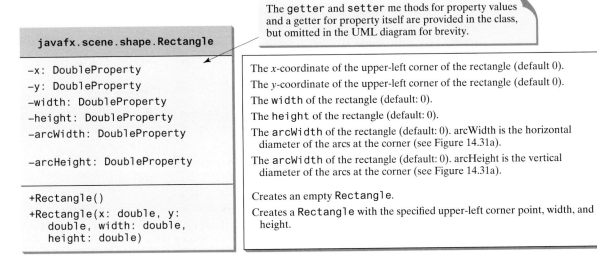

The getter and setter methods for property values and a getter for property itself are provided in the class, but omitted in the UML diagram for brevity.

javafx.scene.shape.Rectangle

-x: DoubleProperty — The x-coordinate of the upper-left corner of the rectangle (default 0).

-y: DoubleProperty — The y-coordinate of the upper-left corner of the rectangle (default 0).

-width: DoubleProperty — The width of the rectangle (default: 0).

-height: DoubleProperty — The height of the rectangle (default: 0).

-arcWidth: DoubleProperty — The arcWidth of the rectangle (default: 0). arcWidth is the horizontal diameter of the arcs at the corner (see Figure 14.31a).

-arcHeight: DoubleProperty — The arcWidth of the rectangle (default: 0). arcHeight is the vertical diameter of the arcs at the corner (see Figure 14.31a).

+Rectangle() — Creates an empty Rectangle.

+Rectangle(x: double, y: double, width: double, height: double) — Creates a Rectangle with the specified upper-left corner point, width, and height.

FIGURE 14.30 Rectangle defines a rectangle.

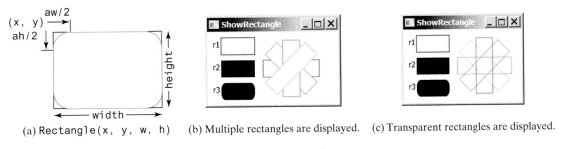

(a) Rectangle(x, y, w, h) (b) Multiple rectangles are displayed. (c) Transparent rectangles are displayed.

FIGURE 14.31 A Rectangle object is created to display a rectangle.

LISTING 14.16 ShowRectangle.java

```
1   import javafx.application.Application;
2   import javafx.scene.Group;
3   import javafx.scene.Scene;
4   import javafx.scene.layout.BorderPane;
5   import javafx.scene.paint.Color;
6   import javafx.stage.Stage;
7   import javafx.scene.text.Text;
8   import javafx.scene.shape.Rectangle;
9
10  public class ShowRectangle extends Application {
11    @Override // Override the start method in the Application class
12    public void start(Stage primaryStage) {
13      // Create rectangles
14      Rectangle r1 = new Rectangle(25, 10, 60, 30);
15      r1.setStroke(Color.BLACK);
16      r1.setFill(Color.WHITE);
17      Rectangle r2 = new Rectangle(25, 50, 60, 30);
18      Rectangle r3 = new Rectangle(25, 90, 60, 30);
19      r3.setArcWidth(15);
20      r3.setArcHeight(25);
21
```

create a rectangle r1
set r1's properties

create rectangle r2

create rectangle r3
set r3's arc width
set r3's arc height

```
22        // Create a group and add nodes to the group
23        Group group = new Group();
24        group.getChildren().addAll(new Text(10, 27, "r1"), r1,
25          new Text(10, 67, "r2"), r2, new Text(10, 107, "r3"), r3);
26
27        for (int i = 0; i < 4; i++) {
28          Rectangle r = new Rectangle(100, 50, 100, 30);
29          r.setRotate(i * 360 / 8);
30          r.setStroke(Color.color(Math.random(), Math.random(),
31            Math.random()));
32          r.setFill(Color.WHITE);
33          group.getChildren().add(r);
34        }
35
36        // Create a scene and place it in the stage
37        Scene scene = new Scene(new BorderPane(group),250, 150);
38        primaryStage.setTitle("ShowRectangle"); // Set the stage title
39        primaryStage.setScene(scene); // Place the scene in the stage
40        primaryStage.show(); // Display the stage
41      }
42    }
```

create a group
add nodes to group

create a rectangle
rotate a rectangle

add rectangle to group

The program creates multiple rectangles. By default, the fill color is black. Thus, a rectangle is filled with black color. The stroke color is white by default. Line 15 sets stroke color of rectangle r1 to black. The program creates rectangle r3 (line 18) and sets its arc width and arc height (lines 19 and 20). Thus, r3 is displayed as a rounded rectangle.

The program creates a Group to hold the nodes (lines 23–25). The program repeatedly creates a rectangle (line 28), rotates it (line 29), sets a random stroke color (lines 30 and 31), its fill color to white (line 32), and adds the rectangle to the group (line 33).

If line 32 is replaced by the following line:

```
r.setFill(null);
```

the rectangle is not filled with a color. Thus, they are displayed as shown in Figure 14.31c.

To center the nodes in the window, the program creates a BorderPane with the group in the center of the pane (line 37). If line 23 is replaced by the following?

```
Pane group = new Pane();
```

the rectangle will not be centered in the window. Therefore, using Group along with the BorderPane displays the contents of the group in the center of the window. Another advantage of using group is you can apply transformation to all nodes in the group. For example, if you add the following two lines in line 35:

```
group.setScaleX(2);
group.setScaleY(2);
```

the sizes of the nodes in the group are doubled.

14.11.4 Circle and Ellipse

You have used circles in several examples early in this chapter. A circle is defined by its parameters centerX, centerY, and radius. The Circle class defines a circle. The UML diagram for the Circle class is shown in Figure 14.32.

An ellipse is defined by its parameters centerX, centerY, radiusX, and radiusY, as shown in Figure 14.34a. The Ellipse class defines an ellipse. The UML diagram for the Ellipse class is shown in Figure 14.33. Listing 14.17 gives an example that demonstrates ellipses, as shown in Figure 14.34b.

The getter and setter methods for property values
and a getter for property itself are provided in the class,
but omitted in the UML diagram for brevity.

javafx.scene.shape.Circle	
−centerX: DoubleProperty	The *x*-coordinate of the center of the circle (default 0).
−centerY: DoubleProperty	The *y*-coordinate of the center of the circle (default 0).
−radius: DoubleProperty	The radius of the circle (default: 0).
+Circle()	Creates an empty Circle.
+Circle(x: double, y: double)	Creates a Circle with the specified center.
+Circle(x: double, y: double, radius: double)	Creates a Circle with the specified center and radius.

FIGURE 14.32 The Circle class defines circles.

The getter and setter methods for property values
and a getter for property itself are provided in the class,
but omitted in the UML diagram for brevity.

javafx.scene.shape.Ellipse	
−centerX: DoubleProperty	The *x*-coordinate of the center of the ellipse (default 0).
−centerY: DoubleProperty	The *y*-coordinate of the center of the ellipse (default 0).
−radiusX: DoubleProperty	The horizontal radius of the ellipse (default: 0).
−radiusY: DoubleProperty	The vertical radius of the ellipse (default: 0).
+Ellipse()	Creates an empty Ellipse.
+Ellipse(x: double, y: double)	Creates an Ellipse with the specified center.
+Ellipse(x: double, y: double, radiusX: double, radiusY: double)	Creates an Ellipse with the specified center and radiuses.

FIGURE 14.33 The Ellipse class defines ellipses.

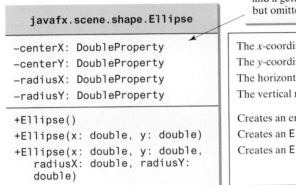

(a) Ellipse(centerX, centerY, radiusX, radiusY)

(b) Multiple ellipses are displayed.

FIGURE 14.34 An Ellipse object is created to display an ellipse.

LISTING 14.17 ShowEllipse.java

```
1  import javafx.application.Application;
2  import javafx.scene.Scene;
3  import javafx.scene.layout.Pane;
4  import javafx.scene.paint.Color;
5  import javafx.stage.Stage;
6  import javafx.scene.shape.Ellipse;
```

```
 7
 8    public class ShowEllipse extends Application {
 9      @Override // Override the start method in the Application class
10      public void start(Stage primaryStage) {
11        // Create a scene and place it in the stage
12        Scene scene = new Scene(new MyEllipse(), 300, 200);
13        primaryStage.setTitle("ShowEllipse"); // Set the stage title
14        primaryStage.setScene(scene); // Place the scene in the stage
15        primaryStage.show(); // Display the stage
16      }
17    }
18
19    class MyEllipse extends Pane {
20      private void paint() {
21        getChildren().clear();
22        for (int i = 0; i < 16; i++) {
23          // Create an ellipse and add it to pane
24          Ellipse e1 = new Ellipse(getWidth() / 2, getHeight() / 2,
25            getWidth() / 2 - 50, getHeight() / 2 - 50);
26          e1.setStroke(Color.color(Math.random(), Math.random(),
27            Math.random()));
28          e1.setFill(Color.WHITE);
29          e1.setRotate(i * 180 / 16);
30          getChildren().add(e1);
31        }
32      }
33
34      @Override
35      public void setWidth(double width) {
36        super.setWidth(width);
37        paint();
38      }
39
40      @Override
41      public void setHeight(double height) {
42        super.setHeight(height);
43        paint();
44      }
45    }
```

create a pane

create an ellipse

set random color for stroke

set fill color
rotate ellipse
add ellipse to pane

The program defines the MyEllipse class to draw the ellipses (lines 19–45) rather than creating ellipses directly in the start method (line 10) for two reasons. First, by defining the MyEllipse class for displaying the ellipses, you can easily reuse the code. Second, the MyEllipse class extends Pane. The contents in the pane can be resized when the stage is resized.

The MyEllipse class extends Pane and overrides the setWidth and setHeight methods (lines 34–44). A MyEllipse object's width and height are automatically set by invoking its setWidth and setHeight methods when it is displayed. When you resize the stage that contains a MyEllipse, the MyEllipse's width and height are automatically resized by again invoking the setWidth and setHeight methods. The setWidth and setHeight methods invoke the paint() method for displaying the ellipses (lines 37 and 43). The paint() method first clears the contents in the pane (line 21), then repeatedly creates ellipses (lines 24 and 25), sets a random stroke color (lines 26 and 27), sets its fill color to white (line 28), rotates it (line 29), and adds the rectangle to the pane (line 30). Thus, when the stage that contains a MyEllipse object is resized, the contents in MyEllipse are redisplayed.

14.11.5 Arc

An arc is conceived as part of an ellipse, defined by the parameters centerX, centerY, radiusX, radiusY, startAngle, length, and an arc type (ArcType.OPEN, ArcType.CHORD, or ArcType.ROUND). The parameter startAngle is the starting angle, and length is the spanning angle (i.e., the angle covered by the arc). Angles are measured in degrees and follow the usual mathematical conventions (i.e., 0 degrees is in the easterly direction and positive angles indicate counterclockwise rotation from the easterly direction), as shown in Figure 14.36a.

The Arc class defines an arc. The UML diagram for the Arc class is shown in Figure 14.35. Listing 14.18 gives an example that demonstrates ellipses, as shown in Figure 14.36b.

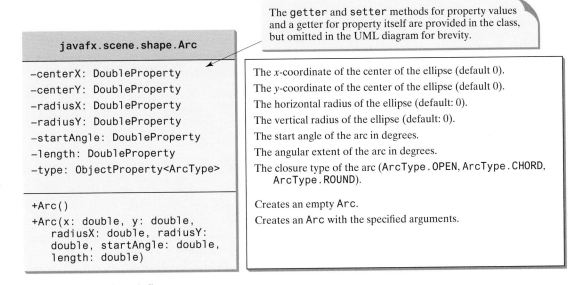

FIGURE 14.35 The Arc class defines an arc.

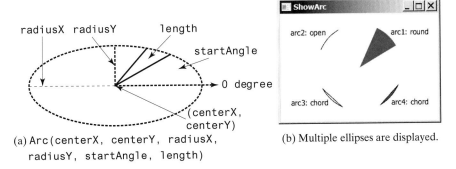

(a) Arc(centerX, centerY, radiusX, radiusY, startAngle, length)

(b) Multiple ellipses are displayed.

FIGURE 14.36 An Arc object is created to display an arc.

LISTING 14.18 ShowArc.java

```
1  import javafx.application.Application;
2  import javafx.scene.Scene;
3  import javafx.scene.Group;
4  import javafx.scene.layout.BorderPane;
5  import javafx.scene.paint.Color;
```

```
 6    import javafx.stage.Stage;
 7    import javafx.scene.shape.Arc;
 8    import javafx.scene.shape.ArcType;
 9    import javafx.scene.text.Text;
10
11    public class ShowArc extends Application {
12      @Override // Override the start method in the Application class
13      public void start(Stage primaryStage) {
14        Arc arc1 = new Arc(150, 100, 80, 80, 30, 35); // Create an arc
15        arc1.setFill(Color.RED); // Set fill color
16        arc1.setType(ArcType.ROUND); // Set arc type
17
18        Arc arc2 = new Arc(150, 100, 80, 80, 30 + 90, 35);
19        arc2.setFill(Color.WHITE);
20        arc2.setType(ArcType.OPEN);
21        arc2.setStroke(Color.BLACK);
22
23        Arc arc3 = new Arc(150, 100, 80, 80, 30 + 180, 35);
24        arc3.setFill(Color.WHITE);
25        arc3.setType(ArcType.CHORD);
26        arc3.setStroke(Color.BLACK);
27
28        Arc arc4 = new Arc(150, 100, 80, 80, 30 + 270, 35);
29        arc4.setFill(Color.GREEN);
30        arc4.setType(ArcType.CHORD);
31        arc4.setStroke(Color.BLACK);
32
33        // Create a group and add nodes to the group
34        Group group = new Group();
35        group.getChildren().addAll(new Text(210, 40, "arc1: round"),
36          arc1, new Text(20, 40, "arc2: open"), arc2,
37          new Text(20, 170, "arc3: chord"), arc3,
38          new Text(210, 170, "arc4: chord"), arc4);
39
40        // Create a scene and place it in the stage
41        Scene scene = new Scene(new BorderPane(group), 300, 200);
42        primaryStage.setTitle("ShowArc"); // Set the stage title
43        primaryStage.setScene(scene); // Place the scene in the stage
44        primaryStage.show(); // Display the stage
45      }
46    }
```

Margin notes:
- create arc1 (line 14)
- set fill color for arc1 (line 15)
- set arc1 as round arc (line 16)
- create arc2 (line 18)
- set fill color for arc2 (line 19)
- set arc2 as round arc (line 20)
- create arc3 (line 23)
- set fill color for arc3 (line 24)
- set arc3 as chord arc (line 25)
- create arc4 (line 28)
- create a group (line 34)
- add arcs and text to group (line 35)

The program creates an arc arc1 centered at (150, 100) with radiusX 80 and radiusY 80. The starting angle is 30 with length 35 (line 14). arc1's arc type is set to ArcType.ROUND (line 16). Since arc1's fill color is red, arc1 is displayed filled with red round.

The program creates an arc arc3 centered at (150, 100) with radiusX 80 and radiusY 80. The starting angle is 30+180 with length 35 (line 23). Arc3's arc type is set to ArcType.CHORD (line 25). Since arc3's fill color is white and stroke color is black, arc3 is displayed with black outline as a chord.

negative degrees

Angles may be negative. A negative starting angle sweeps clockwise from the easterly direction, as shown in Figure 14.37. A negative spanning angle sweeps clockwise from the starting angle. The following two statements define the same arc:

```
new Arc(x, y, radiusX, radiusY, -30, -20);
new Arc(x, y, radiusX, radiusY, -50, 20);
```

The first statement uses negative starting angle -30 and negative spanning angle −20, as shown in Figure 14.37a. The second statement uses negative starting angle −50 and positive spanning angle 20, as shown in Figure 14.37b.

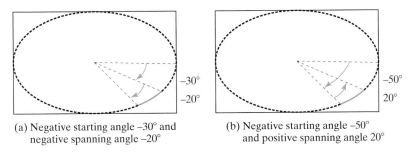

(a) Negative starting angle –30° and   (b) Negative starting angle –50°
   negative spanning angle –20°   and positive spanning angle 20°

FIGURE 14.37   Angles may be negative.

Note the trigonometric methods in the `Math` class use the angles in radians, but the angles in the `Arc` class are in degrees.

14.11.6   `Polygon` and `Polyline`

The `Polygon` class defines a polygon that connects a sequence of points, as shown in Figure 14.38a. The `Polyline` class is similar to the `Polygon` class except that the `Polyline` class is not automatically closed, as shown in Figure 14.38b.

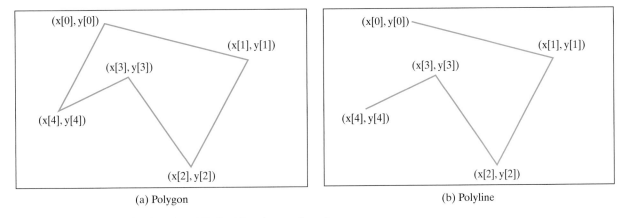

(a) Polygon   (b) Polyline

FIGURE 14.38   `Polygon` is closed and `Polyline` is not closed.

The UML diagram for the `Polygon` class is shown in Figure 14.39. Listing 14.19 gives an example that creates a hexagon, as shown in Figure 14.40.

`javafx.scene.shape.Polygon`	
`+Polygon()`	Creates an empty `Polygon`.
`+Polygon(double... points)`	Creates a `Polygon` with the given points.
`+getPoints():` `  ObservableList<Double>`	Returns a list of double values as *x*- and *y*-coordinates of the points.

FIGURE 14.39   The `Polygon` class defines a polygon.

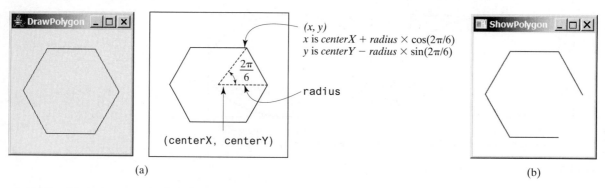

FIGURE 14.40 (a) A `Polygon` is displayed. (b) A `Polyline` is displayed.

LISTING 14.19 ShowPolygon.java

```
1   import javafx.application.Application;
2   import javafx.collections.ObservableList;
3   import javafx.scene.Scene;
4   import javafx.scene.layout.Pane;
5   import javafx.scene.paint.Color;
6   import javafx.stage.Stage;
7   import javafx.scene.shape.Polygon;
8
9   public class ShowPolygon extends Application {
10    @Override // Override the start method in the Application class
11    public void start(Stage primaryStage) {
12      // Create a scene and place it in the stage
13      Scene scene = new Scene(new MyPolygon(), 400, 400);
14      primaryStage.setTitle("ShowPolygon"); // Set the stage title
15      primaryStage.setScene(scene); // Place the scene in the stage
16      primaryStage.show(); // Display the stage
17    }
18  }
19
20  class MyPolygon extends Pane {
21    private void paint() {
22      // Create a polygon and place polygon to pane
23      Polygon polygon = new Polygon();
24      polygon.setFill(Color.WHITE);
25      polygon.setStroke(Color.BLACK);
26      ObservableList<Double> list = polygon.getPoints();
27
28      double centerX = getWidth() / 2, centerY = getHeight() / 2;
29      double radius = Math.min(getWidth(), getHeight()) * 0.4;
30
31      // Add points to the polygon list
32      for (int i = 0; i < 6; i++) {
33        list.add(centerX + radius * Math.cos(2 * i * Math.PI / 6));
34        list.add(centerY - radius * Math.sin(2 * i * Math.PI / 6));
35      }
36
37      getChildren().clear();
38      getChildren().add(polygon);
39    }
40
41    @Override
```

add pane to scene

extends Pane

create a polygon

get a list of points

add *x*-coordinate of a point
add *y*-coordinate of a point

```
42     public void setWidth(double width) {
43       super.setWidth(width);
44       paint();
45     }
46
47     @Override
48     public void setHeight(double height) {
49       super.setHeight(height);
50       paint();
51     }
52   }
```

The program defines the `MyPolygon` class that extends `Pane` (lines 20–52). The `setWidth` and `setHeight` methods in the `Pane` class are overridden in `MyPolygon` to invoke the `paint()` method.

override `setWidth` and `setHeight`

The `paint()` method creates a polygon (line 23) and adds it to a pane (line 38). The `polygon.getPoints()` method returns an `ObservableList<Double>` (line 26), which contains the `add` method for adding an element to the list (lines 33 and 34). Note the value passed to `add(value)` must be a `double` value. If an `int` value is passed, the `int` value would be automatically boxed into an `Integer`. This would cause an error, because the `ObservableList<Double>` consists of `Double` elements.

The `centerX`, `centerY`, and `radius` are obtained in proportion to the width and height of the pane (lines 28 and 29). The loop adds six points to the polygon (lines 32–35). Each point is represented by its *x*- and *y*-coordinates, computed using `centerX`, `centerY`, and `radius`. For each point, its *x*-coordinate is added to the polygon's list (line 33) then its *y*-coordinate is added to the list (line 34). The formula for computing the *x*- and *y*-coordinates for a point in the hexagon is illustrated in Figure 14.40a.

If you replace `Polygon` by `Polyline` (line 23), the program displays a polyline as shown in Figure 14.40b. The `Polyline` class is used in the same way as `Polygon`, except that the starting and ending points are not connected in `Polyline`.

14.11.1 How do you display a text, line, rectangle, circle, ellipse, arc, polygon, and polyline?

14.11.2 Write code fragments to display a string rotated 45 degrees in the center of the pane.

14.11.3 Write code fragments to display a thick line of 10 pixels from (10, 10) to (70, 30).

14.11.4 Write code fragments to fill red color in a rectangle of width 100 and height 50 with the upper-left corner at (10, 10).

14.11.5 Write code fragments to display a round-cornered rectangle with width 100, height 200 with the upper-left corner at (10, 10), corner horizontal diameter 40, and corner vertical diameter 20.

14.11.6 Write code fragments to display an ellipse with horizontal radius 50 and vertical radius 100.

14.11.7 Write code fragments to display the outline of the upper half of a circle with radius 50.

14.11.8 Write code fragments to display the lower half of a circle with radius 50 filled with the red color.

14.11.9 Write code fragments to display a polygon connecting the following points: (20, 40), (30, 50), (40, 90), (90, 10), and (10, 30), and fill the polygon with green color.

14.11.10 Write code fragments to display a polyline connecting the following points: (20, 40), (30, 50), (40, 90), (90, 10), and (10, 30).

14.11.11 What is wrong in the following code?

```java
public void start(Stage primaryStage) {
  // Create a polygon and place it in the scene
  Scene scene = new Scene(new Polygon(), 400, 400);
  primaryStage.setScene(scene); // Place the scene in the stage
  primaryStage.show(); // Display the stage
}
```

14.12 Case Study: The ClockPane Class

Key Point

This case study develops a class that displays a clock on a pane.

The contract of the ClockPane class is shown in Figure 14.41.

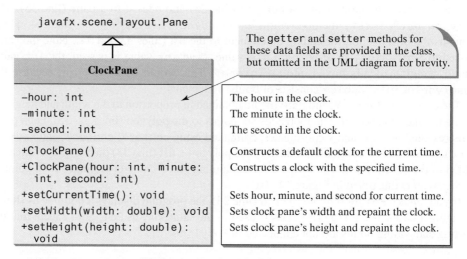

FIGURE 14.41 ClockPane displays an analog clock.

Assume ClockPane is available; we write a test program in Listing 14.20 to display an analog clock and use a label to display the hour, minute, and second, as shown in Figure 14.42.

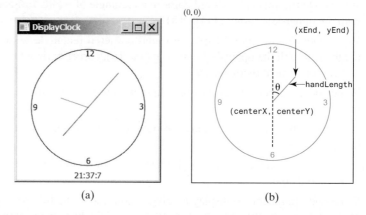

FIGURE 14.42 (a) The DisplayClock program displays a clock that shows the current time. (b) The endpoint of a clock hand can be determined, given the spanning angle, the hand length, and the center point.

LISTING 14.20 `DisplayClock.java`

```
1   import javafx.application.Application;
2   import javafx.geometry.Pos;
3   import javafx.stage.Stage;
4   import javafx.scene.Scene;
5   import javafx.scene.control.Label;
6   import javafx.scene.layout.BorderPane;
7
8   public class DisplayClock extends Application {
9     @Override // Override the start method in the Application class
10    public void start(Stage primaryStage) {
11      // Create a clock and a label
12      ClockPane clock = new ClockPane();                          create a clock
13      String timeString = clock.getHour() + ":" + clock.getMinute()
14        + ":" + clock.getSecond();
15      Label lblCurrentTime = new Label(timeString);               create a label
16
17      // Place clock and label in border pane
18      BorderPane pane = new BorderPane();
19      pane.setCenter(clock);                                      add a clock
20      pane.setBottom(lblCurrentTime);                             add a label
21      BorderPane.setAlignment(lblCurrentTime, Pos.TOP_CENTER);
22
23      // Create a scene and place it in the stage
24      Scene scene = new Scene(pane, 250, 250);
25      primaryStage.setTitle("DisplayClock"); // Set the stage title
26      primaryStage.setScene(scene); // Place the scene in the stage
27      primaryStage.show(); // Display the stage
28    }
29  }
```

The rest of this section explains how to implement the `ClockPane` class. Since you can use the class without knowing how it is implemented, you may skip the implementation if you wish.

skip implementation?
implementation

To draw a clock, you need to draw a circle and three hands for the second, minute, and hour. To draw a hand, you need to specify the two ends of the line. As shown in Figure 14.42b, one end is the center of the clock at `(centerX, centerY)`; the other end, at `(endX, endY)`, is determined by the following formula:

```
endX = centerX + handLength × sin(θ)
endY = centerY − handLength × cos(θ)
```

Since there are 60 seconds in one minute, the angle for the second hand is

```
second × (2π/60)
```

The position of the minute hand is determined by the minute and second. The exact minute value combined with seconds is `minute + second/60`. For example, if the time is 3 minutes and 30 seconds, the total minutes are 3.5. Since there are 60 minutes in one hour, the angle for the minute hand is

$$(minute + second/60) \times (2\pi/60)$$

Since one circle is divided into 12 hours, the angle for the hour hand is

$$(hour + minute/60 + second/(60 \times 60)) \times (2\pi/12)$$

For simplicity in computing the angles of the minute and hour hands, you can omit the seconds because they are negligibly small. Therefore, the endpoints for the second, minute, and hour hands can be computed as follows:

$$\text{secondX} = \text{centerX} + \text{secondHandLength} \times \sin(\text{second} \times (2\pi/60))$$
$$\text{secondY} = \text{centerY} - \text{secondHandLength} \times \cos(\text{second} \times (2\pi/60))$$
$$\text{minuteX} = \text{centerX} + \text{minuteHandLength} \times \sin(\text{minute} \times (2\pi/60))$$
$$\text{minuteY} = \text{centerY} - \text{minuteHandLength} \times \cos(\text{minute} \times (2\pi/60))$$
$$\text{hourX} = \text{centerX} + \text{hourHandLength} \times \sin((\text{hour} + \text{minute}/60) \times (2\pi/12))$$
$$\text{hourY} = \text{centerY} - \text{hourHandLength} \times \cos((\text{hour} + \text{minute}/60) \times (2\pi/12))$$

The `ClockPane` class is implemented in Listing 14.21.

LISTING 14.21 ClockPane.java

```java
import java.util.Calendar;
import java.util.GregorianCalendar;
import javafx.scene.layout.Pane;
import javafx.scene.paint.Color;
import javafx.scene.shape.Circle;
import javafx.scene.shape.Line;
import javafx.scene.text.Text;

public class ClockPane extends Pane {
  private int hour;
  private int minute;
  private int second;

  /** Construct a default clock with the current time*/
  public ClockPane() {
    setCurrentTime();
  }

  /** Construct a clock with specified hour, minute, and second */
  public ClockPane(int hour,int minute,int second) {
    this.hour = hour;
    this.minute = minute;
    this.second = second;
  }

  /** Return hour */
  public int getHour() {
    return hour;
  }

  /** Set a new hour */
  public void setHour(int hour) {
    this.hour = hour;
    paintClock();
  }

  /** Return minute */
  public int getMinute() {
    return minute;
  }

  /** Set a new minute */
  public void setMinute(int minute) {
    this.minute = minute;
```

Margin notes:

clock properties (line 10)
no-arg constructor (line 15)
constructor (line 20)
set a new hour (line 32)
paint clock (line 34)
set a new minute (line 38)

```
45        paintClock();                                                  paint clock
46    }
47
48    /** Return second */
49    public int getSecond() {
50      return second;
51    }
52
53    /** Set a new second */
54    public void setSecond(int second) {                                set a new second
55      this.second = second;
56      paintClock();                                                    paint clock
57    }
58
59    /* Set the current time for the clock */
60    public void setCurrentTime() {                                     set current time
61      // Construct a calendar for the current date and time
62      Calendar calendar = new GregorianCalendar();
63
64      // Set current hour, minute and second
65      this.hour = calendar.get(Calendar.HOUR_OF_DAY);
66      this.minute = calendar.get(Calendar.MINUTE);
67      this.second = calendar.get(Calendar.SECOND);
68
69      paintClock(); // Repaint the clock                               paint clock
70    }
71
72    /** Paint the clock */
73    private void paintClock() {                                        paint clock
74      // Initialize clock parameters
75      double clockRadius =                                             get radius
76        Math.min(getWidth(), getHeight()) * 0.8 * 0.5;
77      double centerX = getWidth() /2;                                  get center
78      double centerY = getHeight() /2;
79
80      // Draw circle
81      Circle circle = new Circle(centerX, centerY, clockRadius);       create a circle
82      circle.setFill(Color.WHITE);
83      circle.setStroke(Color.BLACK);
84      Text t1 = new Text(centerX - 5, centerY - clockRadius + 12, "12"); create texts
85      Text t2 = new Text(centerX - clockRadius + 3, centerY + 5, "9");
86      Text t3 = new Text(centerX + clockRadius - 10, centerY + 3, "3");
87      Text t4 = new Text(centerX - 3, centerY + clockRadius - 3, "6");
88
89      // Draw second hand
90      double sLength = clockRadius * 0.8;
91      double secondX = centerX + sLength *
92        Math.sin(second * (2 * Math.PI / 60));
93      double secondY = centerY - sLength *
94        Math.cos(second * (2 * Math.PI / 60));
95      Line sLine = new Line(centerX, centerY, secondX, secondY);       create second hand
96      sLine.setStroke(Color.RED);
97
98      // Draw minute hand
99      double mLength = clockRadius * 0.65;
100     double xMinute = centerX + mLength *
101       Math.sin(minute * (2 * Math.PI / 60));
102     double minuteY = centerY - mLength *
103       Math.cos(minute * (2 * Math.PI / 60));
104     Line mLine = new Line(centerX, centerY, xMinute, minuteY);       create minute hand
```

create hour hand; clear pane; add nodes to pane; set a new width; paint clock; set a new height; paint clock

```
105      mLine.setStroke(Color.BLUE);
106
107      // Draw hour hand
108      double hLength = clockRadius * 0.5;
109      double hourX = centerX + hLength *
110        Math.sin((hour % 12 + minute / 60.0) * (2 * Math.PI / 12));
111      double hourY = centerY - hLength *
112        Math.cos((hour % 12 + minute / 60.0) * (2 * Math.PI / 12));
113      Line hLine = new Line(centerX, centerY, hourX, hourY);
114      hLine.setStroke(Color.GREEN);
115
116      getChildren().clear();
117      getChildren().addAll(circle, t1, t2, t3, t4, sLine, mLine, hLine);
118    }
119
120    @Override
121    public void setWidth(double width) {
122      super.setWidth(width);
123      paintClock();
124    }
125
126    @Override
127    public void setHeight(double height) {
128      super.setHeight(height);
129      paintClock();
130    }
131  }
```

The program displays a clock for the current time using the no-arg constructor (lines 15–17) and displays a clock for the specified hour, minute, and second using the other constructor (lines 20–24).

The class defines the properties `hour`, `minute`, and `second` to store the time represented in the clock (lines 10–12). The current hour, minute, and second are obtained by using the `GregorianCalendar` class (lines 62–67). The `GregorianCalendar` class in the Java API enables you to create a `Calendar` instance for the current time using its no-arg constructor. You can then use its methods `get(Calendar.HOUR)`, `get(Calendar.MINUTE)`, and `get(Calendar.SECOND)` to return the hour, minute, and second from a `Calendar` object.

The `paintClock()` method paints the clock (lines 73–118). The clock radius is proportional to the width and height of the pane (lines 75–78). A circle for the clock is created at the center of the pane (line 81). The text for showing the hours 12, 3, 6, and 9 are created in lines 84–87. The second, minute, and hour hands are the lines created in lines 90–114. The `paintClock()` method places all these shapes in the pane using the `addAll` method (line 117). Before adding new contents into the pane, the old contents are cleared from the pane (line 116).

override `setWidth` and `setHeight`

The `setWidth` and `setHeight` methods defined in the `Pane` class are overridden in the `ClockPane` class to repaint the clock after the width or height is changed in the clock pane (lines 120–130). The `paintClock()` method is invoked whenever a new property (`hour`, `minute`, `second`, `width`, and `height`) is set (lines 34, 45, 56, 69, 123, and 129).

In Listing 14.20, the clock is placed inside a border pane, the border pane is placed in the scene, and the scene is placed in the stage. When a stage is displayed or resized, all these components inside the stage are automatically resized by invoking their respective `setWidth` and `setHeight` methods. Since the `setWidth` and `setHeight` methods are overridden to invoke the `paintClock()` method, the clock is automatically resized in response to the change of the stage size.

14.12.1 What will happen if lines 120–130 are removed in Listing 14.21? Run the DisplayClock class in Listing 14.20 to test it.

Check Point

Key Terms

AWT   542
bidirectional binding   551
bindable object   548
binding object   548
binding property   548
JavaFX   551
node   545
observable object   548
pane   545

primary stage   543
property getter method   549
shape   545
Swing   542
UI control   545
unidirectional binding   551
value getter method   549
value setter method   549

Chapter Summary

1. JavaFX is the new framework for developing rich GUI applications. JavaFX completely replaces Swing and AWT.

2. A main JavaFX class must extend `javafx.application.Application` and implement the `start` method. The primary stage is automatically created by the JVM and passed to the `start` method.

3. A stage is a window for displaying a scene. You can add nodes to a scene. Panes, groups, controls, and shapes are nodes. Panes can be used as the containers for nodes.

4. A binding property can be bound to an observable source object. A change in the source object will be automatically reflected in the binding property. A binding property has a value getter method, value setter method, and property getter method.

5. The `Node` class defines many properties that are common to all nodes. You can apply these properties to panes, groups, controls, and shapes.

6. You can create a `Color` object with the specified red, green, blue components, and opacity value.

7. You can create a `Font` object and set its name, size, weight, and posture.

8. The `javafx.scene.image.Image` class can be used to load an image, and this image can be displayed in an `ImageView` object.

9. JavaFX provides many types of panes for automatically laying out nodes in a desired location and size. The `Pane` is the base class for all panes. It contains the `getChildren()` method to return an `ObservableList`. You can use `ObservableList`'s `add(node)` and `addAll(node1, node2,...)` methods for adding nodes into a pane.

10. A `FlowPane` arranges the nodes in the pane horizontally from left to right or vertically from top to bottom, in the order in which they were added. A `GridPane` arranges nodes

in a grid (matrix) formation. The nodes are placed in the specified column and row indices. A BorderPane can place nodes in five regions: top, bottom, left, right, and center. An HBox lays out its children in a single horizontal row. A VBox lays out its children in a single vertical column.

11. JavaFX provides many shape classes for drawing texts, lines, circles, rectangles, ellipses, arcs, polygons, and polylines.

QUIZ

Answer the quiz for this chapter online at the book Companion Website.

MyProgrammingLab™

PROGRAMMING EXERCISES

download image files

 Note
The image files used in the exercises can be obtained from liveexample.pearsoncmg.com/resource/image.zip under the image folder.

Sections 14.2–14.9

14.1 (*Display images*) Write a program that displays four images in a grid pane, as shown in Figure 14.43a.

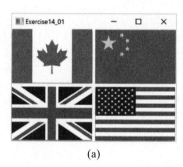 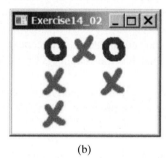 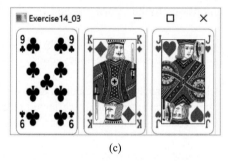

(a) (b) (c)

FIGURE 14.43 (a) Exercise 14.1 displays four images. *Source*: booka/Fotolia. Figure 14.43a4: United States Government. (b) Exercise 14.2 displays a tic-tac-toe board with images. (c) Three cards are randomly selected. *Source*: pandawild/Fotolia.

VideoNote

Display a tic-tac-toe board

*14.2 (*Tic-tac-toe board*) Write a program that displays a tic-tac-toe board, as shown in Figure 14.43b. A cell may be X, O, or empty. What to display at each cell is randomly decided. The X and O are the image files **x.gif** and **o.gif**.

*14.3 (*Display three cards*) Write a program that displays three cards randomly selected from a deck of 52, as shown in Figure 14.43c. The card image files are named **1.png**, **2.png**, . . . , **52.png** and stored in the **image/card** directory. All three cards are distinct and selected randomly. (*Hint*: You can select random cards by storing the numbers 1–52 to an array list, perform a random shuffle introduced in Section 11.12, and use the first three numbers in the array list as the file names for the image.)

14.4 (*Color and font*) Write a program that displays five texts vertically, as shown in Figure 14.44a. Set a random color and opacity for each text and set the font of each text to Times Roman, bold, italic, and 22 pixels.

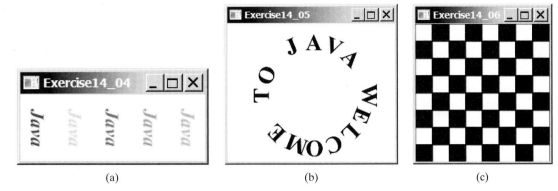

(a)   (b)   (c)

FIGURE 14.44   (a) Five texts are displayed with a random color and a specified font. (b) A string is displayed around the circle. (c) A checkerboard is displayed using rectangles.

14.5   (*Characters around circle*) Write a program that displays a string "Welcome to Java" around the circle, as shown in Figure 14.44b. (*Hint*: You need to display each character in the right location with appropriate rotation using a loop.)

*14.6   (*Game: display a checkerboard*) Write a program that displays a checkerboard in which each white and black cell is a `Rectangle` with a fill color black or white, as shown in Figure 14.44c.

Sections 14.10 and 14.11

*14.7   (*Display random 0 or 1*) Write a program that displays a 10-by-10 square matrix, as shown in Figure 14.45a. Each element in the matrix is 0 or 1, randomly generated. Display each number centered in a text field. Use `TextField`'s `setText` method to set value 0 or 1 as a string.   Display a random matrix

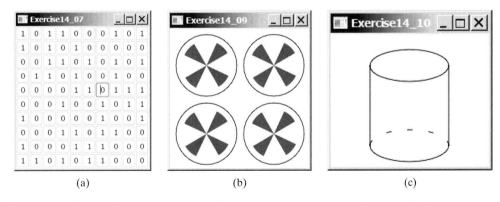

(a)   (b)   (c)

FIGURE 14.45   (a) The program randomly generates 0s and 1s. (b) Exercise 14.9 draws four fans. (c) Exercise 14.10 draws a cylinder.

14.8   (*Display 54 cards*) Expand Exercise 14.3 to display all 54 cards (including two jokers), nine per row. The image files are jokers and are named 53.png and 54.png.

*14.9   (*Create four fans*) Write a program that places four fans in a `GridPane` with two rows and two columns, as shown in Figure 14.45b.

*14.10   (*Display a cylinder*) Write a program that draws a cylinder, as shown in Figure 14.45b. You can use the following method to set the dashed stroke for an arc:

```
arc.getStrokeDashArray().addAll(6.0, 21.0);
```

The solution posted on the website enables the cylinder to resize horizontally. Can you revise it to resize vertically as well?

*14.11 (*Paint a smiley face*) Write a program that paints a smiley face, as shown in Figure 14.46a.

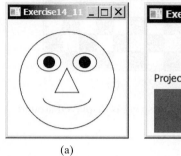
(a)

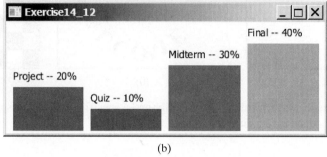
(b)

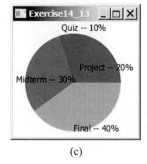
(c)

FIGURE 14.46 (a) Exercise 14.11 paints a smiley face. (b) Exercise 14.12 paints a bar chart. (c) Exercise 14.13 paints a pie chart.

VideoNote

Display a bar chart

14.12 (*Display a bar chart*) Write a program that uses a bar chart to display the percentages of the overall grade represented by projects, quizzes, midterm exams, and the final exam, as shown in Figure 14.46b. Suppose projects take 20% and are displayed in red, quizzes take 10% and are displayed in blue, midterm exams take 30% and are displayed in green, and the final exam takes 40% and is displayed in orange. Use the `Rectangle` class to display the bars. Interested readers may explore the JavaFX `BarChart` class for further study.

14.13 (*Display a pie chart*) Write a program that uses a pie chart to display the percentages of the overall grade represented by projects, quizzes, midterm exams, and the final exam, as shown in Figure 14.46c. Suppose projects take 20% and are displayed in red, quizzes take 10% and are displayed in blue, midterm exams take 30% and are displayed in green, and the final exam takes 40% and is displayed in orange. Use the `Arc` class to display the pies. Interested readers may explore the JavaFX `PieChart` class for further study.

14.14 (*Display a rectanguloid*) Write a program that displays a rectanguloid, as shown in Figure 14.47a. The cube should grow and shrink as the window grows or shrinks.

(a)

(b)

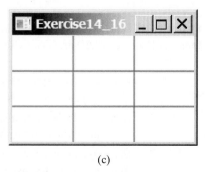
(c)

FIGURE 14.47 (a) Exercise 14.14 paints a rectanguloid. (b) Exercise 14.15 paints a STOP sign. (c) Exercise 14.16 paints a grid.

*14.15 (*Display a STOP sign*) Write a program that displays a STOP sign, as shown in Figure 14.47b. The octagon is in red and the sign is in white. (*Hint*: Place an octagon and a text in a stack pane.)

*14.16 (*Display a 3 × 3 grid*) Write a program that displays a 3 × 3 grid, as shown in Figure 14.47c. Use red color for vertical lines and blue for horizontals. The lines are automatically resized when the window is resized.

14.17 (*Game: hangman*) Write a program that displays a drawing for the popular hangman game, as shown in Figure 14.48a.

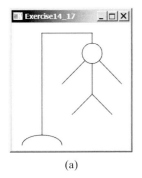 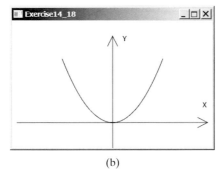 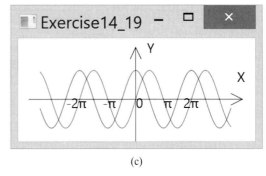

(a)   (b)   (c)

FIGURE 14.48 (a) Exercise 14.17 draws a sketch for the hangman game. (b) Exercise 14.18 plots the quadratic function. (c) Exercise 14.19 plots the sine/cosine functions.

*14.18 (*Plot the square function*) Write a program that draws a diagram for the function $f(x) = x^2$ (see Figure 14.48b).

Hint: Add points to a polyline using the following code:

```
Polyline polyline = new Polyline();
ObservableList<Double> list = polyline.getPoints();
double scaleFactor = 0.0125;
for (int x = -100; x <= 100; x++) {
  list.add(x + 200.0);
  list.add(scaleFactor * x * x);
}
```

**14.19 (*Plot the sine and cosine functions*) Write a program that plots the sine function in red and cosine in blue, as shown in Figure 14.48c.

Hint: The Unicode for π is \u03c0. To display -2π, use Text(x, y, "-2\u03c0"). For a trigonometric function like sin(x), x is in radians. Use the following loop to add the points to a polyline:

```
Polyline polyline = new Polyline();
ObservableList<Double> list = polyline.getPoints();
double scaleFactor = 50;
for (int x = -170; x <= 170; x++) {
  list.add(x + 200.0);
  list.add(100 - 50 * Math.sin((x / 100.0) * 2 * Math.PI));
}
```

**14.20 (*Draw an arrow line*) Write a static method that draws an arrow line from a starting point to an ending point in a pane using the following method header:

```
public static void drawArrowLine(double startX, double startY,
  double endX, double endY, Pane pane)
```

Write a test program that randomly draws an arrow line, as shown in Figure 14.49a.

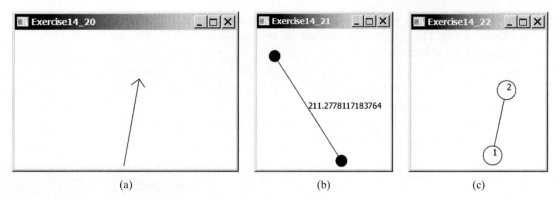

FIGURE 14.49 (a) The program displays an arrow line. (b) Exercise 14.21 connects the centers of two filled circles. (c) Exercise 14.22 connects two circles from their perimeter.

*14.21 (*Two circles and their distance*) Write a program that draws two circles with radius 15 pixels, centered at random locations, with a line connecting the two circles. The distance between the two centers is displayed on the line, as shown in Figure 14.49b.

*14.22 (*Connect two circles*) Write a program that draws two filled circles with radius 15 pixels, centered at random locations, with a line connecting the two circles. The line should not cross inside the circles, as shown in Figure 14.49c.

*14.23 (*Geometry: two rectangles*) Write a program that prompts the user to enter the center coordinates, width, and height of two rectangles from the command line. The program displays the rectangles and a text indicating whether the two are overlapping, whether one is contained in the other, or whether they don't overlap, as shown in Figure 14.50. See Programming Exercise 10.13 for checking the relationship between two rectangles.

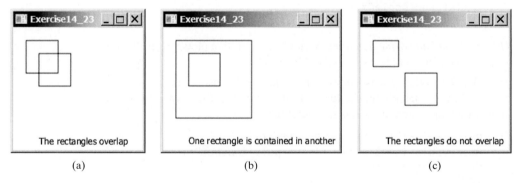

FIGURE 14.50 Two rectangles are displayed.

*14.24 (*Geometry: Inside a polygon?*) Write a program that prompts the user to enter the coordinates of five points from the command line. The first four points form a polygon, and the program displays the polygon and a text that indicates whether the fifth point is inside the polygon, as shown in Figure 14.51a. (*Hint*: Use the Node's contains method to test whether a point is inside a node.)

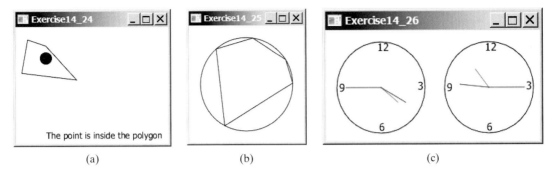

(a) (b) (c)

FIGURE 14.51 (a) The polygon and a point are displayed. (b) Exercise 14.25 connects five random points on a circle. (b) Exercise 14.26 displays two clocks.

*14.25 (*Random points on a circle*) Modify Programming Exercise 4.6 to create five random points on a circle, form a polygon by connecting the points clockwise, and display the circle and the polygon, as shown in Figure 14.51b.

Section 14.12

14.26 (*Use the* `ClockPane` *class*) Write a program that displays two clocks. The hour, minute, and second values are 4, 20, 45 for the first clock, and 22, 46, 15 for the second clock, as shown in Figure 14.51c.

*14.27 (*Draw a detailed clock*) Modify the `ClockPane` class in Section 14.12 to draw the clock with more details on the hours and minutes, as shown in Figure 14.52a.

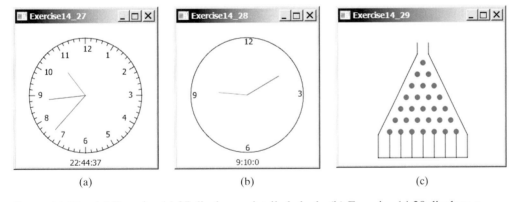

(a) (b) (c)

FIGURE 14.52 (a) Exercise 14.27 displays a detailed clock. (b) Exercise 14.28 displays a clock with random hour and minute values. (c) Exercise 14.29 displays a bean machine.

*14.28 (*Random time*) Modify the `ClockPane` class with three new Boolean properties— `hourHandVisible`, `minuteHandVisible`, and `secondHandVisible`—and their associated accessor and mutator methods. You can use the `set` methods to make a hand visible or invisible. Write a test program that displays only the hour and minute hands. The hour and minute values are randomly generated. The hour is between 0 and 11, and the minute is either 0 or 30, as shown in Figure 14.52b.

**14.29 (*Game: bean machine*) Write a program that displays a bean machine introduced in Programming Exercise 7.37, as shown in Figure 14.52c.

EVENT-DRIVEN PROGRAMMING AND ANIMATIONS

Objectives

- To get a taste of event-driven programming (§15.1).
- To describe events, event sources, and event classes (§15.2).
- To define handler classes, register handler objects with the source object, and write the code to handle events (§15.3).
- To define handler classes using inner classes (§15.4).
- To define handler classes using anonymous inner classes (§15.5).
- To simplify event handling using lambda expressions (§15.6).
- To develop a GUI application for a loan calculator (§15.7).
- To write programs to deal with MouseEvents (§15.8).
- To write programs to deal with KeyEvents (§15.9).

- To create listeners for processing a value change in an observable object (§15.10).
- To use the Animation, PathTransition, FadeTransition, and Timeline classes to develop animations (§15.11).
- To develop an animation for simulating a bouncing ball (§15.12).
- To draw, color, and resize a US map (§15.13).

15.1 Introduction

You can write code to process events such as a button click, mouse movement, and keystrokes.

problem

Suppose you wish to write a GUI program that lets the user enter a loan amount, annual interest rate, and number of years then click the *Calculate* button to obtain the monthly payment and total payment, as shown in Figure 15.1. How do you accomplish the task? You have to use *event-driven programming* to write the code to respond to the button-clicking event.

FIGURE 15.1 The program computes loan payments.

problem

Before delving into event-driven programming, it is helpful to get a taste using a simple example. The example displays two buttons in a pane, as shown in Figure 15.2.

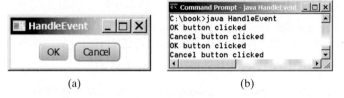

(a)   (b)

FIGURE 15.2 (a) The program displays two buttons. (b) A message is displayed in the console when a button is clicked.

To respond to a button click, you need to write the code to process the button-clicking action. The button is an *event source object*—where the action originates. You need to create an object capable of handling the action event on a button. This object is called an *event handler*, as shown in Figure 15.3.

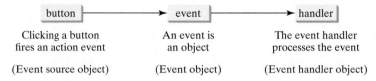

button		event		handler
Clicking a button fires an action event		An event is an object		The event handler processes the event
(Event source object)		(Event object)		(Event handler object)

FIGURE 15.3 An event handler processes the event fired from the source object.

Not all objects can be handlers for an action event. To be a handler of an action event, two requirements must be met:

`EventHandler` interface

1. The object must be an instance of the `EventHandler<T extends Event>` interface. This interface defines the common behavior for all handlers. `<T extends Event>` denotes that `T` is a generic type that is a subtype of `Event`.

2. The `EventHandler` object `handler` must be registered with the event source object using the method `source.setOnAction(handler)`.

`setOnAction(handler)`

The `EventHandler<ActionEvent>` interface contains the `handle(ActionEvent)` method for processing the action event. Your handler class must override this method to respond to the event. Listing 15.1 gives the code that processes the `ActionEvent` on the two buttons. When you click the *OK* button, the message "OK button clicked" is displayed. When you click the *Cancel* button, the message "Cancel button clicked" is displayed, as shown in Figure 15.2.

LISTING 15.1   HandleEvent.java

```java
 1  import javafx.application.Application;
 2  import javafx.geometry.Pos;
 3  import javafx.scene.Scene;
 4  import javafx.scene.control.Button;
 5  import javafx.scene.layout.HBox;
 6  import javafx.stage.Stage;
 7  import javafx.event.ActionEvent;
 8  import javafx.event.EventHandler;
 9
10  public class HandleEvent extends Application {
11    @Override // Override the start method in the Application class
12    public void start(Stage primaryStage) {
13      // Create a pane and set its properties
14      HBox pane = new HBox(10);
15      pane.setAlignment(Pos.CENTER);
16      Button btOK = new Button("OK");
17      Button btCancel = new Button("Cancel");
18      OKHandlerClass handler1 = new OKHandlerClass();        create handler
19      btOK.setOnAction(handler1);                            register handler
20      CancelHandlerClass handler2 = new CancelHandlerClass(); create handler
21      btCancel.setOnAction(handler2);                        register handler
22      pane.getChildren().addAll(btOK, btCancel);
23
24      // Create a scene and place it in the stage
25      Scene scene = new Scene(pane);
26      primaryStage.setTitle("HandleEvent"); // Set the stage title
27      primaryStage.setScene(scene); // Place the scene in the stage
28      primaryStage.show(); // Display the stage
29    }
30  }
31
32  class OKHandlerClass implements EventHandler<ActionEvent> {   handler class
33    @Override
34    public void handle(ActionEvent e) {                        handle event
35      System.out.println("OK button clicked");
36    }
37  }
38
39  class CancelHandlerClass implements EventHandler<ActionEvent> { handler class
40    @Override
41    public void handle(ActionEvent e) {                        handle event
42      System.out.println("Cancel button clicked");
43    }
44  }
```

Two handler classes are defined in lines 32–44. Each handler class implements `EventHandler<ActionEvent>` to process `ActionEvent`. The object `handler1` is an instance of `OKHandlerClass` (line 18), which is registered with the button `btOK` (line 19). When the *OK* button is clicked, the `handle(ActionEvent)` method (line 34) in `OKHandlerClass` is invoked to process the event. The object `handler2` is an instance of `CancelHandlerClass` (line 20), which is registered with the button `btCancel` in line 21. When the *Cancel* button is clicked, the `handle(ActionEvent)` method (line 41) in `CancelHandlerClass` is invoked to process the event.

You now have seen a glimpse of event-driven programming in JavaFX. You probably have many questions, such as why a handler class is defined to implement the `EventHandler<ActionEvent>`. The following sections will give you all the answers.

15.2 Events and Event Sources

Key
Point

An event is an object created from an event source. Firing an event means to create an event and delegate the handler to handle the event.

event-driven programming
event

When you run a Java GUI program, the program interacts with the user and the events drive its execution. This is called *event-driven programming*. An *event* can be defined as a signal to the program that something has happened. Events are triggered by external user actions, such as mouse movements, mouse clicks, and keystrokes. The program can choose to respond to or ignore an event. The example in the preceding section gave you a taste of event-driven programming.

fire event
event source object
source object

The component that creates an event and fires it is called the *event source object*, or simply *source object* or *source component*. For example, a button is the source object for a button-clicking action event. An event is an instance of an event class. The root class of the Java event classes is `java.util.EventObject`. The root class of the JavaFX event classes is `javafx.event.Event`. The hierarchical relationships of some event classes are shown in Figure 15.4.

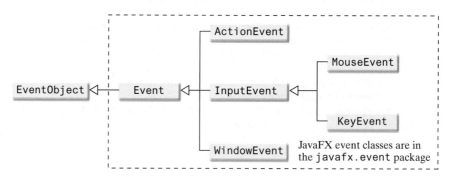

FIGURE 15.4 An event in JavaFX is an object of the `javafx.event.Event` class.

event object
getSource()

An *event object* contains whatever properties are pertinent to the event. You can identify the source object of an event using the `getSource()` instance method in the `EventObject` class. The subclasses of `EventObject` deal with specific types of events, such as action events, window events, mouse events, and key events. The first three columns in Table 15.1 list some external user actions, source objects, and event types fired. For example, when clicking a button, the button creates and fires an `ActionEvent`, as indicated in the first line of this table. Here, the button is an event source object, and an `ActionEvent` is the event object fired by the source object, as shown in Figure 15.3.

 Note

If a component can fire an event, any subclass of the component can fire the same type of event. For example, every JavaFX shape, layout pane, and control can fire `MouseEvent` and `KeyEvent` since `Node` is the superclass for shapes, layout panes, and controls and `Node` can fire `MouseEvent` and `KeyEvent`.

TABLE 15.1 User Action, Source Object, Event Type, Handler Interface, and Handler

User Action	Source Object	Event Type Fired	Event Registration Method
Click a button	`Button`	`ActionEvent`	`setOnAction(EventHandler<ActionEvent>)`
Press Enter in a text field	`TextField`	`ActionEvent`	`setOnAction(EventHandler<ActionEvent>)`
Check or uncheck	`RadioButton`	`ActionEvent`	`setOnAction(EventHandler<ActionEvent>)`
Check or uncheck	`CheckBox`	`ActionEvent`	`setOnAction(EventHandler<ActionEvent>)`
Select a new item	`ComboBox`	`ActionEvent`	`setOnAction(EventHandler<ActionEvent>)`
Mouse pressed	`Node, Scene`	`MouseEvent`	`setOnMousePressed(EventHandler<MouseEvent>)`
Mouse released			`setOnMouseReleased(EventHandler<MouseEvent>)`
Mouse clicked			`setOnMouseClicked(EventHandler<MouseEvent>)`
Mouse entered			`setOnMouseEntered(EventHandler<MouseEvent>)`
Mouse exited			`setOnMouseExited(EventHandler<MouseEvent>)`
Mouse moved			`setOnMouseMoved(EventHandler<MouseEvent>)`
Mouse dragged			`setOnMouseDragged(EventHandler<MouseEvent>)`
Key pressed	`Node, Scene`	`KeyEvent`	`setOnKeyPressed(EventHandler<KeyEvent>)`
Key released			`setOnKeyReleased(EventHandler<KeyEvent>)`
Key typed			`setOnKeyTyped(EventHandler<KeyEvent>)`

15.2.1 What is an event source object? What is an event object? Describe the relationship between an event source object and an event object.

15.2.2 Can a button fire a `MouseEvent`? Can a button fire a `KeyEvent`? Can a button fire an `ActionEvent`?

Check Point

15.3 Registering Handlers and Handling Events

A handler is an object that must be registered with an event source object and it must be an instance of an appropriate event-handling interface.

Key Point

Java uses a delegation-based model for event handling: A source object fires an event, and an object interested in the event handles it. The latter object is called an *event handler* or an event *listener*. For an object to be a handler for an event on a source object, two things are needed, as shown in Figure 15.5.

1. *The handler object must be an instance of the corresponding event–handler interface* to ensure the handler has the correct method for processing the event. JavaFX defines a unified handler interface `EventHandler<T extends Event>` for an event `T`. The handler interface contains the `handle(T e)` method for processing the event. For example, the handler interface for `ActionEvent` is `EventHandler<ActionEvent>`; each handler for `ActionEvent` should implement the `handle(ActionEvent e)` method for processing an `ActionEvent`.

2. *The handler object must be registered by the source object*. Registration methods depend on the event type. For `ActionEvent`, the method is `setOnAction`. For a mouse-pressed event, the method is `setOnMousePressed`. For a key-pressed event, the method is `setOnKeyPressed`.

Let's revisit Listing 15.1, HandleEvent.java. Since a `Button` object fires `ActionEvent`, a handler object for `ActionEvent` must be an instance of `EventHandler<ActionEvent>`, so

(margin notes)
event delegation
event handler

event–handler interface

`EventHandler<T extends Event>`

event handler

register handler

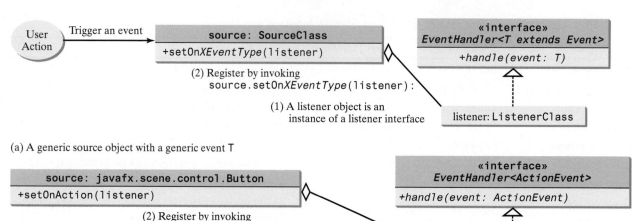

(a) A generic source object with a generic event T

(b) A Button source object with an ActionEvent

FIGURE 15.5 A listener must be an instance of a listener interface and must be registered with a source object.

the handler class implements EventHandler<ActionEvent> in line 32. The source object invokes setOnAction(handler) to register a handler, as follows:

create source object
create handler object
register handler

```
Button btOK = new Button("OK"); // Line 16 in Listing 15.1
OKHandlerClass handler1 = new OKHandlerClass(); // Line 18 in Listing 15.1
btOK.setOnAction(handler1); // Line 19 in Listing 15.1
```

When you click the button, the Button object fires an ActionEvent and passes it to invoke the handler's handle(ActionEvent) method to handle the event. The event object contains information pertinent to the event, which can be obtained using the methods. For example, you can use e.getSource() to obtain the source object that fired the event.

We now write a program that uses two buttons to enlarge and shrink a circle, as shown in Figure 15.6. We will develop this program incrementally. First, we write the program in Listing 15.2 that displays the user interface with a circle in the center (lines 15–19) and two buttons on the bottom (lines 21–27).

first version

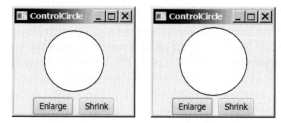

FIGURE 15.6 The user clicks the *Enlarge* and *Shrink* buttons to enlarge and shrink the circle.

LISTING 15.2 ControlCircleWithoutEventHandling.java

```
1  import javafx.application.Application;
2  import javafx.geometry.Pos;
3  import javafx.scene.Scene;
4  import javafx.scene.control.Button;
```

```
 5  import javafx.scene.layout.StackPane;
 6  import javafx.scene.layout.HBox;
 7  import javafx.scene.layout.BorderPane;
 8  import javafx.scene.paint.Color;
 9  import javafx.scene.shape.Circle;
10  import javafx.stage.Stage;
11
12  public class ControlCircleWithoutEventHandling extends Application {
13    @Override // Override the start method in the Application class
14    public void start(Stage primaryStage) {
15      StackPane pane = new StackPane();
16      Circle circle = new Circle(50);                                         circle
17      circle.setStroke(Color.BLACK);
18      circle.setFill(Color.WHITE);
19      pane.getChildren().add(circle);
20
21      HBox hBox = new HBox();
22      hBox.setSpacing(10);
23      hBox.setAlignment(Pos.CENTER);
24      Button btEnlarge = new Button("Enlarge");                               buttons
25      Button btShrink = new Button("Shrink");
26      hBox.getChildren().add(btEnlarge);
27      hBox.getChildren().add(btShrink);
28
29      BorderPane borderPane = new BorderPane();
30      borderPane.setCenter(pane);
31      borderPane.setBottom(hBox);
32      BorderPane.setAlignment(hBox, Pos.CENTER);
33
34      // Create a scene and place it in the stage
35      Scene scene = new Scene(borderPane, 200, 150);
36      primaryStage.setTitle("ControlCircle"); // Set the stage title
37      primaryStage.setScene(scene); // Place the scene in the stage
38      primaryStage.show(); // Display the stage
39    }
49  }
```

How do you use the buttons to enlarge or shrink the circle? When the *Enlarge* button is clicked, you want the circle to be repainted with a larger radius. How can you accomplish this? You can expand and modify the program in Listing 15.2 into Listing 15.3 with the following features: second version

1. Define a new class named `CirclePane` for displaying the circle in a pane (lines 51–68). This new class displays a circle and provides the `enlarge` and `shrink` methods for increasing and decreasing the radius of the circle (lines 60–62 and 64–67). It is a good strategy to design a class to model a circle pane with supporting methods so these related methods along with the circle are coupled in one object.

2. Create a `CirclePane` object and declare `circlePane` as a data field to reference this object (line 15) in the `ControlCircle` class. The methods in the `ControlCircle` class can now access the `CirclePane` object through this data field.

3. Define a handler class named `EnlargeHandler` that implements `EventHandler<ActionEvent>` (lines 43–48). To make the reference variable `circlePane` accessible from the `handle` method, define `EnlargeHandler` as an inner class of the `ControlCircle` class. (*Inner classes* are defined inside another class. We   inner class use an inner class here and will introduce it fully in the next section.)

4. Register the handler for the *Enlarge* button (line 29) and implement the `handle` method in `EnlargeHandler` to invoke `circlePane.enlarge()` (line 46).

VideoNote

Handler and its registration

LISTING 15.3 ControlCircle.java

```java
1  import javafx.application.Application;
2  import javafx.event.ActionEvent;
3  import javafx.event.EventHandler;
4  import javafx.geometry.Pos;
5  import javafx.scene.Scene;
6  import javafx.scene.control.Button;
7  import javafx.scene.layout.StackPane;
8  import javafx.scene.layout.HBox;
9  import javafx.scene.layout.BorderPane;
10 import javafx.scene.paint.Color;
11 import javafx.scene.shape.Circle;
12 import javafx.stage.Stage;
13
14 public class ControlCircle extends Application {
15   private CirclePane circlePane = new CirclePane();
16
17   @Override // Override the start method in the Application class
18   public void start(Stage primaryStage) {
19     // Hold two buttons in an HBox
20     HBox hBox = new HBox();
21     hBox.setSpacing(10);
22     hBox.setAlignment(Pos.CENTER);
23     Button btEnlarge = new Button("Enlarge");
24     Button btShrink = new Button("Shrink");
25     hBox.getChildren().add(btEnlarge);
26     hBox.getChildren().add(btShrink);
27
28     // Create and register the handler
29     btEnlarge.setOnAction(new EnlargeHandler());
30
31     BorderPane borderPane = new BorderPane();
32     borderPane.setCenter(circlePane);
33     borderPane.setBottom(hBox);
34     BorderPane.setAlignment(hBox, Pos.CENTER);
35
36     // Create a scene and place it in the stage
37     Scene scene = new Scene(borderPane, 200, 150);
38     primaryStage.setTitle("ControlCircle"); // Set the stage title
39     primaryStage.setScene(scene); // Place the scene in the stage
40     primaryStage.show(); // Display the stage
41   }
42
43   class EnlargeHandler implements EventHandler<ActionEvent> {
44     @Override // Override the handle method
45     public void handle(ActionEvent e) {
46       circlePane.enlarge();
47     }
48   }
49 }
50
51 class CirclePane extends StackPane {
52   private Circle circle = new Circle(50);
53
54   public CirclePane() {
55     getChildren().add(circle);
56     circle.setStroke(Color.BLACK);
57     circle.setFill(Color.WHITE);
58   }
```

create/register handler

handler class

CirclePane class

```
59
60    public void enlarge() {                                              enlarge method
61      circle.setRadius(circle.getRadius() + 2);
62    }
63
64    public void shrink() {
65      circle.setRadius(circle.getRadius() > 2 ?
66        circle.getRadius() - 2 : circle.getRadius());
67    }
68  }
```

As an exercise, add the code for handling the *Shrink* button to display a smaller circle when   the *Shrink* button
the *Shrink* button is clicked.

15.4 Inner Classes

An inner class, or nested class, is a class defined within the scope of another class.
Inner classes are useful for defining handler classes.

Key
Point

The approach of this book is to introduce difficult programming concepts using practical
examples. We introduce inner classes, anonymous inner classes, and lambda expressions using
practical examples in this section and following two sections.

Inner classes are used in the preceding section. This section introduces inner classes in
detail. First, let us see the code in Figure 15.7. The code in Figure 15.7a defines two separate
classes, `Test` and `A`. The code in Figure 15.7b defines `A` as an inner class in `Test`.

```
public class Test {
   ...
}

public class A {
   ...
}
```
(a)

```
public class Test {
   ...

   // Inner class
   public class A {
     ...
   }
}
```
(b)

```
// OuterClass.java: inner class demo
public class OuterClass {
  private int data;

  /** A method in the outer class */
  public void m() {
    // Do something
  }

  // An inner class
  class InnerClass {
    /** A method in the inner class */
    public void mi() {
      // Directly reference data and method
      // defined in its outer class
      data++;
      m();
    }
  }
}
```
(c)

FIGURE 15.7 An inner class is defined as a member of another class.

The class `InnerClass` defined inside `OuterClass` in Figure 15.7c is another example
of an inner class. An inner class may be used just like a regular class. Normally, you define

a class as an inner class if it is used only by its outer class. An inner class has the following features:

- An inner class is compiled into a class named `OuterClassName$InnerClassName.class`. For example, the inner class `A` in `Test` is compiled into `Test$A.class` in Figure 15.7b.

- An inner class can reference the data and the methods defined in the outer class in which it nests, so you need not pass the reference of an object of the outer class to the constructor of the inner class. For this reason, inner classes can make programs simple and concise. For example, `circlePane` is defined in `ControlCircle` in Listing 15.3 (line 15). It can be referenced in the inner class `EnlargeHandler` in line 46.

- An inner class can be defined with a visibility modifier subject to the same visibility rules applied to a member of the class.

- An inner class can be defined as `static`. A `static` inner class can be accessed using the outer class name. A `static` inner class cannot access nonstatic members of the outer class.

- Objects of an inner class are often created in the outer class. However, you can also create an object of an inner class from another class. If the inner class is nonstatic, you must first create an instance of the outer class, then use the following syntax to create an object for the inner class:

  ```
  OuterClass.InnerClass innerObject = outerObject.new InnerClass();
  ```

- If the inner class is static, use the following syntax to create an object for it:

  ```
  OuterClass.InnerClass innerObject = new OuterClass.InnerClass();
  ```

A simple use of inner classes is to combine dependent classes into a primary class. This reduces the number of source files. It also makes class files easy to organize since they are all named with the primary class as the prefix. For example, rather than creating the two source files **Test.java** and **A.java** as shown in Figure 15.7a, you can merge class `A` into class `Test` and create just one source file, **Test.java** as shown in Figure 15.7b. The resulting class files are **Test.class** and **Test$A.class**.

Another practical use of inner classes is to avoid class-naming conflicts. Two versions of `A` are defined in Figure 15.7a and 15.7b. You can define them as inner classes to avoid a conflict.

A handler class is designed specifically to create a handler object for a GUI component (e.g., a button). The handler class will not be shared by other applications and therefore is appropriate to be defined inside the main class as an inner class.

15.4.1 Can an inner class be used in a class other than the class in which it nests?

15.4.2 Can the modifiers `public`, `protected`, `private`, and `static` be used for inner classes?

15.5 Anonymous Inner-Class Handlers

An anonymous inner class is an inner class without a name. It combines defining an inner class and creating an instance of the class into one step.

anonymous inner class

Inner-class handlers can be shortened using *anonymous inner classes*. The inner class in Listing 15.3 can be replaced by an anonymous inner class as shown below. The complete code is available at liveexample.pearsoncmg.com/html/ControlCircleWithAnonymousInnerClass.html.

```
public void start(Stage primaryStage) {
  // Omitted

  btEnlarge.setOnAction(
    new EnlargeHandler());
}

class EnlargeHandler
    implements EventHandler<ActionEvent> {
  public void handle(ActionEvent e) {
    circlePane.enlarge();
  }
}
```

(a) Inner class `EnlargeListener`

```
public void start(Stage primaryStage) {
  // Omitted

  btEnlarge.setOnAction(
    new class EnlargeHandler
      implements EventHandler<ActionEvent>() {
      public void handle(ActionEvent e) {
        circlePane.enlarge();
      }
    });
}
```

(b) Anonymous inner class

The syntax for an anonymous inner class is shown below.

```
new SuperClassName/InterfaceName() {
  // Implement or override methods in superclass or interface

  // Other methods if necessary
}
```

Since an anonymous inner class is a special kind of inner class, it is treated like an inner class with the following features:

■ An anonymous inner class must always extend a superclass or implement an interface, but it cannot have an explicit `extends` or `implements` clause.

■ An anonymous inner class must implement all the abstract methods in the superclass or in the interface.

■ An anonymous inner class always uses the no-arg constructor from its superclass to create an instance. If an anonymous inner class implements an interface, the constructor is `Object()`.

■ An anonymous inner class is compiled into a class named `OuterClassName$n.class`. For example, if the outer class `Test` has two anonymous inner classes, they are compiled into `Test$1.class` and `Test$2.class`.

Listing 15.4 gives an example that displays a text and uses four buttons to move a text up, down, left, and right, as shown in Figure 15.8.

FIGURE 15.8 The program handles the events from four buttons.

LISTING 15.4 AnonymousHandlerDemo.java

```
1  import javafx.application.Application;
2  import javafx.event.ActionEvent;
3  import javafx.event.EventHandler;
4  import javafx.geometry.Pos;
```

VideoNote

Anonymous handler

```
 5   import javafx.scene.Scene;
 6   import javafx.scene.control.Button;
 7   import javafx.scene.layout.BorderPane;
 8   import javafx.scene.layout.HBox;
 9   import javafx.scene.layout.Pane;
10   import javafx.scene.text.Text;
11   import javafx.stage.Stage;
12
13   public class AnonymousHandlerDemo extends Application {
14     @Override // Override the start method in the Application class
15     public void start(Stage primaryStage) {
16       Text text = new Text(40, 40, "Programming is fun");
17       Pane pane = new Pane(text);
18
19       // Hold four buttons in an HBox
20       Button btUp = new Button("Up");
21       Button btDown = new Button("Down");
22       Button btLeft = new Button("Left");
23       Button btRight = new Button("Right");
24       HBox hBox = new HBox(btUp, btDown, btLeft, btRight);
25       hBox.setSpacing(10);
26       hBox.setAlignment(Pos.CENTER);
27
28       BorderPane borderPane = new BorderPane(pane);
29       borderPane.setBottom(hBox);
30
31       // Create and register the handler
32       btUp.setOnAction(new EventHandler<ActionEvent>() {
33         @Override // Override the handle method
34         public void handle(ActionEvent e) {
35           text.setY(text.getY() > 10 ? text.getY() - 5 : 10);
36         }
37       });
38
39       btDown.setOnAction(new EventHandler<ActionEvent>() {
40         @Override // Override the handle method
41         public void handle(ActionEvent e) {
42           text.setY(text.getY() < pane.getHeight() ?
43             text.getY() + 5 : pane.getHeight());
44         }
45       });
46
47       btLeft.setOnAction(new EventHandler<ActionEvent>() {
48         @Override // Override the handle method
49         public void handle(ActionEvent e) {
50           text.setX(text.getX() > 0 ? text.getX() - 5 : 0);
51         }
52       });
53
54       btRight.setOnAction(new EventHandler<ActionEvent>() {
55         @Override // Override the handle method
56         public void handle(ActionEvent e) {
57           text.setX(text.getX() < pane.getWidth() - 100?
58             text.getX() + 5 : pane.getWidth() - 100);
59         }
60       });
61
62       // Create a scene and place it in the stage
63       Scene scene = new Scene(borderPane, 400, 350);
64       primaryStage.setTitle("AnonymousHandlerDemo"); // Set title
```

anonymous handler

handle event

```
65        primaryStage.setScene(scene); // Place the scene in the stage
66        primaryStage.show(); // Display the stage
67    }
68  }
```

The program creates four handlers using anonymous inner classes (lines 32–60). Without using anonymous inner classes, you would have to create four separate classes. An anonymous handler works the same way as that of an inner-class handler. The program is condensed using an anonymous inner class. Another benefit of using anonymous inner class is the handler can access local variables. In this example, the event handler references local variable `text` (lines 35, 42, 50, and 57).

The anonymous inner classes in this example are compiled into `AnonymousHandlerDemo$1.class`, `AnonymousHandlerDemo$2.class`, `AnonymousHandlerDemo$3.class`, and `AnonymousHandlerDemo$4.class`.

15.5.1 If class `A` is an inner class in class `B`, what is the .class file for `A`? If class `B` contains two anonymous inner classes, what are the .class file names for these two classes?

Check
Point

15.5.2 What is wrong in the following code?

```
public class Test extends Application {
  public void start(Stage stage) {
    Button btOK = new Button("OK");
  }

  private class Handler implements
      EventHandler<ActionEvent> {
    public void handle(Action e) {
      System.out.println(e.getSource());
    }
  }
}
```

(a)

```
public class Test extends Application {
  public void start(Stage stage) {
    Button btOK = new Button("OK");

    btOK.setOnAction(
      new EventHandler<ActionEvent> {
        public void handle
            (ActionEvent e) {
          System.out.println
            (e.getSource());
        }
    } // Something missing here
  }
}
```

(b)

15.6 Simplifying Event Handling Using Lambda Expressions

Lambda expressions can be used to greatly simplify coding for event handling.

Lambda expression is a new feature in Java 8. Lambda expressions can be viewed as an anonymous class with a concise syntax. For example, the following code in (a) can be greatly simplified using a lambda expression in (b) in three lines. The complete code that contains the lambda expression in (b) can be seen at liveexample.pearsoncmg.com/html/ControlCircle-WithLambdaExpression.html.

Key
Point

lambda expression

```
btEnlarge.setOnAction {
  new EventHandler<ActionEvent>() {
    @Override
    public void handle(ActionEvent e) {
      // Code for processing event e
    }
  }
});
```

(a) Anonymous inner class event handler

```
btEnlarge.setOnAction(e -> {
  // Code for processing event e
});
```

(b) Lambda expression event handler

The basic syntax for a lambda expression is either

```
(type1 param1, type2 param2, . . . ) -> expression
```

or

```
(type1 param1, type2 param2, . . . ) -> { statements; }
```

The data type for a parameter may be explicitly declared or implicitly inferred by the compiler. The parentheses can be omitted if there is only one parameter without an explicit data type. The curly braces can be omitted if there is only one statement. For example, the following lambda expressions are all equivalent. *Note there is no semicolon after the statement in (d).*

```
(ActiionEvent e) -> {
   circlePane.enlarge(); }
```

(a) Lambda expression with one statement

```
(e) -> {
   circlePane.enlarge(); }
```

(b) Omit parameter data type

```
e -> {
   circlePane.enlarge(); }
```

(c) Omit parentheses

```
e ->
   circlePane.enlarge()
```

(d) Omit braces

The compiler treats a lambda expression as if it is an object created from an anonymous inner class. The compiler processes a lambda expression in three steps: (1) identify the lambda expression type, (2) identify the parameter types, and (3) identify statements. Consider the following lambda expression:

```
btEnlarge.setOnAction(
   e -> {
   // Code for processing event e
   }
);
```

It is processed as follows:

Step 1: The compiler recognizes that the object must be an instance of EventHandler <ActionEvent>, since the expression is an argument of the setOnAction method as shown in the following figure:

```
btEnlarge.setOnAction(
   e -> {
   // code for processing event e
   }
);
```

(1) The compiler recognizes that the lambda expression is an object of the EventHandler<ActionEvent> type, because the expression is an argument in the setOnAction method.

(2) The compiler recognizes that e is a parameter of the ActionEvent type, since the EventHandler<ActionEvent> interface defines the handle method with a parameter of the ActionEvent type.

(3) The compiler recognizes that the code for processing event e are the statements in the handle method.

Step 2: Since the EventHandler interface defines the handle method with a parameter of the ActionEvent type, the compiler recognizes that e is a parameter of the ActionEvent type.

Step 3: The compiler recognizes that the code for processing e is the statements in the body of the handle method.

The EventHandler interface contains just one method named handle. The statements in the lambda expression are all for that method. If it contains multiple methods, the compiler will not be able to compile the lambda expression. Therefore, for the compiler to understand lambda expressions, the interface must contain exactly one abstract method. Such an interface is known as a *Single Abstract Method* (SAM) *interface*.

SAM interface

In essence, a lambda expression creates an object and the object performs a function by invoking this single method. Thus, a SAM interface is also known as a *functional interface*, and an instance of a functional interface is known as a *function object*. Since a lambda expression is squarely on defining a function, a lambda expression is also called a *lambda function*. The terms lambda expression and lambda function are interchangeable.

functional interface
function object
lambda function
functional programming

Listing 15.4 can be simplified using lambda expressions as shown in Listing 15.5.

LISTING 15.5   LambdaHandlerDemo.java

```
1  import javafx.application.Application;
2  import javafx.event.ActionEvent;
3  import javafx.event.EventHandler;
4  import javafx.geometry.Pos;
5  import javafx.scene.Scene;
6  import javafx.scene.control.Button;
7  import javafx.scene.layout.BorderPane;
8  import javafx.scene.layout.HBox;
9  import javafx.scene.layout.Pane;
10 import javafx.scene.text.Text;
11 import javafx.stage.Stage;
12
13 public class LambdaHandlerDemo extends Application {
14   @Override // Override the start method in the Application class
15   public void start(Stage primaryStage) {
16     Text text = new Text(40, 40, "Programming is fun");
17     Pane pane = new Pane(text);
18
19     // Hold four buttons in an HBox
20     Button btUp = new Button("Up");
21     Button btDown = new Button("Down");
22     Button btLeft = new Button("Left");
23     Button btRight = new Button("Right");
24     HBox hBox = new HBox(btUp, btDown, btLeft, btRight);
25     hBox.setSpacing(10);
26     hBox.setAlignment(Pos.CENTER);
27
28     BorderPane borderPane = new BorderPane(pane);
29     borderPane.setBottom(hBox);
30
31     // Create and register the handler
32     btUp.setOnAction((ActionEvent e) -> {
33       text.setY(text.getY() > 10 ? text.getY() - 5 : 10);
34     });
35
36     btDown.setOnAction((e) -> {
37       text.setY(text.getY() < pane.getHeight() ?
38         text.getY() + 5 : pane.getHeight());
39     });
40
41     btLeft.setOnAction(e -> {
42       text.setX(text.getX() > 0 ? text.getX() - 5 : 0);
43     });
44
45     btRight.setOnAction(e ->
46       text.setX(text.getX() < pane.getWidth() - 100?
47         text.getX() + 5 : pane.getWidth() - 100)
```

lambda handler (line 32)
lambda handler (line 36)
lambda handler (line 41)
lambda handler (line 45)

```
48        );
49
50        // Create a scene and place it in the stage
51        Scene scene = new Scene(borderPane, 400, 350);
52        primaryStage.setTitle("AnonymousHandlerDemo"); // Set title
53        primaryStage.setScene(scene); // Place the scene in the stage
54        primaryStage.show(); // Display the stage
55      }
56    }
```

The program creates four handlers using lambda expressions (lines 32–48). Using lambda expressions, the code is shorter and cleaner. As seen in this example, lambda expressions may have many variations. Line 32 uses a declared type. Line 36 uses an inferred type since the type can be determined by the compiler. Line 41 omits the parentheses for a single inferred type. Line 45 omits the braces for a single statement in the body.

inner class, anonymous class, or Lambda?

You can handle events by defining handler classes using inner classes, anonymous inner classes, or lambda expressions. We recommend you use lambda expressions because it produces a shorter, clearer, and cleaner code.

simplify syntax
simplify concept

Using lambda expressions not only simplifies the syntax, but also simplifies the event-handling concept. For the statement in line 45,

(1) When the button is clicked   (2) This function is performed

```
btRight.setOnAction(e -> move the text right);
```

you can now simply say that when the btRight button is clicked, the lambda function is invoked to move the text right.

You can define a custom functional interface and use it in a lambda expression. Consider the following example:

```
1  public class TestLambda {
2    public static void main(String[] args) {
3      TestLambda test = new TestLambda();
4      test.setAction1(() -> System.out.print("Action 1! "));
5      test.setAction2(e -> System.out.print(e + " "));
6      System.out.println(test.getValue((e1, e2) -> e1 + e2));
7    }
8
9    public void setAction1(T1 t) {
10     t.m1();
11   }
12
13   public void setAction2(T2 t) {
14     t.m2(4.5);
15   }
16
17   public int getValue(T3 t) {
18     return t.m3(5, 2);
19   }
20 }
21
22 @FunctionalInterface
23 interface T1 {
24   public void m1();
25 }
26
27 @FunctionalInterface
28 interface T2 {
```

```
29     public void m2(Double d);
30   }
31
32   @FunctionalInterface
33   interface T3 {
34     public int m3(int d1, int d2);
35   }
```

The annotation `@FunctionalInterface` tells the compiler that the interface is a functional interface. Since `T1`, `T2`, and `T3` are all functional interfaces, a lambda expression can be used with the methods `setAction1(T1)`, `setAction2(T2)`, and `getValue(T3)`. The statement in line 4 is equivalent to using an anonymous inner class, as follows:

```
test.setAction1(new T1() {
  @Override
  public void m1() {
    System.out.print("Action 1! ");
  }
});
```

15.6.1 What is a lambda expression? What is the benefit of using lambda expressions for event handling? What is the syntax of a lambda expression?

15.6.2 What is a functional interface? Why is a functional interface required for a lambda expression?

15.6.3 Replace the code in lines 5 and 6 in `TestLambda.java` using anonymous inner classes.

15.7 Case Study: Loan Calculator

This case study develops a loan calculator using event-driven programming with GUI controls.

Now, we will write the program for the loan-calculator problem presented at the beginning of this chapter. Here are the major steps in the program:

1. Create the user interface, as shown in Figure 15.9.

   a. Create a `GridPane`. Add labels, text fields, and button to the pane.

   b. Set the alignment of the button to the right.

2. Process the event.

   Create and register the handler for processing the button-clicking action event. The handler obtains the user input on the loan amount, interest rate, and number of years, computes the monthly and total payments, and displays the values in the text fields.

FIGURE 15.9 The program computes loan payments.

The complete program is given in Listing 15.6.

LISTING 15.6 LoanCalculator.java

```
1  import javafx.application.Application;
2  import javafx.geometry.Pos;
3  import javafx.geometry.HPos;
4  import javafx.scene.Scene;
5  import javafx.scene.control.Button;
6  import javafx.scene.control.Label;
7  import javafx.scene.control.TextField;
8  import javafx.scene.layout.GridPane;
9  import javafx.stage.Stage;
10
11 public class LoanCalculator extends Application {
12   private TextField tfAnnualInterestRate = new TextField();
13   private TextField tfNumberOfYears = new TextField();
14   private TextField tfLoanAmount = new TextField();
15   private TextField tfMonthlyPayment = new TextField();
16   private TextField tfTotalPayment = new TextField();
17   private Button btCalculate = new Button("Calculate");
18
19   @Override // Override the start method in the Application class
20   public void start(Stage primaryStage) {
21     // Create UI
22     GridPane gridPane = new GridPane();
23     gridPane.setHgap(5);
24     gridPane.setVgap(5);
25     gridPane.add(new Label("Annual Interest Rate:"), 0, 0);
26     gridPane.add(tfAnnualInterestRate, 1, 0);
27     gridPane.add(new Label("Number of Years:"), 0, 1);
28     gridPane.add(tfNumberOfYears, 1, 1);
29     gridPane.add(new Label("Loan Amount:"), 0, 2);
30     gridPane.add(tfLoanAmount, 1, 2);
31     gridPane.add(new Label("Monthly Payment:"), 0, 3);
32     gridPane.add(tfMonthlyPayment, 1, 3);
33     gridPane.add(new Label("Total Payment:"), 0, 4);
34     gridPane.add(tfTotalPayment, 1, 4);
35     gridPane.add(btCalculate, 1, 5);
36
37     // Set properties for UI
38     gridPane.setAlignment(Pos.CENTER);
39     tfAnnualInterestRate.setAlignment(Pos.BOTTOM_RIGHT);
40     tfNumberOfYears.setAlignment(Pos.BOTTOM_RIGHT);
41     tfLoanAmount.setAlignment(Pos.BOTTOM_RIGHT);
42     tfMonthlyPayment.setAlignment(Pos.BOTTOM_RIGHT);
43     tfTotalPayment.setAlignment(Pos.BOTTOM_RIGHT);
44     tfMonthlyPayment.setEditable(false);
45     tfTotalPayment.setEditable(false);
46     GridPane.setHalignment(btCalculate, HPos.RIGHT);
47
48     // Process events
49     btCalculate.setOnAction(e -> calculateLoanPayment());
50
51     // Create a scene and place it in the stage
52     Scene scene = new Scene(gridPane, 400, 250);
53     primaryStage.setTitle("LoanCalculator"); // Set title
54     primaryStage.setScene(scene); // Place the scene in the stage
55     primaryStage.show(); // Display the stage
56   }
```

Margin notes:
- text fields (line 12)
- button (line 17)
- create a grid pane (line 22)
- add to grid pane (line 25)
- register handler (line 49)

```
57
58    private void calculateLoanPayment() {
59      // Get values from text fields
60      double interest =
61        Double.parseDouble(tfAnnualInterestRate.getText());          get input
62      int year = Integer.parseInt(tfNumberOfYears.getText());
63      double loanAmount =
64        Double.parseDouble(tfLoanAmount.getText());
65
66      // Create a loan object. Loan defined in Listing 10.2
67      Loan loan = new Loan(interest, year, loanAmount);            create loan
68
69      // Display monthly payment and total payment
70      tfMonthlyPayment.setText(String.format("$%.2f",             set result
71        loan.getMonthlyPayment()));
72      tfTotalPayment.setText(String.format("$%.2f",
73        loan.getTotalPayment()));
74    }
75  }
```

The user interface is created in the `start` method (lines 22–46). The button is the source of the event. A handler is created and registered with the button (line 49). The button handler invokes the `calculateLoanPayment()` method to get the interest rate (line 60), number of years (line 62), and loan amount (line 64). Invoking `tfAnnualInterestRate.getText()` returns the string text in the `tfAnnualInterestRate` text field. The `Loan` class is used for computing the loan payments. This class was introduced in Listing 10.2, Loan.java. Invoking `loan.getMonthlyPayment()` returns the monthly payment for the loan (line 71). The `String.format` method, introduced in Section 10.10.7, is used to format a number into a desirable format and returns it as a string (lines 70 and 72). Invoking the `setText` method on a text field sets a string value in the text field.

15.8 Mouse Events

A `MouseEvent` is fired whenever a mouse button is pressed, released, clicked, moved, or dragged on a node or a scene.

Key
Point

The `MouseEvent` object captures the event, such as the number of clicks associated with it, the location (the *x*- and *y*-coordinates) of the mouse, or which mouse button was pressed, as shown in Figure 15.10.

javafx.scene.input.MouseEvent	
+getButton(): MouseButton	Indicates which mouse button has been clicked.
+getClickCount(): int	Returns the number of mouse clicks associated with this event.
+getX(): double	Returns the *x*-coordinate of the mouse point in the event source node.
+getY(): double	Returns the *y*-coordinate of the mouse point in the event source node.
+getSceneX(): double	Returns the *x*-coordinate of the mouse point in the scene.
+getSceneY(): double	Returns the *y*-coordinate of the mouse point in the scene.
+getScreenX(): double	Returns the *x*-coordinate of the mouse point in the screen.
+getScreenY(): double	Returns the *y*-coordinate of the mouse point in the screen.
+isAltDown(): boolean	Returns true if the Alt key is pressed on this event.
+isControlDown(): boolean	Returns true if the Control key is pressed on this event.
+isMetaDown(): boolean	Returns true if the mouse Meta button is pressed on this event.
+isShiftDown(): boolean	Returns true if the Shift key is pressed on this event.

FIGURE 15.10 The `MouseEvent` class encapsulates information for mouse events.

Four constants—PRIMARY, SECONDARY, MIDDLE, and NONE—are defined in MouseButton to indicate the left, right, middle, and none mouse buttons, respectively. You can use the getButton() method to detect which button is pressed. For example, getButton() == MouseButton.SECONDARY tests if the right button was pressed. You can also use the isPrimaryButtonDown(), isSecondaryButtonDown(), and isMiddleButtonDown() to test if the primary button, second button, or middle button is pressed.

detect mouse buttons

The mouse events and their corresponding registration methods for handlers are listed in Table 15.1. To demonstrate using mouse events, we give an example that displays a message in a pane and enables the message to be moved using a mouse. The message moves as the mouse is dragged, and it is always displayed at the mouse point. Listing 15.7 gives the program. A sample run of the program is shown in Figure 15.11.

FIGURE 15.11 You can move the message by dragging the mouse.

VideoNote

Move message using the mouse

LISTING 15.7 MouseEventDemo.java

```
1  import javafx.application.Application;
2  import javafx.scene.Scene;
3  import javafx.scene.layout.Pane;
4  import javafx.scene.text.Text;
5  import javafx.stage.Stage;
6
7  public class MouseEventDemo extends Application {
8    @Override // Override the start method in the Application class
9    public void start(Stage primaryStage) {
10     // Create a pane and set its properties
11     Pane pane = new Pane();
12     Text text = new Text(20, 20, "Programming is fun");
13     pane.getChildren().addAll(text);
14     text.setOnMouseDragged(e -> {
15       text.setX(e.getX());
16       text.setY(e.getY());
17     });
18
19     // Create a scene and place it in the stage
20     Scene scene = new Scene(pane, 300, 100);
21     primaryStage.setTitle("MouseEventDemo"); // Set the stage title
22     primaryStage.setScene(scene); // Place the scene in the stage
23     primaryStage.show(); // Display the stage
24   }
25 }
```

create a pane
create a text
add text to a pane
lambda handler
reset text position

Each node or scene can fire mouse events. The program creates a Text (line 12) and registers a handler to handle move dragged event (line 14). Whenever a mouse is dragged, the text's *x*- and *y*-coordinates are set to the mouse position (lines 15 and 16).

Check Point

15.8.1 What method do you use to get the mouse-point position for a mouse event?

15.8.2 What methods do you use to register a handler for mouse-pressed, -released, -clicked, -entered, -exited, -moved, and -dragged events?

15.9 Key Events

A KeyEvent *is fired whenever a key is pressed, released, or typed on a node or a scene.*

Key
Point

Key events enable the use of the keys to control and perform actions, or get input from the keyboard. The KeyEvent object describes the nature of the event (namely, that a key has been pressed, released, or typed) and the value of the key, as shown in Figure 15.12.

javafx.scene.input.KeyEvent	
+getCharacter(): String	Returns the character associated with the key in this event.
+getCode(): KeyCode	Returns the key code associated with the key in this event.
+getText(): String	Returns a string describing the key code.
+isAltDown(): boolean	Returns true if the Alt key is pressed on this event.
+isControlDown(): boolean	Returns true if the Control key is pressed on this event.
+isMetaDown(): boolean	Returns true if the mouse Meta button is pressed on this event.
+isShiftDown(): boolean	Returns true if the Shift key is pressed on this event.

FIGURE 15.12 The KeyEvent class encapsulates information about key events.

The key events key pressed, key released, and key typed and their corresponding registration methods for handlers are listed in Table 15.1. The key pressed handler is invoked when a key is pressed, the key released handler is invoked when a key is released, and the key typed handler is invoked when a Unicode character is entered. If a key does not have a Unicode (e.g., function keys, modifier keys, action keys, arrow keys, and control keys), the key typed handler will not be invoked.

Every key event has an associated code that is returned by the getCode() method in KeyEvent. The *key codes* are constants defined in KeyCode. Table 15.2 lists some constants. KeyCode is an enum type. For use of enum types, see Appendix I. For the key-pressed and key-released events, getCode() returns the value as defined in the table, getText() returns a string that describes the key code, and getCharacter() returns an empty string. For the key-typed event, getCode() returns UNDEFINED and getCharacter() returns the Unicode character or a sequence of characters associated with the key-typed event.

key code

TABLE 15.2 KeyCode Constants

Constant	Description	Constant	Description
HOME	The Home key	CONTROL	The Control key
END	The End key	SHIFT	The Shift key
PAGE_UP	The Page Up key	BACK_SPACE	The Backspace key
PAGE_DOWN	The Page Down key	CAPS	The Caps Lock key
UP	The up-arrow key	NUM_LOCK	The Num Lock key
DOWN	The down-arrow key	ENTER	The Enter key
LEFT	The left-arrow key	UNDEFINED	The keyCode unknown
RIGHT	The right-arrow key	F1 to F12	The function keys from F1 to F12
ESCAPE	The Esc key	0 to 9	The number keys from 0 to 9
TAB	The Tab key	A to Z	The letter keys from A to Z

The program in Listing 15.8 displays a user-input character. The user can move the character up, down, left, and right, using the up-, down-, left-, and right-arrow keys, respectively. Figure 15.13 contains a sample run of the program.

FIGURE 15.13 The program responds to key events by displaying a character and moving it up, down, left, or right.

LISTING 15.8 KeyEventDemo.java

```
1  import javafx.application.Application;
2  import javafx.scene.Scene;
3  import javafx.scene.layout.Pane;
4  import javafx.scene.text.Text;
5  import javafx.stage.Stage;
6
7  public class KeyEventDemo extends Application {
8    @Override // Override the start method in the Application class
9    public void start(Stage primaryStage) {
10     // Create a pane and set its properties
11     Pane pane = new Pane();
12     Text text = new Text(20, 20, "A");
13
14     pane.getChildren().add(text);
15     text.setOnKeyPressed(e -> {
16       switch (e.getCode()) {
17         case DOWN: text.setY(text.getY() + 10); break;
18         case UP: text.setY(text.getY() - 10); break;
19         case LEFT: text.setX(text.getX() - 10); break;
20         case RIGHT: text.setX(text.getX() + 10); break;
21         default:
22           if (e.getText().length > 0)
23             text.setText(e.getText());
24       }
25     });
26
27     // Create a scene and place it in the stage
28     Scene scene = new Scene(pane);
29     primaryStage.setTitle("KeyEventDemo"); // Set the stage title
30     primaryStage.setScene(scene); // Place the scene in the stage
31     primaryStage.show(); // Display the stage
32
33     text.requestFocus(); // text is focused to receive key input
34   }
35 }
```

Margin notes: create a pane (line 11); register handler, get the key pressed, move a character (lines 15–20); set a new character (line 23); request focus on text (line 33).

The program creates a pane (line 11), creates a text (line 12), and places the text into the pane (line 14). The text registers the handler for the key-pressed event in lines 15–25. When a key is pressed, the handler is invoked. The program uses `e.getCode()` (line 16) to obtain the key code and `e.getText()` (line 23) to get the character for the key. Note for a nonprintable character such as a CTRL key or SHIFT key, `e.getText()` returns an empty string. When a non-arrow key is pressed, the character is displayed (lines 22 and 23). When an arrow key is pressed, the character moves in the direction indicated by the arrow key (lines 17–20). Note in a switch statement for an enum-type value, the cases are for the enum constants (lines 16–24). The constants are unqualified. For example, using KeyCode.DOWN in the case clause would be wrong (see Appendix I).

Only a focused node can receive KeyEvent. Invoking requestFocus() on text enables text to receive key input (line 33). This method must be invoked after the stage is displayed. The program would work fine if text is replaced by scene in line 21 as follows:

```
scene.setOnKeyPressed(e -> { ... });
```

You don't need to invoke scene.requestFocus() because scene is a top-level container for receiving key events.

We can now add more control for our ControlCircle example in Listing 15.3 to increase/decrease the circle radius by clicking the left/right mouse button or by pressing the up and down arrow keys. The new program is given in Listing 15.9.

requestFocus()

LISTING 15.9 ControlCircleWithMouseAndKey.java

```java
1  import javafx.application.Application;
2  import javafx.geometry.Pos;
3  import javafx.scene.Scene;
4  import javafx.scene.control.Button;
5  import javafx.scene.input.KeyCode;
6  import javafx.scene.input.MouseButton;
7  import javafx.scene.layout.HBox;
8  import javafx.scene.layout.BorderPane;
9  import javafx.stage.Stage;
10
11 public class ControlCircleWithMouseAndKey extends Application {
12   private CirclePane circlePane = new CirclePane();
13
14   @Override // Override the start method in the Application class
15   public void start(Stage primaryStage) {
16     // Hold two buttons in an HBox
17     HBox hBox = new HBox();
18     hBox.setSpacing(10);
19     hBox.setAlignment(Pos.CENTER);
20     Button btEnlarge = new Button("Enlarge");
21     Button btShrink = new Button("Shrink");
22     hBox.getChildren().add(btEnlarge);
23     hBox.getChildren().add(btShrink);
24
25     // Create and register the handler
26     btEnlarge.setOnAction(e -> circlePane.enlarge());
27     btShrink.setOnAction(e -> circlePane.shrink());
28
29     BorderPane borderPane = new BorderPane();
30     borderPane.setCenter(circlePane);
31     borderPane.setBottom(hBox);
32     BorderPane.setAlignment(hBox, Pos.CENTER);
33
34     // Create a scene and place it in the stage
35     Scene scene = new Scene(borderPane, 200, 150);
36     primaryStage.setTitle("ControlCircle"); // Set the stage title
37     primaryStage.setScene(scene); // Place the scene in the stage
38     primaryStage.show(); // Display the stage
39
40     circlePane.setOnMouseClicked(e -> {
41       if (e.getButton() == MouseButton.PRIMARY) {
42         circlePane.enlarge();
43       }
```

button handler

mouse-click handler

```
44              else if (e.getButton() == MouseButton.SECONDARY) {
45                  circlePane.shrink();
46              }
47          });
48
49          scene.setOnKeyPressed(e -> {
50              if (e.getCode() == KeyCode.UP) {
51                  circlePane.enlarge();
52              }
53              else if (e.getCode() == KeyCode.DOWN) {
54                  circlePane.shrink();
55              }
56          });
57      }
58  }
```

key-pressed handler
Up-arrow key pressed

Down-arrow key pressed

The `CirclePane` class (line 12) is already defined in Listing 15.3 and can be reused in this program.

A handler for mouse-clicked events is created in lines 40–47. If the left mouse button is clicked, the circle is enlarged (lines 41–43); if the right mouse button is clicked, the circle is shrunk (lines 44–46).

mouse-clicked event

A handler for key-pressed events is created in lines 49–56. If the up arrow key is pressed, the circle is enlarged (lines 50–52); if the down arrow key is pressed, the circle is shrunk (lines 53–55).

key-pressed event

✓Check Point

15.9.1 What methods do you use to register handlers for key-pressed, key-released, and key-typed events? In which classes are these methods defined? (See Table 15.1.)

15.9.2 What method do you use to get the key character for a key-typed event? What method do you use to get the key code for a key-pressed or key-released event?

15.9.3 How do you set focus on a node so it can listen for key events?

15.9.4 If the following code is inserted in line 57 in Listing 15.9, what is the output if the user presses the key for letter A? What is the output if the user presses the up arrow key?

```
circlePane.setOnKeyPressed(e ->
    System.out.println("Key pressed " + e.getCode()));
circlePane.setOnKeyTyped(e ->
    System.out.println("Key typed " + e.getCode()));
```

15.10 Listeners for Observable Objects

You can add a listener to process a value change in an observable object.

Key Point

An instance of `Observable` is known as an *observable object*, which contains the `addListener(InvalidationListener listener)` method for adding a listener. The listener class must implement the functional interface `InvalidationListener` to override the `invalidated(Observable o)` method for handling the value change. Once the value is changed in the `Observable` object, the listener is notified by invoking its `invalidated(Observable o)` method. Every binding property is an instance of `Observable`. Listing 15.10 gives an example of observing and handling a change in a `DoubleProperty` object `balance`.

observable object

LISTING 15.10 `ObservablePropertyDemo.java`

```
1  import javafx.beans.InvalidationListener;
2  import javafx.beans.Observable;
3  import javafx.beans.property.DoubleProperty;
```

```
 4   import javafx.beans.property.SimpleDoubleProperty;
 5
 6   public class ObservablePropertyDemo {
 7     public static void main(String[] args) {
 8       DoubleProperty balance = new SimpleDoubleProperty();      observable property
 9       balance.addListener(new InvalidationListener() {          add listener
10         public void invalidated(Observable ov) {                handle change
11           System.out.println("The new value is " +
12             balance.doubleValue());
13         }
14       });
15
16       balance.set(4.5);
17     }
18   }
```

```
The new value is 4.5
```

When line 16 is executed, it causes a change in balance, which notifies the listener by invoking the listener's `invalidated` method.

Note the anonymous inner class in lines 9–14 can be simplified using a lambda expression as follows:

```
balance.addListener(ov -> {
  System.out.println("The new value is " +
    balance.doubleValue());
});
```

Listing 15.11 gives a program that displays a circle with its bounding rectangle, as shown in Figure 15.14. The circle and rectangle are automatically resized when the user resizes the window.

LISTING 15.11 ResizableCircleRectangle.java

```
 1   import javafx.application.Application;
 2   import javafx.scene.paint.Color;
 3   import javafx.scene.shape.Circle;
 4   import javafx.scene.shape.Rectangle;
 5   import javafx.stage.Stage;
 6   import javafx.scene.Scene;
 7   import javafx.scene.control.Label;
 8   import javafx.scene.layout.StackPane;
 9
10   public class ResizableCircleRectangle extends Application {
11     // Create a circle and a rectangle
12     private Circle circle = new Circle(60);
13     private Rectangle rectangle = new Rectangle(120, 120);
14
15     // Place clock and label in border pane
16     private StackPane pane = new StackPane();
17
18     @Override // Override the start method in the Application class
19     public void start(Stage primaryStage) {
20       circle.setFill(Color.GRAY);
21       rectangle.setFill(Color.WHITE);
22       rectangle.setStroke(Color.BLACK);
23       pane.getChildren().addAll(rectangle, circle);
```

```
24
25      // Create a scene and place the pane in the stage
26      Scene scene = new Scene(pane, 140, 140);
27      primaryStage.setTitle("ResizableCircleRectangle");
28      primaryStage.setScene(scene); // Place the scene in the stage
29      primaryStage.show(); // Display the stage
30
31      pane.widthProperty().addListener(ov -> resize());
32      pane.heightProperty().addListener(ov -> resize());
33    }
34
35    private void resize() {
36      double length = Math.min(pane.getWidth(), pane.getHeight());
37      circle.setRadius(length / 2 - 15);
38      rectangle.setWidth(length - 30);
39      rectangle.setHeight(length - 30);
40    }
41  }
```

set a new width for clock
set a new height for clock

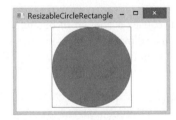

FIGURE 15.14 The program places a rectangle and a circle inside a stack pane, and automatically sets their sizes when the window is resized.

The program registers the listeners for the stack pane's `width` and `height` properties (lines 31 and 32). When the user resizes the window, the pane's size is changed, so the listeners are called to invoke the `resize()` method to change the size of the circle and rectangle (lines 35–40).

15.10.1 What would happen if you replace `pane` with `scene` or `primaryStage` in lines 31–32?

VideoNote

Animate a rising flag

15.11 Animation

JavaFX provides the `Animation` class with the core functionality for all animations.

Suppose you want to write a program that animates a rising flag, as shown in Figure 15.15. How do you accomplish the task? There are several ways to program this. An effective one is to use the subclasses of the JavaFX `Animation` class, which is the subject of this section.

FIGURE 15.15 The animation simulates a flag rising. *Source*: booka/Fotolia.

The abstract `Animation` class provides the core functionalities for animations in JavaFX, as shown in Figure 15.16. Many concrete subclasses of `Animation` are provided in JavaFX. This section introduces `PathTransition`, `FadeTransition,` and `Timeline`.

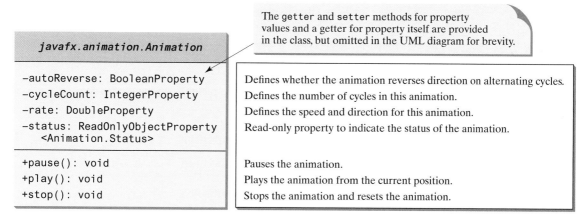

FIGURE 15.16   The abstract `Animation` class is the root class for JavaFX animations.

The `autoReverse` is a Boolean property that indicates whether an animation will reverse its direction on the next cycle. The `cycleCount` indicates the number of the cycles for the animation. You can use the constant `Timeline.INDEFINITE` to indicate an indefinite number of cycles. The `rate` defines the speed of the animation. A negative rate value indicates the opposite direction for the animation. The `status` is a read-only property that indicates the status of the animation (`Animation.Status.PAUSED`, `Animation.Status.RUNNING`, and `Animation.Status.STOPPED`). The methods `pause()`, `play()`, and `stop()` pause, play, and stop an animation, respectively.

15.11.1   PathTransition

The `PathTransition` class animates the moves of a node along a path from one end to the other over a given time. `PathTransition` is a subtype of `Animation`. The UML class diagram for the class is shown in Figure 15.17.

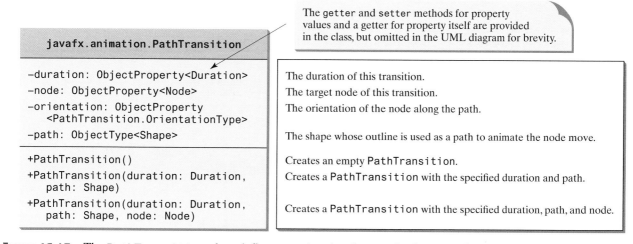

FIGURE 15.17   The `PathTransition` class defines an animation for a node along a path.

The `Duration` class defines a duration of time. It is an immutable class. The class defines constants `INDEFINITE`, `ONE`, `UNKNOWN`, and `ZERO` to represent an indefinte duration, one millisecond, unknown, and zero duration, respectively. You can use `new Duration(double millis)` to create an instance of `Duration`, the `add`, `subtract`, `multiply`, and `divide` methods to perform arithmetic operations, and the `toHours()`, `toMinutes()`, `toSeconds()`, and `toMillis()` to return the number of hours, minutes, seconds, and milliseconds in this duration, respectively. You can also use `compareTo` to compare two durations.

The constants `NONE` and `ORTHOGONAL_TO_TANGENT` are defined in `PathTransition .OrientationType`. The latter specifies that the node is kept perpendicular to the path's tangent along the geometric path.

Listing 15.12 gives an example that moves a rectangle along the outline of a circle, as shown in Figure 15.18a.

LISTING 15.12 PathTransitionDemo.java

```java
 1  import javafx.animation.PathTransition;
 2  import javafx.animation.Timeline;
 3  import javafx.application.Application;
 4  import javafx.scene.Scene;
 5  import javafx.scene.layout.Pane;
 6  import javafx.scene.paint.Color;
 7  import javafx.scene.shape.Rectangle;
 8  import javafx.scene.shape.Circle;
 9  import javafx.stage.Stage;
10  import javafx.util.Duration;
11
12  public class PathTransitionDemo extends Application {
13    @Override // Override the start method in the Application class
14    public void start(Stage primaryStage) {
15      // Create a pane
16      Pane pane = new Pane();
17
18      // Create a rectangle
19      Rectangle rectangle = new Rectangle (0, 0, 25, 50);
20      rectangle.setFill(Color.ORANGE);
21
22      // Create a circle
23      Circle circle = new Circle(125, 100, 50);
24      circle.setFill(Color.WHITE);
25      circle.setStroke(Color.BLACK);
26
27      // Add circle and rectangle to the pane
28      pane.getChildren().add(circle);
29      pane.getChildren().add(rectangle);
30
31      // Create a path transition
32      PathTransition pt = new PathTransition();
33      pt.setDuration(Duration.millis(4000));
34      pt.setPath(circle);
35      pt.setNode(rectangle);
36      pt.setOrientation(
37        PathTransition.OrientationType.ORTHOGONAL_TO_TANGENT);
38      pt.setCycleCount(Timeline.INDEFINITE);
39      pt.setAutoReverse(true);
40      pt.play(); // Start animation
41
42      circle.setOnMousePressed(e -> pt.pause());
43      circle.setOnMouseReleased(e -> pt.play());
```

Margin notes (left column):
- create a pane
- create a rectangle
- create a circle
- add circle to pane
- add rectangle to pane
- create a PathTransition
- set transition duration
- set path in transition
- set node in transition
- set orientation
- set cycle count indefinite
- set auto reverse true
- play animation
- pause animation
- resume animation

```
44
45      // Create a scene and place it in the stage
46      Scene scene = new Scene(pane, 250, 200);
47      primaryStage.setTitle("PathTransitionDemo"); // Set the stage title
48      primaryStage.setScene(scene); // Place the scene in the stage
49      primaryStage.show(); // Display the stage
50    }
51  }
```

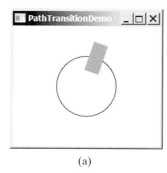 

(a)   (b)

FIGURE 15.18 The `PathTransition` animates a rectangle moving along the circle.

The program creates a pane (line 16), a rectangle (line 19), and a circle (line 23). The circle and rectangle are placed in the pane (lines 28 and 29). If the circle was not placed in the pane, you will see the screen shot as shown in Figure 15.18b.

The program creates a path transition (line 32), sets its duration to 4 seconds for one cycle of animation (line 33), sets circle as the path (line 34), sets rectangle as the node (line 35), and sets the orientation to orthogonal to tangent (line 36).

The cycle count is set to indefinite (line 38) so the animation continues forever. The auto reverse is set to true (line 39) so the direction of the move is reversed in the alternating cycle. The program starts animation by invoking the `play()` method (line 40).

If the `pause()` method is replaced by the `stop()` method in line 42, the animation will start over from the beginning when it restarts.

Listing 15.13 gives the program that animates a flag rising, as shown in Figure 15.14.

LISTING 15.13 FlagRisingAnimation.java

```
1   import javafx.animation.PathTransition;
2   import javafx.application.Application;
3   import javafx.scene.Scene;
4   import javafx.scene.image.ImageView;
5   import javafx.scene.layout.Pane;
6   import javafx.scene.shape.Line;
7   import javafx.stage.Stage;
8   import javafx.util.Duration;
9
10  public class FlagRisingAnimation extends Application {
11    @Override // Override the start method in the Application class
12    public void start(Stage primaryStage) {
13      // Create a pane
14      Pane pane = new Pane();                                          create a pane
15
16      // Add an image view and add it to pane
17      ImageView imageView = new ImageView("image/us.gif");            create an image view
18      pane.getChildren().add(imageView);                              add image view to pane
```

```
19
20      // Create a path transition
21      PathTransition pt = new PathTransition(Duration.millis(10000),
22        new Line(100, 200, 100, 0), imageView);
23      pt.setCycleCount(5);
24      pt.play(); // Start animation
25
26      // Create a scene and place it in the stage
27      Scene scene = new Scene(pane, 250, 200);
28      primaryStage.setTitle("FlagRisingAnimation"); // Set the stage title
29      primaryStage.setScene(scene); // Place the scene in the stage
30      primaryStage.show(); // Display the stage
31    }
32  }
```

create a path transition (line 21)

set cycle count (line 23)
play animation (line 24)

The program creates a pane (line 14), an image view from an image file (line 17), and places the image view to the pane (line 18). A path transition is created with a duration of 10 seconds using a line as a path and the image view as the node (lines 21 and 22). The image view will move along the line. Since the line is not placed in the scene, you will not see the line in the window.

The cycle count is set to 5 (line 23) so the animation is repeated five times.

15.11.2 FadeTransition

The FadeTransition class animates the change of the opacity in a node over a given time. FadeTransition is a subtype of Animation. The UML class diagram for the class is shown in Figure 15.19.

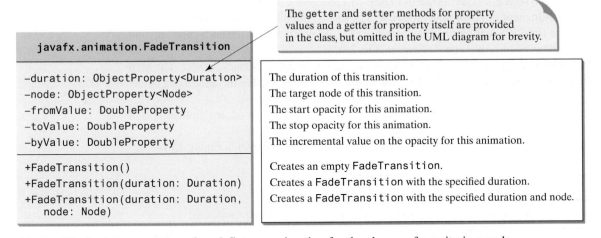

The getter and setter methods for property values and a getter for property itself are provided in the class, but omitted in the UML diagram for brevity.

javafx.animation.FadeTransition	
-duration: ObjectProperty<Duration>	The duration of this transition.
-node: ObjectProperty<Node>	The target node of this transition.
-fromValue: DoubleProperty	The start opacity for this animation.
-toValue: DoubleProperty	The stop opacity for this animation.
-byValue: DoubleProperty	The incremental value on the opacity for this animation.
+FadeTransition()	Creates an empty FadeTransition.
+FadeTransition(duration: Duration)	Creates a FadeTransition with the specified duration.
+FadeTransition(duration: Duration, node: Node)	Creates a FadeTransition with the specified duration and node.

FIGURE 15.19 The FadeTransition class defines an animation for the change of opacity in a node.

Listing 15.14 gives an example that applies a fade transition to the filled color in an ellipse, as shown in Figure 15.20.

LISTING 15.14 FadeTransitionDemo.java

```
1  import javafx.animation.FadeTransition;
2  import javafx.animation.Timeline;
3  import javafx.application.Application;
4  import javafx.scene.Scene;
5  import javafx.scene.layout.Pane;
6  import javafx.scene.paint.Color;
7  import javafx.scene.shape.Ellipse;
8  import javafx.stage.Stage;
```

```
 9  import javafx.util.Duration;
10
11  public class FadeTransitionDemo extends Application {
12    @Override // Override the start method in the Application class
13    public void start(Stage primaryStage) {
14      // Place an ellipse to the pane
15      Pane pane = new Pane();                                              create a pane
16      Ellipse ellipse = new Ellipse(10, 10, 100, 50);                     create an ellipse
17      ellipse.setFill(Color.RED);                                         set ellipse fill color
18      ellipse.setStroke(Color.BLACK);                                     set ellipse stroke color
19      ellipse.centerXProperty().bind(pane.widthProperty().divide(2));     bind ellipse properties
20      ellipse.centerYProperty().bind(pane.heightProperty().divide(2));
21      ellipse.radiusXProperty().bind(
22        pane.widthProperty().multiply(0.4));
23      ellipse.radiusYProperty().bind(
24        pane.heightProperty().multiply(0.4));
25      pane.getChildren().add(ellipse);                                    add ellipse to pane
26
27      // Apply a fade transition to ellipse
28      FadeTransition ft =                                                 create a FadeTransition
29        new FadeTransition(Duration.millis(3000), ellipse);
30      ft.setFromValue(1.0);                                               set start opaque value
31      ft.setToValue(0.1);                                                 set end opaque value
32      ft.setCycleCount(Timeline.INDEFINITE);                             set cycle count
33      ft.setAutoReverse(true);                                            set auto reverse true
34      ft.play(); // Start animation                                       play animation
35
36      // Control animation
37      ellipse.setOnMousePressed(e -> ft.pause());                        pause animation
38      ellipse.setOnMouseReleased(e -> ft.play());                        resume animation
39
40      // Create a scene and place it in the stage
41      Scene scene = new Scene(pane, 200, 150);
42      primaryStage.setTitle("FadeTransitionDemo"); // Set the stage title
43      primaryStage.setScene(scene); // Place the scene in the stage
44      primaryStage.show(); // Display the stage
45    }
46  }
```

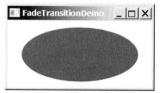

FIGURE 15.20 The `FadeTransition` animates the change of opacity in the ellipse.

The program creates a pane (line 15) and an ellipse (line 16) and places the ellipse into the pane (line 25). The ellipse's `centerX`, `centerY`, `radiusX`, and `radiusY` properties are bound to the pane's size (lines 19–24).

A fade transition is created with a duration of 3 seconds for the ellipse (line 29). It sets the start opaque to 1.0 (line 30) and the stop opaque to 0.1 (line 31). The cycle count is set to infinite so the animation is repeated indefinitely (line 32). When the mouse is pressed, the animation is paused (line 37). When the mouse is released, the animation resumes from where it was paused (line 38).

15.12.3 Timeline

PathTransition and FadeTransition define specialized animations. The Timeline class can be used to program any animation using one or more KeyFrames. Each KeyFrame is executed sequentially at a specified time interval. Timeline inherits from Animation. You can construct a Timeline using the constructor new Timeline(KeyFrame...keyframes). A KeyFrame can be constructed using

```
new KeyFrame(Duration duration, EventHandler<ActionEvent> onFinished)
```

The handler onFinished is called when the duration for the key frame is elapsed.

Listing 15.15 gives an example that displays a flashing text, as shown in Figure 15.21. The text is on and off alternating to animate flashing.

VideoNote

Flashing text

LISTING 15.15 TimelineDemo.java

```
1  import javafx.animation.Animation;
2  import javafx.application.Application;
3  import javafx.stage.Stage;
4  import javafx.animation.KeyFrame;
5  import javafx.animation.Timeline;
6  import javafx.event.ActionEvent;
7  import javafx.event.EventHandler;
8  import javafx.scene.Scene;
9  import javafx.scene.layout.StackPane;
10 import javafx.scene.paint.Color;
11 import javafx.scene.text.Text;
12 import javafx.util.Duration;
13
14 public class TimelineDemo extends Application {
15   @Override // Override the start method in the Application class
16   public void start(Stage primaryStage) {
17     StackPane pane = new StackPane();
18     Text text = new Text(20, 50, "Programming is fun");
19     text.setFill(Color.RED);
20     pane.getChildren().add(text); // Place text into the stack pane
21
22     // Create a handler for changing text
23     EventHandler<ActionEvent> eventHandler = e -> {
24       if (text.getText().length() != 0) {
25         text.setText("");
26       }
27       else {
28         text.setText("Programming is fun");
29       }
30     };
31
32     // Create an animation for alternating text
33     Timeline animation = new Timeline(
34       new KeyFrame(Duration.millis(500), eventHandler));
35     animation.setCycleCount(Timeline.INDEFINITE);
36     animation.play(); // Start animation
37
38     // Pause and resume animation
39     text.setOnMouseClicked(e -> {
40       if (animation.getStatus() == Animation.Status.PAUSED) {
41         animation.play();
42       }
43       else {
44         animation.pause();
```

create a stack pane
create a text

add text to pane

handler for changing text

set text empty

set text

create a Timeline
create a KeyFrame for handler
set cycle count indefinite
play animation

resume animation

pause animation

```
45          }
46      });
47
48      // Create a scene and place it in the stage
49      Scene scene = new Scene(pane, 250, 250);
50      primaryStage.setTitle("TimelineDemo"); // Set the stage title
51      primaryStage.setScene(scene); // Place the scene in the stage
52      primaryStage.show(); // Display the stage
53    }
54  }
```

FIGURE 15.21   The handler is called to set the text to "Programming is fun" or empty in turn.

The program creates a stack pane (line 17) and a text (line 18) and places the text into the pane (line 20). A handler is created to change the text to empty (lines 24–26) if it is not empty or to `Progrmming is fun` if it is empty (lines 27–29). A `KeyFrame` is created to run an action event in every half second (line 34). A `Timeline` animation is created to contain a key frame (lines 33 and 34). The animation is set to run indefinitely (line 35).

The mouse-clicked event is set for the text (lines 39–46). A mouse click on the text resumes the animation if the animation is paused (lines 40–42), and a mouse click on the text pauses the animation if the animation is running (lines 43–45).

In Section 14.12, Case Study: The `ClockPane` Class, you drew a clock to show the current time. The clock does not tick after it is displayed. What can you do to make the clock display a new current time every second? The key to making the clock tick is to repaint it every second with a new current time. You can use a `Timeline` to control the repainting of the clock with the code in Listing 15.16. The sample run of the program is shown in Figure 15.22.

LISTING 15.16   ClockAnimation.java

```
1   import javafx.application.Application;
2   import javafx.stage.Stage;
3   import javafx.animation.KeyFrame;
4   import javafx.animation.Timeline;
5   import javafx.event.ActionEvent;
6   import javafx.event.EventHandler;
7   import javafx.scene.Scene;
8   import javafx.util.Duration;
9
10  public class ClockAnimation extends Application {
11    @Override // Override the start method in the Application class
12    public void start(Stage primaryStage) {
13      ClockPane clock = new ClockPane(); // Create a clock        create a clock
14
15      // Create a handler for animation
16      EventHandler<ActionEvent> eventHandler = e -> {             create a handler
17        clock.setCurrentTime(); // Set a new clock time
18      };
19
20      // Create an animation for a running clock
21      Timeline animation = new Timeline(                          create a time line
```

create a key frame
set cycle count indefinite
play animation

```
22            new KeyFrame(Duration.millis(1000), eventHandler));
23         animation.setCycleCount(Timeline.INDEFINITE);
24         animation.play(); // Start animation
25
26         // Create a scene and place it in the stage
27         Scene scene = new Scene(clock, 250, 50);
28         primaryStage.setTitle("ClockAnimation"); // Set the stage title
29         primaryStage.setScene(scene); // Place the scene in the stage
30         primaryStage.show(); // Display the stage
31     }
32 }
```

FIGURE 15.22 A live clock is displayed in the window.

The program creates an instance `clock` of `ClockPane` for displaying a clock (line 13). The `ClockPane` class is defined in Listing 14.21. The clock is placed in the scene in line 27. An event handler is created for setting the current time in the clock (lines 16–18). This handler is called every second in the key frame in the time line animation (lines 21–24). Thus, the clock time is updated every second in the animation.

15.11.1 How do you set the cycle count of an animation to infinite? How do you auto reverse an animation? How do you start, pause, and stop an animation?

15.11.2 Are `PathTransition`, `FadeTransition`, and `Timeline` subtypes of `Animation`?

15.11.3 How do you create a `PathTransition`? How do you create a `FadeTransition`? How do you create a `Timeline`?

15.11.4 How do you create a `KeyFrame`?

15.12 Case Study: Bouncing Ball

This section presents an animation that displays a ball bouncing in a pane.

The program uses `Timeline` to animate ball bouncing, as shown in Figure 15.23.

FIGURE 15.23 A ball is bouncing in a pane.

Here are the major steps to write this program:

1. Define a subclass of Pane named BallPane to display a ball bouncing, as shown in Listing 15.17.

2. Define a subclass of Application named BounceBallControl to control the bouncing ball with mouse actions, as shown in Listing 15.18. The animation pauses when the mouse is pressed, and resumes when the mouse is released. Pressing the up and down arrow keys increases/decreases the animation speed.

The relationship among these classes is shown in Figure 15.24.

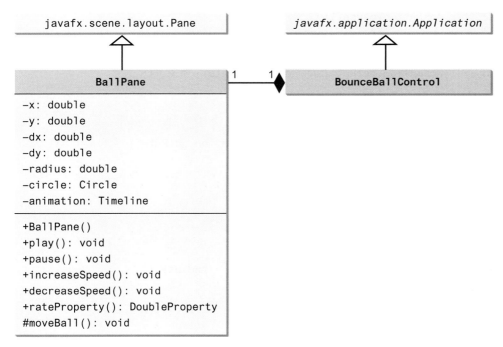

FIGURE 15.24 BounceBallControl contains BallPane.

LISTING 15.17 BallPane.java

```
1  import javafx.animation.KeyFrame;
2  import javafx.animation.Timeline;
3  import javafx.beans.property.DoubleProperty;
4  import javafx.scene.layout.Pane;
5  import javafx.scene.paint.Color;
6  import javafx.scene.shape.Circle;
7  import javafx.util.Duration;
8
9  public class BallPane extends Pane {
10    public final double radius = 20;
11    private double x = radius, y = radius;
12    private double dx = 1, dy = 1;
13    private Circle circle = new Circle(x, y, radius);
14    private Timeline animation;
15
16    public BallPane() {
17      circle.setFill(Color.GREEN); // Set ball color
18      getChildren().add(circle); // Place a ball into this pane
```

```
19
20        // Create an animation for moving the ball
21        animation = new Timeline(
22          new KeyFrame(Duration.millis(50), e -> moveBall()));
23        animation.setCycleCount(Timeline.INDEFINITE);
24        animation.play(); // Start animation
25      }
26
27      public void play() {
28        animation.play();
29      }
30
31      public void pause() {
32        animation.pause();
33      }
34
35      public void increaseSpeed() {
36        animation.setRate(animation.getRate() + 0.1);
37      }
38
39      public void decreaseSpeed() {
40        animation.setRate(
41          animation.getRate() > 0 ? animation.getRate() - 0.1 : 0);
42      }
43
44      public DoubleProperty rateProperty() {
45        return animation.rateProperty();
46      }
47
48      protected void moveBall() {
49        // Check boundaries
50        if (x < radius || x > getWidth() - radius) {
51          dx *= -1; // Change ball move direction
52        }
53        if (y < radius || y > getHeight() - radius) {
54          dy *= -1; // Change ball move direction
55        }
56
57        // Adjust ball position
58        x += dx;
59        y += dy;
60        circle.setCenterX(x);
61        circle.setCenterY(y);
62      }
63    }
```

create animation (line 21)
keep animation running (line 23)
start animation (line 24)

play animation (line 28)

pause animation (line 32)

increase animation rate (line 36)

decrease animation rate (line 40)

change horizontal direction (line 51)

change vertical direction (line 54)

set new ball position (line 58)

BallPane extends Pane to display a moving ball (line 9). An instance of Timeline is created to control animation (lines 21 and 22). This instance contains a KeyFrame object that invokes the moveBall() method at a fixed rate. The moveBall() method moves the ball to simulate animation. The center of the ball is at (x, y), which changes to (x + dx, y + dy) on the next move (lines 58–61). When the ball is out of the horizontal boundary, the sign of dx is changed (from positive to negative or vice versa) (lines 50–52). This causes the ball to change its horizontal movement direction. When the ball is out of the vertical boundary, the sign of dy is changed (from positive to negative or vice versa) (lines 53–55). This causes the ball to change its vertical movement direction. The pause and play methods (lines 27–33) can be used to pause and resume the animation. The increaseSpeed() and decreaseSpeed() methods (lines 35–42) can be used to increase and decrease animation speed. The rateProperty()

method (lines 44–46) returns a binding property value for rate. This binding property will be useful for binding the rate in future applications in the next chapter.

LISTING 15.18   BounceBallControl.java

```
1   import javafx.application.Application;
2   import javafx.stage.Stage;
3   import javafx.scene.Scene;
4   import javafx.scene.input.KeyCode;
5
6   public class BounceBallControl extends Application {
7     @Override // Override the start method in the Application class
8     public void start(Stage primaryStage) {
9       BallPane ballPane = new BallPane(); // Create a ball pane          create a ball pane
10
11      // Pause and resume animation
12      ballPane.setOnMousePressed(e -> ballPane.pause());              pause animation
13      ballPane.setOnMouseReleased(e -> ballPane.play());              resume animation
14
15      // Increase and decrease animation
16      ballPane.setOnKeyPressed(e -> {
17        if (e.getCode() == KeyCode.UP) {
18          ballPane.increaseSpeed();                                   increase speed
19        }
20        else if (e.getCode() == KeyCode.DOWN) {
21          ballPane.decreaseSpeed();                                   decrease speed
22        }
23      });
24
25      // Create a scene and place it in the stage
26      Scene scene = new Scene(ballPane, 250, 150);
27      primaryStage.setTitle("BounceBallControl"); // Set the stage title
28      primaryStage.setScene(scene); // Place the scene in the stage
29      primaryStage.show(); // Display the stage
30
31      // Must request focus after the primary stage is displayed
32      ballPane.requestFocus();                                        request focus on pane
33    }
34  }
```

The `BounceBallControl` class is the main JavaFX class that extends `Application` to display the ball pane with control functions. The mouse-pressed and mouse-released handlers are implemented for the ball pane to pause the animation and resume the animation (lines 12 and 13). When the UP arrow key is pressed, the ball pane's `increaseSpeed()` method is invoked to increase the ball's movement (line 18). When the down arrow key is pressed, the ball pane's `decreaseSpeed()` method is invoked to reduce the ball's movement (line 21).

Invoking `ballPane.requestFocus()` in line 32 sets the input focus to `ballPane`.

15.12.1 How does the program make the ball appear to be moving?

15.12.2 How does the code in Listing 15.17, BallPane.java, change the direction of the ball movement?

15.12.3 What does the program do when the mouse is pressed on the ball pane? What does the program do when the mouse is released on the ball pane?

15.12.4 If line 32 in Listing 15.18, BounceBall.java, is not in the program, what would happen when you press the up or the down arrow key?

15.12.5 If line 23 is not in Listing 15.17, what would happen?

Check Point

Key
Point

15.13 Case Study: US Map

This section presents a program that draws, colors, and resizes a US map.

The program reads the GPS coordinates for each state in the 48 continental United States, and draws a polygon to connect the coordinates and displays all the polygons, as shown in Figure 15.25.

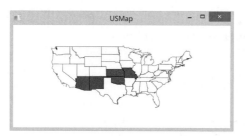

FIGURE 15.25 The program displays, colors, and resizes the US map.

The coordinates are contained in a file at https://liveexample.pearsoncmg.com/data/usmap.txt. For each state, the file contains the state name (e.g., Alabama) and all the coordinates (latitude and longitude) for the state. For example, the following is an example for Alabama and Arkansas:

```
Alabama
    35.0041 -88.1955
    34.9918 -85.6068
    ...
    34.9479 -88.1721
    34.9107 -88.1461
Arkansas
    33.0225 -94.0416
    33.0075 -91.2057
    ...
```

A polygon is displayed in red, blue, or white when the primary, secondary, or middle mouse button is clicked in the polygon. The map size is increased when the up arrow key is pressed, and decreased when the down arrow key is pressed. Listing 15.19 gives the code for this program.

LISTING 15.19 USMap.java

```
1  import javafx.application.Application;
2  import javafx.scene.Scene;
3  import javafx.scene.paint.Color;
4  import javafx.stage.Stage;
5  import javafx.scene.shape.Polygon;
6  import javafx.scene.Group;
7  import javafx.scene.layout.BorderPane;
8  import javafx.scene.input.*;
9  import javafx.geometry.Point2D;
10 import java.util.*;
11
12 public class USMap extends Application {
13   @Override // Override the start method in the Application class
14   public void start(Stage primaryStage) {
15     MapPane map = new MapPane();
```
create a map

```
16        Scene scene = new Scene(map, 1200, 800);
17        primaryStage.setTitle("USMap"); // Set the stage title
18        primaryStage.setScene(scene); // Place the scene in the stage
19        primaryStage.show(); // Display the stage
20
21        map.setOnKeyPressed(e -> {                              listen to key event
22          if (e.getCode() == KeyCode.UP) {
23            map.enlarge(); // Enlarge the map                   enlarge map
24          }
25          else if (e.getCode() == KeyCode.DOWN) {
26            map.shrink(); // SHrink the map                     shrink map
27          }
28        });
29        map.requestFocus();                                     request focus
30      }
31
32      class MapPane extends BorderPane {                        extends BorderPane
33        private Group group = new Group();                      create a Group
34
35        MapPane() {
36          // Load coordinates from a file
37          ArrayList<ArrayList<Point2D>> points = getPoints();   get coordinates for state
38
39          // Add points to the polygon list
40          for (int i = 0; i < points.size(); i++) {
41            Polygon polygon = new Polygon();
42            // Add points to the polygon list
43            for (int j = 0; j < points.get(i).size(); j++)
44              polygon.getPoints().addAll(points.get(i).get(j).getX(),    add coordinates
45                -points.get(i).get(j).getY());
46            polygon.setFill(Color.WHITE);
47            polygon.setStroke(Color.BLACK);
48            polygon.setStrokeWidth(1 / 14.0);                   set polygon stroke width
49
50            polygon.setOnMouseClicked(e -> {                    set listener for mouse click
51              if (e.getButton() == MouseButton.PRIMARY) {       color polygon
52                polygon.setFill(Color.RED);
53              }
54              else if (e.getButton() == MouseButton.SECONDARY) {
55                polygon.setFill(Color.BLUE);
56              }
57              else {
58                polygon.setFill(Color.WHITE);
59              }
60            });
61
62            group.getChildren().add(polygon);                   add a polygon to group
63          }
64
65          group.setScaleX(14);                                  scale polygon
66          group.setScaleY(14);
67          this.setCenter(group);                                center group in the map
68        }
69
70        public void enlarge() {                                 enlarge map
71          group.setScaleX(1.1 * group.getScaleX());
72          group.setScaleY(1.1 * group.getScaleY());
73        }
74
75        public void shrink() {                                  shrink map
```

create array list

try-with-resource
open an Internet resource

read a string
start a state
create a state list

read latitude value
read longitude value
add a point to list

return list of points

```
76          group.setScaleX(0.9 * group.getScaleX());
77          group.setScaleY(0.9 * group.getScaleY());
78        }
79
80        private ArrayList<ArrayList<Point2D>> getPoints() {
81          ArrayList<ArrayList<Point2D>> points = new ArrayList<>();
82
83          try (Scanner input = new Scanner(new java.net.URL(
84            "https://liveexample.pearsoncmg.com/data/usmap.txt")
85              .openStream())) {
86            while (input.hasNext()) {
87              String s = input.nextLine();
88              if (Character.isAlphabetic(s.charAt(0))) {
89                points.add(new ArrayList<>()); // For a new state
90              }
91              else {
92                Scanner scanAString = new Scanner(s); // Scan one point
93                double y = scanAString.nextDouble();
94                double x = scanAString.nextDouble();
95                points.get(points.size() - 1).add(new Point2D(x, y));
96              }
97            }
98          }
99          catch (Exception ex) {
100            ex.printStackTrace();
101          }
102
103          return points;
104        }
105      }
106    }
```

the Group class

the scaleX property
the scaleY property

the scaleX property
the scaleY property

The program defines `MapPane` that extends `BorderPane` to display a map in the center of the border pane (line 32). The program needs to resize the polygons in the map. An instance of the `Group` class is created to hold all the polygons (line 33). Grouping the polygons enables all polygons to be resized in one operation. Resizing the group will cause all polygons in the group to resize accordingly. Resizing can be done by applying the `scaleX` and `scaleY` properties in the group (lines 65 and 66).

The `getPoints()` method is used to return all the coordinates in an array list (line 80). The array list consists of sublists. Each sublist contains the coordinates for a state and is added to the array list (line 89). A `Point2D` object represents the *x*- and *y*-coordinates of the point (line 81). The method creates a `Scanner` object to read data for the map coordinates from a file on the Internet (lines 83–85). The program reads lines from the file. For each line, if the first character is an alphabet, the line is for a new state name (line 88) and a new sublist is created and added to the `points` array list (line 89). Otherwise, the line contains the two coordinates. The latitude becomes the *y*-coordinate for the point (line 93), and the longitude corresponds to the *x*-coordinate of the point (line 94). The program stores the points for a state in a sublist (line 95). `points` is an array list that contains **48** sublists.

The constructor of `MapPane` obtains sublists of the coordinates from the file (line 37). For each sublist of the points, a polygon is created (line 41). The points are added to the polygon (lines 43–45). Since the *y*-coordinates increase upward in the conventional coordinate system, but downward in the Java coordinate system, the program changes the sign for the *y*-coordinates in line 45. The polygon properties are set in lines 46–48. Note the `strokeWidth` is set to **1 / 14.0** (line 48) because all the polygons are scaled up **14** times in lines 65 and 66. If the `strokeWidth` is not set to this value, the stroke width will be very thick. Since polygons are very small, applying the `setScaleX` and `setScaleY` methods on the group causes all the nodes inside the group to be enlarged (lines 65 and 66). `MapPane` is a `BorderPane`. The group is placed in the center of the border pane (line 67).

The `enlarge()` and `shrink()` methods are defined in `MapPane` (lines 70–78). They can be called to enlarge or shrink the group to cause all the polygons in the group to scale up or down.

Each polygon is set to listen to mouse-clicked event (lines 50–60). When clicking the primary/secondary/middle mouse button on a polygon, the polygon is filled red/blue/white.

The program creates an instance of `MapPane` (line 15) and places it in the scene (line 16). The map listens to the key-pressed event to enlarge or shrink the map upon pressing the up and down arrow key (lines 21–28). Since the map is inside the scene, invoking `map.requestFocus()` enables the map to receive key events (line 29).

15.13.1 What would happen if line 29 in Listing 15.19 is removed?

15.13.2 What would happen if `map` is replaced by `scene` in line 21 in Listing 15.19?

15.13.3 What would happen if `map` is replaced by `primaryStage` in line 21 in Listing 15.19?

KEY TERMS

anonymous inner class   602
event   596
event-driven programming   596
event handler   597
event–handler interface   597
event object   596
event source object   596

functional interface   607
inner class   599
key code   613
lambda expression   605
observable object   616
single abstract method interface   607

CHAPTER SUMMARY

1. The root class of the JavaFX event classes is `javafx.event.Event`, which is a subclass of `java.util.EventObject`. The subclasses of `Event` deal with special types of events, such as action events, window events, mouse events, and key events. If a node can fire an event, any subclass of the node can fire the same type of event.

2. The handler object's class must implement the corresponding *event–handler interface*. JavaFX provides a handler interface `EventHandler<T extends Event>` for every event class `T`. The handler interface contains the `handle(T e)` method for handling event `e`.

3. The handler object must be registered by the *source object*. Registration methods depend on the event type. For an action event, the method is `setOnAction`. For a mouse-pressed event, the method is `setOnMousePressed`. For a key-pressed event, the method is `setOnKeyPressed`.

4. An *inner class*, or *nested class*, is defined within the scope of another class. An inner class can reference the data and methods defined in the outer class in which it nests, so you need not pass the reference of the outer class to the constructor of the inner class.

5. An anonymous inner class can be used to shorten the code for event handling. Furthermore, a lambda expression can be used to greatly simplify the event-handling code for functional interface handlers.

6. A *functional interface* is an interface with exactly one abstract method. This is also known as a single abstract method (SAM) interface.

7. A `MouseEvent` is fired whenever a mouse button is pressed, released, clicked, moved, or dragged on a node or a scene. The `getButton()` method can be used to detect which mouse button is pressed for the event.

8. A `KeyEvent` is fired whenever a key is pressed, released, or typed on a node or a scene. The `getCode()` method can be used to return the code value for the key.

9. An instance of `Observable` is known as an observable object, which contains the `add-Listener(InvalidationListener listener)` method for adding a listener. Once the value is changed in the property, a listener is notified. The listener class should implement the `InvalidationListener` interface, which uses the `invalidated` method to handle the property value change.

10. The abstract `Animation` class provides the core functionalities for animations in JavaFX. `PathTransition`, `FadeTransition`, and `Timeline` are specialized classes for implementing animations.

QUIZ

Answer the quiz for this chapter online at the book Companion Website.

MyProgrammingLab ## PROGRAMMING EXERCISES

Sections 15.2–15.7

*15.1   (*Pick four cards*) Write a program that lets the user click the *Refresh* button to display four cards from a deck of 52 cards, as shown in Figure 15.26a. (See the hint in Programming Exercise 14.3 on how to obtain four random cards.)

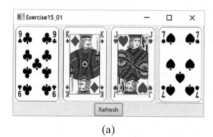
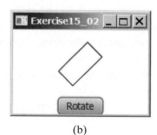
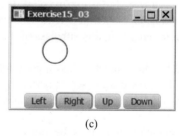

(a)   (b)   (c)

FIGURE 15.26   (a) Exercise 15.1 displays four cards randomly. *Source*: Fotolia. (b) Exercise 15.2 rotates the rectangle. (c) Exercise 15.3 uses the buttons to move the ball.

15.2   (*Rotate a rectangle*) Write a program that rotates a rectangle 15 degrees to the right when the *Rotate* button is clicked, as shown in Figure 15.26b.

*15.3   (*Move the ball*) Write a program that moves the ball in a pane. You should define a pane class for displaying the ball and provide the methods for moving the ball left, right, up, and down, as shown in Figure 15.26c. Check the boundary to prevent the ball from moving out of sight completely.

VideoNote

Simple calculator

*15.4   (*Create a simple calculator*) Write a program to perform addition, subtraction, multiplication, and division, as shown in Figure 15.27a.

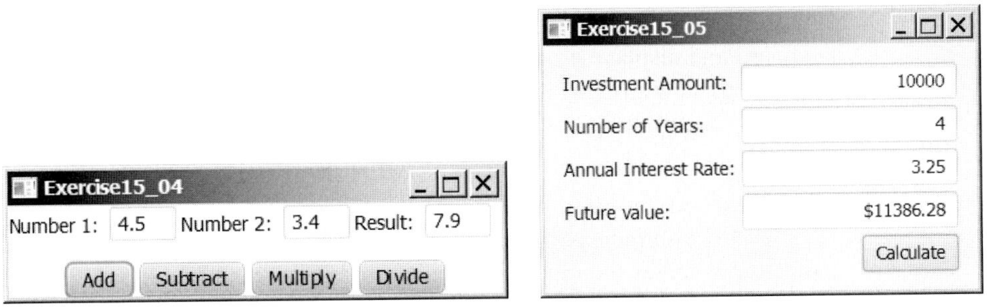

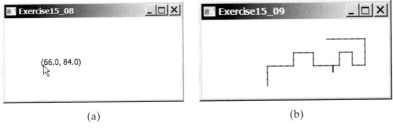

FIGURE 15.27 (a) Exercise 15.4 performs addition, subtraction, multiplication, and division on double numbers. (b) The user enters the investment amount, years, and interest rate to compute future value.

*15.5 (*Create an investment-value calculator*) Write a program that calculates the future value of an investment at a given interest rate for a specified number of years. The formula for the calculation is

```
futureValue = investmentAmount * (1 + monthlyInterestRate)^years*12
```

Use text fields for the investment amount, number of years, and annual interest rate. Display the future amount in a text field when the user clicks the *Calculate* button, as shown in Figure 15.27b.

Sections 15.8 and 15.9

**15.6 (*Alternate two messages*) Write a program to display the text Java is fun and Java is powerful alternately with a mouse click.

*15.7 (*Change color using a mouse*) Write a program that displays the color of a circle as black when the mouse button is pressed, and as white when the mouse button is released.

*15.8 (*Display the mouse position*) Write two programs, such that one displays the mouse position when the mouse button is clicked (see Figure 15.28a), and the other displays the mouse position when the mouse button is pressed and ceases to display it when the mouse button is released.

*15.9 (*Draw lines using the arrow keys*) Write a program that draws line segments using the arrow keys. The line starts from (100, 100) in the pane and draws toward east, north, west, or south when the right-arrow key, up-arrow key, left-arrow key, or down-arrow key is pressed, as shown in Figure 15.28b.

FIGURE 15.28 (a) Exercise 15.8 displays the mouse position. (b) Exercise 15.9 uses the arrow keys to draw the lines.

**15.10 (*Enter and display a string*) Write a program that receives a string from the keyboard and displays it on a pane. The *Enter* key signals the end of a string. Whenever a new string is entered, it is displayed on the pane.

*15.11 (*Move a circle using keys*) Write a program that moves a circle up, down, left, or right using the arrow keys.

VideoNote

Check mouse-point location

**15.12 (*Geometry: inside a circle?*) Write a program that draws a fixed circle centered at (100, 60) with radius 50. Whenever the mouse is moved, display a message indicating whether the mouse point is inside the circle at the mouse point or outside of it, as shown in Figure 15.29a.

**15.13 (*Geometry: inside a rectangle?*) Write a program that draws a fixed rectangle centered at (100, 60) with width 100 and height 40. Whenever the mouse is moved, display a message indicating whether the mouse point is inside the rectangle at the mouse point or outside of it, as shown in Figure 15.29b. To detect whether a point is inside a polygon, use the contains method defined in the Node class.

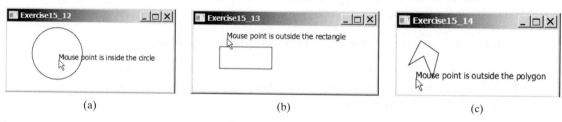

(a)   (b)   (c)

FIGURE 15.29   Detect whether a point is inside a circle, a rectangle, or a polygon.

**15.14 (*Geometry: inside a polygon?*) Write a program that draws a fixed polygon with points at (40, 20), (70, 40), (60, 80), (45, 45), and (20, 60). Whenever the mouse is moved, display a message indicating whether the mouse point is inside the polygon at the mouse point or outside of it, as shown in Figure 15.29c. To detect whether a point is inside a polygon, use the contains method defined in the Node class.

**15.15 (*Geometry: add and remove points*) Write a program that lets the user click on a pane to dynamically create and remove points (see Figure 15.30a). When the user left-clicks the mouse (primary button), a point is created and displayed at the mouse point. The user can remove a point by pointing to it and right-clicking the mouse (secondary button).

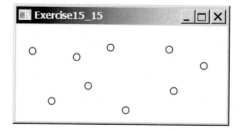
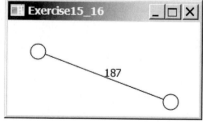

FIGURE 15.30   (a) Exercise 15.15 allows the user to create/remove points dynamically. (b) Exercise 15.16 displays two vertices and a connecting edge.

*15.16　(*Two movable vertices and their distances*) Write a program that displays two circles with radius 10 at location (40, 40) and (120, 150) with a line connecting the two circles, as shown in Figure 15.30b. The distance between the circles is displayed along the line. The user can drag a circle. When that happens, the circle and its line are moved, and the distance between the circles is updated.

**15.17　(*Geometry: find the bounding rectangle*) Write a program that enables the user to add and remove points in a two-dimensional plane dynamically, as shown in Figure 15.31a. A minimum bounding rectangle is updated as the points are added and removed. Assume the radius of each point is 10 pixels.

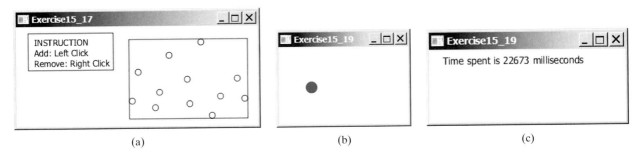

(a)　　　　　　(b)　　　　　　(c)

FIGURE 15.31　(a) Exercise 15.17 enables the user to add/remove points dynamically and displays the bounding rectangle. (b) When you click a circle, a new circle is displayed at a random location. (c) After 20 circles are clicked, the time spent is displayed in the pane.

**15.18　(*Move a rectangle using mouse*) Write a program that displays a rectangle. You can point the mouse inside the rectangle and drag (i.e., move with mouse pressed) the rectangle wherever the mouse goes. The mouse point becomes the center of the rectangle.

**15.19　(*Game: eye–hand coordination*) Write a program that displays a circle of radius 10 pixels filled with a random color at a random location on a pane, as shown in Figure 15.31b. When you click the circle, it disappears and a new random-color circle is displayed at another random location. After 20 circles are clicked, display the time spent in the pane, as shown in Figure 15.31c.

**15.20　(*Geometry: display angles*) Write a program that enables the user to drag the vertices of a triangle and displays the angles dynamically as the triangle shape changes, as shown in Figure 15.32a. The formula to compute angles is given in Listing 4.1.

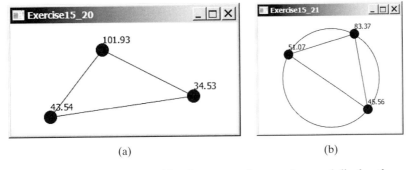

(a)　　　　　　(b)

FIGURE 15.32　(a) Exercise 15.20 enables the user to drag vertices and display the angles dynamically. (b) Exercise 15.21 enables the user to drag vertices and display the angles in the triangle dynamically.

*15.21   (*Drag points*) Draw a circle with three random points on the circle. Connect the points to form a triangle. Display the angles in the triangle. Use the mouse to drag a point along the perimeter of the circle. As you drag it, the triangle and angles are redisplayed dynamically, as shown in Figure 15.32b. For computing angles in a triangle, see Listing 4.1.

Section 15.10

*15.22   (*Auto resize cylinder*) Rewrite Programming Exercise 14.10 so the cylinder's width and height are automatically resized when the window is resized.

*15.23   (*Auto resize stop sign*) Rewrite Programming Exercise 14.15 so the stop sign's width and height are automatically resized when the window is resized.

Section 15.11

**15.24   (*Animation: pendulum swing*) Write a program that animates a pendulum swing, as shown in Figure 15.33. Press/release the mouse to pause/resume the animation.

 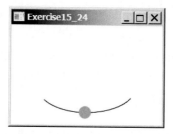 

FIGURE 15.33   The program animates a pendulum swing.

**15.25   (*Animation: ball on curve*) Write a program that animates a ball moving along a sine curve, as shown in Figure 15.34. When the ball gets to the right border, it starts over from the left. Enable the user to resume/pause the animation with a click on the left/right mouse button.

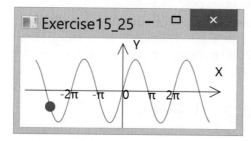 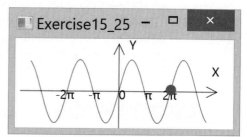

FIGURE 15.34   The program animates a ball traveling along a sine curve.

*15.26   (*Change opacity*) Rewrite Programming Exercise 15.24 so the ball's opacity is changed as it swings.

*15.27   (*Control a moving text*) Write a program that displays a moving text, as shown in Figures 15.35a and b. The text moves from left to right circularly. When it disappears in the right, it reappears from the left. The text freezes when the mouse is pressed, and moves again when the button is released.

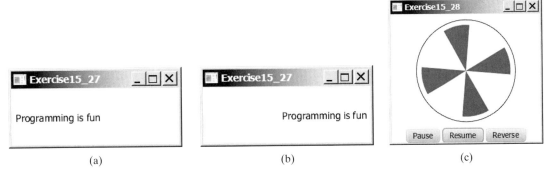

FIGURE 15.35   (a and b) A text is moving from left to right circularly. (c) The program simulates a fan running.

**15.28   (*Display a running fan*) Write a program that displays a running fan, as shown in Figure 15.35c. Use the *Pause*, *Resume*, and *Reverse* buttons to pause, resume, and reverse fan running.

VideoNote

Display a running fan

**15.29   (*Racing car*) Write a program that simulates car racing, as shown in Figure 15.36a. The car moves from left to right. When it hits the right end, it restarts from the left and continues the same process. You can use a timer to control animation. Redraw the car with new base coordinates (x, y), as shown in Figure 15.36b. Also let the user pause/resume the animation with a button press/release and increase/decrease the car speed by pressing the up and down arrow keys.

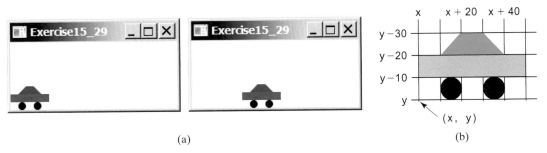

FIGURE 15.36   (a) The program displays a moving car. (b) You can redraw a car with a new base point.

15.30   (*Slide show*) Twenty-five slides are stored as image files (slide0.jpg**, **slide1.jpg**, . . . , **slide24.jpg**) in the **image** directory downloadable along with the source code in the book. The size of each image is 800×600. Write a program that automatically displays the slides repeatedly. Each slide is shown for two seconds. The slides are displayed in order. When the last slide finishes, the first slide is redisplayed, and so on. Click to pause if the animation is currently playing. Click to resume if the animation is currently paused.

**15.31   (*Geometry: pendulum*) Write a program that animates a pendulum swinging, as shown in Figure 15.37. Press the up arrow key to increase the speed, and the down arrow key to decrease it. Press the *S* key to stop animation of and the *R* key to resume it.

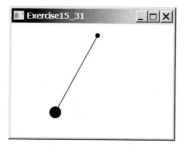 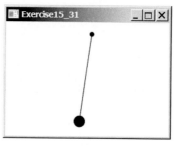 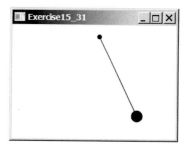

FIGURE 15.37 Exercise 15.31 animates a pendulum swinging.

*15.32 (*Control a clock*) Modify Listing 14.21, ClockPane.java, to add the animation into this class and add two methods `start()` and `stop()` to start and stop the clock, respectively. Write a program that lets the user control the clock with the *Start* and *Stop* buttons, as shown in Figure 15.38a.

***15.33 (*Game: bean-machine animation*) Write a program that animates the bean machine introduced in Programming Exercise 7.37. The animation terminates after 10 balls are dropped, as shown in Figures 15.38b and c.

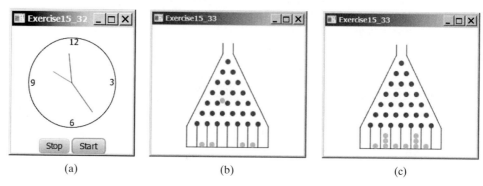

(a)   (b)   (c)

FIGURE 15.38 (a) Exercise 15.32 allows the user to start and stop a clock. (b and c) The balls are dropped into the bean machine.

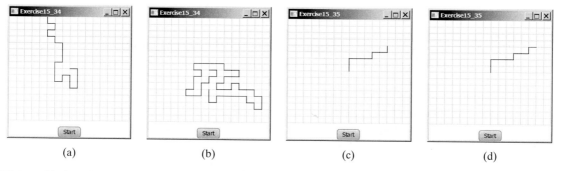

(a)   (b)   (c)   (d)

FIGURE 15.39 (a) A path ends at a boundary point. (b) A path ends at dead-end point. (c and d) Animation shows the progress of a path step by step.

***15.34 (*Simulation: self-avoiding random walk*) A self-avoiding walk in a lattice is a path from one point to another that does not visit the same point twice. Self-avoiding walks have applications in physics, chemistry, and mathematics. They can be used to model chain-like entities such as solvents and polymers. Write a program that displays a random path that starts from the center and ends at a point on the boundary, as shown in Figure 15.39a, or ends at a dead-end point (i.e., surrounded by four points that have already been visited), as shown in Figure 15.39b. Assume the size of the lattice is 16 by 16.

***15.35 (*Animation: self-avoiding random walk*) Revise the preceding exercise to display the walk step by step in an animation, as shown in Figures 15.39c and d.

**15.36 (*Simulation: self-avoiding random walk*) Write a simulation program to show that the chance of getting dead-end paths increases as the grid size increases. Your program simulates lattices with size from 10 to 80 with increments of 5. For each lattice size, simulate a self-avoiding random walk 10,000 times and display the probability of the dead-end paths, as shown in the following sample output:

```
For a lattice of size 10, the probability of dead-end paths is 10.6%
For a lattice of size 15, the probability of dead-end paths is 14.0%
...
For a lattice of size 80, the probability of dead-end paths is 99.5%
```

JavaFX UI Controls and Multimedia

Objectives

- To create graphical user interfaces with various user-interface controls (§§16.2–16.11).

- To create a label with text and graphics using the Label class, and explore properties in the abstract Labeled class (§16.2).

- To create a button with text and graphic using the Button class, and set a handler using the setOnAction method in the abstract ButtonBase class (§16.3).

- To create a check box using the CheckBox class (§16.4).

- To create a radio button using the RadioButton class, and group radio buttons using a ToggleGroup (§16.5).

- To enter data using the TextField class and password using the PasswordField class (§16.6).

- To enter data in multiple lines using the TextArea class (§16.7).

- To select a single item using ComboBox (§16.8).

- To select a single or multiple items using ListView (§16.9).

- To select a range of values using ScrollBar (§16.10).

- To select a range of values using Slider and explore differences between ScrollBar and Slider (§16.11).

- To develop a tic-tac-toe game (§16.12).

- To view and play video and audio using the Media, MediaPlayer, and MediaView (§16.13).

- To develop a case study for showing the national flag and playing the national anthem (§16.14).

16.1 Introduction

JavaFX provides many UI controls for developing a comprehensive user interface.

GUI

A graphical user interface (GUI) makes a program user-friendly and easy to use. Creating a GUI requires creativity and knowledge of how UI controls work. Since the UI controls in JavaFX are very flexible and versatile, you can create a wide assortment of useful user interfaces for rich GUI applications.

Oracle provides tools for visually designing and developing GUIs. This enables the programmer to rapidly assemble the elements of a GUI with minimum coding. Tools, however, cannot do everything. You have to modify the programs they produce. Consequently, before you begin to use the visual tools, you must understand the basic concepts of JavaFX GUI programming.

Previous chapters used UI controls such as `Button`, `Label`, and `TextField`. This chapter introduces the frequently used UI controls in detail (see Figure 16.1).

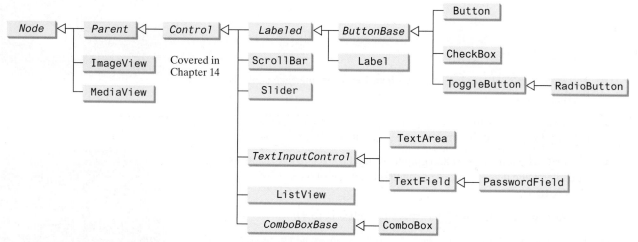

FIGURE 16.1 These UI controls are frequently used to create user interfaces.

naming convention for
controls

 Note

Throughout this book, the prefixes `lbl`, `bt`, `chk`, `rb`, `tf`, `pf`, `ta`, `cbo`, `lv`, `scb`, `sld`, and `mp` are used to name reference variables for `Label`, `Button`, `CheckBox`, `RadioButton`, `TextField`, `PasswordField`, `TextArea`, `ComboBox`, `ListView`, `ScrollBar`, `Slider`, and `MediaPlayer`, respectively.

16.2 Labeled and Label

A label is a display area for a short text, a node, or both. It is often used to label other controls (usually text fields).

Labels and buttons share many common properties. These common properties are defined in the `Labeled` class, as shown in Figure 16.2.

A `Label` can be constructed using one of the three constructors shown in Figure 16.3.

The `graphic` property can be any node such as a shape, an image, or a control. Listing 16.1 gives an example that displays several labels with text and images in the label, as shown in Figure 16.4.

LISTING 16.1 LabelWithGraphic.java

```
1  import javafx.application.Application;
2  import javafx.stage.Stage;
3  import javafx.scene.Scene;
4  import javafx.scene.control.ContentDisplay;
```

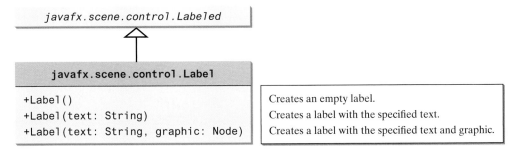

The getter and setter methods for property values and a getter for property itself are provided in the class, but omitted in the UML diagram for brevity.

javafx.scene.control.Labeled	
−alignment: ObjectProperty<Pos>	Specifies the alignment of the text and node in the labeled.
−contentDisplay: ObjectProperty<ContentDisplay>	Specifies the position of the node relative to the text using the constants TOP, BOTTOM, LEFT, and RIGHT defined in ContentDisplay.
−graphic: ObjectProperty<Node>	A graphic for the label.
−graphicTextGap: DoubleProperty	The gap between the graphic and the text.
−textFill: ObjectProperty<Paint>	The paint used to fill the text.
−text: StringProperty	A text for the label.
−underline: BooleanProperty	Whether text should be underlined.
−wrapText: BooleanProperty	Whether text should be wrapped if the text exceeds the width.

FIGURE 16.2 Labeled defines common properties for Label, Button, CheckBox, and RadioButton.

javafx.scene.control.Labeled

javafx.scene.control.Label	
+Label()	Creates an empty label.
+Label(text: String)	Creates a label with the specified text.
+Label(text: String, graphic: Node)	Creates a label with the specified text and graphic.

FIGURE 16.3 Label is created to display a text or a node, or both.

```
5  import javafx.scene.control.Label;
6  import javafx.scene.image.Image;
7  import javafx.scene.image.ImageView;
8  import javafx.scene.layout.HBox;
9  import javafx.scene.layout.StackPane;
10 import javafx.scene.paint.Color;
11 import javafx.scene.shape.Circle;
12 import javafx.scene.shape.Rectangle;
13 import javafx.scene.shape.Ellipse;
14
15 public class LabelWithGraphic extends Application {
16   @Override // Override the start method in the Application class
17   public void start(Stage primaryStage) {
18     ImageView us = new ImageView(new Image("image/us.gif"));
19     Label lb1 = new Label("US\n50 States", us);                    create a label
20     lb1.setStyle("-fx-border-color: green; -fx-border-width: 2");
21     lb1.setContentDisplay(ContentDisplay.BOTTOM);                   set node position
22     lb1.setTextFill(Color.RED);
23
24     Label lb2 = new Label("Circle", new Circle(50, 50, 25));        create a label
25     lb2.setContentDisplay(ContentDisplay.TOP);
26     lb2.setTextFill(Color.ORANGE);                                  set node position
27
28     Label lb3 = new Label("Rectangle", new Rectangle(10, 10, 50, 25));  create a label
29     lb3.setContentDisplay(ContentDisplay.RIGHT);
30
31     Label lb4 = new Label("Ellipse", new Ellipse(50, 50, 50, 25));  create a label
32     lb4.setContentDisplay(ContentDisplay.LEFT);
33
```

create a label

add labels to pane

```
34        Ellipse ellipse = new Ellipse(50, 50, 50, 25);
35        ellipse.setStroke(Color.GREEN);
36        ellipse.setFill(Color.WHITE);
37        StackPane stackPane = new StackPane();
38        stackPane.getChildren().addAll(ellipse, new Label("JavaFX"));
39        Label lb5 = new Label("A pane inside a label", stackPane);
40        lb5.setContentDisplay(ContentDisplay.BOTTOM);
41
42        HBox pane = new HBox(20);
43        pane.getChildren().addAll(lb1, lb2, lb3, lb4, lb5);
44
45        // Create a scene and place it in the stage
46        Scene scene = new Scene(pane, 450, 150);
47        primaryStage.setTitle("LabelWithGraphic"); // Set the stage title
48        primaryStage.setScene(scene); // Place the scene in the stage
49        primaryStage.show(); // Display the stage
50    }
60  }
```

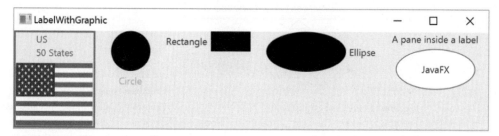

FIGURE 16.4 The program displays labels with texts and nodes. *Source*: booka/Fotolia.

The program creates a label with a text and an image (line 19). The text is US\n50 States, so it is displayed in two lines. Line 21 specifies that the image is placed at the bottom of the text.

The program creates a label with a text and a circle (line 24). The circle is placed on top of the text (line 25). The program creates a label with a text and a rectangle (line 28). The rectangle is placed on the right of the text (line 29). The program creates a label with a text and an ellipse (line 31). The ellipse is placed on the left of the text (line 32).

The program creates an ellipse (line 34), places it along with a label to a stack pane (line 38), and creates a label with a text and the stack pane as the node (line 39). As seen from this example, you can place any node in a label.

The program creates an HBox (line 42) and places all five labels into the HBox (line 43).

16.2.1 How do you create a label with a node without a text?

16.2.2 How do you place a text on the right of the node in a label?

16.2.3 Can you display multiple lines of text in a label?

16.2.4 Can the text in a label be underlined?

16.3 Button

A button is a control that triggers an action event when clicked.

JavaFX provides regular buttons, toggle buttons, check box buttons, and radio buttons. The common features of these buttons are defined in ButtonBase and Labeled classes as shown in Figure 16.5.

The Labeled class defines the common properties for labels and buttons. A button is just like a label, except that the button has the onAction property defined in the ButtonBase class, which sets a handler for handling a button's action.

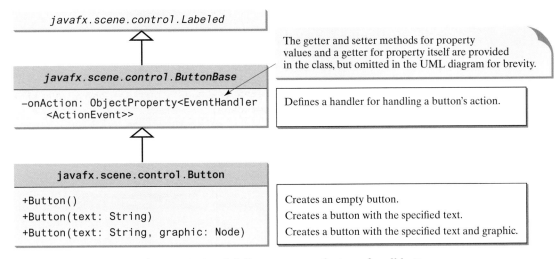

FIGURE 16.5 `ButtonBase` extends `Labeled` and defines common features for all buttons.

Listing 16.2 gives a program that uses the buttons to control the movement of a text, as shown in Figure 16.6.

LISTING 16.2 ButtonDemo.java

```
1   import javafx.application.Application;
2   import javafx.stage.Stage;
3   import javafx.geometry.Pos;
4   import javafx.scene.Scene;
5   import javafx.scene.control.Button;
6   import javafx.scene.image.ImageView;
7   import javafx.scene.layout.BorderPane;
8   import javafx.scene.layout.HBox;
9   import javafx.scene.layout.Pane;
10  import javafx.scene.text.Text;
11
12  public class ButtonDemo extends Application {
13    protected Text text = new Text(50, 50, "JavaFX Programming");
14
15    protected BorderPane getPane() {
16      HBox paneForButtons = new HBox(20);
17      Button btLeft = new Button("Left",                      create a button
18        new ImageView("image/left.gif"));
19      Button btRight = new Button("Right",
20        new ImageView("image/right.gif"));
21      paneForButtons.getChildren().addAll(btLeft, btRight);   add buttons to pane
22      paneForButtons.setAlignment(Pos.CENTER);
23      paneForButtons.setStyle("-fx-border-color: green");
24
25      BorderPane pane = new BorderPane();                     create a border pane
26      pane.setBottom(paneForButtons);                         add buttons to the bottom
27
28      Pane paneForText = new Pane();
29      paneForText.getChildren().add(text);
30      pane.setCenter(paneForText);
31
32      btLeft.setOnAction(e -> text.setX(text.getX() - 10));   add an action handler
33      btRight.setOnAction(e -> text.setX(text.getX() + 10));
34
35      return pane;                                            return a pane
```

```
36      }
37
38      @Override // Override the start method in the Application class
39      public void start(Stage primaryStage) {
40        // Create a scene and place it in the stage
41        Scene scene = new Scene(getPane(), 450, 200);
42        primaryStage.setTitle("ButtonDemo"); // Set the stage title
43        primaryStage.setScene(scene); // Place the scene in the stage
44        primaryStage.show(); // Display the stage
45      }
46    }
```

set pane to scene

FIGURE 16.6 The program demonstrates using buttons. *Source*: Copyright © 1995–2016 Oracle and/or its affiliates. All rights reserved. Used with permission.

The program creates two buttons, `btLeft` and `btRight`, with each button containing a text and an image (lines 17–20). The buttons are placed in an `HBox` (line 21) and the `HBox` is placed in the bottom of a border pane (line 26). A text is created in line 13 and is placed in the center of the border pane (line 30). The action handler for `btLeft` moves the text to the left (line 32). The action handler for `btRight` moves the text to the right (line 33).

getPane() protected

The program purposely defines a protected `getPane()` method to return a pane (line 15). This method will be overridden by subclasses in the upcoming examples to add more nodes in the pane. The text is declared protected so it can be accessed by subclasses (line 13).

16.3.1 How do you create a button with a text and a node? Can you apply all the methods for `Labeled` to `Button`?

16.3.2 Why is the `getPane()` method protected in Listing 16.2? Why is the data field `text` protected?

16.3.3 How do you set a handler for processing a button-clicked action?

16.4 CheckBox

A `CheckBox` is used for the user to make a selection.

Like `Button`, `CheckBox` inherits all the properties such as `onAction`, `text`, `graphic`, `alignment`, `graphicTextGap`, `textFill`, and `contentDisplay` from `ButtonBase` and `Labeled`, as shown in Figure 16.7. In addition, it provides the `selected` property to indicate whether a check box is selected.

Here is an example of a check box with text US, a graphic image, green text color, black border, and initially selected.

```
CheckBox chkUS = new CheckBox("US");
chkUS.setGraphic(new ImageView("image/usIcon.gif"));
chkUS.setTextFill(Color.GREEN);
chkUS.setContentDisplay(ContentDisplay.LEFT);
chkUS.setStyle("-fx-border-color: black");
chkUS.setSelected(true);
chkUS.setPadding(new Insets(5, 5, 5, 5));
```

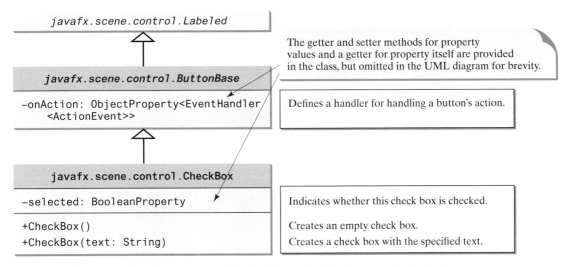

FIGURE 16.7 `CheckBox` contains the properties inherited from `ButtonBase` and `Labeled`.

When a check box is clicked (checked or unchecked), it fires an `ActionEvent`. To see if a check box is selected, use the `isSelected()` method.

We now write a program that adds two check boxes named Bold and Italic to the preceding example to let the user specify whether the message is in bold or italic, as shown in Figure 16.8.

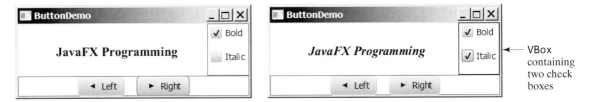

FIGURE 16.8 The program demonstrates check boxes. *Source*: Copyright © 1995–2016 Oracle and/or its affiliates. All rights reserved. Used with permission.

There are at least two approaches to writing this program. The first is to revise the preceding `ButtonDemo` class to insert the code for adding the check boxes and processing their events. The second is to define a subclass that extends `ButtonDemo`. Please implement the first approach as an exercise. Listing 16.3 gives the code to implement the second approach.

LISTING 16.3 CheckBoxDemo.java

```
1   import javafx.event.ActionEvent;
2   import javafx.event.EventHandler;
3   import javafx.geometry.Insets;
4   import javafx.scene.control.CheckBox;
5   import javafx.scene.layout.BorderPane;
6   import javafx.scene.layout.VBox;
7   import javafx.scene.text.Font;
8   import javafx.scene.text.FontPosture;
9   import javafx.scene.text.FontWeight;
10
11  public class CheckBoxDemo extends ButtonDemo {
12    @Override // Override the getPane() method in the super class
13    protected BorderPane getPane() {
14      BorderPane pane = super.getPane();
15
16      Font fontBoldItalic = Font.font("Times New Roman",
17        FontWeight.BOLD, FontPosture.ITALIC, 20);
```

override getPane()
invoke super.getPane()

create fonts

```
18        Font fontBold = Font.font("Times New Roman",
19          FontWeight.BOLD, FontPosture.REGULAR, 20);
20        Font fontItalic = Font.font("Times New Roman",
21          FontWeight.NORMAL, FontPosture.ITALIC, 20);
22        Font fontNormal = Font.font("Times New Roman",
23          FontWeight.NORMAL, FontPosture.REGULAR, 20);
24
25        text.setFont(fontNormal);
26
```

pane for check boxes
```
27        VBox paneForCheckBoxes = new VBox(20);
28        paneForCheckBoxes.setPadding(new Insets(5, 5, 5, 5));
29        paneForCheckBoxes.setStyle("-fx-border-color: green");
```
create check boxes
```
30        CheckBox chkBold = new CheckBox("Bold");
31        CheckBox chkItalic = new CheckBox("Italic");
32        paneForCheckBoxes.getChildren().addAll(chkBold, chkItalic);
33        pane.setRight(paneForCheckBoxes);
34
```
create a handler
```
35        EventHandler<ActionEvent> handler = e -> {
36          if (chkBold.isSelected() && chkItalic.isSelected()) {
37            text.setFont(fontBoldItalic); // Both check boxes checked
38          }
39          else if (chkBold.isSelected()) {
40            text.setFont(fontBold); // The Bold check box checked
41          }
42          else if (chkItalic.isSelected()) {
43            text.setFont(fontItalic); // The Italic check box checked
44          }
45          else {
46            text.setFont(fontNormal); // Both check boxes unchecked
47          }
48        };
49
```
set handler for action
```
50        chkBold.setOnAction(handler);
51        chkItalic.setOnAction(handler);
52
```
return a pane
```
53        return pane; // Return a new pane
54      }
55
56      public static void main(String[] args) {
57        launch(args);
58      }
59    }
```

`CheckBoxDemo` extends `ButtonDemo` and overrides the `getPane()` method (line 13). The new `getPane()` method invokes the `super.getPane()` method from the `ButtonDemo` class to obtain a border pane that contains the buttons and a text (line 14). The check boxes are created and added to `paneForCheckBoxes` (lines 30–32). `paneForCheckBoxes` is added to the border pane (lines 33).

The handler for processing the action event on check boxes is created in lines 35–48. It sets the appropriate font based on the status of the check boxes.

The `start` method for this JavaFX program is defined in `ButtonDemo` and inherited in `CheckBoxDemo`. Therefore, when you run `CheckBoxDemo`, the `start` method in `ButtonDemo` is invoked. Since the `getPane()` method is overridden in `CheckBoxDemo`, the method in `CheckBoxDemo` is invoked from line 41 in Listing 16.2, ButtonDemo.java. For additional information, see CheckPoint question 16.4.1.

Check
Point

16.4.1 What is the output of the following code?

```
public class Test {
  public static void main(String[] args) {
```

```
      Test test = new Test();
      test.new B().start();
    }

    class A {
      public void start() {
        System.out.println(getP());
      }

      public int getP() {
        return 1;
      }
    }

    class B extends A {
      public int getP() {
        return 2 + super.getP();
      }
    }
  }
```

16.4.2 How do you test if a check box is selected?

16.4.3 Can you apply all the methods for `Labeled` to `CheckBox`?

16.4.4 Can you set a node for the `graphic` property in a check box?

16.5 RadioButton

Radio buttons, also known as option buttons, *enable you to choose a single item from a group of choices.*

Key Point

In appearance, radio buttons resemble check boxes, but check boxes display a square that is either checked or blank, whereas radio buttons display a circle that is either filled (if selected) or blank (if not selected).

    `RadioButton` is a subclass of `ToggleButton`. The difference between a radio button and a toggle button is that a radio button displays a circle, but a toggle button is rendered similar to a button. The UML diagrams for `ToggleButton` and `RadioButton` are shown in Figure 16.9.

option buttons

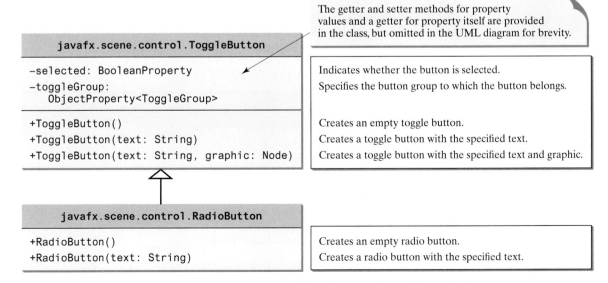

FIGURE 16.9 `ToggleButton` and `RadioButton` are specialized buttons for making selections.

Here is an example of a radio button with text US, a graphic image, green text color, black border, and initially selected.

```
RadioButton rbUS = new RadioButton("US");
rbUS.setGraphic(new ImageView("image/usIcon.gif"));
rbUS.setTextFill(Color.GREEN);
rbUS.setContentDisplay(ContentDisplay.LEFT);
rbUS.setStyle("-fx-border-color: black");
rbUS.setSelected(true);
rbUS.setPadding(new Insets(5, 5, 5, 5));
```

To group radio buttons, you need to create an instance of ToggleGroup and set a radio button's toggleGroup property to join the group, as follows:

```
ToggleGroup group = new ToggleGroup();
rbRed.setToggleGroup(group);
rbGreen.setToggleGroup(group);
rbBlue.setToggleGroup(group);
```

This code creates a button group for radio buttons rbRed, rbGreen, and rbBlue so buttons rbRed, rbGreen, and rbBlue are selected mutually exclusively. Without grouping, these buttons would be independent.

When a radio button is changed (selected or deselected), it fires an ActionEvent. To see if a radio button is selected, use the isSelected() method.

We now give a program that adds three radio buttons named Red, Green, and Blue to the preceding example to let the user choose the color of the message, as shown in Figure 16.10.

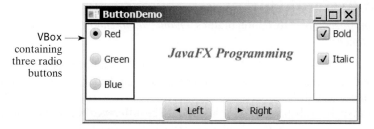

FIGURE 16.10 The program demonstrates using radio buttons. *Source*: Copyright © 1995–2016 Oracle and/or its affiliates. All rights reserved. Used with permission.

Again, there are at least two approaches to writing this program. The first is to revise the preceding CheckBoxDemo class to insert the code for adding the radio buttons and processing their events. The second is to define a subclass that extends CheckBoxDemo. Listing 16.4 gives the code to implement the second approach.

LISTING 16.4 RadioButtonDemo.java

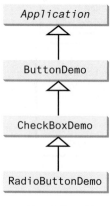

override getPane()
invoke super.getPane()

pane for radio buttons

```
1  import javafx.geometry.Insets;
2  import javafx.scene.control.RadioButton;
3  import javafx.scene.control.ToggleGroup;
4  import javafx.scene.layout.BorderPane;
5  import javafx.scene.layout.VBox;
6  import javafx.scene.paint.Color;
7
8  public class RadioButtonDemo extends CheckBoxDemo {
9    @Override // Override the getPane() method in the super class
10     protected BorderPane getPane() {
11       BorderPane pane = super.getPane();
12
13       VBox paneForRadioButtons = new VBox(20);
14       paneForRadioButtons.setPadding(new Insets(5, 5, 5, 5));
15       paneForRadioButtons.setStyle
```

```
16                  ("-fx-border-width: 2px; -fx-border-color: green");
17
18       RadioButton rbRed = new RadioButton("Red");                        create radio buttons
19       RadioButton rbGreen = new RadioButton("Green");
20       RadioButton rbBlue = new RadioButton("Blue");
21       paneForRadioButtons.getChildren().addAll(rbRed, rbGreen, rbBlue);
22       pane.setLeft(paneForRadioButtons);                                 add to border pane
23
24       ToggleGroup group = new ToggleGroup();                             group radio buttons
25       rbRed.setToggleGroup(group);
26       rbGreen.setToggleGroup(group);
27       rbBlue.setToggleGroup(group);
28
29       rbRed.setOnAction(e -> {                                           handle radio button
30         if (rbRed.isSelected()) {
31           text.setFill(Color.RED);
32         }
33       });
34
35       rbGreen.setOnAction(e -> {
36         if (rbGreen.isSelected()) {
37           text.setFill(Color.GREEN);
38         }
39       });
40
41       rbBlue.setOnAction(e -> {
42         if (rbBlue.isSelected()) {
43           text.setFill(Color.BLUE);
44         }
45       });
46
47       return pane;                                                       return border pane
48     }
49
50     public static void main(String[] args) {
51       launch(args);
52     }
53   }
```

RadioButtonDemo extends CheckBoxDemo and overrides the getPane() method (line 10). The new getPane() method invokes the getPane() method from the CheckBoxDemo class to create a border pane that contains the check boxes, buttons, and a text (line 11). This border pane is returned from invoking super.getPane(). The radio buttons are created and added to paneForRadioButtons (lines 18–21). paneForRadioButtons is added to the border pane (line 22).

The radio buttons are grouped together in lines 24–27. The handlers for processing the action event on radio buttons are created in lines 29–45. It sets the appropriate color based on the status of the radio buttons.

The start method for this JavaFX program is defined in ButtonDemo and inherited in CheckBoxDemo then in RadioButtonDemo. Thus, when you run RadioButtonDemo, the start method in ButtonDemo is invoked. Since the getPane() method is overridden in RadioButtonDemo, the method in RadioButtonDemo is invoked from line 41 in Listing 16.2, ButtonDemo.java.

16.5.1 How do you test if a radio button is selected?

16.5.2 Can you apply all the methods for Labeled to RadioButton?

16.5.3 Can you set any node in the graphic property in a radio button?

16.5.4 How do you group radio buttons?

Check
Point

Key Point

16.6 TextField

A text field can be used to enter or display a string.

TextField is a subclass of TextInputControl. Figure 16.11 lists the properties and constructors in TextField.

Here is an example of creating a noneditable text field with red text color, a specified font, and right horizontal alignment:

```
TextField tfMessage = new TextField("T-Storm");
tfMessage.setEditable(false);
tfMessage.setStyle("-fx-text-fill: red");
tfMessage.setFont(Font.font("Times", 20));
tfMessage.setAlignment(Pos.BASELINE_RIGHT);
```

| T-Storm |

When you move the cursor in the text field and press the *Enter* key, it fires an ActionEvent.

Listing 16.5 gives a program that adds a text field to the preceding example to let the user set a new message, as shown in Figure 16.12.

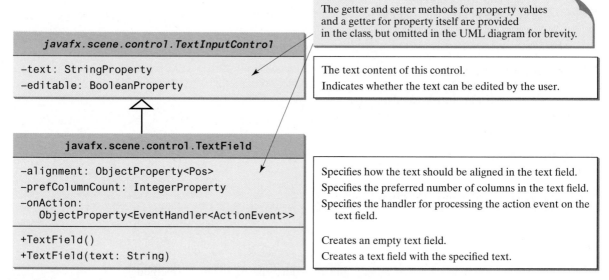

FIGURE 16.11 TextField enables the user to enter or display a string.

FIGURE 16.12 The program demonstrates using text fields. *Source*: Copyright © 1995–2016 Oracle and/or its affiliates. All rights reserved. Used with permission.

LISTING 16.5 TextFieldDemo.java

```java
 1  import javafx.geometry.Insets;
 2  import javafx.geometry.Pos;
 3  import javafx.scene.control.Label;
 4  import javafx.scene.control.TextField;
 5  import javafx.scene.layout.BorderPane;
 6
 7  public class TextFieldDemo extends RadioButtonDemo {
 8    @Override // Override the getPane() method in the super class
 9    protected BorderPane getPane() {
10      BorderPane pane = super.getPane();
11
12      BorderPane paneForTextField = new BorderPane();
13      paneForTextField.setPadding(new Insets(5, 5, 5, 5));
14      paneForTextField.setStyle("-fx-border-color: green");
15      paneForTextField.setLeft(new Label("Enter a new message: "));
16
17      TextField tf = new TextField();
18      tf.setAlignment(Pos.BOTTOM_RIGHT);
19      paneForTextField.setCenter(tf);
20      pane.setTop(paneForTextField);
21
22      tf.setOnAction(e -> text.setText(tf.getText()));
23
24      return pane;
25    }
26
27    public static void main(String[] args) {
28      launch(args);
29    }
30  }
```

override getPane()
invoke super.getPane()

pane for label and text field

create text field

add to border pane

handle text field action

return border pane

TextFieldDemo extends RadioButtonDemo (line 7) and adds a label and a text field to let the user enter a new text (lines 12–20). After you set a new text in the text field and press the *Enter* key, a new message is displayed (line 22). Pressing the *Enter* key on the text field triggers an action event.

Note

If a text field is used for entering a password, use `PasswordField` to replace `TextField`. `PasswordField` extends `TextField` and hides the input text with echo characters ******.

PasswordField

16.6.1 Can you disable editing of a text field?

16.6.2 Can you apply all the methods for `TextInputControl` to `TextField`?

16.6.3 Can you set a node as the `graphic` property in a text field?

16.6.4 How do you align the text in a text field to the right?

✓ **Check Point**

16.7 TextArea

A `TextArea` enables the user to enter multiple lines of text.

If you want to let the user enter multiple lines of text, you may create several instances of `TextField`. A better alternative, however, is to use `TextArea`, which enables the user to enter multiple lines of text. Figure 16.13 lists the properties and constructors in `TextArea`.

Here is an example of creating a text area with 5 rows and 20 columns, wrapped to the next line, red text color, and `Courier` font 20 pixels.

Key Point

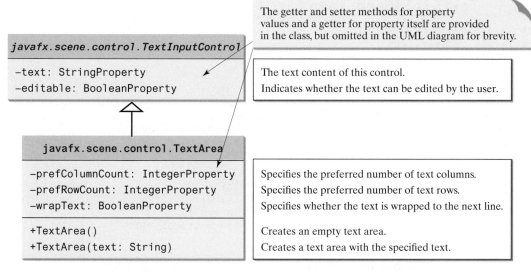

The getter and setter methods for property values and a getter for property itself are provided in the class, but omitted in the UML diagram for brevity.

The text content of this control.
Indicates whether the text can be edited by the user.

Specifies the preferred number of text columns.
Specifies the preferred number of text rows.
Specifies whether the text is wrapped to the next line.

Creates an empty text area.
Creates a text area with the specified text.

FIGURE 16.13 TextArea enables the user to enter or display multiple lines of characters.

```
TextArea taNote = new TextArea("This is a text area");
taNote.setPrefColumnCount(20);
taNote.setPrefRowCount(5);
taNote.setWrapText(true);
taNote.setStyle("-fx-text-fill: red");
taNote.setFont(Font.font("Times", 20));
```

TextArea provides scrolling, but often it is useful to create a ScrollPane object to hold an instance of TextArea and let ScrollPane handle scrolling for TextArea, as follows:

```
// Create a scroll pane to hold text area
ScrollPane scrollPane = new ScrollPane(taNote);
```

ScrollPane

> **Tip**
> You can place any node in a ScrollPane. ScrollPane automatically provides vertical and horizontal scrolling if the node is too large to fit in the viewing area.

We now give a program that displays an image and a short text in a label, and a long text in a text area, as shown in Figure 16.14.

A label showing an image and a text

DescriptionPane

A text area inside a scroll pane

FIGURE 16.14 The program displays an image in a label, a title in a label, and text in the text area. *Source*: Copyright © 1995–2016 Oracle and/or its affiliates. All rights reserved. Used with permission.

Here are the major steps in the program:

1. Define a class named DescriptionPane that extends BorderPane, as shown in Listing 16.6. This class contains a text area inside a scroll pane and a label for displaying an image icon and a title. The class DescriptionPane will be reused in later examples.

2. Define a class named `TextAreaDemo` that extends `Application`, as shown in Listing 16.7. Create an instance of `DescriptionPane` and add it to the scene. The relationship between `DescriptionPane` and `TextAreaDemo` is shown in Figure 16.15.

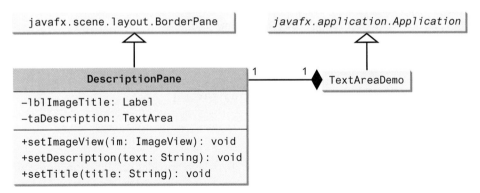

FIGURE 16.15 `TextAreaDemo` uses `DescriptionPane` to display an image, title, and text description of a national flag.

LISTING 16.6 `DescriptionPane.java`

```
1   import javafx.geometry.Insets;
2   import javafx.scene.control.Label;
3   import javafx.scene.control.ContentDisplay;
4   import javafx.scene.control.ScrollPane;
5   import javafx.scene.control.TextArea;
6   import javafx.scene.image.ImageView;
7   import javafx.scene.layout.BorderPane;
8   import javafx.scene.text.Font;
9
10  public class DescriptionPane extends BorderPane {
11    /** Label for displaying an image and a title */
12    private Label lblImageTitle = new Label();                        label
13
14    /** Text area for displaying text */
15    private TextArea taDescription = new TextArea();                  text area
16
17    public DescriptionPane() {
18      // Center the icon and text and place the text under the icon
19      lblImageTitle.setContentDisplay(ContentDisplay.TOP);           label properties
20      lblImageTitle.setPrefSize(200, 100);
21
22      // Set the font in the label and the text field
23      lblImageTitle.setFont(new Font("SansSerif", 16));
24      taDescription.setFont(new Font("Serif", 14));
25
26      taDescription.setWrapText(true);                               wrap text
27      taDescription.setEditable(false);                              read only
28
29      // Create a scroll pane to hold the text area
30      ScrollPane scrollPane = new ScrollPane(taDescription);         scroll pane
31
32      // Place label and scroll pane in the border pane
33      setLeft(lblImageTitle);
34      setCenter(scrollPane);
35      setPadding(new Insets(5, 5, 5, 5));
36    }
37
38    /** Set the title */
```

```
39    public void setTitle(String title) {
40      lblImageTitle.setText(title);
41    }
42
43    /** Set the image view */
44    public void setImageView(ImageView icon) {
45      lblImageTitle.setGraphic(icon);
46    }
47
48    /** Set the text description */
49    public void setDescription(String text) {
50      taDescription.setText(text);
51    }
52  }
```

The text area is inside a `ScrollPane` (line 30), which provides scrolling functions for the text area.

The `wrapText` property is set to `true` (line 26) so the line is automatically wrapped when the text cannot fit in one line. The text area is set as noneditable (line 27), so you cannot edit the description in the text area.

It is not necessary to define a separate class for `DescriptionPane` in this example. However, this class was defined for reuse in the next section, where you will use it to display a description pane for various images.

LISTING 16.7 TextAreaDemo.java

```
1   import javafx.application.Application;
2   import javafx.stage.Stage;
3   import javafx.scene.Scene;
4   import javafx.scene.image.ImageView;
5
6   public class TextAreaDemo extends Application {
7     @Override // Override the start method in the Application class
8     public void start(Stage primaryStage) {
9       // Declare and create a description pane
10      DescriptionPane descriptionPane = new DescriptionPane();
11
12      // Set title, text, and image in the description pane
13      descriptionPane.setTitle("Canada");
14      String description = "The Canadian national flag ... ";
15      descriptionPane.setImageView(new ImageView("image/ca.gif"));
16      descriptionPane.setDescription(description);
17
18      // Create a scene and place it in the stage
19      Scene scene = new Scene(descriptionPane, 450, 200);
20      primaryStage.setTitle("TextAreaDemo"); // Set the stage title
21      primaryStage.setScene(scene); // Place the scene in the stage
22      primaryStage.show(); // Display the stage
23    }
24  }
```

create descriptionPane — line 10

set title — line 13

set image — line 15

add descriptionPane to scene — line 19

The program creates an instance of `DescriptionPane` (line 10) and sets the title (line 13), image (line 15), and text (line 16) in the description pane. `DescriptionPane` is a subclass of `Pane`. `DescriptionPane` contains a label for displaying an image, a title, and a text area for displaying a description of the image.

16.7.1 How do you create a text area with **10** rows and **20** columns?

16.7.2 How do you obtain the text from a text area?

16.7.3   Can you disable editing of a text area?

16.7.4   What method do you use to wrap text to the next line in a text area?

16.8 ComboBox

A combo box, also known as a choice list or drop-down list, contains a list of items from which the user can choose.

Key Point

A combo box is useful for limiting a user's range of choices and avoids the cumbersome validation of data input. Figure 16.16 lists several frequently used properties and constructors in `ComboBox`. `ComboBox` is defined as a generic class like the `ArrayList` class. The generic type `T` specifies the element type for the elements stored in a combo box.

The following statements create a combo box with four items, red color, and value set to the first item:

```
ComboBox<String> cbo = new ComboBox<>();
cbo.getItems().addAll("Item 1", "Item 2",
  "Item 3", "Item 4");
cbo.setStyle("-fx-color: red");
cbo.setValue("Item 1");
```

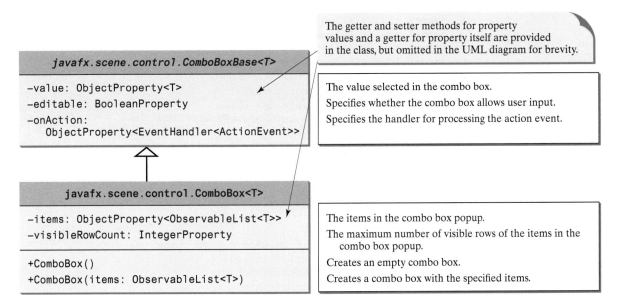

FIGURE 16.16   `ComboBox` enables the user to select an item from a list of items. *Source*: Copyright © 1995–2016 Oracle and/or its affiliates. All rights reserved. Used with permission.

`ComboBox` inherits from `ComboBoxBase`. `ComboBox` can fire an `ActionEvent`. Whenever an item is selected, an `ActionEvent` is fired. `ObservableList` is a subinterface of `java.util.List`. Therefore, you can apply all the methods defined in `List` for an `ObservableList`. For convenience, JavaFX provides the static method `FXCollections.observableArrayList(arrayOfElements)` for creating an `ObservableList` from an array of elements.

Listing 16.8 gives a program that lets the user view an image and a description of a country's flag by selecting the country from a combo box, as shown in Figure 16.17.

Here are the major steps in the program:

1. Create the user interface.
    Create a combo box with country names as its selection values. Create a `DescriptionPane` object (the `DescriptionPane` class was introduced in the preceding section). Place the combo box at the top of the border pane, and the description pane in the center of the border pane.

FIGURE 16.17 Information about a country, including an image and a description of its flag, is displayed when the country is selected in the combo box. *Source*: Copyright © 1995–2016 Oracle and/or its affiliates. All rights reserved. Used with permission.

2. Process the event.
   Create a handler for handling action event from the combo box to set the flag title, image, and text in the description pane for the selected country name.

LISTING 16.8 ComboBoxDemo.java

```
1   import javafx.application.Application;
2   import javafx.stage.Stage;
3   import javafx.collections.FXCollections;
4   import javafx.collections.ObservableList;
5   import javafx.scene.Scene;
6   import javafx.scene.control.ComboBox;
7   import javafx.scene.control.Label;
8   import javafx.scene.image.ImageView;
9   import javafx.scene.layout.BorderPane;
10
11  public class ComboBoxDemo extends Application {
12    // Declare an array of Strings for flag titles
13    private String[] flagTitles = {"Canada", "China", "Denmark",
14      "France", "Germany", "India", "Norway", "United Kingdom",
15      "United States of America"};
16
17    // Declare an ImageView array for the national flags of 9 countries
18    private ImageView[] flagImage = {new ImageView("image/ca.gif"),
19      new ImageView("image/china.gif"),
20      new ImageView("image/denmark.gif"),
21      new ImageView("image/fr.gif"),
22      new ImageView("image/germany.gif"),
23      new ImageView("image/india.gif"),
24      new ImageView("image/norway.gif"),
25      new ImageView("image/uk.gif"), new ImageView("image/us.gif")};
26
27    // Declare an array of strings for flag descriptions
28    private String[] flagDescription = new String[9];
29
30    // Declare and create a description pane
31    private DescriptionPane descriptionPane = new DescriptionPane();
32
33    // Create a combo box for selecting countries
34    private ComboBox<String> cbo = new ComboBox<>(); // flagTitles;
35
36    @Override // Override the start method in the Application class
37    public void start(Stage primaryStage) {
38      // Set text description
```

countries (line 13)

image views (line 18)

description (line 28)

combo box (line 31)

```
39        flagDescription[0] = "The Canadian national flag ... ";
40        flagDescription[1] = "Description for China ... ";
41        flagDescription[2] = "Description for Denmark ... ";
42        flagDescription[3] = "Description for France ... ";
43        flagDescription[4] = "Description for Germany ... ";
44        flagDescription[5] = "Description for India ... ";
45        flagDescription[6] = "Description for Norway ... ";
46        flagDescription[7] = "Description for UK ... ";
47        flagDescription[8] = "Description for US ... ";
48
49        // Set the first country (Canada) for display
50        setDisplay(0);
51
52        // Add combo box and description pane to the border pane
53        BorderPane pane = new BorderPane();
54
55        BorderPane paneForComboBox = new BorderPane();
56        paneForComboBox.setLeft(new Label("Select a country: "));
57        paneForComboBox.setCenter(cbo);
58        pane.setTop(paneForComboBox);
59        cbo.setPrefWidth(400);
60        cbo.setValue("Canada");                                              set combo box value
61
62        ObservableList<String> items =                                      observable list
63          FXCollections.observableArrayList(flagTitles);
64        cbo.getItems().addAll(items);                                       add to combo box
65        pane.setCenter(descriptionPane);
66
67        // Display the selected country
68        cbo.setOnAction(e -> setDisplay(items.indexOf(cbo.getValue())));
69
70        // Create a scene and place it in the stage
71        Scene scene = new Scene(pane, 450, 170);
72        primaryStage.setTitle("ComboBoxDemo"); // Set the stage title
73        primaryStage.setScene(scene); // Place the scene in the stage
74        primaryStage.show(); // Display the stage
75      }
76
77      /** Set display information on the description pane */
78      public void setDisplay(int index) {
79        descriptionPane.setTitle(flagTitles[index]);
80        descriptionPane.setImageView(flagImage[index]);
81        descriptionPane.setDescription(flagDescription[index]);
82      }
83    }
```

The program stores the flag information in three arrays: flagTitles, flagImage, and flagDescription (lines 13–28). The array flagTitles contains the names of nine countries, the array flagImage contains image views of each of the nine countries' flags, and the array flagDescription contains descriptions of the flags.

The program creates an instance of DescriptionPane (line 31), which was presented in Listing 16.6, DescriptionPane.java. The program creates a combo box with values from flagTitles (lines 62 and 63). The getItems() method returns a list from the combo box (line 64) and the addAll method adds multiple items into the list.

When the user selects an item in the combo box, the action event triggers the execution of the handler. The handler finds the selected index (line 68) and invokes the setDisplay(int index) method to set its corresponding flag title, flag image, and flag description on the pane (lines 78–82).

16.8.1 How do you create a combo box and add three items to it?

16.8.2 How do you retrieve an item from a combo box? How do you retrieve a selected item from a combo box?

16.8.3 How do you get the number of items in a combo box? How do you retrieve an item at a specified index in a combo box?

16.8.4 What events would a ComboBox fire upon selecting a new item?

16.9 ListView

VideoNote

Use ListView

A list view is a control that basically performs the same function as a combo box, but it enables the user to choose a single value or multiple values.

Figure 16.18 lists several frequently used properties and constructors in ListView. ListView is defined as a generic class like the ArrayList class. The generic type T specifies the element type for the elements stored in a list view.

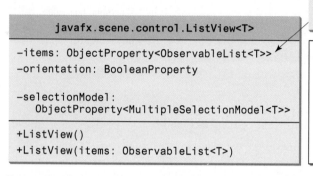

The getter and setter methods for property values and a getter for property itself are provided in the class, but omitted in the UML diagram for brevity.

```
javafx.scene.control.ListView<T>
```

-items: ObjectProperty<ObservableList<T>>	The items in the list view.
-orientation: BooleanProperty	Indicates whether the items are displayed horizontally or vertically in the list view.
-selectionModel: ObjectProperty<MultipleSelectionModel<T>>	Specifies how items are selected. The SelectionModel is also used to obtain the selected items.
+ListView()	Creates an empty list view.
+ListView(items: ObservableList<T>)	Creates a list view with the specified items.

FIGURE 16.18 ListView enables the user to select one or multiple items from a list of items.

The getSelectionModel() method returns an instance of SelectionModel, which contains the methods for setting a selection mode and obtaining selected indices and items. The selection mode is defined in one of the two constants SelectionMode.MULTIPLE and SelectionMode.SINGLE, which indicates whether a single item or multiple items can be selected. The default value is SelectionMode.SINGLE. Figure 16.19a shows a single selection and Figures 16.19b and c show multiple selections.

(a) Single selection   (b) Multiple selection   (c) Multiple selection

FIGURE 16.19 SelectionMode has two selection modes: single selection and multiple-interval selection. *Source*: Copyright © 1995–2016 Oracle and/or its affiliates. All rights reserved. Used with permission.

The following statements create a list view of six items with multiple selections allowed:

```
ObservableList<String> items =
  FXCollections.observableArrayList("Item 1", "Item 2",
    "Item 3", "Item 4", "Item 5", "Item 6");
ListView<String> lv = new ListView<>(items);
lv.getSelectionModel().setSelectionMode(SelectionMode.MULTIPLE);
```

The selection model in a list view has the `selectedItemProperty` property, which is an instance of `Observable`. As discussed in Section 15.10, you can add a listener to this property for handling the property change as follows:

```
lv.getSelectionModel().selectedItemProperty().addListener(
  new InvalidationListener() {
    public void invalidated(Observable ov) {
      System.out.println("Selected indices: "
        + lv.getSelectionModel().getSelectedIndices());
      System.out.println("Selected items: "
        + lv.getSelectionModel().getSelectedItems());
    }
  });
```

This anonymous inner class can be simplified using a lambda expression as follows:

```
lv.getSelectionModel().selectedItemProperty().addListener(ov -> {
  System.out.println("Selected indices: "
    + lv.getSelectionModel().getSelectedIndices());
  System.out.println("Selected items: "
    + lv.getSelectionModel().getSelectedItems());
});
```

Listing 16.9 gives a program that lets users select the countries in a list and displays the flags of the selected countries in the image views. Figure 16.20 shows a sample run of the program.

FIGURE 16.20 When the countries in the list are selected, corresponding images of their flags are displayed in the image views. *Source*: booka/Fotolia.

Here are the major steps in the program:

1. Create the user interface.
   Create a list view with nine country names as selection values and place the list view inside a scroll pane. Place the scroll pane on the left of a border pane. Create nine image views to be used to display the countries' flag images. Create a flow pane to hold the image views and place the pane in the center of the border pane.

2. Process the event.
   Create a listener to implement the `invalidated` method in the `InvalidationListener` interface to place the selected countries' flag image views in the pane.

LISTING 16.9 ListViewDemo.java

```java
1  import javafx.application.Application;
2  import javafx.stage.Stage;
3  import javafx.collections.FXCollections;
4  import javafx.scene.Scene;
5  import javafx.scene.control.ListView;
6  import javafx.scene.control.ScrollPane;
7  import javafx.scene.control.SelectionMode;
8  import javafx.scene.image.ImageView;
9  import javafx.scene.layout.BorderPane;
10 import javafx.scene.layout.FlowPane;
11
12 public class ListViewDemo extends Application {
13   // Declare an array of Strings for flag titles
14   private String[] flagTitles = {"Canada", "China", "Denmark",
15     "France", "Germany", "India", "Norway", "United Kingdom",
16     "United States of America"};
17
18   // Declare an ImageView array for the national flags of 9 countries
19   private ImageView[] ImageViews = {
20     new ImageView("image/ca.gif"),
21     new ImageView("image/china.gif"),
22     new ImageView("image/denmark.gif"),
23     new ImageView("image/fr.gif"),
24     new ImageView("image/germany.gif"),
25     new ImageView("image/india.gif"),
26     new ImageView("image/norway.gif"),
27     new ImageView("image/uk.gif"),
28     new ImageView("image/us.gif")
29   };
30
31   @Override // Override the start method in the Application class
32   public void start(Stage primaryStage) {
```
create a list view
```java
33     ListView<String> lv = new ListView<>
34       (FXCollections.observableArrayList(flagTitles));
```
set list view properties
```java
35     lv.setPrefSize(400, 400);
36     lv.getSelectionModel().setSelectionMode(SelectionMode.MULTIPLE);
37
38     // Create a pane to hold image views
39     FlowPane imagePane = new FlowPane(10, 10);
40     BorderPane pane = new BorderPane();
```
place list view in pane
```java
41     pane.setLeft(new ScrollPane(lv));
42     pane.setCenter(imagePane);
43
```
listen to item selected
```java
44     lv.getSelectionModel().selectedItemProperty().addListener(
45       ov -> {
46         imagePane.getChildren().clear();
47         for (Integer i: lv.getSelectionModel().getSelectedIndices()) {
```
add image views of selected items
```java
48           imagePane.getChildren().add(ImageViews[i]);
49         }
50     });
51
52     // Create a scene and place it in the stage
53     Scene scene = new Scene(pane, 450, 170);
54     primaryStage.setTitle("ListViewDemo"); // Set the stage title
55     primaryStage.setScene(scene); // Place the scene in the stage
56     primaryStage.show(); // Display the stage
57   }
58 }
```

The program creates an array of strings for countries (lines 14–16) and an array of nine image views for displaying flag images for nine countries (lines 19–29) in the same order as in the array of countries. The items in the list view are from the array of countries (line 34). Thus, the index 0 of the image view array corresponds to the first country in the list view.

The list view is placed in a scroll pane (line 41) so it can be scrolled when the number of items in the list extends beyond the viewing area.

By default, the selection mode of the list view is single. The selection mode for the list view is set to multiple (line 36), which allows the user to select multiple items in the list view. When the user selects countries in the list view, the listener's handler (lines 44–50) is executed, which gets the indices of the selected items and adds their corresponding image views to the flow pane.

16.9.1 How do you create an observable list with an array of strings?

16.9.2 How do you set the orientation in a list view?

16.9.3 What selection modes are available for a list view? What is the default selection mode? How do you set a selection mode?

16.9.4 How do you obtain the selected items and selected indices?

16.10 ScrollBar

ScrollBar is a control that enables the user to select from a range of values.

Figure 16.21 shows a scroll bar. Normally, the user changes the value of a scroll bar by making a gesture with the mouse. For example, the user can drag the scroll bar's thumb, click on the scroll bar track, or the scroll bar's left or right buttons.

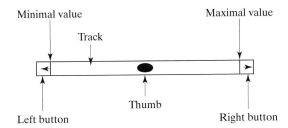

FIGURE 16.21 A scroll bar graphically represents a range of values.

ScrollBar has the following properties, as shown in Figure 16.22.

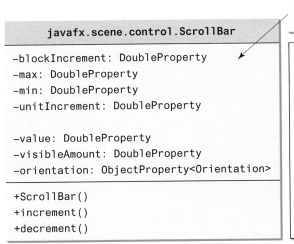

The getter and setter methods for property values and a getter for property itself are provided in the class, but omitted in the UML diagram for brevity.

javafx.scene.control.ScrollBar	
−blockIncrement: DoubleProperty	The amount to adjust the scroll bar if the track of the bar is clicked (default: 10).
−max: DoubleProperty	The maximum value represented by this scroll bar (default: 100).
−min: DoubleProperty	The minimum value represented by this scroll bar (default: 0).
−unitIncrement: DoubleProperty	The amount to adjust the scroll bar when the increment() and decrement() methods are called (default: 1).
−value: DoubleProperty	Current value of the scroll bar (default: 0).
−visibleAmount: DoubleProperty	The width of the scroll bar (default: 15).
−orientation: ObjectProperty<Orientation>	Specifies the orientation of the scroll bar (default: HORIZONTAL).
+ScrollBar()	Creates a default horizontal scroll bar.
+increment()	Increments the value of the scroll bar by unitIncrement.
+decrement()	Decrements the value of the scroll bar by unitIncrement.

FIGURE 16.22 ScrollBar enables the user to select from a range of values.

Note
The width of the scroll bar's track corresponds to `max + visibleAmount`. When a scroll bar is set to its maximum value, the left side of the bubble is at `max`, and the right side is at `max + visibleAmount`.

When the user changes the value of the scroll bar, it notifies the listener of the change. You can register a listener on the scroll bar's `valueProperty` for responding to this change as follows:

```
ScrollBar sb = new ScrollBar();
sb.valueProperty().addListener(ov -> {
  System.out.println("old value: " + oldVal);
  System.out.println("new value: " + newVal);
});
```

Listing 16.10 gives a program that uses horizontal and vertical scroll bars to move a text displayed on a pane. The horizontal scroll bar is used to move the text to the left and the right, and the vertical scroll bar to move it up and down. A sample run of the program is shown in Figure 16.23.

FIGURE 16.23 The scroll bars move the message on a pane horizontally and vertically. *Source*: Copyright © 1995–2016 Oracle and/or its affiliates. All rights reserved. Used with permission.

Here are the major steps in the program:

1. Create the user interface.
   Create a `Text` object and place it in a pane and place the pane in the center of the border pane. Create a vertical scroll bar and place it on the right of the border pane. Create a horizontal scroll bar and place it at the bottom of the border pane.

2. Process the event.
   Create listeners to move the text according to the bar movement in the scroll bars upon the change of the `value` property.

LISTING 16.10 `ScrollBarDemo.java`

```
1   import javafx.application.Application;
2   import javafx.stage.Stage;
3   import javafx.geometry.Orientation;
4   import javafx.scene.Scene;
5   import javafx.scene.control.ScrollBar;
6   import javafx.scene.layout.BorderPane;
7   import javafx.scene.layout.Pane;
8   import javafx.scene.text.Text;
9
10  public class ScrollBarDemo extends Application {
11    @Override // Override the start method in the Application class
12    public void start(Stage primaryStage) {
13      Text text = new Text(20, 20, "JavaFX Programming");
14
15      ScrollBar sbHorizontal = new ScrollBar();
16      ScrollBar sbVertical = new ScrollBar();
17      sbVertical.setOrientation(Orientation.VERTICAL);
18
19      // Create a text in a pane
```

horizontal scroll bar
vertical scroll bar

```
20        Pane paneForText = new Pane();
21        paneForText.getChildren().add(text);                              add text to a pane
22
23        // Create a border pane to hold text and scroll bars
24        BorderPane pane = new BorderPane();                               border pane
25        pane.setCenter(paneForText);
26        pane.setBottom(sbHorizontal);
27        pane.setRight(sbVertical);
28
29        // Listener for horizontal scroll bar value change
30        sbHorizontal.valueProperty().addListener(ov ->
31          text.setX(sbHorizontal.getValue() * paneForText.getWidth() /    set new location for text
32            sbHorizontal.getMax()));
33
34        // Listener for vertical scroll bar value change
35        sbVertical.valueProperty().addListener(ov ->
36          text.setY(sbVertical.getValue() * paneForText.getHeight() /      set new location for text
37            sbVertical.getMax()));
38
39        // Create a scene and place it in the stage
40        Scene scene = new Scene(pane, 450, 170);
41        primaryStage.setTitle("ScrollBarDemo"); // Set the stage title
42        primaryStage.setScene(scene); // Place the scene in the stage
43        primaryStage.show(); // Display the stage
44    }
45 }
```

The program creates a text (line 13) and two scroll bars (`sbHorizontal` and `sbVertical`) (lines 15 and 16). The text is placed in a pane (line 21) that is then placed in the center of the border pane (line 25). If the text were directly placed in the center of the border pane, the position of the text could not be changed by resetting its *x* and *y* properties. The `sbHorizontal` and `sbVertical` are placed on the right and at the bottom of the border pane (lines 26 and 27), respectively.

You can specify the properties of the scroll bar. By default, the property value is `100` for `max`, 0 for `min`, 10 for `blockIncrement`, and `15` for `visibleAmount`.

A listener is registered to listen for the `sbHorizontal value` property change (lines 30–32). When the value of the scroll bar changes, the listener is notified by invoking the handler to set a new *x* value for the text that corresponds to the current value of `sbHorizontal` (lines 31 and 32).

A listener is registered to listen for the `sbVertical value` property change (lines 35–37). When the value of the scroll bar changes, the listener is notified by invoking the handler to set a new *y* value for the text that corresponds to the current value of `sbVertical` (lines 36 and 37).

Alternatively, the code in lines 30–37 can be replaced by using binding properties as follows:

```
text.xProperty().bind(sbHorizontal.valueProperty().
  multiply(paneForText.widthProperty()).
  divide(sbHorizontal.maxProperty()));

text.yProperty().bind(sbVertical.valueProperty().multiply(
  paneForText.heightProperty().divide(
  sbVertical.maxProperty())));
```

16.10.1 How do you create a horizontal scroll bar? How do you create a vertical scroll bar?

16.10.2 How do you write the code to respond to the `value` property change of a scroll bar?

16.10.3 How do you get the value from a scroll bar? How do you get the maximum value from a scroll bar?

Check
Point

16.11 Slider

VideoNote

Use Slider

Slider is similar to ScrollBar, *but* Slider *has more properties and can appear in many forms.*

Figure 16.24 shows two sliders. Slider lets the user graphically select a value by sliding a knob within a bounded interval. The slider can show both major and minor tick marks between them. The number of pixels between the tick marks is specified by the majorTickUnit and minorTickUnit properties. Sliders can be displayed horizontally or vertically, with or without ticks, and with or without labels.

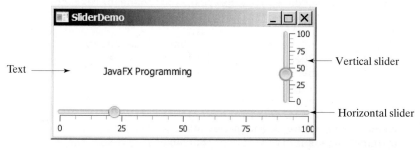

FIGURE 16.24 The sliders move the message on a pane horizontally and vertically. *Source*: Copyright © 1995–2016 Oracle and/or its affiliates. All rights reserved. Used with permission.

The frequently used constructors and properties in Slider are shown in Figure 16.25.

The getter and setter methods for property values and a getter for property itself are provided in the class, but omitted in the UML diagram for brevity.

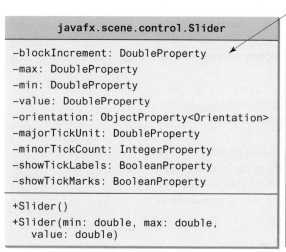

javafx.scene.control.Slider	
−blockIncrement: DoubleProperty	The amount to adjust the slider if the track of the bar is clicked (default: 10).
−max: DoubleProperty	The maximum value represented by this slider (default: 100).
−min: DoubleProperty	The minimum value represented by this slider (default: 0).
−value: DoubleProperty	Current value of the slider (default: 0).
−orientation: ObjectProperty<Orientation>	Specifies the orientation of the slider (default: HORIZONTAL).
−majorTickUnit: DoubleProperty	The unit distance between major tick marks.
−minorTickCount: IntegerProperty	The number of minor ticks to place between two major ticks.
−showTickLabels: BooleanProperty	Specifies whether the labels for tick marks are shown.
−showTickMarks: BooleanProperty	Specifies whether the tick marks are shown.
+Slider()	Creates a default horizontal slider.
+Slider(min: double, max: double, value: double)	Creates a slider with the specified min, max, and value.

FIGURE 16.25 Slider enables the user to select from a range of values.

Note
The values of a vertical scroll bar increase from top to bottom, but the values of a vertical slider decrease from top to bottom.

You can add a listener to listen for the value property change in a slider in the same way as in a scroll bar. We now rewrite the program in the preceding section using the sliders to move a text displayed on a pane in Listing 16.11. A sample run of the program is shown in Figure 16.24.

LISTING 16.11   SliderDemo.java

```
1   import javafx.application.Application;
2   import javafx.stage.Stage;
3   import javafx.geometry.Orientation;
4   import javafx.scene.Scene;
5   import javafx.scene.control.Slider;
6   import javafx.scene.layout.BorderPane;
7   import javafx.scene.layout.Pane;
8   import javafx.scene.text.Text;
9
10  public class SliderDemo extends Application {
11    @Override // Override the start method in the Application class
12    public void start(Stage primaryStage) {
13      Text text = new Text(20, 20, "JavaFX Programming");
14
15      Slider slHorizontal = new Slider();                              horizontal slider
16      slHorizontal.setShowTickLabels(true);                            set slider properties
17      slHorizontal.setShowTickMarks(true);
18
19      Slider slVertical = new Slider();                                vertical slider
20      slVertical.setOrientation(Orientation.VERTICAL);                 set slider properties
21      slVertical.setShowTickLabels(true);
22      slVertical.setShowTickMarks(true);
23      slVertical.setValue(100);
24
25      // Create a text in a pane
26      Pane paneForText = new Pane();
27      paneForText.getChildren().add(text);                             add text to a pane
28
29      // Create a border pane to hold text and scroll bars
30      BorderPane pane = new BorderPane();                              border pane
31      pane.setCenter(paneForText);
32      pane.setBottom(slHorizontal);
33      pane.setRight(slVertical);
34
35      slHorizontal.valueProperty().addListener(ov ->
36        text.setX(slHorizontal.getValue() * paneForText.getWidth() /   set new location for text
37          slHorizontal.getMax()));
38
39      slVertical.valueProperty().addListener(ov ->
40        text.setY((slVertical.getMax() - slVertical.getValue())        set new location for text
41          * paneForText.getHeight() / slVertical.getMax()));
42
43      // Create a scene and place it in the stage
44      Scene scene = new Scene(pane, 450, 170);
45      primaryStage.setTitle("SliderDemo"); // Set the stage title
46      primaryStage.setScene(scene); // Place the scene in the stage
47      primaryStage.show(); // Display the stage
48    }
49  }
```

Slider is similar to ScrollBar but has more features. As shown in this example, you can specify labels, major ticks, and minor ticks on a Slider (lines 16 and 17).

A listener is registered to listen for the slHorizontal value property change (lines 35–37) and another one is for the sbVertical value property change (lines 39–41). When the value of the slider changes, the listener is notified by invoking the handler to set a new position for the text (lines 36 and 37 and 40 and 41). Note since the value of a vertical slider decreases from top to bottom, the corresponding *y* value for the text is adjusted accordingly.

The code in lines 35–41 can be replaced by using binding properties as follows:

```
text.xProperty().bind(slHorizontal.valueProperty().
  multiply(paneForText.widthProperty()).
  divide(slHorizontal.maxProperty()));

text.yProperty().bind((slVertical.maxProperty().subtract(
  slVertical.valueProperty()).multiply(
  paneForText.heightProperty().divide(
  slVertical.maxProperty())))));
```

Listing 15.17 gives a program that displays a bouncing ball. You can add a slider to control the speed of the ball movement, as shown in Figure 16.26. The new program is given in Listing 16.12.

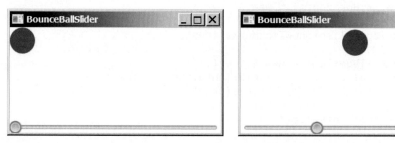

FIGURE 16.26 You can increase or decrease the speed of the ball using a slider. *Source*: Copyright © 1995–2016 Oracle and/or its affiliates. All rights reserved. Used with permission.

LISTING 16.12 BounceBallSlider.java

```
 1  import javafx.application.Application;
 2  import javafx.stage.Stage;
 3  import javafx.scene.Scene;
 4  import javafx.scene.control.Slider;
 5  import javafx.scene.layout.BorderPane;
 6
 7  public class BounceBallSlider extends Application {
 8    @Override // Override the start method in the Application class
 9    public void start(Stage primaryStage) {
10      BallPane ballPane = new BallPane();
11      Slider slSpeed = new Slider();
12      slSpeed.setMax(20);
13      ballPane.rateProperty().bind(slSpeed.valueProperty());
14
15      BorderPane pane = new BorderPane();
16      pane.setCenter(ballPane);
17      pane.setBottom(slSpeed);
18
19      // Create a scene and place it in the stage
20      Scene scene = new Scene(pane, 250, 250);
21      primaryStage.setTitle("BounceBallSlider"); // Set the stage title
22      primaryStage.setScene(scene); // Place the scene in the stage
23      primaryStage.show(); // Display the stage
24    }
25  }
```

create a ball pane
create a slider
set max value for slider
bind rate with slider value

create a border pane
add ball pane to center
add slider to the bottom

The `BallPane` class defined in Listing 15.17 animates a ball bouncing in a pane. The `rateProperty()` method in `BallPane` returns a property value for the animation rate.

The animation stops if the rate is 0. If the rate is greater than 20, the animation will be too fast. Therefore, we purposely set the rate to a value between 0 and 20. This value is bound to the slider value (line 13). Thus, the slider max value is set to 20 (line 12).

16.11.1 How do you create a horizontal slider? How do you create a vertical slider?

16.11.2 How do you add a listener to handle the property value change of a slider?

16.11.3 How do you get the value from a slider? How do you get the maximum value from a slider?

16.12 Case Study: Developing a Tic-Tac-Toe Game

This section develops a program for playing tic-tac-toe game.

Key Point

VideoNote
Tic-Tac-Toe

From the many examples in this and earlier chapters, you have learned about objects, classes, arrays, class inheritance, GUI, and event-driven programming. Now it is time to put what you have learned to work in developing comprehensive projects. In this section, we will develop a JavaFX program with which to play the popular game of tic-tac-toe.

Two players take turns marking an available cell in a 3 × 3 grid with their respective tokens (either X or O). When one player has placed three tokens in a horizontal, vertical, or diagonal row on the grid, the game is over and that player has won. A draw (no winner) occurs when all the cells on the grid have been filled with tokens and neither player has achieved a win. Figure 16.27 shows the representative sample runs of the game.

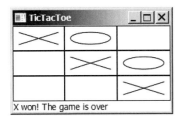 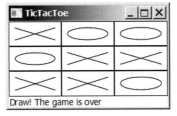 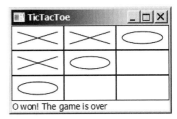

(a) The X player won the game   (b) Draw—no winners   (c) The O player won the game

FIGURE 16.27 Two players play a tic-tac-toe game. *Source*: Copyright © 1995–2016 Oracle and/or its affiliates. All rights reserved. Used with permission.

All the examples you have seen so far show simple behaviors that are easy to model with classes. The behavior of the tic-tac-toe game is somewhat more complex. To define classes that model the behavior, you need to study and understand the game.

Assume all the cells are initially empty, and that the first player takes the X token and the second player the O token. To mark a cell, the player points the mouse to the cell and clicks it. If the cell is empty, the token (X or O) is displayed. If the cell is already filled, the player's action is ignored.

From the preceding description, it should be obvious that a cell is a GUI object that handles the mouse-click event and displays tokens. There are many choices for this object. We will use a pane to model a cell and to display a token (X or O). How do you know the state of the cell (empty, X, or O)? You use a property named `token` of the `char` type in the `Cell` class. The `Cell` class is responsible for drawing the token when an empty cell is clicked, so you need to write the code for listening to the mouse-clicked action and for painting the shapes for tokens X and O. The `Cell` class can be defined as shown in Figure 16.28.

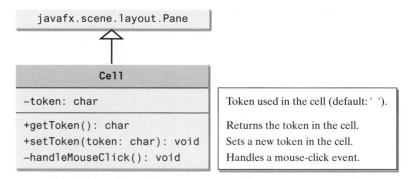

FIGURE 16.28 The `Cell` class displays the token in a cell.

The tic-tac-toe board consists of nine cells, created using `new Cell[3][3]`. To determine which player's turn it is, you can introduce a variable named `whoseTurn` of the `char` type. `whoseTurn` is initially `'X'`, then changes to `'O'`, and subsequently changes between `'X'` and `'O'` whenever a new cell is occupied. When the game is over, set `whoseTurn` to `' '`.

How do you know whether the game is over, whether there is a winner, and who is the winner, if any? You can define a method named `isWon(char token)` to check whether a specified token has won and a method named `isFull()` to check whether all the cells are occupied.

Clearly, two classes emerge from the foregoing analysis. One is the `Cell` class, which handles operations for a single cell; the other is the `TicTacToe` class, which plays the whole game and deals with all the cells. The relationship between these two classes is shown in Figure 16.29.

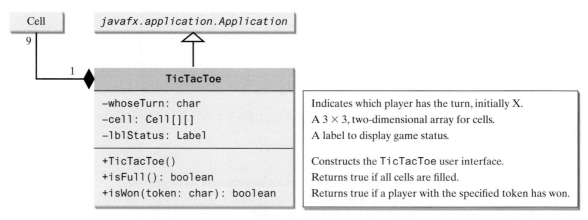

FIGURE 16.29 The `TicTacToe` class contains nine cells.

Since the `Cell` class is only to support the `TicTacToe` class, it can be defined as an inner class in `TicTacToe`. The complete program is given in Listing 16.13.

LISTING 16.13 TicTacToe.java

```
1  import javafx.application.Application;
2  import javafx.stage.Stage;
3  import javafx.scene.Scene;
4  import javafx.scene.control.Label;
5  import javafx.scene.layout.BorderPane;
```

```
6   import javafx.scene.layout.GridPane;
7   import javafx.scene.layout.Pane;
8   import javafx.scene.paint.Color;
9   import javafx.scene.shape.Line;
10  import javafx.scene.shape.Ellipse;
11
12  public class TicTacToe extends Application {                              main class TicTacToe
13    // Indicate which player has a turn, initially it is the X player
14    private char whoseTurn = 'X';
15
16    // Create and initialize cell
17    private Cell[][] cell = new Cell[3][3];
18
19    // Create and initialize a status label
20    private Label lblStatus = new Label("X's turn to play");
21
22    @Override // Override the start method in the Application class
23    public void start(Stage primaryStage) {
24      // Pane to hold cell
25      GridPane pane = new GridPane();                                      hold nine cells
26      for (int i = 0; i < 3; i++)
27        for (int j = 0; j < 3; j++)
28          pane.add(cell[i][j] = new Cell(), j, i);                        create a cell
29
30      BorderPane borderPane = new BorderPane();
31      borderPane.setCenter(pane);                                         tic-tac-toe cells in center
32      borderPane.setBottom(lblStatus);                                    label at bottom
33
34      // Create a scene and place it in the stage
35      Scene scene = new Scene(borderPane, 450, 170);
36      primaryStage.setTitle("TicTacToe"); // Set the stage title
37      primaryStage.setScene(scene); // Place the scene in the stage
38      primaryStage.show(); // Display the stage
39    }
40
41    /** Determine if the cell are all occupied */
42    public boolean isFull() {                                             check isFull
43      for (int i = 0; i < 3; i++)
44        for (int j = 0; j < 3; j++)
45          if (cell[i][j].getToken() == ' ')
46            return false;
47
48      return true;
49    }
50
51    /** Determine if the player with the specified token wins */
52    public boolean isWon(char token) {
53      for (int i = 0; i < 3; i++)                                         check rows
54        if (cell[i][0].getToken() == token
55            && cell[i][1].getToken() == token
56            && cell[i][2].getToken() == token) {
57          return true;
58        }
59
60      for (int j = 0; j < 3; j++)                                         check columns
61        if (cell[0][j].getToken() == token
62            && cell[1][j].getToken() == token
63            && cell[2][j].getToken() == token) {
64          return true;
65        }
```

```
                          66
check major diagonal      67      if (cell[0][0].getToken() == token
                          68          && cell[1][1].getToken() == token
                          69          && cell[2][2].getToken() == token) {
                          70        return true;
                          71      }
                          72
check subdiagonal         73      if (cell[0][2].getToken() == token
                          74          && cell[1][1].getToken() == token
                          75          && cell[2][0].getToken() == token) {
                          76        return true;
                          77      }
                          78
                          79      return false;
                          80    }
                          81
                          82    // An inner class for a cell
inner class Cell          83    public class Cell extends Pane {
                          84      // Token used for this cell
                          85      private char token = ' ';
                          86
                          87      public Cell() {
                          88        setStyle("-fx-border-color: black");
                          89        this.setPrefSize(2000, 2000);
register listener         90        this.setOnMouseClicked(e -> handleMouseClick());
                          91      }
                          92
                          93      /** Return token */
                          94      public char getToken() {
                          95        return token;
                          96      }
                          97
                          98      /** Set a new token */
                          99      public void setToken(char c) {
                         100        token = c;
                         101
display X                102        if (token == 'X') {
                         103          Line line1 = new Line(10, 10,
                         104            this.getWidth() - 10, this.getHeight() - 10);
                         105          line1.endXProperty().bind(this.widthProperty().subtract(10));
                         106          line1.endYProperty().bind(this.heightProperty().subtract(10));
                         107          Line line2 = new Line(10, this.getHeight() - 10,
                         108            this.getWidth() - 10, 10);
                         109          line2.startYProperty().bind(
                         110            this.heightProperty().subtract(10));
                         111          line2.endXProperty().bind(this.widthProperty().subtract(10));
                         112
                         113          // Add the lines to the pane
                         114          this.getChildren().addAll(line1, line2);
                         115        }
display O                116        else if (token == 'O') {
                         117          Ellipse ellipse = new Ellipse(this.getWidth() / 2,
                         118            this.getHeight() / 2, this.getWidth() / 2 - 10,
                         119            this.getHeight() / 2 - 10);
                         120          ellipse.centerXProperty().bind(
                         121            this.widthProperty().divide(2));
                         122          ellipse.centerYProperty().bind(
                         123            this.heightProperty().divide(2));
                         124          ellipse.radiusXProperty().bind(
                         125            this.widthProperty().divide(2).subtract(10));
```

```
126            ellipse.radiusYProperty().bind(
127              this.heightProperty().divide(2).subtract(10));
128            ellipse.setStroke(Color.BLACK);
129            ellipse.setFill(Color.WHITE);
130
131            getChildren().add(ellipse); // Add the ellipse to the pane
132          }
133        }
134
135        /* Handle a mouse click event */
136        private void handleMouseClick() {                        handle mouse click
137          // If cell is empty and game is not over
138          if (token == ' ' && whoseTurn != ' ') {
139            setToken(whoseTurn); // Set token in the cell
140
141            // Check game status
142            if (isWon(whoseTurn)) {
143              lblStatus.setText(whoseTurn + " won! The game is over");
144              whoseTurn = ' '; // Game is over
145            }
146            else if (isFull()) {
147              lblStatus.setText("Draw! The game is over");
148              whoseTurn = ' '; // Game is over
149            }
150            else {
151              // Change the turn
152              whoseTurn = (whoseTurn == 'X') ? 'O' : 'X';
153              // Display whose turn
154              lblStatus.setText(whoseTurn + "'s turn");
155            }
156          }
157        }
158      }
159    }
```

The TicTacToe class initializes the user interface with nine cells placed in a grid pane (lines 25–28). A label named lblStatus is used to show the status of the game (line 20). The variable whoseTurn (line 14) is used to track the next type of token to be placed in a cell. The methods isFull (lines 42–49) and isWon (lines 52–80) are for checking the status of the game.

Since Cell is an inner class in TicTacToe, the variable whoseTurn and methods isFull and isWon defined in TicTacToe can be referenced from the Cell class. The inner class makes programs simple and concise. If Cell were not defined as an inner class of TicTacToe, you would have to pass an object of TicTacToe to Cell in order for the variables and methods in TicTacToe to be used in Cell.

The listener for the mouse-click action is registered for the cell (line 90). If an empty cell is clicked and the game is not over, a token is set in the cell (line 138). If the game is over, whoseTurn is set to ' ' (lines 144 and 148). Otherwise, whoseTurn is alternated to a new turn (line 152).

 Tip
Use an incremental approach in developing and testing a Java project of this kind. For   incremental development and
example, this program can be divided into five steps: testing

1. Lay out the user interface and display a fixed token X on a cell.
2. Enable the cell to display a fixed token X upon a mouse click.
3. Coordinate between the two players so as to display tokens X and O alternately.
4. Check whether a player wins, or whether all the cells are occupied without a winner.
5. Implement displaying a message on the label upon each move by a player.

Check Point

16.12.1 When the game starts, what value is in `whoseTurn`? When the game is over, what value is in `whoseTurn`?

16.12.2 What happens when the user clicks on an empty cell if the game is not over? What happens when the user clicks on an empty cell if the game is over?

16.12.3 How does the program check whether a player wins? How does the program check whether all cells are filled?

16.13 Video and Audio

Key Point

You can use the `Media` class to obtain the source of the media, the `MediaPlayer` class to play and control the media, and the `MediaView` class to display the video.

VideoNote

Use `Media`, `MediaPlayer`, and `MediaView`

Media (video and audio) is essential in developing rich GUI applications. JavaFX provides the `Media`, `MediaPlayer`, and `MediaView` classes for working with media. Currently, JavaFX supports MP3, AIFF, WAV, and MPEG-4 audio formats and FLV and MPEG-4 video formats.

The `Media` class represents a media source with properties `duration`, `width`, and `height`, as shown in Figure 16.30. You can construct a `Media` object from an Internet URL string.

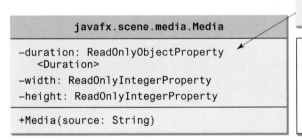

The getter methods for property values are provided in the class, but omitted in the UML diagram for brevity.

javafx.scene.media.Media	
-duration: ReadOnlyObjectProperty<Duration>	The duration in seconds of the source media.
-width: ReadOnlyIntegerProperty	The width in pixels of the source video.
-height: ReadOnlyIntegerProperty	The height in pixels of the source video.
+Media(source: String)	Creates a Media from a URL source.

FIGURE 16.30 `Media` represents a media source such as a video or an audio.

The `MediaPlayer` class plays and controls the media with properties such as `autoPlay`, `currentCount`, `cycleCount`, `mute`, `volume`, and `totalDuration`, as shown in Figure 16.31. You can construct a `MediaPlayer` object from a media and use the `pause()` and `play()` methods to pause and resume playing.

The getter and setter methods for property values and a getter for property itself are provided in the class, but omitted in the UML diagram for brevity.

javafx.scene.media.MediaPlayer	
-autoPlay: BooleanProperty	Specifies whether the playing should start automatically.
-currentCount: ReadOnlyIntegerProperty	The number of completed playback cycles.
-cycleCount: IntegerProperty	Specifies the number of time the media will be played.
-mute: BooleanProperty	Specifies whether the audio is muted.
-volume: DoubleProperty	The volume for the audio.
-totalDuration: ReadOnlyObjectProperty<Duration>	The amount of time to play the media from start to finish.
+MediaPlayer(media: Media)	Creates a player for a specified media.
+play(): void	Plays the media.
+pause(): void	Pauses the media.
+seek(): void	Seeks the player to a new playback time.

FIGURE 16.31 `MediaPlayer` plays and controls a media.

The `MediaView` class is a subclass of `Node` that provides a view of the `Media` being played by a `MediaPlayer`. The `MediaView` class provides the properties for viewing the media, as shown in Figure 16.32.

The getter and setter methods for property values and a getter for property itself are provided in the class, but omitted in the UML diagram for brevity.

javafx.scene.media.MediaView	
–x: DoubleProperty	Specifies the current *x*-coordinate of the media view.
–y: DoubleProperty	Specifies the current *y*-coordinate of the media view.
–mediaPlayer: ObjectProperty<MediaPlayer>	Specifies a media player for the media view.
–fitWidth: DoubleProperty	Specifies the width of the view for the media to fit.
–fitHeight: DoubleProperty	Specifies the height of the view for the media to fit.
+MediaView()	Creates an empty media view.
+MediaView(mediaPlayer: MediaPlayer)	Creates a media view with the specified media player.

FIGURE 16.32 `MediaView` provides the properties for viewing the media.

Listing 16.14 gives an example that displays a video in a view, as shown in Figure 16.33. You can use the play/pause button to play or pause the video and use the rewind button to restart the video, and use the slider to control the volume of the audio.

FIGURE 16.33 The program controls and plays a video.

LISTING 16.14 MediaDemo.java

```
1  import javafx.application.Application;
2  import javafx.stage.Stage;
3  import javafx.geometry.Pos;
4  import javafx.scene.Scene;
5  import javafx.scene.control.Button;
6  import javafx.scene.control.Label;
7  import javafx.scene.control.Slider;
8  import javafx.scene.layout.BorderPane;
9  import javafx.scene.layout.HBox;
10 import javafx.scene.layout.Region;
11 import javafx.scene.media.Media;
```

```
12  import javafx.scene.media.MediaPlayer;
13  import javafx.scene.media.MediaView;
14  import javafx.util.Duration;
15
16  public class MediaDemo extends Application {
17    private static final String MEDIA_URL =
18      "http://liveexample.pearsoncmg.com/common/sample.mp4";
19
20    @Override // Override the start method in the Application class
21    public void start(Stage primaryStage) {
22      Media media = new Media(MEDIA_URL);
23      MediaPlayer mediaPlayer = new MediaPlayer(media);
24      MediaView mediaView = new MediaView(mediaPlayer);
25
26      Button playButton = new Button(">");
27      playButton.setOnAction(e -> {
28        if (playButton.getText().equals(">")) {
29          mediaPlayer.play();
30          playButton.setText("||");
31        } else {
32          mediaPlayer.pause();
33          playButton.setText(">");
34        }
35      });
36
37      Button rewindButton = new Button("<<");
38      rewindButton.setOnAction(e -> mediaPlayer.seek(Duration.ZERO));
39
40      Slider slVolume = new Slider();
41      slVolume.setPrefWidth(150);
42      slVolume.setMaxWidth(Region.USE_PREF_SIZE);
43      slVolume.setMinWidth(30);
44      slVolume.setValue(50);
45      mediaPlayer.volumeProperty().bind(
46        slVolume.valueProperty().divide(100));
47
48      HBox hBox = new HBox(10);
49      hBox.setAlignment(Pos.CENTER);
50      hBox.getChildren().addAll(playButton, rewindButton,
51        new Label("Volume"), slVolume);
52
53      BorderPane pane = new BorderPane();
54      pane.setCenter(mediaView);
55      pane.setBottom(hBox);
56
57      // Create a scene and place it in the stage
58      Scene scene = new Scene(pane, 650, 500);
59      primaryStage.setTitle("MediaDemo"); // Set the stage title
60      primaryStage.setScene(scene); // Place the scene in the stage
61      primaryStage.show(); // Display the stage
62    }
63  }
```

Annotations in left margin:
- create a media (line 22)
- create a media player (line 23)
- create a media view (line 24)
- create a play/pause button (line 26)
- add handler for button action (line 27)
- play media (line 29)
- pause media (line 32)
- create a rewind button (line 37)
- create a handler for rewinding (line 38)
- create a slider for volume (line 40)
- set current volume (line 44)
- bind volume with slider (line 45)
- add buttons, slider to hBox (line 50)
- place media view in a pane (line 54)

The source of the media is a URL string defined in lines 17 and 18. The program creates a `Media` object from this URL (line 22), a `MediaPlayer` from the `Media` object (line 23), and a `MediaView` from the `MediaPlayer` object (line 24). The relationship among these three objects is shown in Figure 16.34.

FIGURE 16.34 The media represents the source, the media player controls the playing, and the media view displays the video.

A `Media` object supports live streaming. You can now download a large media file and play it in the same time. A `Media` object can be shared by multiple media players and different views can use the same `MediaPlayer` object.

A play button is created (line 26) to play/pause the media (line 29). The button's text is changed to | | (line 30) if the button's current text is > (line 28). If the button's current text is | |, it is changed to > (line 33) and the player is paused (line 32).

A rewind button is created (line 37) to reset the playback time to the beginning of the media stream by invoking `seek(Duration.ZERO)` (line 38).

A slider is created (line 40) to set the volume. The media player's volume property is bound to the slider (lines 45 and 46).

The buttons and slider are placed in an `HBox` (lines 48–51) and the media view is placed in the center of the border pane (line 54) and the `HBox` is placed at the bottom of the border pane (line 55).

16.13.1 How do you create a `Media` from a URL? How do you create a `MediaPlayer`? How do you create a `MediaView`?

16.13.2 If the URL is typed as liveexample.pearsoncmg.com/common/sample.mp4 without http:// in front of it, will it work?

16.13.3 Can you place a `Media` in multiple `MediaPlayer`s? Can you place a `MediaPlayer` in multiple `MediaView`s? Can you place a `MediaView` in multiple `Pane`s?

✓ **Check Point**

16.14 Case Study: National Flags and Anthems

This case study presents a program that displays a nation's flag and plays its anthem.

Key Point

The images for seven national flags, named **flag0.gif**, **flag1.gif**, . . . , **flag6.gif** for Denmark, Germany, China, India, Norway, the United Kingdom, and the United States are stored under http://liveexample.pearsoncmg.com/common/image. The audio consists of national anthems for these seven nations, named **anthem0.mp3**, **anthem1.mp3**, . . . , **anthem6.mp3**. They are stored under http://liveexample.pearsoncmg.com/common/audio.

The program enables the user to select a nation from a combo box, then displays its flag and plays its anthem. The user can suspend the audio by clicking the | | button, and resume it by clicking the < button, as shown in Figure 16.35.

FIGURE 16.35 The program displays a national flag and plays its anthem. *Source*: booka/ Fotolia.

The program is given in Listing 16.15.

LISTING 16.15 FlagAnthem.java

```
1  import javafx.application.Application;
2  import javafx.collections.FXCollections;
3  import javafx.collections.ObservableList;
4  import javafx.stage.Stage;
5  import javafx.geometry.Pos;
6  import javafx.scene.Scene;
7  import javafx.scene.control.Button;
8  import javafx.scene.control.ComboBox;
9  import javafx.scene.control.Label;
10 import javafx.scene.image.Image;
11 import javafx.scene.image.ImageView;
12 import javafx.scene.layout.BorderPane;
13 import javafx.scene.layout.HBox;
14 import javafx.scene.media.Media;
15 import javafx.scene.media.MediaPlayer;
16
17 public class FlagAnthem extends Application {
18   private final static int NUMBER_OF_NATIONS = 7;
19   private final static String URLBase =
20     "https://liveexample.pearsoncmg.com/common";
21   private int currentIndex = 0;
22
23   @Override // Override the start method in the Application class
24   public void start(Stage primaryStage) {
25     Image[] images = new Image[NUMBER_OF_NATIONS];
26     MediaPlayer[] mp = new MediaPlayer[NUMBER_OF_NATIONS];
27
28     // Load images and audio
29     for (int i = 0; i < NUMBER_OF_NATIONS; i++) {
30       images[i] = new Image(URLBase + "/image/flag" + i + ".gif");
31       mp[i] = new MediaPlayer(new Media(
32         URLBase + "/audio/anthem/anthem" + i + ".mp3"));
33     }
34
35     Button btPlayPause = new Button("||");
36     btPlayPause.setOnAction(e -> {
37       if (btPlayPause.getText().equals(">")) {
38         btPlayPause.setText("||");
39         mp[currentIndex].play();
40       }
41       else {
42         btPlayPause.setText(">");
43         mp[currentIndex].pause();
44       }
45     });
46
47     ImageView imageView = new ImageView(images[currentIndex]);
48     ComboBox<String> cboNation = new ComboBox<>();
49     ObservableList<String> items = FXCollections.observableArrayList
50       ("Denmark", "Germany", "China", "India", "Norway", "UK", "US");
51     cboNation.getItems().addAll(items);
52     cboNation.setValue(items.get(0));
53     cboNation.setOnAction(e -> {
54       mp[currentIndex].stop();
55       currentIndex = items.indexOf(cboNation.getValue());
56       imageView.setImage(images[currentIndex]);
57       mp[currentIndex].play();
```

Margin notes: URLBase for image and audio; track current image/audio; image array; media player array; load image; load audio; create play button; handle button action; play audio; pause audio; create image view; create combo box; create observable list; process combo selection; choose a new nation; play audio

```
58        btPlayPause.setText("||");
59      });
60
61      HBox hBox = new HBox(10);
62      hBox.getChildren().addAll(btPlayPause,
63        new Label("Select a nation: "), cboNation);
64      hBox.setAlignment(Pos.CENTER);
65
66      // Create a pane to hold nodes
67      BorderPane pane = new BorderPane();
68      pane.setCenter(imageView);
69      pane.setBottom(hBox);
70
71      // Create a scene and place it in the stage
72      Scene scene = new Scene(pane, 350, 270);
73      primaryStage.setTitle("FlagAnthem"); // Set the stage title
74      primaryStage.setScene(scene); // Place the scene in the stage
75      primaryStage.show(); // Display the stage
76      mp[currentIndex].play(); // Play the current selected anthem
77    }
78  }
```

The program loads the image and audio from the Internet (lines 29–33). A play/pause button is created to control the playing of the audio (line 35). When the button is clicked, if the button's current text is > (line 37), its text is changed to || (line 38) and the player is paused (line 39); If the button's current text is ||, it is changed to > (line 42) and the player is paused (line 43).

An image view is created to display a flag image (line 47). A combo box is created for selecting a nation (line 48–51). When a new country name in the combo box is selected, the current audio is stopped (line 54), the newly selected nation's image is displayed (line 56) and the new anthem is played (line 57).

JavaFX also provides the `AudioClip` class for creating auto clips. An `AudioClip` object can be created using `new AudioClip(URL)`. An audio clip stores the audio in memory. `AudioClip` is more efficient for playing a small audio clip in the program than using `MediaPlayer`. `AudioClip` has the similar methods as in the `MediaPlayer` class.

16.14.1 In Listing 16.15, which code sets the initial image icon and which code plays the audio?

16.14.2 In Listing 16.15, what does the program do when a new nation is selected in the combo box?

Check
Point

CHAPTER SUMMARY

1. The abstract `Labeled` class is the base class for `Label`, `Button`, `CheckBox`, and `RadioButton`. It defines properties `alignment`, `contentDisplay`, `text`, `graphic`, `graphicTextGap`, `textFill`, `underline`, and `wrapText`.

2. The abstract `ButtonBase` class is the base class for `Button`, `CheckBox`, and `RadioButton`. It defines the `onAction` property for specifying a handler for action events.

3. The abstract `TextInputContorl` class is the base class for `TextField` and `TextArea`. It defines the properties `text` and `editable`.

4. A `TextField` fires an action event when clicking the *Enter* key with the text field focused. A `TextArea` is often used for editing a multiline text.

5. `ComboBox<T>` and `ListView<T>` are generic classes for storing elements of type `T`. The elements in a combo box or a list view are stored in an observable list.

6. A `ComboBox` fires an action event when a new item is selected.

7. You can set a single item or multiple items selection for a `ListView` and add a listener for processing selected items.

8. You can use a `ScrollBar` or `Slider` to select a range of values and add a listener to the `value` property to respond to the change of the value.

9. JavaFX provides the `Media` class for loading a media, the `MediaPlayer` class for controlling a media, and the `MediaView` for displaying a media.

QUIZ

Answer the quiz for this chapter online at the book Companion Website.

MyProgrammingLab™ **PROGRAMMING EXERCISES**

Sections 16.2–16.5

*16.1 (*Use radio buttons*) Write a GUI program as shown in Figure 16.36a. You can use buttons to move the message to the left and right and use the radio buttons to change the color for the message displayed.

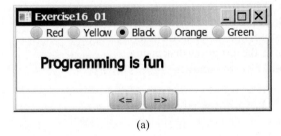
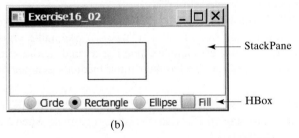

FIGURE 16.36 (a) The <= and => buttons move the message, and the radio buttons change the color for the message. (b) The program displays a circle, rectangle, and ellipse when you select a shape type. *Source*: Copyright © 1995–2016 Oracle and/or its affiliates. All rights reserved. Used with permission.

*16.2 (*Select geometric figures*) Write a program that draws various figures, as shown in Figure 16.36b. The user selects a figure from a radio button and uses a check box to specify whether it is filled.

**16.3 (*Traffic lights*) Write a program that simulates a traffic light. The program lets the user select one of three lights: red, yellow, or green. When a radio button is selected, the light is turned on. Only one light can be on at a time (see Figure 16.37a). No light is on when the program starts.

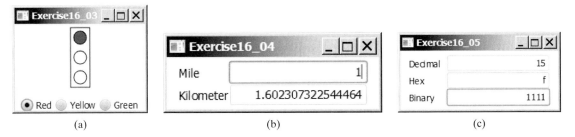

FIGURE 16.37 (a) The radio buttons are grouped to let you turn only one light on at a time. (b) The program converts miles to kilometers and vice versa. (c) The program converts among decimal, hex, and binary numbers. *Source*: Copyright © 1995–2016 Oracle and/or its affiliates. All rights reserved. Used with permission.

*16.4 (*Create a miles/kilometers converter*) Write a program that converts miles and kilometers, as shown in Figure 16.37b. If you enter a value in the Mile text field and press the *Enter* key, the corresponding kilometer measurement is displayed in the Kilometer text field. Likewise, if you enter a value in the Kilometer text field and press the *Enter* key, the corresponding miles is displayed in the Mile text field.

*16.5 (*Convert numbers*) Write a program that converts among decimal, hex, and binary numbers, as shown in Figure 16.37c. When you enter a decimal value in the decimal-value text field and press the *Enter* key, its corresponding hex and binary numbers are displayed in the other two text fields. Likewise, you can enter values in the other fields and convert them accordingly. (*Hint*: Use the `Integer.parseInt(s, radix)` method to parse a string to a decimal and use `Integer.toHexString(decimal)` and `Integer.toBinaryString(decimal)` to obtain a hex number or a binary number from a decimal.)

*16.6 (*Demonstrate `TextField` properties*) Write a program that sets the horizontal-alignment and column-size properties of a text field dynamically, as shown in Figure 16.38a.

VideoNote

Use radio buttons and text fields

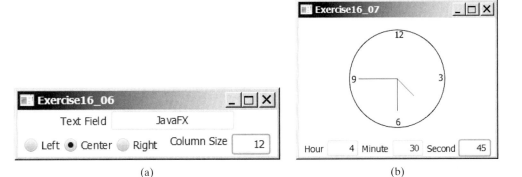

FIGURE 16.38 (a) You can set a text field's properties for the horizontal alignment and column size dynamically. (b) The program displays the time specified in the text fields. *Source*: Copyright © 1995–2016 Oracle and/or its affiliates. All rights reserved. Used with permission.

*16.7 *(Set clock time)* Write a program that displays a clock and sets the time with the input from three text fields, as shown in Figure 16.38b. Use the `ClockPane` in Listing 14.21. Resize the clock to the center of the pane.

**16.8 *(Geometry: two circles intersect?)* Write a program that enables the user to specify the location and size of the circles, and displays whether the two circles intersect, as shown in Figure 16.39a. Enable the user to point the mouse inside a circle and drag it. As the circle is being dragged, the circle's center coordinates in the text fields are updated.

**16.9 *(Geometry: two rectangles intersect?)* Write a program that enables the user to specify the location and size of the rectangles and displays whether the two rectangles intersect, as shown in Figure 16.39b. Enable the user to point the mouse inside a rectangle and drag it. As the rectangle is being dragged, the rectangle's center coordinates in the text fields are updated.

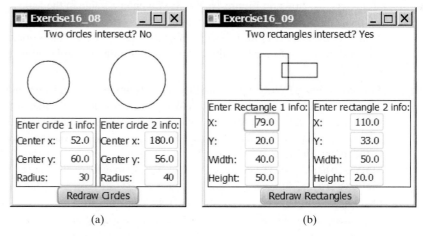

(a)   (b)

FIGURE 16.39 Check whether two circles and two rectangles are overlapping. *Source:* Copyright © 1995–2016 Oracle and/or its affiliates. All rights reserved. Used with permission.

Sections 16.6–16.8

**16.10 *(Text viewer)* Write a program that displays a text file in a text area, as shown in Figure 16.40a. The user enters a file name in a text field and clicks the *View* button; the file is then displayed in a text area.

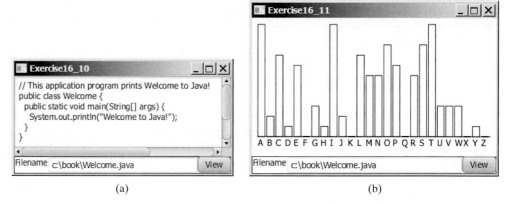

(a)   (b)

FIGURE 16.40 (a) The program displays the text from a file in a text area. (b) The program displays a histogram that shows the occurrences of each letter in the file. *Source:* Copyright © 1995–2016 Oracle and/or its affiliates. All rights reserved. Used with permission.

**16.11 *(Create a histogram for occurrences of letters)* Write a program that reads a file and displays a histogram to show the occurrences of each letter in the file, as shown in Figure 16.40b. The file name is entered from a text field. Pressing the *Enter* key on the text field causes the program to start to read, process the file, and display the histogram. The histogram is displayed in the center of the window. Define a class named `Histogram` that extends `Pane`. The class contains the property `counts` that is an array of 26 elements. `counts[0]` stores the number of `A`, `counts[1]` the number of `B`, and so on. The class also contains a setter method for setting a new `counts` and displaying the histogram for the new `counts`.

*16.12 *(Demonstrate `TextArea` properties)* Write a program that demonstrates the properties of a text area. The program uses a check box to indicate whether the text is wrapped onto next line, as shown in Figure 16.41a.

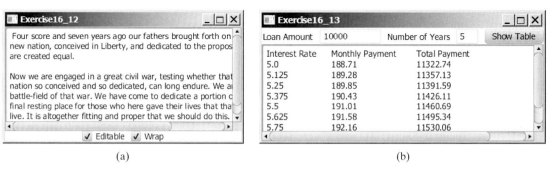

(a) (b)

FIGURE 16.41 (a) You can set the options to enable text editing and text wrapping. (b) The program displays a table for monthly payments and total payments on a given loan based on various interest rates. *Source*: Copyright © 1995–2016 Oracle and/or its affiliates. All rights reserved. Used with permission.

*16.13 *(Compare loans with various interest rates)* Rewrite Programming Exercise 5.21 to create a GUI, as shown in Figure 16.41b. Your program should let the user enter the loan amount and loan period in the number of years from text fields, and it should display the monthly and total payments for each interest rate starting from 5% to 8%, with increments of one-eighth, in a text area.

**16.14 *(Select a font)* Write a program that can dynamically change the font of a text in a label displayed on a stack pane. The text can be displayed in bold and italic at the same time. You can select the font name or font size from combo boxes, as shown in Figure 16.42a. The available font names can be obtained using `Font .getFontNames()`. The combo box for the font size is initialized with numbers from 1 to 100.

VideoNote

Set fonts

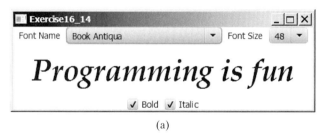
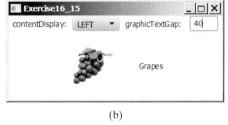

(a) (b)

FIGURE 16.42 You can dynamically set the font for the message. (b) You can set the alignment and text-position properties of a label dynamically. *Source*: Copyright © 1995–2016 Oracle and/or its affiliates. All rights reserved. Used with permission.

**16.15 *(Demonstrate `Label` properties)* Write a program to let the user dynamically set the properties `contentDisplay` and `graphicTextGap`, as shown in Figure 16.42b.

*16.16 *(Use `ComboBox` and `ListView`)* Write a program that demonstrates selecting items in a list. The program uses a combo box to specify a selection mode, as shown in Figure 16.43a. When you select items, they are displayed in a label below the list.

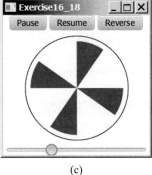

(a)   (b)   (c)

FIGURE 16.43 (a) You can choose single or multiple selection modes in a list. (b) The color changes in the text as you adjust the scroll bars. (c) The program simulates a running fan. *Source:* Copyright © 1995–2016 Oracle and/or its affiliates. All rights reserved. Used with permission.

Sections 16.6–16.8

**16.17 *(Use `ScrollBar` and `Slider`)* Write a program that uses scroll bars or sliders to select the color for a text, as shown in Figure 16.43b. Four horizontal scroll bars are used for selecting the colors: red, green, blue, and opacity percentages.

**16.18 *(Simulation: a running fan)* Rewrite Programming Exercise 15.28 to add a slider to control the speed of the fan, as shown in Figure 16.43c.

**16.19 *(Control a group of fans)* Write a program that displays three fans in a group, with control buttons to start and stop all of them, as shown in Figure 16.44.

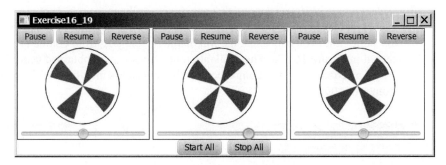

FIGURE 16.44 The program runs and controls a group of fans. *Source:* Copyright © 1995–2016 Oracle and/or its affiliates. All rights reserved. Used with permission.

*16.20 *(Count-up stopwatch)* Write a program that simulates a stopwatch, as shown in Figure 16.45a. When the user clicks the *Start* button, the button's label is changed to *Pause,* as shown in Figure 16.45b. When the user clicks the *Pause* button, the button's label is changed to *Resume,* as shown in Figure 16.45c. The *Clear* button resets the count to 0 and resets the button's label to *Start.*

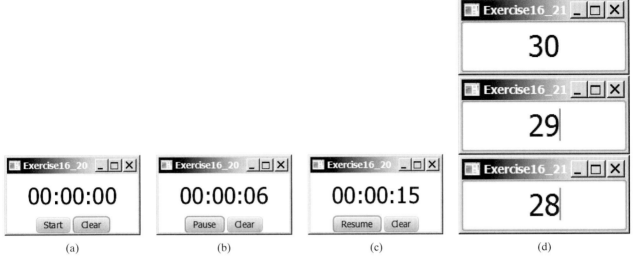

FIGURE 16.45 (a–c) The program counts up the time. (d) The program counts down the time. *Source*: Copyright © 1995–2016 Oracle and/or its affiliates. All rights reserved. Used with permission.

*16.21 *(Count-down stopwatch)* Write a program that allows the user to enter time in seconds in the text field and press the *Enter* key to count down the seconds, as shown in Figure 16.45d. The remaining seconds are redisplayed every second. When the seconds are expired, the program starts to play music continuously.

16.22 *(Play, loop, and stop a sound clip)* Write a program that meets the following requirements:

- Get an audio file from the class directory using `AudioClip`.
- Place three buttons labeled *Play*, *Loop*, and *Stop*, as shown in Figure 16.46a.
- If you click the *Play* button, the audio file is played once. If you click the *Loop* button, the audio file keeps playing repeatedly. If you click the *Stop* button, the playing stops.

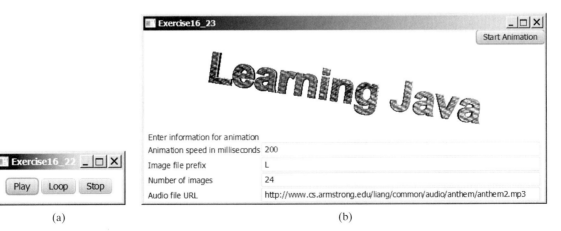

FIGURE 16.46 (a) Click *Play* to play an audio clip once, click *Loop* to play an audio repeatedly, and click *Stop* to terminate playing. *Source*: Copyright © 1995–2016 Oracle and/or its affiliates. All rights reserved. Used with permission. (b) The program lets the user specify image files, an audio file, and the animation speed.

**16.23 *(Create an image animator with audio)* Create animation in Figure 16.46b to meet the following requirements:

- Allow the user to specify the animation speed in a text field.
- Get the number of images and image's file-name prefix from the user. For example, if the user enters **n** for the number of images and **L** for the image prefix, then the files are **L1.gif**, **L2.gif**, and so on, to **L*n*.gif**. Assume the images are stored in the **image** directory, a subdirectory of the program's class directory. The animation displays the images one after the other.
- Allow the user to specify an audio file URL. The audio is played while the animation runs.

**16.24 *(Revise Listing 16.14 MediaDemo.java)* Add a slider to enable the user to set the current time for the video and a label to display the current time and the total time for the video. As shown in Figure 16.47a, the total time is 5 minutes and 3 seconds and the current time is 3 minutes and 58 seconds. As the video plays, the slider value and current time are continuously updated.

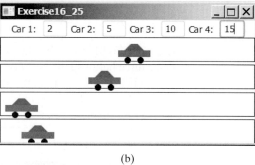

(a)

(b)

FIGURE 16.47 (a) A slider for current video time and a label to show the current time and total time are added. (b) You can set the speed for each car. *Source*: Copyright © 1995–2016 Oracle and/or its affiliates. All rights reserved. Used with permission.

**16.25 *(Racing cars)* Write a program that simulates four cars racing, as shown in Figure 16.47b. You can set the speed for each car, with a maximum of 100.

**16.26 *(Simulation: raise flag and play anthem)* Write a program that displays a flag rising up, as shown in Figure 15.15. As the national flag rises, play the national anthem. (You may use a flag image and anthem audio file from Listing 16.15.)

Comprehensive

16.27 *(Display country flag and flag description)* Listing 16.8, ComboBoxDemo. java, gives a program that lets the user view a country's flag image and description by selecting the country from a combo box. The description is a string coded in the program. Rewrite the program to read the text description from a file. Suppose the descriptions are stored in the files **description0.txt, . . . , and **description8.txt** under the **text** directory for the nine countries Canada, China, Denmark, France, Germany, India, Norway, the United Kingdom, and the United States, in this order.

16.28 *(Slide show)* Programming Exercise 15.30 developed a slide show using images. Rewrite that program to develop a slide show using text files. Suppose that 10 text files named **slide0.txt, **slide1.txt**, . . . , **slide9.txt** are stored in the **text** directory. Each slide displays the text from one file. Each slide is shown for one second, and the slides are displayed in order. When the last slide finishes, the first slide is redisplayed, and so on. Use a text area to display the slide.

***16.29 *(Display a calendar)* Write a program that displays the calendar for the current month. You can use the *Prior* and *Next* buttons to show the calendar of the previous or next month. Display the dates in the current month in black and display the dates in the previous month and next month in gray, as shown in Figure 16.48.

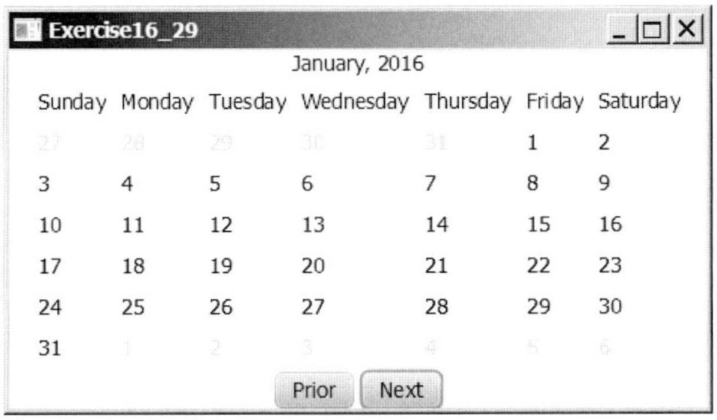

FIGURE 16.48 The program displays the calendar for the current month. *Source*: Copyright © 1995–2016 Oracle and/or its affiliates. All rights reserved. Used with permission.

**16.30 *(Pattern recognition: consecutive four equal numbers)* Write a GUI program for Programming Exercise 8.19, as shown in Figures 16.49a–b. Let the user enter the numbers in the text fields in a grid of 6 rows and 7 columns. The user can click the *Solve* button to highlight a sequence of four equal numbers, if it exists. Initially, the values in the text fields are randomly filled with numbers from 0 to 9.

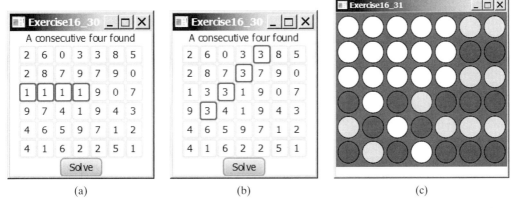

FIGURE 16.49 (a and b) Clicking the *Solve* button highlights the four consecutive numbers in a row, a column, or a diagonal. *Source*: Copyright © 1995–2016 Oracle and/or its affiliates. All rights reserved. Used with permission. (c) The program enables two players to play the connect-four game.

***16.31 *(Game: connect four)* Programming Exercise 8.20 enables two players to play the connect-four game on the console. Rewrite a GUI version for the program, as shown in Figure 16.49c. The program enables two players to place red and yellow discs in turn. To place a disk, the player needs to click an available cell. An *available cell* is unoccupied and its downward neighbor is occupied. The program flashes the four winning cells if a player wins, and reports no winners if all cells are occupied with no winners.

CHAPTER 17

BINARY I/O

Objectives

- To discover how I/O is processed in Java (§17.2).

- To distinguish between text I/O and binary I/O (§17.3).

- To read and write bytes using `FileInputStream` and `FileOutputStream` (§17.4.1).

- To filter data using the base classes `FilterInputStream` and `FilterOutputStream` (§17.4.2).

- To read and write primitive values and strings using `DataInputStream` and `DataOutputStream` (§17.4.3).

- To improve I/O performance by using `BufferedInputStream` and `BufferedOutputStream` (§17.4.4).

- To write a program that copies a file (§17.5).

- To store and restore objects using `ObjectOutputStream` and `ObjectInputStream` (§17.6).

- To implement the `Serializable` interface to make objects serializable (§17.6.1).

- To serialize arrays (§17.6.2).

- To read and write files using the `RandomAccessFile` class (§17.7).

17.1 Introduction

Java provides many classes for performing text I/O and binary I/O.

Files can be classified as either text or binary. A file that can be processed (read, created, or modified) using a text editor such as Notepad on Windows or vi on UNIX is called a *text file*. All other files are called *binary files*. You cannot read binary files using a text editor—they are designed to be read by programs. For example, Java source programs are text files and can be read by a text editor, but Java class files are binary files and are read by the JVM.

Although it is not technically precise and correct, you can envision a text file as consisting of a sequence of characters, and a binary file as consisting of a sequence of bits. Characters in a text file are encoded using a character-encoding scheme such as ASCII or Unicode. For example, the decimal integer 199 is stored as a sequence of three characters 199 in a text file, and the same integer is stored as a byte-type value C7 in a binary file, because decimal 199 equals hex C7 ($199 = 12 \times 16^1 + 7$). The advantage of binary files is that they are more efficient to process than text files.

Java offers many classes for performing file input and output. These can be categorized as *text I/O classes* and *binary I/O classes*. In Section 12.11, File Input and Output, you learned how to read and write strings and numeric values from/to a text file using Scanner and PrintWriter. This chapter introduces the classes for performing binary I/O.

17.2 How Is Text I/O Handled in Java?

Text data are read using the Scanner class and written using the PrintWriter class.

Recall that a File object encapsulates the properties of a file or a path but does not contain the methods for reading/writing data from/to a file. In order to perform I/O, you need to create objects using appropriate Java I/O classes. The objects contain the methods for reading/writing data from/to a file. For example, to write text to a file named **temp.txt**, you can create an object using the PrintWriter class as follows:

```
PrintWriter output = new PrintWriter("temp.txt");
```

You can now invoke the print method on the object to write a string to the file. For example, the following statement writes Java 101 to the file:

```
output.print("Java 101");
```

The following statement closes the file:

```
output.close();
```

There are many I/O classes for various purposes. In general, these can be classified as input classes and output classes. An *input class* contains the methods to read data, and an *output class* contains the methods to write data. PrintWriter is an example of an output class, and Scanner is an example of an input class. The following code creates an input object for the file **temp.txt** and reads data from the file.

```
Scanner input = new Scanner(new File("temp.txt"));
System.out.println(input.nextLine());
```

If **temp.txt** contains the text Java 101, input.nextLine() returns the string "Java 101".

Figure 17.1 illustrates Java I/O programming. An input object reads a *stream* of data from a file, and an output object writes a stream of data to a file. An input object is also called an *input stream* and an output object an *output stream*.

text file
binary file

why binary I/O?

text I/O
binary I/O

stream
input stream
output stream

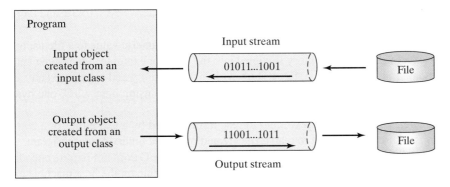

FIGURE 17.1 The program receives data through an input object and sends data through an output object.

17.2.1 What is a text file and what is a binary file? Can you view a text file or a binary file using a text editor?

17.2.2 How do you read or write text data in Java? What is a stream?

17.3 Text I/O vs. Binary I/O

Binary I/O does not involve encoding or decoding and thus is more efficient than text I/O.

Computers do not differentiate between binary files and text files. All files are stored in binary format, and thus all files are essentially binary files. Text I/O is built upon binary I/O to provide a level of abstraction for character encoding and decoding, as shown in Figure 17.2a. Encoding and decoding are automatically performed for text I/O. The JVM converts Unicode to a file-specific encoding when writing a character, and converts a file-specific encoding to Unicode when reading a character. For example, suppose you write the string `"199"` using text I/O to a file, each character is written to the file. Since the Unicode for character `1` is `0x0031`, the Unicode `0x0031` is converted to a code that depends on the encoding scheme for the file. (Note the prefix `0x` denotes a hex number.) In the United States, the default encoding for text files on Windows is ASCII. The ASCII code for character `1` is `49` (`0x31` in hex) and for character `9` is

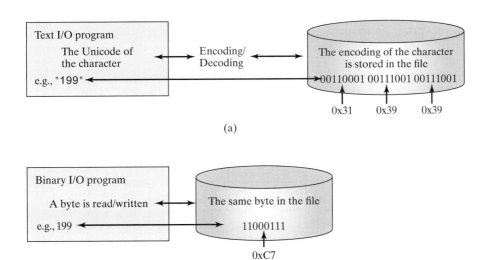

FIGURE 17.2 Text I/O requires encoding and decoding, whereas binary I/O does not.

57 (`0x39` in hex). Thus, to write the characters `199`, three bytes—`0x31`, `0x39`, and `0x39`—are sent to the output, as shown in Figure 17.2a.

Binary I/O does not require conversions. If you write a numeric value to a file using binary I/O, the exact value in the memory is copied into the file. For example, a byte-type value `199` is represented as `0xC7` ($199 = 12 \times 16^1 + 7$) in the memory and appears exactly as `0xC7` in the file, as shown in Figure 17.2b. When you read a byte using binary I/O, one byte value is read from the input.

In general, you should use text input to read a file created by a text editor or a text output program, and use binary input to read a file created by a Java binary output program.

Binary I/O is more efficient than text I/O because binary I/O does not require encoding and decoding. Binary files are independent of the encoding scheme on the host machine and thus are portable. Java programs on any machine can read a binary file created by a Java program. This is why Java class files are binary files. Java class files can run on a JVM on any machine.

 Note

.txt and .dat

For consistency, this book uses the extension **.txt** to name text files and **.dat** to name binary files.

 Check Point

17.3.1 What are the differences between text I/O and binary I/O?

17.3.2 How is a Java character represented in the memory, and how is a character represented in a text file?

17.3.3 If you write the string `"ABC"` to an ASCII text file, what values are stored in the file?

17.3.4 If you write the string `"100"` to an ASCII text file, what values are stored in the file? If you write a numeric byte-type value `100` using binary I/O, what values are stored in the file?

17.3.5 What is the encoding scheme for representing a character in a Java program? By default, what is the encoding scheme for a text file on Windows?

17.4 Binary I/O Classes

 Key Point

The abstract `InputStream` *is the root class for reading binary data, and the abstract* `OutputStream` *is the root class for writing binary data.*

The design of the Java I/O classes is a good example of applying inheritance, where common operations are generalized in superclasses, and subclasses provide specialized operations. Figure 17.3 lists some of the classes for performing binary I/O. `InputStream` is the root for

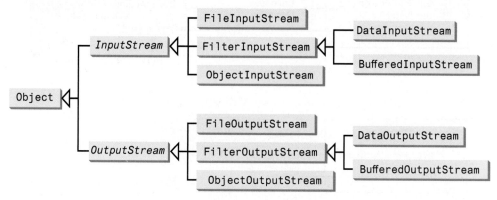

Figure 17.3   `InputStream`, `OutputStream`, and their subclasses are for performing binary I/O.

java.io.InputStream	
+read(): int	Reads the next byte of data from the input stream. The value byte is returned as an int value in the range 0–255. If no byte is available because the end of the stream has been reached, the value –1 is returned.
+read(b: byte[]): int	Reads up to b.length bytes into array b from the input stream and returns the actual number of bytes read. Returns –1 at the end of the stream.
+read(b: byte[], off: int, len: int): int	Reads bytes from the input stream and stores them in b[off], b[off+1],..., b[off+len-1]. The actual number of bytes read is returned. Returns –1 at the end of the stream.
+close(): void	Closes this input stream and releases any system resources occupied by it.
+skip(n: long): long	Skips over and discards n bytes of data from this input stream. The actual number of bytes skipped is returned.

FIGURE 17.4 The abstract InputStream class defines the methods for the input stream of bytes.

binary input classes, and OutputStream is the root for binary output classes. Figures 17.4 and 17.5 list all the methods in the classes InputStream and OutputStream.

 Note
All the methods in the binary I/O classes are declared to throw java.io.IOException or a subclass of java.io.IOException.

throws IOException

java.io.OutputStream	
+write(int b): void	Writes the specified byte to this output stream. The parameter b is an int value. (byte)b is written to the output stream.
+write(b: byte[]): void	Writes all the bytes in array b to the output stream.
+write(b: byte[], off: int, len: int): void	Writes b[off], b[off+1],..., b[off+len-1] into the output stream.
+close(): void	Closes this output stream and releases any system resources occupied by it.
+flush(): void	Flushes this output stream and forces any buffered output bytes to be written out.

FIGURE 17.5 The abstract OutputStream class defines the methods for the output stream of bytes.

17.4.1 **FileInputStream/FileOutputStream**

FileInputStream/FileOutputStream are for reading/writing bytes from/to files. All the methods in these classes are inherited from InputStream and OutputStream. FileInputStream/FileOutputStream do not introduce new methods. To construct a FileInputStream, use the constructors shown in Figure 17.6.

A java.io.FileNotFoundException will occur if you attempt to create a FileInputStream with a nonexistent file.

FileNotFoundException

To construct a FileOutputStream, use the constructors shown in Figure 17.7.

If the file does not exist, a new file will be created. If the file already exists, the first two constructors will delete the current content of the file. To retain the current content and append new data into the file, use the last two constructors and pass true to the append parameter.

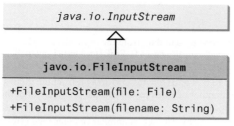

FIGURE 17.6 `FileInputStream` inputs a stream of bytes from a file.

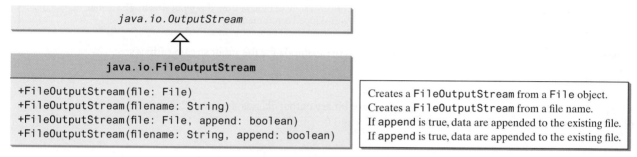

FIGURE 17.7 `FileOutputStream` outputs a stream of bytes to a file.

IOException

Almost all the methods in the I/O classes throw `java.io.IOException`. Therefore, you have to declare to throw `java.io.IOException` in the method or place the code in a try-catch block, as shown below:

Declaring exception in the method

```
public static void main(String[] args)
    throws IOException {
  // Perform I/O operations
}
```

Using try-catch block

```
public static void main(String[] args) {
  try {
    // Perform I/O operations
  }
  catch (IOException ex) {
    ex.printStackTrace();
  }
}
```

Listing 17.1 uses binary I/O to write 10 byte values from **1** to **10** to a file named **temp.dat** and reads them back from the file.

LISTING 17.1 TestFileStream.java

import

output stream

output

```
 1  import java.io.*;
 2
 3  public class TestFileStream {
 4    public static void main(String[] args) throws IOException {
 5      try (
 6        // Create an output stream to the file
 7        FileOutputStream output = new FileOutputStream("temp.dat");
 8      ) {
 9        // Output values to the file
10        for (int i = 1; i <= 10; i++)
11          output.write(i);
12      }
13
14      try (
```

```
15        // Create an input stream for the file
16        FileInputStream input = new FileInputStream("temp.dat");
17      ) {
18        // Read values from the file
19        int value;
20        while ((value = input.read()) != -1)
21          System.out.print(value + " ");
22      }
23    }
24  }
```

input stream

input

```
1 2 3 4 5 6 7 8 9 10
```

The program uses the try-with-resources to declare and create input and output streams so they will be automatically closed after they are used. The `java.io.InputStream` and `java.io.OutputStream` classes implement the `AutoClosable` interface. The `AutoClosable` interface defines the `close()` method that closes a resource. Any object of the `AutoClosable` type can be used with the try-with-resources syntax for automatic closing.

AutoClosable

A `FileOutputStream` is created for the file **temp.dat** in line 7. The `for` loop writes 10 byte values into the file (lines 10 and 11). Invoking `write(i)` is the same as invoking `write((byte)i)`. Line 16 creates a `FileInputStream` for the file **temp.dat**. Values are read from the file and displayed on the console in lines 19–21. The expression `((value = input.read()) != -1)` (line 20) reads a byte from `input.read()`, assigns it to `value`, and checks whether it is −1. The input value of −1 signifies the end of a file.

end of a file

The file **temp.dat** created in this example is a binary file. It can be read from a Java program but not from a text editor, as shown in Figure 17.8.

Binary data →

FIGURE 17.8 A binary file cannot be displayed in text mode. *Source*: Copyright © 1995–2016 Oracle and/or its affiliates. All rights reserved. Used with permission.

Tip
When a stream is no longer needed, always close it using the `close()` method or automatically close it using a try-with-resource statement. Not closing streams may cause data corruption in the output file or other programming errors.

close stream

Note
The root directory for the file is the classpath directory. For the example in this book, the root directory is **c:\book**, so the file **temp.dat** is located at **c:\book**. If you wish to place **temp.dat** in a specific directory, replace line 6 with

where is the file?

```
FileOutputStream output =
  new FileOutputStream ("directory/temp.dat");
```

Note
An instance of `FileInputStream` can be used as an argument to construct a `Scanner`, and an instance of `FileOutputStream` can be used as an argument to construct a `PrintWriter`. You can create a `PrintWriter` to append text into a file using

appending to text file

```
new PrintWriter(new FileOutputStream("temp.txt", true));
```

If **temp.txt** does not exist, it is created. If **temp.txt** already exists, new data are appended to the file. See Programming Exercise 17.1.

17.4.2 `FilterInputStream/FilterOutputStream`

Filter streams are streams that filter bytes for some purpose. The basic byte input stream provides a `read` method that can be used only for reading bytes. If you want to read integers, doubles, or strings, you need a filter class to wrap the byte input stream. Using a filter class enables you to read integers, doubles, and strings instead of bytes and characters. `Filter-InputStream` and `FilterOutputStream` are the base classes for filtering data. When you need to process primitive numeric types, use `DataInputStream` and `DataOutputStream` to filter bytes.

17.4.3 `DataInputStream/DataOutputStream`

`DataInputStream` reads bytes from the stream and converts them into appropriate primitive-type values or strings. `DataOutputStream` converts primitive-type values or strings into bytes and outputs the bytes to the stream.

`DataInputStream` extends `FilterInputStream` and implements the `DataInput` interface, as shown in Figure 17.9. `DataOutputStream` extends `FilterOutputStream` and implements the `DataOutput` interface, as shown in Figure 17.10.

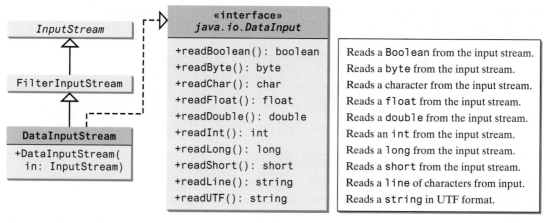

FIGURE 17.9 `DataInputStream` filters an input stream of bytes into primitive data-type values and strings.

`DataInputStream` implements the methods defined in the `DataInput` interface to read primitive data-type values and strings. `DataOutputStream` implements the methods defined in the `DataOutput` interface to write primitive data-type values and strings. Primitive values are copied from memory to the output without any conversions. Characters in a string may be written in several ways, as discussed in the next section.

Characters and Strings in Binary I/O

A Unicode character consists of two bytes. The `writeChar(char c)` method writes the Unicode of character `c` to the output. The `writeChars(String s)` method writes the Unicode for each character in the string `s` to the output. The `writeBytes(String s)` method writes the lower byte of the Unicode for each character in the string `s` to the output. The high byte of the Unicode is discarded. The `writeBytes` method is suitable for strings that consist of

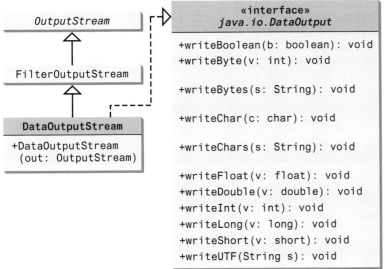

«interface» java.io.DataOutput	
+writeBoolean(b: boolean): void	Writes a Boolean to the output stream.
+writeByte(v: int): void	Writes the eight low-order bits of the argument v to the output stream.
+writeBytes(s: String): void	Writes the lower byte of the characters in a string to the output stream.
+writeChar(c: char): void	Writes a character (composed of 2 bytes) to the output stream.
+writeChars(s: String): void	Writes every character in the string s to the output stream, in order, 2 bytes per character.
+writeFloat(v: float): void	Writes a float value to the output stream.
+writeDouble(v: double): void	Writes a double value to the output stream.
+writeInt(v: int): void	Writes an int value to the output stream.
+writeLong(v: long): void	Writes a long value to the output stream.
+writeShort(v: short): void	Writes a short value to the output stream.
+writeUTF(String s): void	Writes s string in UTF format.

FIGURE 17.10 `DataOutputStream` enables you to write primitive data-type values and strings into an output stream.

ASCII characters, since an ASCII code is stored only in the lower byte of a Unicode. If a string consists of non-ASCII characters, you have to use the `writeChars` method to write the string.

The `writeUTF(String s)` method writes a string using the UTF coding scheme. UTF is efficient for compressing a string with Unicode characters. For more information on UTF, see Supplement III.Z, UTF in Java. The `readUTF()` method reads a string that has been written using the `writeUTF` method.

Creating **DataInputStream/DataOutputStream**

`DataInputStream`/`DataOutputStream` are created using the following constructors (see Figures 17.9 and 17.10):

```
public DataInputStream(InputStream instream)
public DataOutputStream(OutputStream outstream)
```

The following statements create data streams. The first statement creates an input stream for the file **in.dat**; the second statement creates an output stream for the file **out.dat**.

```
DataInputStream input =
  new DataInputStream(new FileInputStream("in.dat"));
DataOutputStream output =
  new DataOutputStream(new FileOutputStream("out.dat"));
```

Listing 17.2 writes student names and scores to a file named **temp.dat** and reads the data back from the file.

LISTING 17.2 TestDataStream.java

```
1  import java.io.*;
2
3  public class TestDataStream {
4    public static void main(String[] args) throws IOException {
5      try ( // Create an output stream for file temp.dat
6        DataOutputStream output =                                    output stream
7          new DataOutputStream(new FileOutputStream("temp.dat"));
8      ) {
```

output

```
 9        // Write student test scores to the file
10        output.writeUTF("John");
11        output.writeDouble(85.5);
12        output.writeUTF("Jim");
13        output.writeDouble(185.5);
14        output.writeUTF("George");
15        output.writeDouble(105.25);
16      }
17
18      try ( // Create an input stream for file temp.dat
```

input stream

```
19        DataInputStream input =
20          new DataInputStream(new FileInputStream("temp.dat"));
21      ) {
22        // Read student test scores from the file
```

input

```
23        System.out.println(input.readUTF() + " " + input.readDouble());
24        System.out.println(input.readUTF() + " " + input.readDouble());
25        System.out.println(input.readUTF() + " " + input.readDouble());
26      }
27    }
28  }
```

```
John 85.5
Susan 185.5
Kim 105.25
```

A DataOutputStream is created for file **temp.dat** in lines 6 and 7. Student names and scores are written to the file in lines 10–15. A DataInputStream is created for the same file in lines 19 and 20. Student names and scores are read back from the file and displayed on the console in lines 23–25.

DataInputStream and DataOutputStream read and write Java primitive-type values and strings in a machine-independent fashion, thereby enabling you to write a data file on one machine and read it on another machine that has a different operating system or file structure. An application uses a data output stream to write data that can later be read by a program using a data input stream.

DataInputStream filters data from an input stream into appropriate primitive-type values or strings. DataOutputStream converts primitive-type values or strings into bytes and outputs the bytes to an output stream. You can view DataInputStream/FileInputStream and DataOutputStream/FileOutputStream working in a pipe line as shown in Figure 17.11.

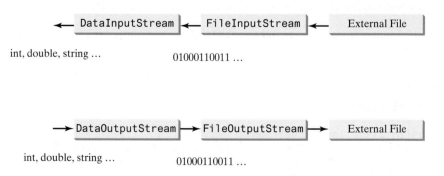

FIGURE 17.11 DataInputStream filters an input stream of byte to data and DataOutputStream converts data into a stream of bytes.

Caution
You have to read data in the same order and format in which they are stored. For example, since names are written in UTF using `writeUTF`, you must read names using `readUTF`.

Detecting the End of a File

If you keep reading data at the end of an `InputStream`, an `EOFException` will occur. This exception can be used to detect the end of a file, as shown in Listing 17.3.

EOFException

LISTING 17.3 DetectEndOfFile.java

```
1   import java.io.*;
2
3   public class DetectEndOfFile {
4     public static void main(String[] args) {
5       try {
6         try (DataOutputStream output =
7           new DataOutputStream(new FileOutputStream("test.dat"))) {
8           output.writeDouble(4.5);
9           output.writeDouble(43.25);
10          output.writeDouble(3.2);
11        }
12
13        try (DataInputStream input =
14          new DataInputStream(new FileInputStream("test.dat"))) {
15          while (true)
16            System.out.println(input.readDouble());
17        }
18      }
19      catch (EOFException ex) {
20        System.out.println("All data were read");
21      }
22      catch (IOException ex) {
23        ex.printStackTrace();
24      }
25    }
26  }
```

output stream

output

input stream

input

EOFException

```
4.5
43.25
3.2
All data were read
```

The program writes three double values to the file using `DataOutputStream` (lines 6–11) and reads the data using `DataInputStream` (lines 13–17). When reading past the end of the file, an `EOFException` is thrown. The exception is caught in line 19.

17.4.4 BufferedInputStream/BufferedOutputStream

`BufferedInputStream`/`BufferedOutputStream` can be used to speed up input and output by reducing the number of disk reads and writes. Using `BufferedInputStream`, the whole block of data on the disk is read into the buffer in the memory once. The individual data are then loaded to your program from the buffer, as shown in Figure 17.12a. Using `BufferedOutputStream`, the individual data are first written to the buffer in the memory. When the buffer is full, all data in the buffer are written to the disk once, as shown in Figure 17.12b.

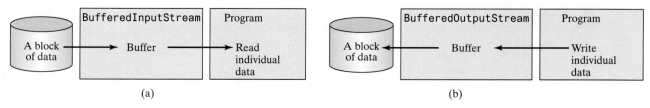

FIGURE 17.12 Buffer I/O places data in a buffer for fast processing.

`BufferedInputStream`/`BufferedOutputStream` does not contain new methods. All the methods in `BufferedInputStream`/`BufferedOutputStream` are inherited from the `InputStream`/`OutputStream` classes. `BufferedInputStream`/`BufferedOutputStream` manages a buffer behind the scene and automatically reads/writes data from/to disk on demand. You can wrap a `BufferedInputStream`/`BufferedOutputStream` on any `InputStream`/`OutputStream` using the constructors shown in Figures 17.13 and 17.14.

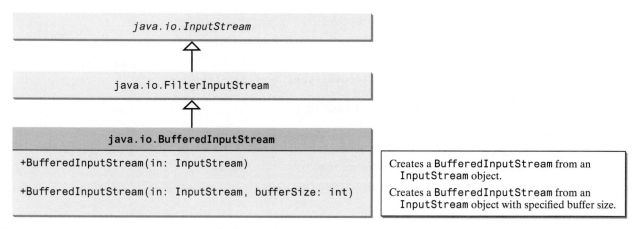

FIGURE 17.13 `BufferedInputStream` buffers an input stream.

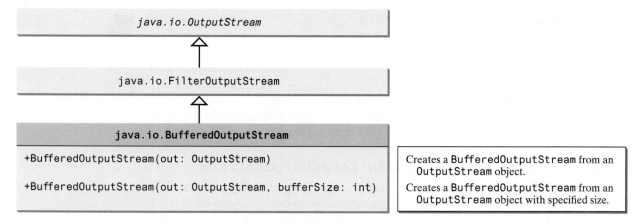

FIGURE 17.14 `BufferedOutputStream` buffers an output stream.

If no buffer size is specified, the default size is 512 bytes. You can improve the performance of the `TestDataStream` program in Listing 17.2 by adding buffers in the stream in lines 6–9 and 19–20, as follows:

```
DataOutputStream output = new DataOutputStream(
  new BufferedOutputStream(new FileOutputStream("temp.dat")));

DataInputStream input = new DataInputStream(
  new BufferedInputStream(new FileInputStream("temp.dat")));
```

Tip
You should always use buffered I/O to speed up input and output. For small files, you may not notice performance improvements. However, for large files—over 100 MB—you will see substantial improvements using buffered I/O.

17.4.1 Why do you have to declare to throw `IOException` in the method or use a try-catch block to handle `IOException` for Java I/O programs?

17.4.2 Why should you always close streams? How do you close streams?

17.4.3 The `read()` method in `InputStream` reads a byte. Why does it return an `int` instead of a `byte`? Find the abstract methods in `InputStream` and `OutputStream`.

17.4.4 Does `FileInputStream`/`FileOutputStream` introduce any new methods beyond the methods inherited from `InputStream`/`OutputStream`? How do you create a `FileInputStream`/`FileOutputStream`?

17.4.5 What will happen if you attempt to create an input stream on a nonexistent file? What will happen if you attempt to create an output stream on an existing file? Can you append data to an existing file?

17.4.6 How do you append data to an existing text file using `java.io.PrintWriter`?

17.4.7 Suppose a file contains an unspecified number of `double` values that were written to the file using the `writeDouble` method using a `DataOutputStream`. How do you write a program to read all these values? How do you detect the end of a file?

17.4.8 What is written to a file using `writeByte(91)` on a `FileOutputStream`?

17.4.9 How do you check the end of a file in an input stream (`FileInputStream`, `DataInputStream`)?

17.4.10 What is wrong in the following code?

```java
import java.io.*;

public class Test {
  public static void main(String[] args) {
    try (
      FileInputStream fis = new FileInputStream("test.dat"); ) {
    }
    catch (IOException ex) {
      ex.printStackTrace();
    }
    catch (FileNotFoundException ex) {
      ex.printStackTrace();
    }
  }
}
```

17.4.11 Suppose you run the following program on Windows using the default ASCII encoding after the program is finished. How many bytes are there in the file **t.txt**? Show the contents of each byte.

```java
public class Test {
  public static void main(String[] args)
      throws java.io.IOException {
    try (java.io.PrintWriter output =
        new java.io.PrintWriter("t.txt"); ) {
      output.printf("%s", "1234");
      output.printf("%s", "5678");
      output.close();
    }
  }
}
```

17.4.12 After the following program is finished, how many bytes are there in the file **t.dat**? Show the contents of each byte.

```java
import java.io.*;

public class Test {
  public static void main(String[] args) throws IOException {
    try (DataOutputStream output = new DataOutputStream(
        new FileOutputStream("t.dat")); ) {
      output.writeInt(1234);
      output.writeInt(5678);
      output.close();
    }
  }
}
```

17.4.13 For each of the following statements on a `DataOutputStream output`, how many bytes are sent to the output?

```java
output.writeChar('A');
output.writeChars("BC");
output.writeUTF("DEF");
```

17.4.14 What are the advantages of using buffered streams? Are the following statements correct?

```java
BufferedInputStream input1 =
  new BufferedInputStream(new FileInputStream("t.dat"));

DataInputStream input2 = new DataInputStream(
  new BufferedInputStream(new FileInputStream("t.dat")));

DataOutputStream output = new DataOutputStream(
  new BufferedOutputStream(new FileOutnputStream("t.dat")));
```

17.5 Case Study: Copying Files

This section develops a useful utility for copying files.

In this section, you will learn how to write a program that lets users copy files. The user needs to provide a source file and a target file as command-line arguments using the command

```
java Copy source target
```

The program copies the source file to the target file and displays the number of bytes in the file. The program should alert the user if the source file does not exist or if the target file already exists. A sample run of the program is shown in Figure 17.15.

VideoNote

Copy file

File exists

Delete file

Copy

Source
does not
exist

FIGURE 17.15 The program copies a file. *Source*: Copyright © 1995–2016 Oracle and/or its affiliates. All rights reserved. Used with permission.

To copy the contents from a source file to a target file, it is appropriate to use an input stream to read bytes from the source file, and an output stream to send bytes to the target file, regardless of the file's contents. The source file and the target file are specified from the command line. Create an `InputFileStream` for the source file, and an `OutputFileStream` for the target file. Use the `read()` method to read a byte from the input stream and then use the `write(b)` method to write the byte to the output stream. Use `BufferedInputStream` and `BufferedOutputStream` to improve the performance. Listing 17.4 gives the solution to the problem.

LISTING 17.4 Copy.java

```java
1   import java.io.*;
2
3   public class Copy {
4     /** Main method
5        @param args[0] for sourcefile
6        @param args[1] for target file
7     */
8     public static void main(String[] args) throws IOException {
9       // Check command-line parameter usage
10      if (args.length != 2) {                                    check usage
11        System.out.println(
12          "Usage: java Copy sourceFile targetfile");
13        System.exit(1);
14      }
15
16      // Check if source file exists
17      File sourceFile = new File(args[0]);                       source file
18      if (!sourceFile.exists()) {
19        System.out.println("Source file " + args[0]
20          + " does not exist");
21        System.exit(2);
22      }
23
24      // Check if target file exists
25      File targetFile = new File(args[1]);                       target file
26      if (targetFile.exists()) {
27        System.out.println("Target file " + args[1]
28          + " already exists");
29        System.exit(3);
30      }
31
```

```
32      try (
33        // Create an input stream
34        BufferedInputStream input =
35          new BufferedInputStream(new FileInputStream(sourceFile));
36
37        // Create an output stream
38        BufferedOutputStream output =
39          new BufferedOutputStream(new FileOutputStream(targetFile));
40      ) {
41        // Continuously read a byte from input and write it to output
42        int r, numberOfBytesCopied = 0;
43        while ((r = input.read()) != -1) {
44          output.write((byte)r);
45          numberOfBytesCopied++;
46        }
47
48        // Display the file size
49        System.out.println(numberOfBytesCopied + " bytes copied");
50      }
51    }
52  }
```

input stream (line 34)
output stream (line 38)
read (line 43)
write (line 44)

The program first checks whether the user has passed the two required arguments from the command line in lines 10–14.

The program uses the `File` class to check whether the source file and target file exist. If the source file does not exist (lines 18–22), or if the target file already exists (lines 25–30), the program ends.

An input stream is created using `BufferedInputStream` wrapped on `FileInputStream` in lines 34–35, and an output stream is created using `BufferedOutputStream` wrapped on `FileOutputStream` in lines 38–39.

The expression `((r = input.read()) != -1)` (line 43) reads a byte from `input.read()`, assigns it to `r`, and checks whether it is `-1`. The input value of `-1` signifies the end of a file. The program continuously reads bytes from the input stream and sends them to the output stream until all of the bytes have been read.

17.5.1 How does the program check if a file already exists?

17.5.2 How does the program detect the end of the file while reading data?

17.5.3 How does the program count the number of bytes read from the file?

17.6 Object I/O

`ObjectInputStream`/`ObjectOutputStream` classes can be used to read/write serializable objects.

VideoNote
Object I/O

`DataInputStream`/`DataOutputStream` enables you to perform I/O for primitive-type values and strings. `ObjectInputStream`/`ObjectOutputStream` enables you to perform I/O for objects in addition to primitive-type values and strings. Since `ObjectInputStream`/`ObjectOutputStream` contains all the functions of `DataInputStream`/`DataOutputStream`, you can replace `DataInputStream`/`DataOutputStream` completely with `ObjectInputStream`/`ObjectOutputStream`.

`ObjectInputStream` extends `InputStream` and implements `ObjectInput` and `ObjectStreamConstants`, as shown in Figure 17.16. `ObjectInput` is a subinterface of `DataInput` (`DataInput` is shown in Figure 17.9). `ObjectStreamConstants` contains the constants to support `ObjectInputStream`/`ObjectOutputStream`.

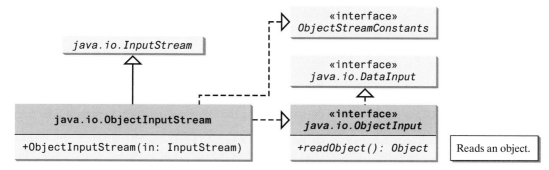

FIGURE 17.16 `ObjectInputStream` can read objects, primitive-type values, and strings.

`ObjectOutputStream` extends `OutputStream` and implements `ObjectOutput` and `ObjectStreamConstants`, as shown in Figure 17.17. `ObjectOutput` is a subinterface of `DataOutput` (`DataOutput` is shown in Figure 17.10).

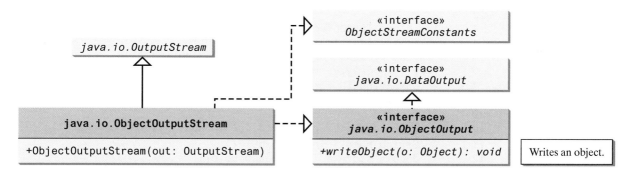

FIGURE 17.17 `ObjectOutputStream` can write objects, primitive-type values, and strings.

You can wrap an `ObjectInputStream`/`ObjectOutputStream` on any `InputStream`/`OutputStream` using the following constructors:

```
// Create an ObjectInputStream
public ObjectInputStream(InputStream in)

// Create an ObjectOutputStream
public ObjectOutputStream(OutputStream out)
```

Listing 17.5 writes students' names, scores, and the current date to a file named **object.dat**.

LISTING 17.5 TestObjectOutputStream.java

```
 1  import java.io.*;
 2
 3  public class TestObjectOutputStream {
 4    public static void main(String[] args) throws IOException {
 5      try ( // Create an output stream for file object.dat
 6        ObjectOutputStream output =
 7          new ObjectOutputStream(new FileOutputStream("object.dat"));
 8      ) {
 9        // Write a string, double value, and object to the file
10        output.writeUTF("John");
11        output.writeDouble(85.5);
```

output stream

output string

output object

```
12          output.writeObject(new java.util.Date());
13      }
14    }
15  }
```

An `ObjectOutputStream` is created to write data into the file **object.dat** in lines 6 and 7. A string, a double value, and an object are written to the file in lines 10–12. To improve performance, you may add a buffer in the stream using the following statement to replace lines 6 and 7:

```
ObjectOutputStream output = new ObjectOutputStream(
  new BufferedOutputStream(new FileOutputStream("object.dat")));
```

Multiple objects or primitives can be written to the stream. The objects must be read back from the corresponding `ObjectInputStream` with the same types and in the same order as they were written. Java's safe casting should be used to get the desired type. Listing 17.6 reads data from **object.dat**.

LISTING 17.6 TestObjectInputStream.java

```
 1  import java.io.*;
 2
 3  public class TestObjectInputStream {
 4    public static void main(String[] args)
 5      throws ClassNotFoundException, IOException {
 6      try ( // Create an input stream for file object.dat
 7        ObjectInputStream input =
 8          new ObjectInputStream(new FileInputStream("object.dat"));
 9      ) {
10        // Read a string, double value, and object from the file
11        String name = input.readUTF();
12        double score = input.readDouble();
13        java.util.Date date = (java.util.Date)(input.readObject());
14        System.out.println(name + " " + score + " " + date);
15      }
16    }
17  }
```

input stream

input string

input object

```
John 85.5 Sun Dec 04 10:35:31 EST 2011
```

ClassNotFoundException

The `readObject()` method may throw `java.lang.ClassNotFoundException` because when the JVM restores an object, it first loads the class for the object if the class has not been loaded. Since `ClassNotFoundException` is a checked exception, the `main` method declares to throw it in line 5. An `ObjectInputStream` is created to read input from **object.dat** in lines 7–8. You have to read the data from the file in the same order and format as they were written to the file. A string, a double value, and an object are read in lines 11–13. Since `readObject()` returns an `Object`, it is cast into `Date` and assigned to a `Date` variable in line 13.

17.6.1 The `Serializable` Interface

Not every object can be written to an output stream. Objects that can be so written are said to be *serializable*. A serializable object is an instance of the `java.io.Serializable` interface, so the object's class must implement `Serializable`.

serializable

The `Serializable` interface is a marker interface. Since it has no methods, you don't need to add additional code in your class that implements `Serializable`. Implementing this interface enables the Java serialization mechanism to automate the process of storing objects and arrays.

To appreciate this automation feature, consider what you otherwise need to do in order to store an object. Suppose that you wish to store an `ArrayList` object. To do this, you need to store all the elements in the list. Each element is an object that may contain other objects. As you can see, this would be a very tedious process. Fortunately, you don't have to go through it manually. Java provides a built-in mechanism to automate the process of writing objects. This process is referred as *object serialization*, which is implemented in `ObjectOutputStream`. In contrast, the process of reading objects is referred as *object deserialization*, which is implemented in `ObjectInputStream`.

serialization
deserialization

Many classes in the Java API implement `Serializable`. All the wrapper classes for primitive-type values, `java.math.BigInteger`, `java.math.BigDecimal`, `java.lang.String`, `java.lang.StringBuilder`, `java.lang.StringBuffer`, `java.util.Date`, and `java.util.ArrayList` implement `java.io.Serializable`. Attempting to store an object that does not support the `Serializable` interface would cause a `NotSerializableException`.

NotSerializableException

When a serializable object is stored, the class of the object is encoded; this includes the class name and the signature of the class, the values of the object's instance variables, and the closure of any other objects referenced by the object. The values of the object's static variables are not stored.

Note
Nonserializable fields

If an object is an instance of `Serializable` but contains nonserializable instance data fields, can it be serialized? The answer is no. To enable the object to be serialized, mark these data fields with the `transient` keyword to tell the JVM to ignore them when writing the object to an object stream. Consider the following class:

```
public class C implements java.io.Serializable {
  private int v1;
  private static double v2;
  private transient A v3 = new A();
}

class A { } // A is not serializable
```

When an object of the `C` class is serialized, only variable `v1` is serialized. Variable `v2` is not serialized because it is a static variable, and variable `v3` is not serialized because it is marked `transient`. If `v3` were not marked `transient`, a `java.io.NotSerializableException` would occur.

transient

Note
Duplicate objects

If an object is written to an object stream more than once, will it be stored in multiple copies? No, it will not. When an object is written for the first time, a serial number is created for it. The JVM writes the complete contents of the object along with the serial number into the object stream. After the first time, only the serial number is stored if the same object is written again. When the objects are read back, their references are the same since only one object is actually created in the memory.

17.6.2 Serializing Arrays

An array is serializable if all its elements are serializable. An entire array can be saved into a file using `writeObject` and later can be restored using `readObject`. Listing 17.7 stores an array of five `int` values and an array of three strings, and reads them back to display on the console.

LISTING 17.7 TestObjectStreamForArray.java

```
1   import java.io.*;
2
3   public class TestObjectStreamForArray {
4     public static void main(String[] args)
5         throws ClassNotFoundException, IOException {
6       int[] numbers = {1, 2, 3, 4, 5};
7       String[] strings = {"John", "Susan", "Kim"};
8
9       try ( // Create an output stream for file array.dat
10        ObjectOutputStream output = new ObjectOutputStream(new
11          FileOutputStream("array.dat", true));
12      ) {
13        // Write arrays to the object output stream
14        output.writeObject(numbers);
15        output.writeObject(strings);
16      }
17
18      try ( // Create an input stream for file array.dat
19        ObjectInputStream input =
20          new ObjectInputStream(new FileInputStream("array.dat"));
21      ) {
22        int[] newNumbers = (int[])(input.readObject());
23        String[] newStrings = (String[])(input.readObject());
24
25        // Display arrays
26        for (int i = 0; i < newNumbers.length; i++)
27          System.out.print(newNumbers[i] + " ");
28        System.out.println();
29
30        for (int i = 0; i < newStrings.length; i++)
31          System.out.print(newStrings[i] + " ");
32      }
33    }
34  }
```

output stream (lines 10–11)
store array (lines 14–15)
input stream (lines 19–20)
restore array (lines 22–23)

```
1 2 3 4 5
John Susan Kim
```

Lines 14–15 write two arrays into file **array.dat**. Lines 22–23 read two arrays back in the same order they were written. Since `readObject()` returns `Object`, casting is used to cast the objects into `int[]` and `String[]`.

Check Point

17.6.1 What types of objects can be stored using the `ObjectOutputStream`? What is the method for writing an object? What is the method for reading an object? What is the return type of the method that reads an object from `ObjectInputStream`?

17.6.2 If you serialize two objects of the same type, will they take the same amount of space? If not, give an example.

17.6.3 Is it true that any instance of `java.io.Serializable` can be successfully serialized? Are the static variables in an object serialized? How do you mark an instance variable not to be serialized?

17.6.4 Can you write an array to an `ObjectOutputStream`?

17.6.5 Is it true that `DataInputStream`/`DataOutputStream` can always be replaced by `ObjectInputStream`/`ObjectOutputStream`?

17.6.6 What will happen when you attempt to run the following code?

```java
import java.io.*;

public class Test {
  public static void main(String[] args) throws IOException {
    try ( ObjectOutputStream output =
        new ObjectOutputStream(new FileOutputStream("object.dat")); ) {
      output.writeObject(new A());
    }
  }
}

class A implements Serializable {
  B b = new B();
}

class B {
}
```

17.7 Random-Access Files

Key Point

Java provides the `RandomAccessFile` *class to allow data to be read from and written to at any locations in the file.*

All of the streams you have used so far are known as *read-only* or *write-only* streams. These streams are called *sequential streams*. A file that is opened using a sequential stream is called a *sequential-access file*. The contents of a sequential-access file cannot be updated. However, it is often necessary to modify files. Java provides the `RandomAccessFile` class to allow data to be read from and written to at any locations in the file. A file that is opened using the `RandomAccessFile` class is known as a *random-access file*.

read-only
write-only
sequential-access file

random-access file

The `RandomAccessFile` class implements the `DataInput` and `DataOutput` interfaces, as shown in Figure 17.18. The `DataInput` interface (see Figure 17.9) defines the methods for reading primitive-type values and strings (e.g., `readInt`, `readDouble`, `readChar`, `read-Boolean`, and `readUTF`) and the `DataOutput` interface (see Figure 17.10) defines the methods for writing primitive-type values and strings (e.g., `writeInt`, `writeDouble`, `writeChar`, `writeBoolean`, and `writeUTF`).

When creating a `RandomAccessFile`, you can specify one of the two modes: `r` or `rw`. Mode `r` means that the stream is read-only, and mode `rw` indicates that the stream allows both read and write. For example, the following statement creates a new stream, `raf`, that allows the program to read from and write to the file **test.dat**:

```java
RandomAccessFile raf = new RandomAccessFile("test.dat", "rw");
```

If **test.dat** already exists, `raf` is created to access it; if **test.dat** does not exist, a new file named **test.dat** is created and `raf` is created to access the new file. The method `raf.length()` returns the number of bytes in **test.dat** at any given time. If you append new data into the file, `raf.length()` increases.

Tip

If the file is not intended to be modified, open it with the `r` mode. This prevents unintentional modification of the file.

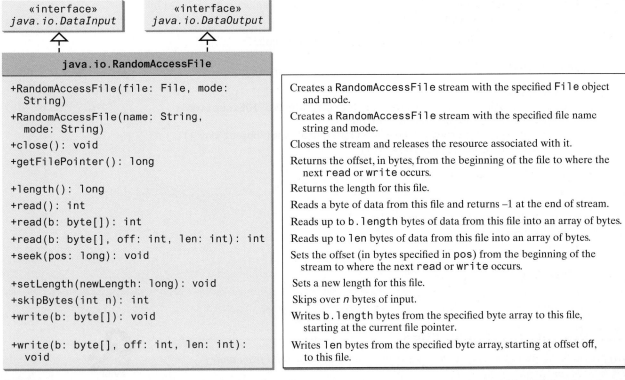

FIGURE 17.18 RandomAccessFile implements the DataInput and DataOutput interfaces with additional methods to support random access.

file pointer

A random-access file consists of a sequence of bytes. A special marker called a *file pointer* is positioned at one of these bytes. A read or write operation takes place at the location of the file pointer. When a file is opened, the file pointer is set at the beginning of the file. When you read from or write data to the file, the file pointer moves forward to the next data item. For example, if you read an int value using readInt(), the JVM reads 4 bytes from the file pointer and now the file pointer is 4 bytes ahead of the previous location, as shown in Figure 17.19.

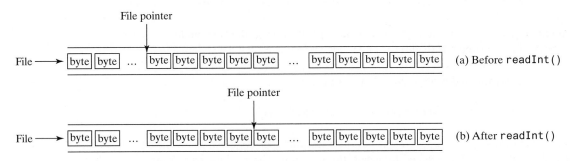

FIGURE 17.19 After an int value is read, the file pointer is moved 4 bytes ahead.

For a RandomAccessFile raf, you can use the raf.seek(position) method to move the file pointer to a specified position. raf.seek(0) moves it to the beginning of the file and raf.seek(raf.length()) moves it to the end of the file. Listing 17.8 demonstrates RandomAccessFile. A large case study of using RandomAccessFile to organize an address book is given in Supplement VI.D.

LISTING 17.8 TestRandomAccessFile.java

```
1   import java.io.*;
2
3   public class TestRandomAccessFile {
4     public static void main(String[] args) throws IOException {
5       try ( // Create a random access file
6         RandomAccessFile inout = new RandomAccessFile("inout.dat", "rw");    RandomAccessFile
7       ) {
8         // Clear the file to destroy the old contents if exists
9         inout.setLength(0);                                                  empty file
10
11        // Write new integers to the file
12        for (int i = 0; i < 200; i++)
13          inout.writeInt(i);                                                 write
14
15        // Display the current length of the file
16        System.out.println("Current file length is " + inout.length());
17
18        // Retrieve the first number
19        inout.seek(0); // Move the file pointer to the beginning             move pointer
20        System.out.println("The first number is " + inout.readInt());        read
21
22        // Retrieve the second number
23        inout.seek(1 * 4); // Move the file pointer to the second number
24        System.out.println("The second number is " + inout.readInt());
25
26        // Retrieve the tenth number
27        inout.seek(9 * 4); // Move the file pointer to the tenth number
28        System.out.println("The tenth number is " + inout.readInt());
29
30        // Modify the eleventh number
31        inout.writeInt(555);
32
33        // Append a new number
34        inout.seek(inout.length()); // Move the file pointer to the end
35        inout.writeInt(999);
36
37        // Display the new length
38        System.out.println("The new length is " + inout.length());
39
40        // Retrieve the new eleventh number
41        inout.seek(10 * 4); // Move the file pointer to the eleventh number
42        System.out.println("The eleventh number is " + inout.readInt());
43      }
44    }
45  }
```

```
Current file length is 800
The first number is 0
The second number is 1
The tenth number is 9
The new length is 804
The eleventh number is 555
```

A RandomAccessFile is created for the file named **inout.dat** with mode rw to allow both read and write operations in line 6.

`inout.setLength(0)` sets the length to 0 in line 9. This, in effect, deletes the old contents of the file.

The `for` loop writes 200 `int` values from 0 to 199 into the file in lines 12–13. Since each `int` value takes 4 bytes, the total length of the file returned from `inout.length()` is now 800 (line 16), as shown in the sample output.

Invoking `inout.seek(0)` in line 19 sets the file pointer to the beginning of the file. `inout.readInt()` reads the first value in line 20 and moves the file pointer to the next number. The second number is read in line 24.

`inout.seek(9 * 4)` (line 27) moves the file pointer to the tenth number. `inout.readInt()` reads the tenth number and moves the file pointer to the eleventh number in line 28. `inout.write(555)` writes a new eleventh number at the current position (line 31). The previous eleventh number is deleted.

`inout.seek(inout.length())` moves the file pointer to the end of the file (line 34). `inout.writeInt(999)` writes a 999 to the file (line 35). Now the length of the file is increased by 4, so `inout.length()` returns 804 (line 38).

`inout.seek(10 * 4)` moves the file pointer to the eleventh number in line 41. The new eleventh number, 555, is displayed in line 42.

Check
Point

17.7.1 Can `RandomAccessFile` streams read and write a data file created by `DataOutputStream`? Can `RandomAccessFile` streams read and write objects?

17.7.2 Create a `RandomAccessFile` stream for the file **address.dat** to allow the updating of student information in the file. Create a `DataOutputStream` for the file **address.dat**. Explain the differences between these two statements.

17.7.3 What happens if the file **test.dat** does not exist when you attempt to compile and run the following code?

```java
import java.io.*;

public class Test {
  public static void main(String[] args) {
    try ( RandomAccessFile raf =
        new RandomAccessFile("test.dat", "r"); ) {
      int i = raf.readInt();
    }
    catch (IOException ex) {
      System.out.println("IO exception");
    }
  }
}
```

KEY TERMS

binary I/O 692	sequential-access file 711
deserialization 709	serialization 709
file pointer 712	stream 692
random-access file 711	text I/O 692

CHAPTER SUMMARY

1. I/O can be classified into *text I/O* and *binary I/O*. Text I/O interprets data in sequences of characters. Binary I/O interprets data as raw binary values. How text is stored in a file depends on the encoding scheme for the file. Java automatically performs encoding and decoding for text I/O.

2. The `InputStream` and `OutputStream` classes are the roots of all binary I/O classes. `FileInputStream`/`FileOutputStream` associates a file for input/output. `Buffered InputStream`/`BufferedOutputStream` can be used to wrap any binary I/O stream to improve performance. `DataInputStream`/`DataOutputStream` can be used to read/write primitive values and strings.

3. `ObjectInputStream`/`ObjectOutputStream` can be used to read/write objects in addition to primitive values and strings. To enable object *serialization*, the object's defining class must implement the `java.io.Serializable` marker interface.

4. The `RandomAccessFile` class enables you to read and write data to a file. You can open a file with the `r` mode to indicate that it is read-only, or with the `rw` mode to indicate that it is updateable. Since the `RandomAccessFile` class implements `DataInput` and `DataOutput` interfaces, many methods in `RandomAccessFile` are the same as those in `DataInputStream` and `DataOutputStream`.

QUIZ

Answer the quiz for this chapter online at the book Companion Website.

PROGRAMMING EXERCISES

MyProgrammingLab™

Section 17.3

*17.1 (*Create a text file*) Write a program to create a file named **Exercise17_01.txt** if it does not exist. Append new data to it if it already exists. Write 100 integers created randomly into the file using text I/O. Integers are separated by a space.

Section 17.4

*17.2 (*Create a binary data file*) Write a program to create a file named **Exercise17_02 .dat** if it does not exist. Append new data to it if it already exists. Write 100 integers created randomly into the file using binary I/O.

*17.3 (*Sum all the integers in a binary data file*) Suppose a binary data file named **Exercise17_02.dat** has been created from Programming Exercise 17.2 and its data are created using `writeInt(int)` in `DataOutputStream`. The file contains an unspecified number of integers. Write a program to find the sum of the integers.

*17.4 (*Convert a text file into UTF*) Write a program that reads lines of characters from a text file and writes each line as a UTF string into a binary file. Display the sizes of the text file and the binary file. Use the following command to run the program:

```
java Exercise17_04 Welcome.java Welcome.utf
```

Section 17.6

*17.5 (*Store objects and arrays in a file*) Write a program that stores an array of the five int values 1, 2, 3, 4, and 5, a Date object for the current time, and the double value 5.5 into the file named **Exercise17_05.dat**. In the same program, write the code to read and display the data.

*17.6 (*Store Loan objects*) The Loan class in Listing 10.2 does not implement Serializable. Rewrite the Loan class to implement Serializable. Write a program that creates five Loan objects and stores them in a file named **Exercise17_06.dat**.

*17.7 (*Restore objects from a file*) Suppose a file named **Exercise17_06.dat** has been created using the ObjectOutputStream from the preceding programming exercises. The file contains Loan objects. The Loan class in Listing 10.2 does not implement Serializable. Rewrite the Loan class to implement Serializable. Write a program that reads the Loan objects from the file and displays the total loan amount. Suppose that you don't know how many Loan objects are there in the file, use EOFException to end the loop.

Section 17.7

*17.8 (*Update count*) Suppose that you wish to track how many times a program has been executed. You can store an int to count the file. Increase the count by 1 each time this program is executed. Let the program be **Exercise17_08.txt** and store the count in **Exercise17_08.dat**.

***17.9 (*Address book*) Write a program that stores, retrieves, adds, and updates addresses as shown in Figure 17.20. Use a fixed-length string for storing each attribute in the address. Use random-access file for reading and writing an address. Assume the sizes of the name, street, city, state, and zip are 32, 32, 20, 2, and 5 bytes, respectively.

Figure 17.20 The application can store, retrieve, and update addresses from a file. *Source*: Copyright © 1995–2016 Oracle and/or its affiliates. All rights reserved. Used with permission.

Comprehensive

*17.10 (*Split files*) Suppose you want to back up a huge file (e.g., a 10-GB AVI file) to a CD-R. You can achieve it by splitting the file into smaller pieces and backing up these pieces separately. Write a utility program that splits a large file into smaller ones using the following command:

```
java Exercise17_10 SourceFile numberOfPieces
```

The command creates the files **SourceFile.1**, **SourceFile.2**, . . . , **SourceFile.n**, where **n** is numberOfPieces and the output files are about the same size.

**17.11 (*Split files GUI*) Rewrite Exercise 17.10 with a GUI, as shown in Figure 17.21a.

*17.12 (*Combine files*) Write a utility program that combines the files together into a new file using the following command:

```
java Exercise17_12 SourceFile1 . . . SourceFilen TargetFile
```

The command combines SourceFile1, . . . , and SourceFilen into TargetFile.

VideoNote

Split a large file

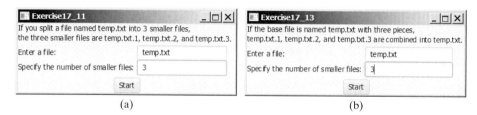

FIGURE 17.21 (a) The program splits a file. *Source*: Copyright © 1995–2016 Oracle and/or its affiliates. All rights reserved. Used with permission. (b) The program combines files into a new file.

*17.13 (*Combine files GUI*) Rewrite Exercise 17.12 with a GUI, as shown in Figure 17.21b.

17.14 (*Encrypt files*) Encode the file by adding 5 to every byte in the file. Write a program that prompts the user to enter an input file name and an output file name and saves the encrypted version of the input file to the output file.

17.15 (*Decrypt files*) Suppose a file is encrypted using the scheme in Programming Exercise 17.14. Write a program to decode an encrypted file. Your program should prompt the user to enter an input file name for the encrypted file and an output file name for the unencrypted version of the input file.

17.16 (*Frequency of characters*) Write a program that prompts the user to enter the name of an ASCII text file and displays the frequency of the characters in the file.

17.17 (*BitOutputStream*) Implement a class named `BitOutputStream`, as shown in Figure 17.22, for writing bits to an output stream. The `writeBit (char bit)` method stores the bit in a byte variable. When you create a `BitOutputStream`, the byte is empty. After invoking `writeBit('1')`, the byte becomes `00000001`. After invoking `writeBit("0101")`, the byte becomes `00010101`. The first three bits are not filled yet. When a byte is full, it is sent to the output stream. Now the byte is reset to empty. You must close the stream by invoking the `close()` method. If the byte is neither empty nor full, the `close()` method first fills the zeros to make a full 8 bits in the byte and then outputs the byte and closes the stream. For a hint, see Programming Exercise 5.44. Write a test program that sends the bits `010000100100001001101` to the file named **Exercise17_17.dat.

BitOutputStream	
+BitOutputStream(file: File)	Creates a BitOutputStream to write bits to the file.
+writeBit(char bit): void	Writes a bit '0' or '1' to the output stream.
+writeBit(String bit): void	Writes a string of bits to the output stream.
+close(): void	This method must be invoked to close the stream.

FIGURE 17.22 `BitOutputStream` outputs a stream of bits to a file.

*17.18 (*View bits*) Write the following method that displays the bit representation for the last byte in an integer:

```
public static String getBits(int value)
```

For a hint, see Programming Exercise 5.44. Write a program that prompts the user to enter a file name, reads bytes from the file, and displays each byte's binary representation.

*17.19 (*View hex*) Write a program that prompts the user to enter a file name, reads bytes from the file, and displays each byte's hex representation. (*Hint*: You can first convert the byte value into an 8-bit string, then convert the bit string into a two-digit hex string.)

**17.20 (*Binary editor*) Write a GUI application that lets the user to enter a file name in the text field and press the *Enter* key to display its binary representation in a text area. The user can also modify the binary code and save it back to the file, as shown in Figure 17.23a.

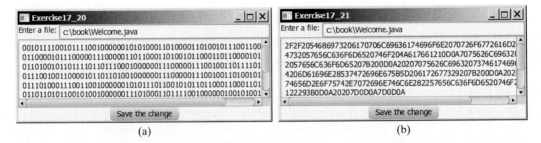

FIGURE 17.23 The programs enable the user to manipulate the contents of the file in (a) binary (b) hex. *Source*:

**17.21 (*Hex editor*) Write a GUI application that lets the user to enter a file name in the text field and press the *Enter* key to display its hex representation in a text area. The user can also modify the hex code and save it back to the file, as shown in Figure 17.23b.

CHAPTER 18

RECURSION

Objectives

- To describe what a recursive method is and the benefits of using recursion (§18.1).

- To develop recursive methods for recursive mathematical functions (§§18.2 and 18.3).

- To explain how recursive method calls are handled in a call stack (§§18.2 and 18.3).

- To solve problems using recursion (§18.4).

- To use an overloaded helper method to design a recursive method (§18.5).

- To implement a selection sort using recursion (§18.5.1).

- To implement a binary search using recursion (§18.5.2).

- To get the directory size using recursion (§18.6).

- To solve the Tower of Hanoi problem using recursion (§18.7).

- To draw fractals using recursion (§18.8).

- To discover the relationship and difference between recursion and iteration (§18.9).

- To know tail-recursive methods and why they are desirable (§18.10).

18.1 Introduction

Key Point

Recursion is a technique that leads to elegant solutions to problems that are difficult to program using simple loops.

search word problem
H-tree problem

Suppose you want to find all the files under a directory that contains a particular word. How do you solve this problem? There are several ways to do so. An intuitive and effective solution is to use recursion by searching the files in the subdirectories recursively.

H-trees, depicted in Figure 18.1, are used in a very large-scale integration (VLSI) design as a clock distribution network for routing timing signals to all parts of a chip with equal propagation delays. How do you write a program to display H-trees? A good approach is to use recursion.

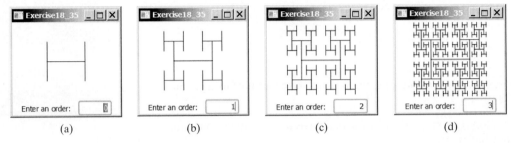

(a)   (b)   (c)   (d)

FIGURE 18.1   An H-tree can be displayed using recursion. *Source*: Copyright © 1995–2016 Oracle and/or its affiliates. All rights reserved. Used with permission.

recursive method

To use recursion is to program using *recursive methods*—that is, to use methods that invoke themselves. Recursion is a useful programming technique. In some cases, it enables you to develop a natural, straightforward, simple solution to an otherwise difficult problem. This chapter introduces the concepts and techniques of recursive programming and illustrates with examples of how to "think recursively."

18.2 Case Study: Computing Factorials

Key Point

A recursive method is one that invokes itself directly or indirectly.

Many mathematical functions are defined using recursion. Let's begin with a simple example. The factorial of a number n can be recursively defined as follows:

```
0! = 1;
n! = n × (n – 1)!; n > 0
```

How do you find $n!$ for a given n? To find $1!$ is easy because you know that $0!$ is 1 and $1!$ is $1 \times 0!$. Assuming that you know $(n - 1)!$, you can obtain $n!$ immediately by using $n \times (n - 1)!$. Thus, the problem of computing $n!$ is reduced to computing $(n - 1)!$. When computing $(n - 1)!$, you can apply the same idea recursively until n is reduced to 0.

Let `factorial(n)` be the method for computing $n!$. If you call the method with $n = 0$, it immediately returns the result. The method knows how to solve the simplest case, which is referred to as the *base case* or the *stopping condition*. If you call the method with $n > 0$, it reduces the problem into a subproblem for computing the factorial of $n - 1$. The *subproblem* is essentially the same as the original problem, but it is simpler or smaller. Because the subproblem has the same property as the original problem, you can call the method with a different argument, which is referred to as a *recursive call*.

base case or stopping condition

recursive call

The recursive algorithm for computing `factorial(n)` can be simply described as follows:

```
if (n == 0)
    return 1;
```

```
    else
      return n * factorial(n - 1);
```

A recursive call can result in many more recursive calls because the method keeps on dividing a subproblem into new subproblems. For a recursive method to terminate, the problem must eventually be reduced to a stopping case, at which point the method returns a result to its caller. The caller then performs a computation and returns the result to its own caller. This process continues until the result is passed back to the original caller. The original problem can now be solved by multiplying n by the result of `factorial(n - 1)`.

Listing 18.1 gives a complete program that prompts the user to enter a nonnegative integer and displays the factorial for the number.

LISTING 18.1 ComputeFactorial.java

```
 1  import java.util.Scanner;
 2
 3  public class ComputeFactorial {
 4    /** Main method */
 5    public static void main(String[] args) {
 6      // Create a Scanner
 7      Scanner input = new Scanner(System.in);
 8      System.out.print("Enter a nonnegative integer: ");
 9      int n = input.nextInt();
10
11      // Display factorial
12      System.out.println("Factorial of " + n + " is " + factorial(n));
13    }
14
15    /** Return the factorial for the specified number */
16    public static long factorial(int n) {
17      if (n == 0)   // Base case                                        base case
18        return 1;
19      else
20        return n *  factorial(n - 1); // Recursive call                 recursion
21    }
22  }
```

```
Enter a nonnegative integer: 4 ⏎Enter
Factorial of 4 is 24
```

```
Enter a nonnegative integer: 10 ⏎Enter
Factorial of 10 is 3628800
```

The `factorial` method (lines 16–21) is essentially a direct translation of the recursive mathematical definition for the factorial into Java code. The call to `factorial` is recursive because it calls itself. The parameter passed to `factorial` is decremented until it reaches the base case of 0.

You see how to write a recursive method. How does recursion work behind the scenes?   how does it work?
Figure 18.2 illustrates the execution of the recursive calls, starting with n = 4. The use of stack space for recursive calls is shown in Figure 18.3.

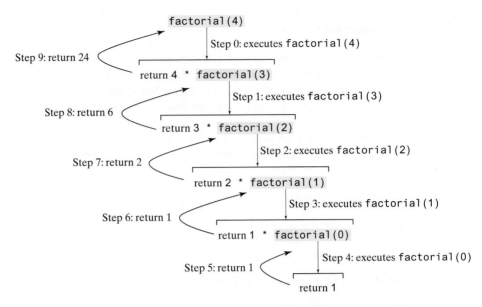

FIGURE 18.2 Invoking `factorial(4)` spawns recursive calls to `factorial`.

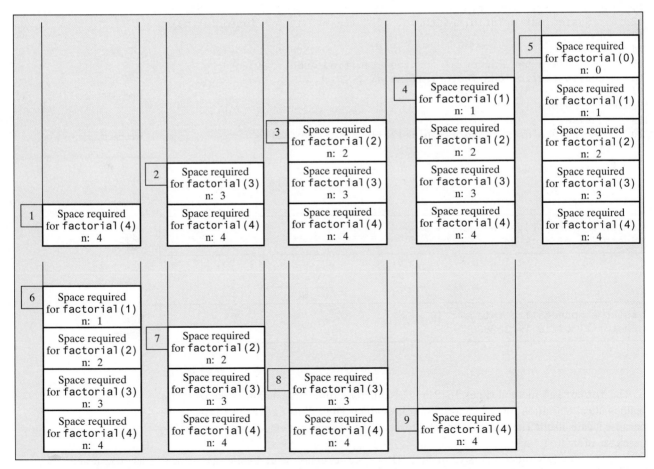

FIGURE 18.3 When `factorial(4)` is being executed, the `factorial` method is called recursively, causing the stack space to dynamically change.

Pedagogical Note

It is simpler and more efficient to implement the `factorial` method using a loop. However, we use the recursive `factorial` method here to demonstrate the concept of recursion. Later in this chapter, we will present some problems that are inherently recursive, and are difficult to solve without using recursion.

Note

If recursion does not reduce the problem in a manner that allows it to eventually converge into the base case or a base case is not specified, *infinite recursion* can occur. For example, suppose you mistakenly write the `factorial` method as follows:

infinite recursion

```
public static long factorial(int n) {
  return n * factorial(n - 1);
}
```

The method runs infinitely and causes a `StackOverflowError`.

The example discussed in this section shows a recursive method that invokes itself. This is known as *direct recursion*. It is also possible to create *indirect recursion*. This occurs when method `A` invokes method `B`, which in turn directly or indirectly invokes method `A`.

direct recursion
indirect recursion

18.2.1 What is a recursive method? What is an infinite recursion?

18.2.2 How many times is the `factorial` method in Listing 18.1 invoked for `factorial(6)`?

18.2.3 Show the output of the following programs and identify base cases and recursive calls.

Check Point

```
public class Test {
  public static void main(String[] args) {
    System.out.println(
      "Sum is " + xMethod(5));
  }

  public static int xMethod(int n) {
    if (n == 1)
      return 1;
    else
      return n + xMethod(n - 1);
  }
}
```

```
public class Test {
  public static void main(String[] args) {
    xMethod(1234567);
  }

  public static void xMethod(int n) {
    if (n > 0) {
      System.out.print(n % 10);
      xMethod(n / 10);
    }
  }
}
```

18.2.4 Write a recursive mathematical definition for computing 2^n for a positive integer n.

18.2.5 Write a recursive mathematical definition for computing x^n for a positive integer n and a real number x.

18.2.6 Write a recursive mathematical definition for computing $1 + 2 + 3 + \cdots + n$ for a positive integer n.

18.3 Case Study: Computing Fibonacci Numbers

In some cases, recursion enables you to create an intuitive, straightforward, simple solution to a problem.

Key Point

The `factorial` method in the preceding section could easily be rewritten without using recursion. In this section, we show an example for creating an intuitive solution to a problem using recursion. Consider the well-known Fibonacci-series problem:

The series:	0	1	1	2	3	5	8	13	21	34	55	89	...
indexes:	0	1	2	3	4	5	6	7	8	9	10	11	

The Fibonacci series begins with 0 and 1, and each subsequent number is the sum of the preceding two. The series can be recursively defined as:

```
fib(0) = 0;
fib(1) = 1;
fib(index) = fib(index - 2) + fib(index - 1); index >= 2
```

The Fibonacci series was named for Leonardo Fibonacci, a medieval mathematician, who originated it to model the growth of the rabbit population. It can be applied in numeric optimization and in various other areas.

How do you find `fib(index)` for a given `index`? It is easy to find `fib(2)` because you know `fib(0)` and `fib(1)`. Assuming you know `fib(index - 2)` and `fib(index - 1)`, you can obtain `fib(index)` immediately. Thus, the problem of computing `fib(index)` is reduced to computing `fib(index - 2)` and `fib(index - 1)`. When doing so, you apply the idea recursively until `index` is reduced to 0 or 1.

The base case is `index = 0` or `index = 1`. If you call the method with `index = 0` or `index = 1`, it immediately returns the result. If you call the method with `index >= 2`, it divides the problem into two subproblems for computing `fib(index - 1)` and `fib(index - 2)` using recursive calls. The recursive algorithm for computing `fib(index)` can be simply described as follows:

```
if (index == 0)
  return 0;
else if (index == 1)
  return 1;
else
  return fib(index - 1) + fib(index - 2);
```

Listing 18.2 gives a complete program that prompts the user to enter an index and computes the Fibonacci number for that index.

LISTING 18.2 ComputeFibonacci.java

```
1  import java.util.Scanner;
2
3  public class ComputeFibonacci {
4    /** Main method */
5    public static void main(String[] args) {
6      // Create a Scanner
7      Scanner input = new Scanner(System.in);
8      System.out.print("Enter an index for a Fibonacci number: ");
9      int index = input.nextInt();
10
11     // Find and display the Fibonacci number
12     System.out.println("The Fibonacci number at index "
13       + index + " is " + fib(index));
14   }
15
16   /** The method for finding the Fibonacci number */
17   public static long fib(long index) {
18     if (index == 0) // Base case
19       return 0;
20     else if (index == 1) // Base case
21       return 1;
22     else // Reduction and recursive calls
23       return fib(index - 1) + fib(index - 2);
24   }
25 }
```

base case
base case
recursion

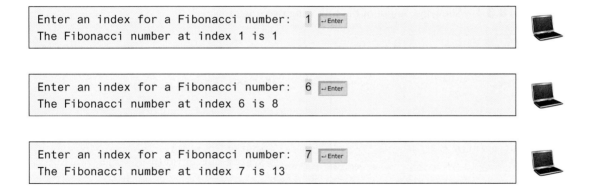

The program does not show the considerable amount of work done behind the scenes by the computer. Figure 18.4, however, shows the successive recursive calls for evaluating `fib(4)`. The original method, `fib(4)`, makes two recursive calls, `fib(3)` and `fib(2)`, and then returns `fib(3) + fib(2)`. However, in what order are these methods called? In Java, operands are evaluated from left to right, so `fib(2)` is called after `fib(3)` is completely evaluated. The labels in Figure 18.4 show the order in which the methods are called.

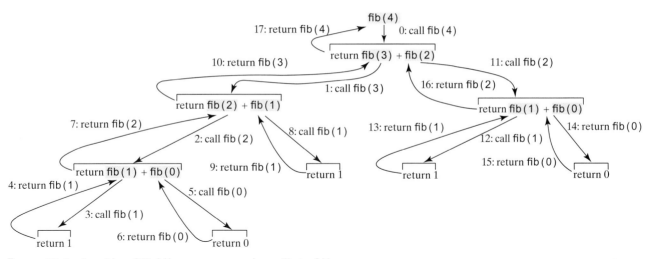

Figure 18.4 Invoking `fib(4)` spawns recursive calls to `fib`.

As shown in Figure 18.4, there are many duplicated recursive calls. For instance, `fib(2)` is called twice, `fib(1)` three times, and `fib(0)` twice. In general, computing `fib(index)` requires roughly twice as many recursive calls as does computing `fib(index - 1)`. As you try larger index values, the number of calls substantially increases, as given in Table 18.1.

TABLE 18.1 Number of Recursive Calls in `fib(index)`

index	2	3	4	10	20	30	40	50
# of calls	3	5	9	177	21,891	2,692,537	331,160,281	2,075,316,483

Pedagogical Note

The recursive implementation of the `fib` method is very simple and straightforward, but it isn't efficient, because it requires more time and memory to run recursive methods. See Programming Exercise 18.2 for an efficient solution using loops. Though it is not practical, the recursive `fib` method is a good example of how to write recursive methods.

18.3.1 Show the output of the following two programs:

```java
public class Test {
  public static void main(String[] args) {
    xMethod(5);
  }

  public static void xMethod(int n) {
    if (n > 0) {
      System.out.print(n + " ");
      xMethod(n - 1);
    }
  }
}
```

```java
public class Test {
  public static void main(String[] args) {
    xMethod(5);
  }

  public static void xMethod(int n) {
    if (n > 0) {
      xMethod(n - 1);
      System.out.print(n + " ");
    }
  }
}
```

18.3.2 What is wrong in the following methods?

```java
public class Test {
  public static void main(String[] args) {
    xMethod(1234567);
  }

  public static void xMethod(double n) {
    if (n != 0) {
      System.out.print(n);
      xMethod(n / 10);
    }
  }
}
```

```java
public class Test {
  public static void main(String[] args) {
    Test test = new Test();
    System.out.println(test.toString());
  }

  public Test() {
    Test test = new Test();
  }
}
```

18.3.3 How many times is the `fib` method in Listing 18.2 invoked for `fib(6)`?

18.4 Problem Solving Using Recursion

If you think recursively, you can solve many problems using recursion.

The preceding sections presented two classic recursion examples. All recursive methods have the following characteristics:

recursion characteristics
if-else

- The method is implemented using an `if-else` or a `switch` statement that leads to different cases.

base cases

- One or more base cases (the simplest case) are used to stop recursion.

reduction

- Every recursive call reduces the original problem, bringing it increasingly closer to a base case until it becomes that case.

In general, to solve a problem using recursion, you break it into subproblems. Each subproblem is the same as the original problem, but smaller in size. You can apply the same approach to each subproblem to solve it recursively.

think recursively

Recursion is everywhere. It is fun to *think recursively*. Consider drinking coffee. You may describe the procedure recursively as follows:

```java
public static void drinkCoffee(Cup cup) {
  if (!cup.isEmpty()) {
    cup.takeOneSip(); // Take one sip
    drinkCoffee(cup);
  }
}
```

Assume `cup` is an object for a cup of coffee with the instance methods `isEmpty()` and `take-OneSip()`. You can break the problem into two subproblems: One is to drink one sip of coffee, and the other is to drink the rest of the coffee in the cup. The second problem is the same as the original problem, but smaller in size. The base case for the problem is when the cup is empty.

Consider the problem of printing a message n times. You can break the problem into two subproblems: One is to print the message one time, and the other is to print it n − 1 times. The second problem is the same as the original problem, but it is smaller in size. The base case for the problem is n == 0. You can solve this problem using recursion as follows:

```
public static void nPrintln(String message, int times) {
  if (times >= 1) {
    System.out.println(message);
    nPrintln(message, times - 1);                           recursive call
  } // The base case is times == 0
}
```

Note the `fib` method in the preceding section returns a value to its caller, but the `drinkCoffee` and `nPrintln` methods are `void` and they do not return a value.

If you *think recursively*, you can use recursion to solve many of the problems presented in earlier chapters of this book. Consider the palindrome problem in Listing 5.14. Recall that a string is a palindrome if it reads the same from the left and from the right. For example, "mom" and "dad" are palindromes, but "uncle" and "aunt" are not. The problem of checking whether a string is a palindrome can be divided into two subproblems:

- Check whether the first character and the last character of the string are equal.

- Ignore the two end characters and check whether the rest of the substring is a palindrome.

The second subproblem is the same as the original problem, but smaller in size. There are two base cases: (1) the two end characters are not the same and (2) the string size is 0 or 1. In case 1, the string is not a palindrome; in case 2, the string is a palindrome. The recursive method for this problem can be implemented as given in Listing 18.3.

LISTING 18.3 RecursivePalindromeUsingSubstring.java

```
1  public class RecursivePalindromeUsingSubstring {
2    public static boolean isPalindrome(String s) {            method header
3      if (s.length() <= 1) // Base case                       base case
4        return true;
5      else if (s.charAt(0) != s.charAt(s.length() - 1)) // Base case   base case
6        return false;
7      else
8        return isPalindrome(s.substring(1, s.length() - 1));   recursive call
9    }
10
11   public static void main(String[] args) {
12     System.out.println("Is moon a palindrome? "
13       + isPalindrome("moon"));
14     System.out.println("Is noon a palindrome? "
15       + isPalindrome("noon"));
16     System.out.println("Is a a palindrome? " + isPalindrome("a"));
17     System.out.println("Is aba a palindrome? " +
18       isPalindrome("aba"));
19     System.out.println("Is ab a palindrome? " + isPalindrome("ab"));
20   }
21 }
```

```
Is moon a palindrome? false
Is noon a palindrome? true
Is a a palindrome? true
Is aba a palindrome? true
Is ab a palindrome? false
```

The substring method in line 8 creates a new string that is the same as the original string except without the first and the last characters. Checking whether a string is a palindrome is equivalent to checking whether the substring is a palindrome if the two end characters in the original string are the same.

18.4.1 Describe the characteristics of recursive methods.

18.4.2 For the isPalindrome method in Listing 18.3, what are the base cases? How many times is this method called when invoking isPalindrome("abdxcxdba")?

18.4.3 Show the call stack for isPalindrome("abcba") using the method defined in Listing 18.3.

18.5 Recursive Helper Methods

Sometimes you can find a solution to the original problem by defining a recursive function to a problem similar to the original problem. This new method is called a recursive helper method. The original problem can be solved by invoking the recursive helper method.

The recursive isPalindrome method in Listing 18.3 is not efficient because it creates a new string for every recursive call. To avoid creating new strings, you can use the low and high indices to indicate the range of the substring. These two indices must be passed to the recursive method. Since the original method is isPalindrome(String s), you have to create the new method isPalindrome(String s, int low, int high) to accept additional information on the string, as given in Listing 18.4.

LISTING 18.4 RecursivePalindrome.java

```
1  public class RecursivePalindrome {
2    public static boolean isPalindrome(String s) {
3      return isPalindrome(s, 0, s.length() - 1);
4    }
5
6    private static boolean isPalindrome(String s, int low, int high) {
7      if (high <= low) // Base case
8        return true;
9      else if (s.charAt(low) != s.charAt(high)) // Base case
10       return false;
11     else
12       return isPalindrome(s, low + 1, high - 1);
13   }
14
15   public static void main(String[] args) {
16     System.out.println("Is moon a palindrome? "
17       + isPalindrome("moon"));
18     System.out.println("Is noon a palindrome? "
19       + isPalindrome("noon"));
20     System.out.println("Is a a palindrome? " + isPalindrome("a"));
21     System.out.println("Is aba a palindrome? " + isPalindrome("aba"));
22     System.out.println("Is ab a palindrome? " + isPalindrome("ab"));
23   }
24 }
```

helper method
base case

base case

Two overloaded `isPalindrome` methods are defined. The first method `isPalindrome` `(String s)` checks whether a string is a palindrome and the second method `isPalindrome` `(String s, int low, int high)` checks whether a substring `s(low..high)` is a palindrome. The first method passes the string `s` with `low = 0` and `high = s.length() − 1` to the second method. The second method can be invoked recursively to check a palindrome in an ever-shrinking substring. It is a common design technique in recursive programming to define a second method that receives additional parameters. Such a method is known as a *recursive helper method.*

recursive helper method

Helper methods are very useful in designing recursive solutions for problems involving strings and arrays. The sections that follow give two more examples.

18.5.1 Recursive Selection Sort

Selection sort was introduced in Section 7.11. Recall that it finds the smallest element in the list and swaps it with the first element. It then finds the smallest element remaining and swaps it with the first element in the remaining list and so on until the remaining list contains only a single element. The problem can be divided into two subproblems:

■ Find the smallest element in the list and swap it with the first element.

■ Ignore the first element and sort the remaining smaller list recursively.

The base case is that the list contains only one element. Listing 18.5 gives the recursive sort method.

LISTING 18.5 `RecursiveSelectionSort.java`

```
1  public class RecursiveSelectionSort {
2    public static void sort(double[] list) {
3      sort(list, 0, list.length - 1); // Sort the entire list
4    }
5
6    private static void sort(double[] list, int low, int high) {
7      if (low < high) {
8        // Find the smallest number and its index in list[low .. high]
9        int indexOfMin = low;
10       double min = list[low];
11       for (int i = low + 1; i <= high; i++) {
12         if (list[i] < min) {
13           min = list[i];
14           indexOfMin = i;
15         }
16       }
17
18       // Swap the smallest in list[low .. high] with list[low]
19       list[indexOfMin] = list[low];
20       list[low] = min;
21
22       // Sort the remaining list[low+1 .. high]
23       sort(list, low + 1, high);
24     }
25   }
26 }
```

helper method
base case

recursive call

Two overloaded `sort` methods are defined. The first method `sort(double[] list)` sorts an array in `list[0..list.length − 1]` and the second method `sort(double[] list, int low, int high)` sorts an array in `list[low..high]`. The second method can be invoked recursively to sort an ever-shrinking subarray.

VideoNote

Binary search

18.5.2   Recursive Binary Search

Binary search was introduced in Section 7.10.2. For binary search to work, the elements in the array must be in increasing order. The binary search first compares the key with the element in the middle of the array. Consider the following three cases:

- Case 1: If the key is less than the middle element, recursively search for the key in the first half of the array.

- Case 2: If the key is equal to the middle element, the search ends with a match.

- Case 3: If the key is greater than the middle element, recursively search for the key in the second half of the array.

Case 1 and Case 3 reduce the search to a smaller list. Case 2 is a base case when there is a match. Another base case is that the search is exhausted without a match. Listing 18.6 gives a clear, simple solution for the binary search problem using recursion.

LISTING 18.6   RecursiveBinarySearch.java

```
 1  public class RecursiveBinarySearch {
 2    public static int recursiveBinarySearch(int[] list, int key) {
 3      int low = 0;
 4      int high = list.length - 1;
 5      return recursiveBinarySearch(list, key, low, high);
 6    }
 7
 8    private static int recursiveBinarySearch(int[] list, int key,
 9        int low, int high) {
10      if (low > high) // The list has been exhausted without a match
11        return -low - 1;
12
13      int mid = (low + high) / 2;
14      if (key < list[mid])
15        return recursiveBinarySearch(list, key, low, mid - 1);
16      else if (key == list[mid])
17        return mid;
18      else
19        return recursiveBinarySearch(list, key, mid + 1, high);
20    }
21  }
```

helper method — line 8

base case — line 10

recursive call — line 15

base case — line 17

recursive call — line 19

The first method finds a key in the whole list. The second method finds a key in the list with index from `low` to `high`.

The first `binarySearch` method passes the initial array with `low = 0` and `high = list.length - 1` to the second `binarySearch` method. The second method is invoked recursively to find the key in an ever-shrinking subarray.

Check Point

18.5.1   Show the call stack for `isPalindrome("abcba")` using the method defined in Listing 18.4.

18.5.2   Show the call stack for `selectionSort(new double[]{2, 3, 5, 1})` using the method defined in Listing 18.5.

18.5.3   What is a recursive helper method?

18.6 Case Study: Finding the Directory Size

Recursive methods are efficient for solving problems with recursive structures.

The preceding examples can easily be solved without using recursion. This section presents a problem that is difficult to solve without using recursion. The problem is to find the size of a directory. The size of a directory is the sum of the sizes of all files in the directory. A directory d may contain subdirectories. Suppose a directory contains files $f_1, f_2, \ldots, f_m$ and subdirectories $d_1, d_2, \ldots, d_n$, as shown in Figure 18.5.

Key Point

VideoNote
Directory size

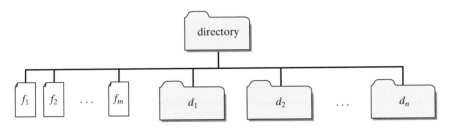

FIGURE 18.5 A directory contains files and subdirectories.

The size of the directory can be defined recursively as follows:

$$size(d) = size(f_1) + size(f_2) + \cdots + size(f_m) + size(d_1) + size(d_2) + \cdots + size(d_n)$$

The `File` class, introduced in Section 12.10, can be used to represent a file or a directory and obtain the properties for files and directories. Two methods in the `File` class are useful for this problem:

- The `length()` method returns the size of a file.

- The `listFiles()` method returns an array of `File` objects under a directory.

Listing 18.7 gives a program that prompts the user to enter a directory or a file and displays its size.

LISTING 18.7 DirectorySize.java

```
1  import java.io.File;
2  import java.util.Scanner;
3
4  public class DirectorySize {
5    public static void main(String[] args) {
6      // Prompt the user to enter a directory or a file
7      System.out.print("Enter a directory or a file: ");
8      Scanner input = new Scanner(System.in);
9      String directory = input.nextLine();
10
11     // Display the size
12     System.out.println(getSize(new File(directory)) + " bytes");
13   }
14
15   public static long getSize(File file) {
16     long size = 0; // Store the total size of all files
17
```

invoke method

getSize method

is directory?
all subitems

recursive call

base case

```
18      if (file.isDirectory()) {
19        File[] files = file.listFiles(); // All files and subdirectories
20        for (int i = 0; files != null && i < files.length; i++) {
21          size += getSize(files[i]); // Recursive call
22        }
23      }
24      else { // Base case
25        size += file.length();
26      }
27
28      return size;
29    }
30  }
```

```
Enter a directory or a file: c:\book ↵Enter
48619631 bytes
```

```
Enter a directory or a file: c:\book\Welcome.java ↵Enter
172 bytes
```

```
Enter a directory or a file: c:\book\NonExistentFile ↵Enter
0 bytes
```

If the `file` object represents a directory (line 18), each subitem (file or subdirectory) in the directory is recursively invoked to obtain its size (line 21). If the `file` object represents a file (line 24), the file size is obtained and added to the total size (line 25).

What happens if an incorrect or a nonexistent directory is entered? The program will detect that it is not a directory and invoke `file.length()` (line 25), which returns 0. Thus, in this case, the `getSize` method will return 0.

testing all cases

Tip
To avoid mistakes, it is a good practice to test all cases. For example, you should test the program for an input of file, an empty directory, a nonexistent directory, and a nonexistent file.

18.6.1 What is the base case for the `getSize` method?

18.6.2 How does the program get all files and directories under a given directory?

18.6.3 How many times will the `getSize` method be invoked for a directory if the directory has three subdirectories and each subdirectory has four files?

18.6.4 Will the program work if the directory is empty (i.e., it does not contain any files)?

18.6.5 Will the program work if line 20 is replaced by the following code?

```
for (int i = 0; i < files.length; i++)
```

18.6.6 Will the program work if lines 20 and 21 are replaced by the following code?

```
for (File file: files)
  size += getSize(file); // Recursive call
```

18.7 Case Study: Tower of Hanoi

The Tower of Hanoi problem is a classic problem that can be solved easily using recursion, but it is difficult to solve otherwise.

Key Point

The problem involves moving a specified number of disks of distinct sizes from one tower to another while observing the following rules:

- There are *n* disks labeled 1, 2, 3, . . . , *n* and three towers labeled A, B, and C.
- No disk can be on top of a smaller disk at any time.
- All the disks are initially placed on tower A.
- Only one disk can be moved at a time and it must be the smallest disk on a tower.

The objective of the problem is to move all the disks from A to B with the assistance of C. For example, if you have three disks, the steps to move all of the disks from A to B are shown in Figure 18.6. For an interactive demo, see liveexample.pearsoncmg.com/dsanimation/TowerOfHanoieBook.html.

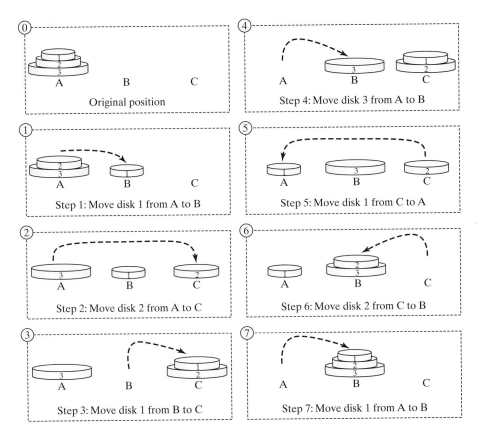

FIGURE 18.6 The goal of the Tower of Hanoi problem is to move disks from tower A to tower B without breaking the rules.

In the case of three disks, you can find the solution manually. For a larger number of disks, however—even for four—the problem is quite complex. Fortunately, the problem has an inherently recursive nature, which leads to a straightforward recursive solution.

The base case for the problem is n = 1. If n == 1, you could simply move the disk from A to B. When n > 1, you could split the original problem into the following three subproblems and solve them sequentially.

1. Move the first n − 1 disks from A to C recursively with the assistance of tower B, as shown in Step 1 in Figure 18.7.

2. Move disk n from A to B, as shown in Step 2 in Figure 18.7.

3. Move n − 1 disks from C to B recursively with the assistance of tower A, as shown in Step 3 in Figure 18.7.

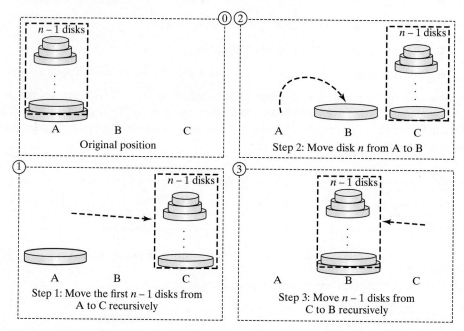

FIGURE 18.7   The Tower of Hanoi problem can be decomposed into three subproblems.

The following method moves *n* disks from the `fromTower` to the `toTower` with the assistance of the `auxTower`:

```
void moveDisks(int n, char fromTower, char toTower, char auxTower)
```

The algorithm for the method can be described as:

```
if (n == 1) // Stopping condition
  Move disk 1 from the fromTower to the toTower;
else {
  moveDisks(n - 1, fromTower, auxTower, toTower);
  Move disk n from the fromTower to the toTower;
  moveDisks(n - 1, auxTower, toTower, fromTower);
}
```

Listing 18.8 gives a program that prompts the user to enter the number of disks and invokes the recursive method `moveDisks` to display the solution for moving the disks.

LISTING 18.8   TowerOfHanoi.java

```
1  import java.util.Scanner;
2
3  public class TowerOfHanoi {
4    /** Main method */
```

```
 5    public static void main(String[] args) {
 6      // Create a Scanner
 7      Scanner input = new Scanner(System.in);
 8      System.out.print("Enter number of disks: ");
 9      int n = input.nextInt();
10
11      // Find the solution recursively
12      System.out.println("The moves are:");
13      moveDisks(n, 'A', 'B', 'C');
14    }
15
16    /** The method for finding the solution to move n disks
17        from fromTower to toTower with auxTower */
18    public static void moveDisks(int n, char fromTower,
19        char toTower, char auxTower) {
20      if (n == 1) // Stopping condition                        base case
21        System.out.println("Move disk " + n + " from " +
22          fromTower + " to " + toTower);
23      else {
24        moveDisks(n - 1, fromTower, auxTower, toTower);         recursion
25        System.out.println("Move disk " + n + " from " +
26          fromTower + " to " + toTower);
27        moveDisks(n - 1, auxTower, toTower, fromTower);         recursion
28      }
29    }
30  }
```

```
Enter number of disks:  4 ↵Enter
The moves are:
Move disk 1 from A to C
Move disk 2 from A to B
Move disk 1 from C to B
Move disk 3 from A to C
Move disk 1 from B to A
Move disk 2 from B to C
Move disk 1 from A to C
Move disk 4 from A to B
Move disk 1 from C to B
Move disk 2 from C to A
Move disk 1 from B to A
Move disk 3 from C to B
Move disk 1 from A to C
Move disk 2 from A to B
Move disk 1 from C to B
```

This problem is inherently recursive. Using recursion makes it possible to find a natural, simple solution. It would be difficult to solve the problem without using recursion.

Consider tracing the program for n = 3. The successive recursive calls are shown in Figure 18.8. As you can see, writing the program is easier than tracing the recursive calls. The system uses stacks to manage the calls behind the scenes. To some extent, recursion provides a level of abstraction that hides iterations and other details from the user.

18.7.1 How many times is the moveDisks method in Listing 18.8 invoked for moveDisks(5, 'A', 'B', 'C')?

Check
Point

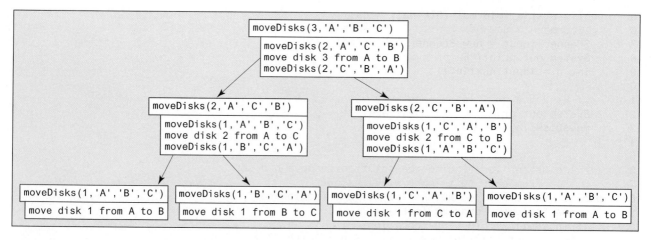

FIGURE 18.8 Invoking `moveDisks(3, 'A', 'B', 'C')` spawns calls to `moveDisks` recursively.

18.8 Case Study: Fractals

Using recursion is ideal for displaying fractals because fractals are inherently recursive.

Key Point

VideoNote

Fractal (Sierpinski triangle)

A *fractal* is a geometrical figure, but unlike triangles, circles, and rectangles, fractals can be divided into parts, each of which is a reduced-size copy of the whole. There are many interesting examples of fractals. This section introduces a simple fractal, the *Sierpinski triangle*, named after a famous Polish mathematician.

A Sierpinski triangle is created as follows:

1. Begin with an equilateral triangle, which is considered to be a Sierpinski fractal of order (or level) 0, as shown in Figure 18.9a.

2. Connect the midpoints of the sides of the triangle of order 0 to create a Sierpinski triangle of order 1 (see Figure 18.9b).

3. Leave the center triangle intact. Connect the midpoints of the sides of the three other triangles to create a Sierpinski triangle of order 2 (see Figure 18.9c).

4. You can repeat the same process recursively to create a Sierpinski triangle of order 3, 4, . . . , and so on (see Figure 18.9d). For an interactive demo, see liveexample.pearsoncmg.com/dsanimation/SierpinskiTriangleUsingHTML.html.

The problem is inherently recursive. How do you develop a recursive solution for it? Consider the base case when the order is 0. It is easy to draw a Sierpinski triangle of order 0. How do you draw a Sierpinski triangle of order 1? The problem can be reduced to drawing three Sierpinski triangles of order 0. How do you draw a Sierpinski triangle of order 2? The problem can be reduced to drawing three Sierpinski triangles of order 1, so the problem of drawing a Sierpinski triangle of order *n* can be reduced to drawing three Sierpinski triangles of order *n* − 1.

Listing 18.9 gives a program that displays a Sierpinski triangle of any order, as shown in Figure 18.9. You can enter an order in a text field to display a Sierpinski triangle of the specified order.

LISTING 18.9 SierpinskiTriangle.java

```
1  import javafx.application.Application;
2  import javafx.geometry.Point2D;
3  import javafx.geometry.Pos;
```

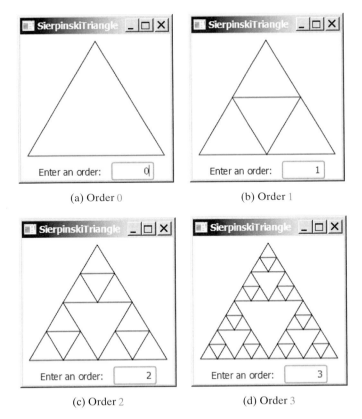

(a) Order 0   (b) Order 1

(c) Order 2   (d) Order 3

FIGURE 18.9 A Sierpinski triangle is a pattern of recursive triangles. *Source*: Copyright © 1995–2016 Oracle and/or its affiliates. All rights reserved. Used with permission.

```
4   import javafx.scene.Scene;
5   import javafx.scene.control.Label;
6   import javafx.scene.control.TextField;
7   import javafx.scene.layout.BorderPane;
8   import javafx.scene.layout.HBox;
9   import javafx.scene.layout.Pane;
10  import javafx.scene.paint.Color;
11  import javafx.scene.shape.Polygon;
12  import javafx.stage.Stage;
13
14  public class SierpinskiTriangle extends Application {
15    @Override // Override the start method in the Application class
16    public void start(Stage primaryStage) {
17      SierpinskiTrianglePane pane = new SierpinskiTrianglePane();       recursive triangle pane
18      TextField tfOrder = new TextField();
19      tfOrder.setOnAction(
20        e -> pane.setOrder(Integer.parseInt(tfOrder.getText())));       listener for text field
21      tfOrder.setPrefColumnCount(4);
22      tfOrder.setAlignment(Pos.BOTTOM_RIGHT);
23
24      // Pane to hold label, text field, and a button
25      HBox hBox = new HBox(10);                                         hold label and text field
26      hBox.getChildren().addAll(new Label("Enter an order: "), tfOrder);
27      hBox.setAlignment(Pos.CENTER);
28
29      BorderPane borderPane = new BorderPane();
30      borderPane.setCenter(pane);
31      borderPane.setBottom(hBox);
32
```

```
33        // Create a scene and place it in the stage
34        Scene scene = new Scene(borderPane, 200, 210);
35        primaryStage.setTitle("SierpinskiTriangle"); // Set the stage title
36        primaryStage.setScene(scene); // Place the scene in the stage
37        primaryStage.show(); // Display the stage
38
```
listener for resizing
```
39        pane.widthProperty().addListener(ov -> pane.paint());
40        pane.heightProperty().addListener(ov -> pane.paint());
41    }
42
43    /** Pane for displaying triangles */
44    static class SierpinskiTrianglePane extends Pane {
45      private int order = 0;
46
47      /** Set a new order */
48      public void setOrder(int order) {
49        this.order = order;
50        paint();
51      }
52
53      SierpinskiTrianglePane() {
54      }
55
56      protected void paint() {
57        // Select three points in proportion to the pane size
```
three initial points
```
58        Point2D p1 = new Point2D(getWidth() / 2, 10);
59        Point2D p2 = new Point2D(10, getHeight() - 10);
60        Point2D p3 = new Point2D(getWidth() - 10, getHeight() - 10);
61
```
clear the pane
```
62        this.getChildren().clear(); // Clear the pane before redisplay
63
```
draw a triangle
```
64        displayTriangles(order, p1, p2, p3);
65      }
66
67      private void displayTriangles(int order, Point2D p1,
68          Point2D p2, Point2D p3) {
69        if (order == 0) {
70          // Draw a triangle to connect three points
```
create a triangle
```
71          Polygon triangle = new Polygon();
72          triangle.getPoints().addAll(p1.getX(), p1.getY(), p2.getX(),
73            p2.getY(), p3.getX(), p3.getY());
74          triangle.setStroke(Color.BLACK);
75          triangle.setFill(Color.WHITE);
76
77          this.getChildren().add(triangle);
78        }
79        else {
80          // Get the midpoint on each edge in the triangle
81          Point2D p12 = p1.midpoint(p2);
82          Point2D p23 = p2.midpoint(p3);
83          Point2D p31 = p3.midpoint(p1);
84
85          // Recursively display three triangles
```
top subtriangle
left subtriangle
right subtriangle
```
86          displayTriangles(order - 1, p1, p12, p31);
87          displayTriangles(order - 1, p12, p2, p23);
88          displayTriangles(order - 1, p31, p23, p3);
89        }
90      }
91    }
92  }
```

The initial triangle has three points set in proportion to the pane size (lines 58–60). If `order == 0`, the `displayTriangles(order, p1, p2, p3)` method displays a triangle that connects the three points `p1`, `p2`, and `p3` (lines 71–77), as shown in Figure 18.10a. Otherwise, it performs the following tasks:

displayTriangle method

1. Obtain the midpoint between `p1` and `p2` (line 81), the midpoint between `p2` and `p3` (line 82), and the midpoint between `p3` and `p1` (line 83), as shown in Figure 18.10b.

2. Recursively invoke `displayTriangles` with a reduced order to display three smaller Sierpinski triangles (lines 86–88). Note each small Sierpinski triangle is structurally identical to the original big Sierpinski triangle except that the order of a small triangle is one less, as shown in Figure 18.10b.

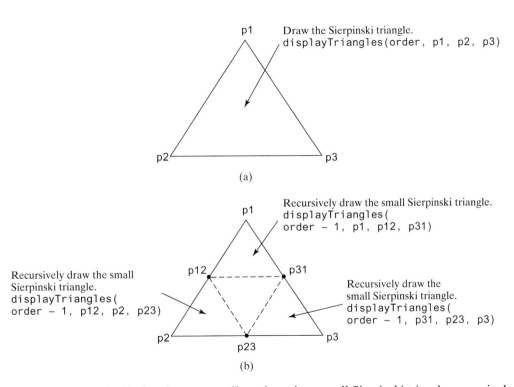

FIGURE 18.10 Drawing a Sierpinski triangle spawns calls to draw three small Sierpinski triangles recursively.

A Sierpinski triangle is displayed in a `SierpinskiTrianglePane`. The `order` property in the inner class `SierpinskiTrianglePane` specifies the order for the Sierpinski triangle. The `Point2D` class, introduced in Section 9.6.3 The `Point2D` Class, represents a point with *x*- and *y*-coordinates. Invoking `p1.midpoint(p2)` returns a new `Point2D` object that is the midpoint between `p1` and `p2` (lines 81–83).

18.8.1 How do you obtain the midpoint between two points?

18.8.2 What is the base case for the `displayTriangles` method?

18.8.3 How many times is the `displayTriangles` method invoked for a Sierpinski triangle of order 0, order 1, order 2, and order n?

18.8.4 What happens if you enter a negative order? How do you fix this problem in the code?

18.8.5 Instead of drawing a triangle using a polygon, rewrite the code to draw a triangle by drawing three lines to connect the points in lines 71–77.

✓Check Point

18.9 Recursion vs. Iteration

Recursion is an alternative form of program control. It is essentially repetition without a loop.

When you use loops, you specify a loop body. The repetition of the loop body is controlled by the loop control structure. In recursion, the method itself is called repeatedly. A selection statement must be used to control whether to call the method recursively or not.

recursion overhead

Recursion bears substantial overhead. Each time the program calls a method, the system must allocate memory for all of the method's local variables and parameters. This can consume considerable memory and requires extra time to manage the memory.

Any problem that can be solved recursively can be solved nonrecursively with iterations. Recursion has some negative aspects: It uses up too much time and too much memory. Why, then, should you use it? In some cases, using recursion enables you to specify a clear, simple solution for an inherently recursive problem that would otherwise be difficult to obtain. Examples are the directory-size problem, the Tower of Hanoi problem, and the fractal problem, which are rather difficult to solve without using recursion.

recursion advantages

recursion or iteration?

The decision whether to use recursion or iteration should be based on the nature of, and your understanding of, the problem you are trying to solve. The rule of thumb is to use whichever approach can best develop an intuitive solution that naturally mirrors the problem. If an iterative solution is obvious, use it. It will generally be more efficient than the recursive option.

Note

StackOverflowError

Recursive programs can run out of memory, causing a `StackOverflowError`.

Tip

performance concern

If you are concerned about your program's performance, avoid using recursion because it takes more time and consumes more memory than iteration. In general, recursion can be used to solve the inherent recursive problems such as Tower of Hanoi, recursive directories, and Sierpinski triangles.

18.9.1 Which of the following statements are true?

a. Any recursive method can be converted into a nonrecursive method.

b. Recursive methods take more time and memory to execute than nonrecursive methods.

c. Recursive methods are *always* simpler than nonrecursive methods.

d. There is always a selection statement in a recursive method to check whether a base case is reached.

18.9.2 What is a cause for a stack-overflow exception?

18.10 Tail Recursion

A tail-recursive method is efficient.

tail recursion

A recursive method is said to be *tail recursive* if there are no pending operations to be performed on return from a recursive call, as illustrated in Figure 18.11a. However, method B in Figure 18.11b is not tail recursive because there are pending operations after a method call is returned.

For example, the recursive `isPalindrome` method (lines 6–13) in Listing 18.4 is tail recursive because there are no pending operations after recursively invoking `isPalindrome` in line 12. However, the recursive `factorial` method (lines 16–21) in Listing 18.1 is not tail recursive because there is a pending operation, namely multiplication, to be performed on return from each recursive call.

Recursive method A	Recursive method B
. . . . Invoke method A recursively	. . . . . . Invoke method B recursively . . . . . .

| (a) Tail recursion | (b) Nontail recursion |

FIGURE 18.11 A tail-recursive method has no pending operations after a recursive call.

Tail recursion is desirable because the method ends when the last recursive call ends, and there is no need to store the intermediate calls in the stack. Compilers can optimize tail recursion to reduce stack size.

A nontail-recursive method can often be converted to a tail-recursive method by using auxiliary parameters. These parameters are used to contain the result. The idea is to incorporate the pending operations into the auxiliary parameters in such a way that the recursive call no longer has a pending operation. You can define a new auxiliary recursive method with the auxiliary parameters. This method may overload the original method with the same name but a different signature. For example, the `factorial` method in Listing 18.1 is written in a tail-recursive way in Listing 18.10.

LISTING 18.10 ComputeFactorialTailRecursion.java

```
1  public class ComputeFactorialTailRecursion {
2    /** Return the factorial for a specified number */
3    public static long factorial(int n) {                    original method
4      return factorial(n, 1); // Call auxiliary method        invoke auxiliary method
5    }
6
7    /** Auxiliary tail-recursive method for factorial */
8    private static long factorial(int n, int result) {       auxiliary method
9      if (n == 0)
10       return result;
11     else
12       return factorial(n - 1, n * result); // Recursive call  recursive call
13   }
14 }
```

The first `factorial` method (line 3) simply invokes the second auxiliary method (line 4). The second method contains an auxiliary parameter `result` that stores the result for the factorial of `n`. This method is invoked recursively in line 12. There is no pending operation after a call is returned. The final result is returned in line 10, which is also the return value from invoking `factorial(n, 1)` in line 4.

18.10.1 Identify tail-recursive methods in this chapter.

18.10.2 Rewrite the `fib` method in Listing 18.2 using tail recursion.

Check
Point

KEY TERMS

base case 720
direct recursion 723
indirect recursion 723
infinite recursion 723

recursive helper method 729
recursive method 720
stopping condition 720
tail recursion 740

CHAPTER SUMMARY

1. A *recursive method* is one that directly or indirectly invokes itself. For a recursive method to terminate, there must be one or more *base cases*.

2. *Recursion* is an alternative form of program control. It is essentially repetition without a loop control. It can be used to write simple, clear solutions for inherently recursive problems that would otherwise be difficult to solve.

3. Sometimes the original method needs to be modified to receive additional parameters in order to be invoked recursively. A *recursive helper method* can be defined for this purpose.

4. Recursion bears substantial overhead. Each time the program calls a method, the system must allocate memory for all of the method's local variables and parameters. This can consume considerable memory and requires extra time to manage the memory.

5. A recursive method is said to be *tail recursive* if there are no pending operations to be performed on return from a recursive call. Some compilers can optimize tail recursion to reduce stack size.

QUIZ

Answer the quiz for this chapter online at the book Companion Website.

MyProgrammingLab™ ## PROGRAMMING EXERCISES

Sections 18.2 and 18.3

*18.1 (*Factorial*) Using the `BigInteger` class introduced in Section 10.9, you can find the factorial for a large number (e.g., `100!`). Implement the `factorial` method using recursion. Write a program that prompts the user to enter an integer and displays its factorial.

*18.2 (*Fibonacci numbers*) Rewrite the `fib` method in Listing 18.2 using iterations.

Hint: To compute `fib(n)` without recursion, you need to obtain `fib(n - 2)` and `fib(n - 1)` first. Let `f0` and `f1` denote the two previous Fibonacci numbers. The current Fibonacci number would then be `f0 + f1`. The algorithm can be described as follows:

```
f0 = 0; // For fib(0)
f1 = 1; // For fib(1)

for (int i = 1; i <= n; i++) {
  currentFib = f0 + f1;
  f0 = f1;
  f1 = currentFib;
}
// After the loop, currentFib is fib(n)
```

Write a test program that prompts the user to enter an index and displays its Fibonacci number.

*18.3 (*Compute greatest common divisor using recursion*) The gcd(m, n) can also be defined recursively as follows:

- If m % n is 0, gcd(m, n) is n.
- Otherwise, gcd(m, n) is gcd(n, m % n).

Write a recursive method to find the GCD. Write a test program that prompts the user to enter two integers and displays their GCD.

18.4 (*Sum series*) Write a recursive method to compute the following series:

$$m(i) = 1 + \frac{1}{2} + \frac{1}{3} + \cdots + \frac{1}{i}$$

Write a test program that displays m(i) for i = 1, 2, ..., 10.

18.5 (*Sum series*) Write a recursive method to compute the following series:

$$m(i) = \frac{1}{3} + \frac{2}{5} + \frac{3}{7} + \frac{4}{9} + \frac{5}{11} + \frac{6}{13} + \cdots + \frac{i}{2i + 1}$$

Write a test program that displays m(i) for i = 1, 2, ..., 10.

*18.6 (*Sum series*) Write a recursive method to compute the following series:

$$m(i) = \frac{1}{2} + \frac{2}{3} + \cdots + \frac{i}{i + 1}$$

Write a test program that displays m(i) for i = 1, 2, ..., 10.

*18.7 (*Fibonacci series*) Modify Listing 18.2, ComputeFibonacci.java, so that the program finds the number of times the fib method is called. (*Hint*: Use a static variable and increment it every time the method is called.)

Section 18.4

*18.8 (*Print the digits in an integer reversely*) Write a recursive method that displays an int value reversely on the console using the following header:

```
public static void reverseDisplay(int value)
```

For example, reverseDisplay(12345) displays 54321. Write a test program that prompts the user to enter an integer and displays its reversal.

*18.9 (*Print the characters in a string reversely*) Write a recursive method that displays a string reversely on the console using the following header:

```
public static void reverseDisplay(String value)
```

For example, reverseDisplay("abcd") displays dcba. Write a test program that prompts the user to enter a string and displays its reversal.

*18.10 (*Occurrences of a specified character in a string*) Write a recursive method that finds the number of occurrences of a specified letter in a string using the following method header:

```
public static int count(String str, char a)
```

For example, count("Welcome", 'e') returns 2. Write a test program that prompts the user to enter a string and a character, and displays the number of occurrences for the character in the string.

*18.11   (*Sum the digits in an integer using recursion*) Write a recursive method that computes the sum of the digits in an integer. Use the following method header:

```
public static int sumDigits(long n)
```

For example, sumDigits(234) returns 2 + 3 + 4 = 9. Write a test program that prompts the user to enter an integer and displays its sum.

Section 18.5

**18.12   (*Print the characters in a string reversely*) Rewrite Programming Exercise 18.9 using a helper method to pass the substring high index to the method. The helper method header is

```
public static void reverseDisplay(String value, int high)
```

*18.13   (*Find the largest number in an array*) Write a recursive method that returns the largest integer in an array. Write a test program that prompts the user to enter a list of eight integers and displays the largest element.

*18.14   (*Find the number of uppercase letters in a string*) Write a recursive method to return the number of uppercase letters in a string. Write a test program that prompts the user to enter a string and displays the number of uppercase letters in the string.

*18.15   (*Occurrences of a specified character in a string*) Rewrite Programming Exercise 18.10 using a helper method to pass the substring high index to the method. The helper method header is

```
public static int count(String str, char a, int high)
```

*18.16   (*Find the number of uppercase letters in an array*) Write a recursive method to return the number of uppercase letters in an array of characters. You need to define the following two methods. The second one is a recursive helper method.

```
public static int count(char[] chars)
public static int count(char[] chars, int high)
```

Write a test program that prompts the user to enter a list of characters in one line and displays the number of uppercase letters in the list.

*18.17   (*Occurrences of a specified character in an array*) Write a recursive method that finds the number of occurrences of a specified character in an array. You need to define the following two methods. The second one is a recursive helper method.

```
public static int count(char[] chars, char ch)
public static int count(char[] chars, char ch, int high)
```

Write a test program that prompts the user to enter a list of characters in one line, and a character, and displays the number of occurrences of the character in the list.

Sections 18.6–18.10

*18.18   (*Tower of Hanoi*) Modify Listing 18.8, TowerOfHanoi.java, so the program finds the number of moves needed to move *n* disks from tower A to tower B. (*Hint*: Use a static variable and increment it every time the method is called.)

*18.19   (*Sierpinski triangle*) Revise Listing 18.9 to develop a program that lets the user use the +/− buttons, primary/secondary mouse buttons, and UP/ DOWN arrow keys to increase or decrease the current order by 1, as shown in Figure 18.12a. The initial order is 0. If the current order is 0, the *Decrease* button is ignored.

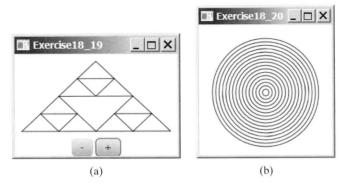

(a)   (b)

FIGURE 18.12   (a) Programming Exercise 18.19 uses the + or − buttons to increase or decrease the current order by 1. *Source*: Copyright © 1995–2016 Oracle and/or its affiliates. All rights reserved. Used with permission. (b) Programming Exercise 18.20 draws ovals using a recursive method.

*18.20   (*Display circles*) Write a Java program that displays ovals, as shown in Figure 18.12b. The circles are centered in the pane. The gap between two adjacent circles is 10 pixels, and the gap between the border of the pane and the largest circle is also 10.

*18.21   (*Decimal to binary*) Write a recursive method that converts a decimal number into a binary number as a string. The method header is

```
public static String dec2Bin(int value)
```

Write a test program that prompts the user to enter a decimal number and displays its binary equivalent.

*18.22   (*Decimal to hex*) Write a recursive method that converts a decimal number into a hex number as a string. The method header is

```
public static String dec2Hex(int value)
```

Write a test program that prompts the user to enter a decimal number and displays its hex equivalent.

*18.23   (*Binary to decimal*) Write a recursive method that parses a binary number as a string into a decimal integer. The method header is

```
public static int bin2Dec(String binaryString)
```

Write a test program that prompts the user to enter a binary string and displays its decimal equivalent.

*18.24   (*Hex to decimal*) Write a recursive method that parses a hex number as a string into a decimal integer. The method header is

```
public static int hex2Dec(String hexString)
```

Write a test program that prompts the user to enter a hex string and displays its decimal equivalent.

**18.25 (*String permutation*) Write a recursive method to print all the permutations of a string. For example, for the string abc, the permutation is

abc
acb
bac
bca
cab
cba

(*Hint*: Define the following two methods. The second is a helper method.)

```
public static void displayPermutation(String s)
public static void displayPermutation(String s1, String s2)
```

The first method simply invokes `displayPermutation(" ", s)`. The second method uses a loop to move a character from s2 to s1 and recursively invokes it with new s1 and s2. The base case is that s2 is empty and prints s1 to the console.

Write a test program that prompts the user to enter a string and displays all its permutations.

**18.26 (*Create a maze*) Write a program that will find a path in a maze, as shown in Figure 18.13a. The maze is represented by a 8 × 8 board. The path must meet the following conditions:

- The path is between the upper-left corner cell and the lower-right corner cell in the maze.

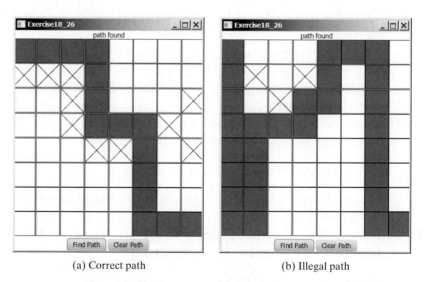

(a) Correct path   (b) Illegal path

FIGURE 18.13 The program finds a path from the upper-left corner to the bottom-right corner. *Source*: Copyright © 1995–2016 Oracle and/or its affiliates. All rights reserved. Used with permission.

- The program enables the user to place or remove a mark on a cell. A path consists of adjacent unmarked cells. Two cells are said to be adjacent if they are horizontal or vertical neighbors.
- The path does not contain cells that form a square. The path in Figure 18.13b, for example, does not meet this condition. (The condition makes a path easy to identify on the board.)

**18.27 (*Koch snowflake fractal*) The text presented the Sierpinski triangle fractal. In this exercise, you will write a program to display another fractal, called the *Koch snowflake*, named after a famous Swedish mathematician. A Koch snowflake is created as follows:

1. Begin with an equilateral triangle, which is considered to be the Koch fractal of order (or level) 0, as shown in Figure 18.14a.
2. Divide each line in the shape into three equal line segments and draw an outward equilateral triangle with the middle line segment as the base to create a Koch fractal of order 1, as shown in Figure 18.14b.
3. Repeat Step 2 to create a Koch fractal of order 2, 3, . . . , and so on, as shown in Figures 18.14c and d.

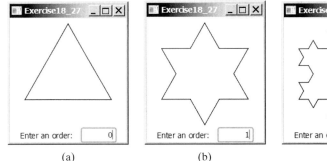 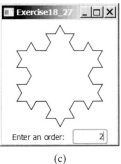 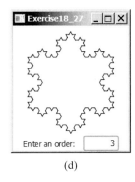

(a)   (b)   (c)   (d)

FIGURE 18.14 A Koch snowflake is a fractal starting with a triangle. *Source*: Copyright © 1995–2016 Oracle and/or its affiliates. All rights reserved. Used with permission.

**18.28 (*Nonrecursive directory size*) Rewrite Listing 18.7, DirectorySize.java, without using recursion.

*18.29 (*Number of files in a directory*) Write a program that prompts the user to enter a directory and displays the number of the files in the directory.

**18.30 (*Find words*) Write a program that finds all occurrences of a word in all the files under a directory, recursively. Pass the parameters from the command line as follows:

```
java Exercise18_30 dirName word
```

VideoNote

Search a string in a directory

**18.31 (*Replace words*) Write a program that replaces all occurrences of a word with a new word in all the files under a directory, recursively. Pass the parameters from the command line as follows:

```
java Exercise18_31 dirName oldWord newWord
```

***18.32 (*Game: Knight's Tour*) The Knight's Tour is an ancient puzzle. The objective is to move a knight, starting from any square on a chessboard, to every other square once, as shown in Figure 18.15a. Note the knight makes only L-shaped moves (two spaces in one direction and one space in a perpendicular direction). As shown in Figure 18.15b, the knight can move to eight squares. Write a program that displays the moves for the knight, as shown in Figure 18.15c. When you click a cell, the knight is placed at the cell. This cell will be the starting point for the knight. Click the *Solve* button to display the path for a solution.

(*Hint*: A brute-force approach for this problem is to move the knight from one square to another available square arbitrarily. Using such an approach, your program will take a long time to finish. A better approach is to employ some

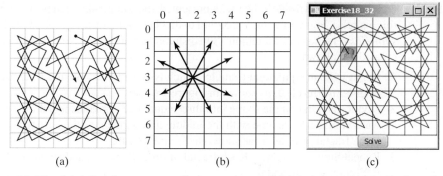

FIGURE 18.15 (a) A knight traverses all squares once. (b) A knight makes an L-shaped move. (c) A program displays a Knight's Tour path. *Source*: Copyright © 1995–2016 Oracle and/or its affiliates. All rights reserved. Used with permission.

heuristics. A knight has two, three, four, six, or eight possible moves, depending on its location. Intuitively, you should attempt to move the knight to the least accessible squares first and leave those more accessible squares open, so there will be a better chance of success at the end of the search.)

***18.33 (*Game: Knight's Tour animation*) Write a program for the Knight's Tour problem. Your program should let the user move a knight to any starting square and click the *Solve* button to animate a knight moving along the path, as shown in Figure 18.16.

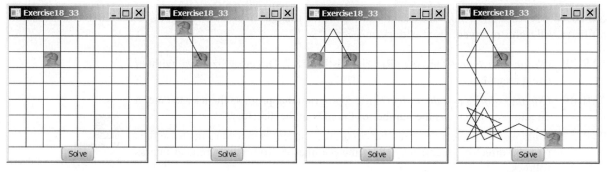

FIGURE 18.16 A knight traverses along the path. *Source*: Copyright © 1995–2016 Oracle and/or its affiliates. All rights reserved. Used with permission.

**18.34 (*Game: Eight Queens*) The Eight Queens problem is to find a solution to place a queen in each row on a chessboard such that no two queens can attack each other. Write a program to solve the Eight Queens problem using recursion and display the result as shown in Figure 18.17.

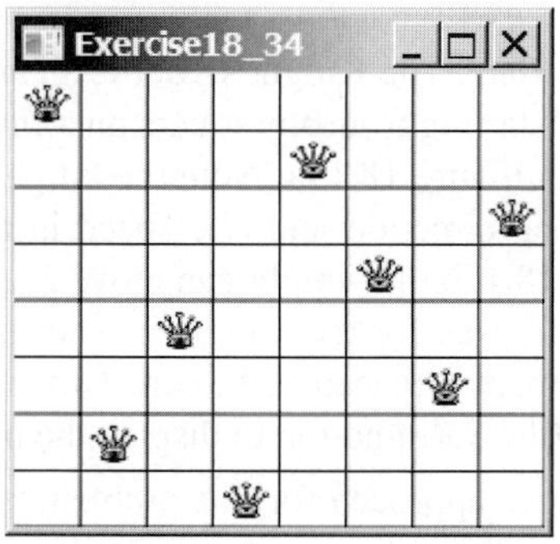

FIGURE 18.17 The program displays a solution to the Eight Queens problem. *Source*: Copyright © 1995–2016 Oracle and/or its affiliates. All rights reserved. Used with permission.

**18.35 (*H-tree fractal*) An H-tree (introduced at the beginning of this chapter in Figure 18.1) is a fractal defined as follows:

1. Begin with a letter H. The three lines of H are of the same length, as shown in Figure 18.1a.
2. The letter H (in its sans-serif form, H) has four endpoints. Draw an H centered at each of the four endpoints to an H-tree of order 1, as shown in Figure 18.1b. These Hs are half the size of the H that contains the four endpoints.
3. Repeat Step 2 to create an H-tree of order 2, 3, . . . , and so on, as shown in Figures 18.1c and d.

Write a program that draws an H-tree, as shown in Figure 18.1.

18.36 (*Sierpinski triangle*) Write a program that lets the user to enter the order and display the filled Sierpinski triangles as shown in Figure 18.18.

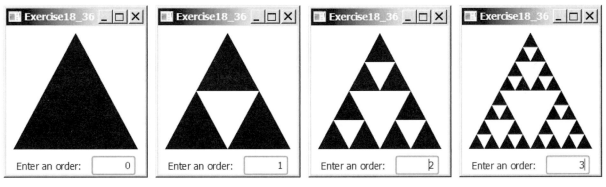

FIGURE 18.18 A filled Sierpinski triangle is displayed. *Source*: Copyright © 1995–2016 Oracle and/or its affiliates. All rights reserved. Used with permission.

**18.37 (*Hilbert curve*) The Hilbert curve, first described by German mathematician David Hilbert in 1891, is a space-filling curve that visits every point in a square grid with a size of 2 × 2, 4 × 4, 8 × 8, 16 × 16, or any other power of 2. Write a program that displays a Hilbert curve for the specified order, as shown in Figure 18.19.

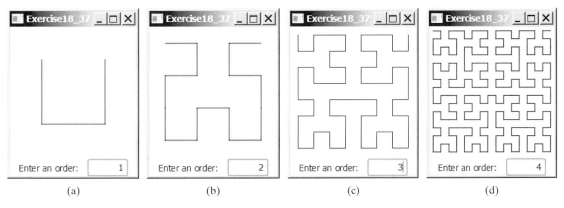

(a)   (b)   (c)   (d)

FIGURE 18.19 A Hilbert curve with the specified order is drawn. *Source*: Copyright © 1995–2016 Oracle and/or its affiliates. All rights reserved. Used with permission.

VideoNote

Recursive tree

**18.38 (*Recursive tree*) Write a program to display a recursive tree as shown in Figure 18.20.

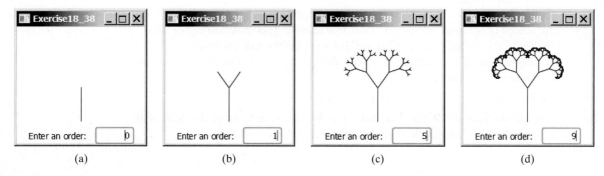

(a) (b) (c) (d)

FIGURE 18.20 A recursive tree with the specified depth is drawn. *Source*: Copyright © 1995–2016 Oracle and/or its affiliates. All rights reserved. Used with permission.

**18.39 (*Drag the tree*) Revise Programming Exercise 18.38 to move the tree to where the mouse is dragged.

CHAPTER 19

GENERICS

Objectives

- To describe the benefits of generics (§19.2).

- To use generic classes and interfaces (§19.2).

- To define generic classes and interfaces (§19.3).

- To explain why generic types can improve reliability and readability (§19.3).

- To define and use generic methods and bounded generic types (§19.4).

- To develop a generic sort method to sort an array of `Comparable` objects (§19.5).

- To use raw types for backward compatibility (§19.6).

- To explain why wildcard generic types are necessary (§19.7).

- To describe generic-type erasure and list certain restrictions and limitations on generic types caused by type erasure (§19.8).

- To design and implement generic matrix classes (§19.9).

19.1 Introduction

Generics enable you to detect errors at compile time rather than at runtime.

what is generics?

You have used a generic class `ArrayList` in Chapter 11, and generic interface `Comparable` in Chapter 13. *Generics* let you parameterize types. With this capability, you can define a class or a method with generic types that the compiler can replace with concrete types. For example, Java defines a generic `ArrayList` class for storing the elements of a generic type. From this generic class, you can create an `ArrayList` object for holding strings, and an `ArrayList` object for holding numbers. Here, strings and numbers are concrete types that replace the generic type.

why generics?

The key benefit of generics is to enable errors to be detected at compile time rather than at runtime. A generic class or method permits you to specify allowable types of objects that the class or method can work with. If you attempt to use an incompatible object, the compiler will detect that error.

This chapter explains how to define and use generic classes, interfaces, and methods and demonstrates how generics can be used to improve software reliability and readability. It can be intertwined with Chapter 13, Abstract Classes and Interfaces.

19.2 Motivations and Benefits

The motivation for using Java generics is to detect errors at compile time.

Java has allowed you to define generic classes, interfaces, and methods since JDK 1.5. Several interfaces and classes in the Java API were modified using generics. For example, prior to JDK 1.5, the `java.lang.Comparable` interface was defined as shown in Figure 19.1a, but since JDK 1.5, it has been modified as shown in Figure 19.1b.

```
package java.lang;

public interface Comparable {
  public int compareTo(Object o)
}
```

(a) Prior to JDK 1.5

```
package java.lang;

public interface Comparable<T> {
  public int compareTo(T o)
}
```

(b) JDK 1.5

FIGURE 19.1 The `java.lang.Comparable` interface was modified in JDK 1.5 with a generic type.

formal generic type
actual concrete type
generic instantiation

Here, `<T>` represents a *formal generic type*, which can be replaced later with an *actual concrete type*. Replacing a generic type is called a *generic instantiation*. By convention, a single capital letter such as `E` or `T` is used to denote a formal generic type.

To see the benefits of using generics, let us examine the code in Figure 19.2. The statement in Figure 19.2a declares that `c` is a reference variable whose type is `Comparable` and invokes the `compareTo` method to compare a `Date` object with a string. The code compiles fine, but it has a runtime error because a string cannot be compared with a date.

```
Comparable c = new Date();
System.out.println(c.compareTo("red"));
```

(a) Prior to JDK 1.5

```
Comparable<Date> c = new Date();
System.out.println(c.compareTo("red"));
```

(b) JDK 1.5

FIGURE 19.2 The new generic type detects possible errors at compile time.

The statement in Figure 19.2b declares that `c` is a reference variable whose type is `Comparable<Date>` and invokes the `compareTo` method to compare a `Date` object with a string. This code has a compile error because the argument passed to the `compareTo` method must be of the `Date` type. Since the errors can be detected at compile time rather than at runtime, the generic type makes the program more reliable.

reliable

`ArrayList` was introduced in Section 11.11, The `ArrayList` Class. This class has been a generic class since JDK 1.5. Figure 19.3 shows the class diagram for `ArrayList` before and since JDK 1.5, respectively.

java.util.ArrayList
+ArrayList()
+add(o: Object): void
+add(index: int, o: Object): void
+clear(): void
+contains(o: Object): boolean
+get(index:int): Object
+indexOf(o: Object): int
+isEmpty(): boolean
+lastIndexOf(o: Object): int
+remove(o: Object): boolean
+size(): int
+remove(index: int): boolean
+set(index: int, o: Object): Object

java.util.ArrayList\<E>
+ArrayList()
+add(o: E): void
+add(index: int, o: E): void
+clear(): void
+contains(o: Object): boolean
+get(index: int): E
+indexOf(o: Object): int
+isEmpty(): boolean
+lastIndexOf(o: Object): int
+remove(o: Object): boolean
+size(): int
+remove(index: int): boolean
+set(index: int, o: E): E

(a) ArrayList before JDK 1.5 (b) ArrayList since JDK 1.5

FIGURE 19.3 `ArrayList` is a generic class since JDK 1.5.

For example, the following statement creates a list for strings:

```
ArrayList<String> list = new ArrayList<>();
```

You can now add *only strings* into the list. For instance,

only strings allowed

```
list.add("Red");
```

If you attempt to add a nonstring, a compile error will occur. For example, the following statement is now illegal because `list` can contain only strings.

```
list.add(new Integer(1));
```

Generic types must be reference types. You cannot replace a generic type with a primitive type such as `int`, `double`, or `char`. For example, the following statement is wrong:

generic reference type

```
ArrayList<int> intList = new ArrayList<>();
```

To create an `ArrayList` object for `int` values, you have to use

```
ArrayList<Integer> intList = new ArrayList<>();
```

You can add an `int` value to `intList`. For example,

```
intList.add(5);
```

Java automatically wraps 5 into `new Integer(5)`. This is called *autoboxing*, as introduced in Section 10.8, Automatic Conversion between Primitive Types and Wrapper Class Types.

autoboxing

no casting needed

Casting is not needed to retrieve a value from a list with a specified element type because the compiler already knows the element type. For example, the following statements create a list that contains strings, add strings to the list, and retrieve strings from the list.

```
1  ArrayList<String> list = new ArrayList<>();
2  list.add("Red");
3  list.add("White");
4  String s = list.get(0); // No casting is needed
```

Prior to JDK 1.5, without using generics, you would have had to cast the return value to `String` as:

```
String s = (String)(list.get(0)); // Casting needed prior to JDK 1.5
```

autounboxing

If the elements are of wrapper types, such as `Integer`, `Double`, and `Character`, you can directly assign an element to a primitive-type variable. This is called *autounboxing*, as introduced in Section 10.8. For example, see the following code:

```
1  ArrayList<Double> list = new ArrayList<>();
2  list.add(5.5); // 5.5 is automatically converted to new Double(5.5)
3  list.add(3.0); // 3.0 is automatically converted to new Double(3.0)
4  Double doubleObject = list.get(0); // No casting is needed
5  double d = list.get(1); // Automatically converted to double
```

In lines 2 and 3, `5.5` and `3.0` are automatically converted into `Double` objects and added to `list`. In line 4, the first element in `list` is assigned to a `Double` variable. No casting is necessary because `list` is declared for `Double` objects. In line 5, the second element in `list` is assigned to a `double` variable. The object in `list.get(1)` is automatically converted into a primitive-type value.

Check Point

19.2.1 Are there any compile errors in (a) and (b)?

```
ArrayList dates = new ArrayList();
dates.add(new Date());
dates.add(new String());
```
(a) Prior to JDK 1.5

```
ArrayList<Date> dates =
    new ArrayList<>();
dates.add(new Date());
dates.add(new String());
```
(b) Since JDK 1.5

19.2.2 What is wrong in (a)? Is the code in (b) correct?

```
ArrayList dates = new ArrayList();
dates.add(new Date());
Date date = dates.get(0);
```
(a) Prior to JDK 1.5

```
ArrayList<Date> dates =
    new ArrayList<>();
dates.add(new Date());
Date date = dates.get(0);
```
(b) Since JDK 1.5

19.2.3 What are the benefits of using generic types?

19.3 Defining Generic Classes and Interfaces

Key Point

A generic type can be defined for a class or interface. A concrete type must be specified when using the class to create an object or using the class or interface to declare a reference variable.

Let us revise the stack class in Section 11.13, Case Study: A Custom Stack Class, to generalize the element type with a generic type. The new stack class, named `GenericStack`, is shown in Figure 19.4 and is implemented in Listing 19.1.

GenericStack<E>	
−list: java.util.ArrayList<E>	An array list to store elements.
+GenericStack()	Creates an empty stack.
+getSize(): int	Returns the number of elements in this stack.
+peek(): E	Returns the top element in this stack.
+pop(): E	Returns and removes the top element in this stack.
+push(o: E): void	Adds a new element to the top of this stack.
+isEmpty(): boolean	Returns true if the stack is empty.

FIGURE 19.4 The `GenericStack` class encapsulates the stack storage and provides the operations for manipulating the stack.

LISTING 19.1 GenericStack.java

```java
public class GenericStack<E> {                                    // generic type E declared
  private java.util.ArrayList<E> list = new java.util.ArrayList<>();  // generic array list

  public int getSize() {                                          // getSize
    return list.size();
  }

  public E peek() {                                               // peek
    return list.get(getSize() - 1);
  }

  public void push(E o) {                                         // push
    list.add(o);
  }

  public E pop() {                                                // pop
    E o = list.get(getSize() - 1);
    list.remove(getSize() - 1);
    return o;
  }

  public boolean isEmpty() {                                      // isEmpty
    return list.isEmpty();
  }

  @Override
  public String toString() {
    return "stack: " + list.toString();
  }
}
```

The following example creates a stack to hold strings and adds three strings to the stack:

```java
GenericStack<String> stack1 = new GenericStack<>();
stack1.push("London");
stack1.push("Paris");
stack1.push("Berlin");
```

This example creates a stack to hold integers and adds three integers to the stack:

```
GenericStack<Integer> stack2 = new GenericStack<>();
stack2.push(1); // autoboxing 1 to new Integer(1)
stack2.push(2);
stack2.push(3);
```

benefits of using generic types

Instead of using a generic type, you could simply make the type element `Object`, which can accommodate any object type. However, using a specific concrete type can improve software reliability and readability because certain errors can be detected at compile time rather than at runtime. For example, because `stack1` is declared `GenericStack<String>`, only strings can be added to the stack. It would be a compile error if you attempted to add an integer to `stack1`.

 Caution

generic class constructor

To create a stack of strings, you use `new GenericStack<String>()` or `new GenericStack<>()`. This could mislead you into thinking that the constructor of `GenericStack` should be defined as

`public GenericStack<E>()`

This is wrong. It should be defined as

`public GenericStack()`

 Note

multiple generic parameters

Occasionally, a generic class may have more than one parameter. In this case, place the parameters together inside the brackets, separated by commas—for example, `<E1, E2, E3>`.

Note

inheritance with generics

You can define a class or an interface as a subtype of a generic class or interface. For example, the `java.lang.String` class is defined to implement the `Comparable` interface in the Java API as follows:

`public class String implements Comparable<String>`

 Check Point

19.3.1 What is the generic definition for `java.lang.Comparable` in the Java API?

19.3.2 Since you create an instance of `ArrayList` of strings using `new ArrayList<String>()`, should the constructor in the `ArrayList` class be defined as

`public ArrayList<E>()`

19.3.3 Can a generic class have multiple generic parameters?

19.3.4 How do you declare a generic type in a class?

19.4 Generic Methods

 Key Point

A generic type can be defined for a static method.

generic method

You can define generic interfaces (e.g., the `Comparable` interface in Figure 19.1b) and classes (e.g., the `GenericStack` class in Listing 19.1). You can also use generic types to define generic methods. For example, Listing 19.2 defines a generic method `print` (lines 10–14) to print an array of objects. Line 6 passes an array of integer objects to invoke the generic `print` method. Line 7 invokes `print` with an array of strings.

LISTING 19.2 GenericMethodDemo.java

```
1  public class GenericMethodDemo {
2    public static void main(String[] args ) {
3      Integer[] integers = {1, 2, 3, 4, 5};
4      String[] strings = {"London", "Paris", "New York", "Austin"};
5
6      GenericMethodDemo.<Integer>print(integers);
7      GenericMethodDemo.<String>print(strings);
8    }
9
10   public static <E> void print(E[] list) {          generic method
11     for (int i = 0; i < list.length; i++)
12       System.out.print(list[i] + " ");
13     System.out.println();
14   }
15 }
```

To declare a generic method, you place the generic type `<E>` immediately after the keyword `static` in the method header. For example, **declare a generic method**

```
public static <E> void print(E[] list)
```

To invoke a generic method, prefix the method name with the actual type in angle brackets. **invoke generic method**
For example,

```
GenericMethodDemo.<Integer>print(integers);
GenericMethodDemo.<String>print(strings);
```

or simply invoke it as follows:

```
print(integers);
print(strings);
```

In the latter case, the actual type is not explicitly specified. The compiler automatically discovers the actual type.

A generic type can be specified as a subtype of another type. Such a generic type is called *bounded*. For example, Listing 19.3 revises the `equalArea` method in Listing 13.4, TestGeometricObject.java, to test whether two geometric objects have the same area. The bounded generic type `<E extends GeometricObject>` (line 10) specifies that E is a generic subtype of `GeometricObject`. You must invoke `equalArea` by passing two instances of `GeometricObject`. **bounded generic type**

LISTING 19.3 BoundedTypeDemo.java

```
1  public class BoundedTypeDemo {
2    public static void main(String[] args ) {
3      Rectangle rectangle = new Rectangle(2, 2);        Rectangle in Listing 13.3
4      Circle circle = new Circle(2);                    Circle in Listing 13.2
5
6      System.out.println("Same area? " +
7        equalArea(rectangle, circle));
8    }
9
10   public static <E extends GeometricObject> boolean equalArea(   bounded generic type
11       E object1, E object2) {
12     return object1.getArea() == object2.getArea();
13   }
14 }
```

Note
An unbounded generic type `<E>` is the same as `<E extends Object>`.

generic class parameter vs.
generic method parameter

Note
To define a generic type for a class, place it after the class name, such as `GenericStack<E>`. To define a generic type for a method, place the generic type before the method return type, such as `<E> void max(E o1, E o2)`.

**Check
Point**

19.4.1   How do you declare a generic method? How do you invoke a generic method?

19.4.2   What is a bounded generic type?

19.5 Case Study: Sorting an Array of Objects

You can develop a generic method for sorting an array of Comparable *objects.*

This section presents a generic method for sorting an array of `Comparable` objects. The objects are instances of the `Comparable` interface and they are compared using the `compareTo` method. To test the method, the program sorts an array of integers, an array of double numbers, an array of characters, and an array of strings. The program is shown in Listing 19.4.

LISTING 19.4   GenericSort.java

```
1  public class GenericSort {
2    public static void main(String[] args) {
3      // Create an Integer array
4      Integer[] intArray = {new Integer(2), new Integer(4),
5        new Integer(3)};
6
7      // Create a Double array
8      Double[] doubleArray = {new Double(3.4), new Double(1.3),
9        new Double(-22.1)};
10
11     // Create a Character array
12     Character[] charArray = {new Character('a'),
13       new Character('J'), new Character('r')};
14
15     // Create a String array
16     String[] stringArray = {"Tom", "Susan", "Kim"};
17
18     // Sort the arrays
19     sort(intArray);
20     sort(doubleArray);
21     sort(charArray);
22     sort(stringArray);
23
24     // Display the sorted arrays
25     System.out.print("Sorted Integer objects: ");
26     printList(intArray);
27     System.out.print("Sorted Double objects: ");
28     printList(doubleArray);
29     System.out.print("Sorted Character objects: ");
30     printList(charArray);
31     System.out.print("Sorted String objects: ");
32     printList(stringArray);
33   }
34
```

sort `Integer` objects
sort `Double` objects
sort `Character` objects
sort `String` objects

```
35    /** Sort an array of comparable objects */
36    public static <E extends Comparable<E>> void sort(E[] list) {        generic sort method
37      E currentMin;
38      int currentMinIndex;
39
40      for (int i = 0; i < list.length - 1; i++) {
41        // Find the minimum in the list[i+1..list.length-2]
42        currentMin = list[i];
43        currentMinIndex = i;
44
45        for (int j = i + 1; j < list.length; j++) {
46          if (currentMin.compareTo(list[j]) > 0) {               compareTo
47            currentMin = list[j];
48            currentMinIndex = j;
49          }
50        }
51
52        // Swap list[i] with list[currentMinIndex] if necessary;
53        if (currentMinIndex != i) {
54          list[currentMinIndex] = list[i];
55          list[i] = currentMin;
56        }
57      }
58    }
59
60    /** Print an array of objects */
61    public static void printList(Object[] list) {
62      for (int i = 0; i < list.length; i++)
63        System.out.print(list[i] + " ");
64      System.out.println();
65    }
66  }
```

```
Sorted Integer objects: 2 3 4
Sorted Double objects: -22.1 1.3 3.4
Sorted Character objects: J a r
Sorted String objects: Kim Susan Tom
```

The algorithm for the sort method is the same as in Listing 7.8, SelectionSort.java. The sort method in that program sorts an array of double values. The sort method in this example can sort an array of any object type, provided that the objects are also instances of the Comparable interface. The generic type is defined as <E extends Comparable<E>> (line 36). This has two meanings. First, it specifies that E is a subtype of Comparable. Second, it specifies that the elements to be compared are of the E type as well.

The sort method uses the compareTo method to determine the order of the objects in the array (line 46). Integer, Double, Character, and String implement Comparable, so the objects of these classes can be compared using the compareTo method. The program creates arrays of Integer objects, Double objects, Character objects, and String objects (lines 4–16) and invokes the sort method to sort these arrays (lines 19–22).

19.5.1 Given int[] list = {1, 2, -1}, can you invoke sort(list) using the sort method in Listing 19.4?

19.5.2 Given int[] list = {new Integer(1), new Integer(2), new Integer (-1)}, can you invoke sort(list) using the sort method in Listing 19.4?

19.6 Raw Types and Backward Compatibility

A generic class or interface used without specifying a concrete type, called a raw type, enables backward compatibility with earlier versions of Java.

You can use a generic class without specifying a concrete type such as the following:

```
GenericStack stack = new GenericStack(); // raw type
```

This is roughly equivalent to

```
GenericStack<Object> stack = new GenericStack<Object>();
```

raw type
backward compatibility

A generic class such as `GenericStack` and `ArrayList` used without a type parameter is called a *raw type*. Using raw types allows for backward compatibility with earlier versions of Java. For example, a generic type has been used in `java.lang.Comparable` since JDK 1.5, but a lot of code still uses the raw type `Comparable`, as given in Listing 19.5:

LISTING 19.5 Max.java

raw type

```
1  public class Max {
2    /** Return the maximum of two objects */
3    public static Comparable max(Comparable o1, Comparable o2) {
4      if (o1.compareTo(o2) > 0)
5        return o1;
6      else
7        return o2;
8    }
9  }
```

`Comparable o1` and `Comparable o2` are raw type declarations. Be careful: *raw types are unsafe*. For example, you might invoke the `max` method using

```
Max.max("Welcome", 23); // 23 is autoboxed into new Integer(23)
```

–Xlint:unchecked

This would cause a runtime error because you cannot compare a string with an integer object. The Java compiler displays a warning on line 3 when compiled with the option *–Xlint:unchecked*, as shown in Figure 19.5.

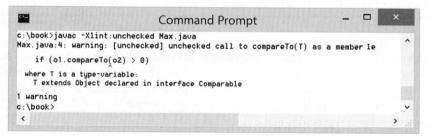

FIGURE 19.5 The unchecked warnings are displayed using the compiler option –Xlint:unchecked. *Source*: Copyright © 1995–2016 Oracle and/or its affiliates. All rights reserved. Used with permission.

A better way to write the `max` method is to use a generic type, as given in Listing 19.6.

LISTING 19.6 MaxUsingGenericType.java

bounded type

```
1  public class MaxUsingGenericType {
2    /** Return the maximum of two objects */
3    public static <E extends Comparable<E>> E max(E o1, E o2) {
4      if (o1.compareTo(o2) > 0)
5        return o1;
```

```
6       else
7         return o2;
8     }
9 }
```

If you invoke the `max` method using

```
// 23 is autoboxed into new Integer(23)
MaxUsingGenericType.max("Welcome", 23);
```

a compile error will be displayed because the two arguments of the `max` method in `MaxUsingGenericType` must have the same type (e.g., two strings or two integer objects). Furthermore, the type `E` must be a subtype of `Comparable<E>`.

As another example, in the following code you can declare a raw type `stack` in line 1, assign `new GenericStack<String>` to it in line 2, and push a string and an integer object to the stack in lines 3 and 4:

```
1 GenericStack stack;
2 stack = new GenericStack<String>();
3 stack.push("Welcome to Java");
4 stack.push(new Integer(2));
```

However, line 4 is unsafe because the stack is intended to store strings, but an `Integer` object is added into the stack. Line 3 should be okay, but the compiler will show warnings for both line 3 and line 4, because it cannot follow the semantic meaning of the program. All the compiler knows is that stack is a raw type, and performing certain operations is unsafe. Therefore, warnings are displayed to alert potential problems.

Tip
Since raw types are unsafe, this book will not use them from here on.

19.6.1 What is a raw type? Why is a raw type unsafe? Why is the raw type allowed in Java?

19.6.2 What is the syntax to declare an `ArrayList` reference variable using the raw type and assign a raw type `ArrayList` object to it?

Check
Point

19.7 Wildcard Generic Types

You can use unbounded wildcards, bounded wildcards, or lower bound wildcards to specify a range for a generic type.

Key
Point

What are wildcard generic types, and why are they needed? Listing 19.7 gives an example to demonstrate the needs. The example defines a generic `max` method for finding the maximum in a stack of numbers (lines 12–22). The main method creates a stack of integer objects, adds three integers to the stack, and invokes the `max` method to find the maximum number in the stack.

LISTING 19.7 `WildCardNeedDemo.java`

```
1  public class WildCardNeedDemo {
2    public static void main(String[] args ) {
3      GenericStack<Integer> intStack = new GenericStack<>();
4      intStack.push(1); // 1 is autoboxed into new Integer(1)
5      intStack.push(2);
6      intStack.push(-2);
7
8      System.out.print("The max number is " + max(intStack));
9    }
10
```

`GenericStack<Integer>`
type

GenericStack<Number>
type

```
11    /** Find the maximum in a stack of numbers */
12    public static double max(GenericStack<Number> stack) {
13      double max = stack.pop().doubleValue(); // Initialize max
14
15      while (!stack.isEmpty()) {
16        double value = stack.pop().doubleValue();
17        if (value > max)
18          max = value;
19      }
20
21      return max;
22    }
23  }
```

The program in Listing 19.7 has a compile error in line 8 because `intStack` is not an instance of `GenericStack<Number>`. Thus, you cannot invoke `max(intStack)`.

The fact is `Integer` is a subtype of `Number`, but `GenericStack<Integer>` is not a subtype of `GenericStack<Number>`. To circumvent this problem, use wildcard generic types. A wildcard generic type has three forms: `?`, `? extends T`, and `? super T`, where `T` is a generic type.

unbounded wildcard
bounded wildcard
lower bound wildcard

The first form, `?`, called an *unbounded wildcard*, is the same as `? extends Object`. The second form, `? extends T`, called a *bounded wildcard*, represents `T` or a subtype of `T`. The third form, `? super T`, called a *lower bound wildcard*, denotes `T` or a supertype of `T`.

You can fix the error by replacing line 12 in Listing 19.7 as follows:

```
public static double max(GenericStack<? extends Number> stack) {
```

`<? extends Number>` is a wildcard type that represents `Number` or a subtype of `Number`, so it is legal to invoke `max(new GenericStack<Integer>())` or `max(new GenericStack<Double>())`.

Listing 19.8 shows an example of using the `?` wildcard in the `print` method that prints objects in a stack and empties the stack. `<?>` is a wildcard that represents any object type. It is equivalent to `<? extends Object>`. What happens if you replace `GenericStack<?>` with `GenericStack<Object>`? It would be wrong to invoke `print(intStack)` because `intStack` is not an instance of `GenericStack<Object>`. Note that `GenericStack<Integer>` is not a subtype of `GenericStack<Object>` even though `Integer` is a subtype of `Object`.

LISTING 19.8   AnyWildCardDemo.java

GenericStack<Integer>
type

wildcard type

```
1  public class AnyWildCardDemo {
2    public static void main(String[] args) {
3      GenericStack<Integer> intStack = new GenericStack<>();
4      intStack.push(1); // 1 is autoboxed into new Integer(1)
5      intStack.push(2);
6      intStack.push(-2);
7
8      print(intStack);
9    }
10
11    /** Prints objects and empties the stack */
12    public static void print(GenericStack<?> stack) {
13      while (!stack.isEmpty()) {
14        System.out.print(stack.pop() + " ");
15      }
16    }
17  }
```

When is the wildcard `<? super T>` needed? Consider the example in Listing 19.9. The example creates a stack of strings in `stack1` (line 3) and a stack of objects in `stack2` (line 4) and invokes `add(stack1, stack2)` (line 8) to add the strings in `stack1` into `stack2`. `GenericStack<? super T>` is used to declare `stack2` in line 13. If `<? super T>` is replaced by `<T>`, a compile error will occur on `add(stack1, stack2)` in line 8 because `stack1`'s type is `GenericStack<String>` and `stack2`'s type is `GenericStack<Object>`. `<? super T>` represents type `T` or a supertype of `T`. `Object` is a supertype of `String`.

why `<? Super T>`

LISTING 19.9 `SuperWildCardDemo.java`

```
1  public class SuperWildCardDemo {
2    public static void main(String[] args) {
3      GenericStack<String> stack1 = new GenericStack<>();
4      GenericStack<Object> stack2 = new GenericStack<>();
5      stack2.push("Java");
6      stack2.push(2);
7      stack1.push("Sun");
8      add(stack1, stack2);
9      AnyWildCardDemo.print(stack2);
10   }
11
12   public static <T> void add(GenericStack<T> stack1,
13       GenericStack<? super T> stack2) {
14     while (!stack1.isEmpty())
15       stack2.push(stack1.pop());
16   }
17 }
```

GenericStack<String> type

<? Super T> type

This program will also work if the method header in lines 12 and 13 is modified as follows:

```
public static <T> void add(GenericStack<? extends T> stack1,
    GenericStack<T> stack2)
```

The inheritance relationship involving generic types and wildcard types is summarized in Figure 19.6. In this figure, `A` and `B` represent classes or interfaces, and `E` is a generic-type parameter.

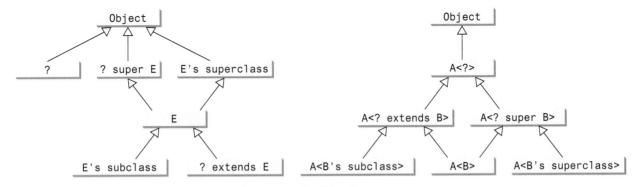

FIGURE 19.6 The relationship between generic types and wildcard types.

19.7.1 Is `GenericStack` the same as `GenericStack<Object>`?

19.7.2 What is an unbounded wildcard, a bounded wildcard, and a lower bound wildcard?

19.7.3 What happens if lines 12 and 13 in Listing 19.9 are changed to

```
public static <T> void add(GenericStack<T> stack1,
    GenericStack<T> stack2)
```

✓**Check Point**

19.7.4 What happens if lines 12 and 13 in Listing 19.9 are changed to

```
public static <T> void add(GenericStack<? extends T> stack1,
    GenericStack<T> stack2)
```

19.8 Erasure and Restrictions on Generics

Key Point

The information on generics is used by the compiler but is not available at runtime.
This is called type erasure.

type erasure

Generics are implemented using an approach called *type erasure*: The compiler uses the generic-type information to compile the code, but erases it afterward. Thus, the generic information is not available at runtime. This approach enables the generic code to be backward compatible with the legacy code that uses raw types.

erase generics

The generics are present at compile time. Once the compiler confirms that a generic type is used safely, it converts the generic type to a raw type. For example, the compiler checks whether the following code in (a) uses generics correctly, then translates it into the equivalent code in (b) for runtime use. The code in (b) uses the raw type.

```
ArrayList<String> list = new ArrayList<>();
list.add("Oklahoma");
String state = list.get(0);
```

(a)

```
ArrayList list = new ArrayList();
list.add("Oklahoma");
String state = (String)(list.get(0));
```

(b)

replace generic type

When generic classes, interfaces, and methods are compiled, the compiler replaces the generic type with the `Object` type. For example, the compiler would convert the following method in (a) into (b).

```
public static <E> void print(E[] list) {
  for (int i = 0; i < list.length; i++)
    System.out.print(list[i] + " ");
  System.out.println();
}
```

(a)

```
public static void print(Object[] list) {
  for (int i = 0; i < list.length; i++)
    System.out.print(list[i] + " ");
  System.out.println();
}
```

(b)

replace bounded type

If a generic type is bounded, the compiler replaces it with the bounded type. For example, the compiler would convert the following method in (a) into (b).

```
public static <E extends GeometricObject>
    boolean equalArea(
      E object1,
      E object2) {
  return object1.getArea() ==
    object2.getArea();
}
```

(a)

```
public static
    boolean equalArea(
      GeometricObject object1,
      GeometricObject object2) {
  return object1.getArea() ==
    object2.getArea();
}
```

(b)

important fact

It is important to note a generic class is shared by all its instances regardless of its actual concrete type. Suppose `list1` and `list2` are created as follows:

```
ArrayList<String> list1 = new ArrayList<>();
ArrayList<Integer> list2 = new ArrayList<>();
```

Although `ArrayList<String>` and `ArrayList<Integer>` are two types at compile time, only one `ArrayList` class is loaded into the JVM at runtime. `list1` and `list2` are both instances of `ArrayList`, so the following statements display `true`:

```
System.out.println(list1 instanceof ArrayList);
System.out.println(list2 instanceof ArrayList);
```

However, the expression `list1 instanceof ArrayList<String>` is wrong. Since `ArrayList<String>` is not stored as a separate class in the JVM, using it at runtime makes no sense.

Because generic types are erased at runtime, there are certain restrictions on how generic types can be used. Here are some of the restrictions:

Restriction 1: Cannot Use *new E()*

You cannot create an instance using a generic-type parameter. For example, the following statement is wrong:

```
E object = new E();
```

no new E()

The reason is `new E()` is executed at runtime, but the generic type `E` is not available at runtime.

Restriction 2: Cannot Use *new E[]*

You cannot create an array using a generic type parameter. For example, the following statement is wrong:

```
E[] elements = new E[capacity];
```

no new E[capacity]

You can circumvent this limitation by creating an array of the `Object` type then casting it to `E[]`, as follows:

```
E[] elements = (E[])new Object[capacity];
```

However, casting to `(E[])` causes an unchecked compile warning. The warning occurs because the compiler is not certain that casting will succeed at runtime. For example, if `E` is `String` and `new Object[]` is an array of `Integer` objects, `(String[])(new Object[])` will cause a `ClassCastException`. This type of compile warning is a limitation of Java generics and is unavoidable.

unavoidable compile warning

Generic array creation using a generic class is not allowed, either. For example, the following code is wrong:

```
ArrayList<String>[] list = new ArrayList<String>[10];
```

You can use the following code to circumvent this restriction:

```
ArrayList<String>[] list = (ArrayList<String>[])new
    ArrayList[10];
```

However, you will still get a compile warning.

Restriction 3: A Generic Type Parameter of a Class Is Not Allowed in a Static Context

Since all instances of a generic class have the same runtime class, the static variables and methods of a generic class are shared by all its instances. Therefore, it is illegal to refer to a generic-type parameter for a class in a static method, field, or initializer. For example, the following code is illegal:

```
public class Test<E> {
  public static void m(E o1) {  // Illegal
  }

  public static E o1; // Illegal

  static {
    E o2; // Illegal
  }
}
```

Restriction 4: Exception Classes Cannot Be Generic

A generic class may not extend `java.lang.Throwable`, so the following class declaration would be illegal:

```
public class MyException<T> extends Exception {
}
```

Why? If it were allowed, you would have a `catch` clause for `MyException<T>` as follows:

```
try {
  ...
}
catch (MyException<T> ex) {
  ...
}
```

The JVM has to check the exception thrown from the `try` clause to see if it matches the type specified in a `catch` clause. This is impossible, because the type information is not present at runtime.

19.8.1   What is erasure? Why are Java generics implemented using erasure?

19.8.2   If your program uses `ArrayList<String>` and `ArrayList<Date>`, does the JVM load both of them?

19.8.3   Can you create an instance using `new E()` for a generic type `E`? Why?

19.8.4   Can a method that uses a generic class parameter be static? Why?

19.8.5   Can you define a custom generic exception class? Why?

19.9 Case Study: Generic Matrix Class

This section presents a case study on designing classes for matrix operations using generic types.

The addition and multiplication operations for all matrices are similar except that their element types differ. Therefore, you can design a superclass that describes the common operations shared by matrices of all types regardless of their element types, and you can define subclasses tailored to specific types of matrices. This case study gives implementations for two types: `int` and `Rational`. For the `int` type, the wrapper class `Integer` should be used to wrap an `int` value into an object, so the object is passed in the methods for operations.

The class diagram is shown in Figure 19.7. The methods `addMatrix` and `multiplyMatrix` add and multiply two matrices of a generic type `E[][]`. The static method `printResult` displays the matrices, the operator, and their result. The methods `add`, `multiply`, and `zero` are abstract because their implementations depend on the specific type of the array elements. For example, the

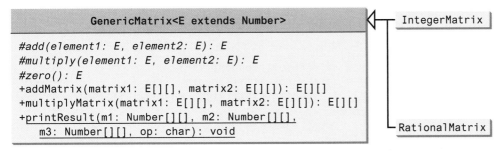

FIGURE 19.7 The GenericMatrix class is an abstract superclass for IntegerMatrix and RationalMatrix.

zero() method returns 0 for the Integer type and 0/1 for the Rational type. These methods will be implemented in the subclasses in which the matrix element type is specified.

IntegerMatrix and RationalMatrix are concrete subclasses of GenericMatrix. These two classes implement the add, multiply, and zero methods defined in the GenericMatrix class.

Listing 19.10 implements the GenericMatrix class. <E extends Number> in line 1 specifies the generic type is a subtype of Number. Three abstract methods—add, multiply, and zero—are defined in lines 3, 6, and 9. These methods are abstract because we cannot implement them without knowing the exact type of the elements. The addMaxtrix (lines 12–30) and multiplyMatrix (lines 33–57) methods implement the methods for adding and multiplying two matrices. All these methods must be nonstatic because they use generic-type E for the class. The printResult method (lines 60–84) is static because it is not tied to specific instances.

The matrix element type is a generic subtype of Number. This enables you to use an object of any subclass of Number as long as you can implement the abstract add, multiply, and zero methods in subclasses.

The addMatrix and multiplyMatrix methods (lines 12–57) are concrete methods. They are ready to use as long as the add, multiply, and zero methods are implemented in the subclasses.

The addMatrix and multiplyMatrix methods check the bounds of the matrices before performing operations. If the two matrices have incompatible bounds, the program throws an exception (lines 16 and 36).

LISTING 19.10 GenericMatrix.java

```
1  public abstract class GenericMatrix<E extends Number> {          bounded generic type
2    /** Abstract method for adding two elements of the matrices */
3    protected abstract E add(E o1, E o2);                          abstract method
4
5    /** Abstract method for multiplying two elements of the matrices */
6    protected abstract E multiply(E o1, E o2);                     abstract method
7
8    /** Abstract method for defining zero for the matrix element */
9    protected abstract E zero();                                   abstract method
10
11   /** Add two matrices */
12   public E[][] addMatrix(E[][] matrix1, E[][] matrix2) {         add two matrices
13     // Check bounds of the two matrices
14     if ((matrix1.length != matrix2.length) ||
15         (matrix1[0].length != matrix2[0].length)) {
16       throw new RuntimeException(
17         "The matrices do not have the same size");
18     }
19
```

```
20      E[][] result =
21        (E[][])new Number[matrix1.length][matrix1[0].length];
22
23      // Perform addition
24      for (int i = 0; i < result.length; i++)
25        for (int j = 0; j < result[i].length; j++) {
26          result[i][j] = add(matrix1[i][j], matrix2[i][j]);
27        }
28
29      return result;
30    }
31
32    /** Multiply two matrices */
33    public E[][] multiplyMatrix(E[][] matrix1, E[][] matrix2) {
34      // Check bounds
35      if (matrix1[0].length != matrix2.length) {
36        throw new RuntimeException(
37          "The matrices do not have compatible size");
38      }
39
40      // Create result matrix
41      E[][] result =
42        (E[][])new Number[matrix1.length][matrix2[0].length];
43
44      // Perform multiplication of two matrices
45      for (int i = 0; i < result.length; i++) {
46        for (int j = 0; j < result[0].length; j++) {
47          result[i][j] = zero();
48
49          for (int k = 0; k < matrix1[0].length; k++) {
50            result[i][j] = add(result[i][j],
51              multiply(matrix1[i][k], matrix2[k][j]));
52          }
53        }
54      }
55
56      return result;
57    }
58
59    /** Print matrices, the operator, and their operation result */
60    public static void printResult(
61        Number[][] m1, Number[][] m2, Number[][] m3, char op) {
62      for (int i = 0; i < m1.length; i++) {
63        for (int j = 0; j < m1[0].length; j++)
64          System.out.print(" " + m1[i][j]);
65
66        if (i == m1.length / 2)
67          System.out.print("  " + op + "  ");
68        else
69          System.out.print("     ");
70
71        for (int j = 0; j < m2.length; j++)
72          System.out.print(" " + m2[i][j]);
73
74        if (i == m1.length / 2)
75          System.out.print("  =  ");
76        else
77          System.out.print("     ");
78
79        for (int j = 0; j < m3.length; j++)
```

multiply two matrices *(margin note, line 33)*

display result *(margin note, line 60)*

```
80              System.out.print(m3[i][j] + " ");
81
82          System.out.println();
83       }
84    }
85 }
```

Listing 19.11 implements the IntegerMatrix class. The class extends GenericMatrix<Integer> in line 1. After the generic instantiation, the add method in GenericMatrix<Integer> is now Integer add(Integer o1, Integer o2). The add, multiply, and zero methods are implemented for Integer objects. These methods are still protected because they are invoked only by the addMatrix and multiplyMatrix methods.

LISTING 19.11 IntegerMatrix.java

```
1  public class IntegerMatrix extends GenericMatrix<Integer> {          extends generic type
2     @Override /** Add two integers */
3     protected Integer add(Integer o1, Integer o2) {                   implement add
4       return o1 + o2;
5     }
6
7     @Override /** Multiply two integers */
8     protected Integer multiply(Integer o1, Integer o2) {              implement multiply
9       return o1 * o2;
10    }
11
12    @Override /** Specify zero for an integer */
13    protected Integer zero() {                                        implement zero
14      return 0;
15    }
16 }
```

Listing 19.12 implements the RationalMatrix class. The Rational class was introduced in Listing 13.13, Rational.java. Rational is a subtype of Number. The RationalMatrix class extends GenericMatrix<Rational> in line 1. After the generic instantiation, the add method in GenericMatrix<Rational> is now Rational add(Rational r1, Rational r2). The add, multiply, and zero methods are implemented for Rational objects. These methods are still protected because they are invoked only by the addMatrix and multiplyMatrix methods.

LISTING 19.12 RationalMatrix.java

```
1  public class RationalMatrix extends GenericMatrix<Rational> {        extends generic type
2     @Override /** Add two rational numbers */
3     protected Rational add(Rational r1, Rational r2) {
4       return r1.add(r2);                                              implement add
5     }
6
7     @Override /** Multiply two rational numbers */
8     protected Rational multiply(Rational r1, Rational r2) {
9       return r1.multiply(r2);                                         implement multiply
10    }
11
12    @Override /** Specify zero for a Rational number */
13    protected Rational zero() {
14      return new Rational(0, 1);                                      implement zero
15    }
16 }
```

Listing 19.13 gives a program that creates two `Integer` matrices (lines 4 and 5) and an `IntegerMatrix` object (line 8), and adds and multiplies two matrices in lines 12 and 16.

LISTING 19.13 TestIntegerMatrix.java

```
1  public class TestIntegerMatrix {
2    public static void main(String[] args) {
3      // Create Integer arrays m1, m2
4      Integer[][] m1 = new Integer[][]{{1, 2, 3}, {4, 5, 6}, {1, 1, 1}};
5      Integer[][] m2 = new Integer[][]{{1, 1, 1}, {2, 2, 2}, {0, 0, 0}};
6
7      // Create an instance of IntegerMatrix
8      IntegerMatrix integerMatrix = new IntegerMatrix();
9
10     System.out.println("\nm1 + m2 is ");
11     GenericMatrix.printResult(
12       m1, m2, integerMatrix.addMatrix(m1, m2), '+');
13
14     System.out.println("\nm1 * m2 is ");
15     GenericMatrix.printResult(
16       m1, m2, integerMatrix.multiplyMatrix(m1, m2), '*');
17   }
18 }
```

create matrices

create `IntegerMatrix`

add two matrices

multiply two matrices

```
m1 + m2 is
  1 2 3     1 1 1     2 3 4
  4 5 6  +  2 2 2  =  6 7 8
  1 1 1     0 0 0     1 1 1

m1 * m2 is
  1 2 3     1 1 1     5  5  5
  4 5 6  *  2 2 2  =  14 14 14
  1 1 1     0 0 0     3  3  3
```

Listing 19.14 gives a program that creates two `Rational` matrices (lines 4–10) and a `RationalMatrix` object (line 13) and adds and multiplies two matrices in lines 17 and 19.

LISTING 19.14 TestRationalMatrix.java

```
1  public class TestRationalMatrix {
2    public static void main(String[] args) {
3      // Create two Rational arrays m1 and m2
4      Rational[][] m1 = new Rational[3][3];
5      Rational[][] m2 = new Rational[3][3];
6      for (int i = 0; i < m1.length; i++)
7        for (int j = 0; j < m1[0].length; j++) {
8          m1[i][j] = new Rational(i + 1, j + 5);
9          m2[i][j] = new Rational(i + 1, j + 6);
10       }
11
12     // Create an instance of RationalMatrix
13     RationalMatrix rationalMatrix = new RationalMatrix();
14
15     System.out.println("\nm1 + m2 is ");
16     GenericMatrix.printResult(
17       m1, m2, rationalMatrix.addMatrix(m1, m2), '+');
18
19     System.out.println("\nm1 * m2 is ");
```

create matrices

create `RationalMatrix`

add two matrices

```
20        GenericMatrix.printResult(
21          m1, m2, rationalMatrix.multiplyMatrix(m1, m2), '*');          multiply two matrices
22      }
23    }
```

```
m1 + m2 is
  1/5 1/6 1/7      1/6 1/7 1/8        11/30 13/42 15/56
  2/5 1/3 2/7  +   1/3 2/7 1/4  =     11/15 13/21 15/28
  3/5 1/2 3/7      1/2 3/7 3/8        11/10 13/14 45/56

m1 * m2 is
  1/5 1/6 1/7      1/6 1/7 1/8        101/630 101/735 101/840
  2/5 1/3 2/7  *   1/3 2/7 1/4  =     101/315 202/735 101/420
  3/5 1/2 3/7      1/2 3/7 3/8        101/210 101/245 101/280
```

19.9.1 Why are the add, multiple, and zero methods defined abstract in the GenericMatrix class?

19.9.2 How are the add, multiple, and zero methods implemented in the IntegerMatrix class?

19.9.3 How are the add, multiple, and zero methods implemented in the RationalMatrix class?

19.9.4 What would be wrong if the printResult method is defined as follows?

```
public static void printResult(
  E[][] m1, E[][] m2, E[][] m3, char op)
```

Check
Point

KEY TERMS

actual concrete type   752
bounded generic type   757
bounded wildcard
   (<? extends E>)   762
formal generic type   752
generic instantiation   752

lower bound wildcard
   (<? super E>)   762
raw type   760
unbounded wildcard (<?>)   762
type erasure (<?>)   764

CHAPTER SUMMARY

1. *Generics* give you the capability to parameterize types. You can define a class or a method with generic types, which are substituted with concrete types.

2. The key benefit of generics is to enable errors to be detected at compile time rather than at runtime.

3. A generic class or method permits you to specify allowable types of objects that the class or method can work with. If you attempt to use a class or method with an incompatible object, the compiler will detect the error.

4. A generic type defined in a class, interface, or a static method is called a *formal generic type*, which can be replaced later with an *actual concrete type*. Replacing a generic type is called a *generic instantiation*.

5. A generic class such as `ArrayList` used without a type parameter is called a *raw type*. Use of raw types allows for backward compatibility with the earlier versions of Java.

6. A wildcard generic type has three forms: `?`, `? extends T`, and `? super T`, where `T` is a generic type. The first form, `?`, called an *unbounded wildcard*, is the same as `? extends Object`. The second form, `? extends T`, called a *bounded wildcard*, represents `T` or a subtype of `T`. The third form, `? super T`, called a *lower bound wildcard*, denotes `T` or a supertype of `T`.

7. Generics are implemented using an approach called *type erasure*. The compiler uses the generic-type information to compile the code but erases it afterward, so the generic information is not available at runtime. This approach enables the generic code to be backward compatible with the legacy code that uses raw types.

8. You cannot create an instance using a generic-type parameter such as `new E()`.

9. You cannot create an array using a generic-type parameter such as `new E[10]`.

10. You cannot use a generic-type parameter of a class in a static context.

11. Generic-type parameters cannot be used in exception classes.

QUIZ

Answer the quiz for this chapter online at the book Companion Website.

MyProgrammingLab™ **PROGRAMMING EXERCISES**

19.1 (*Revising Listing 19.1*) Revise the `GenericStack` class in Listing 19.1 to implement it using an array rather than an `ArrayList`. You should check the array size before adding a new element to the stack. If the array is full, create a new array that doubles the current array size and copy the elements from the current array to the new array.

19.2 (*Implement `GenericStack` using inheritance*) In Listing 19.1, `GenericStack` is implemented using composition. Define a new stack class that extends `ArrayList`.

Draw the UML diagram for the classes then implement `GenericStack`. Write a test program that prompts the user to enter five strings and displays them in reverse order.

19.3 (*Distinct elements in `ArrayList`*) Write the following method that returns a new `ArrayList`. The new list contains the nonduplicate elements from the original list.

```
public static <E> ArrayList<E> removeDuplicates(ArrayList<E> list)
```

19.4 (*Generic linear search*) Implement the following generic method for linear search:

```
public static <E extends Comparable<E>>
    int linearSearch(E[] list, E key)
```

19.5 (*Maximum element in an array*) Implement the following method that returns the maximum element in an array:

```
public static <E extends Comparable<E>> E max(E[] list)
```

19.6 (*Maximum element in a two-dimensional array*) Write a generic method that returns the maximum element in a two-dimensional array.

```
public static <E extends Comparable<E>> E max(E[][] list)
```

19.7 (*Generic binary search*) Implement the following method using binary search:

```
public static <E extends Comparable<E>>
  int binarySearch(E[] list, E key)
```

19.8 (*Shuffle ArrayList*) Write the following method that shuffles an ArrayList:

```
public static <E> void shuffle(ArrayList<E> list)
```

19.9 (*Sort ArrayList*) Write the following method that sorts an ArrayList:

```
public static <E extends Comparable<E>>
  void sort(ArrayList<E> list)
```

19.10 (*Largest element in an ArrayList*) Write the following method that returns the largest element in an ArrayList:

```
public static <E extends Comparable<E>> E max(ArrayList<E> list)
```

19.11 (*ComplexMatrix*) Use the Complex class introduced in Programming Exercise 13.17 to develop the ComplexMatrix class for performing matrix operations involving complex numbers. The ComplexMatrix class should extend the GenericMatrix class and implement the add, multiple, and zero methods. You need to modify GenericMatrix and replace every occurrence of Number by Object because Complex is not a subtype of Number. Write a test program that creates the following two matrices and displays the result of addition and multiplication of the matrices by invoking the printResult method.

LISTS, STACKS, QUEUES, AND PRIORITY QUEUES

Objectives

- To explore the relationship between interfaces and classes in the Java Collections Framework hierarchy (§20.2).

- To use the common methods defined in the `Collection` interface for operating collections (§20.2).

- To use the `Iterator` interface to traverse the elements in a collection (§20.3).

- To use a foreach loop to traverse the elements in a collection (§20.3).

- To use a `forEach` method to perform an action on each element in a collection (§20.4).

- To explore how and when to use `ArrayList` or `LinkedList` to store a list of elements (§20.5).

- To compare elements using the `Comparable` interface and the `Comparator` interface (§20.6).

- To use the static utility methods in the `Collections` class for sorting, searching, shuffling lists, and finding the largest and smallest element in collections (§20.7).

- To develop a multiple bouncing balls application using `ArrayList` (§20.8).

- To distinguish between `Vector` and `ArrayList` and to use the `Stack` class for creating stacks (§20.9).

- To explore the relationships among `Collection`, `Queue`, `LinkedList`, and `PriorityQueue` and to create priority queues using the `PriorityQueue` class (§20.10).

- To use stacks to write a program to evaluate expressions (§20.11).

20.1 Introduction

Choosing the best data structures and algorithms for a particular task is one of the keys to developing high-performance software.

data structure

Chapters 18–29 are typically taught in a data structures course. A *data structure* is a collection of data organized in some fashion. The structure not only stores data, but also supports operations for accessing and manipulating the data. Without knowing data structures, you can still write programs, but your program may not be efficient. With a good knowledge of data structures, you can build efficient programs, which are important for practical applications.

why learning data structure

container

In object-oriented thinking, a data structure, also known as a *container* or *container object*, is an object that stores other objects, referred to as data or elements. To define a data structure is essentially to define a class. The class for a data structure should use data fields to store data and provide methods to support such operations as search, insertion, and deletion. To create a data structure is therefore to create an instance from the class. You can then apply the methods on the instance to manipulate the data structure, such as inserting an element into or deleting an element from the data structure.

Section 11.11 introduced the `ArrayList` class, which is a data structure to store elements in a list. Java provides several more data structures (lists, vectors, stacks, queues, priority queues, sets, and maps) that can be used to organize and manipulate data efficiently. These are commonly known as *Java Collections Framework*. We will introduce the applications of lists, vectors, stacks, queues, and priority queues in this chapter, and sets and maps in the next chapter. The implementation of these data structures will be discussed in Chapters 24–27. Through implementation, students gain a deep understanding on the efficiency of data structures and on how and when to use certain data structures. Finally, we will introduce design and implement data structures and algorithms for graphs in Chapters 28 and 29.

Java Collections Framework

20.2 Collections

The `Collection` *interface defines the common operations for lists, vectors, stacks, queues, priority queues, and sets.*

The Java Collections Framework supports two types of containers:

collection

■ One for storing a collection of elements is simply called a *collection*.

map

■ The other, for storing key/value pairs, is called a *map*.

Maps are efficient data structures for quickly searching an element using a key. We will introduce maps in the next chapter. Now we turn our attention to the following collections.

Set

■ `Set`s store a group of nonduplicate elements.

List

■ `List`s store an ordered collection of elements.

Stack

■ `Stack`s store objects that are processed in a last-in, first-out fashion.

Queue

■ `Queue`s store objects that are processed in a first-in, first-out fashion.

PrioriryQueue

■ `PriorityQueue`s store objects that are processed in the order of their priorities.

The common operations of these collections are defined in the interfaces, and implementations are provided in concrete classes, as shown in Figure 20.1.

Note
All the interfaces and classes defined in the Java Collections Framework are grouped in the `java.util` package.

Design Guide
The design of the Java Collections Framework is an excellent example of using interfaces, abstract classes, and concrete classes. The interfaces define the common operations.

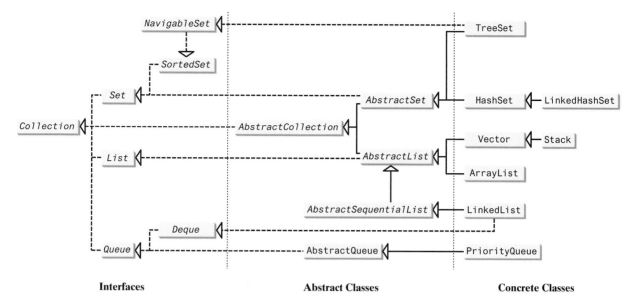

FIGURE 20.1 A collection is a container that stores objects.

The abstract classes provide partial implementation. The concrete classes implement the interfaces with concrete data structures. Providing an abstract class that partially implements an interface makes it convenient for the user to write the code. The user can simply define a concrete class that extends the abstract class rather than implementing all the methods in the interface. The abstract classes such as `AbstractCollection` are provided for convenience. For this reason, they are called *convenience abstract classes*.

convenience abstract class

The `Collection` interface is the root interface for manipulating a collection of objects. Its public methods are listed in Figure 20.2. The `AbstractCollection` class provides partial implementation for the `Collection` interface. It implements all the methods in `Collection` except the `add`, `size`, and `iterator` methods. These are implemented in the concrete subclasses.

The `Collection` interface provides the basic operations for adding and removing elements in a collection. The `add` method adds an element to the collection. The `addAll` method adds all the elements in the specified collection to this collection. The `remove` method removes an element from the collection. The `removeAll` method removes the elements from this collection that are present in the specified collection. The `retainAll` method retains the elements in this collection that are also present in the specified collection. All these methods return `boolean`. The return value is `true` if the collection is changed as a result of the method execution. The `clear()` method simply removes all the elements from the collection.

basic operations

 Note
The methods `addAll`, `removeAll`, and `retainAll` are similar to the set union, difference, and intersection operations.

set operations

The `Collection` interface provides various query operations. The `size` method returns the number of elements in the collection. The `contains` method checks whether the collection contains the specified element. The `containsAll` method checks whether the collection contains all the elements in the specified collection. The `isEmpty` method returns `true` if the collection is empty.

query operations

The `Collection` interface provides the `toArray()` method, which returns an array of `Object` for the collection. It also provides the `toArray(T[])` method, which returns an array of the `T[]` type.

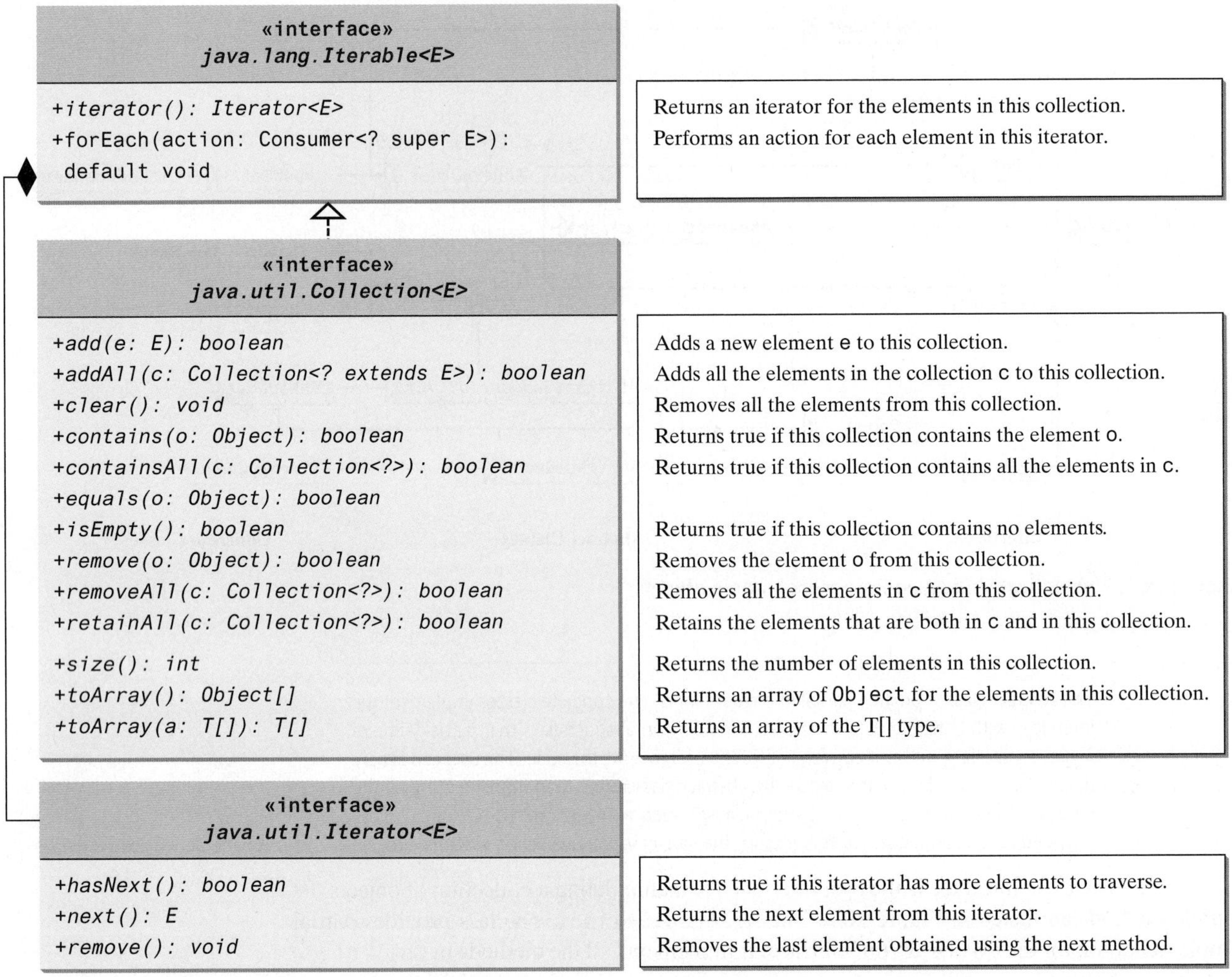

FIGURE 20.2 The `Collection` interface contains the methods for manipulating the elements in a collection, and you can obtain an iterator object for traversing elements in the collection.

Design Guide

Some of the methods in the `Collection` interface cannot be implemented in the concrete subclass. In this case, the method would throw `java.lang.UnsupportedOperation Exception`, a subclass of `RuntimeException`. This is a good design you can use in your project. If a method has no meaning in the subclass, you can implement it as follows:

unsupported operations

```
public void someMethod() {
  throw new UnsupportedOperationException
    ("Method not supported");
}
```

Listing 20.1 gives an example to use the methods defined in the `Collection` interface.

LISTING 20.1 `TestCollection.java`

```
1  import java.util.*;
2
3  public class TestCollection {
4    public static void main(String[] args) {
5      ArrayList<String> collection1 = new ArrayList<>();
```

create an array list

```
 6          collection1.add("New York");                                    add elements
 7          collection1.add("Atlanta");
 8          collection1.add("Dallas");
 9          collection1.add("Madison");
10
11          System.out.println("A list of cities in collection1:");
12          System.out.println(collection1);
13
14          System.out.println("\nIs Dallas in collection1? "
15            + collection1.contains("Dallas"));                            contains?
16
17          collection1.remove("Dallas");
18          System.out.println("\n" + collection1.size() +                 size?
19            " cities are in collection1 now");
20
21          Collection<String> collection2 = new ArrayList<>();
22          collection2.add("Seattle");
23          collection2.add("Portland");
24          collection2.add("Los Angeles");
25          collection2.add("Atlanta");
26
27          System.out.println("\nA list of cities in collection2:");
28          System.out.println(collection2);
29
30          ArrayList<String> c1 = (ArrayList<String>)(collection1.clone()); clone
31          c1.addAll(collection2);                                         addAll
32          System.out.println("\nCities in collection1 or collection2: ");
33          System.out.println(c1);
34
35          c1 = (ArrayList<String>)(collection1.clone());
36          c1.retainAll(collection2);                                      retainAll
37          System.out.print("\nCities in collection1 and collection2: ");
38          System.out.println(c1);
39
40          c1 = (ArrayList<String>)(collection1.clone());
41          c1.removeAll(collection2);                                      removeAll
42          System.out.print("\nCities in collection1, but not in 2: ");
43          System.out.println(c1);
44      }
45  }
```

```
A list of cities in collection1:
[New York, Atlanta, Dallas, Madison]
Is Dallas in collection1? true
3 cities are in collection1 now
A list of cities in collection2:
[Seattle, Portland, Los Angeles, Atlanta]
Cities in collection1 or collection2:
[New York, Atlanta, Madison, Seattle, Portland, Los Angeles, Atlanta]
Cities in collection1 and collection2: [Atlanta]
Cities in collection1, but not in 2: [New York, Madison]
```

The program creates a concrete collection object using ArrayList (line 5) and invokes the Collection interface's contains method (line 15), remove method (line 17), size method (line 18), addAll method (line 31), retainAll method (line 36), and removeAll method (line 41).

For this example, we use `ArrayList`. You can use any concrete class of `Collection` such as `HashSet` and `LinkedList` to replace `ArrayList` to test these methods defined in the `Collection` interface.

The program creates a copy of an array list (lines 30, 35, and 40). The purpose of this is to keep the original array list intact and use its copy to perform `addAll`, `retainAll`, and `removeAll` operations.

Note

Cloneable
Serializable

All the concrete classes in the Java Collections Framework implement the `java.lang` `.Cloneable` and `java.io.Serializable` interfaces except that `java.util` `.PriorityQueue` does not implement the `Cloneable` interface. Thus, all instances of `Collection` except priority queues can be cloned and all instances of `Collection` can be serialized.

20.2.1 What is a data structure?

20.2.2 Describe the Java Collections Framework. List the interfaces, convenience abstract classes, and concrete classes under the `Collection` interface.

20.2.3 Can a collection object be cloned and serialized?

20.2.4 What method do you use to add all the elements from one collection to another collection?

20.2.5 When should a method throw an `UnsupportedOperationException`?

20.3 Iterators

Key
Point

Each collection is `Iterable`. You can obtain its `Iterator` object to traverse all the elements in the collection.

`Iterator` is a classic design pattern for walking through a data structure without having to expose the details of how data is stored in the data structure.

The `Collection` interface extends the `Iterable` interface. The `Iterable` interface defines the `iterator` method, which returns an iterator. The `Iterator` interface provides a uniform way for traversing elements in various types of collections. The `iterator()` method in the `Iterable` interface returns an instance of `Iterator`, as shown in Figure 20.2, which provides sequential access to the elements in the collection using the `next()` method. You can also use the `hasNext()` method to check whether there are more elements in the iterator, and the `remove()` method to remove the last element returned by the iterator.

Listing 20.2 gives an example that uses the iterator to traverse all the elements in an array list.

Listing 20.2 TestIterator.java

create an array list
add elements

iterator
hasNext()
next()

```
1  import java.util.*;
2
3  public class TestIterator {
4    public static void main(String[] args) {
5      Collection<String> collection = new ArrayList<>();
6      collection.add("New York");
7      collection.add("Atlanta");
8      collection.add("Dallas");
9      collection.add("Madison");
10
11     Iterator<String> iterator = collection.iterator();
12     while (iterator.hasNext()) {
13       System.out.print(iterator.next().toUpperCase() + " ");
14     }
15     System.out.println();
16   }
17 }
```

```
NEW YORK ATLANTA DALLAS MADISON
```

The program creates a concrete collection object using `ArrayList` (line 5) and adds four strings into the list (lines 6–9). The program then obtains an iterator for the collection (line 11) and uses the iterator to traverse all the strings in the list and displays the strings in uppercase (lines 12–14).

Tip
You can simplify the code in lines 11–14 using a foreach loop without using an iterator, as follows:

```
for (String element: collection)
  System.out.print(element.toUpperCase() + " ");
```
foreach loop

This loop is read as "for each element in the collection, do the following." The foreach loop can be used for arrays (see Section 7.2.7) as well as any instance of `Iterable`.

20.3.1 How do you obtain an iterator from a collection object?

20.3.2 What method do you use to obtain an element in the collection from an iterator?

20.3.3 Can you use a foreach loop to traverse the elements in any instance of `Collection`?

20.3.4 When using a foreach loop to traverse all elements in a collection, do you need to use the `next()` or `hasNext()` methods in an iterator?

20.4 Using the **forEach** Method

You can use the `forEach` *method to perform an action for each element in a collection.*

Java 8 added a new default method `forEach` in the `Iterable` interface. The method takes an argument for specifying the action, which is an instance of a functional interface `Consumer<? super E>`. The `Consumer` interface defines the `accept(E e)` method for performing an action on the element `e`. You can rewrite the preceding example using a `forEach` method in Listing 20.3.

LISTING 20.3 `TestForEach.java`

```
1  import java.util.*;
2
3  public class TestForEach {
4    public static void main(String[] args) {
5      Collection<String> collection = new ArrayList<>();
6      collection.add("New York");
7      collection.add("Atlanta");
8      collection.add("Dallas");
9      collection.add("Madison");
10
11     collection.forEach(e -> System.out.print(e.toUpperCase() + " "));
12   }
13 }
```
create an array list
add elements

forEach method

```
NEW YORK ATLANTA DALLAS MADISON
```

The statement in line 11 uses a lambda expression in (a), which is equivalent to using an anonymous inner class as shown in (b). Using a lambda expression not only simplifies the syntax but also simplifies the semantics.

```
forEach(e ->
   System.out.print(e.toUppserCase() + " "))
```

```
forEach(
   new java.util.function.Consumer<String>() {
      public void accept(String e) {
         System.out.print(e.toUpperCase() + " ");
      }
   }
)
```

(a) Use a lambda expression

(b) Use an anonymous inner class

You can write the code using a foreach loop or using a `forEach` method. Using a `forEach` is simpler in most cases.

20.4.1 Can you use the `forEach` method on any instance of `Collection`? Where is the `forEach` method defined?

20.4.2 Suppose each element in `list` is a `StringBuilder`, write a statement using a `forEach` method to change the first character to uppercase for each element in `list`.

20.5 Lists

The `List` interface extends the `Collection` interface and defines a collection for storing elements in a sequential order. To create a list, use one of its two concrete classes: `ArrayList` or `LinkedList`.

We used `ArrayList` to test the methods in the `Collection` interface in the preceding sections. Now, we will examine `ArrayList` in more depth. We will also introduce another useful list, `LinkedList`, in this section.

20.5.1   The Common Methods in the `List` Interface

`ArrayList` and `LinkedList` are defined under the `List` interface. The `List` interface extends `Collection` to define an ordered collection with duplicates allowed. The `List` interface adds position-oriented operations as well as a new list iterator that enables a list to be traversed bidirectionally. The methods introduced in the `List` interface are shown in Figure 20.3.

The `add(index, element)` method is used to insert an element at a specified index and the `addAll(index, collection)` method to insert a collection of elements at a specified index. The `remove(index)` method is used to remove an element at the specified index from the list. A new element can be set at the specified index using the `set(index, element)` method.

The `indexOf(element)` method is used to obtain the index of the specified element's first occurrence in the list and the `lastIndexOf(element)` method to obtain the index of its last occurrence. A sublist can be obtained by using the `subList(fromIndex, toIndex)` method.

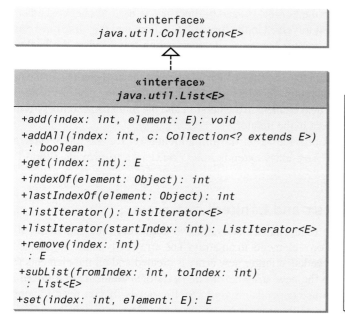

FIGURE 20.3 The `List` interface stores elements in sequence and permits duplicates.

The `listIterator()` or `listIterator(startIndex)` method returns an instance of `ListIterator`. The `ListIterator` interface extends the `Iterator` interface to add bidirectional traversal of the list. The methods in `ListIterator` are listed in Figure 20.4.

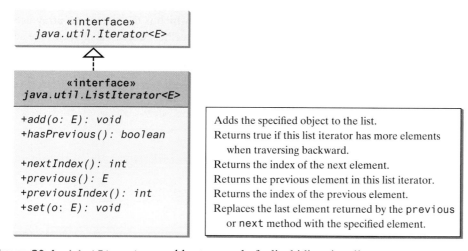

FIGURE 20.4 `ListIterator` enables traversal of a list bidirectionally.

The `add(element)` method inserts the specified element into the list. The element is inserted immediately before the next element that would be returned by the `next()` method defined in the `Iterator` interface, if any, and after the element that would be returned by the `previous()` method, if any. If the list doesn't contain any elements, the new element becomes the sole element in the list. The `set(element)` method can be used to replace the last element returned by the `next` method, or the `previous` method with the specified element.

The `hasNext()` method defined in the `Iterator` interface is used to check whether the iterator has more elements when traversed in the forward direction, and the `hasPrevious()` method to check whether the iterator has more elements when traversed in the backward direction.

The `next()` method defined in the `Iterator` interface returns the next element in the iterator, and the `previous()` method returns the previous element in the iterator. The `nextIndex()` method returns the index of the next element in the iterator, and the `previousIndex()` returns the index of the previous element in the iterator.

The `AbstractList` class provides a partial implementation for the `List` interface. The `AbstractSequentialList` class extends `AbstractList` to provide support for linked lists.

20.5.2   The `ArrayList` and `LinkedList` Classes

ArrayList vs. LinkedList

The `ArrayList` class and the `LinkedList` class are two concrete implementations of the `List` interface. `ArrayList` stores elements in an array. The array is dynamically created. If the capacity of the array is exceeded, a larger new array is created and all the elements from the current array are copied to the new array. `LinkedList` stores elements in a *linked list*. Which of the two classes you use depends on your specific needs. If you need to support random access through an index without inserting or removing elements at the beginning of the list, `ArrayList` is the most efficient. If, however, your application requires the insertion or deletion of elements at the beginning of the list, you should choose `LinkedList`. A list can grow or shrink dynamically. Once it is created, an array is fixed. If your application does not require the insertion or deletion of elements, an array is the most efficient data structure.

linked list

`ArrayList` is a resizable-array implementation of the `List` interface. It also provides methods for manipulating the size of the array used internally to store the list, as shown in Figure 20.5. Each `ArrayList` instance has a capacity, which is the size of the array used to store the elements in the list. It is always at least as large as the list size. As elements are added to an `ArrayList`, its capacity grows automatically. An `ArrayList` does not automatically shrink. You can use the `trimToSize()` method to reduce the array capacity to the size of the list. An `ArrayList` can be constructed using its no-arg constructor, `ArrayList(Collection)`, or `ArrayList(initialCapacity)`.

trimToSize()

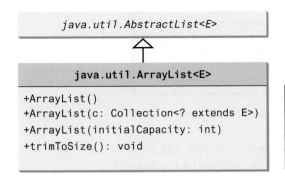

FIGURE 20.5   `ArrayList` implements `List` using an array.

`LinkedList` is a linked list implementation of the `List` interface. In addition to implementing the `List` interface, this class provides the methods for retrieving, inserting, and removing elements from both ends of the list, as shown in Figure 20.6. A `LinkedList` can be constructed using its no-arg constructor or `LinkedList(Collection)`.

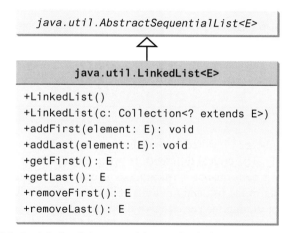

FIGURE 20.6 LinkedList provides methods for adding and inserting elements at both ends of the list.

Listing 20.4 gives a program that creates an array list filled with numbers and inserts new elements into specified locations in the list. The example also creates a linked list from the array list and inserts and removes elements from the list. Finally, the example traverses the list forward and backward.

LISTING 20.4 TestArrayAndLinkedList.java

```
1  import java.util.*;
2
3  public class TestArrayAndLinkedList {
4    public static void main(String[] args) {
5      List<Integer> arrayList = new ArrayList<>();          array list
6      arrayList.add(1); // 1 is autoboxed to new Integer(1)
7      arrayList.add(2);
8      arrayList.add(3);
9      arrayList.add(1);
10     arrayList.add(4);
11     arrayList.add(0, 10);
12     arrayList.add(3, 30);
13
14     System.out.println("A list of integers in the array list:");
15     System.out.println(arrayList);
16
17     LinkedList<Object> linkedList = new LinkedList<Object>(arrayList);   linked list
18     linkedList.add(1, "red");
19     linkedList.removeLast();
20     linkedList.addFirst("green");
21
22     System.out.println("Display the linked list forward:");
23     ListIterator<Object> listIterator = linkedList.listIterator();    list iterator
24     while (listIterator.hasNext()) {
25       System.out.print(listIterator.next() + " ");
26     }
27     System.out.println();
28
29     System.out.println("Display the linked list backward:");
30     listIterator = linkedList.listIterator(linkedList.size());    list iterator
31     while (listIterator.hasPrevious()) {
32       System.out.print(listIterator.previous() + " ");
33     }
34   }
35 }
```

```
A list of integers in the array list:
[10, 1, 2, 30, 3, 1, 4]
Display the linked list forward:
green 10 red 1 2 30 3 1
Display the linked list backward:
1 3 30 2 1 red 10 green
```

A list can hold identical elements. Integer 1 is stored twice in the list (lines 6 and 9). `ArrayList` and `LinkedList` operate similarly. The critical difference between them pertains to internal implementation, which affects their performance. `LinkedList` is efficient for inserting and removing elements at the beginning of the list, and `ArrayList` is more efficient for all other operations. For examples of demonstrating the performance differences between `ArrayList` and `LinkedList`, see liveexample.pearsoncmg.com/supplement/ArrayListvsLinkedList.pdf.

The `get(i)` method is available for a linked list, but it is a time-consuming operation. Do not use it to traverse all the elements in a list as shown in (a). Instead, you should use a foreach loop as shown in (b) or a `forEach` method as shown in (c). Note (b) and (c) use an iterator implicitly. You will know the reason when you learn how to implement a linked list in Chapter 24.

```
for (int i = 0; i < list.size(); i++)
  process list.get(i);
}
```
(a) Very inefficient

```
for (listElementType e: list) {
  process e;
}
```
(b) Efficient

```
list.forEach(e ->
  process e
)
```
(c) Efficient

`Arrays.asList(T... a)`
method

Tip
Java provides the static `asList` method for creating a list from a variable-length list of arguments. Thus, you can use the following code to create a list of strings and a list of integers:

```
List<String> list1 = Arrays.asList("red", "green", "blue");
List<Integer> list2 = Arrays.asList(10, 20, 30, 40, 50);
```

Check
Point

20.5.1 How do you add and remove elements from a list? How do you traverse a list in both directions?

20.5.2 Suppose `list1` is a list that contains the strings red, yellow, and green and `list2` is another list that contains the strings red, yellow, and blue. Answer the following questions:

a. What are `list1` and `list2` after executing `list1.addAll(list2)`?

b. What are `list1` and `list2` after executing `list1.add(list2)`?

c. What are `list1` and `list2` after executing `list1.removeAll(list2)`?

d. What are `list1` and `list2` after executing `list1.remove(list2)`?

e. What are `list1` and `list2` after executing `list1.retainAll(list2)`?

f. What is `list1` after executing `list1.clear()`?

20.5.3 What are the differences between `ArrayList` and `LinkedList`? Which list should you use to insert and delete elements at the beginning of a list?

20.5.4 Are all the methods in `ArrayList` also in `LinkedList`? What methods are in `LinkedList` but not in `ArrayList`?

20.5.5 How do you create a list from an array of objects?

20.6 The **Comparator** Interface

*Comparator can be used to compare the objects of a class that doesn't implement
Comparable or define a new criteria for comparing objects.*

You have learned how to compare elements using the `Comparable` interface (introduced in
Section 13.6). Several classes in the Java API, such as `String`, `Date`, `Calendar`, `BigInteger`,
`BigDecimal`, and all the numeric wrapper classes for the primitive types, implement the `Com-
parable` interface. The `Comparable` interface defines the `compareTo` method, which is used
to compare two elements of the same class that implements the `Comparable` interface.

What if the elements' classes do not implement the `Comparable` interface? Can these
elements be compared? You can define a *comparator* to compare the elements of different   comparator
classes. To do so, define a class that implements the `java.util.Comparator<T>` interface
and overrides its `compare` method.

> **`public int compare(T element1, T element2)`**
>
> Returns a negative value if `element1` is less than `element2`, a positive value if
> `element1` is greater than `element2`, and zero if they are equal.

The `GeometricObject` class was introduced in Section 13.2, Abstract Classes. The
`GeometricObject` class does not implement the `Comparable` interface. To compare the
objects of the `GeometricObject` class, you can define a comparator class, as given in
Listing 20.5.

LISTING 20.5 GeometricObjectComparator.java

```
1  import java.util.Comparator;
2
3  public class GeometricObjectComparator
4      implements Comparator<GeometricObject>, java.io.Serializable {
5    public int compare(GeometricObject o1, GeometricObject o2) {
6      double area1 = o1.getArea();
7      double area2 = o2.getArea();
8
9      if (area1 < area2)
10       return -1;
11     else if (area1 == area2)
12       return 0;
13     else
14       return 1;
15   }
16 }
```

implements Comparator
implements compare

Line 4 implements `Comparator<GeometricObject>`. Line 5 overrides the `compare` method
to compare two geometric objects. The class also implements `Serializable`. It is generally
a good idea for comparators to implement `Serializable` so they can be serialized.

Listing 20.6 gives a method that returns a larger object between two geometric objects. The
objects are compared using the `GeometricObjectComparator`.

LISTING 20.6 TestComparator.java

```
1  import java.util.Comparator;
2
3  public class TestComparator {
4    public static void main(String[] args) {
5      GeometricObject g1 = new Rectangle(5, 5);
6      GeometricObject g2 = new Circle(5);
7
```

invoke max

```
 8       GeometricObject g =
 9         max(g1, g2, new GeometricObjectComparator());
10
11       System.out.println("The area of the larger object is " +
12         g.getArea());
13     }
14
15     public static GeometricObject max(GeometricObject g1,
16       GeometricObject g2, Comparator<GeometricObject> c) {
17       if (c.compare(g1, g2) > 0)
18         return g1;
19       else
20         return g2;
21     }
22   }
```

the max method (line 15)

invoke compare (line 17)

```
The area of the larger object is 78.53981633974483
```

The program creates a `Rectangle` and a `Circle` object in lines 5 and 6 (the `Rectangle` and `Circle` classes were defined in Section 13.2, Abstract Classes). They are all subclasses of `GeometricObject`. The program invokes the `max` method to obtain the geometric object with the larger area (lines 8 and 9).

The `GeometricObjectComparator` is created and passed to the `max` method (line 9) and this comparator is used in the `max` method to compare the geometric objects in line 17.

Since the `Comparator` interface is a single abstract method interface, you can use a lambda expression to simplify the program by replacing line 9 with the following code:

```
max(g1, g2, (o1, o2) -> o1.getArea() > o2.getArea() ?
  1 : o1.getArea() == o2.getArea() ? 0 : -1);
```

Here, `o1` and `o2` are two parameters in the `compare` method in the `Comparator` interface. The method returns 1 if `o1.getArea() > o2.getArea()`, 0 if `o1.getArea() == o2.getArea()`, and −1 otherwise.

Comparable vs. Comparator
natural order
using comparator

Note

Comparing elements using the `Comparable` interface is referred to as comparing using *natural order*, and comparing elements using the `Comparator` interface is referred to as comparing using *comparator*.

The preceding example defines a comparator for comparing two geometric objects since the `GeometricObject` class does not implement the `Comparable` interface. Sometimes a class implements the `Comparable` interface, but if you would like to compare their objects using a different criteria, you can define a custom comparator. Listing 20.7 gives an example that compares string by their length.

LISTING 20.7 SortStringByLength.java

sort using comparator

```
1  public class SortStringByLength {
2    public static void main(String[] args) {
3      String[] cities = {"Atlanta", "Savannah", "New York", "Dallas"};
4      java.util.Arrays.sort(cities, new MyComparator());
5
6      for (String s : cities) {
7        System.out.print(s + " ");
8      }
9    }
```

```
10
11   public static class MyComparator implements
12       java.util.Comparator<String> {
13     @Override
14     public int compare(String s1, String s2) {
15       return s1.length() - s2.length();
16     }
17   }
18 }
```

define custom comparator

override compare method

```
Dallas Atlanta Savannah New York
```

The program defines a comparator class by implementing the `Comparator` interface (lines 11 and 12). The `compare` method is implemented to compare two strings by their lengths (lines 14–16). The program invokes the `sort` method to sort an array of strings using a comparator (line 4).

Since `Comparator` is a functional interface, the code can be simplified using a lambda expression as follows:

```
java.util.Arrays.sort(cities,
  (s1, s2) -> {return s1.length() - s2.length();});
```

or simply

```
java.util.Arrays.sort(cities,
  (s1, s2) -> s1.length() - s2.length());
```

The `List` interface defines the `sort(comparator)` method that can be used to sort the elements in a list using a specified comparator. Listing 20.8 gives an example of using a comparator to sort strings in a list by ignoring cases.

LISTING 20.8 SortStringIgnoreCase.java

```
1  public class SortStringIgnoreCase {
2    public static void main(String[] args) {
3      java.util.List<String> cities = java.util.Arrays.asList
4        ("Atlanta", "Savannah", "New York", "Dallas");
5      cities.sort((s1, s2) -> s1.compareToIgnoreCase(s2));
6
7      for (String s: cities) {
8        System.out.print(s + " ");
9      }
10   }
11 }
```

lambda comparator

```
Atlanta dallas new York Savannah
```

The program sorts a list of strings using a comparator that compares strings ignoring case (line 5). If you invoke `list.sort(null)`, the list will be sorted using its natural order.

The comparator is created using a lambda expression. Note the lambda expression here does nothing but simply invokes the `compareToIgnoreCase` method. In the case like this, you can use a simpler and clearer syntax to replace the lambda expression as follows:

```
cities.sort(String::compareToIgnoreCase);
```

Here `String::compareToIgnoreCase` is known as *method reference*, which is equivalent to a lambda expression. The compiler automatically translates a method reference to an equivalent lambda expression.

method reference

Comparator.comparing
method

The `Comparator` interface also contains several useful static methods and default methods. You can use the static `comparing(Function<? sup T, ? sup R> keyExtracter)` method to create a `Comparator<T>` that compares the elements using the key extracted from a `Function` object. The `Function` object's `apply(T)` method returns the key of type `R` for the object `T`. For example, the following code in (a) creates a `Comparator` that compares strings by their length using a lambda expression, which is equivalent to the code using an anonymous inner class in (b) and a method reference in (c).

```
Comparator.comparing(e -> e.length())
```
(a) Use a lambda expression

```
Comparator.comparing(String::length)
```
(c) Use a method reference

```
Comparator.comparing(
  new java.util.function.Function<String, Integer>() {
    public Integer apply(String s) {
      return s.length();
    }
  })
```
(b) Use an anonymous inner class

The `comparing` method in the `Comparator` interface is implemented essentially as follows for the preceding example:

```
// comparing returns a Comparator
public static Comparator<String> comparing(Function<String, Integer> f) {
  return (s1, s2) -> f.apply(s1).compareTo(f.apply(s2));
}
```

You can replace the comparator in Listing 20.7 using the following code:

```
java.util.Arrays.sort(cities, Comparator.comparing(String::length));
```

The `Comparator.comparing` method is particularly useful to create a `Comparator` using a property from an object. For example, the following code sorts a list of `Loan` objects (see Listing 10.2) based on their `loanAmount` property.

```
Loan[] list = {new Loan(5.5, 10, 2323), new Loan(5, 10, 1000)};
Arrays.sort(list, Comparator.comparing(Loan::getLoanAmount));
```

thenComparing method

You can sort using a primary criteria, second, third, and so on using the `Comparator`'s default `thenComparing` method. For example, the following code sorts a list of `Loan` objects first on their `loanAmount` then on `annualInterestRate`.

```
Loan[] list = {new Loan(5.5, 10, 100), new Loan(5, 10, 1000)};
Arrays.sort(list, Comparator.comparing(Loan::getLoanAmount)
  .thenComparing(Loan::getAnnualInterestRate));
```

The default `reverse()` method can be used to reverse the order for a comparator. For example, the following code sorts a list of `Loan` objects on their `loanAmount` property in a decreasing order.

```
Arrays.sort(list, Comparator.comparing(Loan::getLoanAmount).
  reverse());
```

Check
Point

20.6.1 What are the differences between the `Comparable` interface and the `Comparator` interface? In which package is `Comparable`, and in which package is `Comparator`?

20.6.2 How do you define a class `A` that implements the `Comparable` interface? Are two instances of class `A` comparable? How do you define a class `B` that implements the `Comparator` interface, and override the `compare` method to compare two objects of type `B1`? How do you invoke the `sort` method to sort a list of objects of the type `B1` using a comparator?

20.6.3 Write a lambda expression to create a comparator that compares two Loan objects by their annualInterestRate. Create a comparator using the Comparator.comparing method to compare Loan objects on annualInterestRate. Create a comparator to compare Loan objects first on annualInterestRate then on loanAmount.

20.6.4 Create a comparator using a lambda expression and the Comparator.comparing method, respectively, to compare Collection objects on their size.

20.6.5 Write a statement that sorts an array of Point2D objects on their *y* values and then on their *x* values.

20.6.6 Write a statement that sorts an ArrayList of strings named list in increasing order of their last character.

20.6.7 Write a statement that sorts a two-dimensional array of double[][] in increasing order of their second column. For example, if the array is double[][] x = {{3, 1}, {2, -1}, {2, 0}}, the sorted array will be {{2, -1}, {2, 0}, {3, 1}}.

20.6.8 Write a statement that sorts a two-dimensional array of double[][] in increasing order of their second column as the primary order and the first column as the secondary order. For example, if the array is double[][] x = {{3, 1}, {2, -1}, {2, 0}, {1, -1}}, the sorted array will be {{1, -1}, {2, -1}, {2, 0}, {3, 1}}.

20.7 Static Methods for Lists and Collections

The Collections class contains static methods to perform common operations in a collection and a list.

Key Point

Section 11.12 introduced several static methods in the Collections class for array lists. The Collections class contains the sort, binarySearch, reverse, shuffle, copy, and fill methods for lists and max, min, disjoint, and frequency methods for collections, as shown in Figure 20.7.

java.util.Collections	
List	
+sort(list: List): void	Sorts the specified list.
+sort(list: List, c: Comparator): void	Sorts the specified list with the comparator.
+binarySearch(list: List, key: Object): int	Searches the key in the sorted list using binary search.
+binarySearch(list: List, key: Object, c: Comparator): int	Searches the key in the sorted list using binary search with the comparator.
+reverse(list: List): void	Reverses the specified list.
+reverseOrder(): Comparator	Returns a comparator with the reverse ordering.
+shuffle(list: List): void	Shuffles the specified list randomly.
+shuffle(list: List, rmd: Random): void	Shuffles the specified list with a random object.
+copy(des: List, src: List): void	Copies from the source list to the destination list.
+nCopies(n: int, o: Object): List	Returns a list consisting of *n* copies of the object.
+fill(list: List, o: Object): void	Fills the list with the object.
Collection	
+max(c: Collection): Object	Returns the max object in the collection.
+max(c: Collection, c: Comparator): Object	Returns the max object using the comparator.
+min(c: Collection): Object	Returns the min object in the collection.
+min(c: Collection, c: Comparator): Object	Returns the min object using the comparator.
+disjoint(c1: Collection, c2: Collection): boolean	Returns true if c1 and c2 have no elements in common.
+frequency(c: Collection, o: Object): int	Returns the number of occurrences of the specified element in the collection.

FIGURE 20.7 The Collections class contains static methods for manipulating lists and collections.

sort list

You can sort the comparable elements in a list in its natural order with the `compareTo` method in the `Comparable` interface. You may also specify a comparator to sort elements. For example, the following code sorts strings in a list:

```
List<String> list = Arrays.asList("red", "green", "blue");
Collections.sort(list);
System.out.println(list);
```

The output is `[blue, green, red]`.

ascending order

descending order

The preceding code sorts a list in ascending order. To sort it in descending order, you can simply use the `Collections.reverseOrder()` method to return a `Comparator` object that orders the elements in reverse of natural order. For example, the following code sorts a list of strings in descending order:

```
List<String> list = Arrays.asList("yellow", "red", "green", "blue");
Collections.sort(list, Collections.reverseOrder());
System.out.println(list);
```

The output is `[yellow, red, green, blue]`.

binarySearch

You can use the `binarySearch` method to search for a key in a list. To use this method, the list must be sorted in increasing order. If the key is not in the list, the method returns − (*insertion point* + 1). Recall that the insertion point is where the item would fall in the list if it were present. For example, the following code searches the keys in a list of integers and a list of strings:

```
List<Integer> list1 =
    Arrays.asList(2, 4, 7, 10, 11, 45, 50, 59, 60, 66);
System.out.println("(1) Index: " + Collections.binarySearch(list1, 7));
System.out.println("(2) Index: " + Collections.binarySearch(list1, 9));

List<String> list2 = Arrays.asList("blue", "green", "red");
System.out.println("(3) Index: " +
    Collections.binarySearch(list2, "red"));
System.out.println("(4) Index: " +
    Collections.binarySearch(list2, "cyan"));
```

The output of the preceding code is:

```
(1) Index: 2
(2) Index: -4
(3) Index: 2
(4) Index: -2
```

reverse

You can use the `reverse` method to reverse the elements in a list. For example, the following code displays `[blue, green, red, yellow]`:

```
List<String> list = Arrays.asList("yellow", "red", "green", "blue");
Collections.reverse(list);
System.out.println(list);
```

shuffle

You can use the `shuffle(List)` method to randomly reorder the elements in a list. For example, the following code shuffles the elements in `list`:

```
List<String> list = Arrays.asList("yellow", "red", "green", "blue");
Collections.shuffle(list);
System.out.println(list);
```

You can also use the `shuffle(List, Random)` method to randomly reorder the elements in a list with a specified `Random` object. Using a specified `Random` object is useful to generate a list with identical sequences of elements for the same original list. For example, the following code shuffles the elements in `list`:

```
List<String> list1 = Arrays.asList("yellow", "red", "green", "blue");
List<String> list2 = Arrays.asList("yellow", "red", "green", "blue");
Collections.shuffle(list1, new Random(20));
Collections.shuffle(list2, new Random(20));
System.out.println(list1);
System.out.println(list2);
```

You will see that `list1` and `list2` have the same sequence of elements before and after the shuffling.

You can use the `copy(det, src)` method to copy all the elements from a source list to a destination list on the same index. The destination list must be as long as the source list. If it is longer, the remaining elements in the source list are not affected. For example, the following code copies `list2` to `list1`:

copy

```
List<String> list1 = Arrays.asList("yellow", "red", "green", "blue");
List<String> list2 = Arrays.asList("white", "black");
Collections.copy(list1, list2);
System.out.println(list1);
```

The output for `list1` is `[white, black, green, blue]`. The `copy` method performs a shallow copy: Only the references of the elements from the source list are copied.

You can use the `nCopies(int n, Object o)` method to create an immutable list that consists of n copies of the specified object. For example, the following code creates a list with five `Calendar` objects:

nCopies

```
List<GregorianCalendar> list1 = Collections.nCopies
    (5, new GregorianCalendar(2005, 0, 1));
```

The list created from the `nCopies` method is immutable, so you cannot add, remove, or update elements in the list. All the elements have the same references.

You can use the `fill(List list, Object o)` method to replace all the elements in the list with the specified element. For example, the following code displays `[black, black, black]`:

fill

```
List<String> list = Arrays.asList("red", "green", "blue");
Collections.fill(list, "black");
System.out.println(list);
```

max and min methods

You can use the `max` and `min` methods for finding the maximum and minimum elements in a collection. The elements must be comparable using the `Comparable` interface or the `Comparator` interface. See the following code for examples:

```
Collection<String> collection = Arrays.asList("red", "green", "blue");
System.out.println(Collections.max(collection));     // Use Comparable
System.out.println(Collections.min(collection,
        Comparator.comparing(String::length)));   // Use Comparator
```

The `disjoint(collection1, collection2)` method returns `true` if the two collections have no elements in common. For example, in the following code, `disjoint(collection1, collection2)` returns `false`, but `disjoint(collection1, collection3)` returns `true`:

disjoint method

```
Collection<String> collection1 = Arrays.asList("red", "cyan");
Collection<String> collection2 = Arrays.asList("red", "blue");
Collection<String> collection3 = Arrays.asList("pink", "tan");
System.out.println(Collections.disjoint(collection1, collection2));
System.out.println(Collections.disjoint(collection1, collection3));
```

frequency method

The `frequency(collection, element)` method finds the number of occurrences of the element in the collection. For example, `frequency(collection, "red")` returns 2 in the following code:

```
Collection<String> collection = Arrays.asList("red", "cyan", "red");
System.out.println(Collections.frequency(collection, "red"));
```

20.7.1 Are all the methods in the `Collections` class static?

20.7.2 Which of the following static methods in the `Collections` class are for lists and which are for collections?

sort, binarySearch, reverse, shuffle, max, min, disjoint, frequency

20.7.3 Show the output of the following code:

```
import java.util.*;

public class Test {
  public static void main(String[] args) {
    List<String> list =
      Arrays.asList("yellow", "red", "green", "blue");
    Collections.reverse(list);
    System.out.println(list);

    List<String> list1 =
      Arrays.asList("yellow", "red", "green", "blue");
    List<String> list2 = Arrays.asList("white", "black");
    Collections.copy(list1, list2);
    System.out.println(list1);

    Collection<String> c1 = Arrays.asList("red", "cyan");
    Collection<String> c2 = Arrays.asList("red", "blue");
    Collection<String> c3 = Arrays.asList("pink", "tan");
    System.out.println(Collections.disjoint(c1, c2));
    System.out.println(Collections.disjoint(c1, c3));

    Collection<String> collection =
      Arrays.asList("red", "cyan", "red");
    System.out.println(Collections.frequency(collection, "red"));
  }
}
```

20.7.4 Which method can you use to sort the elements in an `ArrayList` or a `LinkedList`? Which method can you use to sort an array of strings?

20.7.5 Which method can you use to perform binary search for elements in an `ArrayList` or a `LinkedList`? Which method can you use to perform binary search for an array of strings?

20.7.6 Write a statement to find the largest element in an array of comparable objects.

20.8 Case Study: Bouncing Balls

This section presents a program that displays bouncing balls and enables the user to add and remove balls.

Section 15.12 presents a program that displays one bouncing ball. This section presents a program that displays multiple bouncing balls. You can use two buttons to suspend and resume the movement of the balls, a scroll bar to control the ball speed, and the + or − button to add or remove a ball, as shown in Figure 20.8.

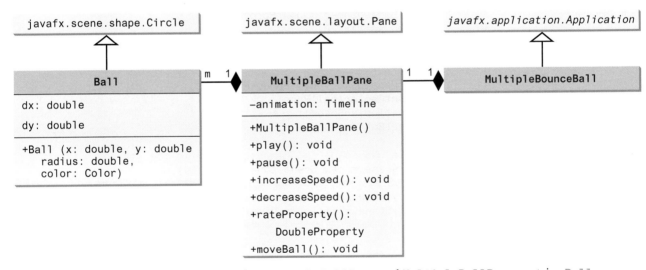

FIGURE 20.8 Pressing the + or − button adds or removes a ball. *Source*: Copyright © 1995–2016 Oracle and/or its affiliates. All rights reserved. Used with permission.

The example in Section 15.12 only had to store one ball. How do you store multiple balls in this example? The `Pane`'s `getChildren()` method returns an `ObservableList<Node>`, a subtype of `List<Node>`, for storing the nodes in the pane. Initially, the list is empty. When a new ball is created, add it to the end of the list. To remove a ball, simply remove the last one in the list.

Each ball has its state: the *x*-, *y*-coordinates, color, and direction to move. You can define a class named `Ball` that extends `javafx.scene.shape.Circle`. The *x*-, *y*-coordinates and the color are already defined in `Circle`. When a ball is created, it starts from the upper-left corner and moves downward to the right. A random color is assigned to a new ball.

The `MultiplBallPane` class is responsible for displaying the ball and the `MultipleBounceBall` class places the control components and implements the control. The relationship of these classes is shown in Figure 20.9. Listing 20.9 gives the program.

```
┌──────────────────────────────┐   ┌──────────────────────────────┐   ┌────────────────────────────────────┐
│ javafx.scene.shape.Circle    │   │ javafx.scene.layout.Pane     │   │ javafx.application.Application     │
└──────────────────────────────┘   └──────────────────────────────┘   └────────────────────────────────────┘
              △                                 △                                      △
              │                                 │                                      │
┌──────────────────────────┐  m 1 ┌──────────────────────────┐ 1  1 ┌──────────────────────────────┐
│          Ball            │──────◆│    MultipleBallPane      │◆─────│    MultipleBounceBall        │
├──────────────────────────┤      ├──────────────────────────┤      └──────────────────────────────┘
│ dx: double               │      │ −animation: Timeline     │
│ dy: double               │      ├──────────────────────────┤
├──────────────────────────┤      │ +MultipleBallPane()      │
│ +Ball (x: double, y: double│     │ +play(): void            │
│    radius: double,       │      │ +pause(): void           │
│    color: Color)         │      │ +increaseSpeed(): void   │
└──────────────────────────┘      │ +decreaseSpeed(): void   │
                                  │ +rateProperty():         │
                                  │     DoubleProperty       │
                                  │ +moveBall(): void        │
                                  └──────────────────────────┘
```

FIGURE 20.9 `MultipleBounceBall` contains `MultipleBallPane` and `MultipleBallPane` contains `Ball`.

LISTING 20.9 MultipleBounceBall.java

```java
1  import javafx.animation.KeyFrame;
2  import javafx.animation.Timeline;
3  import javafx.application.Application;
4  import javafx.beans.property.DoubleProperty;
5  import javafx.geometry.Pos;
6  import javafx.scene.Node;
7  import javafx.stage.Stage;
8  import javafx.scene.Scene;
9  import javafx.scene.control.Button;
10 import javafx.scene.control.ScrollBar;
11 import javafx.scene.layout.BorderPane;
12 import javafx.scene.layout.HBox;
```

```
13  import javafx.scene.layout.Pane;
14  import javafx.scene.paint.Color;
15  import javafx.scene.shape.Circle;
16  import javafx.util.Duration;
17
18  public class MultipleBounceBall extends Application {
19    @Override // Override the start method in the Application class
20    public void start(Stage primaryStage) {
21      MultipleBallPane ballPane = new MultipleBallPane();
22      ballPane.setStyle("-fx-border-color: yellow");
23
24      Button btAdd = new Button("+");
25      Button btSubtract = new Button("-");
26      HBox hBox = new HBox(10);
27      hBox.getChildren().addAll(btAdd, btSubtract);
28      hBox.setAlignment(Pos.CENTER);
29
30      // Add or remove a ball
31      btAdd.setOnAction(e -> ballPane.add());
32      btSubtract.setOnAction(e -> ballPane.subtract());
33
34      // Pause and resume animation
35      ballPane.setOnMousePressed(e -> ballPane.pause());
36      ballPane.setOnMouseReleased(e -> ballPane.play());
37
38      // Use a scroll bar to control animation speed
39      ScrollBar sbSpeed = new ScrollBar();
40      sbSpeed.setMax(20);
41      sbSpeed.setValue(10);
42      ballPane.rateProperty().bind(sbSpeed.valueProperty());
43
44      BorderPane pane = new BorderPane();
45      pane.setCenter(ballPane);
46      pane.setTop(sbSpeed);
47      pane.setBottom(hBox);
48
49      // Create a scene and place the pane in the stage
50      Scene scene = new Scene(pane, 250, 150);
51      primaryStage.setTitle("MultipleBounceBall"); // Set the stage title
52      primaryStage.setScene(scene); // Place the scene in the stage
53      primaryStage.show(); // Display the stage
54    }
55
56    private class MultipleBallPane extends Pane {
57      private Timeline animation;
58
59      public MultipleBallPane() {
60        // Create an animation for moving the ball
61        animation = new Timeline(
62          new KeyFrame(Duration.millis(50), e -> moveBall()));
63        animation.setCycleCount(Timeline.INDEFINITE);
64        animation.play(); // Start animation
65      }
66
67      public void add() {
68        Color color = new Color(Math.random(),
69          Math.random(), Math.random(), 0.5);
70        getChildren().add(new Ball(30, 30, 20,color));
71      }
72
```

Margin notes (left column):

create a ball pane
set ball pane border

create buttons

add buttons to HBox

add a ball
remove a ball

pause animation
resume animation

create a scroll bar

bind animation rate

add a ball to pane

```
73        public void subtract() {
74          if (getChildren().size() > 0) {
75            getChildren().remove(getChildren().size() - 1);        remove a ball
76          }
77        }
78
79        public void play() {
80          animation.play();
81        }
82
83        public void pause() {
84          animation.pause();
85        }
86
87        public void increaseSpeed() {
88          animation.setRate(animation.getRate() + 0.1);
89        }
90
91        public void decreaseSpeed() {
92          animation.setRate(
93            animation.getRate() > 0 ? animation.getRate() - 0.1 : 0);
94        }
95
96        public DoubleProperty rateProperty() {
97          return animation.rateProperty();
98        }
99
100       protected void moveBall() {
101         for (Node node: this.getChildren()) {                    move all balls
102           Ball ball = (Ball)node;
103           // Check boundaries
104           if (ball.getCenterX() < ball.getRadius() ||
105               ball.getCenterX() > getWidth() - ball.getRadius()) {
106             ball.dx *= -1; // Change ball move direction             change x-direction
107           }
108           if (ball.getCenterY() < ball.getRadius() ||
109               ball.getCenterY() > getHeight() - ball.getRadius()) {
110             ball.dy *= -1; // Change ball move direction             change y-direction
111           }
112
113           // Adjust ball position
114           ball.setCenterX(ball.dx + ball.getCenterX());            adjust ball positions
115           ball.setCenterY(ball.dy + ball.getCenterY());
116         }
117       }
118     }
119
120     class Ball extends Circle {
121       private double dx = 1, dy = 1;                              declare dx and dy
122
123       Ball(double x, double y, double radius, Color color) {      create a ball
124         super(x, y, radius);
125         setFill(color); // Set ball color
126       }
127     }
128   }
```

The `add()` method creates a new ball with a random color and adds it to the pane (line 70). The pane stores all the balls in a list. The `subtract()` method removes the last ball in the list (line 75).

When the user clicks the + button, a new ball is added to the pane (line 31). When the user clicks the − button, the last ball in the array list is removed (line 32).

The `moveBall()` method in the `MultipleBallPane` class gets every ball in the pane's list and adjusts the balls' positions (lines 114 and 115).

20.8.1 What is the return value from invoking `pane.getChildren()` for a pane?

20.8.2 How do you modify the code in the `MutilpleBallApp` program to remove the first ball in the list when the − button is clicked?

20.8.3 How do you modify the code in the `MutilpleBallApp` program so each ball will get a random radius between 10 and 20?

20.9 Vector and Stack Classes

Vector is a subclass of AbstractList and Stack is a subclass of Vector in the Java API.

The Java Collections Framework was introduced in Java 2. Several data structures were supported earlier, among them the `Vector` and `Stack` classes. These classes were redesigned to fit into the Java Collections Framework, but all their old-style methods are retained for compatibility.

`Vector` is the same as `ArrayList`, except that it contains synchronized methods for accessing and modifying the vector. Synchronized methods can prevent data corruption when a vector is accessed and modified by two or more threads concurrently. We will discuss synchronization in Chapter 32, Multithreading and Parallel Programming. For the many applications that do not require synchronization, using `ArrayList` is more efficient than using `Vector`.

The `Vector` class extends the `AbstractList` class. It also has the methods contained in the original `Vector` class defined prior to Java 2, as shown in Figure 20.10.

```
java.util.AbstractList<E>
          △
          |
     java.util.Vector<E>
```

+Vector()	Creates a default empty vector with initial capacity 10.
+Vector(c: Collection<? extends E>)	Creates a vector from an existing collection.
+Vector(initialCapacity: int)	Creates a vector with the specified initial capacity.
+Vector(initCapacity: int, capacityIncr: int)	Creates a vector with the specified initial capacity and increment.
+addElement(o: E): void	Appends the element to the end of this vector.
+capacity(): int	Returns the current capacity of this vector.
+copyInto(anArray: Object[]): void	Copies the elements in this vector to the array.
+elementAt(index: int): E	Returns the object at the specified index.
+elements(): Enumeration<E>	Returns an enumeration of this vector.
+ensureCapacity(): void	Increases the capacity of this vector.
+firstElement(): E	Returns the first element in this vector.
+insertElementAt(o: E, index: int): void	Inserts o into this vector at the specified index.
+lastElement(): E	Returns the last element in this vector.
+removeAllElements(): void	Removes all the elements in this vector.
+removeElement(o: Object): boolean	Removes the first matching element in this vector.
+removeElementAt(index: int): void	Removes the element at the specified index.
+setElementAt(o: E, index: int): void	Sets a new element at the specified index.
+setSize(newSize: int): void	Sets a new size in this vector.
+trimToSize(): void	Trims the capacity of this vector to its size.

FIGURE 20.10 Starting in Java 2, the `Vector` class extends `AbstractList` and also retains all the methods in the original `Vector` class.

Most of the methods in the `Vector` class listed in the UML diagram in Figure 20.10 are similar to the methods in the `List` interface. These methods were introduced before the Java Collections Framework. For example, `addElement(Object element)` is the same as the `add(Object element)` method, except that the `addElement` method is synchronized. Use the `ArrayList` class if you don't need synchronization. It works much faster than `Vector`.

Note

The `elements()` method returns an `Enumeration`. The `Enumeration` interface was introduced prior to Java 2 and was superseded by the `Iterator` interface.

Note

`Vector` is widely used in Java legacy code because it was the Java resizable-array implementation before Java 2.

In the Java Collections Framework, `Stack` is implemented as an extension of `Vector`, as illustrated in Figure 20.11.

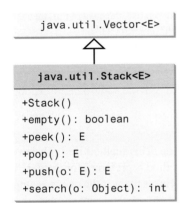

+Stack()	Creates an empty stack.
+empty(): boolean	Returns true if this stack is empty.
+peek(): E	Returns the top element in this stack.
+pop(): E	Returns and removes the top element in this stack.
+push(o: E): E	Adds a new element to the top of this stack.
+search(o: Object): int	Returns the position of the specified element in this stack.

FIGURE 20.11 The `Stack` class extends `Vector` to provide a last-in, first-out data structure.

The `Stack` class was introduced prior to Java 2. The methods shown in Figure 20.11 were used before Java 2. The `empty()` method is the same as `isEmpty()`. The `peek()` method looks at the element at the top of the stack without removing it. The `pop()` method removes the top element from the stack and returns it. The `push(Object element)` method adds the specified element to the stack. The `search(Object element)` method checks whether the specified element is in the stack.

20.9.1 How do you create an instance of `Vector`? How do you add or insert a new element into a vector? How do you remove an element from a vector? How do you find the size of a vector?

20.9.2 How do you create an instance of `Stack`? How do you add a new element to a stack? How do you remove an element from a stack? How do you find the size of a stack?

20.9.3 Does Listing 20.1, TestCollection.java, compile and run if all the occurrences of `ArrayList` are replaced by `LinkedList`, `Vector`, or `Stack`?

Check Point

20.10 Queues and Priority Queues

In a priority queue, the element with the highest priority is removed first.

Key Point

A *queue* is a first-in, first-out data structure. Elements are appended to the end of the queue and are removed from the beginning of the queue. In a *priority queue*, elements are assigned priorities. When accessing elements, the element with the highest priority is removed first. This section introduces queues and priority queues in the Java API.

queue
priority queue

20.10.1 The Queue Interface

The Queue interface extends `java.util.Collection` with additional insertion, extraction, and inspection operations, as shown in Figure 20.12.

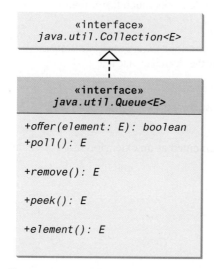

«interface» java.util.Queue\<E>	
+offer(element: E): boolean	Inserts an element into the queue.
+poll(): E	Retrieves and removes the head of this queue, or null if this queue is empty.
+remove(): E	Retrieves and removes the head of this queue and throws an exception if this queue is empty.
+peek(): E	Retrieves, but does not remove, the head of this queue, returning null if this queue is empty.
+element(): E	Retrieves, but does not remove, the head of this queue, throws an exception if this queue is empty.

FIGURE 20.12 The Queue interface extends Collection to provide additional insertion, extraction, and inspection operations.

The offer method is used to add an element to the queue. This method is similar to the add method in the Collection interface, but the offer method is preferred for queues. The poll and remove methods are similar, except that poll() returns null if the queue is empty, whereas remove() throws an exception. The peek and element methods are similar, except that peek() returns null if the queue is empty, whereas element() throws an exception.

20.10.2 Deque and LinkedList

The LinkedList class implements the Deque interface, which extends the Queue interface, as shown in Figure 20.13. Therefore, you can use LinkedList to create a queue. LinkedList is ideal for queue operations because it is efficient for inserting and removing elements from both ends of a list.

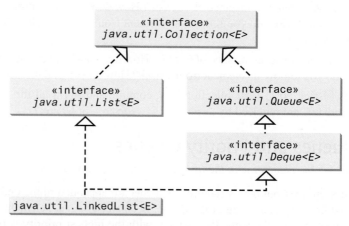

FIGURE 20.13 LinkedList implements List and Deque.

`Deque` supports element insertion and removal at both ends. The name *deque* is short for "double-ended queue" and is usually pronounced "deck." The `Deque` interface extends `Queue` with additional methods for inserting and removing elements from both ends of the queue. The methods `addFirst(e)`, `removeFirst()`, `addLast(e)`, `removeLast()`, `getFirst()`, and `getLast()` are defined in the `Deque` interface.

Listing 20.10 shows an example of using a queue to store strings. Line 3 creates a queue using `LinkedList`. Four strings are added to the queue in lines 4–7. The `size()` method defined in the `Collection` interface returns the number of elements in the queue (line 9). The `remove()` method retrieves and removes the element at the head of the queue (line 10).

LISTING 20.10   `TestQueue.java`

```
 1  public class TestQueue {
 2    public static void main(String[] args) {
 3      java.util.Queue<String> queue = new java.util.LinkedList<>();   creates a queue
 4      queue.offer("Oklahoma");                                        inserts an element
 5      queue.offer("Indiana");
 6      queue.offer("Georgia");
 7      queue.offer("Texas");
 8
 9      while (queue.size() > 0)                                        queue size
10        System.out.print(queue.remove() + " ");                      remove element
11    }
12  }
```

```
Oklahoma Indiana Georgia Texas
```

The `PriorityQueue` class implements a priority queue, as shown in Figure 20.14. By default, the priority queue orders its elements according to their natural ordering using `Comparable`. The element with the least value is assigned the highest priority, and thus is removed from the queue first. If there are several elements with the same highest priority, the tie is broken arbitrarily. You can also specify an ordering using `Comparator` in the constructor `PriorityQueue(initialCapacity, comparator)`.

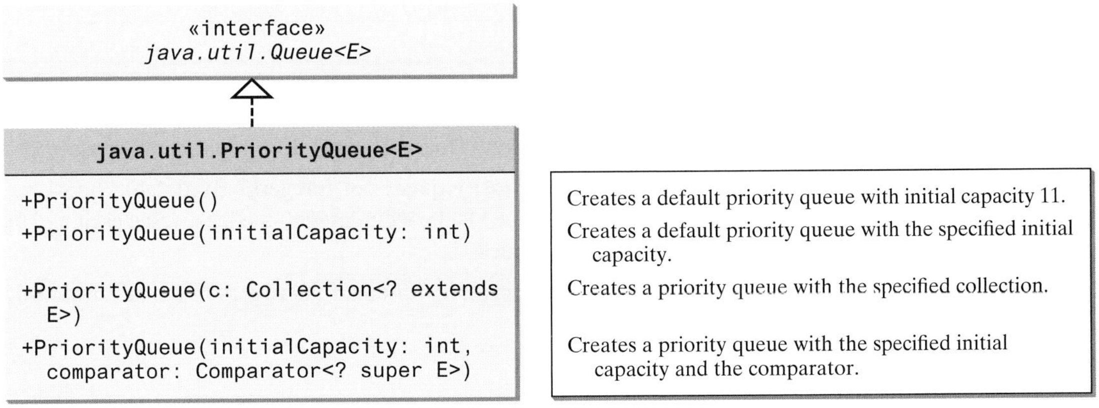

PriorityQueue class

«interface» *java.util.Queue<E>*

△

java.util.PriorityQueue<E>
+PriorityQueue()
+PriorityQueue(initialCapacity: int)
+PriorityQueue(c: Collection<? extends E>)
+PriorityQueue(initialCapacity: int, comparator: Comparator<? super E>)

Creates a default priority queue with initial capacity 11.

Creates a default priority queue with the specified initial capacity.

Creates a priority queue with the specified collection.

Creates a priority queue with the specified initial capacity and the comparator.

FIGURE 20.14   The `PriorityQueue` class implements a priority queue.

Listing 20.11 shows an example of using a priority queue to store strings. Line 5 creates a priority queue for strings using its no-arg constructor. This priority queue orders the strings using their natural order, so the strings are removed from the queue in increasing order. Lines 16 and 17 create a priority queue using the comparator obtained from `Collections.reverseOrder()`, which orders the elements in reverse order, so the strings are removed from the queue in decreasing order.

LISTING 20.11 `PriorityQueueDemo.java`

```
1   import java.util.*;
2
3   public class PriorityQueueDemo {
4     public static void main(String[] args) {
5       PriorityQueue<String> queue1 = new PriorityQueue<>();
6       queue1.offer("Oklahoma");
7       queue1.offer("Indiana");
8       queue1.offer("Georgia");
9       queue1.offer("Texas");
10
11      System.out.println("Priority queue using Comparable:");
12      while (queue1.size() > 0) {
13        System.out.print(queue1.remove() + " ");
14      }
15
16      PriorityQueue<String> queue2 = new PriorityQueue<>(
17        4, Collections.reverseOrder());
18      queue2.offer("Oklahoma");
19      queue2.offer("Indiana");
20      queue2.offer("Georgia");
21      queue2.offer("Texas");
22
23      System.out.println("\nPriority queue using Comparator:");
24      while (queue2.size() > 0) {
25        System.out.print(queue2.remove() + " ");
26      }
27    }
28  }
```

a default queue
inserts an element

a queue with comparator

```
Priority queue using Comparable:
Georgia Indiana Oklahoma Texas
Priority queue using Comparator:
Texas Oklahoma Indiana Georgia
```

**Check
Point**

20.10.1 Is `java.util.Queue` a subinterface of `java.util.Collection`, `java.util.Set`, or `java.util.List`? Does `LinkedList` implement `Queue`?

20.10.2 How do you create a priority queue for integers? By default, how are elements ordered in a priority queue? Is the element with the least value assigned the highest priority in a priority queue?

20.10.3 How do you create a priority queue that reverses the natural order of the elements?

20.11 Case Study: Evaluating Expressions

Stacks can be used to evaluate expressions.

Stacks and queues have many applications. This section gives an application that uses stacks to evaluate expressions. You can enter an arithmetic expression from Google to evaluate the expression, as shown in Figure 20.15.

Key Point

FIGURE 20.15 You can evaluate an arithmetic expression using a Google search engine. *Source*: Google and the Google logo are registered trademarks of Google Inc., used with permission.

How does Google evaluate an expression? This section presents a program that evaluates a *compound expression* with multiple operators and parentheses (e.g., (15 + 2) * 34 − 2). For simplicity, assume the operands are integers, and the operators are of four types: +, −, *, and /.

compound expression

The problem can be solved using two stacks, named `operandStack` and `operator-Stack`, for storing operands and operators, respectively. Operands and operators are pushed into the stacks before they are processed. When an *operator is processed*, it is popped from `operatorStack` and applied to the first two operands from `operandStack` (the two operands are popped from `operandStack`). The resultant value is pushed back to `operandStack`.

process an operator

The algorithm proceeds in two phases:

Phase 1: Scanning the expression
The program scans the expression from left to right to extract operands, operators, and the parentheses.

    1.1. If the extracted item is an operand, push it to `operandStack`.

    1.2. If the extracted item is a + or − operator, process all the operators at the top of `operatorStack` and push the extracted operator to `operatorStack`.

    1.3. If the extracted item is a * or / operator, process the * or / operators at the top of `operatorStack` and push the extracted operator to `operatorStack`.

    1.4. If the extracted item is a (symbol, push it to `operatorStack`.

    1.5. If the extracted item is a) symbol, repeatedly process the operators from the top of `operatorStack` until seeing the (symbol on the stack.

Phase 2: Clearing the stack

Repeatedly process the operators from the top of `operatorStack` until `operatorStack` is empty.

Table 20.1 shows how the algorithm is applied to evaluate the expression (1 + 2) * 4 − 3.

TABLE 20.1 Evaluating an Expression

Expression	Scan	Action	operandStack	operatorStack
(1 + 2) * 4 − 3 ↑	(	Phase 1.4		(
(1 + 2) * 4 − 3 ↑	1	Phase 1.1	1	(
(1 + 2) * 4 − 3 ↑	+	Phase 1.2	1	+ (
(1 + 2) * 4 − 3 ↑	2	Phase 1.1	2 1	(
(1 + 2) * 4 − 3 ↑	)	Phase 1.5	3	
(1 + 2) * 4 − 3 ↑	*	Phase 1.3	3	*
(1 + 2) * 4 − 3 ↑	4	Phase 1.1	4 3	*
(1 + 2) * 4 − 3 ↑	−	Phase 1.2	12	-
(1 + 2) * 4 − 3 ↑	3	Phase 1.1	3 12	-
(1 + 2) * 4 − 3 ↑	none	Phase 2	9	

Listing 20.12 gives the program, and Figure 20.16 shows some sample output.

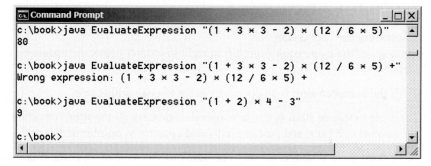

FIGURE 20.16 The program takes an expression as command-line arguments. *Source:* Copyright © 1995–2016 Oracle and/or its affiliates. All rights reserved. Used with permission.

LISTING 20.12 EvaluateExpression.java

```
1  import java.util.Stack;
2
3  public class EvaluateExpression {
4    public static void main(String[] args) {
```

```
5        // Check number of arguments passed
6        if (args.length != 1) {                                         check usage
7          System.out.println(
8            "Usage: java EvaluateExpression \"expression\"");
9          System.exit(1);
10       }
11
12       try {
13         System.out.println(evaluateExpression(args[0]));              evaluate expression
14       }
15       catch (Exception ex) {
16         System.out.println("Wrong expression: " + args[0]);          exception
17       }
18     }
19
20     /** Evaluate an expression */
21     public static int evaluateExpression(String expression) {
22       // Create operandStack to store operands
23       Stack<Integer> operandStack = new Stack<>();                    operandStack
24
25       // Create operatorStack to store operators
26       Stack<Character> operatorStack = new Stack<>();                 operatorStack
27
28       // Insert blanks around (, ), +, -, /, and *
29       expression = insertBlanks(expression);                          prepare for extraction
30
31       // Extract operands and operators
32       String[] tokens = expression.split(" ");                       extract tokens
33
34       // Phase 1: Scan tokens
35       for (String token: tokens) {                                   process tokens
36         if (token.length() == 0) // Blank space
37           continue; // Back to the while loop to extract the next token
38         else if (token.charAt(0) == '+' || token.charAt(0) == '-') { + or - scanned
39           // Process all +, -, *, / in the top of the operator stack
40           while (!operatorStack.isEmpty() &&
41             (operatorStack.peek() == '+' ||
42              operatorStack.peek() == '-' ||
43              operatorStack.peek() == '*' ||
44              operatorStack.peek() == '/')) {
45             processAnOperator(operandStack, operatorStack);
46           }
47
48           // Push the + or - operator into the operator stack
49           operatorStack.push(token.charAt(0));
50         }
51         else if (token.charAt(0) == '*' || token.charAt(0) == '/') { * or / scanned
52           // Process all *, / in the top of the operator stack
53           while (!operatorStack.isEmpty() &&
54             (operatorStack.peek() == '*' ||
55              operatorStack.peek() == '/')) {
56             processAnOperator(operandStack, operatorStack);
57           }
58
59           // Push the * or / operator into the operator stack
60           operatorStack.push(token.charAt(0));
61         }
62         else if(token.trim().charAt(0) =='(') {                      ( scanned
63           operatorStack.push('('); // Push '(' to stack
64         }
```

```
65        else if (token.trim().charAt(0) ==')') {
66          // Process all the operators in the stack until seeing '('
67          while (operatorStack.peek() != '(') {
68            processAnOperator(operandStack, operatorStack);
69          }
70
71          operatorStack.pop(); // Pop the '(' symbol from the stack
72        }
73        else {  // An operand scanned
74          // Push an operand to the stack
75          operandStack.push(new Integer(token));
76        }
77      }
78
79      // Phase 2: Process all the remaining operators in the stack
80      while (!operatorStack.isEmpty()) {
81        processAnOperator(operandStack, operatorStack);
82      }
83
84      // Return the result
85      return operandStack.pop();
86    }
87
88    /** Process one operator: Take an operator from operatorStack and
89     *  apply it on the operands in the operandStack */
90    public static void processAnOperator(
91        Stack<Integer> operandStack, Stack<Character> operatorStack) {
92      char op = operatorStack.pop();
93      int op1 = operandStack.pop();
94      int op2 = operandStack.pop();
95      if (op == '+')
96        operandStack.push(op2 + op1);
97      else if (op == '-')
98        operandStack.push(op2 - op1);
99      else if (op == '*')
100       operandStack.push(op2 * op1);
101     else if (op == '/')
102       operandStack.push(op2 / op1);
103   }
104
105   public static String insertBlanks(String s) {
106     String result = "";
107
108     for (int i = 0; i < s.length(); i++) {
109       if (s.charAt(i) == '(' || s.charAt(i) == ')' ||
110           s.charAt(i) == '+' || s.charAt(i) == '-' ||
111           s.charAt(i) == '*' || s.charAt(i) == '/')
112         result += " " + s.charAt(i) + " ";
113       else
114         result += s.charAt(i);
115     }
116
117     return result;
118   }
119 }
```

Marginal notes (left column):
-) scanned (line 65)
- an operand scanned (line 75)
- clear operatorStack (line 80)
- return result (line 85)
- process + (line 95)
- process − (line 97)
- process * (line 99)
- process / (line 101)
- insert blanks (line 105)

You can use the GenericStack class provided by the book, or the java.util.Stack class defined in the Java API for creating stacks. This example uses the java.util.Stack class. The program will work if it is replaced by GenericStack.

The program takes an expression as a command-line argument in one string.

The `evaluateExpression` method creates two stacks, `operandStack` and `operatorStack` (lines 23 and 26), and extracts operands, operators, and parentheses delimited by space (lines 29–32). The `insertBlanks` method is used to ensure that operands, operators, and parentheses are separated by at least one blank (line 29).

The program scans each token in the `for` loop (lines 35–77). If a token is empty, skip it (line 37). If a token is an operand, push it to `operandStack` (line 75). If a token is a + or − operator (line 38), process all the operators from the top of `operatorStack`, if any (lines 40–46), and push the newly scanned operator into the stack (line 49). If a token is a * or / operator (line 51), process all the * and / operators from the top of `operatorStack`, if any (lines 53–57), and push the newly scanned operator to the stack (line 60). If a token is a (symbol (line 62), push it into `operatorStack`. If a token is a) symbol (line 65), process all the operators from the top of `operatorStack` until seeing the) symbol (lines 67–69) and pop the) symbol from the stack.

After all tokens are considered, the program processes the remaining operators in `operatorStack` (lines 80–82).

The `processAnOperator` method (lines 90–103) processes an operator. The method pops the operator from `operatorStack` (line 92) and pops two operands from `operandStack` (lines 93 and 94). Depending on the operator, the method performs an operation and pushes the result of the operation back to `operandStack` (lines 96, 98, 100, and 102).

20.11.1 Can the `EvaluateExpression` program evaluate the following expressions `"1 + 2"`, `"1 + 2"`, `"(1) + 2"`, `"((1)) + 2"`, and `"(1 + 2)"`?

20.11.2 Show the change of the contents in the stacks when evaluating `"3 + (4 + 5) * (3 + 5) + 4 * 5"` using the `EvaluateExpression` program.

20.11.3 If you enter an expression `"4 + 5 5 5"`, the program will display 10. How do you fix this problem?

KEY TERMS

CHAPTER SUMMARY

1. The `Collection` interface defines the common operations for lists, vectors, stacks, queues, priority queues, and sets.

2. Each collection is `Iterable`. You can obtain its `Iterator` object to traverse all the elements in the collection.

3. All the concrete classes except `PriorityQueue` in the Java Collections Framework implement the `Cloneable` and `Serializable` interfaces. Thus, their instances can be cloned and serialized.

4. A list stores an ordered collection of elements. To allow duplicate elements to be stored in a collection, you need to use a list. A list not only can store duplicate elements but also allows the user to specify where they are stored. The user can access elements by an index.

5. Two types of lists are supported: `ArrayList` and `LinkedList`. `ArrayList` is a resizable-array implementation of the `List` interface. All the methods in `ArrayList` are defined in `List`. `LinkedList` is a *linked-list* implementation of the `List` interface. In addition to implementing the `List` interface, this class provides the methods for retrieving, inserting, and removing elements from both ends of the list.

6. `Comparator` can be used to compare the objects of a class that doesn't implement `Comparable`.

7. The `Vector` class extends the `AbstractList` class. Starting with Java 2, `Vector` has been the same as `ArrayList`, except that the methods for accessing and modifying the vector are synchronized. The `Stack` class extends the `Vector` class and provides several methods for manipulating the stack.

8. The `Queue` interface represents a queue. The `PriorityQueue` class implements `Queue` for a *priority queue*.

QUIZ

Answer the quiz for this chapter online at the book Companion Website.

MyProgrammingLab™ ## PROGRAMMING EXERCISES

Sections 20.2–20.7

*20.1 (*Display words in ascending alphabetical order*) Write a program that reads words from a text file and displays all the words (duplicates allowed) in ascending alphabetical order. The words must start with a letter. The text file is passed as a command-line argument.

*20.2 (*Store numbers in a linked list*) Write a program that lets the user enter numbers from a graphical user interface and displays them in a text area, as shown in Figure 20.17a. Use a linked list to store the numbers. Do not store duplicate numbers. Add the buttons *Sort*, *Shuffle*, and *Reverse* to sort, shuffle, and reverse the list.

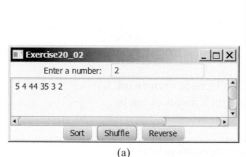

(a)

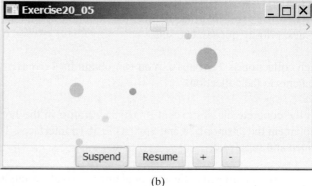

(b)

FIGURE 20.17 (a) The numbers are stored in a list and displayed in the text area. *Source*: Copyright © 1995–2016 Oracle and/or its affiliates. All rights reserved. Used with permission. (b) The colliding balls are combined.

*20.3 (*Guessing the capitals*) Rewrite Programming Exercise 8.37 to store the pairs of states and capitals so that the questions are displayed randomly.

*20.4 (*Sort points in a plane*) Write a program that meets the following requirements. Randomly create `100` points using `Point2D` and apply the `Arrays.sort(list, Comparator)` method to sort the points in increasing order of their *y*-coordinates and then in increasing order of their *x*-coordinates. Display the *x*- and *y*-coordinates of the first five points.

***20.5 (*Combine colliding bouncing balls*) The example in Section 20.8 displays multiple bouncing balls. Extend the example to detect collisions. Once two balls collide, remove the later ball that was added to the pane and add its radius to the other ball, as shown in Figure 20.17b. Use the *Suspend* button to suspend the animation, and the *Resume* button to resume the animation. Add a mouse-pressed handler that removes a ball when the mouse is pressed on the ball.

20.6 (*Use iterators on linked lists*) Write a test program that stores 5 million integers in a linked list and test the time to traverse the list using an `iterator` vs. using the `get(index)` method.

***20.7 (*Game: hangman*) Programming Exercise 7.35 presents a console version of the popular hangman game. Write a GUI program that lets a user play the game. The user guesses a word by entering one letter at a time, as shown in Figure 20.18. If the user misses seven times, a hanging man swings. Once a word is finished, the user can press the *Enter* key to continue to guess another word.

**20.8 (*Game: lottery*) Revise Programming Exercise 3.15 to add an additional $2,000 award if two digits from the user input are in the lottery number. (*Hint*: Sort the three digits in the lottery number and three digits in the user input into two lists, and use the `Collection`'s `containsAll` method to check whether the two digits in the user input are in the lottery number.)

Sections 20.8–20.10

***20.9 (*Remove the largest ball first*) Modify Listing 20.10, `MultipleBallApp.java` to assign a random radius between 2 and 20 when a ball is created. When the − button is clicked, one of largest balls is removed.

20.10 (*Perform set operations on priority queues*) Create two priority queues, `{"George", "Jim", "John", "Blake", "Kevin", "Michael"}` and `{"George", "Katie", "Kevin", "Michelle", "Ryan"}` and find their union, difference, and intersection.

*20.11 (*Match grouping symbols*) A Java program contains various pairs of grouping symbols, such as:

■ Parentheses: (and)
■ Braces: { and }
■ Brackets: [and]

Note the grouping symbols cannot overlap. For example, `(a{b})` is illegal. Write a program to check whether a Java source-code file has correct pairs of grouping symbols. Pass the source-code file name as a command-line argument.

20.12 (*Clone `PriorityQueue`*) Define `MyPriorityQueue` class that extends `PriorityQueue` to implement the `Cloneable` interface and implement the `clone()` method to clone a priority queue.

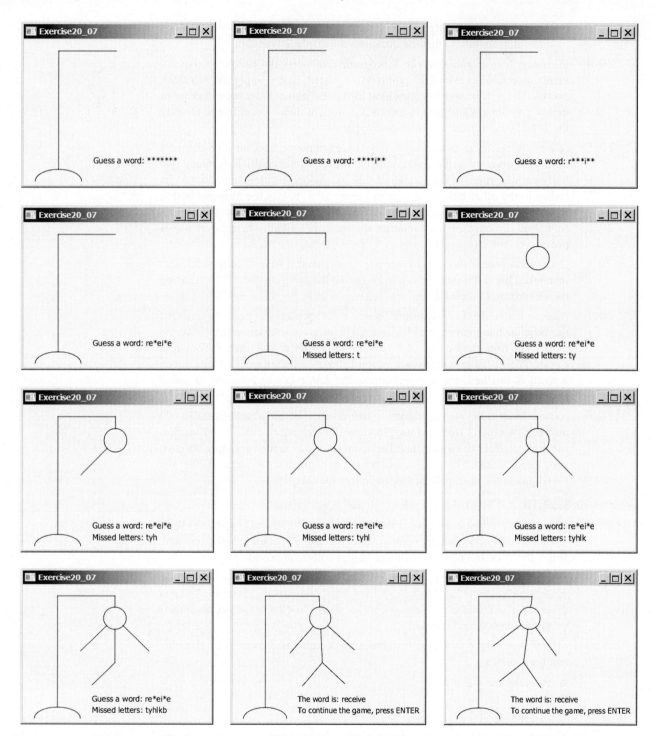

FIGURE 20.18 The program displays a hangman game. *Source*: Copyright © 1995–2016 Oracle and/or its affiliates. All rights reserved. Used with permission.

20.13 (*Game: the 24-point card game*) The 24-point card game is to pick any four cards from 52 cards, as shown in Figure 20.19. Note the Jokers are excluded. Each card represents a number. An Ace, King, Queen, and Jack represent 1, 13, 12, and 11, respectively. You can click the *Shuffle* button to get four new cards. Enter an expression that uses the four numbers from the four selected cards. Each number must be used once and only once. You can use the operators (addition, subtraction, multiplication, and division) and parentheses in the expression. The expression must evaluate to 24. After entering the expression, click the *Verify* button to check whether the numbers in the expression are currently selected and whether the result of the expression is correct. Display the verification in a label before the *Shuffle* button. Assume that images are stored in files named **1.png, **2.png**, . . . , **52.png**, in the order of spades, hearts, diamonds, and clubs. Thus, the first 13 images are for spades 1, 2, 3, . . . , and 13.

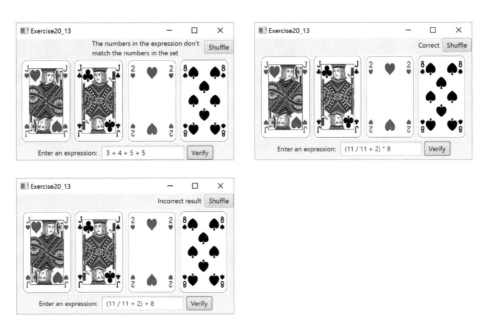

FIGURE 20.19   The user enters an expression consisting of the numbers in the cards and clicks the Verify button to check the answer. *Source*: Fotolia.

**20.14   (*Postfix notation*) Postfix notation is a way of writing expressions without using parentheses. For example, the expression (1 + 2) * 3 would be written as 1 2 + 3 *. A postfix expression is evaluated using a stack. Scan a postfix expression from left to right. A variable or constant is pushed into the stack. When an operator is encountered, apply the operator with the top two operands in the stack and replace the two operands with the result. The following diagram shows how to evaluate 1 2 + 3 *:

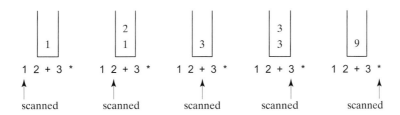

Write a program to evaluate postfix expressions. Pass the expression as a command-line argument in one string.

***20.15 (*Game: the 24-point card game*) Improve Programming Exercise 20.13 to enable the computer to display the expression if one exists, as shown in Figure 20.20. Otherwise, report that the expression does not exist. Place the label for verification result at the bottom of the UI. The expression must use all four cards and evaluated to 24.

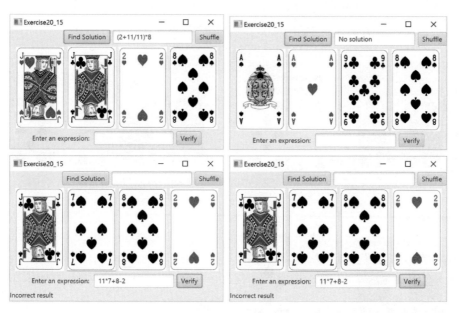

FIGURE 20.20 The program can automatically find a solution if one exists. *Source*: Fotolia.

**20.16 (*Convert infix to postfix*) Write a method that converts an infix expression into a postfix expression using the following header:

```
public static String infixToPostfix(String expression)
```

For example, the method should convert the infix expression (1 + 2) * 3 to 1 2 + 3 * and 2 * (1 + 3) to 2 1 3 + *. Write a program that accepts an expression in one argument from the command line and displays its corresponding postfix expression.

***20.17 (*Game: the 24-point card game*) This exercise is a variation of the 24-point card game described in Programming Exercise 20.13. Write a program to check whether there is a 24-point solution for the four specified numbers. The program lets the user enter four values, each between 1 and 13, as shown in Figure 20.21. The user can then click the *Solve* button to display the solution or display "No solution" if none exists:

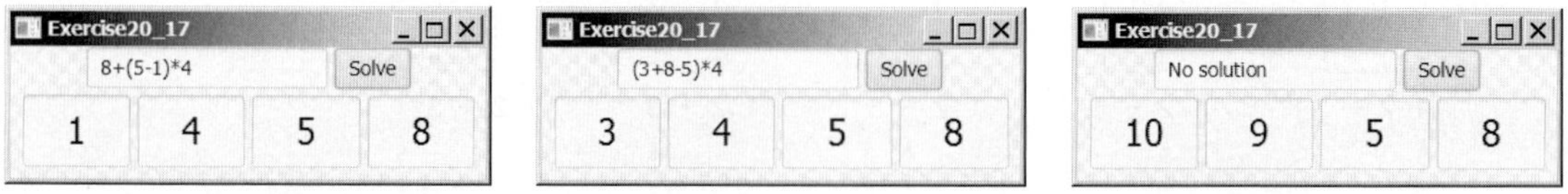

FIGURE 20.21 The user enters four numbers and the program finds a solution. *Source*: Copyright © 1995–2016 Oracle and/or its affiliates. All rights reserved. Used with permission.

*20.18 (*Directory size*) Listing 18.10, DirectorySize.java, gives a recursive method for finding a directory size. Rewrite this method without using recursion. Your program should use a queue to store the subdirectories under a directory. The algorithm can be described as follows:

```
long getSize(File directory) {
  long size = 0;
  add directory to the queue;

  while (queue is not empty) {
    Remove an item from the queue into t;
    if (t is a file)
      size += t.length();
    else
      add all the files and subdirectories under t into the
        queue;
  }

  return size;
}
```

***20.19 (*Game: solution ratio for 24-point card game*) When you pick four cards from a deck of 52 cards for the 24-point card game introduced in Programming Exercise 20.13, the four cards may not have a 24-point solution. What is the number of all possible picks of four cards from 52 cards? Among all possible picks, how many of them have 24-point solutions? What is the success ratio—that is, (number of picks with solutions)/(number of all possible picks of four cards)? Write a program to find these answers.

*20.20 (*Directory size*) Rewrite Programming Exercise 18.28 using a stack instead of a queue.

*20.21 (*Use Comparator*) Write the following generic method using selection sort and a comparator:

```
public static <E> void selectionSort(E[] list,
  Comparator<? super E> comparator)
```

Write a test program that creates an array of 10 GeometricObjects and invokes this method using the GeometricObjectComparator introduced in Listing 20.5 to sort the elements. Display the sorted elements. Use the following statement to create the array:

```
GeometricObject[] list1 = {new Circle(5), new Rectangle(4, 5),
  new Circle(5.5), new Rectangle(2.4, 5), new Circle(0.5),
  new Rectangle(4, 65), new Circle(4.5), new Rectangle(4.4, 1),
  new Circle(6.5), new Rectangle(4, 5)};
```

Also in the same program, write the code that sorts six strings by their last character. Use the following statement to create the array:

```
String[] list2 = {"red", "blue", "green", "yellow", "orange",
  "pink"};
```

*20.22 (*Nonrecursive Tower of Hanoi*) Implement the moveDisks method in Listing 18.8 using a stack instead of using recursion.

**20.23 (*Evaluate expression*) Modify Listing 20.12, EvaluateExpression.java to add operators ^ for exponent and % for remainder. For example, 3 ^ 2 is 9 and 3 % 2 is 1. The ^ operator has the highest precedence and the % operator has the same precedence as the * and / operators. Your program should prompt the user to enter an expression. Here is a sample run of the program:

```
Enter an expression: (5 * 2 ^ 3 + 2 * 3 % 2) * 4  ←Enter
(5 * 2 ^ 3 + 2 * 3 % 2) * 4 = 160
```

SETS AND MAPS

Objectives

- To store unordered, nonduplicate elements using a set (§21.2).

- To explore how and when to use `HashSet` (§21.2.1), `LinkedHashSet` (§21.2.2), or `TreeSet` (§21.2.3) to store a set of elements.

- To compare the performance of sets and lists (§21.3).

- To use sets to develop a program that counts the keywords in a Java source file (§21.4).

- To tell the differences between `Collection` and `Map` and describe when and how to use `HashMap`, `LinkedHashMap`, or `TreeMap` to store values associated with keys (§21.5).

- To use maps to develop a program that counts the occurrence of the words in a text (§21.6).

- To obtain singleton sets, lists, and maps and unmodifiable sets, lists, and maps, use the static methods in the `Collections` class (§21.7).

CHAPTER 21

21.1 Introduction

A set is an efficient data structure for storing and processing nonduplicate elements. A map is like a dictionary that provides a quick lookup to retrieve a value using a key.

The "**No-Fly**" **list** is a list, created and maintained by the U.S. government's Terrorist Screening Center, of people who are not permitted to board a commercial aircraft for travel in or out of the United States. Suppose we need to write a program that checks whether a person is on the No-Fly list. You can use a list to store names in the No-Fly list. However, a more efficient data structure for this application is a *set*.

Suppose your program also needs to store detailed information about terrorists in the No-Fly list. The detailed information such as gender, height, weight, and nationality can be retrieved using the name as the key. A *map* is an efficient data structure for such a task.

This chapter introduces sets and maps in the Java Collections Framework.

21.2 Sets

You can create a set using one of its three concrete classes: `HashSet`*,* `LinkedHashSet`*, or* `TreeSet`*.*

The `Set` interface extends the `Collection` interface, as shown in Figure 20.1. It does not introduce new methods or constants, but it stipulates that an instance of `Set` contains no duplicate elements. The concrete classes that implement `Set` must ensure that no duplicate elements can be added to the set. That is, no two elements `e1` and `e2` can be in the set such that `e1.equals(e2)` is `true`.

The `AbstractSet` class extends `AbstractCollection` and partially implements `Set`. The `AbstractSet` class provides concrete implementations for the `equals` method and the `hashCode` method. The hash code of a set is the sum of the hash codes of all the elements in the set. Since the `size` method and `iterator` method are not implemented in the `Abstract-Set` class, `AbstractSet` is an abstract class.

Three concrete classes of `Set` are `HashSet`, `LinkedHashSet`, and `TreeSet`, as shown in Figure 21.1.

21.2.1   HashSet

The `HashSet` class is a concrete class that implements `Set`. You can create an empty *hash set* using its no-arg constructor, or create a hash set from an existing collection. By default, the initial capacity is `16` and the load factor is `0.75`. If you know the size of your set, you can specify the initial capacity and load factor in the constructor. Otherwise, use the default setting. The load factor is a value between `0.0` and `1.0`.

The load factor measures how full the set is allowed to be before its capacity is increased. When the number of elements exceeds the product of the capacity and load factor, the capacity is automatically doubled. For example, if the capacity is `16` and load factor is `0.75`, the capacity will be doubled to `32` when the size reaches `12` ($16 * 0.75 = 12$). A higher load factor decreases the space costs but increases the search time. Generally, the default load factor `0.75` is a good trade-off between time and space costs. We will discuss more on the load factor in Chapter 27, Hashing.

A `HashSet` can be used to store *duplicate-free* elements. For efficiency, objects added to a hash set need to implement the `hashCode` method in a manner that properly disperses the hash code. The `hashCode` method is defined in the `Object` class. The hash codes of two objects must be the same if the two objects are equal. Two unequal objects may have the same hash code, but you should implement the `hashCode` method to avoid too many such cases. Most of the classes in the Java API implement the `hashCode` method. For example, the `hashCode` in the `Integer` class returns its `int` value. The `hashCode` in the `Character` class returns the Unicode of the character. The `hashCode` in the `String` class returns $s_0 * 31^{(n-1)} + s_1 * 31^{(n-2)} + \cdots + s_{n-1}$, where s_i is `s.charAt(i)`.

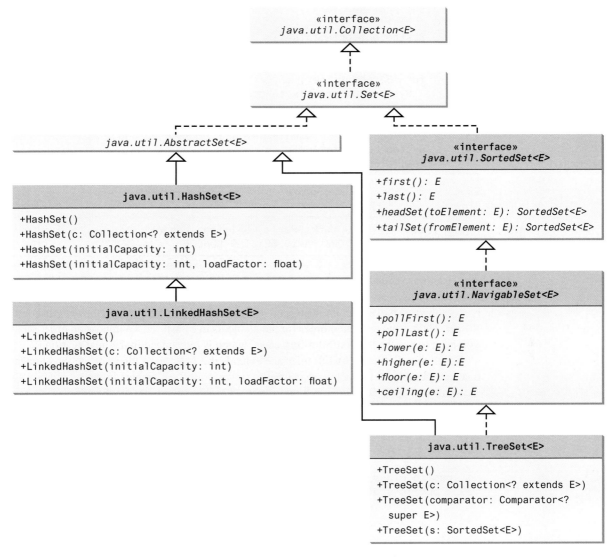

Figure 21.1 The Java Collections Framework provides three concrete set classes.

Listing 21.1 gives a program that creates a hash set to store strings and uses a foreach loop and a `forEach` method to traverse the elements in the set.

Listing 21.1   TestHashSet.java

```java
1   import java.util.*;
2
3   public class TestHashSet {
4     public static void main(String[] args) {
5       // Create a hash set
6       Set<String> set = new HashSet<>();                          create a set
7
8       // Add strings to the set
9       set.add("London");                                          add element
10      set.add("Paris");
11      set.add("New York");
12      set.add("San Francisco");
13      set.add("Beijing");
```

```
14        set.add("New York");
15
16        System.out.println(set);
17
18        // Display the elements in the hash set
19        for (String s: set) {
20          System.out.print(s.toUpperCase() + " ");
21        }
22
23        // Process the elements using a forEach method
24        System.out.println();
25        set.forEach(e -> System.out.print(e.toLowerCase() + " "));
26      }
27    }
```

traverse elements (line 19)

forEach method (line 25)

```
[San Francisco, New York, Paris, Beijing, London]
SAN FRANCISCO NEW YORK PARIS BEIJING LONDON
```

The strings are added to the set (lines 9–14). New York is added to the set more than once, but only one string is stored because a set does not allow duplicates.

As shown in the output, the strings are not stored in the order in which they are inserted into the set. There is no particular order for the elements in a hash set. To impose an order on them, you need to use the LinkedHashSet class, which is introduced in the next section.

Recall that the Collection interface extends the Iterable interface, so the elements in a set are iterable. A foreach loop is used to traverse all the elements in the set (lines 19–21). You can also use a forEach method to process each element in a set (line 25).

Since a set is an instance of Collection, all methods defined in Collection can be used for sets. Listing 21.2 gives an example that applies the methods in the Collection interface on sets.

LISTING 21.2 TestMethodsInCollection.java

```
1   public class TestMethodsInCollection {
2     public static void main(String[] args) {
3       // Create set1
4       java.util.Set<String> set1 = new java.util.HashSet<>();
5
6       // Add strings to set1
7       set1.add("London");
8       set1.add("Paris");
9       set1.add("New York");
10      set1.add("San Francisco");
11      set1.add("Beijing");
12
13      System.out.println("set1 is " + set1);
14      System.out.println(set1.size() + " elements in set1");
15
16      // Delete a string from set1
17      set1.remove("London");
18      System.out.println("\nset1 is " + set1);
19      System.out.println(set1.size() + " elements in set1");
20
21      // Create set2
22      java.util.Set<String> set2 = new java.util.HashSet<>();
23
24      // Add strings to set2
25      set2.add("London");
26      set2.add("Shanghai");
27      set2.add("Paris");
```

create a set (line 4)

add element (line 7)

get size (line 14)

remove element (line 17)

create a set (line 22)

add element (line 25)

```
28        System.out.println("\nset2 is " + set2);
29        System.out.println(set2.size() + " elements in set2");
30
31        System.out.println("\nIs Taipei in set2? "
32          + set2.contains("Taipei"));                                    contains element?
33
34        set1.addAll(set2);                                               addAll
35        System.out.println("\nAfter adding set2 to set1, set1 is "
36          + set1);
37
38        set1.removeAll(set2);                                            removeAll
39        System.out.println("After removing set2 from set1, set1 is "
40          + set1);
41
42        set1.retainAll(set2);                                            retainAll
43        System.out.println("After retaining common elements in set2 "
44          + "and set2, set1 is " + set1);
45      }
46    }
```

```
set1 is [San Francisco, New York, Paris, Beijing, London]
5 elements in set1

set1 is [San Francisco, New York, Paris, Beijing]
4 elements in set1

set2 is [Shanghai, Paris, London]
3 elements in set2

Is Taipei in set2? false

After adding set2 to set1, set1 is
  [San Francisco, New York, Shanghai, Paris, Beijing, London]

After removing set2 from set1, set1 is
  [San Francisco, New York, Beijing]

After retaining common elements in set1 and set2, set1 is []
```

The program creates two sets (lines 4 and 22). The `size()` method returns the number of the elements in a set (line 14). Line 17

```
set1.remove("London");
```

removes London from set1.

The `contains` method (line 32) checks whether an element is in the set.

Line 34

```
set1.addAll(set2);
```

adds set2 to set1. Therefore, set1 becomes [San Francisco, New York, Shanghai, Paris, Beijing, London].

Line 38

```
set1.removeAll(set2);
```

removes set2 from set1. Thus, set1 becomes [San Francisco, New York, Beijing].

Line 42

```
set1.retainAll(set2);
```

retains the common elements in `set1` and `set2`. Since `set1` and `set2` have no common elements, `set1` becomes empty.

21.2.2 LinkedHashSet

`LinkedHashSet` extends `HashSet` with a linked-list implementation that supports an ordering of the elements in the set. The elements in a `HashSet` are not ordered, but the elements in a `LinkedHashSet` can be retrieved in the order in which they were inserted into the set. A `LinkedHashSet` can be created by using one of its four constructors, as shown in Figure 21.1. These constructors are similar to the constructors for `HashSet`.

linked hash set

Listing 21.3 gives a test program for `LinkedHashSet`. The program simply replaces `HashSet` by `LinkedHashSet` in Listing 21.1.

LISTING 21.3 TestLinkedHashSet.java

```
 1  import java.util.*;
 2
 3  public class TestLinkedHashSet {
 4    public static void main(String[] args) {
 5      // Create a hash set
 6      Set<String> set = new LinkedHashSet<>();
 7
 8      // Add strings to the set
 9      set.add("London");
10      set.add("Paris");
11      set.add("New York");
12      set.add("San Francisco");
13      set.add("Beijing");
14      set.add("New York");
15
16      System.out.println(set);
17
18      // Display the elements in the hash set
19      for (String element: set)
20        System.out.print(element.toLowerCase() + " ");
21    }
22  }
```

create linked hash set

add element

display elements

```
[London, Paris, New York, San Francisco, Beijing]
london paris new york san francisco beijing
```

A `LinkedHashSet` is created in line 6. As shown in the output, the strings are stored in the order in which they are inserted. Since `LinkedHashSet` is a set, it does not store duplicate elements.

The `LinkedHashSet` maintains the order in which the elements are inserted. To impose a different order (e.g., increasing or decreasing order), you can use the `TreeSet` class, which is introduced in the next section.

Tip

If you don't need to maintain the order in which the elements are inserted, use `HashSet`, which is more efficient than `LinkedHashSet`.

21.2.3 TreeSet

As shown in Figure 21.1, `SortedSet` is a subinterface of `Set`, which guarantees that the elements in the set are sorted. In addition, it provides the methods `first()` and `last()` for returning the first and last elements in the set, and `headSet(toElement)` and `tailSet(fromElement)` for returning a portion of the set whose elements are less than `toElement` and greater than or equal to `fromElement`, respectively.

`NavigableSet` extends `SortedSet` to provide navigation methods `lower(e)`, `floor(e)`, `ceiling(e)`, and `higher(e)` that return elements, respectively, less than, less than or equal, greater than or equal, and greater than a given element and return `null` if there is no such element. The `pollFirst()` and `pollLast()` methods remove and return the first and last element in the tree set, respectively.

`TreeSet` implements the `SortedSet` interface. To create a `TreeSet`, use a constructor, as shown in Figure 21.1. You can add objects into a *tree set* as long as they can be compared with each other.

tree set

As discussed in Section 20.5, the elements can be compared in two ways: using the `Comparable` interface or the `Comparator` interface.

Listing 21.4 gives an example of ordering elements using the `Comparable` interface. The preceding example in Listing 21.3 displays all the strings in their insertion order. This example rewrites the preceding example to display the strings in alphabetical order using the `TreeSet` class.

LISTING 21.4 `TestTreeSet.java`

```
 1  import java.util.*;
 2
 3  public class TestTreeSet {
 4    public static void main(String[] args) {
 5      // Create a hash set
 6      Set<String> set = new HashSet<>();
 7
 8      // Add strings to the set
 9      set.add("London");
10      set.add("Paris");
11      set.add("New York");
12      set.add("San Francisco");
13      set.add("Beijing");
14      set.add("New York");
15
16      TreeSet<String> treeSet = new TreeSet<>(set);
17      System.out.println("Sorted tree set: " + treeSet);
18
19      // Use the methods in SortedSet interface
20      System.out.println("first(): " + treeSet.first());
21      System.out.println("last(): " + treeSet.last());
22      System.out.println("headSet(\"New York\"): " +
23        treeSet.headSet("New York"));
24      System.out.println("tailSet(\"New York\"): " +
25        treeSet.tailSet("New York"));
26
27      // Use the methods in NavigableSet interface
28      System.out.println("lower(\"P\"): " + treeSet.lower("P"));
29      System.out.println("higher(\"P\"): " + treeSet.higher("P"));
30      System.out.println("floor(\"P\"): " + treeSet.floor("P"));
31      System.out.println("ceiling(\"P\"): " + treeSet.ceiling("P"));
32      System.out.println("pollFirst(): " + treeSet.pollFirst());
33      System.out.println("pollLast(): " + treeSet.pollLast());
34      System.out.println("New tree set: " + treeSet);
35    }
36  }
```

create hash set

create tree set

display elements

```
Sorted tree set: [Beijing, London, New York, Paris, San Francisco]
first(): Beijing
last(): San Francisco
```

```
headSet("New York"): [Beijing, London]
tailSet("New York"): [New York, Paris, San Francisco]
lower("P"): New York
higher("P"): Paris
floor("P"): New York
ceiling("P"): Paris
pollFirst(): Beijing
pollLast(): San Francisco
New tree set: [London, New York, Paris]
```

The example creates a hash set filled with strings, then creates a tree set for the same strings. The strings are sorted in the tree set using the compareTo method in the Comparable interface.

The elements in the set are sorted once you create a TreeSet object from a HashSet object using new TreeSet<>(set) (line 16). You may rewrite the program to create an instance of TreeSet using its no-arg constructor and add the strings into the TreeSet object.

treeSet.first() returns the first element in treeSet (line 20) and treeSet.last() returns the last element in treeSet (line 21). treeSet.headSet("New York") returns the elements in treeSet before New York (lines 22–23). treeSet.tailSet("New York") returns the elements in treeSet after New York, including New York (lines 24–25).

treeSet.lower("P") returns the largest element less than P in treeSet (line 28). treeSet.higher("P") returns the smallest element greater than P in treeSet (line 29). treeSet.floor("P") returns the largest element less than or equal to P in treeSet (line 30). treeSet.ceiling("P") returns the smallest element greater than or equal to P in treeSet (line 31). treeSet.pollFirst() removes the first element in treeSet and returns the removed element (line 32). treeSet.pollLast() removes the last element in treeSet and returns the removed element (line 33).

Note

All the concrete classes in Java Collections Framework (see Figure 20.1) have at least two constructors. One is the no-arg constructor that constructs an empty collection. The other constructs instances from a collection. Thus the TreeSet class has the constructor TreeSet(Collection c) for constructing a TreeSet from a collection c. In this example, new TreeSet<>(set) creates an instance of TreeSet from the collection set.

Tip

If you don't need to maintain a sorted set when updating a set, you should use a hash set because it takes less time to insert and remove elements in a hash set. When you need a sorted set, you can create a tree set from the hash set.

If you create a TreeSet using its no-arg constructor, the compareTo method is used to compare the elements in the set, assuming the class of the elements implements the Comparable interface. To use a comparator, you have to use the constructor TreeSet(Comparator comparator) to create a sorted set that uses the compare method in the comparator to order the elements in the set.

Listing 21.5 gives a program that demonstrates how to sort elements in a tree set using the Comparator interface.

LISTING 21.5 TestTreeSetWithComparator.java

```
1  import java.util.*;
2
```

```
3   public class TestTreeSetWithComparator {
4     public static void main(String[] args) {
5       // Create a tree set for geometric objects using a comparator
6       Set<GeometricObject> set =
7         new TreeSet<>(new GeometricObjectComparator());
8       set.add(new Rectangle(4, 5));
9       set.add(new Circle(40));
10      set.add(new Circle(40));
11      set.add(new Rectangle(4, 1));
12
13      // Display geometric objects in the tree set
14      System.out.println("A sorted set of geometric objects");
15      for (GeometricObject element: set)
16        System.out.println("area = " + element.getArea());
17    }
18  }
```

tree set

display elements

```
A sorted set of geometric objects
area = 4.0
area = 20.0
area = 5021.548245743669
```

The `GeometricObjectComparator` class is defined in Listing 20.4. The program creates a tree set of geometric objects using the `GeometricObjectComparator` for comparing the elements in the set (lines 6 and 7).

The `Circle` and `Rectangle` classes were defined in Section 13.2, Abstract Classes. They are all subclasses of `GeometricObject`. They are added to the set (lines 8–11).

Two circles of the same radius are added to the tree set (lines 9 and 10), but only one is stored because the two circles are equal (determined by the comparator in this case) and the set does not allow duplicates.

21.2.1 How do you create an instance of `Set`? How do you insert a new element in a set? How do you remove an element from a set? How do you find the size of a set?

21.2.2 If two objects o1 and o2 are equal, what is `o1.equals(o2)` and `o1.hashCode() == o2.hashCode()`?

21.2.3 What are the differences among `HashSet`, `LinkedHashSet`, and `TreeSet`?

21.2.4 How do you traverse the elements in a set?

21.2.5 How do you sort the elements in a set using the `compareTo` method in the `Comparable` interface? How do you sort the elements in a set using the `Comparator` interface? What would happen if you added an element that could not be compared with the existing elements in a tree set?

21.2.6 Suppose `set1` is a set that contains the strings `red`, `yellow`, and `green` and that `set2` is another set that contains the strings `red`, `yellow`, and `blue`. Answer the following questions:

- What are in `set1` and `set2` after executing `set1.addAll(set2)`?
- What are in `set1` and `set2` after executing `set1.add(set2)`?
- What are in `set1` and `set2` after executing `set1.removeAll(set2)`?
- What are in `set1` and `set2` after executing `set1.remove(set2)`?

- What are in `set1` and `set2` after executing `set1.retainAll(set2)`?
- What is in `set1` after executing `set1.clear()`?

21.2.7   Show the output of the following code:

```java
import java.util.*;

public class Test {
  public static void main(String[] args) {
    LinkedHashSet<String> set1 = new LinkedHashSet<>();
    set1.add("New York");
    LinkedHashSet<String> set2 = set1;
    LinkedHashSet<String> set3 =
      (LinkedHashSet<String>)(set1.clone());
    set1.add("Atlanta");
    System.out.println("set1 is " + set1);
    System.out.println("set2 is " + set2);
    System.out.println("set3 is " + set3);
    set1.forEach(e -> System.out.print(e + " "));
  }
}
```

21.2.8   Show the output of the following code:

```java
Set<String> set = new LinkedHashSet<>();
set.add("ABC");
set.add("ABD");
System.out.println(set);
```

21.2.9   What will the output be if lines 6–7 in Listing 21.5 are replaced by the following code:

```java
Set<GeometricObject> set = new HashSet<>();
```

21.2.10   Show the output of the following code:

```java
Set<String> set = new TreeSet<>(
  Comparator.comparing(String::length));
set.add("ABC");
set.add("ABD");
System.out.println(set);
```

21.3 Comparing the Performance of Sets and Lists

Key Point

Sets are more efficient than lists for storing nonduplicate elements. Lists are useful for accessing elements through the index.

The elements in a list can be accessed through the index. However, sets do not support indexing because the elements in a set are unordered. To traverse all elements in a set, use a foreach loop. We now conduct an interesting experiment to test the performance of sets and lists. Listing 21.6 gives a program that shows the execution time of (1) testing whether an element is in a hash set, linked hash set, tree set, array list, or linked list and (2) removing elements from a hash set, linked hash set, tree set, array list, and linked list.

LISTING 21.6 SetListPerformanceTest.java

```java
import java.util.*;

public class SetListPerformanceTest {
  static final int N = 50000;

  public static void main(String[] args) {
    // Add numbers 0, 1, 2, ..., N - 1 to the array list
    List<Integer> list = new ArrayList<>();          create test data
    for (int i = 0; i < N; i++)
      list.add(i);
    Collections.shuffle(list); // Shuffle the array list    shuffle

    // Create a hash set, and test its performance
    Collection<Integer> set1 = new HashSet<>(list);       a hash set
    System.out.println("Member test time for hash set is " +
      getTestTime(set1) + " milliseconds");
    System.out.println("Remove element time for hash set is " +
      getRemoveTime(set1) + " milliseconds");

    // Create a linked hash set, and test its performance
    Collection<Integer> set2 = new LinkedHashSet<>(list);   a linked hash set
    System.out.println("Member test time for linked hash set is " +
      getTestTime(set2) + " milliseconds");
    System.out.println("Remove element time for linked hash set is "
      + getRemoveTime(set2) + " milliseconds");

    // Create a tree set, and test its performance
    Collection<Integer> set3 = new TreeSet<>(list);        a tree set
    System.out.println("Member test time for tree set is " +
      getTestTime(set3) + " milliseconds");
    System.out.println("Remove element time for tree set is " +
      getRemoveTime(set3) + " milliseconds");

    // Create an array list, and test its performance
    Collection<Integer> list1 = new ArrayList<>(list);     an array list
    System.out.println("Member test time for array list is " +
      getTestTime(list1) + " milliseconds");
    System.out.println("Remove element time for array list is " +
      getRemoveTime(list1) + " milliseconds");

    // Create a linked list, and test its performance
    Collection<Integer> list2 = new LinkedList<>(list);    a linked list
    System.out.println("Member test time for linked list is " +
      getTestTime(list2) + " milliseconds");
    System.out.println("Remove element time for linked list is " +
      getRemoveTime(list2) + " milliseconds");
  }

  public static long getTestTime(Collection<> c) {
    long startTime = System.currentTimeMillis();         start time

    // Test if a number is in the collection
    for (int i = 0; i < N; i++)
      c.contains((int)(Math.random() * 2 * N));          test membership

    return System.currentTimeMillis() - startTime;       return execution time
```

```
57      }
58
59      public static long getRemoveTime(Collection<Integer> c) {
60        long startTime = System.currentTimeMillis();
61
62        for (int i = 0; i < N; i++)
63          c.remove(i);
64
65        return System.currentTimeMillis() - startTime;
66      }
67  }
```

remove from container

return execution time

```
Member test time for hash set is 20 milliseconds
Remove element time for hash set is 27 milliseconds
Member test time for linked hash set is 27 milliseconds
Remove element time for linked hash set is 26 milliseconds
Member test time for tree set is 47 milliseconds
Remove element time for tree set is 34 milliseconds
Member test time for array list is 39802 milliseconds
Remove element time for array list is 16196 milliseconds
Member test time for linked list is 52197 milliseconds
Remove element time for linked list is 14870 milliseconds
```

The program creates a list for numbers from 0 to N-1 (for N = 50000) (lines 8–10) and shuffles the list (line 11). From this list, the program creates a hash set (line 14), a linked hash set (line 21), a tree set (line 28), an array list (line 35), and a linked list (line 42). The program obtains the execution time for testing whether a number is in the hash set (line 16), linked hash set (line 23), tree set (line 30), array list (line 37), or linked list (line 44) and obtains the execution time for removing the elements from the hash set (line 18), linked hash set (line 25), tree set (line 32), array list (line 39), and linked list (line 46).

The getTestTime method invokes the contains method to test whether a number is in the container (line 54) and the getRemoveTime method invokes the remove method to remove an element from the container (line 63).

sets are better

As these runtimes illustrate, sets are much more efficient than lists for testing whether an element is in a set or a list. Therefore, the No-Fly list should be implemented using a hash set instead of a list, because it is much faster to test whether an element is in a hash set than in a list.

You may wonder why sets are more efficient than lists. The questions will be answered in Chapters 24 and 27 when we introduce the implementations of lists and sets.

Check Point

21.3.1 Suppose you need to write a program that stores unordered, nonduplicate elements, what data structure should you use?

21.3.2 Suppose you need to write a program that stores nonduplicate elements in the order of insertion, what data structure should you use?

21.3.3 Suppose you need to write a program that stores nonduplicate elements in increasing order of the element values, what data structure should you use?

21.3.4 Suppose you need to write a program that stores a fixed number of the elements (possibly duplicates), what data structure should you use?

21.3.5 Suppose you need to write a program that stores the elements in a list with frequent operations to append and delete elements at the end of the list, what data structure should you use?

21.3.6 Suppose you need to write a program that stores the elements in a list with frequent operations to insert and delete elements at the beginning of the list, what data structure should you use?

21.4 Case Study: Counting Keywords

This section presents an application that counts the number of keywords in a Java source file.

Key
Point

For each word in a Java source file, we need to determine whether the word is a keyword. To handle this efficiently, store all the keywords in a `HashSet` and use the `contains` method to test if a word is in the keyword set. Listing 21.7 gives this program.

LISTING 21.7 `CountKeywords.java`

```java
1  import java.util.*;
2  import java.io.*;
3
4  public class CountKeywords {
5    public static void main(String[] args) throws Exception {
6      Scanner input = new Scanner(System.in);
7      System.out.print("Enter a Java source file: ");
8      String filename = input.nextLine();
9
10     File file = new File(filename);
11     if (file.exists()) {
12       System.out.println("The number of keywords in " + filename
13         + " is " + countKeywords(file));
14     }
15     else {
16       System.out.println("File " + filename + " does not exist");
17     }
18   }
19
20   public static int countKeywords(File file) throws Exception {
21     // Array of all Java keywords + true, false and null
22     String[] keywordString = {"abstract", "assert", "boolean",
23       "break", "byte", "case", "catch", "char", "class", "const",
24       "continue", "default", "do", "double", "else", "enum",
25       "extends", "for", "final", "finally", "float", "goto",
26       "if", "implements", "import", "instanceof", "int",
27       "interface", "long", "native", "new", "package", "private",
28       "protected", "public", "return", "short", "static",
29       "strictfp", "super", "switch", "synchronized", "this",
30       "throw", "throws", "transient", "try", "void", "volatile",
31       "while", "true", "false", "null"};
32
33     Set<String> keywordSet =
34       new HashSet<>(Arrays.asList(keywordString));
35     int count = 0;
36
37     Scanner input = new Scanner(file);
38
39     while (input.hasNext()) {
40       String word = input.next();
41       if (keywordSet.contains(word))
42         count++;
43     }
44
45     return count;
46   }
47 }
```

enter a filename

file exists?

count keywords

keywords

keyword set

is a keyword?

```
Enter a Java source file: c:\ Welcome.java  ↵Enter
The number of keywords in c:\ Welcome.java is 5
```

```
Enter a Java source file: c:\ TTT.java  ↵Enter
File c:\ TTT.java does not exist
```

The program prompts the user to enter a Java source filename (line 7) and reads the filename (line 8). If the file exists, the `countKeywords` method is invoked to count the keywords in the file (line 13).

The `countKeywords` method creates an array of strings for the keywords (lines 22–31) and creates a hash set from this array (lines 33–34). It then reads each word from the file and tests if the word is in the set (line 41). If so, the program increases the count by 1 (line 42).

You may rewrite the program to use a `LinkedHashSet`, `TreeSet`, `ArrayList`, or `LinkedList` to store the keywords. However, using a `HashSet` is the most efficient for this program.

21.4.1 Will the `CountKeywords` program work if lines 33–34 are changed to

```
Set<String> keywordSet =
  new LinkedHashSet<>(Arrays.asList(keywordString));
```

21.4.2 Will the `CountKeywords` program work if lines 33–34 are changed to

```
List<String> keywordSet =
  new ArrayList<>(Arrays.asList(keywordString));
```

21.5 Maps

You can create a map using one of its three concrete classes: `HashMap`, `LinkedHashMap`, *or* `TreeMap`.

map

A *map* is a container object that stores a collection of key/value pairs. It enables fast retrieval, deletion, and updating of the pair through the key. A map stores the values along with the keys. The keys are like indexes. In `List`, the indexes are integers. In `Map`, the keys can be any objects. A map cannot contain duplicate keys. Each key maps to one value. A key and its corresponding value form an entry stored in a map, as shown in Figure 21.2a. Figure 21.2b shows a map in which each entry consists of a Social Security number as the key and a name as the value.

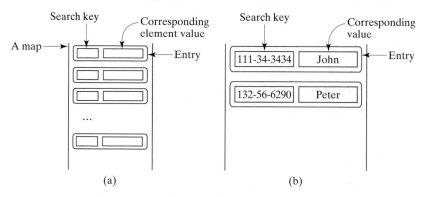

FIGURE 21.2 The entries consisting of key/value pairs are stored in a map.

There are three types of maps: `HashMap`, `LinkedHashMap`, and `TreeMap`. The common features of these maps are defined in the `Map` interface. Their relationship is shown in Figure 21.3.

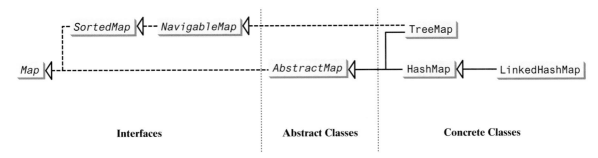

FIGURE 21.3   A map stores key/value pairs.

The `Map` interface provides the methods for querying, updating, and obtaining a collection of values and a set of keys, as shown in Figure 21.4.

«interface» java.util.Map<K,V>	
+clear(): void	Removes all entries from this map.
+containsKey(key: Object): boolean	Returns true if this map contains an entry for the specified key.
+containsValue(value: Object): boolean	Returns true if this map maps one or more keys to the specified value.
+entrySet(): Set<Map.Entry<K,V>>	Returns a set consisting of the entries in this map.
+get(key: Object): V	Returns the value for the specified key in this map.
+isEmpty(): boolean	Returns true if this map contains no entries.
+keySet(): Set<K>	Returns a set consisting of the keys in this map.
+put(key: K, value: V): V	Puts an entry into this map.
+putAll(m: Map<? extends K,? extends V>): void	Adds all the entries from m to this map.
+remove(key: Object): V	Removes the entries for the specified key.
+size(): int	Returns the number of entries in this map.
+values(): Collection<V>	Returns a collection consisting of the values in this map.
+forEach(action: Consumer<? super K, ? super V): default void	Performs an action for each entry in this map.

FIGURE 21.4   The `Map` interface maps keys to values.

The *update methods* include `clear`, `put`, `putAll`, and `remove`. The `clear()` method removes all entries from the map. The `put(K key, V value)` method adds an entry for the specified key and value in the map. If the map formerly contained an entry for this key, the old value is replaced by the new value, and the old value associated with the key is returned. The `putAll(Map m)` method adds all entries in `m` to this map. The `remove(Object key)` method removes the entry for the specified key from the map.

The *query methods* include `containsKey`, `containsValue`, `isEmpty`, and `size`. The `containsKey(Object key)` method checks whether the map contains an entry for the specified key. The `containsValue(Object value)` method checks whether the map contains an entry for this value. The `isEmpty()` method checks whether the map contains any entries. The `size()` method returns the number of entries in the map.

update methods

query methods

keySet()
values()
entrySet()

You can obtain a set of the keys in the map using the `keySet()` method, and a collection of the values in the map using the `values()` method. The `entrySet()` method returns a set of entries. The entries are instances of the `Map.Entry<K, V>` interface, where `Entry` is an inner interface for the `Map` interface, as shown in Figure 21.5. Each entry in the set is a key/value pair in the underlying map.

«interface»
java.util.Map.Entry<K,V>

+getKey(): K
+getValue(): V
+setValue(value: V): void

Returns the key from this entry.
Returns the value from this entry.
Replaces the value in this entry with a new value.

FIGURE 21.5 The `Map.Entry` interface operates on an entry in the map.

forEach method

Java 8 added a default `forEach` method in the `Map` interface for performing an action on each entry in the map. This method can be used like an iterator for traversing the entries in the map.

AbstractMap

The `AbstractMap` class is a convenience abstract class that implements all the methods in the `Map` interface except the `entrySet()` method.

concrete implementation

The `HashMap`, `LinkedHashMap`, and `TreeMap` classes are three *concrete implementations* of the `Map` interface, as shown in Figure 21.6.

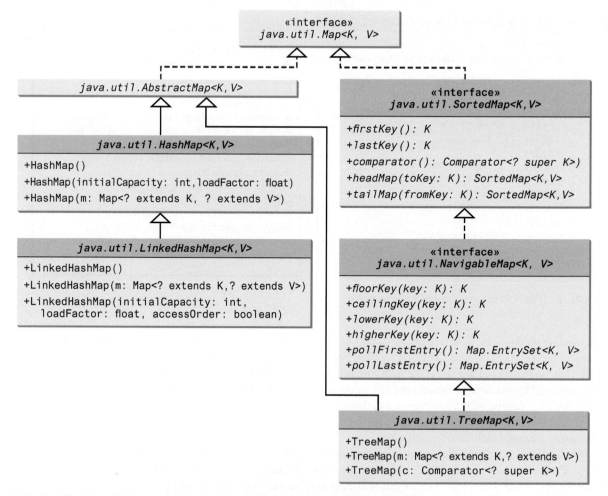

FIGURE 21.6 The Java Collections Framework provides three concrete map classes.

The `HashMap` class is efficient for locating a value, inserting an entry, and deleting an entry.

`LinkedHashMap` extends `HashMap` with a linked-list implementation that supports an ordering of the entries in the map. The entries in a `HashMap` are not ordered, but the entries in a `LinkedHashMap` can be retrieved either in the order in which they were inserted into the map (known as the *insertion order*) or in the order in which they were last accessed, from least recently to most recently accessed (*access order*). The no-arg constructor constructs a `LinkedHashMap` with the insertion order. To construct a `LinkedHashMap` with the access order, use `LinkedHashMap(initialCapacity, loadFactor, true)`.

The `TreeMap` class is efficient for traversing the keys in a sorted order. The keys can be sorted using the `Comparable` interface or the `Comparator` interface. If you create a `TreeMap` using its no-arg constructor, the `compareTo` method in the `Comparable` interface is used to compare the keys in the map, assuming the class for the keys implements the `Comparable` interface. To use a comparator, you have to use the `TreeMap(Comparator comparator)` constructor to create a sorted map that uses the `compare` method in the comparator to order the entries in the map based on the keys.

`SortedMap` is a subinterface of `Map`, which guarantees the entries in the map are sorted. In addition, it provides the methods `firstKey()` and `lastKey()` for returning the first and the last keys in the map, and `headMap(toKey)` and `tailMap(fromKey)` for returning a portion of the map whose keys are less than `toKey` and greater than or equal to `fromKey`, respectively.

`NavigableMap` extends `SortedMap` to provide the navigation methods `lowerKey(key)`, `floorKey(key)`, `ceilingKey(key)`, and `higherKey(key)` that return keys, respectively, less than, less than or equal, greater than or equal, and greater than a given key and return `null` if there is no such key. The `pollFirstEntry()` and `pollLastEntry()` methods remove and return the first and the last entry in the tree map, respectively.

> **Note**
>
> Prior to Java 2, `java.util.Hashtable` was used for mapping keys with values. `Hashtable` was redesigned to fit into the Java Collections Framework with all its methods retained for compatibility. `Hashtable` implements the `Map` interface and is used in the same way as `HashMap`, except that the update methods in `Hashtable` are synchronized.

(margin notes: HashMap, LinkedHashMap, insertion order, access order, TreeMap, SortedMap, NavigableMap, Hashtable)

Listing 21.8 gives an example that creates a *hash map*, a *linked hash map*, and a *tree map* for mapping students to ages. The program first creates a hash map with the student's name as its key and the age as its value. The program then creates a tree map from the hash map and displays the entries in ascending order of the keys. Finally, the program creates a linked hash map, adds the same entries to the map, and displays the entries.

(margin notes: hash map, linked hash map, tree map)

LISTING 21.8 TestMap.java

```
 1  import java.util.*;
 2
 3  public class TestMap {
 4    public static void main(String[] args) {
 5      // Create a HashMap
 6      Map<String, Integer> hashMap = new HashMap<>();
 7      hashMap.put("Smith", 30);
 8      hashMap.put("Anderson", 31);
 9      hashMap.put("Lewis", 29);
10      hashMap.put("Cook", 29);
11
12      System.out.println("Display entries in HashMap");
13      System.out.println(hashMap + "\n");
14
15      // Create a TreeMap from the preceding HashMap
16      Map<String, Integer> treeMap = new TreeMap<>(hashMap);
17      System.out.println("Display entries in ascending order of key");
```

(margin notes: create map, add entry, tree map)

```
18          System.out.println(treeMap);
19
20          // Create a LinkedHashMap
21          Map<String, Integer> linkedHashMap =
22            new LinkedHashMap<>(16, 0.75f, true);
23          linkedHashMap.put("Smith", 30);
24          linkedHashMap.put("Anderson", 31);
25          linkedHashMap.put("Lewis", 29);
26          linkedHashMap.put("Cook", 29);
27
28          // Display the age for Lewis
29          System.out.println("\nThe age for " + "Lewis is " +
30            linkedHashMap.get("Lewis"));
31
32          System.out.println("Display entries in LinkedHashMap");
33          System.out.println(linkedHashMap);
34
35          // Display each entry with name and age
36          System.out.print("\nNames and ages are ");
37          treeMap.forEach(
38            (name, age) -> System.out.print(name + ": " + age + " "));
39        }
40      }
```

linked hash map *(margin note, line 21–22)*

forEach method *(margin note, line 37)*

```
Display entries in HashMap
{Cook=29, Smith=30, Lewis=29, Anderson=31}

Display entries in ascending order of key
{Anderson=31, Cook=29, Lewis=29, Smith=30}

The age for Lewis is 29
Display entries in LinkedHashMap
{Smith=30, Anderson=31, Cook=29, Lewis=29}

Names and ages are Anderson: 31 Cook: 29 Lewis: 29 Smith: 30
```

As shown in the output, the entries in the `HashMap` are in random order. The entries in the `TreeMap` are in increasing order of the keys. The entries in the `LinkedHashMap` are in the order of their access, from least recently accessed to most recently.

All the concrete classes that implement the `Map` interface have at least two constructors. One is the no-arg constructor that constructs an empty map, and the other constructs a map from an instance of `Map`. Thus, `new TreeMap<>(hashMap)` (line 16) constructs a tree map from a hash map.

You can create an insertion- or access-ordered linked hash map. An access-ordered linked hash map is created in lines 21–22. The most recently accessed entry is placed at the end of the map. The entry with the key `Lewis` is last accessed in line 30, so it is displayed last in line 33.

It is convenient to process all the entries in the map using the `forEach` method. The program uses a `forEach` method to display a name and its age (lines 37–38).

Tip

If you don't need to maintain an order in a map when updating it, use a `HashMap`. When you need to maintain the insertion order or access order in the map, use a `LinkedHashMap`. When you need the map to be sorted on keys, use a `TreeMap`.

21.5.1 How do you create an instance of `Map`? How do you add an entry to a map consisting of a key and a value? How do you remove an entry from a map? How do you find the size of a map? How do you traverse entries in a map?

21.5.2 Describe and compare `HashMap`, `LinkedHashMap`, and `TreeMap`.

21.5.3 Show the output of the following code:

```
import java.util.*;
public class Test {
  public static void main(String[] args) {
    Map<String, String> map = new LinkedHashMap<>();
    map.put("123", "John Smith");
    map.put("111", "George Smith");
    map.put("123", "Steve Yao");
    map.put("222", "Steve Yao");
    System.out.println("(1) " + map);
    System.out.println("(2) " + new TreeMap<String, String>(map));
    map.forEach((k, v) -> {
      if (k.equals("123")) System.out.println(v);});
  }
}
```

21.6 Case Study: Occurrences of Words

This case study writes a program that counts the occurrences of words in a text and displays the words and their occurrences in alphabetical order of the words.

Key
Point

The program uses a `TreeMap` to store an entry consisting of a word and its count. For each word, check whether it is already a key in the map. If not, add an entry to the map with the word as the key and value `1`. Otherwise, increase the value for the word (key) by `1` in the map. Assume the words are case insensitive; for example, `Good` is treated the same as `good`.

Listing 21.9 gives the solution to the problem.

LISTING 21.9 `CountOccurrenceOfWords.java`

```
1  import java.util.*;
2
3  public class CountOccurrenceOfWords {
4    public static void main(String[] args) {
5      // Set text in a string
6      String text = "Good morning. Have a good class. " +
7        "Have a good visit. Have fun!";
8
9      // Create a TreeMap to hold words as key and count as value
10     Map<String, Integer> map = new TreeMap<>();                          tree map
11
12     String[] words = text.split("[\\s+\\p{P}]");                         split string
13     for (int i = 0; i < words.length; i++) {
14       String key = words[i].toLowerCase();
15
16       if (key.length() > 0) {
17         if (!map.containsKey(key)) {
18           map.put(key, 1);                                               add entry
19         }
20         else {
21           int value = map.get(key);
22           value++;
23           map.put(key, value);                                          update entry
24         }
25       }
26     }
27
28     // Display key and value for each entry
```

display entry

```
29        map.forEach((k, v) -> System.out.println(k + "\t" + v));
30     }
31  }
```

```
a            2
class        1
fun          1
good         3
have         3
morning      1
visit        1
```

The program creates a `TreeMap` (line 10) to store pairs of words and their occurrence counts. The words serve as the keys. Since all values in the map must be stored as objects, the count is wrapped in an `Integer` object.

The program extracts a word from a text using the `split` method (line 12) in the `String` class (see Section 10.10.4 and Appendix H). The text is split into words using a whitespace `\s` or punctuation `\p{P}` as a delimiter. For each word extracted, the program checks whether it is already stored as a key in the map (line 17). If not, a new pair consisting of the word and its initial count (`1`) is stored in the map (line 18). Otherwise, the count for the word is incremented by `1` (lines 21–23).

The program displays the count and the key in each entry using the `forEach` method in the `Map` class (line 29).

Since the map is a tree map, the entries are displayed in increasing order of words. To display them in ascending order of the occurrence counts, see Programming Exercise 21.8.

Now sit back and think how you would write this program without using map. Your new program would be longer and more complex. You will find that map is a very efficient and powerful data structure for solving problems such as this.

Java Collections Framework provides comprehensive support of organizing and manipulating data. Suppose you wish to display the words in increasing order of their occurrence values, how do you modify the program? This can be done simply by creating a list of map entries and creating a `Comparator` for sorting the entries on their values as follows:

```
List<Map.Entry<String, Integer>> entries =
  new ArrayList<>(map.entrySet());
Collections.sort(entries, (entry1, entry2) -> {
  return entry1.getValue().compareTo(entry2.getValue()); });
for (Map.Entry<String, Integer> entry: entries) {
  System.out.println(entry.getKey() + "\t" + entry.getValue());
}
```

Check Point

21.6.1 Will the `CountOccurrenceOfWords` program work if line 10 is changed to

```
Map<String, int> map = new TreeMap<>();
```

21.6.2 Will the `CountOccurrenceOfWords` program work if line 17 is changed to

```
if (map.get(key) == null) {
```

21.6.3 Will the `CountOccurrenceOfWords` program work if line 29 is changed to

```
for (String key: map)
  System.out.println(key + "\t" + map.getValue(key));
```

21.6.4 How do you simplify the code in lines 17–24 in Listing 21.9 in one line using a conditional expression?

21.7 Singleton and Unmodifiable Collections and Maps

You can create singleton sets, lists, and maps and unmodifiable sets, lists, and maps using the static methods in the Collections *class.*

Key
Point

The Collections class contains the static methods for lists and collections. It also contains the methods for creating immutable singleton sets, lists, and maps and for creating read-only sets, lists, and maps, as shown in Figure 21.7.

java.util.Collections	
+singleton(o: Object): Set	Returns an immutable set containing the specified object.
+singletonList(o: Object): List	Returns an immutable list containing the specified object.
+singletonMap(key: Object, value: Object): Map	Returns an immutable map with the key and value pair.
+unmodifiableCollection(c: Collection): Collection	Returns a read-only view of the collection.
+unmodifiableList(list: List): List	Returns a read-only view of the list.
+unmodifiableMap(m: Map): Map	Returns a read-only view of the map.
+unmodifiableSet(s: Set): Set	Returns a read-only view of the set.
+unmodifiableSortedMap(s: SortedMap): SortedMap	Returns a read-only view of the sorted map.
+unmodifiableSortedSet(s: SortedSet): SortedSet	Returns a read-only view of the sorted set.

FIGURE 21.7 The Collections class contains the static methods for creating singleton and read-only sets, lists, and maps.

The Collections class defines three constants—EMPTY_SET, EMPTY_LIST, and EMPTY_MAP—for an empty set, an empty list, and an empty map. These collections are immutable. The class also provides the singleton(Object o) method for creating an immutable set containing only a single item, the singletonList(Object o) method for creating an immutable list containing only a single item, and the singletonMap(Object key, Object value) method for creating an immutable map containing only a single entry.

The Collections class also provides six static methods for returning *read-only views for collections*: unmodifiableCollection(Collection c), unmodifiableList(List list), unmodifiableMap(Map m), unmodifiableSet(Set set), unmodifiableSortedMap(SortedMap m), and unmodifiableSortedSet(SortedSet s). This type of view is like a reference to the actual collection. However, you cannot modify the collection through a read-only view. Attempting to modify a collection through a read-only view will cause an UnsupportedOperationException.

read-only view

21.7.1 What is wrong in the following code?

Check
Point

```
Set<String> set = Collections.singleton("Chicago");
set.add("Dallas");
```

21.7.2 What happens when you run the following code?

```
List list = Collections.unmodifiableList(Arrays.asList("Chicago",
    "Boston"));
list.remove("Dallas");
```

KEY TERMS

CHAPTER SUMMARY

1. A set stores nonduplicate elements. To allow duplicate elements to be stored in a collection, you need to use a list.

2. A *map* stores key/value pairs. It provides a quick lookup for a value using a key.

3. Three types of sets are supported: `HashSet`, `LinkedHashSet`, and `TreeSet`. `HashSet` stores elements in an unpredictable order. `LinkedHashSet` stores elements in the order they were inserted. `TreeSet` stores elements sorted. `HashSet`, `LinkedHashSet`, and `TreeSet` are subtypes of `Collection`.

4. The `Map` interface maps keys to the elements. The keys are like indexes. In `List`, the indexes are integers. In `Map`, the keys can be any objects. A map cannot contain duplicate keys. Each key can map to at most one value. The `Map` interface provides the methods for querying, updating, and obtaining a collection of values and a set of keys.

5. Three types of maps are supported: `HashMap`, `LinkedHashMap`, and `TreeMap`. `HashMap` is efficient for locating a value, inserting an entry, and deleting an entry. `LinkedHashMap` supports ordering of the entries in the map. The entries in a `HashMap` are not ordered, but the entries in a `LinkedHashMap` can be retrieved either in the order in which they were inserted into the map (known as the *insertion order*) or in the order in which they were last accessed, from least recently accessed to most recently (*access order*). `TreeMap` is efficient for traversing the keys in a sorted order. The keys can be sorted using the `Comparable` interface or the `Comparator` interface.

QUIZ

Answer the quiz for this chapter online at the book Companion Website.

MyProgrammingLab™ ## PROGRAMMING EXERCISES

Sections 21.2–21.4

21.1 (*Perform set operations on hash sets*) Create two linked hash sets {`"George"`, `"Jim"`, `"John"`, `"Blake"`, `"Kevin"`, `"Michael"`} and {`"George"`, `"Katie"`, `"Kevin"`, `"Michelle"`, `"Ryan"`} and find their union, difference, and intersection. (You can clone the sets to preserve the original sets from being changed by these set methods.)

21.2 (*Display nonduplicate words in ascending order*) Write a program that reads words from a text file and displays all the nonduplicate words in ascending order. The text file is passed as a command-line argument.

**21.3 (*Count the keywords in Java source code*) Revise the program in Listing 21.7. If a keyword is in a comment or in a string, don't count it. Pass the Java file name from the command line. Assume the Java source code is correct and line comments and paragraph comments do not overlap.

*21.4 (*Count consonants and vowels*) Write a program that prompts the user to enter a text file name and displays the number of vowels and consonants in the file. Use a set to store the vowels A, E, I, O, and U.

***21.5 (*Syntax highlighting*) Write a program that converts a Java file into an HTML file. In the HTML file, the keywords, comments, and literals are displayed in bold navy, green, and blue, respectively. Use the command line to pass a Java file and an HTML file. For example, the following command

```
java Exercise21_05 Welcome.java Welcome.html
```

converts **Welcome.java** into **Welcome.html**. Figure 21.8a shows a Java file. The corresponding HTML file is shown in Figure 21.8b.

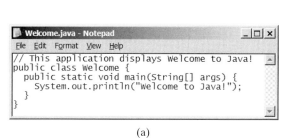
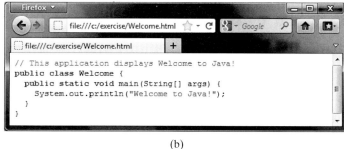

FIGURE 21.8 The Java code in plain text in (a) is displayed in HTML with syntax highlighted in (b). *Source*: Copyright © 1995–2016 Oracle and/or its affiliates. All rights reserved. Used with permission.

Sections 21.5–21.7

*21.6 (*Count the occurrences of numbers entered*) Write a program that reads an unspecified number of integers and finds the one that has the most occurrences. The input ends when the input is 0. For example, if you entered 2 3 40 3 5 4 –3 3 3 2 0, the number 3 occurred most often. If not one but several numbers have the most occurrences, all of them should be reported. For example, since 9 and 3 appear twice in the list 9 30 3 9 3 2 4, both occurrences should be reported.

**21.7 (*Revise Listing 21.9, CountOccurrenceOfWords.java*) Rewrite Listing 21.9 to display the words in ascending order of occurrence counts.

**21.8 (*Count the occurrences of words in a text file*) Rewrite Listing 21.9 to read the text from a text file. The text file is passed as a command-line argument. Words are delimited by whitespace characters, punctuation marks (, ; . : ?), quotation marks (' "), and parentheses. Count words in case-insensitive fashion (e.g., consider Good and good to be the same word). The words must start with a letter. Display the output in alphabetical order of words, with each word preceded by its occurrence count.

**21.9 (*Guess the capitals using maps*) Rewrite Programming Exercise 8.37 to store pairs of each state and its capital in a map. Your program should prompt the user to enter a state, and should display the capital for the state.

*21.10 (*Count the occurrences of each keyword*) Rewrite Listing 21.7, CountKeywords.java to read in a Java source-code file and count the occurrence of each keyword in the file, but don't count the keyword if it is in a comment or in a string literal.

**21.11 (*Baby name popularity ranking*) Use the data files from Programming Exercise 12.31 to write a program that enables the user to select a year, gender, and enter a name to display the ranking of the name for the selected year and gender, as shown in Figure 21.9. To achieve the best efficiency, create two arrays for boy's names and girl's names, respectively. Each array has 10 elements for 10 years. Each element is a map that stores a name and its ranking in a pair with the name as the key.

FIGURE 21.9 The user selects a year and gender, enters a year, and clicks the Find Ranking button to display the ranking. *Source*: Copyright © 1995–2016 Oracle and/or its affiliates. All rights reserved. Used with permission.

**21.12 (*Name for both genders*) Write a program that prompts the user to enter one of the filenames described in Programming Exercise 12.31 and displays the names that are used for both genders in the file. Use sets to store names and find common names in two sets. Here is a sample run:

```
Enter a file name for baby name ranking: babynamesranking2001.txt  ↵Enter
69 names used for both genders
They are Tyler Ryan Christian ...
```

**21.13 (*Baby name popularity ranking*) Revise Programming Exercise 21.11 to prompt the user to enter year, gender, and name and display the ranking for the name. Prompt the user to enter another inquiry or exit the program. Here is a sample run:

```
Enter the year: 2010  ↵Enter
Enter the gender: M  ↵Enter
Enter the name: Javier  ↵Enter
Boy name Javier is ranked #190 in year 2010
Enter another inquiry? Y  ↵Enter
Enter the year: 2001  ↵Enter
Enter the gender: F  ↵Enter
Enter the name: Emily  ↵Enter
Girl name Emily is ranked #1 in year 2001
Enter another inquiry? N  ↵Enter
```

**21.14 (*Web crawler*) Rewrite Listing 12.18, WebCrawler.java, to improve the performance by using appropriate new data structures for `listOfPendingURLs` and `listofTraversedURLs`.

**21.15 (*Addition quiz*) Rewrite Programming Exercise 11.16 to store the answers in a set rather than a list.

DEVELOPING EFFICIENT ALGORITHMS

Objectives

- To estimate algorithm efficiency using the Big O notation (§22.2).

- To explain growth rates and why constants and nondominating terms can be ignored in the estimation (§22.2).

- To determine the complexity of various types of algorithms (§22.3).

- To analyze the binary search algorithm (§22.4.1).

- To analyze the selection sort algorithm (§22.4.2).

- To analyze the Tower of Hanoi algorithm (§22.4.3).

- To describe common growth functions (constant, logarithmic, log-linear, quadratic, cubic, and exponential) (§22.4.4).

- To design efficient algorithms for finding Fibonacci numbers using dynamic programming (§22.5).

- To find the GCD using Euclid's algorithm (§22.6).

- To find prime numbers using the sieve of Eratosthenes (§22.7).

- To design efficient algorithms for finding the closest pair of points using the divide-and-conquer approach (§22.8).

- To solve the Eight Queens problem using the backtracking approach (§22.9).

- To design efficient algorithms for finding a convex hull for a set of points (§22.10).

CHAPTER 22

22.1 Introduction

Algorithm design is to develop a mathematical process for solving a problem. Algorithm analysis is to predict the performance of an algorithm.

The preceding two chapters introduced classic data structures (lists, stacks, queues, priority queues, sets, and maps) and applied them to solve problems. This chapter will use a variety of examples to introduce common algorithmic techniques (dynamic programming, divide-and-conquer, and backtracking) for developing efficient algorithms. Later in the book, we will introduce efficient algorithms in Chapters 23–29. Before introducing developing efficient algorithms, we need to address the question on how to measure algorithm efficiency.

22.2 Measuring Algorithm Efficiency Using Big *O* Notation

The Big O notation obtains a function for measuring algorithm time complexity based on the input size. You can ignore multiplicative constants and nondominating terms in the function.

Suppose two algorithms perform the same task, such as search (linear search vs. binary search). Which one is better? To answer this question, you might implement these algorithms and run the programs to get execution times. However, there are two problems with this approach:

what is algorithm efficiency?

- First, many tasks run concurrently on a computer. The execution time of a particular program depends on the system load.

- Second, the execution time depends on specific input. Consider, for example, linear search and binary search. If an element to be searched happens to be the first in the list, linear search will find the element quicker than binary search.

It is very difficult to compare algorithms by measuring their execution times. To overcome these problems, a theoretical approach was developed to analyze algorithms independent of computers and specific input. This approach approximates the effect of a change on the size of the input. In this way, you can see how fast an algorithm's execution time increases as the input size increases, so you can compare two algorithms by examining their *growth rates*.

growth rates

Consider linear search. The linear search algorithm compares the key with the elements in the array sequentially until the key is found or the array is exhausted. If the key is not in the array, it requires n comparisons for an array of size n. If the key is in the array, it requires $n/2$ comparisons on average. The algorithm's execution time is proportional to the size of the array. If you double the size of the array, you will expect the number of comparisons to double. The algorithm grows at a linear rate. The growth rate has an order of magnitude of n. Computer scientists use the Big *O* notation to represent the "order of magnitude." Using this notation,

Big *O* notation

the complexity of the linear search algorithm is $O(n)$, pronounced as "*order of n.*" We call an algorithm with a time complexity of $O(n)$ linear algorithm, and it exhibits a linear growth rate.

For the same input size, an algorithm's execution time may vary, depending on the

best-case input
worst-case input

input. An input that results in the shortest execution time is called the *best-case input*, and an input that results in the longest execution time is the *worst-case input*. Best-and worst-case analyses are to analyze the algorithms for their best- and worst-case inputs. Best- and worst-case analyses are not representative, but worst-case analysis is very useful. You can be assured that the algorithm will never be slower than the worst case. An *average-case*

average-case analysis

analysis attempts to determine the average amount of time among all possible inputs of the same size. Average-case analysis is ideal, but difficult to perform because for many problems it is hard to determine the relative probabilities and distributions of various input instances. Worst-case analysis is easier to perform, so the analysis is generally conducted for the worst case.

The linear search algorithm requires n comparisons in the worst case and $n/2$ comparisons in the average case if you are nearly always looking for something known to be in the list. Using the Big *O* notation, both the cases require $O(n)$ time. The multiplicative constant $(1/2)$ can be omitted. Algorithm analysis is focused on growth rate. The multiplicative constants have no impact on growth rates. The growth rate for $n/2$ or $100n$ is the same as for n, as illustrated in Table 22.1. Therefore, $O(n) = O(n/2) = O(100n)$.

ignoring multiplicative constants

TABLE 22.1 Growth Rates

n \ $f(n)$	n	$n/2$	$100n$	
100	100	50	10000	
200	200	100	20000	
	2	2	2	$f(200)\,/\,f(100)$

Consider the algorithm for finding the maximum number in an array of n elements. To find the maximum number if n is 2, it takes one comparison and if n is 3, it takes two comparisons. In general, it takes $n - 1$ comparisons to find the maximum number in a list of n elements. Algorithm analysis is for large input size. If the input size is small, there is no significance in estimating an algorithm's efficiency. As n grows larger, the n part in the expression $n - 1$ dominates the complexity. The Big *O* notation allows you to ignore the nondominating part (e.g., -1 in the expression $n - 1$) and highlight the important part (e.g., n in the expression $n - 1$). Therefore, the complexity of this algorithm is $O(n)$.

large input size

ignoring nondominating terms

The Big *O* notation estimates the execution time of an algorithm in relation to the input size. If the time is not related to the input size, the algorithm is said to take *constant time* with the notation $O(1)$. For example, a method that retrieves an element at a given index in an array takes constant time because the time does not grow as the size of the array increases.

constant time

The following mathematical summations are often useful in algorithm analysis:

useful summations

$$1 + 2 + 3 + \cdots + (n - 2) + (n - 1) = \frac{n(n - 1)}{2} = O(n^2)$$

$$1 + 2 + 3 + \cdots + (n - 1) + n = \frac{n(n + 1)}{2} = O(n^2)$$

$$a^0 + a^1 + a^2 + a^3 + \cdots + a^{(n-1)} + a^n = \frac{a^{n+1} - 1}{a - 1} = O(a^n)$$

$$2^0 + 2^1 + 2^2 + 2^3 + \cdots + 2^{(n-1)} + 2^n = \frac{2^{n+1} - 1}{2 - 1} = 2^{n+1} - 1 = O(2^n)$$

Note

Time complexity is a measure of execution time using the Big *O* notation. Similarly, you can also measure *space complexity* using the Big *O* notation. *Space complexity* measures the amount of memory space used by an algorithm. The space complexity for most algorithms presented in this book is $O(n)$, that is, they exhibit linear growth rate to the input size. For example, the space complexity for linear search is $O(n)$.

time complexity

space complexity

22.2.1 Why is a constant factor ignored in the Big *O* notation? Why is a nondominating term ignored in the Big *O* notation?

Check Point

22.2.2 What is the order of each of the following functions?

$$\frac{(n^2 + 1)^2}{n}, \frac{(n^2 + \log^2 n^2)}{n}, n^3 + 100n^2 + n, 2^n + 100n^2 + 45n, n2^n + n^2 2^n$$

22.3 Examples: Determining Big O

This section gives several examples of determining Big O for repetition, sequence, and selection statements.

Example 1

Consider the time complexity for the following loop:

```
for (int i = 1; i <= n; i++) {
  k = k + 5;
}
```

It is a constant time, *c*, for executing

```
k = k + 5;
```

Since the loop is executed *n* times, the time complexity for the loop is

$$T(n) = (\text{a constant } c) * n = O(n).$$

The theoretical analysis predicts the performance of the algorithm. To see how this algorithm performs, we run the code in Listing 22.1 to obtain the execution time for $n = 1,000,000, 10,000,000, 100,000,000,$ and $1,000,000,000$.

LISTING 22.1   `PerformanceTest.java`

```
1  public class PerformanceTest {
2    public static void main(String[] args) {
3      getTime(1000000);
4      getTime(10000000);
5      getTime(100000000);
6      getTime(1000000000);
7    }
8
9    public static void getTime(long n) {
10     long startTime = System.currentTimeMillis();
11     long k = 0;
12     for (long i = 1; i <= n; i++) {
13       k = k + 5;
14     }
15     long endTime = System.currentTimeMillis();
16     System.out.println("Execution time for n = " + n
17       + " is " + (endTime - startTime) + " milliseconds");
18   }
19 }
```

input size 1,000,000
input size 10,000,000
input size 100,000,000
input size 1,000,000,000

time before execution

time after execution

```
Execution time for n = 1,000,000 is 6 milliseconds
Execution time for n = 10,000,000 is 61 milliseconds
Execution time for n = 100,000,000 is 610 milliseconds
Execution time for n = 1,000,000,000 is 6048 milliseconds
```

Our analysis predicts a linear time complexity for this loop. As shown in the sample output, when the input size increases 10 times, the runtime increases roughly 10 times. The execution confirms to the prediction.

Example 2

What is the time complexity for the following loop?

```
for (int i = 1; i <= n; i++) {
  for (int j = 1; j <= n; j++) {
```

```
      k = k + i + j;
    }
  }
```

It is a constant time, c, for executing

```
k = k + i + j;
```

The outer loop executes n times. For each iteration in the outer loop, the inner loop is executed n times. Thus, the time complexity for the loop is

$$T(n) = \text{(a constant } c) * n * n = O(n^2)$$

An algorithm with the $O(n^2)$ time complexity is called a *quadratic algorithm* and it exhibits a quadratic growth rate. The quadratic algorithm grows quickly as the problem size increases. If you double the input size, the time for the algorithm is quadrupled. Algorithms with a nested loop are often quadratic.

quadratic time

Example 3

Consider the following loop:

```
for (int i = 1; i <= n; i++) {
  for (int j = 1; j <= i; j++) {
    k = k + i + j;
  }
}
```

The outer loop executes n times. For $i = 1, 2, \ldots$, the inner loop is executed one time, two times, and n times. Thus, the time complexity for the loop is

$$T(n) = c + 2c + 3c + 4c + \cdots + nc$$
$$= cn(n + 1)/2$$
$$= (c/2)\, n^2 + (c/2)n$$
$$= O(n^2)$$

Example 4

Consider the following loop:

```
for (int i = 1; i <= n; i++) {
  for (int j = 1; j <= 20; j++) {
    k = k + i + j;
  }
}
```

The inner loop executes 20 times and the outer loop n times. Therefore, the time complexity for the loop is

$$T(n) = 20 * c * n = O(n)$$

Example 5

Consider the following sequences:

```
for (int j = 1; j <= 10; j++) {
  k = k + 4;
}
for (int i = 1; i <= n; i++) {
  for (int j = 1; j <= 20; j++) {
```

```
        k = k + i + j;
    }
}
```

The first loop executes 10 times and the second loop 20 * n times. Thus, the time complexity for the loop is

$$T(n) = 10 * c + 20 * c * n = O(n)$$

Example 6

Consider the following selection statement:

```
if (list.contains(e)) {
  System.out.println(e);
}
else
    for (Object t: list) {
      System.out.println(t);
    }
```

Suppose the list contains n elements. The execution time for `list.contains(e)` is $O(n)$. The loop in the `else` clause takes $O(n)$ time. Hence, the time complexity for the entire statement is

$$T(n) = \text{if test time} + \text{worst-case time (if clause, else clause)}$$

$$= O(n) + O(n) = O(n)$$

Example 7

Consider the computation of a^n for an integer n. A simple algorithm would multiply a n times, as follows:

```
result = 1;
for (int i = 1; i <= n; i++)
   result *= a;
```

The algorithm takes $O(n)$ time. Without loss of generality, assume that $n = 2^k$. You can improve the algorithm using the following scheme:

```
result = a;
for (int i = 1; i <= k; i++)
   result = result * result;
```

The algorithm takes $O(\log n)$ time. For an arbitrary n, you can revise the algorithm and prove that the complexity is still $O(\log n)$. (See CheckPoint Question 22.3.5.)

Note

An algorithm with the O(logn) time complexity is called a logarithmic algorithm and it exhibits a logarithmic growth rate. The base of the log is 2, but the base does not affect a logarithmic growth rate, so it can be omitted. In algorithm analysis, the base is usually 2.

omitting base

Check
Point

22.3.1 Count the number of iterations in the following loops.

```
int count = 1;
while (count < 30) {
  count = count * 2;
}
```
(a)

```
int count = 15;
while (count < 30) {
  count = count * 3;
}
```
(b)

```
int count = 1;
while (count < n) {
   count = count *  2;
}
```
(c)

```
int count = 15;
while (count < n) {
   count = count *  3;
}
```
(d)

22.3.2 How many stars are displayed in the following code if n is 10? How many if n is 20? Use the Big *O* notation to estimate the time complexity.

```
for (int i = 0; i < n; i++) {
   System.out.print('*');
}
```
(a)

```
for (int i = 0; i < n; i++) {
   for (int j = 0; j < n; j++) {
      System.out.print('*');
   }
}
```
(b)

```
for (int k = 0; k < n; k++) {
   for (int i = 0; i < n; i++) {
      for (int j = 0; j < n; j++) {
         System.out.print('*');
      }
   }
}
```
(c)

```
for (int k = 0; k < 10; k++) {
   for (int i = 0; i < n; i++) {
      for (int j = 0; j < n; j++) {
         System.out.print('*');
      }
   }
}
```
(d)

22.3.3 Use the Big *O* notation to estimate the time complexity of the following methods:

```
public static void mA(int n) {
   for (int i = 0; i < n; i++) {
      System.out.print(Math.random());
   }
}
```
(a)

```
public static void mB(int n) {
   for (int i = 0; i < n; i++) {
      for (int j = 0; j < i; j++)
         System.out.print(Math.random());
   }
}
```
(b)

```
public static void mC(int[ ] m) {
   for (int i = 0; i < m.length; i++) {
      System.out.print(m[i]);
   }

   for (int i = m.length - 1; i >= 0; )
   {
      System.out.print(m[i]);
      i--;
   }
}
```
(c)

```
public static void mD(int[] m) {
   for (int i = 0; i < m.length; i++) {
      for (int j = 0; j < i; j++)
         System.out.print(m[i] * m[j]);
   }
}
```
(d)

22.3.4 Design an $O(n)$ time algorithm for computing the sum of numbers from $n1$ to $n2$ for ($n1 < n2$). Can you design an $O(1)$ for performing the same task?

22.3.5 Example 7 in Section 22.3 assumes $n = 2^k$. Revise the algorithm for an arbitrary n and prove that the complexity is still $O(\log n)$.

22.4 Analyzing Algorithm Time Complexity

Key Point

This section analyzes the complexity of several well-known algorithms: binary search, selection sort, and Tower of Hanoi.

22.4.1   Analyzing Binary Search

binary search animation on the Companion Website

The binary search algorithm presented in Listing 7.7, BinarySearch.java, searches for a key in a sorted array. Each iteration in the algorithm contains a fixed number of operations, denoted by c. Let $T(n)$ denote the time complexity for a binary search on a list of n elements. Without loss of generality, assume n is a power of 2 and $k = \log n$. Since a binary search eliminates half of the input after two comparisons,

$$T(n) = T\left(\frac{n}{2}\right) + c = T\left(\frac{n}{2^2}\right) + c + c = T\left(\frac{n}{2^k}\right) + kc$$

$$= T(1) + c \log n = 1 + (\log n)c$$

$$= O(\log n)$$

logarithmic time

Ignoring constants and nondominating terms, the complexity of the binary search algorithm is $O(\log n)$. This is a logarithmic algorithm. The logarithmic algorithm grows slowly as the problem size increases. In the case of binary search, each time you double the array size, at most one more comparison will be required. If you square the input size of any logarithmic-time algorithm, you only double the time of execution. Therefore, a logarithmic-time algorithm is very efficient.

22.4.2   Analyzing Selection Sort

selection sort animation on the Companion Website

The selection sort algorithm presented in Listing 7.8, SelectionSort.java, finds the smallest element in the list and swaps it with the first element. It then finds the smallest element remaining and swaps it with the first element in the remaining list, and so on until the remaining list contains only one element left to be sorted. The number of comparisons is $n - 1$ for the first iteration, $n - 2$ for the second iteration, and so on. Let $T(n)$ denote the complexity for selection sort and c denote the total number of other operations such as assignments and additional comparisons in each iteration. Thus,

$$T(n) = (n - 1) + c + (n - 2) + c + \cdots + 2 + c + 1 + c$$

$$= \frac{(n - 1)(n - 1 + 1)}{2} + c(n - 1) = \frac{n^2}{2} - \frac{n}{2} + cn - c$$

$$= O(n^2)$$

Therefore, the complexity of the selection sort algorithm is $O(n^2)$.

22.4.3   Analyzing the Tower of Hanoi Problem

The Tower of Hanoi problem presented in Listing 18.8, TowerOfHanoi.java, recursively moves n disks from tower A to tower B with the assistance of tower C as follows:

1. Move the first $n - 1$ disks from A to C with the assistance of tower B.

2. Move disk n from A to B.

3. Move $n - 1$ disks from C to B with the assistance of tower A.

The complexity of this algorithm is measured by the number of moves. Let $T(n)$ denote the number of moves for the algorithm to move n disks from tower A to tower B with $T(1) = 1$. Thus,

$$
\begin{aligned}
T(n) &= T(n - 1) + 1 + T(n - 1) \\
&= 2T(n - 1) + 1 \\
&= 2(2T(n - 2) + 1) + 1 \\
&= 2(2(2T(n - 3) + 1) + 1) + 1 \\
&= 2^{n-1}T(1) + 2^{n-2} + \cdots + 2 + 1 \\
&= 2^{n-1} + 2^{n-2} + \cdots + 2 + 1 = (2^n - 1) = O(2^n)
\end{aligned}
$$

An algorithm with $O(2^n)$ time complexity is called an *exponential algorithm* and it exhibits an exponential growth rate. As the input size increases, the time for the exponential algorithm grows exponentially. Exponential algorithms are not practical for large input size. Suppose the disk is moved at a rate of 1 per second. It would take $2^{32}/(365 * 24 * 60 * 60) = 136$ years to move 32 disks and $2^{64}/(365 * 24 * 60 * 60) = 585$ billion years to move 64 disks.

$O(2^n)$
exponential time

22.4.4 Common Recurrence Relations

Recurrence relations are a useful tool for analyzing algorithm complexity. As shown in the preceding examples, the complexity for binary search, selection sort, and the Tower of Hanoi is

$$T(n) = T\left(\frac{n}{2}\right) + c, \ T(n) = T(n - 1) + O(n), \text{ and } T(n) = 2T(n - 1) + O(1), \text{ respectively.}$$

Table 22.2 summarizes the common recurrence relations.

TABLE 22.2 Common Recurrence Functions

Recurrence Relation	Result	Example
$T(n) = T(n/2) + O(1)$	$T(n) = O(\log n)$	Binary search, Euclid's GCD
$T(n) = T(n - 1) + O(1)$	$T(n) = O(n)$	Linear search
$T(n) = 2T(n/2) + O(1)$	$T(n) = O(n)$	CheckPoint Question 22.8.2
$T(n) = 2T(n/2) + O(n)$	$T(n) = O(n \log n)$	Merge sort (Chapter 23)
$T(n) = T(n - 1) + O(n)$	$T(n) = O(n^2)$	Selection sort
$T(n) = 2T(n - 1) + O(1)$	$T(n) = O(2^n)$	Tower of Hanoi
$T(n) = T(n - 1) + T(n - 2) + O(1)$	$T(n) = O(2^n)$	Recursive Fibonacci algorithm

22.4.5 Comparing Common Growth Functions

The preceding sections analyzed the complexity of several algorithms. Table 22.3 lists some common growth functions and shows how growth rates change as the input size doubles from $n = 25$ to $n = 50$.

TABLE 22.3 Change of Growth Rates

Function	Name	$n = 25$	$n = 50$	$f(50)$ and $f(25)$
$O(1)$	Constant time	1	1	1
$O(\log n)$	Logarithmic time	4.64	5.64	1.21
$O(n)$	Linear time	25	50	2
$O(n \log n)$	Log-linear time	116	282	2.43
$O(n^2)$	Quadratic time	625	2,500	4
$O(n^3)$	Cubic time	15,625	125,000	8
$O(2^n)$	Exponential time	3.36×10^7	1.27×10^{15}	3.35×10^7

These functions are ordered as follows, as illustrated in Figure 22.1.

$$O(1) < O(\log n) < O(n) < O(n \log n) < O(n^2) < O(n^3) < O(2^n)$$

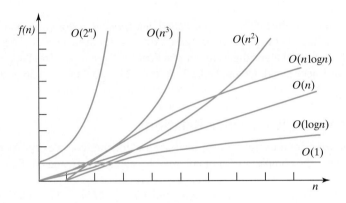

FIGURE 22.1 As the size n increases, the function grows.

Check Point

22.4.1 Put the following growth functions in order:

$$\frac{5n^3}{4{,}032}, \; 44 \log n, \; 10n \log n, \; 500, \; 2n^2, \; \frac{2^n}{45}, \; 3n$$

22.4.2 Estimate the time complexity for adding two $n \times m$ matrices and multiplying an $n \times m$ matrix by an $m \times k$ matrix.

22.4.3 Describe an algorithm for finding the occurrence of the max element in an array. Analyze the complexity of the algorithm.

22.4.4 Describe an algorithm for removing duplicates from an array. Analyze the complexity of the algorithm.

22.4.5 Analyze the following sorting algorithm:

```
for (int i = 0; i < list.length - 1; i++) {
  if (list[i] > list[i + 1]) {
    swap list[i] with list[i + 1];
    i = -1;
  }
}
```

22.4.6 Analyze the complexity for computing a polynomial $f(x)$ of degree n for a given x value using a brute-force approach and the Horner's approach, respectively. A brute-force approach is to compute each term in the polynomial and add them together. The Horner's approach was introduced in Section 6.7.

$$f(x) = a_n x^n + a_{n-1} x^{n-1} + a_{n-2} x^{n-2} + \cdots + a_1 x^1 + a_0$$

22.5 Finding Fibonacci Numbers Using Dynamic Programming

This section analyzes and designs an efficient algorithm for finding Fibonacci numbers using dynamic programming.

Key
Point

Section 18.3, Case Study: Computing Fibonacci Numbers, gave a recursive method for finding the Fibonacci number, as follows:

```java
/** The method for finding the Fibonacci number */
public static long fib(long index) {
  if (index == 0) // Base case
    return 0;
  else if (index == 1) // Base case
    return 1;
  else // Reduction and recursive calls
    return fib(index - 1) + fib(index - 2);
}
```

We can now prove that the complexity of this algorithm is $O(2^n)$. For convenience, let the index be n. Let $T(n)$ denote the complexity for the algorithm that finds fib(n), and c denote the constant time for comparing the index with 0 and 1. Thus,

$$T(n) = T(n - 1) + T(n - 2) + c$$

$$\leq 2T(n - 1) + c$$

$$\leq 2(2T(n - 2) + c) + c$$

$$= 2^2 T(n - 2) + 2c + c$$

Similar to the analysis of the Tower of Hanoi problem, we can show that $T(n)$ is $O(2^n)$.

This algorithm is not efficient. Is there an efficient algorithm for finding a Fibonacci number? The trouble with the recursive `fib` method is that the method is invoked redundantly with the same arguments. For example, to compute `fib(4)`, `fib(3)` and `fib(2)` are invoked. To compute `fib(3)`, `fib(2)` and `fib(1)` are invoked. Note `fib(2)` is redundantly invoked. We can improve it by avoiding repeatedly calling of the `fib` method with the same argument. Note a new Fibonacci number is obtained by adding the preceding two numbers in the sequence. If you use the two variables `f0` and `f1` to store the two preceding numbers, the new number, `f2`, can be immediately obtained by adding `f0` with `f1`. Now you should update `f0` and `f1` by assigning `f1` to `f0` and assigning `f2` to `f1`, as shown in Figure 22.2.

```
                    f0 f1  f2
Fibonacci series: 0  1   1   2   3   5   8   13   21   34   55   89 ...
         indices: 0  1   2   3   4   5   6   7    8    9    10   11

                        f0  f1  f2
Fibonacci series: 0  1   1   2   3   5   8   13   21   34   55   89 ...
         indices: 0  1   2   3   4   5   6   7    8    9    10   11

                                 f0   f1   f2
Fibonacci series: 0  1   1   2   3   5   8   13   21   34   55   89 ...
         indices: 0  1   2   3   4   5   6   7    8    9    10   11
```

FIGURE 22.2 Variables `f0`, `f1`, and `f2` store three consecutive Fibonacci numbers in the series.

The new method is implemented in Listing 22.2.

LISTING 22.2 ImprovedFibonacci.java

```java
 1  import java.util.Scanner;
 2
 3  public class ImprovedFibonacci {
 4    /** Main method */
 5    public static void main(String args[]) {
 6      // Create a Scanner
 7      Scanner input = new Scanner(System.in);
 8      System.out.print("Enter an index for the Fibonacci number: ");
 9      int index = input.nextInt();
10
11      // Find and display the Fibonacci number
12      System.out.println(
13        "Fibonacci number at index " + index + " is " + fib(index));
14    }
15
16    /** The method for finding the Fibonacci number */
17    public static long fib(long n) {
18      long f0 = 0; // For fib(0)
19      long f1 = 1; // For fib(1)
20      long f2 = 1; // For fib(2)
21
22      if (n == 0)
23        return f0;
24      else if (n == 1)
25        return f1;
26      else if (n == 2)
27        return f2;
28
29      for (int i = 3; i <= n; i++) {
30        f0 = f1;
31        f1 = f2;
32        f2 = f0 + f1;
33      }
34
35      return f2;
36    }
37  }
```

input

invoke fib

f0
f1
f2

update f0, f1, f2

```
Enter an index for the Fibonacci number: 6 ⏎Enter
Fibonacci number at index 6 is 8
```

```
Enter an index for the Fibonacci number: 7 ⏎Enter
Fibonacci number at index 7 is 13
```

$O(n)$

Obviously, the complexity of this new algorithm is $O(n)$. This is a tremendous improvement over the recursive $O(2^n)$ algorithm.

dynamic programming

The algorithm for computing Fibonacci numbers presented here uses an approach known as *dynamic programming*. Dynamic programming is the process of solving subproblems, then combining the solutions of the subproblems to obtain an overall solution. This naturally leads to a recursive solution. However, it would be inefficient to use recursion because the subproblems overlap. The key idea behind dynamic programming is to solve each subproblem only once and store the results for subproblems for later use to avoid redundant computing of the subproblems.

22.5.1 What is dynamic programming? Give an example of dynamic programming.

22.5.2 Why is the recursive Fibonacci algorithm inefficient, but the nonrecursive Fibonacci algorithm efficient?

Check Point

22.6 Finding Greatest Common Divisors Using Euclid's Algorithm

Key Point

This section presents several algorithms in the search for an efficient algorithm for finding the greatest common divisor of two integers.

GCD

The greatest common divisor (GCD) of two integers is the largest number that can evenly divide both integers. Listing 5.9, GreatestCommonDivisor.java, presented a brute-force algorithm for finding the GCD of two integers m and n. *Brute force* refers to an algorithmic approach that solves a problem in the simplest or most direct or obvious way. As a result, such an algorithm can end up doing far more work to solve a given problem than a cleverer or more sophisticated algorithm might do. On the other hand, a brute-force algorithm is often easier to implement than a more sophisticated one and, because of this simplicity, sometimes it can be more efficient.

brute force

The brute-force algorithm checks whether k (for k = 2, 3, 4, and so on) is a common divisor for n1 and n2, until k is greater than n1 or n2. The algorithm can be described as follows:

```java
public static int gcd(int m, int n) {
  int gcd = 1;

  for (int k = 2; k <= m && k <= n; k++) {
    if (m % k == 0 && n % k == 0)
      gcd = k;
  }

  return gcd;
}
```

Assuming $m \geq n$, the complexity of this algorithm is obviously $O(n)$.

assume $m \geq n$

$O(n)$

Is there a better algorithm for finding the GCD? Rather than searching a possible divisor from 1 up, it is more efficient to search from n down. Once a divisor is found, the divisor is the GCD. Therefore, you can improve the algorithm using the following loop:

improved solutions

```java
for (int k = n; k >= 1; k--) {
  if (m % k == 0 && n % k == 0) {
    gcd = k;
    break;
  }
}
```

This algorithm is better than the preceding one, but its worst-case time complexity is still $O(n)$.

A divisor for a number n cannot be greater than n / 2, so you can further improve the algorithm using the following loop:

```java
for (int k = m / 2; k >= 1; k--) {
  if (m % k == 0 && n % k == 0) {
    gcd = k;
    break;
  }
}
```

However, this algorithm is incorrect because n can be a divisor for m. This case must be considered. The correct algorithm is shown in Listing 22.3.

LISTING 22.3 GCD.java

```
 1  import java.util.Scanner;
 2
 3  public class GCD {
 4    /** Find GCD for integers m and n */
 5    public static int gcd(int m, int n) {
 6      int gcd = 1;
 7
 8      if (m % n == 0)  return n;
 9
10      for (int k = n / 2; k >= 1; k--) {
11        if (m % k == 0 && n % k == 0) {
12          gcd = k;
13          break;
14        }
15      }
16
17      return gcd;
18    }
19
20    /** Main method */
21    public static void main(String[] args) {
22      // Create a Scanner
23      Scanner input = new Scanner(System.in);
24
25      // Prompt the user to enter two integers
26      System.out.print("Enter first integer: ");
27      int m = input.nextInt();
28      System.out.print("Enter second integer: ");
29      int n = input.nextInt();
30
31      System.out.println("The greatest common divisor for " + m +
32        " and " + n + " is " + gcd(m, n));
33    }
34  }
```

check divisor (line 8)

GCD found (line 12)

input (line 27)

input (line 29)

```
Enter first integer: 2525 ↵Enter
Enter second integer: 125 ↵Enter
The greatest common divisor for 2525 and 125 is 25
```

```
Enter first integer: 3 ↵Enter
Enter second integer: 3 ↵Enter
The greatest common divisor for 3 and 3 is 3
```

O(n)

Assuming $m \geq n$, the `for` loop is executed at most $n/2$ times, which cuts the time by half from the previous algorithm. The time complexity of this algorithm is still $O(n)$, but practically, it is much faster than the algorithm in Listing 5.9.

Note

The Big O notation provides a good theoretical estimate of algorithm efficiency. However, two algorithms of the same time complexity are not necessarily equally efficient. As shown in the preceding example, both algorithms in Listings 5.9 and 22.3 have the same complexity, but in practice, the one in Listing 22.3 is obviously better.

practical consideration

A more efficient algorithm for finding the GCD was discovered by Euclid around 300 B.C. This is one of the oldest known algorithms. It can be defined recursively as follows:

Euclid's algorithm

Let `gcd(m, n)` denote the GCD for integers `m` and `n`:

- If `m % n` is `0`, `gcd(m, n)` is `n`.

- Otherwise, `gcd(m, n)` is `gcd(n, m % n)`.

It is not difficult to prove the correctness of this algorithm. Suppose `m % n = r`. Thus, `m = qn + r`, where `q` is the quotient of `m / n`. Any number that divides `m` and `n` evenly must also divide `r` evenly. Therefore, `gcd(m, n)` is the same as `gcd(n, r)`, where `r = m % n`. The algorithm can be implemented as in Listing 22.4.

LISTING 22.4 `GCDEuclid.java`

```
1   import java.util.Scanner;
2
3   public class GCDEuclid {
4     /** Find GCD for integers m and n */
5     public static int gcd(int m, int n) {
6       if (m % n == 0)                                    base case
7         return n;
8       else
9         return gcd(n, m % n);                            reduction
10    }
11
12    /** Main method */
13    public static void main(String[] args) {
14      // Create a Scanner
15      Scanner input = new Scanner(System.in);
16
17      // Prompt the user to enter two integers
18      System.out.print("Enter first integer: ");
19      int m = input.nextInt();                           input
20      System.out.print("Enter second integer: ");
21      int n = input.nextInt();                           input
22
23      System.out.println("The greatest common divisor for " + m +
24        " and " + n + " is " + gcd(m, n));
25    }
26  }
```

```
Enter first integer: 2525 ⏎Enter
Enter second integer: 125 ⏎Enter
The greatest common divisor for 2525 and 125 is 25
```

```
Enter first integer: 3 ⏎Enter
Enter second integer: 3 ⏎Enter
The greatest common divisor for 3 and 3 is 3
```

In the best case when `m % n` is `0`, the algorithm takes just one step to find the GCD. It is difficult to analyze the average case. However, we can prove that the worst-case time complexity is $O(\log n)$.

Assuming $m \geq n$, we can show that `m % n < m / 2`, as follows:

- If `n <= m / 2`, `m % n < m / 2`, since the remainder of m divided by n is always less than n.

- If `n > m / 2`, `m % n = m - n < m / 2`. Therefore, `m % n < m / 2`.

Euclid's algorithm recursively invokes the `gcd` method. It first calls `gcd(m, n)`, then calls `gcd(n, m % n)` and `gcd(m % n, n % (m % n))`, and so on, as follows:

```
  gcd(m, n)
= gcd(n, m % n)
= gcd(m % n, n % (m % n))
= . . .
```

Since `m % n < m / 2` and `n % (m % n) < n / 2`, the argument passed to the `gcd` method is reduced by half after every two iterations. After invoking `gcd` two times, the second parameter is less than $n/2$. After invoking `gcd` four times, the second parameter is less than $n/4$. After invoking `gcd` six times, the second parameter is less than $\frac{n}{2^3}$. Let k be the number of times the `gcd` method is invoked. After invoking `gcd` k times, the second parameter is less than $\frac{n}{2^{(k/2)}}$, which is greater than or equal to 1. That is,

$$\frac{n}{2^{(k/2)}} \geq 1 \quad \Rightarrow \quad n \geq 2^{(k/2)} \quad \Rightarrow \quad \log n \geq k/2 \quad \Rightarrow \quad k \leq 2 \log n$$

Therefore, $k \leq 2 \log n$. Thus, the time complexity of the `gcd` method is $O(\log n)$.

The worst case occurs when the two numbers result in the most divisions. It turns out that two successive Fibonacci numbers will result in the most divisions. Recall that the Fibonacci series begins with 0 and 1, and each subsequent number is the sum of the preceding two numbers in the series, such as:

$$0 \ 1 \ 1 \ 2 \ 3 \ 5 \ 8 \ 13 \ 21 \ 34 \ 55 \ 89 \ldots$$

The series can be recursively defined as

```
fib(0) = 0;
fib(1) = 1;
fib(index) = fib(index - 2) + fib(index - 1); index >= 2
```

For two successive Fibonacci numbers `fib(index)` and `fib(index - 1)`,

```
  gcd(fib(index), fib(index - 1))
= gcd(fib(index - 1), fib(index - 2))
= gcd(fib(index - 2), fib(index - 3))
= gcd(fib(index - 3), fib(index - 4))
= . . .
= gcd(fib(2), fib(1))
= 1
```

For example,

```
  gcd(21, 13)
= gcd(13, 8)
= gcd(8, 5)
= gcd(5, 3)
```

```
= gcd(3, 2)
= gcd(2, 1)
= 1
```

Therefore, the number of times the `gcd` method is invoked is the same as the index. We can prove that *index* ≤ 1.44 log*n*, where *n* = fib (index − 1). This is a tighter bound than index ≤ 2 log*n*.

Table 22.4 summarizes the complexity of three algorithms for finding the GCD.

TABLE 22.4 Comparisons of GCD Algorithms

Algorithm	Complexity	Description
Listing 5.9	$O(n)$	Brute-force, checking all possible divisors
Listing 22.3	$O(n)$	Checking half of all possible divisors
Listing 22.4	$O(\log n)$	Euclid's algorithm

22.6.1 Prove the following algorithm for finding the GCD of the two integers `m` and `n` is incorrect:

```
int gcd = 1;
for (int k = Math.min(Math.sqrt(n), Math.sqrt(m)); k >= 1; k--) {
  if (m % k == 0 && n % k == 0) {
    gcd = k;
    break;
  }
}
```

22.7 Efficient Algorithms for Finding Prime Numbers

This section presents several algorithms in the search for an efficient algorithm for finding prime numbers.

A \$150,000 award awaits the first individual or group who discovers a prime number with at least 100,000,000 decimal digits (w2.eff.org/awards/coop-prime-rules.php).

Can you design a fast algorithm for finding prime numbers?

An integer greater than 1 is *prime* if its only positive divisor is 1 or itself. For example, 2, 3, 5, and 7 are prime numbers, but 4, 6, 8, and 9 are not.

what is prime?

How do you determine whether a number `n` is prime? Listing 5.15 presented a brute-force algorithm for finding prime numbers. The algorithm checks whether 2, 3, 4, 5, . . . , or n − 1 is divisible by n. If not, n is prime. This algorithm takes $O(n)$ time to check whether n is prime. Note you need to check only whether 2, 3, 4, 5, . . . , and n/2 is divisible by n. If not, n is prime. This algorithm is slightly improved, but it is still of $O(n)$.

In fact, we can prove that if n is not a prime, n must have a factor that is greater than 1 and less than or equal to $\sqrt{n}$. Here is the proof. Since n is not a prime, there exist two numbers p and q such that n = pq with $1 < p \le q$. Note that $n = \sqrt{n}\sqrt{n}$. p must be less than or equal to $\sqrt{n}$. Hence, you need to check only whether 2, 3, 4, 5, . . . , or $\sqrt{n}$ is divisible by n. If not, n is prime. This significantly reduces the time complexity of the algorithm to $O(\sqrt{n})$.

Now consider the algorithm for finding all the prime numbers up to `n`. A straightforward implementation is to check whether `i` is prime for $i = $ 2, 3, 4, . . . , `n`. The program is given in Listing 22.5.

LISTING 22.5 PrimeNumbers.java

```
1   import java.util.Scanner;
2
3   public class PrimeNumbers {
4     public static void main(String[] args) {
5       Scanner input = new Scanner(System.in);
6       System.out.print("Find all prime numbers <= n, enter n: ");
7       int n = input.nextInt();
8
9       final int NUMBER_PER_LINE = 10; // Display 10 per line
10      int count = 0; // Count the number of prime numbers
11      int number = 2; // A number to be tested for primeness
12
13      System.out.println("The prime numbers are:");
14
15      // Repeatedly find prime numbers
16      while (number <= n) {
17        // Assume the number is prime
18        boolean isPrime = true; // Is the current number prime?
19
20        // Test if number is prime
21        for (int divisor = 2; divisor <= (int)(Math.sqrt(number));
22             divisor++) {
23          if (number % divisor == 0) {  // If true, number is not prime
24            isPrime = false; // Set isPrime to false
25            break; // Exit the for loop
26          }
27        }
28
29        // Print the prime number and increase the count
30        if (isPrime) {
31          count++; // Increase the count
32
33          if (count % NUMBER_PER_LINE == 0) {
34            // Print the number and advance to the new line
35            System.out.printf("%7d\n", number);
36          }
37          else
38            System.out.printf("%7d", number);
39        }
40
41        // Check if the next number is prime
42        number++;
43      }
44
45      System.out.println("\n" + count +
46        " prime(s) less than or equal to " + n);
47    }
48  }
```

check prime — (line 21)

increase count — (line 30)

check next number — (line 42)

```
Find all prime numbers <= n, enter n: 1000 ↵Enter
The prime numbers are:
        2     3     5     7    11    13    17    19    23    29
       31    37    41    43    47    53    59    61    67    71
...
...
168 prime(s) less than or equal to 1000
```

The program is not efficient if you have to compute `Math.sqrt(number)` for every iteration of the `for` loop (line 21). A good compiler should evaluate `Math.sqrt(number)` only once for the entire `for` loop. To ensure this happens, you can explicitly replace line 21 with the following two lines:

```java
int squareRoot = (int)(Math.sqrt(number));
for (int divisor = 2; divisor <= squareRoot; divisor++) {
```

In fact, there is no need to actually compute `Math.sqrt(number)` for every `number`. You need to look only for the perfect squares such as 4, 9, 16, 25, 36, 49, and so on. Note for all the numbers between 36 and 48, inclusively, their `(int)(Math.sqrt(number))` is 6. With this insight, you can replace the code in lines 16–26 with the following:

```java
...
int squareRoot = 1;

// Repeatedly find prime numbers
while (number <= n) {
  // Assume the number is prime
  boolean isPrime = true; // Is the current number prime?

  if (squareRoot * squareRoot < number) squareRoot++;

  // Test if number is prime
  for (int divisor = 2; divisor <= squareRoot; divisor++) {
    if (number % divisor == 0) { // If true, number is not prime
      isPrime = false; // Set isPrime to false
      break; // Exit the for loop
    }
  }
}
...
```

Now we turn our attention to analyzing the complexity of this program. Since it takes $\sqrt{i}$ steps in the `for` loop (lines 21–27) to check whether number i is prime, the algorithm takes $\sqrt{2} + \sqrt{3} + \sqrt{4} + \cdots + \sqrt{n}$ steps to find all the prime numbers less than or equal to n. Observe that

$$\sqrt{2} + \sqrt{3} + \sqrt{4} + \cdots + \sqrt{n} \le n\sqrt{n}$$

Therefore, the time complexity for this algorithm is $O\left(n\sqrt{n}\right)$.

To determine whether i is prime, the algorithm checks whether 2, 3, 4, 5, ..., and $\sqrt{i}$ are divisible by i. This algorithm can be further improved. In fact, you need to check only whether the prime numbers from 2 to $\sqrt{i}$ are possible divisors for i.

We can prove that if i is not prime, there must exist a prime number p such that $i = pq$ and $p \le q$. Here is the proof. Assume i is not prime; let p be the smallest factor of i. p must be prime, otherwise, p has a factor k with $2 \le k < p$. k is also a factor of i, which contradicts that p be the smallest factor of i. Therefore, if i is not prime, you can find a prime number from 2 to $\sqrt{i}$ that is divisible by i. This leads to a more efficient algorithm for finding all prime numbers up to n, as given in Listing 22.6.

LISTING 22.6 `EfficientPrimeNumbers.java`

```java
1  import java.util.Scanner;
2
3  public class EfficientPrimeNumbers {
4    public static void main(String[] args) {
5      Scanner input = new Scanner(System.in);
6      System.out.print("Find all prime numbers <= n, enter n: ");
```

```
 7          int n = input.nextInt();
 8
 9          // A list to hold prime numbers
10          java.util.List<Integer> list =
11            new java.util.ArrayList<>();
12
13          final int NUMBER_PER_LINE = 10; // Display 10 per line
14          int count = 0; // Count the number of prime numbers
15          int number = 2; // A number to be tested for primeness
16          int squareRoot = 1; // Check whether number <= squareRoot
17
18          System.out.println("The prime numbers are \n");
19
20          // Repeatedly find prime numbers
21          while (number <= n) {
22            // Assume the number is prime
23            boolean isPrime = true; // Is the current number prime?
24
25            if (squareRoot * squareRoot < number) squareRoot++;
26
27            // Test whether number is prime
28            for (int k = 0; k < list.size()
29                            && list.get(k) <= squareRoot; k++) {
30              if (number % list.get(k) == 0) {  // If true, not prime
31                isPrime = false; // Set isPrime to false
32                break; // Exit the for loop
33              }
34            }
35
36            // Print the prime number and increase the count
37            if (isPrime) {
38              count++; // Increase the count
39              list.add(number); // Add a new prime to the list
40              if (count % NUMBER_PER_LINE == 0) {
41                // Print the number and advance to the new line
42                System.out.println(number);
43              }
44              else
45                System.out.print(number + " ");
46            }
47
48            // Check whether the next number is prime
49            number++;
50          }
51
52        System.out.println("\n" + count +
53          " prime(s) less than or equal to " + n);
54      }
55  }
```

check prime (line 28)

increase count (line 38)

check next number (line 49)

```
Find all prime numbers <= n, enter n: 1000 ↵Enter
The prime numbers are:
     2       3       5       7      11      13      17      19      23      29
    31      37      41      43      47      53      59      61      67      71
...
...
168 prime(s) less than or equal to 1000
```

Let $\pi(i)$ denote the number of prime numbers less than or equal to i. The primes under 20 are 2, 3, 5, 7, 11, 13, 17, and 19. Therefore, $\pi(2)$ is 1, $\pi(3)$ is 2, $\pi(6)$ is 3, and $\pi(20)$ is 8.

It has been proved that $\pi(i)$ is approximately $\dfrac{i}{\log i}$ (see primes.utm.edu/howmany.shtml).

For each number i, the algorithm checks whether a prime number less than or equal to $\sqrt{i}$ is divisible by i. The number of the prime numbers less than or equal to $\sqrt{i}$ is

$$\frac{\sqrt{i}}{\log \sqrt{i}} = \frac{2\sqrt{i}}{\log i}$$

Thus, the complexity for finding all prime numbers up to n is

$$\frac{2\sqrt{2}}{\log 2} + \frac{2\sqrt{3}}{\log 3} + \frac{2\sqrt{4}}{\log 4} + \frac{2\sqrt{5}}{\log 5} + \frac{2\sqrt{6}}{\log 6} + \frac{2\sqrt{7}}{\log 7} + \frac{2\sqrt{8}}{\log 8} + \cdots + \frac{2\sqrt{n}}{\log n}$$

Since $\dfrac{\sqrt{i}}{\log i} < \dfrac{\sqrt{n}}{\log n}$ for $i < n$ and $n \geq 16$,

$$\frac{2\sqrt{2}}{\log 2} + \frac{2\sqrt{3}}{\log 3} + \frac{2\sqrt{4}}{\log 4} + \frac{2\sqrt{5}}{\log 5} + \frac{2\sqrt{6}}{\log 6} + \frac{2\sqrt{7}}{\log 7} + \frac{2\sqrt{8}}{\log 8} + \cdots + \frac{2\sqrt{n}}{\log n} < \frac{2n\sqrt{n}}{\log n}$$

Therefore, the complexity of this algorithm is $O\left(\dfrac{n\sqrt{n}}{\log n}\right)$.

This algorithm is another example of dynamic programming. The algorithm stores the results of the subproblems in the array list and uses them later to check whether a new number is prime.

dynamic programming

Is there any algorithm better than $O\left(\dfrac{n\sqrt{n}}{\log n}\right)$? Let us examine the well-known Eratosthenes

algorithm for finding prime numbers. Eratosthenes (276–194 B.C.) was a Greek mathematician who devised a clever algorithm, known as the *Sieve of Eratosthenes*, for finding all prime numbers $\leq n$. His algorithm is to use an array named `primes` of n Boolean values. Initially, all elements in `primes` are set `true`. Since the multiples of 2 are not prime, set `primes[2 * i]` to `false` for all $2 \leq i \leq n/2$, as shown in Figure 22.3. Since we don't care about `primes[0]` and `primes[1]`, these values are marked $\times$ in the figure.

Sieve of Eratosthenes

primes array

index	0	1	2	3	4	5	6	7	8	9	10	11	12	13	14	15	16	17	18	19	20	21	22	23	24	25	26	27
initial	×	×	T	T	T	T	T	T	T	T	T	T	T	T	T	T	T	T	T	T	T	T	T	T	T	T	T	T
k = 2	×	×	T	T	F	T	F	T	F	T	F	T	F	T	F	T	F	T	F	T	F	T	F	T	F	T	F	T
k = 3	×	×	T	T	F	T	F	T	F	F	F	T	F	T	F	F	F	T	F	T	F	F	F	T	F	T	F	F
k = 5	×	×	Ⓣ	Ⓣ	F	Ⓣ	F	Ⓣ	F	F	F	Ⓣ	F	Ⓣ	F	F	F	Ⓣ	F	Ⓣ	F	F	F	Ⓣ	F	F	F	F

FIGURE 22.3 The values in `primes` are changed with each prime number `k`.

Since the multiples of 3 are not prime, set `primes[3 * i]` to `false` for all $3 \leq i \leq n/3$. Because the multiples of 5 are not prime, set `primes[5 * i]` to `false` for all $5 \leq i \leq n/5$. Note you don't need to consider the multiples of 4 because the multiples of 4 are also the multiples of 2, which have already been considered. Similarly, multiples of 6, 8, and 9 need not be considered. You only need to consider the multiples of a prime number k = 2, 3, 5, 7, 11, . . . , and set the corresponding element in `primes` to `false`. Afterward, if `primes[i]` is still true, then i is a prime number. As shown in Figure 22.3, 2, 3, 5, 7, 11, 13, 17, 19, and 23 are prime numbers. Listing 22.7 gives the program for finding the prime numbers using the Sieve of Eratosthenes algorithm.

LISTING 22.7 SieveOfEratosthenes.java

```
1   import java.util.Scanner;
2
3   public class SieveOfEratosthenes {
4     public static void main(String[] args) {
5       Scanner input = new Scanner(System.in);
6       System.out.print("Find all prime numbers <= n, enter n: ");
7       int n = input.nextInt();
8
9       boolean[] primes = new boolean[n + 1]; // Prime number sieve
10
11      // Initialize primes[i] to true
12      for (int i = 0; i < primes.length; i++) {
13        primes[i] = true;
14      }
15
16      for (int k = 2; k <= n / k; k++) {
17        if (primes[k]) {
18          for (int i = k; i <= n / k; i++) {
19            primes[k * i] = false; // k * i is not prime
20          }
21        }
22      }
23
24      final int NUMBER_PER_LINE = 10; // Display 10 per line
25      int count = 0; // Count the number of prime numbers found so far
26      // Print prime numbers
27      for (int i = 2; i < primes.length; i++) {
28        if (primes[i]) {
29          count++;
30          if (count % NUMBER_PER_LINE == 0)
31            System.out.printf("%7d\n", i);
32          else
33            System.out.printf("%7d", i);
34        }
35      }
36
37      System.out.println("\n" + count +
38        " prime(s) less than or equal to " + n);
39    }
40  }
```

sieve (line 9)

initialize sieve (line 12)

nonprime (line 19)

```
Find all prime numbers <= n, enter n: 1000 ⏎Enter
The prime numbers are:
    2     3     5     7    11    13    17    19    23    29
   31    37    41    43    47    53    59    61    67    71
...
...
168 prime(s) less than or equal to 1000
```

Note k <= n / k (line 16). Otherwise, k * i would be greater than n (line 19). What is the time complexity of this algorithm?

For each prime number `k` (line 17), the algorithm sets `primes[k * i]` to `false` (line 19). This is performed `n / k - k + 1` times in the `for` loop (line 18). Thus, the complexity for finding all prime numbers up to `n` is

$$\frac{n}{2} - 2 + 1 + \frac{n}{3} - 3 + 1 + \frac{n}{5} - 5 + 1 + \frac{n}{7} - 7 + 1 + \frac{n}{11} - 11 + 1 \ldots$$

$$= O\left(\frac{n}{2} + \frac{n}{3} + \frac{n}{5} + \frac{n}{7} + \frac{n}{11} + \cdots\right) < O(n\pi(n))$$

$$= O\left(n\frac{\sqrt{n}}{\log n}\right)$$

The number of items in the series is $\pi(n)$.

This upper bound $O\left(\dfrac{n\sqrt{n}}{\log n}\right)$ is very loose. The actual time complexity is much better than $O\left(\dfrac{n\sqrt{n}}{\log n}\right)$. The Sieve of Eratosthenes algorithm is good for a small `n` such that the array `primes` can fit in the memory.

Table 22.5 summarizes the complexity of these three algorithms for finding all prime numbers up to *n*.

TABLE 22.5 Comparisons of Prime-Number Algorithms

Algorithm	Complexity	Description
Listing 5.15	$O(n^2)$	Brute-force, checking all possible divisors
Listing 22.5	$O(n\sqrt{n})$	Checking divisors up to $\sqrt{n}$
Listing 22.6	$O\left(\dfrac{n\sqrt{n}}{\log n}\right)$	Checking prime divisors up to $\sqrt{n}$
Listing 22.7	$O\left(\dfrac{n\sqrt{n}}{\log n}\right)$	Sieve of Eratosthenes

22.7.1 Prove that if *n* is not prime, there must exist a prime number *p* such that $p <= \sqrt{n}$ and *p* is a factor of *n*.

 Check Point

22.7.2 Describe how the sieve of Eratosthenes is used to find the prime numbers.

 Pedagogical Note

The following sections present interesting and challenging problems. It is time that you begin to study advanced algorithms to become a proficient programmer. We recommend that you study the algorithms and implement them in the exercises.

22.8 Finding the Closest Pair of Points Using Divide-and-Conquer

This section presents efficient algorithms for finding the closest pair of points using divide-and-conquer.

 Key Point

Given a set of points, the closest-pair problem is to find the two points that are nearest to each other. As shown in Figure 22.4, a line is drawn to connect the two nearest points in the closest-pair animation.

Section 8.6, Case Study: Finding the Closest Pair, presented a brute-force algorithm for finding the closest pair of points. The algorithm computes the distances between all pairs of

 closest-pair animation on Companion Website

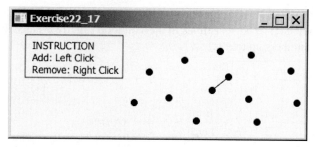

FIGURE 22.4 The closet-pair animation draws a line to connect the closest pair of points dynamically as points are added and removed interactively. *Source*: Copyright © 1995–2016 Oracle and/or its affiliates. All rights reserved. Used with permission.

points and finds the one with the minimum distance. Clearly, the algorithm takes $O(n^2)$ time. Can we design a more efficient algorithm?

divide-and-conquer

We will use an approach called *divide-and-conquer* to solve this problem. The approach divides the problem into subproblems, solves the subproblems, then combines the solutions of the subproblems to obtain the solution for the entire problem. Unlike the dynamic programming approach, the subproblems in the divide-and-conquer approach don't overlap. A subproblem is like the original problem with a smaller size, so you can apply recursion to solve the problem. In fact, all the solutions for recursive problems follow the divide-and-conquer approach.

Listing 22.8 describes how to solve the closest pair problem using the divide-and-conquer approach.

LISTING 22.8 Algorithm for Finding the Closest Pair

Step 1: Sort the points in increasing order of x-coordinates. For the points with the same x-coordinates, sort on y-coordinates. This results in a sorted list S of points.

Step 2: Divide S into two subsets, S_1 and S_2, of equal size using the midpoint in the sorted list. Let the midpoint be in S_1. Recursively find the closest pair in S_1 and S_2. Let d_1 and d_2 denote the distance of the closest pairs in the two subsets, respectively.

Step 3: Find the closest pair between a point in S_1 and a point in S_2 and denote their distance as d_3. The closest pair is the one with the distance $\min(d_1, d_2, d_3)$.

Selection sort takes $O(n^2)$ time. In Chapter 23, we will introduce merge sort and heap sort. These sorting algorithms take $O(n \log n)$ time. Step 1 can be done in $O(n \log n)$ time.

Step 3 can be done in $O(n)$ time. Let $d = \min(d_1, d_2)$. We already know that the closest-pair distance cannot be larger than d. For a point in S_1 and a point in S_2 to form the closest pair in S, the left point must be in stripL and the right point in stripR, as illustrated in Figure 22.5a.

For a point p in stripL, you need only consider a right point within the $d \times 2d$ rectangle, as shown in 22.5b. Any right point outside the rectangle cannot form the closest pair with p. Since the closest-pair distance in S_2 is greater than or equal to d, there can be at most six points in the rectangle. Thus, for each point in stripL, at most six points in stripR need to be considered.

For each point p in stripL, how do you locate the points in the corresponding $d \times 2d$ rectangle area in stripR? This can be done efficiently if the points in stripL and stripR are sorted in increasing order of their y-coordinates. Let pointsOrderedOnY be the list of the points sorted in increasing order of y-coordinates. pointsOrderedOnY can be obtained beforehand in the algorithm. stripL and stripR can be obtained from pointsOrderedOnY in Step 3 as given in Listing 22.9.

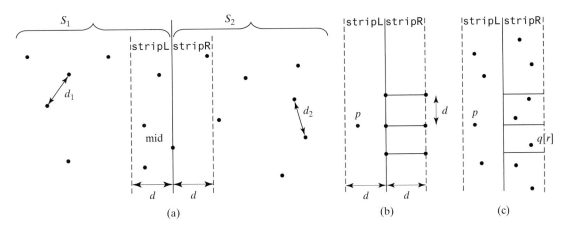

FIGURE 22.5 The midpoint divides the points into two sets of equal size.

LISTING 22.9 Algorithm for Obtaining stripL and stripR

```
1  for each point p in pointsOrderedOnY
2    if (p is in S1 and mid.x - p.x <= d)
3      append p to stripL;                      stripL
4    else if (p is in S2 and p.x - mid.x <= d)
5      append p to stripR;                      stripR
```

Let the points in stripL and stripR be $\{p_0, p_1, \ldots, p_k\}$ and $\{q_0, q_1, \ldots, q_t\}$, as shown in Figure 22.5c. The closest pair between a point in stripL and a point in stripR can be found using the algorithm described in Listing 22.10.

LISTING 22.10 Algorithm for Finding the Closest Pair in Step 3

```
1  d = min(d1, d2);
2  r = 0; // r is the index of a point in stripR
3  for (each point p in stripL) {
4    // Skip the points in stripR below p.y - d
5    while (r < stripR.length && q[r].y <= p.y - d)
6      r++;
7
8    let r1 = r;
9    while (r1 < stripR.length && |q[r1].y - p.y| <= d) {
10     // Check if (p, q[r1]) is a possible closest pair
11     if (distance(p, q[r1]) < d) {
12       d = distance(p, q[r1]);                       update closest pair
13       (p, q[r1]) is now the current closest pair;
14     }
15
16     r1 = r1 + 1;
17   }
18 }
```

The points in stripL are considered from $p_0, p_1, \ldots, p_k$ in this order. For a point p in stripL, skip the points in stripR that are below p.y - d (lines 5–6). Once a point is skipped, it will no longer be considered. The while loop (lines 9–17) checks whether (p, q[r1]) is a possible closest pair. There are at most six such q[r1] pairs, because the distance between two points in stripR cannot be less than d. Thus, the complexity for finding the closest pair in Step 3 is $O(n)$.

Note Step 1 in Listing 22.8 is performed only once to presort the points. Assume all the points are presorted. Let $T(n)$ denote the time complexity for this algorithm. Thus,

$$\overset{\text{Step 2}}{\underset{\downarrow}{}} \quad \overset{\text{Step 3}}{\underset{\downarrow}{}}$$
$$T(n) = 2T(n/2) + O(n) = O(n \log n)$$

Therefore, the closest pair of points can be found in $O(n \log n)$ time. The complete implementation of this algorithm is left as an exercise (see Programming Exercise 22.7).

Check Point

22.8.1 What is divide-and-conquer approach? Give an example.

22.8.2 What is the difference between divide-and-conquer and dynamic programming?

22.8.3 Can you design an algorithm for finding the minimum element in a list using divide-and-conquer? What is the complexity of this algorithm?

22.9 Solving the Eight Queens Problem Using Backtracking

Key Point

This section solves the Eight Queens problem using the backtracking approach.

backtracking

The Eight Queens problem is to find a solution to place a queen in each row on a chessboard such that no two queens can attack each other. The problem can be solved using recursion (see Programming Exercise 18.34). In this section, we will introduce a common algorithm design technique called *backtracking* for solving this problem. The backtracking approach searches for a candidate solution incrementally, abandoning that option as soon as it determines that the candidate cannot possibly be a valid solution, and then looks for a new candidate.

You can use a two-dimensional array to represent a chessboard. However, since each row can have only one queen, it is sufficient to use a one-dimensional array to denote the position of the queen in the row. Thus, you can define the `queens` array as

```
int[] queens = new int[8];
```

Assign `j` to `queens[i]` to denote that a queen is placed in row `i` and column `j`. Figure 22.6a shows the contents of the `queens` array for the chessboard in Figure 22.6b.

queens[0]	0
queens[1]	4
queens[2]	7
queens[3]	5
queens[4]	2
queens[5]	6
queens[6]	1
queens[7]	3

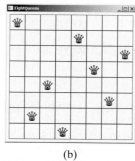

(a)   (b)

FIGURE 22.6 `queens[i]` denotes the position of the queen in row `i`. *Source*: Copyright © 1995–2016 Oracle and/or its affiliates. All rights reserved. Used with permission.

search algorithm

The search starts from the first row with $k = 0$, where k is the index of the current row being considered. The algorithm checks whether a queen can be possibly placed in the jth column in the row for $j = 0, 1, \ldots, 7$, in this order. The search is implemented as follows:

■ If successful, it continues to search for a placement for a queen in the next row. If the current row is the last row, a solution is found.

■ If not successful, it backtracks to the previous row and continues to search for a new placement in the next column in the previous row.

■ If the algorithm backtracks to the first row and cannot find a new placement for a queen in this row, no solution can be found.

Eight Queens animation on the Companion Website

To see how the algorithm works, go to http://liveexample.pearsoncmg.com/dsanimation/
EightQueens.html.

Listing 22.11 gives the program that displays a solution for the Eight Queens problem.

LISTING 22.11 EightQueens.java

```java
import javafx.application.Application;
import javafx.geometry.Pos;
import javafx.stage.Stage;
import javafx.scene.Scene;
import javafx.scene.control.Label;
import javafx.scene.image.Image;
import javafx.scene.image.ImageView;
import javafx.scene.layout.GridPane;

public class EightQueens extends Application {
  public static final int SIZE = 8; // The size of the chessboard
  // queens are placed at (i, queens[i])
  // -1 indicates that no queen is currently placed in the ith row
  // Initially, place a queen at (0, 0) in the 0th row
  private int[] queens = {-1, -1, -1, -1, -1, -1, -1, -1};    // queen positions

  @Override // Override the start method in the Application class
  public void start(Stage primaryStage) {
    search(); // Search for a solution    // search for solution

    // Display chessboard
    GridPane chessBoard = new GridPane();
    chessBoard.setAlignment(Pos.CENTER);
    Label[][] labels = new Label[SIZE][SIZE];
    for (int i = 0; i < SIZE; i++)
      for (int j = 0; j < SIZE; j++) {
        chessBoard.add(labels[i][j] = new Label(), j, i);    // create cells
        labels[i][j].setStyle("-fx-border-color: black");
        labels[i][j].setPrefSize(55, 55);
      }

    // Display queens
    Image image = new Image("image/queen.jpg");
    for (int i = 0; i < SIZE; i++)
      labels[i][queens[i]].setGraphic(new ImageView(image));    // set queen image

    // Create a scene and place it in the stage
    Scene scene = new Scene(chessBoard, 55 * SIZE, 55 * SIZE);
    primaryStage.setTitle("EightQueens"); // Set the stage title
    primaryStage.setScene(scene); // Place the scene in the stage
    primaryStage.show(); // Display the stage
  }

  /** Search for a solution */
  private boolean search() {
    // k - 1 indicates the number of queens placed so far
    // We are looking for a position in the kth row to place a queen
    int k = 0;
    while (k >= 0 && k < SIZE) {
      // Find a position to place a queen in the kth row
      int j = findPosition(k);    // find a column
      if (j < 0) {
        queens[k] = -1;
        k--; // Backtrack to the previous row    // backtrack
      } else {
```

place a queen
search the next row

```
56              queens[k] = j;
57              k++;
58            }
59          }
60
61      if (k == -1)
62        return false; // No solution
63      else
64        return true; // A solution is found
65    }
66
67    public int findPosition(int k) {
68      int start = queens[k] + 1; // Search for a new placement
69
70      for (int j = start; j < SIZE; j++) {
71        if (isValid(k, j))
72          return j; // (k, j) is the place to put the queen now
73      }
74
75      return -1;
76    }
77
78    /** Return true if a queen can be placed at (row, column) */
79    public boolean isValid(int row, int column) {
80      for (int i = 1; i <= row; i++)
81        if (queens[row - i] == column // Check column
82          || queens[row - i] == column - i // Check upleft diagonal
83          || queens[row - i] == column + i)  // Check upright diagonal
84          return false; // There is a conflict
85      return true; // No conflict
86    }
87  }
```

The program invokes `search()` (line 19) to search for a solution. Initially, no queens are placed in any rows (line 15). The search now starts from the first row with `k = 0` (line 48) and finds a place for the queen (line 51). If successful, place it in the row (line 56) and consider the next row (line 57). If not successful, backtrack to the previous row (lines 53–54).

The `findPosition(k)` method searches for a possible position to place a queen in row k starting from `queen[k] + 1` (line 68). It checks whether a queen can be placed at `start`, `start + 1,...`, and 7, in this order (lines 70–73). If possible, return the column index (line 72); otherwise, return −1 (line 75).

The `isValid(row, column)` method is called to check whether placing a queen at the specified position causes a conflict with the queens placed earlier (line 71). It ensures that no queen is placed in the same column (line 81), in the upper-left diagonal (line 82), or in the upper-right diagonal (line 83), as shown in Figure 22.7.

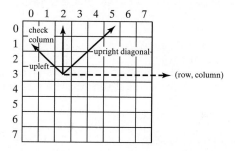

FIGURE 22.7 Invoking `isValid(row, column)` checks whether a queen can be placed at (row, column).

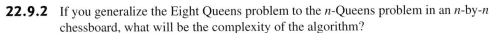

22.9.1 What is backtracking? Give an example.

22.9.2 If you generalize the Eight Queens problem to the *n*-Queens problem in an *n*-by-*n* chessboard, what will be the complexity of the algorithm?

Check Point

22.10 Computational Geometry: Finding a Convex Hull

This section presents efficient geometric algorithms for finding a convex hull for a set of points.

Key Point

Computational geometry is to study the algorithms for geometrical problems. It has applications in computer graphics, games, pattern recognition, image processing, robotics, geographical information systems, and computer-aided design and manufacturing. Section 22.8 presented a geometrical algorithm for finding the closest pair of points. This section introduces geometrical algorithms for finding a convex hull.

Given a set of points, a *convex hull* is the smallest convex polygon that encloses all these points, as shown in Figure 22.8a. A polygon is convex if every line connecting two vertices is inside the polygon. For example, the vertices v0, v1, v2, v3, v4, and v5 in Figure 22.8a form a convex polygon, but not in Figure 22.8b, because the line that connects v3 and v1 is not inside the polygon.

convex hull

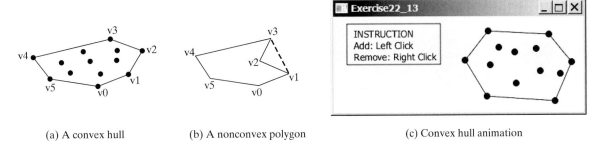

(a) A convex hull (b) A nonconvex polygon (c) Convex hull animation

FIGURE 22.8 A convex hull is the smallest convex polygon that contains a set of points. *Source*: Copyright © 1995–2016 Oracle and/or its affiliates. All rights reserved. Used with permission.

A convex hull has many applications in game programming, pattern recognition, and image processing. Before we introduce the algorithms, it is helpful to get acquainted with the concept using an interactive tool from liveexample.pearsoncmg.com/dsanimation/ConvexHull.html, as shown in Figure 22.8c. This tool allows you to add and remove points and displays the convex hull dynamically.

convex hull animation on the Companion Website

Many algorithms have been developed to find a convex hull. This section introduces two popular algorithms: the gift-wrapping algorithm and Graham's algorithm.

22.10.1 Gift-Wrapping Algorithm

An intuitive approach called the *gift-wrapping algorithm* works as described in Listing 22.12.

LISTING 22.12 Finding a Convex Hull Using Gift-Wrapping Algorithm

Step 1: Given a list of points S, let the points in S be labeled s_0, s_1, . . . , s_k. Select the rightmost lowest point S. As shown in Figure 22.9a, h_0 is such a point. Add h_0 to list H. (H is initially empty. H will hold all points in the convex hull after the algorithm is finished.) Let t_0 be h_0.

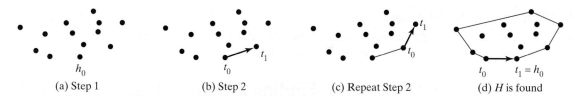

FIGURE 22.9 (a) h_0 is the rightmost lowest point in S. (b) Step 2 finds point t_1. (c) A convex hull is expanded repeatedly. (d) A convex hull is found when t_1 becomes h_0.

```
Step 2: Let t₁ be s₀.
        For every point p in S,
            if p is on the right side of the direct line from t₀ to t₁, then
                let t₁ be p.
```
(After Step 2, no points lie on the right side of the direct line from t_0 to t_1, as shown in Figure 22.9b.)

```
Step 3: If t₁ is h₀ (see Figure 22.9d), the points in H form a convex
        hull for S. Otherwise, add t₁ to H, let t₀ be t₁, and go back to Step 2
        (see Figure 22.9c).
```

correctness of the algorithm

The convex hull is expanded incrementally. The correctness is supported by the fact that no points lie on the right side of the direct line from t_0 to t_1 after Step 2. This ensures that every line segment with two points in S falls inside the polygon.

time complexity of the algorithm

Finding the rightmost lowest point in Step 1 can be done in $O(n)$ time. Whether a point is on the left side of a line, right side, or on the line can be determined in $O(1)$ time (see Programming Exercise 3.32). Thus, it takes $O(n)$ time to find a new point t_1 in Step 2. Step 2 is repeated h times, where h is the size of the convex hull. Therefore, the algorithm takes $O(hn)$ time. In the worst-case, h is n.

The implementation of this algorithm is left as an exercise (see Programming Exercise 22.9).

22.10.2 Graham's Algorithm

A more efficient algorithm was developed by Ronald Graham in 1972, as given in Listing 22.13.

LISTING 22.13 Finding a Convex Hull Using Graham's Algorithm

```
Step 1: Given a list of points S, select the rightmost lowest point and
name it p₀. As shown in Figure 22.10a, p₀ is such a point.
```

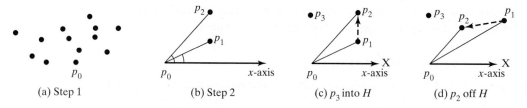

FIGURE 22.10 (a) p_0 is the rightmost lowest point in S. (b) Points are sorted by their angles. (c–d) A convex hull is discovered incrementally.

```
Step 2: Sort the points in S angularly along the x-axis with p₀ as the
center, as shown in Figure 22.10b. If there is a tie and two points have
the same angle, discard the one that is closer to p₀. The points in S are
now sorted as p₀, p₁, p₂, . . . . , pₙ₋₁.
```

Step 3: Push p_0, p_1, and p_2 into stack H. (After the algorithm finishes, H contains all the points in the convex hull.)

Step 4:

```
i = 3;
while (i < n) {
  Let t₁ and t₂ be the top first and second element in stack H;
  if (pᵢ is on the left side of the direct line from t₂ to t₁) {
    Push pᵢ to H;
    i++; // Consider the next point in S.
  }
  else
    Pop the top element off stack H.
}
```

Step 5: The points in H form a convex hull.

The convex hull is discovered incrementally. Initially, p_0, p_1, and p_2 form a convex hull. Consider p_3. p_3 is outside of the current convex hull since points are sorted in increasing order of their angles. If p_3 is strictly on the left side of the line from p_1 to p_2 (see Figure 22.10c), push p_3 into H. Now p_0, p_1, p_2, and p_3 form a convex hull. If p_3 is on the right side of the line from p_1 to p_2 (see Figure 22.10d), pop p_2 out of H and push p_3 into H. Now p_0, p_1, and p_3 form a convex hull and p_2 is inside this convex hull. You can prove by induction that all the points in H in Step 5 form a convex hull for all the points in the input list S. correctness of the algorithm

Finding the rightmost lowest point in Step 1 can be done in $O(n)$ time. The angles can be computed using trigonometry functions. However, you can sort the points without actually computing their angles. Observe p_2 would make a greater angle than p_1 if and only if p_2 lies on the left side of the line from p_0 to p_1. Whether a point is on the left side of a line can be determined in $O(1)$ time, as shown in Programming Exercise 3.32. Sorting in Step 2 can be done in $O(n \log n)$ time using the merge-sort or heap-sort algorithms that will be introduced in Chapter 23. Step 4 can be done in $O(n)$ time. Therefore, the algorithm takes $O(n \log n)$ time. time complexity of the algorithm

The implementation of this algorithm is left as an exercise (see Programming Exercise 22.11).

22.10.1 What is a convex hull?

22.10.2 Describe the gift-wrapping algorithm for finding a convex hull. Should list H be implemented using an `ArrayList` or a `LinkedList`?

22.10.3 Describe Graham's algorithm for finding a convex hull. Why does the algorithm use a stack to store the points in a convex hull?

Check Point

KEY TERMS

average-case analysis 840
backtracking approach 864
best-case input 840
Big *O* notation 840
brute force 851
constant time 841
convex hull 867
divide-and-conquer approach 862

dynamic programming approach 850
exponential time 847
growth rate 840
logarithmic time 846
quadratic time 843
space complexity 841
time complexity 841
worst-case input 840

CHAPTER SUMMARY

1. The *Big O notation* is a theoretical approach for analyzing the performance of an algorithm. It estimates how fast an algorithm's execution time increases as the input size increases, which enables you to compare two algorithms by examining their *growth rates*.

2. An input that results in the shortest execution time is called the *best-case* input, and one that results in the longest execution time is called the *worst-case* input. Best- and worst-case analyses are not representative, but worst-case analysis is very useful. You can be assured that the algorithm will never be slower than the worst case.

3. An *average-case analysis* attempts to determine the average amount of time among all possible input of the same size. Average-case analysis is ideal, but difficult to perform because for many problems, it is hard to determine the relative probabilities and distributions of various input instances.

4. If the time is not related to the input size, the algorithm is said to take *constant time* with the notation $O(1)$.

5. Linear search takes $O(n)$ time. An algorithm with the $O(n)$ time complexity is called a *linear algorithm* and it exhibits a linear growth rate. Binary search takes $O(\log n)$ time. An algorithm with the $O(\log n)$ time complexity is called a *logarithmic algorithm* and it exhibits a logarithmic growth rate.

6. The worst-time complexity for selection sort is $O(n^2)$. An algorithm with the $O(n^2)$ time complexity is called a *quadratic algorithm* and it exhibits a quadratic growth rate.

7. The time complexity for the Tower of Hanoi problem is $O(2^n)$. An algorithm with the $O(2^n)$ time complexity is called an *exponential algorithm*, and it exhibits an exponential growth rate.

8. A Fibonacci number at a given index can be found in $O(n)$ time using dynamic programming approach.

9. Dynamic programming is the process of solving subproblems, then combining the solutions of the subproblems to obtain an overall solution. The key idea behind dynamic programming is to solve each subproblem only once and store the results for subproblems for later use to avoid redundant computing of the subproblems.

10. Euclid's GCD algorithm takes $O(\log n)$ time.

11. All prime numbers less than or equal to n can be found in $O\left(\dfrac{n\sqrt{n}}{\log n}\right)$ time.

12. The closest pair can be found in $O(n \log n)$ time using the *divide-and-conquer approach*.

13. The divide-and-conquer approach divides the problem into subproblems, solves the subproblems, and then combines the solutions of the subproblems to obtain the solution for the entire problem. Unlike the dynamic programming approach, the subproblems in the divide-and-conquer approach don't overlap. A subproblem is like the original problem with a smaller size, so you can apply recursion to solve the problem.

14. The Eight Queens problem can be solved using backtracking.

15. The backtracking approach searches for a candidate solution incrementally, abandoning that option as soon as it determines the candidate cannot possibly be a valid solution, then looks for a new candidate.

16. A *convex hull* for a set of points can be found in $O(n^2)$ time using the gift-wrapping algorithm, and in $O(n \log n)$ time using the Graham's algorithm.

QUIZ

Answer the quiz for this chapter online at the book Companion Website.

PROGRAMMING EXERCISES

MyProgrammingLab™

*22.1 (*Maximum consecutive increasingly ordered substring*) Write a program that prompts the user to enter a string and displays the maximum consecutive increasingly ordered substring. Analyze the time complexity of your program. Here is a sample run:

```
Enter a string: abcabcdgabxy  ↵Enter
abcdg
```

```
Enter a string: abcabcdgabmnsxy  ↵Enter
abmnsxy
```

**22.2 (*Maximum increasingly ordered subsequence*) Write a program that prompts the user to enter a string and displays the maximum increasingly ordered subsequence of characters. Analyze the time complexity of your program. Here is a sample run:

```
Enter a string: Welcome  ↵Enter
Welo
```

*22.3 (*Pattern matching*) Write an `O(n)` time program that prompts the user to enter two strings and tests whether the second string is a substring of the first string. *Suppose the neighboring characters in the string are distinct.* (Don't use the `indexOf` method in the `String` class.) Here is a sample run of the program:

```
Enter a string s1: Welcome to Java  ↵Enter
Enter a string s2: come  ↵Enter
matched at index 3
```

*22.4 (*Pattern matching*) Write a program that prompts the user to enter two strings and tests whether the second string is a substring of the first string. (Don't use the `indexOf` method in the `String` class.) Analyze the time complexity of your algorithm. Here is a sample run of the program:

```
Enter a string s1: Mississippi  ↵Enter
Enter a string s2: sip  ↵Enter
matched at index 6
```

*22.5   (*Same-number subsequence*) Write an $O(n)$ time program that prompts the user to enter a sequence of integers ending with 0 and finds the longest subsequence with the same number. Here is a sample run of the program:

```
Enter a series of numbers ending with 0:
2 4 4 8 8 8 8 2 4 4 0  ↵Enter
The longest same number sequence starts at index 3 with 4 values of 8
```

*22.6   (*Execution time for GCD*) Write a program that obtains the execution time for finding the GCD of every two consecutive Fibonacci numbers from the index 40 to index 45 using the algorithms in Listings 22.3 and 22.4. Your program should print a table like this:

	40	41	42	43	44	45
Listing 22.3 GCD						
Listing 22.4 GCDEuclid						

(*Hint*: You can use the following code template to obtain the execution time.)

```java
long startTime = System.currentTimeMillis();
perform the task;
long endTime = System.currentTimeMillis();
long executionTime = endTime - startTime;
```

**22.7   (*Closest pair of points*) Section 22.8 introduced an algorithm for finding the closest pair of points using a divide-and-conquer approach. Implement the algorithm to meet the following requirements:

■ Define a class named `Pair` with the data fields `p1` and `p2` to represent two points and a method named `getDistance()` that returns the distance between the two points.

■ Implement the following methods:

```java
/** Return the distance of the closest pair of points */
public static Pair getClosestPair(double[][] points)
```

```java
/** Return the distance of the closest pair of points */
public static Pair getClosestPair(Point2D[] points)
```

```java
/** Return the distance of the closest pair of points
 * in pointsOrderedOnX[low..high]. This is a recursive
 * method. pointsOrderedOnX and pointsOrderedOnY are
 * not changed in the subsequent recursive calls.
 */
public static Pair distance(Point2D[] pointsOrderedOnX,
    int low, int high, Point2D[] pointsOrderedOnY)
```

```java
/** Compute the distance between two points p1 and p2 */
public static double distance(Point2D p1, Point2D p2)
```

```java
/** Compute the distance between points (x1, y1) and (x2, y2) */
public static double distance(double x1, double y1,
    double x2, double y2)
```

**22.8 (*All prime numbers up to* 10,000,000,000) Write a program that finds all prime numbers up to 10,000,000,000. There are approximately 455,052,511 such prime numbers. Your program should meet the following requirements:

- Your program should store the prime numbers in a binary data file, named **PrimeNumbers.dat**. When a new prime number is found, the number is appended to the file.
- To find whether a new number is prime, your program should load the prime numbers from the file to an array of the long type of size 10000. If no number in the array is a divisor for the new number, continue to read the next 10000 prime numbers from the data file, until a divisor is found or all numbers in the file are read. If no divisor is found, the new number is prime.
- Since this program takes a long time to finish, you should run it as a batch job from a UNIX machine. If the machine is shut down and rebooted, your program should resume by using the prime numbers stored in the binary data file rather than start over from scratch.

**22.9 (*Geometry: gift-wrapping algorithm for finding a convex hull*) Section 22.10.1 introduced the gift-wrapping algorithm for finding a convex hull for a set of points. Assume Java's coordinate system is used for the points. Implement the algorithm using the following method:

```
/** Return the points that form a convex hull */
public static ArrayList<Point2D> getConvexHull(double[][] s)
```

Point2D is defined in Section 9.6.3.

Write a test program that prompts the user to enter the set size and the points, and displays the points that form a convex hull. Here is a sample run:

```
How many points are in the set?  6  ↵Enter
Enter 6 points:  1 2.4 2.5 2 1.5 34.5 5.5 6 6 2.4 5.5 9  ↵Enter
The convex hull is
  (1.5, 34.5) (5.5, 9.0) (6.0, 2.4) (2.5, 2.0) (1.0, 2.4)
```

22.10 (*Number of prime numbers*) Programming Exercise 22.8 stores the prime numbers in a file named **PrimeNumbers.dat**. Write a program that finds the number of prime numbers that are less than or equal to 10, 100, 1,000, 10,000, 100,000, 1,000,000, 10,000,000, 100,000,000, 1,000,000,000, and 10,000,000,000. Your program should read the data from **PrimeNumbers.dat**.

**22.11 (*Geometry: Graham's algorithm for finding a convex hull*) Section 22.10.2 introduced Graham's algorithm for finding a convex hull for a set of points. Assume Java's coordinate system is used for the points. Implement the algorithm using the following method:

```
/** Return the points that form a convex hull */
public static ArrayList<MyPoint> getConvexHull(double[][] s)
```

MyPoint is a static inner class defined as follows:
```
private static class MyPoint implements Comparable<MyPoint> {
  double x, y;

  MyPoint rightMostLowestPoint;
```

```
MyPoint(double x, double y) {
  this.x = x; this.y = y;
}

public void setRightMostLowestPoint(MyPoint p) {
  rightMostLowestPoint = p;
}

@Override
public int compareTo(MyPoint o) {
  // Implement it to compare this point with point o
  // angularly along the x-axis with rightMostLowestPoint
  // as the center, as shown in Figure 22.10b. By implementing
  // the Comparable interface, you can use the Array.sort
  // method to sort the points to simplify coding.
}
}
```

Write a test program that prompts the user to enter the set size and the points, and displays the points that form a convex hull. Here is a sample run:

```
How many points are in the set? 6 ↵Enter
Enter six points: 1 2.4 2.5 2 1.5 34.5 5.5 6 6 2.4 5.5 9 ↵Enter
The convex hull is
  (1.5, 34.5) (5.5, 9.0) (6.0, 2.4) (2.5, 2.0) (1.0, 2.4)
```

*22.12 (*Last 100 prime numbers*) Programming Exercise 22.8 stores the prime numbers in a file named **PrimeNumbers.dat.** Write an efficient program that reads the last **100** numbers in the file. (*Hint*: Don't read all numbers from the file. Skip all numbers before the last 100 numbers in the file.)

*22.13 (*Geometry: convex hull animation*) Programming Exercise 22.11 finds a convex hull for a set of points entered from the console. Write a program that enables the user to add or remove points by clicking the left or right mouse button and displays a convex hull, as shown in Figure 22.8c.

*22.14 (*Execution time for prime numbers*) Write a program that obtains the execution time for finding all the prime numbers less than 8,000,000, 10,000,000, 12,000,000, 14,000,000, 16,000,000, and 18,000,000 using the algorithms in Listings 22.5–22.7. Your program should print a table like this:

	8,000,000	10,000,000	12,000,000	14,000,000	16,000,000	18,000,000
Listing 22.5						
Listing 22.6						
Listing 22.7						

**22.15 (*Geometry: noncrossed polygon*) Write a program that enables the user to add or remove points by clicking the left or right mouse button and displays a non-crossed polygon that links all the points, as shown in Figure 22.11a. A polygon is crossed if two or more sides intersect, as shown in Figure 22.11b. Use the following algorithm to construct a polygon from a set of points:

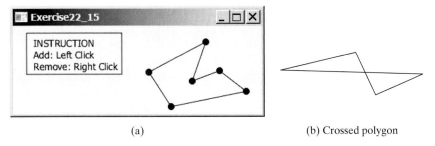

(a)   (b) Crossed polygon

FIGURE 22.11   (a) Programming Exercise 22.15 displays a noncrossed polygon for a set of points. *Source*: Copyright © 1995–2016 Oracle and/or its affiliates. All rights reserved. Used with permission. (b) Two or more sides intersect in a crossed polygon.

> Step 1: Given a set of points S, select the rightmost lowest point p_0 in the set S.
>
> Step 2: Sort the points in S angularly along the x-axis with p_0 as the center. If there is a tie and two points have the same angle, the one that is closer to p_0 is considered greater. The points in S are now sorted as p_0, p_1, p_2, ..., p_{n-1}.
>
> Step 3: The sorted points form a noncrossed polygon.

**22.16   (*Linear search animation*) Write a program that animates the linear search algorithm. Create an array that consists of 20 distinct numbers from 1 to 20 in a random order. The array elements are displayed in a histogram, as shown in Figure 22.12. You need to enter a search key in the text field. Clicking the *Step* button causes the program to perform one comparison in the algorithm and repaints the histogram with a bar indicating the search position. This button also freezes the text field to prevent its value from being changed. When the algorithm is finished, display the status in the label at the top of the border pane to inform the user. Clicking the *Reset* button creates a new random array for a new start. This button also makes the text field editable.

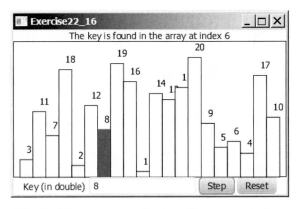
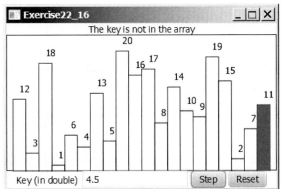

FIGURE 22.12   The program animates a linear search. *Source*: Copyright © 1995–2016 Oracle and/or its affiliates. All rights reserved. Used with permission.

**22.17   (*Closest-pair animation*) Write a program that enables the user to add/remove points by clicking the left/right mouse button and displays a line that connects the pair of nearest points, as shown in Figure 22.4.

**22.18   (*Binary search animation*) Write a program that animates the binary search algorithm. Create an array with numbers from 1 to 20 in this order. The array elements are displayed in a histogram, as shown in Figure 22.13. You need to enter a search key in the text field. Clicking the *Step* button causes the program to perform one comparison in the algorithm. Use a light-gray color to paint the bars for the numbers in the current search range, and use a black color to paint the bar indicating the middle number in the search range. The *Step* button also freezes the text field to prevent its value from being changed. When the algorithm is finished, display the status in a label at the top of a border pane. Clicking the *Reset* button enables a new search to start. This button also makes the text field editable.

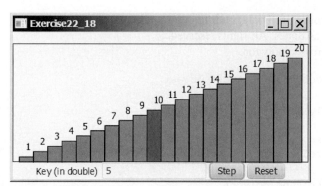

FIGURE 22.13 The program animates a binary search. *Source*: Copyright © 1995–2016 Oracle and/or its affiliates. All rights reserved. Used with permission.

*22.19 (*Largest block*) The problem for finding a largest block is described in Programming Exercise 8.35. Design a dynamic programming algorithm for solving this problem in $O(n^2)$ time. Write a test program that displays a 10-by-10 square matrix, as shown in Figure 22.14a. Each element in the matrix is 0 or 1, randomly generated with a click of the *Refresh* button. Display each number centered in a text field. *Use a text field for each entry. Allow the user to change the entry value.* Click the *Find Largest Block* button to find a largest square submatrix that consists of 1s. Highlight the numbers in the block, as shown in Figure 22.14b. See liveexample.pearsoncmg.com/dsanimation/LargestBlock.html for an interactive test.

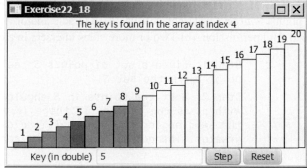

FIGURE 22.14 The program finds the largest block of 1s. *Source*: Copyright © 1995–2016 Oracle and/or its affiliates. All rights reserved. Used with permission.

***22.20 (*Game: multiple Sudoku solutions*) The complete solution for the Sudoku problem is given in Supplement VI.A. A Sudoku problem may have multiple solutions. Modify Sudoku.java in Supplement VI.A to display the total number of solutions. Display two solutions if multiple solutions exist.

***22.21 (*Game: Sudoku*) The complete solution for the Sudoku problem is given in Supplement VI.C. Write a program that lets the user enter the input from the text fields, as shown in Figure 22.15a. Clicking the *Solve* button displays the result, as shown in Figures 22.15b and c.

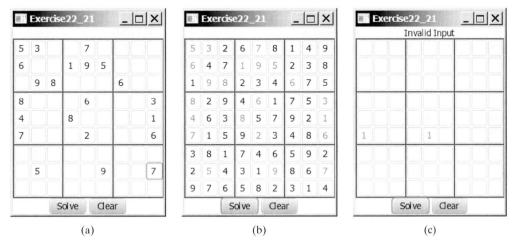

FIGURE 22.15 The program solves the Sudoku problem. *Source*: Copyright © 1995–2016 Oracle and/or its affiliates. All rights reserved. Used with permission.

***22.22 (*Game: recursive Sudoku*) Write a recursive solution for the Sudoku problem.

***22.23 (*Game: multiple Eight Queens solution*) Write a program to display all possible solutions for the Eight Queens puzzle in a scroll pane, as shown in Figure 22.16. For each solution, put a label to denote the solution number. (*Hint*: Place all solution panes into an `HBox` and place this one pane into a `ScrollPane`. If you run into a `StackOverflowError`, run the program using **java –Xss200m Exercise22_23** from the command window.)

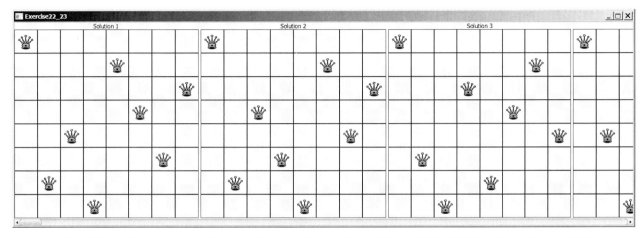

FIGURE 22.16 All solutions are placed in a scroll pane. *Source*: Copyright © 1995–2016 Oracle and/or its affiliates. All rights reserved. Used with permission.

*22.24 (*Find the smallest number*) Write a method that uses the divide-and-conquer approach to find the smallest number in a list.

***22.25 (*Game: Sudoku*) Revise Programming Exercise 22.21 to display all solutions for the Sudoku game, as shown in Figure 22.17a. When you click the *Solve* button, the program stores all solutions in an `ArrayList`. Each element in the list is a two-dimensional 9-by-9 grid. If the program has multiple solutions, the *Next* button appears as shown in Figure 22.17b. You can click the *Next* button to display the next solution and also add a label to show the solution count. When the *Clear* button is clicked, the cells are cleared and the *Next* button is hidden as shown in Figure 22.17c.

FIGURE 22.17 The program can display multiple Sudoku solutions. *Source*: Copyright © 1995–2016 Oracle and/or its affiliates. All rights reserved. Used with permission.

*22.26 (*Bin packing with smallest object first*) The bin packing problem is to pack the objects of various weights into containers. Assume each container can hold a maximum of 10 pounds. The program uses an algorithm that places an object with the *smallest weight* into the first bin in which it would fit. Your program should prompt the user to enter the total number of objects and the weight of each object. The program displays the total number of containers needed to pack the objects, and the contents of each container. Here is a sample run of the program:

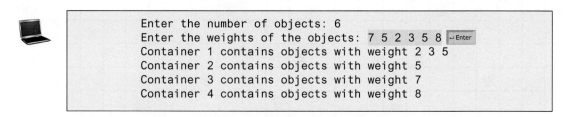

```
Enter the number of objects: 6
Enter the weights of the objects: 7 5 2 3 5 8  ↵Enter
Container 1 contains objects with weight 2 3 5
Container 2 contains objects with weight 5
Container 3 contains objects with weight 7
Container 4 contains objects with weight 8
```

Does this program produce an optimal solution, that is, finding the minimum number of containers to pack the objects?

**22.27 (*Optimal bin packing*) Rewrite the preceding program so that it finds an optimal solution that packs all objects using the smallest number of containers. Here is a sample run of the program:

```
Enter the number of objects: 6 ↵Enter
Enter the weights of the objects: 7 5 2 3 5 8 ↵Enter
Container 1 contains objects with weight 7 3
Container 2 contains objects with weight 5 5
Container 3 contains objects with weight 2 8
The optimal number of bins is 3
```

What is the time complexity of your program?

SORTING

Objectives

- To study and analyze time complexity of various sorting algorithms (§§23.2–23.7).

- To design, implement, and analyze insertion sort (§23.2).

- To design, implement, and analyze bubble sort (§23.3).

- To design, implement, and analyze merge sort (§23.4).

- To design, implement, and analyze quick sort (§23.5).

- To design and implement a binary heap (§23.6).

- To design, implement, and analyze heap sort (§23.6).

- To design, implement, and analyze bucket and radix sorts (§23.7).

- To design, implement, and analyze external sort for files that have a large amount of data (§23.8).

23.1 Introduction

Sorting algorithms are good examples for studying algorithm design and analysis.

Key Point

When president Barack Obama visited Google in 2007, Google as a candidate CEO Eric Schmidt asked Obama the most efficient way to sort a million 32-bit integers (www.youtube .com/watch?v=k4RRi_ntQc8). Obama answered that the bubble sort would be the wrong way to go. Was he right? We will examine different sorting algorithms in this chapter and see if he was correct.

why study sorting?

Sorting is a classic subject in computer science. There are three reasons to study sorting algorithms.

■ First, sorting algorithms illustrate many creative approaches to problem solving, and these approaches can be applied to solve other problems.

■ Second, sorting algorithms are good for practicing fundamental programming techniques using selection statements, loops, methods, and arrays.

■ Third, sorting algorithms are excellent examples to demonstrate algorithm performance.

what data to sort?

The data to be sorted might be integers, doubles, characters, or objects. Section 7.11, Sorting Arrays, presented selection sort. The selection-sort algorithm was extended to sort an array of objects in Section 19.5, Case Study: Sorting an Array of Objects. The Java API contains several overloaded sort methods for sorting primitive-type values and objects in the `java .util.Arrays` and `java.util.Collections` classes. For simplicity, this chapter assumes

1. data to be sorted are integers,

2. data are stored in an array, and

3. data are sorted in ascending order.

The programs can be easily modified to sort other types of data, to sort in descending order, or to sort data in an `ArrayList` or a `LinkedList`.

There are many algorithms for sorting. You have already learned selection sort. This chapter introduces insertion sort, bubble sort, merge sort, quick sort, bucket sort, radix sort, and external sort.

23.2 Insertion Sort

The insertion-sort algorithm sorts a list of values by repeatedly inserting a new element into a sorted sublist until the whole list is sorted.

Key Point

insertion-sort animation on Companion Website

Figure 23.1 shows how to sort the list {2, 9, 5, 4, 8, 1, 6} using insertion sort. For an interactive demo on how insertion sort works, go to liveexample.pearsoncmg.com/dsanimation/ InsertionSortNeweBook.html.

The algorithm can be described as follows:

```
for (int i = 1; i < list.length; i++) {
  insert list[i] into a sorted sublist list[0..i-1] so that
  list[0..i] is sorted.
}
```

To insert `list[i]` into `list[0..i-1]`, save `list[i]` into a temporary variable, say `currentElement`. Move `list[i-1]` to `list[i]` if `list[i-1]` > `currentElement`, move `list[i-2]` to `list[i-1]` if `list[i-2]` > `currentElement`, and so on, until `list[i-k]` <= `currentElement` or k > i (we pass the first element of the sorted list). Assign `currentElement` to `list[i-k+1]`. For example, to insert 4 into {2, 5, 9} in Step 4 in Figure 23.2, move `list[2]` (9) to `list[3]` since 9 > 4 and move `list[1]` (5) to `list[2]` since 5 > 4. Finally, move `currentElement` (4) to `list[1]`.

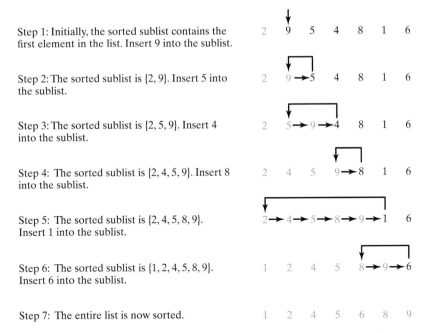

Step 1: Initially, the sorted sublist contains the first element in the list. Insert 9 into the sublist.

Step 2: The sorted sublist is {2, 9}. Insert 5 into the sublist.

Step 3: The sorted sublist is {2, 5, 9}. Insert 4 into the sublist.

Step 4: The sorted sublist is {2, 4, 5, 9}. Insert 8 into the sublist.

Step 5: The sorted sublist is {2, 4, 5, 8, 9}. Insert 1 into the sublist.

Step 6: The sorted sublist is {1, 2, 4, 5, 8, 9}. Insert 6 into the sublist.

Step 7: The entire list is now sorted.

FIGURE 23.1   Insertion sort repeatedly inserts a new element into a sorted sublist.

Step 1: Save 4 to a temporary variable currentElement

currentElement: 4

Step 2: Move list[2] to list[3]

Step 3: Move list[1] to list[2]

Step 4: Assign currentElement to list[1]

FIGURE 23.2   A new element is inserted into a sorted sublist.

The algorithm can be expanded and implemented as in Listing 23.1.

LISTING 23.1   InsertionSort.java

```
1  public class InsertionSort {
2    /** The method for sorting the numbers */
3    public static void insertionSort(int[] list) {
4      for (int i = 1; i < list.length; i++) {
5        /** Insert list[i] into a sorted sublist list[0..i-1] so that
6            list[0..i] is sorted. */
7        int currentElement = list[i];
8        int k;
9        for (k = i - 1; k >= 0 && list[k] > currentElement; k--) {      shift
10         list[k + 1] = list[k];
```

insert

```
11          }
12
13              // Insert the current element into list[k + 1]
14              list[k + 1] = currentElement;
15          }
16      }
17  }
```

The `insertionSort(int[] list)` method sorts an array of `int` elements. The method is implemented with a nested `for` loop. The outer loop (with the loop control variable `i`) (line 4) is iterated in order to obtain a sorted sublist, which ranges from `list[0]` to `list[i]`. The inner loop (with the loop control variable `k`) inserts `list[i]` into the sublist from `list[0]` to `list[i-1]`.

To better understand this method, trace it with the following statements:

```
int[] list = {1, 9, 4, 6, 5, -4};
InsertionSort.insertionSort(list);
```

insertion-sort time complexity

The insertion-sort algorithm presented here sorts a list of elements by repeatedly inserting a new element into a sorted partial array until the whole array is sorted. At the kth iteration, to insert an element into an array of size k, it may take k comparisons to find the insertion position and k moves to insert the element. Let $T(n)$ denote the complexity for insertion sort, and c denote the total number of other operations such as assignments and additional comparisons in each iteration. Thus,

$$
\begin{aligned}
T(n) &= (2 + c) + (2 \times 2 + c) + \cdots + (2 \times (n - 1) + c) \\
&= 2(1 + 2 + \cdots + n - 1) + c(n - 1) \\
&= 2\frac{(n - 1)n}{2} + cn - c = n^2 - n + cn - c \\
&= O(n^2)
\end{aligned}
$$

Therefore, the complexity of the insertion-sort algorithm is $O(n^2)$. Hence, the selection and insertion sorts are of the same time complexity.

 23.2.1 Describe how an insertion sort works. What is the time complexity for an insertion sort?

23.2.2 Use Figure 23.1 as an example to show how to apply an insertion sort on {45, 11, 50, 59, 60, 2, 4, 7, 10}.

23.2.3 If a list is already sorted, how many comparisons will the `insertionSort` method perform?

23.3 Bubble Sort

A bubble sort sorts the array in multiple passes. Each pass successively swaps the neighboring elements if the elements are not in order.

bubble sort

The bubble-sort algorithm makes several passes through the array. On each pass, successive neighboring pairs are compared. If a pair is in decreasing order, its values are swapped; otherwise, the values remain unchanged. The technique is called a *bubble sort* or *sinking sort* because the smaller values gradually "bubble" their way to the top and the larger values sink to the bottom. After the first pass, the last element becomes the largest in the array. After the second pass, the second-to-last element becomes the second largest in the array. This process is continued until all elements are sorted.

Figure 23.3a shows the first pass of a bubble sort on an array of six elements (2 9 5 4 8 1). Compare the elements in the first pair (2 and 9) and no swap is needed because they are already in order. Compare the elements in the second pair (9 and 5) and swap 9 with 5 because 9 is greater than 5. Compare the elements in the third pair (9 and 4) and swap 9 with 4. Compare the elements in the fourth pair (9 and 8) and swap 9 with 8. Compare the elements in the fifth pair (9 and 1) and swap 9 with 1. The pairs being compared are highlighted and the numbers already sorted are italicized in Figure 23.3. For an interactive demo on how bubble sort works, go to liveexample.pearsoncmg.com/dsanimation/BubbleSortNeweBook.html.

bubble-sort illustration

bubble sort animation on the Companion Website

```
2 9 5 4 8 1    2 5 4 8 1 9    2 4 5 1 8 9    2 4 1 5 8 9    1 2 4 5 8 9
2 5 9 4 8 1    2 4 5 8 1 9    2 4 5 1 8 9    2 1 4 5 8 9
2 5 4 9 8 1    2 4 5 8 1 9    2 4 1 5 8 9
2 5 4 8 9 1    2 4 5 1 8 9
2 5 4 8 1 9
```

(a) 1st pass   (b) 2nd pass   (c) 3rd pass   (d) 4th pass   (e) 5th pass

FIGURE 23.3 Each pass compares and orders the pairs of elements sequentially.

The first pass places the largest number (9) as the last in the array. In the second pass, as shown in Figure 23.3b, you compare and order pairs of elements sequentially. There is no need to consider the last pair because the last element in the array is already the largest. In the third pass, as shown in Figure 23.3c, you compare and order pairs of elements sequentially except the last two elements because they are already in order. Thus, in the *k*th pass, you don't need to consider the last $k - 1$ elements because they are already ordered.

The algorithm for a bubble sort is described in Listing 23.2.

algorithm

LISTING 23.2 Bubble-Sort Algorithm

```
1  for (int k = 1; k < list.length; k++) {
2    // Perform the kth pass
3    for (int i = 0; i < list.length - k; i++) {
4      if (list[i] > list[i + 1])
5        swap list[i] with list[i + 1];
6    }
7  }
```

Note if no swap takes place in a pass, there is no need to perform the next pass because all the elements are already sorted. You can use this property to improve the algorithm in Listing 23.2, as in Listing 23.3.

LISTING 23.3 Improved Bubble-Sort Algorithm

```
1  boolean needNextPass = true;
2  for (int k = 1; k < list.length && needNextPass; k++) {
3    // Array may be sorted and next pass not needed
4    needNextPass = false;
5    // Perform the kth pass
6    for (int i = 0; i < list.length - k; i++) {
7      if (list[i] > list[i + 1]) {
8        swap list[i] with list[i + 1];
9        needNextPass = true; // Next pass still needed
10     }
11   }
12 }
```

The algorithm can be implemented in Listing 23.4.

LISTING 23.4   BubbleSort.java

```
 1  public class BubbleSort {
 2    /** Bubble sort method */
 3    public static void bubbleSort(int[] list) {
 4      boolean needNextPass = true;
 5
 6      for (int k = 1; k < list.length && needNextPass; k++) {
 7        // Array may be sorted and next pass not needed
 8        needNextPass = false;
 9        for (int i = 0; i < list.length - k; i++) {
10          if (list[i] > list[i + 1]) {
11            // Swap list[i] with list[i + 1]
12            int temp = list[i];
13            list[i] = list[i + 1];
14            list[i + 1] = temp;
15
16            needNextPass = true; // Next pass still needed
17          }
18        }
19      }
20    }
21
22    /** A test method */
23    public static void main(String[] args) {
24      int[] list = {2, 3, 2, 5, 6, 1, -2, 3, 14, 12};
25      bubbleSort(list);
26      for (int i = 0; i < list.length; i++)
27        System.out.print(list[i] + " ");
28    }
29  }
```

perform one pass *(margin note at line 9)*

```
-2 1 2 2 3 3 5 6 12 14
```

In the best case, the bubble-sort algorithm needs just the first pass to find that the array is already sorted—no next pass is needed. Since the number of comparisons is $n - 1$ in the first pass, the best-case time for a bubble sort is $O(n)$.

bubble-sort time complexity (margin note)

In the worst case, the bubble-sort algorithm requires $n - 1$ passes. The first pass makes $n - 1$ comparisons, the second pass makes $n - 2$ comparisons, and so on; the last pass makes 1 comparison. Thus, the total number of comparisons is as follows:

$$(n - 1) + (n - 2) + \cdots + 2 + 1$$

$$= \frac{(n - 1)n}{2} = \frac{n^2}{2} - \frac{n}{2} = O(n^2)$$

Therefore, the worst-case time for a bubble sort is $O(n^2)$.

23.3.1 Describe how a bubble sort works. What is the time complexity for a bubble sort?

23.3.2 Use Figure 23.3 as an example to show how to apply a bubble sort on {45, 11, 50, 59, 60, 2, 4, 7, 10}.

23.3.3 If a list is already sorted, how many comparisons will the bubbleSort method perform?

23.4 Merge Sort

The merge-sort algorithm can be described recursively as follows: The algorithm divides the array into two halves and applies a merge sort on each half recursively. After the two halves are sorted, the algorithm then merges them.

Key Point

The algorithm for a *merge sort* is given in Listing 23.5.

merge sort

LISTING **23.5** Merge-Sort Algorithm

```
1  public static void mergeSort(int[] list) {
2    if (list.length > 1) {
3      mergeSort(list[0 ... list.length / 2]);
4      mergeSort(list[list.length / 2 + 1 ... list.length]);
5      merge list[0 ... list.length / 2] with
6        list[list.length / 2 + 1 ... list.length];
7    }
8  }
```

base condition
sort first half
sort second half
merge two halves

Figure 23.4 illustrates a merge sort of an array of eight elements (2 9 5 4 8 1 6 7). The original array is split into (2 9 5 4) and (8 1 6 7). Apply a merge sort on these two subarrays recursively to split (2 9 5 4) into (2 9) and (5 4) and (8 1 6 7) into (8 1) and (6 7). This process continues until the subarray contains only one element. For example, array (2 9) is split into the subarrays (2) and (9). Since array (2) contains a single element, it cannot be further split. Now merge (2) with (9) into a new sorted array (2 9) and (5) with (4) into a new sorted array (4 5). Merge (2 9) with (4 5) into a new sorted array (2 4 5 9) and finally merge (2 4 5 9) with (1 6 7 8) into a new sorted array (1 2 4 5 6 7 8 9).

merge-sort illustration

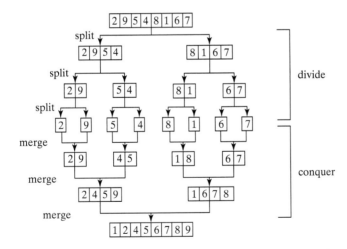

FIGURE 23.4 Merge sort employs a divide-and-conquer approach to sort the array.

The recursive call continues dividing the array into subarrays until each subarray contains only one element. The algorithm then merges these small subarrays into larger sorted subarrays until one sorted array results.

The merge-sort algorithm is implemented in Listing 23.6.

LISTING **23.6** MergeSort.java

```
1  public class MergeSort {
2    /** The method for sorting the numbers */
3    public static void mergeSort(int[] list) {
4      if (list.length > 1) {
```

base case

```
                5           // Merge sort the first half
                6           int[] firstHalf = new int[list.length / 2];
                7           System.arraycopy(list, 0, firstHalf, 0, list.length / 2);
sort first half 8           mergeSort(firstHalf);
                9
                10          // Merge sort the second half
                11          int secondHalfLength = list.length - list.length / 2;
                12          int[] secondHalf = new int[secondHalfLength];
                13          System.arraycopy(list, list.length / 2,
                14            secondHalf, 0, secondHalfLength);
sort second half 15         mergeSort(secondHalf);
                16
                17          // Merge firstHalf with secondHalf into list
merge two halves 18         merge(firstHalf, secondHalf, list);
                19        }
                20      }
                21
                22      /** Merge two sorted lists */
                23      public static void merge(int[] list1, int[] list2, int[] temp) {
                24        int current1 = 0; // Current index in list1
                25        int current2 = 0; // Current index in list2
                26        int current3 = 0; // Current index in temp
                27
                28        while (current1 < list1.length && current2 < list2.length) {
                29          if (list1[current1] < list2[current2])
list1 to temp    30            temp[current3++] = list1[current1++];
                31          else
list2 to temp    32            temp[current3++] = list2[current2++];
                33        }
                34
rest of list1 to temp 35    while (current1 < list1.length)
                36          temp[current3++] = list1[current1++];
                37
rest of list2 to temp 38    while (current2 < list2.length)
                39          temp[current3++] = list2[current2++];
                40      }
                41
                42      /** A test method */
                43      public static void main(String[] args) {
                44        int[] list = {2, 3, 2, 5, 6, 1, -2, 3, 14, 12};
                45        mergeSort(list);
                46        for (int i = 0; i < list.length; i++)
                47          System.out.print(list[i] + " ");
                48      }
                49    }
```

The mergeSort method (lines 3–20) creates a new array firstHalf, which is a copy of the first half of list (line 7). The algorithm invokes mergeSort recursively on firstHalf (line 8). The length of the firstHalf is list.length / 2 and the length of the second-Half is list.length - list.length / 2. The new array secondHalf was created to contain the second part of the original array list. The algorithm invokes mergeSort recursively on secondHalf (line 15). After firstHalf and secondHalf are sorted, they are merged to list (line 18). Thus, array list is now sorted.

The merge method (lines 23–40) merges two sorted arrays list1 and list2 into array temp. current1 and current2 point to the current element to be considered in list1 and list2 (lines 24–26). The method repeatedly compares the current elements from list1 and list2 and moves the smaller one to temp. current1 is increased by 1 (line 30) if the smaller one is in list1, and current2 is increased by 1 (line 32) if the smaller one is in list2.

Finally, all the elements in one of the lists are moved to `temp`. If there are still unmoved elements in `list1`, copy them to `temp` (lines 35–36). If there are still unmoved elements in `list2`, copy them to `temp` (lines 38–39).

Figure 23.5 illustrates how to merge the two arrays `list1` (2 4 5 9) and `list2` (1 6 7 8). Initially, the current elements to be considered in the arrays are 2 and 1. Compare them and move the smaller element 1 to `temp`, as shown in Figure 23.5a. `current2` and `current3` are increased by 1. Continue to compare the current elements in the two arrays and move the smaller one to `temp` until one of the arrays is completely moved. As shown in Figure 23.5b, all the elements in `list2` are moved to `temp` and `current1` points to element 9 in `list1`. Copy 9 to `temp`, as shown in Figure 23.5c. For an interactive demo on how merge works, go to liveexample.pearsoncmg.com/dsanimation/MergeSortNeweBook.html.

merge animation on
Companion Website

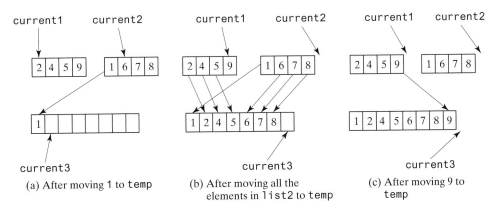

FIGURE 23.5 Two sorted arrays are merged into one sorted array.

The `mergeSort` method creates two temporary arrays (lines 6 and 12) during the dividing process, copies the first half and the second half of the array into the temporary arrays (lines 7 and 13), sorts the temporary arrays (lines 8 and 15), then merges them into the original array (line 18), as shown in Figure 23.6a. You can rewrite the code to recursively sort the first half of the array and the second half of the array without creating new temporary arrays, then merge the two arrays into a temporary array and copy its contents to the original array, as shown in Figure 23.6b. This is left for you to do in Programming Exercise 23.20.

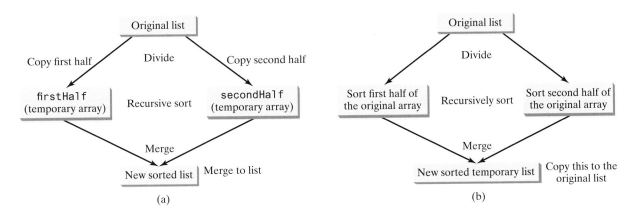

FIGURE 23.6 Temporary arrays are created to support a merge sort.

Note

A merge sort can be implemented efficiently using parallel processing. See Section 32.16, Parallel Programming, for a parallel implementation of a merge sort.

merge-sort time complexity

Let $T(n)$ denote the time required for sorting an array of n elements using a merge sort. Without loss of generality, assume n is a power of 2. The merge-sort algorithm splits the array into two subarrays, sorts the subarrays using the same algorithm recursively, then merges the subarrays. Therefore,

$$T(n) = T\left(\frac{n}{2}\right) + T\left(\frac{n}{2}\right) + mergetime$$

The first $T\left(\frac{n}{2}\right)$ is the time for sorting the first half of the array and the second $T\left(\frac{n}{2}\right)$ is the time for sorting the second half. To merge two subarrays, it takes at most $n - 1$ comparisons to compare the elements from the two subarrays, and n moves to move elements to the temporary array. Thus, the total time is $2n - 1$. Therefore,

$$T(n) = T\left(\frac{n}{2}\right) + T\left(\frac{n}{2}\right) + 2n - 1 = O(n \log n)$$

$O(n \log n)$ merge sort

The complexity of a merge sort is $O(n \log n)$. This algorithm is better than selection sort, insertion sort, and bubble sort because the time complexity of these algorithms is $O(n^2)$. The `sort` method in the `java.util.Arrays` class is implemented using a variation of the merge-sort algorithm.

23.4.1 Describe how a merge sort works. What is the time complexity for a merge sort?

23.4.2 Use Figure 23.4 as an example to show how to apply a merge sort on {45, 11, 50, 59, 60, 2, 4, 7, 10}.

23.4.3 What is wrong if lines 6–15 in Listing 23.6, MergeSort.java, are replaced by the following code?

```
// Merge sort the first half
int[] firstHalf = new int[list.length /  2 + 1];
System.arraycopy(list, 0, firstHalf, 0, list.length / 2 + 1);
mergeSort(firstHalf);

// Merge sort the second half
int secondHalfLength = list.length - list.length / 2 - 1;
int[] secondHalf = new int[secondHalfLength];
System.arraycopy(list, list.length / 2 + 1,
  secondHalf, 0, secondHalfLength);
mergeSort(secondHalf);
```

23.5 Quick Sort

A quick sort works as follows: The algorithm selects an element, called the pivot, in the array. It divides the array into two parts so all the elements in the first part are less than or equal to the pivot, and all the elements in the second part are greater than the pivot. The quick-sort algorithm is then recursively applied to the first part and then the second part.

quick sort

The quick-sort algorithm, developed by C.A.R. Hoare in 1962, is described in Listing 23.7.

LISTING 23.7 Quick-Sort Algorithm

base condition
select the pivot
partition the list

```
1  public static void quickSort(int[] list) {
2    if (list.length > 1) {
3      select a pivot;
4      partition list into list1 and list2 such that
```

```
 5          all elements in list1 <= pivot and
 6          all elements in list2 > pivot;
 7      quickSort(list1);
 8      quickSort(list2);
 9   }
10 }
```

sort first part
sort second part

Each partition places the pivot in the right place. The selection of the pivot affects the performance of the algorithm. Ideally, the algorithm should choose the pivot that divides the two parts evenly. For simplicity, assume that the first element in the array is chosen as the pivot. (Programming Exercise 23.4 proposes an alternative strategy for selecting the pivot.)

how to partition

Figure 23.7 illustrates how to sort an array (5 2 9 3 8 4 0 1 6 7) using quick sort. Choose the first element, 5, as the pivot. The array is partitioned into two parts, as shown in Figure 23.7b. The highlighted pivot is placed in the right place in the array. Apply quick sort on two subarrays (4 2 1 3 0) then (8 9 6 7). The pivot 4 partitions (4 2 1 3 0) into just one subarrays (0 2 1 3), as shown in Figure 23.7c. Apply quick sort on (0 2 1 3). The pivot 0 partitions it into just one subarrays (2 1 3), as shown in Figure 23.7d. Apply quick sort on (2 1 3). The pivot 2 partitions it into (1) and (3), as shown in Figure 23.7e. Apply quick sort on (1). Since the array contains just one element, no further partition is needed.

quick-sort illustration

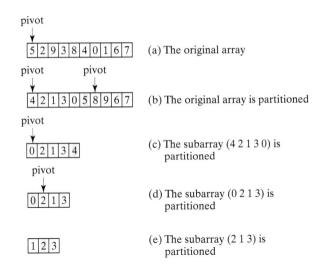

FIGURE 23.7 The quick-sort algorithm is recursively applied to subarrays.

The quick-sort algorithm is implemented in Listing 23.8. There are two overloaded quickSort methods in the class. The first method (line 2) is used to sort an array. The second is a helper method (line 6) that sorts a subarray with a specified range.

LISTING 23.8 QuickSort.java

```
 1  public class QuickSort {
 2    public static void quickSort(int[] list) {
 3      quickSort(list, 0, list.length - 1);
 4    }
 5
 6    public static void quickSort(int[] list, int first, int last) {
 7      if (last > first) {
 8        int pivotIndex = partition(list, first, last);
 9        quickSort(list, first, pivotIndex - 1);
10        quickSort(list, pivotIndex + 1, last);
11      }
```

sort method

helper method

recursive call

```
12     }
13
14     /** Partition the array list[first..last] */
15     public static int partition(int[] list, int first, int last) {
16       int pivot = list[first]; // Choose the first element as the pivot
17       int low = first + 1; // Index for forward search
18       int high = last; // Index for backward search
19
20       while (high > low) {
21         // Search forward from left
22         while (low <= high && list[low] <= pivot)
23           low++;
24
25         // Search backward from right
26         while (low <= high && list[high] > pivot)
27           high--;
28
29         // Swap two elements in the list
30         if (high > low) {
31           int temp = list[high];
32           list[high] = list[low];
33           list[low] = temp;
34         }
35       }
36
37       while (high > first && list[high] >= pivot)
38         high--;
39
40       // Swap pivot with list[high]
41       if (pivot > list[high]) {
42         list[first] = list[high];
43         list[high] = pivot;
44         return high;
45       }
46       else {
47         return first;
48       }
49     }
50
51     /** A test method */
52     public static void main(String[] args) {
53       int[] list = {2, 3, 2, 5, 6, 1, -2, 3, 14, 12};
54       quickSort(list);
55       for (int i = 0; i < list.length; i++)
56         System.out.print(list[i] + " ");
57     }
58   }
```

forward

backward

swap

place pivot
pivot's new index

pivot's original index

```
-2 1 2 2 3 3 5 6 12 14
```

The partition method (lines 15–49) partitions the array list[first..last] using the pivot. The first element in the partial array is chosen as the pivot (line 16). Initially, low points to the second element in the subarrays (line 17) and high points to the last element in the subarrays (line 18).

Starting from the left, the method searches forward in the array for the first element that is greater than the pivot (lines 22–23), then searches from the right backward for the first element in the array that is less than or equal to the pivot (lines 26–27). It then swaps these two elements and repeats the same search and swap operations until all the elements are searched in a `while` loop (lines 20–35).

The method returns the new index for the pivot that divides the subarrays into two parts if the pivot has been moved (line 44). Otherwise, it returns the original index for the pivot (line 47).

Figure 23.8 illustrates how to partition an array (5 2 9 3 8 4 0 1 6 7). Choose the first element, 5, as the pivot. Initially, `low` is the index that points to element 2 and `high` points to element 7, as shown in Figure 23.8a. Advance index `low` forward to search for the first element (9) that is greater than the pivot, and move index `high` backward to search for the first element (1) that is less than or equal to the pivot, as shown in Figure 23.8b. Swap 9 with 1, as shown in Figure 23.8c. Continue the search and move `low` to point to element 8 and `high` to point to element 0, as shown in Figure 23.8d. Swap element 8 with 0, as shown in Figure 23.8e. Continue to move `low` until it passes `high`, as shown in Figure 23.8f. Now all the elements are examined. Swap the pivot with element 4 at index `high`. The final partition is shown in Figure 23.8g. The index of the pivot is returned when the method is finished. For an interactive demo on how partition works, go to liveexample.pearsoncmg.com/dsanimation/QuickSortNeweBook.html.

partition illustration

partition animation on Companion Website

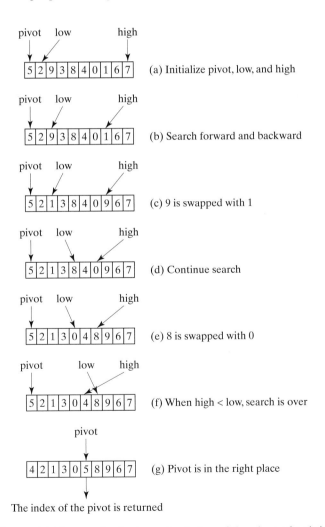

pivot	low						high		
5	2	9	3	8	4	0	1	6	7

(a) Initialize pivot, low, and high

pivot	low						high		
5	2	9	3	8	4	0	1	6	7

(b) Search forward and backward

pivot	low						high		
5	2	1	3	8	4	0	9	6	7

(c) 9 is swapped with 1

pivot	low					high			
5	2	1	3	8	4	0	9	6	7

(d) Continue search

pivot	low				high				
5	2	1	3	0	4	8	9	6	7

(e) 8 is swapped with 0

pivot					high low				
5	2	1	3	0	4	8	9	6	7

(f) When high < low, search is over

					pivot				
4	2	1	3	0	5	8	9	6	7

(g) Pivot is in the right place

The index of the pivot is returned

FIGURE 23.8 The `partition` method returns the index of the pivot after it is put in the correct place.

To partition an array of n elements, it takes n comparisons and n moves in the worst case. Thus, the time required for partition is $O(n)$.

$O(n)$ partition time

$O(n^2)$ worst-case time

In the worst case, the pivot divides the array each time into one big subarray with the other array empty. The size of the big subarray is one less than the one before divided. The algorithm requires $(n - 1) + (n - 2) + \cdots + 2 + 1 = O(n^2)$ time.

$O(n \log n)$ best-case time

In the best case, the pivot divides the array each time into two parts of about the same size. Let $T(n)$ denote the time required for sorting an array of n elements using quick sort. Thus,

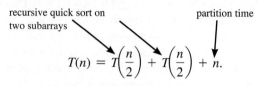

$$T(n) = T\left(\frac{n}{2}\right) + T\left(\frac{n}{2}\right) + n.$$

Similar to the merge-sort analysis, $T(n) = O(n \log n)$.

$O(n \log n)$ average-case time

On the average, the pivot will not divide the array into two parts of the same size or one empty part each time. Statistically, the sizes of the two parts are very close. Therefore, the average time is $O(n \log n)$. The exact average-case analysis is beyond the scope of this book.

Both merge and quick sorts employ the divide-and-conquer approach. For merge sort, the bulk of the work is to merge two sublists, which takes place *after* the sublists are sorted. For quick sort, the bulk of the work is to partition the list into two sublists, which takes place *before* the sublists are sorted. Merge sort is more efficient than quick sort in the worst case, but the two are equally efficient in the average case. Merge sort requires a temporary array for sorting two subarrays. Quick sort does not need additional array space. Thus, quick sort is more space efficient than merge sort.

quick sort vs. merge sort

 Check Point

23.5.1 Describe how quick sort works. What is the time complexity for a quick sort?

23.5.2 Why is quick sort more space efficient than merge sort?

23.5.3 Use Figure 23.7 as an example to show how to apply a quick sort on {45, 11, 50, 59, 60, 2, 4, 7, 10}.

23.5.4 If lines 37–38 in the QuickSort program is removed, will it still work? Give a counter example to show that it will not work.

 Key Point

23.6 Heap Sort

A heap sort uses a binary heap. It first adds all the elements to a heap and then removes the largest elements successively to obtain a sorted list.

heap sort
root
left subtree
right subtree
length
depth
leaf

Heap sorts use a binary heap, which is a complete binary tree. A binary tree is a hierarchical structure. It either is empty or it consists of an element, called the *root*, and two distinct binary trees, called the *left subtree* and *right subtree*. The *length* of a path is the number of the edges in the path. The *depth* of a node is the length of the path from the root to the node. A node is called a *leaf* if it does not have subtrees.

A *binary heap* is a binary tree with the following properties:

■ Shape property: It is a complete binary tree.

■ Heap property: Each node is greater than or equal to any of its children.

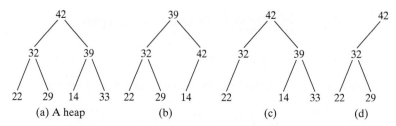

FIGURE 23.9 A binary heap is a special complete binary tree.

A binary tree is *complete* if each of its levels is full, except that the last level may not be full and all the leaves on the last level are placed leftmost. For example, in Figure 23.9, the binary trees in (a) and (b) are complete, but the binary trees in (c) and (d) are not complete. Further, the binary tree in (a) is a heap, but the binary tree in (b) is not a heap because the root (39) is less than its right child (42).

complete binary tree

Note
Heap is a term with many meanings in computer science. In this chapter, heap means a binary heap.

heap

Pedagogical Note
A heap can be implemented efficiently for inserting keys and deleting the root. For an interactive demo on how a heap works, go to liveexample.pearsoncmg.com/dsanimation/ HeapeBook.html, as shown in Figure 23.10.

heap animation on Companion Website

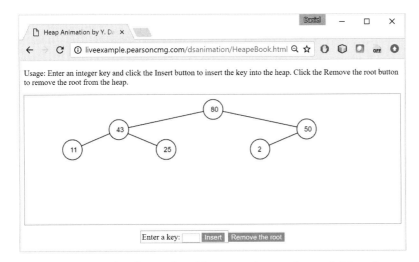

FIGURE 23.10 The heap animation tool enables you to insert a key and delete the root visually. *Source*: Copyright © 1995–2016 Oracle and/or its affiliates. All rights reserved. Used with permission.

23.6.1 Storing a Heap

A heap can be stored in an `ArrayList` or an array if the heap size is known in advance. The heap in Figure 23.11a can be stored using the array in Figure 23.11b. The root is at position 0, and its two children are at positions 1 and 2. For a node at position i, its left child is at position $2i + 1$, its right child is at position $2i + 2$, and its parent is $(i - 1)/2$. For example, the node for element 39 is at position 4, so its left child (element 14) is at 9 ($2 \times 4 + 1$), its right child (element 33) is at 10 ($2 \times 4 + 2$), and its parent (element 42) is at 1 ($(4 - 1)/2$).

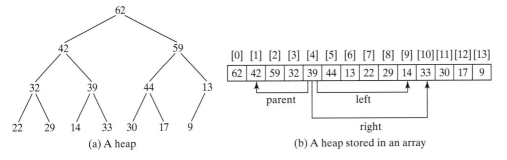

(a) A heap   (b) A heap stored in an array

FIGURE 23.11 A binary heap can be implemented using an array.

23.6.2 Adding a New Node

To add a new node to the heap, first add it to the end of the heap then rebuild the tree as follows:

```
Let the last node be the current node;
while (the current node is greater than its parent) {
    Swap the current node with its parent;
    Now the current node is one level up;
}
```

Suppose a heap is initially empty. That heap is shown in Figure 23.12, after adding numbers 3, 5, 1, 19, 11, and 22 in this order.

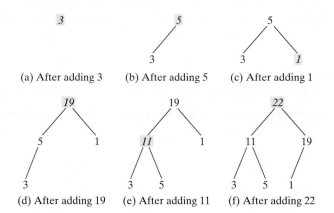

(a) After adding 3   (b) After adding 5   (c) After adding 1

(d) After adding 19   (e) After adding 11   (f) After adding 22

FIGURE 23.12   Elements 3, 5, 1, 19, 11, and 22 are inserted into the heap.

Now consider adding 88 into the heap. Place the new node 88 at the end of the tree, as shown in Figure 23.13a. Swap 88 with 19, as shown in Figure 23.13b. Swap 88 with 22, as shown in Figure 23.13c.

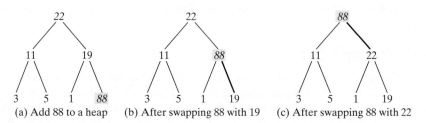

(a) Add 88 to a heap   (b) After swapping 88 with 19   (c) After swapping 88 with 22

FIGURE 23.13   Rebuild the heap after adding a new node.

23.6.3 Removing the Root

Often you need to remove the maximum element, which is the root in a heap. After the root is removed, the tree must be rebuilt to maintain the heap property. The algorithm for rebuilding the tree can be described as follows:

```
Move the last node to replace the root;
Let the root be the current node;
while (the current node has children and the current node is
        smaller than one of its children) {
    Swap the current node with the larger of its children;
    Now the current node is one level down;
}
```

Figure 23.14 shows the process of rebuilding a heap after the root 62 is removed from Figure 23.11a. Move the last node 9 to the root, as shown in Figure 23.14a. Swap 9 with 59, as shown in Figure 23.14b; swap 9 with 44, as shown in Figure 23.14c; and swap 9 with 30, as shown in Figure 23.14d.

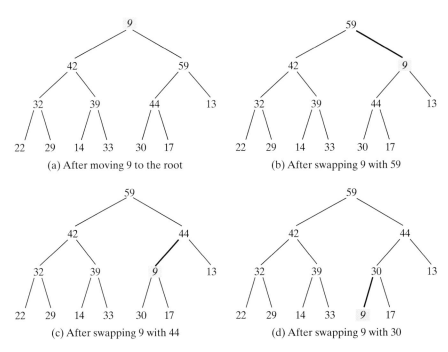

FIGURE 23.14   Rebuild the heap after the root 62 is removed.

Figure 23.15 shows the process of rebuilding a heap after the root 59 is removed from Figure 23.14d. Move the last node 17 to the root, as shown in Figure 23.15a. Swap 17 with 44, as shown in Figure 23.15b, then swap 17 with 30, as shown in Figure 23.15c.

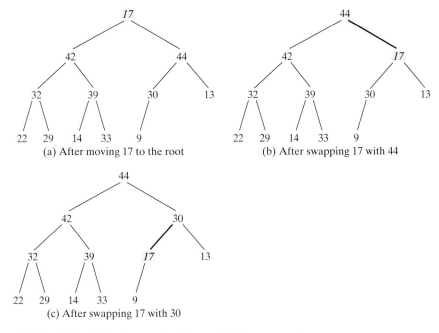

FIGURE 23.15   Rebuild the heap after the root 59 is removed.

23.6.4 The Heap Class

Now you are ready to design and implement the Heap class. The class diagram is shown in Figure 23.16. Its implementation is given in Listing 23.9.

```
┌─────────────────────────────────────────┐
│ Heap<E extends Comparable<E>>            │
├─────────────────────────────────────────┤
│ -list: java.util.ArrayList<E>            │
├─────────────────────────────────────────┤
│ +Heap()                                  │    Creates a default empty Heap.
│ +Heap(objects: E[])                      │    Creates a Heap with the specified objects.
│ +add(newObject: E): void                 │    Adds a new object to the heap.
│ +remove(): E                             │    Removes the root from the heap and returns it.
│ +getSize(): int                          │    Returns the size of the heap.
│ +isEmpty(): boolean                      │    Returns true if the heap is empty.
└─────────────────────────────────────────┘
```

FIGURE 23.16 The Heap class provides operations for manipulating a heap.

LISTING 23.9 Heap.java

```java
 1  public class Heap<E extends Comparable<E>> {
 2    private java.util.ArrayList<E> list = new java.util.ArrayList<>();
 3
 4    /** Create a default heap */
 5    public Heap() {
 6    }
 7
 8    /** Create a heap from an array of objects */
 9    public Heap(E[] objects) {
10      for (int i = 0; i < objects.length; i++)
11        add(objects[i]);
12    }
13
14    /** Add a new object into the heap */
15    public void add(E newObject) {
16      list.add(newObject); // Append to the heap
17      int currentIndex = list.size() - 1; // The index of the last node
18
19      while (currentIndex > 0) {
20        int parentIndex = (currentIndex - 1) / 2;
21        // Swap if the current object is greater than its parent
22        if (list.get(currentIndex).compareTo(
23             list.get(parentIndex)) > 0) {
24          E temp = list.get(currentIndex);
25          list.set(currentIndex, list.get(parentIndex));
26          list.set(parentIndex, temp);
27        }
28        else
29          break; // The tree is a heap now
30
31        currentIndex = parentIndex;
32      }
33    }
34
35    /** Remove the root from the heap */
36    public E remove() {
```

Margin notes:
internal heap representation (line 2)
no-arg constructor (line 5)
constructor (line 9)
add a new object (line 15)
append the object (line 16)
swap with parent (line 24)
heap now (line 29)
remove the root (line 36)

```
37        if (list.size() == 0)  return null;                              empty heap
38
39        E removedObject = list.get(0);                                   root
40        list.set(0, list.get(list.size() - 1));                          new root
41        list.remove(list.size() - 1);                                    remove the last
42
43        int currentIndex = 0;
44        while (currentIndex < list.size()) {                             adjust the tree
45          int leftChildIndex = 2 * currentIndex + 1;
46          int rightChildIndex = 2 * currentIndex + 2;
47
48          // Find the maximum between two children
49          if (leftChildIndex >= list.size()) break; // The tree is a heap
50          int maxIndex = leftChildIndex;
51          if (rightChildIndex < list.size()) {
52            if (list.get(maxIndex).compareTo(                            compare two children
53                list.get(rightChildIndex)) < 0) {
54              maxIndex = rightChildIndex;
55            }
56          }
57
58          // Swap if the current node is less than the maximum
59          if (list.get(currentIndex).compareTo(
60              list.get(maxIndex)) < 0) {
61            E temp = list.get(maxIndex);                                 swap with the larger child
62            list.set(maxIndex, list.get(currentIndex));
63            list.set(currentIndex, temp);
64            currentIndex = maxIndex;
65          }
66          else
67            break; // The tree is a heap
68        }
69
70        return removedObject;
71    }
72
73    /** Get the number of nodes in the tree */
74    public int getSize() {
75      return list.size();
76    }
77  }
```

A heap is represented using an array list internally (line 2). You can change the array list to other data structures, but the Heap class contract will remain unchanged.

The add(E newObject) method (lines 15–33) appends the object to the tree then swaps the object with its parent if the object is greater than its parent. This process continues until the new object becomes the root or is not greater than its parent.

The remove() method (lines 36–71) removes and returns the root. To maintain the heap property, the method moves the last object to the root position and swaps it with its larger child if it is less than the larger child. This process continues until the last object becomes a leaf or is not less than its children.

23.6.5 Sorting Using the Heap Class

To sort an array using a heap, first create an object using the Heap class, add all the elements to the heap using the add method, and remove all the elements from the heap using the remove method. The elements are removed in descending order. Listing 23.10 gives a program for sorting an array using a heap.

LISTING 23.10 HeapSort.java

```
 1  public class HeapSort {
 2    /** Heap sort method */
 3    public static <E extends Comparable<E>> void heapSort(E[] list) {
 4      // Create a Heap of integers
 5      Heap<E> heap = new Heap<>();
 6
 7      // Add elements to the heap
 8      for (int i = 0; i < list.length; i++)
 9        heap.add(list[i]);
10
11      // Remove elements from the heap
12      for (int i = list.length - 1; i >= 0; i--)
13        list[i] = heap.remove();
14    }
15
16    /** A test method */
17    public static void main(String[] args) {
18      Integer[] list = {-44, -5, -3, 3, 3, 1, -4, 0, 1, 2, 4, 5, 53};
19      heapSort(list);
20      for (int i = 0; i < list.length; i++)
21        System.out.print(list[i] + " ");
22    }
23  }
```

create a Heap (line 5)

add element (line 9)

remove element (line 13)

invoke sort method (line 19)

```
-44 -5 -4 -3 0 1 1 2 3 3 4 5 53
```

23.6.6 Heap Sort Time Complexity

height of a heap

Let us turn our attention to analyzing the time complexity for the heap sort. Let h denote the *height* for a heap of n elements. The height of a nonempty tree is the length of the path from the root node to its furthest leaf. The *height* of a tree that contains a single node is 0. Conventionally, the height of an empty tree is -1. Since a heap is a complete binary tree, the first level has 1 (2^0) node, the second level has 2 (2^1) nodes, the kth level has 2^{k-1} nodes, the h level has 2^{h-1} nodes, and the last ($h + 1$)th level has at least 1 and at most 2^h nodes. Therefore,

$$1 + 2 + \cdots + 2^{h-1} < n \le 1 + 2 + \cdots + 2^{h-1} + 2^h$$

That is,

$$2^h - 1 < n \le 2^{h+1} - 1$$
$$2^h < n + 1 \le 2^{h+1}$$
$$h < \log(n + 1) \le h + 1$$

Thus, $h < \log(n + 1)$ and $h \ge \log(n + 1) - 1$. Therefore, $\log(n + 1) - 1 \le h < \log(n + 1)$. Hence, the height of a heap is $O(\log n)$. More precisely, you can prove that $h = \lfloor \log n \rfloor$ for a non-empty tree.

O(n log n) worst-case time

Since the add method traces a path from a leaf to a root, it takes at most h steps to add a new element to the heap. Thus, the total time for constructing an initial heap is $O(n \log n)$ for an array of n elements. Since the remove method traces a path from a root to a leaf, it takes at most h steps to rebuild a heap after removing the root from the heap. Since the remove method is invoked n times, the total time for producing a sorted array from a heap is $O(n \log n)$.

heap sort vs. merge sort

Both merge and heap sorts require $O(n \log n)$ time. A merge sort requires a temporary array for merging two subarrays; a heap sort does not need additional array space. Therefore, a heap sort is more space efficient than a merge sort.

23.6.1 What is a complete binary tree? What is a heap? Describe how to remove the root from a heap and how to add a new object to a heap.

23.6.2 What is the return value from invoking the `remove` method if the heap is empty?

23.6.3 Add the elements 4, 5, 1, 2, 9, and 3 into a heap in this order. Draw the diagrams to show the heap after each element is added.

23.6.4 Show the heap after the root in the heap in Figure 23.15c is removed.

23.6.5 What is the time complexity of inserting a new element into a heap, and what is the time complexity of deleting an element from a heap?

23.6.6 Show the steps of creating a heap using {45, 11, 50, 59, 60, 2, 4, 7, 10}.

23.6.7 Given the following heap, show the steps of removing all nodes from the heap.

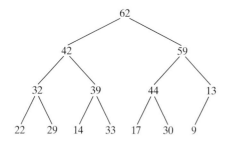

23.6.8 Which of the following statements are wrong?

```
1  Heap<Object> heap1 = new Heap<>();
2  Heap<Number> heap2 = new Heap<>();
3  Heap<BigInteger> heap3 = new Heap<>();
4  Heap<Calendar> heap4 = new Heap<>();
5  Heap<String> heap5 = new Heap<>();
```

23.6.9 What is the height of a nonempty heap? What is the height of a heap with 16, 17, and 512 elements? If the height of a heap is 5, what is the maximum number of nodes in the heap?

23.7 Bucket and Radix Sorts

Bucket and radix sorts are efficient for sorting integers.

Key
Point

All sort algorithms discussed so far are general sorting algorithms that work for any types of keys (e.g., integers, strings, and any comparable objects). These algorithms sort the elements by comparing their keys. It has been proven that no sorting algorithms based on comparisons can perform better than $O(n \log n)$. However, if the keys are integers, you can use a bucket sort without having to compare the keys.

The *bucket sort* algorithm works as follows. Assume the keys are in the range from 0 to t. We need t + 1 buckets labeled 0, 1, . . . , and t. If an element's key is i, the element is put into the bucket i. Each bucket holds the elements with the same key value.

bucket sort

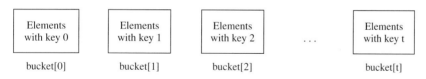

You can use an `ArrayList` to implement a bucket. The bucket-sort algorithm for sorting a list of elements can be described as follows:

```
public static void bucketSort(E[] list) {
  E[] bucket = (E[])new java.util.ArrayList[t+1];

  // Distribute the elements from list to buckets
  for (int i = 0; i < list.length; i++) {
    int key = list[i].getKey(); // Assume element has the getKey() method

    if (bucket[key] == null)
      bucket[key] = new java.util.ArrayList<>();

    bucket[key].add(list[i]);
  }

  // Now move the elements from the buckets back to list
  int k = 0; // k is an index for list
  for (int i = 0; i < bucket.length; i++) {
    if (bucket[i] != null) {
      for (int j = 0; j < bucket[i].size(); j++)
        list[k++] = bucket[i].get(j);
    }
  }
}
```

Clearly, it takes $O(n + t)$ time to sort the list and uses $O(n + t)$ space, where n is the list size.

Note if t is too large, using the bucket sort is not desirable. Instead, you can use a radix sort. The radix sort is based on the bucket sort, but a radix sort uses only 10 buckets.

stable

It is worthwhile to note a bucket sort is *stable*, meaning that if two elements in the original list have the same key value, their order is not changed in the sorted list. That is, if element e_1 and element e_2 have the same key and e_1 precedes e_2 in the original list, e_1 still precedes e_2 in the sorted list.

radix sort

Assume the keys are positive integers. The idea for the *radix sort* is to divide the keys into subgroups based on their radix positions. It applies a bucket sort repeatedly for the key values on radix positions, starting from the least-significant position.

radix sort on Companion Website

Consider sorting the elements with the following keys:

331, 454, 230, 34, 343, 45, 59, 453, 345, 231, 9

queue

Apply the bucket sort on the last radix position, and the elements are put into the buckets as follows:

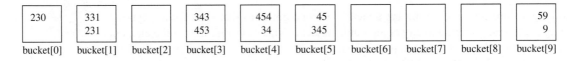

After collecting the elements from the buckets, the elements are in the following order:

230, 331, 231, 343, 453, 454, 34, 45, 345, 59, 9

queue

Apply the bucket sort on the second-to-last radix position, and the elements are put into the buckets as follows:

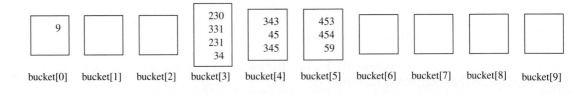

After collecting the elements from the buckets, the elements are in the following order:

9, 230, 331, 231, 34, 343, 45, 345, 453, 454, 59

(Note 9 is 009.)

Apply the bucket sort on the third-to-last radix position, and the elements are put into the buckets as follows:

queue

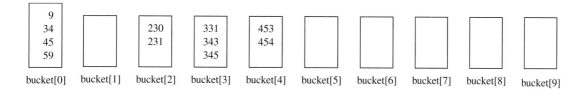

After collecting the elements from the buckets, the elements are in the following order:

9, 34, 45, 59, 230, 231, 331, 343, 345, 453, 454

The elements are now sorted.

Radix sort takes $O(dn)$ time to sort n elements with integer keys, where d is the maximum number of the radix positions among all keys.

23.7.1 Can you sort a list of strings using a bucket sort?

23.7.2 Show how the radix sort works using the numbers 454, 34, 23, 43, 74, 86, and 76.

23.8 External Sort

You can sort a large amount of data using an external sort.

All the sort algorithms discussed in the preceding sections assume all the data to be sorted are available at one time in internal memory, such as in an array. To sort data stored in an external file, you must first bring the data to the memory then sort it internally. However, if the file is too large, all the data in the file cannot be brought to memory at one time. This section discusses how to sort data in a large external file. This is called an *external sort*.

external sort

For simplicity, assume two million `int` values are stored in a binary file named **largedata .dat**. This file was created using the program in Listing 23.11.

LISTING 23.11 CreateLargeFile.java

```
 1  import java.io.*;
 2
 3  public class CreateLargeFile {
 4    public static void main(String[] args)  throws Exception {
 5      DataOutputStream output = new DataOutputStream(
 6        new BufferedOutputStream(
 7        new FileOutputStream("largedata.dat"));
 8
 9      for (int i = 0; i < 2_000_000; i++)
10        output.writeInt((int)(Math.random() * 1000000)));
11
12      output.close();
13
14      // Display first 100 numbers
15      DataInputStream input = new DataInputStream(
16        new BufferedInputStream(new FileInputStream("largedata.dat")));
17      for (int i = 0; i < 100; i++)
```

a binary output stream

output an int value

close output file

read an int value
```
18          System.out.print(input.readInt() + " ");
19
```
close input file
```
20      input.close();
21  }
22 }
```

```
569193 131317 608695 776266 767910 624915 458599 5010 ... (omitted)
```

A variation of merge sort can be used to sort this file in two phases:

Phase I: Repeatedly bring data from the file to an array, sort the array using an internal sorting algorithm, and output the data from the array to a temporary file. This process is shown in Figure 23.17. Ideally, you want to create a large array, but its maximum size depends on how much memory is allocated to the JVM by the operating system. Assume the maximum array size is 100,000 `int` values. In the temporary file, every 100,000 `int` values are sorted. They are denoted as S_1, S_2, ... , and S_k, where the last segment, S_k, may contain less than 100,000 values.

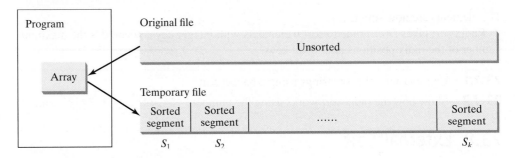

FIGURE 23.17 The original file is sorted in segments.

Phase II: Merge a pair of sorted segments (e.g., S_1 with S_2, S_3 with S_4, ... , and so on) into a larger sorted segment and save the new segment into a new temporary file. Continue the same process until only one sorted segment results. Figure 23.18 shows how to merge eight segments.

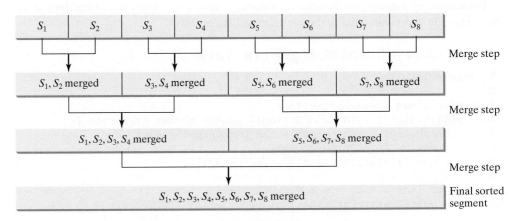

FIGURE 23.18 Sorted segments are merged iteratively.

Note

It is not necessary to merge two successive segments. For example, you can merge S_1 with S_5, S_2 with S_6, S_3 with S_7, and S_4 with S_8, in the first merge step. This observation is useful in implementing Phase II efficiently.

23.8.1 Implementing Phase I

Listing 23.12 gives the method that reads each segment of data from a file, sorts the segment, and stores the sorted segments into a new file. The method returns the number of segments.

LISTING 23.12 Creating Initial Sorted Segments

```
1   /** Sort original file into sorted segments */
2   private static int initializeSegments
3       (int segmentSize, String originalFile, String f1)
4       throws Exception {
5     int[] list = new int[segmentSize];
6     DataInputStream input = new DataInputStream(
7       new BufferedInputStream(new FileInputStream(originalFile)));      original file
8     DataOutputStream output = new DataOutputStream(
9       new BufferedOutputStream(new FileOutputStream(f1)));            file with sorted segments
10
11    int numberOfSegments = 0;
12    while (input.available() > 0) {
13      numberOfSegments++;
14      int i = 0;
15      for ( ; input.available() > 0 && i < segmentSize; i++) {
16        list[i] = input.readInt();
17      }
18
19      // Sort an array list[0..i-1]
20      java.util.Arrays.sort(list, 0, i);                              sort a segment
21
22      // Write the array to f1.dat
23      for (int j = 0; j < i; j++) {
24        output.writeInt(list[j]);                                     output to file
25      }
26    }
27
28    input.close();                                                    close file
29    output.close();
30
31    return numberOfSegments;                                          return # of segments
32  }
```

The method creates an array with the maximum size in line 5, a data input stream for the original file in line 6, and a data output stream for a temporary file in line 8. Buffered streams are used to improve performance.

Lines 14–17 read a segment of data from the file into the array. Line 20 sorts the array. Lines 23–25 write the data in the array to the temporary file.

The number of segments is returned in line 31. Note every segment has `MAX_ARRAY_SIZE` number of elements except the last segment, which may have fewer elements.

23.8.2 Implementing Phase II

In each merge step, two sorted segments are merged to form a new segment. The size of the new segment is doubled. The number of segments is reduced by half after each merge step. A segment is too large to be brought to an array in memory. To implement a merge step, copy half the number of segments from the file **f1.dat** to a temporary file **f2.dat**. Then, merge the first remaining segment in **f1.dat** with the first segment in **f2.dat** into a temporary file named **f3.dat**, as shown in Figure 23.19.

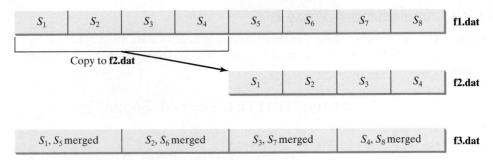

FIGURE 23.19   Sorted segments are merged iteratively.

> **Note**
> **f1.dat** may have one segment more than **f2.dat**. If so, move the last segment into
> **f3.dat** after the merge.

Listing 23.13 gives a method that copies the first half of the segments in **f1.dat** to **f2.dat**.
Listing 23.14 gives a method that merges a pair of segments in **f1.dat** and **f2.dat**. Listing 23.15
gives a method that merges two segments.

LISTING 23.13   Copying First Half Segments

```
1  private static void copyHalfToF2(int numberOfSegments,
2    int segmentSize, DataInputStream f1, DataOutputStream f2)
3    throws Exception {
4    for (int i = 0; i < (numberOfSegments / 2) * segmentSize; i++) {
5      f2.writeInt(f1.readInt());
6    }
7  }
```
input stream f1
output stream f2

segments copied

LISTING 23.14   Merging All Segments

```
1  private static void mergeSegments(int numberOfSegments,
2    int segmentSize, DataInputStream f1, DataInputStream f2,
3    DataOutputStream f3)  throws Exception {
4    for (int i = 0; i < numberOfSegments; i++) {
5      mergeTwoSegments(segmentSize, f1, f2, f3);
6    }
7
8    // If f1 has one extra segment, copy it to f3
9    while (f1.available() > 0) {
10     f3.writeInt(f1.readInt());
11   }
12 }
```
input stream f1 and f2
output stream f3

merge two segments

extra segment in f1?

LISTING 23.15   Merging Two Segments

```
1  private static void mergeTwoSegments(int segmentSize,
2    DataInputStream f1, DataInputStream f2,
3    DataOutputStream f3) throws Exception {
4    int intFromF1 = f1.readInt();
5    int intFromF2 = f2.readInt();
6    int f1Count = 1;
7    int f2Count = 1;
8
9    while (true) {
10     if (intFromF1 < intFromF2) {
11       f3.writeInt(intFromF1);
```
input stream f1 and f2
output stream f3
read from f1
read from f2

write to f3

```
12        if (f1.available() == 0 || f1Count++ >= segmentSize) {
13          f3.writeInt(intFromF2);
14          break;                                                    segment in f1 finished
15        }
16        else {
17          intFromF1 = f1.readInt();
18        }
19      }
20      else {
21        f3.writeInt(intFromF2);                                     write to f3
22        if (f2.available() == 0 || f2Count++ >= segmentSize) {
23          f3.writeInt(intFromF1);
24          break;                                                    segment in f2 finished
25        }
26        else {
27          intFromF2 = f2.readInt();
28        }
29      }
30    }
31
32    while (f1.available() > 0 && f1Count++ < segmentSize) {         remaining f1 segment
33      f3.writeInt(f1.readInt());
34    }
35
36    while (f2.available() > 0 && f2Count++ < segmentSize) {         remaining f2 segment
37      f3.writeInt(f2.readInt());
38    }
39  }
```

23.8.3 Combining Two Phases

Listing 23.16 gives the complete program for sorting `int` values in **largedata.dat** and storing the sorted data in **sortedfile.dat**.

LISTING 23.16 SortLargeFile.java

```
1  import java.io.*;
2
3  public class SortLargeFile {
4    public static final int MAX_ARRAY_SIZE = 100000;              max array size
5    public static final int BUFFER_SIZE = 100000;                 I/O stream buffer size
6
7    public static void main(String[] args)  throws Exception {
8      // Sort largedata.dat to sortedfile.dat
9      sort("largedata.dat", "sortedfile.dat");
10
11     // Display the first 100 numbers in the sorted file
12     displayFile("sortedfile.dat");
13   }
14
15   /** Sort data in source file and into target file */
16   public static void sort(String sourcefile, String targetfile)
17       throws Exception {
18     // Implement Phase 1: Create initial segments
19     int numberOfSegments =
20       initializeSegments(MAX_ARRAY_SIZE, sourcefile, "f1.dat");   create initial segments
21
22     // Implement Phase 2: Merge segments recursively
23     merge(numberOfSegments, MAX_ARRAY_SIZE,                       merge recursively
24       "f1.dat", "f2.dat", "f3.dat", targetfile);
```

```
25        }
26
27        /** Sort original file into sorted segments */
28        private static int initializeSegments
29            (int segmentSize, String originalFile, String f1)
30            throws Exception {
31          // Same as Listing 23.12, so omitted
32        }
33
34        private static void merge(int numberOfSegments, int segmentSize,
35            String f1, String f2, String f3, String targetfile)
36            throws Exception {
37          if (numberOfSegments > 1) {
38            mergeOneStep(numberOfSegments, segmentSize, f1, f2, f3);
39            merge((numberOfSegments + 1) / 2, segmentSize * 2,
40              f3, f1, f2, targetfile);
41          }
42          else {  // Rename f1 as the final sorted file
43            File sortedFile = new File(targetfile);
44            if (sortedFile.exists()) sortedFile.delete();
45            new File(f1).renameTo(sortedFile);
46          }
47        }
48
49        private static void mergeOneStep(int numberOfSegments,
50            int segmentSize, String f1, String f2, String f3)
51            throws Exception {
52          DataInputStream f1Input = new DataInputStream(
53            new BufferedInputStream(new FileInputStream(f1), BUFFER_SIZE));
54          DataOutputStream f2Output = new DataOutputStream(
55            new BufferedOutputStream(new FileOutputStream(f2), BUFFER_SIZE));
56
57          // Copy half number of segments from f1.dat to f2.dat
58          copyHalfToF2(numberOfSegments, segmentSize, f1Input, f2Output);
59          f2Output.close();
60
61          // Merge remaining segments in f1 with segments in f2 into f3
62          DataInputStream f2Input = new DataInputStream(
63            new BufferedInputStream(new FileInputStream(f2), BUFFER_SIZE));
64          DataOutputStream f3Output = new DataOutputStream(
65            new BufferedOutputStream(new FileOutputStream(f3), BUFFER_SIZE));
66
67          mergeSegments(numberOfSegments / 2,
68            segmentSize, f1Input, f2Input, f3Output);
69
70          f1Input.close();
71          f2Input.close();
72          f3Output.close();
73        }
74
75        /** Copy first half number of segments from f1.dat to f2.dat */
76        private static void copyHalfToF2(int numberOfSegments,
77            int segmentSize, DataInputStream f1, DataOutputStream f2)
78            throws Exception {
79          // Same as Listing 23.13, so omitted
80        }
81
82        /** Merge all segments */
83        private static void mergeSegments(int numberOfSegments,
84            int segmentSize, DataInputStream f1, DataInputStream f2,
```

```
85           DataOutputStream f3)  throws Exception {
86       // Same as Listing 23.14, so omitted
87     }
88
89     /** Merges two segments */
90     private static void mergeTwoSegments(int segmentSize,
91       DataInputStream f1, DataInputStream f2,
92       DataOutputStream f3)  throws Exception {
93       // Same as Listing 23.15, so omitted
94     }
95
96     /** Display the first 100 numbers in the specified file */
97     public static void displayFile(String filename) {
98       try {
99         DataInputStream input =
100          new DataInputStream(new FileInputStream(filename));
101        for (int i = 0; i < 100; i++)
102          System.out.print(input.readInt() + " ");
103        input.close();
104      }
105      catch (IOException ex) {
106        ex.printStackTrace();
107      }
108    }
109  }
```

display file

```
0 1 1 1 2 2 2 3 3 4 5 6 8 8 9 9 9 10 10 11...(omitted)
```

Before you run this program, first run Listing 23.11, CreateLargeFile.java, to create the file **largedata.dat**. Invoking sort("largedata.dat", "sortedfile.dat") (line 9) reads data from largedata.dat and writes sorted data to sortedfile.dat. Invoking displayFile("sortedfile.dat") (line 12) displays the first 100 numbers in the specified file. Note the files are created using binary I/O. You cannot view them using a text editor such as Notepad.

The sort method first creates initial segments from the original array and stores the sorted segments in a new file, **f1.dat** (lines 19–20), then produces a sorted file in targetfile (lines 23–24).

The merge method

```
merge(int numberOfSegments, int segmentSize,
   String f1, String f2, String f3, String targetfile)
```

merges the segments in f1 into f3 using f2 to assist the merge. The merge method is invoked recursively with many merge steps. Each merge step reduces the numberOfSegments by half and doubles the sorted segment size. After the completion of one merge step, the next merge step merges the new segments in f3 to f2 using f1 to assist the merge. The statement to invoke the new merge method is

```
merge((numberOfSegments + 1) / 2, segmentSize * 2,
   f3, f1, f2, targetfile);
```

The numberOfSegments for the next merge step is (numberOfSegments + 1) / 2. For example, if numberOfSegments is 5, numberOfSegments is 3 for the next merge step because every two segments are merged but one is left unmerged.

The recursive merge method ends when numberOfSegments is 1. In this case, f1 contains sorted data. File f1 is renamed to targetfile (line 45).

23.8.4 External Sort Complexity

In the external sort, the dominating cost is that of I/O. Assume n is the number of elements to be sorted in the file. In Phase I, n number of elements are read from the original file and output to a temporary file. Therefore, the I/O for Phase I is $O(n)$.

In Phase II, before the first merge step, the number of sorted segments is $\frac{n}{c}$, where c is MAX_ARRAY_SIZE. Each merge step reduces the number of segments by half. Thus, after the first merge step, the number of segments is $\frac{n}{2c}$. After the second merge step, the number of segments is $\frac{n}{2^2c}$, and after the third merge step the number of segments is $\frac{n}{2^3c}$. After $\log\left(\frac{n}{c}\right)$ merge steps, the number of segments is reduced to 1. Therefore, the total number of merge steps is $\log\left(\frac{n}{c}\right)$.

In each merge step, half the number of segments are read from file f1 then written into a temporary file f2. The remaining segments in f1 are merged with the segments in f2. The number of I/Os in each merge step is $O(n)$. Since the total number of merge steps is $\log\left(\frac{n}{c}\right)$, the total number of I/Os is

$$O(n) \times \log\left(\frac{n}{c}\right) = O(n \log n)$$

Therefore, the complexity of the external sort is $O(n \log n)$.

23.8.1 Describe how external sort works. What is the complexity of the external sort algorithm?

23.8.2 Ten numbers {2, 3, 4, 0, 5, 6, 7, 9, 8, 1} are stored in the external file **largedata.dat**. Trace the SortLargeFile program by hand with MAX_ARRAY_SIZE 2.

KEY TERMS

bubble sort 884
bucket sort 901
complete binary tree 895
external sort 903
heap 895

heap sort 894
height of a heap 900
merge sort 900
quick sort 890
radix sort 902

CHAPTER SUMMARY

1. The worst-case complexity for a *selection sort, insertion sort, bubble sort*, and *quick sort* is $O(n^2)$.

2. The average- and worst-case complexity for a *merge sort* is $O(n \log n)$. The average time for a quick sort is also $O(n \log n)$.

3. *Heaps* are a useful data structure for designing efficient algorithms such as sorting. You learned how to define and implement a heap class, and how to insert and delete elements to/from a heap.

4. The time complexity for a *heap sort* is $O(n \log n)$.

5. *Bucket* and *radix sorts* are specialized sorting algorithms for integer keys. These algorithms sort keys using buckets rather than by comparing keys. They are more efficient than general sorting algorithms.

6. A variation of the merge sort—called an *external sort*—can be applied to sort large amounts of data from external files.

QUIZ

Answer the quiz for this chapter online at the book Companion Website.

PROGRAMMING EXERCISES

MyProgrammingLab™

Sections 23.3–23.5

23.1 (*Generic bubble sort*) Write the following two generic methods using bubble sort. The first method sorts the elements using the `Comparable` interface, and the second uses the `Comparator` interface.

```
public static <E extends Comparable<E>>
  void bubbleSort(E[] list)
public static <E> void bubbleSort(E[] list,
  Comparator<? super E> comparator)
```

23.2 (*Generic merge sort*) Write the following two generic methods using merge sort. The first method sorts the elements using the `Comparable` interface and the second uses the `Comparator` interface.

```
public static <E extends Comparable<E>>
  void mergeSort(E[] list)
public static <E> void mergeSort(E[] list,
  Comparator<? super E> comparator)
```

23.3 (*Generic quick sort*) Write the following two generic methods using quick sort. The first method sorts the elements using the `Comparable` interface, and the second uses the `Comparator` interface.

```
public static <E extends Comparable<E>>
  void quickSort(E[] list)
public static <E> void quickSort(E[] list,
  Comparator<? super E> comparator)
```

23.4 (*Improve quick sort*) The quick-sort algorithm presented in the book selects the first element in the list as the pivot. Revise it by selecting the median among the first, middle, and the last elements in the list.

*23.5 (*Generic Heap using Comparator*) Revise `Heap` in Listing 23.9, using a generic parameter and a `Comparator` for comparing objects. Define the class as follows:

```
class HeapWithComparator<E> {
  private Comparator<? super E> comparator; // For comparing elements

  public HeapWithComparator() {
    // Implement no-arg constructor by creating a comparator for
      natural order
  }

  public HeapWithComparator(Comparator<? super E> comparator) {
    this.comparator = comparator;
  }
  // Implement all add, remove, and getSize method
}
```

23.6 (*Check order*) Write the following overloaded methods that check whether an array is ordered in ascending order or descending order. By default, the method checks ascending order. To check descending order, pass `false` to the ascending argument in the method.

```
public static boolean ordered(int[] list)
public static boolean ordered(int[] list, boolean ascending)
public static boolean ordered(double[] list)
public static boolean ordered
   (double[] list, boolean ascending)
public static <E extends Comparable<E>>
   boolean ordered(E[] list)
public static <E extends Comparable<E>> boolean ordered
   (E[] list, boolean ascending)
public static <E> boolean ordered(E[] list,
   Comparator<? super E> comparator)
public static <E> boolean ordered(E[] list,
   Comparator<? super E> comparator, boolean ascending)
```

Section 23.6

max-heap
min-heap

23.7 (*Min-heap*) The heap presented in the text is also known as a *max-heap*, in which each node is greater than or equal to any of its children. A *min-heap* is a heap in which each node is less than or equal to any of its children. Min-heaps are often used to implement priority queues. Revise the `Heap` class in Listing 23.9 to implement a min-heap.

23.8 (*Generic insertion sort*) Write the following two generic methods using insertion sort. The first method sorts the elements using the `Comparable` interface, and the second uses the `Comparator` interface.

```
public static <E extends Comparable<E>>
   void insertionSort(E[] list)
public static <E> void insertionSort(E[] list,
   Comparator<? super E> comparator)
```

23.9 (*Generic heap sort*) Write the following two generic methods using heap sort. The first method sorts the elements using the `Comparable` interface, and the second uses the `Comparator` interface. (*Hint:* Use the `Heap` class in Programming Exercise 23.5.)

```
public static <E extends Comparable<E>>
   void heapSort(E[] list)
public static <E> void heapSort(E[] list,
   Comparator<? super E> comparator)
```

***23.10** (*Heap visualization*) Write a program that displays a heap graphically, as shown in Figure 23.10. The program lets you insert and delete an element from the heap.

23.11 (*Heap clone and equals*) Implement the `clone` and `equals` method in the `Heap` class.

Section 23.7

23.12 (*Radix sort*) Write a program that randomly generates 1,000,000 integers and sorts them using radix sort.

23.13 (*Execution time for sorting*) Write a program that obtains the execution time of selection sort, bubble sort, merge sort, quick sort, heap sort, and radix sort for

input size 50,000, 100,000, 150,000, 200,000, 250,000, and 300,000. Your program should create data randomly and print a table like this:

Array size	Selection Sort	Bubble Sort	Merge Sort	Quick Sort	Heap Sort	Radix Sort
50,000						
100,000						
150,000						
200,000						
250,000						
300,000						

(*Hint:* You can use the following code template to obtain the execution time.)

```
long startTime = System.nanoTime();
perform the task;
long endTime = System.nanoTime();
long executionTime = endTime - startTime;
```

Section 23.8

*23.14 (*Execution time for external sorting*) Write a program that obtains the execution time of external sorts for integers of size 5,000,000, 10,000,000, 15,000,000, 20,000,000, 25,000,000, and 30,000,000. Your program should print a table like this:

File size	5,000,000	10,000,000	15,000,000	20,000,000	25,000,000	30,000,000
Time						

Comprehensive

*23.15 (*Selection-sort animation*) Write a program that animates the selection-sort algorithm. Create an array that consists of 20 distinct numbers from 1 to 20 in a random order. The array elements are displayed in a histogram, as shown in Figure 23.20a. Clicking the *Step* button causes the program to perform an iteration of the outer loop in the algorithm and repaints the histogram for the new array. Color the last bar in the sorted subarray. When the algorithm is finished, display a message to inform the user. Clicking the *Reset* button creates a new random array for a new start. (You can easily modify the program to animate the insertion algorithm.)

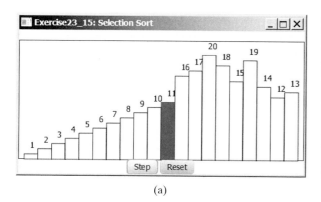
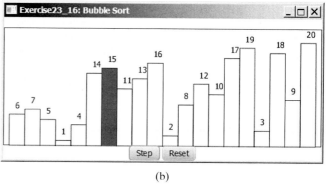

(a)   (b)

FIGURE 23.20   (a) The program animates selection sort. *Source:* Copyright © 1995–2016 Oracle and/or its affiliates. All rights reserved. Used with permission. (b) The program animates bubble sort.

*23.16 (*Bubble-sort animation*) Write a program that animates the bubble-sort algorithm. Create an array that consists of 20 distinct numbers from 1 to 20 in a random order. The array elements are displayed in a histogram, as shown in Figure 23.20b. Clicking the *Step* button causes the program to perform one comparison in the algorithm and repaints the histogram for the new array. Color the bar that represents the number being considered in the swap. When the algorithm is finished, display a message to inform the user. Clicking the *Reset* button creates a new random array for a new start.

*23.17 (*Radix-sort animation*) Write a program that animates the radix-sort algorithm. Create an array that consists of 20 random numbers from 0 to 1,000. The array elements are displayed, as shown in Figure 23.21. Clicking the *Step* button causes the program to place a number in a bucket. The number that has just been placed is displayed in red. Once all the numbers are placed in the buckets, clicking the *Step* button collects all the numbers from the buckets and moves them back to the array. When the algorithm is finished, clicking the *Step* button displays a message to inform the user. Clicking the *Reset* button creates a new random array for a new start.

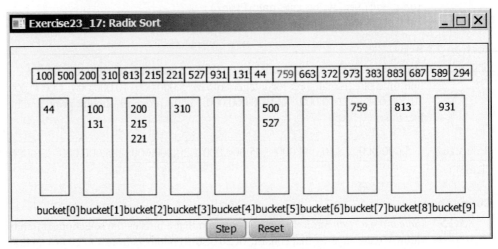

FIGURE 23.21 The program animates radix sort. *Source*: Copyright © 1995–2016 Oracle and/or its affiliates. All rights reserved. Used with permission.

*23.18 (*Merge animation*) Write a program that animates the merge of two sorted lists. Create two arrays, `list1` and `list2`, each of which consists of 8 random numbers from 1 to 999. The array elements are displayed, as shown in Figure 23.22a. Clicking the *Step* button causes the program to move an element from `list1` or `list2` to `temp`. Clicking the *Reset* button creates two new random arrays for a new start. When the algorithm is finished, clicking the *Step* button displays a message to inform the user.

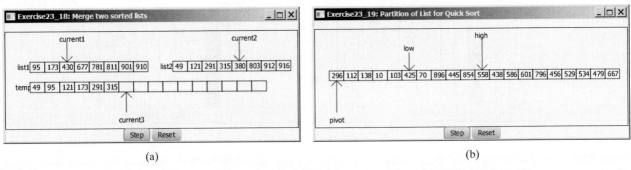

(a)   (b)

FIGURE 23.22 The program animates a merge of two sorted lists. *Source*: Copyright © 1995–2016 Oracle and/or its affiliates. All rights reserved. Used with permission. (b) The program animates a partition for quick sort.

*23.19   (*Quick-sort partition animation*) Write a program that animates the partition for a quick sort. The program creates a list that consists of 20 random numbers from 1 to 999. The list is displayed, as shown in Figure 23.22b. Clicking the *Step* button causes the program to move `low` to the right or `high` to the left, or swap the elements at `low` and `high`. Clicking the *Reset* button creates a new list of random numbers for a new start. When the algorithm is finished, clicking the *Step* button displays a message to inform the user.

*23.20   (*Modify merge sort*) Rewrite the `mergeSort` method to recursively sort the first half of the array and the second half of the array without creating new temporary arrays, then merge the two into a temporary array and copy its contents to the original array, as shown in Figure 23.6b.

Implementing Lists, Stacks, Queues, and Priority Queues

Objectives

- To design common operations of lists in an interface and make the interface a subtype of `Collection` (§24.2).

- To design and implement an array list using an array (§24.3).

- To design and implement a linked list using a linked structure (§24.4).

- To design and implement a stack class using an array list and a queue class using a linked list (§24.5).

- To design and implement a priority queue using a heap (§24.6).

24.1 Introduction

Key Point

This chapter focuses on implementing data structures.

Lists, stacks, queues, and priority queues are classic data structures typically covered in a data structures course. They are supported in the Java API, and their uses were presented in Chapter 20, Lists, Stacks, Queues, and Priority Queues. This chapter will examine how these data structures are implemented under the hood. Implementation of sets and maps will be covered in Chapter 27. Through these implementations, you will gain valuable insight on data structures and learn how to design and implement custom data structures.

24.2 Common Operations for Lists

Key Point

Common operations of lists are defined in the `List` *interface.*

A list is a popular data structure for storing data in sequential order—for example, a list of students, a list of available rooms, a list of cities, and a list of books. You can perform the following operations on a list:

- Retrieve an element from the list.

- Insert a new element into the list.

- Delete an element from the list.

- Find out how many elements are in the list.

- Determine whether an element is in the list.

- Check whether the list is empty.

There are two ways to implement a list. One is to use an *array* to store the elements. Array size is fixed. If the capacity of the array is exceeded, you need to create a new, larger array and copy all the elements from the current array to the new array. The other approach is to use a *linked structure*. A linked structure consists of nodes. Each node is dynamically created to hold an element. All the nodes are linked together to form a list. Thus, you can define two classes for lists. For convenience, let's name these two classes `MyArrayList` and `MyLinkedList`. These two classes have common operations but different implementations.

default methods in interfaces

Design Guide

Prior to Java 8, a popular design strategy for Java data structures is to define common operations in interfaces and provide convenient abstract classes for partially implementing the interfaces. So, the concrete classes can simply extend the convenient abstract classes without implementing the full interfaces. Java 8 enables you to define default methods. You can provide default implementation for some of the methods in the interfaces rather than in convenient abstract classes. Using default methods eliminate the need for convenient abstract classes.

list animation on Companion Website

Pedagogical Note

For an interactive demo on how array lists and linked lists work, go to liveexample .pearsoncmg.com/dsanimation/ArrayListeBook.html and liveexample.pearsoncmg.com/ dsanimation/LinkedListeBook.html, as shown in Figure 24.1.

Let us name the interface `MyList` and define it as a subtype of `Collection` so the common operations in the `Collection` interface are also available in `MyList`. Figure 24.2

shows the relationship of `Collection`, `MyList`, `MyArrayList`, and `MyLinkedList`.
The methods in `MyList` are shown in Figure 24.3. Listing 24.1 gives the source code for
`MyList`.

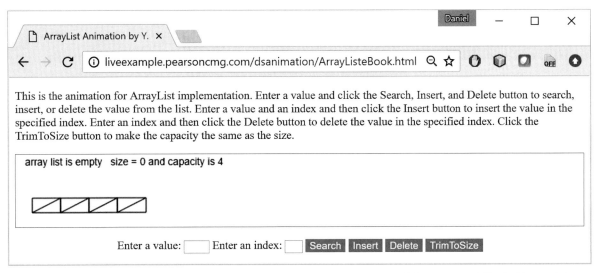

(a) ArrayList animation. *Source*: Copyright © 1995–2016 Oracle and/or its affiliates. All rights reserved. Used with permission.

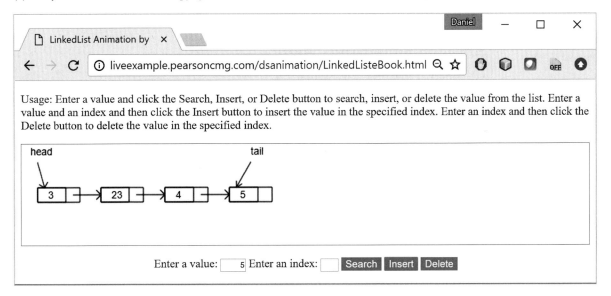

(b) LinkedList animation

FIGURE 24.1 The animation tool enables you to see how array lists and linked lists work.

```
java.util.Iterable <----- java.util.Collection <----- MyList <----+---- MyArrayList
                                                                    |
                                                                    +---- MyLinkedList
```

FIGURE 24.2 `MyList` defines a common interface for `MyArrayList` and `MyLinkedList`.

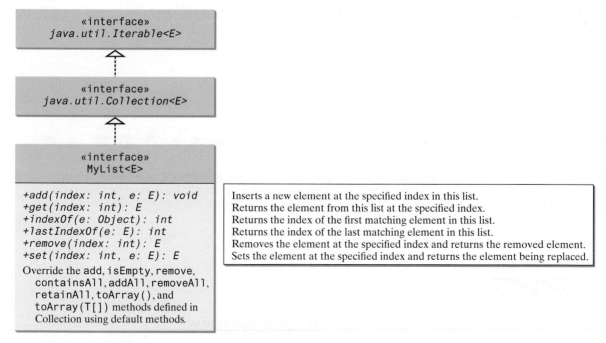

FIGURE 24.3 `MyList` defines the methods for manipulating a list and partially implements some of the methods defined in the `Collection` interface.

LISTING 24.1 MyList.java

```
 1  import java.util.Collection;
 2
 3  public interface MyList<E> extends Collection<E> {
 4    /** Add a new element at the specified index in this list */
 5    public void add(int index, E e);
 6
 7    /** Return the element from this list at the specified index */
 8    public E get(int index);
 9
10    /** Return the index of the first matching element in this list.
11     * Return -1 if no match. */
12    public int indexOf(Object e);
13
14    /** Return the index of the last matching element in this list
15     * Return -1 if no match. */
16    public int lastIndexOf(E e);
17
18    /** Remove the element at the specified position in this list
19     * Shift any subsequent elements to the left.
20     * Return the element that was removed from the list. */
21    public E remove(int index);
22
23    /** Replace the element at the specified position in this list
24     * with the specified element and returns the new set. */
25    public E set(int index, E e);
26
27    @Override /** Add a new element at the end of this list */
28    public default boolean add(E e) {
29      add(size(), e);
30      return true;
```

add(index, e)

get(index)

indexOf(e)

lastIndexOf(e)

remove(e)

set(index, e)

default add(e)

```
31    }
32
33    @Override /** Return true if this list contains no elements */
34    public default boolean isEmpty() {                                    default isEmpty()
35      return size() == 0;
36    }
37
38    @Override /** Remove the first occurrence of the element e
39     * from this list. Shift any subsequent elements to the left.
40     * Return true if the element is removed. */
41    public default boolean remove(Object e) {                             implement remove(E e)
42      if (indexOf(e) >= 0) {
43        remove(indexOf(e));
44        return true;
45      }
46      else
47        return false;
48    }
49
50    @Override
51    public default boolean containsAll(Collection<?> c) {                 implement containsAll
52      // Left as an exercise
53      return true;
54    }
55
56    @Override
57    public default boolean addAll(Collection<?  extends E> c) {           implement addAll
58      // Left as an exercise
59      return true;
60    }
61
62    @Override
63    public default boolean removeAll(Collection<?> c) {                   implement removeAll
64      // Left as an exercise
65      return true;
66    }
67
68    @Override
69    public default boolean retainAll(Collection<?> c) {                   implement retainAll
70      // Left as an exercise
71      return true;
72    }
73
74    @Override
75    public default Object[] toArray() {                                   implement toArray()
76      // Left as an exercise
77      return null;
78    }
79
80    @Override
81    public default <T> T[] toArray(T[] array) {                           implement toArray(T[])
82      // Left as an exercise
83      return null;
84    }
85 }
```

The methods `isEmpty()`, `add(E)`, `remove(E)`, `containsAll`, `addAll`, `removeAll`, `retainAll`, `toArray()`, and `toArray(T[])` are defined in the `Collection` interface. Since these methods are implementable in `MyList`, they are overridden in the `MyList` interface as default methods. The implementation for `isEmpty()`, `add(E)`, and `remove(E)` are provided and the implementation for other default methods are left as exercises in Programming Exercise 24.1.

The following sections give the implementation for `MyArrayList` and `MyLinkedList`, respectively.

24.2.1 Suppose `list` is an instance of `MyList`, can you get an iterator for list using `list.iterator()`?

24.2.2 Can you create a list using `new MyList()`?

24.2.3 What methods in `Collection` are overridden as default methods in `MyList`?

24.2.4 What are the benefits of overriding the methods in `Collection` as default methods in `MyList`?

24.3 Array Lists

An array list is implemented using an array.

An array is a fixed-size data structure. Once an array is created, its size cannot be changed. Nevertheless, you can still use arrays to implement dynamic data structures. The trick is to create a larger new array to replace the current array, if the current array cannot hold new elements in the list.

Initially, an array, say `data` of `E[]` type, is created with a default size. When inserting a new element into the array, first make sure there is enough room in the array. If not, create a new array twice as large as the current one. Copy the elements from the current array to the new array. The new array now becomes the current array. Before inserting a new element at a specified index, shift all the elements after the index to the right and increase the list size by `1`, as shown in Figure 24.4.

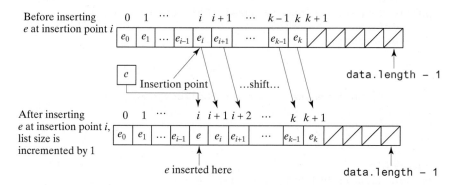

FIGURE 24.4 Inserting a new element into the array requires that all the elements after the insertion point be shifted one position to the right, so the new element can be inserted at the insertion point.

 Note

The data array is of type `E[]`. Each cell in the array actually stores the reference of an object.

To remove an element at a specified index, shift all the elements after the index to the left by one position and decrease the list size by `1`, as shown in Figure 24.5.

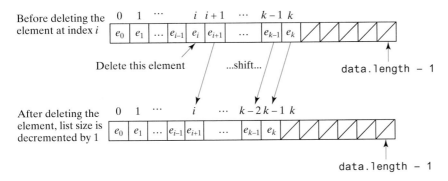

FIGURE 24.5 Deleting an element from the array requires that all the elements after the deletion point be shifted one position to the left.

MyArrayList uses an array to implement MyList, as shown in Figure 24.6. Its implementation is given in Listing 24.2.

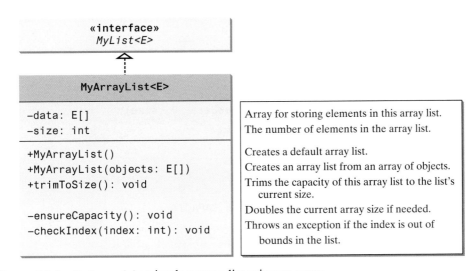

FIGURE 24.6 MyArrayList implements a list using an array.

LISTING 24.2 MyArrayList.java

```
1  public class MyArrayList<E> implements MyList<E> {
2    public static final int INITIAL_CAPACITY = 16;
3    private E[] data = (E[])new Object[INITIAL_CAPACITY];
4    private int size = 0; // Number of elements in the list
5
6    /** Create an empty list */
7    public MyArrayList() {
8    }
9
10   /** Create a list from an array of objects */
```

initial capacity
create an array
number of elements

no-arg constructor

constructor

```
11    public MyArrayList(E[] objects) {
12      for (int i = 0; i < objects.length; i++)
13        add(objects[i]); // Warning: don't use super(objects)!
14    }
15
16    @Override /** Add a new element at the specified index */
17    public void add(int index, E e) {
18      // Ensure the index is in the right range
19      if (index < 0 || index > size)
20        throw new IndexOutOfBoundsException
21          ("Index: " + index + ", Size: " + size);
22
23      ensureCapacity();
24
25      // Move the elements to the right after the specified index
26      for (int i = size - 1; i >= index; i--)
27        data[i + 1] = data[i];
28
29      // Insert new element to data[index]
30      data[index] = e;
31
32      // Increase size by 1
33      size++;
34    }
35
36    /** Create a new larger array, double the current size + 1 */
37    private void ensureCapacity() {
38      if (size >= data.length) {
39        E[] newData = (E[])(new Object[size * 2 + 1]);
40        System.arraycopy(data, 0, newData, 0, size);
41        data = newData;
42      }
43    }
44
45    @Override /** Clear the list */
46    public void clear() {
47      data = (E[])new Object[INITIAL_CAPACITY];
48      size = 0;
49    }
50
51    @Override /** Return true if this list contains the element */
52    public boolean contains(Object e) {
53      for (int i = 0; i < size; i++)
54        if (e.equals(data[i])) return true;
55
56      return false;
57    }
58
59    @Override /** Return the element at the specified index */
60    public E get(int index) {
61      checkIndex(index);
62      return data[index];
63    }
64
65    private void checkIndex(int index) {
66      if (index < 0 || index >= size)
67        throw new IndexOutOfBoundsException
68          ("Index: " + index + ", Size: " + size);
69    }
70
```

add

ensureCapacity

double capacity + 1

clear

contains

get

checkIndex

```
71    @Override /** Return the index of the first matching element
72     * in this list. Return -1 if no match. */
73    public int indexOf(Object e) {                                      indexOf
74      for (int i = 0; i < size; i++)
75        if (e.equals(data[i]))  return i;
76
77      return -1;
78    }
79
80    @Override /** Return the index of the last matching element
81     * in this list. Return -1 if no match. */
82    public int lastIndexOf(E e) {                                       lastIndexOf
83      for (int i = size - 1; i >= 0; i--)
84        if (e.equals(data[i])) return i;
85
86      return -1;
87    }
88
89    @Override /** Remove the element at the specified position
90     * in this list. Shift any subsequent elements to the left.
91     * Return the element that was removed from the list. */
92    public E remove(int index) {                                        remove
93      checkIndex(index);
94
95      E e = data[index];
96
97      // Shift data to the left
98      for (int j = index; j < size - 1; j++)
99        data[j] = data[j + 1];
100
101     data[size - 1] = null; // This element is now null
102
103     // Decrement size
104     size--;
105
106     return e;
107   }
108
109   @Override /** Replace the element at the specified position
110    * in this list with the specified element. */
111   public E set(int index, E e) {                                      set
112     checkIndex(index);
113     E old = data[index];
114     data[index] = e;
115     return old;
116   }
117
118   @Override
119   public String toString() {                                          toString
120     StringBuilder result = new StringBuilder("[");
121
122     for (int i = 0; i < size; i++) {
123       result.append(data[i]);
124       if (i < size - 1) result.append(", ");
125     }
126
127     return result.toString() + "]";
128   }
129
130   /** Trims the capacity to current size */
```

trimToSize

```
131   public void trimToSize() {
132     if (size != data.length) {
133       E[] newData = (E[])(new Object[size]);
134       System.arraycopy(data, 0, newData, 0, size);
135       data = newData;
136     }  // If size == capacity, no need to trim
137   }
138
139   @Override /** Override iterator() defined in Iterable */
140   public java.util.Iterator<E> iterator() {
141     return new ArrayListIterator();
142   }
143
144   private class ArrayListIterator
145       implements java.util.Iterator<E> {
146     private int current = 0; // Current index
147
148     @Override
149     public boolean hasNext() {
150       return current < size;
151     }
152
153     @Override
154     public E next() {
155       return data[current++];
156     }
157
158     @Override // Remove the element returned by the last next()
159     public void remove() {
160       if (current == 0)  // next() has not been called yet
161         throw new IllegalStateException();
162       MyArrayList.this.remove(--current);
163     }
164   }
165
166   @Override /** Return the number of elements in this list */
167   public int size() {
168     return size;
169   }
170 }
```

iterator (margin label at line 140)

size (margin label at line 167)

The constant `INITIAL_CAPACITY` (line 2) is used to create an initial array `data` (line 3). Owing to generics type erasure (see Restriction 2 in Section 19.8), you cannot create a generic array using the syntax `new e[INITIAL_CAPACITY]`. To circumvent this limitation, an array of the `Object` type is created in line 3 and cast into `E[]`. The `size` data field tracks the number of elements in the list (line 4).

add

The `add(int index, E e)` method (lines 17–34) inserts the element `e` at the specified `index` in the array. This method first invokes `ensureCapacity()` (line 23), which ensures that there is a space in the array for the new element. It then shifts all the elements after the index one position to the right before inserting the element (lines 26 and 27). After the element is added, `size` is incremented by 1 (line 33).

ensureCapacity

The `ensureCapacity()` method (lines 37–43) checks whether the array is full. If so, the program creates a new array that doubles the current array size + 1, copies the current array to the new array using the `System.arraycopy` method, and sets the new array as the current array. Note the current size might be 0 after invoking the `trimToSize()` method. `new Object[2 * size + 1]` (line 39) ensures that the new size is not 0.

clear

The `clear()` method (lines 46–49) creates a new array using the size as `INITIAL_CAPACITY` and resets the variable `size` to 0. The class will work if line 47 is deleted. However, the class will have a memory leak because the elements are still in the array, although they are no longer needed. By creating a new array and assigning it to `data`, the old array and the elements stored in the old array become garbage, which will be automatically collected by the JVM.

The `contains(Object e)` method (lines 52–57) checks whether element `e` is contained in the array by comparing `e` with each element in the array using the `equals` method.

The `get(int index)` method (lines 60–63) checks if `index` is within the range and returns `data[index]` if `index` is in the range.

The `checkIndex(int index)` method (lines 65–69) checks if `index` is within the range. If not, the method throws an `IndexOutOfBoundsException` (line 67).

The `indexOf(Object e)` method (lines 73–78) compares element `e` with the elements in the array, starting from the first one. If a match is found, the index of the element is returned; otherwise, −1 is returned.

The `lastIndexOf(Object e)` method (lines 82–87) compares element `e` with the elements in the array, starting from the last one. If a match is found, the index of the element is returned; otherwise, −1 is returned.

The `remove(int index)` method (lines 92–107) shifts all the elements after the index one position to the left (lines 98 and 99) and decrements `size` by 1 (line 104). The last element is not used anymore and is set to `null` (line 101).

The `set(int index, E e)` method (lines 111–116) simply assigns `e` to `data[index]` to replace the element at the specified index with element `e`.

The `toString()` method (lines 119–128) overrides the `toString` method in the `Object` class to return a string representing all the elements in the list.

The `trimToSize()` method (lines 131–137) creates a new array whose size matches the current array-list size (line 133), copies the current array to the new array using the `System.arraycopy` method (line 134), and sets the new array as the current array (line 135). Note if `size == capacity`, there is no need to trim the size of the array.

The `iterator()` method defined in the `java.lang.Iterable` interface is implemented to return an instance on `java.util.Iterator` (lines 140–142). The `ArrayListIterator` class implements `Iterator` with concrete methods for `hasNext`, `next`, and `remove` (lines 144–164). It uses `current` to denote the current position of the element being traversed (line 146).

The `size()` method simply returns the number of elements in the array list (lines 167–169).

Listing 24.3 gives an example that creates a list using `MyArrayList`. It uses the `add` method to add strings to the list, and the `remove` method to remove strings. Since `MyArrayList` implements `Iterable`, the elements can be traversed using a foreach loop (lines 35 and 36).

LISTING 24.3   TestMyArrayList.java

```
 1   public class TestMyArrayList {
 2     public static void main(String[] args) {
 3       // Create a list
 4       MyList<String> list = new MyArrayList<>();
 5
 6       // Add elements to the list
 7       list.add("America"); // Add it to the list
 8       System.out.println("(1) " + list);
 9
10       list.add(0, "Canada"); // Add it to the beginning of the list
11       System.out.println("(2) " + list);
12
13       list.add("Russia"); // Add it to the end of the list
14       System.out.println("(3) " + list);
15
16       list.add("France"); // Add it to the end of the list
17       System.out.println("(4) " + list);
```

```
18
19        list.add(2, "Germany"); // Add it to the list at index 2
20        System.out.println("(5) " + list);
21
22        list.add(5, "Norway"); // Add it to the list at index 5
23        System.out.println("(6) " + list);
24
25        // Remove elements from the list
26        list.remove("Canada"); // Same as list.remove(0) in this case
27        System.out.println("(7) " + list);
28
29        list.remove(2); // Remove the element at index 2
30        System.out.println("(8) " + list);
31
32        list.remove(list.size() -  1); // Remove the last element
33        System.out.print("(9) " + list + "\n(10) ");
34
35      for (String s: list)
36        System.out.print(s.toUpperCase() + " ");
37    }
38  }
```

remove from list *(margin note at line 29)*

use iterator *(margin note at line 35)*

```
(1)  [America]
(2)  [Canada, America]
(3)  [Canada, America, Russia]
(4)  [Canada, America, Russia, France]
(5)  [Canada, America, Germany, Russia, France]
(6)  [Canada, America, Germany, Russia, France, Norway]
(7)  [America, Germany, Russia, France, Norway]
(8)  [America, Germany, France, Norway]
(9)  [America, Germany, France]
(10) AMERICA GERMANY FRANCE
```

24.3.1 What are the limitations of the array data type?

24.3.2 MyArrayList is implemented using an array, and an array is a fixed-size data structure. Why is MyArrayList considered a dynamic data structure?

24.3.3 Show the length of the array in MyArrayList after each of the following statements is executed:

```
1  MyArrayList<Double> list = new MyArrayList<>();
2  list.add(1.5);
3  list.trimToSize();
4  list.add(3.4);
5  list.add(7.4);
6  list.add(17.4);
```

24.3.4 What is wrong if lines 11 and 12 in Listing 24.2, MyArrayList.java,

```
for (int i = 0; i < objects.length; i++)
  add(objects[i]);
```

are replaced by

```
data = objects;
size = objects.length;
```

24.3.5 If you change the code in line 33 in Listing 24.2, MyArrayList.java, from

```
E[] newData = (E[])(new Object[size * 2 + 1]);
```

to

```
E[] newData = (E[])(new Object[size * 2]);
```

the program is incorrect. Can you find the reason?

24.3.6 Will the MyArrayList class have memory leak if the following code in line 41 is deleted?

```
data = (E[])new Object[INITIAL_CAPACITY];
```

24.3.7 The get(index) method invokes the checkIndex(index) method (lines 59–63 in Listing 24.2) to throw an IndexOutOfBoundsException if the index is out of bounds. Suppose the add(index, e) method is implemented as follows:

```
public void add(int index, E e) {
  checkIndex(index);

  // Same as lines 23-33 in Listing 24.2 MyArrayList.java
}
```

What will happen if you run the following code?

```
MyArrayList<String> list = new MyArrayList<>();
list.add("New York");
```

24.4 Linked Lists

A linked list is implemented using a linked structure.

Key
Point

Since MyArrayList is implemented using an array, the methods get(int index) and set(int index, E e) for accessing and modifying an element through an index and the add(E e) method for adding an element at the end of the list are efficient. However, the methods add(int index, E e) and remove(int index) are inefficient because they require shifting a potentially large number of elements. You can use a linked structure to implement a list to improve efficiency for adding and removing an element at the beginning of a list.

24.4.1 Nodes

In a linked list, each element is contained in an object, called the *node*. When a new element is added to the list, a node is created to contain it. Each node is linked to its next neighbor, as shown in Figure 24.7.

A node can be created from a class defined as follows:

```
class Node<E> {
  E element;
  Node<E> next;

  public Node(E e) {
    element = e;
  }
}
```

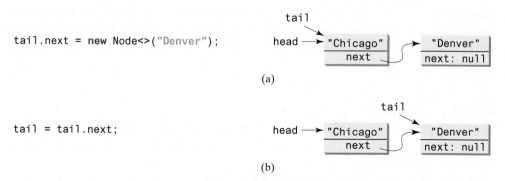

FIGURE 24.7   A linked list consists of any number of nodes chained together.

We use the variable head to refer to the first node in the list and the variable tail to the last node. If the list is empty, both head and tail are null. Here is an example that creates a linked list to hold three nodes. Each node stores a string element.

Step 1: Declare head and tail.

```
Node<String> head = null;    The list is empty now
Node<String> tail = null;
```

head and tail are both null. The list is empty.

Step 2: Create the first node and append it to the list, as shown in Figure 24.8. After the first node is inserted in the list, head and tail point to this node.

```
head = new Node<>("Chicago");    After the first node is inserted
tail = head;
```

FIGURE 24.8   Append the first node to the list.

Step 3: Create the second node and append it into the list, as shown in Figure 24.9a. To append the second node to the list, link the first node with the new node. The new node is now the tail node, so you should move tail to point to this new node, as shown in Figure 24.9b.

```
tail.next = new Node<>("Denver");
```

(a)

```
tail = tail.next;
```

(b)

FIGURE 24.9   Append the second node to the list.

Step 4: Create the third node and append it to the list, as shown in Figure 24.10a. To append the new node to the list, link the last node in the list with the new node. The new node is now the tail node, so you should move tail to point to this new node, as shown in Figure 24.10b.

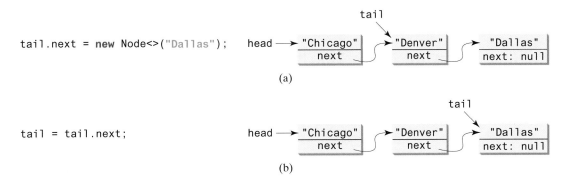

FIGURE 24.10 Append the third node to the list.

Each node contains the element and a data field named `next` that points to the next element. If the node is the last in the list, its pointer data field `next` contains the value `null`. You can use this property to detect the last node. For example, you can write the following loop to traverse all the nodes in the list:

```
1  Node<E> current = head;
2  while (current != null) {
3    System.out.println(current.element);
4    current = current.next;
5  }
```

current pointer
check last node

next node

The variable `current` points initially to the first node in the list (line 1). In the loop, the element of the current node is retrieved (line 3) then `current` points to the next node (line 4). The loop continues until the current node is `null`.

24.4.2 The `MyLinkedList` Class

The `MyLinkedList` class uses a linked structure to implement a dynamic list. It implements `MyList`. In addition, it provides the methods `addFirst`, `addLast`, `removeFirst`, `removeLast`, `getFirst`, and `getLast`, as shown in Figure 24.11.

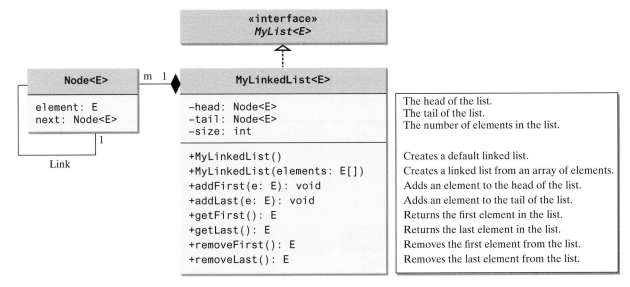

FIGURE 24.11 `MyLinkedList` implements a list using a linked list of nodes.

Assuming the class has been implemented, Listing 24.4 gives a test program that uses the class.

LISTING 24.4   TestMyLinkedList.java

```
 1  public class TestMyLinkedList {
 2    /** Main method */
 3    public static void main(String[] args) {
 4      // Create a list for strings
 5      MyLinkedList<String> list = new MyLinkedList<>();
 6
 7      // Add elements to the list
 8      list.add("America"); // Add it to the list
 9      System.out.println("(1) " + list);
10
11      list.add(0, "Canada"); // Add it to the beginning of the list
12      System.out.println("(2) " + list);
13
14      list.add("Russia"); // Add it to the end of the list
15      System.out.println("(3) " + list);
16
17      list.addLast("France"); // Add it to the end of the list
18      System.out.println("(4) " + list);
19
20      list.add(2, "Germany"); // Add it to the list at index 2
21      System.out.println("(5) " + list);
22
23      list.add(5, "Norway"); // Add it to the list at index 5
24      System.out.println("(6) " + list);
25
26      list.add(0, "Poland"); // Same as list.addFirst("Poland")
27      System.out.println("(7) " + list);
28
29      // Remove elements from the list
30      list.remove(0); // Same as list.remove("Poland") in this case
31      System.out.println("(8) " + list);
32
33      list.remove(2); // Remove the element at index 2
34      System.out.println("(9) " + list);
35
36      list.remove(list.size() - 1); // Remove the last element
37      System.out.print("(10) " + list + "\n(11) ");
38
39      for (String s: list)
40        System.out.print(s.toUpperCase() + " ");
41
42      list.clear();
43      System.out.println("\nAfter clearing the list, the list size is "
44        + list.size());
45    }
46  }
```

create list — line 5
append element — line 8
print list — line 9
insert element — line 11
append element — line 14
append element — line 17
insert element — line 20
insert element — line 23
insert element — line 26
remove element — line 30
remove element — line 33
remove element — line 36
traverse using iterator — line 39

```
(1) [America]
(2) [Canada, America]
(3) [Canada, America, Russia]
(4) [Canada, America, Russia, France]
(5) [Canada, America, Germany, Russia, France]
(6) [Canada, America, Germany, Russia, France, Norway]
(7) [Poland, Canada, America, Germany, Russia, France, Norway]
```

```
(8)  [Canada, America, Germany, Russia, France, Norway]
(9)  [Canada, America, Russia, France, Norway]
(10) [Canada, America, Russia, France]
(11) CANADA AMERICA RUSSIA FRANCE
After clearing the list, the list size is 0
```

24.4.3 Implementing MyLinkedList

Now let us turn our attention to implementing the MyLinkedList class. We will discuss how to implement the methods addFirst, addLast, add(index, e), removeFirst, removeLast, and remove(index) and leave the other methods in the MyLinkedList class as exercises.

24.4.3.1 Implementing addFirst(e)

The addFirst(e) method creates a new node for holding element e. The new node becomes the first node in the list. It can be implemented as follows:

```
1  public void addFirst(E e) {
2    Node<E> newNode = new Node<>(e); // Create a new node          create a node
3    newNode.next = head; // link the new node with the head        link with head
4    head = newNode; // head points to the new node                 head to new node
5    size++; // Increase list size                                  increase size
6
7    if (tail == null) // The new node is the only node in list     was empty?
8      tail = head;
9  }
```

The addFirst(e) method creates a new node to store the element (line 2) and inserts the node at the beginning of the list (line 3), as shown in Figure 24.12a. After the insertion, head should point to this new element node (line 4), as shown in Figure 24.12b.

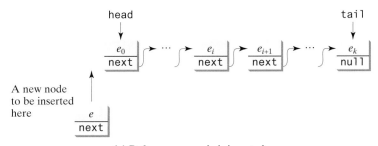

(a) Before a new node is inserted.

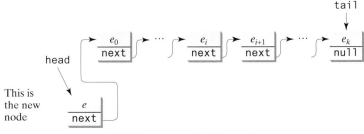

(b) After a new node is inserted.

FIGURE 24.12 A new element is added to the beginning of the list.

If the list is empty (line 7), both head and tail will point to this new node (line 8). After the node is created, size should be increased by 1 (line 5).

24.4.3.2 Implementing `addLast(e)`

The `addLast(e)` method creates a node to hold the element and appends the node at the end of the list. It can be implemented as follows:

```
1  public void addLast(E e) {
2    Node<E> newNode = new Node<>(e); // Create a new node for e
3
4    if (tail == null) {
5      head = tail = newNode; // The only node in list
6    }
7    else {
8      tail.next = newNode; // Link the new node with the last node
9      tail = newNode; // tail now points to the last node
10   }
11
12   size++; // Increase size
13 }
```

create a node

increase size

The `addLast(e)` method creates a new node to store the element (line 2) and appends it to the end of the list. Consider two cases:

1. If the list is empty (line 4), both `head` and `tail` will point to this new node (line 5);

2. Otherwise, link the node with the last node in the list (line 8). `tail` should now point to this new node (line 9). Figures 24.13a and 13b show the new node for element `e` before and after the insertion.

In any case, after the node is created, the `size` should be increased by 1 (line 12).

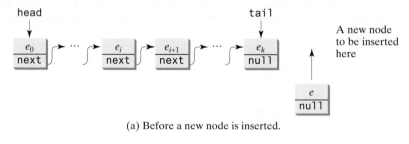

(a) Before a new node is inserted.

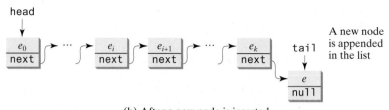

(b) After a new node is inserted.

FIGURE 24.13 A new element is added at the end of the list.

24.4.3.3 Implementing `add(index, e)`

The `add(index, e)` method inserts an element into the list at the specified index. It can be implemented as follows:

```
1  public void add(int index, E e) {
2    if (index == 0) addFirst(e); // Insert first
3    else if (index >= size) addLast(e); // Insert last
4    else { // Insert in the middle
5      Node<E> current = head;
```

insert first
insert last

```
 6        for (int i = 1; i < index; i++)
 7          current = current.next;
 8        Node<E> temp = current.next;
 9        current.next = new Node<>(e);                          create a node
10        (current.next).next = temp;
11        size++;                                                increase size
12      }
13    }
```

There are three cases when inserting an element into the list:

1. If index is 0, invoke addFirst(e) (line 2) to insert the element at the beginning of the list.

2. If index is greater than or equal to size, invoke addLast(e) (line 3) to insert the element at the end of the list.

3. Otherwise, create a new node to store the new element and locate where to insert it. As shown in Figure 24.14a, the new node is to be inserted between the nodes current and temp. The method assigns the new node to current.next and assigns temp to the new node's next, as shown in Figure 24.14b. The size is now increased by 1 (line 11).

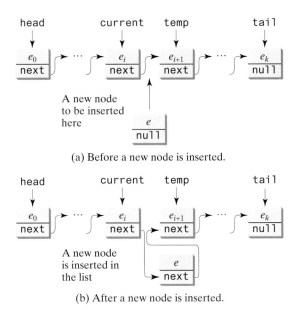

(a) Before a new node is inserted.

(b) After a new node is inserted.

FIGURE 24.14 A new element is inserted in the middle of the list.

24.4.3.4 Implementing removeFirst()

The removeFirst() method removes the first element from the list. It can be implemented as follows:

```
1  public E removeFirst() {
2    if (size == 0) return null; // Nothing to delete              nothing to remove
3    else {
4      Node<E> temp = head; // Keep the first node temporarily      keep old head
5      head = head.next; // Move head to point to next node         new head
6      size--; // Reduce size by 1                                  decrease size
7      if (head == null) tail = null; // List becomes empty         destroy the node
```

```
 8       return temp.element; // Return the deleted element
 9   }
10  }
```

Consider two cases:

1. If the list is empty, there is nothing to delete, so return `null` (line 2).

2. Otherwise, remove the first node from the list by pointing `head` to the second node. Figures 24.15a and 15b show the linked list before and after the deletion. The size is reduced by `1` after the deletion (line 6). If the list becomes empty, after removing the element, `tail` should be set to `null` (line 7).

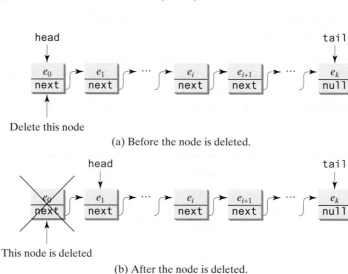

(a) Before the node is deleted.

(b) After the node is deleted.

FIGURE 24.15 The first node is deleted from the list.

24.4.3.5 Implementing `removeLast()`

The `removeLast()` method removes the last element from the list. It can be implemented as follows:

empty?
size 1?

head and tail null
size is 0
return element

size > 1

move tail

reduce size
return element

```
 1  public E removeLast() {
 2    if (size == 0) return null; // Nothing to remove
 3    else if (size == 1) { // Only one element in the list
 4      Node<E> temp = head;
 5      head = tail = null; // list becomes empty
 6      size = 0;
 7      return temp.element;
 8    }
 9    else {
10      Node<E> current = head;
11
12      for (int i = 0; i < size - 2; i++)
13        current = current.next;
14
15      Node<E> temp = tail;
16      tail = current;
17      tail.next = null;
18      size--;
19      return temp.element;
20    }
21  }
```

Consider three cases:

1. If the list is empty, return `null` (line 2).

2. If the list contains only one node, this node is destroyed; `head` and `tail` both become `null` (line 5). The size becomes `0` after the deletion (line 6) and the element value of the deleted node is returned (line 7).

3. Otherwise, the last node is destroyed (line 17) and the `tail` is repositioned to point to the second-to-last node. Figures 24.16a and 16b show the last node before and after it is deleted. The size is reduced by `1` after the deletion (line 18) and the element value of the deleted node is returned (line 19).

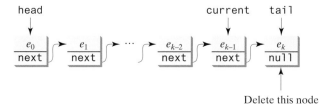

(a) Before the node is deleted.

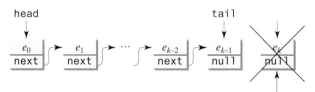

(b) After the node is deleted.

FIGURE 24.16 The last node is deleted from the list.

24.4.3.6 Implementing `remove(index)`

The `remove(index)` method finds the node at the specified index then removes it. It can be implemented as follows:

```
1  public E remove(int index) {
2    if (index < 0 || index >= size) return null; // Out of range      out of range
3    else if (index == 0) return removeFirst(); // Remove first          remove first
4    else if (index == size - 1) return removeLast(); // Remove last     remove last
5    else {
6      Node<E> previous = head;
7
8      for (int i = 1; i < index; i++) {                                 locate previous
9        previous = previous.next;
10     }
11
12     Node<E> current = previous.next;                                  locate current
13     previous.next = current.next;                                     remove from list
14     size--;                                                           reduce size
15     return current.element;                                           return element
16   }
17 }
```

Consider four cases:

1. If `index` is beyond the range of the list (i.e., `index < 0 || index >= size`), return `null` (line 2).

2. If `index` is `0`, invoke `removeFirst()` to remove the first node (line 3).

3. If `index` is `size - 1`, invoke `removeLast()` to remove the last node (line 4).

4. Otherwise, locate the node at the specified `index`. Let `current` denote this node and `previous` denote the node before this node, as shown in Figure 24.17a. Assign `current.next` to `previous.next` to eliminate the current node, as shown in Figure 24.17b.

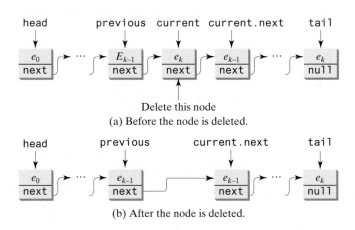

(a) Before the node is deleted.

(b) After the node is deleted.

FIGURE 24.17 A node is deleted from the list.

Listing 24.5 gives the implementation of `MyLinkedList`. The implementation of `get(index)`, `indexOf(e)`, `lastIndexOf(e)`, `contains(e)`, and `set(index, e)` is omitted and left as an exercise. The `iterator()` method defined in the `java.lang.Iterable` interface is implemented to return an instance on `java.util.Iterator` (lines 128–130). The `LinkedListIterator` class implements `Iterator` with concrete methods for `hasNext`, `next`, and `remove` (lines 132–152). This implementation uses `current` to point to the current position of the element being traversed (line 134). Initially, `current` points to the head of the list.

iterator

LISTING 24.5 MyLinkedList.java

```
 1  public class MyLinkedList<E> implements MyList<E> {
 2    private Node<E> head, tail;
 3    private int size = 0; // Number of elements in the list
 4
 5    /** Create an empty list */
 6    public MyLinkedList() {
 7    }
 8
 9    /** Create a list from an array of objects */
10    public MyLinkedList(E[] objects) {
11      for (int i = 0; i < objects.length; i++)
12        add(objects[i]);
13    }
14
15    /** Return the head element in the list */
16    public E getFirst() {
17      if (size == 0) {
18        return null;
19      }
20      else {
```

head, tail
number of elements

no-arg constructor

constructor

getFirst

```
21          return head.element;
22        }
23      }
24
25      /** Return the last element in the list */
26      public E getLast() {                                          getLast
27        if (size == 0) {
28          return null;
29        }
30        else {
31          return tail.element;
32        }
33      }
34
35      /** Add an element to the beginning of the list */
36      public void addFirst(E e) {                                   addFirst
37        // Implemented in Section 24.4.3.1, so omitted here
38      }
39
40      /** Add an element to the end of the list */
41      public void addLast(E e) {                                    addLast
42        // Implemented in Section 24.4.3.2, so omitted here
43      }
44
45      @Override /** Add a new element at the specified index
46       * in this list. The index of the head element is 0 */
47      public void add(int index, E e) {                             add
48        // Implemented in Section 24.4.3.3, so omitted here
49      }
50
51      /** Remove the head node and
52       * return the object that is contained in the removed node. */
53      public E removeFirst() {                                      removeFirst
54        // Implemented in Section 24.4.3.4, so omitted here
55      }
56
57      /** Remove the last node and
58       * return the object that is contained in the removed node. */
59      public E removeLast() {                                       removeLast
60        // Implemented in Section 24.4.3.5, so omitted here
61      }
62
63      @Override /** Remove the element at the specified position in this
64       * list. Return the element that was removed from the list. */
65      public E remove(int index) {                                  remove
66        // Implemented earlier in Section 24.4.3.6, so omitted
67      }
68
69      @Override /** Override toString() to return elements in the list */
70      public String toString() {                                    toString
71        StringBuilder result = new StringBuilder("[");
72
73        Node<E> current = head;
74        for (int i = 0; i < size; i++) {
75          result.append(current.element);
76          current = current.next;
77          if (current != null) {
78            result.append(", "); // Separate two elements with a comma
79          }
80          else {
81            result.append("]"); // Insert the closing ] in the string
```

```
82          }
83        }
84
85      return result.toString();
86    }
87
```

clear
```
88    @Override /** Clear the list */
89    public void clear() {
90      size = 0;
91      head = tail = null;
92    }
93
```

contains
```
94    @Override /** Return true if this list contains the element e */
95    public boolean contains(Object e) {
96      // Left as an exercise
97      return true;
98    }
99
```

get
```
100   @Override /** Return the element at the specified index */
101   public E get(int index) {
102     // Left as an exercise
103     return null;
104   }
105
```

indexOf
```
106   @Override /** Return the index of the head matching element in
107    * this list. Return -1 if no match. */
108   public int indexOf(Object e) {
109     // Left as an exercise
110     return 0;
111   }
112
```

lastIndexOf
```
113   @Override /** Return the index of the last matching element in
114    * this list. Return -1 if no match. */
115   public int lastIndexOf(E e) {
116     // Left as an exercise
117     return 0;
118   }
119
```

set
```
120   @Override /** Replace the element at the specified position
121    * in this list with the specified element. */
122   public E set(int index, E e) {
123     // Left as an exercise
124     return null;
125   }
126
```

iterator
```
127   @Override /** Override iterator() defined in Iterable */
128   public java.util.Iterator<E> iterator() {
129     return new LinkedListIterator();
130   }
131
```

LinkedListIterator class
```
132   private class LinkedListIterator
133       implements java.util.Iterator<E> {
134     private Node<E> current = head; // Current index
135
136     @Override
137     public boolean hasNext() {
138       return (current != null);
139     }
140
141     @Override
```

```
142    public E next() {
143      E e = current.element;
144      current = current.next;
145      return e;
146    }
147
148    @Override
149    public void remove() {
150      // Left as an exercise
151    }
152  }
153
154  private static class Node<E> {
155    E element;
156    Node<E> next;
157
158    public Node(E element) {
159      this.element = element;
160    }
161  }
162
163  @Override /** Return the number of elements in this list */
164  public int size() {
165    return size;
166  }
167 }
```

Node inner class

24.6.4 MyArrayList vs. MyLinkedList

Both MyArrayList and MyLinkedList can be used to store a list. MyArrayList is implemented using an array, and MyLinkedList is implemented using a linked list. The overhead of MyArrayList is smaller than that of MyLinkedList. However, MyLinkedList is more efficient if you need to insert elements into and delete elements from the beginning of the list. Table 24.1 summarizes the complexity of the methods in MyArrayList and MyLinkedList. Note MyArrayList is the same as java.util.ArrayList, and MyLinkedList is the same as java.util.LinkedList.

TABLE 24.1 Time Complexities for Methods in MyArrayList and MyLinkedList

Methods	MyArrayList/ArrayList	MyLinkedList/LinkedList
add(e: E)	$O(1)$	$O(1)$
add(index: int, e: E)	$O(n)$	$O(n)$
clear()	$O(1)$	$O(1)$
contains(e: E)	$O(n)$	$O(n)$
get(index: int)	$O(1)$	$O(n)$
indexOf(e: E)	$O(n)$	$O(n)$
isEmpty()	$O(1)$	$O(1)$
lastIndexOf(e: E)	$O(n)$	$O(n)$
remove(e: E)	$O(n)$	$O(n)$
size()	$O(1)$	$O(1)$
remove(index: int)	$O(n)$	$O(n)$
set(index: int, e: E)	$O(n)$	$O(n)$
addFirst(e: E)	$O(n)$	$O(1)$
removeFirst()	$O(n)$	$O(1)$

24.4.5 Variations of Linked Lists

The linked list introduced in the preceding sections is known as a *singly linked list*. It contains a pointer to the list's first node, and each node contains a pointer to the next node sequentially. Several variations of the linked list are useful in certain applications.

A *circular, singly linked list* is like a singly linked list, except that the pointer of the last node points back to the first node, as shown in Figure 24.18a. Note `tail` is not needed for circular linked lists. `head` points to the current node in the list. Insertion and deletion take place at the current node. A good application of a circular linked list is in the operating system that serves multiple users in a timesharing fashion. The system picks a user from a circular list and grants a small amount of CPU time then moves on to the next user in the list.

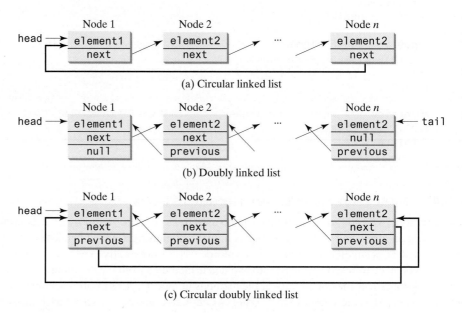

(a) Circular linked list

(b) Doubly linked list

(c) Circular doubly linked list

FIGURE 24.18 Linked lists may appear in various forms.

A *doubly linked list* contains nodes with two pointers. One points to the next node and the other to the previous node, as shown in Figure 24.18b. These two pointers are conveniently called *a forward pointer* and *a backward pointer*. Thus, a doubly linked list can be traversed forward and backward. The `java.util.LinkedList` class is implemented using a doubly linked list, and it supports traversing of the list forward and backward using the `ListIterator`.

A *circular, doubly linked list* is like a doubly linked list, except that the forward pointer of the last node points to the first node, and the backward pointer of the first pointer points to the last node, as shown in Figure 24.18c.

The implementations of these linked lists are left as exercises.

24.4.1 If a linked list does not contain any nodes, what are the values in `head` and `tail`?

24.4.2 If a linked list has only one node, is `head == tail` true? List all cases in which `head == tail` is true.

24.4.3 When a new node is inserted to the head of a linked list, will the `head` and the `tail` be changed?

24.4.4 When a new node is appended to the end of a linked list, will the `head` and the `tail` be changed?

24.4.5 Both `MyArrayList` and `MyLinkedList` are used to store a list of objects. Why do we need both types of lists?

24.4.6 Draw a diagram to show the linked list after each of the following statements is executed:

```
MyLinkedList<Double> list = new MyLinkedList<>();
list.add(1.5);
list.add(6.2);
list.add(3.4);
list.add(7.4);
list.remove(1.5);
list.remove(2);
```

24.4.7 What is the time complexity of the `addFirst(e)` and `removeFirst()` methods in `MyLinkedList`?

24.4.8 Suppose you need to store a list of elements. If the number of elements in the program is fixed, what data structure should you use? If the number of elements in the program changes, what data structure should you use?

24.4.9 If you have to add or delete the elements at the beginning of a list, should you use `MyArrayList` or `MyLinkedList`? If most of the operations on a list involve retrieving an element at a given index, should you use `MyArrayList` or `MyLinkedList`?

24.4.10 Simplify the code in lines 77–82 in Listing 24.5 using a conditional expression.

24.4.11 Simplify the code for the `removeLast()` method by invoking the `removeFirst()` method when the size is less than or equal to `1`. Is the new code more efficient in execution time?

24.5 Stacks and Queues

Stacks can be implemented using array lists and queues can be implemented using linked lists.

A stack can be viewed as a special type of list whose elements are accessed, inserted, and deleted only from the end (top), as shown in Figure 10.11. A queue represents a waiting list. It can be viewed as a special type of list whose elements are inserted into the end (tail) of the queue and are accessed and deleted from the beginning (head), as shown in Figure 24.19.

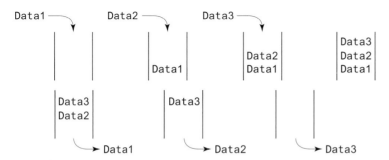

FIGURE 24.19 A queue holds objects in a first-in, first-out fashion.

 Pedagogical Note

For an interactive demo on how stacks and queues work, go to liveexample.pearsoncmg.com/dsanimation/StackeBook.html, and liveexample.pearsoncmg.com/dsanimation/QueueeBook.html, as shown in Figure 24.20.

 stack and queue animation on Companion Website

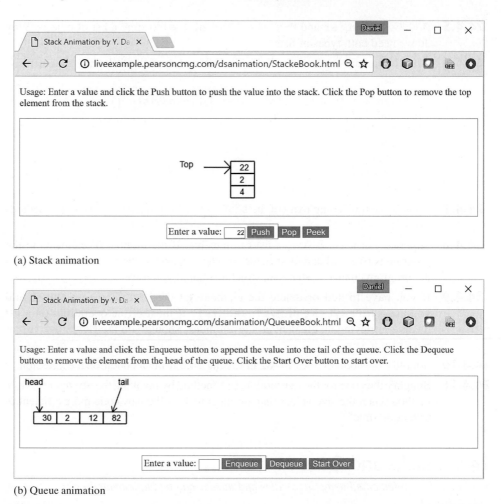

(a) Stack animation

(b) Queue animation

FIGURE 24.20 The animation tool enables you to see how stacks and queues work. *Source*: Copyright © 1995–2016 Oracle and/or its affiliates. All rights reserved. Used with permission.

Since the insertion and deletion operations on a stack are made only at the end of the stack, it is more efficient to implement a stack with an array list than a linked list. Since deletions are made at the beginning of the list, it is more efficient to implement a queue using a linked list than an array list. This section implements a stack class using an array list and a queue class using a linked list. There are two ways to design the stack and queue classes:

inheritance

■ Using inheritance: You can define a stack class by extending `ArrayList`, and a queue class by extending `LinkedList`, as shown in Figure 24.21a.

composition

■ Using composition: You can define an array list as a data field in the stack class and a linked list as a data field in the queue class, as shown in Figure 24.21b.

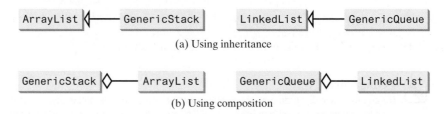

(a) Using inheritance

(b) Using composition

FIGURE 24.21 `GenericStack` and `GenericQueue` may be implemented using inheritance or composition.

Both designs are fine, but using composition is better because it enables you to define a completely new stack class and queue class without inheriting the unnecessary and inappropriate methods from the array list and linked list. The implementation of the stack class using the composition approach was given in Listing 19.1, GenericStack.java. Listing 24.6 implements the GenericQueue class using the composition approach. Figure 24.22 shows the UML of the class.

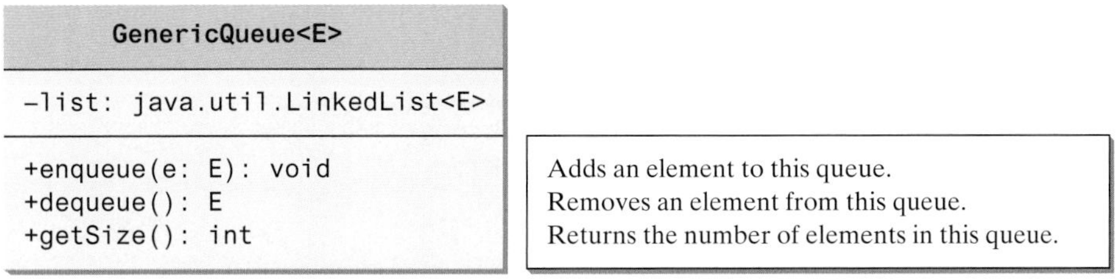

FIGURE 24.22   GenericQueue uses a linked list to provide a first-in, first-out data structure.

LISTING 24.6   GenericQueue.java

```java
1  public class GenericQueue<E> {
2    private java.util.LinkedList<E> list
3      = new java.util.LinkedList<>();
4
5    public void enqueue(E e) {
6      list.addLast(e);
7    }
8
9    public E dequeue() {
10     return list.removeFirst();
11   }
12
13   public int getSize() {
14     return list.size();
15   }
16
17   @Override
18   public String toString() {
19     return "Queue: " + list.toString();
20   }
21 }
```

linked list

enqueue

dequeue

getSize

toString

A linked list is created to store the elements in a queue (lines 2 and 3). The enqueue(e) method (lines 5–7) adds element e into the tail of the queue. The dequeue() method (lines 9–11) removes an element from the head of the queue and returns the removed element. The getSize() method (lines 13–15) returns the number of elements in the queue.

Listing 24.7 gives an example that creates a stack using GenericStack and a queue using GenericQueue. It uses the push (enqueue) method to add strings to the stack (queue) and the pop (dequeue) method to remove strings from the stack (queue).

LISTING 24.7   TestStackQueue.java

```java
1  public class TestStackQueue {
2    public static void main(String[] args) {
3      // Create a stack
4      GenericStack<String> stack = new GenericStack<>();
5
```

```
 6      // Add elements to the stack
 7      stack.push("Tom"); // Push it to the stack
 8      System.out.println("(1) " + stack);
 9
10      stack.push("Susan"); // Push it to the the stack
11      System.out.println("(2) " + stack);
12
13      stack.push("Kim"); // Push it to the stack
14      stack.push("Michael"); // Push it to the stack
15      System.out.println("(3) " + stack);
16
17      // Remove elements from the stack
18      System.out.println("(4) " + stack.pop());
19      System.out.println("(5) " + stack.pop());
20      System.out.println("(6) " + stack);
21
22      // Create a queue
23      GenericQueue<String> queue = new GenericQueue<>();
24
25      // Add elements to the queue
26      queue.enqueue("Tom"); // Add it to the queue
27      System.out.println("(7) " + queue);
28
29      queue.enqueue("Susan"); // Add it to the queue
30      System.out.println("(8) " + queue);
31
32      queue.enqueue("Kim"); // Add it to the queue
33      queue.enqueue("Michael"); // Add it to the queue
34      System.out.println("(9) " + queue);
35
36      // Remove elements from the queue
37      System.out.println("(10) " + queue.dequeue());
38      System.out.println("(11) " + queue.dequeue());
39      System.out.println("(12) " + queue);
40    }
41  }
```

```
(1) stack: [Tom]
(2) stack: [Tom, Susan]
(3) stack: [Tom, Susan, Kim, Michael]
(4) Michael
(5) Kim
(6) stack: [Tom, Susan]
(7) Queue: [Tom]
(8) Queue: [Tom, Susan]
(9) Queue: [Tom, Susan, Kim, Michael]
(10) Tom
(11) Susan
(12) Queue: [Kim, Michael]
```

stack time complexity

For a stack, the push(e) method adds an element to the top of the stack, and the pop() method removes the top element from the stack and returns the removed element. It is easy to see that the time complexity for the push and pop methods is $O(1)$.

queue time complexity

For a queue, the enqueue(e) method adds an element to the tail of the queue, and the dequeue() method removes the element from the head of the queue. It is easy to see that the time complexity for the enqueue and dequeue methods is $O(1)$.

24.5.1 You can use inheritance or composition to design the data structures for stacks and queues. Discuss the pros and cons of these two approaches.

24.5.2 If `LinkedList` is replaced by `ArrayList` in lines 2 and 3 in Listing 24.6, GenericQueue.java, what will be the time complexity for the `enqueue` and `dequeue` methods.

24.5.3 Which lines of the following code are wrong?

```
1  List<String> list = new ArrayList<>();
2  list.add("Tom");
3  list = new LinkedList<>();
4  list.add("Tom");
5  list = new GenericStack<>();
6  list.add("Tom");
```

24.6 Priority Queues

Priority queues can be implemented using heaps.

An ordinary queue is a first-in, first-out data structure. Elements are appended to the end of the queue and removed from the beginning. In a *priority queue*, elements are assigned with priorities. When accessing elements, the element with the highest priority is removed first. For example, the emergency room in a hospital assigns priority numbers to patients; the patient with the highest priority is treated first.

Key Point

A priority queue can be implemented using a heap, in which the root is the object with the highest priority in the queue. Heaps were introduced in Section 23.6, Heap Sort. The class diagram for the priority queue is shown in Figure 24.23. Its implementation is given in Listing 24.8.

MyPriorityQueue <E extends Comparable<E>>	
–heap: Heap<E>	
+enqueue(element: E): void	Adds an element to this queue.
+dequeue(): E	Removes an element from this queue.
+getSize(): int	Returns the number of elements in this queue.

FIGURE 24.23 `MyPriorityQueue` uses a heap to provide a largest-in, first-out data structure.

LISTING 24.8 `MyPriorityQueue.java`

```
1  public class MyPriorityQueue<E extends Comparable<E>> {
2    private Heap<E> heap = new Heap<>();              heap for priority queue
3
4    public void enqueue(E newObject) {                enqueue
5      heap.add(newObject);
6    }
7
8    public E dequeue() {                              dequeue
9      return heap.remove();
10   }
11
12   public int getSize() {                            getsize
13     return heap.getSize();
14   }
15 }
```

Listing 24.9 gives an example of using a priority queue for patients. The `Patient` class is defined in lines 19–37. Four patients are created with associated priority values in lines 3–6. Line 8 creates a priority queue. The patients are enqueued in lines 10–13. Line 16 dequeues a patient from the queue.

LISTING **24.9**   TestPriorityQueue.java

```
 1  public class TestPriorityQueue {
 2    public static void main(String[] args) {
 3      Patient patient1 = new Patient("John", 2);
 4      Patient patient2 = new Patient("Jim", 1);
 5      Patient patient3 = new Patient("Tim", 5);
 6      Patient patient4 = new Patient("Cindy", 7);
 7
 8      MyPriorityQueue<Patient> priorityQueue
 9        = new MyPriorityQueue<>();
10      priorityQueue.enqueue(patient1);
11      priorityQueue.enqueue(patient2);
12      priorityQueue.enqueue(patient3);
13      priorityQueue.enqueue(patient4);
14
15      while (priorityQueue.getSize() > 0)
16        System.out.print(priorityQueue.dequeue() + " ");
17    }
18
19    static class Patient implements Comparable<Patient> {
20      private String name;
21      private int priority;
22
23      public Patient(String name, int priority) {
24        this.name = name;
25        this.priority = priority;
26      }
27
28      @Override
29      public String toString() {
30        return name + "(priority:" + priority + ")";
31      }
32
33      @Override
34      public int compareTo(Patient patient) {
35        return this.priority - patient.priority;
36      }
37    }
38  }
```

create a patient

create a priority queue

add to queue

remove from queue

inner class `Patient`

compareTo

```
Cindy(priority:7) Tim(priority:5) John(priority:2) Jim(priority:1)
```

24.6.1 What is a priority queue?

24.6.2 What are the time complexity of the `enqueue`, `dequeue`, and `getSize` methods in `MyPriorityQueue`?

24.6.3 Which of the following statements are wrong?

```
1  MyPriorityQueue<Object> q1 = new MyPriorityQueue<>();
2  MyPriorityQueue<Number> q2 = new MyPriorityQueue<>();
3  MyPriorityQueue<Integer> q3 = new MyPriorityQueue<>();
4  MyPriorityQueue<Date> q4 = new MyPriorityQueue<>();
5  MyPriorityQueue<String> q5 = new MyPriorityQueue<>();
```

CHAPTER SUMMARY

1. You learned how to implement array lists, linked lists, stacks, and queues.

2. To define a data structure is essentially to define a class. The class for a data structure should use data fields to store data and provide methods to support operations such as insertion and deletion.

3. To create a data structure is to create an instance from the class. You can then apply the methods on the instance to manipulate the data structure, such as inserting an element into the data structure or deleting an element from the data structure.

4. You learned how to implement a priority queue using a heap.

QUIZ

Answer the quiz for this chapter online at the book Companion Website.

PROGRAMMING EXERCISES

MyProgrammingLab™

24.1 (*Implement set operations in* `MyList`) The implementations of the methods `addAll`, `removeAll`, `retainAll`, `toArray()`, and `toArray(T[])` are omitted in the `MyList` interface. Implement these methods. Test your new `MyList` class using the code at liveexample.pearsoncmg.com/test/Exercise24_01Test.txt.

*24.2 (*Implement* `MyLinkedList`) The implementations of the methods `contains(E e)`, `get(int index)`, `indexOf(E e)`, `lastIndexOf(E e)`, and `set(int index, E e)` are omitted in the `MyLinkedList` class. Implement these methods.

*24.3 (*Implement a doubly linked list*) The `MyLinkedList` class used in Listing 24.5 is a one-way directional linked list that enables one-way traversal of the list. Modify the `Node` class to add the new data field name `previous` to refer to the previous node in the list, as follows:

```
public class Node<E> {
  E element;
  Node<E> next;
  Node<E> previous;

  public Node(E e) {
    element = e;
  }
}
```

Implement a new class named `TwoWayLinkedList` that uses a doubly linked list to store elements. Define `TwoWayLinkedList` to implements `MyList`. You need to implement all the methods defined in `MyLinkedList` as well as the methods `listIterator()` and `listIterator(int index)`. Both return an instance of `java.util.ListIterator<E>` (see Figure 20.4). The former sets the cursor to the head of the list and the latter to the element at the specified index.

24.4 (*Use the* `GenericStack` *class*) Write a program that displays the first 50 prime numbers in descending order. Use a stack to store the prime numbers.

24.5 (*Implement* `GenericQueue` *using inheritance*) In Section 24.5, Stacks and Queues, `GenericQueue` is implemented using composition. Define a new queue class that extends `java.util.LinkedList`.

*24.6 (*Generic* `PriorityQueue` *using* `Comparator`) Revise `MyPriorityQueue` in Listing 24.8, using a generic parameter for comparing objects. Define a new constructor with a `Comparator` as its argument as follows:

```
PriorityQueue(Comparator<? super E> comparator)
```

**24.7 (*Animation: linked list*) Write a program to animate search, insertion, and deletion in a linked list, as shown in Figure 24.1b. The *Search* button searches the specified value in the list. The *Delete* button deletes the specified value from the list. The *Insert* button appends the value into the list if the index is not specified; otherwise, it inserts the value into the specified index in the list.

*24.8 (*Animation: array list*) Write a program to animate search, insertion, and deletion in an array list, as shown in Figure 24.1a. The *Search* button searches the specified value in the list. The *Delete* button deletes the specified value from the list. The *Insert* button appends the value into the list if the index is not specified; otherwise, it inserts the value into the specified index in the list.

*24.9 (*Animation: array list in slow motion*) Improve the animation in the preceding programming exercise by showing the insertion and deletion operations in a slow motion.

*24.10 (*Animation: stack*) Write a program to animate push and pop in a stack, as shown in Figure 24.20a.

*24.11 (*Animation: doubly linked list*) Write a program to animate search, insertion, and deletion in a doubly linked list, as shown in Figure 24.24. The *Search* button searches the specified value in the list. The *Delete* button deletes the specified value from the list. The *Insert* button appends the value into the list if the index is not specified; otherwise, it inserts the value into the specified index in the list. Also add two buttons named *Forward Traversal* and *Backward Traversal* for displaying the elements in a forward and backward order, respectively, using iterators, as shown in Figure 24.24. The elements are displayed in a label.

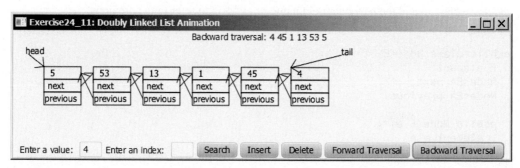

FIGURE 24.24 The program animates the work of a doubly linked list. *Source*: Copyright © 1995–2016 Oracle and/or its affiliates. All rights reserved. Used with permission.

*24.12 (*Animation: queue*) Write a program to animate the `enqueue` and `dequeue` operations on a queue, as shown in Figure 24.20b.

*24.13 (*Fibonacci number iterator*) Define an iterator class named `Fibonacci Iterator` for iterating Fibonacci numbers. The constructor takes an argument that specifies the limit of the maximum Fibonacci number. For example, new

`FibonacciIterator(23302)` creates an iterator that iterates Fibonacci numbers less than or equal to `23302`. Write a test program that uses this iterator to display all Fibonacci numbers less than or equal to `100000`.

*24.14 (*Prime number iterator*) Define an iterator class named `PrimeIterator` for iterating prime numbers. The constructor takes an argument that specifies the limit of the maximum prime number. For example, new `PrimeIterator(23302)` creates an iterator that iterates prime numbers less than or equal to `23302`. Write a test program that uses this iterator to display all prime numbers less than or equal to `100000`.

**24.15 (*Test* `MyArrayList`) Design and write a complete test program to test if the `MyArrayList` class in Listing 24.2 meets all requirements.

**24.16 (*Test* `MyLinkedList`) Design and write a complete test program to test if the `MyLinkedList` class in Listing 24.5 meets all requirements.

**24.17 (*Revise* `MyPriorityQueue`) Listing 24.8 uses a heap to implement the priority queue. Revise the implementation using a sorted array list to store the elements and name the new class `PriorityUsingSortedArrayList`. The elements in the array list are sorted in increasing order of their priority with the last element having the highest priority. Write a test program that generates 5 million integers and enqueues them to the priority and dequeues from the queue. Use the same numbers for `MyPriorityQueue` and `PriorityUsingSortedArrayList` and display their execution times.

BINARY SEARCH TREES

Objectives

- To design and implement a binary search tree (§25.2).

- To represent binary trees using linked data structures (§25.2.1).

- To search an element in a binary search tree (§25.2.2).

- To insert an element into a binary search tree (§25.2.3).

- To traverse elements in a binary tree (§25.2.4).

- To design and implement the `Tree` interface and the `BST` class (§25.2.5).

- To delete elements from a binary search tree (§25.3).

- To display a binary tree graphically (§25.4).

- To create iterators for traversing a binary tree (§25.5).

- To implement Huffman coding for compressing data using a binary tree (§25.6).

25.1 Introduction

A binary search tree is more efficient than a list for search, insertion, and deletion operations.

The preceding chapter gives the implementation for array lists and linked lists. The time complexity of search, insertion, and deletion operations in these data structures is $O(n)$. This chapter presents a new data structure called binary search tree, which takes $O(\log n)$ average time for search, insertion, and deletion of elements.

25.2 Binary Search Trees

A binary search tree can be implemented using a linked structure.

binary tree
root
left subtree
right subtree

Recall that lists, stacks, and queues are linear structures that consist of a sequence of elements. A *binary tree* is a hierarchical structure. It either is empty or consists of an element, called the *root*, and two distinct binary trees, called the *left subtree* and *right subtree*, either or both of which may be empty, as shown in Figure 25.1a. Examples of binary trees are shown in Figures 25.1a and b.

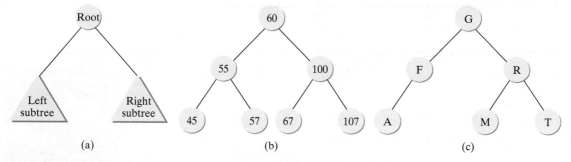

FIGURE 25.1 Each node in a binary tree has zero, one, or two subtrees.

length
depth
level
sibling
leaf
height

The *length* of a path is the number of the edges in the path. The *depth* of a node is the length of the path from the root to the node. The set of all nodes at a given depth is sometimes called a *level* of the tree. *Siblings* are nodes that share the same parent node. The root of a left (right) subtree of a node is called a *left (right) child* of the node. A node without children is called a *leaf*. The height of a nonempty tree is the length of the path from the root node to its furthest leaf. The *height* of a tree that contains a single node is `0`. Conventionally, the height of an empty tree is `-1`. Consider the tree in Figure 25.1b. The length of the path from node 60 to 45 is `2`. The depth of node 60 is `0`, the depth of node 55 is `1`, and the depth of node 45 is `2`. The height of the tree is `2`. Nodes 45 and 57 are siblings. Nodes 45, 57, 67, and 107 are at the same level.

binary search tree

A special type of binary tree called a *binary search tree* (BST) is often useful. A BST (with no duplicate elements) has the property that for every node in the tree, the value of any node in its left subtree is less than the value of the node, and the value of any node in its right subtree is greater than the value of the node. The binary trees in Figures 25.1b-c are all BSTs.

BST animation on Companion Website

Pedagogical Note

For an interactive GUI demo to see how a BST works, go to liveexample.pearsoncmg. com/dsanimation/BSTeBook.html, as shown in Figure 25.2.

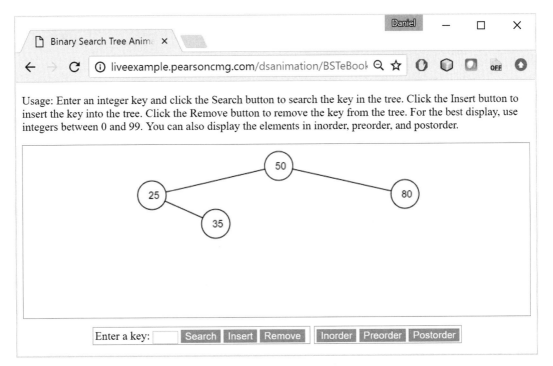

FIGURE 25.2 The animation tool enables you to insert, delete, and search elements. *Source*: Copyright © 1995–2016 Oracle and/or its affiliates. All rights reserved. Used with permission.

25.2.1 Representing Binary Search Trees

A binary tree can be represented using a set of linked nodes. Each node contains a value and two links named *left* and *right* that reference the left child and right child, respectively, as shown in Figure 25.3.

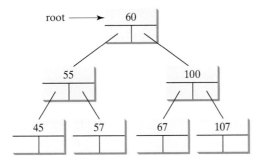

FIGURE 25.3 A binary tree can be represented using a set of linked nodes.

A node can be defined as a class, as follows:

```
class TreeNode<E> {
  protected E element;
  protected TreeNode<E> left;
  protected TreeNode<E> right;

  public TreeNode(E e) {
    element = e;
  }
}
```

We use the variable `root` to refer to the root node of the tree. If the tree is empty, `root` is `null`. The following code creates the first three nodes of the tree in Figure 25.3:

```
// Create the root node
TreeNode<Integer> root = new TreeNode<>(60);

// Create the left child node
root.left = new TreeNode<>(55);

// Create the right child node
root.right = new TreeNode<>(100);
```

25.2.2 Searching for an Element

To search for an element in the BST, you start from the root and scan down from it until a match is found or you arrive at an empty subtree. The algorithm is described in Listing 25.1. Let `current` point to the root (line 2). Repeat the following steps until `current` is `null` (line 4) or the element matches `current.element` (line 12):

- If `element` is less than `current.element`, assign `current.left` to `current` (line 6).

- If `element` is greater than `current.element`, assign `current.right` to `current` (line 9).

- If `element` is equal to `current.element`, return `true` (line 12).

If `current` is `null`, the subtree is empty and the element is not in the tree (line 14).

LISTING 25.1 Searching for an Element in a BST

```
1  public boolean search(E element) {
2    TreeNode<E> current = root; // Start from the root
3
4    while (current != null)
5      if (element < current.element) {
6        current = current.left; // Go left
7      }
8      else if (element > current.element) {
9        current = current.right; // Go right
10     }
11     else // Element matches current.element
12       return true; // Element is found
13
14   return false; // Element is not in the tree
15 }
```

start from root (line 2)
left subtree (line 6)
right subtree (line 9)
found (line 12)
not found (line 14)

25.2.3 Inserting an Element into a BST

To insert an element into a BST, you need to locate where to insert it in the tree. The key idea is to locate the parent for the new node. Listing 25.2 gives the algorithm.

LISTING 25.2 Inserting an Element into a BST

```
1  boolean insert(E e) {
2    if (tree is empty)
3      // Create the node for e as the root;
4    else {
5      // Locate the parent node
6      parent = current = root;
7      while (current != null)
8        if (e < the value in current.element) {
```

create a new node (line 3)
locate parent (line 6)

```
 9            parent = current; // Keep the parent
10            current = current.left; // Go left                          left child
11          }
12          else if (e > the value in current.element) {
13            parent = current; // Keep the parent
14            current = current.right; // Go right                        right child
15          }
16          else
17            return false; // Duplicate node not inserted
18
19        // Create a new node for e and attach it to parent
20
21        return true; // Element inserted
22     }
23  }
```

If the tree is empty, create a root node with the new element (lines 2 and 3). Otherwise, locate the parent node for the new element node (lines 6–17). Create a new node for the element and link this node to its parent node. If the new element is less than the parent element, the node for the new element will be the left child of the parent. If the new element is greater than the parent element, the node for the new element will be the right child of the parent.

For example, to insert 101 into the tree in Figure 25.3, after the while loop finishes in the algorithm, parent points to the node for 107, as shown in Figure 25.4a. The new node for 101 becomes the left child of the parent. To insert 59 into the tree, after the while loop finishes in the algorithm, the parent points to the node for 57, as shown in Figure 25.4b. The new node for 59 becomes the right child of the parent.

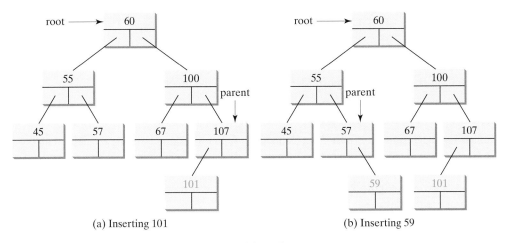

(a) Inserting 101   (b) Inserting 59

FIGURE 25.4   Two new elements are inserted into the tree.

25.2.4 Tree Traversal

Tree traversal is the process of visiting each node in the tree exactly once. There are several ways to traverse a tree. This section presents *inorder, postorder, preorder, depth-first,* and *breadth-first* traversals.

tree traversal

With *inorder traversal*, the left subtree of the current node is visited first recursively, then the current node, and finally the right subtree of the current node recursively. The inorder traversal displays all the nodes in a BST in increasing order.

inorder traversal

With *postorder traversal*, the left subtree of the current node is visited recursively first, then recursively the right subtree of the current node, and finally the current node itself.

postorder traversal

With *preorder traversal*, the current node is visited first, then recursively the left subtree of the current node, and finally the right subtree of the current node recursively.

preorder traversal

reconstruct a tree

Note
You can reconstruct a binary search tree by inserting the elements in their preorder. The reconstructed tree preserves the parent and child relationship for the nodes in the original binary search tree.

depth-first traversal

Depth-first traversal is to visit the root then recursively visit its left subtree and right subtree in an arbitrary order. The preorder traversal can be viewed as a special case of depth-first traversal, which recursively visits its left subtree then its right subtree.

breadth-first traversal

With *breadth-first traversal*, the nodes are visited level by level. First the root is visited, then all the children of the root from left to right, then the grandchildren of the root from left to right, and so on.

For example, in the tree in Figure 25.4b, the inorder is

45 55 57 59 60 67 100 101 107

The postorder is

45 59 57 55 67 101 107 100 60

The preorder is

60 55 45 57 59 100 67 107 101

The breadth-first traversal is

60 55 100 45 57 67 107 59 101

You can use the following simple tree to help remember inorder, postorder, and preorder.

The inorder is `1 + 2`, the postorder is `1 2 +`, and the preorder is `+ 1 2`.

25.2.5 The BST Class

Following the design pattern for Java Collections Framework and utilizing the default methods in Java 8, we use an interface named `Tree` to define all common operations for trees and define `Tree` to be a subtype of `Collection` so we can use common operations in `Collection` for trees, as shown in Figure 25.5. A concrete `BST` class can be defined to implement `Tree`, as shown in Figure 25.6.

Listing 25.3 gives the implementation for `Tree`. It provides default implementations for the `add`, `isEmpty`, `remove`, `containsAll`, `addAll`, `removeAll`, `retainAll`, `toArray()`, and `toArray(T[])` methods inherited from the `Collection` interface as well as the `inorder()`, `preorder()`, and `postorder()` defined in the `Tree` interface.

LISTING 25.3 Tree.java

interface

search

insert

```
 1  import java.util.Collection;
 2
 3  public interface Tree<E> extends Collection<E> {
 4    /** Return true if the element is in the tree */
 5    public boolean search(E e);
 6
 7    /** Insert element e into the binary tree
 8     * Return true if the element is inserted successfully */
 9    public boolean insert(E e);
10
```

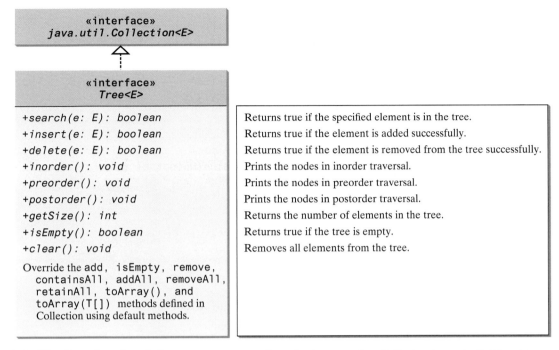

FIGURE 25.5 The `Tree` interface defines common operations for trees, and partially implements `Collection`.

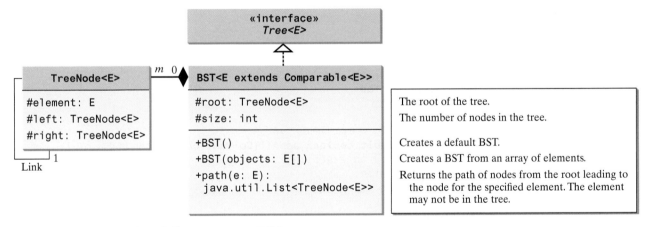

FIGURE 25.6 The `BST` class defines a concrete BST.

```
11      /** Delete the specified element from the tree
12       * Return true if the element is deleted successfully */
13      public boolean delete(E e);                                    delete
14
15      /** Get the number of elements in the tree */
16      public int getSize();                                          getSize
17
18      /** Inorder traversal from the root*/
19      public default void inorder() {                                inorder
20      }
21
22      /** Postorder traversal from the root */
23      public default void postorder() {                              postorder
24      }
```

```
25
26      /** Preorder traversal from the root */
27      public default void preorder() {
28      }
29
30      @Override /** Return true if the tree is empty */
31      public default boolean isEmpty() {
32        return size() == 0;
33      }
34
35      @Override
36      public default boolean contains(Object e) {
37        return search((E)e);
38      }
39
40      @Override
41      public default boolean add(E e) {
42        return insert(e);
43      }
44
45      @Override
46      public default boolean remove(Object e) {
47        return delete((E)e);
48      }
49
50      @Override
51      public default int size() {
52        return getSize();
53      }
54
55      @Override
56      public default boolean containsAll(Collection<?> c) {
57        // Left as an exercise
58        return false;
59      }
60
61      @Override
62      public default boolean addAll(Collection<? extends E> c) {
63        // Left as an exercise
64        return false;
65      }
66
67      @Override
68      public default boolean removeAll(Collection<?> c) {
69        // Left as an exercise
70        return false;
71      }
72
73      @Override
74      public default boolean retainAll(Collection<?> c) {
75        // Left as an exercise
76        return false;
77      }
78
79      @Override
80      public default Object[] toArray() {
81        // Left as an exercise
82        return null;
83      }
84
```

Margin labels:

- preorder (line 27)
- default isEmpty (line 31)
- default contains (line 36)
- default add (line 41)
- default remove (line 46)
- default size (line 51)
- default containsAll (line 56)
- default addAll (line 62)
- default removeAll (line 68)
- default retainAll (line 74)
- default toArray() (line 80)

```
85     @Override
86     public default <T> T[] toArray(T[] array) {                          default toArray(T[])
87       // Left as an exercise
88       return null;
89     }
90   }
```

Listing 25.4 gives the implementations for the BST class.

LISTING 25.4   BST.java

```
1   public class BST<E  extends Comparable<E>> implements Tree<E> {        BST class
2     protected TreeNode<E> root;                                          root
3     protected int size = 0                                               size
4
5     /** Create an empty binary tree */
6     public BST() {                                                       no-arg constructor
7     }
8
9     /** Create a binary tree from an array of objects */
10    public BST(E[] objects) {
11      for (int i = 0; i < objects.length; i++)                           constructor
12        add(objects[i]);
13    }
14
15    @Override /** Returns true if the element is in the tree */
16    public boolean search(E e) {                                         search
17      TreeNode<E> current = root; // Start from the root
18
19      while (current != null) {
20        if (e.compareTo(current.element) < 0) {                          compare objects
21          current = current.left;
22        }
23        else if (e.compareTo(current.element) > 0) {
24          current = current.right;
25        }
26        else // element matches current.element
27          return true; // Element is found
28      }
29
30      return false;
31    }
32
33    @Override /** Insert element e into the binary tree
34      * Return true if the element is inserted successfully */
35    public boolean insert(E e) {                                         insert
36      if (root == null)
37        root = createNewNode(e); // Create a new root                    new root
38      else {
39        // Locate the parent node
40        TreeNode<E> parent = null;
41        TreeNode<E> current = root;
42        while (current != null)
43          if (e.compareTo(current.element) < 0) {                        compare objects
44            parent = current;
45            current = current.left;
46          }
47          else if (e.compareTo(current.element) > 0) {
48            parent = current;
49            current = current.right;
```

```
50          }
51          else
52            return false; // Duplicate node not inserted
53
54        // Create the new node and attach it to the parent node
55        if (e.compareTo(parent.element) < 0)
56          parent.left = createNewNode(e);
57        else
58          parent.right = createNewNode(e);
59      }
60
61      size++;
62      return true; // Element inserted successfully
63    }
64
65    protected TreeNode<E> createNewNode(E e) {
66      return new TreeNode<>(e);
67    }
68
69    @Override /** Inorder traversal from the root */
70    public void inorder() {
71      inorder(root);
72    }
73
74    /** Inorder traversal from a subtree */
75    protected void inorder(TreeNode<E> root) {
76      if (root == null) return;
77      inorder(root.left);
78      System.out.print(root.element + " ");
79      inorder(root.right);
80    }
81
82    @Override /** Postorder traversal from the root */
83    public void postorder() {
84      postorder(root);
85    }
86
87    /** Postorder traversal from a subtree */
88    protected void postorder(TreeNode<E> root) {
89      if (root == null) return;
90      postorder(root.left);
91      postorder(root.right);
92      System.out.print(root.element + " ");
93    }
94
95    @Override /** Preorder traversal from the root */
96    public void preorder() {
97      preorder(root);
98    }
99
100   /** Preorder traversal from a subtree */
101   protected void preorder(TreeNode<E> root) {
102     if (root == null) return;
103     System.out.print(root.element + " ");
104     preorder(root.left);
105     preorder(root.right);
106   }
107
108   /** This inner class is static, because it does not access
109       any instance members defined in its outer class */
```

Left margin annotations:

link to parent (line 55)

increase size (line 61)

create new node (line 65)

inorder (line 70)

recursive helper method (line 75)

postorder (line 83)

recursive helper method (line 88)

preorder (line 96)

recursive helper method (line 101)

```
110    public static class TreeNode<E> {                              inner class
111      protected E element;
112      protected TreeNode<E> left;                                   getSize
113      protected TreeNode<E> right;
114
115      public TreeNode(E e) {
116        element = e;
117      }
118    }
119
120    @Override /** Get the number of nodes in the tree */
121    public int getSize() {
122      return size;
123    }
124
125    /** Returns the root of the tree */
126    public TreeNode<E> getRoot() {                                   getRoot
127      return root;
128    }
129
130    /** Returns a path from the root leading to the specified element */
131    public java.util.ArrayList<TreeNode<E>> path(E e) {              path
132      java.util.ArrayList<TreeNode<E>> list =
133        new java.util.ArrayList<>();
134      TreeNode<E> current = root; // Start from the root
135
136      while (current != null) {
137        list.add(current); // Add the node to the list
138        if (e.compareTo(current.element) < 0) {
139          current = current.left;
140        }
141        else if (e.compareTo(current.element) > 0) {
142          current = current.right;
143        }
144        else
145          break;
146      }
147
148      return list; // Return an array list of nodes
149    }
150
151    @Override /** Delete an element from the binary tree.
152     * Return true if the element is deleted successfully
153     * Return false if the element is not in the tree */
154    public boolean delete(E e) {                                     delete
155      // Locate the node to be deleted and also locate its parent node
156      TreeNode<E> parent = null;                                     locate parent
157      TreeNode<E> current = root;                                    locate current
158      while (current != null) {
159        if (e.compareTo(current.element) < 0) {
160          parent = current;
161          current = current.left;
162        }
163        else if (e.compareTo(current.element) > 0) {
164          parent = current;
165          current = current.right;
166        }
167        else
168          break; // Element is in the tree pointed at by current    current found
169      }
```

```
170
171        if (current == null)
172          return false; // Element is not in the tree
173
174        // Case 1: current has no left child
175        if (current.left == null) {
176          // Connect the parent with the right child of the current node
177          if (parent == null) {
178            root = current.right;
179          }
180          else {
181            if (e.compareTo(parent.element) < 0)
182              parent.left = current.right;
183            else
184              parent.right = current.right;
185          }
186        }
187        else {
188          // Case 2: The current node has a left child
189          // Locate the rightmost node in the left subtree of
190          // the current node and also its parent
191          TreeNode<E> parentOfRightMost = current;
192          TreeNode<E> rightMost = current.left;
193
194          while (rightMost.right != null) {
195            parentOfRightMost = rightMost;
196            rightMost = rightMost.right; // Keep going to the right
197          }
198
199          // Replace the element in current by the element in rightMost
200          current.element = rightMost.element;
201
202          // Eliminate rightmost node
203          if (parentOfRightMost.right == rightMost)
204            parentOfRightMost.right = rightMost.left;
205          else
206            // Special case: parentOfRightMost == current
207            parentOfRightMost.left = rightMost.left;
208        }
209
210        size--;
211        return true; // Element deleted successfully
212      }
213
214      @Override /** Obtain an iterator. Use inorder. */
215      public java.util.Iterator<E> iterator() {
216        return new InorderIterator();
217      }
218
219      // Inner class InorderIterator
220      private class InorderIterator implements java.util.Iterator<E> {
221        // Store the elements in a list
222        private java.util.ArrayList<E> list =
223          new java.util.ArrayList<>();
224        private int current = 0; // Point to the current element in list
225
226        public InorderIterator() {
227          inorder(); // Traverse binary tree and store elements in list
228        }
229
```

Margin notes:
- not found (line 171)
- Case 1 (line 175)
- reconnect parent (line 182)
- reconnect parent (line 184)
- Case 2 (line 188)
- locate parentOfRightMost (line 191)
- locate rightMost (line 192)
- replace current (line 200)
- reconnect parentOfRightMost (line 205)
- reduce size (line 210)
- successful deletion (line 211)
- iterator (line 215)
- iterator class (line 220)
- internal list (line 222)
- current position (line 224)

```
230        /** Inorder traversal from the root*/
231        private void inorder() {
232          inorder(root);
233        }
234
235        /** Inorder traversal from a subtree */
236        private void inorder(TreeNode<E> root) {
237          if (root == null)return;
238          inorder(root.left);
239          list.add(root.element);
240          inorder(root.right);
241        }
242
243        @Override /** More elements for traversing? */
244        public boolean hasNext() {
245          if (current < list.size())
246            return true;
247
248          return false;
249        }
250
251        @Override /** Get the current element and move to the next */
252        public E next() {
253          return list.get(current++);
254        }
255
256        @Override /** Remove the current element */
257        public void remove() {
258          if (current == 0) // next() has not been called yet
259            throw new IllegalStateException();
260
261          delete(list.get(--current));
262          list.clear(); // Clear the list
263          inorder(); // Rebuild the list
264        }
265      }
266
267      @Override /** Remove all elements from the tree */
268      public void clear() {
269        root = null;
270        size = 0;
271      }
272    }
```

obtain inorder list

hasNext in iterator?

get next element

remove the current

refresh list
clear list

tree clear method

The `insert(E e)` method (lines 35–63) creates a node for element `e` and inserts it into the tree. If the tree is empty, the node becomes the root. Otherwise, the method finds an appropriate parent for the node to maintain the order of the tree. If the element is already in the tree, the method returns `false`; otherwise it returns `true`.

The `inorder()` method (lines 70–80) invokes `inorder(root)` to traverse the entire tree. The method `inorder(TreeNode root)` traverses the tree with the specified root. This is a recursive method. It recursively traverses the left subtree, then the root, and finally the right subtree. The traversal ends when the tree is empty.

The `postorder()` method (lines 83–93) and the `preorder()` method (lines 96–106) are implemented similarly using recursion.

The `path(E e)` method (lines 131–149) returns a path of the nodes as an array list. The path starts from the root leading to the element. The element may not be in the tree. For example, in Figure 25.4a, `path(45)` contains the nodes for elements 60, 55, and 45, and `path(58)` contains the nodes for elements 60, 55, and 57.

The implementation of `delete()` and `iterator()` (lines 154–265) will be discussed in Sections 25.3 and 25.5.

Listing 25.5 gives an example that creates a binary search tree using BST (line 4). The program adds strings into the tree (lines 5–11), traverses the tree in inorder, postorder, and preorder (lines 14–20), searches for an element (line 24), and obtains a path from the node containing Peter to the root (lines 28–31).

LISTING 25.5 TestBST.java

```
 1  public class TestBST {
 2    public static void main(String[] args) {
 3      // Create a BST
 4      BST<String> tree = new BST<>();
 5      tree.insert("George");
 6      tree.insert("Michael");
 7      tree.insert("Tom");
 8      tree.insert("Adam");
 9      tree.insert("Jones");
10      tree.insert("Peter");
11      tree.insert("Daniel");
12
13      // Traverse tree
14      System.out.print("Inorder (sorted): ");
15      tree.inorder();
16      System.out.print("\nPostorder: ");
17      tree.postorder();
18      System.out.print("\nPreorder: ");
19      tree.preorder();
20      System.out.print("\nThe number of nodes is " + tree.getSize());
21
22      // Search for an element
23      System.out.print("\nIs Peter in the tree? " +
24        tree.search("Peter"));
25
26      // Get a path from the root to Peter
27      System.out.print("\nA path from the root to Peter is: ");
28      java.util.ArrayList<BST.TreeNode<String>> path
29        = tree.path("Peter");
30      for (int i = 0; path != null && i < path.size(); i++)
31        System.out.print(path.get(i).element + " ");
32
33      Integer[] numbers = {2, 4, 3, 1, 8, 5, 6, 7};
34      BST<Integer> intTree = new BST<>(numbers);
35      System.out.print("\nInorder (sorted): ");
36      intTree.inorder();
37    }
38  }
```

The marginal notes (left of listing) read, top to bottom: create tree, insert, inorder, postorder, preorder, getSize, search.

```
Inorder (sorted): Adam Daniel George Jones Michael Peter Tom
Postorder: Daniel Adam Jones Peter Tom Michael George
Preorder: George Adam Daniel Michael Jones Tom Peter
The number of nodes is 7
Is Peter in the tree? true
A path from the root to Peter is: George Michael Tom Peter
Inorder (sorted): 1 2 3 4 5 6 7 8
```

The program checks `path != null` in line 30 to ensure that the path is not `null` before invoking `path.get(i)`. This is an example of defensive programming to avoid potential runtime errors.

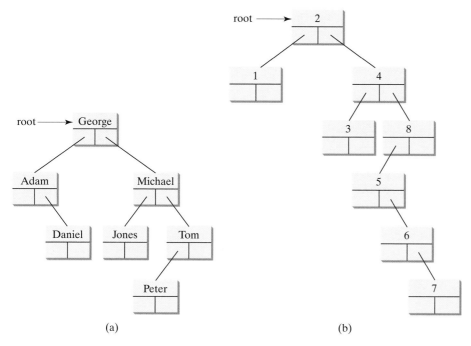

(a)   (b)

FIGURE 25.7 The BSTs in Listing 25.5 are pictured here after they are created.

The program creates another tree for storing `int` values (line 34). After all the elements are inserted in the trees, the trees should appear as shown in Figure 25.7.

If the elements are inserted in a different order (e.g., Daniel, Adam, Jones, Peter, Tom, Michael, and George), the tree will look different. However, the inorder traversal prints elements in the same order as long as the set of elements is the same. The inorder traversal displays a sorted list.

25.2.1 Show the result of inserting 44 into Figure 25.4b.

25.2.2 Show the inorder, preorder, and postorder of traversing the elements in the binary tree shown in Figure 25.1c.

25.2.3 If a set of elements is inserted into a BST in two different orders, will the two corresponding BSTs look the same? Will the inorder traversal be the same? Will the postorder traversal be the same? Will the preorder traversal be the same?

25.2.4 What is the time complexity of inserting an element into a BST?

25.2.5 Implement the `search(element)` method using recursion.

Check Point

25.3 Deleting Elements from a BST

To delete an element from a BST, first locate it in the tree then consider two cases—whether or not the node has a left child—before deleting the element and reconnecting the tree.

Key Point

The `insert(element)` method is presented in Section 25.2.3. Often, you need to delete an element from a binary search tree. Doing so is far more complex than adding an element into a binary search tree.

To delete an element from a binary search tree, you need to first locate the node that contains the element and also its parent node. Let `current` point to the node that contains the element in the binary search tree and `parent` point to the parent of the `current` node. The `current` node may be a left child or a right child of the `parent` node. There are two cases to consider.

locating element

Case 1: The current node does not have a left child, as shown in Figure 25.8a. In this case, simply connect the parent with the right child of the current node, as shown in Figure 25.8b.

For example, to delete node `10` in Figure 25.9a, you would connect the parent of node `10` with the right child of node `10`, as shown in Figure 25.9b.

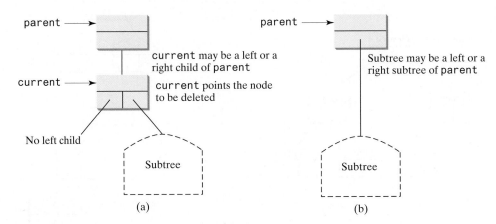

FIGURE 25.8   Case 1: The current node has no left child.

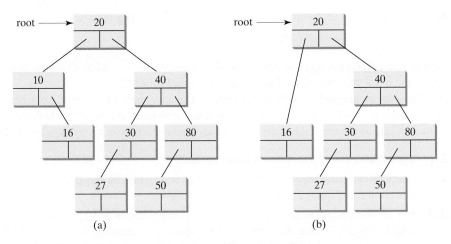

FIGURE 25.9   Case 1: Deleting node `10` from (a) results in (b).

delete a leaf

Note

If the current node is a leaf, it falls into Case 1. For example, to delete element `16` in Figure 25.9a, connect its right child (in this case, it is `null`) to the parent of node `16`.

Case 2: The `current` node has a left child. Let `rightMost` point to the node that contains the largest element in the left subtree of the `current` node and `parentOfRightMost` point to the parent node of the `rightMost` node, as shown in Figure 25.10a. Note the `rightMost` node cannot have a right child but may have a left child. Replace the element value in the `current` node with the one in the `rightMost` node, connect the `parentOfRightMost` node with the left child of the `rightMost` node, and delete the `rightMost` node, as shown in Figure 25.10b.

For example, consider deleting node `20` in Figure 25.11a. The `rightMost` node has the element value `16`. Replace the element value `20` with `16` in the `current` node and make node `10` the parent for node `14`, as shown in Figure 25.11b.

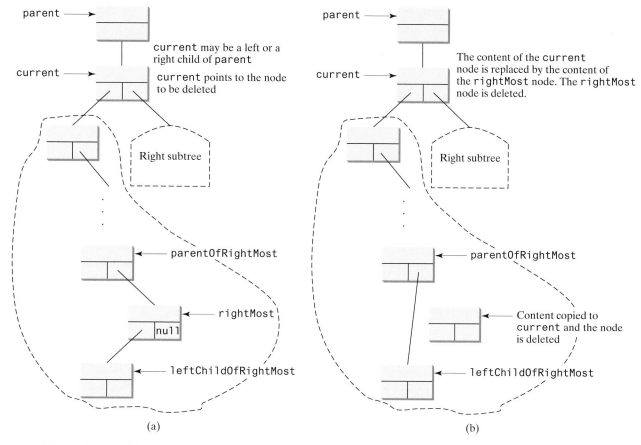

FIGURE 25.10 Case 2: The current node has a left child.

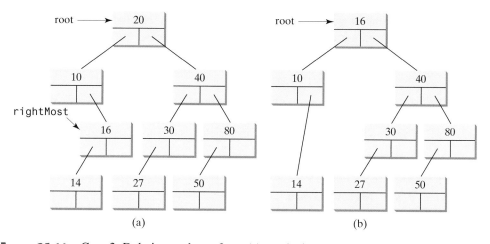

FIGURE 25.11 Case 2: Deleting node 20 from (a) results in (b).

 Note
If the left child of `current` does not have a right child, `current.left` points to the largest element in the left subtree of `current`. In this case, `rightMost` is `current.left` and `parentOfRightMost` is `current`. You have to take care of this special case to reconnect the left child of `rightMost` with `parentOfRightMost`.

special case

delete method

The algorithm for deleting an element from a binary search tree can be described in Listing 25.6.

LISTING 25.6 Deleting an Element from a BST

```
1  boolean delete(E e) {
2    Locate element e in the tree;
3    if element e is not found
4      return true;
5
6    Let current be the node that contains e and parent be
7      the parent of current;
8
9    if (current has no left child)  // Case 1
10     Connect the right child of current with parent;
11       Now current is not referenced, so it is eliminated;
12   else // Case 2
13     Locate the rightmost node in the left subtree of current.
14     Copy the element value in the rightmost node to current.
15     Connect the parent of the rightmost node to the left child
16       of rightmost node;
17
18   return true; // Element deleted
19 }
```

not in the tree

locate current
locate parent

Case 1

Case 2

The complete implementation of the `delete` method is given in lines 154–212 in Listing 25.4. The method locates the node (named `current`) to be deleted and also locates its parent (named `parent`) in lines 156–169. If `current` is `null`, the element is not in the tree. Therefore, the method returns `false` (line 172). Please note that if `current` is `root`, `parent` is `null`. If the tree is empty, both `current` and `parent` are `null`.

Case 1 of the algorithm is covered in lines 175–186. In this case, the `current` node has no left child (i.e., `current.left == null`). If `parent` is `null`, assign `current.right` to `root` (lines 177–179). Otherwise, assign `current.right` to either `parent.left` or `parent.right`, depending on whether `current` is a left or a right child of `parent` (181–184).

Case 2 of the algorithm is covered in lines 187–208. In this case, `current` has a left child. The algorithm locates the rightmost node (named `rightMost`) in the left subtree of the current node and also its parent (named `parentOfRightMost`) (lines 194–197). Replace the element in `current` by the element in `rightMost` (line 200); assign `rightMost.left` to either `parentOfRightMost.right` or `parentOfRightMost.left` (lines 203–207), depending on whether `rightMost` is a right or a left child of `parentOfRightMost`.

Listing 25.7 gives a test program that deletes the elements from the binary search tree.

LISTING 25.7 TestBSTDelete.java

```
1  public class TestBSTDelete {
2    public static void main(String[] args) {
3      BST<String> tree = new BST<>();
4      tree.insert("George");
5      tree.insert("Michael");
6      tree.insert("Tom");
7      tree.insert("Adam");
8      tree.insert("Jones");
9      tree.insert("Peter");
10     tree.insert("Daniel");
11     printTree(tree);
12
13     System.out.println("\nAfter delete George:");
```

```
14      tree.delete("George");                                          delete an element
15      printTree(tree);
16
17      System.out.println("\nAfter delete Adam:");
18      tree.delete("Adam");                                            delete an element
19      printTree(tree);
20
21      System.out.println("\nAfter delete Michael:");
22      tree.delete("Michael");                                         delete an element
23      printTree(tree);
24    }
25
26    public static void printTree(BST tree) {
27      // Traverse tree
28      System.out.print("Inorder (sorted): ");
29      tree.inorder();
30      System.out.print("\nPostorder: ");
31      tree.postorder();
32      System.out.print("\nPreorder: ");
33      tree.preorder();
34      System.out.print("\nThe number of nodes is " + tree.getSize());
35      System.out.println();
36    }
37  }
```

```
Inorder (sorted): Adam Daniel George Jones Michael Peter Tom
Postorder: Daniel Adam Jones Peter Tom Michael George
Preorder: George Adam Daniel Michael Jones Tom Peter
The number of nodes is 7

After delete George:
Inorder (sorted): Adam Daniel Jones Michael Peter Tom
Postorder: Adam Jones Peter Tom Michael Daniel
Preorder: Daniel Adam Michael Jones Tom Peter
The number of nodes is 6

After delete Adam:
Inorder (sorted): Daniel Jones Michael Peter Tom
Postorder: Jones Peter Tom Michael Daniel
Preorder: Daniel Michael Jones Tom Peter
The number of nodes is 5

After delete Michael:
Inorder (sorted): Daniel Jones Peter Tom
Postorder: Peter Tom Jones Daniel
Preorder: Daniel Jones Tom Peter
The number of nodes is 4
```

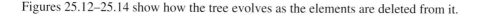

Figures 25.12–25.14 show how the tree evolves as the elements are deleted from it.

Note

It is obvious that the time complexity for the inorder, preorder, and postorder is $O(n)$, since each node is traversed only once. The time complexity for search, insertion, and deletion is the height of the tree. In the worst case, the height of the tree is $O(n)$. On average, the height of the tree is $O(\log n)$. So, the average time for search, insertion, deletion in a BST is $O(\log n)$.

BST time complexity

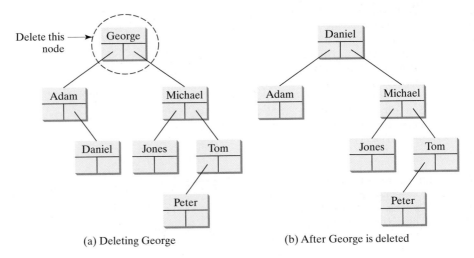

(a) Deleting George   (b) After George is deleted

FIGURE 25.12 Deleting George falls into Case 2.

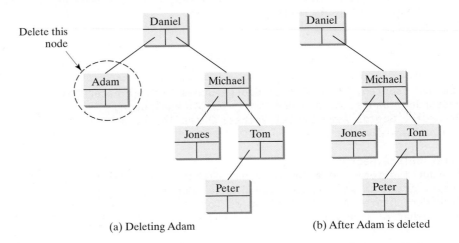

(a) Deleting Adam   (b) After Adam is deleted

FIGURE 25.13 Deleting Adam falls into Case 1.

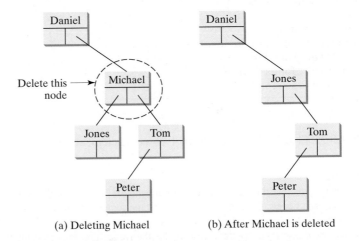

(a) Deleting Michael   (b) After Michael is deleted

FIGURE 25.14 Deleting Michael falls into Case 2.

25.3.1 Show the result of deleting 55 from the tree in Figure 25.4b.

25.3.2 Show the result of deleting 60 from the tree in Figure 25.4b.

25.3.3 What is the time complexity of deleting an element from a BST?

25.3.4 Is the algorithm correct if lines 203–207 in Listing 25.4 in Case 2 of the `delete()` method are replaced by the following code?

```
parentOfRightMost.right = rightMost.left;
```

25.4 Tree Visualization and MVC

You can use recursion to display a binary tree.

 Pedagogical Note

One challenge facing the data-structure course is to motivate students. Displaying a binary tree graphically will not only help you understand the working of a binary tree but perhaps also stimulate your interest in programming. This section introduces the techniques to visualize binary trees. You can also apply visualization techniques to other projects.

How do you display a binary tree? It is a recursive structure, so you can display a binary tree using recursion. You can simply display the root, then display the two subtrees recursively. The techniques for displaying the Sierpinski triangle in Listing 18.9 can be applied to displaying a binary tree. For simplicity, we assume that the keys are positive integers less than 100. Listings 25.8 and 25.9 give the program, and Figure 25.15 shows some sample runs of the program.

 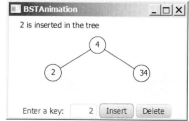 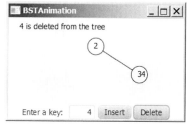

FIGURE 25.15 A binary tree is displayed graphically. *Source*: Copyright © 1995–2016 Oracle and/or its affiliates. All rights reserved. Used with permission.

LISTING 25.8 BSTAnimation.java

```
1  import javafx.application.Application;
2  import javafx.geometry.Pos;
3  import javafx.stage.Stage;
4  import javafx.scene.Scene;
5  import javafx.scene.control.Button;
6  import javafx.scene.control.Label;
7  import javafx.scene.control.TextField;
8  import javafx.scene.layout.BorderPane;
9  import javafx.scene.layout.HBox;
10
11 public class BSTAnimation extends Application {
12   @Override // Override the start method in the Application class
13   public void start(Stage primaryStage) {
14     BST<Integer> tree = new BST<>(); // Create a tree          create a tree
15
16     BorderPane pane = new BorderPane();
17     BTView view = new BTView(tree); // Create a View          view for tree
```

place tree view	18	`pane.setCenter(view);`

```
18      pane.setCenter(view);
19
20      TextField tfKey = new TextField();
21      tfKey.setPrefColumnCount(3);
22      tfKey.setAlignment(Pos.BASELINE_RIGHT);
23      Button btInsert = new Button("Insert");
24      Button btDelete = new Button("Delete");
25      HBox hBox = new HBox(5);
26      hBox.getChildren().addAll(new Label("Enter a key: "),
27        tfKey, btInsert, btDelete);
28      hBox.setAlignment(Pos.CENTER);
29      pane.setBottom(hBox);
30
31      btInsert.setOnAction(e -> {
32        int key = Integer.parseInt(tfKey.getText());
33        if (tree.search(key)) { // key is in the tree already
34          view.displayTree();
35          view.setStatus(key + " is already in the tree");
36        }
37        else {
38          tree.insert(key); // Insert a new key
39          view.displayTree();
40          view.setStatus(key + " is inserted in the tree");
41        }
42      });
43
44      btDelete.setOnAction(e -> {
45        int key = Integer.parseInt(tfKey.getText());
46        if (!tree.search(key)) {  // key is not in the tree
47          view.displayTree();
48          view.setStatus(key + " is not in the tree");
49        }
50        else {
51          tree.delete(key); // Delete a key
52          view.displayTree();
53          view.setStatus(key + " is deleted from the tree");
54        }
55      });
56
57      // Create a scene and place the pane in the stage
58      Scene scene = new Scene(pane, 450, 250);
59      primaryStage.setTitle("BSTAnimation"); // Set the stage title
60      primaryStage.setScene(scene); // Place the scene in the stage
61      primaryStage.show(); // Display the stage
62    }
63  }
```

LISTING 25.9 BTView.java

```
1  import javafx.scene.layout.Pane;
2  import javafx.scene.paint.Color;
3  import javafx.scene.shape.Circle;
4  import javafx.scene.shape.Line;
5  import javafx.scene.text.Text;
6
7  public class BTView extends Pane {
8    private BST<Integer> tree = new BST<>();
9    private double radius = 15; // Tree node radius
10   private double vGap = 50; // Gap between two levels in a tree
11
```

Side notes: handle insertion, insert key, display the tree, handle deletion, delete key, display the tree, place hBox, tree to display.

```
12      BTView(BST<Integer> tree) {
13        this.tree = tree;
14        setStatus("Tree is empty");
15      }
16
17      public void setStatus(String msg) {
18        getChildren().add(new Text(20, 20, msg));
19      }
20
21      public void displayTree() {
22        this.getChildren().clear(); // Clear the pane
23        if (tree.getRoot() != null) {
24          // Display tree recursively
25          displayTree(tree.getRoot(), getWidth() / 2, vGap,
26            getWidth() / 4);
27        }
28      }
29
30      /** Display a subtree rooted at position (x, y) */
31      private void displayTree(BST.TreeNode<Integer> root,
32          double x, double y, double hGap) {
33        if (root.left != null) {
34          // Draw a line to the left node
35          getChildren().add(new Line(x - hGap, y + vGap, x, y));
36          // Draw the left subtree recursively
37          displayTree(root.left, x - hGap, y + vGap, hGap / 2);
38        }
39
40        if (root.right != null) {
41          // Draw a line to the right node
42          getChildren().add(new Line(x + hGap, y + vGap, x, y));
43          // Draw the right subtree recursively
44          displayTree(root.right, x + hGap, y + vGap, hGap / 2);
45        }
46
47        // Display a node
48        Circle circle = new Circle(x, y, radius);
49        circle.setFill(Color.WHITE);
50        circle.setStroke(Color.BLACK);
51        getChildren().addAll(circle,
52          new Text(x - 4, y + 4, root.element + ""));
53      }
54    }
```

- set a tree
- clear the display
- display tree recursively
- connect two nodes
- draw left subtree
- connect two nodes
- draw right subtree
- display a node

In Listing 25.8, BSTAnimation.java, a tree is created (line 14) and a tree view is placed in the pane (line 18). After a new key is inserted into the tree (line 38), the tree is repainted (line 39) to reflect the change. After a key is deleted (line 51), the tree is repainted (line 52) to reflect the change.

In Listing 25.9, BTView.java, the node is displayed as a circle with radius 15 (line 48). The distance between two levels in the tree is defined in vGap 50 (line 25). hGap (line 32) defines the distance between two nodes horizontally. This value is reduced by half (hGap / 2) in the next level when the displayTree method is called recursively (lines 37 and 44). Note that vGap is not changed in the tree.

The method displayTree is recursively invoked to display a left subtree (lines 33–38) and a right subtree (lines 40–45) if a subtree is not empty. A line is added to the pane to connect two nodes (lines 35 and 42). Note the method first adds the lines to the pane then adds the circle into the pane (line 52) so the circles will be painted on top of the lines to achieve desired visual effects.

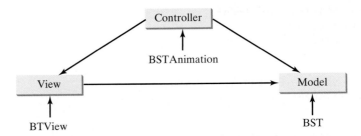

FIGURE 25.16 The controller obtains data and stores it in a model. The view displays the data stored in the model.

The program assumes the keys are integers. You can easily modify the program with a generic type to display keys of characters or short strings.

Tree visualization is an example of the model-view-controller (MVC) software architecture. This is an important architecture for software development. The model is for storing and handling data. The view is for visually presenting the data. The controller handles the user interaction with the model and controls the view, as shown in Figure 25.16.

The MVC architecture separates data storage and handling from the visual representation of the data. It has two major benefits:

■ It makes multiple views possible so data can be shared through the same model. For example, you can create a new view that displays the tree with the root on the left and the tree grows horizontally to the right (see Programming Exercise 25.11).

■ It simplifies the task of writing complex applications and makes the components scalable and easy to maintain. Changes can be made to the view without affecting the model, and vice versa.

25.4.1 How many times will the `displayTree` method be invoked if the tree is empty? How many times will the `displayTree` method be invoked if the tree has **100** nodes?

25.4.2 In what order are the nodes in the tree visited by the `displayTree` method: inorder, preorder, or postorder?

25.4.3 What would happen if the code in lines 47–52 in Listing 25.9, BTView.java is moved to line 33?

25.4.4 What is MVC? What are the benefits of the MVC?

25.4.5 Write one statement that displays the maximum and minimum element in a BST object named `tree`.

25.5 Iterators

BST is iterable because it is defined as a subtype of the `java.lang.Iterable` *interface.*

The methods `inorder()`, `preorder()`, and `postorder()` display the elements in `inorder`, `preorder`, and `postorder` in a binary tree. These methods are limited to displaying the elements in a tree. If you wish to process the elements in a binary tree rather than display them, these methods cannot be used. Recall that an iterator is provided for traversing the elements in a set or list. You can apply the same approach in a binary tree to provide a uniform way of traversing the elements in a binary tree.

iterator

The `java.lang.Iterable` interface defines the `iterator` method, which returns an instance of the `java.util.Iterator` interface. The `java.util.Iterator` interface (see Figure 25.17) defines the common features of iterators.

«interface» java.util.Iterator<E>	
+hasNext(): boolean	Returns true if the iterator has more elements.
+next(): E	Returns the next element in the iterator.
+remove(): void	Removes from the underlying container the last element returned by the iterator (optional operation).

FIGURE 25.17 The Iterator interface defines a uniform way of traversing the elements in a container.

The Tree interface extends java.util.Collection. Since Collection extends java.lang.Iterable, BST is also a subclass of Iterable. The Iterable interface contains the iterator() method that returns an instance of java.util.Iterator.

You can traverse a binary tree in inorder, preorder, or postorder. Since inorder is used frequently, we will use inorder for traversing the elements in a binary tree. We define an iterator class named InorderIterator to implement the java.util.Iterator interface in Listing 25.4 (lines 220–265). The iterator method simply returns an instance of InorderIterator (line 216).

> how to create an iterator

The InorderIterator constructor invokes the inorder method (line 227). The inorder(root) method (lines 236–241) stores all the elements from the tree in list. The elements are traversed in inorder.

Once an Iterator object is created, its current value is initialized to 0 (line 224), which points to the first element in the list. Invoking the next() method returns the current element and moves current to point to the next element in the list (line 252).

The hasNext() method checks whether current is still in the range of list (line 245).

The remove() method removes the element returned by the last next() (line 258). Afterward, a new list is created (lines 261–262). Note that current does not need to be changed.

Listing 25.10 gives a test program that stores the strings in a BST and displays all strings in uppercase.

LISTING 25.10 TestBSTWithIterator.java

```java
1  public class TestBSTWithIterator {
2    public static void main(String[] args) {
3      BST<String> tree = new BST<>();
4      tree.insert("George");
5      tree.insert("Michael");
6      tree.insert("Tom");
7      tree.insert("Adam");
8      tree.insert("Jones");
9      tree.insert("Peter");
10     tree.insert("Daniel");
11
12     for (String s: tree)
13       System.out.print(s.toUpperCase() + " ");
14   }
15 }
```

> use an iterator
> get uppercase letters

The foreach loop (lines 12 and 13) uses an iterator to traverse all elements in the tree.

```
ADAM DANIEL GEORGE JONES MICHAEL PETER TOM
```

iterator pattern
advantages of iterators

Design Guide

Iterator is an important software design pattern. It provides a uniform way of traversing the elements in a container, while hiding the container's structural details. By implementing the same interface `java.util.Iterator`, you can write a program that traverses the elements of all containers in the same way.

variations of iterators

Note

`java.util.Iterator` defines a forward iterator, which traverses the elements in the iterator in a forward direction, and each element can be traversed only once. The Java API also provides the `java.util.ListIterator`, which supports traversing in both forward and backward directions. If your data structure warrants flexible traversing, you may define iterator classes as a subtype of `java.util.ListIterator`.

The implementation of the iterator is not efficient. Every time you remove an element through the iterator, the whole list is rebuilt (line 263 in Listing 25.4, BST.java). The client should always use the `delete` method in the `BST` class to remove an element. To prevent the user from using the `remove` method in the iterator, implement the iterator as follows:

```java
public void remove() {
  throw new UnsupportedOperationException
    ("Removing an element from the iterator is not supported");
}
```

After making the `remove` method unsupported by the iterator class, you can implement the iterator more efficiently without having to maintain a list for the elements in the tree. You can use a stack to store the nodes, and the node on the top of the stack contains the element that is to be returned from the `next()` method. If the tree is well balanced, the maximum stack size will be $O(\log n)$.

25.5.1 What is an iterator?

25.5.2 What method is defined in the `java.lang.Iterable<E>` interface?

25.5.3 Suppose you delete `implements Collection<E>` from line 3 in Listing 25.3, Tree.java. Will Listing 25.10 still compile?

25.5.4 What is the benefit of being a subtype of `Iterable<E>`?

25.5.5 Write one statement that displays the maximum and minimum element in a `BST` object named `tree`.

25.6 Case Study: Data Compression

Huffman coding compresses data by using fewer bits to encode characters that occur more frequently. The codes for the characters are constructed based on the occurrence of the characters in the text using a binary tree, called the Huffman coding tree.

Compressing data is a common task. There are many utilities available for compressing files. This section introduces Huffman coding, invented by David Huffman in 1952.

In ASCII, every character is encoded in 8 bits. If a text consists of 100 characters, it will take 800 bits to represent the text. The idea of Huffman coding is to use a fewer bits to encode frequently used characters in the text and more bits to encode less frequently used characters to reduce the overall size of the file. In Huffman coding, the characters' codes are constructed based on the characters' occurrence in the text using a binary tree, called the *Huffman coding tree*. Suppose the text is `Mississippi`. Its Huffman tree is as shown in Figure 25.18a. The left and right edges of a node are assigned the values 0 and 1, respectively. Each character is a leaf in the tree. The code for the character consists of the edge values in the path from the

Huffman coding

root to the leaf, as shown in Figure 25.18b. Since i and s appear more than M and p in the text, they are assigned shorter codes.

The coding tree is also used for decoding a sequence of bits into characters. To do so, start with the first bit in the sequence and determine whether to go to the left or right branch of the tree's root based on the bit value. Consider the next bit and continue to go down to the left or right branch based on the bit value. When you reach a leaf, you have found a character. The next bit in the stream is the first bit of the next character. For example, the stream 011001 is decoded to sip, with 01 matching s, 1 matching i, and 001 matching p.

decoding

Based on the coding scheme in Figure 25.18,

```
             is encoded to                              is decoded to
Mississippi =========> 00010101101011011001 ==========> Mississippi
```

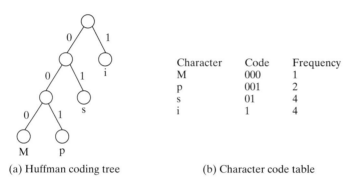

Character	Code	Frequency
M	000	1
p	001	2
s	01	4
i	1	4

(a) Huffman coding tree   (b) Character code table

FIGURE 25.18 The codes for characters are constructed based on the occurrence of characters in the text using a coding tree.

To construct a *Huffman coding tree*, use the following algorithm:

construct coding tree

1. Begin with a forest of trees. Each tree contains a node for a character. The weight of the node is the frequency of the character in the text.

2. Repeat the following action to combine trees until there is only one tree: Choose two trees with the smallest weight and create a new node as their parent. The weight of the new tree is the sum of the weight of the subtrees.

3. For each interior node, assign its left edge a value 0 and right edge a value 1. All leaf nodes represent characters in the text.

Here is an example of building a coding tree for the text Mississippi. The frequency table for the characters is shown in Figure 25.18b. Initially, the forest contains single-node trees, as shown in Figure 25.19a. The trees are repeatedly combined to form large trees until only one tree is left, as shown in Figures 25.19b–d.

It is worth noting that no code is a prefix of another code. This property ensures that the streams can be decoded unambiguously.

prefix property

The algorithm used here is an example of a *greedy algorithm*. A greedy algorithm is often used in solving optimization problems. The algorithm makes the choice that is optimal locally in the hope that this choice will lead to a globally optimal solution. In this case, the algorithm always chooses two trees with the smallest weight and creates a new node as their parent. This intuitive optimal local solution indeed leads to a final optimal solution for constructing a Huffman tree. As another example, consider changing money into the fewest possible coins. A greedy algorithm would take the largest possible coin first. For example, for 98¢, you would use three quarters to make 75¢, additional two dimes to make 95¢, and additional three pennies to make the 98¢. The greedy algorithm finds an optimal solution for this problem. However,

greedy algorithm

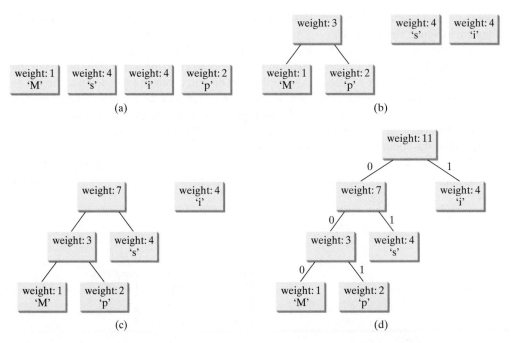

FIGURE 25.19 The coding tree is built by repeatedly combining the two smallest-weighted trees.

a greedy algorithm is not always going to find the optimal result; see the bin packing problem in Programming Exercise 11.19.

Listing 25.11 gives a program that prompts the user to enter a string, displays the frequency table of the characters in the string, and displays the Huffman code for each character.

LISTING 25.11 HuffmanCode.java

```
1  import java.util.Scanner;
2
3  public class HuffmanCode {
4    public static void main(String[] args) {
5      Scanner input = new Scanner(System.in);
6      System.out.print("Enter text: ");
7      String text = input.nextLine();
8
9      int[] counts = getCharacterFrequency(text); // Count frequency
10
11     System.out.printf("%-15s%-15s%-15s%-15s\n",
12       "ASCII Code", "Character", "Frequency", "Code");
13
14     Tree tree = getHuffmanTree(counts); // Create a Huffman tree
15     String[] codes = getCode(tree.root); // Get codes
16
17     for (int i = 0; i < codes.length; i++)
18       if (counts[i] != 0) // (char)i is not in text if counts[i] is 0
19         System.out.printf("%-15d%-15s%-15d%-15s\n",
20           i, (char)i + "", counts[i], codes[i]);
21   }
22
23   /** Get Huffman codes for the characters
24    * This method is called once after a Huffman tree is built
```

count frequency

get Huffman tree
code for each character

```
25     */
26     public static String[] getCode(Tree.Node root) {                    getCode
27       if (root == null)  return null;
28       String[] codes = new String[2 *  128];
29       assignCode(root, codes);
30       return codes;
31     }
32
33     /* Recursively get codes to the leaf node */
34     private static void assignCode(Tree.Node root, String[] codes) {    assignCode
35       if (root.left != null) {
36         root.left.code = root.code + "0";
37         assignCode(root.left, codes);
38
39         root.right.code = root.code + "1";
40         assignCode(root.right, codes);
41       }
42       else {
43         codes[(int)root.element] = root.code;
44       }
45     }
46
47     /** Get a Huffman tree from the codes */
48     public static Tree getHuffmanTree(int[] counts) {                   getHuffmanTree
49       // Create a heap to hold trees
50       Heap<Tree> heap = new Heap<>(); // Defined in Listing 23.9
51       for (int i = 0; i < counts.length; i++) {
52         if (counts[i] > 0)
53           heap.add(new Tree(counts[i], (char)i)); // A leaf node tree
54       }
55
56       while (heap.getSize() > 1) {
57         Tree t1 = heap.remove(); // Remove the smallest-weight tree
58         Tree t2 = heap.remove(); // Remove the next smallest
59         heap.add(new Tree(t1, t2)); // Combine two trees
60       }
61
62       return heap.remove(); // The final tree
63     }
64
65     /** Get the frequency of the characters */
66     public static int[] getCharacterFrequency(String text) {            getCharacterFrequency
67       int[] counts = new int[256]; // 256 ASCII characters
68
69       for (int i = 0; i < text.length(); i++)
70         counts[(int)text.charAt(i)]++; // Count the characters in text
71
72       return counts;
73     }
74
75     /** Define a Huffman coding tree */
76     public static class Tree implements Comparable<Tree> {              Huffman tree
77       Node root; // The root of the tree
78
79       /** Create a tree with two subtrees */
80       public Tree(Tree t1, Tree t2) {
81         root = new Node();
82         root.left = t1.root;
83         root.right = t2.root;
84         root.weight = t1.root.weight + t2.root.weight;
```

```
85        }
86
87        /** Create a tree containing a leaf node */
88        public Tree(int weight, char element) {
89          root = new Node(weight, element);
90        }
91
92        @Override /** Compare trees based on their weights */
93        public int compareTo(Tree t) {
94          if (root.weight < t.root.weight) // Purposely reverse the order
95            return 1;
96          else if (root.weight == t.root.weight)
97            return 0;
98          else
99            return -1;
100       }
101
```

tree node
```
102       public class Node {
103         char element; // Stores the character for a leaf node
104         int weight; // weight of the subtree rooted at this node
105         Node left; // Reference to the left subtree
106         Node right; // Reference to the right subtree
107         String code = ""; // The code of this node from the root
108
109         /** Create an empty node */
110         public Node() {
111         }
112
113         /** Create a node with the specified weight and character */
114         public Node(int weight, char element) {
115           this.weight = weight;
116           this.element = element;
117         }
118       }
119     }
120   }
```

```
Enter text: Welcome  ↵Enter

ASCII Code    Character    Frequency    Code
87            W            1            110
99            c            1            111
101           e            2            10
108           l            1            011
109           m            1            010
111           o            1            00
```

The program prompts the user to enter a text string (lines 5–7) and counts the frequency of the characters in the text (line 9). The `getCharacterFrequency` method (lines 66–73) creates an array `counts` to count the occurrences of each of the 256 ASCII characters in the text. If a character appears in the text, its corresponding count is increased by 1 (line 70).

getCharacterFrequency

The program obtains a Huffman coding tree based on `counts` (line 14). The tree consists of linked nodes. The `Node` class is defined in lines 102–118. Each node consists of properties element (storing character), weight (storing weight of the subtree under this node), left (linking to the left subtree), right (linking to the right subtree), and code (storing the Huffman code for the character). The Tree class (lines 76–119) contains the root property. From the root, you can access all the nodes in the tree. The Tree class implements Comparable. The trees are comparable based on their weights. The compare order is purposely reversed (lines 93–100) so the smallest-weight tree is removed first from the heap of trees.

The getHuffmanTree method returns a Huffman coding tree. Initially, the single-node trees are created and added to the heap (lines 50–54). In each iteration of the while loop (lines 56–60), two smallest-weight trees are removed from the heap and are combined to form a big tree, then the new tree is added to the heap. This process continues until the heap contains just one tree, which is our final Huffman tree for the text.

The assignCode method assigns the code for each node in the tree (lines 34–45). The getCode method gets the code for each character in the leaf node (lines 26–31). The element codes[i] contains the code for character (char)i, where i is from 0 to 255. Note codes[i] is null if (char)i is not in the text.

Node class

Tree class

getHuffmanTree

assignCode
getCode

25.6.1 Every internal node in a Huffman tree has two children. Is it true?

25.6.2 What is a greedy algorithm? Give an example.

25.6.3 If the Heap class in line 50 in Listing 25.9 is replaced by java.util. PriorityQueue, will the program still work?

25.6.4 How do you replace lines 94–99 in Listing 25.11 using one line?

Check Point

KEY TERMS

CHAPTER SUMMARY

1. A *binary search tree* (BST) is a hierarchical data structure. You learned how to define and implement a BST class, how to insert and delete elements into/from a BST, and how to traverse a BST using *inorder*, *postorder*, *preorder*, depth-first, and breadth-first searches.

2. An iterator is an object that provides a uniform way of traversing the elements in a container, such as a set, a list, or a *binary tree*. You learned how to define and implement iterator classes for traversing the elements in a binary tree.

3. *Huffman coding* is a scheme for compressing data by using fewer bits to encode characters that occur more frequently. The codes for characters are constructed based on the occurrence of characters in the text using a binary tree, called the *Huffman coding tree*.

QUIZ

Answer the quiz for this chapter online at the book Companion Website.

PROGRAMMING EXERCISES

Sections 25.2–25.6

*25.1 (*Add new methods in BST*) Add the following new methods in BST.

```
/** Display the nodes in a breadth-first traversal */
public void breadthFirstTraversal()

/** Return the height of this binary tree */
public int height()
```

*25.2 (*Test perfect binary tree*) A perfect binary tree is a complete binary tree with all levels fully filled. Add a method in the BST class to return true if the tree is a perfect binary tree. (*Hint*: The number of nodes in a nonempty perfect binary tree is $2^{\text{height}} - 1$)

```
/** Returns true if the tree is a perfect binary tree */
boolean isPerfectBST()
```

**25.3 (*Implement inorder traversal without using recursion*) Implement the inorder method in BST using a stack instead of recursion. Write a test program that prompts the user to enter 10 integers, stores them in a BST, and invokes the inorder method to display the elements.

**25.4 (*Implement preorder traversal without using recursion*) Implement the preorder method in BST using a stack instead of recursion. Write a test program that prompts the user to enter 10 integers, stores them in a BST, and invokes the preorder method to display the elements.

**25.5 (*Implement postorder traversal without using recursion*) Implement the postorder method in BST using a stack instead of recursion. Write a test program that prompts the user to enter 10 integers, stores them in a BST, and invokes the postorder method to display the elements.

**25.6 (*Find the leaves*) Add a method in the BST class to return the number of the leaves as follows:

```
/** Return the number of leaf nodes */
public int getNumberOfLeaves()
```

**25.7 (*Find the nonleaves*) Add a method in the BST class to return the number of the nonleaves as follows:

```
/** Return the number of nonleaf nodes */
public int getNumberofNonLeaves()
```

***25.8 (*Implement bidirectional iterator*) The java.util.Iterator interface defines a forward iterator. The Java API also provides the java.util.ListIterator interface that defines a bidirectional iterator. Study ListIterator and define a bidirectional iterator for the BST class.

**25.9 (*Tree clone and equals*) Implement the clone and equals methods in the BST class. Two BST trees are equal if they contain the same elements. The clone method returns an identical copy of a BST.

25.10 (*Preorder iterator*) Add the following method in the BST class that returns an iterator for traversing the elements in a BST in preorder.

```
/** Return an iterator for traversing the elements in preorder */
java.util.Iterator<E> preorderIterator()
```

25.11 (*Display tree*) Write a new view class that displays the tree horizontally with the root on the left as shown in Figure 25.20.

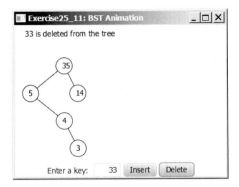

FIGURE 25.20   A binary tree is displayed horizontally.

**25.12 (*Test BST*) Design and write a complete test program to test if the BST class in Listing 25.4 meets all requirements.

**25.13 (*Add new buttons in BSTAnimation*) Modify Listing 25.8, BSTAnimation.java, to add three new buttons—*Show Inorder, Show Preorder, and Show Postorder*— to display the result in a label, as shown in Figure 25.21. You need also to modify Listing 25.4, BST.java to implement the `inorderList()`, `preorderList()`, and `postorderList()` methods so each of these methods returns a `List` of the node elements in inorder, preorder, and postorder, as follows:

```
public java.util.List<E> inorderList();
public java.util.List<E> preorderList();
public java.util.List<E> postorderList();
```

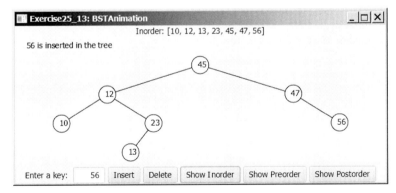

FIGURE 25.21   When you click the Show Inorder, Show Preorder, or Show Postorder button, the elements are displayed in an inorder, preorder, or postorder in a label. *Source*: Copyright © 1995–2016 Oracle and/or its affiliates. All rights reserved. Used with permission.

*25.14 (*Modify BST using Comparator*) Revise BST in Listing 25.4 using a `Comparator` for comparing objects. Define the new class as `BST<E>` with two constructors:

```
BST(); // Compare elements using their natural order
BST(Comparator<? super E> comparator)
```

Hint: You need to add a data field for `Comparator` in the `BST` class as follows:

```
protected Comparator<E> c = (e1, e2) ->
  ((Comparable<E>)e1).compareTo(e2);
```

The lambda expression gives the default comparator using a natural order. You need to use comparator `c` to replace `e.compareTo(anotherElement)` with `c.compare(e, anotherElement)` in Listing 25.4.

*25.15 (*Parent reference for BST*) Redefine `TreeNode` by adding a reference to a node's parent, as shown below:

BST.TreeNode<E>
#element: E
#left: TreeNode<E>
#right: TreeNode<E>
#parent: TreeNode<E>

Reimplement the `insert` and `delete` methods in the `BST` class to update the parent for each node in the tree. Add the following new method in `BST`:

```
/** Return the node for the specified element.
  * Return null if the element is not in the tree. */
private TreeNode<E> getNode(E element)

/** Return true if the node for the element is a leaf */
private boolean isLeaf(E element)

/** Return the path of elements from the specified element
  * to the root in an array list. */
public ArrayList<E> getPath(E e)
```

Write a test program that prompts the user to enter 10 integers, adds them to the tree, deletes the first integer from the tree, and displays the paths for all leaf nodes. Here is a sample run:

```
Enter 10 integers:  45 54 67 56 50 45 23 59 23 67  ⏎Enter
[50, 54, 23]
[59, 56, 67, 54, 23]
```

***25.16 (*Data compression: Huffman coding*) Write a program that prompts the user to enter a file name, then displays the frequency table of the characters in the file and the Huffman code for each character.

***25.17 (*Data compression: Huffman coding animation*) Write a program that enables the user to enter text and displays the Huffman coding tree based on the text, as shown in Figure 25.22a. Display the weight of the subtree inside the subtree's root circle. Display each leaf node's character. Display the encoded bits for the text in a label. When the user clicks the *Decode Text* button, a bit string is decoded into text displayed in the label, as shown in Figure 25.22b.

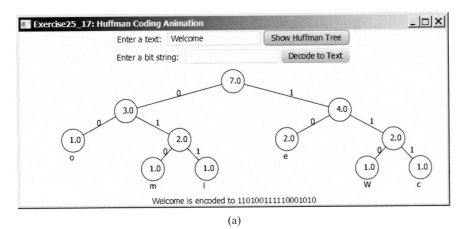

(a)

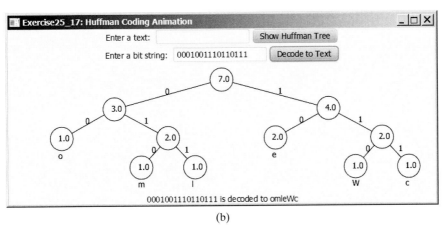

(b)

FIGURE 25.22 (a) The animation shows the coding tree for a given text string and the encoded bits for the text are displayed in the label; (b) You can enter a bit string to display its text in the label. *Source*: Copyright © 1995–2016 Oracle and/or its affiliates. All rights reserved. Used with permission.

***25.18** (*Compress a file*) Write a program that compresses a source file into a target file using the Huffman coding method. First, use `ObjectOutputStream` to output the Huffman codes into the target file, then use `BitOutputStream` in Programming Exercise 17.17 to output the encoded binary contents to the target file. Pass the files from the command line using the following command:

```
java Exercise25_18 sourcefile targetfile
```

***25.19** (*Decompress a file*) The preceding exercise compresses a file. The compressed file contains the Huffman codes and the compressed contents. Write a program that decompresses a source file into a target file using the following command:

```
java Exercise25_19 sourcefile targetfile
```

CHAPTER

26

ΛVL Trees

Objectives

■ To know what an AVL tree is (§26.1).

■ To understand how to rebalance a tree using the LL rotation, LR rotation, RR rotation, and RL rotation (§26.2).

■ To design the `AVLTree` class by extending the `BST` class (§26.3).

■ To insert elements into an AVL tree (§26.4).

■ To implement tree rebalancing (§26.5).

■ To delete elements from an AVL tree (§26.6).

■ To implement the `AVLTree` class (§26.7).

■ To test the `AVLTree` class (§26.8).

■ To analyze the complexity of search, insertion, and deletion operations in AVL trees (§26.9).

26.1 Introduction

AVL Tree is a balanced binary search tree.

perfectly balanced tree

well-balanced tree

AVL tree

$O(\log n)$

balance factor

balanced
left-heavy
right-heavy

Chapter 25 introduced binary search trees. The search, insertion, and deletion times for a binary tree depend on the height of the tree. In the worst case, the height is $O(n)$. If a tree is *perfectly balanced*—that is, a complete binary tree—its height is log n. Can we maintain a perfectly balanced tree? Yes, but doing so will be costly. The compromise is to maintain a *well-balanced tree*—that is, the heights of every node's two subtrees are about the same. This chapter introduces AVL trees. Web Chapters 40 and 41 will introduce 2–4 trees and red–black trees.

AVL trees are well balanced. AVL trees were invented in 1962 by two Russian computer scientists, G. M. Adelson-Velsky and E. M. Landis (hence the name *AVL*). In an AVL tree, the difference between the heights of every node's two subtrees is 0 or 1. It can be shown that the maximum height of an AVL tree is $O(\log n)$.

The process for inserting or deleting an element in an AVL tree is the same as in a binary search tree, except that you may have to rebalance the tree after an insertion or deletion operation. The *balance factor* of a node is the height of its right subtree minus the height of its left subtree. For example, the balance factor for the node 87 in Figure 26.1a is 0, for the node 67 is 1, and for the node 55 is −1. A node is said to be *balanced* if its balance factor is −1, 0, or 1. A node is considered *left-heavy* if its balance factor is −1 or less, and *right-heavy* if its balance factor is +1 or greater.

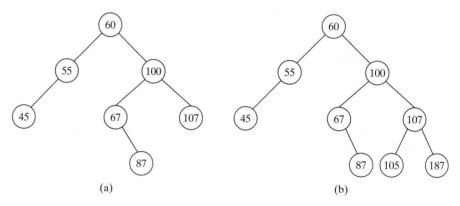

(a)   (b)

FIGURE 26.1 A balance factor determines whether a node is balanced.

AVL tree animation on Companion Website

Pedagogical Note

For an interactive GUI demo to see how an AVL tree works, go to liveexample .pearsoncmg.com/dsanimation/AVLTreeeBook.html, as shown in Figure 26.2.

26.2 Rebalancing Trees

After inserting or deleting an element from an AVL tree, if the tree becomes unbalanced, perform a rotation operation to rebalance the tree.

rotation
LL rotation
LL imbalance

RR rotation
RR imbalance

If a node is not balanced after an insertion or deletion operation, you need to rebalance it. The process of rebalancing a node is called *rotation*. There are four possible rotations: LL, RR, LR, and RL.

LL rotation: An *LL imbalance* occurs at a node A, such that A has a balance factor of −2 and a left child B with a balance factor of −1 or 0, as shown in Figure 26.3a. This type of imbalance can be fixed by performing a single right rotation at A, as shown in Figure 26.3b.

RR rotation: An *RR imbalance* occurs at a node A, such that A has a balance factor of +2 and a right child B with a balance factor of +1 or 0, as shown in Figure 26.4a. This type of imbalance can be fixed by performing a single left rotation at A, as shown in Figure 26.4b.

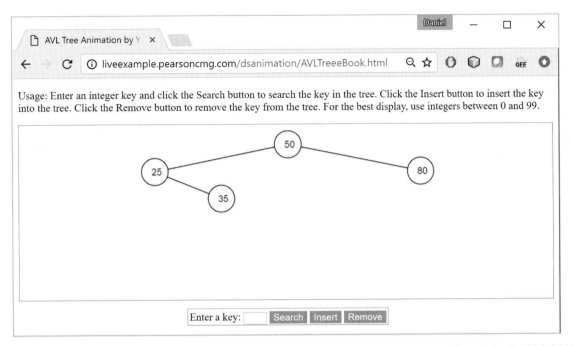

FIGURE 26.2 The animation tool enables you to insert, delete, and search elements. *Source*: Copyright © 1995–2016 Oracle and/or its affiliates. All rights reserved. Used with permission.

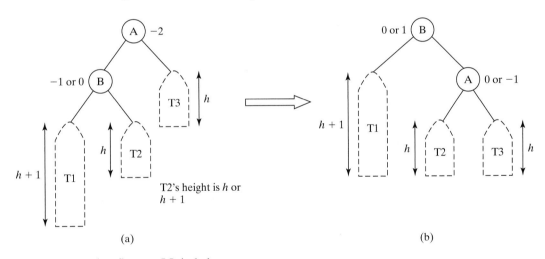

FIGURE 26.3 An LL rotation fixes an LL imbalance.

LR rotation: An *LR imbalance* occurs at a node A, such that A has a balance factor of −2 and a left child B with a balance factor of +1, as shown in Figure 26.5a. Assume B's right child is C. This type of imbalance can be fixed by performing a double rotation (first a single left rotation at B, then a single right rotation at A), as shown in Figure 26.5b.

LR rotation

LR imbalance

RL rotation: An *RL imbalance* occurs at a node A, such that A has a balance factor of +2 and a right child B with a balance factor of −1, as shown in Figure 26.6a. Assume B's left child is C. This type of imbalance can be fixed by performing a double rotation (first a single right rotation at B, then a single left rotation at A), as shown in Figure 26.6b.

RL rotation

RL imbalance

26.2.1 What is an AVL tree? Describe the following terms: balance factor, left-heavy, and right-heavy.

26.2.2 Show the balance factor of each node in the trees shown in Figure 26.1.

26.2.3 Describe LL rotation, RR rotation, LR rotation, and RL rotation for an AVL tree.

Check Point

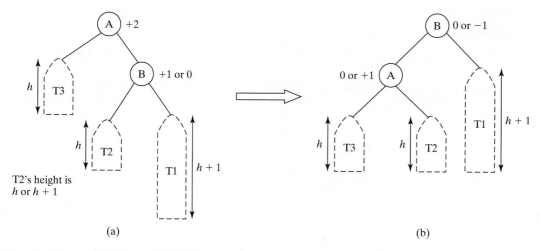

FIGURE 26.4 An RR rotation fixes an RR imbalance.

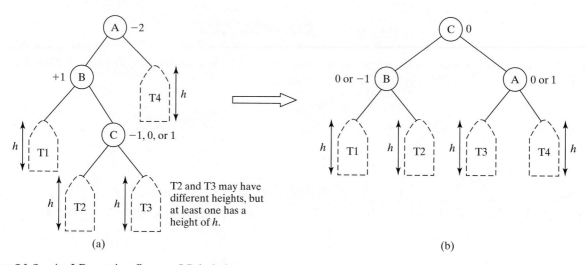

FIGURE 26.5 An LR rotation fixes an LR imbalance.

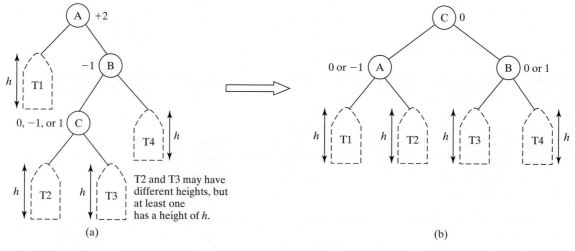

FIGURE 26.6 An RL rotation fixes an RL imbalance.

26.3 Designing Classes for AVL Trees

Since an AVL tree is a binary search tree, AVLTree *is designed as a subclass of* BST.

An AVL tree is a binary tree, so you can define the AVLTree class to extend the BST class, as shown in Figure 26.7. The BST and TreeNode classes were defined in Section 25.2.5.

Key
Point

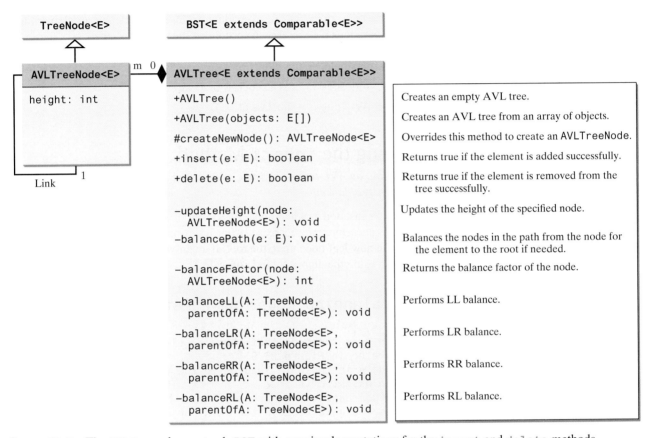

FIGURE 26.7 The AVLTree class extends BST with new implementations for the insert and delete methods.

In order to balance the tree, you need to know each node's height. For convenience, store the height of each node in AVLTreeNode and define AVLTreeNode to be a subclass of BST.TreeNode. Note that TreeNode is defined as a static inner class in BST. AVLTreeNode will be defined as a static inner class in AVLTree. TreeNode contains the data fields element, left, and right, which are inherited by AVLTreeNode. Thus, AVLTreeNode contains four data fields, as shown in Figure 26.8.

AVLTreeNode

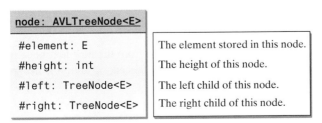

FIGURE 26.8 An AVLTreeNode contains the protected data fields element, height, left, and right.

createNewNode()

In the BST class, the createNewNode() method creates a TreeNode object. This method is overridden in the AVLTree class to create an AVLTreeNode. Note the return type of the createNewNode() method in the BST class is TreeNode, but the return type of the createNewNode() method in the AVLTree class is AVLTreeNode. This is fine, since AVLTreeNode is a subclass of TreeNode.

Searching for an element in an AVLTree is the same as searching in a binary search tree, so the search method defined in the BST class also works for AVLTree.

The insert and delete methods are overridden to insert and delete an element and perform rebalancing operations if necessary to ensure that the tree is balanced.

26.3.1 What are the data fields in the AVLTreeNode class?

26.3.2 True or false: AVLTreeNode is a subclass of TreeNode.

26.3.3 True or false: AVLTree is a subclass of BST.

26.4 Overriding the insert Method

Inserting an element into an AVL tree is the same as inserting it to a BST, except that the tree may need to be rebalanced.

A new element is always inserted as a leaf node. As a result of adding a new node, the heights of the new leaf node's ancestors may increase. After inserting a new node, check the nodes along the path from the new leaf node up to the root. If an unbalanced node is found, perform an appropriate rotation using the algorithm in Listing 26.1.

LISTING 26.1 Balancing Nodes on a Path

```
 1  balancePath(E e) {
 2    Get the path from the node that contains element e to the root,
 3      as illustrated in Figure 26.9;
 4    for each node A in the path leading to the root {
 5      Update the height of A;
 6      Let parentOfA denote the parent of A,
 7        which is the next node in the path, or null if A is the root;
 8
 9      switch (balanceFactor(A)) {
10        case -2:  if balanceFactor(A.left) == -1 or 0
11                    Perform LL rotation; // See Figure 26.3
12                  else
13                    Perform LR rotation; // See Figure 26.5
14                  break;
15        case +2:  if balanceFactor(A.right) == +1 or 0
16                    Perform RR rotation; // See Figure 26.4
17                  else
18                    Perform RL rotation; // See Figure 26.6
19      } // End of switch
20    } // End of for
21  } // End of method
```

get the path

update node height
get parent node

is balanced?

LL rotation

LR rotation

RR rotation

RL rotation

The algorithm considers each node in the path from the new leaf node to the root. Update the height of the node on the path. If a node is balanced, no action is needed. If a node is not balanced, perform an appropriate rotation.

26.4.1 For the AVL tree in Figure 26.1a, show the new AVL tree after adding element 40. What rotation do you perform in order to rebalance the tree? Which node was unbalanced?

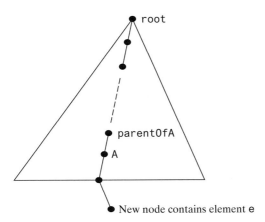

FIGURE 26.9 The nodes along the path from the new leaf node may become unbalanced.

26.4.2 For the AVL tree in Figure 26.1a, show the new AVL tree after adding element 50. What rotation do you perform in order to rebalance the tree? Which node was unbalanced?

26.4.3 For the AVL tree in Figure 26.1a, show the new AVL tree after adding element 80. What rotation do you perform in order to rebalance the tree? Which node was unbalanced?

26.4.4 For the AVL tree in Figure 26.1a, show the new AVL tree after adding element 89. What rotation do you perform in order to rebalance the tree? Which node was unbalanced?

26.5 Implementing Rotations

An unbalanced tree becomes balanced by performing an appropriate rotation operation.

Section 26.2, Rebalancing Trees, illustrated how to perform rotations at a node. Listing 26.2 gives the algorithm for the LL rotation, as illustrated in Figure 26.3.

LISTING 26.2 LL Rotation Algorithm

```
 1  balanceLL(TreeNode A, TreeNode parentOfA) {
 2    Let B be the left child of A.                                    left child of A
 3
 4    if (A is the root)                                               reconnect B's parent
 5      Let B be the new root
 6    else {
 7      if (A is a left child of parentOfA)
 8        Let B be a left child of parentOfA;
 9      else
10        Let B be a right child of parentOfA;
11    }
12
13    Make T2 the left subtree of A by assigning B.right to A.left;    move subtrees
14    Make A the right child of B by assigning A to B.right;
15    Update the height of node A and node B;                          adjust height
16  } // End of method
```

Note the height of nodes A and B can be changed, but the heights of other nodes in the tree are not changed. You can implement the RR, LR, and RL rotations in a similar manner.

26.5.1 Use Listing 26.2 as a template to describe the algorithms for implementing the RR, LR, and RL rotations.

Check Point

26.6 Implementing the `delete` Method

Deleting an element from an AVL tree is the same as deleting it from a BST, except that the tree may need to be rebalanced.

As discussed in Section 25.3, Deleting Elements from a BST, to delete an element from a binary tree, the algorithm first locates the node that contains the element. Let `current` point to the node that contains the element in the binary tree and `parent` point to the parent of the `current` node. The `current` node may be a left child or a right child of the `parent` node. Two cases arise when deleting an element.

Case 1: The `current` node does not have a left child, as shown in Figure 25.10a. To delete the `current` node, simply connect the `parent` node with the right child of the `current` node, as shown in Figure 25.10b.

The height of the nodes along the path from the `parent` node up to the `root` may have decreased. To ensure that the tree is balanced, invoke

```
balancePath(parent.element); // Defined in Listing 26.1
```

Case 2: The `current` node has a left child. Let `rightMost` point to the node that contains the largest element in the left subtree of the `current` node and `parentOfRightMost` point to the parent node of the `rightMost` node, as shown in Figure 25.12a. The `rightMost` node cannot have a right child, but may have a left child. Replace the element value in the `current` node with the one in the `rightMost` node, connect the `parentOfRightMost` node with the left child of the `rightMost` node, and delete the `rightMost` node, as shown in Figure 25.12b.

The height of the nodes along the path from `parentOfRightMost` up to the root may have decreased. To ensure the tree is balanced, invoke

```
balancePath(parentOfRightMost); // Defined in Listing 26.1
```

26.6.1 For the AVL tree in Figure 26.1a, show the new AVL tree after deleting element 107. What rotation do you perform in order to rebalance the tree? Which node was unbalanced?

26.6.2 For the AVL tree in Figure 26.1a, show the new AVL tree after deleting element 60. What rotation do you perform in order to rebalance the tree? Which node was unbalanced?

26.6.3 For the AVL tree in Figure 26.1a, show the new AVL tree after deleting element 55. What rotation did you perform in order to rebalance the tree? Which node was unbalanced?

26.6.4 For the AVL tree in Figure 26.1b, show the new AVL tree after deleting elements 67 and 87. What rotation did you perform in order to rebalance the tree? Which node was unbalanced?

26.7 The `AVLTree` Class

The AVLTree class extends the BST class to override the insert and delete methods to rebalance the tree if necessary.

Listing 26.3 gives the complete source code for the `AVLTree` class.

LISTING 26.3 `AVLTree.java`

```
1  public class AVLTree<E extends Comparable<E>> extends BST<E> {
2    /** Create an empty AVL tree */
3    public AVLTree() {
```

no-arg constructor

```
4    }
5
6    /** Create an AVL tree from an array of objects */
7    public AVLTree(E[] objects) {                                    constructor
8      super(objects);
9    }
10
11   @Override /** Override createNewNode to create an AVLTreeNode */
12   protected AVLTreeNode<E> createNewNode(E e) {                    create AVL tree node
13     return new AVLTreeNode<E>(e);
14   }
15
16   @Override /** Insert an element and rebalance if necessary */
17   public boolean insert(E e) {                                    override insert
18     boolean successful = super.insert(e);
19     if (!successful)
20       return false; // e is already in the tree
21     else {
22       balancePath(e); // Balance from e to the root if necessary  balance tree
23     }
24
25     return true; // e is inserted
26   }
27
28   /** Update the height of a specified node */
29   private void updateHeight(AVLTreeNode<E> node) {                update node height
30     if (node.left == null && node.right == null) // node is a leaf
31       node.height = 0;
32     else if (node.left == null)  // node has no left subtree
33       node.height = 1 + ((AVLTreeNode<E>)(node.right)).height;
34     else if (node.right == null)   // node has no right subtree
35       node.height = 1 + ((AVLTreeNode<E>)(node.left)).height;
36     else
37       node.height = 1 +
38         Math.max(((AVLTreeNode<E>)(node.right)).height,
39         ((AVLTreeNode<E>)(node.left)).height);
40   }
41
42   /** Balance the nodes in the path from the specified
43    * node to the root if necessary
44    */
45   private void balancePath(E e) {                                 balance nodes
46     java.util.ArrayList<TreeNode<E>> path = path(e);              get path
47     for (int i = path.size() - 1; i >= 0; i--) {
48       AVLTreeNode<E> A = (AVLTreeNode<E>)(path.get(i));           consider a node
49       updateHeight(A);                                           update height
50       AVLTreeNode<E> parentOfA = (A == root) ? null :            get height
51         (AVLTreeNode<E>)(path.get(i - 1));
52
53       switch (balanceFactor(A)) {
54         case -2:                                                left-heavy
55           if (balanceFactor((AVLTreeNode<E>)A.left) <= 0) {
56             balanceLL(A, parentOfA); // Perform LL rotation       LL rotation
57           }
58           else {
59             balanceLR(A, parentOfA); // Perform LR rotation       LR rotation
60           }
61           break;
```

right-heavy

RR rotation

RL rotation

get balance factor

LL rotation

update height

LR rotation

```
62        case +2:
63          if (balanceFactor((AVLTreeNode<E>)A.right) >= 0) {
64            balanceRR(A, parentOfA); // Perform RR rotation
65          }
66          else {
67            balanceRL(A, parentOfA); // Perform RL rotation
68          }
69        }
70      }
71    }
72
73    /** Return the balance factor of the node */
74    private int balanceFactor(AVLTreeNode<E> node) {
75      if (node.right == null)  // node has no right subtree
76        return -node.height;
77      else if (node.left == null)  // node has no left subtree
78        return +node.height;
79      else
80        return ((AVLTreeNode<E>)node.right).height -
81          ((AVLTreeNode<E>)node.left).height;
82    }
83
84    /** Balance LL (see Figure 26.3) */
85    private void balanceLL(TreeNode<E> A, TreeNode<E> parentOfA) {
86      TreeNode<E> B = A.left; // A is left-heavy and B is left-heavy
87
88      if (A == root) {
89        root = B;
90      }
91      else {
92        if (parentOfA.left == A) {
93          parentOfA.left = B;
94        }
95        else {
96          parentOfA.right = B;
97        }
98      }
99
100     A.left = B.right; // Make T2 the left subtree of A
101     B.right = A; // Make A the left child of B
102     updateHeight((AVLTreeNode<E>)A);
103     updateHeight((AVLTreeNode<E>)B);
104   }
105
106   /** Balance LR (see Figure 26.5) */
107   private void balanceLR(TreeNode<E> A, TreeNode<E> parentOfA) {
108     TreeNode<E> B = A.left; // A is left-heavy
109     TreeNode<E> C = B.right; // B is right-heavy
110
111     if (A == root) {
112       root = C;
113     }
114     else {
115       if (parentOfA.left == A) {
116         parentOfA.left = C;
117       }
118       else {
119         parentOfA.right = C;
```

```
120          }
121       }
122
123     A.left = C.right; // Make T3 the left subtree of A
124     B.right = C.left; // Make T2 the right subtree of B
125     C.left = B;
126     C.right = A;
127
128     // Adjust heights
129     updateHeight((AVLTreeNode<E>)A);                              update height
130     updateHeight((AVLTreeNode<E>)B);
131     updateHeight((AVLTreeNode<E>)C);
132   }
133
134   /** Balance RR (see Figure 26.4) */
135   private void balanceRR(TreeNode<E> A, TreeNode<E> parentOfA) {   RR rotation
136     TreeNode<E> B = A.right; // A is right-heavy and B is right-heavy
137
138     if (A == root) {
139       root = B;
140     }
141     else {
142       if (parentOfA.left == A) {
143         parentOfA.left = B;
144       }
145       else {
146         parentOfA.right = B;
147       }
148     }
149
150     A.right = B.left; // Make T2 the right subtree of A
151     B.left = A;
152     updateHeight((AVLTreeNode<E>)A);                              update height
153     updateHeight((AVLTreeNode<E>)B);
154   }
155
156   /** Balance RL (see Figure 26.6) */
157   private void balanceRL(TreeNode<E> A, TreeNode<E> parentOfA) {   RL rotation
158     TreeNode<E> B = A.right; // A is right-heavy
159     TreeNode<E> C = B.left; // B is left-heavy
160
161     if (A == root) {
162       root = C;
163     }
164     else {
165       if (parentOfA.left == A) {
166         parentOfA.left = C;
167       }
168       else {
169         parentOfA.right = C;
170       }
171     }
172
173     A.right = C.left; // Make T2 the right subtree of A
174     B.left = C.right; // Make T3 the left subtree of B
175     C.left = A;
176     C.right = B;
177
```

update height

override delete

balance nodes

```
178      // Adjust heights
179      updateHeight((AVLTreeNode<E>)A);
180      updateHeight((AVLTreeNode<E>)B);
181      updateHeight((AVLTreeNode<E>)C);
182    }
183
184    @Override /** Delete an element from the AVL tree.
185     * Return true if the element is deleted successfully
186     * Return false if the element is not in the tree */
187    public boolean delete(E element) {
188      if (root == null)
189        return false; // Element is not in the tree
190
191      // Locate the node to be deleted and also locate its parent node
192      TreeNode<E> parent = null;
193      TreeNode<E> current = root;
194      while (current != null) {
195        if (element.compareTo(current.element) < 0) {
196          parent = current;
197          current = current.left;
198        }
199        else if (element.compareTo(current.element) > 0) {
200          parent = current;
201          current = current.right;
202        }
203        else
204          break; // Element is in the tree pointed by current
205      }
206
207      if (current == null)
208        return false; // Element is not in the tree
209
210      // Case 1: current has no left children (see Figure 25.10)
211      if (current.left == null) {
212        // Connect the parent with the right child of the current node
213        if (parent == null) {
214          root = current.right;
215        }
216        else {
217          if (element.compareTo(parent.element) < 0)
218            parent.left = current.right;
219          else
220            parent.right = current.right;
221
222          // Balance the tree if necessary
223          balancePath(parent.element);
224        }
225      }
226      else {
227        // Case 2: The current node has a left child
228        // Locate the rightmost node in the left subtree of
229        // the current node and also its parent
230        TreeNode<E> parentOfRightMost = current;
231        TreeNode<E> rightMost = current.left;
232
233        while (rightMost.right != null) {
234          parentOfRightMost = rightMost;
235          rightMost = rightMost.right; // Keep going to the right
236        }
```

```
237
238        // Replace the element in current by the element in rightMost
239        current.element = rightMost.element;
240
241        // Eliminate rightmost node
242        if (parentOfRightMost.right == rightMost)
243          parentOfRightMost.right = rightMost.left;
244        else
245          // Special case: parentOfRightMost is current
246          parentOfRightMost.left = rightMost.left;
247
248        // Balance the tree if necessary
249        balancePath(parentOfRightMost.element);                    balance nodes
250      }
251
252    size--;
253    return true; // Element inserted
254    }
255
256    /** AVLTreeNode is TreeNode plus height */
257    protected static class AVLTreeNode<E> extends BST.TreeNode<E> {    inner AVLTreeNode class
258      protected int height = 0; // New data field
259                                                                      node height
260      public AVLTreeNode(E e) {
261        super(e);
262      }
263    }
264  }
```

The AVLTree class extends BST. Like the BST class, the AVLTree class has a no-arg constructor that constructs an empty AVLTree (lines 3 and 4) and a constructor that creates an initial AVLTree from an array of elements (lines 7–9). *(constructors)*

The createNewNode() method defined in the BST class creates a TreeNode. This method is overridden to return an AVLTreeNode (lines 12–14).

The insert method in AVLTree is overridden in lines 17–26. The method first invokes the insert method in BST, then invokes balancePath(e) (line 22) to ensure that the tree is balanced. *(insert)*

The balancePath method first gets the nodes on the path from the node that contains element e to the root (line 46). For each node in the path, update its height (line 49), check its balance factor (line 53), and perform appropriate rotations if necessary (lines 53–69). *(balancePath)*

Four methods for performing rotations are defined in lines 85–182. Each method is invoked with two TreeNode arguments—A and parentOfA—to perform an appropriate rotation at node A. How each rotation is performed is illustrated in Figures 26.3–26.6. After the rotation, the heights of nodes A, B, and C are updated (lines 102, 129, 152, and 179). *(rotations)*

The delete method in AVLTree is overridden in lines 187–254. The method is the same as the one implemented in the BST class, except that you have to rebalance the nodes after deletion in two cases (lines 223, 249). *(delete)*

Check Point

26.7.1 Why is the createNewNode method defined protected? When is it invoked?

26.7.2 When is the updateHeight method invoked? When is the balanceFactor method invoked? When is the balancePath method invoked? Will the program work if you replace the break in line 61 in the AVLTree class with a return and add a return at line 69?

26.7.3 What are data fields in the AVLTree class?

26.7.4 In the insert and delete methods, once you have performed a rotation to balance a node in the tree, is it possible there are still unbalanced nodes?

26.8 Testing the `AVLTree` Class

Key Point

This section gives an example of using the AVLTree class.

Listing 26.4 gives a test program. The program creates an `AVLTree` initialized with an array of the integers 25, 20, and 5 (lines 4 and 5), inserts elements in lines 9–18, and deletes elements in lines 22–28. Since `AVLTree` is a subclass of `BST` and the elements in a `BST` are iterable, the program uses a foreach loop to traverse all the elements in lines 33–35.

LISTING 26.4 TestAVLTree.java

create an AVLTree

insert 34
insert 50

insert 30

insert 10

delete 34
delete 30
delete 50

delete 5

foreach loop

```
1   public class TestAVLTree {
2     public static void main(String[] args) {
3       // Create an AVL tree
4       AVLTree<Integer> tree = new AVLTree<Integer>(new Integer[]{25,
5         20, 5});
6       System.out.print("After inserting 25, 20, 5:");
7       printTree(tree);
8
9       tree.insert(34);
10      tree.insert(50);
11      System.out.print("\nAfter inserting 34, 50:");
12      printTree(tree);
13
14      tree.insert(30);
15      System.out.print("\nAfter inserting 30");
16      printTree(tree);
17
18      tree.insert(10);
19      System.out.print("\nAfter inserting 10");
20      printTree(tree);
21
22      tree.delete(34);
23      tree.delete(30);
24      tree.delete(50);
25      System.out.print("\nAfter removing 34, 30, 50:");
26      printTree(tree);
27
28      tree.delete(5);
29      System.out.print("\nAfter removing 5:");
30      printTree(tree);
31
32      System.out.print("\nTraverse the elements in the tree: ");
33      for (int e: tree) {
34        System.out.print(e + " ");
35      }
36    }
37
38    public static void printTree(BST tree) {
39      // Traverse tree
40      System.out.print("\nInorder (sorted): ");
41      tree.inorder();
42      System.out.print("\nPostorder: ");
43      tree.postorder();
44      System.out.print("\nPreorder: ");
45      tree.preorder();
46      System.out.print("\nThe number of nodes is " + tree.getSize());
```

```
47        System.out.println();
48    }
49 }
```

```
After inserting 25, 20, 5:
Inorder (sorted): 5 20 25
Postorder: 5 25 20
Preorder: 20 5 25
The number of nodes is 3

After inserting 34, 50:
Inorder (sorted): 5 20 25 34 50
Postorder: 5 25 50 34 20
Preorder: 20 5 34 25 50
The number of nodes is 5

After inserting 30
Inorder (sorted): 5 20 25 30 34 50
Postorder: 5 20 30 50 34 25
Preorder: 25 20 5 34 30 50
The number of nodes is 6

After inserting 10
Inorder (sorted): 5 10 20 25 30 34 50
Postorder: 5 20 10 30 50 34 25
Preorder: 25 10 5 20 34 30 50
The number of nodes is 7

After removing 34, 30, 50:
Inorder (sorted): 5 10 20 25
Postorder: 5 20 25 10
Preorder: 10 5 25 20
The number of nodes is 4

After removing 5:
Inorder (sorted): 10 20 25
Postorder: 10 25 20
Preorder: 20 10 25
The number of nodes is 3
Traverse the elements in the tree: 10 20 25
```

Figure 26.10 shows how the tree evolves as elements are added to the tree. After 25 and 20 are added, the tree is as shown in Figure 26.10a. 5 is inserted as a left child of 20, as shown in Figure 26.10b. The tree is not balanced. It is left-heavy at node 25. Perform an LL rotation to result in an AVL tree as shown in Figure 26.10c.

After inserting 34, the tree is as shown in Figure 26.10d. After inserting 50, the tree is as shown in Figure 26.10e. The tree is not balanced. It is right-heavy at node 25. Perform an RR rotation to result in an AVL tree as shown in Figure 26.10f.

After inserting 30, the tree is as shown in Figure 26.10g. The tree is not balanced. Perform an RL rotation to result in an AVL tree as shown in Figure 26.10h.

After inserting 10, the tree is as shown in Figure 26.10i. The tree is not balanced. Perform an LR rotation to result in an AVL tree as shown in Figure 26.10j.

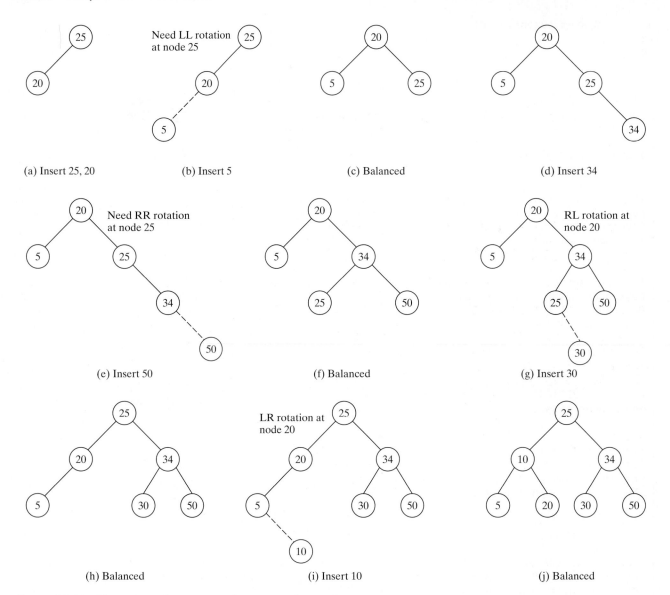

(a) Insert 25, 20   (b) Insert 5   (c) Balanced   (d) Insert 34

(e) Insert 50   (f) Balanced   (g) Insert 30

(h) Balanced   (i) Insert 10   (j) Balanced

FIGURE 26.10 The tree evolves as new elements are inserted.

Figure 26.11a shows how the tree evolves as elements are deleted. After deleting 34, 30, and 50, the tree is as shown in Figure 26.11b. The tree is not balanced. Perform an LL rotation to result in an AVL tree as shown in Figure 26.11c.

After deleting 5, the tree is as shown in Figure 26.11d. The tree is not balanced. Perform an RL rotation to result in an AVL tree as shown in Figure 26.11e.

26.8.1 Show the change of an AVL tree when inserting 1, 2, 3, 4, 10, 9, 7, 5, 8, 6 into the tree, in this order.

26.8.2 For the tree built in the preceding question, show its change after 1, 2, 3, 4, 10, 9, 7, 5, 8, 6 are deleted from the tree in this order.

26.8.3 Can you traverse the elements in an AVL tree using a foreach loop?

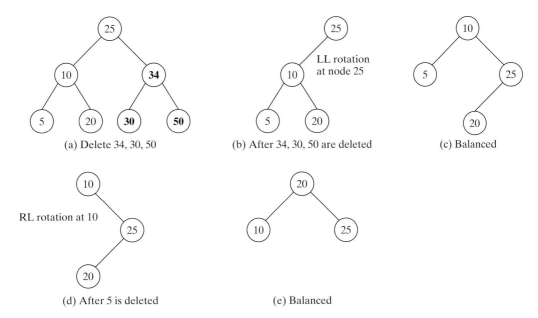

(a) Delete 34, 30, 50   (b) After 34, 30, 50 are deleted   (c) Balanced

(d) After 5 is deleted   (e) Balanced

FIGURE 26.11   The tree evolves as elements are deleted from the tree.

26.9 AVL Tree Time Complexity Analysis

Since the height of an AVL tree is O(log n), the time complexity of the `search`, `insert`, *and* `delete` *methods in* `AVLTree` *is O(log n).*

Key Point

The time complexity of the `search`, `insert`, and `delete` methods in `AVLTree` depends on the height of the tree. We can prove that the height of the tree is $O(\log n)$.

tree height

    Let $G(h)$ denote the minimum number of nodes in an AVL tree with height h. Obviously, $G(1)$ is 1 and $G(2)$ is 2. The minimum number of nodes in an AVL tree with height $h \geq 3$ must have two minimum subtrees: one with height $h - 1$ and the other with height $h - 2$. Thus,

$$G(h) = G(h - 1) + G(h - 2) + 1$$

Recall that a Fibonacci number at index i can be described using the recurrence relation $F(i) = F(i - 1) + F(i - 2)$. Therefore, the function $G(h)$ is essentially the same as $F(i)$. It can be proven that

$$h < 1.4405 \log(n + 2) - 1.3277$$

where n is the number of nodes in the tree. Hence, the height of an AVL tree is $O(\log n)$.

    The `search`, `insert`, and `delete` methods involve only the nodes along a path in the tree. The `updateHeight` and `balanceFactor` methods are executed in a constant time for each node in the path. The `balancePath` method is executed in a constant time for a node in the path. Thus, the time complexity for the `search`, `insert`, and `delete` methods is $O(\log n)$.

26.9.1   What is the maximum/minimum height for an AVL tree of 3 nodes, 5 nodes, and 7 nodes?

Check Point

26.9.2   If an AVL tree has a height of 3, what maximum number of nodes can the tree have? What minimum number of nodes can the tree have?

26.9.3   If an AVL tree has a height of 4, what maximum number of nodes can the tree have? What minimum number of nodes can the tree have?

KEY TERMS

AVL tree 990	right-heavy 990
balance factor 990	RL rotation 991
left-heavy 990	rotation 990
LL rotation 990	RR rotation 990
LR rotation 991	well-balanced tree 990
perfectly balanced tree 990	

CHAPTER SUMMARY

1. An *AVL tree* is a *well-balanced* binary tree. In an AVL tree, the difference between the heights of two subtrees for every node is 0 or 1.

2. The process for inserting or deleting an element in an AVL tree is the same as in a binary search tree. The difference is that you may have to rebalance the tree after an insertion or deletion operation.

3. Imbalances in the tree caused by insertions and deletions are rebalanced through subtree rotations at the node of the imbalance.

4. The process of rebalancing a node is called a *rotation*. There are four possible rotations: *LL rotation*, *LR rotation*, *RR rotation*, and *RL rotation*.

5. The height of an AVL tree is $O(\log n)$. Therefore, the time complexities for the `search`, `insert`, and `delete` methods are $O(\log n)$.

QUIZ

Answer the quiz for this chapter online at the book Companion Website.

MyProgrammingLab™ ## PROGRAMMING EXERCISES

*26.1   (*Display AVL tree graphically*) Write a program that displays an AVL tree along with its balance factor for each node.

26.2   (*Compare performance*) Write a test program that randomly generates 500,000 numbers and inserts them into a `BST`, reshuffles the 500,000 numbers and performs a search, and reshuffles the numbers again before deleting them from the tree. Write another test program that does the same thing for an `AVLTree`. Compare the execution times of these two programs.

***26.3   (*AVL tree animation*) Write a program that animates the AVL tree `insert`, `delete`, and `search` methods, as shown in Figure 26.2.

**26.4   (*Parent reference for BST*) Suppose the `TreeNode` class defined in `BST` contains a reference to the node's parent, as shown in Programming Exercise 25.15. Implement the `AVLTree` class to support this change. Write a test program that adds numbers 1, 2, . . . , 100 to the tree and displays the paths for all leaf nodes.

**26.5   (*The kth smallest element*) You can find the kth smallest element in a BST in $O(n)$ time from an inorder iterator. For an AVL tree, you can find it in $O(\log n)$ time. To achieve this, add a new data field named `size` in `AVLTreeNode` to store the number of nodes in the subtree rooted at this node. Note the size of a node *v* is one more than the sum of the sizes of its two children. Figure 26.12 shows an AVL tree and the `size` value for each node in the tree.

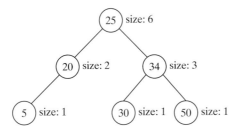

FIGURE 26.12 The `size` data field in `AVLTreeNode` stores the number of nodes in the subtree rooted at the node:

In the `AVLTree` class, add the following method to return the *k*th smallest element in the tree:

```
public E find(int k)
```

The method returns `null` if `k < 1` or `k > the size of the tree`. This method can be implemented using the recursive method `find(k, root)`, which returns the *k*th smallest element in the tree with the specified root. Let `A` and `B` be the left and right children of the root, respectively. Assuming the tree is not empty and $k \le root.size$, `find(k, root)` can be recursively defined as follows:

$$
find(k, root) = \begin{cases}
root.element, & \text{if } A \text{ is null and } k \text{ is 1;} \\
B.element, & \text{if } A \text{ is null and } k \text{ is 2;} \\
find(k, A), & \text{if } k <= A.size; \\
root.element, & \text{if } k = A.size + 1; \\
find(k - A.size - 1, B), & \text{if } k > A.size + 1;
\end{cases}
$$

Modify the `insert` and `delete` methods in `AVLTree` to set the correct value for the `size` property in each node. The `insert` and `delete` methods will still be in $O(\log n)$ time. The `find(k)` method can be implemented in $O(\log n)$ time. Therefore, you can find the *k*th smallest element in an AVL tree in $O(\log n)$ time.

Test your program using the code at

liveexample.pearsoncmg.com/test/Exercise26_05Test.txt.

**26.6 (*Test* `AVLTree`) Design and write a complete test program to test if the `AVLTree` class in Listing 26.3 meets all requirements.

HASHING

Objectives

- To understand what hashing is and for what hashing is used (§27.2).
- To obtain the hash code for an object and design the hash function to map a key to an index (§27.3).
- To handle collisions using open addressing (§27.4).
- To know the differences among linear probing, quadratic probing, and double hashing (§27.4).
- To handle collisions using separate chaining (§27.5).
- To understand the load factor and the need for rehashing (§27.6).
- To implement `MyHashMap` using hashing (§27.7).
- To implement `MyHashSet` using hashing (§27.8).

27.1 Introduction

Hashing is superefficient. It takes O(1) time to search, insert, and delete an element using hashing.

why hashing?

The preceding chapter introduced binary search trees. An element can be found in $O(\log n)$ time in a well-balanced search tree. Is there a more efficient way to search for an element in a container? This chapter introduces a technique called *hashing*. You can use hashing to implement a map or a set to search, insert, and delete an element in $O(1)$ time.

27.2 What Is Hashing?

Hashing uses a hashing function to map a key to an index.

map
key
value

Before introducing hashing, let us review map, which is a data structure that is implemented using hashing. Recall that a *map* (introduced in Section 21.5) is a container object that stores entries. Each entry contains two parts: a *key* and a *value*. The key, also called a *search key*, is used to search for the corresponding value. For example, a dictionary can be stored in a map, in which the words are the keys and the definitions of the words are the values.

Note

dictionary
hash table
associative array

A map is also called a *dictionary*, a *hash table*, or an *associative array*.

The Java Collections Framework defines the `java.util.Map` interface for modeling maps. Three concrete implementations are `java.util.HashMap`, `java.util.LinkedHashMap`, and `java.util.TreeMap`. `java.util.HashMap` is implemented using hashing, `java.util.LinkedHashMap` using `LinkedList`, and `java.util.TreeMap` using red–black trees. (Bonus Chapter 41 will introduce red–black trees.) You will learn the concept of hashing and use it to implement a hash map in this chapter.

If you know the index of an element in the array, you can retrieve the element using the index in $O(1)$ time. So does that mean we can store the values in an array and use the key as the index to find the value? The answer is yes—if you can map a key to an index. The array that stores the values is called a *hash table*. The function that maps a key to an index in the hash table is called a *hash function*. As shown in Figure 27.1, a hash function obtains an index from a key and uses the index to retrieve the value for the key. *Hashing* is a technique that retrieves the value using the index obtained from the key without performing a search.

hash table
hash function
hashing

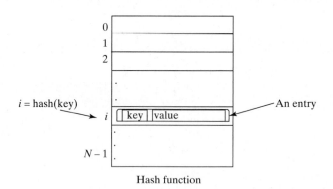

FIGURE 27.1 A hash function maps a key to an index in the hash table.

How do you design a hash function that produces an index from a key? Ideally, we would like to design a function that maps each search key to a different index in the hash table. Such a function is called a *perfect hash function*. However, it is difficult to find a perfect hash

perfect hash function

function. When two or more keys are mapped to the same hash value, we say a *collision* has occurred. Although there are ways to deal with collisions, which will be are discussed later in this chapter, it is better to avoid collisions in the first place. Thus, you should design a fast and easy-to-compute hash function that minimizes collisions.

collision

27.2.1 What is a hash function? What is a perfect hash function? What is a collision?

27.3 Hash Functions and Hash Codes

A typical hash function first converts a search key to an integer value called a hash code, then compresses the hash code into an index to the hash table.

Java's root class `Object` has the `hashCode` method, which returns an integer *hash code*. By default, the method returns the memory address for the object. The general contract for the `hashCode` method is as follows:

hash code
hashCode()

1. You should override the `hashCode` method whenever the `equals` method is overridden to ensure two equal objects return the same hash code.

2. During the execution of a program, invoking the `hashCode` method multiple times returns the same integer, provided that the object's data are not changed.

3. Two unequal objects may have the same hash code, but you should implement the `hashCode` method to avoid too many such cases.

27.3.1 Hash Codes for Primitive Types

For search keys of the type `byte`, `short`, `int`, and `char`, simply cast them to `int`. Therefore, two different search keys of any one of these types will have different hash codes.

byte, short, int, char

For a search key of the type `float`, use `Float.floatToIntBits(key)` as the hash code. Note `floatToIntBits(float f)` returns an `int` value whose bit representation is the same as the bit representation for the floating number `f`. Thus, two different search keys of the `float` type will have different hash codes.

float

For a search key of the type `long`, simply casting it to `int` would not be a good choice, because all keys that differ in only the first 32 bits will have the same hash code. To take the first 32 bits into consideration, divide the 64 bits into two halves and perform the exclusive-or operation to combine the two halves. This process is called *folding*. The hash code for a `long` key is

long

folding

```
int hashCode = (int)(key ^ (key >> 32));
```

Note `>>` is the right-shift operator that shifts the bits 32 positions to the right. For example, `1010110 >> 2` yields `0010101`. The `^` is the bitwise exclusive-or operator. It operates on two corresponding bits of the binary operands. For example, `1010110 ^ 0110111` yields `1100001`. For more on bitwise operations, see Appendix G, Bitwise Operations.

For a search key of the type `double`, first convert it to a `long` value using the `Double.doubleToLongBits` method, then perform a folding as follows:

double
folding

```
long bits = Double.doubleToLongBits(key);
int hashCode = (int)(bits ^ (bits >> 32));
```

27.3.2 Hash Codes for Strings

Search keys are often strings, so it is important to design a good hash function for strings. An intuitive approach is to sum the Unicode of all characters as the hash code for the string. This approach may work if two search keys in an application don't contain the same letters, but it will produce a lot of collisions if the search keys contain the same letters, such as `tod` and `dot`.

A better approach is to generate a hash code that takes the position of characters into consideration. Specifically, let the hash code be

$$s_0 * b^{(n-1)} + s_1 * b^{(n-2)} + \cdots + s_{n-1}$$

polynomial hash code

where s_i is `s.charAt(i)`. This expression is a polynomial for some positive b, so this is called a *polynomial hash code*. Using Horner's rule for polynomial evaluation (see Section 6.7), the hash code can be calculated efficiently as follows:

$$(\cdots ((s_0 * b + s_1) * b + s_2) * b + \cdots + s_{n-2}) * b + s_{n-1}$$

This computation can cause an overflow for long strings, but arithmetic overflow is ignored in Java. You should choose an appropriate value b to minimize collisions. Experiments show that good choices for b are 31, 33, 37, 39, and 41. In the `String` class, the `hashCode` is overridden using the polynomial hash code with b being 31.

27.3.3 Compressing Hash Codes

The hash code for a key can be a large integer that is out of the range for the hash-table index, so you need to scale it down to fit in the index's range. Assume the index for a hash table is between 0 and N-1. The most common way to scale an integer to between 0 and N-1 is to use

```
index = hashCode % N;
```

Ideally, you should choose a prime number for N to ensure the indices are spread evenly. However, it is time consuming to find a large prime number. In the Java API implementation for `java.util.HashMap`, N is set to an integer power of 2. There is a good reason for this choice. When N is an integer power of 2, you can use the & operator to compress a hash code to an index on the hash table as follows:

```
index = hashCode & (N - 1);
```

`index` will be between 0 and N - 1. The ampersand, &, is a bitwise AND operator (see Appendix G, Bitwise Operations). The AND of two corresponding bits yields a 1 if both bits are 1. For example, assume N = 4 and hashCode = 11. Thus, 11 & (4 - 1) = 1011 & 0011 = 0011.

To ensure the hashing is evenly distributed, a supplemental hash function is also used along with the primary hash function in the implementation of `java.util.HashMap`. This function is defined as:

```
private static int supplementalHash(int h) {
  h ^= (h >>> 20) ^ (h >>> 12);
  return h ^ (h >>> 7) ^ (h >>> 4);
}
```

`>>>` is unsigned right-shift operations (also introduced in Appendix G). The bitwise operations are much faster than the multiplication, division, and remainder operations. You should replace these operations with the bitwise operations whenever possible.

The complete hash function is defined as:

```
h(hashCode) = supplementalHash(hashCode) & (N - 1)
```

The supplemental hash function helps avoid collisions for two numbers with the same lower bits. For example, both 11100101 & 00000111 and 11001101 & 00000111 yield 00000111. But supplementalHash(11100101) & 00000111 and supplemental-Hash(11001101) & 00000111 will be different. Using a supplemental function reduces this type of collision.

Note
In Java, an `int` is a 32-bit signed integer. The `hashCode()` method returns an `int` and it may be negative. If a hash code is negative, `hashCode % N` would be negative. But `hashCode & (N - 1)` will be non-negative because the maximum hash-table size in Java is limited to 2^{30}, which is positive in a 32-bit `int`. `anyInt & aNonNegativeInt` will always be non-negative.

27.3.1 What is a hash code? What is the hash code for `Byte`, `Short`, `Integer`, and `Character`?
27.3.2 How is the hash code for a `Float` object computed?
27.3.3 How is the hash code for a `Long` object computed?
27.3.4 How is the hash code for a `Double` object computed?
27.3.5 How is the hash code for a `String` object computed?
27.3.6 How is a hash code compressed to an integer representing the index in a hash table?
27.3.7 If `N` is an integer power of the power of `2`, is `N / 2` same as `N >> 1`?
27.3.8 If `N` is an integer power of the power of `2`, is `m % N` same as `m & (N - 1)` for a positive integer `m`?
27.3.9 What is `new Integer("-98").hashCode()` and what is `"ABCDEFGHIJK."` `hashCode()`?

Check Point

27.4 Handling Collisions Using Open Addressing

A collision occurs when two keys are mapped to the same index in a hash table. Generally, there are two ways for handling collisions: open addressing and separate chaining.

Open addressing is the process of finding an open location in the hash table in the event of a collision. Open addressing has several variations: *linear probing*, *quadratic probing*, and *double hashing*.

open addressing

27.4.1 Linear Probing

When a collision occurs during the insertion of an entry to a hash table, *linear probing* finds the next available location sequentially. For example, if a collision occurs at `hashTable[k % N]`, check whether `hashTable[(k+1) % N]` is available. If not, check `hashTable[(k+2) % N]` and so on, until an available cell is found, as shown in Figure 27.2.

add entry
linear probing

Note
When probing reaches the end of the table, it goes back to the beginning of the table. Thus, the hash table is treated as if it were circular.

circular hash table

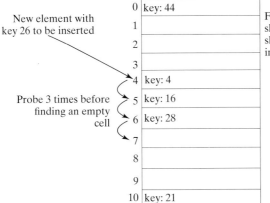

FIGURE 27.2 Linear probing finds the next available location sequentially.

search entry

To search for an entry in the hash table, obtain the index, say `k`, from the hash function for the key. Check whether `hashTable[k % N]` contains the entry. If not, check whether `hashTable[(k+1) % N]` contains the entry, and so on, until it is found, or an empty cell is reached.

remove entry

To remove an entry from the hash table, search the entry that matches the key. If the entry is found, place a special marker to denote that the entry is available. Each cell in the hash table has three possible states: occupied, marked, or empty. Note a marked cell is also available for insertion.

cluster

Linear probing tends to cause groups of consecutive cells in the hash table to be occupied. Each group is called a *cluster*. Each cluster is actually a probe sequence that you must search when retrieving, adding, or removing an entry. As clusters grow in size, they may merge into even larger clusters, further slowing down the search time. This is a big disadvantage of linear probing.

linear probing animation on Companion Website

 Pedagogical Note

For an interactive GUI demo to see how linear probing works, go to http://liveexample. pearsoncmg.com/dsanimation/LinearProbingeBook.html, as shown in Figure 27.3.

27.4.2 Quadratic Probing

quadratic probing

Quadratic probing can avoid the clustering problem that can occur in linear probing. Linear probing looks at the consecutive cells beginning at index k. Quadratic probing, on the other hand, looks at the cells at indices $(k + j^2)$ % N, for $j \geq 0$, that is, k % N, $(k + 1)$ % N, $(k + 4)$ % n, $(k + 9)$ % N, and so on, as shown in Figure 27.4.

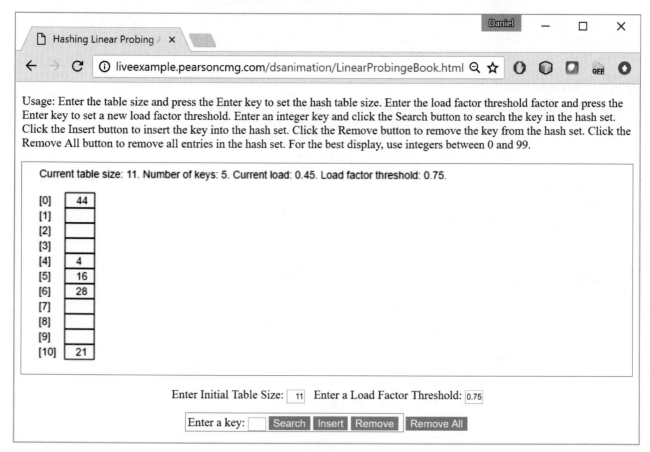

FIGURE 27.3 The animation tool shows how linear probing works.

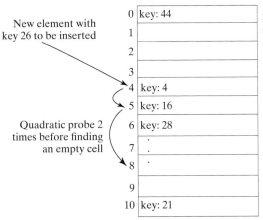

FIGURE 27.4 Quadratic probing increases the next index in the sequence by j^2 for $j = 1, 2, 3, \ldots$.

Quadratic probing works in the same way as linear probing except for a change in the search sequence. Quadratic probing avoids linear probing's clustering problem, but it has its own clustering problem, called *secondary clustering*; that is, the entries that collide with an occupied entry use the same probe sequence.

secondary clustering

Linear probing guarantees that an available cell can be found for insertion as long as the table is not full. However, there is no such guarantee for quadratic probing.

> ✏️ **Pedagogical Note**
> For an interactive GUI demo to see how quadratic probing works, go to http://liveexample
> .pearsoncmg.com/dsanimation/QuadraticProbingeBook.html, as shown in Figure 27.5.

quadratic probing animation on Companion Website

27.4.3 Double Hashing

Another open addressing scheme that avoids the clustering problem is known as *double hashing*. Starting from the initial index k, both linear probing and quadratic probing add an increment to k to define a search sequence. The increment is `1` for linear probing and j^2 for quadratic probing. These increments are independent of the keys. Double hashing uses a secondary hash function $h'(key)$ on the keys to determine the increments to avoid the clustering problem. Specifically, double hashing looks at the cells at indices $(k + j * h'(key)) \% N$, for $j \geq 0$, that is, $k \% N$, $(k + h'(key)) \% N$, $(k + 2 * h'(key)) \% N$, $(k + 3 * h'(key)) \% N$, and so on.

double hashing

For example, let the primary hash function h and secondary hash function h' on a hash table of size `11` be defined as follows:

```
h(key)  = key %  11;
h'(key) = 7 - key % 7;
```

For a search key of `12`, we have

```
h(12)  = 12 % 11 = 1;
h'(12) = 7 - 12 % 7 = 2;
```

Suppose the elements with the keys `45`, `58`, `4`, `28`, and `21` are already placed in the hash table as shown in Figure 27.6. We now insert the element with key `12`. The probe sequence for key `12` starts at index `1`. Since the cell at index `1` is already occupied, search the next cell at index `3` (`1 + 1 * 2`). Since the cell at index `3` is already occupied, search the next cell at index `5` (`1 + 2 * 2`). Since the cell at index `5` is empty, the element for key `12` is now inserted at this cell.

The indices of the probe sequence are as follows: 1, 3, 5, 7, 9, 0, 2, 4, 6, 8, 10. This sequence reaches the entire table. You should design your functions to produce a probe sequence that

FIGURE 27.5 The animation tool shows how quadratic probing works.

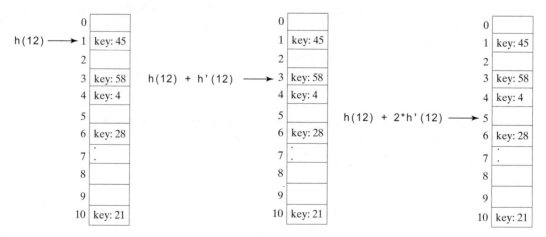

FIGURE 27.6 The secondary hash function in a double hashing determines the increment of the next index in the probe sequence.

reaches the entire table. Note the second function should never have a zero value, since zero is not an increment.

Check Point

27.4.1 What is open addressing? What is linear probing? What is quadratic probing? What is double hashing?

27.4.2 Describe the clustering problem for linear probing.

27.4.3 What is secondary clustering?

27.4.4 Show the hash table of size 11 after inserting entries with keys 34, 29, 53, 44, 120, 39, 45, and 40, using linear probing.

27.4.5 Show the hash table of size 11 after inserting entries with keys 34, 29, 53, 44, 120, 39, 45, and 40, using quadratic probing.

27.4.6 Show the hash table of size 11 after inserting entries with keys 34, 29, 53, 44, 120, 39, 45, and 40, using double hashing with the following functions:

```
h(k) = k %  11;
h'(k) = 7 - k % 7;
```

27.5 Handling Collisions Using Separate Chaining

The separate chaining scheme places all entries with the same hash index in the same location, rather than finding new locations. Each location in the separate chaining scheme uses a bucket to hold multiple entries.

Key Point

You can implement a bucket using an array, `ArrayList`, or `LinkedList`. We will use `LinkedList` for demonstration. You can view each cell in the hash table as the reference to the head of a linked list, and elements in the linked list are chained starting from the head, as shown in Figure 27.7.

separate chaining

implementing bucket

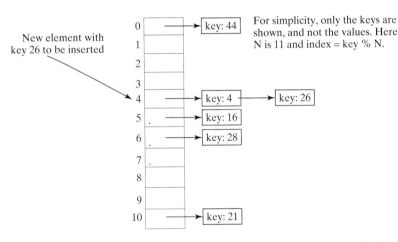

FIGURE 27.7 Separate chaining scheme chains the entries with the same hash index in a bucket.

27.5.1 Show the hash table of size 11 after inserting entries with the keys 34, 29, 53, 44, 120, 39, 45, and 40, using separate chaining.

Check Point

27.6 Load Factor and Rehashing

The load factor measures how full a hash table is. If the load factor is exceeded, increase the hash-table size and reload the entries into a new larger hash table. This is called rehashing.

Key Point

rehashing

Load factor λ (*lambda*) measures how full a hash table is. It is the ratio of the number of elements to the size of the hash table, that is, $\lambda = \dfrac{n}{N}$, where n denotes the number of elements and N the number of locations in the hash table.

load factor

Note λ is zero if the hash table is empty. For the open addressing scheme, λ is between 0 and 1; λ is 1 if the hash table is full. For the separate chaining scheme, λ can be any value. As

λ increases, the probability of a collision also increases. Studies show you should maintain the load factor under `0.5` for the open addressing scheme, and under `0.9` for the separate chaining scheme.

threshold

Keeping the load factor under a certain threshold is important for the performance of hashing. In the implementation of the `java.util.HashMap` class in the Java API, the threshold `0.75` is used. Whenever the load factor exceeds the threshold, you need to increase the hash-table size and *rehash* all the entries in the map into a new larger hash table. Notice you need to change the hash functions, since the hash-table size has been changed. To reduce the likelihood of rehashing, since it is costly, you should at least double the hash-table size. Even with periodic rehashing, hashing is an efficient implementation for map.

rehash

separate chaining animation
on Companion Website

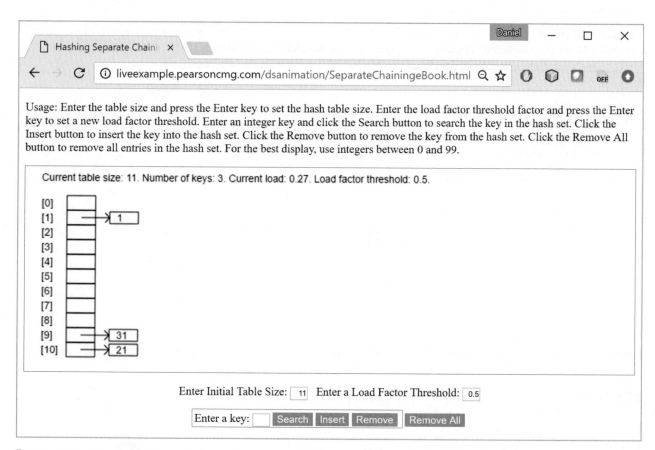

Pedagogical Note

For an interactive GUI demo to see how separate chaining works, go to http://liveexample .pearsoncmg.com/dsanimation/SeparateChainingeBook.html, as shown in Figure 27.8.

FIGURE 27.8 The animation tool shows how separate chaining works.

Check Point

27.6.1 What is load factor? Assume the hash table has the initial size 4 and its load factor is 0.5; show the hash table after inserting entries with the keys 34, 29, 53, 44, 120, 39, 45, and 40, using linear probing.

27.6.2 Assume the hash table has the initial size 4 and its load factor is 0.5; show the hash table after inserting entries with the keys 34, 29, 53, 44, 120, 39, 45, and 40, using quadratic probing.

27.6.3 Assume the hash table has the initial size 4 and its load factor is 0.5; show the hash table after inserting entries with the keys 34, 29, 53, 44, 120, 39, 45, and 40, using separate chaining.

27.7 Implementing a Map Using Hashing

A map can be implemented using hashing.

Key Point

Now you understand the concept of hashing. You know how to design a good hash function to map a key to an index in a hash table, how to measure performance using the load factor, and how to increase the table size and rehash to maintain the performance. This section demonstrates how to implement a map using separate chaining.

We design our custom `Map` interface to mirror `java.util.Map` and name the interface `MyMap` and a concrete class `MyHashMap`, as shown in Figure 27.9.

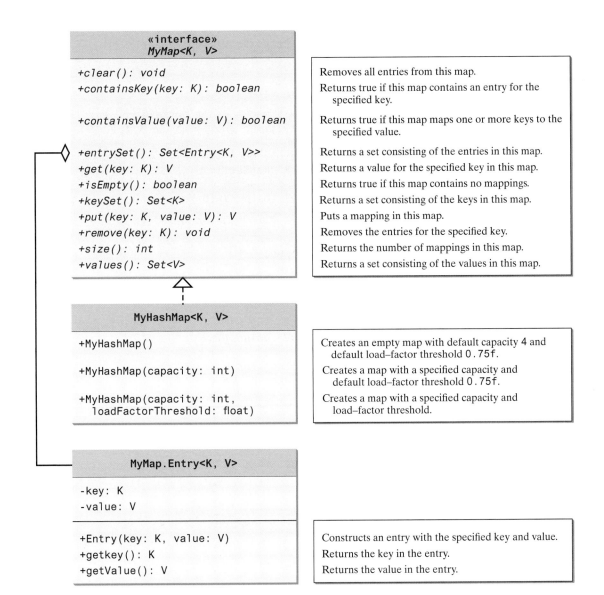

FIGURE 27.9 `MyHashMap` implements the `MyMap` interface.

How do you implement MyHashMap? If you use an ArrayList and store a new entry at the end of the list, the search time will be $O(n)$. If you implement MyHashMap using a binary tree, the search time will be $O(\log n)$ if the tree is well balanced. Nevertheless, you can implement MyHashMap using hashing to obtain an $O(1)$ time search algorithm. Listing 27.1 shows the MyMap interface, and Listing 27.2 implements MyHashMap using separate chaining.

LISTING 27.1   MyMap.java

interface MyMap

clear

containsKey

containsValue

entrySet

get

isEmpty

keySet

put

remove

size

values

Entry inner class

```java
 1  public interface MyMap<K, V> {
 2    /** Remove all of the entries from this map */
 3    public void clear();
 4
 5    /** Return true if the specified key is in the map */
 6    public boolean containsKey(K key);
 7
 8    /** Return true if this map contains the specified value */
 9    public boolean containsValue(V value);
10
11    /** Return a set of entries in the map */
12    public java.util.Set<Entry<K, V>> entrySet();
13
14    /** Return the value that matches the specified key */
15    public V get(K key);
16
17    /** Return true if this map doesn't contain any entries */
18    public boolean isEmpty();
19
20    /** Return a set consisting of the keys in this map */
21    public java.util.Set<K> keySet();
22
23    /** Add an entry (key, value) into the map */
24    public V put(K key, V value);
25
26    /** Remove an entry for the specified key */
27    public void remove(K key);
28
29    /** Return the number of mappings in this map */
30    public int size();
31
32    /** Return a set consisting of the values in this map */
33    public java.util.Set<V> values();
34
35    /** Define an inner class for Entry */
36    public static class Entry<K, V> {
37      K key;
38      V value;
39
40      public Entry(K key, V value) {
41        this.key = key;
42        this.value = value;
43      }
44
45      public K getKey() {
46        return key;
47      }
48
49      public V getValue() {
50        return value;
51      }
52
```

```
53       @Override
54       public String toString() {
55          return "[" + key + ", " + value + "]";
56       }
57    }
58  }
```

LISTING 27.2 MyHashMap.java

```
1   import java.util.LinkedList;
2
3   public class MyHashMap<K, V> implements MyMap<K, V> {          class MyHashMap
4      // Define the default hash-table size. Must be a power of 2
5      private static int DEFAULT_INITIAL_CAPACITY = 4;           default initial capacity
6
7      // Define the maximum hash-table size. 1 << 30 is same as 2^30
8      private static int MAXIMUM_CAPACITY = 1 << 30;             maximum capacity
9
10     // Current hash-table capacity. Capacity is a power of 2
11     private int capacity;                                      current capacity
12
13     // Define default load factor
14     private static float DEFAULT_MAX_LOAD_FACTOR = 0.75f;      default load factor
15
16     // Specify a load factor used in the hash table
17     private float loadFactorThreshold;                         load-factor threshold
18
19     // The number of entries in the map
20     private int size = 0;                                      size
21
22     // Hash table is an array with each cell being a linked list
23     LinkedList<MyMap.Entry<K,V>>[] table;                      hash table
24
25     /** Construct a map with the default capacity and load factor */
26     public MyHashMap() {                                       no-arg constructor
27        this(DEFAULT_INITIAL_CAPACITY, DEFAULT_MAX_LOAD_FACTOR);
28     }
29
30     /** Construct a map with the specified initial capacity and
31      * default load factor */
32     public MyHashMap(int initialCapacity) {                    constructor
33        this(initialCapacity, DEFAULT_MAX_LOAD_FACTOR);
34     }
35
36     /** Construct a map with the specified initial capacity
37      * and load factor */
38     public MyHashMap(int initialCapacity, float loadFactorThreshold) {   constructor
39        if (initialCapacity > MAXIMUM_CAPACITY)
40           this.capacity = MAXIMUM_CAPACITY;
41        else
42           this.capacity = trimToPowerOf2(initialCapacity);
43
44        this.loadFactorThreshold = loadFactorThreshold;
45        table = new LinkedList[capacity];
46     }
47
48     @Override /** Remove all of the entries from this map */
49     public void clear() {                                      clear
50        size = 0;
51        removeEntries();
```

```
 52        }
 53
 54        @Override /** Return true if the specified key is in the map */
 55        public boolean containsKey(K key) {
 56          if (get(key) != null)
 57            return true;
 58          else
 59            return false;
 60        }
 61
 62        @Override /** Return true if this map contains the value */
 63        public boolean containsValue(V value) {
 64          for (int i = 0; i < capacity; i++) {
 65            if (table[i] != null) {
 66              LinkedList<Entry<K, V>> bucket = table[i];
 67              for (Entry<K, V> entry: bucket)
 68                if (entry.getValue().equals(value))
 69                  return true;
 70            }
 71          }
 72
 73          return false;
 74        }
 75
 76        @Override /** Return a set of entries in the map */
 77        public java.util.Set<MyMap.Entry<K,V>> entrySet() {
 78          java.util.Set<MyMap.Entry<K, V>> set =
 79            new java.util.HashSet<>();
 80
 81          for (int i = 0; i < capacity; i++) {
 82            if (table[i] != null) {
 83              LinkedList<Entry<K, V>> bucket = table[i];
 84              for (Entry<K, V> entry: bucket)
 85                set.add(entry);
 86            }
 87          }
 88
 89          return set;
 90        }
 91
 92        @Override /** Return the value that matches the specified key */
 93        public V get(K key) {
 94          int bucketIndex = hash(key.hashCode());
 95          if (table[bucketIndex] != null) {
 96            LinkedList<Entry<K, V>> bucket = table[bucketIndex];
 97            for (Entry<K, V> entry: bucket)
 98              if (entry.getKey().equals(key))
 99                return entry.getValue();
100          }
101
102          return null;
103        }
104
105        @Override /** Return true if this map contains no entries */
106        public boolean isEmpty() {
107          return size == 0;
108        }
109
110        @Override /** Return a set consisting of the keys in this map */
111        public java.util.Set<K> keySet() {
```

Margin labels:
- containsKey (line 55)
- containsValue (line 63)
- entrySet (line 77)
- get (line 93)
- isEmpty (line 106)
- keySet (line 111)

```
112        java.util.Set<K> set = new java.util.HashSet<>();
113
114      for (int i = 0; i < capacity; i++) {
115        if (table[i] != null) {
116          LinkedList<Entry<K, V>> bucket = table[i];
117          for (Entry<K, V> entry: bucket)
118            set.add(entry.getKey());
119        }
120      }
121
122      return set;
123    }
124
125    @Override /** Add an entry (key, value) into the map */
126    public V put(K key, V value) {                                  put
127      if (get(key) != null) {  // The key is already in the map
128        int bucketIndex = hash(key.hashCode());
129        LinkedList<Entry<K, V>> bucket = table[bucketIndex];
130        for (Entry<K, V> entry: bucket)
131          if (entry.getKey().equals(key)) {
132            V oldValue = entry.getValue();
133            // Replace old value with new value
134            entry.value = value;
135            // Return the old value for the key
136            return oldValue;
137          }
138      }
139
140      // Check load factor
141      if (size >= capacity * loadFactorThreshold) {
142        if (capacity == MAXIMUM_CAPACITY)
143          throw new RuntimeException("Exceeding maximum capacity");
144
145        rehash();
146      }
147
148      int bucketIndex = hash(key.hashCode());
149
150      // Create a linked list for the bucket if not already created
151      if (table[bucketIndex] == null) {
152        table[bucketIndex] = new LinkedList<Entry<K, V>>();
153      }
154
155      // Add a new entry (key, value) to hashTable[index]
156      table[bucketIndex].add(new MyMap.Entry<K, V>(key, value));
157
158      size++; // Increase size
159
160      return value;
161    }
162
163    @Override /** Remove the entries for the specified key */
164    public void remove(K key) {                                     remove
165      int bucketIndex = hash(key.hashCode());
166
167      // Remove the first entry that matches the key from a bucket
168      if (table[bucketIndex] != null) {
169        LinkedList<Entry<K, V>> bucket = table[bucketIndex];
170        for (Entry<K, V> entry: bucket)
171          if (entry.getKey().equals(key)) {
```

```
172              bucket.remove(entry);
173              size--; // Decrease size
174              break; // Remove just one entry that matches the key
175          }
176        }
177      }
178
179      @Override /** Return the number of entries in this map */
180      public int size() {
181        return size;
182      }
183
184      @Override /** Return a set consisting of the values in this map */
185      public java.util.Set<V> values() {
186        java.util.Set<V> set = new java.util.HashSet<>();
187
188        for (int i = 0; i < capacity; i++) {
189          if (table[i] != null) {
190            LinkedList<Entry<K, V>> bucket = table[i];
191            for (Entry<K, V> entry: bucket)
192              set.add(entry.getValue());
193          }
194        }
195
196        return set;
197      }
198
199      /** Hash function */
200      private int hash(int hashCode) {
201        return supplementalHash(hashCode) & (capacity - 1);
202      }
203
204      /** Ensure the hashing is evenly distributed */
205      private static int supplementalHash(int h) {
206        h ^= (h >>> 20) ^ (h >>> 12);
207        return h ^ (h >>> 7) ^ (h >>> 4);
208      }
209
210      /** Return a power of 2 for initialCapacity */
211      private int trimToPowerOf2(int initialCapacity) {
212        int capacity = 1;
213        while (capacity < initialCapacity) {
214          capacity <<= 1; // Same as capacity *= 2. <= is more efficient
215        }
216
217        return capacity;
218      }
219
220      /** Remove all entries from each bucket */
221      private void removeEntries() {
222        for (int i = 0; i < capacity; i++) {
223          if (table[i] != null) {
224            table[i].clear();
225          }
226        }
227      }
228
229      /** Rehash the map */
230      private void rehash() {
231        java.util.Set<Entry<K, V>> set = entrySet(); // Get entries
```

size — 180

values — 185

hash — 200

supplementalHash — 205

trimToPowerOf2 — 211

removeEntries — 221

rehash — 230

```
232        capacity <<= 1; // Same as capacity *= 2. <= is more efficient
233        table = new LinkedList[capacity]; // Create a new hash table
234        size = 0; // Reset size to 0
235
236        for (Entry<K, V> entry: set) {
237          put(entry.getKey(), entry.getValue()); // Store to new table
238        }
239      }
240
241      @Override /** Return a string representation for this map */
242      public String toString() {                                    toString
243        StringBuilder builder = new StringBuilder("[");
244
245        for (int i = 0; i < capacity; i++) {
246          if (table[i] != null && table[i].size() > 0)
247            for (Entry<K, V> entry: table[i])
248              builder.append(entry);
249        }
250
251        builder.append("]");
252        return builder.toString();
253      }
254  }
```

The `MyHashMap` class implements the `MyMap` interface using separate chaining. The parameters that determine the hash-table size and load factors are defined in the class. The default   hash-table parameters
initial capacity is 4 (line 5) and the maximum capacity is 2^{30} (line 8). The current hash-table capacity is designed as a value of the power of 2 (line 11). The default load-factor threshold is 0.75f (line 14). You can specify a custom load-factor threshold when constructing a map. The custom load-factor threshold is stored in `loadFactorThreshold` (line 17). The data field `size` denotes the number of entries in the map (line 20). The hash table is an array. Each cell in the array is a linked list (line 23).

Three constructors are provided to construct a map. You can construct a default map with   three constructors
the default capacity and load-factor threshold using the no-arg constructor (lines 26–28), a map with the specified capacity and a default load-factor threshold (lines 32–34), and a map with the specified capacity and load-factor threshold (lines 38–46).

The `clear` method removes all entries from the map (lines 49–52). It invokes   clear
`removeEntries()`, which deletes all entries in the buckets (lines 221–227). The `removeEntries()` method takes $O(capacity)$ time to clear all entries in the table.

The `containsKey(key)` method checks whether the specified key is in the map by invoking   containsKey
the `get` method (lines 55–60). Since the `get` method takes $O(1)$ time, the `containsKey(key)` method takes $O(1)$ time.

The `containsValue(value)` method checks whether the value is in the map (lines 63–74).   containsValue
This method takes $O(capacity + size)$ time. It is actually $O(capacity)$, since $capacity > size$.

The `entrySet()` method returns a set that contains all entries in the map (lines 77–90).   entrySet
This method takes $O(capacity)$ time.

The `get(key)` method returns the value of the first entry with the specified key (lines   get
93–103). This method takes $O(1)$ time.

The `isEmpty()` method simply returns true if the map is empty (lines 106–108). This   isEmpty
method takes $O(1)$ time.

The `keySet()` method returns all keys in the map as a set. The method finds the keys from   keySet
each bucket and adds them to a set (lines 111–123). This method takes $O(capacity)$ time.

The `put(key, value)` method adds a new entry into the map. The method first tests if the   put
key is already in the map (line 127), if so, it locates the entry and replaces the old value with the new value in the entry for the key (line 134) and the old value is returned (line 136). If the key is

new in the map, the new entry is created in the map (line 156). Before inserting the new entry, the method checks whether the size exceeds the load-factor threshold (line 141). If so, the program invokes rehash() (line 145) to increase the capacity and store entries into a new larger hash table.

The rehash() method first copies all entries in a set (line 231), doubles the capacity (line 232), creates a new hash table (line 233), and resets the size to 0 (line 234). The method then copies the entries into the new hash table (lines 236–238). The rehash method takes $O(capacity)$ time. If no rehash is performed, the put method takes $O(1)$ time to add a new entry.

The remove(key) method removes the entry with the specified key in the map (lines 164–177). This method takes $O(1)$ time.

The size() method simply returns the size of the map (lines 180–182). This method takes $O(1)$ time.

The values() method returns all values in the map. The method examines each entry from all buckets and adds it to a set (lines 185–197). This method takes $O(capacity)$ time.

The hash() method invokes the supplementalHash to ensure the hashing is evenly distributed to produce an index for the hash table (lines 200–208). This method takes $O(1)$ time.

Table 27.1 summarizes the time complexities of the methods in MyHashMap.

margin notes: rehash, remove, size, values, hash

TABLE 27.1 Time Complexities for Methods in MyHashMap

Methods	Time
clear()	$O(capacity)$
containsKey(key: Key)	$O(1)$
containsValue(value: V)	$O(capacity)$
entrySet()	$O(capacity)$
get(key: K)	$O(1)$
isEmpty()	$O(1)$
keySet()	$O(capacity)$
put(key: K, value: V)	$O(1)$
remove(key: K)	$O(1)$
size()	$O(1)$
values()	$O(capacity)$
rehash()	$O(capacity)$

Since rehashing does not happen very often, the time complexity for the put method is $O(1)$. Note the complexities of the clear, entrySet, keySet, values, and rehash methods depend on capacity, so to avoid poor performance for these methods, you should choose an initial capacity carefully.

Listing 27.3 gives a test program that uses MyHashMap.

LISTING 27.3 TestMyHashMap.java

margin notes: create a map, put entries

```
1  public class TestMyHashMap {
2    public static void main(String[] args) {
3      // Create a map
4      MyMap<String, Integer> map = new MyHashMap<>();
5      map.put("Smith", 30);
6      map.put("Anderson", 31);
7      map.put("Lewis", 29);
8      map.put("Cook", 29);
```

```
9       map.put("Smith", 65);
10
11      System.out.println("Entries in map: " + map);
12
13      System.out.println("The age for Lewis is " +
14        map.get("Lewis"));
15
16      System.out.println("Is Smith in the map? " +
17        map.containsKey("Smith"));
18      System.out.println("Is age 33 in the map? " +
19        map.containsValue(33));
20
21      map.remove("Smith");
22      System.out.println("Entries in map: " + map);
23
24      map.clear();
25      System.out.println("Entries in map: " + map);
26    }
27  }
```

display entries

get value

is key in map?

is value in map?

remove entry

```
Entries in map: [[Anderson, 31][Smith, 65][Lewis, 29][Cook, 29]]
The age for Lewis is 29
Is Smith in the map? true
Is age 33 in the map? false
Entries in map: [[Anderson, 31][Lewis, 29][Cook, 29]]
Entries in map: []
```

The program creates a map using MyHashMap (line 4) and adds five entries into the map (lines 5–9). Line 5 adds key Smith with value 30 and line 9 adds Smith with value 65. The latter value replaces the former value. The map actually has only four entries. The program displays the entries in the map (line 11), gets a value for a key (line 14), checks whether the map contains the key (line 17) and a value (line 19), removes an entry with the key Smith (line 21), and redisplays the entries in the map (line 22). Finally, the program clears the map (line 24) and displays an empty map (line 25).

27.7.1 What is 1 << 30 in line 8 in Listing 27.2? What are the integers resulted from 1 << 1, 1 << 2, and 1 << 3?

27.7.2 What are the integers resulted from 32 >> 1, 32 >> 2, 32 >> 3, and 32 >> 4?

27.7.3 In Listing 27.2, will the program work if LinkedList is replaced by ArrayList? In Listing 27.2, how do you replace the code in lines 56–59 using one line of code?

27.7.4 Describe how the put(key, value) method is implemented in the MyHashMap class.

27.7.5 In Listing 27.2, the supplementalHash method is declared static. Can the hash method be declared static?

27.7.6 Show the output of the following code:

```
MyMap<String, String> map = new MyHashMap<>();
map.put("Texas", "Dallas");
map.put("Oklahoma", "Norman");
map.put("Texas", "Austin");
map.put("Oklahoma", "Tulsa");

System.out.println(map.get("Texas"));
System.out.println(map.size());
```

27.7.7 If x is a negative int value, will x & (N − 1) be negative?

27.8 Implementing Set Using Hashing

A hash set can be implemented using a hash map.

hash set
hash map
set

A *set* (introduced in Chapter 21) is a data structure that stores distinct values. The Java Collections Framework defines the `java.util.Set` interface for modeling sets. Three concrete implementations are `java.util.HashSet`, `java.util.LinkedHashSet`, and `java.util.TreeSet`. `java.util.HashSet` is implemented using hashing, `java.util.LinkedHashSet` using `LinkedList`, and `java.util.TreeSet` using binary search trees.

You can implement `MyHashSet` using the same approach as for implementing `MyHashMap`. The only difference is that key/value pairs are stored in the map, while elements are stored in the set.

MyHashSet

Since all the methods in `HashSet` are inherited from `Collection`, we design our custom `HashSet` by implementing the `Collection` interface, as shown in Figure 27.10.

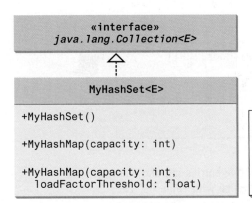

FIGURE 27.10 `MyHashSet` implements the `Collection` interface.

Listing 27.4 implements `MyHashSet` using separate chaining.

LISTING 27.4 MyHashSet.java

```
1  import java.util.*;
2
3  public class MyHashSet<E> implements Collection<E> {
4    // Define the default hash-table size. Must be a power of 2
5    private static int DEFAULT_INITIAL_CAPACITY = 4;
6
7    // Define the maximum hash-table size. 1 << 30 is same as 2^30
8    private static int MAXIMUM_CAPACITY = 1 << 30;
9
10   // Current hash-table capacity. Capacity is a power of 2
11   private int capacity;
12
13   // Define default load factor
14   private static float DEFAULT_MAX_LOAD_FACTOR = 0.75f;
15
16   // Specify a load-factor threshold used in the hash table
17   private float loadFactorThreshold;
18
19   // The number of elements in the set
20   private int size = 0;
```

class MyHashSet

default initial capacity

maximum capacity

current capacity

default max load factor

load-factor threshold

size

```
21
22     // Hash table is an array with each cell being a linked list
23     private LinkedList<E>[] table;                                         hash table
24
25     /** Construct a set with the default capacity and load factor */
26     public MyHashSet() {                                                   no-arg constructor
27       this(DEFAULT_INITIAL_CAPACITY, DEFAULT_MAX_LOAD_FACTOR);
28     }
29
30     /** Construct a set with the specified initial capacity and
31      * default load factor */
32     public MyHashSet(int initialCapacity) {                                constructor
33       this(initialCapacity, DEFAULT_MAX_LOAD_FACTOR);
34     }
35
36     /** Construct a set with the specified initial capacity
37      * and load factor */
38     public MyHashSet(int initialCapacity, float loadFactorThreshold) {     constructor
39       if (initialCapacity > MAXIMUM_CAPACITY)
40         this.capacity = MAXIMUM_CAPACITY;
41       else
42         this.capacity = trimToPowerOf2(initialCapacity);
43
44       this.loadFactorThreshold = loadFactorThreshold;
45       table = new LinkedList[capacity];
46     }
47
48     @Override /** Remove all elements from this set */
49     public void clear() {                                                  clear
50       size = 0;
51       removeElements();
52     }
53
54     @Override /** Return true if the element is in the set */
55     public boolean contains(E e) {                                         contains
56       int bucketIndex = hash(e.hashCode());
57       if (table[bucketIndex] != null) {
58         LinkedList<E> bucket = table[bucketIndex];
59         return bucket.contains(e);
60       }
61
62       return false;
63     }
64
65     @Override /** Add an element to the set */
66     public boolean add(E e) {                                              add
67       if (contains(e))  // Duplicate element not stored
68         return false;
69
70       if (size + 1 > capacity * loadFactorThreshold) {
71         if (capacity == MAXIMUM_CAPACITY)
72           throw new RuntimeException("Exceeding maximum capacity");
73
74         rehash();
75       }
76
77       int bucketIndex = hash(e.hashCode());
78
79       // Create a linked list for the bucket if not already created
80       if (table[bucketIndex] == null) {
```

```
81          table[bucketIndex] = new LinkedList<E>();
82        }
83
84        // Add e to hashTable[index]
85        table[bucketIndex].add(e);
86
87        size++; // Increase size
88
89        return true;
90      }
91
92      @Override /** Remove the element from the set */
93      public boolean remove(E e) {
94        if (!contains(e))
95          return false;
96
97        int bucketIndex = hash(e.hashCode());
98
99        // Create a linked list for the bucket if not already created
100       if (table[bucketIndex] != null) {
101         LinkedList<E> bucket = table[bucketIndex];
102         bucket.removed(e);
103       }
104
105       size--; // Decrease size
106
107       return true;
108     }
109
110     @Override /** Return true if the set contain no elements */
111     public boolean isEmpty() {
112       return size == 0;
113     }
114
115     @Override /** Return the number of elements in the set */
116     public int size() {
117       return size;
118     }
119
120     @Override /** Return an iterator for the elements in this set */
121     public java.util.Iterator<E> iterator() {
122       return new MyHashSetIterator(this);
123     }
124
125     /** Inner class for iterator */
126     private class MyHashSetIterator implements java.util.Iterator<E> {
127       // Store the elements in a list
128       private java.util.ArrayList<E> list;
129       private int current = 0; // Point to the current element in list
130       private MyHashSet<E> set;
131
132       /** Create a list from the set */
133       public MyHashSetIterator(MyHashSet<E> set) {
134         this.set = set;
135         list = setToList();
136       }
137
138       @Override /** Next element for traversing? */
139       public boolean hasNext() {
140         return current < list.size();
141       }
```

remove — line 93
isEmpty — line 111
size — line 116
iterator — line 121
inner class — line 126

```
142
143       @Override /** Get current element and move cursor to the next */
144       public E next() {
145         return list.get(current++);
146       }
147
148       /** Remove the current element returned by the last next() */
149       public void remove() {
150         // Left as an exercise
151         // You need to remove the element from the set
152         // You also need to remove it from the list
153       }
154     }
155
156     /** Hash function */
157     private int hash(int hashCode) {                                   hash
158       return supplementalHash(hashCode) & (capacity - 1);
159     }
160
161     /** Ensure the hashing is evenly distributed */
162     private static int supplementalHash(int h) {                       supplementalHash
163       h ^= (h >>> 20) ^ (h >>> 12);
164       return h ^ (h >>> 7) ^ (h >>> 4);
165     }
166
167     /** Return a power of 2 for initialCapacity */
168     private int trimToPowerOf2(int initialCapacity) {
169       int capacity = 1;                                                trimToPowerOf2
170       while (capacity < initialCapacity) {
171         capacity <<= 1; // Same as capacity *= 2. <= is more efficient
172       }
173
174       return capacity;
175     }
176
177     /** Remove all e from each bucket */
178     private void removeElements() {
179       for (int i = 0; i < capacity; i++) {
180         if (table[i] != null) {
181           table[i].clear();
182         }
183       }
184     }
185
186     /** Rehash the set */
187     private void rehash() {                                            rehash
188       java.util.ArrayList<E> list = setToList(); // Copy to a list
189       capacity <<= 1; // Same as capacity *= 2. <= is more efficient
190       table = new LinkedList[capacity]; // Create a new hash table
191       size = 0;
192
193       for (E element: list) {
194         add(element); // Add from the old table to the new table
195       }
196     }
197
198     /** Copy elements in the hash set to an array list */
199     private java.util.ArrayList<E> setToList() {                       setToList
200       java.util.ArrayList<E> list = new java.util.ArrayList<>();
201
202       for (int i = 0; i < capacity; i++) {
```

```
203          if (table[i] != null) {
204            for (E e: table[i]) {
205              list.add(e);
206            }
207          }
208        }
209
210        return list;
211      }
212
213      @Override /** Return a string representation for this set */
214      public String toString() {
215        java.util.ArrayList<E> list = setToList();
216        StringBuilder builder = new StringBuilder("[");
217
218        // Add the elements except the last one to the string builder
219        for (int i = 0; i < list.size() - 1; i++) {
220          builder.append(list.get(i) + ", ");
221        }
222
223        // Add the last element in the list to the string builder
224        if (list.size() == 0)
225          builder.append("]");
226        else
227          builder.append(list.get(list.size() - 1) + "]");
228
229        return builder.toString();
230      }
231
232      @Override
233      public boolean addAll(Collection<? extends E> arg0) {
234        // Left as an exercise
235        return false;
236      }
237
238      @Override
239      public boolean containsAll(Collection<?> arg0) {
240        // Left as an exercise
241        return false;
242      }
243
244      @Override
245      public boolean removeAll(Collection<?> arg0) {
246        // Left as an exercise
247        return false;
248      }
249
250      @Override
251      public boolean retainAll(Collection<?> arg0) {
252        // Left as an exercise
253        return false;
254      }
255
256      @Override
257      public Object[] toArray() {
258        // Left as an exercise
259        return null;
260      }
261
262      @Override
```

toString

override addAll

override containsAll

override removeAll

override retainAll

override toArray()

```
263    public <T> T[] toArray(T[] arg0) {
264       // Left as an exercise
265       return null;
266    }
267 }
```

override toArray(T[])

The `MyHashSet` class implements the `MySet` interface using separate chaining. Implementing `MyHashSet` is very similar to implementing `MyHashMap` except for the following differences:

MyHashSet vs. MyHashMap

1. The elements are stored in the hash table for `MyHashSet`, but the entries (key/value pairs) are stored in the hash table for `MyHashMap`.

2. `MyHashSet` implements `Collection`. Since `Collection` implements `Iterable`, the elements in `MyHashSet` are iterable.

Three constructors are provided to construct a set. You can construct a default set with the default capacity and load factor using the no-arg constructor (lines 26–28), a set with the specified capacity and a default load factor (lines 32–34), and a set with the specified capacity and load factor (lines 38–46).

three constructors

The `clear` method removes all elements from the set (lines 49–52). It invokes `removeElements()`, which clears all table cells (line 181). Each table cell is a linked list that stores the elements with the same hash table index. The `removeElements()` method takes $O(capacity)$ time.

clear

The `contains(element)` method checks whether the specified element is in the set by examining whether the designated bucket contains the element (line 59). This method takes $O(1)$ time because the bucket size is considered very small.

contains

The `add(element)` method adds a new element into the set. The method first checks if the element is already in the set (line 67). If so, the method returns false. The method then checks whether the size exceeds the load-factor threshold (line 70). If so, the program invokes `rehash()` (line 74) to increase the capacity and store elements into a new larger hash table.

add

The `rehash()` method first copies all elements to a list (line 188), doubles the capacity (line 189), creates a new hash table (line 190), and resets the size to `0` (line 191). The method then copies the elements into the new larger hash table (lines 193–195). The `rehash` method takes $O(capacity)$ time. If no rehash is performed, the `add` method takes $O(1)$ time to add a new element.

rehash

The `remove(element)` method removes the specified element in the set (lines 93–108). This method takes $O(1)$ time.

remove

The `size()` method simply returns the number of elements in the set (lines 116–118). This method takes $O(1)$ time.

size

The `iterator()` method returns an instance of `java.util.Iterator`. The `MyHashSetIterator` class implements `java.util.Iterator` to create a forward iterator. When a `MyHashSetIterator` is constructed, it copies all the elements in the set to a list (line 135). The variable `current` points to the element in the list. Initially, `current` is `0` (line 129), which points to the first element in the list. `MyHashSetIterator` implements the methods `hasNext()`, `next()`, and `remove()` in `java.util.Iterator`. Invoking `hasNext()` returns true if `current < list.size()`. Invoking `next()` returns the current element and moves `current` to point to the next element (line 145). Invoking `remove()` removes the element called by the last `next()`.

iterator

The `hash()` method invokes the `supplementalHash` to ensure the hashing is evenly distributed to produce an index for the hash table (lines 157–159). This method takes $O(1)$ time.

hash

The methods `containsAll`, `addAll`, `removeAll`, `retainAll`, `toArray()`, and `toArray(T[])` defined in the `Collection` interface are overridden in `MyHashSet`. Their implementations are left as exercises in Programming Exercise 27.11.

Table 27.2 summarizes the time complexity of the methods in MyHashSet.

TABLE 27.2 Time Complexities for Methods in MyHashSet

Methods	Time
clear()	O(capacity)
contains(e: E)	O(1)
add(e: E)	O(1)
remove(e: E)	O(1)
isEmpty()	O(1)
size()	O(1)
iterator()	O(capacity)
rehash()	O(capacity)

Listing 27.5 gives a test program that uses MyHashSet.

LISTING 27.5 TestMyHashSet.java

```
 1  public class TestMyHashSet {
 2    public static void main(String[] args) {
 3      // Create a MyHashSet
 4      java.util.Collection<String> set = new MyHashSet<>();
 5      set.add("Smith");
 6      set.add("Anderson");
 7      set.add("Lewis");
 8      set.add("Cook");
 9      set.add("Smith");
10
11      System.out.println("Elements in set: " + set);
12      System.out.println("Number of elements in set: " + set.size());
13      System.out.println("Is Smith in set? " + set.contains("Smith"));
14
15      set.remove("Smith");
16      System.out.print("Names in set in uppercase are ");
17      for (String s: set)
18        System.out.print(s.toUpperCase() + " ");
19
20      set.clear();
21      System.out.println("\nElements in set: " + set);
22    }
23  }
```

create a set
add elements

display elements
set size

remove element

foreach loop

clear set

```
Elements in set: [Cook, Anderson, Smith, Lewis]
Number of elements in set: 4
Is Smith in set? true
Names in set in uppercase are COOK ANDERSON LEWIS
Elements in set: []
```

The program creates a set using MyHashSet (line 4) and adds five elements to the set (lines 5–9). Line 5 adds Smith and line 9 adds Smith again. Since only nonduplicate elements are stored in the set, Smith appears in the set only once. The set actually has four elements. The program displays the elements (line 11), gets its size (line 12), checks whether the set contains a specified element (line 13), and removes an element (line 15). Since the elements in a set are iterable, a foreach loop is used to traverse all elements in the set (lines 17–18). Finally, the program clears the set (line 20) and displays an empty set (line 21).

27.8.1 Why can you use a foreach loop to traverse the elements in a set?

27.8.2 Describe how the `add(e)` method is implemented in the `MyHashSet` class.

27.8.3 Can lines 100–103 in Listing 27.4 be removed?

27.8.4 Implement the `remove()` method in lines 150–152?

Check Point

KEY TERMS

associative array   1010
cluster   1014
dictionary   1010
double hashing   1015
hash code   1011
hash function   1010
hash map   1028
hash set   1028
hash table   1029

linear probing   1013
load factor   1017
open addressing   1013
perfect hash function   1010
polynomial hash code   1012
quadratic probing   1014
rehashing   1017
separate chaining   1017

CHAPTER SUMMARY

1. A *map* is a data structure that stores entries. Each entry contains two parts: a *key* and a *value*. The key is also called a *search key*, which is used to search for the corresponding value. You can implement a map to obtain $O(1)$ time complexity on searching, retrieval, insertion, and deletion using the hashing technique.

2. A *set* is a data structure that stores elements. You can use the hashing technique to implement a set to achieve $O(1)$ time complexity on searching, insertion, and deletion for a set.

3. *Hashing* is a technique that retrieves the value using the index obtained from a key without performing a search. A typical *hash function* first converts a search key to an integer value called a *hash code*, then compresses the hash code into an index to the *hash table*.

4. A *collision* occurs when two keys are mapped to the same index in a hash table. Generally, there are two ways for handling collisions: *open addressing* and *separate chaining*.

5. Open addressing is the process of finding an open location in the hash table in the event of collision. Open addressing has several variations: *linear probing*, *quadratic probing*, and *double hashing*.

6. The *separate chaining* scheme places all entries with the same hash index into the same location, rather than finding new locations. Each location in the separate chaining scheme is called a *bucket*. A bucket is a container that holds multiple entries.

QUIZ

Answer the quiz for this chapter online at the book Companion Website.

PROGRAMMING EXERCISES

**27.1 (*Implement* MyMap *using open addressing with linear probing*) Create a new concrete class that implements MyMap using open addressing with linear probing. For simplicity, use f(key) = key % size as the hash function, where size is the hash-table size. Initially, the hash-table size is 4. The table size is doubled whenever the load factor exceeds the threshold (0.5).

**27.2 (*Implement* MyMap *using open addressing with quadratic probing*) Create a new concrete class that implements MyMap using open addressing with quadratic probing. For simplicity, use f(key) = key % size as the hash function, where size is the hash-table size. Initially, the hash-table size is 4. The table size is doubled whenever the load factor exceeds the threshold (0.5).

**27.3 (*Implement* MyMap *using open addressing with double hashing*) Create a new concrete class that implements MyMap using open addressing with double hashing. For simplicity, use f(key) = key % size as the hash function, where size is the hash-table size. Initially, the hash-table size is 4. The table size is doubled whenever the load factor exceeds the threshold (0.5).

**27.4 (*Modify* MyHashMap *with duplicate keys*) Modify MyHashMap to allow duplicate keys for entries. You need to modify the implementation for the put(key, value) method. Also add a new method named getAll(key) that returns a set of values that match the key in the map.

**27.5 (*Implement* MyHashSet *using* MyHashMap) Implement MyHashSet using MyHashMap. Note you can create entries with (key, key), rather than (key, value).

**27.6 (*Animate linear probing*) Write a program that animates linear probing, as shown in Figure 27.3. You can change the initial size of the hash table in the program. Assume the load-factor threshold is 0.75.

**27.7 (*Animate separate chaining*) Write a program that animates MyHashMap, as shown in Figure 27.8. You can change the initial size of the table. Assume the load-factor threshold is 0.75.

**27.8 (*Animate quadratic probing*) Write a program that animates quadratic probing, as shown in Figure 27.5. You can change the initial size of the hash table in program. Assume the load-factor threshold is 0.75.

**27.9 (*Implement hashCode for string*) Write a method that returns a hash code for string using the approach described in Section 27.3.2 with b value 31. The function header is as follows:

```
public static int hashCodeForString(String s)
```

**27.10 (*Compare* MyHashSet *and* MyArrayList) MyArrayList is defined in Listing 24.2. Write a program that generates 1000000 random double values between 0 and 999999 and stores them in a MyArrayList and in a MyHashSet. Generate a list of 1000000 random double values between 0 and 1999999. For each number in the list, test if it is in the array list and in the hash set. Run your program to display the total test time for the array list and for the hash set.

**27.11 (*Implement set operations in* MyHashSet) The implementations of the methods addAll, removeAll, retainAll, toArray(), and toArray(T[]) are omitted in the MyHashSet class. Implement these methods. Also add a new constructor MyHashSet(E[] list) in the MyHashSet class. Test your new MyHashSet class using the code at liveexample.pearsoncmg.com/test/Exercise27_11Test.txt.

**27.12 (`setToList`) Write the following method that returns an `ArrayList` from a set:

```
public static <E> ArrayList<E> setToList(Set<E> s)
```

*27.13 (*The `Date` class*) Design a class named `Date` that meets the following requirements:

- Three data fields `year`, `month`, and `day` for representing a date
- A constructor that constructs a date with the specified year, month, and day
- Override the `equals` method
- Override the `hashCode` method. (For reference, see the implementation of the `Date` class in the Java API)

*27.14 (*The `Point` class*) Design a class named `Point` that meets the following requirements:

- Two data fields `x` and `y` for representing a point with getter methods
- A no-arg constructor that constructs a point for (`0`, `0`)
- A constructor that constructs a point with the specified `x` and `y` values
- Override the `equals` method. Point `p1` is said to be equal to point `p2` if `p1.x == p2.x` and `p1.y == p2.y`.
- Override the `hashCode` method. (For reference, see the implementation of the `Point2D` class in the Java API.)

*27.15 (*Modify Listing 27.4 MyHashSet.java*) The book uses `LinkedList` for buckets. Replace `LinkedList` with `AVLTree`. Assume `E` is `Comparable`. Redefine `MyHashSet` as follows:

```
public class MyHashSet<E extends Comparable<E>> implements
    Collection {
    ...
}
```

Test your program using the main method in Listing 27.5.

GRAPHS AND
APPLICATIONS

Objectives

- To model real-world problems using graphs and explain the Seven Bridges of Königsberg problem (§28.1).

- To describe the graph terminologies: vertices, edges, simple graphs, weighted/unweighted graphs, and directed/undirected graphs (§28.2).

- To represent vertices and edges using lists, edge arrays, edge objects, adjacency matrices, and adjacency lists (§28.3).

- To model graphs using the `Graph` interface and the `UnweightedGraph` class (§28.4).

- To display graphs visually (§28.5).

- To represent the traversal of a graph using the `UnweightedGraph.SearchTree` class (§28.6).

- To design and implement depth-first search (§28.7).

- To solve the connected-circle problem using depth-first search (§28.8).

- To design and implement breadth-first search (§28.9).

- To solve the nine tails problem using breadth-first search (§28.10).

CHAPTER 28

28.1 Introduction

Many real-world problems can be solved using graph algorithms.

problem

Graphs are useful in modeling and solving real-world problems. For example, the problem to find the least number of flights between two cities can be modeled using a graph, where the vertices represent cities and the edges represent the flights between two adjacent cities, as shown in Figure 28.1. The problem of finding the minimal number of connecting flights between two cities is reduced to finding the shortest path between two vertices in a graph. At United Parcel Service, each driver makes an average 120 stops per day. There are many possible ways for ordering these stops. UPS spent hundreds of millions of dollars for 10 years to develop a system called Orion, which stands for On-Road Integrated Optimization and Navigation. The system uses graph algorithms to plan the most cost-efficient routes for each driver. This chapter studies the algorithms for unweighted graphs, and the next chapter studies those for weighted graphs.

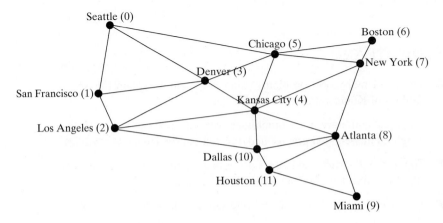

FIGURE 28.1 A graph can be used to model the flights between the cities.

graph theory

Seven Bridges of Königsberg

The study of graph problems is known as *graph theory*. Graph theory was founded by Leonhard Euler in 1736, when he introduced graph terminology to solve the famous *Seven Bridges of Königsberg* problem. The city of Königsberg, Prussia (now Kaliningrad, Russia), was divided by the Pregel River. There were two islands on the river. The city and islands were connected by seven bridges, as shown in Figure 28.2a. The question is, can one take a walk, cross each bridge exactly once, and return to the starting point? Euler proved that it is not possible.

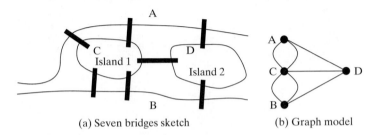

(a) Seven bridges sketch   (b) Graph model

FIGURE 28.2 Seven bridges connected islands and land.

To establish a proof, Euler first abstracted the Königsberg city map by eliminating all streets, producing the sketch shown in Figure 28.2a. Next, he replaced each land mass with a dot, called a *vertex* or a *node*, and each bridge with a line, called an *edge*, as shown in Figure 28.2b. This structure with vertices and edges is called a *graph*.

Looking at the graph, we ask whether there is a path starting from any vertex, traversing all edges exactly once, and returning to the starting vertex. Euler proved that for such a path to exist, each vertex must have an even number of edges. Therefore, the Seven Bridges of Königsberg problem has no solution.

Graphs have many applications in various areas, such as in computer science, mathematics, biology, engineering, economics, genetics, and social sciences. This chapter presents the algorithms for depth-first search and breadth-first search, and their applications. The next chapter presents the algorithms for finding a minimum spanning tree and shortest paths in weighted graphs, and their applications.

28.2 Basic Graph Terminologies

A graph consists of vertices, and edges that connect the vertices.

Key Point

This chapter does not assume that you have any prior knowledge of graph theory or discrete mathematics. We use plain and simple terms to define graphs.

what is a graph?

What is a graph? A *graph* is a mathematical structure that represents relationships among entities in the real world. For example, the graph in Figure 28.1 represents the flights among cities, and the graph in Figure 28.2b represents the bridges among land masses.

A graph consists of a nonempty set of vertices (also known as *nodes* or *points*), and a set of edges that connect the vertices. For convenience, we define a graph as G = (V, E), where V represents a set of vertices and E represents a set of edges. For example, V and E for the graph in Figure 28.1 are as follows:

define a graph

```
V = {"Seattle", "San Francisco", "Los Angeles",
     "Denver", "Kansas City", "Chicago", "Boston", "New York",
     "Atlanta", "Miami", "Dallas", "Houston"};

E = {{"Seattle", "San Francisco"},{"Seattle", "Chicago"},
     {"Seattle", "Denver"}, {"San Francisco", "Denver"},
     ...
     };
```

A graph may be directed or undirected. In a *directed graph*, each edge has a direction, which indicates you can move from one vertex to the other through the edge. You can model parent/child relationships using a directed graph, where an edge from vertex A to B indicates that A is a parent of B. Figure 28.3a shows a directed graph.

directed vs. undirected graphs

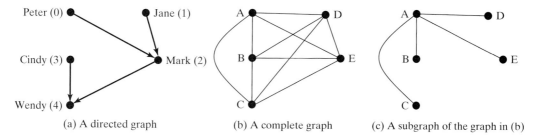

(a) A directed graph   (b) A complete graph   (c) A subgraph of the graph in (b)

FIGURE 28.3 Graphs may appear in many forms.

In an *undirected graph*, you can move in both directions between vertices. The graph in Figure 28.1 is undirected.

weighted vs. unweighted
  graphs

adjacent vertices
incident edges
degree
neighbor

loop
parallel edge
simple graph
complete graph
connected graph
subgraph

cycle
tree
spanning tree

Edges may be weighted or unweighted. For example, you can assign a weight for each edge in the graph in Figure 28.1 to indicate the flight time between the two cities.

Two vertices in a graph are said to be *adjacent* if they are connected by the same edge. Similarly, two edges are said to be *adjacent* if they are connected to the same vertex. An edge in a graph that joins two vertices is said to be *incident* to both vertices. The *degree* of a vertex is the number of edges incident to it.

Two vertices are called *neighbors* if they are adjacent. Similarly, two edges are called *neighbors* if they are adjacent.

A *loop* is an edge that links a vertex to itself. If two vertices are connected by two or more edges, these edges are called *parallel edges*. A *simple graph* is one that doesn't have any loops or parallel edges. In a *complete graph*, every two pairs of vertices are connected, as shown in Figure 28.3b.

A graph is *connected* if there exists a path between any two vertices in the graph. A *subgraph* of a graph *G* is a graph whose vertex set is a subset of that of *G* and whose edge set is a subset of that of *G*. For example, the graph in Figure 28.3c is a subgraph of the graph in Figure 28.3b.

Assume the graph is connected and undirected. A *cycle* is a closed path that starts from a vertex and ends at the same vertex. A connected graph is a *tree* if it does not have cycles. A *spanning tree* of a graph *G* is a connected subgraph of *G*, and the subgraph is a tree that contains all vertices in *G*.

graph learning tool on
Companion Website

 Pedagogical Note

Before we introduce graph algorithms and applications, it is helpful to get acquainted with graphs using the interactive tool at liveexample.pearsoncmg.com/dsanimation /GraphLearningTooleBook.html, as shown in Figure 28.4. The tool allows you to add/ remove/move vertices and draw edges using mouse gestures. You can also find depth-first search (DFS) trees and breadth-first search (BFS) trees, and the shortest path between two vertices.

 Check Point

28.2.1 What is the famous *Seven Bridges of Königsberg* problem?

28.2.2 What is a graph? Explain the following terms: undirected graph, directed graph, weighted graph, degree of a vertex, parallel edge, simple graph, complete graph, connected graph, cycle, subgraph, tree, and spanning tree.

28.2.3 How many edges are in a complete graph with 5 vertices? How many edges are in a tree of 5 vertices?

28.2.4 How many edges are in a complete graph with *n* vertices? How many edges are in a tree of *n* vertices?

28.3 Representing Graphs

 Key Point

Representing a graph is to store its vertices and edges in a program. The data structure for storing a graph is arrays or lists.

To write a program that processes and manipulates graphs, you have to store or represent data for the graphs in the computer.

28.3.1   Representing Vertices

The vertices can be stored in an array or a list. For example, you can store all the city names in the graph in Figure 28.1 using the following array:

```
String[] vertices = {"Seattle", "San Francisco", "Los Angeles",
    "Denver", "Kansas City", "Chicago", "Boston", "New York",
    "Atlanta", "Miami", "Dallas", "Houston"};
```

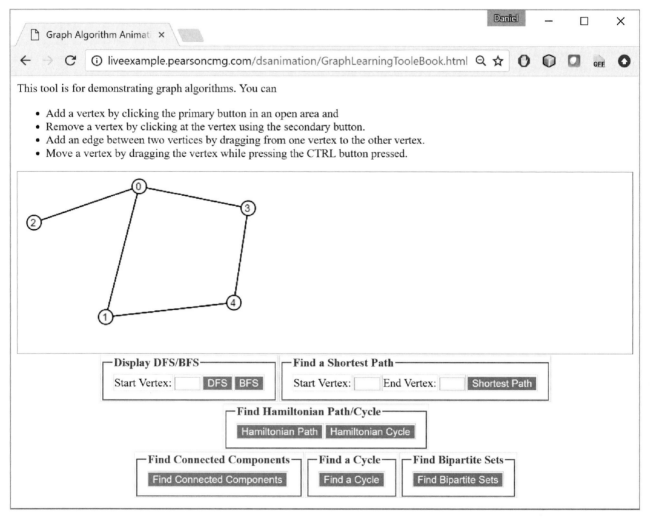

FIGURE 28.4 You can use the tool to create a graph with mouse gestures and show DFS/BFS trees and shortest paths.

 Note

The vertices can be objects of any type. For example, you can consider cities as objects that contain the information such as its name, population, and mayor. Thus, you may define vertices as follows:

vertex type

```
City city0 = new City("Seattle", 608660, "Mike McGinn");
. . .
City city11 = new City("Houston", 2099451, "Annise Parker");
City[] vertices = {city0, city1, . . . , city11};

public class City {
  private String cityName;
  private int population;
  private String mayor;

  public City(String cityName, int population, String mayor) {
    this.cityName = cityName;
    this.population = population;
    this.mayor = mayor;
  }
```

```
    public String getCityName() {
      return cityName;
    }

    public int getPopulation() {
      return population;
    }

    public String getMayor() {
      return mayor;
    }

    public void setMayor(String mayor) {
      this.mayor = mayor;
    }

    public void setPopulation(int population) {
      this.population = population;
    }
  }
```

The vertices can be conveniently labeled using natural numbers $0, 1, 2, \ldots, n-1$, for a graph of n vertices. Thus, `vertices[0]` represents `"Seattle"`, `vertices[1]` represents `"San Francisco"`, and so on, as shown in Figure 28.5.

vertices[0]	Seattle
vertices[1]	San Francisco
vertices[2]	Los Angeles
vertices[3]	Denver
vertices[4]	Kansas City
vertices[5]	Chicago
vertices[6]	Boston
vertices[7]	New York
vertices[8]	Atlanta
vertices[9]	Miami
vertices[10]	Dallas
vertices[11]	Houston

FIGURE 28.5 An array stores the vertex names.

reference vertex

 Note

You can reference a vertex by its name or its index, whichever is more convenient. Obviously, it is easy to access a vertex via its index in a program.

28.3.2 Representing Edges: Edge Array

The edges can be represented using a two-dimensional array. For example, you can store all the edges in the graph in Figure 28.1 using the following array:

```
int[][] edges = {
  {0, 1}, {0, 3}, {0, 5},
  {1, 0}, {1, 2}, {1, 3},
  {2, 1}, {2, 3}, {2, 4}, {2, 10},
  {3, 0}, {3, 1}, {3, 2}, {3, 4}, {3, 5},
  {4, 2}, {4, 3}, {4, 5}, {4, 7}, {4, 8}, {4, 10},
  {5, 0}, {5, 3}, {5, 4}, {5, 6}, {5, 7},
  {6, 5}, {6, 7},
  {7, 4}, {7, 5}, {7, 6}, {7, 8},
  {8, 4}, {8, 7}, {8, 9}, {8, 10}, {8, 11},
  {9, 8}, {9, 11},
  {10, 2}, {10, 4}, {10, 8}, {10, 11},
  {11, 8}, {11, 9}, {11, 10}
};
```

This representation is known as the *edge array*. The vertices and edges in Figure 28.3a can be represented as follows:

edge array

```
String[] vertices = {"Peter", "Jane", "Mark", "Cindy", "Wendy"};

int[][] edges = {{0, 2}, {1, 2}, {2, 4}, {3, 4}};
```

28.3.3 Representing Edges: Edge Objects

Another way to represent the edges is to define edges as objects and store the edges in a `java.util.ArrayList`. The `Edge` class can be defined as in Listing 28.1.

LISTING 28.1 Edge.java

```
public class Edge {
  int u;
  int v;

  public Edge(int u, int v) {
    this.u = u;
    this.v = v;
  }

  public boolean equals(Object o) {
    return u == ((Edge)o).u && v == ((Edge)o).v;
  }
}
```

For example, you can store all the edges in the graph in Figure 28.1 using the following list:

```
java.util.ArrayList<Edge> list = new java.util.ArrayList<>();
list.add(new Edge(0, 1));
list.add(new Edge(0, 3));
list.add(new Edge(0, 5));
...
```

Storing `Edge` objects in an `ArrayList` is useful if you don't know the edges in advance.

While representing edges using an edge array or `Edge` objects may be intuitive for input, it's not efficient for internal processing. The next two sections introduce the representation of graphs using *adjacency matrices* and *adjacency lists*. These two data structures are efficient for processing graphs.

28.3.4   Representing Edges: Adjacency Matrices

Assume the graph has *n* vertices. You can use a two-dimensional *n* × *n* matrix, say `adjacencyMatrix`, to represent the edges. Each element in the array is `0` or `1`. `adjacencyMatrix[i][j]` is `1` if there is an edge from vertex *i* to vertex *j*; otherwise, `adjacencyMatrix[i][j]` is `0`. If the graph is undirected, the matrix is symmetric, because `adjacencyMatrix[i][j]` is the same as `adjacencyMatrix[j][i]`. For exam-ple, the edges in the graph in Figure 28.1 can be represented using an *adjacency matrix* as follows:

adjacency matrix

```
int[][] adjacencyMatrix = {
  {0, 1, 0, 1, 0, 1, 0, 0, 0, 0, 0, 0}, // Seattle
  {1, 0, 1, 1, 0, 0, 0, 0, 0, 0, 0, 0}, // San Francisco
  {0, 1, 0, 1, 1, 1, 0, 0, 0, 0, 0, 0}, // Los Angeles
  {1, 1, 1, 0, 1, 1, 0, 0, 0, 0, 0, 0}, // Denver
  {0, 0, 1, 1, 0, 1, 0, 1, 1, 0, 1, 0}, // Kansas City
  {1, 0, 0, 1, 1, 0, 1, 1, 0, 0, 0, 0}, // Chicago
  {0, 0, 0, 0, 0, 1, 0, 1, 0, 0, 0, 0}, // Boston
  {0, 0, 0, 0, 1, 1, 1, 0, 1, 0, 0, 0}, // New York
  {0, 0, 0, 1, 1, 0, 0, 1, 0, 1, 1, 1}, // Atlanta
  {0, 0, 0, 0, 0, 0, 0, 0, 1, 0, 0, 1}, // Miami
  {0, 0, 1, 0, 1, 0, 0, 0, 1, 0, 0, 1}, // Dallas
  {0, 0, 0, 0, 0, 0, 0, 0, 1, 1, 1, 0}  // Houston
};
```

> **Note**
> Since the matrix is symmetric for an undirected graph, to save storage you can use a ragged array.

ragged array

The adjacency matrix for the directed graph in Figure 28.3a can be represented as follows:

```
int[][] a = {{0, 0, 1, 0, 0}, // Peter
             {0, 0, 1, 0, 0}, // Jane
             {0, 0, 0, 0, 1}, // Mark
             {0, 0, 0, 0, 1}, // Cindy
             {0, 0, 0, 0, 0}  // Wendy
            };
```

28.3.5   Representing Edges: Adjacency Lists

adjacency vertex lists
adjacency edge lists

You can represent edges using *adjacency vertex lists* or *adjacency edge lists*. An adjacency vertex list for a vertex *i* contains the vertices that are adjacent to *i* and an adjacency edge list for a vertex *i* contains the edges that are adjacent to *i*. You may define an array of lists. The array has *n* entries, and each entry is a list. The adjacency vertex list for vertex *i* contains all the vertices *j* such that there is an edge from vertex *i* to vertex *j*. For example, to represent the edges in the graph in Figure 28.1, you can create an array of lists as follows:

```
java.util.List<Integer>[] neighbors = new java.util.List[12];
```

`neighbors[0]` contains all vertices adjacent to vertex `0` (i.e., Seattle), `neighbors[1]` contains all vertices adjacent to vertex `1` (i.e., San Francisco), and so on, as shown in Figure 28.6.

To represent the adjacency edge lists for the graph in Figure 28.1, you can create an array of lists as follows:

```
java.util.List<Edge>[] neighbors = new java.util.List[12];
```

`neighbors[0]` contains all edges adjacent to vertex `0` (i.e., Seattle), `neighbors[1]` contains all edges adjacent to vertex `1` (i.e., San Francisco), and so on, as shown in Figure 28.7.

Seattle	neighbors[0]	1	3	5			
San Francisco	neighbors[1]	0	2	3			
Los Angeles	neighbors[2]	1	3	4	10		
Denver	neighbors[3]	0	1	2	4	5	
Kansas City	neighbors[4]	2	3	5	7	8	10
Chicago	neighbors[5]	0	3	4	6	7	
Boston	neighbors[6]	5	7				
New York	neighbors[7]	4	5	6	8		
Atlanta	neighbors[8]	4	7	9	10	11	
Miami	neighbors[9]	8	11				
Dallas	neighbors[10]	2	4	8	11		
Houston	neighbors[11]	8	9	10			

FIGURE 28.6 Edges in the graph in Figure 28.1 are represented using adjacency vertex lists.

Seattle	neighbors[0]	Edge(0, 1)	Edge(0, 3)	Edge(0, 5)			
San Francisco	neighbors[1]	Edge(1, 0)	Edge(1, 2)	Edge(1, 3)			
Los Angeles	neighbors[2]	Edge(2, 1)	Edge(2, 3)	Edge(2, 4)	Edge(2, 10)		
Denver	neighbors[3]	Edge(3, 0)	Edge(3, 1)	Edge(3, 2)	Edge(3, 4)	Edge(3, 5)	
Kansas City	neighbors[4]	Edge(4, 2)	Edge(4, 3)	Edge(4, 5)	Edge(4, 7)	Edge(4, 8)	Edge(4, 10)
Chicago	neighbors[5]	Edge(5, 0)	Edge(5, 3)	Edge(5, 4)	Edge(5, 6)	Edge(5, 7)	
Boston	neighbors[6]	Edge(6, 5)	Edge(6, 7)				
New York	neighbors[7]	Edge(7, 4)	Edge(7, 5)	Edge(7, 6)	Edge(7, 8)		
Atlanta	neighbors[8]	Edge(8, 4)	Edge(8, 7)	Edge(8, 9)	Edge(8, 10)	Edge(8, 11)	
Miami	neighbors[9]	Edge(9, 8)	Edge(9, 11)				
Dallas	neighbors[10]	Edge(10, 2)	Edge(10, 4)	Edge(10, 8)	Edge(10, 11)		
Houston	neighbors[11]	Edge(11, 8)	Edge(11, 9)	Edge(11, 10)			

FIGURE 28.7 Edges in the graph in Figure 28.1 are represented using adjacency edge lists.

Note

You can represent a graph using an adjacency matrix or adjacency lists. Which one is better? If the graph is dense (i.e., there are a lot of edges), using an adjacency matrix is preferred. If the graph is very sparse (i.e., very few edges), using adjacency lists is better, because using an adjacency matrix would waste a lot of space.

adjacency matrices vs. adjacency lists

Both adjacency matrices and adjacency lists can be used in a program to make algorithms more efficient. For example, it takes $O(1)$ constant time to check whether two vertices are connected using an adjacency matrix, and it takes linear time $O(m)$ to print all edges in a graph using adjacency lists, where m is the number of edges.

adjacency vertex lists vs. adjacency edge lists

Note

Adjacency vertex list is simpler for representing unweighted graphs. However, adjacency edge lists are more flexible for a wide range of graph applications. It is easy to add additional constraints on edges using adjacency edge lists. For this reason, this book will use adjacency edge lists to represent graphs.

using `ArrayList`

You can use arrays, array lists, or linked lists to store adjacency lists. We will use lists instead of arrays, because the lists are easily expandable to enable you to add new vertices. Further we will use array lists instead of linked lists, because our algorithms only require searching for adjacent vertices in the list. Using array lists is more efficient for our algorithms. Using array lists, the adjacency edge list in Figure 28.6 can be built as follows:

```
List<ArrayList<Edge>> neighbors = new ArrayList<>();
neighbors.add(new ArrayList<Edge>());
neighbors.get(0).add(new Edge(0, 1));
neighbors.get(0).add(new Edge(0, 3));
neighbors.get(0).add(new Edge(0, 5));
neighbors.add(new ArrayList<Edge>());
neighbors.get(1).add(new Edge(1, 0));
neighbors.get(1).add(new Edge(1, 2));
neighbors.get(1).add(new Edge(1, 3));
...
...
neighbors.get(11).add(new Edge(11, 8));
neighbors.get(11).add(new Edge(11, 9));
neighbors.get(11).add(new Edge(11, 10));
```

Check Point

28.3.1 How do you represent vertices in a graph? How do you represent edges using an edge array? How do you represent an edge using an edge object? How do you represent edges using an adjacency matrix? How do you represent edges using adjacency lists?

28.3.2 Represent the following graph using an edge array, a list of edge objects, an adjacency matrix, an adjacency vertex list, and an adjacency edge list, respectively.

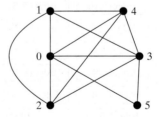

28.4 Modeling Graphs

The `Graph` *interface defines the common operations for a graph.*

Key Point

The Java Collections Framework serves as a good example for designing complex data structures. The common features of data structures are defined in the interfaces (e.g., `Collection`, `Set`, `List`, `Queue`), as shown in Figure 20.1. This design pattern is useful for modeling graphs. We will define an interface named `Graph` that contains all the common operations of graphs. Many concrete graphs can be added to the design. For example, we will define such graphs named `UnweightedGraph` and `WeightedGraph`. The relationships of these interfaces and classes are illustrated in Figure 28.8.

FIGURE 28.8 Common operations of graphs are defined in the interface and concrete classes define concrete graphs.

What are the common operations for a graph? In general, you need to get the number of vertices in a graph, get all vertices in a graph, get the vertex object with a specified index, get the index of the vertex with a specified name, get the neighbors for a vertex, get the degree for a vertex, clear the graph, add a new vertex, add a new edge, perform a depth-first search, and perform a breadth-first search. Depth-first search and breadth-first search will be introduced in the next section. Figure 28.9 illustrates these methods in the UML diagram.

`UnweightedGraph` does not introduce any new methods. A list of vertices and an edge adjacency list are defined in the class. With these data fields, it is sufficient to implement all the methods defined in the `Graph` interface. For convenience, we assume the graph is a simple graph, that is, a vertex has no edge to itself and there are no parallel edges from vertex *u* to *v*.

«interface» Graph<V>	The generic type V is the type for vertices.
+getSize(): int	Returns the number of vertices in the graph.
+getVertices(): List<V>	Returns the vertices in the graph.
+getVertex(index: int): V	Returns the vertex object for the specified vertex index.
+getIndex(v: V): int	Returns the index for the specified vertex and return –1 if *v* is not in the graph.
+getNeighbors(index: int): List<Integer>	Returns the neighbors of vertex with the specified index.
+getDegree(index: int): int	Returns the degree for a specified vertex index.
+printEdges(): void	Prints the edges.
+clear(): void	Clears the graph.
+addVertex(v: V): boolean	Returns true if *v* is added to the graph. Returns false if *v* is already in the graph.
+addEdge(u: int, v: int): boolean	Adds an edge from *u* to *v* to the graph. Throws `IllegalArgumentException` if *u* or *v* is invalid. Returns true if the edge is added and false if (*u*, *v*) is already in the graph.
+addEdge(e: Edge): boolean	Adds an edge into the adjacency edge list.
+remove(v: V): boolean	Removes a vertex from the graph.
+remove(u: int, v: int): boolean	Removes an edge from the graph.
+dfs(v: int): UnWeightedGraph<V>.SearchTree	Obtains a depth-first search tree starting from *v*.
+bfs(v: int): UnWeightedGraph<V>.SearchTree	Obtains a breadth-first search tree starting from *v*.

UnweightedGraph<V>	
#vertices: List<V>	Vertices in the graph.
#neighbors: List<List<Edge>>	Neighbors for each vertex in the graph.
+UnweightedGraph()	Constructs an empty graph.
+UnweightedGraph(vertices: V[], edges: int[][])	Constructs a graph with the specified edges and vertices stored in arrays.
+UnweightedGraph(vertices: List<V>, edges: List<Edge>)	Constructs a graph with the specified edges and vertices stored in lists.
+UnweightedGraph(edges: int[][], numberOfVertices: int)	Constructs a graph with the specified edges in an array and the integer vertices 1, 2, ...
+UnweightedGraph(edges: List<Edge>, numberOfVertices: int)	Constructs a graph with the specified edges in a list and the integer vertices 1, 2, ...

FIGURE 28.9 The `Graph` interface defines the common operations for all types of graphs.

vertices and their indices

Note

You can create a graph with any type of vertices. Each vertex is associated with an index, which is the same as the index of the vertex in the vertices list. If you create a graph without specifying the vertices, the vertices are the same as their indices.

Assume the `Graph` interface and the `UnweightedGraph` class are available. Listing 28.2 gives a test program that creates the graph in Figure 28.1 and another graph for the one in Figure 28.3a.

LISTING 28.2 TestGraph.java

```java
 1  public class TestGraph {
 2    public static void main(String[] args) {
 3      String[] vertices = {"Seattle", "San Francisco", "Los Angeles",
 4        "Denver", "Kansas City", "Chicago", "Boston", "New York",
 5        "Atlanta", "Miami", "Dallas", "Houston"};
 6
 7      // Edge array for graph in Figure 28.1
 8      int[][] edges = {
 9        {0, 1}, {0, 3}, {0, 5},
10        {1, 0}, {1, 2}, {1, 3},
11        {2, 1}, {2, 3}, {2, 4}, {2, 10},
12        {3, 0}, {3, 1}, {3, 2}, {3, 4}, {3, 5},
13        {4, 2}, {4, 3}, {4, 5}, {4, 7}, {4, 8}, {4, 10},
14        {5, 0}, {5, 3}, {5, 4}, {5, 6}, {5, 7},
15        {6, 5}, {6, 7},
16        {7, 4}, {7, 5}, {7, 6}, {7, 8},
17        {8, 4}, {8, 7}, {8, 9}, {8, 10}, {8, 11},
18        {9, 8}, {9, 11},
19        {10, 2}, {10, 4}, {10, 8}, {10, 11},
20        {11, 8}, {11, 9}, {11, 10}
21      };
22
23      Graph<String> graph1 = new UnweightedGraph<>(vertices, edges);
24      System.out.println("The number of vertices in graph1: "
25        + graph1.getSize());
26      System.out.println("The vertex with index 1 is "
27        + graph1.getVertex(1));
28      System.out.println("The index for Miami is " +
29        graph1.getIndex("Miami"));
30      System.out.println("The edges for graph1:");
31      graph1.printEdges();
32
33      // List of Edge objects for graph in Figure 28.3a
34      String[] names = {"Peter", "Jane", "Mark", "Cindy", "Wendy"};
35      java.util.ArrayList<Edge> edgeList
36        = new java.util.ArrayList<>();
37      edgeList.add(new Edge(0, 2));
38      edgeList.add(new Edge(1, 2));
39      edgeList.add(new Edge(2, 4));
40      edgeList.add(new Edge(3, 4));
41      // Create a graph with 5 vertices
42      Graph<String> graph2 = new UnweightedGraph<>
43        (java.util.Arrays.asList(names), edgeList);
44      System.out.println("\nThe number of vertices in graph2: "
45        + graph2.getSize());
46      System.out.println("The edges for graph2:");
47      graph2.printEdges();
48    }
49  }
```

Margin notes (left column): vertices · edges · create a graph · number of vertices · get vertex · get index · print edges · list of Edge objects · create a graph · print edges

```
The number of vertices in graph1: 12
The vertex with index 1 is San Francisco
The index for Miami is 9
The edges for graph1:
Seattle (0): (0, 1) (0, 3) (0, 5)
San Francisco (1): (1, 0) (1, 2) (1, 3)
Los Angeles (2): (2, 1) (2, 3) (2, 4) (2, 10)
Denver (3): (3, 0) (3, 1) (3, 2) (3, 4) (3, 5)
Kansas City (4): (4, 2) (4, 3) (4, 5) (4, 7) (4, 8) (4, 10)
Chicago (5): (5, 0) (5, 3) (5, 4) (5, 6) (5, 7)
Boston (6): (6, 5) (6, 7)
New York (7): (7, 4) (7, 5) (7, 6) (7, 8)
Atlanta (8): (8, 4) (8, 7) (8, 9) (8, 10) (8, 11)
Miami (9): (9, 8) (9, 11)
Dallas (10): (10, 2) (10, 4) (10, 8) (10, 11)
Houston (11): (11, 8) (11, 9) (11, 10)

The number of vertices in graph2: 5
The edges for graph2:
Peter (0): (0, 2)
Jane (1): (1, 2)
Mark (2): (2, 4)
Cindy (3): (3, 4)
Wendy (4):
```

The program creates `graph1` for the graph in Figure 28.1 in lines 3–23. The vertices for `graph1` are defined in lines 3–5. The edges for `graph1` are defined in 8–21. The edges are represented using a two-dimensional array. For each row `i` in the array, `edges[i][0]` and `edges[i][1]` indicate there is an edge from vertex `edges[i][0]` to vertex `edges[i][1]`. For example, the first row, {0, 1}, represents the edge from vertex 0 (`edges[0][0]`) to vertex 1 (`edges[0][1]`). The row {0, 5} represents the edge from vertex 0 (`edges[2][0]`) to vertex 5 (`edges[2][1]`). The graph is created in line 23. Line 31 invokes the `printEdges()` method on `graph1` to display all edges in `graph1`.

The program creates `graph2` for the graph in Figure 28.3a in lines 34–43. The edges for `graph2` are defined in lines 37–40. `graph2` is created using a list of `Edge` objects in line 43. Line 47 invokes the `printEdges()` method on `graph2` to display all edges in `graph2`.

Note both `graph1` and `graph2` contain the vertices of strings. The vertices are associated with indices 0, 1, . . . , n–1. The index is the location of the vertex in `vertices`. For example, the index of vertex `Miami` is 9.

Now, we turn our attention to implementing the interface and classes. Listings 28.3 and 28.4 give the `Graph` interface and the `UnweightedGraph` class, respectively.

LISTING 28.3   Graph.java

```
1  public interface Graph<V> {
2    /** Return the number of vertices in the graph */
3    public int getSize();
4
5    /** Return the vertices in the graph */
6    public java.util.List<V> getVertices();
7
8    /** Return the object for the specified vertex index */
9    public V getVertex(int index);
10
11   /** Return the index for the specified vertex object */
```
getSize

getVertices

getVertex

getIndex

```
12    public int getIndex(V v);
13
14    /** Return the neighbors of vertex with the specified index */
```

getNeighbors

```
15    public java.util.List<Integer> getNeighbors(int index);
16
17    /** Return the degree for a specified vertex */
```

getDegree

```
18    public int getDegree(int v);
19
20    /** Print the edges */
```

printEdges

```
21    public void printEdges();
22
23    /** Clear the graph */
```

clear

```
24    public void clear();
25
26    /** Add a vertex to the graph */
```

addVertex

```
27    public boolean addVertex(V vertex);
28
29    /** Add an edge to the graph */
```

addEdge

```
30    public boolean addEdge(int u, int v);
31
32    /** Add an edge to the graph */
```

addEdge

```
33    public boolean addEdge(Edge e);
34
35    /** Remove a vertex v from the graph, return true if successful */
```

remove vertex

```
36    public boolean remove(V v);
37
38    /** Remove an edge (u, v) from the graph, return true if successful */
```

remove edge

```
39    public boolean remove(int u, int v);
40
41    /** Obtain a depth-first search tree */
```

dfs

```
42    public UnweightedGraph<V>.SearchTree dfs(int v);
43
44    /** Obtain a breadth-first search tree */
```

bfs

```
45    public UnweightedGraph<V>.SearchTree bfs(int v);
46  }
```

LISTING 28.4   UnweightedGraph.java

```
1    import java.util.*;
2
3    public class UnweightedGraph<V> implements Graph<V> {
4      protected List<V> vertices = new ArrayList<>(); // Store vertices
5      protected List<List<Edge>> neighbors
6        = new ArrayList<>(); // Adjacency Edge lists
7
8      /** Construct an empty graph */
```

no-arg constructor

```
9      protected UnweightedGraph() {
10     }
11
12     /** Construct a graph from vertices and edges stored in arrays */
```

constructor

```
13     protected UnweightedGraph(V[] vertices, int[][] edges) {
14       for (int i = 0; i < vertices.length; i++)
15         addVertex(vertices[i]);
16
17       createAdjacencyLists(edges, vertices.length);
18     }
19
20     /** Construct a graph from vertices and edges stored in List */
```

constructor

```
21     protected UnweightedGraph(List<V> vertices, List<Edge> edges) {
22       for (int i = 0; i < vertices.size(); i++)
```

```
23         addVertex(vertices.get(i));
24
25       createAdjacencyLists(edges, vertices.size());
26     }
27
28     /** Construct a graph for integer vertices 0, 1, 2 and edge list */
29     protected UnweightedGraph(List<Edge> edges, int numberOfVertices) {    constructor
30       for (int i = 0; i < numberOfVertices; i++)
31         addVertex((V)(new Integer(i))); // vertices is {0, 1, . . . }
32
33       createAdjacencyLists(edges, numberOfVertices);
34     }
35
36     /** Construct a graph from integer vertices 0, 1, and edge array */
37     protected UnweightedGraph(int[][] edges, int numberOfVertices) {    constructor
38       for (int i = 0; i < numberOfVertices; i++)
39         addVertex((V)(new Integer(i))); // vertices is {0, 1, . . . }
40
41       createAdjacencyLists(edges, numberOfVertices);
42     }
43
44     /** Create adjacency lists for each vertex */
45     private void createAdjacencyLists(
46         int[][] edges, int numberOfVertices) {
47       for (int i = 0; i < edges.length; i++) {
48         addEdge(edges[i][0], edges[i][1]);
49       }
50     }
51
52     /** Create adjacency lists for each vertex */
53     private void createAdjacencyLists(
54         List<Edge> edges, int numberOfVertices) {
55       for (Edge edge: edges) {
56         addEdge(edge.u, edge.v);
57       }
58     }
59
60     @Override /** Return the number of vertices in the graph */
61     public int getSize() {                                      getSize
62       return vertices.size();
63     }
64
65     @Override /** Return the vertices in the graph */
66     public List<V> getVertices() {                              getVertices
67       return vertices;
68     }
69
70     @Override /** Return the object for the specified vertex */
71     public V getVertex(int index) {                             getVertex
72       return vertices.get(index);
73     }
74
75     @Override /** Return the index for the specified vertex object */
76     public int getIndex(V v) {                                  getIndex
77       return vertices.indexOf(v);
78     }
79
80     @Override /** Return the neighbors of the specified vertex */
81     public List<Integer> getNeighbors(int index) {              getNeighbors
82       List<Integer> result = new ArrayList<>();
```

```
83        for (Edge e: neighbors.get(index))
84          result.add(e.v);
85
86        return result;
87    }
88
89    @Override /** Return the degree for a specified vertex */
90    public int getDegree(int v) {
91      return neighbors.get(v).size();
92    }
93
94    @Override /** Print the edges */
95    public void printEdges() {
96      for (int u = 0; u < neighbors.size(); u++) {
97        System.out.print(getVertex(u) + " (" + u + "): ");
98        for (Edge e: neighbors.get(u)) {
99          System.out.print("(" + getVertex(e.u) + ", " +
100             getVertex(e.v) + ") ");
101        }
102        System.out.println();
103      }
104    }
105
106    @Override /** Clear the graph */
107    public void clear() {
108      vertices.clear();
109      neighbors.clear();
110    }
111
112    @Override /** Add a vertex to the graph */
113    public boolean addVertex(V vertex) {
114      if (!vertices.contains(vertex)) {
115        vertices.add(vertex);
116        neighbors.add(new ArrayList<Edge>());
117        return true;
118      }
119      else {
120        return false;
121      }
122    }
123
124    @Override /** Add an edge to the graph */
125    public boolean addEdge(Edge e) {
126      if (e.u < 0 || e.u > getSize() - 1)
127        throw new IllegalArgumentException("No such index: " + e.u);
128
129      if (e.v < 0 || e.v > getSize() - 1)
130        throw new IllegalArgumentException("No such index: " + e.v);
131
132      if (!neighbors.get(e.u).contains(e)) {
133        neighbors.get(e.u).add(e);
134        return true;
135      }
136      else {
137        return false;
138      }
139    }
140
141    @Override /** Add an edge to the graph */
142    public boolean addEdge(int u, int v) {
```

getDegree

printEdges

clear

addVertex

addEdge

addEdge overloaded

```
143        return addEdge(new Edge(u, v));
144      }
145
146      @Override /** Obtain a DFS tree starting from vertex v */
147      /** To be discussed in Section 28.7 */
148      public SearchTree dfs(int v) {
149        List<Integer> searchOrder = new ArrayList<>();
150        int[] parent = new int[vertices.size()];
151        for (int i = 0; i < parent.length; i++)
152          parent[i] = -1; // Initialize parent[i] to -1
153
154        // Mark visited vertices
155        boolean[] isVisited = new boolean[vertices.size()];
156
157        // Recursively search
158        dfs(v, parent, searchOrder, isVisited);
159
160        // Return a search tree
161        return new SearchTree(v, parent, searchOrder);
162      }
163
164      /** Recursive method for DFS search */
165      private void dfs(int v, int[] parent, List<Integer> searchOrder,
166          boolean[] isVisited) {
167        // Store the visited vertex
168        searchOrder.add(v);
169        isVisited[v] = true; // Vertex v visited
170
171        for (Edge e : neighbors.get(v)) {// e.u is v
172          if (!isVisited[e.v]) {// e.v is w in Listing 28.8
173            parent[e.v] = v; // The parent of vertex w is v
174            dfs(e.v, parent, searchOrder, isVisited); // Recursive search
175          }
176        }
177      }
178
179      @Override /** Starting bfs search from vertex v */
180      /** To be discussed in Section 28.9 */
181      public SearchTree bfs(int v) {
182        List<Integer> searchOrder = new ArrayList<>();
183        int[] parent = new int[vertices.size()];
184        for (int i = 0; i < parent.length; i++)
185          parent[i] = -1; // Initialize parent[i] to -1
186
187        java.util.LinkedList<Integer> queue =
188          new java.util.LinkedList<>(); // list used as a queue
189        boolean[] isVisited = new boolean[vertices.size()];
190        queue.offer(v); // Enqueue v
191        isVisited[v] = true; // Mark it visited
192
193        while (!queue.isEmpty()) {
194          int u = queue.poll(); // Dequeue to u
195          searchOrder.add(u); // u searched
196          for (Edge e: neighbors.get(u)) {// Note that e.u is u
197            if (!isVisited[e.v]) {// e.v is w in Listing 28.11
198              queue.offer(e.v); // Enqueue w
199              parent[e.v] = u; // The parent of w is u
200              isVisited[e.v] = true; // Mark it visited
201            }
202          }
```

dfs method

bfs method

SearchTree inner class

```
203        }
204
205        return new SearchTree(v, parent, searchOrder);
206      }
207
208      /** Tree inner class inside the UnweightedGraph class */
209      /** To be discussed in Section 28.6 */
210      public class SearchTree {
211        private int root; // The root of the tree
212        private int[] parent; // Store the parent of each vertex
213        private List<Integer> searchOrder; // Store the search order
214
215        /** Construct a tree with root, parent, and searchOrder */
216        public SearchTree(int root, int[] parent,
217          List<Integer> searchOrder) {
218          this.root = root;
219          this.parent = parent;
220          this.searchOrder = searchOrder;
221        }
222
223        /** Return the root of the tree */
224        public int getRoot() {
225          return root;
226        }
227
228        /** Return the parent of vertex v */
229        public int getParent(int v) {
230          return parent[v];
231        }
232
233        /** Return an array representing search order */
234        public List<Integer> getSearchOrder() {
235          return searchOrder;
236        }
237
238        /** Return number of vertices found */
239        public int getNumberOfVerticesFound() {
240          return searchOrder.size();
241        }
242
243        /** Return the path of vertices from a vertex to the root */
244        public List<V> getPath(int index) {
245          ArrayList<V> path = new ArrayList<>();
246
247          do {
248            path.add(vertices.get(index));
249            index = parent[index];
250          }
251          while (index != -1);
252
253          return path;
254        }
255
256        /** Print a path from the root to vertex v */
257        public void printPath(int index) {
258          List<V> path = getPath(index);
259          System.out.print("A path from " + vertices.get(root) + " to " +
260            vertices.get(index) + ": ");
261          for (int i = path.size() - 1; i >= 0; i--)
262            System.out.print(path.get(i) + " ");
263        }
```

```
264
265        /** Print the whole tree */
266        public void printTree() {
267          System.out.println("Root is: " + vertices.get(root));
268          System.out.print("Edges: ");
269          for (int i = 0; i < parent.length; i++) {
270            if (parent[i] != -1) {
271              // Display an edge
272              System.out.print("(" + vertices.get(parent[i]) + ", " +
273                vertices.get(i) + ") ");
274            }
275          }
276          System.out.println();
277        }
278      }
279
280      @Override /** Remove vertex v and return true if successful */
281      public boolean remove(V v) {
282        return true; // Implementation left as an exercise
283      }
284
285      @Override /** Remove edge (u, v) and return true if successful */
286      public boolean remove(int u, int v) {
287        return true; // Implementation left as an exercise
289      }
290    }
```

The code in the `Graph` interface in Listing 28.3 is straightforward. Let us digest the code in the `UnweightedGraph` class in Listing 28.4.

The `UnweightedGraph` class defines the data field `vertices` (line 4) to store vertices and `neighbors` (line 5) to store edges in adjacency `edges` lists. `neighbors.get(i)` stores all edges adjacent to vertex `i`. Four overloaded constructors are defined in lines 9–42 to create a default graph, or a graph from arrays or lists of edges and vertices. The `createAdjacencyLists(int[][] edges, int numberOfVertices)` method creates adjacency lists from edges in an array (lines 45–50). The `createAdjacencyLists (List<Edge> edges, int numberOfVertices)` method creates adjacency lists from edges in a list (lines 53–58).

The `getNeighbors(u)` method (lines 81–87) returns a list of vertices adjacent to vertex `u`. The `clear()` method (lines 106–110) removes all vertices and edges from the graph. The `addVertex(u)` method (lines 112–122) adds a new vertex to `vertices` and returns true. It returns false if the vertex is already in the graph (line 120).

The `addEdge(e)` method (lines 124–139) adds a new edge to the adjacency edge list and returns true. It returns false if the edge is already in the graph. This method may throw `IllegalArgumentExcepiton` if the edge is invalid (lines 126–130).

The `addEdge(u, v)` method (lines 141–144) adds an edge (u, v) to the graph. If a graph is undirected, you should invoke `addEdge(u, v)` and `addEdge(v, u)` to add an edge between u and v.

The `printEdges()` method (lines 95–104) displays all vertices and edges adjacent to each vertex.

The code in lines 148–278 gives the methods for finding a depth-first search tree and a breadth-first search tree, which will be introduced in Sections 28.7 and 28.9, respectively.

28.4.1 Describe the methods in `Graph` and `UnweightedGraph`.

28.4.2 For the code in Listing 28.2, TestGraph.java, what is `graph1.getIndex("Seattle")`? What is `graph1.getDegree(5)`? What is `graph1.getVertex(4)`?

Check
Point

28.4.3 Show the output of the following code:

```java
public class Test {
  public static void main(String[] args) {
    Graph<Character> graph = new UnweightedGraph<>();
    graph.addVertex('U');
    graph.addVertex('V');
    int indexForU = graph.getIndex('U');
    int indexForV = graph.getIndex('V');
    System.out.println("indexForU is " + indexForU);
    System.out.println("indexForV is " + indexForV);
    graph.addEdge(indexForU, indexForV);
    System.out.println("Degree of U is " +
      graph.getDegree(indexForU));
    System.out.println("Degree of V is " +
      graph.getDegree(indexForV));
  }
}
```

28.4.4 What will getIndex(v) return if v is not in the graph? What happens to getVertex(index) if index is not in the graph? What happens to addVertex(v) if v is already in the graph? What happens to addEdge(u, v) if u or v is not in the graph?

28.5 Graph Visualization

Key Point

To display a graph visually, each vertex must be assigned a location.

The preceding section introduced the Graph interface and the UnweightedGraph class. This section discusses how to display graphs graphically. In order to display a graph, you need to know where each vertex is displayed and the name of each vertex. To ensure a graph can be displayed, we define an interface named Displayable that has the methods for obtaining the x- and y-coordinates and their names, and make vertices instances of Displayable, in Listing 28.5.

LISTING 28.5 Displayable.java

Displayable interface

```java
1  public interface Displayable {
2    public double getX(); // Get x-coordinate of the vertex
3    public double getY(); // Get y-coordinate of the vertex
4    public String getName(); // Get display name of the vertex
5  }
```

A graph with Displayable vertices can now be displayed on a pane named GraphView, as shown in Listing 28.6.

LISTING 28.6 GraphView.java

extends BorderPane
Displayable vertices

```java
1  import javafx.scene.Group;
2  import javafx.scene.layout.BorderPane;
3  import javafx.scene.shape.Circle;
4  import javafx.scene.shape.Line;
5  import javafx.scene.text.Text;
6
7  public class GraphView extends BorderPane {
8    private Graph<? extends Displayable> graph;
9    private Group group = new Group();
10
11   public GraphView(Graph<? extends Displayable> graph) {
12     this.graph = graph;
13     this.setCenter(group); // Center the group
```

```
14          repaintGraph();
15      }
16
17      private void repaintGraph() {
18        group.getChildren().clear(); // Clear group for a new display
19
20        // Draw vertices and text for vertices
21        java.util.List<? extends Displayable> vertices
22          = graph.getVertices();
23        for (int i = 0; i < graph.getSize(); i++) {
24          double x = vertices.get(i).getX();
25          double y = vertices.get(i).getY();
26          String name = vertices.get(i).getName();
27
28          group.getChildren().add(new Circle(x, y, 16));          display a vertex
29          group.getChildren().add(new Text(x - 8, y - 18, name));  display a text
30        }
31
32        // Draw edges for pairs of vertices
33        for (int i = 0; i < graph.getSize(); i++) {
34          java.util.List<Integer> neighbors = graph.getNeighbors(i);
35          double x1 = graph.getVertex(i).getX();
36          double y1 = graph.getVertex(i).getY();
37          for (int v: neighbors) {
38            double x2 = graph.getVertex(v).getX();
39            double y2 = graph.getVertex(v).getY();
40
41            // Draw an edge for (i, v)
42            group.getChildren().add(new Line(x1, y1, x2, y2));       draw an edge
43          }
44        }
45      }
46  }
```

To display a graph on a pane, simply create an instance of `GraphView` by passing the graph as an argument in the constructor (line 11). The class for the graph's vertex must implement the `Displayable` interface in order to display the vertices (lines 21–44). For each vertex index `i`, invoking `graph.getNeighbors(i)` returns its adjacency list (line 34). From this list, you can find all vertices that are adjacent to `i` and draw a line to connect `i` with its adjacent vertex (lines 35–42).

Listing 28.7 gives an example of displaying the graph in Figure 28.1, as shown in Figure 28.10.

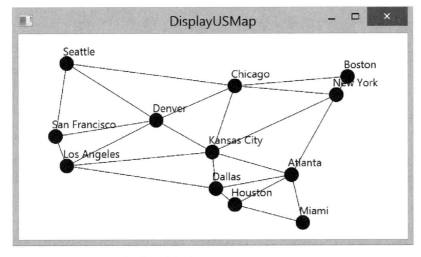

FIGURE 28.10   The graph is displayed in the pane.

LISTING 28.7 DisplayUSMap.java

```
1   import javafx.application.Application;
2   import javafx.scene.Scene;
3   import javafx.stage.Stage;
4
5   public class DisplayUSMap extends Application {
6     @Override // Override the start method in the Application class
7     public void start(Stage primaryStage) {
8       City[] vertices = {new City("Seattle", 75, 50),
9         new City("San Francisco", 50, 210),
10        new City("Los Angeles", 75, 275), new City("Denver", 275, 175),
11        new City("Kansas City", 400, 245),
12        new City("Chicago", 450, 100), new City("Boston", 700, 80),
13        new City("New York", 675, 120), new City("Atlanta", 575, 295),
14        new City("Miami", 600, 400), new City("Dallas", 408, 325),
15        new City("Houston", 450, 360) };
16
17      // Edge array for graph in Figure 28.1
18      int[][] edges = {
19        {0, 1}, {0, 3}, {0, 5}, {1, 0}, {1, 2}, {1, 3},
20        {2, 1}, {2, 3}, {2, 4}, {2, 10},
21        {3, 0}, {3, 1}, {3, 2}, {3, 4}, {3, 5},
22        {4, 2}, {4, 3}, {4, 5}, {4, 7}, {4, 8}, {4, 10},
23        {5, 0}, {5, 3}, {5, 4}, {5, 6}, {5, 7},
24        {6, 5}, {6, 7}, {7, 4}, {7, 5}, {7, 6}, {7, 8},
25        {8, 4}, {8, 7}, {8, 9}, {8, 10}, {8, 11},
26        {9, 8}, {9, 11}, {10, 2}, {10, 4}, {10, 8}, {10, 11},
27        {11, 8}, {11, 9}, {11, 10}
28      };
29
30      Graph<City> graph = new UnweightedGraph<>(vertices, edges);
31
32      // Create a scene and place it in the stage
33      Scene scene = new Scene(new GraphView(graph), 750, 450);
34      primaryStage.setTitle("DisplayUSMap"); // Set the stage title
35      primaryStage.setScene(scene); // Place the scene in the stage
36      primaryStage.show(); // Display the stage
37    }
38
39    static class City implements Displayable {
40      private double x, y;
41      private String name;
42
43      City(String name, double x, double y) {
44        this.name = name;
45        this.x = x;
46        this.y = y;
47      }
48
49      @Override
50      public double getX() {
51        return x;
52      }
53
54      @Override
55      public double getY() {
56        return y;
57      }
58
```

create a graph

create a GraphView

City class

```
59      @Override
60      public String getName() {
61        return name;
62      }
63    }
64  }
```

The class `City` is defined to model the vertices with their coordinates and names (lines 39–63). The program creates a graph with the vertices of the `City` type (line 30). Since `City` implements `Displayable`, a `GraphView` object created for the graph displays the graph in the pane (line 33).

As an exercise to get acquainted with the graph classes and interfaces, add a city (e.g., Savannah) with appropriate edges into the graph.

28.5.1   Will Listing 28.7, DisplayUSMap.java work, if the code in lines 38–42 in Listing 28.6, GraphView.java is replaced by the following code?

```
if (i < v) {
  double x2 = graph.getVertex(v).getX();
  double y2 = graph.getVertex(v).getY();

  // Draw an edge for (i, v)
  getChildren().add(new Line(x1, y1, x2, y2));
}
```

28.5.2   For the `graph1` object created in Listing 28.1, TestGraph.java, can you create a `GraphView` object as follows?

```
GraphView view = new GraphView(graph1);
```

28.6 Graph Traversals

Depth-first and breadth-first are two common ways to traverse a graph.

Graph traversal is the process of visiting each vertex in the graph exactly once. There are two popular ways to traverse a graph: *depth-first traversal* (or *depth-first search*) and *breadth-first traversal* (or *breadth-first search*). Both traversals result in a spanning tree, which can be modeled using a class, as shown in Figure 28.11. Note `SearchTree` is an inner class defined in the `UnweightedGraph` class. `UnweightedGraph<V>.SearchTree` is different from the `Tree` interface defined in Section 25.2.5. `UnweightedGraph<V>.SearchTree` is a specialized class designed for describing the parent–child relationship of the nodes, whereas the `Tree` interface defines common operations such as searching, inserting, and deleting in a tree. Since there is no need to perform these operations for a spanning tree, `UnweightedGraph<V>.SearchTree` is not defined as a subtype of `Tree`.

The `SearchTree` class is defined as an inner class in the `UnweightedGraph` class in lines 210–278 in Listing 28.4. The constructor creates a tree with the root, edges, and a search order.

The `SearchTree` class defines seven methods. The `getRoot()` method returns the root of the tree. You can get the order of the vertices searched by invoking the `getSearchOrder()` method. You can invoke `getParent(v)` to find the parent of vertex `v` in the search. Invoking `getNumberOfVerticesFound()` returns the number of vertices searched. The method `getPath(index)` returns a list of vertices from the specified vertex index to the root. Invoking `printPath(v)` displays a path from the root to `v`. You can display all edges in the tree using the `printTree()` method.

Sections 28.7 and 28.9 will introduce depth-first search and breadth-first search, respectively. Both searches will result in an instance of the `SearchTree` class.

28.6.1   Does `UnweightedGraph<V>.SearchTree` implement the `Tree` interface defined in Listing 25.3, Tree.java?

28.6.2   What method do you use to find the parent of a vertex in the tree?

Key Point

depth-first search
breadth-first search

UnweightedGraph<V>.SearchTree	
−root: int −parent: int[] −searchOrder: List<Integer>	The root of the tree. The parents of the vertices. The orders for traversing the vertices.

+SearchTree(root: int, parent: int[],
   searchOrder: List<Integer>)
	Constructs a tree with the specified root, parent, and
	   searchOrder.

+getRoot(): int	Returns the root of the tree.
+getSearchOrder(): List<Integer>	Returns the order of vertices searched.
+getParent(index: int): int	Returns the parent for the specified vertex index.
+getNumberOfVerticesFound(): int	Returns the number of vertices searched.
+getPath(index: int): List<V>	Returns a list of vertices from the specified vertex index to the root.
+printPath(index: int): void	Displays a path from the root to the specified vertex.
+printTree(): void	Displays tree with the root and all edges.

FIGURE 28.11 The SearchTree class describes the nodes with parent–child relationships.

28.7 Depth-First Search (DFS)

Key Point

The depth-first search of a graph starts from a vertex in the graph and visits all vertices in the graph as far as possible before backtracking.

The depth-first search of a graph is like the depth-first search of a tree discussed in Section 25.2.4, Tree Traversal. In the case of a tree, the search starts from the root. In a graph, the search can start from any vertex.

A depth-first search of a tree first visits the root, then recursively visits the subtrees of the root. Similarly, the depth-first search of a graph first visits a vertex, then it recursively visits all the vertices adjacent to that vertex. The difference is that the graph may contain cycles, which could lead to an infinite recursion. To avoid this problem, you need to track the vertices that have already been visited.

The search is called *depth-first* because it searches "deeper" in the graph as much as possible. The search starts from some vertex *v*. After visiting *v*, it visits an unvisited neighbor of *v*. If *v* has no unvisited neighbor, the search backtracks to the vertex from which it reached *v*. We assume that the graph is connected and the search starting from any vertex can reach all the vertices. If this is not the case, see Programming Exercise 28.4 for finding connected components in a graph.

28.7.1 Depth-First Search Algorithm

The algorithm for the depth-first search is described in Listing 28.8.

LISTING 28.8 Depth-First Search Algorithm

```
Input: G = (V, E) and a starting vertex v
Output: a DFS tree rooted at v

1  SearchTree dfs(vertex v) {
2    visit v;
3    for each neighbor w of v
4      if (w has not been visited) {
5        set v as the parent for w in the tree;
6        dfs(w);
7      }
8  }
```

visit v

check a neighbor
set a parent in the tree
recursive search

You can use an array named `isVisited` to denote whether a vertex has been visited. Initially, `isVisited[i]` is `false` for each vertex *i*. Once a vertex, say *v*, is visited, `isVisited[v]` is set to `true`.

Consider the graph in Figure 28.12a. Suppose we start the depth-first search from vertex 0. First visit 0, then any of its neighbors, say 1. Now 1 is visited, as shown in Figure 28.12b. Vertex 1 has three neighbors—0, 2, and 4. Since 0 has already been visited, you will visit either 2 or 4. Let us pick 2. Now 2 is visited, as shown in Figure 28.12c. Vertex 2 has three neighbors: 0, 1, and 3. Since 0 and 1 have already been visited, pick 3. 3 is now visited, as shown in Figure 28.12d. At this point, the vertices have been visited in this order:

```
0, 1, 2, 3
```

Since all the neighbors of 3 have been visited, backtrack to 2. Since all the vertices of 2 have been visited, backtrack to 1. 4 is adjacent to 1, but 4 has not been visited. Therefore, visit 4, as shown in Figure 28.12e. Since all the neighbors of 4 have been visited, backtrack to 1. Since all the neighbors of 1 have been visited, backtrack to 0. Since all the neighbors of 0 have been visited, the search ends.

Since each edge and each vertex is visited only once, the time complexity of the `dfs` method is $O(|E| + |V|)$, where $|E|$ denotes the number of edges and $|V|$ the number of vertices.

DFS time complexity

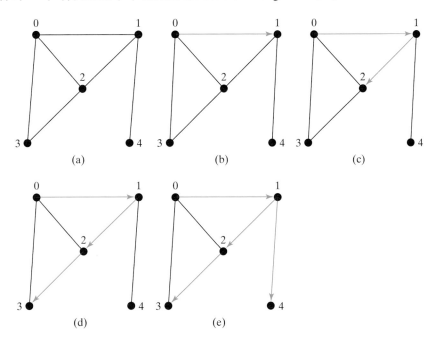

FIGURE 28.12   Depth-first search visits a node and its neighbors recursively.

28.7.2   Implementation of Depth-First Search

The algorithm for DFS in Listing 28.8 uses recursion. It is natural to use recursion to implement it. Alternatively, you can use a stack (see Programming Exercise 28.3).

The `dfs(int v)` method is implemented in lines 148–177 in Listing 28.4. It returns an instance of the `SearchTree` class with vertex `v` as the root. The method stores the vertices searched in the list `searchOrder` (line 149), the parent of each vertex in the array `parent` (line 150), and uses the `isVisited` array to indicate whether a vertex has been visited (line 155). It invokes the helper method `dfs(v, parent, searchOrder, isVisited)` to perform a depth-first search (line 158).

In the recursive helper method, the search starts from vertex `v`. `v` is added to `searchOrder` in line 168 and is marked as visited (line 169). For each unvisited neighbor of `v`, the method is recursively invoked to perform a depth-first search. When a vertex `e.v` is visited, the parent

U.S. Map Search

of `e.v` is stored in `parent[e.v]` (line 173). The method returns when all vertices are visited for a connected graph, or in a connected component.

Listing 28.9 gives a test program that displays a DFS for the graph in Figure 28.1 starting from Chicago. The graphical illustration of the DFS starting from Chicago is shown in Figure 28.13.

LISTING 28.9 TestDFS.java

```java
 1  public class TestDFS {
 2    public static void main(String[] args) {
 3      String[] vertices = {"Seattle", "San Francisco", "Los Angeles",
 4        "Denver", "Kansas City", "Chicago", "Boston", "New York",
 5        "Atlanta", "Miami", "Dallas", "Houston"};
 6
 7      int[][] edges = {
 8        {0, 1}, {0, 3}, {0, 5},
 9        {1, 0}, {1, 2}, {1, 3},
10        {2, 1}, {2, 3}, {2, 4}, {2, 10},
11        {3, 0}, {3, 1}, {3, 2}, {3, 4}, {3, 5},
12        {4, 2}, {4, 3}, {4, 5}, {4, 7}, {4, 8}, {4, 10},
13        {5, 0}, {5, 3}, {5, 4}, {5, 6}, {5, 7},
14        {6, 5}, {6, 7},
15        {7, 4}, {7, 5}, {7, 6}, {7, 8},
16        {8, 4}, {8, 7}, {8, 9}, {8, 10}, {8, 11},
17        {9, 8}, {9, 11},
18        {10, 2}, {10, 4}, {10, 8}, {10, 11},
19        {11, 8}, {11, 9}, {11, 10}
20      };
21
22      Graph<String> graph = new UnweightedGraph<>(vertices, edges);
23      UnweightedGraph<String>.SearchTree dfs =
24        graph.dfs(graph.getIndex("Chicago"));
25
26      java.util.List<Integer> searchOrders = dfs.getSearchOrder();
27      System.out.println(dfs.getNumberOfVerticesFound() +
28        " vertices are searched in this DFS order:");
29      for (int i = 0; i < searchOrders.size(); i++)
30        System.out.print(graph.getVertex(searchOrders.get(i)) + " ");
31      System.out.println();
32
33      for (int i = 0; i < searchOrders.size(); i++)
34        if (dfs.getParent(i) != -1)
35          System.out.println("parent of " + graph.getVertex(i) +
36            " is " + graph.getVertex(dfs.getParent(i)));
37    }
38  }
```

vertices

edges

create a graph

get DFS

get search order

```
12 vertices are searched in this DFS order:
  Chicago Seattle San Francisco Los Angeles Denver
  Kansas City New York Boston Atlanta Miami Houston Dallas
parent of Seattle is Chicago
parent of San Francisco is Seattle
parent of Los Angeles is San Francisco
parent of Denver is Los Angeles
parent of Kansas City is Denver
parent of Boston is New York
parent of New York is Kansas City
parent of Atlanta is New York
parent of Miami is Atlanta
parent of Dallas is Houston
parent of Houston is Miami
```

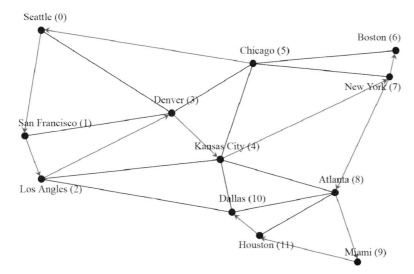

FIGURE 28.13 A DFS search starts from Chicago. *Source*: © Mozilla Firefox.

28.7.3 Applications of the DFS

The depth-first search can be used to solve many problems, such as the following:

- Detecting whether a graph is connected. Search the graph starting from any vertex. If the number of vertices searched is the same as the number of vertices in the graph, the graph is connected. Otherwise, the graph is not connected. (See Programming Exercise 28.1.)

- Detecting whether there is a path between two vertices (see Programming Exercise 28.5).

- Finding a path between two vertices (see Programming Exercise 28.5).

- Finding all connected components. A connected component is a maximal connected subgraph in which every pair of vertices are connected by a path (see Programming Exercise 28.4).

- Detecting whether there is a cycle in the graph (see Programming Exercise 28.6).

- Finding a cycle in the graph (see Programming Exercise 28.7).

- Finding a Hamiltonian path/cycle. A *Hamiltonian path* in a graph is a path that visits each vertex in the graph exactly once. A *Hamiltonian cycle* visits each vertex in the graph exactly once and returns to the starting vertex (see Programming Exercise 28.17).

The first six problems can be easily solved using the `dfs` method in Listing 28.4. To find a Hamiltonian path/cycle, you have to explore all possible DFSs to find the one that leads to the longest path. The Hamiltonian path/cycle has many applications, including for solving the well-known Knight's Tour problem, which is presented in Supplement VI.E on the Companion Website.

28.7.1 What is depth-first search?

28.7.2 Draw a DFS tree for the graph in Figure 28.3b starting from node `A`.

28.7.3 Draw a DFS tree for the graph in Figure 28.1 starting from vertex `Atlanta`.

28.7.4 What is the return type from invoking `dfs(v)`?

Check Point

28.7.5 The depth-first search algorithm described in Listing 28.8 uses recursion. Alternatively, you can use a stack to implement it, as shown below. Point out the error in this algorithm and give a correct algorithm.

```
// Wrong version
SearchTree dfs(vertex v) {
  push v into the stack;
  mark v visited;

  while (the stack is not empty) {
    pop a vertex, say u, from the stack
    visit u;
    for each neighbor w of u
      if (w has not been visited)
        push w into the stack;
  }
}
```

28.8 Case Study: The Connected Circles Problem

The connected circles problem is to determine whether all circles in a two-dimensional plane are connected. This problem can be solved using a depth-first traversal.

The DFS algorithm has many applications. This section applies the DFS algorithm to solve the connected circles problem.

In the connected circles problem, you determine whether all the circles in a two-dimensional plane are connected. If all the circles are connected, they are painted as filled circles, as shown in Figure 28.14a. Otherwise, they are not filled, as shown in Figure 28.14b.

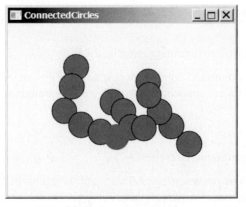
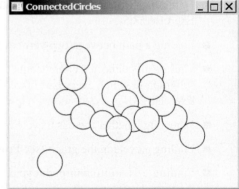

(a) Circles are connected   (b) Circles are not connected

FIGURE 28.14 You can apply DFS to determine whether the circles are connected.
Source: Copyright © 1995–2016 Oracle and/or its affiliates. All rights reserved. Used with permission.

We will write a program that lets the user create a circle by clicking a mouse in a blank area that is not currently covered by a circle. As the circles are added, the circles are repainted filled if they are connected or unfilled otherwise.

We will create a graph to model the problem. Each circle is a vertex in the graph. Two circles are connected if they overlap. We apply the DFS in the graph, and if all vertices are found in the depth-first search, the graph is connected.

The program is given in Listing 28.10.

LISTING 28.10 ConnectedCircles.java

```java
import javafx.application.Application;
import javafx.geometry.Point2D;
import javafx.scene.Node;
import javafx.scene.Scene;
import javafx.scene.layout.Pane;
import javafx.scene.paint.Color;
import javafx.scene.shape.Circle;
import javafx.stage.Stage;

public class ConnectedCircles extends Application {
  @Override // Override the start method in the Application class
  public void start(Stage primaryStage) {
    // Create a scene and place it in the stage
    Scene scene = new Scene(new CirclePane(), 450, 350);        create a circle pane
    primaryStage.setTitle("ConnectedCircles"); // Set the stage title
    primaryStage.setScene(scene); // Place the scene in the stage
    primaryStage.show(); // Display the stage
  }

  /** Pane for displaying circles */
  class CirclePane extends Pane {                               pane for showing circles
    public CirclePane() {
      this.setOnMouseClicked(e -> {                             handle mouse clicked
        if (!isInsideACircle(new Point2D(e.getX(), e.getY()))) {  is it inside another circle?
          // Add a new circle
          getChildren().add(new Circle(e.getX(), e.getY(), 20));  add a new circle
          colorIfConnected();                                  color if all connected
        }
      });
    }

    /** Returns true if the point is inside an existing circle */
    private boolean isInsideACircle(Point2D p) {
      for (Node circle: this.getChildren())
        if (circle.contains(p))                                contains the point?
          return true;

      return false;
    }

    /** Color all circles if they are connected */
    private void colorIfConnected() {
      if (getChildren().size() == 0)
        return; // No circles in the pane

      // Build the edges
      java.util.List<Edge> edges                               create edges
        = new java.util.ArrayList<>();
      for (int i = 0; i < getChildren().size(); i++)
        for (int j = i + 1; j < getChildren().size(); j++)
          if (overlaps((Circle)(getChildren().get(i)),
              (Circle)(getChildren().get(j)))) {
            edges.add(new Edge(i, j));
            edges.add(new Edge(j, i));
          }

      // Create a graph with circles as vertices
```

create a graph

get a search tree
connected?

connected

not connected

two circles overlap?

```
58        Graph<Node> graph = new UnweightedGraph<>
59          ((java.util.List<Node>)getChildren(), edges);
60        UnweightedGraph<Node>.SearchTree tree = graph.dfs(0);
61        boolean isAllCirclesConnected = getChildren().size() == tree
62          .getNumberOfVerticesFound();
63
64        for (Node circle: getChildren()) {
65          if (isAllCirclesConnected) {  // All circles are connected
66            ((Circle)circle).setFill(Color.RED);
67          }
68          else {
69            ((Circle)circle).setStroke(Color.BLACK);
70            ((Circle)circle).setFill(Color.WHITE);
71          }
72        }
73      }
74    }
75
76    public static boolean overlaps(Circle circle1, Circle circle2) {
77      return new Point2D(circle1.getCenterX(), circle1.getCenterY()).
78        distance(circle2.getCenterX(), circle2.getCenterY())
79        <= circle1.getRadius() + circle2.getRadius();
80    }
81  }
```

The JavaFX `Circle` class contains the data fields x, y, and `radius`, which specify the circle's center location and radius. It also defines the `contains` method for testing whether a point is inside the circle. The `overlaps` method (lines 76–80) checks whether two circles overlap.

When the user clicks the mouse outside of any existing circle, a new circle is created centered at the mouse point and the circle is added to the list `circles` (line 26).

To detect whether the circles are connected, the program constructs a graph (lines 46–59). The circles are the vertices of the graph. The edges are constructed in lines 47–55. Two circle vertices are connected if they overlap (line 51). The DFS of the graph results in a tree (line 60). The tree's `getNumberOfVerticesFound()` returns the number of vertices searched. If it is equal to the number of circles, all circles are connected (lines 61–62).

28.8.1 How is a graph created for the connected circles problem?

28.8.2 When you click the mouse inside a circle, does the program create a new circle?

28.8.3 How does the program know if all circles are connected?

28.9 Breadth-First Search (BFS)

The breadth-first search of a graph visits the vertices level by level. The first level consists of the starting vertex. Each next level consists of the vertices adjacent to the vertices in the preceding level.

The breadth-first traversal of a graph is like the breadth-first traversal of a tree discussed in Section 25.2.4, Tree Traversal. With breadth-first traversal of a tree, the nodes are visited level by level. First the root is visited, then all the children of the root, then the grandchildren of the root, and so on. Similarly, the breadth-first search of a graph first visits a vertex, then all its adjacent vertices, then all the vertices adjacent to those vertices, and so on. To ensure each vertex is visited only once, it skips a vertex if it has already been visited.

28.9.1 Breadth-First Search Algorithm

The algorithm for the breadth-first search starting from vertex *v* in a graph is described in Listing 28.11.

LISTING 28.11   Breadth-First Search Algorithm

```
    Input: G = (V, E) and a starting vertex v
    Output: a BFS tree rooted at v

1   SearchTree bfs(vertex v) {
2     create an empty queue for storing vertices to be visited;      create a queue
3     add v into the queue;                                          enqueue v
4     mark v visited;
5
6     while (the queue is not empty) {
7       dequeue a vertex, say u, from the queue;                     dequeue into u
8       add u into a list of traversed vertices;                     u traversed
9       for each neighbor w of u                                     check a neighbor w
10        if w has not been visited {                                is w visited?
11          add w into the queue;                                    enqueue w
12          set u as the parent for w in the tree;
13          mark w visited;
14        }
15    }
16  }
```

Consider the graph in Figure 28.15a. Suppose you start the breadth-first search from vertex 0. First visit 0, then visit all its neighbors, 1, 2, and 3, as shown in Figure 28.15b. Vertex 1 has three neighbors: 0, 2, and 4. Since 0 and 2 have already been visited, you will now visit just 4, as shown in Figure 28.15c. Vertex 2 has three neighbors, 0, 1, and 3, which have all been visited. Vertex 3 has three neighbors, 0, 2, and 4, which have all been visited. Vertex 4 has two neighbors, 1 and 3, which have all been visited. Hence, the search ends.

Since each edge and each vertex is visited only once, the time complexity of the bfs method is $O(|E| + |V|)$, where $|E|$ denotes the number of edges and $|V|$ the number of vertices.

BFS time complexity

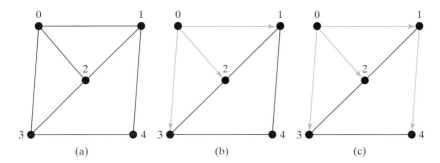

FIGURE 28.15   Breadth-first search visits a node, then its neighbors, then its neighbors's neighbors, and so on.

28.9.2   Implementation of Breadth-First Search

The bfs(int v) method is defined in the Graph interface and implemented in the UnweightedGraph class in Listing 28.4 (lines 181–206). It returns an instance of the SearchTree class with vertex v as the root. The method stores the vertices searched in the list searchOrder (line 182), the parent of each vertex in the array parent (line 183), uses a linked list for a queue (lines 187–188), and uses the isVisited array to indicate whether a vertex has been visited (line 191). The search starts from vertex v. v is added to the queue in line 190 and is marked as visited (line 191). The method now examines each vertex u in the queue (line 193) and adds it to searchOrder (line 195). The method adds each unvisited neighbor e.v of u to the queue (line 198), sets its parent to u (line 199), and marks it as visited (line 200).

Listing 28.12 gives a test program that displays a BFS for the graph in Figure 28.1 starting from Chicago. The graphical illustration of the BFS starting from Chicago is shown in Figure 28.16.

LISTING 28.12 TestBFS.java

vertices

edges

create a graph
create a BFS tree

get search order

```
 1  public class TestBFS {
 2    public static void main(String[] args) {
 3      String[] vertices = {"Seattle", "San Francisco", "Los Angeles",
 4        "Denver", "Kansas City", "Chicago", "Boston", "New York",
 5        "Atlanta", "Miami", "Dallas", "Houston"};
 6
 7      int[][] edges = {
 8        {0, 1}, {0, 3}, {0, 5},
 9        {1, 0}, {1, 2}, {1, 3},
10        {2, 1}, {2, 3}, {2, 4}, {2, 10},
11        {3, 0}, {3, 1}, {3, 2}, {3, 4}, {3, 5},
12        {4, 2}, {4, 3}, {4, 5}, {4, 7}, {4, 8}, {4, 10},
13        {5, 0}, {5, 3}, {5, 4}, {5, 6}, {5, 7},
14        {6, 5}, {6, 7},
15        {7, 4}, {7, 5}, {7, 6}, {7, 8},
16        {8, 4}, {8, 7}, {8, 9}, {8, 10}, {8, 11},
17        {9, 8}, {9, 11},
18        {10, 2}, {10, 4}, {10, 8}, {10, 11},
19        {11, 8}, {11, 9}, {11, 10}
20      };
21
22      Graph<String> graph = new UnweightedGraph<>(vertices, edges);
23      UnweightedGraph<String>.SearchTree bfs =
24        graph.bfs(graph.getIndex("Chicago"));
25
26      java.util.List<Integer> searchOrders = bfs.getSearchOrder();
27      System.out.println(bfs.getNumberOfVerticesFound() +
28        " vertices are searched in this order:");
29      for (int i = 0; i < searchOrders.size(); i++)
30        System.out.println(graph.getVertex(searchOrders.get(i)));
31
32      for (int i = 0; i < searchOrders.size(); i++)
33        if (bfs.getParent(i) != -1)
34          System.out.println("parent of " + graph.getVertex(i) +
35            " is " + graph.getVertex(bfs.getParent(i)));
36    }
37  }
```

```
12 vertices are searched in this order:
  Chicago Seattle Denver Kansas City Boston New York
  San Francisco Los Angeles Atlanta Dallas Miami Houston
parent of Seattle is Chicago
parent of San Francisco is Seattle
parent of Los Angeles is Denver
parent of Denver is Chicago
parent of Kansas City is Chicago
parent of Boston is Chicago
parent of New York is Chicago
parent of Atlanta is Kansas City
parent of Miami is Atlanta
parent of Dallas is Kansas City
parent of Houston is Atlanta
```

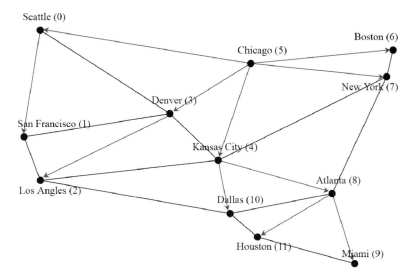

Seattle (0)

Boston (6)

Chicago (5)

New York (7)

Denver (3)

San Francisco (1)

Kansas City (4)

Atlanta (8)

Los Angles (2)

Dallas (10)

Houston (11)

Miami (9)

FIGURE 28.16 BFS search starts from Chicago. *Source*: © Mozilla Firefox.

28.9.3 Applications of the BFS

Many of the problems solved by the DFS can also be solved using the BFS. Specifically, the BFS can be used to solve the following problems:

- Detecting whether a graph is connected. A graph is connected if there is a path between any two vertices in the graph.
- Detecting whether there is a path between two vertices.
- Finding the shortest path between two vertices. You can prove that the path between the root and any node in the BFS tree is the shortest path between the root and the node. (See CheckPoint Question 28.9.5.)
- Finding all connected components. A connected component is a maximal connected subgraph in which every pair of vertices are connected by a path.
- Detecting whether there is a cycle in the graph (see Programming Exercise 28.6).
- Finding a cycle in the graph (see Programming Exercise 28.7).
- Testing whether a graph is bipartite. (A graph is bipartite if the vertices of the graph can be divided into two disjoint sets such that no edges exist between vertices in the same set.) (See Programming Exercise 28.8.)

28.9.1 What is the return type from invoking `bfs(v)`?

28.9.2 What is breadth-first search?

28.9.3 Draw a BFS tree for the graph in Figure 28.3b starting from node `A`.

28.9.4 Draw a BFS tree for the graph in Figure 28.1 starting from vertex `Atlanta`.

28.9.5 Prove the path between the root and any node in the BFS tree is the shortest path between the root and the node.

Check
Point

28.10 Case Study: The Nine Tails Problem

The nine tails problem can be reduced to the shortest path problem.

Key
Point

The nine tails problem is as follows. Nine coins are placed in a 3 × 3 matrix, with some face up and some face down. A legal move is to take any coin that is face up and reverse it, together with the coins adjacent to it (this does not include coins that are diagonally adjacent).

Your task is to find the minimum number of moves that lead to all coins being face down. For example, start with the nine coins as shown in Figure 28.17a. After you flip the second coin in the last row, the nine coins are now as shown in Figure 28.17b. After you flip the second coin in the first row, the nine coins are all face down, as shown in Figure 28.17c. See liveexample .pearsoncmg.com/dsanimation/NineCoin.html for an interactive demo.

H	H	H
T	T	T
H	H	H

(a)

H	H	H
T	H	T
T	T	T

(b)

T	T	T
T	T	T
T	T	T

(c)

FIGURE 28.17 The problem is solved when all coins are face down.

We will write a program that prompts the user to enter an initial state of the nine coins and displays the solution, as shown in the following sample run:

```
Enter the initial nine coins Hs and Ts:   HHHTTTHHH  ↵Enter

The steps to flip the coins are
HHH
TTT
HHH

HHH
THT
TTT

TTT
TTT
TTT
```

Each state of the nine coins represents a node in the graph. For example, the three states in Figure 28.17 correspond to three nodes in the graph. For convenience, we use a 3×3 matrix to represent all nodes and use 0 for heads and 1 for tails. Since there are nine cells and each cell is either 0 or 1, there are a total of 2^9 (512) nodes, labeled 0, 1, . . . , and 511, as shown in Figure 28.18.

0	0	0
0	0	0
0	0	0

0

0	0	0
0	0	0
0	0	1

1

0	0	0
0	0	0
0	1	0

2

0	0	0
0	0	0
0	1	1

3

.....

1	1	1
1	1	1
1	1	1

511

FIGURE 28.18 There are total of 512 nodes labeled in this order: 0, 1, 2, . . . , 511.

We assign an edge from node v to u if there is a legal move from u to v. Figure 28.19 shows a partial graph. Note there is an edge from 511 to 47, since you can flip a cell in node 47 to become node 511.

The last node in Figure 28.18 represents the state of nine face-down coins. For convenience, we call this last node the *target node*. Thus, the target node is labeled 511. Suppose the initial state of the nine tails problem corresponds to the node s. The problem is reduced to finding the shortest path from node s to the target node, which is equivalent to finding the path from node s to the target node in a BFS tree rooted at the target node.

Now the task is to build a directed graph that consists of 512 nodes labeled 0, 1, 2, . . . , 511, and edges among the nodes. Once the graph is created, obtain a BFS tree rooted at node 511. From the BFS tree, you can find the shortest path from the root to any vertex. We will create a class named `NineTailModel`, which contains the method to get the shortest path from the target node to any other node. The class UML diagram is shown in Figure 28.19.

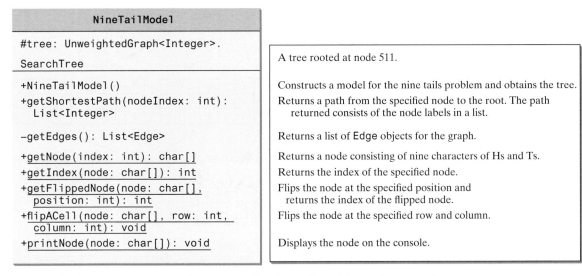

FIGURE 28.19 The `NineTailModel` class models the nine tails problem using a graph.

Visually, a node is represented in a 3 × 3 matrix with the letters `H` and `T`. In our program, we use a single-dimensional array of nine characters to represent a node. For example, the node for vertex `1` in Figure 28.18 is represented as {`'H'`, `'H'`, `'H'`, `'H'`, `'H'`, `'H'`, `'H'`, `'H'`, `'T'`} in the array.

The `getEdges()` method returns a list of `Edge` objects.

The `getNode(index)` method returns the node for the specified index. For example, `getNode(0)` returns the node that contains nine `H`s. `getNode(511)` returns the node that contains nine `T`s. The `getIndex(node)` method returns the index of the node.

Note the data field `tree` is defined as protected so it can be accessed from the `WeightedNineTail` subclass in the next chapter.

The `getFlippedNode(char[] node, int position)` method flips the node at the specified position and its adjacent positions. This method returns the index of the new node. The position is a value from 0 to 8, which points to a coin in the node, as shown in the following figure.

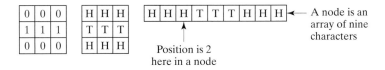

For example, for node `56` in Figure 28.20, flip it at position `0`, and you will get node `51`. If you flip node `56` at position `1`, you will get node `47`.

The `flipACell(char[] node, int row, int column)` method flips a node at the specified row and column. For example, if you flip node `56` at row `0` and column `0`, the new node is `408`. If you flip node `56` at row `2` and column `0`, the new node is `30`.

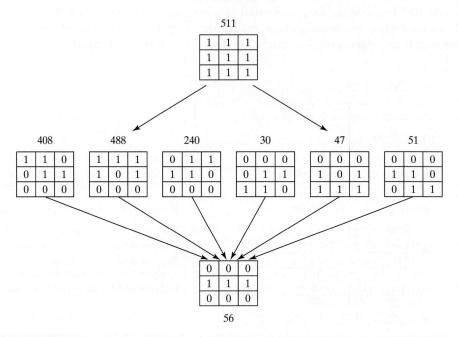

FIGURE 28.20 If node u becomes node v after cells are flipped, assign an edge from v to u.

Listing 28.13 shows the source code for NineTailModel.java.

LISTING 28.13   NineTailModel.java

```
1   import java.util.*;
2
3   public class NineTailModel {
4     public final static int NUMBER_OF_NODES = 512;
5     protected UnweightedGraph<Integer>.SearchTree tree;
6
7     /** Construct a model */
8     public NineTailModel() {
9       // Create edges
10      List<Edge> edges = getEdges();
11
12      // Create a graph
13      UnweightedGraph<Integer> graph = new UnweightedGraph<>(
14        edges, NUMBER_OF_NODES);
15
16      // Obtain a BSF tree rooted at the target node
17      tree = graph.bfs(511);
18    }
19
20    /** Create all edges for the graph */
21    private List<Edge> getEdges() {
22      List<Edge> edges =
23        new ArrayList<>(); // Store edges
24
25      for (int u = 0; u < NUMBER_OF_NODES; u++) {
26        for (int k = 0; k < 9; k++) {
27          char[] node = getNode(u); // Get the node for vertex u
```

declare a tree — line 5

create edges — line 10

create graph — line 13

create tree — line 17

get edges — line 21

```
28            if (node[k] == 'H') {
29              int v = getFlippedNode(node, k);
30              // Add edge (v, u) for a legal move from node u to node v
31              edges.add(new Edge(v, u));                                add an edge
32            }
33          }
34        }
35
36        return edges;
37      }
38
39      public static int getFlippedNode(char[] node, int position) {    flip cells
40        int row = position / 3;
41        int column = position % 3;
42
43        flipACell(node, row, column);
44        flipACell(node, row - 1, column);
45        flipACell(node, row + 1, column);
46        flipACell(node, row, column - 1);
47        flipACell(node, row, column + 1);
48
49        return getIndex(node);
50      }
51
52      public static void flipACell(char[] node, int row, int column) {  flip a cell
53        if (row >= 0 && row <= 2 && column >= 0 && column <= 2) {
54          // Within the boundary
55          if (node[row * 3 + column] == 'H')
56            node[row * 3 + column] = 'T'; // Flip from H to T
57          else
58            node[row * 3 + column] = 'H'; // Flip from T to H
59        }
60      }
61
62      public static int getIndex(char[] node) {                        get index for a node
63        int result = 0;
64
65        for (int i = 0; i < 9; i++)
66          if (node[i] == 'T')
67            result = result * 2 + 1;
68          else
69            result = result * 2 + 0;
70
71        return result;
72      }
73
74      public static char[] getNode(int index) {                        get node for an index
75        char[] result = new char[9];
76
77        for (int i = 0; i < 9; i++) {
78          int digit = index % 2;
79          if (digit == 0)
80            result[8 - i] = 'H';
81          else
82            result[8 - i] = 'T';
83          index = index / 2;
84        }
85
86        return result;
87      }
```

shortest path

```
88
89    public List<Integer> getShortestPath(int nodeIndex) {
90      return tree.getPath(nodeIndex);
91    }
92
```

display a node

```
93    public static void printNode(char[] node) {
94      for (int i = 0; i < 9; i++)
95        if (i % 3 != 2)
96          System.out.print(node[i]);
97        else
98          System.out.println(node[i]);
99
100     System.out.println();
101   }
102 }
```

For example:
node: THHHHHHTT
Output:

```
T H H
H H H
H T T
```

The constructor (lines 8–18) creates a graph with 512 nodes, and each edge corresponds to the move from one node to the other (line 10). From the graph, a BFS tree rooted at the target node `511` is obtained (line 17).

To create edges, the `getEdges` method (lines 21–37) checks each node `u` to see if it can be flipped to another node `v`. If so, add (`v`, `u`) to the `Edge` list (line 31). The `getFlippedNode(node, position)` method finds a flipped node by flipping an `H` cell and its neighbors in a node (lines 43–47). The `flipACell(node, row, column)` method actually flips an `H` cell and its neighbors in a node (lines 52–60).

The `getIndex(node)` method is implemented in the same way as converting a binary number to a decimal number (lines 62–72). The `getNode(index)` method returns a node consisting of the letters `H` and `T` (lines 74–87).

The `getShortestpath(nodeIndex)` method invokes the `getPath(nodeIndex)` method to get the vertices in a shortest path from the specified node to the target node (lines 89–91).

The `printNode(node)` method displays a node on the console (lines 93–101).

Listing 28.14 gives a program that prompts the user to enter an initial node and displays the steps to reach the target node.

LISTING 28.14   NineTail.java

```
1   import java.util.Scanner;
2
3   public class NineTail {
4     public static void main(String[] args) {
5       // Prompt the user to enter nine coins' Hs and Ts
6       System.out.print("Enter the initial nine coins Hs and Ts: ");
7       Scanner input = new Scanner(System.in);
8       String s = input.nextLine();
9       char[] initialNode = s.toCharArray();
10
11      NineTailModel model = new NineTailModel();
12      java.util.List<Integer> path =
13        model.getShortestPath(NineTailModel.getIndex(initialNode));
14
15      System.out.println("The steps to flip the coins are ");
16      for (int i = 0; i < path.size(); i++)
17        NineTailModel.printNode(
18          NineTailModel.getNode(path.get(i).intValue()));
19    }
20  }
```

initial node — line 9

create model — line 11

get shortest path — line 13

The program prompts the user to enter an initial node with nine letters with a combination of Hs and Ts as a string in line 8, obtains an array of characters from the string (line 9), creates a graph model to get a BFS tree (line 11), obtains the shortest path from the initial node to the target node (lines 12–13), and displays the nodes in the path (lines 16–18).

28.10.1 How are the nodes created for the graph in `NineTailModel`?

28.10.2 How are the edges created for the graph in `NineTailModel`?

28.10.3 What is returned after invoking `getIndex("HTHTTTHHH".toCharArray())` in Listing 28.13? What is returned after invoking `getNode(46)` in Listing 28.13?

28.10.4 If lines 26 and 27 are swapped in Listing 28.13, NineTailModel.java, will the program work? Why not?

KEY TERMS

adjacency list   1047
adjacency matrix   1047
adjacent vertices   1042
breadth-first search   1061
complete graph   1042
cycle   1042
degree   1042
depth-first search   1061
directed graph   1041
graph   1040

incident edges   1042
parallel edge   1042
Seven Bridges of Königsberg   1040
simple graph   1042
spanning tree   1042
tree   1042
undirected graph   1041
unweighted graph   1042
weighted graph   1042

CHAPTER SUMMARY

1. A *graph* is a useful mathematical structure that represents relationships among entities in the real world. You learned how to model graphs using classes and interfaces, how to represent vertices and edges using arrays and linked lists, and how to implement operations for graphs.

2. Graph traversal is the process of visiting each vertex in the graph exactly once. You learned two popular ways for traversing a graph: the *depth-first search* (DFS) and *breadth-first search* (BFS).

3. DFS and BFS can be used to solve many problems such as detecting whether a graph is connected, detecting whether there is a cycle in the graph, and finding the shortest path between two vertices.

QUIZ

Answer the quiz for this chapter online at the book Companion Website.

PROGRAMMING EXERCISES

MyProgrammingLab

Sections 28.6–28.10

*28.1 (*Test whether a graph is connected*) Write a program that reads a graph from a file and determines whether the graph is connected. The first line in the file contains a number that indicates the number of vertices (n). The vertices are labeled as 0, 1, . . . , n−1. Each subsequent line, with the format u v1 v2 . . . , describes edges (u, v1), (u, v2), and so on. Figure 28.21 gives the examples of two files for their corresponding graphs.

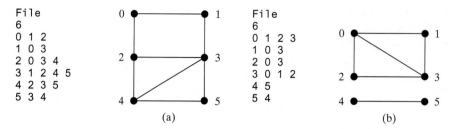

```
File                        0 ●————————● 1        File                        0 ●————————● 1
6                                                  6                               |\       |
0 1 2                                              0 1 2 3                         | \      |
1 0 3                       2 ●————————● 3         1 0 3                           |  \     |
2 0 3 4                       |      ╱ |           2 0 3                           |   \    |
3 1 2 4 5                     |    ╱   |           3 0 1 2      2 ●————————● 3      |    \   |
4 2 3 5                       |  ╱     |           4 5                             |     \  |
5 3 4                       4 ●————————● 5         5 4          4 ●————————● 5
                              (a)                                (b)
```

FIGURE 28.21   The vertices and edges of a graph can be stored in a file.

Your program should prompt the user to enter a URL for the file, then it should read data from the file, create an instance g of `UnweightedGraph`, invoke `g.printEdges()` to display all edges, and invoke `dfs()` to obtain an instance `tree` of `UnweightedGraph<V>.SearchTree`. If `tree.getNumberOfVerticesFound()` is the same as the number of vertices in the graph, the graph is connected. Here is a sample run of the program:

```
Enter a URL:
https://liveexample.pearsoncmg.com/test/GraphSample1.txt ↵Enter
The number of vertices is 6
Vertex 0: (0, 1) (0, 2)
Vertex 1: (1, 0) (1, 3)
Vertex 2: (2, 0) (2, 3) (2, 4)
Vertex 3: (3, 1) (3, 2) (3, 4) (3, 5)
Vertex 4: (4, 2) (4, 3) (4, 5)
Vertex 5: (5, 3) (5, 4)
The graph is connected
```

(*Hint*: Use `new UnweightedGraph(list, numberOfVertices)` to create a graph, where `list` contains a list of `Edge` objects. Use `new Edge(u, v)` to create an edge. Read the first line to get the number of vertices. Read each subsequent line into a string s and use `s.split("[\\;\\s+]")` to extract the vertices from the string and create edges from the vertices.)

*28.2   (*Create a file for a graph*) Modify Listing 28.2, TestGraph.java to create a file representing `graph1`. The file format is described in Programming Exercise 28.1. Create the file from the array defined in lines 8–21 in Listing 28.2. The number of vertices for the graph is 12, which will be stored in the first line of the file. The contents of the file should be as follows:

```
12
0 1 3 5
1 0 2 3
2 1 3 4 10
3 0 1 2 4 5
4 2 3 5 7 8 10
5 0 3 4 6 7
6 5 7
7 4 5 6 8
8 4 7 9 10 11
9 8 11
10 2 4 8 11
11 8 9 10
```

*28.3   (*Implement DFS using a stack*) The depth-first search algorithm described
in Listing 28.8, Depth-First Search Algorithm uses recursion. Design a new
algorithm without using recursion. Describe it using pseudocode. Implement it
by defining a new class named UnweightedGraphWithNonrecursiveDFS
that extends UnweightedGraph and overriding the dfs method. Write a test
program same as Listing 28.9, TestPFS.java except that UnweightedGraph is
replaced by UnweightedGraphWithNonrecursiveDFS.

*28.4   (*Find connected components*) Create a new class named MyGraph as a subclass
of UnweightedGraph that contains a method for finding all connected components in a graph with the following header:

```
public List<List<Integer>> getConnectedComponents();
```

The method returns a List<List<Integer>>. Each element in the list is
another list that contains all the vertices in a connected component. For example, for the graph in Figure 28.21b, getConnectedComponents() returns
[[0, 1, 2, 3], [4, 5]].

*28.5   (*Find paths*) Define a new class named UnweightedGraphWithGetPath that
extends UnweightedGraph with a new method for finding a path between two
vertices with the following header:

```
public List<Integer> getPath(int u, int v);
```

The method returns a List<Integer> that contains all the vertices in a
path from u to v in this order. Using the BFS approach, you can obtain
the shortest path from u to v. If there isn't a path from u to v, the method
returns null. Write a test program that creates a graph for Figure 28.1. The
program prompts the user to enter two cities and displays their paths. Here
is a sample run:

```
Enter a starting city: Seattle  ↵Enter
Enter an ending city: Miami  ↵Enter
The path is Seattle Denver Kansas City Atlanta Miami
```

*28.6   (*Detect cycles*) Define a new class named UnweightedGraphDetectCycle
that extends UnweightedGraph with a new method for determining whether
there is a cycle in the graph with the following header:

```
public boolean isCyclic();
```

Describe the algorithm in pseudocode and implement it. Note the graph may
be a directed graph.

*28.7   (*Find a cycle*) Define a new class named UnweightedGraphFindCycle that
extends UnweightedGraph with a new method for finding a cycle starting at
vertex u with the following header:

```
public List<Integer> getACycle(int u);
```

The method returns a List that contains all the vertices in a cycle starting from
u. If the graph doesn't have any cycles, the method returns null. Describe the
algorithm in pseudocode and implement it.

**28.8 (*Test bipartite*) Recall that a graph is bipartite if its vertices can be divided into two disjoint sets such that no edges exist between vertices in the same set. Define a new class named `UnweightedGraphTestBipartite` with the following method to detect whether the graph is bipartite:

```
public boolean isBipartite();
```

**28.9 (*Get bipartite sets*) Add a new method in `UnweightedGraph` with the following header to return two bipartite sets if the graph is bipartite:

```
public List<List<Integer>> getBipartite();
```

The method returns a `List` that contains two sublists, each of which contains a set of vertices. If the graph is not bipartite, the method returns `null`.

*28.10 (*Find the shortest path*) Write a program that reads a connected graph from a file. The graph is stored in a file using the same format specified in Programming Exercise 28.1. Your program should prompt the user to enter the name of the file, then two vertices, and should display the shortest path between the two vertices. For example, for the graph in Figure 28.21a, the shortest path between 0 and 5 may be displayed as 0 1 3 5.

Here is a sample run of the program:

```
Enter a file name: c:\exercise\GraphSample1.txt  ↵Enter
Enter two vertices (integer indexes): 0 5  ↵Enter
The number of vertices is 6
Vertex 0: (0, 1) (0, 2)
Vertex 1: (1, 0) (1, 3)
Vertex 2: (2, 0) (2, 3) (2, 4)
Vertex 3: (3, 1) (3, 2) (3, 4) (3, 5)
Vertex 4: (4, 2) (4, 3) (4, 5)
Vertex 5: (5, 3) (5, 4)
The path is 0 1 3 5
```

**28.11 (*Revise Listing 28.14, NineTail.java*) The program in Listing 28.14 lets the user enter an input for the nine tails problem from the console and displays the result on the console. Write a program that lets the user set an initial state of the nine coins (see Figure 28.22a) and click the *Solve* button to display the solution, as shown in Figure 28.22b. Initially, the user can click the mouse button to flip a coin. Set a red color on the flipped cells.

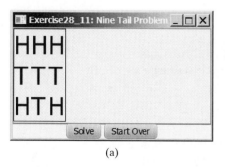

(a)

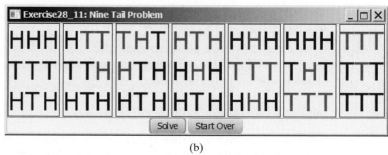

(b)

Figure 28.22 The program solves the nine tails problem. *Source*: Copyright © 1995–2016 Oracle and/or its affiliates. All rights reserved. Used with permission.

**28.12 (*Variation of the nine tails problem*) In the nine tails problem, when you flip a coin, the horizontal and vertical neighboring cells are also flipped. Rewrite the program, assuming all neighboring cells including the diagonal neighbors are also flipped.

**28.13 (*4 × 4 16 tails problem*) Listing 28.14, NineTail.java, presents a solution for the nine tails problem. Revise this program for the 4 × 4 16 tails problem. Note it is possible that a solution may not exist for a starting pattern. If so, report that no solution exists.

**28.14 (*4 × 4 16 tails analysis*) The nine tails problem in the text uses a 3 × 3 matrix. Assume you have 16 coins placed in a 4 × 4 matrix. Write a program to find out the number of the starting patterns that don't have a solution.

*28.15 (*4 × 4 16 tails GUI*) Rewrite Programming Exercise 28.14 to enable the user to set an initial pattern of the 4 × 4 16 tails problem (see Figure 28.23a). The user can click the *Solve* button to display the solution, as shown in Figure 28.23b. Initially, the user can click the mouse button to flip a coin. If a solution does not exist, display a message dialog to report it.

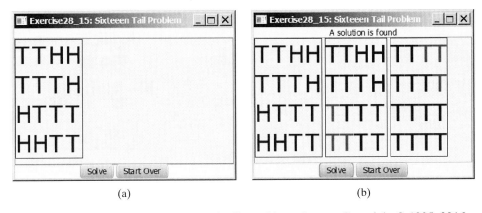

(a)   (b)

FIGURE 28.23   The problem solves the 16 tails problem. *Source*: Copyright © 1995–2016 Oracle and/or its affiliates. All rights reserved. Used with permission.

**28.16 (*Induced subgraph*) Given an undirected graph G = (V, E) and an integer k, find an induced subgraph H of G of maximum size such that all vertices of H have a degree $>= k$, or conclude that no such induced subgraph exists. Implement the method with the following header:

```
public static <V> Graph<V> maxInducedSubgraph(Graph<V> g, int k)
```

The method returns an empty graph if such a subgraph does not exist.

(*Hint*: An intuitive approach is to remove vertices whose degree is less than k. As vertices are removed with their adjacent edges, the degrees of other vertices may be reduced. Continue the process until no vertices can be removed, or all the vertices are removed.)

***28.17 (*Hamiltonian cycle*) The Hamiltonian path algorithm is implemented in Supplement VI.E. Add the following `getHamiltonianCycle` method in the `Graph` interface and implement it in the `UnweightedGraph` class:

```
/** Return a Hamiltonian cycle
 * Return null if the graph doesn't contain a Hamiltonian cycle */
public List<Integer> getHamiltonianCycle()
```

***28.18 (*Knight's Tour cycle*) Rewrite KnightTourApp.java in the case study in Supplement VI.E to find a knight's tour that visits each square in a chessboard and returns to the starting square. Reduce the Knight's Tour cycle problem to the problem of finding a Hamiltonian cycle.

**28.19 (*Display a DFS/BFS tree in a graph*) Modify GraphView in Listing 28.6 to add a new data field tree with a setter method. The edges in the tree are displayed in red. Write a program that displays the graph in Figure 28.1 and the DFS/BFS tree starting from a specified city, as shown in Figures 28.13 and 28.16. If a city not in the map is entered, the program displays an error message in the label.

*28.20 (*Display a graph*) Write a program that reads a graph from a file and displays it. The first line in the file contains a number that indicates the number of vertices (n). The vertices are labeled 0, 1, . . . , n-1. Each subsequent line, with the format u x y v1 v2 . . . , describes the position of u at (x, y) and edges (u, v1), (u, v2), and so on. Figure 28.24a gives an example of the file for their corresponding graph. Your program prompts the user to enter the name of the file, reads data from the file, and displays the graph on a pane using GraphView, as shown in Figure 28.24b.

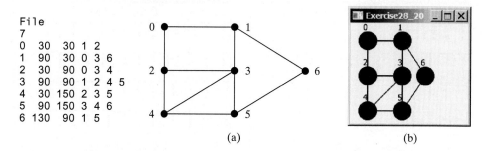

FIGURE 28.24 The program reads the information about the graph and displays it visually. *Source*: Copyright © 1995–2016 Oracle and/or its affiliates. All rights reserved. Used with permission.

**28.21 (*Display sets of connected circles*) Modify Listing 28.10, ConnectedCircles.java to display sets of connected circles in different colors. That is, if two circles are connected, they are displayed using the same color; otherwise, they are not in same color, as shown in Figure 28.25. (*Hint*: See Programming Exercise 28.4.)

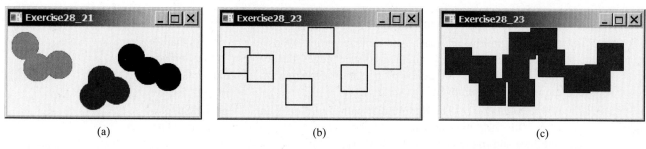

FIGURE 28.25 (a) Connected circles are displayed in the same color. (b) Rectangles are not filled with a color if they are not connected. (c) Rectangles are filled with a color if they are connected. *Source*: Copyright © 1995–2016 Oracle and/or its affiliates. All rights reserved. Used with permission.

*28.22 (*Move a circle*) Modify Listing 28.10, ConnectedCircles.java, to enable the user to drag and move a circle.

**28.23 (*Connected rectangles*) Listing 28.10, ConnectedCircles.java, allows the user to create circles and determine whether they are connected. Rewrite the program for rectangles. The program lets the user create a rectangle by clicking a mouse in a blank area that is not currently covered by a rectangle. As the rectangles are added, the rectangles are repainted as filled if they are connected or are unfilled otherwise, as shown in Figure 28.25b–c.

*28.24 (*Remove a circle*) Modify Listing 28.10, ConnectedCircles.java, to enable the user to remove a circle when the mouse is clicked inside the circle.

*28.25 (*Implement remove(V v)*) Modify Listing 28.4, UnweightedGraph.java, to override the `remove(V v)` method defined in the `Graph` interface.

*28.26 (*Implement remove(int u, int v)*) Modify Listing 28.4, UnweightedGraph.java, to override the `remove(int u, int v)` method defined in the `Graph` interface.

WEIGHTED GRAPHS AND APPLICATIONS

Objectives

- To represent weighted edges using adjacency matrices and adjacency lists (§29.2).

- To model weighted graphs using the `WeightedGraph` class that extends the `UnweightedGraph` class (§29.3).

- To design and implement the algorithm for finding a minimum spanning tree (§29.4).

- To define the `MST` class that extends the `SearchTree` class (§29.4).

- To design and implement the algorithm for finding single-source shortest paths (§29.5).

- To define the `ShortestPathTree` class that extends the `SearchTree` class (§29.5).

- To solve the weighted nine tails problem using the shortest-path algorithm (§29.6).

29.1 Introduction

A graph is a weighted graph if each edge is assigned a weight. Weighted graphs have many practical applications.

Figure 28.1 assumes the graph represents the number of flights among cities. You can apply the Breadth-First Search (BFS) to find the fewest number of flights between two cities. Assume the edges represent the driving distances among the cities as shown in Figure 29.1. How do you find the minimal total distances for connecting all cities? How do you find the shortest path between two cities? This chapter will address these questions. The former is known as the *minimum spanning tree (MST) problem*, and the latter as the *shortest path problem*.

problem

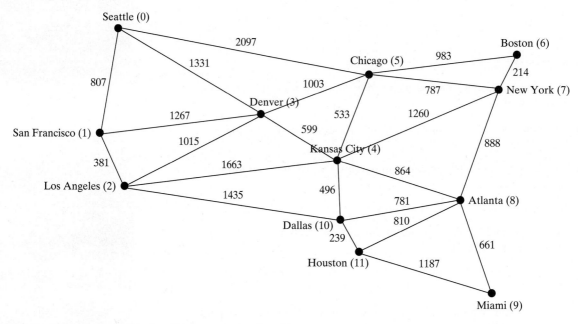

FIGURE 29.1 The graph models the distances among the cities.

The preceding chapter introduced the concept of graphs. You learned how to represent edges using edge arrays, edge lists, adjacency matrices, and adjacency lists, and how to model a graph using the `Graph` interface and the `UnweightedGraph` class. The preceding chapter also introduced two important techniques for traversing graphs: depth-first search and breadth-first search, and applied traversal to solve practical problems. This chapter will introduce weighted graphs. You will learn the algorithm for finding a minimum spanning tree in Section 29.4, and the algorithm for finding shortest paths in Section 29.5.

weighted graph learning tool
on Companion Website

Pedagogical Note

Before we introduce the algorithms and applications for weighted graphs, it is helpful to get acquainted with weighted graphs using the GUI interactive tool at liveexample.pearsoncmg.com/dsanimation/WeightedGraphLearningTooleBook .html, as shown in Figure 29.2. The tool allows you to enter vertices, specify edges and their weights, view the graph, and find an MST and all shortest paths from a single source.

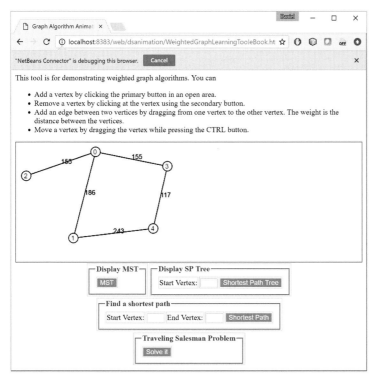

Figure 29.2 You can use the tool to create a weighted graph with mouse gestures and show the MST and shortest paths. *Source:* © Mozilla Firefox.

29.2 Representing Weighted Graphs

Weighted edges can be stored in adjacency lists.

There are two types of weighted graphs: vertex weighted and edge weighted. In a *vertex-weighted graph*, each vertex is assigned a weight. In an *edge-weighted graph*, each edge is assigned a weight. Of the two types, edge-weighted graphs have more applications. This chapter considers edge-weighted graphs.

Weighted graphs can be represented in the same way as unweighted graphs, except that you have to represent the weights on the edges. As with unweighted graphs, the vertices in weighted graphs can be stored in an array. This section introduces three representations for the edges in weighted graphs.

Key Point

vertex-weighted graph
edge-weighted graph

29.2.1 Representing Weighted Edges: Edge Array

Weighted edges can be represented using a two-dimensional array. For example, you can store all the edges in the graph in Figure 29.3a using the array in Figure 29.3b.

Note
Weights can be of any type: `Integer`, `Double`, `BigDecimal`, and so on. You can use a two-dimensional array of the `Object` type to represent weighted edges as follows:

```
Object[][] edges = {
  {new Integer(0), new Integer(1), new SomeTypeForWeight(2)},
  {new Integer(0), new Integer(3), new SomeTypeForWeight(8)},
  ...
};
```

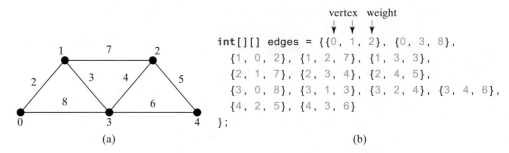

FIGURE 29.3 Each edge is assigned a weight in an edge-weighted graph.

29.2.2 Weighted Adjacency Matrices

Assume the graph has *n* vertices. You can use a two-dimensional $n \times n$ matrix, say `weights`, to represent the weights on edges. `weights[i][j]` represents the weight on edge (i, j). If vertices i and j are not connected, `weights[i][j]` is `null`. For example, the weights in the graph in Figure 29.3a can be represented using an adjacency matrix as follows:

```
Integer[][] adjacencyMatrix = {
  {null, 2, null, 8, null},
  {2, null, 7, 3, null},
  {null, 7, null, 4, 5},
  {8, 3, 4, null, 6},
  {null, null, 5, 6, null}
};
```

	0	1	2	3	4
0	null	2	null	8	null
1	2	null	7	3	null
2	null	7	null	4	5
3	8	3	4	null	6
4	null	null	5	6	null

29.2.3 Adjacency Lists

Another way to represent the edges is to define edges as objects. The `Edge` class was defined to represent an unweighted edge in Listing 28.3. For weighted edges, we define the `WeightedEdge` class as shown in Listing 29.1.

LISTING 29.1 WeightedEdge.java

```
1  public class WeightedEdge extends Edge
2      implements Comparable<WeightedEdge> {
3    public double weight;  // The weight on edge (u, v)
4
5    /** Create a weighted edge on (u, v) */
6    public WeightedEdge(int u, int v, double weight) {
7      super(u, v);
8      this.weight = weight;
9    }
10
11   @Override  /** Compare two edges on weights */
12   public int compareTo(WeightedEdge edge) {
13     if (weight > edge.weight)
14       return 1;
15     else if (weight == edge.weight)
16       return 0;
17     else
18       return -1;
19   }
20 }
```
edge weight

constructor

compare edges

An **Edge** object represents an edge from vertex **u** to **v**. **WeightedEdge** extends **Edge** with a new property **weight**. To create a **WeightedEdge** object, use **new WeightedEdge(i, j, w)**, where **w** is the weight on edge (**i, j**). Often you need to compare the weights of the edges. For this reason, the **WeightedEdge** class implements the **Comparable** interface.

For unweighted graphs, we use adjacency lists to represent edges. For weighted graphs, we still use adjacency lists, the adjacency lists for the vertices in the graph in Figure 29.3a can be represented as follows:

```
java.util.List<WeightedEdge>[] list = new java.util.List[5];
```

list[0]	WeightedEdge(0, 1, 2)	WeightedEdge(0, 3, 8)		
list[1]	WeightedEdge(1, 0, 2)	WeightedEdge(1, 3, 3)	WeightedEdge(1, 2, 7)	
list[2]	WeightedEdge(2, 3, 4)	WeightedEdge(2, 4, 5)	WeightedEdge(2, 1, 7)	
list[3]	WeightedEdge(3, 1, 3)	WeightedEdge(3, 2, 4)	WeightedEdge(3, 4, 6)	WeightedEdge(3, 0, 8)
list[4]	WeightedEdge(4, 2, 5)	WeightedEdge(4, 3, 6)		

list[i] stores all edges adjacent to vertex **i**.

For flexibility, we will use an array list rather than a fixed-sized array to represent **list** as follows:

```
List<List<WeightedEdge>> list = new java.util.ArrayList<>();
```

29.2.1 For the code **WeightedEdge edge = new WeightedEdge(1, 2, 3.5)**, what is **edge.u**, **edge.v**, and **edge.weight**?

Check Point

29.2.2 What is the output of the following code?

```
List<WeightedEdge> list = new ArrayList<>();
list.add(new WeightedEdge(1, 2, 3.5));
list.add(new WeightedEdge(2, 3, 4.5));
WeightedEdge e = java.util.Collections.max(list);
System.out.println(e.u);
System.out.println(e.v);
System.out.println(e.weight);
```

29.3 The **WeightedGraph** Class

The **WeightedGraph** *class extends* **UnweightedGraph**.

Key Point

The preceding chapter designed the **Graph** interface and the **UnweightedGraph** class for modeling graphs. We now design **WeightedGraph** as a subclass of **UnweightedGraph**, as shown in Figure 29.4.

WeightedGraph simply extends **UnweightedGraph** with five constructors for creating concrete **WeightedGraph** instances. **WeightedGraph** inherits all methods from **UnweightedGraph**, overrides the **clear** and **addVertex** methods, implements a new **addEdge** method for adding a weighted edge, and also introduces new methods for obtaining minimum spanning trees and for finding all *single-source shortest paths*. Minimum spanning trees and shortest paths will be introduced in Sections 29.4 and 29.5, respectively.

Listing 29.2 implements **WeightedGraph**. Edge adjacency lists (lines 38–63) are used internally to store adjacent edges for a vertex. When a **WeightedGraph** is constructed, its edge

UnweightedGraph<V>	Defined in Figure 28.9.

WeightedGraph<V>	
+WeightedGraph()	Constructs an empty graph.
+WeightedGraph(vertices: V[], edges: int[][])	Constructs a weighted graph with the specified edges and the vertices in arrays.
+WeightedGraph(vertices: List<V>, edges: List<WeightedEdge>)	Constructs a weighted graph with the specified edges and the number of vertices.
+WeightedGraph(edges: int[][], numberOfVertices: int)	Constructs a weighted graph with the specified edges in an array and the number of vertices.
+WeightedGraph(edges: List<WeightedEdge>, numberOfVertices: int)	Constructs a weighted graph with the specified edges in a list and the number of vertices.
+printWeightedEdges(): void	Displays all edges and weights.
+getWeight(int u, int v): double	Returns the weight on the edge from u to v. Throw an exception if the edge does not exist.
+addEdges(u: int, v: int, weight: double): void	Adds a weighted edge to the graph and throws an IllegalArgumentException if u, v, or w is invalid. If (u, v) is already in the graph, the new weight is set.
+getMinimumSpanningTree(): MST	Returns a minimum spanning tree starting from vertex 0.
+getMinimumSpanningTree(index: int): MST	Returns a minimum spanning tree starting from vertex v.
+getShortestPath(index: int): ShortestPathTree	Returns all single-source shortest paths.

FIGURE 29.4 WeightedGraph extends UnweightedGraph.

adjacency lists are created (lines 47 and 57). The methods getMinimumSpanningTree() (lines 99–138) and getShortestPath() (lines 156–197) will be introduced in upcoming sections.

LISTING 29.2 WeightedGraph.java

```
1   import java.util.*;
2
3   public class WeightedGraph<V>extends UnweightedGraph<V> {
4     /** Construct an empty */
5     public WeightedGraph() {
6     }
7
8     /** Construct a WeightedGraph from vertices and edged in arrays */
9     public WeightedGraph(V[] vertices, int[][] edges) {
10      createWeightedGraph(java.util.Arrays.asList(vertices), edges);
11    }
12
13    /** Construct a WeightedGraph from vertices and edges in list */
14    public WeightedGraph(int[][] edges, int numberOfVertices) {
15      List<V> vertices = new ArrayList<>();
16      for (int i = 0; i < numberOfVertices; i++)
17        vertices.add((V)(new Integer(i)));
18
19      createWeightedGraph(vertices, edges);
20    }
21
```

```
22      /** Construct a WeightedGraph for vertices 0, 1, 2 and edge list */
23      public WeightedGraph(List<V> vertices, List<WeightedEdge> edges) {      constructor
24        createWeightedGraph(vertices, edges);
25      }
26
27      /** Construct a WeightedGraph from vertices 0, 1, and edge array */
28      public WeightedGraph(List<WeightedEdge> edges,                          constructor
29          int numberOfVertices) {
30        List<V> vertices = new ArrayList<>();
31        for (int i = 0; i < numberOfVertices; i++)
32          vertices.add((V)(new Integer(i)));
33
34        createWeightedGraph(vertices, edges);
35      }
36
37      /** Create adjacency lists from edge arrays */
38      private void createWeightedGraph(List<V> vertices, int[][] edges) {
39        this.vertices = vertices;
40
41        for (int i = 0; i < vertices.size(); i++) {
42          neighbors.add(new ArrayList<Edge>()); // Create a list for vertices   create list for vertices
43        }
44
45        for (int i = 0; i < edges.length; i++) {
46          neighbors.get(edges[i][0]).add(
47            new WeightedEdge(edges[i][0], edges[i][1], edges[i][2]));          create a weighted edge
48        }
49      }
50
51      /** Create adjacency lists from edge lists */
52      private void createWeightedGraph(
53          List<V> vertices, List<WeightedEdge> edges) {
54        this.vertices = vertices;
55
56        for (int i = 0; i < vertices.size(); i++) {
57          neighbors.add(new ArrayList<Edge>()); // Create a list for vertices   create list for vertices
58        }
59
60        for (WeightedEdge edge: edges) {
61          neighbors.get(edge.u).add(edge); // Add an edge into the list
62        }
63      }
64
65      /** Return the weight on the edge (u, v) */
66      public double getWeight(int u, int v) throws Exception {               get edge weight
67        for (Edge edge : neighbors.get(u)) {
68          if (edge.v == v) {
69            return ((WeightedEdge)edge).weight;
70          }
71        }
72
73        throw new Exception("Edge does not exit");
74      }
75
76      /** Display edges with weights */
77      public void printWeightedEdges() {                                     print edges
78        for (int i = 0; i < getSize(); i++) {
79          System.out.print(getVertex(i) + " (" + i + "): ");
80          for (Edge edge : neighbors.get(i)) {
81            System.out.print("(" + edge.u +
```

```
82            ", " + edge.v + ", " + ((WeightedEdge)edge).weight + ") ");
83        }
84      System.out.println();
85    }
86  }
87
88  /** Add edges to the weighted graph */
```

add edge

```
89  public boolean addEdge(int u, int v, double weight) {
90    return addEdge(new WeightedEdge(u, v, weight));
91  }
92
93  /** Get a minimum spanning tree rooted at vertex 0 */
```

get an MST
start from vertex 0

```
94  public MST getMinimumSpanningTree() {
95    return getMinimumSpanningTree(0);
96  }
97
98  /** Get a minimum spanning tree rooted at a specified vertex */
```

MST from a starting vertex

```
99  public MST getMinimumSpanningTree(int startingVertex) {
100    // cost[v] stores the cost by adding v to the tree
101    double[] cost = new double[getSize()];
102    for (int i = 0; i < cost.length; i++) {
```

initialize cost

```
103      cost[i] = Double.POSITIVE_INFINITY; // Initial cost
104    }
105    cost[startingVertex] = 0; // Cost of source is 0
106
```

initialize parent

```
107    int[] parent = new int[getSize()]; // Parent of a vertex
108    parent[startingVertex] = -1; // startingVertex is the root
109    double totalWeight = 0; // Total weight of the tree thus far
110
```

minimum spanning tree

```
111    List<Integer> T = new ArrayList<>();
112
113    // Expand T
```

expand MST
update total cost

```
114    while (T.size() < getSize()) {
115      // Find smallest cost u in V - T
116      int u = -1; // Vertex to be determined
117      double currentMinCost = Double.POSITIVE_INFINITY;
118      for (int i = 0; i < getSize(); i++) {
119        if (!T.contains(i) && cost[i] < currentMinCost) {
120          currentMinCost = cost[i];
```

vertex with smallest cost

```
121          u = i;
122        }
123      }
124
```

add to tree

```
125      if (u == -1) break; else T.add(u); // Add a new vertex to T
126      totalWeight += cost[u]; // Add cost[u] to the tree
127
128      // Adjust cost[v] for v that is adjacent to u and v in V - T
```

adjust cost

```
129      for (Edge e: neighbors.get(u)) {
130        if (!T.contains(e.v) && cost[e.v] > ((WeightedEdge)e).weight) {
131          cost[e.v] = ((WeightedEdge)e).weight;
132          parent[e.v] = u;
133        }
134      }
135    } // End of while
136
```

create an MST

```
137    return new MST(startingVertex, parent, T, totalWeight);
138  }
139
140  /** MST is an inner class in WeightedGraph */
```

MST inner class

```
141  public class MST extends SearchTree {
```

```
142       private double totalWeight; // Total weight of all edges in the tree      total weight in tree
143
144       public MST(int root, int[] parent, List<Integer> searchOrder,
145           double totalWeight) {
146         super(root, parent, searchOrder);
147         this.totalWeight = totalWeight;
148       }
149
150       public double getTotalWeight() {
151         return totalWeight;
152       }
153     }
154
155     /** Find single-source shortest paths */
156     public ShortestPathTree getShortestPath(int sourceVertex) {           getShortestPath
157       // cost[v] stores the cost of the path from v to the source
158       double[] cost = new double[getSize()];                             initialize cost
159       for (int i = 0; i < cost.length; i++) {
160         cost[i] = Double.POSITIVE_INFINITY; // Initial cost set to infinity
161       }
162       cost[sourceVertex] = 0; // Cost of source is 0
163
164       // parent[v] stores the previous vertex of v in the path
165       int[] parent = new int[getSize()];
166       parent[sourceVertex] = -1; // The parent of source is set to -1
167
168       // T stores the vertices whose path found so far
169       List<Integer> T = new ArrayList<>();                               shortest-path tree
170
171       // Expand T
172       while (T.size() < getSize()) {                                     expand tree
173         // Find smallest cost u in V - T
174         int u = -1; // Vertex to be determined
175         double currentMinCost = Double.POSITIVE_INFINITY;
176         for (int i = 0; i < getSize(); i++) {
177           if (!T.contains(i) && cost[i] < currentMinCost) {
178             currentMinCost = cost[i];
179             u = i;                                                       vertex with smallest cost
180           }
181         }
182
183         if (u == -1) break; else T.add(u); // Add a new vertex to T      add to T
184
185         // Adjust cost[v] for v that is adjacent to u and v in V - T
186         for (Edge e: neighbors.get(u)) {
187           if (!T.contains(e.v)
188               && cost[e.v] > cost[u] + ((WeightedEdge)e).weight) {
189             cost[e.v] = cost[u] + ((WeightedEdge)e).weight;              adjust cost
190             parent[e.v] = u;                                             adjust parent
191           }
192         }
193       } // End of while
194
195       // Create a ShortestPathTree
196       return new ShortestPathTree(sourceVertex, parent, T, cost);        create a tree
197     }
198
199     /** ShortestPathTree is an inner class in WeightedGraph */
200     public class ShortestPathTree extends SearchTree {                   shortest-path tree
201       private double[] cost; // cost[v] is the cost from v to source      cost
```

```
202
203        /** Construct a path */
204        public ShortestPathTree(int source, int[] parent,
205            List<Integer> searchOrder, double[] cost) {
206          super(source, parent, searchOrder);
207          this.cost = cost;
208        }
209
210        /** Return the cost for a path from the root to vertex v */
211        public double getCost(int v) {
212          return cost[v];
213        }
214
215        /** Print paths from all vertices to the source */
216        public void printAllPaths() {
217          System.out.println("All shortest paths from " +
218            vertices.get(getRoot()) + " are:");
219          for (int i = 0; i < cost.length; i++) {
220            printPath(i); // Print a path from i to the source
221            System.out.println("(cost: " + cost[i] + ")"); // Path cost
222          }
223        }
224      }
225    }
```

constructor — lines 204
get cost — line 211
print all paths — line 216

The `WeightedGraph` class extends the `UnweightedGraph` class (line 3). The properties `vertices` and `neighbors` in `UnweightedGraph` are inherited in `WeightedGraph`. `neighbors` is a list. Each element is the list is another list that contains edges. For unweighted graph, each edge is an instance of `Edge`. For a weighted graph, each edge is an instance of `WeightedEdge`. `WeightedEdge` is a subtype of `Edge`. So you can add a weighted edge into `neighbors.get(i)` for a weighted graph (line 47).

The `addEdge(u, v, weight)` method (lines 88–91) adds an edge (u, v, weight) to the graph. If a graph is undirected, you should invoke `addEdge(u, v, weight)` and `addEdge(v, u, weight)` to add an edge between u and v.

Listing 29.3 gives a test program that creates a graph for the one in Figure 29.1, and another graph for the one in Figure 29.3a.

LISTING 29.3 TestWeightedGraph.java

```
1    public class TestWeightedGraph {
2      public static void main(String[] args) {
3        String[] vertices = {"Seattle", "San Francisco", "Los Angeles",
4          "Denver", "Kansas City", "Chicago", "Boston", "New York",
5          "Atlanta", "Miami", "Dallas", "Houston"};
6
7        int[][] edges = {
8          {0, 1, 807}, {0, 3, 1331}, {0, 5, 2097},
9          {1, 0, 807}, {1, 2, 381}, {1, 3, 1267},
10         {2, 1, 381}, {2, 3, 1015}, {2, 4, 1663}, {2, 10, 1435},
11         {3, 0, 1331}, {3, 1, 1267}, {3, 2, 1015}, {3, 4, 599},
12           {3, 5, 1003},
13         {4, 2, 1663}, {4, 3, 599}, {4, 5, 533}, {4, 7, 1260},
14           {4, 8, 864}, {4, 10, 496},
15         {5, 0, 2097}, {5, 3, 1003}, {5, 4, 533},
16           {5, 6, 983}, {5, 7, 787},
17         {6, 5, 983}, {6, 7, 214},
18         {7, 4, 1260}, {7, 5, 787}, {7, 6, 214}, {7, 8, 888},
19         {8, 4, 864}, {8, 7, 888}, {8, 9, 661},
```

vertices — line 3
edges — line 7

```
20           {8, 10, 781}, {8, 11, 810},
21         {9, 8, 661}, {9, 11, 1187},
22         {10, 2, 1435}, {10, 4, 496}, {10, 8, 781}, {10, 11, 239},
23         {11, 8, 810}, {11, 9, 1187}, {11, 10, 239}
24       };
25
26       WeightedGraph<String> graph1 =
27         new WeightedGraph<>(vertices, edges);                        create graph
28       System.out.println("The number of vertices in graph1: "
29         + graph1.getSize());
30       System.out.println("The vertex with index 1 is "
31         + graph1.getVertex(1));
32       System.out.println("The index for Miami is " +
33         graph1.getIndex("Miami"));
34       System.out.println("The edges for graph1:");
35       graph1.printWeightedEdges();                                   print edges
36
37       edges = new int[][] {                                         edges
38         {0, 1, 2}, {0, 3, 8},
39         {1, 0, 2}, {1, 2, 7}, {1, 3, 3},
40         {2, 1, 7}, {2, 3, 4}, {2, 4, 5},
41         {3, 0, 8}, {3, 1, 3}, {3, 2, 4}, {3, 4, 6},
42         {4, 2, 5}, {4, 3, 6}
43       };
44       WeightedGraph<Integer> graph2 = new WeightedGraph<>(edges, 5);  create graph
45       System.out.println("\nThe edges for graph2:");
46       graph2.printWeightedEdges();                                   print edges
47     }
48   }
```

```
The number of vertices in graph1: 12
The vertex with index 1 is San Francisco
The index for Miami is 9
The edges for graph1:
Vertex 0: (0, 1, 807) (0, 3, 1331) (0, 5, 2097)
Vertex 1: (1, 2, 381) (1, 0, 807) (1, 3, 1267)
Vertex 2: (2, 1, 381) (2, 3, 1015) (2, 4, 1663) (2, 10, 1435)
Vertex 3: (3, 4, 599) (3, 5, 1003) (3, 1, 1267)
  (3, 0, 1331) (3, 2, 1015)
Vertex 4: (4, 10, 496) (4, 8, 864) (4, 5, 533) (4, 2, 1663)
  (4, 7, 1260) (4, 3, 599)
Vertex 5: (5, 4, 533) (5, 7, 787) (5, 3, 1003)
  (5, 0, 2097) (5, 6, 983)
Vertex 6: (6, 7, 214) (6, 5, 983)
Vertex 7: (7, 6, 214) (7, 8, 888) (7, 5, 787) (7, 4, 1260)
Vertex 8: (8, 9, 661) (8, 10, 781) (8, 4, 864)
  (8, 7, 888) (8, 11, 810)
Vertex 9: (9, 8, 661) (9, 11, 1187)
Vertex 10: (10, 11, 239) (10, 4, 496) (10, 8, 781) (10, 2, 1435)
Vertex 11: (11, 10, 239) (11, 9, 1187) (11, 8, 810)

The edges for graph2:
Vertex 0: (0, 1, 2) (0, 3, 8)
Vertex 1: (1, 0, 2) (1, 2, 7) (1, 3, 3)
Vertex 2: (2, 3, 4) (2, 1, 7) (2, 4, 5)
Vertex 3: (3, 1, 3) (3, 4, 6) (3, 2, 4) (3, 0, 8)
Vertex 4: (4, 2, 5) (4, 3, 6)
```

The program creates `graph1` for the graph in Figure 29.1 in lines 3–27. The vertices for `graph1` are defined in lines 3–5. The edges for `graph1` are defined in lines 7–24. The edges are represented using a two-dimensional array. For each row `i` in the array, `edges[i][0]` and `edges[i][1]` indicate there is an edge from vertex `edges[i][0]` to vertex `edges[i][1]` and the weight for the edge is `edges[i][2]`. For example, {0, 1, 807} (line 8) represents the edge from vertex 0 (`edges[0][0]`) to vertex 1 (`edges[0][1]`) with weight 807 (`edges[0][2]`). {0, 5, 2097} (line 8) represents the edge from vertex 0 (`edges[2][0]`) to vertex 5 (`edges[2][1]`) with weight 2097 (`edges[2][2]`). Line 35 invokes the `printWeightedEdges()` method on `graph1` to display all edges in `graph1`.

The program creates the edges for `graph2` for the graph in Figure 29.3a in lines 37–44. Line 46 invokes the `printWeightedEdges()` method on `graph2` to display all edges in `graph2`.

29.3.1 If a priority queue is used to store weighted edges, what is the output of the following code?

```
PriorityQueue<WeightedEdge> q = new PriorityQueue<>();
q.offer(new WeightedEdge(1, 2, 3.5));
q.offer(new WeightedEdge(1, 6, 6.5));
q.offer(new WeightedEdge(1, 7, 1.5));
System.out.println(q.poll().weight);
System.out.println(q.poll().weight);
System.out.println(q.poll().weight);
```

29.3.2 If a priority queue is used to store weighted edges, what is wrong in the following code? Fix it and show the output.

```
List<PriorityQueue<WeightedEdge>> queues = new ArrayList<>();
queues.get(0).offer(new WeightedEdge(0, 2, 3.5));
queues.get(0).offer(new WeightedEdge(0, 6, 6.5));
queues.get(0).offer(new WeightedEdge(0, 7, 1.5));
queues.get(1).offer(new WeightedEdge(1, 0, 3.5));
queues.get(1).offer(new WeightedEdge(1, 5, 8.5));
queues.get(1).offer(new WeightedEdge(1, 8, 19.5));
System.out.println(queues.get(0).peek()
  .compareTo(queues.get(1).peek()));
```

29.3.3 Show the output of the following code:

```
public class Test {
  public static void main(String[] args) {
    WeightedGraph<Character> graph = new WeightedGraph<>();
    graph.addVertex('U');
    graph.addVertex('V');
    int indexForU = graph.getIndex('U');
    int indexForV = graph.getIndex('V');
    System.out.println("indexForU is " + indexForU);
    System.out.println("indexForV is " + indexForV);
    graph.addEdge(indexForU, indexForV, 2.5);
    System.out.println("Degree of U is " +
      graph.getDegree(indexForU));
    System.out.println("Degree of V is " +
      graph.getDegree(indexForV));
    System.out.println("Weight of UV is " +
      graph.getWeight(indexForU, indexOfV));
  }
}
```

29.4 Minimum Spanning Trees

Key
Point

A minimum spanning tree of a graph is a spanning tree with the minimum total weights.

minimum spanning tree

A graph may have many spanning trees. Suppose the edges are weighted. A *minimum spanning tree* has the minimum total weights. For example, the trees in Figures 29.5b, 29.5c, 29.5d are spanning trees for the graph in Figure 29.5a. The trees in Figures 29.5c and 29.5d are minimum spanning trees.

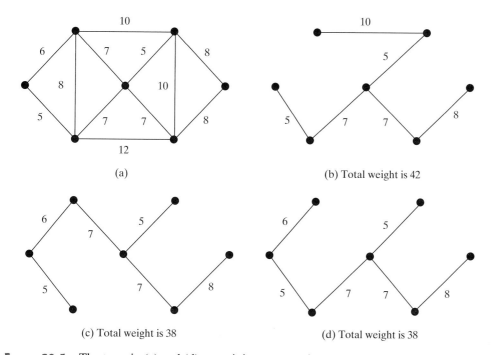

(a)

(b) Total weight is 42

(c) Total weight is 38

(d) Total weight is 38

FIGURE 29.5 The trees in (c) and (d) are minimum spanning trees of the graph in (a).

The problem of finding a minimum spanning tree has many applications. Consider a company with branches in many cities. The company wants to lease telephone lines to connect all the branches together. The phone company charges different rates to connect different pairs of cities. There are many ways to connect all branches together. The cheapest way is to find a spanning tree with the minimum total rates.

29.4.1 Minimum Spanning Tree Algorithms

How do you find a minimum spanning tree? There are several well-known algorithms for doing so. This section introduces *Prim's algorithm*. Prim's algorithm starts with a spanning tree T that contains an arbitrary vertex. The algorithm expands the tree by repeatedly adding a vertex with the *lowest-cost* edge incident to a vertex already in the tree. Prim's algorithm is a greedy algorithm, and it is described in Listing 29.4.

Prim's algorithm

LISTING 29.4 Prim's Minimum Spanning Tree Algorithm

```
Input: A connected undirected weighted G = (V, E) with nonnegative weights
Output: MST (a minimum spanning tree)

1  MST minimumSpanningTree() {
2    Let T be a set for the vertices in the spanning tree;
```

add initial vertex

more vertices?
find a vertex

add to tree

```
3      Initially, add the starting vertex, s, to T;
4
5      while (size of T < n) {
6        Find x in T and y in V - T with the smallest weight
7          on the edge (x, y), as shown in Figure 29.6;
8        Add y to T and set parent[y] = x;
9      }
10   }
```

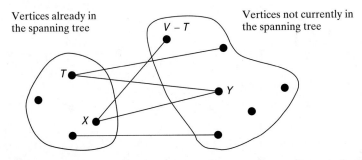

Vertices already in
the spanning tree

V – T

Vertices not currently in
the spanning tree

FIGURE 29.6 Find a vertex x in T that connects a vertex y in V – T with the smallest weight.

The algorithm starts by adding the starting vertex into T. It then continuously adds a vertex (say y) from V – T into T. y is the vertex that is adjacent to a vertex in T with the smallest weight on the edge. For example, there are five edges connecting vertices in T and V – T as shown in Figure 29.6, and (x, y) is the one with the smallest weight. Consider the graph in Figure 29.7. The algorithm adds the vertices to T in this order:

example

1. Add vertex 0 to T.

2. Add vertex 5 to T, since WeightedEdge(5, 0, 5) has the smallest weight among all edges incident to a vertex in T, as shown in Figure 29.7a. The arrow line from 0 to 5 indicates that 0 is the parent of 5.

3. Add vertex 1 to T, since WeightedEdge(1, 0, 6) has the smallest weight among all edges incident to a vertex in T, as shown in Figure 29.7b.

4. Add vertex 6 to T, since WeightedEdge(6, 1, 7) has the smallest weight among all edges incident to a vertex in T, as shown in Figure 29.7c.

5. Add vertex 2 to T, since WeightedEdge(2, 6, 5) has the smallest weight among all edges incident to a vertex in T, as shown in Figure 29.7d.

6. Add vertex 4 to T, since WeightedEdge(4, 6, 7) has the smallest weight among all edges incident to a vertex in T, as shown in Figure 29.7e.

7. Add vertex 3 to T, since WeightedEdge(3, 2, 8) has the smallest weight among all edges incident to a vertex in T, as shown in Figure 29.7f.

unique tree?

 Note
A minimum spanning tree is not unique. For example, both (c) and (d) in Figure 29.5 are minimum spanning trees for the graph in Figure 29.5a. However, if the weights are distinct, the graph has a unique minimum spanning tree.

connected and undirected

Note
Assume the graph is connected and undirected. If a graph is not connected or directed, the algorithm will not work. You can modify the algorithm to find a spanning forest for any undirected graph. A spanning forest is a graph in which each connected component is a tree.

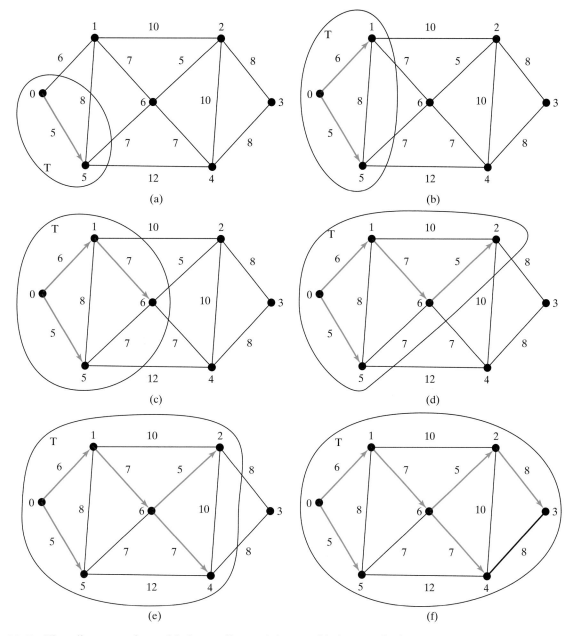

FIGURE 29.7 The adjacent vertices with the smallest weight are added successively to T.

29.4.2 Refining Prim's MST Algorithm

To make it easy to identify the next vertex to add into the tree, we use `cost[v]` to store the cost of adding a vertex `v` to the spanning tree T. Initially, `cost[s]` is `0` for a starting vertex and assign infinity to `cost[v]` for all other vertices. The algorithm repeatedly finds a vertex `u` in V–T with the smallest `cost[u]` and moves `u` to T. The refined version of the alogrithm is given in Listing 29.5.

LISTING 29.5 Refined Version of Prim's Algorithm

```
Input: A connected undirected weighted G = (V, E) with nonnegative weights
Output: a minimum spanning tree with the starting vertex s as the root
```

```
1   MST getMinimumSpanngingTree(s) {
2     Let T be a set that contains the vertices in the spanning tree;
3     Initially T is empty;
4     Set cost[s] = 0 and cost[v] = infinity for all other vertices in V;
5
6     while (size of T < n) {
7       Find u not in T with the smallest cost[u];
8       Add u to T;
9       for (each v not in T and (u, v) in E)
10        if (cost[v] > w(u, v)) { // Adjust cost[v]
11          cost[v] = w(u, v); parent[v] = u;
12        }
13    }
14  }
```

find next vertex
add a vertex to T

adjust cost[v]

For an interactive demo on how the refined Prim's algorithm works, see liveexample
.pearsoncmg.com/dsanimation/RefinedPrim.html.

29.4.3 Implementation of the MST Algorithm

getMinimumSpanningTree()

The `getMinimumSpanningTree(int v)` method is defined in the `WeightedGraph` class,
as shown in Figure 29.4. It returns an instance of the `MST` class. The `MST` class is defined as an
inner class in the `WeightedGraph` class, which extends the `SearchTree` class, as shown in
Figure 29.8. The `SearchTree` class was shown in Figure 28.11. The `MST` class was
implemented in lines 141–153 in Listing 29.2.

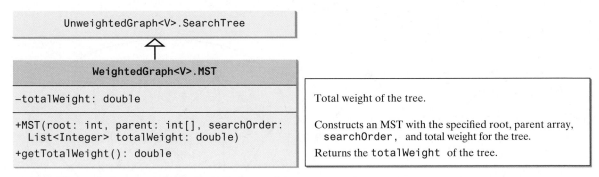

FIGURE 29.8 The `MST` class extends the `SearchTree` class.

The refined version of the Prim's algorithm greatly simplifies the implementation. The
`getMinimumSpanningTree` method was implemented using the refined version of the
Prim's algorithm in lines 99–138 in Listing 29.2. The `getMinimumSpanningTree(int
startingVertex)` method sets `cost[startingVertex]` to 0 (line 105) and `cost[v]` to
infinity for all other vertices (lines 102–104). The parent of `startingVertex` is set to −1
(line 108). `T` is a list that stores the vertices added into the spanning tree (line 111). We use a
list for `T` rather than a set in order to record the order of the vertices added to `T`.

Initially, `T` is empty. To expand `T`, the method performs the following operations:

1. Find the vertex `u` with the smallest `cost[u]` (lines 118–123).

2. If `u` is found, add it to `T` (line 125). Note if `u` is not found (`u == −1`), the graph is not
connected. The `break` statement exits the while loop in this case.

3. After adding `u` in `T`, update `cost[v]` and `parent[v]` for each `v` adjacent to `u` in `V−T` if
`cost[v] > w(u, v)` (lines 129–134).

After a new vertex is added to `T`, `totalWeight` is updated (line 126). Once all vertices are
added to `T`, an instance of `MST` is created (line 137). Note the method will not work if the graph
is not connected. However, you can modify it to obtain a partial MST.

The `MST` class extends the `SearchTree` class (line 141). To create an instance of `MST`, pass `root`, `parent`, `T`, and `totalWeight` (lines 144–145). The data fields `root`, `parent`, and `searchOrder` are defined in the `SearchTree` class, which is an inner class defined in `UnweightedGraph`.

Note testing whether a vertex `i` is in `T` by invoking `T.contains(i)` takes $O(n)$ time, since `T` is a list. Therefore, the overall time complexity for this implementation is $O(n^3)$. Interested readers may see Programming Exercise 29.20 for improving the implementation and reduce the complexity to $O(n^2)$.

time complexity

Listing 29.6 gives a test program that displays minimum spanning trees for the graph in Figure 29.1 and the graph in Figure 29.3a, respectively.

LISTING 29.6 TestMinimumSpanningTree.java

```
1  public class TestMinimumSpanningTree {
2    public static void main(String[] args) {
3      String[] vertices = {"Seattle", "San Francisco", "Los Angeles",
4        "Denver", "Kansas City", "Chicago", "Boston", "New York",
5        "Atlanta", "Miami", "Dallas", "Houston"};
6
7      int[][] edges = {
8        {0, 1, 807}, {0, 3, 1331}, {0, 5, 2097},
9        {1, 0, 807}, {1, 2, 381}, {1, 3, 1267},
10       {2, 1, 381}, {2, 3, 1015}, {2, 4, 1663}, {2, 10, 1435},
11       {3, 0, 1331}, {3, 1, 1267}, {3, 2, 1015}, {3, 4, 599},
12         {3, 5, 1003},
13       {4, 2, 1663}, {4, 3, 599}, {4, 5, 533}, {4, 7, 1260},
14         {4, 8, 864}, {4, 10, 496},
15       {5, 0, 2097}, {5, 3, 1003}, {5, 4, 533},
16         {5, 6, 983}, {5, 7, 787},
17       {6, 5, 983}, {6, 7, 214},
18       {7, 4, 1260}, {7, 5, 787}, {7, 6, 214}, {7, 8, 888},
19       {8, 4, 864}, {8, 7, 888}, {8, 9, 661},
20         {8, 10, 781}, {8, 11, 810},
21       {9, 8, 661}, {9, 11, 1187},
22       {10, 2, 1435}, {10, 4, 496}, {10, 8, 781}, {10, 11, 239},
23       {11, 8, 810}, {11, 9, 1187}, {11, 10, 239}
24     };
25
26     WeightedGraph<String> graph1 =                                    create graph1
27       new WeightedGraph<>(vertices, edges);
28     WeightedGraph<String>.MST tree1 = graph1.getMinimumSpanningTree(); MST for graph1
29     System.out.println("tree1: Total weight is " +                    total weight
30       tree1.getTotalWeight());
31     tree1.printTree();                                                print tree
32
33     edges = new int[][] {                                             create edges
34       {0, 1, 2}, {0, 3, 8},
35       {1, 0, 2}, {1, 2, 7}, {1, 3, 3},
36       {2, 1, 7}, {2, 3, 4}, {2, 4, 5},
37       {3, 0, 8}, {3, 1, 3}, {3, 2, 4}, {3, 4, 6},
38       {4, 2, 5}, {4, 3, 6}
39     };
40
41     WeightedGraph<Integer> graph2 = new WeightedGraph<>(edges, 5);     create graph2
42     WeightedGraph<Integer>.MST tree2 =
43       graph2.getMinimumSpanningTree(1);                               MST for graph2
44     System.out.println("\ntree2: Total weight is " +                 total weight
45       tree2.getTotalWeight());
46     tree2.printTree();                                               print tree
```

display search order

```
47
48        System.out.println("\nShow the search order for tree1:");
49        for (int i: tree1.getSearchOrder())
50          System.out.print(graph1.getVertex(i) + " ");
51      }
52    }
```

```
Total weight is 6513.0
Root is: Seattle
Edges: (Seattle, San Francisco) (San Francisco, Los Angeles)
  (Los Angeles, Denver) (Denver, Kansas City) (Kansas City, Chicago)
  (New York, Boston) (Chicago, New York) (Dallas, Atlanta)
  (Atlanta, Miami) (Kansas City, Dallas) (Dallas, Houston)

Total weight is 14.0
Root is: 1
Edges: (1, 0) (3, 2) (1, 3) (2, 4)

Show the search order for tree1:
Seattle San Francisco Los Angeles Denver Kansas City Dallas

Houston Chicago Atlanta Miami New York Boston
```

The program creates a weighted graph for Figure 29.1 in line 27. It then invokes
`getMinimumSpanningTree()` (line 28) to return an `MST` that represents a minimum spanning tree for the graph. Invoking `printTree()` (line 31) on the `MST` object displays the edges
in the tree. Note that `MST` is a subclass of `Tree`. The `printTree()` method is defined in the
`SearchTree` class.

graphical illustration

The graphical illustration of the minimum spanning tree is shown in Figure 29.9. The
vertices are added to the tree in this order: Seattle, San Francisco, Los Angeles, Denver, Kansas
City, Dallas, Houston, Chicago, Atlanta, Miami, New York, and Boston.

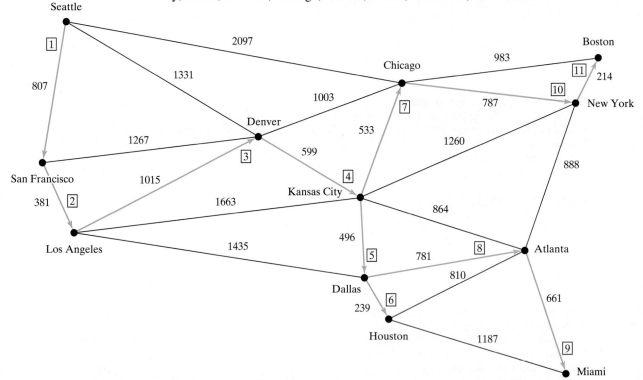

FIGURE 29.9 The edges in a minimum spanning tree for the cities are highlighted.

29.4.1 Find a minimum spanning tree for the following graph:

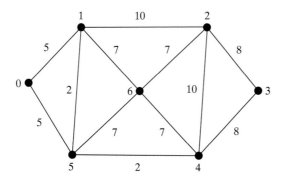

29.4.2 Is a minimum spanning tree unique if all edges have different weights?

29.4.3 If you use an adjacency matrix to represent weighted edges, what will be the time complexity for Prim's algorithm?

29.4.4 What happens to the `getMinimumSpanningTree()` method in `WeightedGraph` if the graph is not connected? Verify your answer by writing a test program that creates an unconnected graph and invokes the `getMinimumSpanningTree()` method. How do you fix the problem by obtaining a partial MST?

29.4.5 Show the output of the following code:

```java
public class Test {
  public static void main(String[] args) {
    WeightedGraph<Character> graph = new WeightedGraph<>();
    graph.addVertex('U');
    graph.addVertex('V');
    graph.addVertex('X');
    int indexForU = graph.getIndex('U');
    int indexForV = graph.getIndex('V');
    int indexForX = graph.getIndex('X');
    System.out.println("indexForU is " + indexForU);
    System.out.println("indexForV is " + indexForV);
    System.out.println("indexForX is " + indexForV);
    graph.addEdge(indexForU, indexForV, 3.5);
    graph.addEdge(indexForV, indexForU, 3.5);
    graph.addEdge(indexForU, indexForX, 2.1);
    graph.addEdge(indexForX, indexForU, 2.1);
    graph.addEdge(indexForV, indexForX, 3.1);
    graph.addEdge(indexForX, indexForV, 3.1);
    WeightedGraph<Character>.MST mst
      = graph.getMinimumSpanningTree();
    graph.printWeightedEdges();
    System.out.println(mst.getTotalWeight());
    mst.printTree();
  }
}
```

29.5 Finding Shortest Paths

The shortest path between two vertices is a path with the minimum total weights.

Given a graph with nonnegative weights on the edges, a well-known algorithm for finding a *shortest path* between two vertices was discovered by Edsger Dijkstra, a Dutch computer scientist. In order to find a shortest path from vertex s to vertex v, *Dijkstra's algorithm* finds the shortest path from s to all vertices. So Dijkstra's algorithm is known as a

Key Point

Dijkstra's algorithm

single-source shortest path

shortest path

single-source shortest-path algorithm. The algorithm uses `cost[v]` to store the cost of a *shortest path* from vertex `v` to the source vertex `s`. `cost[s]` is `0`. Initially assign infinity to `cost[v]` for all other vertices. The algorithm repeatedly finds a vertex `u` in V–T with the smallest `cost[u]` and moves `u` to T.

The algorithm is described in Listing 29.7.

LISTING 29.7 Dijkstra's Single-Source Shortest-Path Algorithm

Input: a graph G = (V, E) with nonnegative weights
Output: a shortest-path tree with the source vertex s as the root

```
1   ShortestPathTree getShortestPath(s) {
2     Let T be a set that contains the vertices whose
3       paths to s are known; Initially T is empty;
4     Set cost[s] = 0; and cost[v] = infinity for all other vertices in V;
5
6     while (size of T < n) {
7       Find u not in T with the smallest cost[u];
8       Add u to T;
9       for (each v not in T and (u, v) in E)
10        if (cost[v] > cost[u] + w(u, v)) {
11          cost[v] = cost[u] + w(u, v); parent[v] = u;
12        }
13    }
14  }
```

find next vertex
add a vertex to T

adjust cost[v]

This algorithm is very similar to Prim's for finding a minimum spanning tree. Both algorithms divide the vertices into two sets: T and V − T. In the case of Prim's algorithm, set T contains the vertices that are already added to the tree. In the case of Dijkstra's, set T contains the vertices whose shortest paths to the source have been found. Both algorithms repeatedly find a vertex from V − T and add it to T. In the case of Prim's algorithm, the vertex is adjacent to some vertex in the set with the minimum weight on the edge. In Dijkstra's algorithm, the vertex is adjacent to some vertex in the set with the minimum total cost to the source.

The algorithm starts by setting `cost[s]` to `0` (line 4), sets `cost[v]` to infinity for all other vertices. It then continuously adds a vertex (say `u`) from V–T into T with smallest `cost[u]` (lines 7–8), as shown in Figure 29.10a. After adding `u` to T, the algorithm updates `cost[v]` and `parent[v]` for each `v` not in T if `(u, v)` is in T and `cost[v] > cost[u] + w(u, v)` (lines 10–12).

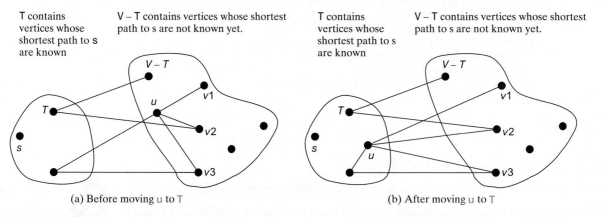

(a) Before moving u to T   (b) After moving u to T

FIGURE 29.10 (a) Find a vertex u in V–T with the smallest `cost[u]`. (b) Update `cost[v]` for v in V–T and v is adjacent to u.

Let us illustrate Dijkstra's algorithm using the graph in Figure 29.11a. Suppose the source vertex is `1`. Therefore, `cost[1]` = `0` and the costs for all other vertices are initially ∞, as shown in Figure 29.11b. We use the `parent[i]` to denote the parent of `i` in the path. For convenience, set the parent of the source node to `−1`.

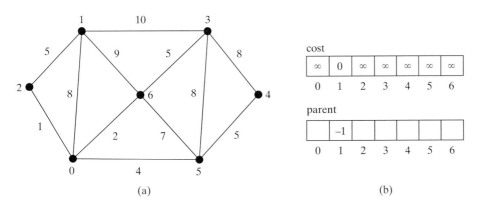

(a)   (b)

FIGURE 29.11   The algorithm will find all shortest paths from source vertex `1`.

Initially set `T` is empty. The algorithm selects the vertex with the smallest cost. In this case, the vertex is `1`. The algorithm adds `1` to `T`, as shown in Figure 29.12a. Afterward, it adjusts the cost for each vertex adjacent to `1`. The cost for vertices 2, 0, 6, and 3 and their parents are now updated, as shown in Figure 29.12b.

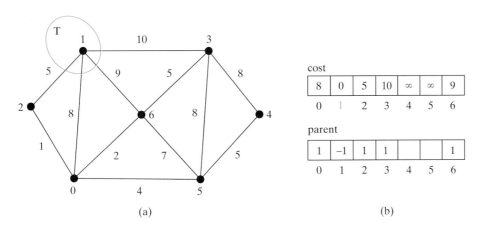

(a)   (b)

FIGURE 29.12   Now vertex `1` is in set `T`.

Vertices `2`, `0`, `6`, and `3` are adjacent to the source vertex, and vertex `2` is the one in `V−T` with the smallest cost, so add `2` to `T`, as shown in Figure 29.13 and update the cost and parent for vertices in `V−T` and adjacent to `2`. `cost[0]` is now updated to `6` and its parent is set to `2`. The arrow line from `1` to `2` indicates `1` is the parent of `2` after `2` is added into `T`.

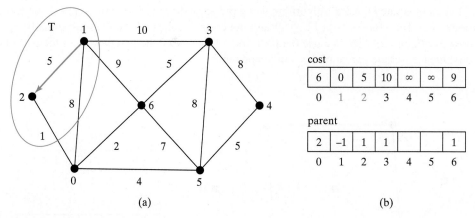

FIGURE 29.13 Now vertices 1 and 2 are in set T.

Now T contains {1, 2}. Vertex 0 is the one in V−T with the smallest cost, so add 0 to T, as shown in Figure 29.14 and update the cost and parent for vertices in V−T and adjacent to 0 if applicable. cost[5] is now updated to 10 and its parent is set to 0 and cost[6] is now updated to 8 and its parent is set to 0.

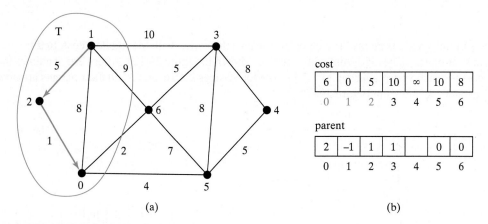

FIGURE 29.14 Now vertices {1, 2, 0} are in set T.

Now T contains {1, 2, 0}. Vertex 6 is the one in V−T with the smallest cost, so add 6 to T, as shown in Figure 29.15 and update the cost and parent for vertices in V−T and adjacent to 6 if applicable.

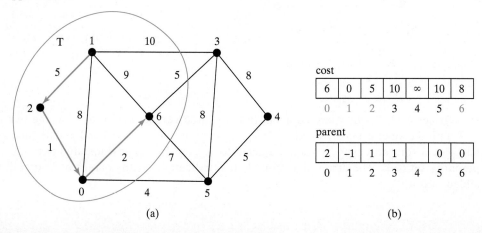

FIGURE 29.15 Now vertices {1, 2, 0, 6} are in set T.

Now T contains {1, 2, 0, 6}. Vertex 3 or 5 is the one in V−T with the smallest cost. You may add either 3 or 5 into T. Let us add 3 to T, as shown in Figure 29.16 and update the cost and parent for vertices in V−T and adjacent to 3 if applicable. cost[4] is now updated to 18 and its parent is set to 3.

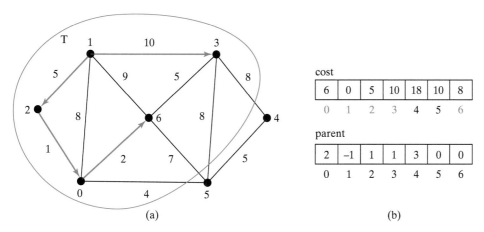

cost

6	0	5	10	18	10	8
0	1	2	3	4	5	6

parent

2	−1	1	1	3	0	0
0	1	2	3	4	5	6

(a) (b)

FIGURE 29.16 Now vertices {1, 2, 0, 6, 3} are in set T.

Now T contains {1, 2, 0, 6, 3}. Vertex 5 is the one in V−T with the smallest cost, so add 5 to T, as shown in Figure 29.17 and update the cost and parent for vertices in V−T and adjacent to 5 if applicable. cost[4] is now updated to 15, and its parent is set to 5.

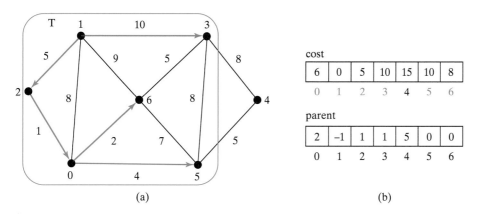

cost

6	0	5	10	15	10	8
0	1	2	3	4	5	6

parent

2	−1	1	1	5	0	0
0	1	2	3	4	5	6

(a) (b)

FIGURE 29.17 Now vertices {1, 2, 0, 6, 3, 5} are in set T. *Source*: Copyright © 1995–2016 Oracle and/or its affiliates. All rights reserved. Used with permission.

Now T contains {1, 2, 0, 6, 3, 5}. Vertex 4 is the one in V−T with the smallest cost, so add 4 to T, as shown in Figure 29.18.

As you can see, the algorithm essentially finds all shortest paths from a source vertex, which produces a tree rooted at the source vertex. We call this tree a *single-source all-shortest-path tree* (or simply a *shortest-path tree*). To model this tree, define a class named ShortestPathTree that extends the SearchTree class, as shown in Figure 29.19. ShortestPathTree is defined as an inner class in WeightedGraph in lines 200–224 in Listing 29.2.

shortest-path tree

The getShortestPath(int sourceVertex) method was implemented in lines 156–197 in Listing 29.2. The method sets cost[sourceVertex] to 0 (line 162) and cost[v] to

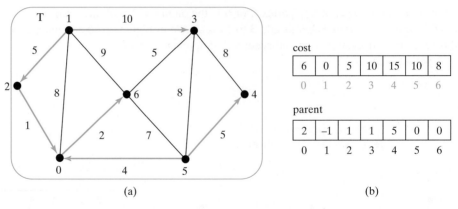

FIGURE 29.18 Now vertices {1, 2, 6, 0, 3, 5, 4} are in set T. *Source*: Copyright © 1995–2016 Oracle and/or its affiliates. All rights reserved. Used with permission.

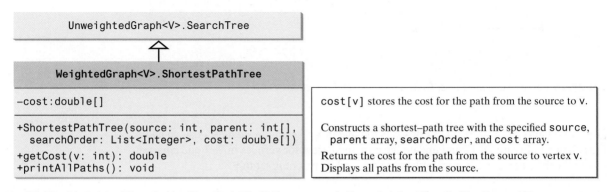

FIGURE 29.19 `WeightedGraph<V>.ShortestPathTree` extends `UnweightedGraph<V>.SearchTree`.
Source: Copyright © 1995–2016 Oracle and/or its affiliates. All rights reserved. Used with permission.

infinity for all other vertices (lines 159–161). The parent of `sourceVertex` is set to −1 (line 166). T is a list that stores the vertices added into the shortest-path tree (line 169). We use a list for T rather than a set in order to record the order of the vertices added to T.

Initially, T is empty. To expand T, the method performs the following operations:

1. Find the vertex u with the smallest `cost[u]` (lines 175–181).

2. If u is found, add it to T (line 183). Note that if u is not found (u == −1), the graph is not connected. The `break` statement exits the while loop in this case.

3. After adding u in T, update `cost[v]` and `parent[v]` for each v adjacent to u in V−T if `cost[v] > cost[u] + w(u, v)` (lines 186–192).

ShortestPathTree class

Once all vertices from s are added to T, an instance of `ShortestPathTree` is created (line 196).

The `ShortestPathTree` class extends the `SearchTree` class (line 200). To create an instance of `ShortestPathTree`, pass `sourceVertex`, `parent`, T, and `cost` (lines 204–205). `sourceVertex` becomes the root in the tree. The data fields `root`, `parent`, and `searchOrder` are defined in the `SearchTree` class, which is an inner class defined in `UnweightedGraph`.

Note testing whether a vertex i is in T by invoking `T.conatins(i)` takes $O(n)$ time, since T is a list. Therefore, the overall time complexity for this implementation is $O(n^3)$. Interested readers may see Programming Exercise 29.20 for improving the implementation and reducing the complexity to $O(n^2)$.

Dijkstra's algorithm time complexity

greedy and dynamic programming

Dijkstra's algorithm is a combination of a greedy algorithm and dynamic programming. It is a greedy algorithm in the sense that it always adds a new vertex that has the shortest distance to the source. It stores the shortest distance of each known vertex to the source, and uses it later to avoid redundant computing, so Dijkstra's algorithm also uses dynamic programming.

Listing 29.8 gives a test program that displays the shortest paths from Chicago to all other cities in Figure 29.1, and the shortest paths from vertex 3 to all vertices for the graph in Figure 29.3a, respectively.

LISTING 29.8   TestShortestPath.java

```
1   public class TestShortestPath {
2     public static void main(String[] args) {
3       String[] vertices = {"Seattle", "San Francisco", "Los Angeles",          vertices
4         "Denver", "Kansas City", "Chicago", "Boston", "New York",
5         "Atlanta", "Miami", "Dallas", "Houston"};
6
7       int[][] edges = {                                                         edges
8         {0, 1, 807}, {0, 3, 1331}, {0, 5, 2097},
9         {1, 0, 807}, {1, 2, 381}, {1, 3, 1267},
10        {2, 1, 381}, {2, 3, 1015}, {2, 4, 1663}, {2, 10, 1435},
11        {3, 0, 1331}, {3, 1, 1267}, {3, 2, 1015}, {3, 4, 599},
12          {3, 5, 1003},
13        {4, 2, 1663}, {4, 3, 599}, {4, 5, 533}, {4, 7, 1260},
14          {4, 8, 864}, {4, 10, 496},
15        {5, 0, 2097}, {5, 3, 1003}, {5, 4, 533},
16          {5, 6, 983}, {5, 7, 787},
17        {6, 5, 983}, {6, 7, 214},
18        {7, 4, 1260}, {7, 5, 787}, {7, 6, 214}, {7, 8, 888},
19        {8, 4, 864}, {8, 7, 888}, {8, 9, 661},
20          {8, 10, 781}, {8, 11, 810},
21        {9, 8, 661}, {9, 11, 1187},
22        {10, 2, 1435}, {10, 4, 496}, {10, 8, 781}, {10, 11, 239},
23        {11, 8, 810}, {11, 9, 1187}, {11, 10, 239}
24      };
25
26      WeightedGraph<String> graph1 =
27        new WeightedGraph<>(vertices, edges);                                   create graph1
28      WeightedGraph<String>.ShortestPathTree tree1 =
29        graph1.getShortestPath(graph1.getIndex("Chicago"));                     shortest path
30      tree1.printAllPaths();
31
32      // Display shortest paths from Houston to Chicago
33      System.out.print("Shortest path from Houston to Chicago: ");
34      java.util.List<String> path
35        = tree1.getPath(graph1.getIndex("Houston"));
36      for (String s: path) {
37        System.out.print(s + " ");
38      }
39                                                                                create edges
40      edges = new int[][] {
41        {0, 1, 2}, {0, 3, 8},
42        {1, 0, 2}, {1, 2, 7}, {1, 3, 3},
43        {2, 1, 7}, {2, 3, 4}, {2, 4, 5},
44        {3, 0, 8}, {3, 1, 3}, {3, 2, 4}, {3, 4, 6},
45        {4, 2, 5}, {4, 3, 6}
46      };
47      WeightedGraph<Integer> graph2 = new WeightedGraph<>(edges, 5);            create graph2
48      WeightedGraph<Integer>.ShortestPathTree tree2 =
49        graph2.getShortestPath(3);
50      System.out.println("\n");
51      tree2.printAllPaths();                                                    print paths
52    }
53  }
```

```
All shortest paths from Chicago are:
A path from Chicago to Seattle: Chicago Seattle (cost: 2097.0)
A path from Chicago to San Francisco: Chicago Denver San Francisco
  (cost: 2270.0)
A path from Chicago to Los Angeles: Chicago Denver Los Angeles
  (cost: 2018.0)
A path from Chicago to Denver: Chicago Denver (cost: 1003.0)
A path from Chicago to Kansas City: Chicago Kansas City (cost: 533.0)
A path from Chicago to Chicago: Chicago (cost: 0.0)
A path from Chicago to Boston: Chicago Boston (cost: 983.0)
A path from Chicago to New York: Chicago New York (cost: 787.0)
A path from Chicago to Atlanta: Chicago Kansas City Atlanta
  (cost: 1397.0)
A path from Chicago to Miami:
  Chicago Kansas City Atlanta Miami (cost: 2058.0)
A path from Chicago to Dallas:
  Chicago Kansas City Dallas (cost: 1029.0)
A path from Chicago to Houston:
  Chicago Kansas City Dallas Houston (cost: 1268.0)
Shortest path from Houston to Chicago:
  Houston Dallas Kansas City Chicago

All shortest paths from 3 are:
A path from 3 to 0: 3 1 0 (cost: 5.0)
A path from 3 to 1: 3 1 (cost: 3.0)
A path from 3 to 2: 3 2 (cost: 4.0)
A path from 3 to 3: 3 (cost: 0.0)
A path from 3 to 4: 3 4 (cost: 6.0)
```

The program creates a weighted graph for Figure 29.1 in line 27. It then invokes the `getShortestPath(graph1.getIndex("Chicago"))` method to return a `Path` object that contains all shortest paths from Chicago. Invoking `printAllPaths()` on the `ShortestPathTree` object displays all the paths (line 30).

The graphical illustration of all shortest paths from Chicago is shown in Figure 29.20. The shortest paths from Chicago to the cities are found in this order: Kansas City, New York, Boston, Denver, Dallas, Houston, Atlanta, Los Angeles, Miami, Seattle, and San Francisco.

29.5.1 Trace Dijkstra's algorithm for finding shortest paths from Boston to all other cities in Figure 29.1.

29.5.2 Is a shortest path between two vertices unique if all edges have different weights?

29.5.3 If you use an adjacency matrix to represent weighted edges, what would be the time complexity for Dijkstra's algorithm?

29.5.4 What happens to the `getShortestPath()` method in `WeightedGraph` if the source vertex cannot reach all vertices in the graph? Verify your answer by writing a test program that creates an unconnected graph and invoke the `getShortestPath()` method. How do you fix the problem by obtaining a partial shortest-path tree?

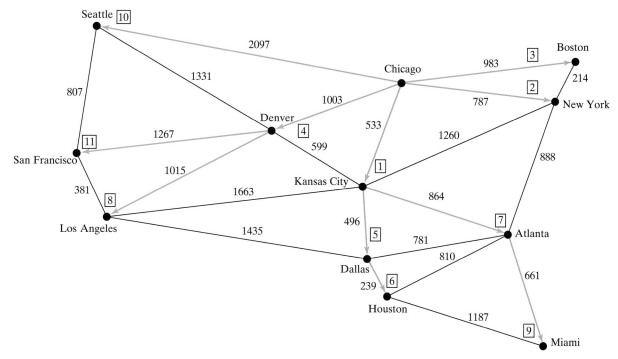

FIGURE 29.20 The shortest paths from Chicago to all other cities are highlighted.

29.5.5 If there is no path from vertex `v` to the source vertex, what will be `cost[v]`?

29.5.6 Assume the graph is connected; will the `getShortestPath` method find the short-est paths correctly if lines 159–161 in `WeightedGraph` are deleted?

29.5.7 Show the output of the following code:

```java
public class Test {
  public static void main(String[] args) {
    WeightedGraph<Character> graph = new WeightedGraph<>();
    graph.addVertex('U');
    graph.addVertex('V');
    graph.addVertex('X');
    int indexForU = graph.getIndex('U');
    int indexForV = graph.getIndex('V');
    int indexForX = graph.getIndex('X');
    System.out.println("indexForU is " + indexForU);
    System.out.println("indexForV is " + indexForV);
    System.out.println("indexForX is " + indexForV);
    graph.addEdge(indexForU, indexForV, 3.5);
    graph.addEdge(indexForV, indexForU, 3.5);
    graph.addEdge(indexForU, indexForX, 2.1);
    graph.addEdge(indexForX, indexForU, 2.1);
    graph.addEdge(indexForV, indexForX, 3.1);
    graph.addEdge(indexForX, indexForV, 3.1);
    WeightedGraph<Character>.ShortestPathTree tree =
      graph.getShortestPath(1);
```

```
                     graph.printWeightedEdges();
                     tree.printTree();
                 }
             }
```

29.6 Case Study: The Weighted Nine Tails Problem

The weighted nine tails problem can be reduced to the weighted shortest path problem.

Key Point

Section 28.10 presented the nine tails problem and solved it using the BFS algorithm. This section presents a variation of the nine tails problem and solves it using the shortest-path algorithm.

The nine tails problem is to find the minimum number of the moves that lead to all coins facing down. Each move flips a head coin and its neighbors. The weighted nine tails problem assigns the number of flips as a weight on each move. For example, you can move from the coins in Figure 29.21a to those in Figure 29.21b by flipping the first coin in the first row and its two neighbors. Thus, the weight for this move is 3. You can move from the coins in Figure 29.21c to Figure 29.21d by flipping the five coins. So the weight for this move is 5.

H	H	H
T	T	T
H	H	H

(a)

T	T	H
H	T	T
H	H	H

(b)

T	T	H
H	H	T
H	H	H

(c)

T	H	H
T	T	H
H	T	H

(d)

FIGURE 29.21 The weight for each move is the number of flips for the move.

The weighted nine tails problem can be reduced to finding a shortest path from a starting node to the target node in an edge-weighted graph. The graph has 512 nodes. Create an edge from node v to u if there is a move from node u to node v. Assign the number of flips to be the weight of the edge.

Recall in Section 28.10, we defined a class NineTailModel for modeling the nine tails problem. We now define a new class named WeightedNineTailModel that extends NineTailModel, as shown in Figure 29.22.

The NineTailModel class creates a Graph and obtains a Tree rooted at the target node 511. WeightedNineTailModel is the same as NineTailModel except that it creates a WeightedGraph and obtains a ShortestPathTree rooted at the target node 511. The method getEdges() finds all edges in the graph. The getNumberOfFlips(int u, int v) method returns the number of flips from node u to node v. The getNumberOfFlips(int u) method returns the number of flips from node u to the target node.

Listing 29.9 implements the WeightedNineTailModel.

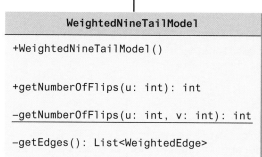

NineTailModel
#tree: UnweightedGraph<Integer>.SeachTree
+NineTailModel()
+getShortestPath(nodeIndex: int): List<Integer>
-getEdges(): List<AbstractGraph.Edge>
+getNode(index: int): char[]
+getIndex(node: char[]): int
+getFlippedNode(node: char[], position: int): int
+flipACell(node: char[], row: int, column: int): void
+printNode(node: char[]): void

A tree rooted at node 511.

Constructs a model for the nine tails problem and obtains the tree.

Returns a path from the specified node to the root. The path returned consists of the node labels in a list.

Returns a list of Edge objects for the graph.

Returns a node consisting of nine characters of Hs and Ts.

Returns the index of the specified node.

Flips the node at the specified position and returns the index of the flipped node.

Flips the node at the specified row and column.

Displays the node to the console.

WeightedNineTailModel
+WeightedNineTailModel()
+getNumberOfFlips(u: int): int
-getNumberOfFlips(u: int, v: int): int
-getEdges(): List<WeightedEdge>

Constructs a model for the weighted nine tails problem and obtains a ShortestPathTree rooted from the target node.

Returns the number of flips from node u to the target node 511.

Returns the number of different cells between the two nodes.

Gets the weighted edges for the weighted nine tail problem.

FIGURE 29.22 The WeightedNineTailModel class extends NineTailModel.

LISTING 29.9 WeightedNineTailModel.java

```java
1   import java.util.*;
2
3   public class WeightedNineTailModel extends NineTailModel {      extends NineTailModel
4     /** Construct a model */
5     public WeightedNineTailModel() {                             constructor
6       // Create edges
7       List<WeightedEdge> edges = getEdges();                     get edges
8
9       // Create a graph
10      WeightedGraph<Integer> graph = new WeightedGraph<Integer>(  create a graph
11        edges, NUMBER_OF_NODES);
12
13      // Obtain a shortest-path tree rooted at the target node
14      tree = graph.getShortestPath(511);                         get a tree
15    }
16
17    /** Create all edges for the graph */
18    private List<WeightedEdge> getEdges() {                      get weighted edges
19      // Store edges
20      List<WeightedEdge> edges = new ArrayList<>();
```

```
21
22      for (int u = 0; u < NUMBER_OF_NODES; u++) {
23        for (int k = 0; k < 9; k++) {
24          char[] node = getNode(u); // Get the node for vertex u
25          if (node[k] == 'H') {
26            int v = getFlippedNode(node, k);
27            int numberOfFlips = getNumberOfFlips(u, v);
28
29            // Add edge (v, u) for a legal move from node u to node v
30            edges.add(new WeightedEdge(v, u, numberOfFlips));
31          }
32        }
33      }
34
35      return edges;
36    }
37
38    private static int getNumberOfFlips(int u, int v) {
39      char[] node1 = getNode(u);
40      char[] node2 = getNode(v);
41
42      int count = 0; // Count the number of different cells
43      for (int i = 0; i < node1.length; i++)
44        if (node1[i] != node2[i]) count++;
45
46      return count;
47    }
48
49    public int getNumberOfFlips(int u) {
50      return (int)((WeightedGraph<Integer>.ShortestPathTree)tree)
51        .getCost(u);
52    }
53  }
```

Line labels: get adjacent node (24), weight (27), add an edge (30), number of flips (38), total number of flips (49).

`WeightedNineTailModel` extends `NineTailModel` to build a `WeightedGraph` to model the weighted nine tails problem (lines 10–11). For each node u, the `getEdges()` method finds a flipped node v and assigns the number of flips as the weight for edge (v, u) (line 30). The `getNumberOfFlips(int u, int v)` method returns the number of flips from node u to node v (lines 38–47). The number of flips is the number of the different cells between the two nodes (line 44).

The `WeightedNineTailModel` obtains a `ShortestPathTree` rooted at the target node 511 (line 14). Note `tree` is a protected data field defined in `NineTailModel` and `ShortestPathTree` is a subclass of `Tree`. The methods defined in `NineTailModel` use the `tree` property.

The `getNumberOfFlips(int u)` method (lines 49–52) returns the number of flips from node u to the target node, which is the cost of the path from node u to the target node. This cost can be obtained by invoking the `getCost(u)` method defined in the `ShortestPathTree` class (line 51).

Listing 29.10 gives a program that prompts the user to enter an initial node and displays the minimum number of flips to reach the target node.

LISTING 29.10 WeightedNineTail.java

```
1  import java.util.Scanner;
2
3  public class WeightedNineTail {
4    public static void main(String[] args) {
5      // Prompt the user to enter the nine coins' Hs and Ts
```

```
6          System.out.print("Enter an initial nine coins' Hs and Ts: ");
7          Scanner input = new Scanner(System.in);
8          String s = input.nextLine();
9          char[] initialNode = s.toCharArray();                                    initial node
10
11         WeightedNineTailModel model = new WeightedNineTailModel();                create model
12         java.util.List<Integer> path =
13            model.getShortestPath(NineTailModel.getIndex(initialNode));            get shortest path
14
15         System.out.println("The steps to flip the coins are ");
16         for (int i = 0; i < path.size(); i++)
17            NineTailModel.printNode(NineTailModel.getNode(path.get(i)));           print node
18
19         System.out.println("The number of flips is " +
20            model.getNumberOfFlips(NineTailModel.getIndex(initialNode)));          number of flips
21     }
22   }
```

```
Enter an initial nine coins Hs and Ts: HHHTTTHHH  ↵Enter

The steps to flip the coins are
HHH
TTT
HHH

HHH
THT
TTT

TTT
TTT
TTT

The number of flips is 8
```

The program prompts the user to enter an initial node with nine letters with a combination of
Hs and Ts as a string in line 8, obtains an array of characters from the string (line 9), creates a
model (line 11), obtains the shortest path from the initial node to the target node (lines 12–13),
displays the nodes in the path (lines 16–17), and invokes getNumberOfFlips to get the
number of flips needed to reach the target node (line 20).

29.6.1 Why is the tree data field in NineTailModel in Listing 28.13 defined
protected?

29.6.2 How are the nodes created for the graph in WeightedNineTailModel?

29.6.3 How are the edges created for the graph in WeightedNineTailModel?

✓ **Check
Point**

KEY TERMS

Dijkstra's algorithm   1103
edge-weighted graph   1087
minimum spanning tree   1097
Prim's algorithm   1097

shortest path   1104
single-source shortest path   1104
vertex-weighted graph   1087

CHAPTER SUMMARY

1. You can use adjacency matrices or lists to store weighted edges in graphs.

2. A spanning tree of a graph is a subgraph that is a tree and connects all vertices in the graph.

3. Prim's algorithm for finding a minimum spanning tree works as follows: the algorithm starts with a spanning tree T that contains an arbitrary vertex. The algorithm expands the tree by adding a vertex with the minimum-weight edge incident to a vertex already in the tree.

4. Dijkstra's algorithm starts the search from the source vertex and keeps finding vertices that have the shortest path to the source until all vertices are found.

 ## QUIZ

Answer the quiz for this chapter online at the book Companion Website.

MyProgrammingLab™ ## PROGRAMMING EXERCISES

*29.1 (*Kruskal's algorithm*) The text introduced Prim's algorithm for finding a minimum spanning tree. Kruskal's algorithm is another well-known algorithm for finding a minimum spanning tree. The algorithm repeatedly finds a minimum-weight edge and adds it to the tree if it does not cause a cycle. The process ends when all vertices are in the tree. Design and implement an algorithm for finding an MST using Kruskal's algorithm.

*29.2 (*Implement Prim's algorithm using an adjacency matrix*) The text implements Prim's algorithm using lists for adjacent edges. Implement the algorithm using an adjacency matrix for weighted graphs.

*29.3 (*Implement Dijkstra's algorithm using an adjacency matrix*) The text implements Dijkstra's algorithm using lists for adjacent edges. Implement the algorithm using an adjacency matrix for weighted graphs.

*29.4 (*Modify weight in the nine tails problem*) In the text, we assign the number of the flips as the weight for each move. Assuming the weight is three times of the number of flips, revise the program.

*29.5 (*Prove or disprove*) The conjecture is that both `NineTailModel` and `WeightedNineTailModel` result in the same shortest path. Write a program to prove or disprove it. (*Hint*: Let `tree1` and `tree2` denote the trees rooted at node `511` obtained from `NineTailModel` and `WeightedNineTailModel`, respectively. If the depth of a node u is the same in `tree1` and in `tree2`, the length of the path from u to the target is the same.)

**29.6 (*Weighted 4 × 4 16 tails model*) The weighted nine tails problem in the text uses a 3 × 3 matrix. Assume that you have 16 coins placed in a 4 × 4 matrix. Create a new model class named `WeightedTailModel16`. Create an instance of the model and save the object into a file named WeightedTailModel16.dat.

**29.7 (*Weighted 4 × 4 16 tails*) Revise Listing 29.9, WeightedNineTail.java, for the weighted 4 × 4 16 tails problem. Your program should read the model object created from the preceding exercise.

**29.8 (*Traveling salesperson problem*) The traveling salesperson problem (TSP) is to find the shortest round-trip route that visits each city exactly once and then returns to the starting city. The problem is similar to finding a shortest Hamiltonian cycle in Programming Exercise 28.17. Add the following method in the `WeightedGraph` class:

```
// Return a shortest cycle
// Return null if no such cycle exists
public List<Integer> getShortestHamiltonianCycle()
```

*29.9 (*Find a minimum spanning tree*) Write a program that reads a connected graph from a file and displays its minimum spanning tree. The first line in the file contains a number that indicates the number of vertices (`n`). The vertices are labeled as `0, 1, ..., n−1`. Each subsequent line describes the edges in the form of `u1, v1, w1 | u2, v2, w2 | . . . .` Each triplet in this form describes an edge and its weight. Figure 29.23 shows an example of the file for the corresponding graph. Note we assume the graph is undirected. If the graph has an edge (`u, v`), it also has an edge (`v, u`). Only one edge is represented in the file. When you construct a graph, both edges need to be added.

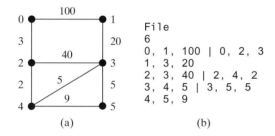

```
File
6
0, 1, 100 | 0, 2, 3
1, 3, 20
2, 3, 40 | 2, 4, 2
3, 4, 5 | 3, 5, 5
4, 5, 9
```

(a)   (b)

FIGURE 29.23   The vertices and edges of a weighted graph can be stored in a file.

Your program should prompt the user to enter a URL for the file, read data from the file, create an instance `g` of `WeightedGraph`, invoke `g.printWeightedEdges()` to display all edges, invoke `getMinimumSpanningTree()` to obtain an instance `tree` of `WeightedGraph.MST`, invoke `tree.getTotalWeight()` to display the weight of the minimum spanning tree, and invoke `tree.printTree()` to display the tree. Here is a sample run of the program:

```
Enter a URL:
  https://liveexample.pearsoncmg.com/test/WeightedGraphSample.txt  ↵Enter
The number of vertices is 6
Vertex 0: (0, 2, 3) (0, 1, 100)
Vertex 1: (1, 3, 20) (1, 0, 100)
Vertex 2: (2, 4, 2) (2, 3, 40) (2, 0, 3)
Vertex 3: (3, 4, 5) (3, 5, 5) (3, 1, 20) (3, 2, 40)
Vertex 4: (4, 2, 2) (4, 3, 5) (4, 5, 9)
Vertex 5: (5, 3, 5) (5, 4, 9)
Total weight in MST is 35
Root is: 0
Edges: (3, 1) (0, 2) (4, 3) (2, 4) (3, 5)
```

(*Hint*: Use `new WeightedGraph(list, numberOfVertices)` to create a graph, where `list` contains a list of `WeightedEdge` objects. Use `new WeightedEdge(u, v, w)` to create an edge. Read the first line to get the number of vertices. Read each subsequent line into a string `s` and use `s.split("[\\|]")` to extract the triplets. For each triplet, use `triplet.split("[,]")` to extract vertices and weight.)

*29.10 (*Create a file for a graph*) Modify Listing 29.3, TestWeightedGraph.java, to create a file for representing `graph1`. The file format is described in Programming Exercise 29.9. Create the file from the array defined in lines 7–24 in Listing 29.3. The number of vertices for the graph is 12, which will be stored in the first line of the file. An edge (u, v) is stored if u < v. The contents of the file should be as follows:

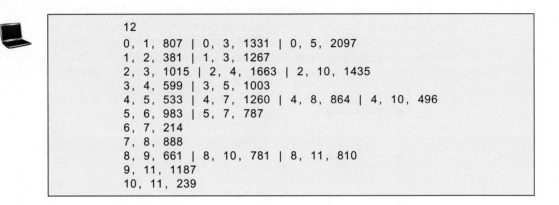

```
12
0, 1, 807 | 0, 3, 1331 | 0, 5, 2097
1, 2, 381 | 1, 3, 1267
2, 3, 1015 | 2, 4, 1663 | 2, 10, 1435
3, 4, 599 | 3, 5, 1003
4, 5, 533 | 4, 7, 1260 | 4, 8, 864 | 4, 10, 496
5, 6, 983 | 5, 7, 787
6, 7, 214
7, 8, 888
8, 9, 661 | 8, 10, 781 | 8, 11, 810
9, 11, 1187
10, 11, 239
```

*29.11 (*Find shortest paths*) Write a program that reads a connected graph from a file. The graph is stored in a file using the same format specified in Programming Exercise 29.9. Your program should prompt the user to enter a URL for the file, then two vertices, and should display a shortest path between the two vertices. For example, for the graph in Figure 29.23, a shortest path between 0 and 1 can be displayed as 0 2 4 3 1.

Here is a sample run of the program:

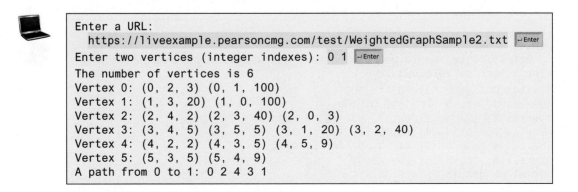

```
Enter a URL:
    https://liveexample.pearsoncmg.com/test/WeightedGraphSample2.txt ↵Enter
Enter two vertices (integer indexes): 0 1 ↵Enter
The number of vertices is 6
Vertex 0: (0, 2, 3) (0, 1, 100)
Vertex 1: (1, 3, 20) (1, 0, 100)
Vertex 2: (2, 4, 2) (2, 3, 40) (2, 0, 3)
Vertex 3: (3, 4, 5) (3, 5, 5) (3, 1, 20) (3, 2, 40)
Vertex 4: (4, 2, 2) (4, 3, 5) (4, 5, 9)
Vertex 5: (5, 3, 5) (5, 4, 9)
A path from 0 to 1: 0 2 4 3 1
```

*29.12 (*Display weighted graphs*) Revise `GraphView` in Listing 28.6 to display a weighted graph. Write a program that displays the graph in Figure 29.1 as shown in Figure 29.24. (Instructors may ask students to expand this program by adding new cities with appropriate edges into the graph).

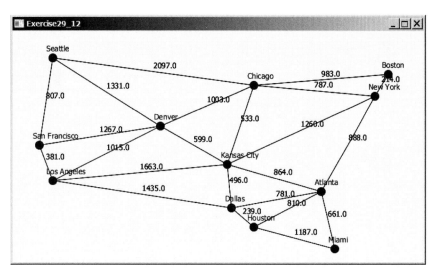

FIGURE 29.24 Programming Exercise 29.12 displays a weighted graph.

*29.13 (*Display shortest paths*) Revise `GraphView` in Listing 28.6 to display a weighted graph and a shortest path between the two specified cities, as shown in Figure 29.25. You need to add a data field `path` in `GraphView`. If a `path` is not null, the edges in the path are displayed in red. If a city not in the map is entered, the program displays a text to alert the user.

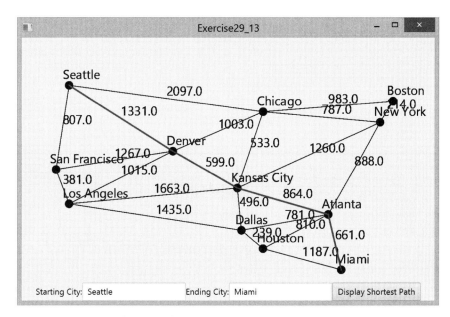

FIGURE 29.25 Programming Exercise 29.13 displays a shortest path.

*29.14 (*Display a minimum spanning tree*) Revise `GraphView` in Listing 28.6 to display a weighted graph and a minimum spanning tree for the graph in Figure 29.1, as shown in Figure 29.26. The edges in the MST are shown in red.

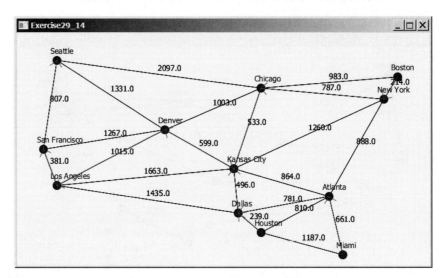

FIGURE 29.26 Programming Exercise 29.14 displays an MST.

***29.15 (*Dynamic graphs*) Write a program that lets the users create a weighted graph dynamically. The user can create a vertex by entering its name and location, as shown in Figure 29.27. The user can also create an edge to connect two vertices. To simplify the program, assume vertex names are the same as vertex indices. You have to add the vertex indices 0, 1, . . . , and n, in this order. The user can specify two vertices and let the program display their shortest path in red.

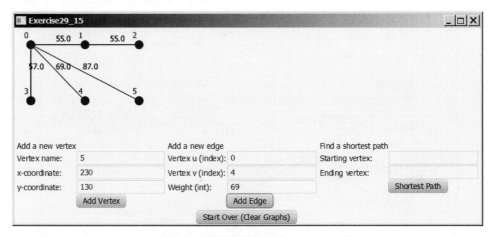

FIGURE 29.27 The program can add vertices and edges and display a shortest path between two specified vertices. *Source*: Copyright © 1995–2016 Oracle and/or its affiliates. All rights reserved. Used with permission.

***29.16 (*Display a dynamic MST*) Write a program that lets the user create a weighted graph dynamically. The user can create a vertex by entering its name and location, as shown in Figure 29.28. The user can also create an edge to connect two vertices. To simplify the program, assume vertex names are the same as those of vertex indices. You have to add the vertex indices 0, 1, . . . , and n, in this order. The edges in the MST are displayed in red. As new edges are added, the MST is redisplayed.

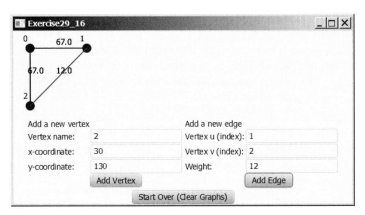

FIGURE 29.28 The program can add vertices and edges and display MST dynamically. *Source*: Copyright © 1995–2016 Oracle and/or its affiliates. All rights reserved. Used with permission.

***29.17   (*Weighted graph visualization tool*) Develop a GUI program as shown in Figure 29.2, with the following requirements: (1) The radius of each vertex is 20 pixels. (2) The user clicks the left mouse button to place a vertex centered at the mouse point, provided the mouse point is not inside or too close to an existing vertex. (3) The user clicks the right mouse button inside an existing vertex to remove the vertex. (4) The user presses a mouse button inside a vertex and drags to another vertex then releases the button to create an edge, and the distance between the two vertices is also displayed. (5) The user drags a vertex while pressing the *CTRL* key to move a vertex. (6) The vertices are numbers starting from 0. When a vertex is removed, the vertices are renumbered. (7) You can click the *Show MST* or *Show All SP From the Source* button to display an MST or SP tree from a starting vertex. (8) You can click the *Show Shortest Path* button to display the shortest path between the two specified vertices.

***29.18   (*Alternative version of Dijkstra algorithm*) An alternative version of the Dijkstra algorithm can be described as follows:

```
Input: a weighted graph G = (V, E) with nonnegative weights
Output: A shortest-path tree from a source vertex s

1   ShortestPathTree getShortestPath(s) {
2     Let T be a set that contains the vertices whose
3       paths to s are known;
4     Initially T contains source vertex s with cost[s] = 0;     add initial vertex
5     for (each u in V - T)
6       cost[u] = infinity;
7
8     while (size of T < n) {                                    more vertex
9       Find v in V - T with the smallest cost[u] + w(u, v) value    find next vertex
10        among all u in T;
11      Add v to T and set cost[v] = cost[u] + w(u, v);          add a vertex
12      parent[v] = u;
13    }
14  }
```

The algorithm uses `cost[v]` to store the cost of a shortest path from vertex `v` to the source vertex `s`. `cost[s]` is `0`. Initially assign infinity to `cost[v]` to indicate that no path is found from `v` to `s`. Let `V` denote all vertices in the graph and `T` denote the set of the vertices whose costs are known. Initially, the source vertex `s` is in `T`. The algorithm repeatedly finds a vertex `u` in `T` and a vertex `v` in `V–T` such that `cost[u] + w(u, v)` is the smallest, and moves `v` to `T`. The shortest-path algorithm given in the text continuously updates the cost and parent for a vertex in `V–T`. This algorithm initializes the cost to infinity for each vertex and then changes the cost for a vertex only once when the vertex is added into `T`. Implement this algorithm and use Listing 29.7, TestShortestPath.java, to test your new algorithm.

***29.19 (*Find `u` with smallest `cost[u]` efficiently*) The `getShortestPath` method finds a `u` with the smallest `cost[u]` using a linear search, which takes $O(|V|)$. The search time can be reduced to $O(\log|V|)$ using an AVL tree. Modify the method using an AVL tree to store the vertices in `V–T`. Use Listing 29.7, TestShortestPath.java, to test your new implementation.

***29.20 (*Test if a vertex `u` is in T efficiently*) Since `T` is implemented using a list in the `getMinimumSpanningTree` and `getShortestPath` methods in Listing 29.2 WeightedGraph.java, testing whether a vertex `u` is in `T` by invoking `T.contains(u)` takes `O(n)` time. Modify these two methods by introducing an array named `isInT`. Set `isInT[u]` to `true` when a vertex `u` is added to `T`. Testing whether a vertex `u` is in `T` can now be done in `O(1)` time. Write a test program using the following code, where `graph1` is created from Figure 29.1:

```
WeightedGraph<String> graph1 = new WeightedGraph<>(edges, vertices);

WeightedGraph<String>.MST tree1 = graph1.getMinimumSpanningTree();

System.out.println("Total weight is " + tree1.getTotalWeight());

tree1.printTree();

WeightedGraph<String>.ShortestPathTree tree2 =
  graph1.getShortestPath(graph1.getIndex("Chicago"));

tree2.printAllPaths();
```

CHAPTER 30

AGGREGATE OPERATIONS FOR COLLECTION STREAMS

Objectives

- To use aggregate operations on collection streams to simplify coding and improve performance (§30.1).

- To create a stream pipeline, apply lazy intermediate methods (`skip`, `limit`, `filter`, `distinct`, `sorted`, `map`, and `mapToInt`), and terminal methods (`count`, `sum`, `average`, `max`, `min`, `forEach`, `findFirst`, `firstAny`, `anyMatch`, `allMatch`, `noneMatch`, and `toArray`) on a stream (§30.2).

- To process primitive data values using the `IntStream`, `LongStream`, and `DoubleStream` (§30.3).

- To create parallel streams for fast execution (§30.4).

- To reduce the elements in a stream into a single result using the `reduce` method (§30.5).

- To place the elements in a stream into a mutable collection using the `collect` method (§30.6).

- To group the elements in a stream and apply aggregate methods for the elements in the groups (§30.7).

- To use a variety of examples to demonstrate how to simplify coding using streams (§30.8).

30.1 Introduction

Using aggregate operations on collection streams can greatly simplify coding and improve performance.

Often, you need to process data in an array or a collection. Suppose, for instance, that you need to count the number of elements in a set that is greater than 60. You may write the code using a foreach loop as follows:

```
Double[] numbers = {2.4, 55.6, 90.12, 26.6};
Set<Double> set = new HashSet<>(Arrays.asList(numbers));
int count = 0;
for (double e: set)
  if (e > 60)
    count++;
System.out.println("Count is " + count);
```

The code is fine. However, Java provides a better and simpler way for accomplishing the task. Using the aggregate operations, you can rewrite the code as follows:

```
System.out.println("Count is "
  + set.stream().filter(e -> e > 60).count());
```

Invoking the `stream()` method on a set returns a `Stream` for the elements from a set. The `filter` method specifies a condition for selecting the elements whose value is greater than 60. The `count()` method returns the number of elements in the stream that satisfy the condition.

stream

aggregate operations

A *collection stream* or simply *stream* is a sequence of elements. The operations on a stream is called *aggregate operations* (also known as *stream operations*) because they apply to all the data in the stream. The `filter` and `count` are the examples of aggregate operations. The code written using a foreach loop describes the process how to obtain the count, i.e., for each element, if it is greater than 60, increase the count. The code written using the aggregate operations tells the program to return the count for the elements greater than 60, but it does not specify how the count is obtained. Clearly, using the aggregate operations leaves the detailed implementation to the computer, therefore, makes the code concise and simpler. Moreover, the aggregate operations on a stream can be executed in parallel to take advantage of multiple processors. So, the code written using aggregate operations usually run faster than the ones using a foreach loop.

why using aggregate operations?

Java provides many aggregate operations and many different ways of using aggregate operations. This chapter gives a comprehensive coverage on aggregate operations and streams.

Check Point

30.1.1 What are the benefits of using aggregate operations on collection streams for processing data?

30.2 Stream Pipelines

A stream pipeline consists of a stream created from a data source, zero or more intermediate methods, and a final terminal method.

An array or a collection is an object for storing data. A stream is a transient object for processing data. After data is processed, the stream is destroyed. Java 8 introduced a new default `stream()` method in the `Collection` interface to return a `Stream` object. The `Stream` interface extends the `BaseStream` interface and contains the aggregate methods and the utility methods as shown in Figure 30.1.

intermediate method

terminal method

static method

The methods in the `Stream` interface are divided into three groups: intermediate methods, terminal methods, and static methods. An *intermediate method* transforms the stream into another stream. A *terminal method* returns a result or performs actions. After a terminal method is executed, the stream is closed automatically. A *static method* creates a stream.

«interface» java.util.stream.BaseStream<T, S extendsBaseStream<T, S>>	
+close(): S	Closes this stream.
+parallel(): S	Returns an equivalent stream that is executed in parallel.
+sequential(): S	Returns an equivalent stream that is executed in sequential.
+isParallel(): boolean	Returns true if this stream is parallel.

△

«interface»
java.util.stream.Stream<T>

Intermediate operations

+distinct(): Stream<T>	Returns a stream consisting of distinct elements from this stream.
+filter(p: Predicate<? super T): Stream<T>	Returns a stream consisting of the elements matching the predicate.
+limit(n: long): Stream<T>	Returns a stream consisting of the first n elements from this stream.
+skip(n: long): Stream<T>	Returns a stream consisting of the remaining elements in this stream after discarding the first n elements.
+sorted(): Stream<T>	Returns a stream consisting of the elements of this stream sorted in a natural order.
+sorted(comparator: Comparator<? super T>): Stream<T>	Returns a stream consisting of the elements of this stream sorted using the comparator.
+map(mapper: Function<? super T, ? extends R>: Stream<R>	Returns a stream consisting of the results of applying the function to the elements of this stream.
+mapToInt(mapper: ToIntFunction<? super T>): IntStream	Returns an IntStream consisting of the results of applying the function to the elements of this stream.
+mapToLong(mapper: ToLongFunction<? super T>): LongStream	Returns a LongStream consisting of the results of applying the function to the elements of this stream.
+mapToDouble(mapper: ToDoubleFunction<? super T>): DoubleStream	Returns a DoubleStream consisting of the results of applying the function to the elements of this stream.

Terminal operations

+count(): long	Returns the number of elements in this stream.
+max(c: Comparator<? super T>): Optional<T>	Returns the maximum element in this stream based on the comparator.
+min(c: Comparator<? super T>): Optional<T>	Returns the minimum element in this stream based on the comparator.
+findFirst(): Optional<T>	Returns the first element from this stream.
+findAny(): Optional<T>	Returns any element from this stream.
+allMatch(p: Predicate<? super T>): boolean	Returns true if all the elements in this stream match the predicate.
+anyMatch(p: Predicate<? super T>): boolean	Returns true if one element in this stream matches the predicate.
+noneMatch(p: Predicate<? super T>): boolean	Returns true if no element in this stream matches the predicate.
+forEach(action: Consumer<? super T>): void	Performs an action for each element of this stream.
+reduce(accumulator: BinaryOperator<T>): Optional<T>	Reduces the elements in the stream to a value using the identity and an associative accumulation function. Return an Optional describing the reduced value.
+reduce(identity: T, accumulator: BinaryOperator<T>): T	Reduces the elements in the stream to a value using the identity and an associative accumulation function. Return the reduced value.
+collect(collector: <? super <T, A, R>>): R	Performs a mutable reduction operation on the elements of this stream using a Collector.
+toArray(): Object[]	Returns an array consisting of the elements in this stream.

Static methods

+empty(): Stream<T>	Returns an empty sequential stream. (static method)
+of(values: T...): Stream<T>	Returns a stream consisting of the specified values. (static method)
+of(values: T): Stream<T>	Returns a stream consisting of a single value. (static method)
+concat(a1: Stream<? extends T>, a2: Stream<? extends T>): Stream<T>	Returns a lazily concatenated stream consisting of the elements in a1 followed by the elements in a2. (static method)

FIGURE 30.1 The Stream class defines the aggregate operations for the elements in a stream.

The methods are invoked using a stream pipeline. A *stream pipeline* consists of a source (e.g., a list, a set, or an array), a method that creates a stream, zero or more intermediate methods, and a final terminal method. The following is a stream pipeline example:

stream pipeline

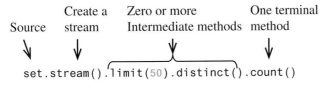

```
Source    Create a   Zero or more           One terminal
          stream     Intermediate methods   method

set.stream().limit(50).distinct().count()
```

Here, `set` is the source of the data, invoking `stream()` creates a stream for the data from the source, invoking `limit(50)` returns the first `50` elements from the stream, invoking `distinct()` obtains a stream of distinct elements from the stream of the `50` elements, and invoking `count()` returns the number of elements in the final stream.

lazy evaluation

Streams are lazy, which means that the computation is performed only when the terminal operation is initiated. This allows the JVM to optimize computation.

Most of the arguments for stream methods are instances of functional interfaces. So the arguments can be created using lambda expressions or method references. Listing 30.1 gives an example that demonstrates creating a stream and applying methods on the streams.

LISTING 30.1 StreamDemo.java

```java
 1  import java.util.stream.Stream;
 2
 3  public class StreamDemo {
 4    public static void main(String[] args) {
 5      String[] names = {"John", "Peter", "Susan", "Kim", "Jen",
 6        "George", "Alan", "Stacy", "Michelle", "john"};
 7
 8      // Display the first four names sorted
 9      Stream.of(names).limit(4).sorted()
10        .forEach(e -> System.out.print(e + " "));
11
12      // Skip four names and dispaly the rest sorted ignore case
13      System.out.println();
14      Stream.of(names).skip(4)
15        .sorted((e1, e2) -> e1.compareToIgnoreCase(e2))
16        .forEach(e -> System.out.print(e + " "));
17
18      System.out.println();
19      Stream.of(names).skip(4)
20        .sorted(String::compareToIgnoreCase)
21        .forEach(e -> System.out.print(e + " "));
22
23      System.out.println("\nLargest string with length > 4: "
24        + Stream.of(names)
25          .filter(e -> e.length() > 4)
26          .max(String::compareTo).get());
27
28      System.out.println("Smallest string alphabetically: "
29        + Stream.of(names).min(String::compareTo).get());
30
31      System.out.println("Stacy is in names? "
32        + Stream.of(names).anyMatch(e -> e.equals("Stacy")));
33
34      System.out.println("All names start with a capital letter? "
35        + Stream.of(names)
36          .allMatch(e -> Character.isUpperCase(e.charAt(0))));
37
38      System.out.println("No name begins with Ko? "
39        + Stream.of(names).noneMatch(e -> e.startsWith("Ko")));
40
41      System.out.println("Number of distinct case-insensitive strings: "
42        + Stream.of(names).map(e -> e.toUpperCase())
43          .distinct().count());
44
45      System.out.println("First element in this stream in lowercase: "
46        + Stream.of(names).map(String::toLowerCase).findFirst().get());
47
```

create an array

Stream.of
forEach

skip
sorted

method reference

filter
method reference

min

anyMatch

allMatch

distinct

findFirst

```
48        System.out.println("Skip 4 and get any element in this stream:"
49          + Stream.of(names).skip(4).sorted().findAny().get());
50
51        Object[] namesInLowerCase =
52          Stream.of(names).map(String::toLowerCase).toArray();
53        System.out.println(java.util.Arrays.toString(namesInLowerCase));
54      }
55   }
```

findAny

toArray
display array

```
John Kim Peter Susan
Alan George Jen john Michelle Stacy
Alan George Jen john Michelle Stacy
Largest string with length > 4: Susan
Smallest string alphabetically: Alan
Stacy is in names? true
All names start with a capital letter? false
No name begins with Ko? true
Number of distinct case-insensitive strings: 9
First element in this stream in lowercase: john
Skip 4 and get any element in this stream: Alan
[john, peter, susan, kim, jen, george, alan, stacy, michelle, john]
```

We now introduce the stream methods through this example.

30.2.1 The `Stream.of`, `limit`, and `forEach` Methods

The program creates an array of strings (lines 5–6). In lines 9–10, invoking the static `Stream.of(names)` returns a `Stream` consisting of strings from the `names` array, invoking `limit(4)` returns a new `Stream` consisting the first four elements in the stream, invoking `sorted()` sorts the stream, and invoking the `forEach` method displays each element in the stream. The argument passed to the `forEach` method is a lambda expression. As introduced in Section 15.6, a lambda expression is a concise syntax to replace an anonymous inner class that implements a functional interface. The argument passed to the `forEach` method is an instance of the functional interface `Consumer<? super T>` with an abstract function `accept(T t)`. The statement in line 10 using a lambda expression in (a) is equivalent to using an anonymous inner class in (b) as shown below. The lambda expression not only simplifies the code, but also the concept of the method. You can now simply say that for each element in the stream, perform the action as specified in the expression.

forEach method

lambda expression

```
forEach(e -> System.out.print(e + " "))
```

```
forEach(
  new java.util.function.Consumer<String>() {
    public void accept(String e) {
      System.out.print(e + " ");
    }
  }
)
```

(a) Using a lambda expression   (b) Using an anonymous inner class

30.2.2 The sorted Method

The `sorted` method in line 15 sorts the strings in the stream using a `Comparator`. The `Comparator` is a functional interface. A lambda expression is used to implement the interface and specifies that two strings are compared ignoring cases. This lambda expression in (a) is

method reference

equivalent to the code using an anonymous inner class in (b). The lambda expression simply invokes a method in this case. So, it can be further simplified using a method reference in line 20 (also see in (c)). The method reference was introduced in Section 20.6.

```
sorted((e1, e2) ->
  e1.compareToIgnoreCase(e2))
```

(a) Using a lambda expression

```
sorted(
  new java.util.Comparator<String>() {
    public int compare(String e1, String e2) {
      return e1.compareToIgnoreCase(e2);
    }
  }
)
```

(b) Using an anonymous inner class

```
sorted(String::compareToIgnoreCase)
```

(c) Using a method reference

30.2.3 The `filter` Method

The `filter` method takes an argument of the `Predicate<? super T>` type, which is a functional interface with an abstract method `test(T t)` that returns a Boolean value. The method selects the elements from the stream that satisfies the predicate. Line 25 uses a lambda expression to implement the `Predicate` interface as shown in (a), which is equivalent to the code using an anonymous inner class as shown in (b).

```
filter(e -> e.length() > 4)
```

(a) Using a lambda expression

```
filter(
  new java.util.function.Predicate<String>() {
    public boolean test(String e) {
      return e.length() > 4;
    }
  }
)
```

(b) Using an anonymous inner class

30.2.4 The `max` and `min` Methods

The `max` and `min` methods take an argument of the `Comparator<? Super T>` type. This argument specifies how the elements are compared in order to obtain the maximum and minimum elements. The program uses the method reference `String::compareTo` to simplify the code for creating a `Comparator` (lines 26 and 29). The `max` and `min` methods return an `Optional<T>` that describes the element. You need to invoke the `get()` method from the `Optional` class to return the element.

Optional <T>
get method

30.2.5 The `anyMatch`, `allMatch`, and `noneMatch` Methods

The `anyMatch`, `allMatch`, and `noneMatch` methods take an argument of the `Predicate<? super T>` type to test if the stream contains an element, all elements, or no element that satisfies the predicate. The program tests whether the name `Stacy` is in the stream (line 32), whether all the names in the stream start with a capital letter (line 36), and whether any names starts with string `Ko` (line 39).

30.2.6 The `map`, `distinct`, and `count` Methods

The `map` method returns a new stream by mapping each element in the stream into a new element. So, the `map` method in line 42 returns a new stream with all uppercase strings. The `distinct()` method obtains a new stream with all distinct elements. The `count()` method counts the number of the elements in the stream. So, the stream pipeline in line 43 counts the number of distinct strings in the array `names`.

The `map` method takes an argument of the `Function<? super T, ? super R>` type to return an instance of the `Stream<R>`. The `Function` is a functional interface with an abstract method `apply(T t)` that maps `t` into a value of the type `R`. Line 42 uses a lambda expression to implement the `Function` interface as shown in (a), which is equivalent to the code using an anonymous inner class as shown in (b). You can further simplify it using a method reference as shown in (c).

```
map(e -> e.toUpperCase())
```

(a) Using a lambda expression

```
map(
  new java.util.function.Function<String, String>() {
    public String apply(String e) {
      return e.toUpperCase();
    }
  }
)
```

(b) Using an anonymous inner class

```
map(String::toUpperCase)
```

(c) Using a method reference

30.2.7 The `findFirst`, `findAny`, and `toArray` Methods

The `findFirst()` method (line 46) returns the first element in the stream wrapped in an instance of `Optional<T>`. The actual element value is then returned by invoking the `get()` method in the `Optional<T>` class. The `findAny()` method (line 49) returns any element in the stream. Which element is selected depends on the internal state of the stream. The `findAny()` method is more efficient than the `findFirst()` method.

The `toArray()` method (line 52) returns an array of objects from the stream.

 Note
The `BaseStream` interface defines the `close()` method, which can be invoked to close a stream. You don't need to use it because the stream is automatically closed after the terminal method is executed.

`close` method

30.2.1 Show the output of the following code:

```
Character[] chars = {'D', 'B', 'A', 'C'};
System.out.println(Stream.of(chars).sorted().findFirst().get());
System.out.println(Stream.of(chars).sorted(
  java.util.Comparator.reverseOrder()).findFirst().get());
System.out.println(Stream.of(chars)
  .limit(2).sorted().findFirst().get());
System.out.println(Stream.of(chars).distinct()
  .skip(2).filter(e -> e > 'A').findFirst().get());
System.out.println(Stream.of(chars)
  .max(Character::compareTo).get());
System.out.println(Stream.of(chars)
  .max(java.util.Comparator.reverseOrder()).get());
System.out.println(Stream.of(chars)
  .filter(e -> e > 'A').findFirst().get());
System.out.println(Stream.of(chars)
  .allMatch(e -> e >= 'A'));
System.out.println(Stream.of(chars)
  .anyMatch(e -> e > 'F'));
System.out.println(Stream.of(chars)
  .noneMatch(e -> e > 'F'));
Stream.of(chars).map(e -> e + "").map(e -> e.toLowerCase())
  .forEach(System.out::println);
```

```
Object[] temp = Stream.of(chars).map(e -> e + "Y")
  .map(e -> e.toLowerCase()).sorted().toArray();
System.out.println(java.util.Arrays.toString(temp));
```

30.2.2 What is wrong in the following code?

```
Character[] chars = {'D', 'B', 'A', 'C'};
Stream<Character> stream = Stream.of(chars).sorted();
System.out.println(stream.findFirst());
System.out.println(stream.skip(2).findFirst());
```

30.2.3 Rewrite (a) using a method reference and an anonymous inner class and (b) using lambda expression and an anonymous inner class:

```
(a) sorted((s1, s2) -> s1.compareToIgnoreCase(s2))
(b) forEach(System.out::println)
```

30.2.4 Given a `map` of the type `Map<String, Double>`, write an expression that returns the sum of all the values in `map`. For example, if the `map` contains `{"john", 1.5}` and `{"Peter", 1.1}`, the sum is `2.6`.

30.3 IntStream, LongStream, and DoubleStream

IntStream, LongStream, and DoubleStream are special type of streams for processing a sequence of primitive int, long, and double values.

IntStream
LongStream
DoubleStream

`Stream` represents a sequence of objects. In addition to `Stream`, Java provides `IntStream`, `LongStream`, and `DoubleStream` for representing a sequence of `int`, `long`, and `double` values. These streams are also subinterfaces of `BaseStream`. You can use these streams in the same way like a `Stream`. Additionally, you can use the `sum()`, `average()`, and `summaryStatistics()` methods for returning the sum, average, various statistics of the elements in the stream. You can use the `mapToInt` method to convert a `Stream` to an `IntStream` and use the `map` method to convert any stream including an `IntStream` to a `Stream`.

Listing 30.2 gives an example of using the `IntStream`.

LISTING 30.2 IntStreamDemo.java

```
 1  import java.util.IntSummaryStatistics;
 2  import java.util.stream.IntStream;
 3  import java.util.stream.Stream;
 4
 5  public class IntStreamDemo {
 6    public static void main(String[] args) {
 7      int[] values = {3, 4, 1, 5, 20, 1, 3, 3, 4, 6};
 8
 9      System.out.println("The average of distinct even numbers > 3: " +
10        IntStream.of(values).distinct()
11          .filter(e -> e > 3 && e % 2 == 0).average().getAsDouble());
12
13      System.out.println("The sum of the first 4 numbers is " +
14        IntStream.of(values).limit(4).sum());
15
16      IntSummaryStatistics stats =
17      IntStream.of(values).summaryStatistics();
18
19      System.out.printf("The summary of the stream is\n%-10s%10d\n" +
20        "%-10s%10d\n%-10s%10d\n%-10s%10d\n%-10s%10.2f\n",
```

create an int array

IntStream.of
average

sum

summaryStatistics

```
21          " Count:", stats.getCount(), " Max:", stats.getMax(),
22          " Min:", stats.getMin(), " Sum:", stats.getSum(),
23          " Average:", stats.getAverage());
24
25      String[] names = {"John", "Peter", "Susan", "Kim", "Jen",
26          "George", "Alan", "Stacy", "Michelle", "john"};
27
28      System.out.println("Total character count for all names is "
29          + Stream.of(names).mapToInt(e -> e.length()).sum());    mapToInt
30
31      System.out.println("The number of digits in array values is " +
32          Stream.of(values).map(e -> e + "")                       map
33              .mapToInt(e -> e.length()).sum());                   mapToInt
34      }
35  }
```

```
The average of distinct even numbers > 3: 10.0
The sum of the first 4 numbers is 13
The summary of the stream is

  Count:        10
  Max:          20
  Min:           1
  Sum:          50
  Average:    5.00

Total character count for all names is 47
The number of digits in array values is 11
```

The program creates an array of `int` values (line 7). The stream pipeline in line 10 applies the intermediate methods `distinct` and `filter` with a terminal method `average`. The `average()` method returns the average value in the stream as an `OptionalDouble` object (line 11). The actual average value is obtained by invoking the `getAsDouble()` method.

`OptionalDouble` class
average method

The stream pipeline in line 14 applies the intermediate method `limit` with a terminal method `sum`. The `sum()` method returns the sum of all values in the stream.

sum method

If you need to obtain multiple summary values from the stream, using the `summaryStatistics()` method is more efficient. This method (line 17) returns an instance of `IntSummaryStatistics` that contains summary values for count, min, max, sum, and average (lines 19–23). Note `sum()`, `average()`, and `summaryStatistics()` methods are only applicable to the `IntStream`, `LongStream`, and `DoubleStream`.

summaryStatistics method

The `mapToInt` method returns an `IntStream` by mapping each element in the stream into an `int` value. The `mapToInt` method in the stream pipeline in line 29 maps each string into an `int` value that is the length of a string, and the `sum` method obtains the sum of all the `int` values in the `IntStream`. The stream pipeline in line 29 obtains the total count for all characters in the stream.

The `mapToInt` method takes an argument of the `ToIntFunction<? super T>` type to return an instance of the `IntStream`. The `ToIntFunction` is a functional interface with an abstract method `applyAsInt(T t)` that maps `t` into a value of the type `int`. Line 33 uses a lambda expression to implement the `ToIntFunction` interface as shown in (a), which is equivalent to the code using an anonymous inner class as shown in (b). You can also further simplify it using a method reference as shown in (c).

mapToInt method

```
mapToInt(e -> e.length())
```

(a) Using a lambda expression

```
mapToInt(String::length)
```

(c) Using a method reference

```
mapToInt(
  new java.util.function.ToIntFunction<String>() {
    public int applyAsInt(String e) {
      return e.length();
    }
  }
)
```

(b) Using an anonymous inner class

The `map` method in line 32 returns a new stream of strings. Each string is converted from an integer in array `values`. The `mapToInt` method in line 33 returns a new stream of integers. Each integer represents the length of a string. The `sum()` method returns the sum of all `int` values in the final stream. So the stream pipeline in lines 32–33 obtains the total number of digits in the array `values`.

Check Point

30.3.1 Show the output of the following code:

```
int[] numbers = {1, 4, 2, 3, 1};
System.out.println(IntStream.of(numbers)
  .sorted().findFirst().getAsInt());
System.out.println(IntStream.of(numbers)
  .limit(2).sorted().findFirst().getAsInt());
System.out.println(IntStream.of(numbers).distinct()
  .skip(1).filter(e -> e > 2).sum());
System.out.println(IntStream.of(numbers).distinct()
  .skip(1).filter(e -> e > 2).average().getAsDouble());
System.out.println(IntStream.of(numbers).max().getAsInt());
System.out.println(IntStream.of(numbers).max().getAsInt());
System.out.println(IntStream.of(numbers)
  .filter(e -> e > 1).findFirst().getAsInt());
System.out.println(IntStream.of(numbers)
  .allMatch(e -> e >= 1));
System.out.println(IntStream.of(numbers)
  .anyMatch(e -> e > 4));
System.out.println(IntStream.of(numbers).noneMatch(e -> e > 4));
IntStream.of(numbers).mapToObj(e -> (char)(e + 50))
  .forEach(System.out::println);

Object[] temp = IntStream.of(numbers)
  .mapToObj(e -> (char)(e + 'A')).toArray();
System.out.println(java.util.Arrays.toString(temp));
```

30.3.2 What is wrong in the following code?

```
int[] numbers = {1, 4, 2, 3, 1};
DoubleSummaryStatistics stats =
  DoubleStream.of(numbers).summaryStatistics();
System.out.printf("The summary of the stream is\n%-10s%10d\n" +
  "%-10s%10.2f\n%-10s%10.2f\n%-10s%10.2f\n%-10s%10.2f\n",
  " Count:", stats.getCount(), " Max:", stats.getMax(),
  " Min:", stats.getMin(), " Sum:", stats.getSum(),
  " Average:", stats.getAverage());
```

30.3.3 Rewrite the following code that maps an `int` to a `Character` using an anonymous inner class:

```
mapToObj(e -> (char)(e + 50))
```

30.3.4 Show the output of the following code:

```
int[][] m = {{1, 2}, {3, 4}, {5, 6}};
System.out.println(Stream.of(m)
  .mapToInt(e -> IntStream.of(e).sum()).sum());
```

30.3.5 Given an array `names` in Listing 30.1, write the code to display the total number of characters in `names`.

30.4 Parallel Streams

Streams can be executed in parallel mode to improve performance.

The widespread use of multicore systems has created a revolution in software. In order to benefit from multiple processors, software needs to run in parallel. All stream operations can execute in parallel to utilize the multicore processors. The `stream()` method in the `Collection` interface returns a sequential stream. To execute operations in parallel, use the `parallelStream()` method in the `Collection` interface to obtain a parallel stream. Any stream can be turned to into a parallel stream by invoking the `parallel()` method defined in tbe `BaseStream` interface. Likewise, you can turn a parallel stream into a sequential stream by invoking the `sequential()` method.

Intermediate methods can be further divided into *stateless* and *stateful* methods. A stateless method such as `filter` and `map` can be executed independently from other elements in the stream. A stateful method such as `distinct` and `sorted` must be executed to take the entire stream into consideration. For example, to produce a result, the `distinct` method must consider all elements in the stream. Stateless methods are inherently parallelizable and can be executed in one pass in parallel. Stateful methods have to be executed in multiple passes in parallel.

stateless methods
stateful methods

Listing 30.3 gives an example to demonstrate the benefits of using parallel streams.

LISTING 30.3 `ParallelStreamDemo.java`

```
1  import java.util.Arrays;
2  import java.util.Random;
3  import java.util.stream.IntStream;
4
5  public class ParallelStreamDemo {
6    public static void main(String[] args) {
7      Random random = new Random();
8      int[] list = random.ints(200_000_000).toArray();
9
10     System.out.println("Number of processors: " +
11       Runtime.getRuntime().availableProcessors());
12
13     long startTime = System.currentTimeMillis();
14     int[] list1 = IntStream.of(list).filter(e -> e > 0).sorted()
15       .limit(5).toArray();
16     System.out.println(Arrays.toString(list1));
17     long endTime = System.currentTimeMillis();
18     System.out.println("Sequential execution time is " +
19       (endTime - startTime) + " milliseconds");
20
21     startTime = System.currentTimeMillis();
22     int[] list2 = IntStream.of(list).parallel().filter(e -> e > 0)
23       .sorted().limit(5).toArray();
24     System.out.println(Arrays.toString(list2));
25     endTime = System.currentTimeMillis();
```

create an array

available processors

sequential stream

parallel stream

```
26        System.out.println("Parallel execution time is " +
27          (endTime - startTime) + " milliseconds");
28      }
29  }
```

```
Number of processors: 8
[4, 9, 38, 42, 52]
Sequential execution time is 12362 milliseconds
[4, 9, 38, 42, 52]
Parallel execution time is 3448 milliseconds
```

The Random class introduced in Section 9.6.2 can be used to generate random numbers. You can use its ints(n) method to generate an IntStream consisting of n number of random int values (line 8). You can also use ints(n, r1, r2) to generate an IntStream with n element in the range from r1 (inclusive) to r2 (exclusive), use doubles(n) and doubles(n, r1, r2) to generate a DoubleStream of random floating-point numbers. Invoking the toArray() method on an IntStream (line 8) returns an array of int values from the stream. Recall that you can use underscores in an integer 200_000_000 to improve readability (see Section 2.10.1).

Invoking Runtime.getRuntim() returns a Runtime object (line 11). Invoking Runtime object's availableProcessors() returns the number of available processors for the JVM. In this case, the system has 8 processors.

An IntStream is created using IntStream.of(list) (line 14). The intermediate filter(e -> e > 0) method selects positive integers from the stream. The intermediate sorted() method sorts the filtered stream. The intermediate limit(5) method selects the first five integers in the sorted stream (line 15). Finally, the terminal method toArray() returns an array from the 5 integers in the stream. This is a sequential stream. To turn it into a parallel stream, simply invoke the parallel() method (line 22), which sets the stream for parallel execution. As you see from the sample run, the parallel execution is much faster than the sequential execution.

Several interesting questions arise.

lazy intermediate methods

1. The intermediate methods are lazy and are executed when the terminal method is initiated. This can be confirmed in the following code:

```
1   long startTime = System.currentTimeMillis();
2   IntStream stream = IntStream.of(list).filter(e -> e > 0).sorted()
3     .limit(5);
4   System.out.println("The time for the preceding method is " +
5     (System.currentTimeMillis() - startTime) + " milliseconds");
6   int[] list1 = stream.toArray();
7   System.out.println("The execution time is " +
8     (System.currentTimeMillis() - startTime) + " milliseconds");
```

When you run the code, you will see that almost no time is spent on lines 2–3 because the intermediate methods are not executed yet. When the terminal method toArray() is invoked, all the methods for the stream pipeline are executed. So, the actual execution time for the stream pipeline is in line 6.

order of methods

2. Does the order of the intermediate methods in a stream pipeline matter? Yes, it matters. For example, if the methods limit(5) and sorted() are swapped, the result will be different. It also matters to the performance even though the result is the same. For example, if the sorted() method is placed before filter(e -> e > 0), the result will be the same, but it would take more time to execute the stream because sorting a

large number of elements takes more time to complete. Applying `filter` before `sorted` would eliminate roughly half of the elements for sorting.

3. Is a parallel stream always faster? Not necessarily. Parallel execution requires synchronization, which carries some overhead. If you replace `IntStream.of(list)` in lines 14 and 22 by `random.ints(200_000_000)`, the parallel stream in lines 22–23 will takes longer time to execute than the sequential stream in lines 14–15. The reason is that the algorithm for generating a sequence of pseudo-random numbers is highly sequential. The overhead of a parallel stream is far greater than the time saving on parallel processing. So, you should test both sequential and parallel streams before choosing parallel streams for deployment.

parallel vs. sequential streams

4. When executing a stream method in parallel, the elements in the stream may be processed in any order. So, the following code may display the numbers in the stream in a random order:

order of parallel execution

```
IntStream.of(1, 2, 3, 4, 5).parallel()
   .forEach(e -> System.out.print(e + " "));
```

However, if it is executed sequentially, the numbers will be displayed as 1 2 3 4 5.

30.4.1 What is a stateless method? What is a stateful method?

30.4.2 How do you create a parallel stream?

30.4.3 Suppose `names` is a set of strings, which of the following two streams is better?

```
Object[] s = set.parallelStream().filter(e -> e.length() > 3)
   .sorted().toArray();

Object[] s = set.parallelStream().sorted()
   .filter(e -> e.length() > 3).toArray();
```

30.4.4 What will be the output of the following code?

```
int[] values = {3, 4, 1, 5, 20, 1, 3, 3, 4, 6};
System.out.print("The values are ");
  IntStream.of(values)
     .forEach(e -> System.out.print(e + " "));
```

30.4.5 What will be the output of the following code?

```
int[] values = {3, 4, 1, 5, 20, 1, 3, 3, 4, 6};
System.out.print("The values are ");
  IntStream.of(values).parallel()
     .forEach(e -> System.out.print(e + " "));
```

30.4.6 Write a statement to obtain an array of `1000` random double values between `0.0` and `1.0`, excluding `1.0`.

Check Point

30.5 Stream Reduction Using the **reduce** Method

You can use the `reduce` *method to reduce the elements in a stream into a single value.*

Key Point

Often you need to process all the elements in a collection to produce a summary value such as the sum, the maximum, or the minimum. For example, the following code obtains the sum of all elements in set `s`:

```
int total = 0;
for (int e: s) {
  total += e;
}
```

reduction

This is a simple code, but it specifies the exact steps on how to obtain the sum and it is highly sequential. The `reduce` method on a stream can be used to write the code in a high level for parallel execution.

A *reduction* takes the elements from a stream to produce a single value by repeated application of a binary operation such as addition, multiplication, or finding the maximum between two elements. Using reduction, you can write the code for finding the sum of all elements in a set as follows:

```
int sum = s.parallelStream().reduce(0, (e1, e2) -> e1 + e2);
```

Here, the `reduce` method takes two arguments. The first is an identity, i.e., the starting value. The second argument is an object of the functional interface `IntBinaryOperator`. This interface contains the abstract method `applyAsInt(int e1, int e2)` that returns an `int` value from applying a binary operation. The preceding lambda expression in (a) is equivalent to the code using an anonymous inner class in (b).

```
reduce(0, e -> (e1, e2) -> e1 + e2)
```

(a) Using a lambda expression

```
reduce(0,
  new java.util.function.IntBinaryOperator() {
    public int applyAsInt(int e1, int e2) {
      return e1 + e2;
    }
  }
)
```

(b) Using an anonymous inner class

The preceding `reduce` method is semantically equivalent to an imperative code as follows:

```
int total = identity (i.e., 0, in this case);
for (int e: s) {
  total = applyAsInt(total, e);
}
```

The `reduce` method makes the code concise. Moreover, the code can be parallelizable, because multiple processors can simultaneously invoke the `applyAsInt` method on two integers repeatedly.

Using the `reduce` method, you can write the following code to return the maximum element in the set:

```
int result = s.parallelStream()
    .reduce(Integer.MIN_VALUE, (e1, e2) -> Math.max(e1, e2));
```

In fact, the `sum`, `max`, and `min` methods are implemented using the `reduce` method.

Listing 30.4 gives an example of using the `reduce` method.

LISTING 30.4 StreamReductionDemo.java

```
 1  import java.util.stream.IntStream;
 2  import java.util.stream.Stream;
 3
 4  public class StreamReductionDemo {
 5    public static void main(String[] args) {
 6      int[] values = {3, 4, 1, 5, 20, 1, 3, 3, 4, 6};
 7
 8      System.out.print("The values are ");
 9      IntStream.of(values).forEach(e -> System.out.print(e + " "));
10
```

create an array

forEach

```
11       System.out.println("\nThe result of multiplying all values is " +
12         IntStream.of(values).parallel().reduce(1, (e1, e2) -> e1 * e2));      reduce
13
14       System.out.print("The values are " +
15         IntStream.of(values).mapToObj(e -> e + "")                             mapToObj
16           .reduce((e1, e2) -> e1 + ", " + e2).get());                         reduce
17
18       String[] names = {"John", "Peter", "Susan", "Kim", "Jen",
19         "George", "Alan", "Stacy", "Michelle", "john"};
20       System.out.print("\nThe names are: ");
21       System.out.println(Stream.of(names)
22         .reduce((x, y) -> x + ", " + y).get());                               reduce
23
24       System.out.print("Concat names: ");
25       System.out.println(Stream.of(names)
26         .reduce((x, y) -> x + y).get());
27
28       System.out.print("Total number of characters: ");
29       System.out.println(Stream.of(names)
30         .reduce((x, y) -> x + y).get().length());
31     }
32   }
```

```
The values are 3, 4, 1, 5, 20, 1, 3, 3, 4, 6
The result of multiplying all values is 259200
The values are 3, 4, 1, 5, 20, 1, 3, 3, 4, 6
The names are John, Peter, Susan, Kim, Jen, George, Alan, Stacy,
  Michelle, john
Concat names: JohnPeterSusanKimJenGeorgeAlanStacyMichellejohn
Total number of characters: 47
```

The program creates an array of `int` values (line 6). The stream pipeline creates an `IntStream` from the `int` array and invokes the `forEach` method to display each integer in the stream (line 9).

The program creates a parallel stream pipeline for the `int` array and applies the `reduce` method to obtain the product of `int` values in the stream (line 12).

The `mapToObj` method returns a stream of string objects from the `IntStream` (line 15). The `reduce` method can be called without an identity. In this case, it returns an object of `Optional<T>`. The `reduce` method in line 16 reduces the strings in the stream into one composite string that consists of all strings in the stream separated by commas.

The `reduce` method in line 26 combines all strings in the stream together into one long string. `Stream.of(names).reduce((x, y) -> x + y).get()` returns a string that concatenates all strings in the stream into one string, and invoking the `length()` method on the string returns the number of characters in the string (line 30).

Note `reduce((x, y) -> x + y)` in line 30 can be simplified using a method reference as `reduce(String::concat)`.

30.5.1 Show the output of the following code:

Check Point

```
int[] values = {1, 2, 3, 4};
System.out.println(IntStream.of(values)
  .reduce(0, (e1, e2) -> e1 + e2));
System.out.println(IntStream.of(values)
  .reduce(1, (e1, e2) -> e1 * e2));
System.out.println(IntStream.of(values).map(e -> e * e)
  .reduce(0, (e1, e2) -> e1 + e2));
```

```
System.out.println(IntStream.of(values).mapToObj(e -> "" + e)
  .reduce((e1, e2) -> e1 + " " + e2).get());
System.out.println(IntStream.of(values).mapToObj(e -> "" + e)
  .reduce((e1, e2) -> e1 + ", " + e2).get());
```

30.5.2 Show the output of the following code:

```
int[][] m = {{1, 2}, {3, 4}, {5, 6}};
System.out.println(Stream.of(m)
  .map(e -> IntStream.of(e).reduce(1, (e1, e2) -> e1 * e2))
  .reduce(1, (e1, e2) -> e1 * e2));
```

30.5.3 Show the output of the following code:

```
int[][] m = {{1, 2}, {3, 4}, {5, 6}, {1, 3}};
Stream.of(m).map(e -> IntStream.of(e))
  .reduce((e1, e2) -> IntStream.concat(e1, e2))
  .get().distinct()
  .forEach(e -> System.out.print(e + " "));
```

30.5.4 Show the output of the following code:

```
int[][] m = {{1, 2}, {3, 4}, {5, 6}, {1, 3}};
System.out.println(
  Stream.of(m).map(e -> IntStream.of(e))
    .reduce((e1, e2) -> IntStream.concat(e1, e2))
    .get().distinct().mapToObj(e -> e + "")
    .reduce((e1, e2) -> e1 + ", " + e2).get());
```

30.6 Stream Reduction Using the `collect` Method

Key Point

You can use the `collect` method to reduce the elements in a stream into a mutable container.

In the preceding example, the `String`'s `concat` method is used in the `reduce` method for `Stream.of(names).reduce((x, y) -> x + y)`. This operation causes a new string to be created when concatenating two strings, which is very inefficient. A better approach is to use a `StringBuilder` and accumulate the result into a `StringBuilder`. This can be accomplished using the `collect` method.

The `collect` method collects the elements in a stream into a mutable container such as a `Collection` object using the following syntax:

```
<R> R collect(Supplier<R> supplier,
              BiConsumer<R, ? super T> accumulator,
              BiConsumer<R, R> combiner)
```

The method takes three functional arguments: 1) a supplier function to construct a new instance of the result container, 2) an accumulator function to incorporate the elements from the stream to the result container, and 3) a combining function to merge the contents of one result container into another.

For example, to combine strings into a `StringBuilder`, you may write the following code using a `collect` method like this:

```
String[] names = {"John", "Peter", "Susan", "Kim", "Jen",
  "George", "Alan", "Stacy", "Michelle", "john"};
StringBuilder sb = Stream.of(names).collect(() -> new StringBuilder(),
  (c, e) -> c.append(e), (c1, c2) -> c1.append(c2));
```

The lambda expression `() -> new StringBuilder()` creates a `StringBuilder` object for storing the result, which can be simplified using the method reference `StringBuilder::new`. The lambda expression `(c, e) -> c.append(e)` adds a string `e` to a `StringBuilder` `c`, which can be simplified using a method reference `StringBuilder::append`. The lambda expression `(c1, c2) -> c1.append(c2)` merges the contents in `c2` into `c1`, which also can be simplified using a method reference `StringBuilder::append`. So, you can simplify the preceding statement as follows:

```
StringBuilder sb = Stream.of(names).collect(StringBuilder::new,
   StringBuilder::append, StringBuilder::append);
```

The sequential foreach loop implementation for this `collect` method might be as follows:

```
StringBuilder sb = new StringBuilder();
for (String s: Stream.of(names)) {
  sb.append(s);
}
```

Note that the combiner function `(c1, c2) -> c1.append(c2)` is not used in the sequential implementation. It is used when the stream pipeline is executed in parallel. When executing a `collect` method in parallel, multiple result `StringBuilder` are created and then merged using a combiner function. So, the purpose of the combiner function is for parallel processing.

Here is another example that creates an `ArrayList` from strings in the stream:

```
ArrayList<String> list = Stream.of(names).collect(ArrayList::new,
   ArrayList::add, ArrayList::addAll);
```

The supplier function is the `ArrayList` constructor. The accumulator is the `add` method that adds an element to the `ArrayList`. The combiner function merges an `ArrayList` into another `ArrayList`. The three arguments—supplier, accumulator, and combiner—are tightly coupled and are defined using standard methods. For simplicity, Java provides another `collect` method that takes an argument of the `Collector` type, called a *collector*. The `Collector` interface defines the methods for returning a supplier, an accumulator, and a combiner. You can use a static factory method `toList()` in the `Collectors` class to create an instance of the `Collector` interface. So, the preceding statement can be simplified using a standard collector as follows:

```
List<String> list = Stream.of(names).collect(Collectors.toList());
```

Listing 30.5 gives an example of using the `collect` methods and the `Collectors`' factory methods.

LISTING 30.5 CollectDemo.java

```
1  import java.util.ArrayList;
2  import java.util.List;
3  import java.util.Map;
4  import java.util.Set;
5  import java.util.stream.Collectors;
6  import java.util.stream.Stream;
7
8  public class CollectDemo {
9    public static void main(String[] args) {
10     String[] names = {"John", "Peter", "Susan", "Kim", "Jen",          create an array
11        "George", "Alan", "Stacy", "Michelle", "john"};
12     System.out.println("The number of characters for all names: " +
13       Stream.of(names).collect(StringBuilder::new,                      collect into StringBuilder
14         StringBuilder::append, StringBuilder::append).length());
```

```
15
16      List<String> list = Stream.of(names).collect(ArrayList::new,
17        ArrayList::add, ArrayList::addAll);
18      System.out.println(list);
19
20      list = Stream.of(names).collect(Collectors.toList());
21      System.out.println(list);
22
23      Set<String> set = Stream.of(names).map(e -> e.toUpperCase()).
24        collect(Collectors.toSet());
25      System.out.println(set);
26
27      Map<String, Integer> map = Stream.of(names).collect(
28        Collectors.toMap(e -> e, e -> e.length()));
29      System.out.println(map);
30
31      System.out.println("The total number of characters is " +
32        Stream.of(names).
33          collect(Collectors.summingInt(e -> e.length())));
34
35      java.util.IntSummaryStatistics stats = Stream.of(names).
36        collect(Collectors.summarizingInt(e -> e.length()));
37      System.out.println("Max is " + stats.getMax());
38      System.out.println("Min is " + stats.getMin());
39      System.out.println("Average is " + stats.getAverage());
40    }
41  }
```

Margin notes:
- collect into ArrayList (lines 16–17)
- Collectors.toList() (line 20)
- Collectors.toSet() (lines 23–24)
- Collectors.toMap() (lines 27–28)
- sum of integers
- summary information

```
The number of characters for all names: 47
[John, Peter, Susan, Kim, Jen, George, Alan, Stacy, Michelle, john]
[John, Peter, Susan, Kim, Jen, George, Alan, Stacy, Michelle, john]
[JEN, GEORGE, ALAN, SUSAN, JOHN, PETER, MICHELLE, KIM, STACY]
{Michelle=8, Stacy=5, Jen=3, George=6, Susan=5, Alan=4, John=4,
  john=4, Peter=5, Kim=3}
The total number of characters is 47
Max is 8
Min is 3
Average is 4.7
```

The program creates an array of strings, names (lines 10–11). The collect method (line 13) specifies a supplier (StringBuilder::new) for creating a StringBuilder, an accumulator (StringBuilder::append) for adding a string to the StringBuilder, and a combiner (StringBuilder::append) for combining two StringBuilders (lines 13–14). The stream pipeline obtains a StringBuilder that contains all strings in the stream. The length() method returns the length of the characters in the StringBuilder.

The collect method (line 16) specifies a supplier (ArrayList::new) for creating an ArrayList, an accumulator (ArrayList::add) for adding a string to the ArrayList, and a combiner (ArrayList:addAll) for combining two ArrayLists (lines 16–17). The stream pipeline obtains an ArrayList that contains all strings in the stream. This statement is simplified using a standard collector Collectors.toList() for a list (line 20).

The program creates a string stream, maps each string to uppercase (line 23), and creates a set using the collect method with a standard collector Collectors.toSet() for a set (lines 24). There are two uppercase strings JOHN in the stream. Since a set contains no duplicate elements, only one JOHN is stored in the set.

The program creates a string stream and creates a map using the `collect` method with a standard collector for a map (lines 28). The key of the map is the string and the value is the length of the string. Note key must be unique. If two strings are identical in the stream, a runtime exception would occur.

The `Collectors` class also contains the method for returning collectors that produce summary information. For example, `Collectors.summingInt` produces the sum of integer values in the stream (line 33), and `Collectors.summarizingInt` produces an `IntSummaryStatistics` for the integer values in the stream (lines 35–36).

30.6.1 Show the output of the following code:

Check Point

```
int[] values = {1, 2, 3, 4, 1};
List<Integer> list = IntStream.of(values).mapToObj(e -> e)
  .collect(Collectors.toList());
System.out.println(list);

Set<Integer> set = IntStream.of(values).mapToObj(e -> e)
  .collect(Collectors.toSet());
System.out.println(set);

Map<Integer, Integer> map = IntStream.of(values).distinct()
  .mapToObj(e -> e)
  .collect(Collectors.toMap(e -> e, e -> e.hashCode()));
System.out.println(map);

System.out.println(
  IntStream.of(values).mapToObj(e -> e)
    .collect(Collectors.summingInt(e -> e)));

System.out.println(
  IntStream.of(values).mapToObj(e -> e)
    .collect(Collectors.averagingDouble(e -> e)));
```

30.7 Grouping Elements Using the `groupingby` Collector

You can use the groupingBy *collector along with the* collect *method to collect the elements by groups.*

Key Point

The elements in a stream can be divided into groups using the groupingBy collector and then applying aggregate collectors on each group. For example, you can group all the strings by their first letter and obtain the count of the elements in the group as follows:

```
String[] names = {"John", "Peter", "Susan", "Kim", "Jen",
  "George", "Alan", "Stacy", "Steve", "john"};
Map<Character, Long> map = Stream.of(names).collect(
  Collectors.groupingBy(e -> e.charAt(0), Collectors.counting()));
```

The first argument in the groupingBy method specifies the criteria for grouping, known as a *classifier*. The second argument specifies how the elements in a group are processed, known as a group *processor*. A processor is commonly a summary collector such as `counting()`. Using the groupingBy collector, the `collect` method returns a map with the classifier as the key. You may also specify a supplier in the groupingBy method such as the following:

group classifier
group processor

```
Map<Character, Long> map = Stream.of(names).collect(
Collectors.groupingBy(e -> e.charAt(0),
  TreeMap::new, Collectors.counting()));
```

In this case, a tree map is used to store the map entries.

Listing 30.6 gives an example of using the `groupingBy` method.

LISTING 30.6 CollectGroupDemo.java

```java
 1  import java.util.Map;
 2  import java.util.TreeMap;
 3  import java.util.stream.Collectors;
 4  import java.util.stream.IntStream;
 5  import java.util.stream.Stream;
 6
 7  public class CollectGroupDemo {
 8    public static void main(String[] args) {
 9      String[] names = {"John", "Peter", "Susan", "Kim", "Jen",
10        "George", "Alan", "Stacy", "Steve", "john"};
11
12      Map<String, Long> map1 = Stream.of(names).
13        map(e -> e.toUpperCase()).collect(
14          Collectors.groupingBy(e -> e, Collectors.counting()));
15      System.out.println(map1);
16
17      Map<Character, Long> map2 = Stream.of(names).collect(
18        Collectors.groupingBy(e -> e.charAt(0), TreeMap::new,
19          Collectors.counting()));
20      System.out.println(map2);
21
22      int[] values = {2, 3, 4, 1, 2, 3, 2, 3, 4, 5, 1, 421};
23      IntStream.of(values).mapToObj(e -> e).collect(
24        Collectors.groupingBy(e -> e, TreeMap::new,
25          Collectors.counting())).
26        forEach((k, v) -> System.out.println(k + " occurs " + v +
27          (v > 1 ? " times " : " time ")));
28
29      MyStudent[] students = {new MyStudent("John", "Lu", "CS", 32, 78),
30        new MyStudent("Susan", "Yao", "Math", 31, 85.4),
31        new MyStudent("Kim", "Johnson", "CS", 30, 78.1)};
32
33      System.out.printf("%10s%10s\n", "Department", "Average");
34      Stream.of(students).collect(Collectors.
35        groupingBy(MyStudent::getMajor, TreeMap::new,
36          Collectors.averagingDouble(MyStudent::getScore))).
37        forEach((k, v) -> System.out.printf("%10s%10.2f\n", k, v));
38    }
39  }
40
41  class MyStudent {
42    private String firstName;
43    private String lastName;
44    private String major;
45    private int age;
46    private double score;
47
48    public MyStudent(String firstName, String lastName, String major,
49        int age, double score) {
50      this.firstName = firstName;
51      this.lastName = lastName;
52      this.major = major;
53      this.age = age;
54      this.score = score;
55    }
```

Margin notes:
- create an array (lines 9–10)
- groupingBy (line 14)
- groupingBy (line 18)
- groupingBy (line 24)
- groupingby (line 35)
- Student class (line 41)

```
56
57    public String getFirstName() {
58       return firstName;
59    }
60
61    public String getLastName() {
62       return lastName;
63    }
64
65    public String getMajor() {
66       return major;
67    }
68
69    public int getAge() {
70       return age;
71    }
72
73    public double getScore() {
74       return score;
75    }
76 }
```

```
{JEN=1, ALAN=1, GEORGE=1, SUSAN=1, JOHN=2, STEVE=1, PETER=1, STACY=1,
   KIM=1}
{A=1, G=1, J=2, K=1, P=1, S=3, j=1}
1 occurs 2 times
2 occurs 3 times
3 occurs 3 times
4 occurs 2 times
5 occurs 1 time
421 occurs 1 time
Department    Average
      CS       78.05
    Math       85.40
```

The program creates a string stream, maps its elements to uppercase (lines 12–13), and collects the elements into a map with the string as the key and the occurrence of the string as the value (line 14). Note the counting() collector uses a value of the Long type. So, the Map is declared Map<String, Long>.

The program creates a string stream and collects the elements into a map with the first character in the string as the key and the occurrence of the first character as the value (lines 17–18). The key and value entries are stored in a TreeMap.

The program creates an int array (line 22). A stream is created from this array and the elements are mapped to Integer objects using the mapToObj method (line 23). The collect method returns a map with the Integer value as the key and the occurrence of the integer as the value (lines 24–25). The forEach method displays the key and value entries. Note the collect method is a terminal method. It returns an instance of TreeMap in this case. TreeMap has the forEach method for performing an action on each element in the collection.

The program creates an array of Student objects (lines 29–31). The Student class is defined with properties firstName, lastName, major, age, and score in lines 41–76. The program creates a stream for the array and the collect method groups the students by their major and returns a map with the major as the key and the average scores for the group as the value (lines 34-36). The method reference MyStudent::getMajor is used to specify the group by classifier. The method reference TreeMap::new specifies a supplier for the result map. The method reference MyStudent:getScore specifies the value for averaging.

30.7.1 Show the output of the following code:

```
int[] values = {1, 2, 2, 3, 4, 2, 1};
IntStream.of(values).mapToObj(e -> e).collect(
  Collectors.groupingBy(e -> e, TreeMap::new,
    Collectors.counting())).
  forEach((k, v) -> System.out.println(k + " occurs " + v
    + (v > 1 ? " times " : " time ")));

IntStream.of(values).mapToObj(e -> e).collect(
  Collectors.groupingBy(e -> e, TreeMap::new,
    Collectors.summingInt(e -> e))).
  forEach((k, v) -> System.out.println(k + ": " + v));

MyStudent[] students = {
  new MyStudent("John", "Johnson", "CS", 23, 89.2),
  new MyStudent("Susan", "Johnson", "Math", 21, 89.1),
  new MyStudent("John", "Peterson", "CS", 21, 92.3),
  new MyStudent("Kim", "Yao", "Math", 22, 87.3),
  new MyStudent("Jeff", "Johnson", "CS", 23, 78.5)};

Stream.of(students)
  .sorted(Comparator.comparing(MyStudent::getLastName)
    .thenComparing(MyStudent::getFirstName))
  .forEach(e -> System.out.println(e.getLastName() + ", " +
            e.getFirstName()));

Stream.of(students).collect(Collectors.
  groupingBy(MyStudent::getAge, TreeMap::new,
    Collectors.averagingDouble(MyStudent::getScore))).
  forEach((k, v) -> System.out.printf("%10s%10.2f\n", k, v));
```

30.8 Case Studies

Many programs for processing arrays and collections can now be simplified and run faster using aggregate methods on streams.

You can write programs without using streams. However, using streams enables you to write shorter and simpler programs that can be executed faster in parallel by utilizing multiple processors. Many of the programs that involve arrays and collections in the early chapters can be simplified using streams. This section presents several case studies.

30.8.1 Case Study: Analyzing Numbers

Section 7.3 gives a program that prompts the user to enter values, obtains their average, and displays the number of values greater than the average. The program can be simplified using a `DoubleStream` as shown in Listing 30.7.

LISTING 30.7 AnalyzeNumbersUsingStream.java

```
1  import java.util.stream.*;
2
3  public class AnalyzeNumbersUsingStream {
4    public static void main(String[] args) {
5      java.util.Scanner input = new java.util.Scanner(System.in);
6      System.out.print("Enter the number of items: ");
7      int n = input.nextInt();
8      double[] numbers = new double[n];
9      double sum = 0;
10
```

create array

```
11       System.out.print("Enter the numbers: ");
12       for (int i = 0; i < n; i++) {
13         numbers[i] = input.nextDouble();                                store number in array
14       }
15
16       double average = DoubleStream.of(numbers).average().getAsDouble();    get average
17       System.out.println("Average is " + average);
18       System.out.println("Number of elements above the average is "
19         + DoubleStream.of(numbers).filter(e -> e > average).count());      above average?
20     }
21   }
```

```
Enter the number of items: 10 ⏎Enter
Enter the numbers: 3.4 5 6 1 6.5 7.8 3.5 8.5 6.3 9.5 ⏎Enter
Average is 5.75
Number of elements above the average is 6
```

The program obtains the input from the user and stores the values in an array (lines 8–14), and obtains the average of the values using a stream (line 16), and finds the number of values greater than the average using a filtered stream (line 19).

30.8.2   Case Study: Counting the Occurrences of Each Letter

Listing 7.4, CountLettersInArrays.java gives a program that randomly generates 100 lowercase letters and counts the occurrences of each letter.

The program can be simplified using a `Stream` as shown in Listing 30.8.

LISTING 30.8   CountLettersUsingStream.java

```java
1   import java.util.Random;
2   import java.util.TreeMap;
3   import java.util.stream.Collectors;
4   import java.util.stream.Stream;
5
6   public class CountLettersUsingStream {
7     private static int count = 0;
8
9     public static void main(String[] args) {
10      Random random = new Random();
11      Object[] chars = random.ints(100, (int)'a', (int)'z' + 1).        create array
12        mapToObj(e -> (char)e).toArray();
13
14      System.out.println("The lowercase letters are:");
15      Stream.of(chars).forEach(e -> {                                   display array
16        System.out.print(e + (++count % 20 == 0 ? "\n" : " "));
17      });
18
19      count = 0; // Reset the count for columns
20      System.out.println("\nThe occurrences of each letter are:");
21      Stream.of(chars).collect(Collectors.groupingBy(e -> e,            count occurrence
22        TreeMap::new, Collectors.counting())).forEach((k, v) -> {
23        System.out.print(v + " " + k
24          + (++count % 10 == 0 ? "\n" : " "));
25      });
26    }
27  }
```

```
The lowercase letters are:
e y l s r i b k j v j h a b z n w b t v
s c c k r d w a m p w v u n q a m p l o
a z g d e g f i n d x m z o u l o z j v
h w i w n t g x w c d o t x h y v z y z
q e a m f w p g u q t r e n n w f c r f

The occurrences of each letter are:
5 a 3 b 4 c 4 d 4 e 4 f 4 g 3 h 3 i 3 j
2 k 3 l 4 m 6 n 4 o 3 p 3 q 4 r 2 s 4 t
3 u 5 v 8 w 3 x 3 y 6 z
```

The program generates a stream of 100 random integers. These integers are in the range between `(char)'a'` and `(char)'z'` (line 11). They are ASCII code for the lowercase letters. The `mapToObj` method maps the integers to their corresponding lowercase letters (line 12). The `toArray()` method returns an array consisting of these lowercase letters.

The program creates a stream of lowercase letters (line 15) and uses the `forEach` method to display each letter (line 16). The letters are displayed 20 per line. The static variable `count` is used to count the letters printed.

The program resets the count to `0` (line 19), creates a stream of lowercase letters (line 21), returns a map with lowercase letters as the key and the occurrences of each letter as the value (lines 21–22), and invokes the `forEach` method to display each key and value 10 per line (lines 23–24).

The code has 66 lines in Listing 7.4. The new code has only 27 lines, which greatly simplified coding. Furthermore, using streams is more efficient.

30.8.3 Case Study: Counting the Occurrences of Each Letter in a String

The preceding example randomly generates lowercase letters and counts the occurrence of each letter. This example counts the occurrence of each letter in a string. The program given in Listing 30.9 prompts the user to enter the string, converts all letters to uppercase, and displays the count of each letter in the string.

LISTING 30.9 CountOccurrenceOfLettersInAString.java

```java
1   import java.util.*;
2   import java.util.stream.Stream;
3   import java.util.stream.Collectors;
4
5   public class CountOccurrenceOfLettersInAString {
6     private static int count = 0;
7
8     public static void main(String[] args) {
9       Scanner input = new Scanner(System.in);
10      System.out.print("Enter a string: ");
11      String s = input.nextLine();
12
13      count = 0; // Reset the count for columns
14      System.out.println("The occurrences of each letter are:");
15      Stream.of(toCharacterArray(s.toCharArray()))
16        .filter(ch -> Character.isLetter(ch))
17        .map(ch -> Character.toUpperCase(ch))
18        .collect(Collectors.groupingBy(e -> e,
```

read a string

convert char[] to Character[]

select letters

map to uppercase

collect and count

```
19                  TreeMap::new, Collectors.counting()))
20                .forEach((k, v) -> { System.out.print(v + " " + k       display value and key
21                  + (++count %  10 == 0 ?  "\n" :  " "));
22              });
23        }
24
25      public static Character[] toCharacterArray(char[] list) {
26          Character[] result = new Character[list.length];
27          for (int i = 0; i < result.length; i++) {
28            result[i] = list[i];
29          }
30          return result;
31      }
32   }
```

```
Enter a string: Welcome to JavaAA  ↵Enter
The occurrences of each letter are:
4 A 1 C 2 E 1 J 1 L 1 M 2 O 1 T 1 V 1 W
```

The program reads a string s and obtains an array of char from the string by invoking s.toCharArray(). To create a stream of characters, you need to convert char[] into Character[]. So, the program defines the toCharacterArray method (lines 25–31) for obtaining a Character[] from char[].

char[] to Character[]

The program creates a stream of Character object (line 15), eliminates nonletters from the stream using the filter method (line 16), coverts all letters to uppercase using the map method (line 17), and obtains a TreeMap using the collect method (lines 18–19). In the TreeMap, the key is the letter and the value is the count for the letter. The forEach method (lines 20–21) in TreeMap is used to display the value and key.

30.8.3 Case Study: Processing All Elements in a Two-Dimensional Array

You can create a stream from a one-dimensional array. Can you create a stream for processing two-dimensional arrays? Listing 30.10 gives an example of processing two-dimensional arrays using streams.

LISTING 30.10   TwoDimensionalArrayStream.java

```
1   import java.util.IntSummaryStatistics;
2   import java.util.stream.IntStream;
3   import java.util.stream.Stream;
4
5   public class TwoDimensionalArrayStream {
6     private static int i = 0;
7     public static void main(String[] args) {
8       int[][] m = {{1, 2}, {3, 4}, {4, 5}, {1, 3}};       create an array
9
10      int[] list = Stream.of(m).map(e -> IntStream.of(e)).
11        reduce((e1, e2) -> IntStream.concat(e1, e2)).get().toArray();   reduce to onedimensional
12
13      IntSummaryStatistics stats =
14        IntStream.of(list).summaryStatistics();           obtain statistical information
15      System.out.println("Max: " + stats.getMax());
16      System.out.println("Min: " + stats.getMin());
```

```
17        System.out.println("Sum: " + stats.getSum());
18        System.out.println("Average: " + stats.getAverage());
19
20        System.out.println("Sum of row ");
21        Stream.of(m).mapToInt(e -> IntStream.of(e).sum())
22          .forEach(e ->
23            System.out.println("Sum of row " + i++ + ": " + e));
24      }
25    }
```

sum of each row

```
Max: 5
Min: 1
Sum: 23
Average: 2.875
Sum of row
Sum of row 0: 3
Sum of row 1: 7
Sum of row 2: 9
Sum of row 3: 4
```

The program creates a two-dimensional array m in line 8. Invoking `Stream.of(m)` creates a stream consisting of rows as elements (line 10). The `map` method maps each row to an `IntStream`. The `reduce` method concatenates these streams into one large stream (line 11). This large stream now contains all the elements in m. Invoking `toArray()` from the stream returns an array consisting of all the integers in the stream (line 11).

The program obtains a statistical summary for an `IntStream` created from the array (lines 13–14) and displays the maximum, minimum, sum, and average of the integers in the stream (lines 15–18).

Finally, the program creates a stream from m that consists of rows in m (line 21). Each row is mapped to an `int` value using the `mapToInt` method (line 21). The `int` value is the sum of the elements in the row. The `forEach` method displays the sum for each row (lines 22–23).

30.8.4 Case Study: Finding the Directory Size

Listing 18.7 gives a recursive program that finds the size of a directory. The size of a directory is the sum of the sizes of all the files in the directory. The program can be implemented using streams as shown in Listing 30.11.

LISTING 30.11 `DirectorySizeStream.java`

```
1   import java.io.File;
2   import java.nio.file.Files;
3   import java.util.Scanner;
4
5   public class DirectorySizeStream {
6     public static void main(String[] args) throws Exception {
7       // Prompt the user to enter a directory or a file
8       System.out.print("Enter a directory or a file: ");
9       Scanner input = new Scanner(System.in);
10      String directory = input.nextLine();
11
12      // Display the size
13      System.out.println(getSize(new File(directory)) + " bytes");
14    }
15
```

invoke method

```
16    public static long getSize(File file) {
17      if (file.isFile()) {
18        return file.length();
19      }
20      else {
21        try {
22          return Files.list(file.toPath()).parallel().
23            mapToLong(e -> getSize(e.toFile())).sum();
24        } catch (Exception ex) {
25          return 0;
26        }
27      }
28    }
29  }
```

getSize method
is file?
return file length

get subpaths
recursive call

```
Enter a directory or a file: c:\book [↵Enter]
48619631 bytes
```

```
Enter a directory or a file: c:\book\Welcome.java [↵Enter]
172 bytes
```

```
Enter a directory or a file: c:\book\NonExistentFile [↵Enter]
0 bytes
```

The program prompts the user to enter a file or a directory name (lines 8–10) and invokes the `getSize(File file)` method to return the size of the file or a directory (line 13). The `File` object can be a directory or a file. If it is a file, the `getSize` method returns the size of the file (lines 17–19). If it is a directory, invoking `Files.list(file.toPath())` returns a stream consisting of the `Path` objects. Each `Path` object represents a subpath in the directory (line 22). Since JDK 1.8, new methods are added in some existing classes to return streams. The `Files` class now has the static `list(Path)` method that returns a stream of subpaths in the path. For each subpath `e`, the `mapToLong` method maps `e` into the size of `e` by invoking `getSize(e)`. Finally, the terminal `sum()` method returns the size of the whole directory.

Both `getSize` methods in Listing 18.7 and Listing 30.9 are recursive. The `getSize` method in Listing 30.9 can be executed in a parallel stream. So, Listing 30.9 has better performance.

30.8.5 Case Study: Counting Keywords

Listing 21.7 gives a program to count the keywords in a Java source file. The program reads the words from a text file and tests if the word is a keyword. You can rewrite the code using streams as shown in Listing 30.12.

LISTING 30.12 CountKeywordStream.java

```
1  import java.util.*;
2  import java.io.*;
3  import java.nio.file.Files;
4  import java.util.stream.Stream;
5
6  public class CountKeywordStream {
7    public static void main(String[] args) throws Exception {
8      Scanner input = new Scanner(System.in);
```

```
 9        System.out.print("Enter a Java source file: ");
10        String filename = input.nextLine();
11
12        File file = new File(filename);
13        if (file.exists()) {
14          System.out.println("The number of keywords in " + filename
15            + " is " + countKeywords(file));
16        }
17        else {
18          System.out.println("File " + filename + " does not exist");
19        }
20      }
21
22      public static long countKeywords(File file) throws Exception {
23        // Array of all Java keywords + true, false and null
24        String[] keywordString = {"abstract", "assert", "boolean",
25          "break", "byte", "case", "catch", "char", "class", "const",
26          "continue", "default", "do", "double", "else", "enum",
27          "extends", "for", "final", "finally", "float", "goto",
28          "if", "implements", "import", "instanceof", "int",
29          "interface", "long", "native", "new", "package", "private",
30          "protected", "public", "return", "short", "static",
31          "strictfp", "super", "switch", "synchronized", "this",
32          "throw", "throws", "transient", "try", "void", "volatile",
33          "while", "true", "false", "null"};
34
35        Set<String> keywordSet =
36          new HashSet<>(Arrays.asList(keywordString));
37
38        return Files.lines(file.toPath()).parallel().mapToLong(line ->
39          Stream.of(line.split("[\\s++]")).
40            filter(word -> keywordSet.contains(word)).count()).sum();
41      }
42    }
```

Margin notes: enter a filename (line 10); file exists? (line 13); count keywords (line 15); keywords (line 24); keyword set (line 35); count keyword (line 40).

```
Enter a Java source file: c:\Welcome.java  ↵Enter
The number of keywords in c:\Welcome.java is 5
```

```
Enter a Java source file: c:\TTT.java  ↵Enter
File c:\TTT.java does not exist
```

The program prompts the user to enter a filename (lines 9–10). If the file exists, it invokes `conutKeywords(file)` to return the number of keywords in the file (line 15). The keywords are stored in a set `keywordSet` (lines 35–36). Invoking `Files.lines(file.toPath())` returns a streams of lines form the file (line 38). Each line in the stream is mapped to a `long` value that counts the number of the keywords in the line. The line is split into an array of words using `line.split("[\\s++]")` and this array is used to create a stream (line 39). The `filter` method is applied to select the keyword from the stream. Invoking `count()` returns the number of the keywords in a line. The `sum()` method returns the total number of keywords in all lines (line 40).

The real benefit of using parallel streams in this example is for improving performance (line 38).

30.8.6 Case Study: Occurrences of Words

Listing 21.9 gives a program that counts the occurrences of words in a text. You can rewrite the code using streams as shown in Listing 30.13.

LISTING 30.13 CountOccurrenceOfWordsStream.java

```
1   import java.util.*;
2   import java.util.stream.Collectors;
3   import java.util.stream.Stream;
4
5   public class CountOccurrenceOfWordsStream {
6     public static void main(String[] args) {
7       // Set text in a string
8       String text = "Good morning. Have a good class. "           text
9         + "Have a good visit. Have fun!";
10
11      Stream.of(text.split("[\\s+\\p{P}]")).parallel()            split into words
12        .filter(e -> e.length() > 0).collect(                     filter empty words
13          Collectors.groupingBy(String::toLowerCase, TreeMap::new,  group by words
14            Collectors.counting()))
15        .forEach((k, v) -> System.out.println(k + " " + v));      display counts
16    }
17  }
```

```
a          2
class      1
fun        1
good       3
have       3
morning    1
visit      1
```

The text is split into words using a whitespace \s or punctuation \p{P} as a delimiter (line 11) and a stream is created for the words. The **filter** method is used to select nonempty words (line 12). The **collect** method groups the words by converting each into lowercase and returns a **TreeMap** with the lowercase words as the key and their count as the value (lines 13–14). The **forEach** method displays the key and its value (line 15).

The code in Listing 30.11 is about half in size as the code in Listing 21.9. The new program greatly simplifies coding and improves performance.

30.8.1 Can the following code be used to replace line 19 in Listing 30.7?

Check Point

```
DoubleStream.of(numbers).filter(e -> e >
  DoubleStream.of(numbers).average()).count());
```

30.8.2 Can the following code be used to replace lines 15–16 in Listing 30.8?

```
Stream.of(chars).forEach(e -> {
  int count = 0;
  System.out.print(e + (++count %  20 == 0 ?  "\n" :  " ")); });
```

30.8.3 Show the output of the following code?

```
String s = "ABC";
Stream.of(s.toCharArray()).forEach(ch ->
  System.out.println(ch));
```

30.8.4 Show the output of the following code (The `toCharacterArray` method is presented in Listing 30.9.)

```
String s = "ABC";
Stream.of(toCharacterArray(s.toCharArray())).forEach(ch ->
  System.out.println(ch));
```

30.8.5 Write the code to obtain a one-dimensional array `list` of strings from a two-dimensional array `matrix` of strings.

CHAPTER SUMMARY

1. Java 8 introduces aggregate methods on collection streams to simplify coding and improve performance.

2. A stream pipeline creates a stream from a data source, consists of zero or more intermediate methods (`skip`, `limit`, `filter`, `distinct`, `sorted`, `map`, and `mapToInt`), and a final terminal method (`count`, `sum`, `average`, `max`,`min`, `forEach`, `findFirst`, `firstAny`, `anyMatch`, `allMatch`, `noneMatch`, and `toArray`).

3. The execution of a stream is lazy, which means that the methods in the stream are not executed until the final terminal method is initiated.

4. The streams are transient objects. They are destroyed once the terminal method is executed.

5. The `Stream<T>` class defines the streams for a sequence of objects of the `T` type. `IntStream`, `LongStream`, and `DoubleStream` are the streams for a sequence of primitive `int`, `long`, and `double` values.

6. An important benefit of using streams is for performance. Streams can be executed in parallel mode to take advantages of multi-core architecture. You can switch a stream into a parallel or sequential mode by invoking the `parallel()` or `sequential()` method.

7. You can use the `reduce` method to reduce a stream into a single value and use the `collect` method to place the elements in the stream into a collection.

8. You can use the `groupingBy` collector to group the elements in the stream and apply aggregate methods for the elements in the group.

QUIZ

Answer the quiz for this chapter online at the book Companion Website.

MyProgrammingLab™ **PROGRAMMING EXERCISES**

30.1 (*Assign grades*) Rewrite Programming Exercise 7.1 using streams.

30.2 (*Count occurrence of numbers*) Rewrite Programming Exercise 7.3 using streams.

30.3 (*Analyze scores*) Rewrite Programming Exercise 7.4 using streams.

30.4 (*Print distinct numbers*) Rewrite Programming Exercise 7.5 using streams. Display the numbers in increasing order.

30.5 (*Count single digits*) Rewrite Programming Exercise 7.7 using streams.

30.6 (*Average an array*) Rewrite Programming Exercise 7.8 using streams.

30.7 (*Find the smallest element*) Rewrite Programming Exercise 7.9 using streams.

30.8 (*Eliminate duplicates*) Rewrite Programming Exercise 7.15 using streams and sort the elements in the new array in increasing order.

30.9 (*Sort students*) Rewrite Programming Exercise 7.17 using streams. Define a class named `Student` with data fields `name` and `score` and their getter methods. Store each student in a `Student` object.

30.10 (*Convert binary to decimal*) Write a program that prompts the user to enter a binary number in string and displays its decimal value. Use `Stream`'s `reduce` method to convert a binary number to decimal.

30.11 (*Convert hex to decimal*) Write a program that prompts the user to enter a hex number in string and displays its decimal value. Use `Stream`'s `reduce` method to convert a hex number to decimal.

30.12 (*Sum the digits in an integer*) Rewrite Programming Exercise 6.2 using streams.

30.13 (*Count the letters in a string*) Rewrite Programming Exercise 6.20 using streams.

30.14 (*Occurrences of a specified character*) Rewrite Programming Exercise 6.23 using streams.

30.15 (*Display words in ascending alphabetical order*) Rewrite Programming Exercise 20.1 using streams.

30.16 (*Distinct scores*) Use streams to write a program that displays the distinct scores in the `scores` array in Section 8.8. Display the scores in increasing order, separated by exactly one space, five numbers per line.

30.17 (*Count consonants and vowels*) Rewrite Programming Exercise 21.4 using streams.

30.18 (*Count the occurrences of words in a text file*) Rewrite Programming Exercise 21.8 using streams.

30.19 (*Summary information*) Suppose the file test.txt contains floating-point numbers separated by spaces. Write a program to obtain the sum, average, maximum, and minimum of the numbers.

APPENDIXES

Java Keywords

The following 50 keywords are reserved for use by the Java language:

abstract	double	int	super
assert	else	interface	switch
boolean	enum	long	synchronized
break	extends	native	this
byte	final	new	throw
case	finally	package	throws
catch	float	private	transient
char	for	protected	try
class	goto	public	void
const	if	return	volatile
continue	implements	short	while
default	import	static	
do	instanceof	strictfp*	

The keywords **goto** and **const** are C++ keywords reserved, but not currently used in Java. This enables Java compilers to identify them and to produce better error messages if they appear in Java programs.

The literal values **true**, **false**, and **null** are not keywords, just like literal value 100. However, you cannot use them as identifiers, just as you cannot use 100 as an identifier.

In the code listing, we use the keyword color for **true**, **false**, and **null** to be consistent with their coloring in Java IDEs.

---

*The **strictfp** keyword is a modifier for a method or class that enables it to use strict floating-point calculations. Floating-point arithmetic can be executed in one of two modes: *strict* or *nonstrict*. The strict mode guarantees that the evaluation result is the same on all Java Virtual Machine implementations. The nonstrict mode allows intermediate results from calculations to be stored in an extended format different from the standard IEEE floating-point number format. The extended format is machine dependent and enables code to be executed faster. However, when you execute the code using the nonstrict mode on different JVMs, you may not always get precisely the same results. By default, the nonstrict mode is used for floating-point calculations. To use the strict mode in a method or a class, add the **strictfp** keyword in the method or the class declaration. Strict floating-point may give you slightly better precision than nonstrict floating-point, but the distinction will only affect some applications. Strictness is not inherited; that is, the presence of **strictfp** on a class or interface declaration does not cause extended classes or interfaces to be strict.

APPENDIX B

The ASCII Character Set

Tables B.1 and B.2 show ASCII characters and their respective decimal and hexadecimal codes. The decimal or hexadecimal code of a character is a combination of its row index and column index. For example, in Table B.1, the letter A is at row 6 and column 5, so its decimal equivalent is 65; in Table B.2, letter A is at row 4 and column 1, so its hexadecimal equivalent is 41.

TABLE B.1 ASCII Character Set in the Decimal Index

	0	1	2	3	4	5	6	7	8	9
0	nul	soh	stx	etx	eot	enq	ack	bel	bs	ht
1	nl	vt	ff	cr	so	si	dle	dc1	dc2	dc3
2	dc4	nak	syn	etb	can	em	sub	esc	fs	gs
3	rs	us	sp	!	"	#	$	%	&	'
4	(	)	*	+	,	-	.	/	0	1
5	2	3	4	5	6	7	8	9	:	;
6	<	=	>	?	@	A	B	C	D	E
7	F	G	H	I	J	K	L	M	N	O
8	P	Q	R	S	T	U	V	W	X	Y
9	Z	[	\	]	^	_	`	a	b	c
10	d	e	f	g	h	i	j	k	l	m
11	n	o	p	q	r	s	t	u	v	w
12	x	y	z	{	|	}	~	del		

TABLE B.2 ASCII Character Set in the Hexadecimal Index

	0	1	2	3	4	5	6	7	8	9	A	B	C	D	E	F
0	nul	soh	stx	etx	eot	enq	ack	bel	bs	ht	nl	vt	ff	cr	so	si
1	dle	dc1	dc2	dc3	dc4	nak	syn	etb	can	em	sub	esc	fs	gs	rs	us
2	sp	!	"	#	$	%	&	'	(	)	*	+	,	-	.	/
3	0	1	2	3	4	5	6	7	8	9	:	;	<	=	>	?
4	@	A	B	C	D	E	F	G	H	I	J	K	L	M	N	O
5	P	Q	R	S	T	U	V	W	X	Y	Z	[	\	]	^	_
6	`	a	b	c	d	e	f	g	h	i	j	k	l	m	n	o
7	p	q	r	s	t	u	v	w	x	y	z	{	|	}	~	del

1159

APPENDIX C

Operator Precedence Chart

The operators are shown in decreasing order of precedence from top to bottom. Operators in the same group have the same precedence, and their associativity is shown in the table.

Operator	Name	Associativity
()	Parentheses	Left to right
()	Function call	Left to right
[]	Array subscript	Left to right
.	Object member access	Left to right
++	Postincrement	Left to right
--	Postdecrement	Left to right
++	Preincrement	Right to left
--	Predecrement	Right to left
+	Unary plus	Right to left
-	Unary minus	Right to left
!	Unary logical negation	Right to left
(type)	Unary casting	Right to left
new	Creating object	Right to left
*	Multiplication	Left to right
/	Division	Left to right
%	Remainder	Left to right
+	Addition	Left to right
-	Subtraction	Left to right
<<	Left shift	Left to right
>>	Right shift with sign extension	Left to right
>>>	Right shift with zero extension	Left to right
<	Less than	Left to right
<=	Less than or equal to	Left to right
>	Greater than	Left to right
>=	Greater than or equal to	Left to right
instanceof	Checking object type	Left to right

Operator	Name	Associativity
==	Equal comparison	Left to right
!=	Not equal	Left to right
&	(Unconditional AND)	Left to right
^	(Exclusive OR)	Left to right
|	(Unconditional OR)	Left to right
&&	Conditional AND	Left to right
||	Conditional OR	Left to right
? :	Ternary condition	Right to left
=	Assignment	Right to left
+=	Addition assignment	Right to left
-=	Subtraction assignment	Right to left
*=	Multiplication assignment	Right to left
/=	Division assignment	Right to left
%=	Remainder assignment	Right to left

APPENDIX D

Java Modifiers

Modifiers are used on classes and class members (constructors, methods, data, and class-level blocks), but the `final` modifier can also be used on local variables in a method. A modifier that can be applied to a class is called a *class modifier*. A modifier that can be applied to a method is called a *method modifier*. A modifier that can be applied to a data field is called a *data modifier*. A modifier that can be applied to a class-level block is called a *block modifier*. The following table gives a summary of the Java modifiers.

Modifier	Class	Constructor	Method	Data	Block	Explanation
(default)*	√	√	√	√	√	A class, constructor, method, or data field is visible in this package.
public	√	√	√	√		A class, constructor, method, or data field is visible to all the programs in any package.
private		√	√	√		A constructor, method, or data field is only visible in this class.
protected		√	√	√		A constructor, method, or data field is visible in this package and in subclasses of this class in any package.
static			√	√	√	Define a class method, a class data field, or a static initialization block.
final	√		√	√		A final class cannot be extended. A final method cannot be modified in a subclass. A final data field is a constant.
abstract	√		√			An abstract class must be extended. An abstract method must be implemented in a concrete subclass.
native			√			A native method indicates that the method is implemented using a language other than Java.

* Default access doesn't have a modifier associated with it. For example: `class Test {}`

Modifier	Class	Constructor	Method	Data	Block	Explanation
synchronized			√		√	Only one thread at a time can execute this method.
strictfp	√		√			Use strict floating-point calculations to guarantee that the evaluation result is the same on all JVMs.
transient				√		Mark a nonserializable instance data field.

The modifiers default (no modifier), `public`, `private`, and `protected` are known as *visibility* or *accessibility modifiers* because they specify how classes and class members are accessed.

The modifiers `public`, `private`, `protected`, `static`, `final`, and `abstract` can also be applied to inner classes.

APPENDIX E

Special Floating-Point Values

Dividing an integer by zero is invalid and throws `ArithmeticException`, but dividing a floating-point value by zero does not cause an exception. Floating-point arithmetic can overflow to infinity if the result of the operation is too large for a `double` or a `float`, or underflow to zero if the result is too small for a `double` or a `float`. Java provides the special floating-point values `POSITIVE_INFINITY`, `NEGATIVE_INFINITY`, and `NaN` (Not a Number) to denote these results. These values are defined as special constants in the `Float` class and the `Double` class.

If a positive floating-point number is divided by zero, the result is `POSITIVE_INFINITY`. If a negative floating-point number is divided by zero, the result is `NEGATIVE_INFINITY`. If a floating-point zero is divided by zero, the result is `NaN`, which means that the result is undefined mathematically. The string representations of these three values are `Infinity`, `-Infinity`, and `NaN`. For example,

```
System.out.print(1.0 / 0); // Print Infinity
System.out.print(-1.0 / 0); // Print -Infinity
System.out.print(0.0 / 0); // Print NaN
```

These special values can also be used as operands in computations. For example, a number divided by `POSITIVE_INFINITY` yields a positive zero. Table E.1 summarizes various combinations of the /, *, %, +, and – operators.

TABLE E.1 Special Floating-Point Values

x	y	x/y	$x*y$	$x\%y$	$x + y$	$x - y$
Finite	± 0.0	± infinity	± 0.0	NaN	Finite	Finite
Finite	± infinity	± 0.0	± 0.0	x	± infinity	infinity
± 0.0	± 0.0	NaN	± 0.0	NaN	± 0.0	± 0.0
± infinity	Finite	± infinity	± 0.0	NaN	± infinity	± infinity
± infinity	± infinity	NaN	± 0.0	NaN	± infinity	infinity
± 0.0	± infinity	± 0.0	NaN	± 0.0	± infinity	± 0.0
NaN	Any	NaN	NaN	NaN	NaN	NaN
Any	NaN	NaN	NaN	NaN	NaN	NaN

Note
If one of the operands is NaN, the result is NaN.

APPENDIX F

Number Systems

F.1 Introduction

Computers use binary numbers internally, because computers are made naturally to store and process 0s and 1s. The binary number system has two digits, 0 and 1. A number or character is stored as a sequence of 0s and 1s. Each 0 or 1 is called a *bit* (binary digit).

    In our daily life, we use decimal numbers. When we write a number such as 20 in a program, it is assumed to be a decimal number. Internally, computer software is used to convert decimal numbers into binary numbers, and vice versa.

    We write computer programs using decimal numbers. However, to deal with an operating system, we need to reach down to the "machine level" by using binary numbers. Binary numbers tend to be very long and cumbersome. Often hexadecimal numbers are used to abbreviate them, with each hexadecimal digit representing four binary digits. The hexadecimal number system has 16 digits: 0–9 and A–F. The letters A, B, C, D, E, and F correspond to the decimal numbers 10, 11, 12, 13, 14, and 15.

    The digits in the decimal number system are 0, 1, 2, 3, 4, 5, 6, 7, 8, and 9. A decimal number is represented by a sequence of one or more of these digits. The value that each digit represents depends on its position, which denotes an integral power of 10. For example, the digits 7, 4, 2, and 3 in decimal number 7423 represent 7000, 400, 20, and 3, respectively, as shown below:

$$\boxed{7\,|\,4\,|\,2\,|\,3} = 7 \times 10^3 + 4 \times 10^2 + 2 \times 10^1 + 3 \times 10^0$$
$$10^3 \ 10^2 \ 10^1 \ 10^0 = 7000 + 400 + 20 + 3 = 7423$$

The decimal number system has 10 digits, and the position values are integral powers of 10. We say that 10 is the *base* or *radix* of the decimal number system. Similarly, since the binary number system has two digits, its base is 2, and since the hex number system has 16 digits, its base is 16.

    If 1101 is a binary number, the digits 1, 1, 0, and 1 represent 1×2^3, 1×2^2, 0×2^1, and 1×2^0, respectively:

$$\boxed{1\,|\,1\,|\,0\,|\,1} = 1 \times 2^3 + 1 \times 2^2 + 0 \times 2^1 + 1 \times 2^0$$
$$2^3 \ 2^2 \ 2^1 \ 2^0 = 8 + 4 + 0 + 1 = 13$$

If 7423 is a hex number, the digits 7, 4, 2, and 3 represent 7×16^3, 4×16^2, 2×16^1, and 3×16^0, respectively:

$$\boxed{7\,|\,4\,|\,2\,|\,3} = 7 \times 16^3 + 4 \times 16^2 + 2 \times 16^1 + 3 \times 16^0$$
$$16^3 \ 16^2 \ 16^1 \ 16^0 = 28672 + 1024 + 32 + 3 = 29731$$

Margin notes: base radix · decimal numbers · hexadecimal number · binary numbers

F.2 Conversions between Binary and Decimal Numbers

Given a binary number $b_n b_{n-1} b_{n-2} \ldots b_2 b_1 b_0$, the equivalent decimal value is

$$b_n \times 2^n + b_{n-1} \times 2^{n-1} + b_{n-2} \times 2^{n-2} + \ldots + b_2 \times 2^2 + b_1 \times 2^1 + b_0 \times 2^0$$

Here are some examples of converting binary numbers to decimals:

Binary	Conversion Formula	Decimal
10	$1 \times 2^1 + 0 \times 2^0$	2
1000	$1 \times 2^3 + 0 \times 2^2 + 0 \times 2^1 + 0 \times 2^0$	8
10101011	$1 \times 2^7 + 0 \times 2^6 + 1 \times 2^5 + 0 \times 2^4 + 1 \times 2^3 + 0 \times 2^2 + 1 \times 2^1 + 1 \times 2^0$	171

To convert a decimal number d to a binary number is to find the bits b_n, b_{n-1}, b_{n-2}, $\ldots$, b_2, b_1 and b_0 such that

$$d = b_n \times 2^n + b_{n-1} \times 2^{n-1} + b_{n-2} \times 2^{n-2} + \ldots + b_2 \times 2^2 + b_1 \times 2^1 + b_0 \times 2^0$$

These bits can be found by successively dividing d by 2 until the quotient is 0. The remainders are b_0, b_1, b_2, $\ldots$, b_{n-2}, b_{n-1}, and b_n.

For example, the decimal number 123 is 1111011 in binary. The conversion is done as follows:

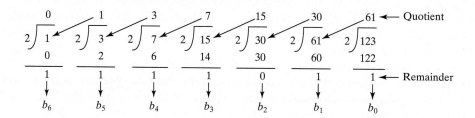

Tip
The Windows Calculator, as shown in Figure F.1, is a useful tool for performing number conversions. To run it, search for *Calculator* from the *Start* button and launch Calculator, then under *View* select *Scientific*.

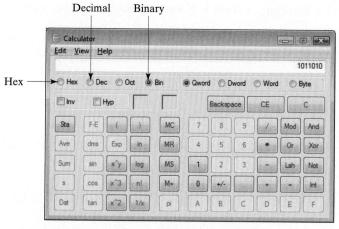

FIGURE F.1 You can perform number conversions using the Windows Calculator.

F.3 Conversions between Hexadecimal and Decimal Numbers

Given a hexadecimal number $h_n h_{n-1} h_{n-2} \ldots h_2 h_1 h_0$, the equivalent decimal value is

hex to decimal

$$h_n \times 16^n + h_{n-1} \times 16^{n-1} + h_{n-2} \times 16^{n-2} + \ldots + h_2 \times 16^2 + h_1 \times 16^1 + h_0 \times 16^0$$

Here are some examples of converting hexadecimal numbers to decimals:

Hexadecimal	Conversion Formula	Decimal
7F	$7 \times 16^1 + 15 \times 16^0$	127
FFFF	$15 \times 16^3 + 15 \times 16^2 + 15 \times 16^1 + 15 \times 16^0$	65535
431	$4 \times 16^2 + 3 \times 16^1 + 1 \times 16^0$	1073

To convert a decimal number d to a hexadecimal number is to find the hexadecimal digits $h_n, h_{n-1}, h_{n-2}, \ldots, h_2, h_1,$ and h_0 such that

decimal to hex

$$d = h_n \times 16^n + h_{n-1} \times 16^{n-1} + h_{n-2} \times 16^{n-2} + \ldots + h_2 \times 16^2$$
$$+ h_1 \times 16^1 + h_0 \times 16^0$$

These numbers can be found by successively dividing d by 16 until the quotient is 0. The remainders are $h_0, h_1, h_2, \ldots, h_{n-2}, h_{n-1},$ and h_n.

For example, the decimal number 123 is 7B in hexadecimal. The conversion is done as follows:

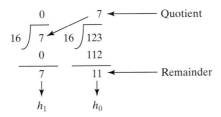

F.4 Conversions between Binary and Hexadecimal Numbers

To convert a hexadecimal number to a binary number, simply convert each digit in the hexadecimal number into a four-digit binary number, using Table F.1.

hex to binary

For example, the hexadecimal number 7B is 1111011, where 7 is 111 in binary and B is 1011 in binary.

To convert a binary number to a hexadecimal number, convert every four binary digits from right to left in the binary number into a hexadecimal number.

binary to hex

For example, the binary number 1110001101 is 38D, since 1101 is D, 1000 is 8, and 11 is 3, as shown below.

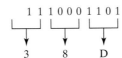

TABLE F.1 Converting Hexadecimal to Binary

Hexadecimal	Binary	Decimal
0	0000	0
1	0001	1
2	0010	2
3	0011	3
4	0100	4
5	0101	5
6	0110	6
7	0111	7
8	1000	8
9	1001	9
A	1010	10
B	1011	11
C	1100	12
D	1101	13
E	1110	14
F	1111	15

Note
Octal numbers are also useful. The octal number system has eight digits, 0 to 7. A decimal number 8 is represented in the octal system as 10.

Here are some good online resources for practicing number conversions:

- http://forums.cisco.com/CertCom/game/binary_game_page.htm
- http://people.sinclair.edu/nickreeder/Flash/binDec.htm
- http://people.sinclair.edu/nickreeder/Flash/binHex.htm

Check
Point

F.1 Convert the following decimal numbers into hexadecimal and binary numbers:
100; 4340; 2000

F.2 Convert the following binary numbers into hexadecimal and decimal numbers:
1000011001; 100000000; 100111

F.3 Convert the following hexadecimal numbers into binary and decimal numbers:
FEFA9; 93; 2000

APPENDIX G

Bitwise Operations

To write programs at the machine-level, often you need to deal with binary numbers directly and perform operations at the bit level. Java provides the bitwise operators and shift operators defined in Table G.1.

The bit operators apply only to integer types (`byte`, `short`, `int`, and `long`). A character involved in a bit operation is converted to an integer. All bitwise operators can form bitwise assignment operators, such as =, |=, <<=, >>=, and >>>=.

TABLE G.1

Operator	Name	Example (using bytes in the example)	Description
&	Bitwise AND	10101110 & 10010010 yields 10000010	The AND of two corresponding bits yields a 1 if both bits are 1.
|	Bitwise inclusive OR	10101110 | 10010010 yields 10111110	The OR of two corresponding bits yields a 1 if either bit is 1.
^	Bitwise exclusive OR	10101110 ^ 10010010 yields 00111100	The XOR of two corresponding bits yields a 1 only if two bits are different.
~	One's complement	~10101110 yields 01010001	The operator toggles each bit from 0 to 1 and from 1 to 0.
<<	Left shift	10101110 << 2 yields 10111000	The operator shifts bits in the first operand left by the number of bits specified in the second operand, filling with 0s on the right.
>>	Right shift with sign extension	10101110 >> 2 yields 11101011 00101110 >> 2 yields 00001011	The operator shifts bit in the first operand right by the number of bits specified in the second operand, filling with the highest (sign) bit on the left.
>>>	Unsigned right shift with zero extension	10101110 >>> 2 yields 00101011 00101110 >>> 2 yields 00001011	The operator shifts bit in the first operand right by the number of bits specified in the second operand, filling with 0s on the left.

APPENDIX H

Regular Expressions

Often, you need to write the code to validate user input such as to check whether the input is a number, a string with all lowercase letters, or a Social Security number. How do you write this type of code? A simple and effective way to accomplish this task is to use the regular expression.

regular expression

A *regular expression* (abbreviated *regex*) is a string that describes a pattern for matching a set of strings. Regular expression is a powerful tool for string manipulations. You can use regular expressions for matching, replacing, and splitting strings.

H.1 Matching Strings

matches

Let us begin with the matches method in the String class. At first glance, the matches method is very similar to the equals method. For example, the following two statements both evaluate to true:

```
"Java".matches("Java");
"Java".equals("Java");
```

However, the matches method is more powerful. It can match not only a fixed string, but also a set of strings that follow a pattern. For example, the following statements all evaluate to true:

```
"Java is fun".matches("Java.*")
"Java is cool".matches("Java.*")
"Java is powerful".matches("Java.*")
```

"Java.*" in the preceding statements is a regular expression. It describes a string pattern that begins with Java followed by any zero or more characters. Here, the substring .* matches any zero or more characters.

H.2 Regular Expression Syntax

A regular expression consists of literal characters and special symbols. Table H.1 lists some frequently used syntax for regular expressions.

Note
Backslash is a special character that starts an escape sequence in a string. So you need to use \\ to represent a literal character \.

Note
Recall that a *whitespace character* is ' ', '\t', '\n', '\r', or '\f'. So \s is the same as [\t\n\r\f], and \S is the same as [^ \t\n\r\f].

TABLE H.1 Frequently Used Regular Expressions

Regular Expression	Matches	Example
x	a specified character x	Java matches Java
.	any single character	Java matches J..a
(ab|cd)	ab or cd	ten matches t(en|im)
[abc]	a, b, or c	Java matches Ja[uvwx]a
[^abc]	any character except a, b, or c	Java matches Ja[^ars]a
[a-z]	a through z	Java matches [A-M]av[a-d]
[^a-z]	any character except a through z	Java matches Jav[^b-d]
[a-e[m-p]]	a through e or m through p	Java matches [A-G[I-M]]av[a-d]
[a-e&&[c-p]]	intersection of a-e with c-p	Java matches [A-P&&[I-M]]av[a-d]
\d	a digit, same as [0-9]	Java2 matches "Java[\\d]"
\D	a non-digit	$Java matches "[\\D][\\ D]ava"
\w	a word character	Java1 matches "[\\w]ava[\\w]"
\W	a non-word character	$Java matches "[\\W][\\ w]ava"
\s	a whitespace character	"Java 2" matches "Java\\s2"
\S	a non-whitespace char	Java matches "[\\S]ava"
p*	zero or more occurrences of pattern p	aaaa matches "a*" abab matches "(ab)*"
p+	one or more occurrences of pattern p	Java matches "a+" bbb matches "a+"
p?	zero or one occurrence of pattern p	Java matches "J?Java" ava matches "J?ava"
p{n}	exactly n occurrences of pattern p	Java matches "a{1}" Java does not match "a{2}"
p{n,}	at least n occurrences of pattern p	Java matches "a{1,}" Java does not match "a{2,}"
p{n,m}	between n and m occurrences (inclusive)	Java matches "a{1,9}" Java does not match "a{2,9}"
\p{P}	a punctuation character !"#$%&'()*+, -./:;<=>?@ [\]^_'{|}~	J?a matches "J\p{P}a" J?a. does not match "J\p{P}a"

Note
A word character is any letter, digit, or the underscore character. So \w is the same as [a-z[A-Z][0-9]_] or simply [a-zA-Z0-9_], and \W is the same as [^a-zA-Z0-9_].

Note
The last six entries *, +, ?, {n}, {n,}, and {n, m} in Table H.1 are called *quantifiers* that specify how many times the pattern before a quantifier may repeat. For example, A* matches zero or more A's, A+ matches one or more A's, A? matches zero or one A, A{3} matches exactly AAA, A{3,} matches at least three A's, and A{3,6} matches between 3 and 6 A's. * is the same as {0,}, + is the same as {1,}, and ? is the same as {0,1}.

quantifier

> ⚠️ **Caution**
> Do not use spaces in the repeat quantifiers. For example, `A{3,6}` cannot be written as `A{3, 6}` with a space after the comma.

> **Note**
> You may use parentheses to group patterns. For example, `(ab){3}` matches `ababab`, but `ab{3}` matches `abbb`.

Let us use several examples to demonstrate how to construct regular expressions.

Example 1
The pattern for Social Security numbers is `xxx-xx-xxxx`, where `x` is a digit. A regular expression for Social Security numbers can be described as

```
[\\d]{3}-[\\d]{2}-[\\d]{4}
```

For example,

```
"111-22-3333".matches("[\\d]{3}-[\\d]{2}-[\\d]{4}") returns true.
"11-22-3333".matches("[\\d]{3}-[\\d]{2}-[\\d]{4}") returns false.
```

Example 2
An even number ends with digits `0`, `2`, `4`, `6`, or `8`. The pattern for even numbers can be described as

```
[\\d]*[02468]
```

For example,

```
"123".matches("[\\d]*[02468]") returns false.
"122".matches("[\\d]*[02468]") returns true.
```

Example 3
The pattern for telephone numbers is `(xxx) xxx-xxxx`, where `x` is a digit and the first digit cannot be zero. A regular expression for telephone numbers can be described as

```
\\ ([1-9][\\ d]{2}\\) [\\d]{3}-[\\d]{4}
```

Note the parentheses symbols (and) are special characters in a regular expression for grouping patterns. To represent a literal (or) in a regular expression, you have to use \\(and \\).
For example,

```
"(912) 921-2728".matches("\\ ([1-9][\\ d]{2}\\) [\\d]{3}-[\\d]{4}")
returns true.
"921-2728".matches("\\ ([1-9][\\ d]{2}\\) [\\d]{3}-[\\d]{4}") returns
false.
```

Example 4
Suppose the last name consists of at most 25 letters, and the first letter is in uppercase. The pattern for a last name can be described as

```
[A-Z][a-zA-Z]{1,24}
```

Note you cannot have arbitrary whitespace in a regular expression. For example, `[A-Z][a-zA-Z]{1, 24}` would be wrong.

For example,

```
"Smith".matches("[A-Z][a-zA-Z]{1,24}") returns true.
"Jones123".matches("[A-Z][a-zA-Z]{1,24}") returns false.
```

Example 5
Java identifiers are defined in Section 2.3, Identifiers.

- An identifier must start with a letter, an underscore (_), or a dollar sign ($). It cannot start with a digit.

- An identifier is a sequence of characters that consists of letters, digits, underscores (_), and dollar signs ($).

The pattern for identifiers can be described as

```
[a-zA-Z_$][\\w$]*
```

Example 6
What strings are matched by the regular expression "Welcome to (Java|HTML)"? The answer is Welcome to Java or Welcome to HTML.

Example 7
What strings are matched by the regular expression ".*"? The answer is any string.

H.3 Replacing and Splitting Strings
The matches method in the String class returns true if the string matches the regular expression. The String class also contains the replaceAll, replaceFirst, and split methods for replacing and splitting strings, as shown in Figure H.1.

java.lang.String	
+matches(regex: String): boolean	Returns true if this string matches the pattern.
+replaceAll(regex: String, replacement: String): String	Returns a new string that replaces all matching substrings with the replacement.
+replaceFirst(regex: String, replacement: String): String	Returns a new string that replaces the first matching substring with the replacement.
+split(regex: String): String[]	Returns an array of strings consisting of the substrings split by the matches.
+split(regex: String, limit: int): String[]	Same as the preceding split method except that the limit parameter controls the number of times the pattern is applied.

FIGURE H.1 The String class contains the methods for matching, replacing, and splitting strings using regular expressions.

The replaceAll method replaces all matching substring, and the replaceFirst method replaces the first matching substring. For example, the code

```
System.out.println("Java Java Java".replaceAll("v\\w", "wi"));
```

displays

```
Jawi Jawi Jawi
```

and this code

```
System.out.println("Java Java Java".replaceFirst("v\\w", "wi"));
```

displays

```
Jawi Java Java
```

There are two overloaded `split` methods. The `split(regex)` method splits a string into substrings delimited by the matches. For example, the statement

```
String[] tokens = "Java1HTML2Perl".split("\\d");
```

splits string `"Java1HTML2Perl"` into `Java`, `HTML`, and `Perl` and saves in `tokens[0]`, `tokens[1]`, and `tokens[2]`.

In the `split(regex, limit)` method, the `limit` parameter determines how many times the pattern is matched. If `limit <= 0`, `split(regex, limit)` is same as `split(regex)`. If `limit > 0`, the pattern is matched at most `limit` −1 times. Here are some examples:

```
"Java1HTML2Perl".split("\\d", 0); splits into Java, HTML, Perl
"Java1HTML2Perl".split("\\d", 1); splits into Java1HTML2Perl
"Java1HTML2Perl".split("\\d", 2); splits into Java, HTML2Perl
"Java1HTML2Perl".split("\\d", 3); splits into Java, HTML, Perl
"Java1HTML2Perl".split("\\d", 4); splits into Java, HTML, Perl
"Java1HTML2Perl".split("\\d", 5); splits into Java, HTML, Perl
```

 Note

By default, all the quantifiers are *greedy*. This means that they will match as many occurrences as possible. For example, the following statement displays JRvaa, since the first match is aaa:

```
System.out.println("Jaaavaa".replaceFirst("a+", "R"));
```

You can change a qualifier's default behavior by appending a question mark (**?**) after it. The quantifier becomes *reluctant* or *lazy*, which means that it will match as few occurrences as possible. For example, the following statement displays JRaavaa, since the first match is a:

```
System.out.println("Jaaavaa".replaceFirst("a+?", "R"));
```

APPENDIX 1

Enumerated Types

1.1 Simple Enumerated Types

An enumerated type defines a list of enumerated values. Each value is an identifier. For example, the following statement declares a type, named MyFavoriteColor, with values RED, BLUE, GREEN, and YELLOW in this order:

```
enum MyFavoriteColor {RED, BLUE, GREEN, YELLOW};
```

A value of an enumerated type is like a constant and so, by convention, is spelled with all uppercase letters. So, the preceding declaration uses RED, not red. By convention, an enumerated type is named like a class with first letter of each word capitalized.

Once a type is defined, you can declare a variable of that type:

```
MyFavoriteColor color;
```

The variable color can hold one of the values defined in the enumerated type MyFavoriteColor or null, but nothing else. Java enumerated type is *type-safe*, meaning that an attempt to assign a value other than one of the enumerated values or null will result in a compile error.

The enumerated values can be accessed using the syntax

```
EnumeratedTypeName.valueName
```

For example, the following statement assigns enumerated value BLUE to variable color:

```
color = MyFavoriteColor.BLUE;
```

Note you have to use the enumerated type name as a qualifier to reference a value such as BLUE.

As with any other type, you can declare and initialize a variable in one statement:

```
MyFavoriteColor color = MyFavoriteColor.BLUE;
```

An enumerated type is treated as a special class. An enumerated type variable is therefore a reference variable. An enumerated type is a subtype of the Object class and the Comparable interface. Therefore, an enumerated type inherits all the methods in the Object class and the compareTo method in the Comparable interface. Additionally, you can use the following methods on an enumerated object:

- ■ public String name();
  Returns a name of the value for the object.

- ■ public int ordinal();
  Returns the ordinal value associated with the enumerated value. The first value in an enumerated type has an ordinal value of 0, the second has an ordinal value of 1, the third one 3, and so on.

Listing I.1 gives a program that demonstrates the use of enumerated types.

LISTING I.1   `EnumeratedTypeDemo.java`

<table>
<tr><td>define an enum type</td><td>

```
1  public class EnumeratedTypeDemo {
2    static enum Day {SUNDAY, MONDAY, TUESDAY, WEDNESDAY, THURSDAY,
3      FRIDAY, SATURDAY};
4
```
</td></tr>
<tr><td>declare an enum variable</td><td>

```
5    public static void main(String[] args) {
6      Day day1 = Day.FRIDAY;
7      Day day2 = Day.THURSDAY;
8
```
</td></tr>
<tr><td>get enum name

get enum ordinal</td><td>

```
9      System.out.println("day1's name is " + day1.name());
10     System.out.println("day2's name is " + day2.name());
11     System.out.println("day1's ordinal is " + day1.ordinal());
12     System.out.println("day2's ordinal is " + day2.ordinal());
13
```
</td></tr>
<tr><td>compare enum values</td><td>

```
14     System.out.println("day1.equals(day2) returns " +
15       day1.equals(day2));
16     System.out.println("day1.toString() returns " +
17       day1.toString());
18     System.out.println("day1.compareTo(day2) returns " +
19       day1.compareTo(day2));
20   }
21 }
```
</td></tr>
</table>

```
day1's name is FRIDAY
day2's name is THURSDAY
day1's ordinal is 5
day2's ordinal is 4
day1.equals(day2) returns false
day1.toString() returns FRIDAY
day1.compareTo(day2) returns 1
```

An enumerated type `Day` is defined in lines 2 and 3. Variables `day1` and `day2` are declared as the `Day` type and assigned enumerated values in lines 6 and 7. Since `day1`'s value is `FRIDAY`, its ordinal value is 5 (line 11). Since `day2`'s value is `THURSDAY`, its ordinal value is 4 (line 12).

Since an enumerated type is a subclass of the `Object` class and the `Comparable` interface, you can invoke the methods `equals`, `toString`, and `compareTo` from an enumerated object reference variable (lines 14–19). `day1.equals(day2)` returns true if `day1` and `day2` have the same ordinal value. `day1.compareTo(day2)` returns the difference between `day1`'s ordinal value and `day2`'s.

Alternatively, you can rewrite the code in Listing I.1 into Listing I.2.

LISTING I.2   `StandaloneEnumTypeDemo.java`

```
1  public class StandaloneEnumTypeDemo {
2    public static void main(String[] args) {
3      Day day1 = Day.FRIDAY;
4      Day day2 = Day.THURSDAY;
5
6      System.out.println("day1's name is " + day1.name());
7      System.out.println("day2's name is " + day2.name());
8      System.out.println("day1's ordinal is " + day1.ordinal());
```

```
 9        System.out.println("day2's ordinal is " + day2.ordinal());
10
11        System.out.println("day1.equals(day2) returns " +
12          day1.equals(day2));
13        System.out.println("day1.toString() returns " +
14          day1.toString());
15        System.out.println("day1.compareTo(day2) returns " +
16          day1.compareTo(day2));
17      }
18  }
19
20  enum Day {SUNDAY, MONDAY, TUESDAY, WEDNESDAY, THURSDAY,
21    FRIDAY, SATURDAY}
```

An enumerated type can be defined inside a class, as shown in lines 2 and 3 in Listing I.1, or standalone as shown in lines 20 and 21 in Listing I.2. In the former case, the type is treated as an inner class. After the program is compiled, a class named EnumeratedTypeDemo$Day.class is created. In the latter case, the type is treated as a stand-alone class. After the program is compiled, a class named Day.class is created.

Note

When an enumerated type is declared inside a class, the type must be declared as a member of the class and cannot be declared inside a method. Furthermore, the type is always `static`. For this reason, the `static` keyword in line 2 in Listing I.1 may be omitted. The visibility modifiers on inner class can be also be applied to enumerated types defined inside a class.

Tip

Using enumerated values (e.g., Day.MONDAY, Day.TUESDAY, and so on) rather than literal integer values (e.g., 0, 1, and so on) can make the program easier to read and maintain.

I.2 Using `if` or `switch` Statements with an Enumerated Variable

An enumerated variable holds a value. Often, your program needs to perform a specific action depending on the value. For example, if the value is Day.MONDAY, play soccer; if the value is Day.TUESDAY, take piano lesson, and so on. You can use an `if` statement or a `switch` statement to test the value in the variable, as shown in (a) and (b).

```
if (day.equals(Day.MONDAY)) {
  // process Monday
}
else if (day.equals(Day.TUESDAY)) {
  // process Tuesday
}
else
  ...
```
(a)

Equivalent

```
switch (day) {
  case MONDAY:
    // process Monday
    break;
  case TUESDAY:
    // process Tuesday
    break;
  ...
}
```
(b)

In the `switch` statement in (b), the case label is an unqualified enumerated value (e.g., MONDAY, but not Day.MONDAY).

I.3 Processing Enumerated Values Using a Foreach Loop

Each enumerated type has a static method `values()` that returns all enumerated values for the type in an array. For example,

```
Day[] days = Day.values();
```

You can use a regular for loop in (a) or an enhanced for loop in (b) to process all the values in the array.

```for (int i = 0; i < days.length; i++)```
```   System.out.println(days[i]);```
 	
(a)
	Equivalent	```for (Day day: days)```
		``` System.out.println(day);```
		
		(b)

I.4 Enumerated Types with Data Fields, Constructors, and Methods

The simple enumerated types introduced in the preceding section define a type with a list of enumerated values. You can also define an enumerate type with data fields, constructors, and methods, as shown in Listing I.3.

LISTING I.3 `TrafficLight.java`

```
1  public enum TrafficLight {
2    RED ("Please stop"), GREEN ("Please go"),
3    YELLOW ("Please caution");
4
5    private String description;
6
7    private TrafficLight(String description) {
8      this.description = description;
9    }
10
11   public String getDescription() {
12     return description;
13   }
14 }
```

The enumerated values are defined in lines 2 and 3. The value declaration must be the first statement in the type declaration. A data field named `description` is declared in line 5 to describe an enumerated value. The constructor `TrafficLight` is declared in lines 7–9. The constructor is invoked whenever an enumerated value is accessed. The enumerated value's argument is passed to the constructor, which is then assigned to `description`.

Listing I.4 gives a test program to use `TrafficLight`.

LISTING I.4 `TestTrafficLight.java`

```
1  public class TestTrafficLight {
2    public static void main(String[] args) {
3      TrafficLight light = TrafficLight.RED;
4      System.out.println(light.getDescription());
5    }
6  }
```

An enumerated value `TrafficLight.red` is assigned to variable `light` (line 3). Accessing `TrafficLight.RED` causes the JVM to invoke the constructor with argument "please stop". The methods in enumerated type are invoked in the same way as the methods in a class. `light.getDescription()` returns the description for the enumerated value (line 4).

 Note

The Java syntax requires that the constructor for enumerated types be private to prevent it from being invoked directly. The private modifier may be omitted. In this case, it is considered private by default.

Java Quick Reference

Console Input

```
Scanner input = new Scanner(System.in);
int intValue = input.nextInt();
long longValue = input.nextLong();
double doubleValue = input.nextDouble();
float floatValue = input.nextFloat();
String string = input.next();
String line = input.nextLine();
```

Console Output

```
System.out.println(anyValue);
```

Conditional Expression

```
boolean-expression ? expression1 :
  expression2

y = (x > 0) ? 1 : -1

System.out.println(number % 2 == 0 ?
  "number is even" : "number is odd");
```

Primitive Data Types

byte	8 bits
short	16 bits
int	32 bits
long	64 bits
float	32 bits
double	64 bits
char	16 bits
boolean	true/false

Arithmetic Operators

+	addition
-	subtraction
*	multiplication
/	division
%	remainder
++var	preincrement
--var	predecrement
var++	postincrement
var--	postdecrement

Assignment Operators

=	assignment
+=	addition assignment
-=	subtraction assignment
*=	multiplication assignment
/=	division assignment
%=	remainder assignment

Relational Operators

<	less than
<=	less than or equal to
>	greater than
>=	greater than or equal to
==	equal to
!=	not equal

Logical Operators

&&	short circuit AND
||	short circuit OR
!	NOT
^	exclusive OR

if Statements

```
if (condition) {
  statements;
}

if (condition) {
  statements;
}
else {
  statements;
}

if (condition1) {
  statements;
}
else if (condition2) {
  statements;
}
else {
  statements;
}
```

switch Statements

```
switch (intExpression) {
  case value1:
    statements;
    break;
  ...
  case valuen:
    statements;
    break;
  default:
    statements;
}
```

loop Statements

```
while (condition) {
  statements;
}

do {
  statements;
} while (condition);

for (init; condition;
  adjustment) {
  statements;
}
```

Java Quick Reference

Frequently Used Static Constants/Methods

```
Math.PI
Math.random()
Math.pow(a, b)
Math.abs(a)
Math.max(a, b)
Math.min(a, b)
Math.sqrt(a)
Math.sin(radians)
Math.asin(a)
Math.toRadians(degrees)
Math.toDegress(radians)
System.currentTimeMillis()
Integer.parseInt(string)
Integer.parseInt(string, radix)
Double.parseDouble(string)
Arrays.sort(type[] list)
Arrays.binarySearch(type[] list, type key)
```

Array/Length/Initializer

```
int[] list = new int[10];
list.length;
int[] list = {1, 2, 3, 4};
```

Multidimensional Array/Length/Initializer

```
int[][] list = new int[10][10];
list.length;
list[0].length;
int[][] list = {{1, 2}, {3, 4}};
```

Ragged Array

```
int[][] m = {{1, 2, 3, 4},
             {1, 2, 3},
             {1, 2},
             {1}};
```

Text File Output

```
PrintWriter output =
  new PrintWriter(filename);
output.print(...);
output.println(...);
output.printf(...);
```

Text File Input

```
Scanner input = new Scanner(
  new File(filename));
```

File Class

```
File file =
  new File(filename);
file.exists()
file.renameTo(File)
file.delete()
```

Object Class

```
Object o = new Object();
o.toString();
o.equals(o1);
```

Comparable Interface

```
c.compareTo(Comparable)
c is a Comparable object
```

String Class

```
String s = "Welcome";
String s = new String(char[]);
int length = s.length();
char ch = s.charAt(index);
int d = s.compareTo(s1);
boolean b = s.equals(s1);
boolean b = s.startsWith(s1);
boolean b = s.endsWith(s1);
boolean b = s.contains(s1);
String s1 = s.trim();
String s1 = s.toUpperCase();
String s1 = s.toLowerCase();
int index = s.indexOf(ch);
int index = s.lastIndexOf(ch);
String s1 = s.substring(ch);
String s1 = s.substring(i,j);
char[] chs = s.toCharArray();
boolean b = s.matches(regex);
String s1 = s.replaceAll(regex,repl);
String[] tokens = s.split(regex);
```

ArrayList Class

```
ArrayList<E> list = new ArrayList<>();
list.add(object);
list.add(index, object);
list.clear();
Object o = list.get(index);
boolean b = list.isEmpty();
boolean b = list.contains(object);
int i = list.size();
list.remove(index);
list.set(index, object);
int i = list.indexOf(object);
int i = list.lastIndexOf(object);
```

printf Method

```
System.out.printf("%b %c %d %f %e %s",
  true, 'A', 45, 45.5, 45.5, "Welcome");
System.out.printf("%-5d %10.2f %10.2e %8s",
  45, 45.5, 45.5, "Welcome");
```

INDEX